PLAY INDEX

1993–1997

PLAY INDEX

VOLUMES IN PRINT

1949–1952
1953–1960
1961–1967
1968–1972
1973–1977
1978–1982
1983–1987
1988–1992

PLAY INDEX

1993–1997

AN INDEX TO 4,617 PLAYS

Edited by
Juliette Yaakov
and
John Greenfieldt

NEW YORK • DUBLIN
THE H. W. WILSON COMPANY
1998

ISSN 0554-3037

Library of Congress Catalog Card Number 64-1054

Printed in the United States of America

CONTENTS

Preface vii

Directions for Use ix

Part I. Author, Title and Subject Index 1

Part II. Cast Analysis 431

Part III. List of Collections Indexed 485

Part IV. Directory of Publishers and Distributors 543

PREFACE

This volume of *Play Index* indexes 4,617 plays that were published during the five-year period 1993–1997. Some plays published before 1993, but which were omitted from the previous volume of *Play Index,* are included. Like its eight predecessors, the present volume contains both separately published plays and plays in collections, written in or translated into English.

Its broad scope—from puppet plays to classical drama—and detailed cast analysis make *Play Index* suitable to a variety of uses. These can be most fully realized by a reading of the Directions for Use and the introduction to Part II, Cast Analysis.

The H. W. Wilson Company is grateful to those publishers who provided copies of their titles for indexing.

DIRECTIONS FOR USE

Part I. Author, Title, and Subject Index. This section provides detailed information about individual plays. Entries are arranged under author, title, and subject in a single alphabet. The author entry for the play is the most inclusive and contains the following information: name of the author, title of the play, a brief descriptive note, the number of acts and scenes, the size and composition of the cast, and the number of sets required. For radio and television plays the size of the cast is given but the number of scenes and settings is omitted. For puppet plays the cast is given only as a number of characters.

In the case of separately published plays the author entry includes the publisher, date of publication, and pagination. If the play is contained in a collection, the name of the collection is given. Further information about the collection may be found in Part III of this volume.

Sample author entry:

Albee, Edward
Three tall women. Dramatists 1994 57p
Dowager, her secretary, and her lawyer depict one woman at three stages of her life. 2 acts 1m 3w 1 interior

—Same
In Plays for actresses; ed. by E. Lane and N. Shengold

This entry shows that a play by Edward Albee entitled *Three Tall Women* was published by Dramatists in 1994 and contains fifty-seven pages. For full information about the publisher see Part IV, Directory of Publishers and Distributors. The play has two acts and requires a cast of one man and three women plus one setting for production. This play also appears in the collection *Plays for Actresses.* For full information about the collection cited see Part III, List of Collections Indexed.

All plays are also listed under their titles followed by the name of the author. Fuller information about the play is obtained by consulting the author entry.

Sample title entry:

Three tall women. Albee, E.

All plays dealing in whole or in part with a particular subject are listed under that subject. Plays in a distinctive form, such as masques, mysteries and miracle plays, one-act plays, pageants, pantomimes, puppet plays, plays in verse, radio plays, television plays, etc., are entered under the appropriate form heading as well as under specific subjects. Full information about the play will be found by consulting the author entry.

Sample subject entry:

Christmas
Lebow, B. Tiny Tim is dead
y Levi, S. Merry Christmas Miss Vickers
Linney, R. A Christmas carol
c Mahlmann, L. and Jones, D. C. The Nutcracker Prince

The symbol *c* preceding an entry indicates that the play is intended for children at elementary school level, through grade six. The symbol *y* indentifies material for grades seven through twelve approximately.

Part II. Cast Analysis. This section is designed to help the user locate plays by type of cast (male, female, mixed, etc.) and number of players or readers. Specific directions for use of this section appear at the beginning of Part II.

Part III. List of Collections Indexed. This section provides information about the collections indexed, including publisher, date, pagination, ISBN designation, and Library of Congress control number when available.

Part IV. Directory of Publishers and Distributors. This section supplies full name and address of the publishers or distributors of the plays and collections cited in Parts I and III.

Play Index, 1993-1997

Part I

Author, Title, and Subject Index

1-900-desperate. Durang, C.

2. Linney, R.

2-2-tango. MacIvor, D.

2B WUT UR. Panych, M.

2 trains running. Wilson, A.

3 out. Bartel, R.

4-H Club. Shepard, S.

5 visits from Mr. Whitcomb. Bays, C. L.

7 blowjobs. Wellman, M.

9th inning wedding. May, B.

12-1-A. Yamauchi, W.

13 bells of Boglewood. Bush, M.

13 past midnight. St. John, B.

21A. Kling, K.

50 . . . and counting. Booth, J.

The **75th**. Horovitz, I.

1837: The Farmers' Revolt. Salutin, R. and Theatre Passe Muraille

1969. Landau, T.

1992: blood speaks. Colorado, E. and Colorado, H.

67201. Shank, A. E.

A

A . . . my name is still Alice. Silver, J. M. and Boyd, J.

Aalmauria: Voyage of the dragonfly. Bush, M.

Aba, Noureddine

Such great hope; or, The new song of a lost country

Former freedom fighter, after thirty year absence, returns to native Algeria torn apart by religious violence. 6 scenes Variable cast 13 characters 1 interior 3 exteriors

In Playwrights of exile: an international anthology

Abbie and Lou, Norman and Rose. O'Donoghue, J.

Abdoh, Reza

The law of remains

Experimental drama. Andy Warhol makes film about serial killer Jeffrey Dahmer in style of Bombay movie. 7 scenes 7m 7w 1 setting

In Plays for the end of the century; ed. by B. Marranca

Abducting Diana. Fo, D.

Abe, Kōbō

The ghost is here

Satire on modern life set in Japanese village. Ghosts exploited by entrepreneurs. 3 acts 18 scenes 7m 2w extras 1 setting

In Abe, K. Three plays

The green stockings

Parable about alienation. Experimental medical procedure turns lingerie fetishist into world's first human herbivore. Slide projections. 14 scenes 3m 3w extras 1 setting

In Abe, K. Three plays

Involuntary homicide

Series of bizarre events involve entire Japanese island community in murder. 11 scenes Variable cast 10 characters 1 setting

In Abe, K. Three plays

Abe and the runaways. See Watson, W. J. Abe Lincoln and the runaways

Abe Lincoln and the runaways. Watson, W. J.

Abe Lincoln for the defense. McCullough, L. E.

Abigail! Harris, R. C.

The **Abolition** Flyer. Lerman, L.

Abolitionists
Aiken, G. L. Uncle Tom's cabin
y Asher, S. F. A woman called Truth
Branch, W. In splendid error
c McCaslin, N. Prelude to fame

Abortion
Martin, J. Keely and Du
O'Neill, E. Abortion
Page, E. Aryan birth
Schwartz, D. Choosing company
Tolins, J. The twilight of the Golds

Abracadabra, Aladdin! Hughes, P.

Abraham. Mitterer, F.

Abraham Lincoln dies at Versailles. Prideaux, J.

Abroad (Split, Part 2). Weller, M.

The **absence** of war. Hare, D.

An **absolute** turkey. Feydeau, G.

Abstinence. Wilson, L.

Absurd, Theater of the. See Experimental theater

Acapulco (Mexico)
Berkoff, S. Acapulco

Accidental death of an anarchist. Fo, D.

According to Hoyle. Gaminara, W.

Accounts. Wilcox, M.

Acetylene. Ramsey, E.

Acharnians. Aristophanes

Ackerman, Marianne
L'affaire Tartuffe; or, The garrison officers rehearse Molière; with an introduction by Guy Spring. NuAge Eds. 1993 111p
Drama about language controversy in Montreal based on historical event. In 1774, British officers stationed in Montreal performed Molière in French. 2 acts 12 scenes 8m 3w extras 2 settings

Ackermann, Joan
The batting cage
Set in Florida Holiday Inn. Two sisters grieving for dead sibling try to reconcile differences. 2 acts 11 scenes 1m 3w 1 interior
In Humana Festival '96

Off the map
Coming-of-age tale. Woman recalls summer she was eleven and living with parents in Nevada desert. 2 acts 27 scenes 3m 2w 1g 1 setting
In Women playwrights: the best plays of 1994

Stanton's Garage. French 1994 94p
Small service station in upstate Missouri setting for interaction between locals and passing motorists. 2 acts 11 scenes 4m 4w 1 setting
—Same
In Humana Festival '93

Zara Spook and other lures. French 1993 88p
Comedy. Woman dreams of winning national women's bass fishing tournament. 2 acts 9 scenes 2m 4w 1 setting
—Same
In A Decade of new comedy: plays from the Humana Festival v1

Acquired immune deficiency syndrome. See AIDS (Disease)

Acrobats. Horovitz, I.

Acrobats and acrobatics
Horovitz, I. Acrobats

An **act** of devotion. Tannen, D.

Act of will. Polsky, M. E.

Acting
Durang, C. The actor's nightmare
MacIvor, D. This is a play

Acting exercise. Barnes, P.

Actors
Adamson, S. Clocks and whistles
Albee, E. Edward Albee's fragments
Barnes, P. Acting exercise
Barnes, P. Last things
Bartram, F. Tiddley pum
Beim, N. Dreams
Beim, N. On a darkling plain
Berkoff, S. Acapulco
Berkoff, S. Actor
Berkoff, S. Dahling you were marvellous
Booth, J. Echo of applause
Chekhov, A. Swan song
Childress, A. Trouble in mind
Dashow, K. Top of 16
Faulkner, A. For England and King George
Fols, C. Buck Simple
Gilroy, F. D. Real to reel
Gotanda, P. K. Yankee dawg you die
Greenberg, R. The author's voice
Guare, J. New York actor
Hardstack, M. The cure
Harper, T. That's the spirit
Harwood, R. The dresser
Linney, R. Yancey
Margulies, D. L.A.
Oates, J. C. The rehearsal

Actors—*Continued*
Phelan, B. Himself
Rattigan, T. Harlequinade
Rudnick, P. Jeffrey
Warner, F. Maquettes for the requiem: Lumen
West, M. The pleasure man
Whelan, P. Shakespeare country
Wyld, H. Night's candles
See also Actresses; Entertainers; Theater; and names of real actors, e.g. Booth, Junius Brutus, 1796-1852

The **actor's** nightmare. Durang, C.

Actresses
Barnes, P. Humour helps
Barrie, J. M. Rosalind
Beard, J. A. Vladivostok blues
Beim, N. Dreams
Beim, N. Jewel thieves!
Bell, N. On the bum
Berkoff, S. Dahling you were marvellous
Booth, J. Sleeping arrangements
Chekhov, A. The seagull
Childress, A. Trouble in mind
Chinn, J. In by the half
Conde, M. The Tropical Breeze Hotel
Cooperman, D. Miss Temptation
Crane, R. Under the stars
De Angelis, A. Playhouse creatures
Friedman, R. All for art
Fuentes, C. Orchids in the moonlight
Gilbert, S. Lola Starr builds her dream home
Granville-Barker, H. Farewell to the theatre
Greth, R. Curtain call
Hare, D. Amy's view
Hughes, L. Scarlet Sister Barry
Kilroy, T. The seagull
Laird, M. Ruthless!
Laughton, V. The mourning after
Linney, R. Juliet
Lloyd Webber, A. Sunset Boulevard
MacLeod, J. The Hope slide
Margulies, D. Pitching to the star
Medoff, M. Stumps
Mercer, D. An afternoon at the festival
Munro, R. The maiden stone
Murray-Smith, J. Love child
Oates, J. C. The rehearsal
Orr, M. The wisdom of Eve
Pedrero, P. A night divided
Pinero, A. W. Trelawny of the 'Wells'
Pintauro, J. Ten-dollar drinks
Rattigan, T. Harlequinade
Shanley, J. P. Four dogs and a bone
Shengold, N. Lives of the great waitresses
Simon, N. London suite: Diana and Sidney
Stroppel, F. Package deal
Taikeff, S. Dolorosa Sanchez
Warner, F. Maquettes for the requiem: Lumen
Winer, D. G. The last girl singer
Wong, E. China doll
Wooten, J. J. The role of Della
See also Actors; Entertainers; Theater; and names of real actresses, e.g. Bernhardt, Sarah

Acts of love and other comedies. Taylor, R. and Bologna, J.

Acworth, Elaine
Composing Venus. Currency Press 1995 86p
Drama portraying lives of three generations of women living in North Queensland outback. 2 parts 4m 7w 1 setting

Adam, Agnes
Between two thieves. Players Press 1996 27p
Drama about old women in Scottish nursing home. 1 act 7w extras 1 interior

Birds of prey. Players Press 1996 32p
Comedy in Scottish dialect about two gossipy women. 1 act 5w 1 interior

A bit of land. Players Press 1996 26p
Comedy set in 1880 Ireland. Farmer enlists friend in scheme to procure inheritance. 1 act 4m 2w 1 interior

Business meeting. Players Press 1996 23p
Comedy about annual business meeting of church women's guild. 6w 1 interior

A cameo from Cranford. Players Press 1996 26p
Comedy revolving around spinsters in 1840 provincial Scottish town. 6w 1 interior

Castles in the air. Players Press 1996 28p
Comedy about two middle-aged spinsters in Scottish village. 1 act 8w 1 interior

Christmas. Players Press 1996 28p
Set in village in Scotland. Christmas night brings understanding to widow and neighbors. 1 act 8w 1 interior

A great occasion. Players Press 1996 30p
Drama in Scottish dialect. Confrontation between elderly woman and niece at birthday party. 1 act 6w 1 interior

A matter of diplomacy. Players Press 1996 26p
Comedy in Scottish dialect about parents bickering over daughter's marriage. 1 act 2m 3w 1 interior

Adam, Agnes—*Continued*

A pearl of great price. Players Press 1996 27p

Comedy in Scottish dialect. When domineering wife's first husband, thought dead, returns from sea, he and present husband decide who will remain with her. 2m 3w 1 interior

Adam (Biblical figure)

y Perry, E. E. Once upon a beginning

Adam. Sobol, J.

Adamov, Arthur

Professor Taranne (Le professeur Taranne); tr. by Albert Bermel

Tragifarce set in police station and hotel office about nightmarish experiences of French professor. 2 scenes 10m 4w 2 interiors

In A Dozen French farces; ed. by A. Bermel

Adams, Gill

Lonely hearts. Warner Chappell Plays 1996 86p

Bittersweet drama about relationships and romance spanning twenty years in lives of four friends. Prologue 2 acts 2m 2w 1 interior

Off out. Warner Chappell Plays 1994 98p

Drama about seedy and dangerous world of male and female prostitution in contemporary Scotland. 2 acts 21 scenes 2m 2w 1 interior

Adams, John, 1735-1826

c Smith, B. S. Adams for the defense

Adams for the defense. Smith, B. S.

Adamson, Samuel

Clocks and whistles. Amber Lane Press 1996 111p

Portrays sexual and emotional confusion among friends in London's artistic community. 20 scenes 3m 2w 1 setting

Grace note. Amber Lane Press 1997 96p

Drama set in West London. Behind facade of genteel senility, woman develops understanding with daughter-in-law as family gathers to protect their inheritance. 2 acts 11 scenes 3m 3w 1 interior

Addison, Joseph

Cato. Players Press 1996 57p

18th century English tragedy in verse. Life and death of Cato the Younger during Roman civil war, 49 B.C. Prologue 5 acts 8 scenes epilogue 8m 2w

Adkins, Donald

c Ready steady go; a play by Sandra Redmond; music by Donald Adkins. Anchorage Press 1995 56p

Musical. Dolls unite to defeat greedy rats. 6m 6w 1 interior

Adler, Marion. See Bohmler, C. jt. auth.

The **admirable** Crichton. Olfson, L.

Adolescence

Ackermann, J. Off the map
y Allaway, B. Makin' it
y Astón, M. Fossils!
Bingham, S. Milk of paradise
y Clark, R. J. Fighting for myself
y Cowell, M. Song for the navigator
Cruz, M. The have-little
y Curran, K. T. The First Time Club
y Deverell, R. Switching places
Donaghy, T. Down the shore
Foote, H. Laura Dennis
y Francoeur, B. The internal machine
y Frost, R.; Olson, G. and Johnson, L. No means no!
y Fuson, D. Clippings
y Gibbs, P. Lockie Leonard, human torpedo
Gurney, A. R. What I did last summer
y Harder, E. Rememberin' stuff
Harvey, J. Beautiful thing
Johanson, R. Charles Dickens' Great expectations
Korder, H. Fun
Kravitz, A. Just thinking
Lane, E. Dancing on Checker's grave
y Lazarus, J. Secrets
y Leader, J. Land slides
MacLeod, J. Little sister
MacLeod, W. The shallow end
Martin, J. The boy who ate the moon
Martin, J. Summer
y Mason, T. Ascension day
y Mason, T. The less than human club
Morris, M. Boss of the pool
Moxley, G. Danti-Dan
Nyswaner, R. Reservoir
Osment, P. What I did in the holidays
y Panych, M. 2B WUT UR
y Panych, M. Cost of living
y Panych, M. Life science
Peterson, L. Take a giant step
y Rideout, G. Texas boy
Sherman, J. M. Serendipity and serenity
y Slaight, B. Class action
y Slaight, B. High tide
y Slaight, B. Sightings
Sod, T. and Grant, S. Three wishes
Solórzano, C. The shoe
y Soto, G. Novio boy
y Tobin, S. Cotton girls
Townsend, S. The secret diary of Adrian Mole aged 13¾
Wedekind, F. Spring awakening
Wilcox, M. Lent
y Williams, B. In the garden of the witch

See also Boys; Girls; Youth

Adoption
Houston, V. H. As sometimes in a dead man's face
Machiavelli, N. Clizia
Murray-Smith, J. Love child

Adrian, Yvonne
Flyboy
Surreal look at world from perspective of eight-year-old boy. Prologue 1 act 12 scenes 3m 2w 1b 1 setting
In EST marathon '95

Adult child/dead child. Dowie, C.

Adultery
Allen, W. Central Park West
Baker, E. A. A dead man's apartment
Barnes, D. An Irish triangle
Barnes, P. Not as bad as they seem
Benfield, D. Anyone for breakfast?
Bruce, L. Keyboard skills
Buzo, A. Rooted
Carr, M. Portia Coughlan
De Filippo, E. Grand magic
Dietz, S. Private eyes
Donnelly, N. The duty master
Edmundson, H. Anna Karenina
Gersten, A. My thing of love
Gilroy, F. D. Match point
Gray, S. Molly
Gray, S. Otherwise engaged
Gray, S. Plaintiffs and defendants
Gray, S. Stage struck
Hare, D. Skylight
Harrower, D. Knives in hens
Havel, V. The increased difficulty of concentration
Huth, A. The trouble with old lovers
Isitt, D. The woman who cooked her husband
Kyle, C. The monogamist
Linney, R. Shotgun
McConnell, J. Late frost
Middleton, T. A mad world, my masters
Minghella, A. A little like drowning
Minghella, A. What if it's raining?
Molière. The imaginary cuckold
Moore, C. M. Love's light in flight
Murray-Smith, J. Honour
Nagy, P. The scarlet letter
O'Neill, E. Recklessness
Otway, T. The soldiers' fortune
Pen, P. Bed and sofa
Pintauro, J. Two eclairs
Pinter, H. Betrayal
Pinter, H. Moonlight
Ranson, R. Blood on blood
Reynolds, J. Dance with me
Sade, Marquis de. The bedroom
Schnitzler, A. The big scene
Shank, A. E. 67201
Slade, B. Same time, another year
Smith, L. Sins of the father
Spence, E. Undertow
Stoppard, T. Teeth
Vago, S. M. An ordinary woman under stress
Vickery, F. Erogenous zones
Warner, F. Lying figures
Waterhouse, K. Our song
Whelan, P. The herbal bed
Wright, D. Watbanaland

Adventure and adventurers
Francis, M. The prisoner of Zenda
Hall, W. The three musketeers
y Leech, M. T. The Scarlet Pimpernel
Rubess, B. Oblivion: a story of Isabelle Eberhardt

Adventures in the country. See Goldoni, C. Villeggiatura: Adventures in the country

The **adventures** of Anansi: "How Anansi helped a fisherman." Gerke, P.

The **adventures** of Anansi: "How the world got wisdom." Gerke, P.

The **adventures** of Anansi: "Why Anansi lives in ceilings." Gerke, P.

The **adventures** of Peter Rabbit and his friends. Robinette, J.

The **adventures** of Pinocchio. Collodi, C. (dramatization) See Roca, M. Pinocchio

The **adventures** of Tom Sawyer. Twain, M. (dramatization) See Hackett, W. Tom Sawyer, whitewasher

Adventures with young King Arthur. Stites, K.

Advertising
Carmichael, F. Meet my husbands
Godber, J. The office party
Shengold, N. Finger food

Advertising Arnold. Law, M.

Aerenson, Benjie
Lighting up the two-year-old
Personal conflicts and shady dealings in horse racing circles. 2 acts 3 scenes 4m 1 setting
In Humana Festival '97

Aeschylus
Agamemnon; tr. by S. H. Landes. Players Press 1995 56p
First play in Oresteia trilogy. Greek classical drama in verse. Based on legend of murder of Agamemnon by his wife and her lover after the Trojan War. Speaking chorus
The Persians (adaptation) See Auletta, R. The Persians

Aeschylus—*Continued*
Seven against Thebes; tr. by Robert Emmet Meagher. Bolchazy-Carducci Pubs. 1996 44p
Greek tragedy in verse. Battle between sons of Oedipus for sovereignty of Thebes. Speaking chorus
About
Aristophanes. Frogs

The **affairs** of Dilys Willis. Walker, D.

Affections of an alley cat. Calhoun, W.

The **affections** of May. Foster, N.

Afghanistan
History—Occupation, 1979-
Mastrosimone, W. Nanawatai!

Africa
c Artist, V. A. The clever Maakafi
Harnetiaux, B. The snows of Kilimanjaro
Mercer, D. The Governor's lady
Native peoples
Onwueme, O. T. Tell it to women

Africa, South. See South Africa

Africa, West. See West Africa

African American soldiers
Brown, C. Buffalo Hair
Burrill, M. P. Aftermath
Fuller, C. A soldier's play
c McCullough, L. E. Ninth Cavalry to the rescue!

African Americans
Aiken, G. L. Uncle Tom's cabin
Alexander, R. I ain't yo' uncle
Baraka, A. Dutchman
Bartley, J. Stephen & Mr. Wilde
Bass, G. H. Black masque: the passion of darkie's bones
Bonner, M. O. The purple flower
Braithwaite, D. Martha and Elvira
Bronson, J. G. Willie & Esther
Brown, C. The African Company presents Richard III
Brown, C. The Little Tommy Parker Celebrated Colored Minstrel Show
Brown, W. W. The escape
Bullins, E. In the wine time
Burrill, M. P. They that sit in darkness
Caldwell, B. Prayer meeting
Carlos, L. White chocolate for my father
Childress, A. Trouble in mind
Childress, A. Wine in the wilderness
Clarke, B. and Dickerson, G. Re/membering Aunt Jemima: a menstrual show
Cleage, P. Chain
Cleage, P. Late bus to Mecca
Corbitt, W. Crying holy
Corthron, K. Cage rhythm
Corthron, K. Come down burning
Cummings, B. Your obituary is a dance
Dashow, K. Sing this
Davis, T. The life and times of Malcolm X
Dean, P. H. Dink's blues
Dean, P. H. The owl killer
Dean, P. H. The Sty of The Blind Pig
Dodson, O. Bayou legend
Dunbar, P. L. and Shipp, J. A. In Dahomey
Edmonds, S. R. Old man Pete
Edward, H. F. V. Job hunters
Edwards, G. The offering
Elder, L. Ceremonies in dark old men
Evans, D. One monkey don't stop no show
Feldshuh, D. Miss Evers' boys
Fornes, M. I. Springtime
Fornes, M. I. What of the night?: Springtime
Franklin, J. E. Christchild
Franklin, J. E. Miss Honey's young'uns
Franklin, J. E. Two mens'es daughter
Freeman, B.; Branner, D. and Gupton, E. Fierce love
Gaines-Shelton, R. A. The church fight
Gardner, H. I'm not Rappaport
Gilbert, M. Environment
Glover, K. Dancing on moonlight
Graham, S. It's morning
Graham, S. Track thirteen
Greer, B. Munda negra
Grimké, A. W. Rachel
Hansberry, L. A raisin in the sun
Harrison, P. C. The great MacDaddy
Hazzard, A. Mother liked it
Heelan, K. Distant fires
Horovitz, I. Morning
Hughes, L. Don't you want to be free?
Hughes, L. The Em-Fuehrer Jones
Hughes, L. Limitations of life
Hughes, L. Mulatto
Hughes, L. Simply heavenly
Hughes, L. Soul gone home
y Hunkins, L. Freedom is my middle name
Jackson, J. A. WOMBmanWARs
Jackson, M. A. Sisters
Jennings, C. S. Sunday dinner
Johnson, J. P. and Hughes, L. The organizer
Jones, L. Combination skin
Jones, R. Big butt girls, hard-headed women
Jones, T. W. The wizard of hip

African Americans—*Continued*
Kai, N. Harvest the frost
Kearns, M. Myron, a fairy tale in black and white
Kennedy, A. Funnyhouse of a Negro
Kennedy, A. P. and Kennedy, A. Sleep deprivation chamber
Lebow, B. The keepers
Lee, L. The first breeze of summer
Livingston, M. S. For unborn children
Mann, E. Having our say
Martin, J. Shasta Rue
Mason, K. A. For black boys who have considered homicide when the streets were too much
Mastrosimone, W. Tamer of horses
McCauley, R. Sally's rape
McClinton, M. Stones and bones
Meadows, K. J. Henrietta
Minjares, J. The king of the kosher grocers
Moore, C. M. Love's light in flight
Oates, J. C. Black
Oates, J. C. Negative
O'Neal, J. and Watkins, N. B. You can't judge a book by looking at the cover: sayings from the life and writings of Junebug Jabbo Jones: v2
O'Neill, E. All God's chillun got wings
Oyamo. I am a man
Parks, S.-L. The America play
Parks, S.-L. The death of the last black man in the whole entire world
Parris-Bailey, L. Dark cowgirls and prairie queens
Penny, R. Good black don't crack
Perry, S. In Dahomey
Rahman, A. The mojo and the sayso
Richardson, W. The chip woman's fortune
Richardson, W. The deacon's awakening
Richardson, W. A pillar of the church
Russell, C. Five on the black hand side
y Satchell, M. The secret gifts
Schmidt, E. Mr. Rickey calls a meeting
Silvera, J. D. and Hill, A. Liberty deferred
Simonson, E. Bang the drum slowly
Smith, A. D. Fires in the mirror: Crown Heights, Brooklyn and other identities
Smith, A. D. Twilight: Los Angeles, 1992
Smith, C. Freefall
Stickney, P. Y. Big Momma 'n 'em
Taylor, R. Inside the belly of the beast
Taylor, R. Mudtracks
Taylor, R. Watermelon rinds
Toomer, J. Balo
United States Food Administration. Why we are at war
Vance, D. Live and in color!
Walker, J. The River Niger
Ward, D. T. Day of absence
Ward, T. Big white fog
Ward, T. Our lan'
Wesley, R. The talented tenth
West, C. L. Before it hits home
West, C. L. Jar the floor
Wilder, T. Bernice
Wilks, T. Tod, the boy Tod
Wilson, A. Joe Turner's come and gone
Wilson, A. Ma Rainey's black bottom
Wilson, A. Seven guitars
Wilson, A. Two trains running
Wolfe, G. C. The colored museum
Wong, E. Kimchee and chitlins
Woodard, C. Pretty fire
Wright, R. and Green, P. Native son
Youngblood, S. Talking bones
Youngblood, S. There are many houses in my tribe
See also Blacks

Civil rights

c Fisher, A. I have a dream
Friedman, S. Freedom days
Nicholas, D. Buses
Shine, T. Contribution
Stetson, J. The meeting

Arkansas

Burris, A. M. You mus' be bo'n ag'in

France

Aldridge, I. The black doctor

Georgia

Matheus, J. F. 'Cruiter
Toomer, J. Balo

Kansas

Cleage, P. Flyin' west

Kentucky

McCarthy, C. The stonemason

Los Angeles (Calif.)

Bullins, E. Goin' a Buffalo

Louisiana

Mason, J. A. Daughters of the mock

Maryland

Davis, O. Escape to freedom
Glover, K. Coming of the Hurricane

Michigan

Medley, C. Dearborn Heights

New England

Peterson, L. Take a giant step

African Americans—*Continued*
New York (N.Y.)
Baldwin, J. The amen corner
Coleman, R. M. The girl from back home
Dunbar-Nelson, A. Mine eyes have seen
Edward, H. F. V. Job hunters
Hill, A. On Strivers Row
Schuyler, G. S. The yellow peril
Spence, E. Undertow
Ward, T. Big white fog
San Francisco
Anderson, G. Appearances
Southern States
Dove, R. The darker face of the earth
Johnson, G. D. A Sunday morning in the South
Johnson, F. H. Run little chillun
Mitchell, J. S. Son-Boy
Seiler, C. Darker brother
Uhry, A. Driving Miss Daisy
Williams, S.-A. Home
Youngblood, S. Shakin' the mess outta misery
Virginia
Pawley, T. The tumult and the shouting
West Virginia
Browne, T. Natural man
y Winther, B. John Henry

The **African** Company presents Richard III. Brown, C.

Africans
France
Tilly. A modest proposal

After all. Canby, V.

After Easter. Devlin, A.

After Magritte. Stoppard, T.

After Miss Julie. Marber, P.

After-play. Meara, A.

After September. Chinn, J.

After the child. Mead, K.

After the dance. Rattigan, T.

After the fall. Miller, A.

After the lions. Harwood, R.

Afterhours. Brownell, R.

Aftermath. Burrill, M. P.

Afternoon at Tavern MacTavish. Hogg, F. A.

An **afternoon** at the festival. Mercer, D.

Afternoon of the elves. York, Y.

Agamemnon (Greek mythology)
Aeschylus. Agamemnon
Euripides. Iphigenia in Aulis
Rabe, D. The orphan

Agnes. LaChiusa, M. J.

Agoraphobia
Dulaney, M. The view from here
Mead, K. Crying out loud
Townsend, S. Bazaar & rummage

Ahearn, John. See Valenti, M. Beauty and the beast

AIDS (Disease)
Blessing, L. Patient A
Berg, R. AIDS! the musical!
Bumbalo, V. Show
Bumbalo, V. What are Tuesdays like?
Corbitt, W. Crying holy
Cummings, B. Your obituary is a dance
y Curran, KT. The First Time Club
Dietz, S. Lonely planet
Donaghy, T. The dadshuttle
Elyot, K. My night with Reg
Finn, W. and Lapine, J. Falsettoland
Fornes, M. I. Enter the night
Harding, A. Blood and honour
Hoffman, W. M. As is
Holsclaw, D. The baddest of boys
Kearns, M. Myron, a fairy tale in black and white
Kramer, L. The destiny of me
Kramer, L. The normal heart
Kushner, T. Angels in America: Pt.1: Millennium approaches
Kushner, T. Angels in America: Pt.2: Perestroika
Lee, J. A. Coming home
Lucas, C. Bad dream
MacLeod, J. The Hope slide
McNally, T. Andre's mother
Miller, T. My queer body
Mitterer, F. Abraham
Oates, J. C. The rehearsal
O'Connor, C. All that he was ...
Pendleton, A. Uncle Bob
Pickett, J. C. Queen of Angels
Rintoul, H. Brave hearts
Rodriguez, Y. Rising sun, falling star
Rudnick, P. Jeffrey
Russell, B. Elegies for angels, punks and raging queens
Schwartz, S. Vito on the beach
Silver, N. Pterodactyls
Silverman, J. L. Correct address

AIDS (Disease)—*Continued*
Sod, T. Satan and Simon Desoto
y Sorensen, K. An endangered species: waking up
Storey, R. The saints and apostles
y Thomas, C. Flesh and blood
Vogel, P. The Baltimore waltz
West, C. L. Before it hits home
Wilson, L. A poster of the cosmos
Yew, C. A language of their own

AIDS! the musical! Berg, R.

Aiken, George L.
Uncle Tom's cabin; or, Life among the lowly
Based on Harriet Beecher Stowe's novel about slavery and freedom. 6 acts 30 scenes 20m 7w 1b 8 interiors 8 exteriors
In Early American drama; ed. by J. H. Richards

Air pilots
Koch, K. The Red Robins

Airplanes
Burns, K. Identity crisis
Burns, K. On hold at 30,000 feet
Burns, K. Terminal terror
Shepard, S. Icarus's mother

Airports
Rector, M. H. The lady and the commissioner of airports

Akerman, Anthony
Somewhere on the border
Anti-war drama dealing with South Africa's 1978 invasion of Angola. 2 acts 9 scenes 7m 2 settings
In South Africa plays; ed. by S. Gray

Akmatova, Anna Andreevna
Linney, R. Three poets: Akhmatova

Aladdin. Cregan, D.

Aladdin. Edgar, K.

Aladdin. Mahlmann, L. and Jones, D. C.

Aladdin and his wonderful lamp (dramatization) See Hughes, P. Abracadabra, Aladdin!

Aladdin and the wonderful lamp. Neary, J.

Alám, Juan Shamsul
Zookeeper
Drama set in East Harlem, 1989. Puerto Rican man caught between needs of dying brother and those of wife and daughters. 1 act 2m 1 interior
In Nuestro New York; ed. by J. V. Antush

al-'Ani, Yusuf
The key; tr. by Salwa Jabsheh and Alan Brownjohn
Series of tableaux based on Arab folklore about young couple's quest for secure life with baby. Incorporates political commentary and folk songs. 2 prologues 2 parts 12 scenes 2m 1w extras 1 setting
In Modern Arabic drama; ed. by S. K. Jayyusi and R. Allen

Alas! Alack! Zorro's back. Reiser, D.

Alaska
c McCullough, L. E. Klondike fever

Albee, Edward
Edward Albee's fragments. Dramatists 1995 57p
Abstract theater piece. Eight actors tell stories in attempt to reveal their characters. 2 acts 4m 4w 1 setting
Edward Albee's Marriage play. Dramatists 1995 41p
Husband and wife discuss dissolution of 30 year marriage that has survived infidelity, familiarity and boredom. 1m 1w 1 interior
Finding the sun. Dramatists 1994 39p
Drama set at beach explores aging, marriage, bisexuality and death. 1 act 21 scenes 4m 4w 1 exterior
Three tall women. Dramatists 1994 57p
Dowager, her secretary, and her lawyer depict one woman at three stages of her life. 2 acts 1m 3w 1 interior
—Same. Dutton 1995 110p
—Same
In Plays for actresses; ed. by E. Lane and N. Shengold
Three tall women (condensation)
In The Best plays of 1993-1994

Albert, Sandra J.
How many to tango?
Romantic comedy about couple who finally meet after having only talked by phone. 3 scenes 1m 1w 3 interiors
In Off-Off Broadway Festival plays, 18th ser.

Albert make us laugh. Chinn, J.

Albert Victor, Duke of Clarence and Avondale, 1864-1892
Pollock, S. Saucy Jack

Albert's bridge. Stoppard, T.

Alcestis. Euripides

Alcoholics
Ayckbourn, A. A chorus of disapproval
y Beechy High School Drama Club. Me 'n' Alfred
Bozzone, B. Sonny DeRee's life flashes before his eyes

Alcoholics—*Continued*
Cardinal, V. J. The Colorado catechism
Cartwright, J. Road
Colón, O. A. Siempre en mi corazón
Crawford, D. W. Tangled garden
Geoghan, J. Light sensitive
Hughes, D. Digging for fire
Lennon, G. Blackout
Lichtig, R. R. Queen for a day
Linney, R. Paradise
McPherson, C. Rum and vodka
Oates, J. C. Black
O'Neill, E. The iceman cometh
y Parker, R. Under the influence
Pollock, D. Doc
Potter, D. Karaoke
Quinn, L. Well done poets
Reddin, K. Brutality of fact
Sears, J. Eddie Lee, Eddie Lee
Smith, W. H. The drunkard
Thomas, E. East from the Gantry
Upton, J. Bruises

Alcoholism. See Alcoholics

Alcott, Louisa May
Little women (dramatization) See Morley, O. J. Little women

Alderete, Betty. See McDonough, J. jt. auth.

Aldrich, Arthur
The housewarming. French (London) 1994 30p

Thriller. Young couple discovers that their new home has history of ghostly intrigue. 2 scenes 1m 3w 1 interior

Aldridge, Ira
The black doctor

Tragedy. Dignified black doctor falls in love and secretly marries French aristocrat, but family and societal conflict lead to his death. 4 acts 7 scenes 7m 6w extras 4 interiors 3 exteriors

In Black theatre USA [vl]; ed. by J. V. Hatch and T. Shine

Alette, Carl
c The secret garden; a musical based on the book by Frances Hodgson Burnett; adapted by R. Eugene Jackson; music by Carl Alette. Clark, I.E. 1993 58p

Orphaned girl and invalid cousin are restored to health and happiness as they tend secret garden. 13 scenes 3m 3w 2b 1g extras 1 setting

Alexander the Great, 356-323 B.C.
Lyly, J. Campaspe

Alexander, Robert
I ain't yo' uncle

Author Harriett Beecher Stowe on trial for creating and perpetuating black stereotypes. Prologue 6 acts 24 scenes 14m 10w settings

In Colored contradictions: an anthology of contemporary African-American plays

Alexandria, Egypt

Siege, 48-47 B.C.

See Alexandrine War, 48-47 B.C.

Alexandrine War, 48-47 B.C.
Shaw, B. Caesar and Cleopatra

Algeria
Aba, N. Such great hope
Gallaire, F. You have come back
Strindberg, A. Simoom
Wertenbaker, T. New anatomies

Ali Baba and the Forty Thieves. Mahlmann, L. and Jones, D. C.

'Ali Janah al-Tabrizi and his servant Quffa. Farag, A.

Alianak, Hrant
Passion and sin

Experimental theater set in 1957 Cuba explores relationship between sex and violence. Background music. 10 scenes 3m 3w 1 setting

In The *CTR* anthology; ed. by A. Filewod

Alice in bed. Sontag, S.

Alice in Wonderland. Rochelle, R.

Alice's adventures in Wonderland. Mahlmann, L. and Jones, D. C.

Alice's adventures under ground. Hampton, C.

An **alien** stole my skateboard. Lewton, R.

Alienation (Social psychology)
Abe, K. The green stockings
Donald, S. The life of stuff
Gray, S. Otherwise engaged
Gray, S. Simply disconnected
Treadwell, S. Machinal
Turrini, P. Shooting rats
Wertenbaker, T. New anatomies

All fall down. Lill, W.

All for art. Friedman, R.

All for love. Dryden, J.

All for one. Weitz, P.

All God's chillun got wings. O'Neill, E.

All he fears. Barker, H.

All in the timing (condensation). Ives, D.

All my husbands. Feydeau, G. and Devalliers, M.

All Souls. Keene, D.

All Souls' Day

c Vigil, A. El Dia de los Muertos. The Fiesta of the Day of the Dead

All that glitters . . . McDonough, V. M.

All that he was . . . O'Connor, C.

All the tricks but one. Segal, G.

All things considered. Brown, B.

Allais, Alphonse

The poor beggar and the fairy godmother (Le pauvre bougre et le bon génie); tr. by Norman R. Shapiro

Tragic farce set in turn of century Paris. Sketch of beggar's state of mind before during and after encounter with fairy godmother. 2m 1w 1 exterior

In A Flea in her rear and other vintage French farces!

Allard, Janet

y Painted rain

Drama. Handicapped teenager faces crisis when younger foster care "brother" is adopted. 1 act 4 scenes 1m 1w 1b 1 interior

In Short plays for young actors; ed. by C. Slaight and J. Sharrar

Allaway, Ben

y Makin' it (the musical); book by Cynthia Mercati; music by Ben Allaway; lyrics by Ben Allaway and Cynthia Mercati. Bakers Plays 1993 106p

Musical. High school students cope with problems of adolescence. 2 acts 11 scenes Large mixed cast

Allegories

Basso, E. Joseph in the underground
Basso, E. Middle distance
Bonner, M. O. The purple flower
Césaire, M. The ship
Dorfman, A. Widows
Everyman
Harrison, P. C. The great MacDaddy
Horovitz, I. Rats
Howles, L. The king's highway
Koch, K. The Red Robins
Lyly, J. Gallathea
Mankind. A critical edition of the medieval play Mankind
Mitterer, F. Dragon thirst
Mitterer, F. One everyman
Murphy, T. Bailegangaire
Németh, Á. Müller's dancers
Shepard, S. States of shock
y Swortzell, L. Lucky Peter's journey
c Thain, P. Stone soup
White, P. Signal driver
Williams, N. William Golding's Lord of the flies

Allen, Claudia

Ripe conditions. Dramatic 1994 54p

Comedy set in rural Michigan during tornado season. Bumbling brothers visited by attractive, widowed sister-in-law. 2 acts 2m 1w 1 interior

Blue cities

Television dance play about the afterlife. Murderer seeks admittance to paradise. 2m 2w

In Allen, R. J. What to name your baby

What to name your baby

Text for video dance piece. Thoughts of expectant parents awaiting birth of child. 7 scenes 1m 1w 1b

In Allen, R. J. What to name your baby

Allen, Woody

Central Park West

Comedy about adultery and May-September affair on Manhattan's Upper West Side. 2m 3w 1 interior

In Death defying acts

Allman, Sheldon, and Pickett, Bob

y Frankenstein unbound; another monster musical. Dramatic 1995 75p

Musical comedy. Sequel to I'm sorry the bridge is out, you'll have to spend the night. Dr. Frankenstein succeeds in transferring boy's brain to monster and vice versa. Music, singing. 2 acts 11m 3w extras 2 interiors

All-wondrous. La Roche-Guilhen, A. de

All's well that ends wrong. Kachejian, G.

Almost done. Mamet, D.

Alpine glow. Turrini, P.

Alvarez, Lynne

y Eddie Mundo Edmundo

Following mother's death Mexican American travels to Mexico to explore his heritage. Singing, dancing. 2 acts 25 scenes 3m 3w 1b 1 setting

In New plays from A.C.T.'S young conservatory v2

The reincarnation of Jaimie Brown

Black comedy about sex, suicide, hair loss and reincarnation. 2 acts 5m 3w settings

In Women playwrights: the best plays of 1994

Who is chasing whom!

Series of scenes without words in which physical expression is sole form of communication. Music. Unidentified cast 2 characters 1 setting

In Short plays for young actors; ed. by C. Slaight and J. Sharrar

Always together. Visdei, A.

Amazing Grace. Pope, R.

Ambition

Hill, A. On Strivers Row
Weitz, P. All for one

Amboyna. Dryden, J.

Ambrosio. Linney, R.

Ambush. High, B. G.

Amelia and the man. Lang, C.

The **amen** corner. Baldwin, J.

Ameriasians
Houston, V. H. As sometimes in a dead man's face

The **America** play. Parks, S.-L.

The **American** century. Guyer, M.

The **American** clock. Miller, A.

American drama

Colonial period

Warren, M. The Group

Revolutionary period

Tyler, R. The contrast

19th century

Aiken, G. L. Uncle Tom's cabin
Barker, J. N. The Indian princess
Bird, R. M. The gladiator
Boucicault, D. Octoroon
Mowatt, A. C. Fashion
Smith, W. H. The drunkard

American dreamers. Mueller, L.

American enterprise (condensation). Sweet, J.

American loyalists
Warren, M. The Group

The **American** plan. Greenberg, R.

An **American** story. Morris, A. J.

Americans

Asia

Koch, K. The Red Robins

Austria

Marans, J. Old wicked songs

Canada

y Rideout, G. Texas boy

Costa Rica

Milner, A. Zero hour

England

Glore, J. The company of heaven
Greer, B. Munda negra
Kennedy, A. The dramatic circle
Simon, N. London suite: Going home
Simon, N. London suite: The man on the floor
Whelan, P. Shakespeare country

France

Horovitz, I. My old lady
Prideaux, J. Abraham Lincoln dies at Versailles

Germany

Horovitz, I. The honest-to-god schnozzola

Hungary

Fornes, M. I. The Danube

India

McNally, T. A perfect Ganesh

Ireland

Cahill, S. Ballycastle

Italy

Crowley, M. For reasons that remain unclear
Guare, J. Four baboons adoring the sun

Japan

Houston, V. H. Asa ga kimashita (Morning has broken)
McDonough, J. Butterfly

Mexico

GeBauer, J. The nip and the bite

Middle East

McGuinness, F. Someone who'll watch over me

Russia

Lawrence, J. and Lee, R. E. A call on Kuprin

Scotland

Hogg, F. A. Afternoon at Tavern MacTavish

South Africa

Baitz, J. R. A fair country

Spain

Winer, D. G. The last girl singer

Americansaint. LeFevre, A.

Amphibious spangulatos. Doust, P.

Amphitryon (Greek mythology)
Dryden, J. Amphitryon
Molière. Amphitryon
Plautus, T. M. Amphitryon

Amusement parks
Horovitz, I. Shooting gallery

Amy's attic. Shurtz, R. K.

Amy's view. Hare, D.

Ancestress. O'Brien, J. T.

Ancient history. Ives, D.

And baby makes seven. Vogel, P.

And death brought forth the light. Solórzano, C.

And Fat Freddy's blues. Barry, P. J.

And go to Innisfree. Toddie, J. L.

And the soul shall dance. Yamauchi, W.

And the tide shall cover the earth. Cole, N.

And who will pay the rent? Mead, K.

Andersen, Hans Christian
The Emperor's nightingale (dramatization) See Mahlmann, L. and Jones, D. C. The Emperor's nightingale
The little fir tree (dramatization) See Woyiwada, A. The little fir tree
The little mermaid (dramatization) See Daugherty, L. The little mermaid
The Nightingale (dramatization) See Lazarus, J. The Nightingale
The princess and the pea (dramatization) See Miller, H. L. The princess and the pea
c The Snow Queen (dramatization) See Kennedy, R. Hans Christian Andersen's The Snow Queen; Nicol, R. The Snow Queen
Thumbelina (dramatization) See Morris, V. Thumbelina
The tinder box (dramatization) See Whelan, P. The tinder box

Anderson, Eliza
That all of us should be fed
Set in New England, 1920. Reclusive woman confides in neighbor. 2w 1 exterior
In Actors Theatre of Louisville. Ten-minute plays: v3

Anderson, Garland
Appearances
Black bellboy's honesty is rewarded when he is exonerated from false accusation in attack of woman. His virtues serve as model for hotel residents in early 20th century San Francisco. Prologue 3 acts 14m 4w 2 exteriors
In Black theatre USA [v1]; ed. by J. V. Hatch and T. Shine

Anderson, James
c The animals' Christmas. New Playwrights Network 1996 16p
Television reporters question animal witnesses to birth of Christ. 2 parts Variable cast 13 characters 1 interior

Anderson, Jane
The last time we saw her
Lesbian employee seeks male supervisor's approval to disclose her sexual orientation. 1m 1w 1 interior
In Actors Theatre of Louisville. Ten-minute plays: v3
In Humana Festival '94

Lynette at 3 AM
Woman having difficulties with boyfriend has supernatural encounter. 1 act 2m 1w 1 interior
In Showtime's Act One Festival of one-act plays, 1994

Lynette has beautiful skin
Three youths hanging out in pizza parlor. 2m 1w 1 interior
In Actors Theatre of Louisville. Ten-minute plays: v3

Tough choices for the new century. French 1996 37p
Black comedy about disaster preparedness seminar. 1m 1w
—Same
In 20/20: twenty one-act plays from twenty years of the Humana Festival
In Humana Festival '95

Anderson, John-Stuart
Tyndale's dream. Miller, J. G. 1994 91p
Drama set in 16th century Britain based on life of William Tyndale, clergyman who translated Bible into English. 3 acts Variable cast 20 characters

Anderson, Marian, 1897-1993
LaChuisa, M. J. First Lady suite: Where's Mamie?

Anderson, Maxwell
Richard and Anne. McFarland & Co. 1995 162p
Verse play about Richard III and Anne Neville, his wife. 2 acts Large mixed cast

Anderson, Poul
Rokuro
Nō play set on comet in far future. 3m extras 1 setting
In Anderson, P. All in one universe

The **Anderson.** Mead, K.

André, John, 1751-1780
Dunlap, W. André

Andre's mother. McNally, T.

Andrews, Betty
No wider than the heart. Dramatic 1994 90p
Dramatic look at life and work of American poet Edna St. Vincent Millay. 2 acts 3m 4w extras 1 interior

Angel of the battlefield. McCaslin, N.

Angelis, April de. See De Angelis, April

Angels
Allen, R. J. Blue cities
Ford, K. Time quest
c Haylock, D. Guardian angels
c Petersen, C. A. If angels were mortal . . .
c Pound, S. R. The Angels' greatest message

Angels—*Continued*
Rivera, J. Marisol
Rodgers, J. W. It's a wonderful life
Solórzano, C. The Angel's forty winks
Waterhouse, J. and Leach, P. Frank's feathered friend

The **Angel's** forty winks. Solórzano, C.

The **Angels'** greatest message. Pound, S. R.

Angels in America: Pt.1: Millennium approaches. Kushner, T.

Angels in America: Pt.2: Perestroika. Kushner, T.

Anger
Osborne, J. Déjàvu
Osborne, J. Look back in anger

Anglican Church of Australia
Kirby, M. My body. My blood

Angwin, Fiona
Beryllium. New Playwrights Network 1996 26p
Romantic comedy about scientific rivalry between male and female scientists. 1 act 1m 1w extras 1 interior

Anima mundi. Nigro, D.

Animal welfare
Walker, D. A quiet night in

Animals
c Anderson, J. The animals' Christmas
c Dawson, J. and Bass, P. The inside story
Neuman, C. Lion and mouse stories
c Peterson, L. The wind in the willows
c Robinette, J. The adventures of Peter Rabbit and his friends
c Rosenberg, J. El gato sin amigos—The cat who had no friends
c Vigil, A. The foolish coyote
c Vigil, A. The littlest ant
c Vigil, A. The smelly feet

The **animals'** Christmas. Anderson, J.

"**Anna** Christie." O'Neill, E.

Anna Karenina. Edmundson, H.

The Anna Project
This is for you, Anna
Performance piece. Woman kills her young daughter's murderer. Background music. Prologue 7 scenes 4w 1 setting
In The *CTR* anthology; ed. by A. Filewod

Anna Rey. See Linney, R. Spain: Anna Rey

Anne, Queen, consort of Richard III, King of England, 1452-1485
Anderson, M. Richard and Anne

Anne Marie's bedroom. Ross, J.

Anne of Green Gables. Sandberg, R. N.

Anne of Green Gables. Turner, J.

Annie Christmas and the Natchez Trace bandits. McCullough, L. E.

Annie G.
Something rotten in Denmark
Farce about 16th century rehearsal of Hamlet with many anachronisms. 4m 2w 1 interior
In Off-Off Broadway Festival plays, 18th ser.

Annie Oakley: little sure-shot. McCullough, L. E.

Anniversaries
Nunn, J. Arrangements
Rooney, T. Flip

The **anniversary.** Chekhov, A.

Annulla. Mann, E.

Anorexia nervosa
Harmer, W. What is the matter with Mary Jane?

Another moon called Earth. Stoppard, T.

Another time. Harwood, R.

Ansky, S.
The dybbuk; or, Between two worlds; tr. by Golda Werman
Yiddish tragedy based on Jewish folk tale concerning Hasidic belief in demoniacal possession and exorcism. 23m 5w extras 2 interiors 1 exterior
In Ansky, S. The dybbuk and other writings

The **answer.** Bamford, S.

Anthony, Susan B.
Stein, G. The mother of us all

Anthony. Margulies, D.

Anthropologists
Bennett, T. Dark rituals

Antigone. Judy, G.

Antigone. Sophocles

Antigone in New York. Glowacki, J.

Antisemitism
Hoffman, A. Welcome stranger
Mamet, D. Goldberg Street
Marlowe, C. The Jew of Malta
Schnitzler, A. Professor Bernhardi
Sherman, J. The God of Isaac

Anton. Standjofski, H.

Antonius, Marcus
Dryden, J. All for love

Antony and Cleopatra. Shakespeare, W. (adaptation) See Dryden, J. All for love

Any given day. Gilroy, F. D.

Anyone for breakfast? Benfield, D.

Aoki, Brenda Wong
The Queen's garden
Autobiographical play set in Hawaii and Southern California. Mixed race woman's coming of age against backdrop of gang violence. 4 parts Variable cast
In Contemporary plays by women of color; ed. by K. A. Perkins and R. Uno

La **aparicion** de Nuestra Senora de Guadalupe. The miracle of Our Lady of Guadalupe. Vigil, A.

Apart from George. Ward, N.

Apartment houses
Congdon, C. Boarders

Ape-God. See Schevill, J. Shadows of memory: Ape-God

Aphasia
Yankowitz, S. Night sky

Apollo (Mythology)
Wilder, T. The drunken sisters

Apology. Emery, S. W.

Appalachian Mountains
Baker, D. and Cocke, D. Red fox/second hangin'
Higgins, F. The sweet by 'n' by
Linney, R. Heathen Valley
Linney, R. Mountain memory
Linney, R. Tennessee
Linney, R. True crimes
Wilson, L. This is the rill speaking

Appearances. Anderson, G.

Appearances. Howe, T.

The **appeasment.** Teschke, H.

Appleseed, Johnny, 1774-1845
c McCaslin, N. Johnny Appleseed
y McCullough, L. E. Johnny Appleseed and Willie Crabgrass

The **appointment.** Jannuzzi, L.

The **appointment.** Ricchi, R.

Approaching Zanzibar. Howe, T.

Approximating mother. Tolan, K.

April Bright. Bolger, D.

April in Paris. Godber, J.

April snow. Linney, R.

Arabian nights
Aladdin and the wonderful lamp (dramatization) See Cregan, D. Aladdin; Hughes, P. Abracadabra, Aladdin!; Mahlmann, L. and Jones, D. C. Aladdin; Neary, J. Aladdin and the wonderful lamp
Ali Baba and the Forty Thieves (dramatization) See Mahlmann, L. and Jones, D. C. Ali Baba and the Forty Thieves

Arabs
Diyab, Mahmud. Strangers don't drink coffee
Ikhlasi, Walid. The path
Ramlī, L. In plain Arabic
Al-Surayyiʿ, ʿAbd aL-ʿAziz. The bird has flown
'Udwan, Mamduh. That's life
Wannus, Sa'dallah. The king is the king

The **Arab's** mouth. MacDonald, A.-M.

Aran Islands
See also Inishmaan (Ireland)

Arblay, Frances Burney d'. See Burney, Fanny

Arcadia. Stoppard, T.

The **Arcata** promise. Mercer, D.

Archaeologists
Wilson, L. The mound builders

Archaeology
Wilson, L. The mound builders

Architects
Greig, D. The architect
Ibsen, H. The master builder
O'Neill, E. The great God Brown

Ardy Fafirsin. Nigro, D.

Are you sure? Bobrick, S.

Arendt, Hannah
Jelinek, E. Totenauberg (Death/Valley/Summit)

Arent, Arthur
Ethiopia
Living newspaper account of Italian intervention in Ethiopia. 14 scenes Variable cast
In Voicings: ten plays from the documentary theatre

Argentina
Gambaro, G. Bad blood
Politics and government
Lawrence, J. and Lee, R. E. Diamond orchid

Aria da capo. Millay, E. St. V.

Arise, Sparta! Nightingale, E. M.

Aristocracy

Desjardins, M.-C. The favorite minister

y Hackett, W. A tale of two cities

Middleton, T. A critical edition of Thomas Middleton's The witch

Middleton, T. The witch

France

Beaumarchais, P. A. C. de. The marriage of Figaro

Great Britain

Barnes, P. The ruling class

North, F. The Kentish barons

Wilde, O. Lady Windermere's fan

Russia

Brustein, R. The cherry orchard

Chekhov, A. The cherry orchard

Chekhov, A. Three sisters

Aristophanes

Acharnians; tr. by Kenneth McLeish

Greek classical comedy satirizing economic and social effects of militarism. Athenian farmer makes private peace treaty with Sparta. Verse play. Speaking chorus

In Aristophanes. Plays: one

Birds; tr. by Kenneth McLeish

Greek classical comedy. Utopian fantasy. Two Athenians persuade birds to build city in the air called Cloud Cuckooland to cut off gods from men and replace them as ruling powers. Verse play. Speaking chorus

In Aristophanes. Plays: two

The clouds; tr. by S. H. Landes. Players Press 1996 31p

Greek classical satire on sophistical system of Socrates' educational methods. Verse play. Speaking chorus

—Same; tr. by Kenneth McLeish

In Aristophanes. Plays: two

Festival time (Thesmophoriazousai); tr. by Kenneth McLeish

Greek classical comedy. Farce which burlesques Euripides and eternal battle of the sexes. Verse play. Speaking chorus

In Aristophanes. Plays: two

Frogs; tr. by R. L. Mila. Players Press 1995 31p

Greek satirical comedy. Dionysus, patron of theater, touring underworld in search of great poet, must choose between Aeschylus and Euripides. Speaking chorus

—Same; tr. by Kenneth McLeish

In Aristophanes. Plays: two

Knights; tr. by Kenneth McLeish

Greek classical comedy in verse. Satirical attack on the Athenian politician Cleon and demagoguery

In Aristophanes. Plays: one

Lysistrata. Players Press 1995 27p

Greek classical farce. To end war Athenian women organize sex strike. Speaking chorus

—Same; tr. by Kenneth McLeish

In Aristophanes. Plays: one

Peace; tr. by Kenneth McLeish

Greek classical comedy. Trygiaos enlists aid of other Athenian farmers to rescue goddess Peace after learning gods have left War in control of heaven to punish Greek cities for their squabbling. Verse play. Speaking chorus

Wasps; tr. by Kenneth McLeish

Greek classical satire on demagogues. Philodeon's passion for lawsuits is checked when his son turns their house into a law court. Verse play. Speaking chorus

In Aristophanes. Plays: two

Arlen, Harold

Sweet and hot: the songs of Harold Arlen; music by Harold Arlen; lyrics by Harold Arlen [et al.] with additional lyrics by Mary Bracken Phillips; conceived and originally directed by Julianne Boyd. French 1996 66p (French's musical library)

Musical revue based on songs of legendary composer. 2 acts 3m 3w 1 setting

Armenian question

Kalinoski, R. Beast on the moon

Armenians

United States

Kalinoski, R. Beast on the moon

Arms and the man. Shaw, G. B.

Armstrong, G. K.

Handcuffs. New Playwrights Network 1995 56p

Following stint as full-time wife and mother, woman returns to workplace to rescue husband's failing business. 3 acts 3m 2w 1 interior 1 exterior

Armstrong, Ian

Fallen heroes. French (London) 1994 32p

Two Irish men of different religious backgrounds serve in Welsh regiment of British Army. 3m 3w 1 exterior

Arnold, Benedict

Nelson, R. The General from America

Aron, Geraldine

Olive and Hilary. French (London) 1996 44p

Comedy with fantastic elements. Woman tries to persuade sister and roommate to abandon their new-age lifestyle. 5 scenes 3w 1m 1 interior

The Stanley Parkers. French (London) 1995 18p

Portrait of long-term relationship between two middle-aged men. 2m 1 interior

Aronson, Billy
Little Red Riding Hood
Sardonic adult version of the fairy tale. 6 scenes epilogue 2m 3w
In The Best American short plays, 1992-1993

Arrangements. Nunn, J.

Arria and Paetus. Barbier, M.-A.

Arson
Tasca, J. Outrageous

Art
Wertenbaker, T. Three birds alighting on a field

Galleries and museums

Plowman, G. Beata Beatrix

The **art** of dating. Elwell, J. S.

The **art** of success. Dear, N.

The **art** of waiting. Shin, R.

The **art** of war. Walker, G. F.

Arthur, King
c Chambers, J. Tales of King Arthur
Dryden, J. King Arthur
c Reakes, P. King Arthur
c Stites, K. Adventures with young King Arthur

Arthur and Leila. Lee, C.

Artificial reality. Essmann, J.

Artist, Virginia A.
c The clever judge
Young African girl earns right to attend school when she captures thief who stole King's pearl. Background music. 4m 3w extras 1 exterior
In Thirty plays from favorite stories; ed. by S. E. Kamerman
c The clever Maakafi
Variant title entered above
In The Big book of large-cast plays; ed. by S. E. Kamerman

The **artist** and the model. Schisgal, M.

The **artist** and the model/2. Schisgal, M.

Artist descending a staircase. Stoppard, T.

Artists
Dear, N. The art of success
Dover, M. and Jarvis, G. Seconds
Ekstrom, P. An O. Henry Christmas: The last leaf
Frost, R. In an art factory
Gems, P. Stanley
c Gerke, P. Ma Lien and the magic paintbrush
MacNeice, L. Persons from Porlock
Margulies, D. Sight unseen
c McCullough, L. E. Great medicine painter
McGuinness, F. Innocence
Schisgal, M. The artist and the model
Schisgal, M. The artist and the model/2
Stoppard, T. Artist descending a staircase
Storey, D. Stages
Wertenbaker, T. Three birds alighting on a field
Wilson, L. Say De Kooning
See also Painters; Sculptors; and names of individual artists, e.g. Goya, Francisco

Arts & leisure. Tesich, S.

Aryan birth. Page, E.

Arzoomanian, Ralph
The Tack Room
Lawyer reluctant to take over uncle's tavern. 3m 1 interior
In The Best American short plays, 1992-1993

As is. Hoffman, W. M.

As sometimes in a dead man's face. Houston, V. H.

As you were. Nestroy, J.

Asa ga kimashita (Morning has broken). Houston, V. H.

Asbrand, Karin
Pandora's box
Based on Greek myth of how evil spirits were released into the world. 4m 5w extras 1 exterior
In Thirty plays from favorite stories; ed. by S. E. Kamerman

Ascension day. Mason T.

Asceticism
Barnes, P. The jumping Mimuses of Byzantium

Asher, Sandra Fenichel
y A woman called Truth; a play in two acts celebrating the life of Sojourner Truth. Dramatic 1993 61p
First produced under title: God and a woman. Drama about life of Sojourner Truth who, born into slavery, became abolitionist and advocate of women's rights. Singing. 2 acts 3m 3w 1 setting

Asher, Sandy. See Asher, Sandra Fenichel

Ashes and sand. Upton, J.

Ashes to ashes. Pinter, H.

Asia
Koch, K. The Red Robins

Asian Americans
Gotanda, P. K. Yankee dawg you die
Omata, G. H. S.A.M. I am
Son, D. R.A.W. ('cause I'm a woman)
Yew, C. A language of their own

Asians

Australia

Harding, A. Blood and honour

England

Yew, C. Porcelain

United States

Yew, C. A language of their own

Asinaria. See Plautus, T. M. Asses galore (Asinaria)

Aspengren, Kate
House of wonders. French 1993 76p

Comedy about family legends and the afterlife. Author visited by ghost of notorious great aunt. 2 acts 5 scenes 3m 5w extra 1 interior

Assassination
McNally, T. Witness
Musset, A. de. Lorenzaccio

Asses galore. Plautus, T. M.

The **assignment.** See Kopit, A. End of the world

Aston, Manuel
y Fossils! Currency Press 1995 84p

Explores relationship between parents and teenagers. Variable cast 10 characters 1 setting

Astronauts
Godfrey, P. The blue ball

Astronauts. Reilly, C.

Astronomers
Hunter, M. Transit of Venus
Yankowitz, S. Night sky

Asylum! Asylum! O'Kelly, D.

At home (Split, Part 1). Weller, M.

At Land's End. Steinour, M.

At the bus stop. Schurman-O'Connor, K.

At the inland sea. Bond, E.

At the root. Eisenstein, L.

At the roots of the stars. Barnes, D.

The **atheist's** tragedy. Tourneur, C.

Athens (Greece)
Lyly, J. Campaspe
Warner, F. Healing nature

Atkins, Eileen
Vita & Virginia. French (London) 1995 42p

Two person play based on letters between novelists Virginia Woolf and Vita Sackville-West. 2 acts 2w 1 setting

Atkins, Greg
y William of Stratford. Bakers Plays 1993 63p

Portrays Shakespeare's pre-London years. Background music. 2 acts 15 scenes 7m 3w 1g extras 3 interiors 1 exterior

Atomic bomb
Congdon, C. No mercy

Atreus, House of (Greek mythology)
Seneca. Thyestes

Attack of the giant grasshoppers. Swift, R.

Attucks, Crispus
c Keats, M. Peter Salem, Minuteman

Auden, W. H.
The dark valley

Radio play. Monologue by old woman haunted by memory of father killed in mining accident. 1w

In Auden, W. H. Libretti, and other dramatic writings

The play of Daniel

Liturgical drama about the prophet

In Auden, W. H. Libretti, and other dramatic writings

Auden, W. H. and Stern, James
The rocking horse winner

Radio dramatization of D. H. Lawrence short story. Variable cast

In Auden, W. H. Libretti, and other dramatic writings

Audience. Havel, V.

August. Mitchell, J.

Augustine, John
Window of opportunity

Unhappy wife learns her close friend and confidante had affair with husband. 2w 1 interior

In The Best American short plays, 1993-1994

Augustus, Emperor of Rome, 63 B.C.-14 A.D.
Warner, F. Virgil and Caesar

Auletta, Robert
The Persians. Sun & Moon Press 1993 94p
Verse drama set in modern-day Iraq. Explores how triumphant nations view recently defeated enemies. 5m 1w 1 setting

Aunt Dan and Lemon. Shawn, W.

Aunt Sophie's latkes. Rumble, P. B.

Auntie Mame. Lawrence, J. and Lee, R. E.

Aunts
Bingham, S. Milk of paradise
Franklin, J. E. Two mens'es daughter
Lawrence, J. and Lee, R. E. Auntie Mame
Linney, R. Paradise
c McGovern, C. The ugly duck
Pintauro, J. Lenten pudding
Rumble, P. B. Aunt Sophie's latkes
Wilson, L. Brontosaurus

Aureng-Zebe. Dryden, J.

Auschwitz (Concentration camp)
y Bond, E. The inland sea

Austen, Jane
Mansfield Park (dramatization) See Hall, W. Mansfield Park
Northanger Abbey (dramatization) See Francis, M. Jane Austen's Northanger Abbey
Pride and prejudice (dramatization) See Morley, O. J. Pride and prejudice

Australia
Acworth, E. Composing Venus
Bell, H. Fortune
Broinowski, A. The gap
Buzo, A. Norm and Ahmed
Buzo, A. Rooted
Buzo, A. The Roy Murphy show
c Davis, J. Moorli and the Leprechauns
Enright, N. Blackrock
Enright, N. Good works
y Enright, N. A property of the clan
Enright, N. St. James Infirmary
Flanagan, N. Burning time
Gow, M. Sweet Phoebe
Graham, G. The boys
Gray, O. The torrents
Gurr, M. Jerusalem
Hibberd, J. Slam dunk
c Holman, D. No worries
Lyssiotis, T. The Forty Lounge Cafe
Morris, M. Boss of the pool
y Murray, P. Spitting chips
Nimmo, H. One small step
Nowra, L. Crow
Nowra, L. The temple
O'Donoghue, J. Abbie and Lou, Norman and Rose
Oswald, D. Gary's house
Rayson, H. Competitive tenderness
Rayson, H. Falling from grace
Roland, B. Feet of clay
Shearer, J. The family
Shepherd, C. Delphiniums
Thomson, K. Barmaids
Weternbaker, T. Our country's good
White, P. Big toys
White, P. Netherwood
White, P. Night on Bald Mountain
White, P. Shepherd on the rocks
White, P. Signal driver
Wilkinson, M. E. The lighthouse keeper's wife
Williamson, D. The club
Williamson, D. The department
Williamson, D. A handful of friends
Williamson, D. Travelling north
See also names of cities, e.g. Sydney (Australia)

Politics and government
Buzo, A. Macquarie
Gurr, M. Underwear, perfume and crash helmet
Nowra, L. The incorruptible

Race relations
Bennett, R. Funerals and circuses
Parsons, N. Dead heart

Australian aborigines
Bennett, R. Funerals and circuses
c Davis, J. Moorli and the Leprechauns
y Hannay, R. Windows
Johnson, E. What do they call me?
Manning, N. Close to the bone
y Manns, D. Heart of the land
Parsons, N. Dead heart
c Roberts, A. V. Ji-da (the bird)

Australians

England
Morris, M. Two weeks with the Queen

Austria
Canetti, V. The Ogre
c McCullough, L. E. Silent night
Mitterer, F. There's not a finer country
Turrini, P. The siege of Vienna

Authors
Aspengren, K. House of wonders
Beckett, S. Eleuthéria

Authors—*Continued*
Bremner, B. Mrs. Coney
Carmichael, F. Coming apart
Carmichael, F. I bet your life
Chayefsky, P. The latent heterosexual
Chinn, J. Something to remember you by
Christian, B. Blue murder
Crews, H. Blood issue
French, D. Silver dagger
Gerstenberg, A. The pot boiler
Gilroy, F. D. Fore!
Gilroy, F. D. Give the bishop my faint regards
Goluboff, B. Big Al
Gow, M. Furious
Gray, S. Hidden laughter
Gray, S. Man in a side-car
Griffin, T. Mrs. Sedgewick's head
Gurney, A. R. The cocktail hour
Handke, P. Walk about the villages
Hare, D. A map of the world
Harnetiaux, B. The snows of Kilimanjaro
Harwood, R. The ordeal of Gilbert Pinfold
Havel, V. Protest
Heiss, R. L. Illegal contact
Katims, J. Who made Robert DeNiro king of America?
Lewis, I. Chinese coffee
Linney, R. The captivity of Pixie Shedman
Linney, R. April snow
Linney, R. F.M.
Lucas, C. The Dying Gaul
Margulies, D. Pitching to the star
Mercer, D. The cellar and the almond tree
Mercer, D. Emma's time
Mercer, D. Find me
Mercer, D. On the eve of publication
Mercer, D. A suitable case for treatment
Norman, P. Love off the shelf
Overmyer, E. In perpetuity throughout the universe
Parnell, P. Flaubert's latest
Plowman, G. Umjana Land
Pogos, A. Strangers in the night
Potter, D. Karaoke
Rattigan, T. After the dance
Reddin, K. Black snow
Rubens, B. Hijack
Sherman, M. A madhouse in Goa
Simon, N. Jake's women
Simon, N. Laughter on the 23rd floor
Simon, N. London suite: Settling accounts
Sroka, J. and Fleming, J. Dying for laughs
y Terson, P. How to write a play
Wilder, T. Such things only happen in books
See also Poets; Women authors; also names of authors, e.g. Shakespeare, William

The **author's** voice. Greenberg, R.

Autobiography
Kennedy, A. P. and Kennedy, A. Sleep deprivation chamber
Linney, R. Gold and silver waltz
Miller, S. My left breast
Miller, T. My queer body
Najera, R. A quiet love
Seremba, G. Come good rain
Williams, T. Something cloudy, something clear
Woodard, C. Pretty fire

Automata
Dinner, W. Logic upside down

Automatic pilot. Ritter, E.

Automobiles
y Bruce, M. Car crazy

Touring
Wilder, T. The happy journey to Camden and Trenton

Autumn leaves. Pflomm, P. N.

Autumn violins. Lanquirand, J.

Avarice
Ayckbourn, A. A small family business
Ayckbourn, A. Wolf at the door
Barnes, P. Leonardo's Last Supper
Godber, J. Lucky sods
Godfrey, P. The modern husband
Hellman, L. The little foxes
Lloyd, P. The scam
Marlowe, C. The Jew of Malta
Mitterer, F. No place for idiots
Nowra, L. The temple
Ravenhill, M. Shopping and fucking
Sade, Marquis de. Truth and treason
c Scanlan, M. Give and take
Tasca, J. The spelling of Coynes
Tourneur, C. The atheist's tragedy
Valle-Inclán, R. del. The paper rose
Vargas Llosa, C. Orchids in the moonlight
Wilder, T. Cement hands
Williams, R. The life of the world to come
See also Greed

Aven'u boys. Pugliese, F.

Avenue X. Leslee, R.

Averill, Ric. See Willmott, K. jt. auth.

Avery, Alan

y Stardust melody. New Playwrights Network 1995 15p

Teenage girls share near-death experience. Music. 1 act 1m 2w

Avery, Charles

y The seven ages of Dan. Clark, I.E. 1993 57p

Comedy. Scenes from lives of high school students based on Shakespeare's Seven ages of man. 2 acts 11 scenes 10m 6w 1 interior

Avi

Nothing but the truth (dramatization) See Smith, R. Nothing but the truth

Avon calling! Olfson, L.

Awake and sing! Odets, C.

Away from me. Champagne, S.

Awkward silence. Reiss, J.

Ayckbourn, Alan

y Callisto 5. French (London) 1995 64p

Science fiction play about young man marooned on moon of Jupiter with robot and computer as his only company. 2 acts Unidentified cast 4 characters extras 1 setting

A chorus of disapproval

Humor and pathos combine in this depiction of human idiosyncrasy. Cautionary tale of rise and fall of young man in world of amateur operatics. Singing. 2 acts 7m 6w 1 setting

In Ayckbourn, A. Plays: one

Communicating doors. Faber & Faber 1995 125p

Time-traveling comedy thriller about three women trying to undo wrongs and alter their destinies. 3 acts 3m 3w 1 interior

—Same. French (London) 1995 87p

Family circles. French 1997 81p

Comedy first produced 1970 with title: The story so far.... Following in parents' footsteps, three daughters chose unsuitable partners. 2 acts 4 scenes 4m 4w 1 interior

Henceforward . . .

Comedy. Man, hoping to gain custody of daughter plots elaborate ruse that is foiled by his computer. 2 acts 2m 2w 1g extras 1 interior

In Ayckbourn, A. Plays: one

Man of the moment

Black comedy. BBC newswoman disrupts life of convicted felon, now a wildly successful media pundit. 2 acts 5m 4w 1g 1 interior

In Ayckbourn, A. Plays: one

c Mr A's amazing maze plays. French (London) 1993 90p

Comedy. Young girl and her dog search sinister neighbor's house for her pet's lost bark. 2 parts 5m 1w 1g extra 1 setting

c My very own story. French (London) 1995 66p

Morality tale about storytelling and reality. Background music. 2 acts 10m 8w extras 1 setting

The revengers' comedies. French (London) 1993 224p

Black comedy. Two suicidal people, one outmaneuvered in business, the other bested in love, meet and form pact to wreak revenge upon each other's oppressors. Prologue 2 parts 4 acts 42 scenes 12m 11w settings

A small family business

Drama about greed. Businessman confronts corruption in family run enterprise. 2 acts 7m 6w 1 interior

In Ayckbourn, A. Plays: one

c This is where we came in. French (London) 1995 86p

Fantasy about story theater. Group of storyteller characters want to be released to tell own tales. 2 acts 6m 4w

Time of my life. Faber & Faber 1993 101p

Drama about decline and fall of successful family business set in London restaurant. Past problems resurface and questions are raised about future as family celebrates mother's birthday. 2 acts 4m 3w 1 interior

—Same. French (London) 1993 92p

Wildest dreams. Faber & Faber 1993 95p

Tragicomedy set in contemporary England. Four unhappy middle-class friends seek to escape their dull lives with homemade role-playing game. 2 acts 3 scenes 5m 3w 3 interiors

—Same. French (London) 1993 101p

Wolf at the door; a play by Henry Becque; tr. by David Walker and adapted by Alan Ayckbourn. French (London) 1993 87p

Variant title: The vultures. Adaptation of Henry Becque play. When patriarch of a wealthy family dies, business partner and attorney swoop down like vultures to enrich themselves on his estate. 4 acts 12m 6w 2 interiors

Aye aye aye I'm integrated. Smith, A. D.

Aynslzey, Elizabeth

'I told you so'. Moorley's 1994 16p

Religious play based on Biblical story of Naaman, the Syrian who was cured of leprosy by the prophet Elisha. 5 scenes 4m 2w extras

y What a weekend! Moorley's 1993 19p

Religious drama about effects of Christ's crucifixion and resurrection on Roman soldiers. 3 scenes 15m 3w 4 interiors

Ayvazian, Leslie. See Mama drama

Aztecs
c Vigil, A. La aparicion de Nuestra Senora de Guadalupe. The miracle of Our Lady Of Guadalupe

B

Babe, the sheep-pig. Wood, D.

Babes in the wood. Webster, P.

Babies. Harvey, J.

Baby with the bathwater. Durang, C.

Babylon gardens. Mason, T.

The **Bacchae.** See Euripides. Bakkhai

The **Bacchanale.** Schnitzler, A.

The Bacchanals. See Euripides. Bakkhai

Bacchides. See Plautus, T. M. Two sisters named Bacchis (Bacchides)

Bachelor holiday. Ball, A.

The **bachelor** party. Chayefsky, P.

Bachelors
Berkoff, S. Harry's Christmas
Sondheim, S. Company

Back bog beast bait. Shepard, S.

Back from the country. See Goldoni, C. Villeggiatura: Back from the country

Bad blood. Gambaro, G.

Bad company. Bent, S.

Bad dream. Lucas, C.

Bad habits: Dunelawn. McNally, T.

Bad habits: Ravenswood. McNally, T.

The **bad** infinity. Wellman, M.

The **baddest** of boys. Holsclaw, D.

Baeck, Leo
Sylvanus, E. Leo Baeck

Baer, Richard
Mixed emotions. Dramatists 1996 68p
Romantic comedy about courtship of Catholic widow and Jewish widower. 2 acts 4 scenes 3m 1w 1 interior

Bag ladies. See Homeless

Bagdasian, Harry Michael. See Joselovitz, E. jt. auth.

Baglady. McGuinness, F.

Bailegangaire. Murphy, T.

Bailey, Michèle
Going all the way. French (London) 1992 24p
Unmarried couple unable to resolve differences over moral responsibility for less fortunate. 7 scenes 3m 2w 1 setting

The **bailiff's** wonderful coat. McCaslin, N.

Baillie, Joanna
De Monfort
Gothic tragedy. Paranoid aristocrat driven to murder when he suspects alliance between beloved sister and hated rival. Prologue 5 acts 14 scenes epilogue 6m 4w extras 9 interiors 2 exteriors
In Seven Gothic dramas, 1789-1825

Baitz, Jon Robin
Broadway
Monologue by dancer touches on musicals, AIDS, and NEA grants. 1m
In Baitz, J. R. Three hotels: plays and monologues

Coq au vin
Short scene of two unemployed actors reduced to working in chicken suits. 3m
In Baitz, J. R. Three hotels: plays and monologues

The end of the day. French 1993 78p
Set in California and England, 1986 and 1992. Expatriate English doctor becomes disillusioned and corrupt. 2 acts 9 scenes 4m 2w settings
—Same
In Baitz, J. R. The substance of fire and other plays

A fair country. Dramatists 1997 60p
United States information officer stationed in South Africa trades sensitive information for cushy job in Hague. Family disintegration follows. 2 acts 7 scenes 6m 2w settings
—Same. Theatre Communications Group 1997 84p
A fair country (condensation)
In The Best plays of 1995-1996

The film society
Dramatic comedy set in South Africa. Tensions in provincial private school reflect those of society at large. 2 acts 15 scenes 4m 2w 1 setting
In Baitz, J. R. The substance of fire and other plays

The girl on the train
Monologue about contemporary values. 1w
In Baitz, J. R. Three hotels: plays and monologues

It changes every year
Gay couple take each other's mother out on Mother's Day. 2m 2w 1 setting
In Baitz, J. R. Three hotels: plays and monologues

Baitz, Jon Robin—*Continued*

Library lady

Monologue on book censorship. 1w

In Baitz, J. R. Three hotels: plays and monologues

Recipe for one; or, A handbook for travelers

Monologue. Nostalgic memories of things and places in one's past. 1m

In Baitz, J. R. Three hotels: plays and monologues

Standards & practices

Satiric monologue about television standards and practices. 1m

In Baitz, J. R. Three hotels: plays and monologues

The substance of fire

Drama revolving around conflict between three young adults and their father, a domineering publisher and Holocaust survivor. 2 acts 3m 2w 2 interiors

In Baitz, J. R. The substance of fire and other plays

In Fruitful and multiplying; ed. by E. Schiff

Three hotels. French 1993 50p

American executive of unscrupulous company selling to Third World countries and his wife present alternate monologues on corporate responsibility. 3 pts 1m 1w 3 interiors

In Baitz, J. R. Three hotels: plays and monologues

Baker, Don, and Cocke, Dudley

Red fox/second hangin'

Three storytellers relate hundred-year-old tale of murder and vengeance in Appalachia. Slide projections. Prologue 2 acts 3m 1 setting

In Alternate roots; ed. by K. deNobriga and V. Anderson

Baker, Edward Allan

A dead man's apartment

Comedy. Adulterous lovers decide not to leave their spouses. 2m 2w 1 interior

In Act One '95

In Baker, E. A. A dead man's apartment; Rosemary with Ginger; Face divided

In EST marathon '95

Face divided

Psychological drama set in Providence, Rhode Island hospital. Husband unable to get wife to admit she abuses daughter. 1m 2w 1 interior

In Baker, E. A. A dead man's apartment; Rosemary with Ginger; Face divided

Rosemary with Ginger

Two sisters, one alcoholic the other in loveless marriage, discover their common bond. 2w 1 interior

In Baker, E. A. A dead man's apartment; Rosemary with Ginger; Face divided

In EST marathon, 1994

A **baker's** dozen. Rowland, E.

Bakkhai. Euripides

Balalin Company of Jerusalem

Darkness

Experimental exploration of Palestinian Arab concerns. 7m 2w 1 setting

In Modern Arabic drama; ed. by S. K. Jayyusi and R. Allen

Balconville. Fennario, D.

Balderston, John L. See Deane, H. jt. auth.

Baldwin, James

The amen corner

Harlem evangelist rejects her own husband and dominates her son in order to answer what she believes is the Lord's call. Singing. 3 acts 5m 9w extras 1 setting

In Black theatre USA [v2]; ed. by J. V. Hatch and T. Shine

Ball, Alan

Bachelor holiday

Comedy. Three male roommates discuss meaning of life. 1 act 3m 1 interior

In Ball, A. Five one-act plays

Five women wearing the same dress. Dramatists 1993 76p

Bridesmaids share confidences during wedding reception. 2 acts 1m 5w 1 interior

The M word

Satire about ambition set in Manhattan. Male and female executives negotiate terms of relationship. 1 act 1m 1w 1 interior

In Ball, A. Five one-act plays

Made for a woman

Satire set in Manhattan. When image conscious young woman's world falls apart she responds with act of random violence. 1 act 1m 1w 1 interior

In Ball, A. Five one-act plays

Power lunch

Satire set in restaurant. Ambitious couple battle for control of their relationship. 1 act 2m 2w 1 interior

In Ball, A. Five one-act plays

Your mother's butt

Satire. Therapist desperately searches for clues to source of young man's problems. 1 act 1m 1w 1 interior

In Ball, A. Five one-act plays

The **ballad** of King Windowglass. Kurtz, J.

Ballad of Yachiyo. Gotanda, P. K.

Ballad opera
Gay, J. Beggar's opera

Ballet dancers. See Dancers

Balls (Parties)
Gurney, A. R. The snow ball
Kipling, R. Mrs. Hauksbee sits out

Ballycastle. Cahill, S.

Balm in Gilead. Wilson, L.

Balo. Toomer, J.

The **Baltimore** waltz. Vogel, P.

Balzac, Honoré de
Mercadet (the Napoleon of finance); tr. by Robert Cornthwaite. Smith & Kraus 1994 81p (Great translations for actors series)

Comedy. Wily financier attempts to outwit his creditors. 3 acts 37 scenes 9m 4w extras 3 interiors

Mercadet (adaptation) See Lewes, G. H. The game of speculation

Bambi. Salten, F. (dramatization) See DeVita, J. A life in the woods

Bamford, Simon
The answer. New Playwrights Network 1996 26p

Young punk takes unhappy office worker on surreal journey through subconscious mind. Background music. 1 act 2m 1 exterior

Just a loving touch. New Playwrights Network 1995 72p

Jilted young man finds solace from next door neighbors, a young polio victim and her father. 2 acts 4 scenes 3m 3w 1 interior

No roses around the door. New Playwrights Network 1996 77p

Black comedy about parents of youth suspected of murdering homosexual. 3 acts 5m 1w 1 extra 1 interior

Scorpio. New Playwrights Network 1995 56p

Terminally ill old man is sent home to be cared for by embittered family members. 2 acts 4 scenes 3m 3w 1 interior

Who's a pretty boy then? New Playwrights Network 1996 30p

Lonely old man grieves over lost pet bird and lost love. 2m 3w 1 exterior

Bandele, 'Biyi
Marching for Fausa. Amber Lane Press 1993 70p

Political drama set in West African republic. Journalist investigates disappearance of group of schoolchildren arrested by state police during demonstration. 2 acts 8m 5w extras 2 interiors

Bandit Ben rides again. Miller, H. L.

Bang! Bang! You're dead. Kelly, T.

Bang the drum slowly. Simonson, E.

Bangkok (Thailand)
Minghella, A. Made in Bangkok

Bank, Diane
Halfway home. French 1994 104p

Comedy. Woman returns to family in Iowa after ten years in New York. Prologue 2 acts 4 scenes 1m 7w 4 interiors

Bankers
Boretz, A. I remember you
Hare, D. Knuckle
Kaiser, G. From morning to midnight

The **bankrupt.** Mercer, D.

Banks and banking
Chekhov, A. The anniversary
Chekhov, A. The festivities

The **banquet.** Koch, K.

Banville, John
The broken jug. Gallery Bks. 1994 84p

Adaptation of comedy by Heinrich von Kleist. Set 1846 in small town in west of Ireland. Corrupt magistrate presides over trial for a crime he committed. 2 acts 9 scenes 6m 5w 2 interiors

Baraka, Amiri
Dutchman

Subway dialogue between white woman and black man ends in murder. 2 scenes 3m 1w extras 1 interior

In Black theatre USA [v2]; ed. by J. V. Hatch and T. Shine

Great goodness of life (a coon show)
In Black drama in America: an anthology; ed. by D. T. Turner

Slave ship

Pageant on horrors of slavery. Music. 7m 3w extras 1 setting

In Crosswinds; ed. by W. B. Branch

Barasch, Norman
Standing by. French 1996 82p

Television writer and attractive young flutist meet on flight from L.A. to New York. Following intense four day affair she learns her leukemia is no longer in remission. 10 scenes 1m 1w 3 interiors

Das **barbecü.** Warrender, S.

The **barber** of Seville. Beaumarchais, P.-A. C. de

Barbers
Beaumarchais, P.-A. C. de. The barber of Seville

Barbier, Marie-Anne
Arria and Paetus (Arrie et Pétus)
Tragedy set in Rome of Claudius celebrates heroic womanhood. 5 acts 5w 4m extras 1 interior
In The Lunatic lover and other plays by French women of the 17th and 18th centuries; ed. by P. Gethner

Barefoot. Compton, J.

Barham, Richard Harris
Pickering, K. The Ingoldsby legends

Barker, Clive
Colossus
Portrait of visionary Spanish artist Francisco Goya. Large mixed cast
In Barker, C. Incarnations
Crazyface
Clown adrift in midst of Europe's Dark Ages discovers fine line between comedy and tragedy. 2 acts 16 scenes Large mixed cast
In Barker, C. Forms of heaven
Frankenstein in love; or, The life of death
Drama inspired by Shelley's horror classic. Depicts depths of human depravity in banana republic under siege. 2 acts 9 scenes 8m 2w extras
In Barker, C. Incarnations
The history of the Devil; or, Scenes from a pretended life
Portrait of evil incarnate. 4 acts Large mixed cast
In Barker, C. Incarnations
Paradise Street
Time travelers, including Elizabeth I, visit contemporary Liverpool. 2 acts 9 scenes 10m 4w 1 setting
In Barker, C. Forms of heaven

Barker, Harley Granville. See Granville-Barker, Harley

Barker, Howard
All he fears. Calder, J./Riverrun Press 1993 28p
Puppet play about philosopher who, through intellectual dishonesty, loses everything. 17 characters
Brutopia
Explores alienation between Thomas More and daughter who has secretly composed counter-text to her father's classic Utopia. 22 scenes 11m 5w extras
In Barker, H. Collected plays v2
Ego in Arcadia
Political refugees from modern times, victims of revolution and disastrous love, seek relief in melancholy landscape of antiquity. 10 scenes 6m 4w 1 setting
In Barker, H. Collected plays v3
The Europeans: struggles to love
Drama set in 1682 Vienna following the Turkish siege about sexual power and the rebirth of Europe. 2 acts 12 scenes 4m 3w extras 1 setting
In Barker, H. Collected plays v3
Hated nightfall
Drama of historical speculation about role played by tutor of Romanoff children on last night of their lives. 2 acts 2m 2w 1b 2g extras 1 setting
In Barker, H. Hated nightfall [and] Wounds to the face
Judith: a parting from the body
Drama about sexuality and betrayal of the body. Retelling of Apocryphal story of Judith and Holofernes. 1m 2w 1 interior
In Barker, H. Collected plays v3
The love of a good man
World War I drama showing how class attitudes affected both casualties and survivors. 3 acts 13 scenes 11m 2w 1 setting
In Barker, H. Collected plays v2
Minna
Conversion of Lessing's 18th century comedy Minna von Bernhelm into tragic love story. Woman lawyer uses questionable tactics in her single-minded pursuit of atrocity. 2 acts 12 scenes 5m 2w extras 1 setting
In Barker, H. Collected plays v3
The possibilities
Ten short pieces on irrationality and limits of logic. 3m 1w 1b 1g
In Barker, H. Collected plays v2
The power of the dog
Historical speculation set in Eastern Europe, 1945. Displaced Scottish comic performing in Kremlin treads murderous line between truth and accommodation. Cast of characters includes Churchill, Stalin and Molotov. 10 scenes 15m 5w extras settings
In Barker, H. Collected plays v3
Rome
Dramatic meditation on siege, pride, and sacrifice comprised of interwoven narratives, interludes, and digressions. 2 parts 26 scenes Large mixed cast
In Barker, H. Collected plays v2
Ten dilemmas
Portrays collective wrath provoked by tragic passion of man and woman of conventionally opposed social viewpoints. 10 scenes 6m 4w extras
In Barker, H. Collected plays v2
Uncle Vanya
Vanya confronts Chekhov when he leads rebellion of characters against coercive restraints of naturalism. 2 acts 3 scenes 5m 4w
In Barker, H. Collected plays v2
Women beware women
Condenses Middleton's Jacobean tragedy while subverting the social context in terms of violence and eroticism. 2 parts 15 scenes 8m 4w
In Barker, H. Collected plays v3

Barker, Howard—*Continued*

Wounds to the face

Philosophical drama about appearances and identity. Variable cast 30 characters 1 setting

In Barker, H. Hated nightfall [and] Wounds to the face

Barker, James Nelson

The Indian princess; or, La belle sauvage

First American drama about Pocahontas based on Smith's General history of Virginia. Accompanying music. 3 acts 12 scenes 12m 5w extras 1 interior 6 exteriors

In Early American drama; ed. by J. H. Richards

Barker, Wayne. See Blum, G. jt. auth.

Barkley, Alben William

Schreiber, W. Burgoo!

Barmaids. Thomson, K.

Barnes, Djuna

At the roots of the stars

British landlady awaits visit from son. 3w 1 interior

In Barnes, D. At the roots of the stars: the short plays

The beauty

Bored Russian princess. 4m 1w

In Barnes, D. At the roots of the stars: the short plays

The death of life

Poverty and despair drive woman to suicide. 2m 1w 1 setting

In Barnes, D. At the roots of the stars: the short plays

The dove

Two sisters' sexual and imaginative frustration. 3w 1 interior

In Barnes, D. At the roots of the stars: the short plays

Five thousand miles

Castaway couple on Pacific island. 1m 1w 1 exterior

In Barnes, D. At the roots of the stars: the short plays

An Irish triangle

Woman recounts husband's extramarital arrangement. 2w

In Barnes, D. At the roots of the stars: the short plays

Kurzy of the sea

Fantasy. Mermaid metamorphoses into barmaid. 2m 3w 1 interior

In Barnes, D. At the roots of the stars: the short plays

Little drops of rain

Generational conflict between two women. 2w

In Barnes, D. At the roots of the stars: the short plays

Madame collects herself

Experimental play set in beauty salon. 1m 3w 1 interior

In Barnes, D. At the roots of the stars: the short plays

Maggie of the saints

Church charwoman and her elderly mother discuss religion. 2w 2b 1 interior

In Barnes, D. At the roots of the stars: the short plays

A passion play

Thieves and prostitutes on Calvary in days of Christ. 5m 2w 1 setting

In Barnes, D. At the roots of the stars: the short plays

She tells her daughter

Mother tells daughter of her murderous past. 2w 1 interior

In Barnes, D. At the roots of the stars: the short plays

Three from the earth

Experimental symbolic play. Three loutish-looking but intelligent brothers visit father's former mistress following his suicide. 1 act 3m 1w 1 interior

In Barnes, D. At the roots of the stars: the short plays

To the dogs

Woman rejects sexual advances of neighbor. 1m 1w 1 interior

In Barnes, D. At the roots of the stars: the short plays

Two ladies take tea

Italian countess takes tea with young American woman. 2w 1 interior

In Barnes, D. At the roots of the stars: the short plays

Water-ice

Celibate woman recalls lost love. 1m 2w 1 interior

In Barnes, D. At the roots of the stars: the short plays

About

Schevill, J. Shadows of memory: The radiator

Barnes, Peter

Acting exercise

Radio play. Jealous husband learns some truths about lying from actor. 2m

In Barnes, P. Corpsing

The bewitched

Satire on authority set in seventeenth century Spain during rule of Carlos II, an epileptic. Singing. Prologue 2 acts 28 scenes epilogue Large mixed cast 9 interiors 1 exterior settings

In Barnes, P. Plays: one

Barnes, Peter—*Continued*

Bye bye Columbus

Television play about exploits of Christopher Columbus. 13m 3w 1 extra

In Barnes, P. Plays: two

Clap hands here comes Charlie

Satirical comedy set in 1960s and 1990s London. Convicted murderer returns to society after thirty years in mental institution. 2 acts 19 scenes epilogue Large mixed cast settings

In Barnes, P. Plays: three

Confessions of a primary terrestrial mental receiver and communicator: Num III Mark I

Barnes' people radio play. Monologue. Man imagines he receives communications from outer space. 1m

In Barnes, P. Plays: one

The end of the world—and after

Barnes' people radio play. Monologue. William Miller whose prophecy of the end of the world proved false, discusses his life and beliefs. 1m

In Barnes, P. Plays: one

Glory

Barnes' people radio play. Monologue. Peregrinus Proteus, Greek philosopher, recalls his life before being burned alive. 1m

In Barnes, P. Plays: one

Heaven's blessings

Epic comedy based on Old Testament apocryphal book of Tobit. Husband, wife, son and cantankerous guardian angel have their faith tested to breaking point. Prologue 7 scenes 11m 2w extras setting

In Barnes, P. Plays: three

Humour helps

Neighbor unwittingly helps actress commit suicide. 1 act 2w 1 interior

In Barnes, P. Corpsing

The jumping Mimuses of Byzantium

Barnes' people radio play. Monologue. Dying old man recalls his meeting with two clowns in Byzantium. 1m

In Barnes, P. Plays: one

Last things

Comedy. Elderly acting couple wake up to find themselves dead. 1 act 1m 1w 1 interior

In Barnes, P. Corpsing

Laughter!

Satire. Part I deals with the tyranny of Ivan the Terrible. Part II mocks the bureaucracy and brutality of Nazi Germany. Non-human characters include a hammer, nail, axe and tree. 2 parts epilogue 14m 2w extras 1 setting 1 interior

In Barnes, P. Plays: one

Leonardo's Last Supper

Satire. Greedy, poor mortician and family murder resurrected body of Leonardo da Vinci in order to receive full payment for services. Music, singing, dancing. 3m 1w 1 interior

In Barnes, P. Plays: one

More than a touch of Zen

Television play about two crippled men trying to learn judo. 3m

In Barnes, P. Plays: two

No end to dreaming

Barnes' people radio play. Monologue. On analyst's couch elderly Jewish widower recounts dream he had as youth in Cracow that changed direction of his life. 1m

In Barnes, P. Plays: one

Nobody here but us chickens

Television play about two men who believe they are chickens. 2m

In Barnes, P. Plays: two

Noonday demons

Satire about pride. Two 4th century ascetic monks challenge each other's holiness and self-deprecation. 2m extra 1 exterior

In Barnes, P. Plays: one

Not as bad as they seem

Television play. Sex farce. Adulterous couple surprised by woman's husband; all three are blind. 2m 1w

In Barnes, P. Plays: two

Red noses

Black comedy. Catholic priest leads comedic theatrical troupe through plague-ridden England. Large mixed cast 1 setting

In Barnes, P. Plays: two

Revolutionary witness

Historical drama. Four monologues delivered by obscure participants in French Revolution. 3m 1w

In Barnes, P. Plays: three

Rosa

Barnes' people radio play. Monologue. English social worker writes official memorandums about elderly poor in her care. 1w

In Barnes, P. Plays: one

The ruling class

Satire. Aristocratic clan in present-day England is headed by cruel young eccentric who is first convinced that he is God and later Jack the Ripper. Prologue 2 acts 27 scenes epilogue 17m 5w 5 interiors 1 exterior

In Barnes, P. Plays: one

The spirit of man: A hand witch of the second stage

Television play set in 1437 France. Woman accused of witchcraft outwits her accusers. 3m 1w

In Barnes, P. Plays: two

The spirit of man: From sleep and shadow

Television play about Ranters religious movement in 17th century England. 2m 1w

In Barnes, P. Plays: two

The spirit of man: The night of the Sinhat [sic] Torah

Television play set in 1812 Lubin, Poland. Rabbis face crisis of faith. 3m

In Barnes, P. Plays: two

Barnes, Peter—*Continued*

Sunsets and glories

Satire set in 13th century Italy about power struggle between church and state. Pope Celestine V provokes bitter crisis of faith. 2 acts 24 scenes 19m 5w

In Barnes, P. Plays: two

The theory and practice of belly-dancing

Barnes' people radio play. Monologue. Student of belly-dancing discusses her marriage and belly-dancing. 1w

In Barnes, P. Plays: one

Waiting for a bus

Pair of lovers apparently interrupted by husband's arrival. 1 act 2m 1w 1 interior

In Barnes, P. Corpsing

Yesterday's news

Barnes' people radio play. Monologue. Old prostitute reminisces about her life. 1w

In Barnes, P. Plays: one

Barnieh, Zina

c A nest of dragons

Based on Italian fairy tale. Dragons help Prince learn life's lessons. Variable cast 10 characters 13 scenes

In Playhouse: six fantasy plays for children

Barnum, P. T. (Phineus Taylor)

Vingoe, M. Living curiosities: a story of Anna Swan

Barr, Nancy

Mrs. Cage. Dramatists 1993 35p

Middle-class woman interrogated by police after shooting yuppie woman in supermarket parking lot. Prologue 1 act 1m 1w 1 interior

Barrie, J. M.

The admirable Crichton (adaptation) See Olfson, L. The admirable Crichton

Pantaloon. Players Press 1993 32p

Play about commedia dell'arte character Pantaloon, his daughter Columbine and her sweetheart Harlequin. 3m 1w 1 setting

Peter Pan (adaptation) See Caird, J. and Nunn, T. Peter Pan; Mahlmann, L. and Jones, D. C. Peter Pan; Webster, P. Peter Panto

Rosalind. Players Press 1993 47p

Drawing-room comedy about human vanity. Actress has difficulty facing middle age. 1m 2w 1 interior

Barrie, Shirley

y Carrying the calf

Four women of different ages and cultural backgrounds meet in self-defense class and help each other cope with violence in their lives. 4 scenes 4w 1 interior

In Wanna play?

Barroga, Jeannie

Talk-story

Past and present intertwine in drama about Filipino father and daughter in 1930s and 1940s California. 2 acts 4m 2w settings

In But still, like air, I'll rise; ed. by V. H. Houston

Walls

Drama about Vietnam War Memorial and its designer Maya Ying Lin. 2 acts 25 scenes 9m 4w extras settings

In Unbroken thread; ed. by R. Uno

Barry, Betty and Bill. Taylor, R. and Bologna, J.

Barry, Lynda

The good times are killing me. French 1993 116p

Autobiographical comic drama about friendship between black girl and white girl living side-by-side in working-class neighborhood in 1960s. Music, singing. 2 acts 36 scenes 8m 14w 1 setting

Barry, P. J.

And Fat Freddy's blues. French 1997 104p

Comedy set in 1952 Rhode Island. Mobster attempts to reunite his daughter with her former boyfriend. 2 acts 6 scenes 2m 2w 1 interior

A distance from Calcutta. French 1993 115p

Part of author's Jericho cycle. Comic drama set in 1923. Catholic woman's love for younger learning-disabled boarder leads to heartbreak. 2 acts 5 scenes 2m 3w 1 setting

Down by the ocean. French 1995 120p

Comic drama set 1946 to 1960 on Rhode Island seashore. Four middle-aged brothers-in-law captivated by fetching neighbor. 3 acts 4m 2w 1 setting

Barry, Sebastian

Boss Grady's boys

Drama about two brothers in their later years living on their small farm in Ireland. 2 acts 4m 4w 1 setting

In Barry, S. Plays: 1

The only true history of Lizzie Finn

Depicts transformation of heroine from English music-hall star to Anglo-Irish lady in the 1890s. Music, singing. 2 acts 5m 3w 1 setting

In Barry, S. The only true history of Lizzie Finn; The steward of Christendom; White Woman Street

In Barry, S. Plays: 1

Prayers of Sherkin

Drama set in 1890s on Sherkin Island off the southwest coast of Ireland. Depicts dwindling of religious sect that hoped to find "New Jerusalem." 2 acts 7m 5w 2 interiors

In Barry, S. Plays: 1

Barry, Sebastian—*Continued*
The Steward of Christendom. Methuen Drama 1996 65p (Methuen modern plays)
Drama set 1932 in County Wicklow old age home. Ex superintendent of Dublin police tries to break free of history. 2 acts 5m 4w 1 interior
—Same
In Barry, S. The only true history of Lizzie Finn; The steward of Christendom; White Woman Street
In Barry, S. Plays: 1
White Woman Street
Drama set in small Ohio town, 1916. Irish outcast participates in struggle and dispossession of Native Americans. 2 acts 6m 1 setting
In Barry, S. The only true history of Lizzie Finn; The steward of Christendom; White Woman Street
In Barry, S. Plays: 1

Barrymore, John
Miller, J. Barrymore's ghost

Barrymore's ghost. Miller, J.

Bars. See Hotels, taverns, etc.

Bartel, Rob
y 3 out
Teenager and his family cope with problems that arise from having professional athlete as father. 8 scenes 2m 2w extras 1 interior 3 exteriors
In Young playwrights; ed. by E. Bray

Bartenders
Thomson, K. Barmaids

Barteve, Reine
The orphanage
European woman runs hotel in corrupt famine-stricken African village. 3 scenes 2m 3w 1g
In Plays by women: an international anthology bk2; ed. by N. Shange

Bartlett, Neil
Night after night. Methuen Drama in association with the Royal Court Theatre 1993 57p (Royal Court Writers series)
Gay man looks back on father's night out in 1958 London. Depicts homosexual role in musical theater. Music, singing. 2 acts 6m 1w extras 1 setting

Bartley, Jim
Stephen & Mr. Wilde. Blizzard Pub. 1994 79p
Drama set in 1882 Toronto. Oscar Wilde is accompanied on lecture tour by black American valet with turbulent past. 2 acts 12 scenes 4m 2w 3 interiors

Barton, Clara
c McCaslin, N. Angel of the battlefield

Bartram, Frances
Tiddley pum. New Playwrights Network 1996 18p
Comedy. Actors rehearse their audition pieces for children's television program. 1 act 3m 3w 1 interior

Barylli, Gabriel
Buttered bread (Butterbrot)
Three men share apartment and their views on women, friendship and love. 11 scenes 3m 1 setting
In Seven contemporary Austrian plays; ed. by R. H. Lawson
Honeymoon (Honigmond)
Women discuss their relationships with men. 3w 1 setting
In Seven contemporary Austrian plays; ed. by R. H. Lawson

Baseball
y Bartel, R. 3 out
c Boiko, C. Yankees vs. Redcoats
Reddin, K. Throwing smoke
Simonson, E. Bang the drum slowly

The **basic** training of Pavlo Hummel. Rabe, D.

Basketball
Dashow, K. Time out
Horovitz, I. The former one-on-one basketball champion

Bass, Eric
c In my grandmother's purse. Anchorage Press 1994 21p
Fantasy takes over when young boy and his mother play memory game about grandmother. Puppets 2w 1b 1 setting

Bass, George Houston
Black masque: the passion of darkie's bones
Ritual drama about African American history. 3m 5w extras 1 setting
In Black drama in America: an anthology; ed. by D. T. Turner

Bass, Philip. See Dawson, J. jt. auth.; Pickering, K. One child at a time

Bassen, Lois Shapley
The month before the moon. French 1996 87p
Four women in their late forties meet at their twenty-fifth reunion of Vassar class of 1969. Music, singing. 2 acts 9 scenes 2m 6w 2 interiors

Basso, Eric
The fall of Prague
Final play in trilogy finds Joseph in seventeenth century Prague assuming identity of Rabbi Judah Loew, creator of Golem. 3 acts 12 scenes Large mixed cast
In Basso, E. The Golem triptych

Basso, Eric—*Continued*
Joseph in the underground
Pt. II of allegorical triptych is set in subterranean city full of outcasts, criminals and enemies of the State. 3 acts 5 scenes 10m 2w settings
In Basso, E. The Golem triptych

Middle distance
Allegorical drama set against rumors of war and plague in unnamed country. In pt. I of triptych Joseph Golem, an old man who died in prison camp is brought back to life. 3 acts 4 scenes 4m 2w settings
In Basso, E. The Golem triptych

La **Batalla** de Cinco de Mayo. Vigil, A.

Bates, H. E.
The darling buds of May. French (London) 1996 83p
Dramatization of the author's comic novel about family in rural England in 1957. 2 acts 6 scenes 6m 7w 3g 1 setting

Baths, Public. See Public baths

The **batting** cage. Ackermann, J.

The **Battle** of Cinco de Mayo. See Vigil, A. La Batalla de Cinco de Mayo

Bauer, Wolfgang
Insalata mista (Insalata mista)
Experimental play about language and theater set in New York City tavern. 9w 1w 1 interior
In Seven contemporary Austrian plays; ed. by R. H. Lawson

Baum, L. Frank
The Wizard of Oz (dramatization) See Francoeur, B. Oz!; Mahlmann, L. and Jones, D. C. The Wizard of Oz; Mapp, E. The wonderful Wizard of Oz

Baum, Thomas
Cold hands
Austrian folk play in verse. Father sexually abuses his twelve-year-old daughter. 10 scenes 3m 4w
In New anthology of contemporary Austrian folk plays; ed. by R. H. Lawson

The **bay** at Nice. Hare, D.

Bayou legend. Dodson, O.

Bays, Carter L.
Five visits from Mr. Whitcomb
Satire. IRS agent harasses man living alone in woods. 5 scenes 4m 1w 1 interior
In Young playwrights; ed. by E. Bray

Bazaar & rummage. Townsend, S.

Be kind to your Mother (Earth). Love, D.

Be smart! Don't start! Simmons, D. W.

The **bear.** Chekhov, A.

Beard, Jocelyn A.
Vladivostok blues
Satire. Mexican soap opera star kidnapped in Vladivostok by man who has her confused with her television role. 4m 3w 1 interior
In Women playwrights: the best plays of 1995

Beard, Paul
Cliff's edge. New Playwrights Network 1996 24p
Black comedy revolving around depressed actor, pub landlord and schizophrenic woman. 1 act 2m 1w 1 exterior

Come the resolution. New Playwrights Network 1995 30p
Comedy. Characters try to remember events of previous night's New Year's Eve party. 1 act 3m 2w 1 interior

Death of a clown. New Playwrights Network 1996 30p
Struggle between clown and estranged half-brother for control of family circus results in murder. 1 act 2m 1 interior

Lavender years. New Playwrights Network 1995 26p
Man and wife consider euthanasia for aged terminally ill mother. 1 act 1m 2w 1 interior

Meat and two veg. French (London) 1996 25p
Retired couple suspect neighbor of doing away with his wife. 2m 1w 1 interior

Swingers. New Playwrights Network 1995 20p
Comedy set in London. Middle class morals and working class values clash when couples attempt wife swapping. 1 act 2m 2w 1 interior

Waiting for Pierrepoint. New Playwrights Network 1996 47p
Drama explores mind of serial killer and necrophile John Christie as he awaits execution in 1953. 1 act 2m 2w

Beast on the moon. Kalinoski, R.

Beata Beatrix. Plowman, G.

Beaumarchais, Pierre Augustin Caron de
The barber of Seville; or, The useless precaution; tr. by Albert Bermel
Romantic comedy set in Spain. Heroine evades advances of amorous guardian with aid of barber Figaro and young count she loves. Singing. 4 acts 8m 1w extras 2 interiors 1 exterior
In A Dozen French farces; ed. by A. Bermel

The marriage of Figaro; tr. by Bernard Sahlins. Dee, I.R. 1994 104p (Plays for performance)
Variant title: Figaro's marriage. Farce. Figaro, erstwhile loyal henchman of Count Almaviva, is about to marry maid-in-waiting Suzanne. Count, through unscrupulous trickery tries to prevent marriage and secure girl as mistress. 5 acts 5 scenes 10m 5w 1g 4 interiors 1 exterior

Beautiful bodies. Cunningham, L.

The **beautiful** stranger. Pohl, K.

Beautiful thing. Harvey, J.

Beauty

Personal

y Hamlett, C. Hairum-scarum

The **beauty**. Barnes, D.

Beauty and the beast. Boswell, L.

Beauty and the beast. Mahlmann, L. and Jones, D. C.

Beauty and the beast. Sachon S.

Beauty and the beast. Valenti, M.

Beauty contests
Martin, J. Shasta Rue
Oates, J. C. Here she is!

The **beauty** queen of Leenane. McDonagh, M.

Beauvoir, Simone de
Kaufman, L. Shooting Simone

The **beaux'** stratagem. Farquhar, G.

The **beaver** coat. Hauptmann, G.

Beber, Neena
Food

Experimental theater piece about unusual eating habits and possible miracle. 2w

In Facing forward; ed. by L. D. Frank

Misreadings

Short scene of teacher student confrontation. 2w 1 interior

In Humana Festival '97

Becher, Ulrich. See Preses, P. jt. auth.

Beck, Susan Baer. See Cole, J. D. Conestoga stories

Becker, Christopher. See Price, J. W. jt. auth.

Beckett, Samuel
Eleuthéria; tr. from the French by Michael Brodsky. Foxrock 1996 196p

Experimental drama about failed writer. 3 acts 11m 6w settings

Ohio impromptu

Experimental play. A drama of the interdependency of the two characters, Reader and Listener, as they read and listen to the story of their relationship. 2m 1 interior

In The Best of Off-Broadway; ed. by R. Wetzsteon

About

Nigro, D. Lucia mad

Beckwourth, James Pierson
c McCullough, L. E. Rocky Mountain rendezvous

Becque, Henry
Wolf at the door (adaptation) See Ayckbourn, A. Wolf at the door

Bed. Cartwright, J.

Bed and sofa. Pen, P.

The **bedroom.** Sade, Marquis de

Bedtime. Gallagher, M.

Beechy High School Drama Club
y Me 'n' Alfred

Flashbacks in life of homeless man who has lost job and family because of drinking. 13 scenes 10m 11w

In Eureka! ed. by J. J. Lewis and D. Warren

Before daybreak. Hauptmann, G.

Before it hits home. West, C. L.

The **beggar** in the blanket. McCullough, L. E.

Beggar's opera. Gay, J.

Behm, Tom. See Cooper, R. M. How things happen in three!

Behn, Aphra
The emperor of the moon

Restoration farce set in Naples combining commedia dell' arte techniques with spectacle. Prologue 3 acts 11 scenes epilogue Large mixed cast

In Behn, A. The rover; The feigned courtesans; The lucky chance; The emperor of the moon

The feigned courtesans; or, A night's intrigue

Comedy of intrigue set in Rome. To gain freedom of action heroines resort to cross-dressing and disguises. Prologue 5 acts 10 scenes epilogues 8m 5w extras settings

In Behn, A. The rover; The feigned courtesans; The lucky chance; The emperor of the moon

The lucky chance; or, An alderman's bargain

Restoration comedy revolving around clandestine affairs, infidelities, love and marriage. 5 acts 19 scenes 12m 7w extras 9 interiors 2 exteriors

In Behn, A. The rover; The feigned courtesans; The lucky chance; The emperor of the moon

The rover; or, The banished cavaliers

Based on Thomaso; or The wanderer. Comedy about the amorous adventures of a band of English cavaliers in

Behn, Aphra—*Continued*

Naples during the exile of Charles II. Prologue 5 acts 15 scenes epilogue 11m 7w extras

In Behn, A. The rover; The feigned courtesans; The lucky chance; The emperor of the moon

In The Sensational Restoration; ed. by H. J. Jensen

Sir Patient Fancy

Risqué comedy about old man with young wife. Prologue 5 acts 17 scenes 15m 9w extras 6 interiors 2 exteriors

In The Meridian anthology of Restoration and eighteenth-century plays by women; ed. by K. M. Rogers

About

Herst, B. A woman's comedy

Behrman, S. N.

The cold wind and the warm

Jewish man, loved by girl, can't forget his love for another woman and finally kills himself. Background music. 3 acts 9 scenes 8m 4w 2 settings

In Awake and singing: 7 classic plays from the American Jewish repertoire; ed. by E. Schiff

Beim, Norman

The deserter

In deserted French chateau during World War II, young deserter guarded by sergeant and visited by priest, awaits execution. 1 act 3m 1 interior

In Beim, N. Six award winning plays

Dreams

Theatrical couple, coming out of semi-retirement, faced with crucial decision. 2 acts 11 scenes 2m 2w 1 interior

In Beim, N. Six award winning plays

Inside

Comedy set in library. Characters do not talk, they think out loud. 1 act 2m 1w 1b 3g 1 interior

In Beim, N. Six award winning plays

Jewel thieves!

Comic mystery about theft of legendary movie star's priceless necklace. 2 acts 2m 2w 1 interior

In Beim, N. Six award winning plays

On a darkling plain

Blacklisted actor considers returning to work for unethical director. 2 acts 4 scenes 3m 1w 1 interior

In Beim, N. Six award winning plays

Shakespeare revisited

Shakespeare returns to earth and tries to come to terms with revisionist production of Richard III. 2m 1 interior

In Beim, N. Six award winning plays

Bein Lochaber. Quayle, T.

Being at home with Claude. Dubois, R. D.

Belasco, David

Madame Butterfly (adaptation) See McDonough, J. Butterfly

Belfast (Northern Ireland)

Gee, S. Never in my lifetime

Reid, C. The belle of the Belfast city

Reid, C. Clowns

Reid, C. Did you hear the one about the Irishman . . . ?

Reid, C. Joyriders

Reid, C. Tea in a china cup

Belgian Congo. See Congo (Democratic Republic)

Belgium

History—1555-1648

Goethe, J. W. von. Egmont

Belinda and the Beast. Boiko, C.

Belinda Braveheart and Billy Barnstorm. See Campbell, E. Hauncho the hamster

Belize

Manet, E. Lady Strass

Bell, Alexander Graham

c Sussman, D. Mystery of the phantom voice

Bell, Hilary

Fortune. Currency Press 1995 90p

Drama about racial prejudice and cultural difference in 1860s Australia. Eleven-year-old seven-foot-tall Chinese boy, exhibited as sideshow freak, turns tables on his exploiters. 2 acts 20 scenes 4m 2w extras 1 setting

Bell, James A.

Prisoner. French 1996 102p

Drama based on Gerald Coffee's autobiographical book Beyond survival. Depicts experiences of American POWs in Vietnam. Slide projections. 2 acts 14m 1w extras 1 setting

Bell, Neal

Drive

Deadly drive in back-streets of inner-city neighborhood. 6 scenes 1m 1w extras

In Actors Theatre of Louisville. Ten-minute plays: v3

On the bum; or, The next train through. Dramatists 1994 93p

Drama set in 1938. Out-of-work New York actress travels to small midwestern town to act in pageant by local author. 2 acts 12 scenes Variable cast 35 characters 1 setting

Out the window

Depicts relationship between wheelchair-bound man and his fiancée. 1m 1w 1 interior

In 20/20: twenty one-act plays from twenty years of the Humana Festival

The **bell** tolls at twelve. Unger, H. R.

The **belle** of the Belfast city. Reid, C.

Les **belles** soeurs. Tremblay, M.

The **belle's** stratagem. Cowley, H. P.

Bellon, Loleh
Bonds of affection
Relationship between Jewish mother and daughter from 1930s to 1960s. 2m 2w
In Plays by women: an international anthology bk3; ed. by N. Shange

The **bells** of Orleans. Gala, A.

Belly dance
Barnes, P. The theory and practice of belly-dancing

Belmont Avenue Social Club. Graham, B.

Below the belt. Dresser, R.

Benet, Stephen Vincent
Johnny Pye and the Foolkiller (dramatization) See Courts, R. Johnny Pye

Benfield, Derek
Anyone for breakfast? French (London) 1994 105p
Comedy of marital mishaps. Misunderstandings ensue when woman lends friend use of house for adulterous rendevous. 2 acts 3m 3w 1 interior

A fly in the ointment. French (London) 1996 84p
Farce revolving around British MP, his ex-mistress, his virtuous wife, an amorous doctor, a frustrated policewoman and a devious pizza delivery boy. 2 acts 3m 3w 1 interior

Up and running! French (London) 1995 85p
Comedy set in London. Veteran talk show host's attempt to impress new producer results in chaos. 2 acts 3m 3w 1 interior

Benjamin falling. Pintauro, J.

Benn, Gottfried
Ithaka; tr. by J. M. Ritchie
Expressionist drama about life, death and medical ethics. 4m extras 1 interior
In German expressionist plays; ed. by E. Schurer

Bennett, Alan
Enjoy
Back-to-back house in north of England setting for drama about elderly Leeds couple facing eviction as transvestite son arrives to supervise removal. 2 acts 10m 3w 1 interior
In Bennett, A. Plays: one

Forty years on
Comedy. Antics and satirical skits at English boy's school underscore generation gap at assembly program honoring retiring and disapproving headmaster. Music, singing. 2 acts 5m 2w extras 1 interior
In Bennett, A. Plays: one

Getting on
Comedy about Labour MP whose nostalgia for stability prevents him from dealing effectively with family and the modern world. 2 acts 4m 3w 1 interior
In Bennett, A. Plays: one

Habeas corpus
Vaudevillian farce focusing on lecherous, aging British physician. Singing. 2 acts 6m 5w 1 setting
In Bennett, A. Plays: one

The madness of George III (condensation)
In The Best plays of 1993-1994

Bennett, Roger
Funerals and circuses. Currency Press 1995 60p
Tragicomedy about race relations in Australia. Small town copper's daughter marries Aboriginal artist. Music, singing. 2 acts 18 scenes 7m 5w 1 setting

Bennett, Rowena
c Rumpelstiltskin
Based on the Grimm fairy tale. To save her baby, miller's daughter who became queen must guess Rumpelstiltskin's name. Verse play. 2 scenes 5m 1w extras 1 interior
In Thirty plays from favorite stories; ed. by S. E. Kamerman

c The shoemaker and the elves
Based on the fairy tale by Brothers Grimm. Needy shoemaker makes clothes for elves who make his Christmas brighter. 2m 1w extras 1 interior
In Thirty plays from favorite stories; ed. by S. E. Kamerman

Bennett, Thom
Dark rituals. French 1994 101p
Thriller. Supernatural blends with murder and ritual death when female anthropologist researches rituals of Native Americans. 2 acts 7 scenes 2m 3w 1 interior

Bensinger, Lenore
A ghost story
Monologue by woman ghostwriter. 1w
In Facing forward; ed. by L. D. Frank
See also Mast, E. jt. auth.

Bent, Simon
Bad company. French (London) 1995 77p
Group of twentysomethings hang out on seafront of northern English resort. 22 scenes 6m 2w 1 setting

Bentley, Eric. See Wedekind, F. The first Lulu

Bentley-Fisher, Tom
c Friends
Children in day care center wait for duck eggs to hatch. 1w 2b 2g Prologue 14 scenes 1 interior
In Playhouse: six fantasy plays for children

Benyon, Lissa
Love seen in laundromat
Unmarried middle-aged urban professionals meet in laundromat. 1m 1w 1 interior
In Passion: six new short plays by Australian women; ed. by R. Horin

Beolco, Angelo. See Ruzzante, 1502?-1542

Berc, Shelley
A girl's guide to the Divine Comedy: a trilogy
Experimental drama. Feminist rewriting of Dante's classic. Singing. 3 parts 4m 4w extras 1 setting
In Plays for the end of the century; ed. by B. Marranca

Berg, Robert
AIDS! the musical!
Musical look at world of AIDS activism. Music, singing, dancing. 2 acts 15 scenes Variable cast 1 setting
In Sharing the delirium; ed. by T. Jones

Bergalis, Kimberly
Blessing, L. Patient A

Berger, John
The three lives of Lucie Cabrol (dramatization) See McBurney, S. and Wheatley, M. The three lives of Lucie Cabrol

Berkoff, Steven
Acapulco
Time itself becomes enemy of group of film actors in Mexico as they attempt to fill their spare time. 5m 1w 1 interior
In Berkoff, S. The collected plays v2

Actor
Monologue about frustrations of actor's life. 1m
In Berkoff, S. The collected plays v2

Brighton beach scumbags
Group of British low-class yobs on beach outing exhibit contempt for traditional values. 4m 2w 1 exterior
In Berkoff, S. The collected plays v2

Dahling you were marvellous
Television parody set in cafe catering to theatrical set. Focuses on pretentious babble of opening night crowd. 14m 5w extras
In Berkoff, S. The collected plays v2

Decadence
Satirical portrayal of decadent life-styles of the British upper classes. 1 act 14 scenes 1m 1w 1 setting
In Berkoff, S. The collected plays v2

Dog
First performed under title: Pitbull. Satiric sketch about pitbull whose ferocity reflects violent nature of its owner. 1m
In Berkoff, S. The collected plays v2

East
Set in London's East End, illustrates anarchic response to frustration and waste in contemporary society utilizing cockney rhyming slang and Shakespearean allusions. Background music, singing. Mime, film 12 scenes 3m 2w 1 setting
In Berkoff, S. The collected plays v1

Greek
Oedipal story set in London's East End. 4 scenes 2m 2w 1 setting
In Berkoff, S. The collected plays v1

Harry's Christmas
Monologue. Friendless 40-year-old bachelor struggles with depression during lonely holiday. 1m 1 interior
In Berkoff, S. The collected plays v2

Kvetch
Black comedy about the deepest hates, fears and anxieties that lie beneath surface of typical family. 2 acts 4 scenes 3m 2w 1 interior
In Berkoff, S. The collected plays v2

Lunch
Brief encounter between strangers seeking excitement in their bored lives, but refusing commitment. 1m 1w 1 setting
In Berkoff, S. The collected plays v1

Massage
Drama examining sexual politics of massage parlours. 2m 1w 1 setting
In Berkoff, S. The collected plays v1

Sink the Belgrano!
Verse satire derived from events of Falklands War about underlying values of English society revealed during the crisis. 4m 1w extras 1 setting
In Berkoff, S. The collected plays v1

West; or, Welcome to Dalston Junction
Set in London's West End. Disaffected teenager in suburban street gang searches for honor and romance, and meets violence. Singing. 7m 2w 1 setting
In Berkoff, S. The collected plays v1

Berlichingen, Götz von
Goethe, J. W. von. Goetz von Berlichingen with the iron hand

Berlin, Eric
The Midnight Moonlight Wedding Chapel
Romantic comedy set in Las Vegas. Drunken tourist marries cocktail waitress planning to divorce her the next day. Problems ensue when she vanishes. 2 scenes 3m 3w 1 interior
In Berlin, E. Babes and brides

Berlin, Eric—*Continued*
The line that's picked up 1000 babes (and how it can work for you!)
Romantic comedy set in singles bar. Men and women in search of companionship. 9 scenes 3m 3w 1 interior
In Berlin, E. Babes and brides

Berlin Bertie. Brenton, H.

Berlin (Germany)
Harwood, R. Taking sides
Piscator, E. and Gasbarra, F. In spite of everything!

Bernard, Catherine
Laodamia, Queen of Epirus (Laodamie reine d'Epire)
Tragedy about hard-working, well-intentioned queen and sister who sacrifice all for public good. 5 acts 4m 4w 1 interior
In The Lunatic lover and other plays; ed. by P. Gethner

Bernardi, Philip, and Havens, Diane
y Twice upon a time. Players Press 1995 24p
Fantasy about time. Hour and minute hands desert clock forcing numbers to seek new occupation. Music. 2 scenes Unidentified cast 15 characters 1 setting

Bernhardt, Sarah
Garrett-Groag, L. The ladies of the camellias
Harwood, R. After the lions
Murrell, J. Memoir

Bernice. Wilder, T.

Bernier, Eric [et. al]
The seven streams of the River Ota. Methuen Drama 1996 147p (Methuen modern plays)
Hiroshima metaphorical setting for exploration of 20th century civilization. Conflicts between East and West, male and female, tragedy and comedy, life and death seen as reflections of same reality. Prologue 7 scenes 5m 5w 1 setting

Bernstein, Douglas, and Krausz, Rob
Hello muddah, hello fadduh! the Allan Sherman musical; conceived and written by Douglas Bernstein & Rob Krausz. French 1994 191p
Musical revue based on the humorous songs of Allan Sherman. Prologue 2 acts 9 scenes epilogue 3m 2w 1 setting

Bernstein, Julianne
Pizza: a love story
Romantic comedy. Knowing her boyfriend is ready to propose, young woman desperately stalls for time. 3m 2w 1 interior
In Off-Off Broadway Festival plays, 19th ser.

Berry, Wendell
The cool of the day
Set in 1910 Kentucky. Farm family faces misfortune. 4m 2w
In By Southern playwrights; ed. by M. B. Dixon and M. Volansky

Bertram. Maturin, C. R.

Beryllium. Angwin, F.

Beside herself. Daniels, S.

The **best** blood of the country. Keithley, G.

The **best** man. Vidal, G.

The **best** of friends. Whitemore, H.

The **best** of strangers. Hunkins, L.

Bethune, Mary McLeod
y Satchell, M. Mary McLeod Bethune, dream maker

Betrayal. Pinter, H.

Betrayed by everyone. Lonergan, K.

Betrothal
Chinn, J. Sylvia's wedding
Russell, W. Stags and hens

The **betrothal.** Suarez, R. R.

A **betrothal.** Wilson, L.

Better living. Walker, G. F.

A **better** mousetrap. Neuman, C.

Betting on the Dust Commander. Parks, S.-L.

Betty the yeti. Klein, J.

Between the lines. Taylor, R.

Between two thieves. Adam, A.

Beulah. Robson, J.

Beuys, Joseph
Garnhum, K. Beuys buoys boys

Beuys buoys boys. Garnhum, K.

Beware the heart. Bonal, D.

The **bewitched.** Barnes, P.

Beyond Mozambique. Walker, G. F.

Beyond our understanding. Mitterer, F.

Beyond survival. Coffee, G. (dramatization) See Bell, J. A. Prisoner

Beyond the ruins. Micone, M.

Beyond therapy. Durang, C.

Bible. N.T.
See also Jesus Christ

Bible N.T. Acts
c Haylock, D. Light on the road to Damascus

Bible. O.T.
y Sloyer, G. Ezekiel saw the . . . what?
See also names of Biblical figures, e.g. Jonah (Biblical figure)

Bible O.T. Apocrypha. Tobit
Barnes, P. Heaven's blessings

Bible O.T. Daniel
Haylock, D. The flaming fiery furnace
c Haylock, D. How to be an alien

Bible. O.T. Genesis
Hurston, Z. N. The first one
O'Brien, J. T. Ancestress

Bible. O.T. Judges
Chayefsky, P. Gideon

Bible. O.T. Kings
Aynsley, E. 'I told you so'
Cross, J. The prophet's cloak

Bible. O.T. Numbers
Miller, M. Graven images

Big Al. Goluboff, B.

The **big** black Box. Haubold, C.

The **big** bun. Campanile, A.

Big burger. Martin, J.

Big butt girls, hard-headed women. Jones, R.

The **big** deal. Chayefsky, P.

Big Mary. Medoff, M.

The **big** mess. Martin, J.

Big Momma 'n 'em. Stickney, P. Y.

The **big** scene. Schnitzler, A.

The **big** stone. Leuser, E.

Big toys. White, P.

Big white fog. Ward, T.

Bigamy
Goethe, J. W. von. Stella
Macdonald, S. When we were women
Miller, A. The ride down Mount Morgan
Miller, J. A light on the landing

Bigger than life! Mercati, C.

Bilingual plays

French-English

Fennario, D. Balconville

Spanish-English

c Conboy, R. Song of the oak—El canto del roble
y Kesselman, W. Maggie Magalita
c Loomer, L. Bocón
McDonough, J. Posadas
Morton, C. Johnny Tenorio
Morton, C. Pancho Diablo
c Rosenberg, J. El gato sin amigos—The cat who had no friends

Bill, Stephen
Curtains. Dramatists 1997 81p
Black comedy. Woman assists death of old, suffering mother and must then face the family. 2 acts 3 scenes 3m 5w 1 interior
Curtains (condensation)
In The Best plays of 1995-1996

Billy Bishop goes to war. Gray, J.

Billy Shaw. Corrie, J.

Billy's problem. Schurman-O'Connor, K.

Bind up the nation's wounds. DuBois, G.

Bingham, Sallie
Milk of paradise
Drama set in 1930s Kentucky. Young girl's coming-of-age accomplished with help of aunt. 2 acts 3m 7w 1 setting
In Playwriting women; ed. by J. Miles

Bingo
Michels, J. and Murphy, P. The queen of bingo

Bird, Robert Montgomery
The gladiator
Tragedy in verse. Revolt of gladiator-slaves in ancient Rome led by Spartacus, Thracian superman. 5 acts 17 scenes 12m 2w extras 3 interiors 8 exteriors
In Early American drama; ed. by J. H. Richards

The **bird** has flown. Al-Surayyiʿ, ʿAbd al-ʿAziz

The **bird** lovers. Bjorneboe, J.

Bird of ill omen. Pintauro, J.

Bird woman of the Shoshones. McCullough, L. E.

Birds. Aristophanes

Birds. Teagarden, J.

The **Birds'** Christmas Carol. Miller, H. L.

Birds in church. Pintauro, J.

Birds of prey. Adam, A.

Birkenhead, Susan. See Wolfe, G. C. Jelly's last jam

Birth and after birth. Howe, T.

Birthday. Saunders, J.

The **birthday** guests. Wartski, M. C.

Birthdays
Adam, A. A great occasion
Howe, T. Birth and after birth
McCusker, P. Pap's place
y Kral, B. One to grow on

Birthdays are not for dying. Osofisan, F.

Bisexuality
Albee, E. Finding the sun
Durang, C. Beyond therapy
Gill, P. Mean tears
McNally, T. Prelude & Liebestod

Bishop, Billy
Gray, J. Billy Bishop goes to war

Bishop, William A. See Bishop, Billy

Bisson, Pat
Is there anybody there? New Playwrights Network 1997 28p

Comedy. Woman haunted by 18th century ghost. 1 act 2 scenes 5m 3w 1 interior

c Little Red Riding Hood. New Playwrights Network 1994 36p

Pantomime with music based on fairy tale about innocent girl and big bad wolf. Singing, dancing. 2 acts 12 scenes 7m 5w 1g extras 1 interior 3 exteriors

Merry widows. New Playwrights Network 1995 16p

Black comedy. Three recent widows celebrate deaths of abusive husbands. 1 act 1m 3w 1 interior

c Simple Simon. New Playwrights Network 1993 42p

Pantomime. Fairy gives Simon Dimwit brain transplant. Music, singing. 2 acts 12 scenes 4m 5w 1b extras 1 interior 3 exteriors

c Spacenapped. New Playwrights Network 1996 36p

English boy rescues mayor's daughter from space aliens. 11 scenes 12m 2w 1b 1g extras 4 interiors 1 exterior

When the clock strikes. New Playwrights Network 1996 24p

Parody of Bram Stoker's Dracula. Devoted housekeeper devises plan to restore vampire's zest for living. 1 act 1m 4w 1 interior

Biswas, Neil
Skin

Young East Indian woman in London mourns death of father. 2 scenes 1m 3w 1 setting

In Young playwrights; ed. by E. Bray

A **bit** of land. Adams, A.

A **bit** on the other side. Booth, J.

Biting the bullet. Vickery, F.

Bitter cane. Lim, G.

Bjorneboe, Jens
The bird lovers; tr. from the Norwegian by Frederick Wasser. Sun & Moon Press 1994 155p (Sun & Moon classics: 43)

Mock trial of German birdwatchers recognized by Italian villagers as former Nazi officers. Catholic priest defends the accused and argues they are boon to economy. 2 parts 29 scenes 10m 3w extras 1 setting

Black. Oates, J. C.

Black Bart. See Boles, Charles E.

Black Beauty. See Harris, A. Young Black Beauty

The **Black** Branch. Hill, G. L.

Black bride. Kelm, A.

Black cloud morning New York. See Nemeth, S. Sally's shorts: Black cloud morning New York

Black damp. Matheus, J. F.

The **black** doctor. Aldridge, I.

Black, green, white and gold. Owen, K.

Black humor. See Comedy—Black humor

Black masque: the passion of darkie's bones. Bass, G. H.

Black nationalism
Baraka, A. Slave ship
Kalamu ya Salaam. Blk love song #1

The **black** sequin dress. Kemp, J.

Black snow. Reddin, K.

Black widow. Thain, P.

Blacker, Terence
y Homebird. Collins. Educ. 1994 74p (Plays plus)

Based on the author's novel. Thirteen-year-old boy runs away from boarding school and becomes homeless in London. 3 acts 8m 7w 1 setting

Blacklisting of entertainers
Sweet, J. The value of names

Blackman, Michael
The Golden Shadows Old West Museum (dramatization) See King, L. L. The Golden Shadows Old West Museum

Blackmore, R. D.
Lorna Doone (dramatization) See Hyem, J. Lorna Doone

Blackout. Gifford, B.

Blackout. Lennon, G.

Blackrock. Enright, N.

Blacks
Boakye, P. Boy with beer
D'Aguiar, F. A Jamaican airman foresees his death
DuBois, W. E. B. Star of Ethiopia
Farmer, B. Irene and Lillian forever
Hurston, Z. N. The first one
Ikoli, T. Scrape off the black
Jackson, C. B. Iago
Maponya, M. The hungry earth
Nascimento, A. do. Sortilege II: Zumbi returns
O'Neill, E. The Emperor Jones
O'Neill, E. Thirst
Parks, S. L. Venus
Pinnock, W. Talking in tongues
Walcott, D. Dream on Monkey Mountain
Yourgrau, T. The song of Jacob Zulu
See also African Americans

Blackwood, Gary L.
Futures. Players Press 1996 39p
Impending remarriage of widow exposes family conflicts. 3 acts 3m 4w 1 interior

Blade to the heat. Mayer, O.

Blame it on the wolf. Love, D.

Blameless. Rosei, P.

Blanc, Esther Silverstein
Wars I have seen
Drama about nurses and doctors caring for casualties of the Spanish Civil War and World War II. 3 acts 23 scenes 8m 6w extras 2 interiors 1 exterior
In Blanc, E. S. Wars I have seen: the play, with selected short stories

Blanca flor. White flower. Vigil, A.

Bland, Joellen
y The squire's daughter
Based on story by Alexander Pushkin set in 19th century Russia. Squire's daughter disguises herself as peasant and falls in love. 4 scenes 3m 3w 1 interior 1 exterior
In The Big book of dramatized classics; ed. by S. E. Kamerman

Blasted. Kane, S.

Bleasdale, Alan
On the ledge. Faber & Faber 1993 63p
Satirical look at British urban life. 2 acts 8m 1w 1 setting

Blecher, Hilary; Cruz, Migdalia, and Rodriguez, Robert X.
Frida: the story of Frida Kahlo
Opera/theater piece about Mexican painter Frida Kahlo. Large mixed cast
In Here to stay: five plays from the Women's Project; ed. by J. Miles

Blessing, Lee
Down the road
Drama. Husband and wife writing team hired to help serial killer with account of his crimes. 22 scenes 2m 1w 1 setting
In Blessing, L. Patient A and other plays

Fortinbras
Comedy about nature of political power. Continues the story of William Shakespeare's Hamlet. Fortinbras, man of action, becomes new king of Denmark. 2 acts 15 scenes 11m 4w
In Blessing, L. Patient A and other plays

Independence
Set in rural Iowa. Emotionally disturbed mother and her three daughters attempt a reconciliation. 2 acts 9 scenes 4w 1 interior
In Plays for actresses; ed. by E. Lane and N. Shengold

Lake Street extension. Dramatists 1993 49p
Drama about sexual abuse. Male prostitute, estranged son of middle-aged man, returns home to find father living with young Salvadoran boy. 13 scenes 3m 1 interior
—Same
In Blessing, L. Patient A and other plays

Patient A. Dramatists 1993 47p
Explores case of Kimberly Bergalis who was infected with AIDS virus during dental treatment. 2m 1w
—Same
In Blessing, L. Patient A and other plays

Two rooms
Drama portrays ordeal of both an American hostage held in Beirut and of his wife, waiting in the United States. 2 acts 8 scenes 2m 2w 1 setting
In Blessing, L. Patient A and other plays

Blind
Barnes, P. Not as bad as they seem
Dean, P. H. The Sty of The Blind Pig
Friel, B. Molly Sweeney
Geoghan, J. Light sensitive
Mack, C. K. In her sight
Marshall, G. and Ganz, L. Wrong turn at Lungfish
Rabe, D. Sticks and bones
Stoppard, T. Artist descending a staircase
Turrini, P. Alpine glow
Valle-Inclan, R. del. Bohemian lights
See also Visually handicapped

Blind date. Sodaro, C.

Blind dates. Fuerstenberg, A.

Blind desire. Members of the Road Company Ensemble

Blinded by the light. Bolger, D.

Blinded by the sun. Poliakoff, S.

Blk love song #1. Kalamu ya Salaam

Block, Simon
Not a game for boys. Hern Bks. 1995 64p (Instant playscript)
Comedy about competitive obsession set in seedy London table tennis club. 3 acts 3m 1 interior

Blood and honour. Harding, A.

Blood guilty. Ó Flatharta, A.

Blood issue. Crews, H.

Blood moon. Lyssiotis, T.

Blood on blood. Ranson, R.

Blood pact. Valle-Inclán, R. del

Blood red roses. McGrath, J.

Blood, sweat and tears. Godber, J.

Blood wedding. García Lorca, F.

The **bloomers.** Sternheim, C.

Blount, Roy
Five Ives get named
Comic monologue. Baseball player phones brother to describe first major league at bat. 1m
In By Southern playwrights; ed. by M. B. Dixon and M. Volansky
That dog isn't fifteen
Satiric sketch about influence of television. 2w 1g
In By Southern playwrights; ed. by M. B. Dixon and M. Volansky

The **blue** ball. Godfrey, P.

Blue cities. Allen, R. J.

Blue heart: Blue kettle. Churchill, C.

Blue heart: Heart's desire. Churchill, C.

Blue kettle. See Churchill, C. Blue heart: Blue kettle

Blue murder. Christian, B.

Blue night in the heart of the West. Stock, J.

Blue remembered hills. Potter, D.

Blue stars. Spencer, S.

Bluebonnets. McCaslin, N.

Blues (Songs, etc.)
Wilson, A. Ma Rainey's black bottom

Blum, Galen; Barker, Wayne, and Martucci, Vinnie
Clue; the musical; based on the board game by Parker Brothers; book by Peter DePietro; lyrics by Tom Chiodo; music by Galen Blum, Wayne Barker [and] Vinnie Martucci. French 1997 81p
Musical murder mystery based on popular board game. Music, singing. 5m 3w 1 interior

Blum, Renon
c California wax museum. Players Press 1994 16p
Children visit wax museum where figures from California's history argue about their relative importance. Large mixed cast 1 setting

Bly, Nellie, 1867-1922
Cooper, B. Nellie Bly: ten days in a madhouse

Blyton, Enid
Parodies, imitations, etc.
c Wood, D. Noddy

Boakye, Paul
Boy with beer
Drama set in London about homosexual relationship between two black men. 3 acts 2m 1 interior
In Black plays: three; ed. by Y. Brewster

Boarder skirmish. Hamlett, C.

Boarders. Congdon, C.

Boarding houses. See Lodging houses

Boardwalk melody hour murders. Chiodo, T.

Bobrick, Sam
Are you sure? French 1993 82p
Comic mystery about shifting realities, gamesmanship, and murky motivations. 2 acts 7 scenes 3m 3w 1 interior
See also Clark, R. jt. auth.

Bocón. Loomer, L.

Body and soul. Mighton, J.

A **body** of water: Foreign bodies. Zark, J.

A **body** of water: Shooting souls. Zark, J.

A **body** of water: White days. Zark, J.

Bogosian, Eric
Drinking in America
Black comedy. Series of short scenes of men pursuing, and being corrupted by the American dream. Background music. 1m extra
In Bogosian, E. The essential Bogosian
Fun house
Satiric monologues on contemporary society. 1m
In Bogosian, E. The essential Bogosian

Bogosian, Eric—*Continued*

Men inside

Monologues by frustrated male character types. 1m

In Bogosian, E. The essential Bogosian

Pounding nails in the floor with my forehead. French 1994 77p

Twelve monologues satirizing contemporary urban and suburban scene. 1m

—Same. Theatre Communications Group 1994 82p

Sex, drugs, rock & roll. Theatre Communications Group 1996 123p

Series of performance monologues reflecting on contemporary society. 1m

—Same

In The Best of Off-Broadway; ed. by R. Wetzsteon

SubUrbia. Dramatists 1995 77p

Drama about youthful disillusionment. Seven twenty-something characters hang out in convenience store parking lot. 2 acts 4 scenes 5m 4w 1 exterior

—Same. Theatre Communications Group 1995 122p

SubUrbia (condensation)

In The Best plays of 1993-1994

Talk radio

Comedy portrays call-in radio program hosted by dissipated and depressed talk-show host. 7m 2w extras 1 interior

In Bogosian, E. The essential Bogosian

Voices of America

Monologues reflecting material nature of American society. 1m

In Bogosian, E. The essential Bogosian

Bohemian lights. Valle-Inclan, R. del

Bohmler, Craig, and Adler, Marion

Gunmetal blues; a musical mystery; book by Scott Wentworth; music and lyrics by Craig Bohmler & Marion Adler. French 1993 70p

Chandleresque private eye musical. Music, singing. 2 acts 2m 1w extras 1 interior

Boiko, Claire

y Belinda and the Beast

Parody of Beauty and the Beast set in American West. Beast is transformed by reading. Dancing, singing. 4 scenes 15m 6w extras 1 interior

In The Big book of large-cast plays; ed. by S. E. Kamerman

c A dog's best friend

Comedy. Dogs purchase people pets. 3m 2w 1b 1g extras 1 interior

In The Big book of skits; ed. by S. E. Kamerman

y Escape to the blue planet

Teenager aids lady from another planet overcome evil aliens. 2 scenes Variable cast 11 characters 1 interior 1 exterior

In The Big book of large-cast plays; ed. by S. E. Kamerman

y Murder on the Orient Express subway

Parody of mystery novels. Detectives and murder suspects ride subway. 4m 2w extras 2 interiors

In The Big book of skits; ed. by S. E. Kamerman

c Once upon a dream

Three young European immigrants come to America in 1910. 3 scenes 11m 6w extras

In Great American events on stage; ed. by S. E. Kamerman

c Persephone

Based on Greek myth of Persephone who was carried off by Hades and made his queen in the underworld. Background music. 4 scenes Variable cast 11 characters extras 1 interior 1 exterior

In Thirty plays from favorite stories; ed. by S. E. Kamerman

c Yankees vs. Redcoats

Yankees and Redcoats enact American Revolution as baseball game. 17m extras 1 exterior

In The Big book of large-cast plays; ed. by S. E. Kamerman

The **boiler** room. Gonzalez, R.

A **bold** stroke for a wife. Centlivre, S.

Boles, Charles E.

c McCullough, L. E. Turquoise Tom, the versifying bandit of Old California

Bolger, Dermot

April Bright

Play set simultaneously in 1940s and 1990s. Young couple in new home experience joys and tragedies of previous residents. 2 acts 2m 5w 1 interior

In Bolger, D. April Bright & Blinded by the light

Blinded by the light

Black comedy. World comes crashing in on solitary Dublin man when he opens his door to Mormon missionaries. 2 acts 9 scenes 11m 2w 1 interior

In Bolger, D. April Bright & Blinded by the light

Bologna, Joseph. See Taylor, R. jt. auth.

Bolt, Carol

Compañeras

Radio play based on life of Karen Ridd, Canadian civil

Bolt, Carol—*Continued*
rights activist. In El Salvador Ridd saves friend from prison. Background music. 19 scenes 7m 3w
In Adventures for (big) girls; ed. by A. Jansen

Bonal, Denise
Beware the heart
Family forever altered when they open their home to apparently ill young man. 3 acts epilogue 3m 4w 1 setting
In Plays by women: an international anthology bk2; ed. by N. Shange

A country wedding
Dream-like staging of large provincial wedding celebration. 26 scenes Large mixed cast 1 setting
In Plays by women: an international anthology bk3; ed. by N. Shange

Bond, Edward
y At the inland sea. Methuen Drama 1997 81p (Methuen modern plays)
While studying for history exam teenage boy takes imaginative journey that forces him to confront horrors of Auschwitz. 6 scenes 2m 3w extras 1 setting

The bundle; or, New narrow road to the deep north
Basho, a 17th century Japanese poet, refuses to save abandoned baby while on solitary journey. Child survives and grows to be liberator of oppressed, ultimately confronting poet. 2 acts 12 scenes 23m 4w 2 interiors 5 exteriors
In Bond, E. Plays: 5

Coffee. Methuen Drama 1995 87p (Methuen modern plays)
Symbolic exploration of historical and psychological issues raised by Holocaust. 5 scenes 7m extras 4 interiors 1 exterior

Human cannon
Drama portraying women's role in the struggle against fascism in Spain. 2 parts 12 scenes Large mixed cast 1 setting
In Bond, E. Plays: 5

In the company of men
Satirical look at corporate values. Differences between successful British tycoon and his ambitious son lead to violence. 9 scenes 6m 5 interiors
In Bond, E. Plays: 5

Jackets; or, The secret hand
Dramatic look at political martyrdom. Part I: The village school, is set in 18th century Japan. Part II: The city, takes place in 20th century Europe. Music, singing. 2 parts 12m 6w extras settings
In Bond, E. Plays: 5

Olly's prison. Methuen 1993 88p (Methuen modern plays)
Television play. British man kills his daughter, serves ten years in prison, attempts to adjust to life after release. Stage version included. 10m 3w extras

y Tuesday. Methuen 1993 77p (Methuen modern plays)
Television drama about political and familial authoritarianism. Violence results when AWOL soldier, haunted by experience in desert war, seeks refuge in girlfriend's house. 7m 2w 1b

See also Wedekind, F. Lulu: a monster tragedy; Wedekind, F. Spring awakenings

Bondage. Hwang, D. H.

Bondagers. Glover, S.

Bonds of affection. Bellon, L.

Bonfire at dawn. Salom, J.

Boniface, Saint, Archbishop of Mainz, ca. 680-754
c McCullough, L. E. O, Christmas tree

Bonner, Marita Odette
The purple flower
Allegorical look at blacks in post-Emancipation America. Background music, dancing. Variable cast 1 exterior
In Black theatre USA [v1]; ed. by J. V. Hatch and T. Shine

The **book** of herself. Hall, F. B.

The **Book** of Leviticus Show. Durang, C.

Bookends. Perry, S.

Books and reading
y Boiko, C. Belinda and the Beast
c Miller, H. L. Name that book!
c Tesh, J. Breakfast at the Bookworm Cafe

Boom, baby, boom! Rubess, B.

Boom bang-a-bang. Harvey, J.

Boone, Daniel, 1734-1820
Norman, M. Loving Daniel Boone

The **boor.** See Chekhov, A. The bear

Booth, Edwin, 1833-1893
Pendleton, A. Booth

Booth, Jack
50 . . . and counting. New Playwrights Network 1996 30p
Comedy revolving around fifty-year-old actress posing nude for magazine. 1 act 2m 5w 1 interior

A bit on the other side. New Playwrights Network 1996 32p
Farce. Englishman's political ambitions jeopardized by nephews who hire woman to pose as illegitimate daughter. 1 act 3m 5w 1 interior

Both worlds. New Playwrights Network 1996 22p
Mother tries to dissuade daughter from Himalayan mountain climbing expedition. Offstage voice. 1 act 1m 2w 1 interior

Booth, Jack—*Continued*
By whose hand? New Playwrights Network 1995 20p
Mystery set in 1940s English country home. German woman seeks revenge for sister's murder during World War II. 5w extras 1 interior

Charley's uncle. New Playwrights Network 1996 38p
Farcical comedy revolving around visiting uncle and window cleaner who impersonates niece's husband. 1 act 3m 3w 1 interior

Dead on time. New Playwrights Network 1994 28p
Mystery. Woman plots to kill unfaithful husband. 3m 3w 1 interior

Dirty weekend. New Playwrights Network 1996 34p
Farce. Chaos ensues when daughter of divorced parents attempts to spend weekend with boyfriend instead of father. 1 act 3m 4w 1 interior

Echo of applause. New Playwrights Network 1995 24p
Actor mourns demolition of English provincial theater. 1 act 3m 2w 1 interior

Face of evil. New Playwrights Network 1997 27p
Mystery. Murder investigation leads to revelations of past infidelities of two couples. 1 act 3m 3w 1 interior

Friendly affair. New Playwrights Network 1995 24p
Comedy. High-strung pregnant wife suspects husband of infidelity. 1 act 5w 1 interior

Little white lies. New Playwrights Network 1995 29p
Comedy. Jealousy between sisters leads to romantic misunderstandings. 1 act 2 scenes 3m 3w 1 interior

The loved one. New Playwrights Network 1995 21p
Man renews acquaintance with old flame and learns that she is probably responsible for her sister's death. 1 act 1m 2w 1 interior

Mirror mirror on the wall. New Playwrights Network 1996 30p
Murder mystery set in isolated house in Norfolk coast. 1 act 1m 2w 1 interior

Or was he pushed? New Playwrights Network 1996 32p
Mystery set in South of France. Mother investigates circumstances of son's death. 1 act 5w 1 exterior

Over his dead body. New Playwrights Network 1996 32p
Woman's one-night-stand turns into comedy of errors involving police, press and a dead body. 1 act 3m 4w 1 interior

A question of identity. New Playwrights Network 1995 77p
Mystery. After man kills twin brother and assumes his identity, he is accused of another murder. 2 acts 4 scenes 3m 3w 1 interior

Season of goodwill. New Playwrights Network 1995 23p
Comedy. Christmas season tarnished by feuding neighbors. 1 act 3m 4w 1 extra 1 interior

Seeing double. New Playwrights Network 1994 20p
Farce. Plot revolves around mistaken identities of twin brothers, their wives and mistress. 1 act 2m 3w 1 interior

Sleeping arrangements. New Playwrights Network 1994 76p
Comedy. Hollywood actress visiting England with prospective third husband unexpectedly encounters two exes. 2 acts 5 scenes 4m 3w 1 interior

Something on his mind. New Playwrights Network 1996 40p
Comedy. English family objects to father's plan to emigrate to Australia. 1 act 3m 3w 1 interior

Tangled web. New Playwrights Network 1995 60p
Mystery. To alleviate gambling debts photojournalist attempts to blackmail British aristocrat. 2 acts 4 scenes 3m 3w 1 interior

Your place or mine? New Playwrights Network 1996 28p
Comedy. Marital infidelity complicated by appearance of mysterious stranger. 3m 3w 1 setting

Booth, Junius Brutus, 1796-1852
Pendleton, A. Booth

Booth, Richard
y Where did you spend the night? Players Press 1993 44p
Horror. Teenagers spend the night in museum, mausoleum, and service station rest room. 3 acts 6m 8w extras 3 interiors

Booth. Pendleton, A.

Booth is back. See Pendleton, A. Booth

Boothe, Clare
The women
Woman resorts to tactics of her malicious, wealthy New York City social circle to recapture former husband. 3 acts 12 scenes Large female cast settings
In Plays by American women, 1930-1960; ed. by J. E. Barlow

Border warfare. McGrath, J.

Borders of paradise. Macdonald, S.

Boretz, Alvin
I remember you. Clark, I.E. 1993 28p
Middle aged ex-lovers meet again accompanied by their younger alter egos. 2 acts 2m 2w 1 interior

Boris Fyodorovich Godunov, Czar of Russia, 1551?-1605
Pushkin, A. Boris Godunov

Boris Godunov. Pushkin, A.

Born guilty. Roth, A.

Borrowed plumage. Crawford, D. W.

Borrowed trouble. McCaslin, N.

Boss Grady's boys. Barry, S.

Boss of the pool. Morris, M.

Boston (Mass.)
Koch, K. The construction of Boston

Boston Massacre, 1770
c Smith, B. S. Adams for the defense

Boswell, Laurence
c Beauty and the beast. Hern Bks. in association with the Young Vic Theatre 1996 67p
Drama based on classic fairy tale. Journey to Beast's palace forces Beauty's family to reexamine materialism of their lives. Music, singing, dancing. 2 acts 15 scenes 4m 4w 1 setting

Botanists
Wilson, L. A betrothal

Both worlds. Booth, J.

Botticelli, Sandro
Warner, F. Living creation

Botticelli. McNally, T.

Bottles with baskets on. Tibbetts, M.

Boubouroche. Courteline, G.

Bouchard, Michel Marc
The orphan muses
Part of the Tangway series of plays. Set in Quebec Province, 1965. Abandoned in youth, brother and three sisters, now dysfunctional adults relive past. 3 acts 19 scenes 1m 3w 1 interior
In New French-language plays

Boucicault, Dion
The Colleen Bawn; or, The brides of Garryowen
Set in nineteenth century Ireland. A man rues his rash first marriage when he realizes a better one with an heiress could have been made. Incidental music. 3 acts 14 scenes 9m 6w extras 6 interiors 6 exteriors
In Great Irish plays

The octoroon; or, Life in Louisiana
Melodrama set in pre-Civil War Mississippi. Octoroon daughter of bankrupt planter commits suicide when she is bought by cunning overseer. 5 acts 8 scenes 14m 6w 3 interiors 4 exteriors
In Early American drama; ed. by J. H. Richards

Bouncers: 1990's REMIX. Godber, J.

Boundary Waters. Field, B.

Bower, Margaret
A fitting finish. Kenyon-Deane 1993 21p
Comedy set early 1900s England about social climbing. Unscrupulous mayor's wife and poor laundry woman patronize same dressmaking shop. 1 act 5w 1 interior

Bowles, Jane
In the summer house
Surrealistic look at mother-daughter relationships. 2 acts 5 scenes 5m 10w extras 1 interior
In Plays by American women, 1930-1960; ed. by J. E. Barlow

Boxing
Glover, K. Coming of the Hurricane
Kwahulé, K. That old black magic
Mayer, O. Blade to the heat

Boy with beer. Boakye, P.

The **boy** who ate the moon. Martin, J.

The **boy** who killed the giant. See Vigil, A. El muchacho que mato al gigante. The boy who killed the giant

The **boy** who left home to find out about the shivers. Bush, M.

The **boy** who tricked the moon. Grauer, R.

Boyd, Belle
c DuBois, G. Bind up the nation's wounds

Boyd, Pamela
Odd fish. Red Deer College Press 1994 94p
Czech woman living comfortably in Canada with her husband and two children forced to confront past when old lover pays unexpected visit. 2 acts 7 scenes 4m 2w 1 setting

Boys
Adrian, Y. Flyboy
y Hackett, W. Tom Sawyer, whitewasher
Margulies, D. Anthony
c Prendergast, S. Little victories
Segal, G. All the tricks but one
Williams, N. William Golding's Lord of the flies
y York, M. A. Treasure Island

The **boys.** Graham, G.

The **boys** in the band. Crowley, M.

Boys mean business. Johnson, C.

Bozzone, Bill
Sonny DeRee's life flashes before his eyes
Black comedy. Alcoholic mother comes to rescue of ne'er-do-well son being menaced by hitman. 1 act 2m 1w 1 interior
In EST marathon '95

Bozzone, Bill, and DiPietro, Joe
Breast men
Comedy set in tacky honeymoon cottage. Two buddies face personal problems. 1 act 3m 1 interior
In Act One '95

Bracken, Brendan Bracken, 1st Viscount
Kilroy, T. Double cross

The **braggart** soldier. Plautus, T. M.

The **braggart** warrior. See Plautus, T. M. The braggart soldier

Brain
Warner, F. Killing time

Braithwaite, Diana
Martha and Elvíra. Sister Vision 1993 46p
Drama about friendship between two elderly women and their journey through Underground Railroad in 1865. Music. 1 act 3 scenes 2w 1 setting

Branch, William
In splendid error
Historical drama. Frederick Douglass rejects John Brown's invitation to participate in raid on Harpers Ferry, but later regrets his decision. 3 acts 5 scenes 10m 2w 1 interior
In Crosswinds; ed. by W. B. Branch

Brand. Hill, G.

Brandl, Dave
Vine and dandy. Players Press 1994 51p
Comedy. Elderly sisters open shop specializing in erotic floral arrangements. 2 acts 5 scenes 6m 5w 1 setting

Branner, Djola. See Freeman, B. jt. auth.

Brassard, Marie. See Lepage, R. jt. auth.

Brave hearts. Rintoul, H.

Brave new banner. McCaslin, N.

Brave smiles . . . another lesbian tragedy. The Five Lesbian Brothers

Braverman, Carole
The Yiddish Trojan women. Dramatists 1996 74p
Originally produced under title: The Brooklyn Trojan women. Interwoven story of four strong-willed Jewish women in 1980s Brooklyn. 2 acts 13 scenes 1m 4w 1 setting

Brazil
Nascimento, A. do. Sortilege II: Zumbi returns

Politics and government

Hampton, C. Savages

Break. LaChiusa, M. J.

The **break** of day. Wertenbaker, T.

Breakfast at the Bookworm Cafe. Tesh, J.

Breakfast at the track. Wilson, L.

Breakfast serial. Terry, M.

Breaking glass. Roberts, D.

Breaking the chain. Dixon, M. B. and Smith, V.

Breaking the silence. Poliakoff, S.

Breast cancer
Miller, S. My left breast

Breast men. Bozzone, B. and DiPietro, J.

Brecht, Bertolt
Mother Courage and her children. Arcade Pub. 1996 93p
Variant title: Mother Courage. Tragedy. Camp follower struggles to make money and keep family alive during Thirty Years' War. Music, singing. 12 scenes Large mixed cast

Breeze, Nick
c The Rochdale Pioneers; a musical play for young people. Co-operative Union 1993 52p
Musical play celebrating founding of Rochdale Equitable Pioneers Society by English factory workers in 1844, signalling birth of modern co-operative movement. Music. 11 scenes Large mixed cast 2 interiors 2 exteriors

A **breeze** from the gulf. Crowley, M.

Breezeblock Park. Russell, W.

The **Brementown** musicians. See Gerke, P. Los mariachis Mexicanos: "The Brementown musicians"

Bremner, Belinda
Mrs. Coney. French 1997 43p
Christmas memory play with music. Writer recalls his boyhood in 1934 dust bowl Oklahoma and rural Kentucky. 3m 3w 1b 1 setting

Brennert, Alan
Her pilgrim soul (dramatization) See Menken, A. Weird romance: Her pilgrim soul

Brenton, Howard
Berlin Bertie. Hern Bks. 1992 76p
Psychological study of two sisters set in 1990. Woman fleeing East Berlin and ruined marriage followed to sister's South London flat by sinister figure. 3 acts 9 scenes 2m 3w 1 interior

Faust, parts I & II; a new version by Howard Brenton; from a literal translation by Christa Weisman. Hern Bks. 1995 277p
Adaptation of Goethe's drama about man who sold his soul to Devil. pt. 1 24 scenes, pt2 5 acts 25 scenes Large mixed cast

Breslin, Jimmy
Contract with Jackie
Short satirical piece on politics and politicians. Congressman visits wife in Atlanta hospital, 1980. 1m 1w 1 interior
In Humana Festival '96

Brett, Simon
Mr. Quigley's revenge. French (London) 1995 109p
Caretaker of English community hall devises scheme to save building from demolition. 2 acts 5 scenes 14m 20w extras 1 interior

Murder in play. French (London) 1994 75p
Play-within-a-play mystery about murder during performance by inept theatrical company. 2 acts 3 scenes 3m 5w 1 interior

Brewer, Elly, and Toksvig, Sandi
The pocket dream. French (London) 1992 107p
Comedy. Amateur theatrical troupe stages problem-riddled production of A midsummer night's dream. 2 acts 10 scenes 4m 2w extras 1 interior

Bricusse, Leslie
The revenge of Sherlock Holmes; a musical mystery; book, music and lyrics by Leslie Bricusse. French (London) 1994 124p
Musical confrontation between the great detective and his arch-enemy Professor Moriarity. Prologue 2 acts 18 scenes 9m 5w 3b extras

A **bride** for Heatherhill. Corrie, J.

Brides are not for burning. Mehta, D.

Brideshead revisited. Parsley, R.

Bridge (Game)
Lauro, S. The coal diamond

Bridges
Stoppard, T. Albert's bridge

A **bright** room called day. Kushner, T.

Brighton (England)
Berkoff, S. Brighton beach scumbags

Brighton Beach memoirs. Simon, N.

Brighton beach scumbags. Berkoff, S.

Bring a torch, Jeannette, Isabella. McCullough, L. E.

Bringing it all back home. McNally, T.

Brinvilliers, Marie Madeleine d'Aubray Gobelin
Churchill, C. Lives of the great poisoners

British

Africa

Churchill, C. Cloud 9
Mercer, D. The Governor's lady
Owen, K. Black, green, white and gold

Canada

Ackerman, M. L'affaire Tartuffe

Congo (Democratic Republic)

Gray, S. The rear column

Egypt

Sherman, M. Some sunny day

France

Booth, J. Or was he pushed?
Godber, J. April in Paris
Hornby, I. A question of innocence

India

Kipling, R. Mrs. Hauksbee sits out
y Thane, A. The moonstone

Indonesia

Dryden, J. Amboyna
Inchbald, Mrs. Such things are

Ireland

Shaw, B. John Bull's other Island

Middle East

McGuinness, F. Someone who'll watch over me

Nigeria

Soyinka, W. Death and the King's Horseman

Spain

Brooks, V. Let's pretend

Thailand

Minghella, A. Made in Bangkok
Smith, S. One-sided triangle

United States

Baitz, J. R. The end of the day
Horovitz, I. Fighting over Beverley
Nelson, R. New England

The **British.** See Hollingsworth, M. The history of the village of the small huts

Brittney, Lynn
A different way to die. French (London) 1993 23p
Psychological drama. Concentration camp survivor struggles to forge new life for herself in 1950 Jerusalem. 2m 2w 1 interior

Failed investments. French (London) 1995 25p
Social comedy. Four women at London tenants meeting condemn male-oriented society for making their lives so difficult. 1m 4w 1 interior

Brittney, Lynn—*Continued*
Have a nice day. French (London) 1994 19p
Television personality about to be fired turns her anger to her advantage. 2m 3w extra 1 interior

The last wife. French (London) 1994 25p
Drama about courtly tyranny. Facing death, Henry VIII ponders fate of wife Catharine Parr. 2m 3w

Properly processed. French (London) 1994 20p
Satirical look at modern bureaucracy. Woman killed in car crash takes job in office processing applicants for afterlife. 3m 1w 1 interior

Broadhurst, Kent
The eye of the beholder
Satire poking fun at pretentiousness of "serious artists". Interpretative dispute between two painters resolved by model in unexpected way. 1 act 3m 1 interior
In 20/20: twenty one-act plays from twenty years of the Humana Festival

Broadway. Baitz, J. R.

Broadway hit. Cheatham, V. R.

Brochu, Jim
Fat chance. French 1994 93p
May-December romance between food-addicted middle-aged sculptress and her handsome young model. 2 acts 4 scenes 2m 3w 1 interior

Brogan, Patricia Burke
Eclipsed. Salmon Pub. 1994 77p (Salmon drama)
Drama set in Irish Magdalen convent in 1963. Portrays life in penitential-home laundries where women were locked away to cleanse their sin of having become pregnant out of wedlock. Prologue 2 acts 12 scenes 8w 1 interior

Broinowski, Anna
The gap. Currency Press 1995 63p
Drama about cultural attitudes set in Australia. Directionless life of female tour guide becomes entwined with that of young Japanese bride facing life crisis. 11 scenes 2w 1 setting

Broken bones. McWeeny, D. and Swan, S.

The **broken** calabash. Onwueme, O. T.

Broken English. Sherman, G.

Broken English. See Yew, C. A language of their own

Broken glass. Miller, A.

The **broken** heart. Ford, J.

Broken hearts. McLeod, K. R.

The **broken** jug. Banville, J.

Bronson, James Graham
Willie & Esther. French 1997 70p
Two middle-aged, blue collar African American lovers fantasize about robbing bank. 2 acts 1m 1w 2 exteriors

Brontë, Charlotte
Jane Eyre (dramatization) See Hall, W. Jane Eyre; Vance, C. Jane Eyre

Brontë, Emily
Wuthering Heights (dramatization) See Olfson, L. Wuthering Heights

About

Hall, F. B. Emily's play

Brontë, Patrick Branwell
Hall, F. B. Emily's play

Brontosaurus. Wilson, L.

Brooker, Blake
Changing bodies
Surreal comedy about personal change. 1m 1 setting
In Brooker, B. Ilsa, queen of the Nazi love camp and other plays

Ilsa, queen of the Nazi love camp
Musical satire on intolerance and paranoia. Man angrily denies Holocaust. 2m 1w 1 setting
In Brooker, B. Ilsa, queen of the Nazi love camp and other plays

The land, the animals
Ecological comedy-dance piece. Three scientists investigate land and animals of future city. 23 scenes 2m 1w 1 setting
In Brooker, B. Ilsa, queen of the Nazi love camp and other plays

Tears of a dinosaur
Satirical look at modern family consisting of mother, father, adopted son and numerous dinosaurs. Prologue 6 scenes 1w 2m 1 setting
In Brooker, B. Ilsa, queen of the Nazi love camp and other plays
See also Millan, J. jt. auth.

Brooklyn. See New York (N.Y.)—Brooklyn

The **Brooklyn** Trojan women. See Braverman, C. The Yiddish Trojan women

Brooks, Daniel. See MacIvor, D. jt. auth.

Brooks, Vanessa
Let's pretend. Warner Chappell Plays 1995 118p
Comedy set in once glamorous hotel. Pretense and deception among British penshioners wintering in Majorca. 2 acts 3m 3w 1 interior 1 exterior

Love me slender. Warner Chappell Plays 1996 107p
Drama about seven women in British dieting club. 2 acts 5 scenes 7w 1 interior

Brooks, Vanessa—*Continued*
Penny Blue. Warner Chappell Plays 1994 122p
Visit of old friends from Australia disrupts life of working class London couple and their rebellious daughter. 2 acts 3m 3w 1 interior

Brothels. See Prostitution

Brother and sister. Goethe, J. W. von

Brother truckers. Osterman, G.

Brothers
Alám, S. A. Zookeeper
Allen, C. Ripe conditions
Barry, S. Boss Grady's boys
Dashow, K. He ain't heavy
Donnelly, N. The duty master
Farquhar, G. The twin rivals
Fishelson, D. The brothers Karamazov
FitzGibbon, G. The rock station
Fletcher, J. and Massinger, P. Rollo, Duke of Normandy
Gray, S. Dog days
Hamilton, G. Kissing Marianne
Huff, K. Leon and Joey
Korder, H. Night maneuver
McDonagh, M. The lonesome West
Milligan, J. Road trip
Morris, M. Two weeks with the Queen
Nelson, G. Castrato
O Flatharta, A. Blood guilty
Osment, P. Flesh and blood
Pernak, A. Killers
Pintauro, J. His dish
Plautus, T. M. The brothers Menaechmus
Plautus, T. M. Stichus
Pugliese, F. The talk
Ranson, R. Blood on blood
Smith, C. Freefall
y Thomas, C. Flesh and blood
Woudstra, K. Burying the dog
York, Y. Life gap
Zuberbuehler, A. Fieldstones

Brothers and sisters
Bouchard, M. M. The orphan muses
Delaney, D. The last ten miles of Avery J. Coping
Dryden, J. Aureng-Zebe
Handke, P. Walk about the villages
Hellman, L. The little foxes
Horovitz, I. Stage directions
Houston, V. H. As sometimes in a dead man's face
c Jones, T. Camping out
c Lazarus, J. Night light
Lee, C. Arthur and Leila
Linney, R. El hermano
Mamet, D. Jolly
Paterson, D. L. Finger painting in a Murphy bed
Rno, S. Cleveland raining
Sanchez, E. Icarus
Silver, N. Raised in captivity
Strindberg, A. The pelican
Taylor, P. Familiar haunts
Tremblay, M. Marcel pursued by the hounds
Triana, J. Night of the assassins
Vogel, P. The Baltimore waltz
Wilson, L. Home free!

Brothers in crime. Feydeau, G.

The **brothers** Karamazov. Fishelson, D.

The **brothers** Menaechmus. Plautus, T. M.

Brown, Alan
c Sleeping Beauty. French (London) 1993 75p
Victorian musical pantomime based on the popular fairy tale. 2 acts 13 scenes Large mixed cast settings

Brown, Ben
All things considered. French (London) 1997 73p
Philosophical comedy of manners about British professor's efforts to control his own death. 2 acts 4m 3w 1 interior

Brown, Carlyle
The African Company presents Richard III. Dramatists 1994 60p
Drama set in 1821 Manhattan focusing on black theatrical groups' troubled production of Shakespeare's Richard III. 2 acts 13 scenes 5m 2w 2 interiors

Buffalo Hair. Dramatists 1995 45p
Historical drama set in 1874 during Red River War on Southern plains. Group of black troopers from Tenth Cavalry sent to supress uprising of Southern Cheyenne. 3 scenes 8m 1 exterior

The Little Tommy Parker Celebrated Colored Minstrel Show
Examines lives of troupe of black minstrels touring the United States in 1895. 2 acts 7m 1 setting
In Colored contradictions: an anthology of contemporary African-American plays

Brown, Carol J.
The Constitution is born
Historical drama depicting activities at the Constitutional Convention. 13m extra 1 interior
In Great American events on stage; ed. by S. E. Kamerman

Brown, Janet
c The lake at the end of the world
Inca girl saves her brothers by finding cure for emperor's son. 5 scenes 7m 3w 1g extras 1 interior
In Thirty plays from favorite stories; ed. by S. E. Kamerman

Brown, John, 1800-1859
Branch, W. In splendid error

Brown, K. C.
Sherlock's veiled secret. Dramatists 1996 87p
Mystery of identity featuring Sherlock Holmes in retirement. Young sculptress discovers startling truth about her heritage. 2 acts 12 scenes 3m 4w 1 setting

Brown, Kent R.
Welcome to Four Way: the town that time forgot. Dramatic 1993 83p
Comedy. Opinionated cross section of small town characters. 2 acts 7m 6w 1 setting
See also Sloyer, G. Ezekiel saw the . . . what?

Brown, Michael Henry
The day the Bronx died. Applause 1996 94p
Depiction of racial and class tensions in integrated Bronx neighborhood in late 1960s. 2 acts 11 scenes 11m 1w 1 setting

Brown, William Wells
The escape; or, A leap for freedom
A hypocritical physician, abolitionists, and runaway slaves are portrayed in this drama about slavery in the United States. Singing. 5 acts 20 scenes Large mixed cast 9 interiors 4 exteriors
In Black theatre USA [v1]; ed. by J. V. Hatch and T. Shine

The **brown** overcoat. Séjour, V.

Brownbread. Doyle, R.

Browne, Theodore
Natural man
Folk drama with ballads based on the legend of John Henry, the black steel driving man victimized by prejudice. Music, singing. 8 episodes 26m 4w extras 3 interiors 3 exteriors
In Black theatre USA [v1]; ed. by J. V. Hatch and T. Shine

Brownell, Richard
Afterhours. French 1997 63p
Comedy. Confusion reigns as man tries to conceal infidelity from his girlfriend. 1 act 3m 4w extras 1 interior

Browning, Robert, 1812-1889
The Pied Piper of Hamelin (dramatization) See Mahlmann, L. and Jones, D. C. The Pied Piper of Hamelin; Norcross, E. B. Pied Piper's land; Nunn, J. The Pied Piper

Parodies, travesties, etc.

c Church, J. The Pied Piper of New Orleans

The **Browning** version. Rattigan, T.

Bruce, Kathleen
Vingoe, M. and Kudelka, J. Hooligans

Bruce, Lesley
Keyboard skills
Philandering British politician's latest fling has career threatening consequences. 2 acts 24 scenes 2m 3w 1 setting
In Bush Theatre plays

Bruce, Mark
y Car crazy
Girlfriend is jealous of teenage boy's love of new car. 1m 1w 1 setting
In The Big book of skits; ed. by S. E. Kamerman
y Caveman blues
Caveman tries making music with sticks but starts fire instead. Singing. 2m 1w 1 interior
In The Big book of skits; ed. by S. E. Kamerman

Bruises. Upton, J.

Brussels (Belgium)
Emond, P. Talk about love!

Brussels sprouts. Neipris, J.

Brustein, Robert
The cherry orchard. Dee, I.R. 1995 85p (Plays for performance)
This adaptation of Chekhov's play is based on a translation by George Calderon. 4 acts 8m 5w extras 2 interiors 1 exterior
The wild duck. Dee, I.R. 1997 146p (Plays for performance)
Adaptation of Ibsen's symbolic tragedy. Idealistic son exposes wealthy father's corruption. 5 acts 7m 3w extras 2 interiors

Brutality of fact. Reddin, K.

The **brute.** See Chekhov, A. The bear

Brutopia. Barker, H.

Buchan, Alex
Conditional surrender. Players Press 1996 39p
Comedy in Scottish dialect based on Lawrence Sterne's The life and opinions of Tristram Shandy. Set in 1713. Naive captain courts attractive widow. 3m 3w 1 exterior

Bucharest (Romania)
Visdei, A. Class photo

Büchner, Georg
Danton's death; tr. by John Reddick
Historical tragedy. Conflict between Robespierre and

Büchner, Georg—*Continued*

Danton during the Reign of Terror of the French Revolution. 4 acts 32 scenes Large mixed cast settings

In Büchner, G. Complete plays, Lenz and other writings

Leonce and Lena; tr. by John Reddick

Romantic comedy exploring social and moral convention. Romance of prince and princess who met while each was seeking to escape arranged marriage. 3 acts 11 scenes 9m 3w 4 interiors 5 exteriors

In Büchner, G. Complete plays, Lenz and other writings

Woyzeck; tr. by John Reddick

Series of related incidents portray simple soldier's inner torment and disintegration leading to murder of his faithless common law wife. 24 scenes 10m 3w 7 interiors 6 exteriors

In Büchner, G. Complete plays, Lenz and other writings

Buck. Ribman, R.

Buck Simple. Fols, C.

The **Buddha** of Ceylon. De Boer, L.

Buenos Aires

Puig, M. Kiss of the spider woman

Buero-Vallejo, Antonio

The music window (Música cercana); tr. by Marion Peter Holt. Estreno 1994 64p (Estreno contemporary Spanish plays 5)

Psychological family drama. Aging financier's veneer of self-deception stripped away when he is drawn home to estranged daughter. 2 parts 3m 3w 1 setting

Buffalo Hair. Brown, C.

The **buffalo** hunters. McCullough, L. E.

The **bug** in her ear. See Feydeau, G. A flea in her rear

Bulgakov, Mikhail

Black snow (dramatization) See Reddin, K. Black snow

The master and Margarita (dramatization) See Van Itallie, J.-C. Master & Margarita

Zoyka's apartment; tr. and adapted by Nicholas Saunders and Frank Dwyer. Rev. ed. Smith & Kraus 1996 154p (Great translation for actors series)

Variant title: Madame Zoyka. Satire on class and corruption in Soviet Russia. Widow uses bribery to avoid sharing "dressmaker's" shop, a front for a brothel. 3 acts 7 scenes 12m 11w 2 interiors

Bulimia

Harmer, W. What is the matter with Mary Jane?

Bullins, Ed

Goin' a Buffalo

Seamy side of black life in Los Angeles in the early 1960's. Trusted accomplice of junkies and pimps informs police of narcotic sale so he can take prostitutes to Buffalo. Music. 3 acts 6 scenes 9m 3w extras 2 interiors

In Black theatre USA [v2]; ed. by J. V. Hatch and T. Shine

In the wine time

Drama set in Philadelphia slum. Black man encourages his nephew to pursue his dreams. Prologue 3 acts 7m 7w

In Black drama in America: an anthology; ed. by D. T. Turner

Bums on seats. Snelgrove, M.

The **bundle.** Bond, E.

Bumbalo, Victor

Show

Homosexual Catholic priest with AIDS visited by male prostitute orderly in institution. 2m

In The Best American short plays, 1992-1993

What are Tuesdays like?

Drama about AIDS set in outpatient waiting room of hospital. 5m 1w 1 interior

In The Actor's book of gay and lesbian plays; ed. by E. Lane and N. Shengold

In Sharing the delirium; ed. by T. Jones

Bunyan, John, 1628-1688

The Pilgrim's progress (dramatization) See Howles, L. The king's highway

Bunyan, Paul (Legendary character)

c McCaslin, N. Paul Bunyan: lumberjack

Bureaucracy

Brittney, L. Properly processed
Clark, S. The trial of Judith K.
Havel, V. The garden party
Havel, V. The memorandum
Havel, V. Temptation
Lumborg, D. One fine day
Rayson, H. Competitive tenderness
Reddin, K. Black snow

Burglary

Caldwell, B. Prayer meeting

Burgoo! Schreiber, W.

Buried child. Shepard, S.

Buried treasure

Shepard, S. The mad dog blues
y York, M. A. Treasure Island

Burke, Johnny

Swinging on a star (the Johnny Burke musical); lyrics by Johnny Burke; music by Johnny Burke [et al.]; written by Michael Leeds. Dramatists 1994 76p

Musical revue. Johnny Burke songs woven into various settings and scenes ranging from 1920s Chicago speakeasy to elegant Manhattan Supper club. 2 acts 7 scenes 3m 4w settings

Burke, Simon
The lodger. Methuen Drama 1994 99p (Methuen modern plays)
Thriller set in suburban London. Violence results when constable rents room to enigmatic woman. 17 scenes 4m 2w 1 setting

Burke, William
Hood, E. A wake for Donald

Burlesque
See also Farces

Burn this. Wilson, L.

Burnett, Frances Hodgson
Sara Crewe (dramatization) See Francoeur, B. A little princess
The secret garden (dramatization) See Alette, C. The secret garden; Francoeur, B. The secret garden; Norman, M. The secret garden

Burney, Fanny
The Witlings
Satirical look at pretensions abounding in women's intellectual circles in 18th century London. 5 acts 6 scenes 6m 7w 6 interiors
In The Meridian anthology of Restoration and eighteenth-century plays by women; ed. by K. M. Rogers

Burnham, Yvette
Everywoman: a modern morality play. Bakers Plays 1994 36p
Facing death, woman reviews life and accepts God. 3m 7w extras

Burning time. Flanagan, N.

Burns, Kitty
Identity crisis
Comedy. Paparazzi's attempt to stage elaborate hoax involving discovery of Amelia Earhart's luggage foiled by airline baggage claim employees. 3m 3w 1 interior
In Burns, K. If God wanted us to fly he would have given us wings!

On hold at 30,000 feet
Comedy. Neurotic airplane passenger alienates other passengers and flight crew. 2m 2w extra 1 interior
In Burns, K. If God wanted us to fly he would have given us wings!

Psycho night at the Paradise Lounge. French 1994 62p
Mystery. Eight people, unaware of each other, arrive at nightclub intent on murdering singer. 2 acts 9m 7w 1 setting

Terminal terror
Passengers reveal past sins on airplane flight to Hell. 3m 2w 1 interior
In Burns, K. If God wanted us to fly he would have given us wings!

Burr, Aaron, 1756-1836
Keithley, G. The best blood of the country

Burns, Robert, 1759-1796
Dunbar, D. A song for Robbie

Burrill, Mary P.
Aftermath
Black soldier returning to South Carolina as hero from World War II learns father was murdered by whites in his absence and determines to fight back. 3m 3w 1 interior
In Black theatre USA [v1]; ed. by J. V. Hatch and T. Shine

They that sit in darkness
Poverty-stricken black woman in rural South during early 20th century works herself to death to support her children. 1 act 1m 3w 2b 1g extras 1 interior
In Black theatre USA [v1]; ed. by J. V. Hatch and T. Shine

Burris, Andrew M.
You mus' be bo'n ag'in
Comedy drama depicting hypocrisy of African American Baptist community in 1900 small town Arkansas. 3 acts 4 scenes 6m 6w extras 2 interiors
In Lost plays of the Harlem Renaissance; ed. by J. V. Hatch and L. Hamalian

Burying the dog. Woudstra, K.

Bus stop diner. Pintauro, J.

Busch, Charles
You should be so lucky. French 1995 115p
Screwball comedy set in Greenwhich Village. Gay electrologist's act of altruism leads to huge inheritance and pop-culture celebrity. Includes alternate scenes. 2 acts 7 scenes 3m 3w 1 interior

Buses. Nicholas, D.

Bush, Max
y 13 bells of Boglewood
Fantasy adventure about greed set in enchanted forest. Singing, dancing. 4m 3w 1 exterior
In Bush, M. Plays for young audiences

y Aalmauria: Voyage of the dragonfly
Fantasy. Queen, magician, and magician's daughter seek magic fire to warm castle. Music, singing. 4 scenes Variable cast 7 characters 1 interior 2 exteriors
In Bush, M. Plays for young audiences

c The boy who left home to find out about the shivers
Fairy tale adventure. Boy's journey to self-awareness. Music, singing. 11 scenes Variable cast 17 characters 3 interiors 2 exteriors
In Bush, M. Plays for young audiences

Bush, Max—*Continued*

y The crystal

Fantasy adventure. Hero utilizes magic crystal in battle with evil. Singing, music. 2 acts 6 scenes 4m 3w 1 interior 4 exteriors

In Bush, M. Plays for young audiences

y The emerald circle

Adolescent boy tormented by girlfriend's rape. 3m 2w 1 setting

In Bush, M. Plays for young audiences

c Ghost of the river house. Anchorage Press 1997 61p

Girl, suffering pain of father's rejection, encounters ghost of ancestor. 2m 1w 1b 1g 1 exterior

—Same

In Bush, M. Plays for young audiences

c Hansel and Gretel, the little brother and sister. Anchorage Press 1994 46p

Based on the Brothers Grimm's fairy tale. Brother and sister abandoned in woods meet a witch who threatens to eat them. 6 scenes 1m 3w 1b 1g 3 exteriors

—Same

In Bush, M. Plays for young audiences

c Puss in boots

Dramatization of fairy tale by Charles Perrault. Talking cat outwits ogre and wins princess for his master. 7 scenes Variable cast 12 characters 3 interiors 3 exteriors

In Bush, M. Plays for young audiences

c Rapunzel

German folktale. Rapunzel's long hair enables prince to rescue her from tower where she is imprisoned. Singing. Variable cast 7 characters 2 interiors 2 exteriors

In Bush, M. Plays for young audiences

y Rockway Cafe

Seeking her own identity, teenaged girl confuses real world with television show about rock singer. 2m 3w 1 setting

In Bush, M. Plays for young audiences

Business

Bond, E. In the company of men
Granville-Barker, H. The Madras House
Weller, M. Fishing

Unscrupulous methods

Ayckbourn, A. A small family business
Baitz, J. R. Three hotels
Chayefsky, P. The latent heterosexual
Elton, B. Gasping
Hare, D. Knuckle
Ibsen, H. Pillars of society
Sterner, J. Other people's money

Business lunch at the Russian Tea Room. Durang, C.

Business meeting. Adam, A.

Businessmen

Bynum, R. C. Interviewee
DiPietro, J. Executive dance
Firth, T. Neville's Island
Jeffreys, S. A going concern
Lloyd, P. The scam
Minjares, J. The king of the kosher grocers
Nowra, L. The temple
O'Neill, E. Fog
Poliakoff, S. Playing with trains
Strand, R. The death of Zukasky

Businesswomen

Armstrong, G. K. Handcuffs

Bussy d'Amboise, Louis de Clermont d'Amboise, sieur de Bussy, called

Chapman, G. The revenge of Bussy d'Ambois

Buster come back. Trott, S.

Buster Keaton enters into paradise. Higgins, D.

The **busy** Santa. Pflomm, P. N.

Butchers

Kroetz, F. X. Through the leaves

Butley. Gray, S.

Butterball. Pintauro, J.

Buttered bread. Barylli, G.

Butterfield, Catherine

Joined at the head. Dramatists 1993 71p

Woman author is drawn into friendship with former high school sweetheart and his cancer-stricken wife. 2 acts 4m 5w 1 setting

—Same

In Women playwrights: the best plays of 1992

Joined at the head (condensation)

In The Best plays of 1992-1993

Life in the trees: Chemistry

Comic drama. Woman's belief in free will over "chemistry" dissolves when she meets jazz musician. 2m 1w 1 interior

In Butterfield, C. Life in the trees

Life in the trees: The last time I saw Timmy Boggs

Visit from childhood friend has surprising impact on sisters. 2m 3w 1 interior

In Butterfield, C. Life in the trees

Life in the trees: No problem

Comedy. Two women who were once in group therapy together meet for lunch at a trendy cafe. 1m 2w 1 interior

In Butterfield, C. Life in the trees

Butterfield, Catherine—*Continued*
Snowing at Delphi. Dramatists 1994 68p
Thirtysomething New York friends gather in upstate country house for Christmas. Woman's tale of her pregnancy by rape jolts two couples away from their obsessive troubles. 3m 3w 1 interior

Where the truth lies. French 1997 78p
Drama set in small town Vermont. Arrival of high-living sister and her problems causes woman to reassess her marriage. 2 acts 3 scenes 2m 5w 1 interior

Butterfly. McDonough, J.

Butterfly kiss. Nagy, P.

Butterscotch. Smith, B. L.

Butterworth, Jez
Mojo. Hern Bks. 1995 85p
Black comedy set in 1958 Soho club about British rock and roll scene. 2 acts 4 scenes 6m 2 interiors

Buttonbush. McMahon, J. P. and Ryan, N.

Buzo, Alex
Macquarie. Currency Press 1993 54p
Set in British colony of New South Wales, Australia in 1810-1822; concerns the early governor whose idealistic liberalism leads to his downfall. 3 acts 14m 2w 1 setting

Norm and Ahmed
Drama set in Sydney, Australia. Conversation between bigoted Aussie worker and Pakistani student. 1 act 2m 1 setting
In Buzo, A. Norm & Ahmed and other plays

Pacific Union. Currency Press 1995 96p (Current theatre series)
Drama about United Nations Conference on International Organization held in 1945 San Francisco. Prologue 23 scenes Variable cast 25 characters extras 1 setting

Rooted
Tragicomedy set in Australia. Having achieved middle class status, young man loses wife, home, possessions, and his dignity. 3 acts 12 scenes 3m 2w 2 interiors
In Buzo, A. Norm & Ahmed and other plays

The Roy Murphy show
Satirical look at empty life of Australian television sports commentator. 7m 1w 1 interior
In Buzo, A. Norm & Ahmed and other plays

By whose hand? Booth, J.

Byars, Betsy
The pinballs (dramatization) See Harris, A. The pinballs

Bye bye Columbus. Barnes, P.

Byerrum, Eliot
A Christmas cactus. French 1995 90p
Comic mystery. Beleaguered female private eye faces myriad of problems on Christmas Eve. 2 acts 4m 2w 1 setting

Bynum, R. Cary
Escapee
Father and daughter held captive by homicidal escapee from mental hospital. 2m 2w 1 interior
In Bynum, R. C. Six short plays

Interviewee
Personnel manager is terrorized by intruder. 3m 1w 1 interior
In Bynum, R. C. Six short plays

Live-in witnesses
Surrealist drama set in department store. 1m 1w 1 interior
In Bynum, R. C. Six short plays

The monkey palace
Surrealist drama about child used as puppet in cabaret. 2m 1g 1 interior
In Bynum, R. C. Six short plays

The sharpshooters
Historical drama about confederate soldiers at battle of Gettysburg. 3m 1 exterior
In Bynum, R. C. Six short plays

Sherwood
Drama set in 1957 South. Small town draftsman struggles to succeed in big city. 3m 1w 1 extra 1 interior
In Bynum, R. C. Six short plays

Byron, George Gordon Byron, 6th Baron
Chappell, E. Haunted
Hall, F. B. Via Reggio revisited
Linney, R. Childe Byron

Byzantium. Warner, F.

C

Cadman, Larry
Peace in our time
Vietnam Veterans Memorial in Washington, D.C. scene of confrontation between veteran and draft dodger. 2m 1 exterior
In Off-Off Broadway Festival plays, 18th ser.

Caesar, Caius Julius
Shaw, B. Caesar and Cleopatra

Caesar and Cleopatra. Shaw, B.

Cage rhythm. Corthron, K.

Cahill, Sylvia
Ballycastle
American girl hitchhiking in Northern Ireland offered ride by Ulster boy. 1m 1w 1 exterior
In Off-Off Braodway Festival plays, 21st ser.

Caird, John, and Nunn, Trevor
c Peter Pan; or, The boy who would not grow up. Dramatists 1993 125p
Adaptation of J. M. Barrie's fantasy about children's adventures in Never-Never Land. Music. Prologue 5 acts 6 scenes Large mixed cast 2 interiors 3 exteriors

Cairo (Egypt)
Sherman, M. Some sunny day

Cajuns
y McCullough, L. E. The flames of hell (Les flammes d'enfer)

Calamity Jane
Thompson, P. Calamity Jane and the fat buffalo moon

Calamity Jane and the fat buffalo moon. Thompson, P.

Calchas. Chekhov, A. (dramatization) See Chekhov, A. Swan song

Caldwell, Ben
Prayer meeting; or, The first militant preacher
Comedy. Burglar convinces nonviolent African American minister to lead protests. 2m 1 interior
In Black theatre USA [v2]; ed. by J. V. Hatch and T. Shine

Calhoun, Wil
Affections of an alley cat
Set in New Orleans. Eddie character from Call it clover makes vain attempt at forming relationship. 1m 1w
In Act One '95

Call it clover
Set in New Orleans. Friction between young partially paralyzed wife, her husband and his friend, Eddie. 1 act 2m 1w 1 interior
In Showtime's Act One Festival of one-act plays, 1994

Caliban, Richard
Gladiator
Journalist's interview with prisoner in federal penitentiary turns deadly. 3m 1 interior
In Act One '95

California
Aoki, B. W. The Queen's garden
c Blum, R. California wax museum

California wax museum. Blum, R.

Call for the lights and sing! Ensco, L. G. and Enscoe, A.

Call it clover. Calhoun, W.

A **call** on Kuprin. Lawrence, J. and Lee, R. E.

Callan, Lyndall
Homebound
Monologue by young woman coping with sea of emotions as she escapes small Texas town and terminally ill father. 8 scenes 1w 1 setting
In Off-Off Broadway Festival plays, 17th ser.

Callas, Maria
McNally, T. Master class

Calling in. Sharrocks, M.

Callisto 5. Ayckbourn, A.

Cambodia
Lipsky, J. The survivor: A Cambodian odyssey

Cambodian odyssey. Haing Ngor. (dramatization) See Lipsky, J. The survivor: a Cambodian odyssey

A **cameo** from Cranford. Adam, A.

Camille and Perdican. See Musset, A. de. Don't play with love

Camp followers
Brecht, B. Mother Courage and her children

Campaign fever. Sandock, F.

Campanile, Achille
The big bun
Comic parable about bourgeois values. 3 scenes 8m 1w 1 interior
In Campanile, A. The inventor of the horse and two other short plays

The inventor of the horse
Absurdist comedy about world of academia. 4 scenes 10m 2w extras 1 setting
In Campanile, A. The inventor of the horse and two other short plays

War
Antiwar sketch. Man, annoyed by its intrusion on his sleep, ends fighting. 1m extra 1 setting
In Campanile, A. The inventor of the horse and two other short plays

Campaspe. Lyly, J.

Campbell, Edward
c Hauncho the hamster. Pioneer Drama Service 1992 47p
Produced under title: Belinda Braveheart and Billy Barnstorm. Adventure fantasy. Boy and his pet hamster search for boy's parents. 2 acts 5 scenes Variable cast 12 characters 1 setting

Campbell, Ken
Jamais vu
Concluding piece of Bald trilogy. Comic discourse in pidgin English about life in Vanuatu. 1m
In Campbell, K. The Bald trilogy

Campbell, Ken—*Continued*
Pigspurt; or, Six pigs from happiness. Methuen Drama 1993 103p
Second play in Bald trilogy. Monologue about subjects ranging from nursery schools and faith healing to obsessions and sex. 1m
—Same
In Campbell, K. The Bald trilogy
The recollections of a furtive nudist
First play in Bald trilogy. One man show comprised of comedic prophecies, dreams, tall tales, and quasi-memories. 1m
In Campbell, K. The Bald trilogy
Violin time; or, The lady from Montségur. Methuen Drama 1996 135p
Comic monologue about Cathar heretics, French book thief, Oriental violinist and the Temple of Mankind in Damanhur, Egypt. 1m

Campbell, Mrs. Patrick
O'Donovan, J. Carlotta

Camping out. Jones, T.

Camping with Henry & Tom. St. Germain, M.

Camps
c Schurman-O'Connor, K. Ghoul Scout camp

Campton, David
The evergreens. French (London) 1994 29p
Comedy. Man and woman who courted in 1940s reunited as members of senior citizens club. 1m 1w 1 setting
Permission to cry. French (London) 1996 20p
Drama about public and private morality set in London. Up-and-coming junior minister's life thrown into turmoil when her lesbian lover is killed. Variable cast 5 characters

Can can. Linney, R.

Can you hear their voices? Flanagan, H. and Clifford, M. E.

Canada
Chislett, A. Yankee notions
Hollingsworth, M. The history of the village of the small huts
Lambert, B. Jennie's story
Ledous, P. and Smyth, D. Cheatin' hearts
Rose, R. and Kugler, D. D. Newhouse
Taylor, D. H. Someday
Thompson, J. Sled
Vanderhaeghe, G. I had a job I liked. Once.
Wyatt, R. Crackpot
See also names of provinces, e.g. Nova Scotia; and names of cities, e.g. Montreal (Québec); Toronto (Ont.)

English-French relations
Fennario, D. Balconville

History—Rebellion, 1837-1838
Salutin, R. and Theatre Passe Muraille. 1837: The Farmer's Revolt

Canadians

Russia
Findley, T. The stillborn lover

Canby, Vincent
After all
Part of trilogy. Scene of elderly couple getting ready for bed sheds light on their life, relationship and indignities of old age. 1m 1w 1 interior
In Act One '95

Cancer
Butterfield, C. Joined at the head
Gillis, C. Caveman rainbow
Goldstein, J. Our baby's first seven years
Harrison, J. Holidays
Morris, M. Two weeks with the Queen
Shaffer, D. Last requests
Shaffer, D. Last respects
Vickery, F. A kiss on the bottom
See also Breast cancer

Cancer. See Weller, M. Moonchildren

Candles and carols. Enscoe, L. G. and Enscoe, A.

Canetti, Veza
The Ogre
Austrian folk play about destructive nature of power and money. Man exhibits excessive cruelty toward wife, children, and business associates. 5 acts 7 scenes 10m 11w extras 4 interiors
In Anthology of contemporary Austrian folk plays

Canker sores and other distractions. Durang, C.

The **cannibal** masque. Ribman, R.

Can't pay? Won't pay! Fo, D.

Canterbury tales. Chaucer, G. (dramatization) See Thomas, E. and Redmond, B. Six Canterbury tales

El **canto** del roble. See Conboy, R. Song of the oak—El canto del roble

Cantrell. Kranes, D.

Cape Town (South Africa)
Harwood, R. Tramway road

Capek, Karel
The Makropoulos secret. International Pocket Lib. 1997 96p
Pessimistic fantasy. Woman suffers burdens of immortality. 3 acts 6m 2w extras 3 interiors

Capitalism
McGrath, J. The Cheviot, the stag and the black, black oil
Shaw, B. Major Barbara
Balzac, H. de. Mercadet
Ibsen, H. Pillars of society
Lewes, G. H. The game of speculation
Sterner, J. Other people's money
Strijards, F. The Stendhal syndrome

Capote, Truman
Gilbert, S. Capote at Yaddo

Capote at Yaddo. Gilbert, S.

Capra, Frank
It's a wonderful life (adaptation) See Rodgers, J. W. It's a wonderful life; Sharkey, T. M. It's a wonderful life

Caprice. Musset, A. de

The **Captain's** daughter. Pushkin, A. (dramatization) See Bland, J. The squire's daughter

The **captive.** Lewis, M. G.

The **captives.** Plautus, T. M.

The **captivity** of Pixie Shedman. Linney, R.

Car crazy. Bruce, M.

The **caramel** crisis. Gray, S.

Caravaggio, Michelangelo Merisi da
McGuinness, F. Innocence

The **caravan.** Colón, A.

The **cardboard** cavaliers. Waterhouse, J.

Cardenio. Shakespeare, W. and Fletcher, J.

Cardiff (Wales)
Gill, P. Cardiff East

Cardiff East. Gill, P.

Cardinal, Vincent J.
The Colorado catechism. French 1993 78p

Comedy-drama. Relationship develops between man and woman in drug and alcohol rehabilitation center. 2 acts 1m 1w 1 interior

Careless love. Jenkin, L.

Caribbean region
Carter, S. Pecong
Colón, O. A. Siempre en mi corazón

Carilli, Theresa
Dolores Street

Dramatic comedy about four lesbian roommates in 1980s San Francisco. 2 acts 7 scenes 4w 1 interior

In Carilli, T. Women as lovers

Wine country

Dramatic comedy about lesbian love triangle. 2 acts 11 scenes 5w settings

In Carilli, T. Women as lovers

Caring. Storey, D.

Carl XII. Strindberg, A.

Carley, Dave
Into

Comedy inspired by Julio Cortazar's story The southern thruway. Relationships develop among people caught in traffic jam. 2m 2w 1 exterior

In Carley, D. Taking liberties & Into

Taking liberties

Drama set in midsize Canadian city 1955 to 1995. Morals of one era impact on events of another as individuals react to social pressures. 3m 2w

In Carley, D. Taking liberties & Into

Carlisle, Barbara
c The crane wife. Anchorage Press 1997 34p

Man rewarded for helping wounded crane. Puppets, dancing, music. Prologue 3m 1w extras

Carlos, Laurie
White chocolate for my father

Depicts multi-generational devastation of rape on African American women. Incorporates stylized gesture and text-based improvisation. 7w 1 setting

In Moon marked and touched by sun; ed. by S. Mahone

Carlos II, King of Spain
Barnes, P. The bewitched

Carlotta. O'Donovan, J.

Carlson, Nancy Kierspe, and Chapman, Betsy
y The magic pebble; book & lyrics by Nancy Kierspe Carlson; music by Nancy Kierspe Carlson & Betsy Chapman. French 1996 63p

Wishing on magic pebble leads to adventure with pirates and ancient Egyptians. 6 scenes 4m 1w 2b 2g extras 3 interiors 2 exteriors

Carmen Kittel. Seidel, G.

Carmichael, Fred
Coming apart. French 1994 80p

Romantic comedy. Two conceited authors review scenes from their marriage as they consider divorce. 2 acts 2m 2w 1 setting

Damsel of the desert; or, A villain foiled by virtue. French 1995 40p

Melodrama set in Western desert about greed, gold, and lost love featuring amnesiac villain. 1 act 2m 3w 1 interior

Don't mention my name. French 1993 94p

Comedy. Award-winning playwright, suffering from amnesia, stumbles into Vermont bed-and-breakfast where it seems he was expected. 2 acts 3 scenes 3m 5w 1 interior

Carmichael, Fred—*Continued*

Frankenstein 1930. French 1996 81p

Version of Shelley's classic set in 1930s small village outside of Vienna. 2 acts 10m 6w 1 setting

I bet your life. French 1995 81p

Comedy. Soap opera writer pens screenplay about hitman. 2 acts 4m 4w 1 interior

Meet my husbands. French 1997 94p

Comic look at advertising industry. Woman executive's pursuit of must-have account threatened by unexpected interference of her opportunistic ex-husband. 2 acts 3 scenes 4m 5w 1 interior

Over the checkerboard. French 1996 94p

Comedy set in small town Vermont. Resident's dismayed after discovering that they were models for characters in steamy unpublished novel. 2 acts 4m 4w 1 interior

Carr, Emily

Marchessault, J. The magnificent voyage of Emily Carr

Carr, Marina

The Mai. Gallery Bks. 1995 72p

Set during summers of 1979 and 1980 in Ireland. Cruel family history revealed in conversations and stories of seven women. 2 acts 1m 7w 1 setting

Portia Coughlan. Faber & Faber 1996 64p

Psychological drama. Unhappily married Irish woman, haunted by spectral twin brothers, seeks solace in soulless affairs. 2 acts 10 scenes 6m 5w 1 setting

—Same

In The Dazzling dark: new Irish plays; ed. by F. McGuinness

Carroll, Lewis

Alice's adventures in Wonderland (dramatization) See Mahlmann, L. and Jones, D. C. Alice's adventures in Wonderland; Rochelle, R. Alice in Wonderland

Parodies, imitations, etc.

Glore, J. What she found there

Hampton, C. Alice's adventures under ground

Carrying the calf. Barrie, S.

Carson, Jo

A preacher with a horse to ride

Historical drama set in 1931. Novelist/activist Theodore Dreiser heads committee investigating union strife in coal mining region of Eastern Kentucky. Music, singing. 2 acts 11m 9w extras 1 setting

In Alternate roots; ed. by K. deNobriga and V. Anderson

Carter, Josephine

The twisted mirror. New Playwrights Network 1995 16p

After death of father, lonely single woman is urged to be adventurous by her alter-ego. 2w 1 interior

Carter, Steve

Pecong. Broadway Play Pub. 1993 87p

Dramatic retelling of Medea story set on Caribbean island. Jilted sorceress seeks revenge on shallow womanizer. Prologue 2 acts 10 scenes epilogue 3m 5w extras

Carter, Vivienne. See Ross, D.; Parker, N. and Mullane, M. A tale of two cities

The **Carthaginian.** See Plautus, T. M. The little Carthaginian

Carthaginians. McGuinness, F.

Cartwright, Jim

Bed

Drama. Eight elderly people share a bed, dreams, and memories. 4m 4w 1 setting

In Cartwright, J. Plays: 1

In Cartwright, J. Two & Bed

The rise and fall of Little Voice. French 1995 86p

Drama set in England's industrial north. Mother's boyfriend exploits painfully shy teenaged daughter's talent for impersonation. 2 acts 3m 3w 1 setting

—Same. French (London) 1992 71p

—Same. Methuen Drama 1992 86p (Methuen modern plays)

—Same

In Cartwright, J. Plays: 1

Road

Tragicomedy. Drunk conducts tour of his derelict Lancashire street. 2 acts 8m 6w extras 1 exterior

In Cartwright, J. Plays: 1

Two

Tragicomic exploration of underlying melancholy of English pub life. 1m 1w 1 interior

In Cartwright, J. Plays: 1

In Cartwright, J. Two & Bed

Carver, George Washington

y Hark, M. and McQueen, N. George Washington Carver

Cary, Elizabeth

The tragedy of Mariam, the fair

17th century verse play. Uses biblical story of Mariam and Herod to explore issues of monarchy, power and gender. 5 acts 22 scenes 7m 5w 2b extras 1 setting

In Renaissance women; ed. by D. Purkiss

Casanova, Giacomo

Congdon, C. Casanova

Casas, Bartolomé de las

Salom, J. Bonfire at dawn

The **case** of the dead flamingo dancer. Oliver, D.

Cash on delivery! Cooney, M.

Cashman, Nellie
c McCaslin, N. The last horizon
c McCullough, L. E. Klondike fever

Casina. See Plautus, T. M. A funny thing happened on the way to the wedding

The **casket.** See Plautus, T. M. The little box

Casler, Lawrence
A night in the theatre. French 1993 63p
Comedy. Secrets emerge and friendships unravel as two couples view production of Hamlet. 2 acts 2m 2w extras 1 setting

The **Cassandra** Complex. Millar, T. P.

Castle, Gerald V.
c Recess! a musical joke-filled spoof. Pioneer Drama Service 1996 25p
Musical version of Laffin' school by Keith Jackson. Class misbehaves for substitute teacher. Variable cast 12 characters extras

The **castle** spectre. Lewis, M. G.

Castles in the air. Adam, A.

The **castrata.** Scribe, E. and Melesville

Castrato. Nelson, G.

The **cat** act. See Nemeth, S. Sally's shorts: The cat act

Cat on the rails. Topol, J.

The **cat** who had no friends. See Rosenberg, J. El gato sin amigos—The cat who had no friends

The **catechism** of Patty Reed. Mayberry, B.

Cater-waiter. Lane, E.

Catfish moon. Sartin, L.

Catharine Parr
Brittney, L. The last wife

Cather, Willa
My Antonia (dramatization) See Jones, C. My Antonia
O pioneers! (dramatization) See Cloud, D. O pioneers!

Catholic Church
Barnes, P. Sunsets and glories
Barry, P. J. A distance from Calcutta
Crawford, J. L. Facelifting at St. Viators
De la Tour, A. The Pope and the witch
Durang, C. The marriage of Bette and Boo
Durang, C. Sister Mary Ignatius explains it all for you
Fo, D. The Pope and the witch
Kilroy, T. Talbot's box
Kurtti, C. Catholic school girls
Lambert, B. Jennie's story
Linney, R. Spain: Anna Rey
Linney, R. Spain: Escobedo de la Aixa
Linney, R. Spain: Torquemada
Minghella, A. A little like drowning
Morton, C. The savior
Murphy, T. The sanctuary lamp
Parsley, R. Brideshead revisited
Pintauro, J. Birds in church
Rivera, J. Marisol
Rubess, B. Pope Joan
Shaffer, D. Sacrilege

Clergy

Crowley, M. For reasons that remain unclear
Enright, N. St. James Infirmary
Fletcher, J. and Massinger, P. The Spanish curate
Keane, J. B. Moll
Pickering, K. The parting of friends
Santareno, B. The judgment of Father Martinho
Tasca, J. A modern proposal
Wilder, T. Someone from Assisi

Catholic faith
Finnegan, S. Mary Maginn

Catholic school girls. Kurtti, C.

Catholics

Australia

Enright, N. Good works

Canada

Reaney, J. The St. Nicholas Hotel, Wm. Donnelly, prop.

Ireland

McGuinness, F. Carthaginians

Japan

Tanaka, C. The head of Mary

Catlin, George
c McCullough, L. E. Great medicine painter

Cato, Marcus Porticus Uticensis
Addison, J. Cato

The **cat's** away. Hornby, I.

Caught on the hop. Foxton, D.

The **Cavalcaders.** Roche, B.

Caveman blues. Bruce, M.

Caveman rainbow. Gillis, C.

Cearley, Buster
y Welcome to Nashville; a musical comedy; book by Eddie Cope; lyrics and music by Buster Cearley; (additional lyrics by Eddie Cope). Clark, I.E. 1993 52p
Aspiring songwriter victimized by unscrupulous music publisher. Prologue 2 acts 3 scenes epilogue 4m 4w 1 interior

Celestine V, Pope, Saint, 1215-1296
Barnes, P. Sunsets and glories

The **cellar** and the almond tree. Mercer, D.

Cellophane. Wellman, M.

Cement hands. Wilder, T.

Cementville. Martin, J.

Cemeteries
Hardstack, M. In the cemetery
Hood, E. A wake for Donald

Cenia. Graffigny, F. D. D. de.

Centlivre, Susanna
A bold stroke for a wife
Romantic comedy. Heiress, victim of will which places her under guardianship of four different opinionated men, cannot marry until all approve. Action follows farcical ruses used by suitor to effect happy ending. Prologue 5 acts 10 scenes 8m 3w extras 4 interiors 1 exterior
In The Meridian anthology of Restoration and eighteenth-century plays by women; ed. by K. M. Rogers

Central America
c Martin, M. The legend of the golden coffee bean

Central Park West. Allen, W.

Cerebral palsy
Freeman, D. Creeps

Ceremonies in dark old men. Elder, L.

Cervantes Saavedra, Miguel de
Parodies, imitations, etc.
Overmyer, E. Don Quixote de La Jolla

Césaire, Ina
Fire's daughters
Set in Martinique. Mother and twin daughters become involved in insurrection of 1870. Music. 2 acts 8 scenes 4w 1 extra 1 setting
In New French-language plays

Césaire, Michèle
The ship
Allegorical drama about characters from various epochs and places on voyage aboard "Ship of Fools." 3 acts 10 scenes 3m 2w 1b 1 setting
In New French-language plays

Chadwick, Charles
The man's shop. Playwrights 1995 59p
Personnel in unsuccessful men's clothing shop face imminent unemployment. 2 acts 4 scenes 4m 1w 1 interior

Chafee, Claire
Why we have a body
Lyrical depiction of lesbian relationships. 2 Prologues 2 acts 23 scenes epilogue 4w 1 setting
In The Actor's book of gay and lesbian plays; ed. by E. Lane and N. Shengold
In Here to stay: five plays from the Women's Project; ed. by J. Miles
In Women playwrights: the best plays of 1993

Chain. Cleage, P.

The **chairman's** wife. Yamauchi, W.

Chambers, John
c Tales of King Arthur. French (London) 1996 73p
Traces Arthur's life from birth to his death at hands of evil Mordred. 2 acts 9 scenes 10m 4w extras 1 setting

Chambers, Whittaker
Can you hear their voices? (dramatization) See Flanagan, H. and Clifford, M. E. Can you hear their voices?

Champagne, Dominic
Playing bare; tr. by Shelley Tepperman. Talonbooks 1993 112p
Satire on relation between theater and life. Troubled actress directing production of Beckett's Waiting for Godot casts lead roles with non-actors. Music. 8 scenes 3m 2w 1 setting

Champagne, Susan
Away from me. French 1996 42p
Comedy. Nerdy psychiatrist loses control of group therapy session. 6 scenes 4m 2w 1 setting

The **Champagne** Charlie Stakes. Graham, B.

Changing bodies. Brooker, B.

Chapman, Betsy. See Carlson, N. K. The magic pebble

Chapman, George
The revenge of Bussy d'Ambois
Elizabethan verse play. In this sequel to: Bussy d'Ambois, Clermont d'Ambois seeks revenge for his brother's murder. 5 acts 17 scenes 20m 4w extras 6 interiors 2 exteriors
In Four revenge tragedies; edited by K. E. Maus

Chappell, Eric
Haunted. French (London) 1995 62p
Neurotic playwright visited by ghost of Lord Byron. 2 acts 4 scenes 4m 2w 1 interior

Chappell, Eric—*Continued*
Theft. French (London) 1996 65p
After being caught red-handed, thief disrupts two seemingly happy marriages and one strong friendship through his caustic observations. 2 acts 4 scenes 3m 2w 1 interior

Charles V, Emperor of the Holy Roman Empire
Hugo, V. Hernani

Charles XII, King of Sweden, 1683-1718
Strindberg, A. Carl XII

Charles, Ron
y A perfect match
Romantic comedy. Young woman's imagination creates "ideal" suitor. 1m 2w 1 interior
In The Big book of skits; ed. by S. E. Kamerman

Charles Dickens' A Christmas carol. Mortimer, J.

Charles Dickens' Great expectations. Johanson, R.

Charley's girl. Goldenthal, J.

Charley's uncle. Booth, J.

Charlie's farewell. Pintauro, J.

The **chase.** Foote, H.

Chase me up Farndale Avenue, s'il vous plaît! McGillivray, D. and Zerlin, W.

Chasidism. See Hasidism

Chat botté: Puss-in-boots. Gerke, P.

Chatfield, Roy
c The great Santa kidnap. French (London) 1994 51p
Boy and girl save Santa Claus from being kidnapped by goblins. Prologue 5 scenes epilogue Unidentified cast 12 characters extras settings

Chaucer, Geoffrey
Canterbury tales (dramatization) See Thomas, E. and Redmond, B. Six Canterbury tales

Chauffeurs
O'Neill, E. Recklessness
Uhry, A. Driving Miss Daisy

Chaurette, Normand
The queens; tr. by Linda Gaboriau. Coach House Press 1992 94p
Drama set in 1483 London. Depicts shifting passions and ambitions of six historical women drawn from Shakespeare's Richard III. 6w 1 setting

Chauvin, Louis, 1881-1908
Overmyer, E. The Heliotrope Bouquet by Scott Joplin & Louis Chauvin

Chayefsky, Paddy
The bachelor party
Television play. Five men go on a night about town in honor of co-worker's impending marriage. 7m 5w
In Chayefsky, P. The television plays
The big deal
Television play. Former successful building contractor, bankrupt for fifteen years, finally accepts building inspector's job in order not to sponge off his daughter. 9m 2w
In Chayefsky, P. The television plays
Gideon
Retelling of biblical story of Gideon and the angel. 2 acts 5 scenes Large mixed cast 2 settings
In Chayefsky, P. The stage plays
Holiday song
Television play. Cantor loses faith in God and refuses to sing for High Holy Days, but his faith is restored when he unwittingly becomes responsible for bringing together couple whom war had separated. 7m 4w extras
In Chayefsky, P. The television plays
The latent heterosexual
Satire on big business tax evasions. Attempts by two ingenious tax lawyers to settle economic affairs of well-adjusted homosexual writer via incorporation and marriage, end disastrously. 6 scenes 8m 3w extras 3 interiors
In Chayefsky, P. The stage plays
Marty
Middle-aged Bronx butcher falls in love with plain Jane schoolteacher. 6m 8w
In Chayefsky, P. The television plays
Middle of the night
Set in 1950s New York City. Lonely middle-aged widower falls in love with young married woman half his age. 3 acts 8 scenes 3m 9w 2 interiors
In Chayefsky, P. The stage plays
The mother
Television play. Married, self-sacrificing daughter tries to take care of aged mother who insists on independence. 2m 8w
In Chayefsky, P. The television plays
The passion of Josef D.
Stalin's power struggle with Lenin and party members from 1917 to 1924. Singing. 3 acts 11 scenes 15m 2w extras 2 settings
In Chayefsky, P. The stage plays
Printer's measure
Television play. Old-time printer refuses to adjust to new technology. 9m 5w extras
In Chayefsky, P. The television plays
The tenth man
Man believing daughter possessed by dybbuk (demon spirit) gathers ten men for exorcism ceremony. 3 acts 4 scenes 12m 1w 1 interior
In Chayefsky, P. The stage plays
—Same
In Awake and singing: 7 classic plays from the American Jewish repertoire; ed. by E. Schiff

Cheatham, Val R.
y Broadway hit
Behind scenes bickering before Broadway musical opening. 2 scenes 5m 3w 1 interior
In The Big book of skits; ed. by S. E. Kamerman
c The Miss Witch contest
Contest to determine vilest fairy tale villain. 2 scenes 5m 5w 1 interior
In The Big book of skits; ed. by S. E. Kamerman
c The Three Little Pigs and friends
Parody of Three Little Pigs as TV program. Unidentified cast 9 characters 1 interior
In The Big book of skits; ed. by S. E. Kamerman

Cheatin' hearts. Ledoux, P. and Smyth, D.

Checkmate. Sands, L.

Checkmate. See Lawrence, J. and Lee, R. E. A call on Kuprin

A **cheery** soul. White, P.

Cheever, John
Parodies, imitations, etc.
Gurney, A. R. A Cheever evening

A **Cheever** evening. Gurney, A. R.

Chekhov, Anton
The anniversary; tr. by Betsy Hulick
Variant title: The festivities. Farce. Dramatized adaptation of the author's short story, A defenceless creature. Director's preparations for his bank's semi-centennial celebration upset by two unexpected female visitors. 1 act 2m 2w extras 1 interior
In Chekhov, A. Uncle Vanya and other plays
The bear; tr. by Betsy Hulick
Variant titles: The boor; The brute. Romantic comedy. Landowner tries to collect debt from neighbor but collects young widow instead. 1 act 11 scenes 2m 1w 1 interior
In Chekhov, A. Uncle Vanya and other plays
—Same; tr. by Paul Schmidt
In Chekhov, A. The plays of Anton Chekhov
Calchas (dramatization) See Chekhov, A. Swan song
The cherry orchard. Players Press 1997 40p
Naive and unrealistic Russian landed gentry fail to comprehend approaching financial collapse. Music. 4 acts 9m 5w extras 2 interiors 1 exterior
—Same; English version by J.-C. Van Itallie
In Chekhov, A. Chekhov: the major plays
—Same; tr. by Betsy Hulick
In Chekhov, A. Uncle Vanya and other plays
—Same; tr. by Carol Rocamora
In Chekhov, A. Chekhov: four plays
—Same; tr. by Karl Kramer and Margaret Booker
In Chekhov, A. Chekhov's major plays
—Same; tr. by Paul Schmidt
In Chekhov, A. The plays of Anton Chekhov
The cherry orchard (adaptation) See Brustein, R. The cherry orchard
The dangers of tobacco; tr. by Paul Schmidt
Variant titles: The evils of tobacco; The harmfulness of tobacco; On the harmfulness of tobacco. Satirical lecture by henpecked husband. 1 act 1m
In Chekhov, A. The plays of Anton Chekhov
A defenceless creature (dramatization) See Chekhov, A. The anniversary; Chekhov, A. The festivities
The festivities; tr. by Paul Schmidt
Variant title: The anniversary, entered above
In Chekhov, A. The plays of Anton Chekhov
Ivanov; tr. by Karl Kramer
Social tragedy. Idealistic, intellectual landowner in Czarist Russia depressed by failure to realize his youthful ambitions, commits suicide. 4 acts 40 scenes 8m 10w extras 3 interiors 1 exterior
In Chekhov, A. Chekhov's major plays
—Same; tr. by Paul Schmidt
In Chekhov, A. The plays of Anton Chekhov
Ivanov (adaptation) See Hare, D. Ivanov
A joke (dramatization) See Gaure, J. The talking dog
The proposal; tr. by Betsy Hulick
Variant title: The marriage proposal. Farce. Hypochondriacal suitor quarrels with the girl he wants to marry, but she accepts him. 1 act 7 scenes 2m 1w 1 interior
In Chekhov, A. Uncle Vanya and other plays
—Same; tr. by Paul Schmidt
In Chekhov, A. The plays of Anton Chekhov
The seagull; a new version by Pam Gems. Hern Bks. 1994 78p (Royal National theatre)

Chekhov, Anton—*Continued*
Tragic outcome of young actress' love for selfish playwright. 4 acts 7m 6w 2 interiors 2 exteriors
—Same; tr. by David French. Talonbooks 1993 112p
—Same; English version by J. C. Van-Itallie
In Chekhov, A. Chekhov: the major plays
—Same; tr. by Betsy Hulick
In Chekhov, A. Uncle Vanya and other plays
—Same; tr. by Carol Rocamora
In Chekhov, A. Chekhov: four plays
—Same; tr. by Karl Kramer
In Chekhov, A. Chekhov's major plays
—Same; tr. by Nicholas Saunders and Frank Dwyer. Smith & Kraus 1994 97p
—Same; tr. by Paul Schmidt
In Chekhov, A. The plays of Anton Chekhov
The seagull (adaptation) See Kilroy, T. The seagull
Swan song; tr. by Paul Schmidt
Dramatized adaptation of the author's short story, Calchas. Study of a life broken by old age. 1 act 2 scenes 2m 1 interior
In Chekhov, A. The plays of Anton Chekhov
Three sisters. Players Press 1996 48p
Life of the intelligentsia in 19th century Russia reflected in unhappy lives of a Moscow family stranded (financially) in a small provincial city. 4 acts 9m 5w 2 interiors 1 exterior
—Same; A newly revised version by Jean-Claude Van Itallie. Dramatists 1995 72p
—Same; English version by J.-C. Van Itallie
In Chekhov, A. Chekhov: the major plays
—Same; tr. by Betsy Hulick
In Chekhov, A. Uncle Vanya and other plays
—Same; tr. by Carol Rocamora
In Chekhov, A. Chekhov: four plays
—Same; tr. by Karl Kramer
In Chekhov, A. Chekhov's major plays
—Same; tr. by Lanford Wilson. Smith & Kraus 1994 82p (Great translations for actors series)
—Same; tr. by Paul Schmidt
In Chekhov, A. The plays of Anton Chekhov
—Same; tr. by Stephen Mulrine. Hern Bks. 1994 99p (Drama classics)
Uncle Vanya. Players Press 1996 38p
Country life in 19th century Russia. Character contrast between intellectual professor and practical farmer. 4 acts 5m 4w 3 interiors 1 exterior
—Same; English version by J. C. Van Itallie
In Chekhov, A. Chekhov: the major plays
—Same; tr. by Betsy Hulick
In Chekhov, A. Uncle Vanya and other plays
—Same; tr. by Carol Rocamora
In Chekhov, A. Chekhov: four plays
—Same; tr. by Karl Kramer
In Chekhov, A. Chekhov's major plays
—Same; tr. by Paul Schmidt
In Chekhov, A. The plays of Anton Chekhov
Uncle Vanya (adaptation) See Mitchell, J. August
The wedding; tr. by Sergius Ponomarov. Players Press 1996 18p
Variant title: The wedding reception. Farce based on author's short story. Satirical portrayal of guests at wedding reception. 1 act 7m 3w extras 1 interior
The wedding reception; tr. by Paul Schmidt
Variant title entered above
In Chekhov, A. The plays of Anton Chekhov
The wood demon (Lyeshiy); tr. by Nicholas Saunders and Frank Dwyer. Smith & Kraus 1993 110p (Great translations for actors)
Tragicomedy. Life of the upper middle class in a late nineteenth century Russian village. 4 acts 47 scenes 9m 4w 2 interiors 2 exteriors

Parodies, imitations, etc.

Barker, H. Uncle Vanya
Gans, S. and Charney, J. A Chekhov concert
Jackson, N. The quick-change room

A **Chekhov** concert. Gans, S. and Charney, J.

Chemical reactions. Foster, A.

Chemistry. See Butterfield, C. Life in the trees: Chemistry

Chen, Kitty
Eating chicken feet. Dramatic 1995 59p
Black comedy about effects of divorce on Chinese American family. Prologue 9 scenes epilogue 3m 4w 1 interior

Cherchez la femme. House, J.

Chernobyl Nuclear Accident, Chernobyl, Ukraine, 1986
Kurginian, S. Compensation

Cherry blend with vanilla. Wilhelm, L.

The **cherry** orchard. Brustein, R.

The **cherry** orchard. Chekhov, A.

Chess
Witten, M. Washington Square moves

Chessman, Peter, et al.
Fight for Shelton Bar
Docudrama opposing British Steel Corporations 1973 decision to close newly renovated works in Stoke-on-Trent. Music, singing. 2 parts Variable cast
In Voicings: ten plays from the documentary theatre; ed. by A. Favorini

The **Cheviot**, the stag and the black, black oil. McGrath, J.

Chiang, Ching. See Jiang Qing, 1914-1991

Chicago (Ill.)
Hansberry, L. A raisin in the sun
Race relations
Wilson, A. Ma Rainey's black bottom

Chicago. Shepard, S.

Chicago. Watkins, M.

Chief Sarah, the Indian Joan of Arc. McCullough, L. E.

Chikao, Tanaka
The head of Mary; tr. by David G. Goodman. Currency Press in association with Playbox Theatre 1995 65p (Current theatre series)
Christian interpretation of atomic destruction set in post-war Nagasaki. Japanese Catholics attempt theft of statue of Virgin Mary, believing only she can understand their suffering. 4 acts 9 scenes 10m 8w extras 5 interiors 2 exteriors

Child abuse
Baker, E. A. Face divided
Dowie, C. Adult child/dead child
Foxton, D. Kenneth
Lill, W. All fall down
MacDonald, B. The weekend healer
Miller, J. A light on the landing
Wilson, L. The moonshot tape

Child custody. See Custody of children

Childbirth
Mama drama

Childe Byron. Linney, R.

Childhood. Wilder, T.

Childlessness
Dowling, C. The Marlboro man
Goldstein, J. The end
Mastrosimone, W. Tamer of horses

Children
c Alette, C. The secret garden
c Francoeur, B. The secret garden
Margulies, D. First love
Mitterer, F. Children of the Devil
Morgan, J. Kids
Norman, M. The secret garden
Pickering, K. One child at a time
Potter, D. Blue remembered hills
c Schurman-O'Connor, K. At the bus stop
c Schurman-O'Connor, K. Grandma Rusnak
Wilder, T. Childhood

Children. Gurney, A. R.

The **children** of Heracles. Euripides

Children of the Devil. Mitterer, F.

Children of the shadows. Tomer, B.-Z.

Childress, Alice
Trouble in mind
Rehearsal of play about lynching in South leads to confrontation between white director and black actress. 2 acts 6m 3w 1 interior
In Black drama in America: an anthology; ed. by D. T. Turner
In Plays by American women, 1930-1960; ed. by J. E. Barlow
Wine in the wilderness
Comedy drama set in 1964 Harlem. Artist exhibits contempt for his "uncultured" model until she proves to be more politically astute than he is. 1 act 3m 2w 1 interior
In Black theatre USA [v2]; ed. by J. V. Hatch and T. Shine

Chile
Parra, M. A. de la. The raw, the cooked, and the rotten
Reyes, G. Chilean holiday

Chilean holiday. Reyes, G.

China
Hare, D. Fanshen
Huynh, Quang Nhuong. Dance of the wandering souls
O'Neill, E. "Marco millions"
History—20th century
Yamauchi, W. The chairman's wife

China—*Continued*

Social conditions

Wong, E. Letters to a student revolutionary

China doll. Wong, E.

The **China** tree. Mahfuz, 'Isam

Chinese

Australia

Bell, H. Fortune

Canada

c Pollock, S. Prairie dragons

Hawaii

Lim, G. Bitter cane

United States

Lim, G. Paper angels

Chinese Americans

Chen, K. Eating chicken feet
Hwang, D. H. Trying to find Chinatown
Lee, C. Arthur and Leila
Wang, L. Junk bonds
Wong, E. China doll
Wong, E. Letters to a student revolutionary
c Yep, L. Dragonwings

Chinese coffee. Lewis, I.

Chinese New Year

c Marshall, S. L. The emperor's New Year

Chinn, Jimmie

After September. French (London) 1994 62p

Play about eccentric staff of British school for girls in early 1960s. 2 acts 1m 10w 1 interior

Albert make us laugh. French (London) 1996 64p

Seemingly backward British schoolboy revealed to be poet and visionary. Background music. 2 acts Variable cast 15 characters

Home before dark. French (London) 1994 77p

Drama set in small Lancashire cotton mill town from 1946 to 1964. Woman struggles to raise illegimate son while family members fall victim to cotton dust. 2 acts 14m 15w extras 1 setting

In by the half. French (London) 1994 35p

Drama set in West London. Once distinguished actress and her estranged daughter forced to face unpleasant truths. 1m 4w 1 interior

Something to remember you by. French (London) 1996 65p

Surreal black comedy. Struggling writer obsessed with pop songstress. 2 acts 2m 3w 1 setting

Sylvia's wedding. French (London) 1996 79p

Man's proposal of marriage after ten year courtship throws girlfriend's family, and his own, into turmoil. 2 acts 4 scenes 3m 4w 1 interior

Chiodo, Tom

Boardwalk melody hour murders. French 1995 72p

Murder a La Carte mystery with audience participation. Kidnapping and murder take place during live radio broadcast in 1932 Atlantic City. Prologue 5 scenes 4m 5w 1 interior

The medieval murders. French 1996 28p

Murder a la Carte mystery with audience participation. Murder and madness in castle full of wenches, thieves, and sorcerers. 7 scenes 3m 3w 1 interior

Murder under the big top. French 1996 39p

Murder a La Carte mystery with audience participation. Deadly escapades at circus when rival trapeze artists face off. 5 scenes 3m 4w 1 setting

The **chip** woman's fortune. Richardson, W.

Chislett, Anne

Yankee notions. Playwrights Canada 1993 141p

Historical drama about decisions faced by two young Canadian women in turbulent year following MacKenzie Rebellion. 2 acts 24 scenes 7m 4w extras 1 setting

Chitra. Tagore, R.

Cho doi (Market of lives). Le, Q. D.

Chocrón, Isaac

Clipper

Father opposes son's artistic endeavors. 2 parts 5m 2w 1 setting

In Chocrón, I. Three plays by Isaac Chocrón

OK

Drama about nontraditional family unit. Two older women and younger man profit from threesome until financial concerns get out of hand. 2 parts 1m 2w 1 interior

In Chocrón, I. Three plays by Isaac Chocrón

The ultimate bliss

Two men and woman form a family and raise child together. 2 parts 2m 1w 1 setting

In Chocrón, I. Three plays by Isaac Chocrón

Choice. Elisha, R.

The choice. Luckham, C.

Choosing company. Schwartz, D.

A **chorus** of disapproval. Ayckbourn, A.

Christchild. Franklin, J. E.

Christian, Beatrix
Blue murder. Currency Press in association with Belvoir Street Theatre 1994 51p (Current theatre series)
Modern gothic romance set in mysterious stone cathedral in Sydney harbour. Writer of children's books serves as mentor to woman on journey of self-discovery. 5 acts 15 scenes 2m 4w 1 setting

Christian life
Burnham, Y. Everywoman: a modern morality play
c Haylock, D. Christian olympics
Paul, S. L. The Rainclouds study the Ten Commandments
c Trott, S. Buster come home
c Trott, S. R.S.V.P.

Christian olympics. Haylock, D.

Christianity
Warner, F. Moving reflections

Christiansen, Arne
y A monster ate my homework; the musical; a crazy comedy in two acts; book by Tim Kelly; music by Arne Christiansen; lyrics by Ole Kittleson. Pioneer Drama Service 1995 61p
High school presents play about Dracula. 2 acts 5 scenes Large mixed cast 1 interior
y Teens in Tinseltown; a musical-comedy spoof in two acts; book by Tim Kelly; music by Arne Christiansen; lyrics of Ole Kittleson. Pioneer Drama Service 1993 63p
Musical version of Hooray for Hollywood by Tim Kelly. 2 acts 7 scenes 9m 16w extras 1 setting
y Wash your troubles away; or, ... Dirty deeds come clean; a musical romp of the gold rush days; book by Tim Kelly; music by Arne Christiansen; lyrics by Ole Kittleson. Pioneer Drama Service 1994 40p
Musical comedy set in California gold mining town. Sheriff defeats avaricious villain and wins heart of local laundress. 2 acts 4m 8w extras 1 interior

Christiansen, Debbie McBeth
Who's mining the mercantile? or, If it's counterfeit, ware it. Pioneer Drama Service 1993 24p
Comedy melodrama set in Old West. Hero risks all to save his love from clutches of counterfeiting criminal. 4 scenes 5m 5w 2b 2g 1 interior

Christie, Agatha
Parodies, imitations, etc.
Gordon, P. Murdered to death
Hornby, I. Hello.... Is there any body there?

Christie, John Reginald Halliday
Beard, P. Waiting for Pierrepoint

Christmas
Adam, A. Christmas
c Bennett, R. The shoemaker and the elves
Berkoff, S. Harry's Christmas
Booth, J. Season of goodwill
Bremner, B. Mrs. Coney
c Chatfield, R. The great Santa kidnap
Ekstrom, P. An O. Henry Christmas: The gift of the Magi
Enscoe, L. G. and Enscoe, A. Call for the lights and sing!
Enscoe, L. G. and Enscoe, A. Candles and carols
Enscoe, L. G. and Enscoe, A. The great Gemdale Christmas tree ornament factory
Enscoe, L. G. and Enscoe, A. The king who hated Christmas
Enscoe, L. G. and Enscoe, A. The towne without a tale
Enscoe, L. G. and Enscoe, A. The wise men had it easy
Foxton, D. Kenneth
Harper, T. Christmas isn't for families
c Haylock, D. The Wallies guide to Christmas
y Horitz, T. Good King Wenceslas and the Chancellor of Bohemia
Hornby, I. One across
y Hurst, Z. B. and Hurst, J. R. The cowhand's Christmas Carol
c Kennedy, R. Hans Christian Andersen's The Snow Queen
King, L. L. The Golden Shadows Old West Museum
c Lawrence, M. 'Twas the night before Columbus day ... I mean Christmas
Lebow, B. Tiny Tim is dead
y Levi, S. Merry Christmas Miss Vickers
Linney, R. A Christmas carol
c Mahlmann, L. and Jones, D. C. The Nutcracker Prince
Marx, P. Old Frost's winter adventure
c McCaslin, N. Christmas fiesta
c McCaslin, N. The Christmas lamb
c McCaslin, N. A miracle in the Christmas city
c McCullough, L. E. Bring a torch, Jeannette, Isabella
c McCullough, L. E. The cobbler's pipe
c McCullough, L. E. Diamonds in the snow

Christmas—*Continued*
c McCullough, L. E. Go tell it on the mountain
c McCullough, L. E. Good King Wenceslas
c McCullough, L. E. Here we come a-wassailing
c McCullough, L. E. Jingle bells
c McCullough, L. E. Let us go, O shepherds
c McCullough, L. E. O, Christmas tree
c McCullough, L. E. O thou joyful day
c McCullough, L. E. Silent night
c McCullough, L. E. The twelve days of Christmas
McDonough, J. Posadas
c Medoff, M. Kringle's window
c Miller, H. L. The Birds' Christmas Carol
Mortimer, J. Charles Dickens' A Christmas carol
Murphy, T. A thief of a Christmas
c Peterson, M. L. How Santa Claus discovered Christmas
c Pflomm, P. N. The busy Santa
c Pflomm, P. N. Silvie the substitute reindeer
Pintauro, J. Seymour in the very heart of winter
Rodgers, J. W. It's a wonderful life
Sadler, C. and Pemberton, S. Christmas balls
c Schario, C. A Christmas carol
Shores, D. Daughters of the Lone Star State
Stickland, E. Some assembly required
c Swortzell, L. A visit from St. Nicholas
c Vigil, A. La flor de la Noche Buena. The flower of the Holy Night
Wilder, T. The long Christmas dinner
Wilhelm, L. The road to Nineveh
Williams, J.; Sears, J. and Howard, E. A Tuna Christmas
c Woyiwada, A. The little fir tree

Christmas. Adam, A.

Christmas balls. Sadler, C. and Pemberton, S.

A **Christmas** cactus. Byerrum, E.

A **Christmas** carol. Dickens, C. (dramatization) See Linney, R. A Christmas carol; Mortimer, J. Charles Dickens' A Christmas carol; Schario, C. A Christmas carol

Christmas fiesta. McCaslin, N.

Christmas isn't for families. Harper, T.

The **Christmas** lamb. McCaslin, N.

Christopher Columbus. MacNeice, L.

Church, Jeff
c The Pied Piper of New Orleans. Anchorage Press 1993 46p

Play based on Robert Browning's poem The Pied Piper of Hamelin set 1930s New Orleans. Piper rids town of rats but leads children away when merchants refuse to pay. Music, singing. 8 scenes 4m 4w 1 exterior

Church
c Haylock, D. A window in the diary
Jamal, D. The highway
White, P. A cheery soul

The **church** fight. Gaines-Shelton, R. A.

Church of England

Clergy

Mercer, D. Flint

Church schools
Wilde, P. What's wrong with angry?

Church societies
Gaines-Shelton, R. A. The church fight

Churchill, Caryl
Blue heart: Blue kettle

Drama about mothers, sons and breakdown of language. Middle-aged man and girlfriend involved in scam. 2m 6w 1 setting

In Churchill, C. Blue heart

Blue heart: Heart's desire

Catastrophe looms in various scenarios as father, mother and aunt await for woman to arrive home after years abroad. 3m 4w extras 1 interior

In Churchill, C. Blue heart

Cloud 9. Theatre Communications Group 1995 87p

Comedy exploring gender roles and sexual politics set in Victorian colonial Africa and present day London. 2 acts 6m 6w 1 setting

Lives of the great poisoners. Methuen 1993 171p

Dance theater piece investigating lives of notorious poisoners Dr. Crippen, Medea, and Madame de Brinvilliers. Music, singing. Variable cast

Mad forest. Theatre Communications Group 1996 87p

Drama focusing on two Romanian families before, during and after the overthrow of the Ceausescus and their secret police. Music, singing. 3 acts 25 scenes Large mixed cast settings

The skriker. Hern Bks. 1994 52p

Drama juxtaposing English folk tales with modern urban life. Shapeshifting being in search of love and revenge insinuates itself into lives of two young London women. 7m 9w 1 setting

—Same. Theatre Communciation Group 1994 52p

Churchill, Caryl—*Continued*
The skriker (condensation)
In The Best plays of 1995-1996
See also Seneca. Thyestes

Ciccotosto, Emma
Pitts, G. Emma

Cider with Rosie. Roose-Evans, J.

Cigarettes and chocolate. Minghella, A.

Cinco de Mayo, Battle of, 1862
c Vigil, A. La Batalla de Cinco de Mayo. The Battle of Cinco de Mayo

Cinderella

Parodies, imitations, etc.

Davis, R. The (revised) Travelling Cinderella show
c Foxton, D. The real story of Puss in boots
c Jackson, M. Unlucky Cinderella

Cinderella. D'Arcy, A.

Cinderella. Mahlmann, L. and Jones, D. C.

Cinderella. Mercati, C.

Cinderella—the sequel. Staite, J.

Cinoman, Susan
Fitting rooms
Three pairs of women converse in fitting room of tony boutique. 6w 1 interior
In The Best American short plays, 1995-1996

Cintas Largas tribe. See Indians of South America—Brazil

Circus
Beard, P. Death of a clown
y Swift, R. Rascals under the big top
Vingoe, M. Living curiosities: a story of Anna Swan

Cistellaria. See Plautus, T. M. The little box

City and town life
Korder, H. The lights

Civil rights
See also African Americans—Civil rights

Civil War. See United States—History—Civil War

Civilians stay put. Hark, M. and McQueen, N.

Clair de Lune. Linney, R.

Clap hands here comes Charlie. Barnes, P.

Clapp, Patricia
c The girl whose fortune sought her
Girl learns true value of flowers she grows. 3m 3w 1 exterior
In Thirty plays from favorite stories; ed. by S. E. Kamerman

Clapp, Tom
Dracula. Players Press 1993 56p
Dramatization of Bram Stoker's classic vampire novel. 3 acts 11m 6w extras 1 setting

The open boat. Players Press 1996 56p
Drama set in 1897 loosely based on Stephen Crane's short story. Four shipwrecked men try to reach land. Singing. 2 acts 2 scenes 5m extras 1 setting

Clara and the gambler. Milligan, J.

Clarence Darrow in hell. Heise, K. and Heise, D.

Clarissa's closet. Ruch, A.

Clark, Badger, 1883-1957
Pierson, K. Mountain thunder

Clark, Finn. See Webster, P. Peter Panto

Clark, Renee J.
y Fighting for myself. Pioneer Drama Service 1996 40p
Series of scenes portray pressures and stresses experienced by today's teenage girls. 2 acts 9 scenes Variable cast 24 characters extras

Clark, Ron, and Bobrick, Sam
Norman, is that you? [Revised] French 1997 87p
Comedy. Father discovers that his son is homosexual. 2 acts 5 scenes 3m 2w 1 interior

Clark, Sally
Jehanne of the witches
Sexuality, power, and religion explored in historical drama about Joan of Arc and Gilles de Rais. 2 acts 21 scenes 4m 4w 1 setting
In Big-time women from way back when

Life without instruction. Talonbooks 1994 168p
Drama about 17th-century Italian painter Artemisia Gentileschi who was raped by her tutor Agostino Tassi and forced to endure torture and public humiliation during the trial. 2 acts 28 scenes 8m 3w

Moo
Comedy about love and obsession. Feisty, rebellious woman relentlessly pursues man she just met. 2 acts 47 scenes 3m 5w 1 setting
In Modern Canadian plays v2; ed. by J. Wasserman

Clark, Sally—*Continued*
Saint Frances of Hollywood. Talonbooks 1996 191p
Drama about unconventional Hollywood star Frances Farmer who, committed to radical political causes, was incarcerated in psychiatric hospital where she was lobotomized and released as "cured" in 1949. 2 acts 51 scenes 4m 4w extras 1 setting

The trial of Judith K. Playwrights Canada 1991 119p
Black comedy loosely based on Kafka's The trial. Businesswoman, accused of unknown crime, thrust into bureaucratic nightmare. 2 acts 21 scenes 3m 4w 1 setting

Clarke, Breena, and Dickerson, Glenda
Re/membering Aunt Jemima: a menstrual show
Postmodern minstrel show about stereotypes faced by African American women. Singing. 2 acts 5w 1 setting
In Colored contradictions: an anthology of contemporary African-American plays
In Contemporary plays by women of color; ed. by K. A. Perkins and R. Uno

Clarke, Terence
The Venetian twins; a musical comedy; book and lyrics by Nick Enright; music by Terence Clarke; based on the play by Carlo Goldoni. Currency Press in association with State Theatre Co. 1996 54p (Australian Playhouse series)
Musical comedy about love and mistaken identity set in eighteenth century Verona. Prologue 2 acts 5 scenes 7m 3w extras 1 interior 1 exterior

Class action. Slaight, B.

Class conflict. See Social conflict

Class distinction
Boucicault, D. The Colleen Bawn
Foote, H. The Prisoner's Song
Miller, A. The last Yankee
y Olfson, L. The admirable Crichton
y Olfson, L. Monsieur Beaucaire
Strindberg, A. Miss Julie
White, P. Big toys

Great Britain

Mercer, D. Where the difference begins
Osborne, J. Déjàvu
Osborne, J. Look back in anger
Pinero, A. W. The second Mrs. Tanqueray
Wallace, N. One flea spare

Class enemy. Williams, N.

Class of '77. Milligan, J.

Class photo. Visdei, A.

Classical drama. See Greek drama (Comedy); Greek drama (Satyr play); Greek drama (Tragedy); Latin drama (Comedy); Latin drama (Tragedy)

Claudius, Emperor of Rome, 10 B.C.-54 A.D.
Barbier, M.-A. Arria and Paetus

Claudius. Gass, K.

Clavigo. Goethe, J. W. von

Cleage, Pearl
Chain
Drama set in Harlem about young black crack addict held prisoner by her parents in desperate attempt to cure her. 1w 1 interior
In Playwriting women; ed. by J. Miles

Flyin' West. Dramatists 1995 79p
Historical drama set in 1898. Story of African American women pioneers who left the South and settled in all-black town of Nicodemus, Kansas. 2 acts 11 scenes 2m 4w 1 setting
—Same
In Black drama in America: an anthology; ed. by D. T. Turner
In Contemporary plays by women of color; ed. by K. A. Perkins and R. Uno

Late bus to Mecca
Drama set in 1970 Detroit bus station. Two young black women form bond while waiting for bus. Slide projections 13 scenes 2w 1 setting
In Playwriting women; ed. by J. Miles

Cleaning women
Santeiro, L. A royal affair

The **clearing.** Edmundson, H.

Cleary, Beverly
Ramona Quimby (dramatization) See Jenkin, L. Ramona Quimby

Clemens, Brian
Inside job. French (London) 1993 58p
Thriller set on the Costa del Sol. Professional criminal, employed by man to kill wife, becomes involved in tangle of murder, greed, and infidelity. 2 acts 6 scenes 2m 1w 1 interior

Cleomenes III, King of Sparta
Dryden, J. Cleomenes, the Spartan heroe

Cleomenes, the Spartan heroe. Dryden, J.

Cleon
Aristophanes. Knights

Cleopatra, Queen of Egypt
Dryden, J. All for love
Shaw, B. Caesar and Cleopatra

Clergy
Caldwell, B. Prayer meeting
Gaines-Shelton, R. A. The church fight
Glover, S. The straw chair
Larson, L.; Lee, L. and Wackler, R. Tent meeting
LeFevre, A. Americansaint
c McCullough, L. E. O, Christmas tree
Mercer, D. Flint
Nunn, J. Stuck
White, P. Shepherd on the rocks

Cleveland, Rick
Tom and Jerry
Activities of two hit-men. 11 scenes 3m 1 setting
In Showtime's Act One Festival of one act plays, 1994

Cleveland. Wellman, M.

Cleveland raining. Rno, S.

The **clever** judge. Artist, V. A.

The **clever** Maakafi. Artist, V. A.

Clever Marya and the Czar. McCaslin, N.

Clever Peter. Pyle, M. T.

Clever pets. Pflomm, P. N.

Clifford, Margaret Ellen. See Flanagan, H. jt. auth.

Cliff's edge. Beard, P.

Clipper. Chocrón, I.

Clippings. Fuson, D.

Clizia. Machiavelli, N.

Clocks and whistles. Adamson, S.

Close of play. Gray, S.

Close to Croydon. Plowman, G.

Close to the bone. Manning, N.

Close to the wind. Everett, R.

Cloud, Darrah
O pioneers!
Dramatization of Willa Cather's novel. Follows life of pioneer woman in late 1890s-early 1900s Nebraska. Music, singing. 3 acts 30 scenes 11m 8w 1 setting
In Playwriting women; ed. by J. Miles

Cloud 9. Churchill, C.

Cloud tectonics. Rivera, J.

The **clouds.** Aristophanes

Clowns
Barker, C. Crazyface

Clowns. Reid, C.

The **club.** Williamson, D.

Club Chernobyl. Warren, D.

Clubs
Epstein, M. How Gertrude stormed the Philosophers' Club
Gurney, A. R. The Middle Ages
Labiche, E. and Delacour, A. The piggy bank
Schmidt, W. F. The Explorators Club

Clue: the musical. Blum, G; Barker, W. and Martucci, V.

Clum, John M.
Randy's house
Drama set in Cobb County, Georgia town in 1993. Homosexuality becomes divisive issue in community. 12 scenes 8m 1w 1 setting
In Staging gay lives; ed. by J. M. Clum

The **coal** diamond. Lauro, S.

Coal mines and mining
Carson, J. A preacher with a horse to ride
Cullen, M. The cut
Lill, W. The Glace Bay Miners' Museum
Matheus, J. F. Black damp
Schenkkan, R. Fire in the hole
Schenkkan, R. Which side are you on?
Tuttle, J. Terminal Cafe

The **cobbler's** pipe. McCullough, L. E.

Cocek, Christina
Stepping off a cloud
Monologue by woman analysand. 1w 1 interior
In Facing forward; ed. by L. D. Frank

Cock-a-doodle dandy. O'Casey, S.

Cocke, Dudley. See Baker, D. jt. auth.

Cockerell, Sir Sydney Carlyle
Whitemore, H. The best of friends

The **cockroach** trilogy. Williams, A.

Cockroaches. Witkiewicz, S. I.

The **cocktail** hour. Gurney, A. R.

Cocteau, Jean
Les parents terribles (Indiscretions); tr. by Jeremy Sams. Hern Bks. 1994 73p (Royal National Theatre)
Overprotective, emotional mother commits suicide when she cannot prevent son from marrying. 3 acts 30 scenes 2m 3w 2 interiors

Coen, Dana
Tinkle time
President and aides make emergency stop at public toilet. 6m 1 interior
In Showtime's Act One Festival of one-act plays, 1994

Coffee, Gerald
Beyond survival (dramatization) See Bell, J. A. Prisoner

Coffee. Bond, E.

The **coffee** shop. Goldoni, C.

Coghlan, Lin

Waking. Hern Bks. 1997 59p (An Instant playscript)

Man returns to Ireland with young son and reopens old wounds between him and his own father. 2 acts 10 scenes 3m 1w 1 setting

Cohen, Frumi

y Try a little Shakespeare. Players Press 1993 44p

Musical based on Shakespeare's Comedy of errors. Modern story of mistaken identity alternates with scenes from Shakespeare's play. Prologue 3 acts 9 scenes Variable cast extras 1 setting

Cohn, Roy

Kushner, T. Angels in America: Pt. 1: Millennium approaches

The **coins** of Lin Foo. McCaslin, N.

Cold Comfort Farm. Doust, P.

Cold face, warm heart. McCaslin, N.

Cold hands. Baum, T.

Cold Lazarus. Potter, D.

The **cold** wind and the warm. Behrman, S. N.

Cole, Jonathan D.

c Conestoga stories, by Susan Baer Beck; music by Jonathan D. Cole. Anchorage Press 1995 50p

Musical based on historical accounts of Western pioneers. Variable cast 42 characters 1 setting

c Ichabod; a new musical adaptation of The legend of Sleepy Hollow by Washington Irving; book and lyrics by Charles Jones; music by Jonathan D. Cole. Anchorage Press 1996 49p

Musical dramatization of tale about superstitious schoolmaster's encounter with ghost of headless horseman. 7m 4w extras 1 setting

Cole, Norma

y And the tide shall cover the earth. Anchorage Press 1994 59p

Dramatization of author's novel The final tide about dam built by TVA which is about to flood Kentucky community. 2 acts 2m 4w 1g 1 setting

The final tide (dramatization) See Cole, N. And the tide shall cover the earth

Coleman, Ralf M.

The girl from back home

Melodrama set in Harlem at height of bootlegging era. Mistress of racketeer seeks to escape her desperate circumstances. 2m 1w 1 interior

In Lost plays of the Harlem Renaissance; ed. by J. V. Hatch and L. Hamalian

Coles, Enid

September revisited. French (London) 1994 21p

English nanny with upper class pretensions is reminded of her youthful cruelty by poor woman in park. 4w extras 1 interior 1 exterior

Collateral damage. Robinson, M.

The **Colleen** Bawn. Boucicault, D.

College students

Beber, N. Misreadings
Franklin, J. E. Miss Honey's young'uns
Gurney, A. R. The Old One-Two
Hallman, B. The women of Theta Kappa
Horovitz, I. It's called the Sugar Plum
y Kachejian, G. All's well that ends wrong
Kelly, T. Yard sale
Oates, J. C. Negative
Quinn, L. Well done poets
Russell, W. Educating Rita
Shaughnessy, D. The manager
Sherman, J. M. Sophistry
Sherman, J. M. Wonderful time
Taikeff, S. Dolorosa Sanchez
Weller, M. Moonchildren

College teachers

Gilbert, S. M. and Gubar, S. Masterpiece theatre
Gotanda, P. K. Day standing on its head
Gray, S. Butley
Gurney, A. R. The Old One-Two
Gurney, A. R. Public affairs: Pt 1 The love course
Kraus, J. H. and Woodward, G. Tenure track
Mamet, D. Oleanna
Neipris, J. Brussels sprouts
Nelson, R. Life sentences
Pawley, T. The tumult and the shouting
Poliakoff, S. Blinded by the sun
Russell, W. Educating Rita
Shawn, W. Aunt Dan and Lemon
Sherman, J. M. Sophistry
Stoppard, T. Professional foul
Tuttle, J. The hammerstone
Williamson, D. Dead white males
Williamson, D. The department
Wine, B. Tenure

Collette, Paul, and Fritzen, Gary

c Toy camp. Pioneer Drama Service 1994 27p

Musical. Toys go to camp to learn how to be toys. 4 scenes Unidentified cast 13 characters extras 1 interior

Collings, John

Kelly & Donald. New Playwrights Network 1996 18p

Two men released from English mental hospital share bed-sit. 1 act 2m 1 interior

Collins, Michael, 1890-1922
Mac Intyre, T. Good evening, Mr Collins

Collins, Wilkie
The moonstone (dramatization) See Thane, A. The moonstone

Collodi, Carlo
The adventures of Pinocchio (dramatization) See Harder, E. Hey ho, Pinocchio; Mahlmann, L. and Jones, D. C. Pinocchio; Roca, M. Pinocchio; Simons, J. Pinocchio commedia

Colón, Alvan
c The caravan

Drama about abuse of power based on poem La elegia del Saltimbanqui by Luis Pales Matos. Traveling magician and assistant trade places. Music, singing, masks 3m 1w

In ¡Aplauso! Hispanic children's theater; ed. by J. Rosenberg

Colón, Oscar A.
Siempre en mi corazón

Alcoholic woman, on verge of mental breakdown, returns to Caribbean island home to track down source of recurrent vision-like dream. 16 scenes 3m 5w 1 setting

In Nuestro New York; ed. by J. V. Antush

Colonial tongues. Robinson, M.

Colonialism. See Great Britain—Colonies

The **color** of August. Pedrero, P.

Colorado, Elvira, and Colorado, Hortensia
1992: blood speaks

Legend, song and poetry illustrate how women of Mexican and Native American ancestry have dealt with oppression. Singing. 13 scenes 4w

In Contemporary plays by women of color; ed. by K. A. Perkins and R. Uno

Colorado, Hortensia. See Colorado, E. jt. auth.

The **colored** museum. Wolfe, G. C.

Colossus. Barker, C.

Columbus, Christopher
Barnes, P. Bye bye Columbus
MacNeice, C. Christopher Columbus
y Suntep Theatre. Wheel of justice

The **Colorado** catechism. Cardinal, V. J.

Colvill, Bill. See Fo, D. Can't pay? Won't pay!

Combination skin. Jones, L.

Come back for light refreshments after the service. Day, J.

Come down burning. Corthron, K.

Come good rain. Seremba, G.

Come on up. Walker, S.

Come the resolution. Beard, P.

Come to leave. Zell, A. E.

The **comeback.** Gurney, A. R.

The **comeback** caper. Martens, A. C.

Comedians
Griffiths, T. Comedians
Johnson, T. Unsuitable for adults
Ritter, E. Automatic pilot
Segal, G. All the tricks but one
St. John, B. Is there a comic in the house?

Comedies in apple blossom time. Taylor, R. and Bologna, J.

Comedies of family life. Witkiewicz, S. I.

Comedy
Ackermann, J. The batting cage
Ackermann, J. Stanton's Garage
Ackermann, J. Zara Spook and other lures
Adam, A. Birds of prey
Adam, A. A bit of land
Adam, A. Business meeting
Adam, A. A cameo from Cranford
Adam, A. Castles in the air
Allen, C. Ripe conditions
Allen, W. Central Park West
Aron, G. Olive and Hilary
Aspengren, K. House of wonders
y Avery, C. The seven ages of Dan
Ayckbourn, A. A chorus of disapproval
Ayckbourn, A. Communicating doors
Ayckbourn, A. Henceforward . . .
c Ayckbourn, A. Mr A's amazing maze plays
Ayckbourn, A. The revengers' comedies
Baitz, J. R. The film society
Ball, A. Bachelor holiday
Balzac, H. de. Mercadet
Bank, D. Halfway home
Banville, J. The broken jug
Barnes, P. Last things
Barrie, J. M. Rosalind
Barry, P. J. And Fat Freddy's blues
Barry, P. J. Down by the ocean
Bartram, F. Tiddley pum
Beard, P. Come the resolution
Beard, P. Meat and two veg
Beard, P. Swingers
Behn, A. The feigned courtesans
Beim, N. Inside

Comedy—*Continued*
Beim, N. Jewel thieves!
Benfield, D. Up and running!
Bennett, A. Forty years on
Bennett, A. Getting on
Berkoff, S. Kvetch
Bernstein, J. Pizza: a love story
Bisson, P. Is there anybody there?
Bisson, P. When the clock strikes
Blessing, L. Fortinbras
Block, S. Not a game for boys
Bobrick, S. Are you sure?
Bogosian, E. Pounding nails in the floor with my forehead
Bogosian, E. Talk radio
c Boiko, C. A dog's best friend
Booth, J. Friendly affair
Booth, J. Little white lies
Booth, J. Over his dead body
Booth, J. Season of goodwill
Booth, J. Sleeping arrangements
Booth, J. Something on his mind
Bozzone, B. and DiPietro, J. Breast men
Brandl, D. Vine and dandy
Brewer, E. and Toksvig, S. The pocket dream
Brittney, L. Failed investments
Brooks, V. Let's pretend
Brown, K. R. Welcome to Four Way: the town that time forgot
Brownell, R. Afterhours
Buchan, A. Conditional surrender
Burns, K. Identity crisis
Burns, K. On hold at 30,000 feet
Burns, K. Terminal terror
Busch, C. You should be so lucky
Butterfield, C. Life in the trees: No problem
Campbell, K. Jamais vu
Campbell, K. The recollections of a furtive nudist
Campton, D. The evergreens
Carmichael, F. Don't mention my name
Carmichael, F. I bet your life
Carmichael, F. Meet my husbands
Carmichael, F. Over the checkerboard
Champagne, S. Away from me
Chappell, E. It can damage your health
Churchill, C. Cloud 9
Conde, M. The Tropical Breeze Hotel
Congdon, C. Dog opera
Corrie, J. Billy Shaw
Courteline, G. Boubouroche
Crane, R. Under the stars
Crump, R. The strange illness
Dashow, K. Thanks
Davies, R. Eros at breakfast
Davis, R. The (revised) Travelling Cinderella show
c Davis, R. The travelling Jekyll & Hyde show
Day, D. M. Possession is . . .
De Filippo, E. Filumena Marturano
De Filippo, E. Grand magic
DePietro, P. The hilarious hillbilly massacre
Dickinson, S. Styx and Bones
Dinner, W. Logic upside down
Donnelly, N. A little like paradise
Donoghue, M. A. Me and Mamie O'Rourke
Doyle, R. Brownbread
Dryden, J. Amphitryon
Dunbar, D. A song for Robbie
Dunn, M. Judge and jury
Durang, C. Baby with the bathwater
Durang, C. Beyond therapy
Durang, C. Business lunch at the Russian Tea Room
Durang, C. DMV tyrant
Durang, C. Funeral parlor
Durang, C. The Hardy Boys and the mystery of where babies come from
Durang, C. Sister Mary Ignatius explains it all for you
Durang, C. Titanic
Durang, C. Wanda's visit
Elyot, K. My night with Reg
Everett, R. Close to the wind
Farrell, B. Forty-four, Sycamore
Farrell, B. The last Apache reunion
Faulkner, A. For England and King George
Feydeau, G. "Hey, cut out the parading around stark naked!"
Feydeau, G. My wife's dead mother
Firbank, R. A disciple from the country
Firbank, R. The Princess Zoubaroff
Firth, T. The end of the food chain
Fischer, M. The gay divorcee
The Five Lesbian Brothers. Brave smiles . . . another lesbian tragedy
Fletcher, J. and Massinger, P. The elder brother
Fletcher, J. and Massinger, P. The little French lawyer
Fletcher, J. and Massinger, P. The Spanish curate
Fletcher, J. and Rowley, W. The maid in the mill
Foster, N. The motor trade
c Foxton, D. The real story of Puss in Boots
Frayn, M. Now you know

Comedy—*Continued*

Friedman, R. All for art
c Gallanar, I. Showdown at the 3-R Ranch
Gardner, H. I'm not Rappaport
Gersten, A. My thing of love
Gerstenberg, A. The pot boiler
Gilroy, F. D. Fore!
Gilroy, F. D. Give the bishop my faint regards
Gilroy, F. D. Real to reel
Godber, J. April in Paris
Godber, J. The office party
Godber, J. Up 'n' under II
Godber, J. and Thornton, J. Shakers re-stirred
Goldoni, C. The coffee shop
Goldstein, C. Last exit before toll
Gorky, M. The summer people
Graham, B. Belmont Avenue Social Club
Granville-Barker, H. The Madras House
Granville-Barker, H. The marrying of Ann-Leete
Granville-Barker, H. Vote by ballot
Gray, S. The common pursuit
Gray, S. Pig in a poke
Greenberg, R. The author's voice
Greenberg, R. Jenny keeps talking
Gregory, L. A. Spreading the news
c Griffiths, D. That's the way to do it
Griffiths, T. Comedians
Gurney, A. R. The cocktail hour
Gurney, A. R. The fourth wall
Gurney, A. R. Sylvia
Guyer, M. The American century
Hallman, B. The women of Theta Kappa
y Hamlett, C. Hairum-scarum
Hampton, C. The philanthropist
Hannan, C. Shining souls
Hatcher, J. Smash
Haubold, C. The big black Box
Hendrick, B. If I can't take it with me ... I'm not going to go
Hillman, B. L. Iron magnolias
Hoffman, A. Welcome stranger
Hogg, F. A. Afternoon at Tavern MacTavish
Hornby, I. Dream, lover!
Hornby, I. Late of this address
Hornby, I. Wait until the ghost is clear
Horovitz, I. Line
Horovitz, I. Play for germs
Horovitz, I. The primary English class
Horovitz, I. Today I am a fountain pen
House, J. Cherchez la femme
House, R. and Shearman, A. The scandalous adventures of Sir Toby Trollope
Howe, T. Appearances
Howe, T. One shoe off
y Huff, B. Spy for a day
Inchbald, Mrs. Such things are
Ives, D. Don Juan in Chicago
Ives, D. Mere mortals
Ives, D. The Philadelphia
Ives, D. Seven menus
Ives, D. Sure thing
Ives, D. The universal language
Ives, D. Variations on the death of Trotsky
Ives, D. Words, words, words
c Jackson, K. Laffin' school reunion
Janes, H. Two of a kind
Jannuzzi, L. The appointment
Jeffreys, S. The libertine
Johnson, T. Dead funny
Johnson, T. Hysteria
Jones, T. W. The wizard of hip
Kass, S. H. Lusting after Pipino's wife
Keane, J. B. Moll
Keillor, G. The midlife crisis of Dionysus
Kelly, C. Excess baggage
Kelly, T. Renfield of the flies and spiders
y Kelly, T. Trick or treat
y Kelly, T. Yard sale
Kemp, R. A trump for Jericho
Kitchen, B. Halfway up the M3 on the way to Basingstoke
Kobler, F. Wild dust
y Kottke, T. G. Deputy Toby
Kovacevic, D. The gathering place
Kravitz, A. Just thinking
y Kukla, D. Sticks and stones
c Kurtz, J. The ballad of King Windowglass
Kushner, T. The illusion
Labiche, E. Eating crow
c LaBounty, D. Jeremy Whistler, mad scientist
Lambert, L. Sunrise at noon
Lane, E. Cater-waiter
Larbey, B. Half an idea
Larbey, B. A small affair
La Roche-Guilhen, A. de. All-wondrous
Lawrence, J. and Lee, R. E. Auntie Mame
Lawrence, J. and Lee, R. E. First Monday in October
Lawrence, J. and Lee, R. E. Only in America
LeFevre, A. Americansaint
LeSage, A. R. Turcaret
y Levi, S. Good morning Miss Vickers
y Levi, S. Merry Christmas Miss Vickers
Lewes, G. H. The game of speculation

Comedy—*Continued*
y Lewton, R. An alien stole my skateboard
c Love, D. Holiday in the rain forest
c Love, D. Kabuki gift
Ludwig, K. Moon over Buffalo
Lyly, J. Campaspe
Machiavelli, N. Clizia
Mamet, D. Glengarry Glen Ross
Mamet, D. An interview
Mander, C. Getting along
Mander, C. World première
Margulies, D. What's wrong with this picture?
Martin, J. Cementville
Martin, J. Criminal hearts
Martin, J. Middle-aged white guys
Martin, J. Shasta Rue
Martin, S. WASP
May, E. Hot line
Mayer, J. Killjoy
c McCaslin, N. The lazy ones
c McCaslin, N. Three meals a day
McConnell, J. Dancers
McConnell, J. Doggies
McConnell, J. A lovesome thing
McGillivray, D. and Zerlin, W. Chase me up Farndale Avenue, s'il vous plaît!
McNally, T. Noon
McNally, T. The Ritz
McNally, T. Whiskey
Mead, K. The other other woman
Mellor, K. A passionate woman
Milligan, J. Clara and the gambler
Milligan, J. Life after Elvis
Milligan, J. Money talks
Milligan, J. Walking on the moon
Minieri, A. Your life is a feature film
Minjares, J. The king of the kosher grocers
Mortimer, J. Edwin
Murphy, T. Conversations on a homecoming
Musset, A. de. Fantasio
Najera, R. Latinologues: Monologues of the Latin experience
Nelson, R. and Gelman, A. Misha's party
Nigro, D. Paganini
Norbury, P. Valparaiso
Nottage, L. Poof!
Nunn, J. Stuck
Oates, J. C. The perfectionist
y O'Brien, J. Wherefore art thou Juliet?
y Olfson, L. The Pickwick papers
O'Neill, E. The movie man
Ornsbo, J. Odysseus from Vraa
Osborne, W. and Herrera, A. Smoke & mirrors
Osterman, G. Brother truckers
Otway, T. The soldiers' fortune
Overmyer, E. On the verge
y Panych, M. 2B WUT UR
Parnell, P. An imaginary life
Pearson, S. Watching the dog
y Perry, E. E. Once upon a beginning
Pinero, A. W. Trelawny of the 'Wells'
Pintauro, J. Bus stop diner
Pinter, H. Victoria Station
y Polsky, M. E. Act of will
Porter, D. No more Medea
Pospisil, C. Somewhere in between
c Pricone, S. A tree grows in Hollywood
c Priore, F. V. Spooks on strike!
Quinton, E. William Shakespeare's A midsummer night's dream
Rattigan, T. French without tears
Rebeck, T. Loose knit
Rebeck, T. Sunday on the rocks
Rector, M. H. The lady and the commissioner of airports
Reddin, K. Throwing smoke
Reilly, C. Astronauts
Reiss, J. Awkward silence
Rensten, M. The skip
Reynolds, J. Dance with me
Ribman, R. The rug merchants of chaos
Richardson, A. A fine gentleman
Richardson, D. McJonah
Robinson, G. and Robinson, C. K. Murder for rent
Roth, A. Oh, the innocents
Rubens, B. Hijack
Rubess, B. Pope Joan
Rudnick, P. Jeffrey
Rumble, P. B. Aunt Sophie's latkes
Russell, W. Breezeblock Park
Russell, W. Educating Rita
y Russell, W. Our day out
Russell, W. Stags and hens
Sade, Marquis de. The self-proclaimed philosopher
Sade, Marquis de. The shyster
Saunders, J. Birthday
Saunders, J. Fashion
Saunders, J. France
Saunders, J. Iso tank
Saunders, J. Magazine
Sawyer, A. V. Life comes to the old maid
Schmidt, W. F. The Explorators Club
Schnitzler, A. Fink and Fliederbusch
Schooleman, S. and Sewell, C. The stars within
Scotland, J. A surgeon for Lucinda
Sears, J. Eddie Lee, Eddie Lee
Serreau, C. Lapin Lapin

Comedy—*Continued*
Sewell, G. Speak of the devil
Shanley, J. P. Four dogs and a bone
Sharrocks, M. Calling in
Shaughnessy, D. The manager
Shaw, B. Caesar and Cleopatra
Shaw, B. John Bull's other Island
Shengold, N. Finger food
Shengold, N. Lives of the great waitresses
Sherman, J. The God of Isaac
Sherman, J. Jest a second!
Sherman, J. The retreat
Sherman, J. M. Serendipity and serenity
Shores, D. Daughters of the Lone Star State
Silver, N. Fit to be tied
Silverstein, S. Dreamers
Simon, N. Laughter on the 23rd floor
Simon, N. London suite: Diana and Sidney
Simon, N. London suite: Going home
Simon, N. London suite: The man on the floor
Simon, N. London suite: Settling accounts
Simpson, E. The comet of St. Loomis
Slade, B. Same time, another year
Slade, B. You say tomatoes
Smith, B. L. Butterscotch
Smith, M. L. An evening of culture: Faith County II, the saga continues
Smith, S. Parentcraft
Snelgrove, M. Bums on seats
Southerne, T. The wives' excuse
Sroka, J. and Fleming, J. Dying for laughs
St. Germain, M. Camping with Henry & Tom
St. John, B. 13 past midnight
y St. John, B. Here comes the judge!
St. John, B. Is there a comic in the house?
y St. John, B. Murder in the House of horrors
c Staite, J. Cinderella—the sequel
Sternheim, C. The bloomers
Stone, T. Hello, Ma!
Stone, T. She needs me
Stone, T. Whatever you say
Stoppard, T. Professional foul
Stroppel, F. Domestic violence
Stroppel, F. The Mamet women
Stroppel, F. Package deal
Stroppel, F. Single and proud
c Summer, A. The just so letter
Svanoe, B. Punch and Judy
y Swartz, L. D. Halloween screams
y Swift, R. The Hunchback of Notre Dame goes West
c Swortzell, L. Jack Fuggler
c Swortzell, L. The love of three oranges
Tasca, J. Gums
Tasca, J. Italian rum cake
Tasca, J. The spelling of Coynes
Taylor, R. and Bologna, J. Barry, Betty and Bill
Teagarden, J. Letting Lucinda down
y Terson, P. How to write a play
Thomas, B. Physical
Thomas, T. Without apologies
Tibbles, G. The turn of the worm
Tolan, K. Approximating mother
Tony n' Tina's wedding
Townsend, S. Bazaar & rummage
Townsend, S. The secret diary of Adrian Mole aged $13\frac{3}{4}$
Townsend, S. Womberang
Tricker, C. Losers
y Ullom, S. Geeks do come from outer space
Vago, S. M. An ordinary woman under stress
Valle, F. I am a winner
Vassallo, P. The spelling bee
Vickery, F. Biting the bullet
Vickery, F. A kiss on the bottom
Vickery, F. Roots and wings
Vickery, F. Spanish lies
Vogel, P. Desdemona
Wadsworth, S. The triumph of love
Walker, G. F. The art of war
Walker, S. Come on up
Warburton, N. The Droitwich discovery
Warburton, N. The last bread pudding
Warburton, N. J. Distracted globe
Ward, D. T. Day of absence
Warner, F. Lying figures
Wasserstein, W. The sisters Rosensweig
y Wells, J. S. Competition piece
Wells, J. S. The ladykiller
West, M. The drag
West, M. Sex
Whyte, P. Tuesday, eight-fifteen
Wilder, T. Such things only happen in books
Wilhelm, L. Cherry blend with vanilla
Wilhelm, L. Whoppers
Williams, N. A little like paradise
Williams, N. Harry and me
Williams, J.; Sears, J. and Howard, E. A Tuna Christmas
Wilson, J. Abstinence
Wilson, L. Ikke, ikke, nye, nye, nye

Comedy—*Continued*
Wilson, L. Ludlow fair
Wine, B. Tenure
Wise, R. Eventide
Wise, R. Some do, some don't
Wise, R. When one door closes
c Witkiewicz, S. I. Cockroaches
c Witkiewicz, S. I. Comedies of family life
Wood, P. Faint sound of a bell
Wreggitt, A. and Shaw, R. The wild guys
Ziegler, T. Grace & Glorie
y Zindel, P. Every seventeen minutes the crowd goes crazy!
Zoshchenko, M. Crime and punishment
See also Farces; Greek drama (Comedy); Latin drama (Comedy)

Black humor

Alvarez, L. The reincarnation of Jaimie Brown
Anderson, J. Tough choices for the new century: a seminar for responsible living
Ayckbourn, A. Man of the moment
Bamford, S. No roses around the door
Barnes, P. Red noses
Beard, P. Cliff's edge
Bill, S. Curtains
Bisson, P. Merry widows
Bogosian, E. Drinking in America
Bolger, D. Blinded by the light
Bozzone, B. Sonny DeRee's life flashes before his eyes
Chen, K. Eating chicken feet
Chinn, J. Something to remember you by
Clark, S. The trial of Judith K.
Congdon, C. Losing father's body
Cullen, A. Self catering
Cunningham, L. Beautiful bodies
Dashow, K. Joey-Boy
Dewberry, E. Flesh and blood
Donald, S. The life of stuff
Doyle, R. War
Dresser, R. Below the belt
Durang, C. Diversions
Egloff, E. The swan
Feuer, J. Eating Raoul
Firth, T. Neville's Island
Gambaro, G. Saying yes
George, M. The most massive woman wins
Gilbert, S. Suzie Goo: private secretary
Gilroy, F. D. Match point
Glowacki, J. Antigone in New York
Glowacki, J. Home section
Godber, J. Lucky sods
Gow, M. Sweet Phoebe
Guare, J. The loveliest afternoon of the year
Hibberd, J. Slam dunk
Holsclaw, D. The baddest of boys
Horovitz, I. Un drôle de mari français
Horovitz, I. One under
Horovitz, I. Rats
Hughes, D. Digging for fire
Isitt, D. Matilda liar!
Isitt, D. Nasty neighbours
Isitt, D. The woman who cooked her husband
Jones, J. M. Love trouble
Kondoleon, H. The houseguests
Kopit, A. Road to Nirvana
Learner, T. Witchplay
Lucie, D. The shallow end
MacIvor, D. House humans
MacLeod, W. The house of yes
Margulies, D. The Loman family picnic
Margulies, D. The model apartment
Martini, C. Life history of the African elephant
McNally, T. Witness
Melfi, M. Sex therapy
Nigro, D. Give us a kiss and show us your knickers
Nigro, D. Major Weir
Panych, M. The ends of the earth
Panych, M. Vigil
Pickett, J. C. Queen of Angels
Pintauro, J. Rex
Reddin, K. Brutality of fact
Ribman, R. The cannibal masque
Ridley, P. Ghost from a perfect place
Ridley, P. The pitchfork Disney
Sherman, G. Broken English
Sherman, J. M. Sons and fathers
Sherman, J. M. Women and Wallace
Silver, N. Fat men in skirts
Silver, N. The food chain
Silver, N. Pterodactyls
Silver, N. Raised in captivity
Sod, T. Satan and Simon Desoto
Starosta, S. The sausage eaters
Stickland, E. Some assembly required
Stock, J. Blue night in the heart of the West
Strelich, T. Dog logic
Stroppel, F. A good man
Tasca, J. Deus-X
Tasca, J. Extraction
Tesich, S. Arts & leisure
Tesich, S. On the open road
Walker, G. F. Escape from happiness
Walker, G. F. Rumours of our death
Ward, N. The present

Comedy—Black humor—*Continued*
Warren, D. Club Chernobyl
Wouldstra, K. Burying the dog
Wright, D. Quills

Domestic

Adam, A. A matter of diplomacy
Adam, A. A pearl of great price
Bates, H. E. The darling buds of May
Booth, J. 50 . . . and counting
Clark, R. and Bobrick, S. Norman, is that you?
Corrie, J. A bride for Heatherhill
Durang, C. Death comes to us all, Mary Agnes
Durang, C. The Vietnamization of New Jersey
Evans, D. One monkey don't stop no show
Gray, S. Close of play
Gurney, A. R. The problem
Harwood, R. A family
Hornby, I. The cat's away
Hornby, I. Situation vacant
May, B. 9th inning wedding
Molière. Amphitryon
Musset, A. de. Caprice
Pinero, A. W. The magistrate
Rowan, A. A. A stitch in time
Sewell, S. The garden of granddaughters
Sturgess, B. Marius's mule
Taylor, R. Watermelon rinds
Walker, D. The affairs of Dilys Willis

Romantic

Albert, S. J. How many to tango?
Angwin, F. Beryllium
Ayckbourn, A. Family circles
Baer, R. Mixed emotions
Baker, E. A. A dead man's apartment
Beaumarchais, P.-A. C. de. The barber of Seville
Behn, A. The lucky chance
Behn, A. The rover
Behn, A. Sir Patient Fancy
Benfield, D. Anyone for breakfast?
Berlin, E. The line that's picked up 1000 babes (and how it can work for you!)
Berlin, E. The Midnight Moonlight Wedding Chapel
Booth, J. Your place or mine?
Brochu, J. Fat chance
Büchner, G. Leonce and Lena
Carmichael, F. Coming apart
Centlivre, S. A bold stroke for a wife
Chekhov, A. The bear
Clark, S. Moo
Coyne, J. Exploding love
Dietz, S. Private eyes
Durang, C. Canker sores and other distractions
Elwell, J. S. The art of dating
Field, B. Boundary Waters
Foster, N. The affections of May
Foster, N. Wrong for each other
y Frankel, R. The Decade Club
Godber, J. Passion killers
Goldsmith, O. She stoops to conquer
Grae, D. Moose mating
Gross, T. D. Them . . . within us
Guare, J. A day for surprises
Gurney, A. R. Later life
Gurney, A. R. The Middle Ages
y Hamlett, C. Once upon a taxi
Hampton, C. Treats
Harvey, J. Rupert Street Lonely Hearts Club
Haywood, C. Table for one?
Hughes, L. Simply heavenly
Ives, D. Ancient history
Ives, D. English made simple
Ives, D. Foreplay
Jannuzzi, L. With or without you
Joselovitz, E. and Bagdasian, H. M. Love by the numbers
Kanin, F. Goodbye, my fancy
Klavan, L. Freud's house
Kluger, G. M. Till death, or whatever, do us part
Lennon, G. Dates and nuts
Lucas, C. Prelude to a kiss
Lyly, J. Gallathea
Marivaux. La dispute
Marivaux. The triumph of love
Mason, T. Sorry
Mastrosimone, W. Shivaree
Mayer, J. A love affair
McNally, T. Frankie and Johnny in the Clair de Lune
Moore, E. The foundling
Moreto, A. Spite for spite
Musset, A. de. You can't think of everything
y Nolan, P. T. The school for wives
Norman, M. Loving Daniel Boone
O'Malley, M. Diverting devotion
Omata, G. H. S.A.M. I am
Paterson, D. L. Finger painting in a Murphy bed
Pix, M. The Spanish wives
Rebeck, T. Spike heels
Rector, M. H. The lady and the mortician
Robson, J. Falling short
Rosenthal, A. Lifelines

Comedy—Romantic—*Continued*
Rubio, J. L. In August we play the Pyrenees
Ruzzante. L'Anconitana: the woman from Ancona
Sade, Marquis de. The twins
y Sarkies, D. Lovepuke
Schave, E. A Texas romance
Shaw, B. Arms and the man
Shaw, B. Man and superman
Sheridan, R. B. The rivals
Siefert, L. Little Egypt
Slade, B. I remember you
Soland, L. The name game
Steele, R. The conscious lovers
Stone, T. One question
Stroppel, F. Fortune's fool
Synge, J. M. The playboy of the Western World
Taylor, R. and Bologna, J. Acts of love and other comedies
Taylor, R. and Bologna, J. Manhattan love songs—Bronx cheers
Taylor, R. and Bologna, J. Paradise follies
Van Zandt, B. and Milmore, J. Infidelities
Vickery, F. Green favours
Weller, M. Abroad (Split, Part 2)
Weller, M. At home (Split, Part 1)
Wilson, L. Burn this

Social

Aristophanes. Acharnians
Aristophanes. Birds
Beaumarchais, P.-A. C. de. The marriage of Figaro
Boothe, C. The women
Bower, M. A fitting finish
Childress, A. Wine in the wilderness
Crimp, M. The misanthrope
Dunsay, E. J. M. D. P. The lost silk hat
Etherege, G. The man of mode
Farquhar, G. The beaux' stratagem
Farquhar, G. The constant couple
Farquhar, G. The recruiting officer
Farquhar, G. The twin rivals
Guare, J. Rich and famous
Gurney, A. R. Public affairs: Pt2 The opening meeting
Harris, A. The importance of being Earnest
Hauptmann, G. The beaver coat
Horovitz, I. The 75th
Kemp, R. Dalwhinnie
Lee, N. The Princess of Cleves
Middleton, T. A mad world, my masters
Middleton, T. No wit, no help like a woman's
Middleton, T. A trick to catch the old one
Molière. The hypochondriac
Molière. The imaginary cuckold
Molière. The imaginary invalid
Molière. The misanthrope
Molière. The miser
Rattigan, T. Harlequinade
Roland, B. Feet of clay
Shaw, B. Getting married
Shaw, B. Major Barbara
Shaw, B. Mrs. Warren's profession
Shaw, B. Pygmalion
Sheridan, R. B. The school for scandal
Strindberg, A. The stronger
Thomas, F. Tartuffe: born again
Tyler, R. The contrast
Weller, M. Moonchildren
White, P. A cheery soul
Wilde, O. An ideal husband
Wilde, O. The importance of being Earnest
Wilde, O. Lady Windermere's fan
Wilde, O. A woman of no importance
Wilson, L. Thymus vulgaris
Wilson, L. Victory on Mrs. Dandywine's island
Wycherley, W. The plain dealer

The **comedy** of asses. See Plautus, T. M. Asses galore

The **comedy** of Oedipus: you're the one who killed the beast. Salim, ʿAli

The **comet** of St. Loomis. Simpson, E.

The **comic** illusion. Corneille, P. (adaptation) See Kushner, T. The illusion

Coming apart. Carmichael, F.

Coming home. Lee, J. A.

Coming of the Hurricane. Glover, K.

Commander Carrigan. Szyszkowitz, G.

Commedia dell'arte
c Griffiths, D. Flavio's disgrace
c Simons, J. Pinocchio commedia

The **commissioner.** See Courteline, G. The police chief's an easygoing guy

The **commissioner** has a big heart. See Courteline, G. The police chief's an easygoing guy

Commodus
Harrison, T. The Kaisers of Carnuntum

The **common** pursuit. Gray, S.

Communicating doors. Ayckbourn, A.

Communication
Shepard, S. Cowboys #2

Communism
Mercer, D. The cellar and the almond tree

China

Hare, D. Fanshen
Yamauchi, W. The chairman's wife

Czechoslovak Republic

Havel, V. Audience

Italy

Griffiths, T. Occupations

Russia

Bulgakov, M. Zoyka's apartment
Kingsley, S. Darkness at noon
Van Itallie, J.-C. Master & Margarita

United States

Flanagan, H. and Clifford, M. E. Can you hear their voices?

Compãneras. Bolt, C.

Company. Sondheim, S.

The **company** of heaven. Glore, J.

Compensation. Kurginian, S.

Competition piece. Wells, J. S.

Competitive tenderness. Rayson, H.

Composers
Martin, J. Pomp and circumstance

Composing Venus. Acworth, E.

Compton, Jennifer
Barefoot

Farce. Widow and two daughters exhibit a passion for passion. 2 scenes 1m 3w 1 interior

In Passion: six new short plays by Australian women; ed. by R. Horin

The **computer.** Jones, T.

Computers
Ayckbourn, A. Henceforward ...
c Jones, T. The computer
Shepard, S. Operation sidewinder

Comrade Brennan. Finnegan, S.

Comrade Briggemann. Szyszkowitz, G.

Conboy, Roy
c Song of the oak—El canto del roble

Fable. Boy learns what goes into making of oak leaves. Dialogue in English and Spanish. Singing, dancing. 6 scenes Unidentified cast 4 characters

In ¡Aplauso! Hispanic children's theater; ed. by J. Rosenberg

Concentration camps
Szumigalski, A. Z: a meditation on oppression, desire and freedom

A **conception** of love. Warner, F.

Conde, Maryse
The Tropical Breeze Hotel

Comedy. Aging black actress romanticizes her past. 5 tableau 8 scenes 1m 1w 1 setting

In Plays by women: an international anthology bk2; ed. by N. Shange

Conditional surrender. Buchan, A.

Condon, Richard
The Manchurian candidate (dramatization) See Lahr, J. The Manchurian candidate

The **conduct** of life. Fornes, M. I.

Conductors (Music)
McNally, T. Prelude & Liebestod
See also names of conductors, e.g. Furtwängler, Wilhelm

Conestoga stories. Cole, J. D.

Coney Island of Dr. Moreau. Francoeur, B.

Confederation and Riel. See Hollingsworth, M. The history of the village of the small huts

Confession (Catholic Church)
Solórzano, C. Mea culpa

Confessions of a primary terrestrial mental receiver and communicator: Num III Mark I. Barnes, P.

The **confirmation.** Peters, K.

Conflict of generations
y Aston, M. Fossils!
Barnes, D. Little drops of rain
Bennett, A. Forty years on
Edmonds, S. R. Old man Pete
Foote, H. The widow Claire
French, D. Leaving home
Fugard, A. Valley song
Gomez, T. Inter-tribal
Gurney, A. R. Children
Harwood, R. A family
Hasenclever, W. The son
Kovacevic, D. A roaring tragedy
c Lee, C. K. Journey to the West
Mercer, D. Where the difference begins
Miller, E. Up rose a burning man
Quayle, T. Bein Lochaber
Richards, G. Dividends
Sessions, G. The return of spring
West, C. L. Jar the floor
Wilson, L. Brontosaurus
Wilson, L. Lemon sky
Wilson, L. Talley & Son

Congdon, Constance
Boarders
Explores lives of landlady and three tenants in apartment house in once-nice neighborhood of mid-size Northeastern city. 3 scenes epilogue 3m 6w 4 interiors
In Facing forward; ed. by L. D. Frank
Casanova
Feminist drama about sexuality and gender based on life of famous lover. 2 acts Large mixed cast 1 setting
In Congdon, C. Tales of the lost Formicans and other plays
Dog opera
Comedy. Intimate friendship between gay man and straight woman. 2 acts 5m 4w extras
In The Actor's book of gay and lesbian plays; ed. by E. Lane and N. Shengold
Losing father's body
Black comedy chronicles reactions of dysfunctional family when father's corpse is stolen. 2 acts 13 scenes 6m 7w 1 setting
In Congdon, C. Tales of the lost Formicans and other plays
No mercy
Drama about first atomic bomb and its after-effects set in 1945 and 1985 simultaneously. J. Robert Oppenheimer, lost in time, represents mankind's loss of faith in science and religion. 5m 3w 1b 1 setting
In Congdon, C. Tales of the lost Formicans and other plays
Tales of the lost Formicans
Satire. Aliens observe foibles of human behavior. Singing. 2 acts 4m 3w 2 settings
In Congdon, C. Tales of the lost Formicans and other plays

Congo (Democratic Republic)
Gray, S. The rear column
Greenland, S. Jungle rot

Congo, Belgian. See Congo (Democratic Republic)

Connie & Sabrina in waiting. Vago, S. M.

Connolly, H.
Daddy's gone a-hunting. French (London) 1994 41p
Thriller about secrets, jealousy, and attempted murder. Sister's new boyfriend turns out to be important figure from young mother's past. 2m 2w extra 1 interior
One careful owner. French (London) 1997 35p
When wealthy man visits couple's working-class home, ostensibly to look at car husband is selling, skeletons start tumbling from everyone's closets. 3m 1w 1 interior
Overtime. French (London) 1994 34p
Raucous retirement party ends in horror when guest of honor hangs himself. 3m 2w 1 interior
Snakes and ladders. New Playwrights Network 1995 71p
Old man who sold his soul to the Devil redeems himself by saving friend. 2 acts 5m 4w 1 interior

Connor, Tony
A couple with a cat
Working-class man feels alienated from wife and college student son. 2m 1w 1 interior
In The Best American short plays, 1992-1993

The **conscious** lovers. Steele, R.

Conscription. See Military service, Compulsory

Consequences. Miller, J. and Miller, S.

Conservationists
Johnson, T. Cries from the mammal house

Conspiracies
Gray, S. Stage struck

The **constant** couple. Farquhar, G.

The **Constitution** is born. Brown, C. J.

The **construction** of Boston. Koch, K.

Construction workers
Kroetz, F. X. Through the leaves

Contract with Jackie. Breslin, J.

The **contractor.** Storey, D.

The **contrast.** Tyler, R.

Contribution. Shine, T.

Convents
Brogan, P. B. Eclipsed

Conversations on a homecoming. Murphy, T.

Conversations with my father. Gardner, H.

The **conversion** of Ka'ahumanu. Kneubuhl, V. N.

Conville, David, and Gooderson, David
c The curse of the Egyptian mummy. French (London) 1993 58p
Dramatization of Pat Hutchin's novel. Hampstead Cub Scouts become embroiled in mystery while on weekend campout. 2 acts 12 scenes Variable cast 20 characters 3 interiors 3 exteriors

Coo, Coarence
y Removing the glove. Bakers Plays 1994 27p
Satire. Teenager faces prejudice when he reveals he is left-handed. 3m 3w extras 1 interior

Cook, Michael
The head, guts and sound bone dance
Wrapped in dreams of fishing and seeking to retain control of family, aging Newfoundland fisherman ignores pleas of boy to save child from drowning. 2 acts 5m 1w 3b 1 interior
In The *CTR* anthology; ed. by A. Filewod

Jacob's wake
Trapped in the house by a winter storm, members of a Newfoundland family express their feelings of love and hatred for each other. The patriarch of the family, an old sailor, dies in the middle of the storm. 2 acts 4 scenes 5m 2w 1 setting
In Modern Canadian plays v1; ed. by J. Wasserman

Cook, Pat
y The whole shebang. Bakers Plays 1995 30p
Comedy. High school drama teacher mounts one-act drama contest. 4m 4w extras 1 interior

Cooke, Christine
Threat. New Playwrights Network 1995 22p
Husband fears wife's divorced friend is threat to his shaky marriage. 1 act 2m 2w 1 interior

The **cool** of the day. Berry, W.

Cooney, Michael
Cash on delivery! French 1997 143p
Farce. Mayhem ensues when man, having defrauded welfare system for years, is visited by investigators. 2 acts 6m 4w 1 interior
—Same. French (London) 1997 99p

Cooney, Ray
Funny money. French 1995 151p
Farce. Chaos ensues when mild-mannered C.P.A. accidentally picks up briefcase filled with money. 2 acts 6m 2w 1 interior
—Same. French (London) 1996 107p

Cooper, Beverley
Nellie Bly: ten days in a madhouse
Radio play. Journalist Nellie Bly exposes conditions in insane asylum. Background music. 20 scenes 4m 9w
In Adventures for (big) girls; ed. by A. Jansen
See also Rubess, B. jt. auth.

Cooper, J. B.
Picnic time. New Playwrights Network 1994 56p
Woman's matchmaking attempts on behalf of divorcing friend go awry. 3 acts 4 scenes 5m 3w 1 interior

Cooper, Rose Marie
c How things happen in three! Words and lyrics by Tom Behm; music by Rose Marie Cooper. Anchorage Press 1992 33p
Musical based on fairy tales and nursery rhymes that incorporate the number three. 3m 3w

Cooperman, David
Miss Temptation. Dramatic 1993 25p
Dramatization of short story by Kurt Vonnegut. Encounter between beautiful young actress and insecure returning soldier in small town Vermont general store. 2 scenes 6m 3w 1 interior

Cop-out. Guare, J.

Cope, Eddie. See Cearley, B. Welcome to Nashville

Copperfaced Jack. O'Donovan, J.

Coq au vin. Baitz, J. R.

Corbitt, Wayne
Crying holy
African American gay poet with AIDS returns home for Labor Day weekend. 2 acts 6 scenes 4w 1m
In Colored contradictions: an anthology of contemporary African-American plays

The **cord** and the track. Duberstein, H.

Cork (Ireland)
Moxley, G. Danti-Dan

Corneille, Pierre
The comic illusion (adaptation) See Kushner, T. The illusion

Corner boys. Coyle, K.

Cornerstone of civil rights. Miranda, J. E.

Cornthwaite, Robert
y Carlo Goldoni's Villeggiatura. Smith & Kraus 1994 102p (Young actors series)
Three act version for young people of Goldoni's trilogy. 3 acts 16 scenes 12m 6w 5 interiors 2 exterior

Cornwallis, Charles Cornwallis
Koch, K. George Washington crossing the Delaware

Correct address. Silverman, J. L.

El **Corrido** de Gregorio Cortez. McCullough, L. E.

Corrie, Joe
Billy Shaw. Players Press 1996 28p
Comedy in Scottish dialect. Old farmworker's unexpected good fortune puzzles son and daughter-in-law. 1 act 2m 4w 1 interior

A bride for Heatherhill. Players Press 1996 27p
Comedy in Scottish dialect. Son resists father's attempts to marry him off. 1 act 2m 2w 1 interior

Corruption (in politics)
Graham, B. Belmont Avenue Social Club
Guare, J. Moon under Miami
Horovitz, I. Henry Lumper

Corruption (in politics)—*Continued*
y Kottke, T. G. Deputy Toby
Lawrence, J. and Lee, R. E. The gang's all here
Nowra, L. The incorruptible
Solórzano, C. And death brought forth the light
Wellman, M. The self-begotten

Cortez, Gregorio
McCullough, L. E. El Corrido de Gregorio Cortez

Corthron, Kia
Cage rhythm
Portrays African American women serving life sentences in prison. 2 scenes 8w extras 1 setting
In Moon marked and touched by sun; ed. by S. Mahone
Come down burning. Dramatists 1995 32p
Drama portraying how prejudice and poverty affect lives of three African-American women and their children. 7 scenes 3w 1b 1g 1 interior
—Same
In The Best American short plays, 1993-1994
In Colored contradictions: an anthology of contemporary African-American plays
In Contemporary plays by women of color; ed. by K. A. Perkins and R. Uno

Cosa Nostra. See Mafia

Così. Nowra, L.

Cosmetic surgery. See Surgery, Plastic

Cost of living. Panych, M.

Costa Rica
Milner, A. Zero hour

Cotter, Joseph Seamon
On the fields of France
Short scene. Two American officers, one white one black, lie mortally wounded on battlefield in Northern France during World War I. 2m
In Lost plays of the Harlem Renaissance; ed. by J. V. Hatch and L. Hamalian

Cotton girls. Tobin, S.

Counsellor-at-law. Rice, E.

The **Count** of Monte Cristo. Eleder, M. V.

Count Oxtiern. Sade, Marquis de

The **Countess** Cathleen. Yeats, W. B.

Countess de Kitchen. Sloate, D.

Countess in Courtland. Sloate, D.

Countess in Thistleland. Sloate, D.

Country life
Martin, J. Travelin' show
Robinson, R. T. The cover of life
Roose-Evans, J. Cider with Rosie
Schnupp, A. The Harper chronicles
Sherman, J. M. Jesus on the oil tank
Smith, M. L. An evening of culture: Faith County II, the saga continues
Williams, J.; Sears, J. and Howard, E. A Tuna Christmas

Country music
Ledoux, P. and Smyth, D. Cheatin' hearts

A **country** wedding. Bonal, D.

The **country** wife. Wycherley, W. (adaptation) See The Heather Brothers. Lust

A **couple** with a cat. Connor, T.

The **courageous** princess. Witkiewicz, S. I.

Courteline, Georges
Boubouroche; tr. by Albert Bermel
Comedy of man with double-dealing mistress. 2 acts 8m 1w 2 interiors
In A Dozen French farces; ed. by A. Bermel
—Same; tr. by Norman R. Shapiro
In A Flea in her rear, and other vintage French farces
The police chief's an easygoing guy (Le commissaire est bon enfant); tr. by Albert Bermel
Variant titles: The commissioner; The commissioner has a big heart. Farce. Police commissioner in Paris, after showing his insensitivity to those seeking his aid and making petty display of authority, is humiliated by madman. 1 act 6m 1w extras 1 interior
In A Dozen French farces; ed. by A. Bermel

Courtesans
Lang, W. Lady of the camellias
Lillo, G. The London merchant
Middleton, T. A mad world, my masters

Courts, Randy
Jack's holiday; a musical; book by Mark St. Germain; music by Randy Courts; lyrics by Mart St. Germain & Randy Courts. French 1997 127p (French's musical library)
Musical set in 1891. Jack the Ripper menaces New York City. 2 acts Prologue 21 scenes Variable cast 27 characters settings

Courts, Randy—*Continued*
Johnny Pye; a musical based on the short story, "Johnny Pye and the Foolkiller" [by] Stephen Vincent Benet; book and lyrics by Mart St. Germain; music and lyrics by Randy Courts. Dramatists 1994 73p
Musical based on Benet's allegorical tale of man's attempts to outrun death. 2 acts 7m 3w 1 setting

Courts. See Justice, Administration of

Courts-martial and courts of inquiry
Fuller, C. A soldier's play
Linney, R. The love suicide at Schofield Barracks

Courtship
Buchan, A. Conditional surrender
Chekhov, A. The bear
Chekhov, A. The proposal
Farquhar, G. The beaux' stratagem
Foote, H. The widow Claire
Granville-Barker, H. The marrying of Ann-Leete
Linney, R. Sand Mountain
Musset, A. de. The moods of Marianne
Musset, A. de. You can't think of everything
y Nolan, P. T. The school for wives
Séjour, V. The brown overcoat

The **courtship** of Morning Star. Schenkkan, R.

Cousins
Schnitzler, A. The gallant Cassian
St. John, B. Rubies: Heirlooms
St. John, B. Rubies: Little gems

The **cover** of life. Robinson, R. T.

Cover your eyes and run! Nordlicht, L.

Cowan, Cindy
A woman from the sea
Symbolic feminist drama about destruction, birth, and power of women's love. Prologue 2 acts 11 scenes 1m 2w 1 setting
In The *CTR* anthology; ed. by A. Filewod

Coward, Noel
Morley, S. Noel and Gertie

The **cowboy,** the Indian and the fervent feminist. Schisgal, M.

Cowboys
y Hurst, Z. B. and Hurst, J. R. The cowhand's Christmas Carol
Lebow, B. Little Joe Monaghan
c McCullough, L. E. "Git along, little dogies!"
c McCullough, L. E. El paseo del vaquero (the ride of the vaquero)
c McCullough, L. E. Vinegar Pete's calico whisker pie
c McCullough, L. E. Zebra dun
c Miller, H. L. Bandit Ben rides again
Shepard, S. Cowboys #2

Cowboys #2. Shepard, S.

Cowboys, Indians and waitresses. Shurtz, R. K.

Cowell, Michael
y Song for the navigator. Dramatic 1993 57p
Teenage boy spends summer with grandfather on small Pacific island of Satawal. 20 scenes 5m 2w

The **cowhand's** Christmas Carol. Hurst, Z. B. and Hurst, J. R.

Cowley, Hannah Parkhouse
The belle's stratagem
Farce set in 18th century London. Clever young woman sets out to win man's heart. 5 acts 12 scenes epilogue 15m 6w extras 8 interiors 1 exterior
In The Meridian anthology of Restoration and eighteenth-century plays by women; ed. by K. M. Rogers

Coxon, Lucinda
Wishbones. Methuen Drama 1997 91p (Methuen modern plays)
Drama set in Derbyshire village. Two friends struggle with legacy of their shared childhood, their current relationships and fate of tragically mismatched neighbors. 2 acts 22 scenes 2m 3w 1 setting

Coyle, Kevin
Corner boys
Street culture and first love of young British males. 3 acts 10 scenes 3m 3w 1 interior 1 exterior
In Coming on strong: new writing from the Royal Court Theatre

Coyne, Joseph
Exploding love. French 1997 64p
Romantic comedy. Husband disrupts ex-wife's marriage ceremony. 5m 3w 1 interior

Coyne, Joseph Stirling
Did you ever send your wife to Camberwell?
Nineteenth-century farce revolving around lowly attorney's mishaps. 1 act 2m 3w 1 interior
In The Lights o' London and other Victorian plays; ed. by M. R. Booth

Crabtree, Howard
Howard Crabtree's Whoop-dee-doo! a musical extravaganza; conceived, created and developed by Howard Crabtree [et al.]; songs & sketches by Dick Gallagher [et al.]; additional material by Jack Feldman, Bruce Sussman [and] David Rambo. French 1995 84p (French's musical library)
Madcap review about mounting of musical. Presents gay slant on life, politics and fashion. 2 acts 20 scenes 9m

Crack (Drug)
Cleage, P. Chain

The **cracked** pot. Morrison, B.

Crackpot. Wyatt, R.

Cracks. Sherman, M.

Craig, Edward Gordon
Vingoe, M. and Kudelka, J. Hooligans

Crane, Richard
Under the stars. French (London) 1994 66p
Comedy about two female understudies in West End production of classical tragedy. 2 acts 12 scenes 2m 3w extras 1 interior

Crane, Stephen
The red badge of courage (dramatization) See Miller, K. S. Red badge of courage

The **crane** wife. Carlisle, B.

Craver, Mike, and Hardwick, Mark
Radio gals; book, music and lyrics by Mike Craver and Mark Hardwick. French 1997 75p (French's musical library)
Musical comedy set in 1920s Arkansas. Government inspector tries to stop piratical radio station broadcasting music and conversation from retired music teacher's parlor. Music, singing. 2 acts 3m 4w 1 interior

Crawford, David Wright
Borrowed plumage. Players Press 1993 22p
Young woman falsely accuses father of sexual abuse. 3m 3w 1 exterior

Tangled garden. Players Press 1994 56p
Set in 1912 Galveston Texas. Alcoholic son of aging Civil War veteran faces up to family responsibilities and reconciles with father. 2 acts 4 scenes 4m 3w 1 exterior

Crawford, Jerry L.
Facelifting at St. Viators
Family drama set in Nevada. Young boy, in attempt to earn father's love, desecrates Catholic sanctuary. 2m 1w 1b 1 interior
In Lucky 13; ed. by R. Shuttleworth

Crazy for the country. See Goldoni, C. Villeggiatura: Crazy for the country

Crazyface. Barker, C.

Cream, Thomas Neill
Fennario, D. Doctor Thomas Neill Cream: mystery at McGill

Cream in my coffee. Potter, D.

Credo. Lucas, C.

Creeps. Freeman, D.

The **creepy** creeps of Pilgrim Road. Reiser, D.

Cregan, David
c Aladdin. French (London) 1993 89p
Pantomime version of Arabian nights tale about Aladdin and magic lamp. Music, singing. 2 acts 22 scenes 7m 6w extras various settings

Creighton, Anthony. See Osborne, J. jt. auth.

Crews, Harry
Blood issue
Novelist son returns to Georgia for reunion, uncovers family secrets. 2 acts 4 scenes 5m 3w 1 interior 1 exterior
In By Southern playwrights; ed. by M. B. Dixon and M. Volansky

Cries from the mammal house. Johnson, T.

Crime and criminals
Bullins, E. Goin' a Buffalo
Clemens, B. Inside job
Edwards, G. The offering
Elder, L. Ceremonies in dark old men
Fishburne, L. Riff raff
Foote, H. The chase
Foster, A. Chemical reactions
Glover, K. Dancing on moonlight
Golden, E. Great expectations
Gray, S. Wise child
Kingsley, S. Dead end
Kingsley, S. Detective story
Kranes, D. Cantrell
Linney, R. True crimes
Martin, J. Criminal hearts
McKelvey, P. House of secrets
McPherson, C. The good thief
McPherson, C. This lime tree bower
Millan, J. and Brooker, B. Serpent kills
Overmyer, E. Dark rapture
Penhall, J. Pale horse
Rabe, D. Those the river keeps
Richards, G. The root
Strindberg, A. Pariah
Valle-Inclán, R. del. Sacrilege
Vassallo, P. The spelling bee
Watkins, M. Chicago
Wilson, L. Eukiah
See also Arson; Assassination; Fugitives from justice; Imposters and imposture;

Crime and criminals—*Continued*
Juvenile delinquency; Kidnapping; Murder; Prisoners; Prostitution; Thieves

Crime and punishment. Zoshchenko, M.

Crime at the tennis club. Maraini, D.

Criminal hearts. Martin, J.

Criminals in love. Walker, G. F.

Crimp, Martin
The misanthrope. Faber & Faber 1996 103p (Young Vic)
Adaptation of Molière's comedy of manners set in contemporary London. Playwright abhors hypocrisy and social pretentions of chattering classes. 5 acts 5m 3w extras 1 interior

The treatment. Hern Bks. in association with Royal Court Theatre 1993 96p
Black comedy set in Manhattan. Woman on run from brutal husband exploited by two sleazy film producers. 4 acts 15 scenes 5m 3w extras 1 setting

Crippen, Hawley Harvey
Churchill, C. Lives of the great poisoners
Dallman, J. The inside story of Dr. Crippen

The **cripple** of Inishmaan. McDonagh, M.

Cripples. See Physically handicapped

Crises intervention telephone service. See Hotlines (Telephone counseling)

A **critical** edition of the medieval play Mankind. Mankind

A **critical** edition of Thomas Middleton's The witch. Middleton, T.

Critics
See also Music critics

Crito. Emery, S. W.

Cross, J. C.
Julia of Louvain; or, Monkish cruelty
Gothic pantomime. Woman entombed beneath convent when she rejects advances of villainous aristocrat. Variable cast settings
In Seven Gothic dramas, 1789-1825

Cross, Janet
The prophet's cloak. Moorley's 1994 20p
Biblical drama. Elijah encounters poor widow, King Ahab, Queen Jezebel, and his successor Elisha. 6 scenes 8m 2w extras

Cross-dressing in the Depression. Wilson, E. C.

Crossroads. Solórzano, C.

Crow. Nowra, L.

Crow & Weasel. Leonard, J.

Crowbar. Wellman, M.

The **crowded** house. Jacob, E.

Crowley, Mart
The boys in the band
Eruption of personal frictions among a group of homosexuals giving a birthday party for one of their number. 2 acts 9m 1 interior
In Crowley, M. 3 plays

A breeze from the gulf
Tragedy revolving around weak asthmatic son's attempts to cope with father's drinking and mother's drug addiction. 2 acts 15 scenes 2m 1w 1 setting
In Crowley, M. 3 plays

For reasons that remain unclear
American screenwriter on all-expenses-paid trip to Rome encounters priest who sexually abused him at the age of nine. 1 act 3m 1 interior
In Crowley, M. 3 plays

The **crucible.** Miller, A.

The **crucified.** Solórzano, C.

The **crucifixion.** See Solórzano, C. The crucified

'Cruiter. Matheus, J. F.

Crump, Rita
The strange illness. Players Press 1995 19p
Commedia dell'arte set in 1543 Venice. In order to be cured of bizarre illness old man must allow his young fiancée to marry man she truly loves. Prologue 4m 2w extras 1 exterior

Crutcher, Julie, and McBride, Vaughn
Diggin in: the farm crisis in Kentucky
Farmers from different regions of Kentucky express opinions on problems of farming in the state. 9m 5w
In By Southern playwrights; ed. by M. B. Dixon and M. Volansky

Cruz, Migdalia
The have-little
Drama of poor adolescent Puerto Rican girl and her family in the South Bronx. 17 scenes 1m 3w 1 setting
In Contemporary plays by women of color; ed. by K. A. Perkins and R. Uno

Telling tales
Series of monologues about Hispanic life. Variable cast
In Telling tales: new one-act plays; ed. by E. Lane
See also Blecher, H. jt. auth.

Cry wolf. Law, M.

Crying holy. Corbitt, W.

Crying out loud. Mead, K.

The **cryptogram.** Mamet, D.

The **crystal.** Bush, M.

Cuba
Machado, E. In the eye of the hurricane

¡**Cuba** si! McNally, T.

Cuchulain (Legendary character)
Yeats, W. B. On Baile's strand

Cul de sac. Martin, J.

La **culebra.** "The snake." Gerke, P.

Cullen, Andrew
Pig's ear. Warner Chappell Plays 1994 138p

Drama exploring effects of political and cultural changes on English family during the Thatcher years. 4 acts 5m 5w 4 interiors

Self catering. Warner Chappell Plays 1993 90p

Black comedy featuring Henry Fonda, Bette Davis, Meryl Streep, Clint Eastwood, and Marilyn Monroe. 12 scenes 2m 3w

Cullen, Mike
The cut

Look at post-strike Scottish coal industry awash in bitterness and cynicism. 2 acts 9 scenes 4m extras 1 setting

In Made in Scotland; ed. by I. Brown and M. Fisher

Cults
Barry, S. Prayers of Sherkin

Culture conflict
Bell, H. Fortune
Broinowski, A. The gap
y Dietz, S. The rememberer
Houston, V. H. Kokoro (true heart)
Khan-Din, A. East is east
Linney, R. El hermano
López, E. I. Spanish eyes
Lyssiotis, T. The Forty Lounge Cafe
Manet, E. Lady Strass
Micone, M. Beyond the ruins
Minghella, A. Made in Bangkok
Roberts, D. Breaking glass
Robinson, M. Collateral damage
Sebbar, L. My mother's eyes
Soyinka, W. Death and the King's Horseman
Al-Surayyiʿ, ʿAbd al-ʿAziz. The bird has flown
Verdecchia, G. Fronteras Americanas (American borders)

Cummings, Benard
Your obituary is a dance

African American man dying of AIDS returns to small East Texas town. 1m 1w 1 setting

In Actors Theatre of Louisville. Ten-minute plays: v3
In Humana Festival '95

Cunningham, Laura
Beautiful bodies

Black comedy. Lower Manhattan baby shower runs amok. 2 acts 6w 1 interior

In Plays for actresses; ed. by E. Lane and N. Shengold

Curculio. See Plautus, T. M. The weevil

The **cure.** Hardstack, M.

Curl up and dye. Pam-Grant, S.

Curran, Colleen
Senetta Boynton visits the Orient

Woman author, addressing church audience about her world travels, has surprise for congregation. Background music. 1m 2w 1 interior

In Escape acts; ed. by C. Curran

Curran, Keith
The stand-in

Comic look at homophobia in Hollywood. 2 acts 7m 3w 2 settings

In The Actor's book of gay and lesbian plays; ed. by E. Lane and N. Shengold

Curran, KT
y The First Time Club. Clark, I.E. 1993 25p

Friendship among four teenage girls tested when one contracts AIDS virus. 12 scenes 4w 1 setting

Currie, Sheldon
The Glace Bay Miners' Museum (dramatization) See Lill, W. The Glace Bay Miners' Museum

The **curse** of the Egyptian mummy. Conville, D. and Gooderson, D.

Curtain call. Greth, R.

Curtains. Bill, S.

Custody of children
Lyssa, A. Pinball

The **cut.** Cullen, M.

The **cycle** of spring. Tagore, R.

The **cyclops.** Euripides

Cyrano de Bergerac, Savanien
Rostand, E. Cyrano de Bergerac

Czechoslovakia
Havel, V. Audience
Havel, V. Tomorrow!

Czechoslovakia—*Continued*
Havel, V. Unveiling
Stoppard, T. Professional foul

Czechs

Canada

Body, P. Odd fish

D

D. Boone. See Norman, M. Loving Daniel Boone

D-Day. Hall, P.

Da-hoos-whee'-whee: The seal-hunting brothers. Gerke, P.

Daddy's gone a-hunting. Connolly, H.

The **dadshuttle.** Donaghy, T.

D'Aguiar, Fred
A Jamaican airman foresees his death
Drama about Jamaican men in Royal Air Force during World War II. 2 acts 26 scenes 5m 2w extras
In Black plays: three; ed. by Y. Brewster

Dahl, Roald
The Giraffe and the Pelly and me (dramatization) See Ireland, V. Roald Dahl's The Giraffe and the Pelly and me
The witches (dramatization) See Wood, D. The witches

Dahling you were marvellous. Berkoff, S.

Dahmer, Jeffrey
Abdoh, R. The law of remains

Dali, Salvador
Johnson, T. Hysteria

Dallman, Jean
The inside story of Dr. Crippen. New Playwrights Network 1996 74p
Surrealist psychological drama about English physician and murderer Hawley Harvey Crippen. 2 acts 5 scenes 3m 3w extras 3 interiors 2 exteriors

Dalwhinnie. Kemp, R.

Daly, Timothy
Kafka dances. Currency Press 1994 78p
Dramatic portrayal of Kafka's romance with Felice Bauer and the impact of Yiddish theater on his imagination. 2 acts 18 scenes 2m 3w 1 setting

Damashek, Barbara. See Newman, M. jt. auth.

Damsel of the desert. Carmichael, F.

The **dance** of death. Strindberg, A.

Dance of the Eland. Hall, F. B.

Dance of the wandering souls. Huynh, Quang Nhuong

Dance piece. Goldenthal, J.

Dance Saturday night. Newsom, J. D.

Dance with me. Reynolds, J.

Dancers
Fyffe, L. The sand
Németh, Á. Müller's dancers
O'Neill, E. Thirst
Reingold, J. Girl gone
Taylor, A. and Devenish, L. Disturbing the dust
Wilson, L. Burn this

The **dancers.** Foote, H.

Dancers. McConnell, J.

Dancing on Checkers' grave. Lane, E.

Dancing on moonlight. Glover, K.

Dancock's dance. Vanderhaeghe, G.

The **dangers** of tobacco. Chekhov, A.

Daniel (Biblical figure)
Auden, W. H. The play of Daniel
c Haylock, D. How to be an alien

Daniel Hale Williams, pioneer surgeon. Satchell, M.

Daniels, Sarah
Beside herself
Drama about lasting psychological scars of sexual abuse of young girls by their fathers or other adult male relatives. Prelude 12 scenes 4m 5w
In Daniels, S. Plays: two

The gut girls. French 1993 115p
Drama set in gutting sheds of late Victorian slaughterhouse. Shows how lives of women employees changed when their jobs were made illegal. 2 acts 23 scenes 2m 6w 1 setting
—Same
In Daniels, S. Plays: two

Head-rot holiday
Examines treatment women receive in psychiatric facilities. 2 acts 24 scenes Variable cast 9 characters 1 setting
In Daniels, S. Plays: two

The madness of Esme and Shaz
Romantic comedy featuring gun-toting woman and her foul-mouthed niece. 2 acts 16 scenes 8w 1 setting
In Daniels, S. Plays: two

Danowski, Christopher
Family values
Estranged relatives yearn for days of nuclear families. 3m 2w 1 exterior
In Lucky 13; ed. by R. Shuttleworth

Dante Alighieri
Heise, K. and Heise, D. Clarence Darrow in hell
Parodies, imitations, etc.
Berc, S. A girl's guide to the Divine Comedy: a trilogy

Danti-Dan. Moxley, G.

Danton, Georges Jacques
Büchner, G. Danton's death
Griffiths, T. Hope in the year two
Griffiths, T. Who shall be happy... ?

Danton's death. Büchner, G.

The **Danube.** Fornes, M. I.

D'Arblay, Frances Burney. See Burney, Fanny

D'Arcy, Alice
c Cinderella
Based on Charles Perrault's fairy tale. 3 scenes 1m 4w extras 2 interiors
In Thirty plays from favorite stories; ed. by S. E. Kamerman

Daring, darling Dolly. McCaslin, N.

The **dark** castle. Netzel, S.

Dark cowgirls and prairie queens. Parris-Bailey, L.

Dark rapture. Overmyer, E.

Dark rituals. Bennett, T.

The **dark** tower. MacNeice, L.

The **dark** valley. Auden, W. H.

Darker brother. Seiler, C.

The **darker** face of the earth. Dove, R.

Darkness. Balalin Company of Jerusalem

Darkness at noon. Kingsley, S.

The **darling** buds of May. Bates, H. E.

Darling Clementine: a tail of old San Francisco. McCullough, L. E.

Darrow, Clarence
Heise, K. and Heise, D. Clarence Darrow in hell

Dashow, Ken
He ain't heavy
Two men at odds at brother's funeral. 3m 1 interior
In Dashow, K. Da-show must go on
Joey-Boy
Black comedy. Pet parrot not amused by practical joke. Variable cast 4 characters 1 interior
In Dashow, K. Da-show must go on
Sing this
Star of community theater group coaxes talented black janitor to join them. 2m
In Dashow, K. Da-show must go on
Thanks
Comedy. Prodigal son returns to eccentric family on Thanksgiving Day. 7m 3w 1 interior
In Dashow, K. Da-show must go on
Time out
After spending four years on bench, basketball player dreams of on-the-court heroics. 3m 1 interior
In Dashow, K. Da-show must go on
Top of 16
When director abandons them for bigger show, actors commit to directing themselves. 2m 3w 1 interior
In Dashow, K. Da-show must go on

Dasvedanya Mama. Eichelberger, E.

Date with a stranger. Vogelstein, C.

Dates and nuts. Lennon, G.

Dating (Social customs)
Albert, S. J. How many to tango?
y Foote, H. The dancers
y Lazarus, J. Secrets
y Mauro, R. Formula for romance
y Mondschein, N. L. Hold on!
Omata, G. H. S.A.M. I am
Shanley, J. P. Kissing Christine
y Soto, G. Novio boy

Daugherty, Linda
c The little mermaid. Anchorage Press 1995 61p
Dramatization of Hans Christian Andersen's fairy tale about mermaid who falls in love with prince. 2 acts 10 scenes 5m 7w

The **daughter.** See Morrison, B. A. A love song for Ulster: The daughter

Daughters. See Mothers and daughters

Daughters of the Lone Star State. Shores, D.

Daughters of the mock. Mason, J. A.

David, King of Israel
Gurney, A. R. The David show
c Haylock, D. Here is the news: Good news and bad news

The **David** show. Gurney, A. R.

David's mother. Randall, B.

David's redhaired death. Kramer, S.

Davies, Robertson

Eros at breakfast

Comic look at affects of first love on the "inner man." 1 act 4m 1w 1 setting

In Davies, R. Fortune, my foe & Eros at breakfast

Fortune, my foe

Satire. Recent immigrant and two literature professors, seeking support for artistic project, greeted with indifference from smug middle-class Canadians. Singing. 3 acts 7m 3w 1 setting

In Davies, R. Fortune, my foe & Eros at breakfast

Davis, Bette

Cullen, A. Self catering

Fuller, E. L. Me and Jezebel

Davis, Jack

c Moorli and the Leprechaun. Currency Press 1994 61p

Australian aboriginal spirit and Irish leprechaun help young girl fulfill her dream and combat prejudices of greedy art dealer. Music, singing. 20 scenes 4m 3w 1b 1g 3 interiors 2 exteriors

Davis, Ossie

c Escape to freedom

Depicts Frederick Douglass' early life as a slave in Maryland, his struggle to learn to read and write, and his escape to freedom. Singing. Prologue 5 scenes 5m 2w 1 setting

In Around the world in 21 plays; ed. by L. Swortzell

Davis, Richard

y Losing it. Heuer 1993 53p

Drama depicting consequences of teenage drug use. 2 acts 9m 6w

Davis, Russell

c The (revised) travelling Cinderella show

Comedy. Travelling players mount problem-laden production of Cinderella. 1m 3w

In Davis, R. A book of travelling shows

c The travelling Jekyll & Hyde show

Comedy. Mishaps occur during travelling players' stage production of Stevenson's classic tale of good and evil. 1m 3w

In Davis, R. A book of travelling shows

Davis, Thulani

The life and times of Malcolm X

Portrays events in life of prominent black activist. 3 acts 12 scenes Large mixed cast

In Moon marked and touched by sun; ed. by S. Mahone

Dawn. Pintauro, J.

Dawson, John, and Bass, Phillip

c The inside story; a zoological musical; book and lyrics by Ken Pickering; music and lyrics by John Dawson and Phillip Bass. Clark, I.E. 1992 21p

Musical. Zoo animals teach humans to live in harmony with nature. 2 acts Variable cast 26 characters extras 1 setting

Day, Doris M.

Possession is ... Kenyon-Deane 1993 60p

Comedy. Female family members vie for inheritance. 2 acts 4 scenes 6w 1 interior

Day, Julie

Come back for light refreshments after the service. French 1997 63p

Comic drama. Woman, after father's death, plans to sell house and go backpacking despite disapproval of others. Prologue 1 scene epilogue 1m 5w 1 interior 1 exterior

Day. Wilson, L.

A **day** for surprises. Guare, J.

Day of absence. Ward, D. T.

Day of wrath. Scotland, J.

Day shift. Woodward, M. B.

Day standing on its head. Gotanda, P. K.

The **day** the Bronx died. Brown, M. H.

The **day** they stole all the colors. Santiago, H.

Days ahead. Wilson, L.

Days like these. Minghella, A.

De Angelis, April

Hush

Explores madness, mysticism, nihilism and pessimism as responses to world without compassionate ideology. Family and friends confront their personal demons on anniversary of woman's death by drowning. 2 parts 3m 3w 1 setting

In Frontline intelligence I; ed. by P. Edwardes

Playhouse creatures. French (London) 1994 67p

Examines lives of English actresses during Restoration. Prologue 2 acts 18 scenes 5w 1 setting

De Boer, Lodewijk

The Buddha of Ceylon

Drama set in 1943 South American Dutch colony. Jewish refugee violinist and Nazi functionary create problems for ambivalent colonial governor. 3 acts 8 scenes 3m 3w 1 interior

In Dutch and Flemish plays; ed. by D. Couling

De Filippo, Eduardo

Filumena Marturano

Comedy set in Naples. Former prostitute assures fi-

De Filippo, Eduardo—*Continued*
nancial future of her three illegitimate sons by tricking lover into marriage. 3 acts 8m 5w 1 interior
In De Filippo, E. Four plays

Grand magic
Comedy about reality, fidelity, and trust. Magician helps woman elude jealous husband. 3 acts 11m 9w extras settings
In De Filippo, E. Four plays

The local authority
Mafia boss withdraws in favor of contender, who eventually kills him. 3 acts 14m 6w 2 interiors
In De Filippo, E. Four plays

Napoli milionaria; adapted by Peter Tinniswood
Moral corruption of family involved in war-time black market activities. 3 acts Large mixed cast settings
In De Filippo, E. Four plays

De Geesewell, Peter
Murder at the asylum. New Playwrights Network 1996 82p
Delusional patients in mental hospital die under mysterious circumstances. 3 acts 13 scenes 7m 7w 1 interior

De Groen, Alma
The girl who saw everything. Currency Press 1993 72p
Drama set in contemporary Australia. Feminist historian and her husband shaken by brutalized young woman's horrific death. 2 acts 2m 4w 1 interior

De la Tour, Andy
The Pope and the witch. Methuen 1992 110p (Methuen modern plays)
Free adaptation of Dario Fo's satire about Catholic Church's stand on social issues. 2 acts 5 scenes 12m 4w

De las Casas, Bartolomé. See Casas, Bartolomé de las, 1474–1566

De Montfort. Baillie, J.

The **deacon's** awakening. Richardson, W.

The dead
Brittney, L. Properly processed
Pittman, A. West moon
Warner, F. Lying figures

Dead end. Kingsley, S.

Dead end. Parson, R.

Dead funny. Johnson, T.

Dead guilty. Harris, R.

Dead heart. Parsons, N.

A **dead** man's apartment. Baker, E. A.

Dead man's hat. Way, C.

Dead mother. Greenspan, D.

Dead on time. Booth, J.

Dead white males. Williamson, D.

Deadly virtues (condensation). Jucha, B.

Deaf
Margulies, D. Louie
O'Neill, E. Warnings
Pintauro, J. Bird of ill omen
c Zeder, S. L. Mother Hicks

Dealer's choice. Marber, P.

Dean, Dell
Mama's girl. Players Press 1993 18p
Sheltered Texas college librarian falls in love with student athlete. 1 act 3m 2w extras 1 interior

Dean, Philip
Long gone lonesome cowgirls. Currency Press 1996 71p
Comic drama set in small Queensland town between 1965 and 1968. Unlikely friendship between two women, united in their abandonment by men in their lives and their love of country music. Music. 2 acts 2w 1 setting

Dean, Phillip Hayes
Dink's blues
Guilt-ridden African American pays drunken late night visit to old friend. 2m 1w 1 interior
In Dean, P. H. Moloch blues

The owl killer
African American father, consumed by guilt, attempts to obliterate all connections to renegade son. 1m 2w 1 setting
In Dean, P. H. Moloch blues

Paul Robeson. Dramatists 1997 72p
Chronicles life of renowned Afro-American performer and social activist. Singing. 2 acts 2m 1 setting

The Sty of The Blind Pig
Life of young African American woman living with mother is changed with arrival of Blind Jordan, a street singer. Set in Chicago of the 50's. Music, singing. 3 acts 9 scenes 2m 2w extras 1 interior
In Classic plays from the Negro Ensemble Company; ed. by P. C. Harrison and G. Edwards

Deane, Hamilton
Dracula (1924)
Original script of Deane's collaboration with Balderston, entered below. Prologue 3 acts epilogue 7m 4w 3 interiors 1 exterior
In Deane, H. and Balderston, J. L. Dracula

Deane, Hamilton, and Balderston, John L.
Dracula: the vampire play (1927)
Dramatization of Stoker's vampire classic. 3 acts 4 scenes 6m 2w 3 interiors
In Deane, H. and Balderston, J. L. Dracula

Dear, Nick
The art of success
Satire. Portrays eventful night in the troubled life of William Hogarth; Henry Fielding, politicians, criminals, and whores form the backdrop. 2 acts 12 scenes 6m 4w setting
In Dear, N. The art of success & In the ruins

In the ruins
Radio play. Mad King George III muses on his life and times. 1m 1b
In Dear, N. The art of success & In the ruins

Zenobia. Faber & Faber 1995 126p
Historical drama, set 267 A.D., about Zenobia, warrior queen of Palmyra and her battles with Rome. 2 acts 28 scenes 22m 2w extras 1 setting

Dear Kenneth Blake. Reingold, J.

Dearborn Heights. Medley, C.

The **dearest** of friends. See Foote, H. The roads to home: The dearest of friends

The **dearly** beloved. Osment, P.

Death
Anderson, J. Lynette at 3 AM
y Avery, A. Stardust melody
Barnes, P. Last things
Biswas, N. Skin
y Booth, R. Where did you spend the night?
c Bush, M. The boy who left home to find out about the shivers
Cook, M. Jacob's wake
Courts, R. Johnny Pye
Dashow, K. He ain't heavy
Day, J. Come back for light refreshments after the service
c Evans, L. Gran
Everett, R. Present from the past
Everyman
Garro, E. The tree
Howe, T. Approaching Zanzibar
Ibsen, H. The master builder
Kovacevic, D. The gathering place
Kramer, L. The normal heart
Levy, J. Old blues
Linney, R. Paradise
Lyssiotis, T. Blood moon
MacLeod, J. Jewel
Margulies, D. Somnambulist
McNally, T. Bringing it all back home
Mitchell, M. Life support
y Murray, P. Spitting chips
Murray-Smith, J. Flame
O'Connor, J. Red roses and petrol
Osofisan, F. Birthdays are not for dying
y Panych, M. Life science
Paz, O. Rappaccini's daughter
Pintauro, J. Benjamin falling
Pintauro, J. Charlie's farewell
Pintauro, J. Easter night
Pintauro, J. Men without wives
Pinter, H. Moonlight
Potter, D. Joe's ark
c Prendergast, S. Little victories
Prideaux, J. Abraham Lincoln dies at Versailles
Ricchi, R. The appointment
Ricchi, R. The promise
Ricchi, R. The scandal
Robson, J. Beulah
Rodriguez Solis, E. The fickle finger of Lady Death
Shepard, S. The holy ghostly
Simonson, E. Bang the drum slowly
y Slaight, C. High tide
Strindberg, A. The ghost sonata
Tagore, R. The Post Office
Thompson, G. M. A time to go home
Valle-Inclán, R. del. The paper rose
Vogel, P. The Baltimore waltz
Zark, J. A body of water: Foreign bodies
Zell, A. E. Come to leave
See also The dead

Death and dancing. Dowie, C.

Death and deceit on the Nile. De Pietro, P.

The **death** and life of Sherlock Holmes. Zeder, S. L.

Death and the Devil. Turrini, P.

Death and the King's Horseman. Soyinka, W.

Death comes to us all, Mary Agnes. Durang, C.

A **death** in Bethany. Williams, G.

Death in the family. Margulies, D.

Death of a clown. Beard, P.

Death of a salesman. Miller, A.

The **death** of Huey Newton. Sturner, L.

The **death** of King Philip. Linney, R.

The **death** of life. Barnes, D.

The **death** of Sir Brian Caitskill. Koch, K.

The **death** of the last black man in the whole entire world. Parks, S. L.

The **death** of Zukasky. Strand, R.

Deborah's daughter. Gems, P.

Debtor and creditor
Balzac, H. de. Mercadet
Lewes, G. H. The game of speculation

The **Decade** Club. Frankel, R.

Decadence. Berkoff, S.

Deer
c DeVita, J. A life in the woods

DeFelice, James
c The merchants of Dazu
Tale of human greed and comeuppance set in ancient China. Singing. 10 characters Variable cast 1 exterior
In Playhouse: six fantasy plays for children

The **defenceless** creature. Chekhov, A. (dramatization) See Chekhov, A. The anniversary; Chekhov, A. The festivities

Defoe, Daniel
Moll Flanders (dramatization) See Stiles, G. Moll Flanders

Degas, Edgar
Ives, D. Degas, c'est moi

Degas, c'est moi. Ives, D.

Degeneration
Barker, H. The power of the dog
Berkoff, S. East
Horovitz, I. Henry Lumper

Déjàvu. Osborne, J.

Del Rio, Dolores
Fuentes, C. Orchids in the moonlight

Del Valle, Peter. See Valenti, M. Beauty and the beast

Delacour, A. See Labiche, E. jt. auth.

Delaney, Bessie. See Delaney, S. jt. auth.

Delaney, Doug
The last ten miles of Avery J. Coping. French 1995 86p
Comic drama set in small town Kansas. After lifetime of adventure aging invalid finds himself under care of domineering sister. Prologue 2 acts 5m 4w 1 interior

Delany, Sarah, and Delany, Bessie
Having our say (dramatization) See Mann, E. Having our say

Delany Family
Mann, E. Having our say

Delilah (Biblical figure)
Perry, E. E. Once upon a beginning

Delisle, Jeanne-Mance
A live bird in its jaws; tr. by Yves Saint-Pierre. NuAge Eds. 1992 71p (Performance series)
Sexual fable about love triangle involving woman and twin brothers. 4 scenes 2m 1w 1 setting

Delphiniums. Shepherd, C.

Demchuk, David
Touch
Naked gay lovers debate merits of pornography. 2m 1 interior
In Making, out; ed. by R. Wallace

The **demon.** Downing, M.

Demoniac possession
Chayefsky, P. The tenth man

Denmark
O'Brien, M. Mad boy chronicle

Dennis, Patrick
Auntie Mame (dramatization) See Lawrence, J. and Lee, R. E. Auntie Mame

Dentists
Feydeau, G. Nothing but the tooth
c McCullough, L. E. "Have floss, will travel" the ever-so-true saga of Hiram T. McRoot, frontier dentist
Mercer, D. Huggy bear
Stoppard, T. Teeth
Tasca, J. Extraction

'dentity crisis. Durang, C.

The **department.** Williamson, D.

DePietro, Peter
Death and deceit on the Nile. French 1996 43p
Murder a La Carte mystery with audience participation. Discovery of Pharoah's tomb leads to murder. 4 scenes 4m 3w extra 1 interior

The hilarious hillbilly massacre. French 1995 47p
Murder a La Carte mystery with audience participation. I.R.S. agent murdered at Tennessee mountain family reunion. 5 scenes 2m 5w

y Murder at the prom. French 1994 55p
Murder a La Carte mystery with audience participation. Vengeful student wrecks havoc at senior prom. 10 scenes 2m 5w extras 1 setting

Depression, Mental
Beard, P. Cliff's edge
Miller, J. and Miller, S. Consequences
Puig, M. Mystery of the rose bouquet
Storey, D. Home

Depressions
1929—Canada
Winter, J. and Smith, C. Ten lost years

Depressions—*Continued*

1929—United States

Edward, H. F. V. Job hunters
Flanagan, H. and Clifford, M. E. Can you hear their voices?
Franklin, J. E. Christchild
Miller, A. The American clock
Odets, C. Awake and sing!
Simon, N. Brighton Beach memoirs
Wilson, E. C. Cross-dressing in the Depression
c Zeder, S. L. Mother Hicks

Deputy Toby. Kottke, T. G.

Desdemona. Vogel, P.

Desert Storm, Operation, 1991. See Persian Gulf War, 1991

The **deserter.** Beim, N.

Desertion, Military
Beim, N. The deserter
Fugard, A. A place with the pigs

The **designated** mourner. Shawn, W.

Desire, desire, desire. Durang, C.

Desire under the elms. O'Neill, E.

Desjardins, Marie-Catherine
The favorite minister (Le favori)

Tragicomedy reflecting change of values between older and younger generations of 17th century French nobility. 5 acts 6m 3w 1 exterior

In The Lunatic lover and other plays; ed. by P. Gethner

Despotism
Barnes, P. Laughter!

Dessalines, Jean Jacques
Hughes, L. Emperor of Haiti

Destination Bethlehem. Trott, S.

The **destiny** of me. Kramer, L.

Detective story. Kingsley, S.

Detectives
Bohmler, C. and Adler, M. Gunmetal blues
Byerrum, E. A Christmas cactus
Dudley, E. The return of Sherlock Holmes
Gray, S. Stage struck
Kingsley, S. Detective story
Manzi, W. Perfect crime
Parra, M. A. de la. Dostoevski goes to the beach
Paul, J. The secret of Sherlock Holmes
y Thum, N. B. The Red-headed League

Deus-x. Tasca, J.

Devalliers, Maurice. See Feydeau, G. jt. auth.

Devenish, Luke. See Taylor, A. jt. auth.

Deverell, Rex
y Switching places

Satirical look at teenage sex, pregnancy and single parenthood. 2m 2w

In Eureka! ed. by J. J. Lewis and D. Warren

Devil
Barker, C. The history of the Devil
Brenton, H. Faust, parts I & II
Connolly, H. Snakes and ladders
Goethe, J. W. von. Faust, part I
Goethe, J. W. von. Faust, part II
Joseph, C. M. The temptations of Jesus
Morton, C. Pancho Diablo
Pickering, K. The Ingoldsby legends
Sod, T. Satan and Simon Desoto
Solórzano, C. The hands of God
Van Itallie, J.-C. Master & Margarita

Devita, James
c A life in the woods. Anchorage Press 1997 60p

Dramatization of Felix Salten's novel about young deer's life in forest. 9 scenes 4m 5w 1 exterior

Devlin, Anne
After Easter. Faber & Faber 1994 76p

Comic drama. Woman returns to Northern Ireland after living for years in England and confronts aspects of identity she has willfully excluded. 8 scenes 6m 6w 5 interiors 2 exteriors

Devon (England)
Osment, P. The dearly beloved
Osment, P. Flesh and blood
Osment, P. What I did in the holidays

Devotees in the garden of love. Parks, S. L.

Dewberry, Elizabeth
Flesh and blood

Macabre Southern tragicomedy revolving around adultery and sibling rivalry. 1 act 1m 3w 1 setting

In Humana Festival '96

Head on

Short sketch of therapist and her patient minutes before appearance on The Oprah Winfrey Show. 2w

In By Southern playwrights; ed. by M. B. Dixon and M. Volansky
In Humana Festival '95

El **Dia** de los Muertos. The Fiesta of the Day of the Dead. Vigil, A.

Dialect

Black

Aiken, G. L. Uncle Tom's cabin

Dialect—Black—*Continued*
Boucicault, D. Octoroon
Brown, W. W. The escape
Burrill, M. P. Aftermath
Burrill, M. P. They that sit in darkness
Graham, S. It's morning
Harrison, P. C. The great MacDaddy
Hughes, L. Mulatto
Hughes, L. Simply heavenly
Hughes, L. Soul gone home
Johnson, G. D. A Sunday morning in the South
Parks, S. L. Imperceptible mutabilities in the Third Kingdom
Richardson, W. The chip woman's fortune
Russell, C. Five on the black hand side
Spence, E. Undertow
Wolfe, G. C. Story in Harlem slang

English—Early modern and Elizabethan

Ford, J. The broken heart
Ford, J. The lover's melancholy
Ford, J. Perkin Warbeck
Ford, J. 'Tis pity she's a whore
Marlowe, C. Edward II
Marlowe, C. The Jew of Malta
The Revenger's tragedy

English—Middle English

Mankind. A critical edition of the medieval play Mankind

English—Yorkshire

Morrison, B. The cracked pot
Storey, D. In celebration

Irish

O'Casey, S. Cock-a-doodle dandy
O'Neill, E. A touch of the poet

New England

O'Neill, E. Desire under the elms

Pidgin English

Khan-Din, A. East is east

Scottish

Adam, A. Birds of prey
Adam, A. A great occasion
Adam, A. A matter of diplomacy
Adam, A. A pearl of great price
Buchan, A. Conditional surrender
Corrie, J. Billy Shaw
Corrie, J. A bride for Heatherhill
Dunbar, D. A song for Robbie
Hood, E. A wake for Donald
House, J. Cherchez la femme
Rowan, A. A. A stitch in time
Scotland, J. Day of wrath
Scotland, J. A surgeon for Lucinda
Silver, R. S. The hert o Scotland
Whyte, P. Tuesday, eight-fifteen

Southern States

c Zeder, S. L. Wiley and the Hairy Man

Swedish

O'Neill, E. "Anna Christie"

West Indian

White, E. Lament for Rastafari

Dialogue between a prostitute and her client. Maraini, D.

Diamond orchid. Lawrence, J. and Lee, R. E.

Diamonds
Dias, E. J. The necklace
y Thane, A. The moonstone

Diamonds in the snow. McCullough, L. E.

Diana and Sidney. See Simon, N. London suite: Diana and Sidney

Dias, Earl J.
y Landslide for Shakespeare
Brilliant teen-ager wins television quiz and donates $5,000 to town for football field. 1 act 2 scenes 4m 4w extras 1 interior
In The Big book of large-cast plays; ed. by S. E. Kamerman

y The necklace
Dramatization of Guy de Maupassant's short story set in 19th century Paris about loss of borrowed necklace. 4 scenes 3m 3w 2 interiors
In The Big book of dramatized classics; ed. by S. E. Kamerman

Dice and cards. Kass, S. H.

Dick Turpin. Reakes, P.

Dick Turpin. Webster, P.

Dickens, Charles
A Christmas carol (dramatization) See Linney, R. A Christmas carol; Mortimer, J. Charles Dickens' A Christmas carol; Schario, C. A Christmas carol
Great expectations (dramatization) See Golden, E. Great expectations; Johanson, R. Charles Dickens' Great expectations
The Pickwick papers (dramatization) See Olfson, L. The Pickwick papers
A tale of two cities (dramatization) See Francis, M. A tale of two cities; Hackett, W. A tale of two cities; Johanson, R. A tale of two cities
Larson, L. and Lee, E. L. The salvation of Iggy Scrooge

Dickerson, Glenda. See Clarke, B. jt. auth.

Dickins, Barry

Remember Ronald Ryan. Currency Press in association with Playbox Theatre 1994 67p (Current theatre series)

Dramatic portrayal of Ronald Ryan, the last felon to be executed in Australia. 2 acts Large mixed cast

Dickinson, Joe

Jack the Ripper, monster of Whitechapel. Bakers Plays 1995 79p

Drama about serial killer in 1888 London. Includes three possible endings each with different characters exposed as murderer. 3 acts 22 scenes 6m 6w settings

Dickinson, John, 1732-1808

c Swajeski, D. M. The revolution machine

Dickinson, Samantha

Styx and Bones

Comedy. Unscrupulous used car salesman opens funeral parlour. 6 scenes 4m 3w 2 interiors

In Young playwrights; ed. by E. Bray

Dictators

Lawrence, J. and Lee, R. E. Diamond orchid

O'Neill, E. The Emperor Jones

Did I miss anything important? Trott, S.

Did you ever send your wife to Camberwell? Coyne, J. S.

Did you hear the one about the Irishman...? Reid, C.

Dierlam, Katy

Helen Melon at the sideshow

Monologue by carnival sideshow fat lady. Slide projections. 1w extra 1 setting

In Facing forward; ed. by L. D. Frank

Dietz, Steven

Dracula. Dramatists 1996 89p

Dramatization of Stoker's classic erotic vampire tale. 2 acts 5m 2w extras 1 setting

Halcyon days. Dramatists 1995 90p

Political satire about 1983 U.S. invasion of Grenada. 2 acts 5m 3w extras 1 interior 1 exterior

Lonely planet. Dramatists 1994 59p

Symbolic drama set in map store. Two gay men ponder fear, death and friendship in age of AIDS. 2 acts 5 scenes 2m 1 interior

—Same

In The Actor's book of gay and lesbian plays; ed. by E. Lane and N. Shengold

Private eyes

Comedy of suspicion and infidelities presented in play within a play format. 2 acts 3m 2w 1 interior

In Humana Festival '97

y The rememberer

Drama set in 1911 Washington State. Squaxin Indian girl struggles to preserve culture of her people. Background music, dancing, singing. 2 acts 7m 7w 2b 1g 1 setting

In Seattle Children's Theatre: six plays for young audiences; ed. by M. Smith

Trust. Dramatists 1995 72p

Dramatic comedy about love, lust and deception set against backdrop of rock music scene. 2 acts 2m 4w 1 setting

A **different** way to die. Brittney, L.

Diggin in: the farm crisis in Kentucky. Crutcher, J. and McBride, V.

Digging for fire. Hughes, D.

The **dining** room. Gurney, A. R.

Dink's blues. Dean, P. H.

Dinner, William

Logic upside down. Miller, J. G. 1993 19p

Comedy. Prospective heirs plot against robot who inherits their fortune. 1 act 3m 4w 1 interior

Dinners and dining

Doctorow, E. L. Drinks before dinner

Dinosaurs

c Mast, E. and Bensinger, L. Dinosaurs

Dionysus

Euripides. Bakkhai

Diocletian

Fletcher, J. and Massinger, P. The prophetess

DiPietro, Joe

Executive dance

A satirical look at two middle-aged executives at corporate social function. 2m 1 interior

In Actors Theatre of Louisville. Ten-minute plays: v3

See also Bozzone, B. jt. auth.

Diplomats

Findley, T. The stillborn lover

Hampton, C. Savages

Hare, D. Plenty

Dirty linen. Stoppard, T.

Dirty talk. Pintauro, J.

Dirty weekend. Booth, J.

Dirty work on the trail. Swift, R.

Disappeared. Nagy, P.

Disc jockeys

Overmyer, E. Native speech

A **disciple** from the country. Firbank, R.

The **discipline** committee. Mason, P. N.

Discrimination, Racial. See Race discrimination

Disguises
Beaumarchais, P. A. C. de. The marriage of Figaro
y Bland, J. The squire's daughter
Farquhar, G. The recruiting officer
Ford, J. The lover's melancholy
Lyly, J. Gallathea
Middleton, T. No wit, no help like a woman's
y Olfson, L. Monsieur Beaucaire
See also Impersonation

The **dismissal** of the Grecian envoys. Kochanowski, J.

La **dispute.** Marivaux

The **dissolution** of Dominic Boot. Stoppard, T.

A **distance** from Calcutta. Barry, P. J.

Distant fires. Heelan, K.

Distracted globe. Warburton, N. J.

Disturbing the dust. Taylor, A. and Devenish, L.

Ditch day. Kelly, T.

Divergent lines. Pearson, C.

A **diversion.** See Musset, A. de. Caprice

Diversions. Durang, C.

Diverting devotion. O'Malley, M.

Dividends. Richards, G.

Dividing the estate. Foote, H.

Divine right. Whelan, P.

Divine words. Valle-Inclan, R. del

Divorce
Carmichael, F. Coming apart
Chen, K. Eating chicken feet
Cooke, C. Threat
Cooper, J. B. Picnic time
Dresser, R. Gun-shy
Durang, C. Canker sores and other distractions
Finn, W. and Lapine, J. March of the falsettos
Gilroy, F. D. A way with words
Goldenthal, J. Wife to Tolstoi
Linney, R. Shotgun
c Lysander, P. and Osten, S. Medea's children
Mann, E. Still life
Mayer, J. Killjoy
Oates, J. C. Black
Pedrero, P. The voucher
Pintauro, J. Fur hat
Smith, L. Sins of the father
Terry, M. Fireworks
Walker, D. Triangle
Weller, M. Spoils of war
Wyld, H. Night's candles
See also Separation (Law)

Dixon, Dorothy
c The snow witch
Dramatization of Russian folktale. Snow Witch offers woman ability to change places with anyone she chooses. Dancing. 2m 4w extras 1 interior
In Thirty plays from favorite stories; ed. by S. E. Kamerman

Dixon, Michael Bigelow, and Smith, Val
Breaking the chain
Disagreement over chain letter spoils friendship of neighbors. 1m 2w
In Actors Theatre of Louisville. Ten-minute plays: v3

Diyab, Mahmud
Strangers don't drink coffee; tr. by Owen Wright and Alan Brownjohn
Drama about ordinary citizen confronted by anonymous authority. Arab man terrorized by series of strange men. 1m extras 1 setting
In Modern Arabic drama; ed. by S. K. Jayyusi and R. Allen

Dizon, Louella
Till voices wake us
Drama about immigrant Filipino family in Brooklyn, N.Y. Singing. 4m 3w extras 1 setting
In Contemporary plays by women of color; ed. by K. A. Perkins and R. Uno

DMV tyrant. Durang, C.

Doc. Pollock, S.

Doctorow, E. L.
Drinks before dinner. Theatre Communications Group 1996 56p
Drama about social responsibility depicting Manhattan dinner party for economically privileged. 2 acts 3 scenes 4m 5w 1b 1g 1 interior

Doctors. See Physicians

The **doctor's** dilemma. Shaw, G. B.

Dodge. Mamet, D.

Dodson, Owen
Bayou legend
Allegorical folk adaptation of Ibsen's Peer Gynt set in Louisiana bayou incorporating elements of African American storytelling tradition. 2 acts Large mixed cast 1 setting
In Black drama in America: an anthology; ed. by D. T. Turner

Dog. Berkoff, S.

Dog and wolf. Fischerová, D.

Dog days. Gray, S.

The **dog** it was that died. Stoppard, T.

Dog logic. Strelich, T.

Dog opera. Congdon, C.

Dogbrain. Weller, M.

Doggies. McConnell, J.

Dogg's Hamlet, Cahoot's Macbeth. Stoppard, T.

Dogs
c Ayckbourn, A. Mr A's amazing maze plays
Berkoff, S. Dog
c Boiko, C. A dog's best friend
Gow, M. Sweet Phoebe
Gurney, A. R. Sylvia
Pedrero, P. The voucher
c Robbins, G. The hundred and one Dalmatians

A **dog's** best friend. Boiko, C.

Dogsbreath Devereaux, the dastardly doctor. St. John, B.

Dolls
c Adkins, D. Ready steady go

A **doll's** house. Ibsen, H.

A **doll's** house. McGuinness, F.

Dolmen, Christopher, and Dolmen, Jean
c The three little pigs. New Playwrights Network 1997 48p

Musical pantomime. Fairy tale characters in play about perils of pig-poaching. 11 scenes Unidentified cast 14 characters

Dolmen, Jean. See Dolmen, C. jt. auth.

Dolores Street. Carilli, T.

Dolorosa Sanchez. Taikeff, S.

Domestic relations. See Family

Domestic violence. Stroppel, F.

Don Juan (Legendary character)
Morton, C. Johnny Tenorio
Shaw, B. Man and superman

Don Juan in Chicago. Ives, D.

Don Quixote de La Jolla. Overmyer, E.

Donaghy, Tom
The dadshuttle

Drama about AIDS. Father and homosexual son speak at cross purpose during drive to train station. 2m

In Donaghy, T. The dadshuttle and Down the shore

Down the shore

Teenage girl waiting to escape suburbia is accosted by man claiming to be her older brother. 3m 1w 1 setting

In Donaghy, T. The dadshuttle and Down the shore

Northeast local. Dramatists 1996 63p

Depicts working-class marriage from 1963 to its desolution thirty years later. 2 acts 10 scenes 2m 2w 1 setting

Donald, Simon
The life of stuff

Black comedy about marginalized Scottish urban life. Prologue 18 scenes 5m 3w 1 setting

In Made in Scotland; ed. by I. Brown and M. Fisher

Donnelly, Neil
The duty master

Drama about personal and national identity set in Leicestershire boys school. Irish-born English master faces dissolution of marriage and unexpected visit by brother. 2 acts 14 scenes 6m 7w extras 4 interiors 2 exteriors

In New plays for the Abbey Theatre, 1993–1995

Donnelly family
Reaney, J. The St. Nicholas Hotel, Wm. Donnelly, prop.

Donner Party
Mayberry, B. The catechism of Patty Reed

Donoghue, Mary Agnes
Me and Mamie O'Rourke. French (London) 1995 64p

Woman escapes unhappy marriage by fantasizing about former lover and forming stormy friendship with troubled young woman. 2 acts 4 scenes 2m 2w 1 interior

Don't care, won't care, couldn't care less. Haylock, D.

Don't go walking around naked. See Feydeau, G. "Hey, cut out the parading around stark naked!"

Don't mention my name. Carmichael, F.

Don't play with love. See Musset, A. de. Don't trifle with love

Don't trifle with love. Musset, A. de

Don't you want to be free? Hughes, L.

Dora: a case of hysteria. Morrissey, K.

Dora and the Pheelguds from the future. Price, J. W.

Dorfman, Ariel
Widows, by Ariel Dorfman in collaboration with Tony Kushner. Hern Bks. in association with the Traverse Theatre 1997 80p

Dorfman, Ariel—*Continued*

Political allegory set in war-torn Latin American village. Mothers, wives, and daughters of the disappeared defy military. 3 acts 31 scenes 8m 14w extras settings

Dorst, Tankred

Fernando Krapp wrote me this letter: an assaying of the truth

Dramatization of Miguel de Unamuno's novella Nothing less than a man (Nada menes que todo un hombre). Man destroys himself and object of his desire in pursuit of unattainable dream. 14 scenes 5m 1w

In DramaContemporary: Germany; ed. by C. Weber

Dostoevski goes to the beach. Parra, M. A. de la

Dostoyevsky, Fyodor

The brothers Karamazov (dramatization) See Fishelson, D. The brothers Karamazov

The idiot (dramatization) See Fishelson, D. The idiot

Parodies, imitations, etc.

Durang, C. The idiots Karamazov

Double cross. Kilroy, T.

The **double** deceiver. Menander. (adaptation) See Plautus, T. M. Two sisters named Bacchis

The **double** marriage. Fletcher, J. and Massinger, P.

The **doubles** according to Plautus. See Plautus, T. M. The brothers Menaechmus

Douglas, Alfred Bruce

Kilroy, T. The secret fall of Constance Wilde

Douglass, Frederick

Branch, W. In splendid error

Davis, O. Escape to freedom

Doust, Paul

Amphibious spangulatos; or, Newt on your Nellie. French (London) 1995 95p

Farce. Drama society, cricket team, country western band, bereaved nuns, and group of protestors all converge on English village hall. 2 acts Large mixed cast 1 interior

Cold Comfort Farm. French (London) 1993 102p

Adaptation of Stella Gibbons' novel set in 1930s England about eccentric farm family. Chorus. 2 acts 14 scenes 5m 5w settings

Dove, Rita

The darker face of the earth. Completely rev. 2nd ed. Story Line Press 1996 161p

Tragedy in blank verse based on Oedipus story set on plantation in antebellum South Carolina. Prologue 2 acts 11 scenes 10m 7w extras settings

—Same. Story Line Press 1994 140p

Original version of drama entered above. 14 scenes 12m 9w extras 1 setting

The **dove.** Barnes, D.

Dover, Mic, and Jarvis, Graham

Seconds. New Playwrights Network 1996 59p

Artist's romance with ex-lover's best friend ends in disaster. 2 acts 12 scenes 2m 2w extras 7 interiors

Dowie, Claire

Adult child/dead child

Monologue. Perceptions of an abused and disturbed child. 1w

In Dowie, C. Why is John Lennon wearing a skirt and other stand-up theatre plays

Death and dancing

Friendship between gay man and lesbian. 2 parts 1m 1w 1 interior

In Dowie, C. Why is John Lennon wearing a skirt and other stand-up theatre plays

Drag act

Monologue by lesbian. 1w

In Dowie, C. Why is John Lennon wearing a skirt and other stand-up theatre plays

Leaking from every orifice

Monologue about lesbianism and motherhood. 1w

In Dowie, C. Why is John Lennon wearing a skirt and other stand-up theatre plays

Why is John Lennon wearing a skirt?

Monologue by adolescent lesbian school girl. 1w

In Dowie, C. Why is John Lennon wearing a skirt and other stand-up theatre plays

Dowling, Clare

The Marlboro man

Tragicomedy set in army barracks about desolation of infertile young Irish couple coping with jeers of his comrades and insensitivity of her family. 1 act 1m 1w extras 1 interior

In Greatest hits: four Irish one-act plays; ed. by D. Bolger

Down by the ocean. Barry, P. J.

Downing, Martin
The demon. French (London) 1993 36p
Thriller. One of six friends seeking shelter from storm in high-rise flat is serial killer possessed by the Devil. 3m 3w 1 interior

Dowry
Plautus, T. M. The thirty-dollar day

Down syndrome
Luckham, C. The choice

Down the road. Blessing, L.

Down the shore. Donaghy, T.

Doyle, Sir Arthur Conan
The Red-headed League (dramatization) See Thum, N. B. The Red-headed League

Parodies, imitations, etc.

Bricusse, L. The revenge of Sherlock Holmes
Brown, K. C. Sherlock's veiled secret
Dudley, E. The return of Sherlock Holmes
Paul, J. The secret of Sherlock Holmes
y Zeder, S. L. The death and life of Sherlock Holmes

Doyle, Roddy
Brownbread
Comedy set in North Dublin suburb. Three young men kidnap bishop and realize their folly when U.S. Marines mount rescue. 2 acts 4 scenes 10m 2w extras 1 interior
In Doyle, R. Brownbread and War
War
Black comedy set in Irish pub. Trivia addicts meet every month to answer questions posed by quizmaster who detests wrong answers and shoots to kill. 2 acts 12 scenes 10m 6w 1 interior
In Doyle, R. Brownbread and War

Dr. Bergen's belief. Schwartz, D.

Dr. Jekyll . . . please don't hyde. Reiser, D.

Dracula. Clapp, T.

Dracula. Dietz, S.

Dracula. Wellman, M.

Dracula (1924). Deane, H.

Dracula: the vampire play (1927). Deane, H. and Balderston, J. L.

Draft, Military. See Military service, Compulsory

The **drag.** West, M.

Drag act. Dowie, C.

Drag queens in outer space. Gilbert, S.

Drag queens on trial. Gilbert, S.

Dragon thirst. Mitterer, F.

Dragons
c Barnieh, Z. A nest of dragons
c Elitzig, F. Seagirl
c Liebert, B. A terrible tale of a dreaded dragon
c Mahlmann, L. and Jones, D. C. The reluctant dragon
c Pollock, S. Prairie dragons
Surface, M. H. The reluctant dragon
c Winther, B. The dreadful dragon of Utrecht

Dragonwings. Yep, L.

Drakesbill. Gerke, P.

The **dramatic** circle. Kennedy, A.

Dramatists
Chekhov, A. The seagull
Duff, J. A quarrel of sparrows
Durang, C. Business lunch at the Russian Tea Room
Enright, N. Mongrels
Feingold, M. Scribe's paradox
Guare, J. Rich and famous
Havel, V. Unveiling
Larbey, B. Half an idea
Lyssiotis, T. A white sports coat
McLure, J. Ghost world
O'Neill, E. Servitude
Osborne, J. and Creighton, A. Epitaph for George Dillon
Parnell, P. An imaginary life
Pintauro, J. Bus stop diner
Schnitzler, A. A procession of shades
Shaffer, P. The gift of the Gorgon
Williams, T. Something cloudy, something clear

Dreadful doings at the cider mill. Mueller, D. A.

The **dreadful** dragon of Utrecht. Winther, B.

Dream, lover! Hornby, I.

Dream of a common language. McDonald, H.

Dream on Monkey Mountain. Walcott, D.

Dreamers. Silverstein, S.

Dreamkeeper. Sinclair, B.

Dreams
Barker, C. Subtle bodies
Colón, O. A. Siempre en mi corazón

Dreams—*Continued*
Dashow, K. Time out
Green, M. Dreams of a drunken Quaker
Lapine, J. Twelve dreams
Silverstein, S. Dreamers
Walcott, D. Dream on Monkey Mountain
Wellman, M. Cleveland
c Westerhout, G. The Zeem dream

Dreams. Beim, N.

Dreams from a summer house. Pattison, J.

Dreams of a drunken Quaker. Green, M.

Dreams of Anne Frank. Kops, B.

Dreams of Clytemnestra. Maraini, D.

Dreiser, Theodore
Carson, J. A preacher with a horse to ride

Dresser, Richard
Below the belt. French 1997 77p
Remote industrial outpost setting for look at loneliness and boredom confronting men employed by faceless corporation. 2 acts 3m 1 setting
—Same
In A Decade of new comedy: plays from the Humana Festival v2
In Humana Festival '95
Gun-shy
Divorced couple unable to stay divorced. 2 acts 25 scenes 3m 2w settings
In Humana Festival '97

The **dresser.** Harwood, R.

The **dressmaker.** Feydeau, G.

Drexler, Rosalyn
Occupational hazard
Experimental drama based on Kafka's fable A hunger artist. Portrait of artist as suicide. 2 acts 11m 4w extras 1 exterior
In Women on the verge: 7 avant-garde American plays; ed. by R. C. Lamont

Drinking in America. Bogosian, E.

Drinks before dinner. Doctorow, E. L.

Drive. Bell, N.

Driving Miss Daisy. Uhry, A.

The **Droitwich** discovery. Warburton, N.

Un **drôle** de mari français. Horovitz, I.

The **drought.** Petsinis, T.

Droughts
Flanagan, H. and Clifford, M. E. Can you hear their voices?
y St. John, B. Heaven help the po'taters!

Drowning
De Angelis, A. Hush

The **drowning** of Manhattan. Noonan, J. F.

Drug abuse
Bogosian, E. Sex, drugs, rock & roll
Davis, R. Losing it
Hare, D. Teeth 'n' smiles
y Parker, R. Under the influence
c Simmons, D. W. Be smart! Don't start!

Drug addicts. See Narcotic addicts

Drug traffic
Smith, S. One-sided triangle

Drugs
Ravenhill, M. Shopping and fucking
Rodriguez, Y. Rising sun, falling star

Drummers. Sierens, A.

The **drunkard.** Smith, W. H.

Drunkards. See Alcoholics

The **drunken** sisters. Wilder, T.

Dry lips oughta move to Kapuskasing. Highway, T.

Dry smoke. Shank, A. E.

Dryden, John
All for love. Players Press 1994 79p
English Restoration tragedy in blank verse. Adaptation of Shakespeare's Antony and Cleopatra. Prologue 5 acts epilogue 6m 4w 2g extras 1 interior
Amboyna
Historical drama set in 1623 Indonesia. Dutch employ rape and torture in their destruction of English trading posts on islands of Ambon and Ceram. Prologue 5 acts 11 scenes epilogue 9m 3w extras
In Dryden, J. The works of John Dryden v12
Amphitryon; or, The two Socias
Comedy based on mythological legend, and drawing heavily from Plautus' and Molière's earlier versions, in which Jupiter assumes likeness of Amphitryon and deceives him with his wife. Music. Prologue 5 acts 7 scenes epilogue 8m 4w 2 interiors 2 exteriors
In Four Restoration marriage plays; ed. by M. Cordner
Aureng-Zebe
Restoration drama in verse. Historical tragedy set in India, dealing with provincial rivalries among Emperor's four sons. Prologue 5 acts 5 scenes epilogue 10m 4w 1 setting
In Dryden, J. The works of John Dryden v12
Cleomenes, the Spartan heroe
Verse tragedy about Spartan King who, after losing battle of Sellasia, took refuge in Egypt where he planned to recover his kingdom. Historical parallels to exiled James II. Songs. Prologue 5 acts 13 scenes epilogue 7m 3w extras
In Dryden, J. The works of John Dryden v16

Dryden, John—*Continued*
King Arthur; or, The British worthy
Dramatic opera based on Arthurian legends. Prologue 5 acts 13 scenes epilogue 8m 4w extras
In Dryden, J. The works of John Dryden v16
Love triumphant; or, Nature will prevail
Tragicomedy in verse. Fornication and incest among Spanish ruling families. Prologue 5 acts 8 scenes epilogue 7m 5w
In Dryden, J. The works of John Dryden v16
The state of innocence and fall of man
Verse version of Milton's Paradise lost. 5 acts 13 scenes Variable cast 1 setting
In Dryden, J. The works of John Dryden v12

Doctor Thomas Neill Cream: mystery at McGill. Fennario, D.

Dual personality
Harwood, R. Poison pen

Duberstein, Helen
The cord and the track
Fiftysomething man discusses his affair with 19-year-old girl with friend. 2m 1 interior
In Facing forward; ed. by L. D. Frank

Dublin (Ireland)
Kilroy, T. Talbot's box
Murphy, J. A picture of paradise
O'Connor, J. Red roses and petrol

Dubois, Graham
c Bind up the nation's wounds
President Lincoln frees Confederate spy Belle Boyd. 3m 4w 1 interior
In Great American events on stage; ed. by S. E. Kamerman

Dubois, René-Daniel
Being at home with Claude
Male prostitute is interrogated about murder of his lover. 4m 1 interior
In The *CTR* anthology; ed. by A. Filewod

DuBois, W. E. B.
Star of Ethiopia
Pageant about black history. Large mixed cast
In Black theatre USA [v1]; ed. by J. V. Hatch and T. Shine

Duchamp, Marcel
Gordon, D. The mysteries and what's so funny?

The **Duchess** of Padua. Wilde, O.

The **Duchess:** pieces of Wallis Simpson. Griffiths, L.

La **Duchesse** de Langeais. Tremblay, M.

Duck-hunting. Vampilov, A.

Duck shooting. See Vampilov, A. Duck-hunting

Duck song. Mercer, D.

Ducks
c Bentley-Fisher, T. Friends

Dudley, Ernest
The return of Sherlock Holmes. Players Press 1995 48p
Adaptation of play by J. E. Harold Terry and Arthur Rose, based on stories of Arthur Conan Doyle. 2 acts 4 scenes 7m 3w 2 interiors

Dueling
Koch, K. The death of Sir Brian Caitskill

Duff, James
A quarrel of sparrows. French 1994 107p
Comic drama about ambition and religion. Young New York playwright experiences vision of God on Fifth Avenue. 2 acts 3 scenes 4m 2w 1 interior

Duffy, Carol Ann
Grimm tales (dramatization). See Supple, T. Grimm tales

Dulaney, Margaret
The view from here. French 1993 86p
Comic drama about agoraphobic woman in small town Kentucky. 2 acts 6 scenes 1m 3w 1 interior

Dumas, Alexandre, 1802–1870
The Count of Monte Cristo (dramatization) See Eleder, M. V. The Count of Monte Cristo
The three musketeers (dramatization) See Hall, W. The three musketeers

Dumas, Alexandre, 1824–1895
The lady of the camellias (dramatization) See Lang, W. Lady of the camellias

DuMaurier, Daphne
Rebecca (adaptation) See Williams, C. Rebecca
September tide; revised version by Mark Rayment. French (London) 1994 65p
Psychological drama originally produced 1948. Cornish widow falls in love with daughter's husband. 2 acts 4 scenes 3m 3w 1 interior

Dunbar, Dorothy
A song for Robbie. Players Press 1996 24p
Historical comedy in Scottish dialect. Poet Robert Burns' visit thrills village women. 2m 4w 1 exterior

Dunbar, Paul Laurence, and Shipp, Jesse A.
In Dahomey
Musical farce about fraudulent land schene designed to bilk African Americans. Prologue 2 acts 4 scenes 15m 4w extras 1 interior 4 exteriors
In Black theatre USA [v1]; ed. by J. V. Hatch and T. Shine

Dunbar-Nelson, Alice
Mine eyes have seen
Young black man is drafted into World War I army but doesn't want to serve a nation in which he is a victim of racial prejudice. 1 act 4m 4w 1 interior
In Black theatre USA [v1]; ed. by J. V. Hatch and T. Shine

Duncan, Isadora
Vingoe, M. and Kudelka, J. Hooligans

Duncombe, Peta
c Robin Hood. New Playwrights' Network 1993 77p
Pantomime based on English legend about outlaw who befriended the poor. Prologue 2 acts 12 scenes 9m 3w extras

Dungeons. Paterson, D. L.

Dunham, Sherrie
c Wanted: one fair damsel
Maiden rescues knight from dragon. 2 scenes 4m 4w 2 exteriors
In The Big book of skits; ed. by S. E. Kamerman

Dunlap, William
André
Tragedy. Several people plead for life of captured spy. Major André, during American Revolutionary War. Verse play. Prologue 5 acts 16 scenes 9m 2w extras 3 interiors 3 exteriors
In Early American drama; ed. by J. H. Richards

Dunn, Mark
Five tellers dancing in the rain. French 1994 97p
Comedy set in Mississippi bank. Five women tellers share confidences. 2 acts 6 scenes 5w 1 interior

Judge and jury. French 1994 91p
Comedic battle of the sexes set in Texas small claims court. 5m 4w 1 interior

Dunsany, Edward John Moreton Drax Plunkett
The glittering gate. Players Press 1994 14p
Two thieves locked out of heaven face a bleak eternity. 1 act 2m 1 setting

The lost silk hat. Players Press 1994 17p
Whimsical comedy. Befuddled man lacks gumption to retrieve hat from girlfriend's home. 5m 1 exterior

Dunsany, Lord. See Dunsany, Edward John Moreton Drax Plunkett

Dunsmuir family
Langley, R. The Dunsmuirs: a promise kept

The **Dunsmuirs:** a promise kept. Langley, R.

The **dupe.** See Feydeau, G. An absolute turkey

Durang, Christopher
1-900-desperate
Satirical look at singles' telephone services. 1m 3w 1b extra 1 setting
In Durang, C. 27 short plays

The actor's nightmare
Make-believe gives way to reality as stranger is forced to take actor's role in confused mix of Coward, Beckett, and Shakespeare. Background music. 1 act 2m 3w 1 setting
In Durang, C. 27 short plays
In Durang, C. Sister Mary Ignatius explains it all for you and The actor's nightmare
In Telling tales: new one-act plays; ed. by E. Lane

Baby with the bathwater
Satiric look at parenthood and sex roles in contemporary society. 2 acts 9 scenes 2m 3w 1 setting
In Durang, C. Complete full-length plays, 1975–1995

Beyond therapy
Satirical look at psychotherapy and its ineffectiveness in dealing with contemporary relationships. 2 acts 9 scenes 4m 2w settings
In Durang, C. Complete full-length plays, 1975–1995

The Book of Leviticus Show
Comedy about public TV access show broadcast from Wheeling, West Virginia motel room. Woman fulminates against homosexuality and adultery. Variable cast 7 characters 1 interior
In Durang, C. 27 short plays

Business lunch at the Russian Tea Room
Comedy. Playwright meets film development person for possible screenwriting job. 2m 2w extras 1 interior
In Durang, C. 27 short plays
In Durang, C. Durang/Durang

Canker sores and other distractions
Comedy. Canker sore and talkative waitress ruin previously married couple's chance at reconciliation. 1m 2w 1 interior
In Durang, C. 27 short plays

Death comes to us all, Mary Agnes
Black comedy set in decaying mansion where family dramatize their problems (incest, homosexuality, hatred, conceit) in highly theatrical style. 1 act 5 scenes 6m 6w 1 setting
In Durang, C. 27 short plays

Durang, Christopher—*Continued*

'dentity crisis

Black comedy attacking pretentions of psychiatry. Patient recovering from nervous breakdown finds her identity interchangeable with those of her doctor and her family. 1 act 2m 3w 1 interior

In Durang, C. 27 short plays

Desire, desire, desire

Parody of several Tennessee Williams' plays. 3m 5w 1 interior

In Durang, C. 27 short plays

Diversions

Black comedy. Man's attempted suicide leads to absurd courtroom spectacle. 7m 3w 1 setting

In Durang, C. 27 short plays

DMV tyrant

Man has frustrating experience with clerk at Division of Motor Vehicles. 1m 1w 1 interior

In Durang, C. 27 short plays

For whom the Southern belle tolls

Parody of Tennessee Williams' The glass menagerie. 2m 2w 1 interior

In The Best American short plays, 1993-1994

In Durang, C. 27 short plays

In Durang, C. Durang/Durang

In EST marathon, 1994

Funeral parlor

Comedy. Widow confronted by crazy mourner at funeral parlor. 1m 1w 1 interior

In Durang, C. 27 short plays

The Hardy Boys and the mystery of where babies come from

Comedy. Boy sleuths uncover facts of life. 3m 1w 1 interior

In Durang, C. 27 short plays

A history of the American film

Musical comedy. Take-off on American films, parodies various Hollywood genres and types of actors. Music, singing. 2 acts 35 scenes 9m 6w 1 setting

In Durang, C. Complete full-length plays, 1975-1995

The idiots Karamazov

Filled with numerous literary allusions and intellectual gamesmanship this parody of Dostoevsky is narrated by famed translator Constance Garnett. 2 acts 19 scenes 7m 6w extras 1 setting

In Durang, C. Complete full-length plays, 1975-1995

John and Mary Doe

Satirical look at problems facing contemporary families. 3m 2w 1 interior

In Durang, C. 27 short plays

Laughing wild. Dramatists 1996 83p

Satirical sketches on contemporary life. 2 acts 1m 1w 1 setting

—Same

In Durang, C. Complete full-length plays, 1975-1995

The marriage of Bette and Boo

Black comedy. Marriage between two Catholic Americans reflects uncertainties and confusions of contemporary life. 2 acts 41 scenes 5m 5w 1 setting

In The Best of Off-Broadway; ed. by R. Wetzsteon

In Durang, C. Complete full-length plays, 1975-1995

Mrs. Sorken

Humorous monologue about theater. 1w

In Durang, C. 27 short plays

In Durang, C. Durang/Durang

Naomi in the living room

Satire. Bizarre scene of son and daughter-in-law's visit with mother. 1m 2w 1 interior

In Durang, C. 27 short plays

The nature and purpose of the universe

Satire on religious fanaticism. New Jersey family becomes embroiled in plot to assassinate the Pope. Singing. 1 act Variable cast 11 characters 1 setting

In Durang, C. 27 short plays

Nina in the morning

Style piece a la Edward Gorey about preposterously narcissistic woman of means. 3m 2w 1 interior

In Durang, C. 27 short plays

In Durang, C. Durang/Durang

One minute play

Troubled man has brief conversation with female acquaintance. 1m 1w

In Durang, C. 27 short plays

Phyllis and Xenobia

Conversation between two eccentric sisters. 2w 1 interior

In Durang, C. 27 short plays

Sister Mary Ignatius explains it all for you

Comedy satirizing rigidity of Catholic dogma. Teaching nun is confronted by former students whose lives she failed to control. 1 act 2m 3w 1b 1 setting

In Durang, C. 27 short plays

In Durang, C. Sister Mary Ignatius explains it all for you and The actor's nightmare

A stye of the eye

Parody of Sam Shepard's play Lie of the mind. 3m 4w 1 exterior

In The Best American short plays, 1994-1995

In Durang, C. 27 short plays

In Durang, C. Durang/Durang

Titanic

Comedy-farce about zany doings and bizarre fetishes of

Durang, Christopher—*Continued*
American family aboard ill-fated liner. 12 scenes 4m 2w 1 setting
In Durang, C. 27 short plays

The Vietnamization of New Jersey
Satiric view of post-Vietnam America incorporating suicide, adultery and homosexuality. Eccentric New Jersey family awaits return of Vietnam veteran son and his native wife. 2 acts 8 scenes 6m 2w 1 setting
In Durang, C. Complete full-length plays, 1975-1995

Wanda's visit
Comedy. Visit by husband's manipulative high school sweetheart disrupts life of Connecticut couple. 2m 2w extras 1 interior
In Durang, C. 27 short plays
In Durang, C. Durang/Durang

Woman stand-up
Sensitive woman's unsuccessful attempt to turn pain and emotional abuse of her life into comedy routine. 1w 1 setting
In Durang, C. 27 short plays

Women in a playground
Two mothers, one an optimist the other a pessimist, meet at playground. 2w 1 exterior
In Durang, C. 27 short plays

Durang, Christopher, and Wasserstein, Wendy
Medea
Comic sketch about Jason and Medea. 3m 4w 1 setting
In Durang, C. 27 short plays

Durbridge, Francis
Sweet revenge. French (London) 1993 87p
Thriller. Prominent cardiologist suspected of killing wife's lover. 2 acts 9 scenes 6m 4w 1 interior

Duse, Eleonora
Garrett-Groag, L. The ladies of the camellias

Dusk. McNally, T.

Dutch

Indonesia

Dryden, J. Amboyna

Dutch uncle. Gray, S.

Dutchman. Baraka, A.

The **duty** master. Donnelly, N.

Dwellings
c Ayckbourn, A. Mr A's amazing maze plays

The **dybbuk.** Ansky, S.

Dying for laughs. Sroka, J. and Fleming, J.

The **dying** Gaul. Lucas, C.

E

Each day dies with sleep. Rivera, J.

Earhart, Amelia, 1898-1937
LaChuisa, M. J. First Lady suite: Eleanor sleeps here

Early blight. McConnell, J.

East. Berkoff, S.

East from the Gantry. Thomas, E.

East Indians

England

Biswas, N. Skin
Townsend, S. The great celestial cow

United States

Hazzard, A. Mother liked it
Horovitz, I. The Indian wants the Bronx

East is east. Khan-Din, A.

East of the sun and west of the moon. Gerke, P.

East Texas hot links. Lee, E.

Easter
Mueller, D. A. Eyes upon the cross

Easter night. Pintauro, J.

Eastwood, Clint
Cullen, A. Self catering

Eating chicken feet. Chen, K.

Eating crow. Labiche, E.

Eating disorders
Mullins, B. Pathological Venus
See also Anorexia nervosa; Bulimia

Eating Raoul. Feuer, J.

Eating sandwiches. See Pope, R. Sandwiches: Eating sandwiches

Eberhardt, Isabelle
Rubess, B. Oblivion: a story of Isabelle Eberhardt

Eccentrics and eccentricities
Barnes, P. The ruling class
Chinn, J. After September
Doust, P. Cold Comfort Farm
Lawrence, J. and Lee, R. E. Auntie Mame

The **echo** box. James, J.

Echo of applause. Booth, J.

Eclipsed. Brogan, P. B.

Ecology
Brooker, B. The land, the animals
c Dawson, J. and Bass, P. The inside story
c Ellison, L. Utter garbage
c Gallanar, I. Showdown at the 3-R Ranch
c Haylock, D. Don't care, won't care, couldn't care less
Klein, J. Betty the yeti
y Lavrakas, P. Escape from Nemotex
c Love, D. Be kind to your Mother (Earth)
c Love, D. Holiday in the rain forest
c Marx, P. The picnic
Moraga, C. Heroes and saints
c Neidermyer, D. The tortoise and the hare race again
c Price, J. W. Rocket recycle
c Price, J. W. and Becker, C. Legend of the lake
Rosenthal, R. Pangaean dreams a shamanic journey

The **ecstasy** of Rita Joe. Ryga, G.

Eddie goes to Poetry City (Part one: Seattle version). Foreman, R.

Eddie goes to Poetry City (Part two: New York version). Foreman, R.

Eddie Lee, Eddie Lee. Sears, J.

Eddie Mundo Edmundo. Alvarez, L.

Edelman, Maurice
A call on Kuprin (dramatization) See Lawrence, J. and Lee, R. E. A call on Kuprin

Edgar, David
Pentecost. Hern Bks. 1995 105p

Political parable set in war torn Eastern Europe. Religious and intellectual aspects of sectarian violence explored. 2 acts 8 scenes 12m 10w extras 1 setting

Edgar, Kate
c Aladdin. Warner Chappell Plays 1996 93p

Pantomime version of tale about Aladdin and magic lamp. Music, singing. 2 acts 15 scenes 6m 4w extras

c Mother Goose; book and lyrics by Colin Wakefield; music by Kate Edgar. Warner Chappell Plays 1996 77p

Musical pantomime with audience participation in Victorian setting. Mother Goose confronts Demoness of Discontent. Prologue 2 acts 12 scenes 3m 5w extras 1 interior 3 exteriors

c The sleeping beauty; book by Colin Wakefield; music and lyrics by Kate Edgar. Warner Chappell Plays 1996 87p

Pantomime with music based on Grimm brothers classic fairy tale of princess under sleeping spell. Singing. 2 acts 13 scenes 4m 6w extras 2 interiors 2 exteriors

Edinburgh (Scotland)
Hood, E. A wake for Donald
Kemp, R. Dalwhinnie
Wilcox, M. Rents

Edison, Thomas A.
St. Germain, M. Camping with Henry & Tom

Edith Wharton's The house of mirth. Keeler, D.

Edmond. Mamet, D.

Edmonds, S. Randolph
Old man Pete

Domestic drama. Southern rural parents of middle-class Harlemites clash with new values of urban blacks. 2 scenes 4m 3w extras 1 interior 1 exterior

In Black theatre USA [v1]; ed. by J. V. Hatch and T. Shine

Edmundson, Helen
Anna Karenina. Hern Bks. 1994 86p

Dramatization of Tolstoy's story of tragic, adulterous love set in 19th century Russia. 2 acts 4m 4w extras

The clearing. Hern Bks. 1994 86p

Historical drama about English suppression of Ireland set 1652–1655 in small farming community in County Kildare. 5 acts 23 scenes 5m 3w

The mill on the floss. Hern Bks. 1994 85p

Dramatization of Eliot's 1860 novel about vain efforts of Maggie Tulliver to adapt to her provincial world. In this free adaptation Maggie is portrayed by three actresses. Music. 36 scenes 3m 4w 1 setting

War and peace. Hern Bks. 1996 118p

Dramatization of Tolstoy's epic account of Napoleon's invasion of Russia and its effect on three aristocratic families. Prologue 7 acts 68 scenes 9m 6w settings

Educating Rita. Russell, W.

Education
Aristophanes. The clouds

Edufa. Sutherland, E.

Edward II, King of England
Marlowe, C. Edward II

Edward, H. F. V.
Job hunters

Public employment office in Harlem during the Depression flooded with destitute men. 1 act 13m 1w extras 1 interior

In Black theatre USA [v1]; ed. by J. V. Hatch and T. Shine

Edward Albee's fragments. Albee, E.

Edward Albee's Marriage play. Albee, E.

Edward and Christine. Koch, K.

Edwards, Gus
The offering
Shabby New York City basement apartment scene of psychological battle of wits as prosperous young African American hired killer and his aging mentor now on welfare struggle for sexual dominance of killer's white girl friend. 2 acts 7 scenes 2m 2w 1 interior
In Classic plays from the Negro Ensemble Company; ed. by P. C. Harrison and G. Edwards
Old West
Shooting in roadside bar. 4m 1w 1 interior
In Lucky 13; ed. by R. Shuttleworth

Edwin. Mortimer, J.

Egloff, Elizabeth
The swan. Dramatists 1994 57p
Dark supernatural comedy incorporating elements of Greek myth. Woman living in Nebraska prairie town encounters charismatic swan. 19 scenes 2m 1w 1 setting

Egmont, Lamoraal
Goethe, J. W. von. Egmont

Ego in Arcadia. Barker, H.

Egypt
History—332-30 B.C.
See also Alexandrine War, 48-47 B.C.

Ehn, Erik
Two altars, ten funerals (all souls)
Experimental theater piece based on life of Quiché Indian Rigoberta Menchú, winner of 1992 Nobel Peace Prize. 1m 4w 1 setting
In Plays for the end of the century; ed. by B. Marranca

Eichelberger, Ethyl
Dasvedanya Mama
Comic performance piece about truth, incest and the theater. 2m 3w 1 setting
In Grove new American theater; ed. by M. Feingold

Einstein, Albert, 1879-1955
Martin, S. Picasso at the Lapin Agile

Eisenhower, Mamie Doud, 1896-1979
LaChuisa, M. J. First Lady suite: Where's Mamie?

Eisenstein, Linda
At the root
Monologue about lesbian mother's sacrifice for her son. 1w
In The Actor's book of gay and lesbian plays; ed. by E. Lane and N. Shengold

Ekstrom, Peter
An O. Henry Christmas: The gift of the Magi
Musical based on O. Henry's ironic Christmas classic. Music, singing. 2 scenes 1m 1w 1 interior
In Ekstrom, P. An O. Henry Christmas
An O. Henry Christmas: The last leaf
Musical version of O. Henry's tale of artists in New York's Greenwich Village. Music, singing. 4 scenes 2m 2w 1 interior
In Ekstrom, P. An O. Henry Christmas

Elder, Lonne
Ceremonies in dark old men
Tragedy. Harlem family facing financial disintegration, attempts to get rich by joining criminal organization which proves to be as vicious as white exploitation. 2 acts 4 scenes 5m 2w 2 interiors
In Black theatre USA [v2]; ed. by J. V. Hatch and T. Shine
In Classic plays from the Negro Ensemble Company; ed. by P. C. Harrison and G. Edwards

The **elder** brother. Fletcher, J. and Massinger, P.

Eleanor sleeps here. See LaChuisa, M. J. First Lady suite: Eleanor sleeps here

Eleazer. See Eliezar, son of Moses

Electra (Greek mythology)
Euripides. Electra
Euripides. Orestes
Sophocles. Electra

Eleder, Maurine V.
y The Count of Monte Cristo
Dramatization of part of Alexandre Dumas' novel set in 19th century France. Dantes is framed and unjustly imprisoned for political crime but escapes. 12m 1w
In The Big book of dramatized classics; ed. by S. E. Kamerman

La **elegia** del Saltimbanqui. Pales Matos, L. (dramatization) See Colon, A. The caravan

Elegies for angels, punks and raging queens. Russell, B.

Elephants. Prideaux, J.

Eleuthéria. Beckett, S.

Elfenbein, Josef A.
c Puss-in-boots
Based on Charles Perrault's fairy tale. Clever cat outwits Ogre and wins fortune for master. 3m 2w extra
In Thirty plays from favorite stories; ed. by S. E. Kamerman

Eliesar. See Eliezar, son of Moses

Eliezar, son of Moses
Miller, M. Graven images

Elijah (Biblical figure)
Cross, J. The prophet's cloak

Eliot, George
The mill on the floss (dramatization) See Edmundson, H. The mill on the floss

Elisha, Ron
Choice. Currency Press in association with N.S.W. State Theatre Project 1994 67p (Current theatre series)
Unfettered choice plays tyrannical role in lives of three generations of women in Australian family. 2 acts 2m 3w 1 setting

Elitzig, Francis
c Seagirl. Anchorage Press 1993 34p
Based on Chinese folktale. Seagirl breaks spell of Dragon King. Variable case 14 characters 1 setting

Elizabeth I, Queen of England, 1533-1603
Fo, D. Elizabeth: almost by chance a woman
Maraini, D. Mary Stuart

Elizabeth: almost by chance a woman. Fo, D.

Ellison, Karen
The Harry and Sam dialogues. Dramatists 1994 51p
Series of dialogues between two old friends who pass time by posing outlandish questions to one another. 2m 1 setting

Ellison, Les
c Utter garbage. French (London) 1996 34p
Play about the environment. Idealistic rat in garbage dump foils evil rat to build better, cleaner world. Singing. 2 acts Unidentified cast 7 characters extras 1 exterior

El-Ramly, Lenin. See Ramlī, Līnīn

El Salvador
Bolt, C. Compañeras
Morton, C. The savior

Elton, Ben
Gasping. French (London) 1997 68p
Satire on big business. Marketing of "designer air" depletes oxygen supply. 2 acts 17 scenes 3m 3w extras settings

Silly cow. Warner Bks. 1993 90p
Satirical look at British tabloid press. Venemous TV columnist tries to keep her past secret. 2 acts 3 scenes 3m 2w 1 interior

Elves. See Fairies

Elwell, Jeffrey Scott
The art of dating
Romantic comedy. Two lawyers meeting for lunch to discuss their respective clients begin to take interest in each other. 2m 1w 1 interior
In Off-Off Broadway Festival plays, 20th ser.

Elyot, Kevin
My night with Reg. Hern Bks. 1997 78p
Comedy about gay manners and morals in age of AIDS. 3 scenes 6m 1 interior

Embezzlement
Granville-Barker, H. The Voysey inheritance
Kaiser, G. From morning to midnight

Emblems. See Warner, F. Maquettes for the requiem: Emblems

The **emerald** circle. Bush, M.

Emery, S. W.
Apology
Dramatic presentation of one of Plato's Dialogues. Socrates on trial. 9m extras 1 setting
In Emery, S. W. Plato's Euthyphro, Apology, and Crito

Crito
Dramatic presentation of one of Plato's Dialogues. Socrates, found guilty of rejecting official gods and corrupting youth, refuses friend's plea to escape. 2m extras 1 setting
In Emery S. W. Plato's Euthyphro, Apology, and Crito

Euthyphro
Dramatic presentation of one of Plato's Dialogues. Socrates explores concept of piety. 2m extras
In Emery, S. W. Plato's Euthyphro, Apology, and Crito

The **Em**-Fuehrer Jones. Hughes, L.

Emigration and immigration
c Boiko, C. Once upon a dream
Dizon, L. Till voices wake us
Horovitz, I. The primary English class
Jones, C. My Antonia
Lim, G. Paper angels
c Loomer, L. Bocón
y McCullough, L. E. The splendid voyage of Kitty Doyle
Micone, M. Beyond the ruins
O'Kelly, D. Asylum! Asylum!
Petsinis, T. The drought

Emily's play. Hall, F. B.

Emin-Pasha Relief Expedition, 1887-1889
Gray, S. The rear column

Emma. Pitts, G.

Emma's child. Thatcher, K.

Emma's time. Mercer, D.

Emond, Paul

Talk about love!

Waitress in Brussels bar and two customers exchange confidences. 2m 1w 1 interior

In New French-language plays

The **Emperor** Jones. O'Neill, E.

Emperor of Haiti. Hughes, L.

The **emperor** of the moon. Behn, A.

The **emperor's** New Year. Marshall, S. L.

The **Emperor's** nightingale. Mahlmann, L. and Jones, D. C.

Emporus. Philemon. (adaptation) See Plautus, T. M. The entrepreneur

The **enchantment** of Beauty and the beast. Francoeur, B.

The **end.** Goldstein, J.

The **end** of the day. Baitz, J. R.

The **end** of the food chain. Firth, T.

End of the world

Barnes, P. The end of the world—and after

Nemeth, S. Sally's shorts: Living in this world

End of the world. Kopit, A.

The **end** of the world—and after. Barnes, P.

An **endangered** species: waking up. Sorensen, K.

The **ends** of the earth. Lan, D.

The **ends** of the earth. Panych, M.

An **enemy** of the people. Ibsen, H.

An **enemy** of the people. Nolan, P. T.

Engagement. See Betrothal

English drama

Medieval

Mankind. A critical edition of the medieval play Mankind

Early modern and Elizabethan

Kyd, T. The Spanish tragedy
Lyly, J. Campaspe
Lyly, J. Gallathea
Marlowe, C. Edward II
Marlowe, C. The Jew of Malta

17th century

Chapman, G. The revenge of Bussy d'Ambois
Fletcher, J. The fair maid of the inn
Fletcher, J. The lover's progress
Fletcher, J. The sea voyage
Fletcher, J. and Massinger, P. The double marriage
Fletcher, J. and Massinger, P. The elder brother
Fletcher, J. and Massinger, P. The little French lawyer
Fletcher, J. and Massinger, P. The prophetess
Fletcher, J. and Rowley, W. The maid in the mill
Ford, J. The broken heart
Ford, J. The lover's melancholy
Ford, J. Perkin Warbeck
Ford, J. 'Tis pity she's a whore
Middleton, T. A critical edition of Thomas Middleton's The witch
Middleton, T. A mad world, my masters
Middleton, T. Michaelmas Term
Middleton, T. No wit, no help like a woman's
Middleton, T. A trick to catch the old one
Middleton, T. The witch
The Revenger's tragedy
Shakespeare, W. and Fletcher, J. Cardenio
Tourneur, C. The atheist's tragedy

Restoration

Behn, A. The emperor of the moon
Behn, A. The feigned courtesans
Behn, A. The lucky chance
Behn, A. The rover
Behn, A. Sir Patient Fancy
Centlivre, S. A bold stroke for a wife
Dryden, J. All for love
Dryden, J. Amboyna
Dryden, J. Amphitryon
Dryden, J. Aureng-Zebe
Dryden, J. Cleomenes the Spartan heroe
Dryden, J. Love triumphant
Dryden, J. The state of innocence and fall of man
Etherege, G. The man of mode
Farquhar, G. The beaux' stratagem
Farquhar, G. The constant couple
Farquhar, G. The recruiting officer
Farquhar, G. The twin rivals
Lee, N. The Princess of Cleves
Otway, T. The soldiers' fortune
Pix, M. The Spanish wives
Shadwell, T. The virtuoso
Southerne, T. The wives' excuse
Wycherley, W. The plain dealer

18th century

Addison, J. Cato
Burney, F. The Witlings

English drama—18th century—*Continued*
Cowley, H. P. The belle's stratagem
Gay, J. Beggar's opera
Goldsmith, O. She stoops to conquer
Inchbald, Mrs. Such things are
Lillo, G. The London merchant
Moore, E. The foundling
Moore, E. The gamester
Sheridan, R. B. The rivals
Sheridan, R. B. The school for scandal
Steele, R. The conscious lovers

English-French relations

Canada

See Canada—English-French relations

English language

Study and teaching

Horovitz, I. The primary English class

English made simple. Ives, D.

Enjoy. Bennett, A.

Enright, Nick
Blackrock. Currency Press 1996 69p
Rowdy birthday party near Australian surf club results in rape and murder of young girl. 24 scenes 6m 5w extras 1 setting

Good works. Currency Press in association with Playbox Theatre Centre 1995 57p (Current theatre series)
Domestic drama set in Australia 1928 to 1981. Explores three generations in lives of two Irish Catholic families. 2 acts 3m 3w 1 setting

Mongrels. Currency Press 1994 77p
Prison playwright strives for tenderness in his work while another writer searches for vigor in his. Loosely based on Australian dramatists Jim McNeil and Peter Kenna. 2 acts 16 scenes 3m 3w extras

y A property of the clan. Currency Press 1994 53p
Drama set in Australian industrial city. Teens react to murder of classmate. Variable cast 8 characters 1 setting

St. James Infirmary. Currency Press 1993 73p
Drama set in 1967 Australia about effect of Vietnam War protests on boys in Catholic boarding school. 2 acts 9 scenes 4m 2w 1 setting

Enscoe, L. G. and Enscoe, Annie
Call for the lights and sing!
Worship program. Medieval knaves interrupt king's party to tell true story of Christmas. Singing. 4 scenes Variable cast
In Enscoe, L. G. and Enscoe, A. Joy to the world!

Candles and carols
Worship program. Dramatization of Biblical account of Christ's nativity. Singing. Variable cast
In Enscoe, L. G. and Enscoe, A. Joy to the world!

The great Gemdale Christmas tree ornament factory
Worship program. Stranger teaches factory workers value of diversity. Singing. 11 scenes Variable cast 1 interior
In Enscoe, L. G. and Enscoe, A. Joy to the world!

The king who hated Christmas
Worship program. Jealous king learns a lesson when he tries to cancel Christmas celebration. Singing. Variable cast
In Enscoe, L. G. and Enscoe, A. Joy to the world!

The towne without a tale
Worship program. Christmas comedy. Medieval town presents holiday pageant. Singing. 7 scenes Variable cast 1 interior
In Enscoe, L. G. and Enscoe, A. Joy to the world!

The wise men had it easy
Worship program. Choir rehearses in mall among harried Christmas shoppers. Singing. 2 acts Variable cast 1 interior
In Enscoe, L. G. and Enscoe, A. Joy to the world!

Ensler, Eve
Floating Rhoda and the glue man
An examination of sexual identities set within New York's art subculture. 2 acts 2 scenes 3m 4w 1 setting
In Women playwrights: the best plays of 1993

Enter the night. Fornes, M. I.

Entertainers
Barry, S. The only true history of Lizzie Finn
Brown, C. The Little Tommy Parker Celebrated Colored Minstrel Show
Franco, C. [et al.] The LA LA Awards
Ingraffia, S. Pasquini the Magnificent
Kenna, P. Mates
Kopit, A. Road to Nirvana
Martin, J. Travelin' show
McNally, T. Whiskey
Slade, B. I remember you
Storey, D. Caring
Sweet, J. The value of names
See also Comedians

Entertaining
Guare, J. In fireworks lie secret codes
Walcott, D. Pantomime

The **entrepreneur.** Plautus, T. M.

Environment. Gilbert, M.

Epidicus. Plautus, T. M.

Epitaph for George Dillon. Osborne, J. and Creighton, A.

Epstein, Martin

How Gertrude stormed the Philosophers' Club

Sanctuary for philosophical males is invaded by progressive, impassioned female. 2 scenes 3m 1w 1 interior

In 20/20: twenty one-act plays from twenty years of the Humana Festival

Erogenous zones. Vickery, F.

Eros at breakfast. Davies, R.

The **escape.** Brown, W. W.

Escape. Kittson, J.

Escape from happiness. Walker, G. F.

Escape from Nemotex. Lavrakas, P.

Escape to freedom. Davis, O.

Escape to the blue planet. Boiko, C.

Escapee. Bynum, R. C.

Escapes

y Eleder, M. V. The Count of Monte Cristo

Escobedo de la Aixa. See Linney, R. Spain: Escobedo de la Aixa

Esenin, Sergie Aleksandrovich, 1895-1925

Vingoe, M. and Kudelka, J. Hooligans

Espionage. See Spies

Essex girls. Prichard, R.

Essmann, Jeffrey

Artificial reality; music composed by Michael John LaChiusa. Dramatists 1993 71p

One man theater piece with music. Satirical look at contemporary stereotypes. 1m

Esther. Swados, E.

La **estrella** de oro. The gold star. Vigil, A.

ESU and the vagabond minstrels. Osofisan, F.

Etherege, George

The man of mode; or, Sir Fopling Flutter

Plotless comedy of manners about love affairs among London aristocracy. Singing, music, dancing. Prologue 5 acts 11 scenes 8m 9w 3 interiors 1 exterior

In The Sensational Restoration; ed. by H. J. Jensen

Ethics, Medical. See Medical ethics

Ethiopia

History—1889-1974

Arent, A. Ethiopia

Eugenics

Stock, J. Star-gazy pie and sauerkraut

Eukiah. Wilson, L.

Eulogy for Mister Hamm. LaChiusa, M. J.

Euripides

Alcestis; tr. by David Kovacs

Greek classical drama. Psychological fantasy, based on the legend of a sacrificing wife who agrees to die so that husband may live. Speaking chorus

In Euripides. Cyclops; Alcestis; Medea

—Same; tr. by John Davie

In Euripides. Alcestis and other plays

The Bacchae; tr. by Nicholas Rudall. Dee, I. R. 1996 60p (Plays for performance)

Bakkhai; translation and commentary by Robert Emmet Meagher. Bolchazy-Carducci Pubs. 1995 97p

Variant titles: The Bacchanals; The Bacchae (entered above). Greek classical tragedy in verse. Punishment of Pentheus, King of Thebes, by Dionysus, god of wine, for his refusal to permit Bacchanaeian revels in Thebes. Speaking chorus

The children of Heracles; tr. by John Davie

Variant title: Heracleides. Greek classical verse tragedy. Legendary account of the war resulting from the refusal of Demophon, King of Athens to surrender the children of Herakles to their enemy, Eursytheus, King of Argos. Speaking chorus

In Euripides. Alcestis and other plays

The Cyclops. Players Press 1996 19p

Greek satyr play in verse. Based on Homer's story of Odysseus' escape from the cave of the Cyclops Polyphemus. Speaking chorus

—Same; tr. by David Kovacs

In Euripides. Cyclops; Alcestis; Medea

Electra; tr. by Janet Lembke and Kenneth J. Rockford. Oxford 1994 89p (Greek tragedy in new translations)

Greek classical tragedy in verse. Legend of Orestes and Electra, son and daughter of Agamemnon, telling how they avenged their father's murder

Hekabe; tr. by Robert Emmet Meagher. Bolchazy-Carducci Pubs. 1995 55p

Greek tragedy in verse based on legend. Hecuba, formerly Queen of Troy, avenges son's murder committed by King of Thrace. Speaking chorus

Euripides—*Continued*

Hippolytus; tr. by John Davie

Verse play. Greek tragedy based on legend. Phaedra, scorned by chaste stepson Hippolytus, arranges his destruction by falsely accusing him to his father Theseus. Speaking chorus

In Euripides. Alcestis and other plays

Iphigenia among the Taurians; tr. by Nicholas Rudall. Dee, I. R. 1997 64p (Plays for performance)

Variant title: Iphigenia in Tauris. Greek classical tragedy in verse. Legend relating how Iphigenia, while serving as priestess of Artemis plots to save her brother, Orestes, from being sacrificed to the goddess

Iphigenia in Aulis; tr. by Nicholas Rudall. Dee, I. R. 1997 66p (Plays for performance)

Greek classical tragedy in verse. Based on legend of sacrifice of Iphigenia, daughter of Agamemnon, to help Greek cause in Trojan War

Medea; tr. by Frederic Raphael and Kenneth McLeish. Hern Bks. 1994 56p

Greek classical tragedy in verse. Based on legend of Medea's revenge against husband Jason for deserting her. Speaking chorus

—Same; tr. by David Kovacs

In Euripides. Cyclops; Alcestis; Medea

—Same; tr. by John Davie

In Euripides. Alcestis and other plays

Medea (adaptation) See Lysander, P. and Osten, S. Medea's children

Orestes; tr. by John Peck and Frank Nisetich. Oxford 1995 111p (Greek tragedy in new translations)

Greek classical tragedy in verse. Apollo intervenes to save Orestes and Electra after they had been condemned to death for revenge slaying of their mother

Suppliant women; tr. by Rosanna Warren and Stephen Scully. Oxford 1995 82p (Greek tragedy in new translations)

Greek classical tragedy in verse. Based on legend of Argive women who invoked aid of the gods in recovering from the Thebans bodies of the Argive warriors slain in battle against Thebes

Trojan woman (adaptation) See Kennelly, B. The Trojan woman

About

Aristophanes. Festival time (Thesmophoriazousai)

Aristophanes. Frogs

Parodies, imitations, etc.

Durang, C. and Wasserstein, W. Medea

Euripides' The Trojan woman. Kennelly, B.

Europe

History—476-1492

Barker, C. Crazyface

Europe. Greig, D.

Europeans

Africa

Barteve, R. The orphanage

Algeria

Wertenbaker, T. New anatomies

The **Europeans:** struggles to love. Barker, H.

Euthanasia

Beard, P. Lavender years

Bill, S. Curtains

Groves, W. Good night, sweet mother

Euthyphro. Emery, S. W.

Evangelists

Baldwin, J. The amen corner

See also Televangelists

Evans, Don

One monkey don't stop no show

Comedy. Examination of life and loves of upwardly mobile middle-class black family in suburban Philadelphia. 3 acts 8 scenes 3m 5w 2 interiors 1 exterior

In Black comedy: nine plays; ed. by P. F. Jackson and Karimah

Evans, Lynda

c Gran. New Playwrights Network 1995 22p

Girl reviews her dying grandmother's life. Background music. 1 act 15 scenes Variable cast 20 characters 1 setting

Eve (Biblical figure)

y Perry, E. E. Once upon a beginning

Ritchie, R. In the beginning

Evelyn and the polka king. Finch, C. and Lucas, B.

An **evening** of culture: Faith County II, the saga continues. Smith, M. L.

Eventide. Wise, R.

Everett, Richard

Close to the wind. French (London) 1994 71p

Comedy about marriage and mid-life crises. After twenty-three years of marriage and child-rearing couple faces future. 2 acts 3m 3w 1 interior

Present from the past. French (London) 1994 68p

Family drama about inheritance, acceptance and forgiveness. Following their mother's death two sisters and brother are reunited with father they thought had died years ago. 2 acts 3m 2w 1 interior

The **evergreens.** Campton, D.

Every seventeen minutes the crowd goes crazy! Zindel, P.

Every young woman's desire. Parra, M. A. de la

Everyman; introduction and edited by William-Alan Landes. Players Press 1995 35p

Also known as The summoning of Everyman; The moral play of Everyman. 15th century morality play. Allegorical verse play about death

Everything under the sun. Spoor, K.

Everywoman. Kárpáti, P.

Everywoman: a modern morality play. Burnham, Y.

Eviction
y Ursell, G. The park

Evidence to the contrary. Pedneault, H.

Evil. See Good and evil

The **evils** of tobacco. See Chekhov, A. The dangers of tobacco

Evolution
Lawrence, J. and Lee, R. E. Inherit the wind

Excess baggage. Kelly, C.

Ex-convicts
Nelson, T. B. Eye of God
Wilder, T. Bernice

The **Execution.** Lee, J. A.

Execution of justice. Mann, E.

Executions and executioners
Dickins, B. Remember Ronald Ryan

Executive dance. DiPietro, J.

Exorcism
Ansky, S. The dybbuk
Chayefsky, P. The tenth man

An **experienced** woman gives advice. Heggie, I.

Experimental theater
Abdoh, R. The law of remains
Alianak, H. Passion and sin
Barker, H. Rome
Barnes, D. Madame collects herself
Barnes, D. Three from the earth
Bauer, W. Insalata mista
Beckett, S. Eleuthéria
Beckett, S. Ohio impromptu
Berc, S. A girl's guide to the Divine Comedy: a trilogy
Campanile, A. The big bun
Campanile, A. The inventor of the horse
Cartwright, J. Bed
Drexler, R. Occupational hazard
Ehn, E. Two altars, ten funerals (all souls)
Eichelberger, E. Dasvedanya Mama
Foreman, R. Eddie goes to Poetry City (Part one: Seattle version)
Foreman, R. Eddie goes to Poetry City (Part two: New York version)
Foreman, R. I've got the shakes
Foreman, R. The mind king
Foreman, R. My head was a sledgehammer
Foreman, R. Samuel's major problem
Fornes, M. I. The Danube
Fornes, M. I. What of the night?: Hunger
Garnhum, K. Surrounded by water
Gilbert, S. Jim Dandy
Gordon, D. The mysteries and what's so funny?
Greenspan, D. Son of an engineer
Guare, J. Marco Polo sings a solo
Handke, P. The hour we knew nothing of each other
Handke, P. Voyage to the sonorous land
Harrison, T. The labourers of Herakles
Higgins, D. Buster Keaton enters into paradise
Horovitz, I. Un drôle de mari français
Horovitz, I. Shooting gallery
Horovitz, I. Stage directions
Jarry, A. Ubu cocu
Kelm, A. Black bride
Koch, K. Edward and Christine
Linney, R. Can can
Malpede, K. US
Mamet, D. A life with no joy in it
Mason, K. A. For black boys who have considered homicide when the streets were too much
Overmyer, E. In perpetuity throughout the universe
Parks, S.-L. The America play
Parks, S.-L. Betting on the Dust Commander
Parks, S.-L. The death of the last black man in the whole entire world
Parks, S.-L. Imperceptible mutabilities in the Third Kingdom
Pintauro, J. Lightning
Pintauro, J. Swans flying
Puig, M. Under a mantle of stars
Rosenthal, R. Pangaean dreams a shamanic journey
Salah, 'Abd al-Sabur. Night traveler

Experimental theater—*Continued*
Schenkar, J. M. The universal wolf
Schevill, J. Lovecraft's follies
Schevill, J. Mother O
Schevill, J. The ushers
Schwab, W. People annihilation
Shepard, S. 4-H Club
Shepard, S. Forensic and the navigators
Son, D. R.A.W. ('cause I'm a woman)
Stein, G. The mother of us all
Stein, G. Three sisters who are not sisters
Stoppard, T. Dogg's Hamlet, Cahoot's Macbeth
Warner, F. Killing time
Warner, F. Maquettes for the requiem: Emblems
Warner, F. Maquettes for the requiem: Lumen
Warner, F. Maquettes for the requiem: Troat
Warner, F. Meeting ends
Wellman, M. Cellophane
Wilson, L. The family continues
Witkiewicz, S. L. The mother
Witkiewicz, S. I. The shoemakers
The Wooster Group. Frank Dell's The temptation of St. Antony
See also Expressionism; Surrealism

Exploding love. Coyne, J.

The **Exploratos** Club. Schmidt, W. F.

Explorers
Overmyer, E. On the verge
See also names of explorers, e.g. Columbus, Christopher

Expressionism
Benn, G. Ithaka
Hasenclever, W. The son
Kaiser, G. From morning to midnight
Kaiser, G. Gas I
Kaiser, G. Gas II
Kokoschka, O. Murderer the women's hope
Stramm, A. Sancta Susanna
Strindberg, A. Carl XII
Strindberg, A. The ghost sonata
Toller, E. Masses and man
Wedekind, F. Lulu: a monster tragedy
See also Experimental theater

Extensions. Schisgal, M.

Extortion
Booth, J. Tangled web
Shields, B. J. Highwire

Extraction. Tasca, J.

Extremities. Mastrosimone, W.

Eye of God. Nelson, T. B.

The **eye** of the beholder. Broadhurst, K.

Eyes upon the cross. Mueller, D. A.

Ezekiel (Biblical figure)
y Sloyer, G. Ezekiel saw the ... what?

Ezekiel saw the ... what? Sloyer, G.

Ezra's Noh for Willie. Hall, F. B.

F

F.M. Linney, R.

Fables
Drexler, R. Occupational hazard
c Leonard, J. Crow & Weasel
Prokofiev, S. The love of three oranges
c Vigil, A. The foolish coyote
c Vigil, A. The littlest ant
c Vigil, A. The smelly feet

Face divided. Baker, E. A.

Face of evil. Booth, J.

Face value. Hamlett, C.

Facelifting at St. Viators. Crawford, J. L.

The **factory** girls. McGuinness, F.

Failed investments. Brittney, L.

Faint sound of a bell. Wood, P.

Faint voices. MacKenna, J.

A **fair** country. Baitz, J. R.

Fair Kirsten. Nissen, K.

Fair ladies at a game of poem cards. Oswald, P.

The **fair** maid of the inn. Fletcher, J.

Fair Rosamund and her murderer. Nigro, D.

Fairies
c Bennett, R. The shoemaker and the elves
y Bush, M. 13 bells of Boglewood

Fairs
Gregory, L. Spreading the news

Fairy tales
c Artist, V. A. The clever judge
c Barnieh, Z. A nest of dragons

Fairy tales—*Continued*
c Bennett, R. Rumpelstiltskin
c Bennett, R. The shoemaker and the elves
c Bisson, P. Little Red Riding Hood
c Boswell, L. Beauty and the beast
c Brown, A. Sleeping Beauty
c Brown, J. The lake at the end of the world
c Bush, M. The boy who left home to find out about the shivers
c Bush, M. Hansel and Gretel, little brother and sister
c Bush, M. Puss in boots
c Bush, M. Rapunzel
c Caird, J. and Nunn, T. Peter Pan
c Cheatham, V. R. The Miss Witch contest
c Clapp, P. The girl whose fortune sought her
c Cooper, R. M. How things happen in three!
c Cregan, D. Aladdin
c D'Arcy, A. Cinderella
c Daugherty, L. The little mermaid
c Dolmen, C. and Dolmen, J. The three little pigs
c Dunham, S. Wanted: one fair damsel
c Edgar, K. Aladdin
c Elfenbein, J. A. Puss-in-boots
Enscoe, L. G. and Enscoe, A. The king who hated Christmas
c Francoeur, B. The enchantment of Beauty and the beast
c Francoeur, B. Snow White and the seven dwarfs
c Goldberg, M. Little Red Riding Hood and The three little pigs
c Green, M. Spring the king
c Hamlett, C. Boarder skirmish
c Hamlett, C. Face value
y Hamlett, C. Hairum-scarum
c Harder, E. Hey ho, Pinocchio
c Hezlep, W. Merlin's cave
c Holmes, R. V. The king and the miller
y Hughes, P. Abracadabra, Aladdin!
c Kennedy, R. Hans Christian Andersen's The Snow Queen
c Lavrakas, P. The princess and the pea
c Lazarus, J. The Nightingale
c Leuser, E. The big stone
y Leznoff, G. The stockbroker and the fairy godmother
c Liebert, B. A terrible tale of a dreaded dragon
c Love, D. Blame it on the wolf
c Mahlmann, L. and Jones, D. C. Aladdin
c Mahlmann, L. and Jones, D. C. Beauty and the Beast
c Mahlmann, L. and Jones, D. C. Cinderella
c Mahlmann, L. and Jones, D. C. The Emperor's nightingale
c Mahlmann, L. and Jones, D. C. The Frog Prince
c Mahlmann, L. and Jones, D. C. Jack and the beanstalk
c Mahlmann, L. and Jones, D. C. The Nutcracker Prince
c Mahlmann, L. and Jones, D. C. Peter Pan
c Mahlmann, L. and Jones, D. C. The Pied Piper of Hamelin
c Mahlmann, L. and Jones, D. C. Pinocchio
c Mahlmann, L. and Jones, D. C. Puss-in-Boots
c Mahlmann, L. and Jones, D. C. Rapunzel's tower
c Mahlmann, L. and Jones, D. C. The reluctant dragon
c Mahlmann, L. and Jones, D. C. Rumpelstiltskin
c Mahlmann, L. and Jones, D. C. Sleeping Beauty
c Mahlmann, L. and Jones, D. C. Snow White and Rose Red
c Mahlmann, L. and Jones, D. C. Snow White and the seven dwarfs
c McLaren, M. Seven with one blow
c Mercati, C. Cinderella
c Miller, H. L. The princess and the pea
c Morris, V. Thumbelina
c Neary, J. Aladdin and the wonderful lamp
c Netzel, S. The dark castle
c Nicol, R. The Snow Queen
c Norcross, E. B. Pied Piper's land
c Nunn, J. The Pied Piper
c Palmer, G. The falcon
c Pflomm, P. N. The leprechaun
c Pflomm, P. N. Lost in a fairy tale
c Poskitt, K. The Rumpelstiltskin racket
Prokofiev, S. The love of three oranges
c Pyle, M. T. Clever Peter
c Robbins, N. Snow White
c Roca, M. Pinocchio
c Sachon, S. Beauty and the beast
Schurman-O'Connor, K. The Wizard of Zoz
c Simons, J. Pinocchio commedia
c Slattery, M. E. The king in the kitchen
c Snipes, L. E. Jack and the wonder beans
Sondheim, S. and Lapine, J. Into the woods
c Staite, J. Cinderella—the sequel
c Supple, T. Grimm tales

Fairy tales—*Continued*
Surface, M. H. The reluctant dragon
c Swintz, M. Panic in the palace
c Swortzell, L. The love of three oranges
c Thane, A. Rapunzel
c Throckmorton, S. L. The forest bride
c Valenti, M. Beauty and the beast
c Vigil, A. Blanca flor. White flower
c Vigil, A. La estrella de oro. The gold star
c Vigil, A. Juan Oso. John the bear
c Vigil, A. The most interesting gift of all
c Vigil, A. El muchacho que mato al gigante. The boy who killed the giant
c Wakefield, C. The sleeping beauty
c Warhurst, M. Peter and the princess
c Webster, P. Peter Panto
c Werner, S. The king's bean soup
c Whelan, P. The tinder box
c Winther, B. The dreadful dragon of Utrecht
y Wood, B. The green snake and the beautiful lily
c Wood, D. Rupert and the green dragon
c Wood, D. The witches
c Woyiwada, A. The little fir tree
Yeats, W. B. The Land of Heart's Desire
See also Fables; Fantasy

Faith
Chayefsky, P. Holiday song
Harwood, R. J. J. Farr
Mitterer, F. Stigma
Pintauro, J. Birds in church
Schwartz, D. Dr. Bergen's belief
Wright, D. The stonewater rapture

Faith. Horovitz, I.

The **falcon.** Palmer, G.

Falkland Islands War, 1982
Berkoff, S. Sink the Belgrano!

The **fall** of Prague. Basso, E.

Fallen heroes. Armstrong, I.

Falling from grace. Rayson, H.

Falling man. Scheffer, W.

Falling over England. Mitchell, J.

Falling short. Robson, J.

False accusation
Euripides. Hippolytus
Lill, W. All fall down

Falsehood. See Truthfulness and falsehood

Falsettoland. Finn, W. and Lapine, J.

Falsettos. See under Finn, W. and Finn, W. and Lapine, J.

Familiar haunts. Taylor, P.

Family
Adam, A. A great occasion
Ayckbourn, A. Time of my life
Baitz, J. R. A fair country
Baldwin, J. The amen corner
Bamford, S. Scorpio
Bank, D. Halfway home
Barry, P. J. A distance from Calcutta
y Bartel, R. 3 out
Bates, H. E. The darling buds of May
Bennett, A. Enjoy
Berkoff, S. Kvetch
Berry, W. The cool of the day
Bill, S. Curtains
Blackwood, G. L. Futures
Bonal, D. Beware the heart
Booth, J. Something on his mind
Brooker, B. Tears of a dinosaur
Carr, M. The Mai
Chen, K. Eating chicken feet
Chocrón, I. The ultimate bliss
Clum, J. M. Randy's house
Congdon, C. Losing father's body
Connor, T. A couple with a cat
Cook, M. Jacob's wake
Crews, H. Blood issue
Cullen, A. Pig's ear
Danowski, C. Family values
De Filippo, E. Napoli milionaria
Dewberry, E. Flesh and blood
Doust, P. Cold Comfort Farm
Durang, C. John and Mary Doe
Durang, C. The marriage of Bette and Boo
Durang, C. Titanic
Enright, N. Good works
Evans, D. One monkey don't stop no show
Finley, K. The theory of total blame
Finnegan, S. It's all blarney
Flanagan, N. Burning time
Foote, H. Dividing the estate
Foote, H. The habitation of dragons
Foote, H. Night seasons
French, D. Leaving home
y Gallagher, M. Windshook
Gilbert, M. Environment
Gill, P. Cardiff East
Gilroy, F. D. Any given day
Gonzalez, R. The boiler room
Gotanda, P. K. Fish head soup
Gotanda, P. K. A song for a Nisei fisherman

Family—*Continued*
Gotanda, P. K. The wash
Granville-Barker, H. Rococo
Greenspan, D. Dead mother
Greenspan, D. Son of an engineer
Grumberg, J.-C. The free zone
Guare, J. Four baboons adoring the sun
Gurney, A. R. Children
Gurney, A. R. The dining room
Gurney, A. R. What I did last summer
Hall, W. Mansfield Park
Hansberry, L. A raisin in the sun
Harper, T. Christmas isn't for families
Harper, T. Requiem for Denys
Harwood, R. Another time
Harwood, R. A family
Hodgson, S. Tunnel vision
Horovitz, I. Unexpected tenderness
Houston, V. H. Asa ga kimashita (Morning has broken)
Howe, T. Approaching Zanzibar
Ikoli, T. Scrape off the black
Isitt, D. Matilda liar!
Ives, D. The land of Cockaigne
Johnson, J. Uganda
Khan-Din, A. East is east
Lebow, B. The keepers
Lee, L. The first breeze of summer
Leonard, H. Moving
Linney, R. True crimes
Machado, E. In the eye of the hurricane
Mamet, D. The cryptogram
Mamet, D. Jolly
Margulies, D. The Loman family picnic
Margulies, D. The model apartment
c Martin, J. Big burger
c Martin, J. Lost in a mall
Martin, S. WASP
May, B. 9th inning wedding
McCarthy, C. The stonemason
McCusker, P. Pap's place
McPherson, S. Marvin's room
Mercer, D. Where the difference begins
Miller, E. Morning shows the day
Minghella, A. A little like drowning
Miranda, J. Italian funerals and other festive occasions
Mitchell, J. Falling over England
y Morley, O. J. Romance for Jo March
Morrison, B. A love song for Ulster: The daughter
Morrison, B. A love song for Ulster: The son
Mouawad, W. Wedding day at the Cro-Magnons'
Murphy, J. A picture of paradise
Najera, R. A quiet love
Nunn, J. Arrangements
Oates, J. C. Tone clusters
Odets, C. Awake and sing!
O'Neill, E. Mourning becomes Electra: Homecoming
O'Neill, E. Mourning becomes Electra: The haunted
O'Neill, E. Mourning becomes Electra: The hunted
Osment, P. The dearly beloved
Oswald, D. Gary's house
Pawley, T. The tumult and the shouting
Pearson, S. Unfinished stories
Pintauro, J. Men's lives
y Pintauro, J. Reindeer soup
Pinter, H. Family voices
Poliakoff, S. Breaking the silence
Pollock, D. Doc
Rabe, D. Sticks and bones
Rahman, A. The mojo and the sayso
Reddin, K. Brutality of fact
Regan, S. Morning star
Reid, C. Did you hear the one about the Irishman... ?
Reid, C. Tea in a china cup
Reyes, G. Chilean holiday
Roberts, D. Breaking glass
Robinson, M. Colonial tongues
Robson, J. Beulah
Rodriguez, Y. Rising sun, falling star
Russell, C. Five on the black hand side
Russell, W. Breezeblock Park
Schenkkan, R. The war on poverty
c Schurman-O'Connor, K. Billy's problem
Schwab, W. People annihilation
Serreau, C. Lapin Lapin
Sessions, G. The return of spring
Sewell, S. The garden of granddaughters
Sharif, B. My ancestor's house
Shepard, S. Buried child
Sherman, J. M. Serendipity and serenity
Shields, Carol, and Shields, Catherine. Fashion, power, guilt and the charity of families
Silver, N. Pterodactyls
Simon, N. Brighton Beach memoirs
Standjofski, H. Anton
Stickland, E. Some assembly required
Storey, D. The march on Russia
y Thane, A. The House of the Seven Gables
Thomas, E. House of America
Tinniswood, P. The village fête
Townsend, S. The secret diary of Adrian Mole aged $13\frac{3}{4}$
Walker, G. F. Better living
Walker, G. F. Escape from happiness

Family—*Continued*
Walker, J. The River Niger
Way, C. Paradise Drive
White, E. Lament for Rastafari
Wilder, T. The long Christmas dinner
Wilson, L. Talley & Son
c Witkiewicz, S. I. Comedies of family life
Wynne, M. The knocky
Yamauchi, W. And the soul shall dance
Yamauchi, W. The music lessons
y Zindel, P. Every seventeen minutes the crowd goes crazy!
See also Brothers; Brothers and sisters; Conflict of generations; Fathers; Fathers and daughters; Fathers and sons; Grandfathers; Grandmothers; Mothers; Mothers and daughters; Mothers and sons; Mothers-in-law; Parent and child

A **family**. Harwood, R.

The **family**. Shearer, J.

Family circles. Ayckbourn, A.

The **family** continues. Wilson, L.

Family names. Pelonero, E.

The **family** of Mann. Rebeck, T.

Family reunions
Gray, S. Close of play
Horovitz, I. Stage directions
Nelson, R. New England
O'Connor, J. Red roses and petrol
Reid, C. The belle of the Belfast city
Storey, D. In celebration
Taylor, R. Watermelon rinds

Family values. Danowski, C.

Family voices. Pinter, H.

The **famous** tragedy of the rich Jew of Malta. See Marlowe, C. The Jew of Malta

Fanaticism
Martin, J. Keely and Du

Fandango! McCullough, L. E.

Fannon, Cecilia
Green icebergs
Drama about modern marriage set in Tuscany. Two couples disentangle with each other and are rematched with surprising results. 2 acts 3m 2w 1 interior 1 exterior
In Women playwrights: the best plays of 1995

Fanshen. Hare, D.

Fantasio. Musset, A. de

Fantasy
Aristophanes. Birds
Aron, G. Olive and Hilary
y Avery, A. Stardust melody
Ayckbourn, A. Communicating doors
c Ayckbourn, A. This is where we came in
Barnes, D. Kurzy of the sea
Barrie, J. M. Pantaloon
c Bass, E. In my grandmother's purse
y Bernadi, P. and Havens, D. Twice upon a time
y Bush, M. 13 bells of Boglewood
y Bush, M. Aalmauria: Voyage of the dragonfly
y Bush, M. The crystal
c Caird, J. and Nunn, T. Peter Pan
Capek, K. The Makropoulos secret
Churchill, C. The Skriker
Dunsany, L. The glittering gate
c Francoeur, B. Oz!
Gilbert, S. Drag queens in outer space
Glore, J. What she found there
Goethe, J. W. von. Faust, part II
Guare, J. A day for surprises
Guare, J. Marco Polo sings a solo
Gurney, A. R. The comeback
Gurney, A. R. The David show
Gurney, A. R. The Golden Fleece
c Ireland, V. Roald Dahl's The Giraffe and the Pelly and me
c Jackson, D. No one will marry a princess with a tree growing out of her head!
Jensen, M. Zombie chick
Klein, J. Betty the yeti
Koch, K. The Red Robins
Kramer, S. David's redhaired death
Kramer, S. Permanent signal
y Lewton, R. An alien stole my skateboard
Lucas, C. Prelude to a kiss
Lyly, J. Gallathea
MacNeice, L. The mad islands
c Mahlmann, L. and Jones, D. C. The Wizard of Oz
y Mapp, F. The wonderful Wizard of Oz
Martin, J. The boy who ate the moon
c Martini, C. Swimmers
McLure, J. Ghost world
c Medoff, M. Stefanie hero
Mitterer, F. Dragon thirst
Murphy, T. The morning after optimism
Norman, M. Loving Daniel Boone
Pattison, J. Dreams from a summer house
c Pflomm, P. N. The loose tooth
Rhodes, N. Ocean dream
Rivera, J. Cloud tectonics
Rivera, J. The winged man

Fantasy—*Continued*
y Rochelle, R. Alice in Wonderland
c Rocklin, B. The Island of Anyplace
Santeiro, L. A royal affair
c Santiago, H. The day they stole all the colors
Schisgal, M. The cowboy, the Indian and the fervent feminist
Shepard, S. The unseen hand
c Shurtz, R. K. Amy's attic
Sloate, D. Countess in Thistleland
Strindberg, A. The ghost sonata
Thompson, E. The Valentine Fairy
Uyehara, D. Hiro
Walcott, D. Dream on Monkey Mountain
c Weller, M. Dogbrain
Wilder, T. The long Christmas dinner
Wilder, T. Pullman car Hiawatha
Wright, D. Lot 13: the bone violin

The '**far**-flung'. McKee, J.

Farag, Alfred
'Ali Janah al-Tabrizi and his servant Quffa
Comic drama based on motif from Thousand and one nights. Merchant accumulates wealth in anticipation of arrival of fictitious caravan. 2 acts 6 scenes 1 interlude 3m extras 2 interiors 2 exteriors
In Modern Arabic drama; ed. by S. K. Jayyusi and R. Allen

Farces
Allais, A. The poor beggar and the fairy godmother
Annie G. Something rotten in Denmark
Aristophanes. Festival time
Aristophanes. Lysistrata
Barnes, P. Not as bad as they seem
Behn, A. The emperor of the moon
Benfield, D. A fly in the ointment
Bennett, A. Habeas corpus
Booth, J. A bit on the other side
Booth, J. Charley's uncle
Booth, J. Dirty weekend
Booth, J. Seeing double
Chekhov, A. The anniversary
Chekhov, A. The bear
Chekhov, A. The festivities
Chekhov, A. The proposal
Chekhov, A. The wedding
Chekhov, A. The wedding reception
Compton, J. Barefoot
Cooney, M. Cash on delivery!
Cooney, R. Funny money
Courteline, G. The police chief's an easygoing guy
Cowley, H. P. The belle's stratagem
Coyne, J. S. Did you ever send your wife to Camberwell?
Doust, P. Amphibious spangulatos
Feydeau, G. An absolute turkey
Feydeau, G. Brothers in crime
Feydeau, G. The dressmaker
Feydeau, G. A fitting confusion
Feydeau, G. A flea in her rear
Feydeau, G. Going to pot
Feydeau, G. "Hey, cut out the parading around stark naked!"
Feydeau, G. Nothing but the tooth
Feydeau, G. That's my girl
Feydeau, G. and Devalliers, M. All my husbands
Fo, D. Abducting Diana
Fo, D. Accidental death of an anarchist
Fo, D. Can't pay? Won't pay!
Fo, D. Elizabeth: almost by chance a woman
Fo, D. One was nude and one wore tails
Fo, D. The open couple
Fo, D. An ordinary day
Fo, D. The Pope and the witch
Fo, D. The virtuous burglar
Foxton, D. Caught on the hop
Freeman, D. Kindly keep it covered
Furse, J. The old rust bucket
Godfrey, P. A bucket of eels
Granville-Barker, H. Rococo
Gray, S. Dutch uncle
Greenland, S. Jungle rot
Greenspan, D. Dead mother
Guare, J. Home fires
Hardstack, M. The cure
Hazzard, A. Mother liked it
Hornby, I. Hello.... Is there any body there?
Hornby, I. Tim'll fix it!
Hornby, I. Where there's a will . . .
Jarry, A. Ubu cocu
Kash, M. and Hughes, D. Who's under where?
y Kelly, T. Ditch Day
Kelly, T. Hide and shriek
y Kelly, T. Trouble in Tumbleweed
Labiche, E. and Delacour, A. The piggy bank
Labiche, E. and Michel, M. It's all relative
Meilhac, H. and Halevy, L. Mardi Gras
Meilhac, H. and Halevy, L. Signor Nicodemo
Milligan, J. The quality of boiled water
Molière. The flying doctor
Morrison, B. The cracked pot
Nestroy, J. As you were
Nigro, D. Ardy Fafirsin
O'Casey, S. Cock-a-doodle dandy

Farces—*Continued*
y Olfson, L. Avon calling!
Pascal, F. The lunatic lover
Pelonero, E. Family names
Pinero, A. W. The magistrate
Pinero, A. W. The schoolmistress
Plautus, T. M. The braggart soldier
Plautus, T. M. The brothers Menaechmus
Plautus, T. M. A funny thing happened on the way to the wedding
Rooney, T. Flaming idiots
Sadler, C. and Pemberton, S. Christmas balls
Sardou, V. For love or monkey
Scribe, E. and Mélesville. The castrata
Sergent, S. Father's prize Poland china
Shepard, S. The mad dog blues
Simon, N. Rumours
Stoppard, T. Dirty linen
Stoppard, T. The real Inspector Hound
Strand, R. The death of Zukasky
Van Zandt, B. and Milmore, J. What the rabbi saw
The Washtub
Waterhouse, J. The cardboard cavaliers
Waterhouse, J. and Leach, P. Frank's feathered friend
y Welsh, D. Mellow drama
Wilder, T. The happy journey to Camden and Trenton

Farewell to the theatre. Granville-Barker, H.

Farhoud, Abla
Game of patience
Plight of Arab women in war-torn Third world country. 6 scenes 3w 1 setting
In Plays by women: an international anthology bk2; ed. by N. Shange

Farm life
Barry, S. Boss Grady's boys
Berry, W. The cool of the day
Cloud, D. O pioneers!
Crutcher, J. and McBride, V. Diggin in: the farm crisis in Kentucky
Doust, P. Cold Comfort Farm
Flanagan, H. and Clifford, M. E. Can you hear their voices?
Glover, S. Bondagers
c Jones, T. Gertie goat
c Jones, T. Scarecrows
Mason, T. The fiery furnace
O'Neill, E. Desire under the elms
Osment, P. Flesh and blood
Osment, P. What I did in the holidays
c Pollock, S. Prairie dragons
c Sandberg, R. N. Anne of Green Gables
y St. John, B. Heaven help the po'taters!
y Turner, J. Anne of Green Gables
Turrini, P. Swine
Wilcox, M. Accounts
Yamauchi, W. And the soul shall dance
Yamauchi, W. The music lessons
Zauner, F. Ch. A handful of earth

Farmer, Bonnie
Irene and Lillian forever
Tragedy set in Nova Scotia. Contentious relationship between poor black women. 2w 1 interior
In Escape acts; ed. by C. Curran

Farmer, Frances, 1913-1970
Clark, S. Saint Frances of Hollywood

Farmers. See Farm life

The **Farndale** Avenue Housing Estate Townspeople's Guild Operatic Society's production of The Mikado. McGillivray, D. and Zerlin, W.

Farquhar, George
The beaux' stratagem
Restoration comedy of manners. Fortune-hunting gentleman uses impersonation to win rich wife. Prologue 5 acts 12 scenes epilogue 11m 6w extras 4 interiors
In Farquhar, G. The recruiting officer and other plays
In Great Irish plays

The constant couple; or, A trip to the jubilee
Late Restoration comedy of manners. A rake's adventures in London. Prologue 5 acts 16 scenes epilogue 8m 4w extras 6 interiors 5 exteriors
In Farquhar, G. The recruiting officer and other plays

The recruiting officer
Late Restoration comedy of manners. Sergeant, disguised as fortune-teller promotes enlistment campaign for the British army during Queen Anne's reign. Prologue 5 acts 15 scenes epilogue 10m 4w extras 7 interiors 4 exteriors
In Farquhar, G. The recruiting officer and other plays

The twin rivals
Late Restoration comedy set in London. Twin brothers argue over inheritance. 5 acts 18 scenes epilogue 9m 4w extras 5 interiors 3 exteriors
In Farquhar, G. The recruiting officer and other plays

Farrell, Bernard
Forty-four, Sycamore
Comedy. Socially ambitious middle-class Irish couple tries to impress and entertain their more established neighbors. 3m 2w 1 interior
In Farrell, B. Forty-four, Sycamore & The last Apache reunion

Farrell, Bernard—*Continued*
The last Apache reunion
Comedy. Men at school reunion attempt to relive past and keep certain secrets from their wives. 2 acts 4 scenes 6m 2w 1 interior
In Farrell, B. Forty-four, Sycamore & The last Apache reunion

Fascism
Bond, E. Human cannon
Kilroy, T. Double cross
See also Totalitarianism

Fashion. Mowatt, A. C.

Fashion. Saunders, J.

Fashion, power, guilt and the charity of families. Shields, Carol, and Shields, Catherine

The **fastest** clock in the universe. Ridley, P.

Fat chance. Brochu, J.

Fat men in skirts. Silver, N.

Father and son. Margulies, D.

Fathers
Baitz, J. R. The substance of fire
Hare, D. Knuckle

Fathers and daughters
Barker, H. Brutopia
Barroga, J. Talk-story
Barry, P. J. And Fat Freddy's blues
Biswas, N. Skin
Bond, E. Olly's prison
Buero-Vallejo, A. The music window
Bynum, R. C. Escapee
Callan, L. Homebound
Day, J. Come back for light refreshments after the service
Granville-Barker, H. The marrying of Ann-Leete
Horovitz, I. Strong-man's weak child
Lan, D. The ends of the earth
Linney, R. Childe Byron
MacDonald, B. What we do with it
Mitterer, F. Wheat on the autobahn
O'Neill, E. "Anna Christie"
Pintauro, J. Easter night
Rivera, J. Each day dies with sleep
Sade, Marquis de. Count Oxtiern
Schwartz, D. Dr. Bergen's belief
Shearer, J. The family
Sweet, J. The value of names
Tannen, D. An act of devotion
Walker, D. Triangle
Wiener, S. D. A place where love is
Wilder, T. The rivers under the earth
Wilson, L. Redwood curtain
Windwick, N. D. A father's daughter

Fathers and sons
y Bartel, R. 3 out
Bartlett, N. Night after night
Blessing, L. Lake Street extension
Bond, E. In the company of men
Chocrón, I. Clipper
Coghlan, L. Waking
Crawford, D. W. Tangled garden
Dean, P. H. The owl killer
Donaghy, T. The dadshuttle
Gardner, H. Conversations with my father
Goldstein, J. Martin Night
Goluboff, B. My side of the story
Gordon, P. Generations apart
Granger, P. Vivien
Gurney, A. R. The cocktail hour
Hasenclever, W. The son
Jeffreys, S. A going concern
Kroetz, F. X. Mensch Meier
Kroetz, F. X. The nest
Kushner, T. The illusion
Lee, J. A. Coming home
Marber, P. Dealer's choice
Margulies, D. Father and son
Margulies, D. What's wrong with this picture?
Mastrosimone, W. A stone carver
Mitterer, F. Abraham
Nelson, G. Castrato
O'Neill, E. Desire under the elms
Pearson, S. Unfinished stories
Pintauro, J. Dirty talk
Pintauro, J. Men without wives
Pintauro, J. Rosen's son
Pintauro, J. Snow orchid
Pinter, H. Moonlight
Ricchi, R. The appointment
Riche, E. Possible maps
Shepard, S. The holy ghostly
Shepard, S. States of shock
Simpatico, D. Wish fulfillment
y Slaight, B. The open road
Upton, J. Bruises
Weiss, M. Hesh
Wiechmann, B. Feeding the moonfish
Wilson, L. Lemon sky
Wilson, L. Talley & Son
Wooten, J. J. Trophies
c Yep, L. Dragonwings

A **father's** daughter. Windwick, N. D.

Fathers-in-law
Smith, B. L. Butterscotch

Father's prize Poland china. Sergent, S.

Faulkner, Alistair
For England and King George. New Playwrights Network 1994 92p
Restoration-style Regency comedy. Swashbuckling actor involves his household in cloak and dagger escapades during Napoleonic Wars. 3 acts 4m 5w 2 interiors

Faulkner, William
McDonald, H. Faulkner's bicycle

Faulkner's bicycle. McDonald, H.

Faust, part I. Goethe, J. W. von

Faust, part II. Goethe, J. W. von

Faust, parts I & II. Brenton, H.

The **favorite** minister. Desjardins, M.-C.

FBI. See United States. Federal Bureau of Investigation

Fear
c Bush, M. The boy who left home to find out about the shivers
Graybill, C. Go look
c Lazarus, J. Night light
Shepard, S. Icarus's mother
Tremblay, M. Marcel pursued by the hounds
Upton, J. The shorewatchers' house
Williams, C. Rebecca

Feeding the moonfish. Wiechmann, B.

Feet. Ross, A.

Feet of clay. Roland, B.

Feffer, Steve
The wizards of quiz. Dramatists 1994 67p
Drama about 1950s quiz show scandals. Focuses on Herbert Stempel contestant who took dive for Charles Van Doren. 2 acts 6m 1w 1 setting

The **feigned** courtesans. Behn, A.

Feingold, Michael
Scribe's paradox; or, The mechanical rabbit
Drama about theater set in 1895 Paris. Playwright is criticized for taking new direction. 3m 2w 1 interior
In The Best American short plays, 1995-1996

Feldshuh, David
Miss Evers' boys. Dramatists 1995 101p
Drama based on the "Tuskegee Study of Untreated Syphilis in the Negro Male." Nurse testifies about men used as guinea pigs in Public Health Service experiment. 2 acts 16 scenes epilogue 6m 1w 1 setting

Felix, Maria
Fuentes, C. Orchids in the moonlight

Fell blow. Trenholme, H.

Feminism
Chafee, C. Why we have a body
Congdon, C. Casanova
Cowan, C. A woman from the sea
De Groen, A. The girl who saw everything
Hare, D. Slag
Jackson, J. A. WOMBmanWARs
Johnson, E. What do they call me?
Kaufman, L. Shooting Simone
Keatley, C. My mother said I never should
Mason, J. A. Daughters of the mock
McCauley, R. Sally's rape
Meyer, M. The odd women
Morrissey, K. Dora: a case of hysteria
Onwueme, O. T. Tell it to women
Rosenthal, R. Pangaean dreams a shamanic journey
Schenkar, J. M. The universal wolf
Silver, J. M. and Boyd, J. A . . . my name is still Alice
Vogel, P. Desdemona
Wilhelm, L. The power and the glory

Feng zhen-zhu: The wind pearl. Gerke, P.

Fennario, David
Balconville
Portrays life in Montreal working class district and comments on French-English relations and politics. Dialogue in English and French. 2 acts 7 scenes 4m 4w 1 exterior
In Modern Canadian plays v2; ed. by J. Wasserman

Doctor Thomas Neill Cream: mystery at McGill. Talonbooks 1993 126p
Fact and speculation mix in drama about Canadian doctor, backstreet abortionist and brothel operator who was hanged 1892 in London for murder of four prostitutes. Music, singing. 6m 4w extras 1 setting

Ferdinand, Val. See Kalamu ya Salaam

Fernandez, Evelina
How else am I supposed to know I'm still alive
Middle-aged Mexican American woman discusses unexpected pregnancy with friend. 2w 1 extra 1 interior
In Contemporary plays by women of color; ed. by K. A. Perkins and R. Uno

Fernando Krapp wrote me this letter: an assaying of the truth. Dorst, T.

Festival time. Aristophanes

Festivals
Rensten, M. Village day

The **festivities.** Chekhov, A.

Feuer, Jed
Eating Raoul; the musical; book by Paul Bartel; music by Jed Feuer; lyrics by Boyd Graham; based on the film "Eating Raoul." French 1993 99p
Musical based on black comedy film about food, lust and murder. Music, singing. 2 acts Variable cast 16 characters extras 1 setting

Feydeau, Georges
An absolute turkey. Absolute Classics 1994 126p
Farce revolving around infidelity, mixed up hotel room assignments, and husband's friend who turns out to be wife's secret admirer. 3 acts 45 scenes 10m 8w 3 interiors

Brothers in crime (Gibier de potence); tr. by J. Paul Marcoux
Variant title: Fit to be tied. Farce revolves around husband suspicious of actress wife's admirer and mistaken identity of visitor. 1 act 4m 3w 1 interior
In Feydeau, G. Five by Feydeau

The dressmaker (Tailleur pour dames); tr. by J. Paul Marcoux
Variant titles: A fitting confusion (entered below); A gown for his mistress; Love by the bolt. Farce. To avoid getting caught, philandering husband involves himself and others in a series of impersonations. 3 acts 6m 4w 2 interiors
In Feydeau, G. Five by Feydeau

A fitting confusion (Tailleur pour dames); tr. by Norman R. Shapiro
In A Flea in her rear, and other vintage French farces!

A flea in her rear; or, Ants in her pants (La puce à l'oreille); tr. by Norman R. Shapiro
Variant titles: The bug in her ear; A flea in her ear. Farce. Woman's arrangement of assignation with her own husband, to test his fidelity, leads to all kinds of complications. 3 acts 10m 5w extras 2 interiors
In A Flea in her rear, and other vintage French farces!

Going to pot (On purge bébé); tr. by Norman R. Shapiro
Farce. Confusion results when porcelain manufacturer and wife entertain. 3m 3w 1b 1 interior
In A Flea in her rear, and other vintage French farces!

"Hey, cut out the parading around stark naked!" ("Mais n'te promène donc pas toute nue!"); tr. by Albert Bermel
Variant title: Don't go walking around naked. Comedy revolving around prudish husband's disapproval of wife's revealing clothing. 1 act 4m 1w extras 1 interior
In A Dozen French farces; ed. by A. Bermel

My wife's dead mother (Feu la mère de madame); tr. by Albert Bermel
Variant title: Madame's late mother. Satirical comedy about young married couple with pretensions. Plot revolves around erroneous information about mother's death. 1 act 2m 2w 1 interior
In A Dozen French farces; ed. by A. Bermel

Nothing but the tooth (Hortense a dit: je m'en fous); tr. by J. Paul Marcoux
Variant title: Tooth and consequences. Farce about weak-willed dentist and his shrewish wife who quarrel over disciplining their maid Hortense while patient sits in dental chair. 1 act 5m 4w 1 interior
In Feydeau, G. Five by Feydeau

That's my girl! (Occupe-toi d'Amélie); tr. by J. Paul Marcoux
Variant title: Keep an eye on Amélie. Everyone keeps getting involved with wrong people in this farce about marriage. 3 acts 2 scenes 16m 9w 1g extras 4 interiors
In Feydeau, G. Five by Feydeau

Feydeau, Georges, and Devallieres, Maurice
All my husbands (Le marriage de Barillon); tr. by J. Paul Marcoux
Variant title: On the merry-go-round. Farce revolving around erroneously issued marriage certificate, return of "drowned" husband and resulting charges of bigamy. 3 acts 7m 3w 1b extras 3 interiors
In Feydeau, G. Five by Feydeau

Fiat. Pintauro, J.

The **fickle** finger of Lady Death. Rodriguez Solis, E.

The **fiddler** and the Dean. O'Donovan, J.

Fidelity. See Faithfulness

Field, Barbara
Boundary Waters. Dramatists 1993 76p
Comedy set in Boundary Waters National Park. After night of romantic encounters group of scientists wake to find they have rediscovered their scientific calling. 2 acts 6 scenes 4m 2w 1 exterior

Field, Nathan. See Fletcher, J. The honest man's fortune

Fielding, Henry
The modern husband (adaptation) See Godfrey, P. The modern husband

Fields, Mary, 1832-1914
y Hunkins, L. Freedom is my middle name

Fieldstones. Zuberbuehler, A.

The **fiendish** firebug strikes again! St. John, B.

Fierce love. Freeman, B.; Branner, D. and Gupton, E.

The **fiery** furnace. Mason, T.

The **Fiesta** of the Day of the Dead. See Vigil, A. El Dia de Los Muertos. The Fiesta of the Day of the Dead

Figaro's marriage. See Beaumarchais, P. A. C. de. The marriage of Figaro

Fight for Shelton Bar. Chessman, P. et al.

Fighting for myself. Clark, R. J.

Fighting over Beverley. Horovitz, I.

Filipino Americans
Barroga, J. Talk-story
Dizon, L. Till voices wake us

The **film** society. Baitz, J. R.

Filumena Marturano. De Filippo, E.

Final passages. Schenkkan, R.

Final placement. Watson, A.

The **final** tide. Cole, N. (dramatization) See Cole, N. And the tide shall cover the earth

Finch, Carl, and Lucas, Bob
Evelyn and the polka king; a play by John Olive; music by Carl Finch & Bob Lucas. French 1996 75p (French's musical library)

Musical. Father and estranged daughter resurrect legendary polka band and hit the road in search of girl's mother. Music, singing. 2 acts 4 scenes epilogue 1m 2w extras 1 setting

Find me. Mercer, D.

Finding the sun. Albee, E.

Findley, Timothy
The stillborn lover. Blizzard Pub. 1993 92p

Drama about loyalty, commitment and love. Canadian ambassador in Moscow, his ailing wife and adult daughter subjected to interrogations by special agents forcing them to unravel the past. Prologue 2 acts 29 scenes epilogue 4m 3w 1 setting

A **fine** gentleman. Richardson, A.

Finger food. Shengold, N.

Finger painting in a Murphy bed. Paterson, D. L.

Fink and Fliederbusch. Schnitzler, A.

Finley, Karen
The theory of total blame

Satiric look at American family dominated by tragic archfiend mother. 4m 2w 1 interior

In Grove new American theater; ed. by M. Feingold

Finn, William
"In trousers"

Musical set chronologically before March of the falsettos. Husband/father struggles with his confused sexuality. 1m 3w 1 setting

In Finn, W. Falsettos

March of the falsettos

Musical following events that took place in author's In trousers. Man decides to divorce wife to be with male lover. Singing. 3m 1w 1b 1 setting

In Finn, W. Falsettos

Finn, William, and Lapine, James
Falsettoland

Musical continuation of March of the falsettos. Gay man reunited with lover as son reaches age of bar mitzvah and reality of AIDS surfaces. 4m 3w 1 setting

In Finn, W. Falsettos
In Fruitful and multiplying; ed. by E. Schiff

Finnegan, Seamus
Comrade Brennan

Scottish socialist faces shattered dreams at end of 20th century. 4m 2w extras 1 interior

In Finnegan, S. It's all blarney: four plays

It's all blarney

Irish family in North London create myths of the past, the old country and themselves. 2 acts 11 scenes 8m 3w 1 setting

In Finnegan, S. It's all blarney: four plays

Mary Maginn

Irish working-class woman's Catholic faith enables her to endure harsh realities. 2 acts 32 scenes 3m 3w extras 1 setting

In Finnegan, S. It's all blarney: four plays

Wild grass

Radio play. Man returns to Ireland for mother's funeral. 2m 2w extras

In Finnegan, S. It's all blarney: four plays

Firbank, Ronald
A disciple from the country

Comedy. Debutante flirts with religion and sainthood in quest for husband. 1 act 2m 5w 1 interior

In Firbank, R. Complete plays

The mauve tower

Dream play about princess fleeing unwanted marriage and prince's wrongful imprisonment. 7 scenes 2m 2w extras 1 setting

In Firbank, R. Complete plays

The Princess Zoubaroff

Comedy about marriage, religion and homosexual separatism. 3 acts 52 scenes 6m 7w 1b 1g 1 exterior

In Firbank, R. Complete plays

Fire in the hole. Schenkkan, R.

The **firebird,** the horse of power, and Czarevna Vasilisa. Gerke, P.

Fires
Shank, A. E. Dry smoke

Fire's daughters. Césaire, I.

Fires in the mirror: Crown Heights, Brooklyn and other identities. Smith, A. D.

Fireworks. Terry, M.

A **first**-born son. Wilson, E.

The **first** breeze of summer. Lee, L.

First Lady suite: Eleanor sleeps here. LaChuisa, M. J.

First Lady suite: Olio. LaChuisa, M. J.

First Lady suite: Over Texas. LaChuisa, M. J.

First Lady suite: Where's Mamie? LaChuisa, M. J.

First love. Margulies, D.

The **first** Lulu. Wedekind, F.

First Monday in October. Lawrence, J. and Lee, R. E.

The **first** one. Hurston, Z. N.

The **First** Time Club. Curran, KT

Firth, Tim
The end of the food chain. French 1995 96p
Comedy. Young woman joins all male night shift in grocery distribution depot. 2 acts 20 scenes 5m 1w 1 interior

Neville's Island. French (London) 1994 98p
Four middle-aged British businessmen participating in corporate team-building exercise are shipwrecked on island in Lake District. 2 acts 14 scenes 4m 1 setting

Fischer, Margaret
The gay divorcee
Comic portrait of Australian Jewish lesbian. 22 scenes 1w extra
In Australian gay and lesbian plays; ed. by B. Parr

Fischerová, Daniela
Dog and wolf
Drama depicting French poet François Villon as exemplum of clash between artist and society. 2 acts 8m 5w extras 1 interior
In Czech plays; modern Czech drama; ed. by B. Day

Fischoff, George
James A. Michener's Sayonara; a new musical adapted from the novel by James A. Michener; book by William Luce; lyrics by Hy Gilbert; music by George Fischoff; orchestration by Joseph Gianono. French 1995 92p
Musical based on James Michener's novel about love between American soldier and Japanese woman. 2 acts 28 scenes Large mixed cast settings

Fish. Mamet, D.

Fish head soup. Gotanda, P. K.

Fishburne, Laurence
Riff raff. Dramatists 1997 58p
Drama set on New York's Lower East Side. Dim-witted thieves try to figure way out of drug rip-off gone bad. 4 scenes 3m 1 interior

Fishelson, David
The brothers Karamazov. Dramatists 1995 131p
Dramatization of Dostoyevsky's novel about lust, patricide and redemption revolving around three brothers in 19th century Russia. 3 acts 22 scenes 12m 4w 1 setting

The idiot. Dramatists 1995 117p
Dramatization of Dostoyevsky novel set in 1869 St. Petersburg. Man of great intellect who retains simplicity and insight of a child confronts society awash in vice, pretence and foolishness. 3 acts 19 scenes 9m 6w 1 setting

Fisher, Aileen
c I have a dream
Vignettes about Martin Luther King's work in the civil rights movement. Singing. 1 act 9m 2w extras 1 setting
In Great American events on stage; ed. by S. E. Kamerman
In Plays of black Americans; ed. by S. E. Kamerman

c Harriet Tubman—the second Moses
Verse play about slave who brought others to freedom via the Underground Railroad. Singing. Variable cast 1 setting
In Plays of black Americans; ed. by S. E. Kamerman

Fisheries. See Fishermen

Fishermen
Gotanda, P. K. A song for a Nisei fisherman
Horovitz, I. Henry Lumper
c Pflomm, P. N. Fishing
Pintauro, J. Men's lives

Canada

Cook, M. The head, guts and sound bone dance

Ireland

Synge, J. M. Riders to the sea

Fishermen—*Continued*

Scotland

Windwick, N. D. A father's daughter

Fishing. Pflomm, P. N.

Fishing. Weller, M.

Fit to be tied. Silver, N.

Fit to be tied. See Feydeau, G. Brothers in crime

A **fitting** confusion. Feydeau, G.

A **fitting** finish. Bower, M.

Fitting rooms. Cinoman, S.

Fitzball, Edward

The inchcape bell; or, The dumb sailor boy

Nineteenth century nautical burletta with cast of smugglers, marines and pirates. 2 acts 8 scenes 7m 3w extra settings

In The Lights o' London and other Victorian plays; ed. by M. R. Booth

Fitzgibbon, Ger

The rock station. Meridian Theatre Co. in association with The Collins Press 1997 84p (Meridian playtext)

Drama set in 1866 Ireland against backdrop of militant Fenianism. Two brothers operate lighthouse off coast of County Clare. 8 scenes 2m 1 interior

Five-dollar drinks. See Pintauro, J. Ten-dollar drinks

Five Ives get named. Blount, R.

The Five Lesbian Brothers

Brave smiles ... another lesbian tragedy

Comedic look at lesbian life. 2 acts 11 scenes 5w 1 setting

In The Actor's book of gay and lesbian plays; ed. by E. Lane and N. Shengold

Five little snowmen. Pflomm, P. N.

Five on the black hand side. Russell, C.

Five tellers dancing in the rain. Dunn, M.

Five thousand miles. Barnes, D.

Five visits from Mr. Whitcomb. Bays, C. L.

Five women wearing the same dress. Ball, A.

Flame. Murray-Smith, J.

The **flames** of hell. McCullough, L. E.

The **flaming** fiery furnace. Haylock, D.

Flaming idiots. Rooney, T.

Flanagan, Hallie, and Clifford, Margaret Ellen

Can you hear their voices?

Based on story by Whittaker Chambers set during depression of 1930. American farmers facing starvation urged to consider communist alternative. Music, dancing, slide projections. 7 scenes 17m 12w extras settings

In Plays by American women, 1930–1960; ed. by J. E. Barlow

Flanagan, Nicholas

Burning time. Currency Press in association with Playbox Theatre 1996 106p (Current theatre series)

Family chronicle set in affluent Melbourne, Australia suburb from 1986 to 1996. 2 acts 29 scenes 6m 6w 1 setting

Flaubert, Gustave

Parnell, P. Flaubert's latest

Flaubert's latest. Parnell, P.

Flavio's disgrace. Griffiths, D.

A **flea** in her ear. See Feydeau, G. A flea in her rear

A **flea** in her rear. Feydeau, G.

Flesh and blood. Dewberry, E.

Flesh and blood. Osment, P.

Flesh and blood. Thomas, C.

Fletcher, John, 1579–1625

The fair maid of the inn

John Ford, Philip Massinger and John Webster have been identified as possible collaborators. Tragicomedy about mistaken identity, virtue and love in Florentine court. Prologue 5 acts 14 scenes 10m 5w extras

In Beaumont, F. and Fletcher, J. The dramatic works in the Beaumont and Fletcher canon v10

The honest man's fortune

Authorship attributed to Fletcher, Nathan Field and Philip Massinger. Tragicomedy about romance, virtue, hypocrisy and social conventions among French aristocrats. 5 acts 16 scenes 9m 3w extras

In Beaumont, F. and Fletcher, J. The dramatic works in the Beaumont and Fletcher canon v10

The lover's progress

Revised by Philip Massinger. Drama about love and friendship set in 17th century France. Contains supernatural elements. Prologue 5 acts 19 scenes epilogue 13m 3w extras

In Beaumont, F. and Fletcher, J. The dramatic works in the Beaumont and Fletcher canon v10

See also Shakespeare, W. jt. auth.

Fletcher, John, 1579-1625, and Massinger, Philip

The double marriage

Political and sexual court intrigue during tyrannous reign of Arragonese King Ferrand of Naples. 5 acts 18 scenes 11m 2w extras

In Beaumont, F. and Fletcher, J. The dramatic works in the Beaumont and Fletcher canon v9

The elder brother

Verse comedy. Courtship of virginal young woman in 17th century France. Prologue 5 acts 17 scenes epilogue 10m 3w extras

In Beaumont, F. and Fletcher, J. The dramatic works in the Beaumont and Fletcher canon v9

The little French lawyer

Verse comedy about love, seduction, honor, and revenge among French aristocrats. Prologue 5 acts 20 scenes epilogue 8m 4w extras

In Beaumont, F. and Fletcher, J. The dramatic works in the Beaumont and Fletcher canon v9

The prophetess

Verse play about Diocletian and role of prophecy in Roman society. 5 acts 28 scenes 8m 4w extras

In Beaumont, F. and Fletcher, J. The dramatic works in the Beaumont and Fletcher canon v9

Rollo, Duke of Normandy

Other possible collaborators include Ben Jonson, Nathan Field and George Chapman. Tragedy about tyranny and corruption. Man slays brother to secure political power. 5 acts 11 scenes 21m 3w extras

In Beaumont, F. and Fletcher, J. The dramatic works in the Beaumont and Fletcher canon v10

The sea voyage

Variant title: The storm. Members of shipwrecked party, stranded on desolate isle, find themselves subject to revenge of former victims. 5 acts 16 scenes 10m 3w extras

In Beaumont, F. and Fletcher, J. The dramatic works in the Beaumont and Fletcher canon v9

The Spanish curate

Comedy, with romantic subplot, about Spanish curate's relations with his parishoners. Prologue 5 acts 21 scenes epilogue 13m 4w extras

In Beaumont, F. and Fletcher, J. The dramatic works in the Beaumont and Fletcher canon v10

Fletcher, John, 1579-1625, and Rowley, William

The maid in the mill

Comic verse play about rivalry and romance in Spanish court. 5 acts 13 scenes 15m 4w extras

In Beaumont, F. and Fletcher, J. The dramatic works in the Beaumont and Fletcher canon v9

Flip. Rooney, T.

The **flight** into Egypt. Garner, J.

Flint. Mercer, D.

Floating Rhoda and the glue man. Ensler, E.

La **flor** de la Noche Buena. The flower of the Holy Night. Vigil, A.

Florence (Italy)

Fletcher, J. The fair maid of the inn

Musset, A. de. Lorenzaccio

Warner, F. Living creation

Wilde, O. A Florentine tragedy

Florence Nightingale. Waddy, L.

A **Florentine** tragedy. Wilde, O.

Flower, Martha, and Follows, Sonia

c Robin's last stand; a musical play. New Playwrights Network 1995 74p

Musical based on Robin Hood legend. To provide for their retirement aging Merry Men ineptly execute one last scheme. 2 acts 18 scenes 8m 5w extras 1 setting

The **flower** of the Holy Night. See Vigil, A. La flor de la Noche Buena. The flower of the Holy Night

Flowers. Porter, D.

Flowers of the dead red sea. Thomas, E.

A **flutter** of lace. Majeski, B.

A **fly** in the ointment. Benfield, D.

Flyboy. Adrian, Y.

Flyer. Nelson, R.

Flyin' west. Cleage, P.

The **flying** doctor. Molière

Fo, Dario

Abducting Diana (Il ratto della Francesca); adapted by Stephen Stenning from a translation by Rupert Lowe. Oberon Bks. 1994 79p

Satirical farce. Kidnapped woman media boss proves more ruthless than her abductors. 2 acts 3 scenes 5m 2w 2 interiors

Accidental death of an anarchist; tr. by Ed Emery

Farce satirizing right-wing bureaucracy. Lunatic conman tricks police into reopening case of anarchist's death. 2 acts 5m 1w 1 interior

In Fo, D. Plays: one

Can't pay? Won't pay! tr. by Lino Pertile; adapted by Bill Colvill and Robert Walker

Variant title: We won't pay! We won't pay! Political farce set in working class suburb of Milan where house-

Fo, Dario—*Continued*
wives struggle with inflation and their communist trade unionist husbands. 2 acts 3m 2w 1 interior

In Fo, D. Plays: two

Elizabeth: almost by chance a woman; tr. by Gillian Hanna

Political farce offering radical interpretation of reign of Elizabeth I. 2 acts 4m 2w 1 setting

In Fo, D. Plays: two

Mistero buffo comic mysteries; tr. by Ed Emery

Series of episodes drawn on counterculture of Middle Ages, on apocryphal gospel stories, legends and tales. Variable cast

In Fo, D. Plays: one

One was nude and one wore tails; tr. by Ed Emery

Farce about old saying "clothes make the man." 1 act 5m 2w 1 exterior

In Fo, D. Plays: one

The open couple; written with Franca Rame; tr. by Joe Farrell

Exchange between husband and wife reveals woman's distaste for marital strictures. 1m 1w 1 interior

In Fo, D. Plays: two

An ordinary day; written with Franca Rame; tr. by Joe Farrell

Farce examines woman's insecurities in male-dominated society. 2m 1w extras 1 interior

In Fo, D. Plays: two

The Pope and the witch; tr. by Joan Holden. French 1997 109p

Farce about Catholicism and Vatican politics. 2 acts 5 scenes 7m 3w extras 3 interiors

The Pope and the witch (adaptation) See De la Tour, A. The Pope and the witch

Trumpets and raspberries; tr. by R. C. McAvoy and A. M. Giugni

Political satire set in Italy. Kidnapped automobile executive is unwittingly rescued by communist shop steward but is badly disfigured in process leading to hopeless confusion of identities. 2 acts 4 scenes 14m 2w 2 interiors

In Fo, D. Plays: one

The virtuous burglar; tr. by Joseph Farrell

Farce revolving around burglary, adultery and mistaken identity. 1 act 4m 3w 1 interior

In Fo, D. Plays: one

Fog

O'Neill, E. Fog

Folk drama

African American

Dodson, O. Bayou legend
Richardson, W. The chip woman's fortune

Austrian

Baum, T. Cold hands
Canetti, V. The Ogre
Jelinek, E. President Evening Breeze
Mitterer, F. No place for idiots
Preses, P. and Becher, U. Our Mr. Bockerer
Szyszkowitz, G. Friedmann Puntigam
Turrini, P. Swine
Unger, H. R. The bell tolls at twelve
Zauner, F. Ch. A handful of earth

Greek

Karagiozis baker

Irish

Synge, J. M. The playboy of the Western World

Spanish

García Lorca, F. Blood wedding
c Vigil, A. Los pastores. The shepherds

Folklore

c Gerke, P. Los mariachis Mexicanos: "The Brementown musicians"
c Jacob, E. The crowded house
c Peterson, M. N. The soup stone
y Poole-Carter, R. Mossy Cape
c Scanlan, M. Give and take
c Throckmorton, S. L. The forest bride

African

c Gerke, P. The adventures of Anansi: "How Anansi helped a fisherman"
c Gerke, P. The adventures of Anansi: "Why Anansi lives in ceilings"
c Gerke, P. Multicultural plays for children
c Kuharski, J. The leopard's noisy drum

African American

c McCullough, L. E. Patches solves a wedding riddle
y McCullough, L. E. When people could fly

American

c Gerke, P. The little red hen
c Kase-Polisini, J. Southern fried cracker tales
y Lerman, L. The Abolition Flyer
c McCaslin, N. Paul Bunyan: lumberjack
y McCullough, L. E. Annie Christmas and the Natchez Trace bandits
y McCullough, L. E. The flames of hell
y McCullough, L. E. Johnny Appleseed and Willie Crabgrass
c McCullough, L. E. Let's have a hoedown!
c McCullough, L. E. Magnus Fourpenny and the black bear birthday bash

Folklore—American—*Continued*
c McCullough, L. E. Mr. & Mrs. Charlie T. Mule
c McCullough, L. E. Return of the Red Phantom
c McCullough, L. E. Tillie Edelpickel's sack of lies
c Mercati, C. Bigger than life!
c Wheeler, J. and Hartsfield, M. G. Tall Betsy and the crackerbarrel tales
y Winther, B. John Henry
c Zeder, S. L. Wiley and the Hairy Man

Arabian

al-'Ani, Yusuf. The key
Farag, A. 'Ali Janah al-Tabrizi and his servant Quffa
c Mahlmann, L. and Jones, D. C. Ali Baba and the forty thieves

Chinese

Elitzig, F. Seagirl
c Gerke, P. Feng zhen-zhu: The wind pearl
c Gerke, P. The great bear
c Gerke, P. Ma Lien and the magic paintbrush
c Lee, C. K. Journey to the West
c McCaslin, N. The coins of Lin Foo
y McCullough, L. E. The seven Chan brothers of Paiute Pass

Colombian

c McCaslin, N. The lazy ones

Czech

c Gerke, P. Tri zlate vlasy Deda Vseveda: "The three golden hairs of Grandfather Know All"

Danish

c McCaslin, N. Borrowed trouble

Dutch

c McCaslin, N. Three meals a day
c McCullough, L. E. The cobbler's pipe

English

c Mahlmann, L. and Jones, D. C. The Gingerbread Boy
c Rowland, E. A baker's dozen

Finnish

c Gerke, P. No hölmöläiset: The silly villagers
c McCullough, L. E. The glass mountain

French

c Elfenbein, J. A. Puss-in-boots
c Gerke, P. Chat botté: Puss-in-boots
Gerke, P. Drakesbill

German

c Mahlmann, L. and Jones, D. C. The table, the donkey and the stick

Hispanic

c Vigil, A. Blanca flor. White flower
c Vigil, A. La estrella de oro. The gold star
c Vigil, A. Juan Oso. John the bear
c Vigil, A. The most interesting gift of all
c Vigil, A. El muchacho que mato al gigante. The boy who killed the giant
c Vigil, A. The three pieces of good advice

Indic

c Simon, S. The tiger and the Brahman
c Winther, B. The Maharajah is bored

Iranian

c McCaslin, N. Humai's secret

Irish

c Gerke, P. The long leather bag
c McCullough, L. E. The laziest girl in the world
Yeats, W. B. The Land of Heart's Desire

Italian

c Gerke, P. I dodici mesi: The twelve months
c Swortzell, L. The love of three oranges

Japanese

c Carlisle, B. The crane wife
Houston, V. H. The Matsuyama mirror
c Hughes, V. Strongman meets his match
Hwang, D. H. The sound of a voice

Jewish

Ansky, S. The dybbuk
c McCullough, L. E. Shlemazl goes to paradise

Maori

c Gerke, P. Mataora and Niwareka in the Underworld

Mexican

c Gerke, P. La culebra: "The snake"
c McCullough, L. E. The honest miller

Norwegian

c Gerke, P. East of the sun and west of the moon

Polish

c McCaslin, N. Who laughs last?

Russian

c Dixon, D. The Snow Witch
c Gerke, P. The firebird, the horse of power, and Czarevna Vasilisa
c Gerke, P. Vasilisa Prekrasnaia: "Vasilisa the beautiful"
McCaslin, N. Clever Marya and the Czar
c Palmer, G. The falcon

Folklore—*Continued*

Scottish

y Gollobin, L. B. Selkie

South American

c Turner, J. The white spider's gift

Swedish

c McCaslin, N. The bailiff's wonderful coat

Vietnamese

c McCullough, L. E. The beggar in the blanket

West African

Osofisan, F. Morountodun

The **follies** of Marianne. See Musset, A. de. The moods of Marianne

Follow the leader. Haylock, D.

Follows, Sonia. See Flower, M. jt. auth.

Fols, Craig

Buck Simple

Actress discovers her romantic leading man is gay. 2m 1w 1 interior

In The Best American short plays, 1994-1995

Fonda, Henry, 1905-1982

Cullen, A. Self catering

Fontaine, Robert

y Graduation address

Satire on high school graduation addresses and valedictorians. 3m 2w

In The Big book of skits; ed. by S. E. Kamerman

Food. Beber, N.

The **food** chain. Silver, N.

The **foolish** Coyote. Vigil, A.

Foon, Dennis

y War. Blizzard Pub. 1995 58p

Realistic exploration of gangs, street justice and aggressive behavior. 4m 1 setting

Football

Tasca, J. Gums

Williamson, D. The club

Foote, Horton

The chase

Tragedy. Honest, kind sheriff involved in pursuit of an escaped convict who had sworn to "get" him. 3 acts 9 scenes 8m 3w 2 interiors

In Foote, H. Collected plays v2

y The dancers

Television play. Teenage boy lacking self-confidence meets girl with similar handicap and together they attend first dance. 3m 7w

In Short plays for young actors; ed. by C. Slaight and J. Sharrar

Dividing the estate

Set in 1987 Texas. Family bickers over settlement of estate. 2 acts 4 scenes 4m 9w 1 interior

In Foote, H. 4 new plays

The habitation of dragons. Dramatists 1993 79p

Set in 1935-1936 Texas. Misfortunes befall Texas family. 2 acts 7 scenes 11m 5w settings

—Same

In Foote, H. 4 new plays

The land of the astronauts

Symbolic drama set in 1983 Texas town about suburban life and false idols. 9m 8w 1b extras 1 interior

In Foote, H. The tears of my sister; The Prisoner's Song; The one-armed man and The land of the astronauts

Laura Dennis. Dramatists 1996 49p

High school senior in 1938 small Texas town confronts truth about her family's sordid past as she contends with her burgeoning sexuality. 5m 8w 1 setting

Night seasons. Dramatists 1996 64p

Set in 1917-1963 Texas. Family saga moving back and forth in time focuses on domineering matriarch's disregard for daughter's prospects for happiness. 2 acts 7m 6w settings

—Same

In Foote, H. 4 new plays

The one-armed man

Symbolic drama set in Texas cotton gin in summer of 1928. Violence erupts when distraught employee who lost arm in accident confronts plant manager. 3m 1 interior

In Foote, H. The tears of my sister; The Prisoner's Song; The one-armed man and The land of the astronauts

The Prisoner's Song

Drama about class distinction in small Texas town ca.1927 focuses on problems of young unemployed ex-alcoholic husband. 2m 2w 1 interior

In Foote, H. The tears of my sister; The Prisoner's Song; The one-armed man and The land of the astronauts

The roads to home: A nightingale

Woman and her neighbor are visited by woman's girlhood acquaintance who is gradually slipping toward insanity. 1 act 1m 3w 1 interior

In Foote, H. Collected plays v2

The roads to home: Spring dance

Exchange of confidences among patients at sanatorium dance reveal their isolation and inability to cope with reality. 1 act 3m 1w 1 interior

In Foote, H. Collected plays v2

Foote, Horton—*Continued*

The roads to home: The dearest of friends

Husband and wife are unable to face implications of friends' marital problems. 1 act 2m 2w 1 interior

In Foote, H. Collected plays v2

Talking pictures. Dramatists 1996 65p

Portrayal of small town Texas in 1929. Single mother is about to lose job playing piano at town's only movie theater. 6m 5w 1 setting

—Same

In Foote, H. 4 new plays

The tears of my sister

Television play. Young woman feels obliged to marry older but wealthy man in order to help her family. 2m 4w

In Foote, H. The tears of my sister; The Prisoner's Song; The one-armed man and The land of the astronauts

Tomorrow. Rev. ed. Dramatists 1996 42p

Tragedy. Television play adapted from William Faulkner's short story about shooting in rural area of deep South. 15m 3w extras

The traveling lady

Wife and daughter, rejected by ex-convict husband, turn to widower. 3 acts 4 scenes 4m 5w 1g 1 exterior

In Foote, H. Collected plays v2

The trip to Bountiful

Aging widow living with son and selfish daughter-in-law, runs away to her former home. 3 acts 4 scenes 6m 3w extras 1 interior 2 exteriors

In Foote, H. Collected plays v2

In Foote, H. Horton Foote's three trips to Bountiful

The trip to Bountiful [television play]

Television version of play entered above. 7m 3w

In Foote, H. Horton Foote's three trips to Bountiful

The widow Claire

Part four of The orphans' home cycle. Man conceives futile passion for comely young widow at his boarding house. 8m 2w 1 setting

In Best American plays: 9th series, 1983-1992

The young man from Atlanta. Dutton 1995 110p

Set in 1950s Texas. Couple face only son's suicide and growing realization of his homosexual life style. 6 scenes 5m 4w 1 interior

The young man from Atlanta (condensation)

In The Best plays of 1994-1995

For black boys who have considered homicide when the streets were too much. Mason, K. A.

For England and King George. Faulkner, A.

For love or monkey. Sardou, V.

For reasons that remain unclear. Crowley, M.

For unborn children. Livingston, M. S.

For whom the Southern belle tolls. Durang, C.

Ford, Henry, 1863-1947

St. Germain, M. Camping with Henry & Tom

Ford, John

The broken heart

Jacobean tragedy in verse set at Spartan court. Orgilus, in love with Renthea, takes revenge on her ambitious brother Ithocles who forces her into unhappy marriage. Songs, music, dancing. Prologue 5 acts 18 scenes epilogue 13m 6w extras 1 setting

In Ford, J. 'Tis pity she's a whore and other plays

The lover's melancholy

Jacobean tragicomedy in verse. Prince's melancholy is dispelled by discovery that strange youth is really beautiful girl in disguise. Includes a masque. 5 acts 12 scenes 12m 4w extras 6 interiors

In Ford, J. 'Tis pity she's a whore and other plays

Perkin Warbeck

Jacobean historical tragedy in verse. Chronicle play about pretender to English throne during reign of Henry VII. Prologue 5 acts 18 scenes epilogue 24m 3w extras 7 interiors 6 exteriors 1 setting

In Ford, J. 'Tis pity she's a whore and other plays

'Tis pity she's a whore

Jacobean tragedy in verse set in Renaissance Italy. Disastrous consequences follow when young man's incestuous love for his sister is revealed. 5 acts 27 scenes 11m 4w extras

In Ford, J. 'Tis pity she's a whore and other plays

See also Fletcher, J. The fair maid of the inn

Ford, Kathleen

Time quest. Moorley's 1995 15p

Religious play. Angels learn about time and eternity. 5 scenes Variable cast

Fore! Gilroy, F. D.

A **foreboding.** Ricchi, R.

Foreign bodies. See Zark, J. A body of water: Foreign bodies

Foreign lands. Hope, K.

Foreman, Richard
Eddie goes to Poetry City (Part one: Seattle version)
Experimental play about language and theater. 2m 3w 1 setting
In Foreman, R. My head was a sledgehammer; six plays
Eddie goes to Poetry City (Part two: New York version)
Companion piece to title entered above. 3m 2w 1 setting
In Foreman, R. My head was a sledgehammer; six plays
I've got the shakes
Experimental play about elusiveness of reality. 1m 3w 1 setting
In Foreman, R. My head was a sledgehammer; six plays
The mind king
Experimental play about man's encounter with angel. 2m 1w 1 setting
In Foreman, R. My head was a sledgehammer; six plays
--Same
In Plays for the end of the century; ed. by B. Marranca
My head was a sledgehammer
Experimental theater piece. Professor and students ponder nature of reality. 2m 1w extras 1 setting
In Foreman, R. My head was a sledgehammer; six plays
Samuel's major problem
Experimental play about memory, death and language. 2m 1w 1 setting
In Foreman, R. My head was a sledgehammer; six plays

Forensic and the navigators. Shepard, S.

Foreplay. Ives, D.

The **forest** bride. Throckmorton, S. L.

The **former** one-on-one basketball champion. Horovitz, I.

Formula for romance. Mauro, R.

Fornes, Maria Irene
The conduct of life
Latin American lieutenant, obsessed with gaining power, intimidates wife and servants while torturing prisoners. 19 scenes 2m 3w 1 setting
In Telling tales: new one-act plays; ed. by E. Lane
The Danube
Produced under title: You can swim in the Danube—but the water is too cold. Experimental play set in Hungary. American's encounter with local girl is in the form of language lessons. 15 scenes 3m 1w 1 setting
In The Best of Off-Broadway; ed. by R. Wetzsteon
Enter the night
Two women who share great affection for each other and gay man whose lover died of AIDS dramatize different kinds of love and fantasy. 2 acts 2m 1w 1 interior
In Plays for the end of the century; ed. by B. Marranca
Springtime
Woman turns to life of crime to support lesbian lover. 1 act 14 scenes 1m 2w 1 setting
In Facing forward; ed. by L. D. Frank
What of the night?: Hunger
Experimental memory play. Ineffectual angel offers no solace to aging characters sinking into greater and greater poverty. 2 scenes 3m 2w 2 interiors
In Women on the verge: 7 avant-garde American plays; ed. by R. C. Lamont
What of the night?: Lust
Experimental drama. Driven, amoral businessmen. 12 scenes 4m 6w 1b 1 setting
In Women on the verge: 7 avant-garde American plays; ed. by R. C. Lamont
What of the night?: Nadine
Two mothers struggle to escape degrading existence in economically depressed Southwest. 3 scenes 3w 2m 1g 1 setting
In Women on the verge: 7 avant-garde American plays; ed. by R. C. Lamont
What of the night?: Springtime
Entered above under Springtime
In Women on the verge: 7 avant-garde American plays; ed. by R. C. Lamont

Fortinbras. Blessing, L.

Fortune. Bell, H.

Fortune and men's eyes. Herbert, J.

Fortune, my foe. Davies, R.

Fortune's fools. Stroppel, F.

Forty-four, Sycamore. Farrell, B.

The **Forty** Lounge Cafe. Lyssiotis, T.

Forty years on. Bennett, A.

Fosca. Tarchetti, I. U. (dramatization) See Sondheim, S. Passion

Fossey, Dian
Schevill, J. Shadows of memory: Ape-God

Fossils! Aston, M.

Foster, Andrew
Chemical reactions
Two small-time hoods discover their trip to dump means burying man alive. 3m 1 exterior
In 20/20: twenty one-act plays from twenty years of the Humana Festival

Foster, James
Play to win; book by James de Jongh and Carles Cleveland; lyrics by James Foster, Jr., James de Jongh and Carles Cleveland; music by James Foster, Jr. French 1993 94p
Musical about how Jackie Robinson broke color barrier in professional baseball. Prologue 5 scenes 4m 1w 1 setting

Foster, Norm
The affections of May
Romantic comedy. City woman, deserted by husband in small town, copes with local men vying for her affections. 2 acts 5 scenes 3m 1w 1 interior
In Foster, N. The motor trade & The affections of May

The motor trade
Comedy about car salesman with disgruntled partner, tax problems and adulterous wife. 2 acts 3 scenes 2m 2w 1 interior
In Foster, N. The motor trade & The affections of May

Wrong for each other. Playwrights Canada 1992 112p
Comedy set in restaurant. Seeing each other for first time in four years, couple recalls ups and downs of their relationship and marriage. 2 acts 3 scenes 1m 1w 1 interior

Foster children
y Allard, J. Painted rain
y Harris, A. The pinballs
c Zeder, S. L. Mother Hicks

Found a peanut. Margulies, D.

Foundlings
Moore, E. The foundling

Four baboons adoring the sun. Guare, J.

Four dogs and a bone. Shanley, J. P.

Four-H Club. Shepard, S.

Fourteen hundred thousand. Shepard, S.

The **fourth** wall. Gurney, A. R.

Foxton, David
Caught on the hop. French (London) 1993 25p
Farce set in Paris 1890-1900. Misunderstandings ensue when philandering husband finds wife in compromising situation. 2m 3w 1 interior

Kenneth. New Playwrights Network 1993 19p
At Christmas, friends, neighbors, and teachers recall plight of poor abused boy. Variable cast 23 characters

c The real story of Puss in boots. French (London) 1997 61p
Comedy merging plots of Perrault's Puss in boots with Cinderella. 3 acts 10 scenes Variable cast 10 characters

France
Sade, Marquis de. Jeanne Laisné

Aristocracy

See Aristocracy—France

History—House of Valois, 1328-1589

Barnes, P. The spirit of man: A hand witch of the second stage
Chapman, G. The revenge of Bussy d'Ambois
Warner, F. King Francis I

History—Louis XIII, 1610-1643

Hall, W. The three musketeers

History—Revolution, 1789-1794

Barnes, P. Revolutionary witness
Büchner, G. Danton's death
Francis, M. A tale of two cities
Goethe, J. W. von. The natural daughter
Griffiths, T. Hope in the year two
Griffiths, T. Who shall be happy . . . ?
y Hackett, W. A tale of two cities
Johanson, R. A tale of two cities
y Leech, M. T. The Scarlet Pimpernel
Schnitzler, A. The Green Cockatoo

History—18th century

Sade, Marquis de. Truth and treason

History—19th century

Eleder, M. V. The Count of Monte Cristo

Race relations

Tilly. A modest proposal

Social life and customs—Bourbons, 1589-1789

Fletcher, J. The honest man's fortune
Fletcher, J. The lover's progress
Graffigny, F. D. D. de. Cenia
c McCullough, L. E. Bring a torch, Jeannette, Isabella
Molière. The hypochondriac
Molière. The imaginary invalid
Molière. The misanthrope
Molière. The miser
y Nolan, P. T. The school for wives
Rostand, E. Cyrano de Bergerac
Sade, Marquis de. The shyster

Social life and customs—1789-1900

Dias, E. J. The necklace
Musset, A. de. Caprice
Musset, A. de. Don't play with love
Musset, A. de. You can't think of everything

France. Saunders, J.

Francis I, King of France
Hugo, V. The king amuses himself
Warner, F. King Francis I

Francis, Matthew
Jane Austen's Northanger Abbey. French (London) 1997 90p

Dramatization of Austen's satirical romantic mystery about feminine self-delusion. Portray's heroine Catherine Morland's fantasy world alongside the real one. Prologue 2 acts 61 scenes 8m 8w extras settings

The prisoner of Zenda. French (London) 1994 84p

Dramatization of Anthony Hope's swashbuckling adventure novel set in imaginary Kingdom of Ruritania. English gallant takes place of crown prince and helps restore crown. 2 acts 22 scenes 11m 2w settings

A tale of two cities. French (London) 1996 95p

Dramatization of Dickens' epic novel of the French Revolution. 2 acts 34 scenes 13m 6w extras

Franco, Cris [et al.]
The LA LA Awards

Satirical look at Latinos in the entertainment industry. 2m 2w extras 1 setting

In Latins anonymous: two plays

Francoeur, Bill
y Coney Island of Dr. Moreau; a musical comedy spoof in two acts—with apologies to H. G. Wells; book by Tim Kelly; music & lyrics by Bill Francoeur. Pioneer Drama Service 1996 64p

Scientist turns animals into humans on jungle island. 2 acts 4 scenes Large mixed cast 1 exterior

c The enchantment of Beauty and the beast; adapted and dramatized from the classic fables of Giovani Francesco Straparola and Madame Laprince de Beaumont. Book by Vera Morris; music & lyrics by Bill Francoeur. Pioneer Drama Service 1993 65p

Musical adaptation of classic fable. Enchanted beast is transformed into prince through love of beautiful woman. Prologue 2 acts 9 scenes 6m 10w extras 1 setting

y Gone with the breeze; book by Tim Kelly; music & lyrics by Bill Francoeur. Pioneer Drama Service 1994 63p

Musical comedy. Complications arise as studio prepares to film best-selling novel. 2 acts 11 scenes Large mixed cast

y Hee haw hayride; book by Tim Kelly; music & lyrics by Bill Francoeur. Pioneer Drama Service 1993 69p

Musical comedy about hillbilly feud. 2 acts 14 scenes Large mixed cast 1 setting

y The internal teen machine; book by Tim Kelly; music & lyrics by Bill Francoeur. Pioneer Drama Service 1993 57p

Musical comedy about boy's high school experience. 2 acts 11 scenes Variable cast 23 characters extras

y Kilroy was here! Book by Tim Kelly; music & lyrics by Bill Francoeur. Pioneer Drama Service 1995 64p

Musical set in 1942 Brooklyn. Spy exposed in U.S.O. club. 2 acts 10 scenes 11m 19w extras 1 interior

c A little princess; the musical adapted from Frances Hodgson Burnett's "Sara Crewe"; book by Tim Kelly; music & lyrics by Bill Francoeur. Pioneer Drama Service 1996 63p

Girl in Victorian London boarding school is rescued from poverty by mysterious benefactor. Prologue 2 acts 6 scenes 5m 4w 7g extras 2 interiors

c Oz! a musical based on the story by L. Frank Baum; book by Tim Kelly; music and lyrics by Bill Francoeur. Pioneer Drama Service 1995 59p

Musical dramatization of The Wizard of Oz. 2 acts 9 scenes 4m 4w extras 2 interiors 5 exteriors

c The secret garden; adapted from the novel by Frances Hodgson Burnett; book by Tim Kelly; music & lyrics by Bill Francoeur. Pioneer Drama Service 1994 53p

Musical set in Victorian England. Orphaned girl and invalid cousin are restored to happiness and health as they tend secret garden. 2 acts 16 scenes 5m 11w 1b 1g extras 1 setting

y Shakespeare comes to Calamity Creek; or, "Curtain call in the corral"; a Wild West, speechifying, sagebrush musical comedy in two acts; book by Tim Kelly; music & lyrics by Bill Francoeur. Pioneer Drama Service 1997 61p

Shakespearean theater company plays mining town in Arizona Territory. 2 acts 5 scenes Variable cast 30 characters extras

Snow White and the seven dwarfs; the musical; book by Tim Kelly; music & lyrics by Bill Francoeur. Pioneer Drama Service 1994 46p

Musical dramatization of Brothers Grimm fairy tale about jealous queen's stepdaughter and the dwarfs who befriend her. 2 acts 8 scenes 9m 5w 1 setting

y Wrangler Ranch; book by Tim Kelly; music & lyrics by Bill Francoeur. Pioneer Drama Service 1995 63p

Musical spoof of westerns. Students in Arizona high school plot to cheat student out of inheritance. 2 acts 8 scenes 9m 18w extras 1 setting

Frandsen, Erick [et al.]
Song of Singapore; book by Allan Katz [et al.]; music and lyrics by Erick Frandsen [et al.]. French 1993 95p

Frandsen, Erick [et al.]—*Continued*
Cabaret recreation of seedy waterfront bar in 1941 Singapore. Music, singing. 2 acts 8m 2w 1 interior

Frank, Anne
y Kops, B. Dreams of Anne Frank

Frank Dell's The temptation of St. Antony. The Wooster Group

Frankel, Robert
y The Decade Club. Pioneer Drama Service 1996 55p
Romantic comedy. High school classmates hold reunion every ten years. Background music. Prologue 2 acts 4 scenes epilogue 6m 5w extras 1 interior 1 exterior

Frankenstein. Shelley, M. W. (dramatization) See Carmichael, F. Frankenstein 1930; Peake, R. B. Presumption

Frankenstein in love. Barker, C.

Frankenstein unbound. Allman, S. and Pickett, B.

Frankie and Johnny in the Clair de Lune. McNally, T.

Franklin, Benjamin
c Mayr, G. A. The printer on Queen Street

Franklin, J. E.
Christchild
Drama about struggles of black family in Texas during the Great Depression. 8 scenes 2m 3w 1b 1g 1 interior 1 exterior
In Women playwrights: the best plays of 1993

Miss Honey's young'uns
Revised version of play first produced 1966 with title: The Mau Mau room. Drama set in 1960s South about undergraduate's spiritual struggle with racially charged atmosphere surrounding university desegregation. 7 scenes 4m 6w 1 interior
In Black drama in America: an anthology; ed. by D. T. Turner

Two mens'es daughter
African American woman raised by black stepfather reacts to death of white father. 2w 1 interior
In The Best American short plays, 1994-1995

Franks, Alan
The mother tongue. French (London) 1993 83p
Snobbish woman, forced out of home by fire, moves to working-class London neighborhood to live with daughter and grandson. 2 acts 3m 4w 1 interior

Frank's feathered friend. Waterhouse, J. and Leach, P.

Fraser, Brad
Poor Super Man. NeWest Press 1995 181p (Prairie play series 14)
Play about moral and sexual ambiguity. Romance between gay painter and straight, married man. 2 acts 2m 3w settings

y Prom night of the living dead
Musical comedy. Zombies attend high school prom. Large mixed cast settings
In Fraser, B. The wolf plays

The ugly man. NeWest Press 1993 158p (Prairie play series 13)
Pop culture exploration of lust and violence loosely based on Middleton and Rowley's The changeling. Femme fatale enlists hired man in plot to murder fiance. 45 scenes 4m 3w 1 setting

Wolfboy
Relationship between two troubled young men in psychiatric hospital ends in violence. 3m 3w 1 setting
In Fraser, B. The wolf plays

Fratricide
Fletcher, J. and Massinger, P. Rollo, Duke of Normandy

Fraud
Poliakoff, S. Blinded by the sun

Frayn, Michael
Here. French 1994 128p
Drama about responsibility and decision-making. Two people move into empty room and begin to construct life together. 2 acts 5 scenes 1m 2w 1 interior
—Same. Methuen 1993 138p (Methuen modern plays)

Now you know. French (London) 1996 88p
Everyone has something to hide in comedy based on author's novel about London freedom-of-information pressure group. 2 acts 4 scenes 4m 4w 1 interior

Fred Menchacha and Filemón. Gaytán, J. G.

Free gift. Horovitz, I.

Free will & wanton lust. Silver, N.

The **free** zone. Grumberg, J.-C.

Freed, Donald
Inquest
Espionage trial of Julius and Ethel Rosenberg. Prologue 2 acts 15m 4w 1 interior
In Voicings: ten plays from the documentary theatre; ed. by A. Favorini

Freedom days. Friedman, S.

Freedom! Freedom! Gregor, H.

Freedom is my middle name. Hunkins, L.

Freedom train. Sodaro, C.

Freefall. Smith, C.

Freeman, Brian; Branner, Djola, and Gupton, Eric

Fierce love

Scenes about gay African American men. Variable cast

In Colored contradictions: an anthology of contemporary African-American plays; ed. by H. J. Elam, Jr. and R. Alexander

Freeman, Dave

Kindly keep it covered. French (London) 1997 74p

Farce set in English health spa. 2 acts 4m 3w 1 interior

Freeman, David, 1945-

Creeps

Drama set in men's washroom of workshop for cerebral palsy victims. 1 act 9m 1w 1 interior

In Modern Canadian plays v1; ed. by J. Wasserman

French, David

Leaving home

Tragedy. Working class Toronto home rocked by father's conflict with his two teenaged sons. 2 acts 4m 3w 1 setting

In Modern Canadian plays v1; ed. by J. Wasserman

Silver dagger. Talonbooks 1993 134p

Thriller. Adultery, blackmail, and murder engulf mystery writer. 2 acts 4 scenes 3m 3w 1 interior

French

England

y Olfson, L. Monsieur Beaucaire

French Canadians

Fennario, D. Balconville

French drama

Medieval

The Washtub

17th century

Bernard, C. Laodamia, Queen of Epirus
Desjardins, M.-C. The favorite minister
La Roche-Guilhen, A. de All-wondrous
Molière. Amphitryon
Molière. The flying doctor
Molière. The hypochondriac
Molière. The imaginary cuckold
Molière. The imaginary invalid
Molière. The misanthrope
Molière. The miser
Pascal, F. The lunatic lover
Racine, J. Phædra

18th century

Graffigny, F. D. D. de Cenia
LeSage, A. R. Turcaret
Marivaux. La dispute
Marivaux. The triumph of love
Labiche, E. Eating crow

French language

Study and teaching

Rattigan, T. French without tears

French without tears. Rattigan, T.

Freud, Sigmund

Johnson, T. Hysteria
Morrissey, K. Dora: a case of hysteria

Freud's house. Klavan, L.

Frida: the story of Frida Kahlo. Blecher, H.; Cruz, M. and Rodriguez, R. X.

Freidemann Puntigam. Szyszkowitz, G.

Friedman, Roy

All for art. French 1993 35p

Comedy. Poet and actress wife are investigated by IRS for claiming outrageous tax deductions. 2m 1w 1 interior

Friedman, Steve

Freedom days. Bakers Plays 1993 43p

Four individuals involved in African American civil rights movement recall their experiences. Singing. 2m 2w 1 setting

Friel, Brian

Molly Sweeney. Dramatists 1996 57p

Middle-aged woman, blind since infancy, undergoes operation to restore sight. 2 acts 2m 1w

—Same. Gallery Bks. 1994 67p
—Same. Penguin Bks. 1995 70p

Molly Sweeney (condensation)

In The Best plays of 1995-1996

A month in the country. Dramatists 1993 105p

Adaptation of Turgenev's play about life on 19th century Russian estate. Music. 2 acts 5 scenes 7m 5w 1 setting

Wonderful Tennessee. Faber & Faber 1993 79p

Symbolic drama about religious, social and moral plight of three middle-class couples on stalled birthday outing in County Donegal, Ireland. 2 acts 3 scenes 3m 3w 1 exterior

—Same. French 1993 110p
—Same. Gallery Bks. 1993 93p

Friendly affair. Booth, J.

Friends. Bentley-Fisher, T.

Friendship

Barry, L. The good times are killing me
c Bentley-Fisher, T. Friends

Friendship—*Continued*
Butterfield, C. Joined at the head
Butterfield, C. Snowing at Delphi
Connolly, H. Snakes and ladders
Cooke, C. Threat
Cooper, J. B. Picnic time
y Curran, KT. The First Time Club
Dean, P. H. Dink's blues
Dietz, S. Lonely planet
Dover, M. and Jarvis, G. Seconds
Dunn, M. Five tellers dancing in the rain
Ellison, K. The Harry and Sam dialogues
Foote, H. The roads to home: A nightingale
Gaminara, W. According to Hoyle
Gilroy, F. D. A way with words
Gray, S. The common pursuit
Gray, S. Two Sundays
y Harris, A. The pinballs
Harvey, J. Boom bang-a-bang
c James, J. The echo box
c James, J. Moving day
c James, J. Willa and Sam
c Jones, T. Scarecrows
Lazarus, J. Schoolyard games
Lewis, I. Chinese coffee
MacLaughlin, W. Watermelon boats
c Martini, C. Swimmers
Mazza, R. N. Parked
Meara, A. After-play
Medley, C. Dearborn Heights
Nishikawa, L. and Talmadge, V. The gate of heaven
O'Malley, M. Three years from "thirty"
Oliensis, A. Ring of men
Paterson, D. L. Pieces of the sky
Pintauro, J. Frozen dog
Pinter, H. Old times
Puig, M. Kiss of the spider woman
Rivera, J. Slaughter in the lake
c Saba, J. A tree with arms
Sartin, L. Catfish moon
Shepard, S. The mad dog blues
y Slaight, B. Sightings
Taylor, R. Between the lines
y Tobin, S. Cotton girls
Vago, S. M. Connie & Sabrina in waiting
Weitz, P. All for one
Weller, M. Abroad (Split, Part 2)
Whitemore, H. The best of friends
Williamson, D. A handful of friends
c York, Y. Afternoon of the elves

Frisby, Terence
Rough justice. French (London) 1995 60p
Courtroom drama. British television commentator admits responsibility but pleads manslaughter when charged with murder of his severely handicapped child. 2 acts 5m 3w 2 interiors

Fritzen, Gary. See Collette, P. jt. auth.

Frockt, Deborah Lynn
Hard-boiled
Sexist views of young lawyer on female lawyer's job success. 2m 1w 1 interior
In Actors Theatre of Louisville. Ten-minute plays: v3

The **Frog** Prince. Mahlmann, L. and Jones, D. C.

Froggie woggies. Jones, T.

Frogs. Aristophanes

From morning to midnight. Kaiser, G.

From sleep and shadow. See Barnes, P. The spirit of man: From sleep and shadow

From the life of the bog people. Kral, B.

Fronteras Americanas (American borders). Verdecchia, G.

Frontier and pioneer life
Kentucky
Schenkkan, R. The courtship of Morning Star
Schenkkan, R. The homecoming
Schenkkan, R. Masters of the trade
Schenkkan, R. Ties that bind
Nebraska
Jones, C. My Antonia
West (U.S.)
Cleage, P. Flyin' west
c Cole, J. D. Conestoga stories
c McCullough, L. E. The little old sod shanty
Newman, M. and Damashek, B. Quilters
Parris-Bailey, L. Dark cowgirls and prairie queens
Way, C. Dead man's hat

Frost, Richard; Olson, Greg, and Johnson, Lyle
y No means no!
Drama examines the effect of date rape on teenagers. Background music. 9 scenes 5m 4w extras
In Eureka! ed. by J. J. Lewis and D. Warren

Frost, Robert
The guardeen
Graduate student comes to guard cider supply from lumberjacks. 5 scenes 7m 1w extras 1 interior 1 exterior
In Frost, R. Collected poems, prose & plays

Frost, Robert—*Continued*

In an art factory

Discontented sculptor's views on his work and the art world. 1m 1w 1 interior

In Frost, R. Collected poems, prose & plays

A way out

Old hermit living in secluded farm house outwits menacing stranger. 2m extras 1 interior

In Frost, R. Collected poems, prose & plays

Frozen dog. Pintauro, J.

Fry, Michael

Tess of the d'Urbervilles. French (London) 1997 83p

Dramatization of Hardy's novel set in 19th century England about young woman driven by circumstances to murder her seducer. 2 acts 3m 4w extras 1 setting

Fuentes, Carlos

Orchids in the moonlight

Various aspects of Mexican national character explored in play about actresses Dolores Del Rio and Maria Felix. 1 act 1m 2w extras 1 interior

In Latin American plays; ed. by S. Doggart

Fuerstenberg, Anna

y Blind dates

Vignettes show young adults dealing with their fears of life after high school. 33 scenes Variable cast 1 setting

In Wanna play?

Fugard, Athol

A place with the pigs

Drama based on story of Pavel Ivanovich Narrotsky, deserter from Soviet army who spent 41 years of his exile in pigsty. 4 scenes 1m 1w 1 setting

In Fugard, A. Playland and A place with the pigs

Playland. Faber & Faber 1993 46p

Drama set New Year's Eve 1989 at traveling amusement park on outskirts of Karoo town in South Africa. Symbolic encounter between young white returnee from the Border and black night watchman. 5 scenes 2m extra 1 setting

—Same. French 1994 63p

—Same

In Fugard, A. Playland and A place with the pigs

Statements after an arrest under the immorality act

Drama depicting how two lives are shattered by South Africa's miscegenation laws. 2m 1w 1 setting

In Telling tales: new one-act plays; ed. by E. Lane

Valley song. French 1997 57p

Effects of political change in present-day South Africa as witnessed by colored tenant-farmer and his ambitious teenaged granddaughter. Written for three characters and 2 performers. 1m 1w

—Same. Theatre Communications Group 1996 60p

Valley song (condensation)

In The Best plays of 1995-1996

Fugue. Munro, R.

Fugitives from justice

O'Neill, E. The web

Fulford, Robin

Lovesong

Monologue by murderer. 1m 1 setting

In Solo; ed. by J. Sherman

Full gallop. Hampton, M. and Wilson, M. L.

Fuller, Charles

A soldier's play

Racial tensions surface as murder investigation is conducted in Southern army camp during World War II. Music, singing. 2 acts 12m 1 setting

In Black drama in America: an anthology; ed. by D. T. Turner

In Black theatre USA [v1]; ed. by J. V. Hatch and T. Shine

In Classic plays from the Negro Ensemble Company; ed. by P. C. Harrison and G. Edwards

Fuller, Elizabeth L.

Me and Jezebel. Dramatists 1995 48p

Based on visit from screen legend Bette Davis to Fuller's Connecticut home in 1985. 2 acts 2w 1 interior

Fun. Korder, H.

Fun house. Bogosian, E.

Funeral parlor. Durang, C.

Funeral rites and ceremonies

Hatcher, J. Three viewings

Miller, J. A light on the landing

Nelson, R. New England

Simon, M. Walking to Waldheim

Strijards, F. The Stendhal syndrome

Stroppel, F. A good man

White, P. The ham funeral

Funerals and circuses. Bennett, R.

Funny money. Cooney, R.

A **funny** thing happened on the way to the wedding. Plautus, T. M.

Funnyhouse of a Negro. Kennedy, A.

Fur hat. Pintauro, J.

Furious. Gow, M.

Furse, John
The old rust bucket. New Playwrights Network 1996 91p
Farce. Sisters stowaway on tramp steamer with oddball crew. 2 acts 4 scenes epilogue 4m 3w 1 interior

Furth, George. See Sondheim, S. Company

Furtwängler, Wilhelm
Harwood, R. Taking sides

Fuson, Deni
y Clippings. French 1997 54p
High school students explore issues of sexual harassment, parental abuse, abortion, teen pregnancy, suicide, drugs, homosexuality, and guilt. Mime. 1 act Variable cast 9 characters extras 1 interior

Future, Plays of the
y Garver, J. The numbers game
Noonan, J. F. The drowning of Manhattan
Overmyer, E. Native speech
Overmyer, E. On the verge
Potter, D. Cold Lazarus

Futures. Blackwood, G. L.

Fyffe, Laurie
The sand
Monologue. Wife of business executive learns to belly-dance. 1w
In Escape acts; ed. by C. Curran

G

Gaines-Shelton, Ruth Ada
The church fight
Satire. Black church group wants to dismiss parson but cannot find good excuse. 1 act 4m 6w 1 interior
In Black theatre USA [v1]; ed. by J. V. Hatch and T. Shine

Gala, Antonio
The Bells of Orleans (Los buenos días perdidós); tr. by Edward W. Borsoi. Estreno 1993 60p (Estreno contemporary Spanish plays 4)
Fable about characters caught in changing and uncaring world. Stranger's promises forever alter household living in abandoned chapel. 2 acts 4 scenes 1m 3w extras 1 interior

Galilei, Galileo
Spoor, K. Everything under the sun

Gallagher, Mary
Bedtime
Explores childhood fears and bond between two young sisters. 2g 1 interior
In Plays for actresses; ed. by E. Lane and N. Shengold

y Windshook
Family's desire to use daughter's beauty to secure them higher social standing leads to jealousy, betrayal and rage. 4m 3w 1 setting
In New plays from A.C.T.'S young conservatory [v1]

Gallaire, Fatima
You have come back
Drama set in Algeria. Woman, returning home after studying abroad, is accused of betraying Islam. Music, singing, dancing. Prologue 2 acts Variable cast 16 characters 1 exterior
In Plays by women: an international anthology bk3; ed. by N. Shange

Gallaire-Bourega, Fatima. See Gallaire, Fatima

Gallanar, Ian
c Showdown at the 3-R Ranch. Pioneer Drama Service 1996 31p
Two educational comedies about reducing, reusing, and recycling. Grades k–3 version has 3m 1w, grades 4–6 version has 4m 1w

The **gallant** Cassian. See Schnitzler, A. Marionettes: The gallant Cassian

Gallathea. Lyly, J.

Gambaro, Griselda
Bad blood (La malasangre); tr. from the Spanish by Marguerite Feitlowitz. Dramatic 1994 69p
Irony, black comedy and Grand Guignol utilized in portrayal of tyranny in 1840s Argentina. 1 act 8 scenes 4m 2w 2 interiors

Saying yes
Black comedy set in hairdressing salon about man's inhumanity to man. 2m 1 interior
In Latin American plays; ed. by S. Doggart

The **gamblers.** Smith, V.

Gambling
Graham, B. The Champagne Charlie Stakes
Moore, E. The gamester
Smith, V. The gamblers

A **game** of inches. Griffiths, L.

Game of patience. Farhoud, A.

The **game** of speculation. Lewes, G. H.

Games
Ayckbourn, A. Wildest dreams
Gurney, A. R. The problem
Klíma, I. Games
c Younghusband, C. Only a game

The **gamester**. Moore, E.

Gaminara, William
According to Hoyle. Hern Bks. 1996 90p
Poker game exposes fissures in friendships among five men. 2 acts 5m 1 interior

Gangs
Aoki, B. W. The Queen's garden
Berkoff, S. West
y Foon, D. War
y Jackson, K. Street story
Upton, J. Ashes and sand
Willmott, K. and Averill, R. T-Money & Wolf

The **gang's** all here. Lawrence, J. and Lee, R. E.

Gans, Sharon, and Charney, Jordon
A Chekhov concert. French 1993 62p
Theatrical piece blending scenes from Chekhov's The sea gull, Uncle Vanya, Three sisters, and The cherry orchard. 2 acts 1m 1w 1 setting

Ganz, Lowell. See Marshall, G. jt. auth.

The **gap**. Broinowski, A.

The **garbage** cantata. Keating, B.

García Lorca, Federico
Blood wedding (Bodas de sangre); tr. by Brendan Kennelly. Bloodaxe Bks. 1996 80p
Symbolic tragic folk drama. Marriage of unwilling bride brings death to both bridegroom and former suitor. 3 acts 7 scenes 3m 7w extras 5 interiors 2 exteriors
—Same. tr. by Michael Dewell and Carmen Zapata
In García Lorca, F. Three plays
—Same; tr. by Langston Hughes
In Garcia Lorca, F. Blood wedding and Yerma
The house of Bernarda Alba; tr. by Michael Sewell and Carmen Zapata
Tragedy. Realistic portrayal of sexual repression among women in villages of rural Spain. 3 acts 8m 12w extras 1 interior 1 exterior
In García Lorca, F. Three plays
Yerma; tr. by Michael Dewell and Carmen Zapata
Tragedy in verse. Woman murders husband who she blames for their childlessness. 3 acts 6 scenes 6m 17w 1b 2 interiors 3 exteriors
In García Lorca, F. Three plays
—Same; tr. by W. S. Merwin
In Garcia Lorca, F. Blood wedding and Yerma

The **garden** of granddaughters. Sewell, S.

The **garden** party. Havel, V.

Gardening
Oakes, M. and Wells, J. Greenfield blooms
c Pflomm, P. N. Gracie's garden

Gardiner, Dennis
Weeds in the wheat. New Playwrights Network 1995 44p
Police investigate murder of crippled man's adulterous wife. 3 acts 5 scenes 4m 3w 1 interior

Gardner, Herb
Conversations with my father. French 1994 160p
Drama set in Lower East Side bar about father-son relationships and the assimilation of New York Jews into American culture. 2 acts 8 scenes 9m 2w 2b 1 interior
—Same. Pantheon Bks. 1994 155p
—Same
In Fruitful and multiplying; ed. by E. Schiff
I'm not Rappaport
Comedy about relationship between two octogenarians, one a lifelong radical, the other, a black apartment super. Both men are fighting attempts to put them out to pasture. 2 acts 4 scenes 4m 3w 1 exterior
In Best American plays: 9th series, 1983–1992

Garner, Julian
The flight into Egypt. Hern Bks. in association with Hampstead Theatre 1996 47p (Instant playscript)
Drama about personal bravery and redemptive power of art set in Poland 1939–1946. Cracow caretaker provides refuge for young Jewish woman artist at great personal risk. 2 acts 12 scenes 4m 3w 2 interiors

Garnhum, Ken
Beuys buoys boys
Monologue about homosexual German artist Joseph Beuys. 1m 1 setting
In Making, out; ed. by R. Wallace
Surrounded by water
Performance piece about creative process. 1m 1 setting
In Solo; ed. by J. Sherman

Garrett-Groag, Lillian
The ladies of the camellias. Dramatists 1996 84p
Farce set in Paris, 1879. Imagined meeting between Eleonora Duse and Sarah Bernhardt. 2 acts 7m 3w 1 interior
The White Rose. Dramatists 1993 71p
Drama based on true story set in Munich, 1942–1943. Group of university students imprisoned for disseminating anti-Nazi leaflets. 7m 1w 1 setting

Garro, Elena
The tree
Symbolic drama incorporating elements of magic realism. Death and guilt define relationship between two women in Mexico City. 2w 1 interior
In The Fickle finger of Lady Death and other plays

Garver, Juliet
y The numbers game
Man and woman rebel against future society which believes in statistics not love. 1m 1w extra 1 interior
In The Big book of skits; ed. by S. E. Kamerman

Gary's house. Oswald, D.

Gas I. Kaiser, G.

Gas II. Kaiser, G.

Gas stations. See Service stations

Gasbarra, Felix. See Piscator, E. jt. auth.

Gasping. Elton, B.

Gass, Ken
Claudius. Playwrights Canada 1995 121p
Comedy of political intrigue. Explores relationship between Hamlet's mother Gertrude and his new stepfather Claudius. 25 scenes 6m 4w 1 setting

The **gate** of heaven. Nishikawa, L. and Talmadge, V.

The **gathering** place. Kovacevic, D.

El **gato** sin amigos—The cat who had no friends. Rosenberg, J.

Gay, John
Beggar's opera. Players Press 1994 60p
Ballad opera. Rogue's comedy satirizing corrupt politics in 18th century England. Singing, music. 3 acts 45 scenes 14m 12w extras 5 interiors

The **gay** detective. Stembridge, G.

The **gay** divorcee. Fischer, M.

Gaytán, José G.
c Fred Menchacha and Filemón
Monologue about Mexican traveller and his mule. Singing. 1m
In ¡Aplauso! Hispanic children's theater; ed. by J. Rosenberg

GeBauer, Judy
The nip and the bite
Corruption in Mexican border town. 9 scenes 3m 2w 1b
In Facing forward; ed. by L. D. Frank

Gee, Shirley
Never in my lifetime. French 1993 86p
Drama set in Belfast. Young Catholic girl and British soldier fall in love. 2m 4w 1 setting

Geeks do come from outer space. Ullom, S.

Gelbart, Larry
Mastergate
Satire about assault on language that occurs during congressional hearing into government scandal. 10m 2w extras 1 interior
In Gelbart, L. Mastergate and Power failure

Power failure
Satirical scenes depicting corruption in contemporary American society. 10 scenes 4m 3w 1 setting
In Gelbart, L. Mastergate and Power failure

Gélinas, Gratien
The passion of Narcisse Mondoux; tr. by Linda Gaboriau. Anansi 1992 85p
Drama set in Quebec village. Man wins widower's love by agreeing to support her mayoral bid. Prologue 2 acts 15 scenes 1m 1w 1 setting

Gems, Pam
Deborah's daughter. Hern Bks. 1995 79p
First produced as radio play. Drama about role of multinational corporations in developing world and relationship between mothers and daughters. Westerners caught up in Third World coup. 2 acts 8 scenes 4m 3w extras 4 exteriors 1 interior

Stanley. Hern Bks. 1996 88p
Scenes from life of Stanley Spencer focus on English painter's relationship with his long-suffering wife. 2 acts 23 scenes 5m 6w 1 setting

See also Chekhov, A. The seagull

The **general** from America. Nelson, R.

Generation gap. See Conflict of generation

Generations apart. Gordon, P.

Gentileschi, Artemisia
Clark, S. Life without instruction

Geoghan, Jim
Light sensitive. French 1993 86p
Dramatic comedy set in New York's Hell's Kitchen. Blind alcoholic, wallowing in self-pity, falls in love with handicapped volunteer reader. 2 acts 2m 1w 1 interior

George III, King of England
Dear, N. In the ruins

George, Madeleine
The most massive woman wins
Black comedy set in waiting room of liposuction clinic. 4w 1 interior
In Plays for actresses; ed. by E. Lane and N. Shengold

George Barnwell. See Lillo, G. The London merchant

George Washington Carver. Hark, M. and McQueen, N.

George Washington crossing the Delaware. Koch, K.

Gerke, Pamela

c The adventures of Anansi: "How Anansi helped a fisherman"

Based on West African folktale. Fisherman tricks lazy spider into doing all his work. Variable cast 1 exterior

In Gerke, P. Multicultural plays for children v1

c The adventures of Anansi: "How the world got wisdom"

Based on West African folktale. Spider tries to keep Sky God's gift of wisdom for himself. Variable cast 1 exterior

In Gerke, P. Multicultural plays for children v1

c The adventures of Anansi: "Why Anansi lives in ceilings"

Based on West African folktale. Spider tricks leopard who wants to eat him. Unidentified cast 3 characters 1 exterior

In Gerke, P. Multicultural plays for children v1

c Chat botté: Puss-in-boots

Based on Charles Perrault's fairy tale. Talking cat outwits ogre. 5 scenes Variable cast

In Gerke, P. Multicultural plays for children v2

c La culebra: "The snake"

Based on Aztec folktale from Mexico. Coyote outsmarts snake who wants to eat farmer. Variable cast

In Gerke, P. Multicultural plays for children v2

c Da-hoos-whee'-whee: The seal-hunting brothers

Based on legend of the Lushootseed Salish people of the Puget Sound region of Washington State. Two brothers are bewitched. Singing. 4 scenes Variable cast

In Gerke, P. Multicultural plays for children v2

c Drakesbill

Based on French folktale. Clever duck outwits king. 3 scenes Variable cast

In Gerke, P. Multicultural plays for children v1

c East of the sun and west of the moon

Based on Norwegian folktale. Girl rescues prince who is under wicked spell. Background music. 10 scenes Variable cast 1 setting

In Gerke, P. Multicultural plays for children v2

c Feng zhen-zhu: The wind pearl

Based on Chinese folktale. Prince's adventures in faraway land. Singing, background music. 5 scenes Variable cast

In Gerke, P. Multicultural plays for children v2

c The firebird, the horse of power, and Czarevna Vasilisa

Based on Russian folktale. Horse helps archer accomplish impossible tasks and become Czar. Background music. 6 scenes Variable cast

In Gerke, P. Multicultural plays for children v1

c The great bear

Based on Mongolian folktale about origin of stars in Ursa Major. 6 scenes Variable cast

In Gerke, P. Multicultural plays for children v1

c Ne hölmöläiset: The silly villagers

Based on three Finnish folktales about foolish arguments among villagers. Variable cast 1 exterior

In Gerke, P. Multicultural plays for children v2

c I dodici mesi: The twelve months

Based on Italian folktale about young girl and wicked stepmother. Singing, dancing. 3 scenes Variable cast

In Gerke, P. Multicultural plays for children v1

c Legend of the seasons

Based on legend of Lushootseed Salish people of Puget Sound region of Washington State. Young man takes spirit journey and finds wife. Background music. 7 scenes Variable cast 1 exterior

In Gerke, P. Multicultural plays for children v2

c The little red hen

Based on American folktale. Animals who refuse to help hen cannot share her Thanksgiving pumpkin pie. 4 scenes Variable cast

In Gerke, P. Multicultural plays for children v1

c The long leather bag

Based on Irish folktale. Three sisters seek fortune and regain gold and silver from witch. 10 scenes Variable cast 1 setting

In Gerke, P. Multicultural plays for children v1

c Ma Lien and the magic paintbrush

Based on Chinese folktale. Artist uses magic paintbrush to defeat greedy mandarin. 3 scenes Variable cast 1 setting

In Gerke, P. Multicultural plays for children v1

c Los mariachis Mexicanos "The Bremen-town musicians"

Based on Grimms' fairy tale The Bremen town musicians. Four old lonely animals in Mexico form a mariachi band, rout robbers, and find place to live. Singing. 2 scenes Variable cast

In Gerke, C. Multicultural plays for children v1

c Mataora and Niwareka in the Underworld

Based on Maori myth from New Zealand. Warrior journeys to Underworld and returns with wife and symbolic

Gerke, Pamela—*Continued*
tatoo. Background music, dancing. 4 scenes Variable cast 1 setting
In Gerke, P. Multicultural plays for children v2

c Star story
Based on legend of the Lushootseed Salish people of the Puget Sound region of Washington State. Brothers become the moon and sun. 6 scenes Variable cast 1 setting
In Gerke, P. Multicultural plays for children v1

c Tri zlate vlasy Deda Vseveda: "The three golden hairs of Grandfather Know All"
Based on Czech folktale. Poor young man learns secrets of youth and becomes king. Background music. 13 scenes Variable cast 1 setting
In Gerke, P. Multicultural plays for children v2

c Vasilisa Prekrasnaia: "Vasilisa the beautiful"
Based on Russian folktale. With help of magic doll, young woman defeats evil witch and stepmother. 9 scenes Variable cast 1 interior 1 exterior
In Gerke, P. Multicultural plays for children v2

German drama

18th century

Goethe, J. W. von. Clavigo
Goethe, J. W. von. Egmont
Goethe, J. W. von. Goetz von Berlichingen with the iron hand
Goethe, J. W. von. Iphigenia in Tauris
Goethe, J. W. von. The natural daughter
Goethe, J. W. von. Pandora
Goethe, J. W. von. Stella
Goethe, J. W. von. Torquato Tasso

19th century

Hauptmann, G. The beaver coat
Hauptmann, G. Before daybreak

Germans

United States

Guare, J. Home fires

Germany

See also Berlin (Germany)

History—1517-1648

Goethe, J. W. von. Goetz von Berlichingen with the iron hand

History—1871-

Piscator, E. and Gasbarra, F. In spite of everything!

History—1933-1945

Barnes, P. Laughter!
Garrett-Groag, L. The White Rose
Kushner, T. A bright room called day
y Williams, K. Gran Webster's war

Moral conditions

Kaiser, G. From morning to midnight

Politics and government

Rubess, B. No, here comes Ulrike Meinhof
Szyszkowitz, G. Comrade Briggemann

Social conditions

Hauptmann, G. The weavers
Pohl, K. The beautiful stranger
Seidel, G. Carmen Kittel

Social life and customs—19th century

Wedekind, F. Spring awakening: a children's tragedy

Social life and customs—20th century

Sternheim, C. The bloomers

Gersten, Alexandra
My thing of love. French 1996 89p
Marital farce about troubled lower middle-class suburban marriage. 2 acts 5 scenes 2m 2w 1 interior

Gerstenberg, Alice
The pot boiler
Vaudevillean comedy about antics occurring during rehearsal of melodrama. 4m 3w 1 setting
In Short plays for young actors; ed. by C. Slaight and J. Sharrar

Gertie goat. Jones, T.

Getting along. Mander, C.

Getting away with murder. Sondheim, S. and Furth, G.

Getting it straight. Pollock, S.

Getting married. Shaw, G. B.

Getting on. Bennett, A.

Ghost from a perfect place. Ridley, P.

The **ghost** is here. Abe, K.

Ghost of the river house. Bush, M.

The **ghost** sonata. Strindberg, A.

A **ghost** story. Bensinger, L.

Ghost world. McLure, J.

Ghosts
Abe, K. The ghost is here
Aspengren, K. House of wonders
Bisson, P. Is there anybody there?
c Bush, M. Ghost of the river house
Carr, M. Portia Coughlan
Chappell, E. Haunted
c Cole, J. D. Ichabod
Fletcher, J. The lover's progress
Harding, M. Hubert Murray's widow
Hatcher, J. The turn of the screw
Heward, L. Or what's a heaven for?

Ghosts—*Continued*
c Hezlep, W. Tower of London
Hischak, T. Murder by the book
Hornby, I. Late of this address
Hornby, I. Wait until the ghost is clear
y Kelly, T. That's the spirit!
Kyd, T. The Spanish tragedy
y Levi, S. Good morning Miss Vickers
Lewis, M. G. The castle spectre
Linney, R. The captivity of Pixie Shedman
Linney, R. A Christmas carol
Miller, D. L. Origami tears
Mortimer, J. Charles Dickens' A Christmas carol
Nigro, D. Major Weir
y Nolan, P. T. The inexperienced ghost
c Nordlicht, L. Cover your eyes and run!
c Priore, F. V. Spooks on strike!
c Schario, C. A Christmas carol
Schenkkan, R. Final passages
Sharpe, T. Shadows
Shepard, S. The holy ghostly
y Sodaro, C. Salem's daughter
y Swartz, L. D. Halloween screams
Taylor, P. Familiar haunts
Taylor, P. Missing person
Taylor, P. A redheaded man
Thompson, J. Lion in the streets
Tirado, C. Some people have all the luck
Warburton, N. The Droitwich discovery
c Wheeler, J. and Hartsfield, M. G. Tall Betsy and the crackerbarrel tales
Wilhelm, L. Cherry blend with vanilla
Wood, P. Faint sound of a bell

Ghosts. Ibsen, H.

Ghoul Scout camp. Schurman-O'Connor, K.

Gibbons, Stella
Cold Comfort Farm (dramatization) See Doust, P. Cold Comfort Farm

Gibbs, Paige
y Lockie Leonard, human torpedo. Currency Press 1996 75p (Currency teenage drama)

Dramatization of Tim Winton's novel about trials and tribulations of teenage son of new cop in Western Australian coastal town. 32 scenes 7m 4w 1 setting

Gideon (Biblical figure)
Chayefsky, P. Gideon

Gifford, Barry
Blackout

Television play set in New York City hotel room, 1936. Oklahoma couple cannot move beyond grief after death of their son. 2m 1w

In Gifford, B. Hotel room trilogy

Mrs. Kashfi

Television play set in big city hotel, 1952. Young boy experiences visitation while mother seeks information from fortune teller. 3m 3w 1b extras

In Gifford, B. Hotel room trilogy

Tricks

Television play set in New York City hotel room, 1969. Two men share prostitute and appropriate each others identity. 5m 2w

In Gifford, B. Hotel room trilogy

A **gift** of music. McCaslin, N.

The **gift** of the Gorgon. Shaffer, P.

The **gift** of the Magi. Henry O. (dramatization) See Ekstrom, P. An O. Henry Christmas: The gift of the Magi

The **Gigli** Concert. Murphy, T.

Gigolos
Sergent, S. Father's prize Poland china

Gilbert, Hy. See Fischoff, G. James A. Michener's Sayonara

Gilbert, Mercedes
Environment

Domestic melodrama. African American family, beset by violence and drugs in Harlem, returns to its rural roots in the South. 3 acts 4 scenes 6m 6w extras 3 interiors

In Lost plays of the Harlem Renaissance; ed. by J. V. Hatch and L. Hamalian

Gilbert, Ronnie
Mother Jones: the most dangerous woman in America

Monologue with songs. On her 100th birthday the labor leader and social activist reflects on her life. 2 acts 1w 1 setting

In Gilbert, R. Ronnie Gilbert on Mother Jones

Gilbert, Sandra M. and Gubar, Susan
Masterpiece theatre. Rutgers Univ. Press 1995 203p

Satirical look at culture wars and contemporary academia. Prologue 3 acts Large mixed cast

Gilbert, Sky
Capote at Yaddo

Musical about Truman Capote set in 1946 in New York writer's colony. 3m 1w 1 setting

In Making, out; ed. by R. Wallace

Drag queens in outer space

Fantasy dreamplay. Three drag queens travel to the stars. 3m 1 setting

In Gilbert, S. Painted, tainted, sainted

Gilbert, Sky—*Continued*

Drag queens on trial

Courtroom melodrama exploring world of Toronto drag queens. 2 acts 4m 1 setting

In Gilbert, S. Painted, tainted, sainted

Jim Dandy

Experimental theater piece about homosexuality. Video. 6m 1w 1 setting

In Gilbert, S. Painted, tainted, sainted

Lola Starr builds her dream home

Gay parody. Life of film star in 1950s Connecticut. Singing. 2 acts 4 scenes 4m 1w extras 1 setting

In The *CTR* anthology; ed. by A. Filewod

Suzie Goo: private secretary

Black comedy. Drag queen becomes secretary to corporate executive. 3 acts 4 scenes 4m 1w extras 2 interiors

In Gilbert, S. Painted, tainted, sainted

Gilbert, W. S.

Parodies, imitations, etc.

McGillivray, D. and Zerlin, W. The Farndale Avenue Housing Estate Townswomen's Guild Operatic Society's production of The Mikado

Gill, Peter

Cardiff East. Faber & Faber 1997 115p

Drama set in Cardiff exploring family life and social conditions of Welsh underclass. 6 scenes 8m 8w extras 1 setting

Mean tears

Satirical look at group of people incapable of real human commitment. Homosexual author infatuated with feckless bisexual. 2 acts 29 scenes 3m 2w 1 setting

In Staging gay lives; ed. by J. M. Clum

Gillis, Caroline

Caveman rainbow

Young woman in small town faces cancer. 1w 1 setting

In Solo; ed. by J. Sherman

Gilroy, Frank D.

Any given day. French 1994 122p

Prelude to the author's The subject was roses. Depicts family tensions in middle-class Bronx family from 1941 to 1943. 2 acts 3 scenes 6m 3w 1 interior

Fore!

Comedy. Two Hollywood writers and secretary share bungalow at major movie studio. 2m 1w 1 setting

In Gilroy, F. D. A way with words: five one act plays

Give the bishop my faint regards

Comedy. Tensions rise as young woman interviews legendary Hollywood screenwriting team. 2m 1w 1 interior

In Gilroy, F. D. A way with words: five one act plays

Match point

Black comedy set at desert resort. Woman drives husband's lover to suicide. 2 scenes 1m 2w 1 exterior

In Gilroy, F. D. A way with words: five one act plays

Real to reel

Comedy. Intellectual film critic saved from Central Park mugging by filmmaker/actor she loathes. 2 scenes 1m 1w 1 interior 1 exterior

In Gilroy, F. D. A way with words: five one act plays

A way with words

Man hopes friend will help him get his wife back. 3 scenes 2m 1w 1 interior 1 exterior

In Gilroy, F. D. A way with words: five one act plays

The **Gingerbread** Boy. Mahlmann, L. and Jones, D. C.

The **gingham** dog. Wilson, L.

The **Giraffe** and the Pelly and me. See Ireland, V. Roald Dahl's The Giraffe and the Pelly and me

The **girl** from back home. Coleman, R. M.

The **girl** from Persia. See Plautus, T. M. The Persian

Girl gone. Reingold, J.

The **girl** on the train. Baitz, J. R.

The **girl** who saw everything. De Groen, A.

The **girl** who was plugged in. See Menken, A. Weird romance: The girl who was plugged in

The **girl** whose fortune sought her. Clapp, P.

Girls

Ackermann, J. Off the map
Barry, L. The good times are killing me
y Clark, R. J. Fighting for myself
y Curran, KT. The First Time Club
Gallagher, M. Bedtime
c Jenkin, L. Ramona Quimby
Kurtti, C. Catholic school girls
Laird, M. Ruthless!
Lapine, J. Twelve dreams
Lazarus, J. Schoolyard games
MacLeod, W. The shallow end
Oates, J. C. Ontological proof of my existence
Prichard, R. Essex girls
Rhodes, N. Ocean dream
c Sandberg, R. N. Anne of Green Gables
c Shurtz, R. K. Amy's attic
y Turner, J. Anne of Green Gables
Upton, J. Ashes and sand

See also Adolescence: Children; Youth

A **girl's** guide to the Divine comedy: a trilogy. Berc, S.

Gissing, George Robert
The odd women (dramatization) See Meyer, M. The odd women

"**Git** along, little doggies!" McCullough, L. E.

Give and take. Scanlan, M.

Give the bishop my faint regards. Gilroy, F. D.

Give us a kiss and show us your knickers. Nigro, D.

Giving up the ghost. Moraga, C.

The **Glace** Bay Miners' Museum. Lill, W.

The **gladiator.** Bird, R. M.

Gladiator. Caliban, R.

Gladiators, War of the, 73–71 B.C.
Bird, R. M. The gladiator

Glamorgan. Nigro, D.

Glancy, Diane
Weebjob
Drama about troubles of middle-aged Apache Indian in New Mexico. 2 acts 8 scenes 4m 2w extras 1 setting
In Contemporary plays by women of color; ed. by K. A. Perkins and R. Uno

Glass, Joanna McClelland
If we are women. Dramatists 1997 70p
Two grandmothers, a daughter, and a granddaughter gather at beach house and discuss their pasts, present and future options. 2 acts 4 scenes 4w 1 setting
—Same. French (London) 1994 61p
—Same. Playwrights Canada 1994 102p

Glass, Philip
Ives, D. Philip Glass buys a loaf of bread

The **glass** mermaid. Learner, T.

The **glass** mountain. McCullough, L. E.

A **glass** of water. Scribe, E.

Gleitzman, Morris
Two weeks with the Queen (dramatization) See Morris, M. Two weeks with the Queen

Glengarry Glen Ross. Mamet, D.

Glenn. Young, D.

The **glittering** gate. Dunsany, L.

Glore, John
The company of heaven. Dramatists 1995 72p
Drama about belief and doubt. Marriage of Air Force colonel, stationed in England, collapses when wife becomes involved in controversy surrounding paranormal sightings. 2 acts 3m 3w 1b
What she found there
Fantasy. After having sex with young man, young woman reveals that a hundred and twenty years ago she traded place with Alice, who took her place in the Looking Glass World. 1m 1w 1 interior
In 20/20: twenty one-act plays from twenty years of the Humana Festival

Glory. Barnes, P.

Gloucester (Mass.)
Horovitz, I. North Shore Fish

Glover, Keith
Coming of the Hurricane. Dramatists 1996 73p
Drama set in Maryland during era of reconstruction. Afro-American boxer struggles to assimilate in corrupt post-war society. 2 acts 12 scenes 7m 1w 1 setting
Dancing on moonlight. Dramatists 1996 78p
Drama about rage and violence it breeds set in Harlem of 1930s and 1960s. Impressionistic portrayal of small-time crooks. Choreographed movement. Singing. Prologue 2 acts 12 scenes 4m 3w 1 setting

Glover, Sue
Bondagers
Drama set 1860 in rural Scotland. Portrays practice of "bonding" female farmhands to their male counterparts to ensure cheap labor. Singing. 2 acts 23 scenes 6w extras 1 setting
In Glover, S. Bondagers & The straw chair
In Made in Scotland; ed. by I. Brown and M. Fisher
The straw chair
Drama set 1735 to 1740 on remote Scottish island of Hirta (St. Kilda). Seventeen-year-old woman and her minister husband encounter island's inhabitants. 2 acts 10 scenes 1m 3w 1 setting
In Glover, S. Bondagers & The straw chair

Glowacki, Janusz.
Antigone in New York. French 1997 86p
Black comedy set in 1989. Adventures of two homeless Eastern European refugees. 2 acts 14 scenes 3m 1w
Home section
Black comedy. Polish immigrants renovate New York apartment. 3m 1 interior
In The Best American short plays, 1995–1996

Gluscabi and his magic game bag. McCullough, L. E.

Go look. Graybill, C.

Go tell it on the mountain. McCullough, L. E.

Goatherds
White, P. Night on Bald Mountain

Goats
c Mahlmann, L. and Jones, D. C. Three Billy Goats Gruff

God and a woman. See Asher, S. F. A woman called Truth

The **God** of Isaac. Sherman, J.

Godber, John
April in Paris. French (London) 1993 54p

Comedy. English couple wins holiday in Paris. 2 acts 1m 1w 1 setting

Blood, sweat and tears. French (London) 1995 76p

Drama about how English waitress' pursuit of black belt in judo changes her life. 2 acts 12 scenes 2m 3w 2 interiors

Bouncers: 1990's REMIX. Warner Chappell Plays 1995 67p

Updated version of play about working class youth first produced 1984. Satirical look at British nightclub scene. Singing. 4m 1 setting

Lucky sods. French (London) 1995 80p

Black comedy about London couple who win lottery. 2 acts 10 scenes 2m 2w 1 setting

—Same
In Godber, J. Lucky sods & Passion killers

The office party. Warner Chappell Plays 1995 127p

Satiric comedy. Facade of advertising business stripped away at office Christmas party. 2 acts 8 scenes 4m 3w 1 interior

Passion killers. French (London) 1995 79p

Romantic comedy. Middle-aged British businessman and journalist, vacationing on the Mediterranean, find themselves torn between sexual promise and commitments back home. 2 acts 10 scenes 4m 3w 1 setting

—Same
In Godber, J. Lucky sods & Passion killers

Up 'n' under II. French (London) 1994 90p

Comedy sequel to 1985 play continues exploits of amateur rugby team in north of England. 2 acts 10 scenes 7m 2w

Godber, John, and Thornton, Jane
Shakers re-stirred. Warner Chappell Plays 1993 93p

Revised version of comedy first produced 1984. Four long-suffering waitresses offer their views of patrons of trendy cocktail lounge. 2 acts 4w 1 interior

Godfrey, Paul
The blue ball. Methuen Drama 1995 79p (Methuen's modern plays)

Depicts cultural and political aspects of space programs. Playwright takes ironic look at myths surrounding astronauts. 21 scenes 8m 5w extras

A bucket of eels

Farce. Bridegroom runs away on eve of wedding setting in motion sequence of bizarre events. 4 acts 2m 4w 1 exterior

In Godfrey, P. A bucket of eels & The modern husband

The modern husband

Freely adapted from 1730 play by Henry Fielding. Depicts society where love and marriage are subordinated to worship of money and sexual gratification. 17 scenes epilogue 3m 3w 1 interior

In Godfrey, P. A bucket of eels & The modern husband

God's great supper. Schenkkan, R.

Godunov, Boris. See Boris Fyodorovich Godunov, Czar of Russia, 1551?–1605

Goering, Herman
Linney, R. 2

Goethe, Johann Wolfgang von
Brother and sister; tr. by Frank Ryder

Woman discovers she is not man's sister but daughter of his dead lover. 3m 1w

In Goethe, J. W. von. Early verse drama and prose plays

Clavigo; tr. by Robert M. Browning

Tragedy set in Madrid based on Beaumarchais' memoirs. Broken promise of marriage leads to dishonor, misunderstanding and death. 5 acts 6m 2w setting

In Goethe, J. W. von. Early verse drama and prose plays

Egmont; tr. by Anna Swanwick

Tragedy. Historical drama of Count Egmont who led 16th century Flemish revolt against the Spanish in the Netherlands. 5 acts 12 scenes 15m 3w extras 5 interiors

In Goethe, J. W. von. Plays

—Same; tr. by Michael Hamburger
In Goethe, J. W. von. Early verse drama and prose plays

Faust, part I; tr. by Stuart Atkins

Aged scholar, transformed by Devil into handsome youth, seduces devout young woman. 25 scenes Prelude Prologue Large mixed cast

In Goethe, J. W. von. Faust I & II

Faust, part II; tr. by Stuart Atkins

Faust tastes every form of intellectual and world power but fails to find way to redeem his soul from Devil until at last he promotes a land reclamation project that will benefit many people. 5 acts Large mixed cast

In Goethe, J. W. von. Faust I & II

Goethe, Johann Wolfgang von
—Continued

Faust (adaptation) See Brenton, H. Faust I & II

Goetz von Berlichingen with the iron hand; tr. by Cyrus Hamlin

Historical drama based on life of 16th century German knight who defended his concept of justice. 5 acts 56 scenes 19m 3w 1b extras 15 interiors 18 exteriors

In Goethe, J. W. von. Early verse drama and prose plays

The green snake and the beautiful lily (dramatization) See Wood, B. The green snake and the beautiful lily

Iphigenia in Tauris; tr. by David Luke

Blank verse. Based on Greek legend of Iphigenia who while serving as priestess of Artemis, saved her brother, Orestes, from being sacrificed to the goddess. 5 acts 4m 1w 1 exterior

In Goethe, J. W. von. Verse plays and epic

—Same; tr. by Frank G. Ryder
In Goethe, J. W. von. Plays

Jery and Betty; tr. by Frank Ryder

Love story in verse. Swiss youth pursues farmer's daughter. Singing. 3m 1w extras 1 exterior

In Goethe, J. W. von. Early verse drama and prose plays

The natural daughter; tr. by Hunter Hannum

Symbolic verse play about the French Revolution. Illegitimate daughter of King's uncle victim of petty intrigues. 5 acts 28 scenes 8m 3w 2 interiors 2 exteriors

In Goethe, J. W. von. Verse plays and epic

Pandora, tr. by Michael Hamburger

Verse play about creation and creativity based on Greek myth of Pandora. Large mixed cast 1 setting

In Goethe, J. W. von. Verse plays and epic

Prometheus; tr. by Frank Ryder

Dramatic verse fragment based on Greek mythology. 2 acts 5m 2w extras 1 setting

In Goethe, J. W. von. Early verse drama and prose plays

Proserpina; tr. by Cyrus Hamlin

Free verse monodrama about the Roman deity. 1w extras 1 setting

In Goethe, J. W. von. Early verse drama and prose plays

Stella; tr. by Robert M. Browning and Frank Ryder

Tragedy of two friends who learn they are married to same man. 5 acts 3m 5w extras setting

In Goethe, J. W. von. Early verse drama and prose plays

Torquato Tasso; tr. by Charles E. Passage

Tragedy in verse. Based on legend about Italian poet whose unrequitted love for a princess drove him insane. 5 acts 3m 2w 1 interior 1 exterior

In Goethe, J. W. von. Plays

—Same; tr. by Michael Hamburger
In Goethe, J. W. von. Verse plays and epic

Goethe's fairy tale The green snake and the beautiful lily. Wood, B.

Goetz von Berlichingen with the iron hand. Goethe, J. W. von

Gogol, Nikolai

Parodies, imitations, etc.

y Kelly, T. Trouble in Tumbleweed

Goin' a Buffalo. Bullins, E.

Going all the way. Bailey, M.

A **going** concern. Jeffreys, S.

Going home. See Simon, N. London suite: Going home

Going to pot. Feydeau, G.

Gold and silver waltz. Linney, R.

Gold mines and mining

y Christiansen, A. Wash your troubles away

c McCullough, L. E. Darling Clementine: a tail of old San Francisco

c McCullough, L. E. Klondike fever

O'Neill, E. A wife for a life

The **gold** standard. Koch, K.

The **gold** star. See Vigil, A. La estrella de oro. The gold star

Gold watch. Iko, M.

Goldberg, Leah

Lady of the Castle; tr. by T. Carmi

Librarian and social worker on mission in central Europe in 1947 encounter Holocaust survivor still hiding in old castle. 3 acts 2m 2w 1 setting

In Israeli Holocaust drama; ed. by M. Taub

Goldberg, Moses

c Little Red Riding Hood and The three little pigs. Anchorage Press 1996 34p

Participation play based on two fairy tales. Music, singing. 2m 2w

Goldberg Street. Mamet, D.

Golden, Edward

y Great expectations

Dramatization of Charles Dickens' novel set in 19th century England. Poor orphan, reared as gentleman, discovers that his benefactor is a convict he once helped. 5m 4w

In The Big book of dramatized classics; ed. by S. E. Kamerman

Golden, Gail. See Golden, G. The magic in me

Golden, Grant

c The magic in me; by Gail Golden; music & lyrics by Grant Golden. Pioneer Drama Service 1993 19p

Various fantastic characters help little wizard discover her magical powers. 6m 8w extras 1 setting

The **golden** door. See Regan, S. Morning star

The **Golden** Fleece. Gurney, A. R.

The **golden** shadows old west museum. King, L. L.

The **golden** spike. McCullough, L. E.

Goldenthal, Jolene

Charley's girl

Monologue by childlike woman awaiting her husband. 1w

In Goldenthal, J. Mequasset by the sea and other plays

Dance piece

Monologue by teenager who seduced her mother's boyfriend. 1w

In Goldenthal, J. Mequasset by the sea and other plays

Mequasset by the sea

Middle-aged women at beach look back on past disappointments. 5w extras 1 exterior

In Goldenthal, J. Mequasset by the sea and other plays

Wife to Tolstoi

Monologue. Woman reacts to husband's request for divorce. 1w

In Goldenthal, J. Mequasset by the sea and other plays

Goldilocks and the three Martians. Staite, J.

Golding, William

Lord of the flies (dramatization) See Williams, N. William Golding's Lord of the flies

Goldoni, Carlo

The coffee shop; tr. by Robert Cornthwaite. Smith & Kraus 1995 92p (Great translation for actors)

Comedy set in 1750 Venice during Carnival season revolving around denizens of quiet piazzetta and coffee shop. 3 acts 10m 3w extras 1 setting

The Venetian twins (adaptation) See Clarke, T. The Venetian twins

Villeggiatura: Adventures in the country

Second play in trilogy. Young man continues efforts to win affections of young woman pledged to another. 5 scenes 9m 6w 1 exterior

In Goldoni, C. Carlo Goldoni's Villeggiatura trilogy

Villeggiatura: Back from the country

Concluding play in trology about jealousy and romance among fashionable youth in 18th century Italy. 6 scenes 10m 6w 4 interiors

In Goldoni, C. Carlo Goldoni's Villeggiatura trilogy

Villeggiatura: Crazy for the country

First play in trilogy satirizing fashionable country life in 18th century Livorno, Italy. 6 scenes 8m 3w 2 interiors

In Goldoni, C. Carlo Goldoni's Villeggiatura trilogy

Villeggiatura (adaptation) See Cornthwaite, R. Carlo Goldoni's Villeggiatura

Goldsmith, Oliver

She stoops to conquer; or, The mistakes of a night

Romantic comedy set in 18th century England revolving around two sets of lovers and the mistaken impression that home of prospective bride is an inn. Prologue 5 acts 8 scenes epilogue 6m 4w extras 3 interiors 1 exterior

In Great Irish plays

Goldstein, Carrie

Last exit before toll

Comic monologue. Woman, unable to pay toll, leaves baby at toll booth as collateral. 1w

In Off-Off Broadway Festival plays, 18th ser.

Goldstein, Joshua

The end

Husband and wife struggle against infertility. 2 acts 19 scenes 5m 1w 1 setting

In Goldstein, J. Four plays

Hate

Monologue delivered by Hitler. 7 scenes 1m

In Goldstein, J. Four plays

Martin Night

Drama set in 1960s New York suburb about troubled family headed by self-hating German-Jewish refugee. 2 acts 3m 2w 1 interior

In Goldstein, J. Four plays

Our baby's first seven years

Dramatic monologue set in 1950s Washington, D.C. Young mother copes with infant son's cancer. 7 scenes 1w

In Goldstein, J. Four plays

Golem

Basso, E. The fall of Prague

Golf

Horovitz, I. One under

Gollobin, Laurie Brooks

Selkie. Anchorage Press 1997 47p

Drama based on Scottish folklore about sealfolk able to assume human form on land. Singing, background music, dancing. 3m 4w 1 setting

Goluboff, Bryan

Big Al

Author is obsessed with writing screenplay for Al Pacino. 2m 1 interior

In Goluboff, B. Big Al and My side of the story

My side of the story

Father confides in son about marriage problems. 2m 1 interior

In Goluboff, B. Big Al and My side of the story

The other five percent

Surreal encounters on Halloween night in Manhattan. 2m 1w

In Showtime's Act One Festival of one-act plays, 1994

Gone fishing. Jones, T.

Gone with the breeze. Francoeur, B.

Gomez, Terry

Inter-tribal

Indian grandmother disapproves of teenaged granddaughter's irresponsible behavior and rejection of Indian culture. 2 acts 6 scenes 3m 3w extras

In Contemporary plays by women of color; ed. by K. A. Perkins and R. Uno

Gonzalez, Reuben

The boiler room

Surreal domestic drama about Puerto Rican family in New York. 2 acts 9 scenes 2m 2w 1 setting

In Nuestro New York; ed. by J. V. Antush

Good and evil

c Haylock, D. Light of the world
c Medoff, M. Stefanie hero
Schwartz, D. Venus in the back room
Shawn, W. Aunt Dan and Lemon
Walker, G. F. Zastrozzi: the master of discipline

Good black don't crack. Penny, R.

Good evening, Mr Collins. Mac Intyre, T.

Good Friday

Solórzano, C. The crucified

Good King Wenceslas. McCullough, L. E.

Good King Wenceslas and the Chancellor of Bohemia. Horitz, T.

A **good** man. Stroppel, F.

Good morning Miss Vickers. Levi, S.

Good news and bad news. See Haylock, D. Here is the news: Good news and bad news

Good night, sweet mother. Groves, W.

A **good** place to come from. Torgov, M. (dramatization) See Horovitz, I. Today, I am a fountain pen

The **good** thief. McPherson, C.

The **good** times are killing me. Barry, L.

Good works. Enright, N.

Goodbye, Howard. Linney, R.

Goodbye Marianne. Watts, I. K.

Goodbye, my fancy. Kanin, F.

Gooderson, David. See Conville, D. jt. auth.

Gordon, David

The mysteries and what's so funny?

Choreographed play about Marcel Duchamp and family history. Music, singing. Prologue 2 parts 6m 8w 1 setting

In Grove new American theater; ed. by M. Feingold

Gordon, Peter

Generations apart. Warner Chappell Plays 1996 101p

Humorous drama set on Isle of Wight exploring how love affair in 1969 affected father-son relationships over three generations. 2 acts 4 scenes Variable cast 8 characters 1 exterior

Murdered to death. Warner Chappell Plays 1996 106p

Spoof of Agatha Christie type murder mystery set in English country house in 1930s. 2 acts 4 scenes 5m 5w 1 interior

Gorky, Maxim

The summer people; tr. by Nicholas Saunders and Frank Dwyer. Smith & Kraus 1995 (Great translations for actors)

Variant title: Summer folk. Summer on lawyer's dacha setting for exploration of bourgeois society in pre-Revolutionary Russia. 4 acts Large mixed cast settings

Gorman, Clem

Manual of trench warfare

Homosexual love in Australian armed forces at Gallipoli in 1915. Prologue 8 scenes 5m 1 setting

In Australian gay and lesbian plays; ed. by B. Parr

Gossip

Adam, A. Birds of prey
Gregory, L. Spreading the news
Lauro, S. The coal diamond
Wilson, L. The Rimers of Eldritch

Gotanda, Philip Kan
Ballad of Yachiyo. Dramatists 1997 64p
Portrays young Japanese girl's sexual awakening and social downfall in Hawaii's plantation system of 1919. Slide projections. 2 acts 3m 4w 1 setting
—Same. Theatre Communications Group 1997 84p
Day standing on its head. Dramatists 1994 51p
Fantasy and reality blur when emotionally inhibited Japanese-American law professor reexamines his role in 1970s campus strike. 5m 4w 1 interior
—Same
In Asian American drama; ed. by B. Nelson
In But still, like air, I'll rise; ed. by V. H. Houston
Fish head soup
Japanese American family torn apart by violent familial and generational conflicts. 3 acts 3m 1w extras 1 setting
In Gotanda, P. K. Fish head soup and other plays
A song for a Nisei fisherman
Set in Stockton, California. Nisei fisherman's life vehicle for examination of frustrations, dilemmas and dreams of second-generation Japanese-Americans. Music, singing. 5 scenes 7m 4w extras 1 setting
In Gotanda, P. K. Fish head soup and other plays
The wash
Drama about love, pride and cultural identity. Middle-aged Japanese American woman leaves her husband after more than 25 years of marriage. 2 acts 26 scenes 3m 5w 1 interior
In Gotanda, P. K. Fish head soup and other plays
Yankee dawg you die
Asian American actors face discrimination and stereotyping. 2 acts 14 scenes 2m 1 setting
In Gotanda, P. K. Fish head soup and other plays

Gotwald, Helen Louise Miller. See Miller, Helen Louise

Gould, Glenn
Young, D. Glenn

Government, Resistance to
Lawrence, J. and Lee, R. E. The night Thoreau spent in jail

The **Governor's** lady. Mercer, D.

Gow, Michael
Furious. Currency Press in association with Playbox Theatre Centre 1994 36p (Current theatre series)
Stranger enters author's life and family secret is revealed. 19 scenes 3m 2w 1 setting
—Same
In Australian gay and lesbian plays; ed. by B. Parr
Sweet Phoebe. Currency Press in association with Playbox Theatre 1995 61p (Current theatre series)
Black comedy. Suburban Australian couple's marriage laid bare when troublesome dog entrusted to their care runs away. 1m 1w

A **gown** for his mistress. See Feydeau, G. The dressmaker; Feydeau, G. A fitting confusion

Goya, Francisco
Barker, C. Colossus
Shamas, L. Portrait of a nude

Gozzi, Carlo
The love for three oranges (adaptation) See Prokofiev, S. The love of three oranges; Swortzell, L. The love of three oranges

Grace. Lucie, D.

Grace & Glorie. Ziegler, T.

Grace note. Adamson, S.

The **grace** of Mary Traverse. Wertenbaker, T.

Gracie's garden. Pflomm, P. N.

Graduation address. Fontaine, R.

Grae, David
Moose mating. Dramatists 1996 57p
Romantic comedy about mating rituals of paranoid New Yorkers. 2m 2w extras 1 setting

Graffigny, Françoise d'Issembourg d'Happoncourt de
Cenia (Cénie)
Bold young woman in 18th century France chooses life of poverty in convent rather than submit to villainous blackmail demands. 5 acts 4m 3w 1 interior
In The Lunatic lover and other plays; ed. by P. Gethner

Grafigny, Mme de. See Graffigny, Françoise d'Issembourg d'Happoncourt de

Graham, Bruce
Belmont Avenue Social Club. Dramatists 1993 76p
Comedy about white male privilege, power and betrayal. Urban politicos meet to fill seat left by death of corrupt councilman. 2 acts 3 scenes 5m 1 interior

Graham, Bruce—*Continued*

The Champagne Charlie Stakes. Dramatists 1993 65p

Comedy drama. Race track regular bets entire savings on long-shot while wife of fifty-three years looks on. 2 acts 3m 2w 1 exterior

Graham, Gordon

The boys. Currency Press 1994 83p

Drama set in Australia about vicious rape and murder of woman by three men who are, nonetheless, loved and cared for by their own women. 2 acts 8 scenes 3m 4w 1 setting

Graham, Shirley

It's morning

Tragedy. Slave woman kills her fourteen-year-old daughter on New Year's morning 1863, rather than see her sold. 6m 8w extras 1 interior

In Plays by American women, 1930-1960; ed. by J. E. Barlow

Track thirteen

Radio comedy about African American employees on cross-country train. 17m 4w extras

In Lost plays of the Harlem Renaissance; ed. by J. V. Hatch and L. Hamalian

Grahame, Kenneth

The reluctant dragon (dramatization) See Mahlmann, L. and Jones, D. C. The reluctant dragon; Surface, M. H. The reluctant dragon

The wind in the willows (dramatization) See Peterson, L. The wind in the willows

Gramsci, Antonio

Griffiths, T. Occupations

Gran. Evans, L.

Gran Webster's war. Williams, K.

Grand magic. De Filippo, E.

Grandchild of kings. Prince, H.

Grandfathers

y Cowell, M. Song for the navigator

Fugard, A. Valley song

y Kral, B. One to grow on

Middleton, T. A mad world, my masters

Ricchi, R. A foreboding

Richards, G. Dividends

Grandma Rusnak. Schurman-O'Connor, K.

Grandmothers

c Bass, E. In my grandmother's purse

y Cole, N. And the tide shall cover the earth

c Evans, L. Gran

Gomez, T. Inter-tribal

y Kesselman, W. Maggie Magalita

c Schurman-O'Connor, K. Grandma Rusnak

Shine, T. Contribution

Toddie, J. L. Late Sunday afternoon, early Sunday evening

Grandparents

Peterson, L. Take a giant step

Granger, Percy

Vivien

Confrontation between mentally disturbed father and anxiety-ridden son. 1 act 2m 1w 1 setting

In Telling tales; new one-act plays; ed. by E. Lane

Granville-Barker, Harley

Farewell to the theatre

Tete à tete between London solicitor and actress he has loved all his life. 1m 1w extra 1 interior

In Granville-Barker, H. Plays: two

His majesty

Political intrigue in Europe after First World War as experienced by deposed monarch of imaginary kingdom of Carpethia. 4 acts 15m 4w settings

In Granville-Barker, H. Plays: two

The Madras House

Comedy. Attitudes toward sex and marriage are aired during and after a meeting to sell the dress business of two feuding brothers. 4 acts 8m 17w 4 interiors

In Granville-Barker, H. Plays: two

The marrying of Ann-Leete

Comedy set at turn of century revolving around politically ambitious father's attempts to arrange advantageous marriage for his daughter. 4 acts 5 scenes 14m 6w 2 interiors 1 exterior

In Granville-Barker, H. Plays: two

Rococo

Farce. English family quarrels over bequest of Rococo vase. 1 act 3m 3w 1 interior

In Granville-Barker, H. Plays: one

The secret life

Soul searching by disillusioned idealist, formerly member of ruling elite in post World War I England. 3 acts 11 scenes 7m 5w settings

In Granville-Barker, H. Plays: one

Vote by ballot

Comedy about local politics set in early 20th century England. 1 act 3m 3w 1 interior

In Granville-Barker, H. Plays: one

The Voysey inheritance (1934 revision)

British melodrama posing questions about honesty. Edward Voysey inherits investment firm whose funds his father has been embezzling, and tries to straighten out his accounts without being detected. 5 acts 9m 7w 1b 2 interiors

In Granville-Barker, H. Plays: one

Waste (1926 revision)

Tragedy. Casual affair results in unwanted pregnancy. Death, political ruin and suicide follow. 4 acts 7 scenes 10m 6w 3 interiors

In Granville-Barker, H. Plays: one

Grauer, Rita
c The boy who tricked the moon. Anchorage Press 1997 45p
Drama with audience participation based on Tlingit Indian folklore. Orphan boy, with help of spirit guides, earns respect of chief's son. Background music. Prologue 3 acts 6 scenes 1m 1w 4b 1g 1 setting

Graven images. Miller, M.

Graveyards. *See* Cemeteries

Gray, Cliff
The shaken reed. New Playwrights Network 1995 64p
Man's secret past is revealed when ex-wife unexpectedly appears with blackmail in mind. 3 acts 4 scenes 3m 5w 1 interior

Gray, John
Billy Bishop goes to war [by] John Gray with Eric Peterson
Canada's role in World War I is examined through the eyes of flying ace Billy Bishop. Music, singing. 2m 1 setting
In Modern Canadian plays v2; ed. by J. Wasserman

Gray, Oriel
The torrents. Currency Press in association with State Theatre Co. 1996 (Australian Playhouse series)
Drama set in Australian goldfields of 1890s. New editor questions ethics of family run newspaper. 3 acts 5 scenes 11m 2w 1 interior

Gray, Simon
Butley
Unsuccessful British professor tries to cope with academia, his divorce, and a dissolving homosexual relationship. 2 acts 4m 3w 1 interior
In Gray, S. The definitive Simon Gray I

The caramel crisis
Television play. Satire about incompetent factory executives. 5m 4w
In Gray, S. The definitive Simon Gray I

Close of play
Black comedy. Aged professor silently witnesses the reunion of sons and daughters-in-law as their interpersonal conflicts and problems are revealed. 2 acts 4m 4w 1 interior
In Gray, S. The definitive Simon Gray III

The common pursuit
Chronicles the lives of six Cambridge University classmates from the 1960s through the next twenty years. 2 acts 4 scenes epilogue 5m 1w 2 interiors
In Gray, S. The definitive Simon Gray IV

Dog days
Disenchanted editor faces truth about himself as result of stormy relationships with his wife and his brother. 2 acts 4 scenes 2m 2w 2 interiors
In Gray, S. The definitive Simon Gray II

Dutch uncle
Comic farce about Mr. Godboy's futile efforts to murder his wife and bring himself to the attention of his idol, Inspector Hawkins. 2 acts 4 scenes 4m 2w 1 interior
In Gray, S. The definitive Simon Gray I

Hidden laughter. French 1993 118p
Satirical look at artistic pretensions of the middle class. Literary agent and his author wife find country life to be opposite of idyll they envisaged. 2 acts 5 scenes 5m 3w 1 interior
—Same
In Gray, S. The definitive Simon Gray IV

The holy terror. French 1993 78p
This revised version of Melon was originally produced as a radio play. Satirical look at nervous breakdown of London publisher. 2 acts 8m 3w 1 interior

—Same
In Gray, S. The definitive Simon Gray IV

Man in a side-car
Television play. Successful woman novelist and her less successful writer husband play cat-and-mouse games with each other and young man living with them. 4m 2w extras
In Gray, S. The definitive Simon Gray II

Molly
Inspired by notorious Rattenburg murder case, this is a stage adaptation of author's television play, Death of a teddy bear. Woman having affair with teenage handyman takes blame when he kills her aging husband. 2 acts 7 scenes 3m 2w extra 1 interior
In Gray, S. The definitive Simon Gray II

Otherwise engaged
British publisher's record listening interrupted by uninvited visitors seeking to involve him in personal problems. He remains outwardly calm and disengaged through attempted seduction, suicide, wife's revelation of adultery, etc. 2 acts 5m 2w 1 interior
In Gray, S. The definitive Simon Gray II

Pig in a poke
Television play. When English couple move into trendy new home they realize that a slovenly tenant is part of the deal. 2m 1w
In Gray, S. The definitive Simon Gray II

Gray, Simon—*Continued*

Plaintiffs and defendants

Television play. Married middle-aged lawyer trying to extricate himself from love affair with unstable young woman, has difficulty communicating with those around him, including wife, teenage son, and student assistant. 8m 3w extras

In Gray, S. The definitive Simon Gray II

Quartermaine's terms

Tragicomedy set in 1960s Cambridge England follows fortunes of staff of school that teaches English to foreigners. 2 acts 5 scenes 5m 2w 1 interior

In Gray, S. The definitive Simon Gray III

The rear column

English officers awaiting supplies in Congo for Henry Stanley's 1880s Emin Pasha Relief Expedition face sickness, starvation, restless native troops, an unreliable Arab ally, and insane commanding officer who feels career threatened by quarrel with Stanley. 3 acts 6 scenes 6m extras 1 interior

In Gray, S. The definitive Simon Gray III

Simply disconnected. Faber & Faber 1996 50p

Sequel to Otherwise engaged. Simon Hench responds to life's catastrophes and absurdities with continuing pressure from others for explanations. 2 acts 5m 2w 1 interior

Sleeping dog

Television play. Retired colonial officer torments West Indians for being too familiar with his wife. 5m 2w

In Gray, S. The definitive Simon Gray I

Spoiled

Television play about married male teacher's feelings for male student. 3m 2w 2 acts 5 scenes

In Gray, S. The definitive Simon Gray I

Stage struck

Comedy thriller. Stage manager's marriage to West End actress destroyed by clumsy intervention of psychiatrist. 2 acts 3 scenes 3m 1w 1 interior

In Gray, S. The definitive Simon Gray III

Two Sundays

Television play. Middle-aged publisher and teacher continue close friendship begun as schoolboys. 7m 2w extras

In Gray, S. The definitive Simon Gray II

Wise child

Two male criminals on the run, one disguised as the other's mother, find refuge in a hotel whose owner is a homosexual. 3 acts 4 scenes 2m 1w 1 interior

In Gray, S. The definitive Simon Gray I

Gray, Spalding

Gray's anatomy. Vintage Bks. 1994 80p

Satirical monologue about alternative medicine, disease, aging and mortality. 1m

It's a slippery slope. Noonday Press 1997 105p

Autobiographical monologue about love, betrayal, divorce, middle-age, fatherhood and skiing. 1m

Graybill, Christopher

Go look

Man and woman on camping trip face their fears. 1m 1w

In Actors Theatre of Louisville. Ten-minute plays v3

Gray's anatomy. Gray, S.

Greasepaint and Ginthons: the medicine show comes to town. McCullough, L. E.

The **great** bear. Gerke, P.

Great Britain

Mitchell, J. Falling over England

Storey, D. The contractor

See also England; Northern Ireland; Scotland; Wales; names of provinces, e.g. Lancashire (England); and names of cities, e.g. Liverpool (England); London (England)

Colonies

Walcott, D. Pantomime

History—Plantagenets, 1154–1399

y Thomas, E. and Redmond, B. Six Canterbury tales

History—13th century

Marlowe, C. Edward II

History—Lancaster and York, 1399–1485

Anderson, M. Richard and Anne

Chaurette, N. The queens

History—Tudors, 1485–1603

Anderson, J.-S. Tyndale's dream

Fo, D. Elizabeth: almost by chance a woman

Ford, J. Perkin Warbeck

Maraini, D. Mary Stuart

y Poskitt, K. Henry the Tudor dude

History—Stuarts, 1603–1714

Barnes, P. The spirit of man: From sleep and shadow

Hyem, J. Lorna Doone

History—19th century

c Breeze, N. The Rochdale Pioneers

Great Britain—*Continued*

History—20th century

Griffiths, L. The Duchess: pieces of Wallis Simpson

Parliament. House of Commons

Stoppard, T. Dirty linen

Politics and government

Campton, D. Permission to cry
Cullen, A. Pig's ear
Granville-Barker, H. The secret life
Granville-Barker, H. Vote by ballot
Griffiths, T. The party
Hare, D. The absence of war
Marber, P. After Miss Julie
Townsend, S. The Queen and I
Whelan, P. Divine right

Race relations

Pinnock, W. Talking in tongues

Royal Air Force

D'Aguiar, F. A Jamaican airman foresees his death

Social conditions

Berkoff, S. Decadence
Chinn, J. Home before dark
Cullen, A. Pig's ear
Daniels, S. The gut girls
Godber, J. Bouncers: 1990's REMIX
Griffiths, T. Thatcher's children
Hare, D. Knuckle
Johnson, C. Boys mean business
Johnson, J. Somewhere
McIntyre, C. The thickness of skin
Poliakoff, S. Playing with trains
Shaw, B. Mrs. Warren's profession
Spencer, D. Hurricane roses
Wallace, N. One flea spare

Social life and customs—Tudors, 1485–1603

c Harris, A. The prince and the pauper
c McCullough, L. E. Here we come a-wassailing
Nigro, D. Ardy Fafirsin

Social life and customs—Early Stuarts, 1603–1649

Middleton, T. A mad world, my masters
Middleton, T. Michaelmas Term
Whelan, P. The herbal bed

Social life and customs—Civil War and Commonwealth, 1642–1660

Behn, A. The rover

Social life and customs—Restoration, 1660–1688

Behn, A. The lucky chance
Etherege, G. The man of mode
The Heather Brothers. Lust
Jeffreys, S. The libertine
Wycherley, W. The plain dealer

Social life and customs—1689–1714

Farquhar, G. The beaux' stratagem
Farquhar, G. The constant couple
Farquhar, G. The recruiting officer
Farquhar, G. The twin rivals

Social life and customs—18th century

Buchan, A. Conditional surrender
Faulkner, A. For England and King George
Goldsmith, O. She stoops to conquer
y Olfson, L. Monsieur Beaucaire
y Olfson, L. Wuthering Heights
Scribe, E. A glass of water
Sheridan, R. B. The rivals
Sheridan, R. B. The school for scandal
Steele, R. The conscious lovers

Social life and customs—19th century

Edmundson, H. The mill on the floss
Francis, M. Jane Austen's Northanger Abbey
c Francoeur, B. A little princess
Golden, E. Great expectations
Hall, W. Jane Eyre
Hall, W. Mansfield Park
Harris, A. The importance of being Earnest
Johanson, R. Charles Dickens' Great expectations
Meyer, M. The odd women
y Morley, O. J. Pride and prejudice
y Nolan, P. T. The inexperienced ghost
y Olfson, L. The admirable Crichton
y Olfson, L. The Pickwick papers
Pinero, A. W. The second Mrs. Tanqueray
Pinero, A. W. Trelawny of the 'Wells'
Sheridan, R. B. The school for scandal
Vance, C. Jane Eyre
Wilde, O. An ideal husband
Wilde, O. The importance of being Earnest
Wilde, O. Lady Windermere's fan

Social life and customs—20th century

c Alette, C. The secret garden
Bleadsdale, A. On the ledge
c Francoeur, B. The secret garden
Leach, K. The mysterious Mr. Love
Norman, M. The secret garden
Parsley, R. Brideshead revisited
Potter, D. Pennies from heaven
Shaw, B. Heartbreak House

The **great** celestial cow. Townsend, S.

Great expectations. Dickens, C. (dramatization) See Golden, E. Great expectations; Johanson, R. Charles Dickens' Great expectations

The **great** Gemdale Christmas tree ornament factory. Enscoe, L. G. and Enscoe, A.

The **great** God Brown. O'Neill, E.

The **great** Labor Day classic. Horovitz, I.

The **great** MacDaddy. Harrison, P. C.

Great medicine painter. McCullough, L. E.

The **Great** Nebula in Orion. Wilson, L.

A **great** occasion. Adam, A.

The **great** puppet show. See Schnitzler, A. Marionettes: The great puppet show.

The **great** Santa kidnap. Chatfield, R.

The **Great** War. See Hollingsworth, M. The history of the village of the small huts

Greatest hits. McLaughlin, T.

Greece
Strauss, B. The tour guide
Wadsworth, S. The triumph of love

History—Peloponnesian War, 431–404 B.C.

Aristophanes. Acharnians
Aristophanes. Lysistrata
Aristophanes. Peace

Greed. See Avarice

Greek. Berkoff, S.

Greek drama (Comedy)
Aristophanes. Acharnians
Aristophanes. Birds
Aristophanes. The clouds
Aristophanes. Festival time
Aristophanes. Frogs
Aristophanes. Knights
Aristophanes. Lysistrata
Aristophanes. Peace
Aristophanes. Wasps

Greek drama (Satyr play)
Euripides. The Cyclops

Greek drama (Tragedy)
Aeschylus. Agamemnon
Aeschylus. Seven against Thebes
Euripides. Alcestis
Euripides. Bakkhai
Euripides. The children of Heracles
Euripedes. Electra
Euripides. Hekabe
Euripides. Hippolytus
Euripides. Iphigenia among the Taurians
Euripides. Iphigenia in Aulis
Euripides. Medea
Euripides. Orestes
Euripides. Suppliant women
Kennelly, B. Euripides' The Trojan woman
Sophocles. Antigone
Sophocles. Electra
Sophocles. Oedipus at Colonus
Sophocles. Oedipus the King

Greek mythology. See Mythology, Greek

Greeks

Australia

Lyssiotis, T. The Forty Lounge Cafe

Green, Mark
c Spring the king. New Playwrights Network 1996 58p

Pantomime. Rescue of gypsy king from evil sorcerer. 2 acts 6 scenes 6m 4w extras 1 interior 2 exteriors

Green, Michael
Dreams of a drunken Quaker

Absurdist comedy with surrealist visions of apocalypse and debauchery. 3 parts 2m 1 setting

In Green, M. Dreams of a drunken Quaker; Naked West & Yowl

Naked West

Absurdist exploration of masculinity. Dancing. 4m 1 setting

In Green, M. Dreams of a drunken Quaker; Naked West & Yowl

Yowl

Experimental monologue. 1m

In Green, M. Dreams of a drunken Quaker; Naked West & Yowl

Green, Paul. See Wright, R. jt. auth.

The **Green** Cockatoo. Schnitzler, A.

Green favours. Vickery, F.

Green icebergs. Fannon, C.

The **green** snake and the beautiful lily. Wood, B.

The **green** stockings. Abe, K.

Greenberg, Richard
The American plan

Drama about loneliness, homosexuality and class distinction set in 1960s Catskill resort. Jewish widow discourages disturbed daughter's romance with young social climber. 2 acts 13 scenes 3m 2w 1 setting

In Grove new American theater: ed. by M. Feingold

The author's voice

Satirical look at publishing world. Editor discovers that her latest protege is taking credit for work of misshapen creature whose physical ugliness forces him to remain in closet. 9 scenes 2m 1w 1 interior

In Telling tales: new one-act plays; ed. by E. Lane

Greenberg, Richard—*Continued*
Jenny keeps talking. Dramatists 1995 46p
Comedy. One-woman show about feuding sisters and grandmother who reconciles them. 3 acts 4 scenes 1w 2 interiors
Night and her stars (condensation)
In The Best plays of 1994-1995

Greenfield blooms. Oakes, M. and Wells, J.

Greenland, Seth
Jungle rot. Dramatists 1997 78p
Political farce set 1960 in Leopoldville. CIA station chief told to assassinate Congo's Prime Minister, Patrice Lumumba. 2 acts 26 scenes 8m 3w 1 setting

Greensboro. Mann, E.

Greenspan, David
Dead mother; or, Shirley not all in vain
Farce set in L.A. about Jewish family life and homosexuality. 5 acts 4m 2w 1 setting
In Grove new American theater; ed. by M. Feingold
Son of an engineer. Sun & Moon Press 1995 102p
Absurdist drama set in suburbia and on Mars about stereotypical family roles imposed by society. 2 acts 2m 2w 1 interior 1 exterior

Greer, Bonnie
Munda negra
Drama about black American woman art lecturer living in England. 3 acts 10 scenes 3m 2w extras 1 setting
In Black plays: three; ed. by Y. Brewster

Gregg, Stephen
A private moment
Siamese twin spends time with young woman he fancies. 2m 2w 1 interior
In Actors Theatre of Louisville. Ten-minute plays v3

Gregor, Henry
Freedom! Freedom!
Concludes author's freedom trilogy. Revolutionists proclaim love of freedom but in reality thirst for power. 1 act 3 scenes 2m 3w 1 interior
In Gregor, H. Prince & plays
The Spanish cape
Second installment in freedom trilogy. Examines role of Christian spirituality as redemptive force in Western European society. 8 scenes 4m 5w 5 interiors
In Gregor, H. Prince & plays
The third death
First play in Trilogy of freedom. Drama about persecutions of Christians in modern totalitarian state. Prologue 2 acts 16 scenes epilogue 10m 6w 1 setting
In Gregor, H. Prince & plays

Gregory, Isabella Augusta Peisse. See Gregory, Lady, 1852-1932

Gregory, Lady, 1852-1932
Spreading the news
Two women come to visit a prisoner only to discover that he had been hanged on the previous day. 1m 2w 1 exterior
In Great Irish plays

About

Hall, F. B. The book of herself

Greig, David
The architect
Portrait of once idealistic and successful architect whose buildings and family crumble in light of harsh reality. 2 acts 49 scenes 4m 3w 1 setting
In Greig, D. Europe & The architect
Europe
Drama about love, loss and longing. Old and new Europeans interact in railway station in unnamed border town. 2 acts 20 scenes 6m 2w 1 interior
In Frontline intelligence 3; ed. by P. Edwardes
In Greig, D. Europe & The architect

Grenada

History—American Invasion, 1983

Dietz, S. Halcyon days

Greta Nilson's magic mare. McCullough, L. E.

Greth, Roma
Curtain call
Monologue by aging actress. 1w extra 1 interior
In Facing forward; ed. by L. D. Frank
Halfway
Two women in halfway house for patients recently released from mental institutions. 2w 1 interior
In Facing forward; ed. by L. D. Frank

Griffin, Tom
Mrs. Sedgewick's head. Dramatists 1997 67p
Drama set in Los Angeles and rural upstate New York town. Ex-con screenwriter clashes with Hollywood moguls over production of his pseudonymously published novel. 2 acts 8m 2w settings

Griffiths, David
c Flavio's disgrace
Traditional commedia dell'arte for young performers. 19 scenes 4m 4w 1 setting
In Griffiths, D. Flavio's disgrace [and another play]
c That's the way to do it
Comedy. Aristocratic English country couple and their servants both have difficulty with their children. 6 scenes 5m 4w 1 setting
In Griffiths, D. Flavio's disgrace [and another play]

Griffiths, Linda

The Duchess: pieces of Wallis Simpson

Radio play based on life of Wallis Simpson, who became Duchess of Windsor when King Edward VIII abdicated the throne to marry her. Background music. 13 scenes 6m 4w

In Adventures for (big) girls; ed. by A. Jansen

A game of inches

Woman reflects on Zen, baseball and sex. 1w 1 interior

In Solo; ed. by J. Sherman

Griffiths, Trevor

Comedians

An evening class of budding comics explores the meaning of comedy and why people laugh at jokes about sex, ethnic groups, and physical disabilities. 3 acts 11m 2 interiors

In Griffiths, T. Plays: one

Hope in the year two

Television play set in Paris at height of Great Terror in 1794. Depicts Georges Jacques Danton, one of the Revolution's most charismatic figures, on eve of his execution. 2m 1w

In Griffiths, T. Hope in the year two and Thatcher's children

Occupations

Political drama set in Italy based on life of Antonio Gramsci. During strike, Gramsci and a colleague differ on methods of achieving revolutionary change. 2 acts 8 scenes 6m 2w 1 setting

In Griffiths, T. Plays: one

The party

During 1968 Paris student uprising, group of people meet in London drawing room of successful television producer to discuss their socialist beliefs. Background music, photographic projections. Prologue 2 acts 3 scenes 10m 5w 2 interiors

In Griffiths, T. Plays: one

Real dreams

Dramatization of Jeremy Pikser's short story Revolution in Cleveland (text included in this volume). Satiric look at young radicals in 1969 Cleveland and their commitment to cause of Third World revolution. 2 acts 3 scenes 9m 3w 1 setting

In Griffiths, T. Plays: one

Thatcher's children

Drama about British society follows lives of seven young people from their primary school days in the 1970s to the turn of the century. 2 acts 3m 4w extras 2 interiors

In Griffiths, T. Hope in the year two and Thatcher's children

Who shall be happy ...? French 1997 55p

Drama set in 1794 Paris. Imprisoned French Revolution leader Danton attempts to convince guard to facilitate his liberation. 2m 1 interior

Grillparzer. Szyszkowitz, G.

Grimké, Angelina Weld

Rachel

Protest drama set in early 20th century. Young woman refuses to marry because she foresees painful future for black children in America. Music, singing. 3 acts 2m 3w 1b 1g extras 1 interior

In Black theatre USA [v1]; ed. by J. V. Hatch and T. Shine

Grimm, Jacob, and Grimm, Wilhelm

Beauty and the beast (dramatization) See Sachon, S. Beauty and the beast

The Brementown musicians (dramatization) See Gerke, P. Los mariachis Mexicanos: "The Brementown musicians"

The Frog Prince (dramatization) See Mahlmann, L. and Jones, D. C. The Frog Prince

Hansel and Gretel (dramatization) See Bush, M. Hansel and Gretel, little brother and little sister

Rapunzel (dramatization) See Thane, A. Rapunzel

Rumpelstiltskin (dramatization) See Bennett, R. Rumpelstiltskin; Mahlman, L. and Jones, D. C. Rumpelstiltskin

Seven with one blow (dramatization) See McLaren, M. Seven with one blow

The shoemaker and the elves (dramatization) See Bennett, R. The shoemaker and the elves

Sleeping beauty (dramatization) See Edgar, K. The sleeping beauty

Snow White and the seven dwarfs (dramatization) See Francoeur, B. Snow White and the seven dwarfs; Mahlmann, L. and Jones, D. C. Snow White and the seven dwarfs; Robbins, N. Snow White

The table, the donkey and the stick (dramatization) See Mahlmann, L. and Jones, D. C. The table, the donkey and the stick

Parodies, imitations, etc.

c Poskitt, K. The Rumpelstiltskin racket

c Stanford, J. Snow White—the purdiest gal in the West

Grimm tales. Grimm, J. and Grimm, W. (dramatization) See Supple, T. Grimm tales

Grimsley, Jim

Mr. Universe

Portrays sexual obsessions and fetishes of marginal characters in underbelly of New Orleans. 2 acts 5 scenes 4m 3w 1 exterior 1 interior

In Alternate roots; ed. by K. deNobriga and V. Anderson

Groping for words. Townsend, S.

Gross, Todd David

Them . . . within us. Broadway Play Pub. 1994 88p

Romantic science fiction comedy. Unmarried couple's bodies inhabited by loving extraterrestrials. 2 acts 2m 2w 1 interior

Grosso, Nick

Peaches

Portrays group of twentysomethings in contemporary London. 2 parts 10 scenes 3m 3w setting

In Coming on strong: new writing from the Royal Court Theatre

The **Group.** Warren, M.

Groves, William

Good night, sweet mother. Clark, I. E. 1993 20p

Old woman suffering from terminal cancer asks son to help her end her life. Prologue 2 scenes 1m 2w 1 interior

Grumberg, Jean-Claude

The free zone

Drama about Jewish family hiding in non-occupied part of France during World War II. Prologue 10 scenes 7m 4w 1b 1 interior

In Grumberg, J.-C. The free zone and The workroom

The workroom

Drama. Scenes in Paris tailoring workroom from 1945-1952 follow lives of seamstresses with focus on their wartime experiences and plight of Jews during the occupation. Singing. 10 scenes 6m 6w 1 interior

In Grumberg, J.-C. The free zone and The workroom

Guadalupe, Our Lady of

c Vigil, A. La aparicion de Nuestra Senora de Guadalupe. The miracle of Our Lady of Guadalupe

The **guardeen.** Frost, R.

Guardian Angels. Haylock, D.

Guare, John

Cop-out

Satire on police power. 1m 1w 1 setting

In Guare, J. The war against the kitchen sink

A day for surprises

Romantic comedy-fantasy about librarians. 1m 1w 1 interior

In Guare, J. Four baboons adoring the sun and other plays

Four baboons adoring the sun. Dramatists 1995 65p

Drama set in Italy about relationships between two archeologists and their children from previous marriages. 2m 2w extras 1 setting

—Same

In Guare, J. Four baboons adoring the sun and other plays

Home fires

Farce set in a funeral parlor on Armistice Day. German family's assimiliation into America's melting pot is traced. 3m 2w extras 1 interior

In Gaure, J. The war against the kitchen sink

In fireworks lie secret codes

Five friends at Manhattan penthouse party on 4th of July make unexpected revelations while watching Macy's fireworks display. 1 act 3m 2w 1 exterior

In Guare, J. Four baboons adoring the sun and other plays

The loveliest afternoon of the year

Absurdist comedy. Park meetings between lonely girl eager to marry and strange young man. 1m 1w 1 setting

In Guare, J. Four baboons adoring the sun and other plays

Marco Polo sings a solo

Absurdist comedy set on iceberg floating off the coast of Norway in 1999 offers disquieting glimpse of the future. 2 acts 3 scenes 6m 2w

In Guare, J. The war against the kitchen sink

Moon under Miami

First produced with title: Moon over Miami. Satire set in Alaska and Miami deals with corrupt practices among FBI agents and politicians. Music, singing. 7m 4w extras 1 setting

In Guare, J. The war against the kitchen sink

Muzeeka

Satire on middle-class values, Muzak, the Vietnam War, and its TV coverage. 6 scenes 2m 2w extras

In Guare, J. Four baboons adoring the sun and other plays

New York actor

Satirical look at New York theater community. 5m 3w 1 interior

In EST marathon, 1994

In Guare, J. Four baboons adoring the sun and other plays

Rich and famous

Comedy. Satire. The trials and tribulations of one of 'the world's oldest living promising young playwrights' and his encounters with lady producer, music collaborator, oddball parents and his old girlfriend. Music, singing. 7 scenes Variable cast 1 setting

In Guare, J. The war against the kitchen sink

Something I'll tell you Tuesday

Story of two couples, one old, one young, each at a point of crises in their lives. 2m 3w 1 setting

In Guare, J. Four baboons adoring the sun and other plays

The talking dog

Dramatization of Chekhov's short story A joke, in which a man whispers tantalizing phrases to woman, but never acknowledges that he spoke. 1 act 1m 1w 1 setting

In Guare, J. Four baboons adoring the sun and other plays

Gubar, Susan. See Gilbert, S. M. jt. auth.

Guerrillas
Hampton, C. Savages

The **guests.** Harwood, R.

Guilt
Abe, K. Involuntary homicide
Garro, E. The tree
Ibsen, H. The master builder
Kroetz, F. X. The nest
Lan, D. The ends of the earth
Lucas, C. Throwing your voice
Medoff, M. The homage that follows
Pearson, S. Unfinished stories
Ramsey, E. Acetylene
Roth, A. Born guilty
Shepard, S. Buried child
Slout, W. L. The trial of Dr. Jekyll
Solórzano, C. The Angel's forty winks
Solórzano, C. Mea culpa
Strindberg, A. The ghost sonata
Swedeen, S. The sleep seeker
Vanderhaeghe, G. Dancock's dance
Walker, G. F. Theatre of the film noir

Gulf War. Oates, J. C.

Gulf War, 1991. See Persian Gulf War, 1991

Gullahs
c McCullough, L. E. Patches solves a wedding riddle

Gums. Tasca, J.

The **gun** in history. Learner, T.

Gunmetal blues. Bohler, C. and Adler, M.

Gun-shy. Dresser, R.

Gupton, Eric. See Freeman, B. jt. auth.

Gurney, A. R.
A Cheever evening. Dramatists 1995 62p
Episodes from seventeen of John Cheever's stories interwoven to portray WASP life in 1950s and 1960s. Music. 2 acts 3m 3w 1 setting

Children
Well-to-do WASP family jolted by mother's decision to remarry. Loosely based on John Cheever story. Background music. 2 acts 8 scenes 2m 3w 1 exterior
In Gurney, A. R. Collected plays v2, 1974-1983

The cocktail hour
Set in 1970s upstate New York. Playwright comes in conflict with elderly father when he writes autobiographical play. 2 acts 2m 2w 1 interior
In Best American plays: 9th series, 1983-1992

The comeback
Odysseus' return to Penelope as news story covered by skeptical modern reporter. 1 act 4m 2w 1 exterior
In Gurney, A. R. Nine early plays, 1961-1973

The David show
This fantasy transports David, Bathsheba, Saul, Samuel to present day television studio for David's coronation. 1 act 5m 1w 1 interior
In Gurney, A. R. Nine early plays, 1961-1973

The dining room
Changing life styles and mores of upper middle class WASP families portrayed in vignettes around dining room table. 2 acts 3m 3w 1 interior
In Gurney, A. R. Collected plays v2, 1974-1983

The fourth wall. Dramatists 1996 63p
Comedy set in Buffalo, New York. Wife's decision to redecorate living room as if it were stage set vehicle for comments on contemporary life, theater, marriage and politics. Music. 2 acts 2m 2w 1 setting

The Golden Fleece
Fantasy. Squabbling suburban couple relate story of Jason and Medea. 1 act 1m 1w
In Gurney, A. R. Nine early plays, 1961-1973

Later life. Dramatists 1994 54p
Romantic comedy. Boston cocktail party setting for divorced middle-aged banker's encounter with woman he nearly had an affair with in his youth. Background music. 2m 2w 1 exterior
—Same
In Gurney, A. R. Later life and two other plays

Later life (condensation)
In The Best plays of 1992-1993

The Middle Ages
Romantic comedy set in trophy room of stuffy men's club steeped in WASP tradition. Scenes follow zany antics of nonconformist son of club's president from teenage rebel to middle age. 2 acts 2m 2w 1 interior
In Gurney, A. R. Collected plays v2, 1974-1983

The old boy
Drama. Politician's return to prep-school to dedicate building to friend dead of AIDS forces crisis of conscience. 2 acts 3m 3w 1 setting
In Gurney, A. R. Later life and two other plays

The Old One-Two
Satire on academic attitudes. Problems faced by classics professor in American university. 2m 1w 1 setting
In Gurney, A. R. Nine early plays, 1961-1973

Overtime. Dramatists 1996 75p
Modern sequel to The merchant of Venice set in contemporary America vehicle for comments on class distinction, ethnicity, wealth, gender, etc. 6m 3w setting

Gurney, A. R.—*Continued*
The problem
Absurdist comedy. Husband and wife pass the evening playing psychological games. 1 act 1m 1w 1 interior
In Gurney, A. R. Nine early plays, 1963-1973

Public affairs: Pt1 The love course
Woman professor, team-teaching with younger male colleague with whom she has fallen in love, attempts to bring their relationship and their class to conclusion. 1 act 2m 2w 1 interior
In Gurney, A. R. Nine early plays, 1961-1973

Public affairs: Pt2 The open meeting
Comedy. Fate of missing participant of meeting is revealed in surprise ending. 1 act 2m 1w 1 interior
In Gurney, A. R. Nine early plays, 1961-1973

The rape of Bunny Stuntz
Efficient suburban matron chairing meeting has to cope with off-stage intruder who claims to know her. 1 act 1m 2w 1 interior
In Gurney, A. R. Nine early plays, 1961-1973

Richard Cory
Revised version of Who killed Richard Cory? An attempt to discover why a successful lawyer, who had wealth, health, good breeding and respect of his fellow men would commit suicide. Variable cast 1 setting
In Gurney, A. R. Collected plays v2, 1974-1983

Scenes from American life
Social satire. Vignettes of WASP life from the Depression into the 1980s. 2 acts 4m 4w 1 setting
In Gurney, A. R. Nine early plays, 1961-1973

The snow ball
Drama depicting middle-aged WASP men attempting to relive their youth by staging mid-winter charity ball. Dancing. 2 acts 5m 5w extras interior
In Gurney, A. R. Later life and two other plays

Sylvia. Dramatists 1996 75p
Comedy. Middle-aged New York couple's marriage put in jeopardy when husband becomes overly attached to stray dog (portrayed by actress) he found in park. Music. 2 acts 2m 2w 1 setting

The Wayside Motor Inn
Motel outside Boston housing five sets of travelers vehicle for commentary on shortcomings of life in contemporary America. 2 acts 6m 4w 1 interior
In Gurney, A. R. Collected plays v2, 1974-1983

What I did last summer
Summer of 1945 setting for memory play about adolescent's rebellion against constraints of WASP mores. Background singing. 2 acts 2m 4w 1 setting
In Gurney, A. R. Collected plays v2, 1974-1983

Gurr, Michael
Jerusalem. Currency Press in association with Playbox Theatre 1996 85p (Current theatre series)
Drama about moral role of individual in society. Australian prison reform activist, parlimentarian husband and son begin to question their ideals. 2 acts 43 scenes 3m 3w 1 setting

Underwear, perfume and crash helmet. Currency Press in association with Playbox Theatre 1994 73p (Current theatre series)
Political thriller set in contemporary Australia. Right-wing philosopher and disturbed young woman forever alter lives of MP and family. 2 acts 38 scenes 3m 3w 1 setting

The **gut** girls. Daniels, S.

Guyer, Murphy
The American century
Absurdist comedy about son who travels back in time to visit his yet childless parents and inform them of unexpected disasters ahead. 1 act 2m 1w 1 interior
In 20/20: twenty one-act plays from twenty years of the Humana Festival

Gwen and Gwen. Kiefer, N.

H

Habeas corpus. Bennett, A.

The **habitation** of dragons. Foote, H.

Hackett, Walter
y The man without a country
Based on Edward Everett Hale's story about patriotism. 14m extras
In The Big book of dramatized classics; ed. by S. E. Kamerman

y A tale of two cities
Dramatization of Charles Dickens' novel set in Paris and London during the French Revolution. 7 scenes 12m 4w extras 5 interiors 1 exterior
In The Big book of dramatized classics; ed. by S. E. Kamerman

y Tom Sawyer, whitewasher
Dramatization of incident from Mark Twain's novel The adventures of Tom Sawyer. Tom tricks friends into whitewashing fence. 1w 6b 1 exterior
In The Big book of dramatized classics; ed. by S. E. Kamerman

Hagger, Nicholas
The warlords. Element 1995 221p
Verse drama about last year of World War II focusing on Montgomery and his conflict with Eisenhower. 2 parts 12 scenes Large mixed cast settings

Haiku. Snodgrass, K.

Haing Ngor
Cambodian odyssey (dramatization) See Lipsky, J. The survivor: a Cambodian odyssey

Hairum-scarum. Hamlett, C.

The **hairy** ape. O'Neill, E.

Haiti

History—To 1791

Hughes, L. Emperor of Haiti

Haiti (a dream). Sunde, K.

Haitian refugees. See Refugees, Haitian

Haitians

Guadeloupe

Schwarz-Bart, S. Your handsome captain

Halcyon days. Dietz, S.

Hale, Edward Everett
The man without a country (dramatization) See Hackett, W. The man without a country

Hale, Nathan
c Martens, A. C. One life to lose

Halevy, Ludovic. See Meilhac, H. jt. auth.

Half an idea. Larbey, B.

Halfway. Greth, R.

Halfway home. Bank, D.

Halfway up the M3 on the way to Basingstoke. Kitchen, B.

Hall, Frances Benn
The book of herself
Life of Irish dramatist Lady Gregory employing conventions of Nō drama. Dancing, music. 2w extras
In Hall, F. B. Ezra's Noh for Willie and other plays

Dance of the Eland
Life of African American poet Phillis Wheatley employing conventions of Nō drama. Background music. 2m 3w
In Hall, F. B. Ezra's Noh for Willie and other plays

Emily's play
Portrayal of Emily and Branwell Bronte employing conventions of Nō drama. Background music. 1m 2w 1b 1g extras
In Hall, F. B. Ezra's Noh for Willie and other plays

Ezra's Noh for Willie
Life of Ezra Pound employing conventions of Nō drama. Background music, dancing. 4m 2w extras
In Hall, F. B. Ezra's Noh for Willie and other plays

Lucia
Explores troubled life of James Joyce's daughter Lucia using conventions of Nō drama. Dancing. 2m 3w extras
In Hall, F. B. Ezra's Noh for Willie and other plays

Nathaniel in Berkshire
Play about Nathaniel Hawthorne employing conventions of Nō drama. Background music. 3m 2w extras
In Hall, F. B. Ezra's Noh for Willie and other plays

Via Reggio revisited
Portrayal of Lord Byron employing conventions of Nō drama. Background music. lm 2w extras
In Hall, F. B. Ezra's Noh for Willie and other plays

Hall, Marjory
c Molly Pitcher meets the General
Molly Pitcher, who provided for weary Revolutionary soldiers, meets General Washington. 2 scenes 7m 1w 1 interior 1 exterior
In Great American events on stage; ed. by S. E. Kamerman

Hall, Paavo
D-Day
Three veterans of seperate wars converse around Las Vegas apartment complex pool. 3m 1w 1 exterior
In Lucky 13; ed. by R. Shuttleworth

Hall, Willis
Jane Eyre. French (London) 1994 99p
Dramatization of Charlotte Bronte's classic 19th century novel of love and madness. Prologue 2 acts 31 scenes Large mixed cast settings

Mansfield Park. French (London) 1994 97p
Dramatization of Austen's classic novel about girl adopted into family of rich uncle. 2 acts 14 scenes 9m 7w extras settings

The three musketeers. French (London) 1995 98p
Dramatization of Dumas' swashbuckling classic. Prologue 2 acts 23 scenes 13m 4w extras

Halliwell, Kenneth
Moore, E. Live with it

Hallman, Bill
The women of Theta Kappa. French 1995 71p
Comedy. Sorority life at University of Texas in 1950s. 1 act 8w 1 interior

Halloween
Goluboff, B. The other five percent
y Kelly, T. Trick or Treat
c Marx, P. The haunting contest
c Nordlicht, L. Cover your eyes and run!
c Pflomm, P. N. Halloween ghosts
c Pflomm, P. N. Witches and ghosts
y Swartz, L. D. Halloween dreams
y Swartz, L. D. Halloween screams

Halloween dreams. Swartz, L. D.

Halloween ghosts. Pflomm, P. N.

Halloween screams. Swartz, L. D.

Hallucinations and illusions
Strindberg, A. Simoom

Halvorson, Kristina
One hundred women
Young woman jealous of time roommate spends with boyfriend. 1m 2w 1 interior
In Actors Theatre of Louisville. Ten minute plays v3

Ham (Biblical figure)
Hurston, Z. N. The first one

The **ham** funeral. White, P.

Hamilton, Alexander, 1757-1804
Keithley, G. The best blood of the country
Kingsley, S. The patriots

Hamilton, Godfrey
Kissing Marianne
Drama about incest and homosexuality. Brothers reunited after thirteen years apart. Music. 16 scenes 2m 1 setting.
In Staging gay lives; ed. by J. M. Clum

Hamlett, Christina
c Boarder skirmish
Fairy tale characters visit boarding house. 2m 4w 2b 2g extras 1 interior
In The Big book of large-cast plays; ed. by S. E. Kamerman

c Face value
Knight breaks spell and turns ugly crone into beautiful lady. 3 scenes 3m 1w extras 1 setting
In The Big book of large-cast plays; ed. by S. E. Kamerman

y Hairum-scarum
Comedy. Fairy tale characters come to beauty parlor to solve their problems. 7w 1 interior
In The Big book of skits; ed. by S. E. Kamerman

y Once upon a taxi
Romantic comedy. Woman claiming to be princess proposes to New York taxi driver. Music. 1m 1w extra
In The Big book of skits; ed. by S. E. Kamerman

The **hammerstone.** Tuttle, J.

Hammond, Wendy
Julie Johnson. Dramatists 1995 62p
After leaving abusive husband, New Jersey housewife falls in love with lady friend, returns to school and adjusts to new found independence. 2 acts 13 scenes 1m 3w 1g 1 setting

—Same
In Humana Festival '94

Hampton, Christopher
Alice's adventures under ground. Faber & Faber 1995 70p
Drama presenting Alice books as private emotional fantasies and dreams of Lewis Carroll. Music, singing. 17 scenes 4m 1g 1 setting

The philanthropist
Comedy about the love life of shy university professor. 2 acts 6 scenes 4m 3w 1 interior
In Hampton, C. Plays: one

Savages
English diplomat's kidnapping by Brazilian revolutionary guerrillas is vehicle for indictment of western man for genocide of Cintas Largas tribe of Brazilian Indians. 2 acts 19 scenes 9m 1w extras 1 setting
In Hampton, C. Plays: one

Total eclipse
Traces relationship between French symbolist poets Rimbaud and Verlaine. 2 acts 12 scenes 10m 5w extras 9 interiors 1 exterior
In Hampton, C. Plays: one

Treats
Comedy about a love triangle. 1 act 9 scenes 2m 1w 1 interior
In Hampton, C. Plays: one

Hampton, Mark, and Wilson, Mary Louise
Full gallop. Dramatists 1997 48p
Drama based on life of Diana Vreeland, legendary editor of Harper's Bazaar and Vogue. 1w 1 extra 1 interior

A **hand** witch of the second stage. See Barnes, P. The spirit of man: A hand witch of the second stage

Handcuffs. Armstrong, G. K.

Handel, George Frederick
O'Donovan, J. The fiddler and the Dean

A **handful** of earth. Zauner, F. Ch.

A **handful** of friends. Williamson, D.

Handke, Peter
The hour we knew nothing of each other
Experimental drama set in city square. More than four hundred characters pass by without uttering single word. Large mixed cast
In Hanke, P. Voyage to the sonorous land and The hour we knew nothing of each other

Voyage to the sonorous land; or, The art of asking
Experimental drama about language. Cock-eyed optimist and spoilsport lead group of characters through hinterlands of imagination. 3 acts 7 scenes 6m 2w 1 setting
In Handke, P. Voyage to the sonorous land and The hour we knew nothing of each other

Handke, Peter—*Continued*
Walk about the villages; a dramatic poem; in a translation for voice with an afterword by Michael Roloff. Ariadne Press 1996 153p (Studies in Austrian literature, culture, and thought. Translation series)
Dramatic meditation on rural roots, modernity and self. Author returns to home village and argues with brother and sister over disposition of family home. 4 parts 6m 3w 1 setting

The **hands** of God. Solórzano, C.

Hands off! don't touch! Martin, J.

The **handyman.** Harwood, R.

Hang up. Minghella, A.

Hanna Senesh. Megged, A.

Hannan, Chris
Shining souls. Hern Bks. 1996 83p
Comedy about love, marriage, idealism, mothers, daughters, and Tarot cards. 2 acts 8 scenes 6m 4w 2 settings

Hannay, Richard
y Windows
Drama set in Australia. Suicidal woman falsely accuses two aborigines of assault. 3m 3w extra
In Young playwrights; ed. by E. Bray

Hans Christian Andersen's The Snow Queen. Kennedy, R.

Hansberry, Lorraine
A raisin in the sun. Modern Lib. 1995 xxvi, 135p
Tensions erupt in middle class Chicago black family when they come into possession of a legacy. 3 acts 6 scenes 5m 3w 1b extras 1 interior
—Same
In Black theatre USA [v2]; ed. by J. V. Hatch and T. Shine
In Hansberry, L. A raisin in the sun and The sign in Sidney Brustein's window

The sign in Sidney Brustein's window
Greenwich Village intellectual and friends support reform candidate who, they later discover is not purely altruistic. Singing. 3 acts 7 scenes 6m 3w 1 setting
In Hansberry, L. A raisin in the sun and The sign in Sidney Brustein's window

Hansel and Gretel, the little brother and sister. Bush, M.

Hanson, Mary E. and Sheldon, David P.
c Madame Zena's séance
Comedy. Kidnapped Arab princess is rescued following bogus séance. 6m 6w 1b 1g 1 interior
In The Big book of large-cast plays; ed. by S. E. Kamerman

Hanukkah
Rumble, P. B. Aunt Sophie's latkes

Hapgood. Stoppard, T.

Happy journey. See Wilder, T. The happy journey to Camden and Trenton

The **happy** journey to Camden and Trenton. Wilder, T.

Hard-boiled. Frockt, D. L.

Hardee, Lewis
The prince and the pauper; a musical comedy; book, lyrics and music by Lewis Hardee; based on the novel by Mark Twain. Dramatic 1995 80p
Musical based on Mark Twain's novel of mistaken identity. 2 acts 10m 6w extras 1 interior 1 exterior

Harder, Eleanor
c Hey ho, Pinocchio; book by Eleanor & Ray Harder; music & lyrics by Eleanor Harder. Pioneer Drama Service 1993 40p
Musical based on Carlo Collodi's tale about marionette who becomes real boy. Variable cast 15 characters extras 1 setting
y Rememberin' stuff. Pioneer Drama Service 1996 37p
Teenagers share memories for high school drama class assignment. 2 acts Variable cast

Harder, Ray. See Harder, E. Hey ho, Pinocchio

Harding, Alex
Blood and honour
Drama about AIDS, homophobia and anti-Asian racism set in contemporary Australia. 2m 1w 1 setting
In Australian gay and lesbian plays; ed. by B. Parr

Harding, Michael
Hubert Murray's widow
Surreal drama about political and sexual passion set in rural Northern Ireland. Protestant youth and senior IRA operative, both ghosts, continue rivalry over older man's widow. 2 acts 5m 3w 1 interior
In New plays from the Abbey Theatre, 1993-1995

Harding, Norah
This year, next year. Playwrights Canada 1996 102p
Drama set in Bournemouth, England, 1944. Three high-spirited sisters and their mother struggle to survive during wartime. 2 acts 5 scenes 1m 5w 1 interior

Harding, Warren G. President
St. Germain, M. Camping with Henry & Tom

Hardstack, Michael

The cure

Farce based on Chekhov's short story A cure for drinking. Troupe of Yiddish actors in turn-of-the-century Cleveland struggle to sober up their star. 4m 1w 1 interior

In Hardstack, M. The last laugh

In the cemetery

Comic drama suggested by Chekhov story. Young businessman hires rabbi to pray at father's grave. 3m 1 exterior

In Hardstack, M. The last laugh

Hardy, Thomas

Tess of the d'Urbervilles (dramatization) See Fry, M. Tess of the d'Urbervilles

The **Hardy** Boys and the mystery of where babies come from. Durang, C.

Hare, David

The absence of war. Faber & Faber 1993 110p

Third play in trilogy about British institutions focuses on Labour Party politics and politicians. 10m 3w 2 acts 23 scenes settings

Amy's view. Faber & Faber 1997 127p

Psychological drama about strained relationship between famous British actress and her dutiful daughter from 1979 to 1995. 4 acts 3m 3w 2 interiors

The bay at Nice

Drama set in 1956 Leningrad about attempt to authenticate a painting. 2m 2w 1 interior

In Hare, D. Plays: two

Fanshen

Dramatization of William Hinton's book detailing effect of Chinese revolution on inhabitants of the village of Long Bow. 2 acts 12 sections 7m 2w

In Hare, D. Plays: two

Ivanov. Methuen Drama 1997 89p (Methuen theatre classic)

Adaptation of Chekhov's satirical look at playwright's world of domestic and philosophical chaos. 4 acts 40 scenes 13m 4w extras 3 interiors 1 exterior

Knuckle

Philosophical mystery examining societal corruption. Arms dealing soldier of fortune returns to England to investigate possible suicide or murder of idealistic sister and possible guilt of banker father. Music. 2 parts 16 scenes 5m 2w extras

In Hare, D. Plays: one

Licking Hitler

Television play. British World War II propaganda unit becomes symbol of society infected by falsehood. Upper class young woman forced to resign when slandered by journalist propagandist. 7m 2w extras

In Hare, D. Plays: one

A map of the world

Set in Bombay during UNESCO conference on world poverty. Relationship of the West to the Third World reflected in ideological and emotional clashes between cynical Indian novelist and idealistic British journalist. 2 acts 10 scenes 6m 4w extras 1 setting

In Hare, D. Plays: two

Murmuring judges. [Rev. ed] Faber & Faber 1993 109p

Second play in trilogy about British institutions. Young lawyer encounters shortcomings of British legal system. 2 acts 15 scenes Large mixed cast settings

Plenty

Drama counterpointing experiences of Englishwoman who aided the French Resistance with her life in the following twenty years. Music. 12 scenes 9m 5w 4 interiors 2 exteriors

In Hare, D. Plays: one

Saigon: year of the cat

Drama focusing on emotional turmoil endured by individuals during United States' withdrawal from Vietnam. 11m 1w extras

In Hare, D. Plays: two

The secret rapture

Political allegory set in Thatcher's England. Following father's death, "good" sister's life is destroyed by ambitious MP sister, her born again Christian husband, and father's destructive young alcoholic widow. 2 acts 8 scenes 2m 4w settings

In Hare, D. Plays: two

Skylight. Faber & Faber 1995 102p

Present day London setting for drama exploring relationship between wealthy middle-aged restaurateur and his much younger former mistress. 2 acts 3 scenes 2m 1w 1 setting

—Same. French 1997 118p

—Same. French (London) 1997 73p

Skylight (condensation)

In The Best plays of 1996-1997

Slag

Three teachers attempt to establish a feminist community in British girl's boarding school. 6 scenes 3w 3 interiors 1 exterior

In Hare, D. Plays: one

Teeth 'n' smiles

A study of disintegrating English rock group at the end of the 1960s. Drugs, alcohol and indiscrimnate fan approval speed its downfall. Music. 8 scenes 10m 2w 1 interior 1 exterior

In Hare, D. Plays: one

See also Brecht, B. Mother Courage and her children; Pirandello, L. The rules of the game

Hare, William

Hood, E. A wake for Donald

Hark, Mildred, and McQueen, Noel

c Civilians stay put

Grandfather remembers his teenage years during World War II. 2 scenes 6m 3w extras 1 interior

In Great American events on stage; ed. by S. E. Kamerman

Hark, Mildred, and McQueen, Noel —*Continued*

y George Washington Carver

Drama illustrating the thirst for knowledge which gained Carver his education and reputation in many fields of science. 3 scenes 7m 3w 3 interiors

In Plays of black Americans; ed. by S. E. Kamerman

Harlem. See New York (N.Y.)—Harlem

Harlequin

Millay, E. St. V. Aria da capo

Harlequinade. Rattigan, T.

Harmer, Wendy

What is the matter with Mary Jane? Currency Press 1996 74p (Currency teenage drama)

One woman drama about anorexia nervosa and bulimia. 1w 1 setting

The **harmfulness** of tobacco. See Chekhov, A. The dangers of tobacco

Harm's way. Wellman, M.

Harnetiaux, Bryan

The snows of Kilimanjaro. Dramatic 1995 77p

Based on story by Ernest Hemingway. Writer seeks redemption on African Serengeti Plain in the 1930s. Prelude 2 acts 9 scenes 5m 5w 1 setting

Harper, Terry

Christmas isn't for families. New Playwrights Network 1996 68p

Christmas celebration highlights family problems. 2 acts 5 scenes 3m 4w 1 interior

Rehearsal for murder. New Playwrights Network 1997 71p

Mystery. Props girl is murdered during amateur drama society rehearsal. 2 acts 4 scenes 4m 4w 1 interior

Requiem for Denys. New Playwrights Network 1996 77p

Mentally handicapped man is cared for by brother and sister-in-law. 2 acts 6 scenes 4m 4w 1 setting

That's the spirit. New Playwrights Network 1995 60p

Actor tricked into murder trap by father-in-law. 2 acts 4 scenes 6m 4w 1 interior

The **Harper** chronicles. Schnupp, A.

Harpers Ferry (W. VA.)

John Brown's Raid, 1859

Branch, W. In splendid error

Harriet. Kenyatta, K.

Harriet Tubman—the second Moses. Fisher, A.

Harris, Aurand

The importance of being Earnest. Anchorage Press 1991 32p

Adaptation of Wilde's drawing room comedy about Victorian society. 2 scenes 5m 4w 2 interiors

c Peter Rabbit and me. Anchorage Press 1994 52p

Dramatization of Peter Rabbit tale by Beatrix Potter interspersed with scenes from Beatrix Potter's life. Variable cast 16 characters 2 interiors 1 exterior

y The pinballs

Dramatization of novel by Betsy Byars. Two teenagers and eight-year-old boy come together in supportive foster home. 6 scenes 2m 2w 1b extras 1 exterior

In Around the world in 21 plays; ed. by L. Swortzell

y The prince and the pauper. Anchorage Press 1995 56p

Dramatization of Mark Twain's novel set in 16th century England. Edward VI and Tom Canty, a beggar boy, exchange identities. Singing, puppets. 4m 4w 2b extras

c Young Black Beauty. Anchorage Press 1996 58p

Dramatization of Anna Sewell's novel Black Beauty set in 1870 England about experiences of horse at hands of many owners. Background music. 2 acts 2 scenes Variable cast 12 characters extras 1 setting

Harris, Bill

Robert Johnson: trick the Devil

Drama about African American blues legend. Music, singing. Prologue 2 acts 3 scenes 4m 1w 1 interior

In The National black drama anthology; ed. by W. King

Harris, Mark, 1922-

Bang the drum slowly (dramatization) See Simonson, E. Bang the drum slowly

Harris, R. C.

Abigail! New Playwrights Network 1995 80p

Series of mysterious deaths occur in English country house when relative returns from Australia. 3 acts 4 scenes 2m 6w 1 interior

Harris, Richard

Dead guilty. French (London) 1996 83p

Revenge thriller. Widow and lover of accident victim find themselves locked in deadly combat. 2 acts 1m 3w extra 1 interior

Harrison, John

Holidays. French (London) 1996 62p

Woman fighting battle with cancer retreats to country cottage to make decisions regarding her future. 2 acts 2m 1w 2 interiors

Harrison, Paul Carter

The great MacDaddy

Allegorical play utilizing Afro-American myths, songs and music. Black bootlegger encounters forces that change his direction in life. Prologue 7 scenes epilogue Variable cast

In Classic plays from the Negro Ensemble Company; ed. by P. C. Harrison and G. Edwards

Harrison, Tony

The Kaisers of Carnuntum

Verse drama portraying Roman Emperor Commodus, son of Marcus Aurelius, as bloodthirsty tyrant. 4m 1w 1 setting

In Harrison, T. Plays: three

The labourers of Herakles

Experimental verse play based on existing fragments of Phrynikos, the earliest Greek tragedian. 5m 1 setting

In Harrison, T. Plays: three

Poetry or bust

Verse drama about Airedale poet John Nicholson. 6m 3w 1 setting

In Harrison, T. Plays: three

Harrower, David

Knives in hens. Methuen Drama 1995 36p (Methuen fast track playscript)

Drama about lust, love and murder set in pre-industrial Scottish village. Lives of passionate young woman, ploughman husband and miller become tragically interwoven. 24 scenes 2m 1w 1 setting

Harry and me. Williams, N.

The **Harry** and Sam dialogues. Ellison, K.

Harry's Christmas. Berkoff, S.

Hartsfield, Mariella Glenn

Tall Betsy and Dunce Baby (dramatization) See Wheeler, J. and Hartsfield, M. G. Tall Betsy and the crackerbarrel tales

See also Wheeler, J. jt. auth.

Harvest the frost. Kai, N.

Harvey, Jonathan

Babies. Methuen Drama in association with the Royal Court Theatre 1994 94p (Royal Court writers series)

Comedy about private and professional life of gay tutor in southeast London comprehensive. 2 acts 16 scenes 6m 7w extras 1 setting

Beautiful thing. Methuen Drama 1994 71p (Methuen modern plays)

Working-class comedy set in 1993 South East London about adolescent self-discovery. Two sixteen-year-old boys fall in love. 2 acts 10 scenes 3m 2w 1 setting

Boom bang-a-bang

Heartbroken homosexual hosts party for select group of friends on night of Eurovision Song Contest, 1995. 3 acts 5m 2w 1 interior

In Harvey, J. Rupert Street Lonely Hearts Club & Boom bang-a-bang

Rupert Street Lonely Hearts Club

Comedy set in 1995 East London. Explores relationships, homosexual and heterosexual, among group of twentysomethings. 2 acts 7 scenes 3m 2w 1 interior

In Harvey, J. Rupert Street Lonely Hearts Club & Boom bang-a-bang

The **Harvey** Milk show. Pruitt, D. and Hutchison, P.

Harwood, Ronald

After the lions

Set in France during first World War. Portrays Sarah Bernhardt near the end of her career. Singing. 2 acts 4m 3w 1 interior

In Harwood, R. Plays: two

Another time

Set in 1950s South Africa and London thirty-five years later. Drama traces family relationship of successful but troubled Jewish pianist. 2 acts 8 scenes 3m 2w extras 4 interiors

In Harwood, R. The collected plays of Ronald Harwood

The dresser

Provincial theater in wartime England setting for drama exploring aging Shakespearean actor's relationship with his devoted dresser. 2 acts 8m 3w 1 setting

In Harwood, R. The collected plays of Ronald Harwood

A family

Domestic comedy. Young woman rebels against constriction of family environment and dominating elders. 2 acts 4m 4w 1 setting

In Harwood, R. The collected plays of Ronald Harwood

The guests

Revealing conversation with imaginary guests. 1w

In Harwood, R. Plays: two

The handyman. Faber & Faber 1996 81p

Drama about guilt, retribution, universal responsibility, and nature of evil. English couple's Ukranian odd-job man accused of participating in Nazi ordered massacre of Jews. 2 acts 5m 3w 1 interior 1 exterior

J. J. Farr

Comedy drama about loss of religious faith by former hostage. 2 acts 6 scenes 6m 1 setting

In Harwood, R. The collected plays of Ronald Harwood

The ordeal of Gilbert Pinfold

Dramatization of Evelyn Waugh's autobiographical novel of writer on sea voyage to Ceylon, who is beset by hallucinations and paranoia. 2 acts 12m 5w 2 interiors

In Harwood, R. Plays: two

Harwood, Ronald—*Continued*
Poison pen. Faber & Faber 1994 96p
Mortal struggle between homosexual music critic and his heterosexual alternate personality. 6m 2w 1 setting
—Same
In Harwood, R. Plays: two
Taking sides. Dramatists 1997 65p
Set in American Zone of occupied Berlin, 1946. Denazifaction Tribunal questions maestro Wilhelm Furtwängler. 2 acts 3 scenes 4m 2w 1 interior
—Same Faber & Faber 1995 60p
—Same
In Harwood, R. Plays: two
Tramway Road
Set in Cape Town suburb. Middle-aged expatriate English couple's marriage of convenience shaken by homosexual husband's latest protégé being re-classified non-white. 2 acts 3m 1w 1 interior
In Harwood, R. Plays: two

Hasenclever, Walter
The son
Expressionist drama exploring generational conflicts. 5 acts 8m 2w 4 interiors
In German expressionist plays; ed. by E. Schurer

Hasidism
Ansky, S. The dybbuk

Hassle in the castle. Schaaf, A. K.

Hastings, Charlotte
The wayward spirit. French (London) 1995 95p
Drama set in East Anglia convent hospital. Nun saves relationship between embittered permanently paralyzed soldier and fiancée. 3 acts 6 scenes 6m 6w 1 interior

Hatcher, Jeffrey
Scotland Road. Dramatists 1996 48p
Psychological drama set in 1990s Maine. Mysterious man interrogates young woman claiming to be survivor of Titanic. 2 acts 20 scenes 1m 3w 1 interior
Smash. Dramatist 1997 79p
Dramatization of Bernard Shaw's novel An unsocial socialist. Political comedy of manners set in 1910 England. Millionaire's quest for socialist ideals sidetracked by love triangles and mistaken identity. 3 acts 4 scenes 5m 5w 2 exteriors
Three viewings. Dramatists 1996 63p
Three comic/dramatic monologues set in midwestern funeral parlor. 1m 2w 1 interior
The turn of the screw. Dramatists 1997 50p
Dramatization of Henry James's tale of horror, suspense and repressed sexuality. Young governess haunted by ghosts of predecessor and sadistic valet. 1m 1w 1 setting

Hate. Goldstein, J.

Hated nightfall. Barker, H.

Hatton, Thomas J.
c Super Dooper Man
Parody of Superman. Super Dooper Man defeats Kryptonite Kid with help of Mary Wonderful. 3m 1w extra 1 interior
In The Big book of skits; ed. by S. E. Kamerman

Haubold, Cleve
The big black Box
Symbolic comedy. Black Box takes advantage of gullible man. 1 act 1m extra 1 exterior
In Short plays for young actors; ed. by C. Slaight and J. Sharrar

Hauncho the hamster. Campbell, E.

Haunted. Chappell, E.

The **haunted.** See O'Neill, E. Mourning becomes Electra: The haunted

The **haunted** house. Plautus, T. M.

The **haunted** tower. Sade, Marquis de

The **haunting** contest. Marx, P.

Hauptmann, Gerhart
The beaver coat; tr. by Theodore H. Lustig
Satire. Ambitious and industrious washerwoman turns to theft to supplement income. 4 acts 8m 4w 1b 2 interiors
In Hauptmann, G. Plays
Before daybreak; tr. by Peter Bauland
Naturalistic drama. Idealistic young socialist is dismayed by corruption of newly wealthy peasant family. Although he loves their daughter, he abandons her to her grim future. 5 acts 10m 9w 1 interior 1 exterior
In Hauptmann, G. Plays
The weavers; tr. by Theodore H. Lustig
Tragedy. Revolt of textile workers in mid-nineteenth century Germany. 5 acts Large mixed cast 5 interiors
In Hauptmann, G. Plays

Have a nice day. Brittney, L.

"**Have** floss, will travel": the ever-so-true saga of Hiram T. McRoot, frontier dentist. McCullough, L. E.

The **have**-little. Cruz, M.

Havel, Václav
Audience
Television play about communism. Ideological and economic pressures exerted upon nonconformist Czech playwright. 2m
In Havel, V. Selected plays, 1963-83

Havel, Václav—*Continued*

The garden party

Satirical look at life under totalitarian regime. Young upstart's success depends on his ability to adjust his speaking habits to fit into various bureaucratic situations. 2 acts 4 scenes 6m 3w 3 interiors

In Havel, V. Selected plays, 1963-83

The increased difficulty of concentration

Satire about dehumanization of modern life. Sociologist becomes hopelessly enmeshed in his erotic conflicts. 2 acts 4m 4w 1 interior

In Havel, V. Selected plays, 1963-83

Largo desolato; English version by Tom Stoppard

Philosopher in totalitarian state is pressed by government to repudiate his work and pressured by friends to take a stand. 7 scenes 5m 3w 1 interior

In Havel, V. Selected plays, 1984-87

The memorandum

In this satire on bureaucratic "efficiency" a new "scientific" language is imposed as the official means of communication in a large organization. 12 scenes 9m 3w extras 3 interiors

In Havel, V. Selected plays, 1963-83

Mistake

Prisoners turn on new cellmate. 5m 1 interior

In Havel, V. Selected plays, 1963-83

Protest

Writer uses logical linguistic evasions when dissident colleague asks for his signature on petition. 1 act 2m 1 interior

In Havel, V. Selected plays, 1963-83

Redevelopment; or, Slum clearance; English version by James Saunders

Political drama using town planning as metaphor of life in Eastern Europe before collapse of communism. 5 acts 9m 4w 1 interior

In Havel, V. Selected plays, 1984-87

Temptation; tr. by George Theiner

Political drama. Variation on Faust theme portraying scientist in police state who meets his downfall when enticed to dabble in magic. 10 scenes 8m 4w extras

In Havel, V. Selected plays, 1984-87

Tomorrow!

Historical comedy about founding of Czechoslovak Republic. 5 acts Variable cast 17 characters extras

In Czech plays; modern Czech drama; ed. by B. Day

Unveiling

Variant title: Private view. Television satire. Dissident Czech playwright is urged by materialistic friends to redirect his supposedly futile life. 2m 1w

In Havel, V. Selected plays, 1963-83

Havens, Diane. See Bernardi, P. jt. auth.

Having our say. Mann, E.

Havis, Allan

A vow of silence

Drama dealing with Israeli-Palestinian conflicts. 30 scenes 10m 1w

In Fruitful and multiplying; ed. by E. Schiff

Hawaii

Aoki, B. W. The Queen's garden

Gotanda, P. K. Ballad of Yachiyo

Kneubuhl, V. N. The conversion of Ka'ahumanu

Lim, G. Bitter cane

Linney, R. The love suicide at Schofield Barracks

Morris, A. Lili'uokalani

Hawkins, Rudolph V. See Higginsen, V. and Wydro, K. Mama, I want to sing

Hawthorne, Nathaniel

The House of the Seven Gables (dramatization) See Thane, A. The House of the Seven Gables

Rappaccini's daughter (dramatization) See Paz, O. Rappaccini's daughter

The scarlet letter (dramatization) See Nagy, P. The scarlet letter

About

Hall, F. B. Nathaniel in Berkshire

Hayes, Elliott

Poison

Husband discovers wife is having affair. 1m 1w 1 interior

In Actors Theatre of Louisville. Ten-minute plays v3

Hayes, Jennifer Fell

Nothing in common

Successful businesswoman offers to adopt baby born to young woman abandoned by boyfriend. 2w 1 setting

In Off-Off Broadway Festival plays, 19th ser.

Haylock, Derek

c Christian olympics

Worship program. Living of Christian life likened to athletic endeavor. Variable cast 8 characters

In Haylock, D. Plays on the word

c Don't care, won't care, couldn't care less

Worship program. Christian response to environmental issues. Variable cast 10 characters

In Haylock, D. Plays on the word

c The flaming fiery furnace

Worship program based on Bible story of three youths saved from death by their faith in God. Large mixed cast

In Haylock, D. Plays on the word

Haylock, Derek—*Continued*

c Follow the leader

Worship program. Silly sheep follow anyone, but sensible sheep follow Good Shepherd. Variable cast

In Haylock, D. Plays on the word

c Guardian Angels

Worship program. Angels observe the Nativity from heaven. Variable cast 3 characters

In Haylock, D. Plays on the word

c Here is the news: Good news and bad news

Worship program. Death of King David's son Absalom related on television news program. 5m 2w 1 interior

In Haylock, D. Plays on the word

c Here is the news: Overseas and underseas news

Worship program. Story of Jonah and the whale told on television news program. 4m 2w 1 interior

In Haylock, D. Plays on the word

c Here is the news: Riot in Nazareth

Worship program. Television news show reports story of Jesus' return to Nazareth. 4m 3w 1 interior

In Haylock, D. Plays on the word

c Here is the news: Sad news and amazing news

Worship program. Television news show covers Story of crucifixion and resurrection of Christ. 4m 3w 1 interior

In Haylock, D. Plays on the word

c How to be an alien

Worship program tells light-hearted version of story of Daniel in the lion's den. Variable cast 6 characters

In Haylock, D. Plays on the word

c Light of the world

Worship program. Contrasts Light of God with darkness of evil. Variable cast

In Haylock, D. Plays on the word

c Light on the road to Damascus

Worship program with mime recounting Biblical story of Saul's conversion. Large mixed cast

In Haylock, D. Plays on the word

c The nativity scene

Worship program about Christ's nativity. 2m 3w

In Haylock, D. Plays on the word

c Rejection

Worship program. Symbolic mime with Bible readings about how Christ has been rejected through the ages. Background music. Variable cast

In Haylock, D. Plays on the word

c The shepherd and the psychiatrist

Worship program. Shepherd describes Nativity to psychiatrist. 1m 2w 1 interior

In Haylock, D. Plays on the word

c The Wallies guide to Christmas

Worship program about real meaning of Christmas. Variable cast 6 characters

In Haylock, D. Plays on the word

c Whoever

Worship program. Christ turns no one away. Audience participation. Large mixed cast

In Haylock, D. Plays on the word

c A window in the diary

Worship program. Pretentious couple misses significance of Christmas church service. 1m 1w 1 interior

In Haylock, D. Plays on the word

Hayman, Ronald

Playing the wife. French (London) 1996 73p

Drama about creative process. August Strindberg directs two actors in autobiographical play about his stormy first marriage. 2 acts 5 scenes 2m 2w 1 interior

Haynes, Harold J.

y Isolation. Clark, I.E. 1993 23p

Confrontation between troubled bully and three other high school boys leads to fatal shootings and suicide. 1 act 5m 3w 1 interior

Haywood, Claire

Table for one? Currency Press 1995 55p (Current theatre series)

Comedy about sexual politics follows four people through contemporary singles scene. 18 scenes 2m 2w 1 setting

Haywood, Dennis

Twisted tape. New Playwrights Network 1994 32p

Woman exposes plot of housekeeper's nephew to gain her aged mother's fortune. 1m 3w 1 interior

Hazzard, Alvira

Mother liked it

Farce. Two young African American girls infatuated by man they believe to be Indian prince. 2 acts 3 scenes 2m 3w 2 interiors

In Lost plays of the Harlem Renaissance; ed. by J. V. Hatch and L. Hamalian

He ain't heavy. Dashow, K.

He had a date. MacNeice, L.

The **head**, guts and sound bone dance. Cook, M.

The **head** of Mary. Chikao, T.

The **head** of the Baptist. Valle-Inclán, R. del

Head on. Dewberry, E.

Head-rot holiday. Daniels, S.

Headmasters. See Teachers

Healing nature. Warner, F.

Health

c Simmons, D. W. Nutricia Goodheart's Body Building Construction Company

Heart of the land. Manns, D.

Heart to heart. Tutt, B.

Heartbreak House. Shaw, B.

Hearts and tarts. Marx, P.

Heart's desire. See Churchill, C. Blue heart: Heart's desire

Heathen Valley, Linney, R.

The Heather Brothers
Lust; a musical; book, music and lyrics by The Heather Brothers; based on William Wycherley's The country wife. French (London) 1994 89p

Musical adaptation of Wycherley's Restoration comedy. Notorious London libertine seduces society ladies while charming their foolish husbands. Music, singing. Prologue 2 acts 14 scenes 7m 5w extras

Heaven
Allen, R. J. Blue cities
Walker, S. Come on up

Heaven help the po'taters! St. John, B.

Heaven's blessings. Barnes, P.

Hecuba, wife of Priam, King of Troy
Euripides. Hekabe
Kennelly, B. Euripides' The Trojan woman

Hedda Gabler. Ibsen, H.

Hee haw hayride. Francoeur, B.

Heelan, Kevin
Distant fires. Dramatists 1993 62p

Drama set in Ocean City Maryland. Relationships among five construction workers, three black and two white, as race riots take place in nearby neighborhood. 2 acts 6m 1 setting

Heggie, Iain
An experienced woman gives advice. Methuen Drama 1995 122p (Methuen modern plays)

Comedy about innocence and experience set in garden of block of flats in London. Woman offers young neighbor advice about men and love. 3 acts 4m 2w 1 exterior

Heidegger, Martin
Jelinek, E. Totenauberg (Death/Valley/Summit)

Heiresses. See Inheritance and succession

Heirlooms. See St. John, B. Rubies: Heirlooms

Heise, Kenan, and Heise, Dan
Clarence Darrow in hell. Chicago Hist. Bookworks 1993 64p

Legal allegory set in Dante's Hell. Clarence Darrow defends famed Chicago madam Minna Everleigh. 2 acts 11 scenes 6m 3w extras 1 setting

Heiss, Rolland L.
Illegal contact. Players Press 1996 67p

Mystery. Novelist uncovers family secrets and murder. 2 acts 4m 4w 1 interior

Hekabe. Euripides

Helen at risk. Yeaton, D.

Helen Melon at the sideshow. Dierlam, K.

Helen of Troy (Greek mythology)
Kochanoswki, J. The dismissal of the Grecian envoys
y Nightingale, E. M. Arise, Sparta!

The **Helitrope** Bouquet by Scott Joplin & Louis Chauvin. Overmyer, E.

Hellman, Lillian
The little foxes

Psychological study of greed. In small Southern town about 1900, two brothers and a sister attempt to swindle each other. 3 acts 6m 4w 1 interior

In Plays by American women, 1930-1960; ed. by J. E. Barlow

Hello . . . Is there any body there? Hornby, I.

Hello again. LaChiusa, M. J.

Hello, Ma! Stone, T.

Hello muddah, hello fadduh! Sherman, A.

Hemingway, Ernest
The snows of Kilimanjaro (dramatization) See Harnetiaux, B. The snows of Kilimanjaro

Hemophiliacs
Mastrosimone, W. Shivaree

Henceforward . . . Ayckbourn, A.

Henderson, Luther. See Wolfe, G. C. Jelly's last jam

Hendrick, Barbara
If I can't take it with me . . . I'm not going to go. New Playwrights Network 1994 18p

Comedy. Irish woman, prematurely pronounced dead, angrily reclaims her possessions. 3m 4w extras 1 interior

Henrietta. Meadows, K. J.

Henrietta and St. Clair. Sade, Marquis de

Henrik Ibsen on the necessity of producing Norwegian drama. Palmer, J.

Henry VIII, King of England
Brittney, L. The last wife
y Poskitt, K. Henry the Tudor dude

Henry, John. See John Henry

Henry, O.
The gift of the Magi (dramatization) See Ekstrom, P. An O. Henry Christmas: The gift of the Magi
The last leaf (dramatization) See Ekstrom, P. An O. Henry Christmas: The last leaf

Henry Lumper. Horovitz, I.

Henry the Tudor dude. Poskitt, K.

Her pilgrim soul. See Menken, A. Weird romance: Her pilgrim soul

Heracleidae. See Euripides. The children of Heracles

The **herbal** bed. Whelan, P.

Herbert, John
Fortune and men's eyes
Four young men in Canadian reform school brutalized by system and other inmates. 2 acts 8 scenes 5m 1 interior
In Modern Canadian plays v1; ed. by J. Wasserman

Here. Frayn, M.

Here come the cows. Kelly, T.

Here comes the judge! St. John, B.

Here is the news: Good news and bad news. Haylock, D.

Here is the news: Overseas and underseas news. Haylock, D.

Here is the news: Riot in Nazareth. Haylock, D.

Here is the news: Sad news and amazing news. Haylock, D.

Here lies Henry. MacIvor, D. and Brooks, D.

Here she is! Oates, J. C.

Here we come a-wassailing. McCullough, L. E.

El **hermano.** Linney, R.

Hermits. See Recluses

Hernani. Hugo, V.

Herod, I, King of Judea, 73-4 B.C.
Cary, E. The tragedy of Mariam, the fair

Heroes
McGuinness, F. Observe the sons of Ulster marching towards the Somme

Heroes and saints. Moraga, C.

Heroin
Harrison, P. C. The great MacDaddy

A **heroine** of the Greek resistance. Koch, K.

Herrera, Anthony. See Osborne, W. jt. auth.

Herst, Beth
A woman's comedy
Drama set in 17th century London about Aphra Behn, England's first professional woman writer. Prologue 2 acts 18 scenes epilogue 4m 2w 1 setting
In Big-time women from way back when

The **hert** o Scotland. Silver, R. S.

Herzberg, Judith
The wedding party
Guests at unhappy wedding party in 1970s Amsterdam are all in one way or another involved in fate of the Jews. 8m 6w 1 setting
In Dutch and Flemish plays; ed. by D. Couling

Hesh. Weiss, M.

Heward, Leslie
Or what's a heaven for? Excalibur Press of London 1993 77p
Jilted woman settles in Devon village where she falls in love with ghostly presence of 18th century poet. 3 acts 6 scenes 6m 6w 1 setting

"Hey, cut out the parading around stark naked!" Feydeau, G.

Hey ho, Pinocchio. Harder, E.

Hezlep, William
c Merlin's cave. Players Press 1996 28p
Welsh brother, sister and their nanny encounter fairies, pixies and the slumbering Merlin. 2m 1w 1b 1g extras 1 exterior
c Red Cloud's revenge. Players Press 1994 22p
Adventure. Sioux chief teaches mischievous boys to respect heritage of Native Americans. 1m 1w 2b 2g 1 exterior
c Tower of London. Players Press 1995 23p
An episode in the Travelers series. In Tower of London two American children meet young ghosts of Richard, Duke of York and Princess Anne of Skye. 1m 1w 2b 2g
c Treasure of the Mayans. Players Press 1994 28p
An adventure in the Travelers series. American children visiting Mayan ruins in Mexico save treasure from thieves. 2m 1w 2b 1g 1 exterior

Hibberd, Jack
Slam dunk. Currency Press in association with La Mama Theatre 1996 50p (Current theatre series)
Black comedy about brutality of contemporary youth. Two young punks terrorize young man in Australian park. 3m 1 setting

Hibbert, Guy
Tilting ground. French (London) 1997 56p
Drama set on Pacific Coast of Mexico. Widow forced to choose between troubled son and sensitive suitor. 2 acts 12 scenes 2m 1w 1 exterior

Hickok, Lorena A., 1893-1968
LaChuisa, M. J. First lady suite: Eleanor sleeps here

Hickok, Wild Bill
Thompson, P. Calamity Jane and the fat buffalo moon

Hidden agendas. McNally, T.

Hidden laughter. Gray, S.

Hide and shriek. Kelly, T.

Higgins, Dick
Buster Keaton enters into paradise. Left Hand Bks. 1994 68p
Experimental meditation on Keaton's impact on 20th century art forms. 11 scenes Variable cast

Higgins, Frank
The sweet by 'n' by. Dramatists 1996 70p
Mythic tale about three generations of Appalachian women. 2 acts 4 scenes 3m 4w 1 interior

Higginsen, Vy, and Wydro, Ken
Mama, I want to sing; book and lyrics by Vy Higginsen and Ken Wydro; original music by Rudolph V. Hawkins [et al.] Broadway Play Pub. 1995 56p
Gospel singer becomes international star. Music, singing. 2 acts 2m 3w extras 1 setting

High, Bernard G.
Ambush. Players Press 1996 36p
Middle-aged woman living alone on moors is terrorized by young female intruder. 1 act 3w 1 interior

High school students. See Students

High schools
y Allaway, B. Makin' it
y Avery, C. The seven ages of Dan
y Cook, P. The whole shebang
y DePietro, P. Murder at the prom
y Francoeur, B. The internal machine
y Francoeur, B. Wrangler Ranch
y Fuson, D. Clippings
y Haynes, H. J. Isolation
y Hoppenstedt, E. M. Shoo fly pudding
y Kelly, T. Ditch Day
y Mason, T. The less than human club
y O'Brien, J. Wherefore art thou Juliet?
y Sandock, F. Campaign fever
y Slaight, B. Class action
y Swift, R. Attack of the giant grasshoppers
y Ullom, S. Geeks do come from outer space
y Wells, J. S. Competition piece

High society. See Society

High tide. Slaight, B.

Highway, Tomson
Dry Lips oughta move to Kapuskasing
Drama set on mythical Canadian Indian reservation. Men's reactions to hockey game reflect their ambivalent feelings toward their place in society. 2 acts 7m 2w 1 setting
In Modern Canadian plays v2; ed. by J. Wasserman

The **highway.** Jamal, D.

Highwire. Shields, B. J.

Hijack. Rubens, B.

The **hilarious** hillbilly massacre. DePietro, P.

Hill, Abram
On Strivers Row
Satire about ambitious black middle-class family in Harlem. Background music, singing, dancing. 2 acts 2 scenes 6m 10w 1 interior
In Black comedy: nine palys; ed. by P. F. Jackson and Karimah
In Black theatre USA [v2]; ed. by J. V. Hatch and T. Shine
See also Silvera, J. D. jt. auth.

Hill, Anita
Hunt, M. Unquestioned integrity: the Hill-Thomas hearings

Hill, Gary Leon
The Black Branch
Inmates of state-run mental institution fight for dignity. 1 act 3m 3w 1 setting
In 20/20: twenty one-act plays from twenty years of the Humana Festival

Hill, Geoffrey
Brand. Penguin Bks. 1996 160p (Penguin classics)
Theatrical adaptation in verse based on a literal translation of Henrik Ibsen's poetic drama Brand. Uncompromising Norwegian priest severs all his human bonds in his pursuit of spiritual perfection. 5 acts 18m 5w 1 interior 4 exteriors

Hill, Ken
The invisible man. French (London) 1996 136p
Dramatization of H. G. Wells' classic as music hall production. 2 acts 20 scenes 13m 4w extras 1 interior

The phantom of the opera; a musical play; book and lyrics by Ken Hill; arrangements and incidental music by Alasdair MacNeill; music by Offenbach [et al.]; based on the novel by Gaston Leroux. French (London) 1994 124p
Musical dramatization of novel about masked man who inhabits cellar of Paris Opera House and his obsessive love for young singer. 2 acts 19 scenes Large mixed cast settings

Hillman, Barry L.
Iron magnolias. French (London) 1994 27p
Comedy. Elderly woman and friends avail themselves of discount day at beauty salon. 7w 1 interior

Himself. Phelan, B.

Hippolytus (Greek mythology)
Euripides. Hippolytus

Hired killers
Cleveland, R. Tom and Jerry

Hiro. Uyehara, D.

Hiroshima (Japan)
History—Bombardment, 1945
Bernier, E. The seven streams of the River Ota

His dish. Pintauro, J.

His majesty. Granville-Barker, H.

Hischak, Thomas
Murder by the book. Bakers Plays 1995 67p
Mystery. Ghosts are suspected in murder at women's literary society. 2 acts 5 scenes 2m 9w 1 interior

Murder on reserve. French 1994 77p
Murder mystery set in reference section of library in midwestern town. 2 acts 5 scenes 5m 5w 1 interior

Hispanic Americans
Cruz, M. Telling tales
Franco, C. [et al.] The LA LA Awards
y Kesselman, W. Maggie Magalita
Leguizamo, J. Mambo mouth
Leschin, L. [et al.] Latins Anonymous
Mayer, O. Blade to the heat
c McDonough, J. and Alderete, B. Posadas
Najera, R. Latinologues: Monologues of the Latin experience
Najera, R. The pain of the macho
Reyes, G. Men on the verge of a hispanic breakdown

History
y Bond, E. At the inland sea

A **history** of the American Film. Durang, C.

The **history** of the Devil. Barker, C.

The **history** of the village of the small huts. Hollingsworth, M.

The **history** of water/huyền thoại một giòng nu'ó'c. Janaczewska, N.

Hitler, Adolf
Goldstein, J. Hate
Stock, J. Star-gazy pie and sauerkraut
Tambori, G. Mein Kampf

Hoaxes
Burns, K. Identity crisis
De Filippo, E. Filumena Marturano
Plautus, T. M. Two sisters named Bacchis

Hockey
Highway, T. Dry Lips oughta move to Kapuskasing

Hodgkin's disease
Simonson, E. Bang the drum slowly

Hodgson, Sheila
Tunnel vision. French (London) 1995 46p
Family secrets revealed when young woman, her parents and boyfriend share London underground station platform with runaway teen girl. 2m 3w 1 setting

Hoffman, Aaron
Welcome stranger
Anti-Semitism in New England town ca. 1918. 4 acts 11m 4w 3 interiors
In Awake and singing: 7 classic plays from the American Jewish repertoire; ed. by E. Schiff

Hoffman, E. T. A.
The Nutcracker and the Mouse King (dramatization) See Mahlmann, L. and Jones, D. C. The Nutcracker Prince

Hoffman, William M.
As is
Portrayal of young homosexual dying of AIDS. 1 act 10m 4w extras 1 setting
In Best American plays: 9th series, 1983-1992

Hogarth, William
Dear, N. The art of success

Hogg, Frances A.
Afternoon at Tavern MacTavish; or, My wallet is in the Highlands. Clark, I.E. 1994 13p
Comedy. Scotsmen profit from gullible American tourists. 1 act 4m 2w 1 extra 1 interior

Hold on! Mondschein, N. L.

Holiday in the rain forest. Love, D.

Holiday song. Chayefsky, P.

Holidays. Harrison, J.

Hollinger, Michael
Two-part invention
Light bulb salesman and client meet in bar. 2m 1 interior
In Actors Theatre of Louisville. Ten-minute plays v3

Hollingsworth, Michael
The history of the village of the small huts; parts I-VIII. Blizzard Pub. 1994 371p
Eight episodes from Canadian history: New France; The British; The Mackenzie-Papineau Rebellion; Confederation and Riel; Laurier; The Great War; The life and times of Mackenzie King; World War II. 8 parts Large mixed cast

Hollywood (Calif.)
y Christiansen, A. Hooray for Hollywood
y Christiansen, A. Teens in Tinseltown
Curran, K. The stand-in
Kopit, A. Road to Nirvana

Holm, Sven
Leonora; tr. by Hans Chr. Andersen
Historical drama set in 17th century Denmark. Leonora Christina Ulfeldt, daughter of Danish King and devoted wife of traitor comes to terms with her fate. 3 scenes 3m 4w extras 1 interior
In New Danish plays; ed. by H. C. Andersen

Holman, David
c No worries
Set in Australia. Country girl feels better about new life in city after making friends in school with empathetic Vietnamese girl. 2 acts 3m 3w extras 1 setting
In Around the world in 21 plays; ed. by L. Swortzell

Holmes, Ruth Vickery
c The king and the miller
Lost in Sherwood Forest, king enjoys hospitality of miller's family. 4 scenes 7m 1w 1 interior 1 exterior
In Thirty plays from favorite stories; ed. by S. E. Kamerman

Ne **hölmöläiset:** The silly villagers. Gerke, P.

Holocaust, Jewish (1933-1945)
y Bond, E. At the inland sea
Bond, E. Coffee
Brooker, B. Ilsa, queen of the Nazi love camp
Garner, J. The flight into Egypt
Grumberg, J.-C. The free zone
Grumberg, J.-C. The workroom
Harwood, R. The handyman
y Kops, B. Dreams of Anne Frank
Lerner, M. Kastner
Megged, A. Hanna Senesh
Miller, A. Broken glass
Mitterer, F. There's not a finer country
Page, E. Aryan birth
Preses, P. and Becher, U. Our Mr. Bockerer
Roth, A. Born guilty
Samuels, D. Kindertransport
Sobol, J. Adam
Sylvanus, E. Leo Baeck
Szumigalski, A. Z: a meditation on oppression, desire and freedom
Tomer, B.-Z. Children of the shadows
c Watts, I. K. Goodbye Marianne

Holocaust survivors
Baitz, J. R. The substance of fire
Brittney, L. A different way to die
Goldberg, L. Lady of the Castle
Learner, T. Witchplay
Lee, J. A. Coming home
Mann, E. Annulla
Margulies, D. Lola
Margulies, D. The model apartment
Nishikawa, L. and Talmadge, V. The gate of heaven
Ravel, A. Vengeance
Samuels, D. Kindertransport
Tomer, B.-Z. Children of the shadows

Holofernes (Biblical figure)
Barker, H. Judith: a parting from the body

Holsclaw, Doug
The baddest of boys
Farcical black comedy set in San Francisco depicting various responses to AIDs within gay community. 3 acts 3m 2w 1 setting
In Sharing the delirium; ed. by T. Jones

The **holy** ghostly. Shepard, S.

The **holy** terror. Gray, S.

The **homage** that follows. Medoff, M.

Home. Mitterer, F.

Home. Storey, D.

Home. Williams, S.-A.

Home before dark. Chinn, J.

Home fires. Guare, J.

Home free! Wilson, L.

Home of the brave. Laurents, A.

Home section. Glowacki, J.

Homebird. Blacker, T.

Homebound. Callan, L.

Homecoming
Gallaire, F. You have come back
Schenkkan, R. The homecoming
Storey, D. In celebration

The **homecoming**. Schenkkan, R.

Homecoming. See O'Neill, E. Mourning becomes Electra: Homecoming

Homeless
y Beechy High School Drama Club. Me 'n' Alfred
y Blacker, T. Homebird
Bogosian, E. Sex, drugs, rock & roll
Glowacki, J. Antigone in New York
Lebow, B. Tiny Tim is dead
Paterson, D. L. Dungeons
Reingold, J. Dear Kenneth Blake
Rensten, M. The skip
Sawyer, A. V. Snow stars
Waterhouse, J. The cardboard cavaliers

Homer
Odyssey—Parodies, imitations, etc.
Gurney, A. R. The comeback
Ornsbo, J. Odysseus from Vraa
Schwartz, D. Paris and Helen

Homesick. Oates, J. C.

Homework. Margulies, D.

Homosexuality
Aron, G. The Stanley Parkers
Bamford, S. No roses around the door
Bartlett, N. Night after night
Berg, R. AIDS! the musical!
Boakye, P. Boy with beer
Bumbalo, V. Show
Chayefsky, P. The latent heterosexual
Churchill, C. Cloud 9
Clark, R. and Bobrick, S. Norman, is that you?
Clum, J. M. Randy's house
Congdon, C. Dog opera
Crabtree, H. Howard Crabtree's Whoop-dee-doo!
Crowley, M. For reasons that remain unclear
Crowley, M. The boys in the band
Curran, K. The stand-in
Demchuk, D. Touch
Dowie, C. Death and dancing
Dubois, R. D. Being at home with Claude
Elyot, K. My night with Reg
Finn, W. "In trousers"
Finn, W. and Lapine, J. Falsettoland
Finn, W. and Lapine, J. March of the falsettos
Firbank, R. The Princess Zoubaroff
Fols, C. Buck Simple
Foote, H. The young man from Atlanta
Fornes, M. I. Enter the night
Fraser, B. Poor Super Man
Freeman, B.; Branner, D. and Gupton, E. Fierce love
Garnhum, K. Beuys buoys boys
Gilbert, S. Capote at Yaddo
Gilbert, S. Drag queens in outer space
Gilbert, S. Drag queens on trial
Gilbert, S. Jim Dandy
Gilbert, S. Suzie Goo: private secretary
Gill, P. Mean tears
Gorman, C. Manual of trench warfare
Gray, S. Butley
Gray, S. Wise child
Green, M. Dreams of a drunken Quaker
Greenberg, R. The American plan
Greenspan, D. Dean mother
Grimsley, J. Mr. Universe
Gurney, A. R. The old boy
Hamilton, G. Kissing Marianne
Hampton, C. Total eclipse
Harding, A. Blood and honour
Harvey, J. Babies
Harvey, J. Beautiful thing
Harvey, J. Boom bang-a-bang
Harvey, J. Rupert Street Lonely Hearts Club
Harwood, R. Poison pen
Herbert, J. Fortune and men's eyes
Hoffman, W. M. As is
Holsclaw, D. The baddest of boys
Kander, J. The kiss of the spider woman
Kearns, M. Myron, a fairy tale in black and white
Kenna, P. Mates
Kramer, L. The destiny of me
Kramer, L. The normal heart
Kravitz, A. Just thinking
Kushner, T. Angels in America: Pt.1: Millennium approaches

Homosexuality—*Continued*
Kushner, T. Angels in America: Pt.2: Perestroika
Landau, T. 1969
Lane, E. Cater-waiter
Lee, J. A. Coming home
Legg, R. Oscar: the Oscar Wilde trials of 1895
Lucas, C. Bad dream
Lucas, C. What I meant was
MacDonald, B. Whale riding weather
MacIvor, D. 2-2-tango
MacIvor, D. and Brooks, D. Here lies Henry
McGuinness, F. Innocence
McNally, T. Andre's mother
McNally, T. Love! Valour! Compassion!
McNally, T. The Ritz
McNally, T. The wibbly, wobbly, wiggly dance that Cleopatterer did
Miller, S. It's our town, too
Miller, T. My queer body
Mitchell, M. Life support
Mitterer, F. Abraham
Moore, E. Live with it
Nagy, P. Weldon rising
Nyswaner, R. Reservoir
Okita, D. The rainy season
Parnell, P. An imaginary life
Peschina, H. Straight as a corkscrew
Pickett, J. C. Queen of Angels
Pintauro, J. Frozen dog
Pintauro, J. Rosen's son
Pintauro, J. Snow orchid
Pintauro, J. Uncle Chick
Pintauro, J. Watchman of the night
Pruitt, D. and Hutchison, P. The Harvey Milk show
Puig, M. Kiss of the spider woman
Rabe, D. Streamers
Reyes, G. Men on the verge of a hispanic breakdown
Ridley, P. The fastest clock in the universe
Rintoul H. Brave hearts
Rudnick, P. Jeffrey
Sánchez, E. Trafficking in broken hearts
Schwartz, D. Venus in the back room
Schwartz, S. Vito on the beach
Sheffer, W. Falling man
Sherman, J. Jest a second!
Sherman, J. M. Sophistry
Sherman, M. A madhouse in Goa
Sickles, S. C. Murmurs
Silver, N. Fit to be tied
Sliverman, J. L. Correct address
Simpatico, D. Wish fulfillment
Sod, T. Satan and Simon Desoto
Stembridge, G. The gay detective
Stoppard, T. The invention of love
Storey, R. The saints and apostles
y Thomas, C. Flesh and blood
Tolins, J. The twilight of the Golds
Tremblay, M. Hosanna
Tremblay, M. La Duchesse de Langeais
Vickery, F. Erogenous zones
Vickery, F. Roots and wings
Vogel, P. And baby makes seven
Wallace, N. In the heart of America
Weiner, S. D. Pavane
West, M. The drag
Wilcox, M. Accounts
Wilcox, M. Rents
Wilde, P. What's wrong with angry?
Williams, T. Something cloudy, something clear
Wilson, L. Balm in Gilead
Wilson, L. The madness of Lady Bright
Wilson, L. A poster of the cosmos
Yew, C. A language of their own
Yew, C. Porcelain

Hondurans

United States

Santeiro, L. A royal affair

The **honest** man's fortune. Fletcher, J.

The **honest** miller. McCullough, L. E.

The **honest**-to-god schnozzola. Horovitz, I.

Honesty
Molière. The misanthrope
Wycherley, W. The plain dealer

Honeymoon. Barylli, G.

Honour. Murray-Smith, J.

Hood, Evelyn
A wake for Donald. Players Press 1996 24p

Set in Edinburgh graveyard, 1820s. Graverobbers, Burke and Hare, kill widow who arrives to watch over husband's body. 2m 1w 1 exterior

Hooligans. Vingoe, M. and Kudelka, J.

Hooray for Hollywood. Kelly, T.

Hope, Anthony
The prisoner of Zenda (dramatization) See Francis, M. The prisoner of Zenda

Hope, Karen
Foreign lands

Psychological thriller set in northern English town. Child murderer, released from prison, returns to scene of her crime. 3 scenes 4w 1 interior

In Frontline intelligence 2; ed. by P. Edwardes

Hope in the year two. Griffiths, T.

The **Hope** slide. MacLeod, J.

Hoppenstedt, Elbert M.

y Shoo fly pudding

High school students put flies in cafeteria's rice pudding to start protest. 3 scenes 6m 5w extras 2 interiors

In The Big book of large-cast plays; ed. by S. E. Kamerman

Hopkins, Sarah Winnemucca

c McCullough, L. E. Chief Sarah, the Indian Joan of Arc

Hopscotch. Horovitz, I.

Horitz, Tony

y Good King Wenceslas and the Chancellor of Bohemia. French (London) 1993 47p

ISBN 0-573-16501-7

Dramatization of the Christmas carol. Singing. 2 acts 8 scenes Variable cast 13 characters extras settings

Hornby, Ian

The cat's away. New Playwrights Network 1995 90p

Comedy. Amnesia prevents man from explaining compromising situation his wife finds him in. 3 acts 4 scenes 4m 5w 1 interior

Dream, lover! New Playwrights Network 1995 90p

Comedy. Man leaves wife for woman who resembles imaginary lover. 3 acts 7 scenes 2m 4w 1 interior

Hello. . . . Is there any body there? New Playwrights Network 1995 68p

Farce. Cast, crew, and audience become integral parts of Agatha Christie murder mystery parody. 3 acts 4m 5w 1 interior

Late of this address. New Playwrights Network 1995 76p

Comedy about jealousy. Ghostly husband and wife haunt newlyweds. 3 acts 6 scenes 2m 3w 1 interior

Murdered, presumed dead. New Playwrights Network 1996 76p

Thriller revolving around successful businesswoman, her playboy husband and his girlfriend. 2 acts 6 scenes 3m 4w 1 interior

One across. New Playwrights Network 1995 16p

Husband knows wife wants eternity ring for Christmas and decides to have some fun with situation. 1 act 1m 2w 1 interior

The price to pay. New Playwrights Network 1995 72p

Domestic happiness of couple shattered when wife is kidnapped. 2 acts 3 scenes 3m 4w 1 setting

A question of innocence. New Playwrights Network 1996 62p

Mystery. English couple's holiday in France is shattered when wife is accused of robbery and murder. 3 acts 5 scenes 4m 6w 1 interior

Situation vacant. New Playwrights Network 1994 36p

Comedy. Woman abandons unemployed husband who then advertises for new wife. Variable cast 7 characters 1 interior

Tim'll fix it! New Playwrights Network 1996 68p

Farce. Inept handyman causes home repair disasters and falls in love. 2 acts 3m 4w 1 interior

Voices. New Playwrights Network 1995 74p

Mystery. Woman questions her sanity when she hears voices after automobile accident. 2 acts 4 scenes 3m 6w extras 1 interior

Wait until the ghost is clear. New Playwrights Network 1994 80p

Comedy. Ghost of husband helps clear wife of suspicion in his murder. 3 acts 4 scenes 3m 3w 1 interior

Where there's a will. . . . New Playwrights Network 1994 88p

Farce. Marital infidelities lead to series of bungled murder attempts. 3 acts 4m 4w 1 interior

Horovitz, Israel

The 75th

Forms part of the Quannapowitt quartet. Comedy about reunion of two ninety-three-year-old classmates at lakeside restaurant. 1m 1w 1 interior

In Horovitz, I. Sixteen short plays

Acrobats

Husband and wife acrobatic team feud while they perform. 1m 1w

In Horovitz, I. Sixteen short plays

Un drôle de mari français

Experimental dark comedy played simultaneously in French and English. 2m 1w 1 interior

In Horovitz, I. The primary English class and six new plays

Faith

Drama set in Central Park. Group of 1960's radicals hold reunion and are confronted by legacy of hopelessness and cynicism which they have passed on. 2m 3w 1 exterior

In Horovitz, I. Sixteen short plays

Fighting over Beverley

Love triangle among three seventy-year-olds. 2 acts 6 scenes 2m 2w 1 interior

In Horovitz, I. The primary English class and six new plays

The former one-on-one basketball champion

On a city playground middle-aged ex-basketball pro and fourteen-year-old youth match skills in a game of 21 during which they unravel the ironic fate that brought them together. 2m

In Horovitz, I. Sixteen short plays

Horovitz, Israel—*Continued*

Free gift

Eccentric woman visited by African American mother of her adopted son. 2w 1 interior

In Horovitz, I. The primary English class and six new plays

The great Labor Day classic

Follows interaction among entrants of different ages and backgrounds as they compete in grueling marathon race. Background music. 3m 3w

In Horovitz, I. Sixteen short plays

Henry Lumper

Drama about social and moral decay in small New England village caused by collapse of local fishing industry. Characters and themes parallel those found in Shakespeare's Henry IV. Prologue 2 acts 15 scenes epilogue 18m 6w extras 1 setting

In Horovitz, I. New England blue: plays for working-class life

The honest-to-god schnozzola

Two American businessmen in Germany patronize prostitutes and discover that one of them is male transvestite. Background music, singing. 5m 2w 1 interior

In Horovitz, I. Sixteen short plays

Hopscotch

Forms part of the Quannapowitt quartet. An unexpected encounter between former lovers. Background music. 1m 1w 1 exterior

In Horovitz, I. Sixteen short plays

The Indian wants the Bronx

East Indian lost on first day in New York assaulted by two teenage toughs. 3m

In Horovitz, I. Sixteen short plays

It's called the Sugar Plum

Tragicomedy. Girl whose fiancé has accidentally been run over by inept student, visits latter to upbraid him, but ends up forgetting dead boy and becoming student's lover. 1m 1w 1 interior

In Horovitz, I. Sixteen short plays

Lebensraum

Drama set at start of 21st century. Family accepts Germany's offer of work and citizenship to 6,000,000 Jews. 2m 1w 1 setting

In Horovitz, I. The primary English class and six new plays

Line

Absurdist comedy. Group of disparate people grapple to be first in line waiting for unspecified event. Singing, dancing. 4m 1w

In Horovitz, I. Sixteen short plays

Morning

Satire. African American family of misfits take pills to turn their skin white. Singing, dancing. 8 scenes 3m 2w 1 interior

In Horovitz, I. Sixteen short plays

My old lady

American inherits Paris apartment occupied by ninety-year-old tenant who refuses to vacate. 2 acts 10 scenes 1m 2w 1 interior

In Horovitz, I. The primary English class and six new plays

North Shore Fish

Drama set in Gloucester fish packing plant examines mundane events in typical working day of mostly female employees. 2 acts 3 scenes 2m 7w 1 interior

In Horovitz, I. New England blue: plays for working-class life

One under

Black comedy about friendship, money, competition, marriage, and suicide. Three men play golf. 3m 1w

In Horovitz, I. The primary English class and six new plays

Park your car in Harvard Yard. French 1993 93p

Comic drama about last year in life of ailing Gloucester teacher who hires former student, who he flunked, as housekeeper. 4 scenes 1m 1w 1 extra 1 setting

—Same

In Horovitz, I. New England blue: plays for working-class life

Play for germs

Comedy. Socrates, a gonorrhea germ confronts Aristotle, a syphillis germ in a humorous play about venereal disease. 2m 1 setting

In Horovitz, I. Sixteen short plays

The primary English class

Comedy. Misunderstandings abound as group of new citizens try to master basic English lesson given by eager but nervous and inexperienced young teacher. Singing. 2 acts 4m 3w extras 1 interior

In Horovitz, I. The primary English class and six new plays

Rats

Black comedy about power struggle between Harlem rat and country cousin from Connecticut. Unidentified cast 1 setting

In Around the world in 21 plays; ed. by L. Swortzell

In Horovitz, I. Sixteen short plays

Shooting gallery

Avant garde comedy. Young man in amusement park shooting gallery has spent all his money, neglected his children, and exhausted wife in effort to hit a mechanical bear. 2m 1w 1 setting

In Horovitz, I. Sixteen short plays

Spared

Forms part of the Quannapowitt quartet. Man's life passes in review as he holds a gun to his head. 1m

In Horovitz, I. Sixteen short plays

Horovitz, Israel—*Continued*

Stage directions

Forms part of the Quannapowitt quartet. Estranged brother and two sisters meet after parents' death; the only communication taking place is via the stage directions. 1m 2w 1 interior

In Horovitz, I. Sixteen short plays

Strong-man's weak child

Father and stepfather, both weight lifters, struggle to come to terms with daughter's terminal illness. 7 scenes 3m 1g 1 interior

In Horovitz, I. New England blue: plays for working-class life

Today, I am a fountain pen. [Rev. ed.] Dramatists 1996 72p

Play based on stories by Morley Torgov. First of trilogy dealing with Jewish home life in Sault Ste. Marie, Ontario in the 1940s. Traces coming of age of precocious, musically gifted pre-teenager. 2 acts 4m 3w 1b 1 setting

Unexpected tenderness. French 1995 101p

Domestic drama set in 1950s North Shore Massachusetts town. Jewish blue collar family living in shadow of abusive father. 5m 2w 1 interior

—Same

In Horovitz, I. New England blue: plays for working-class life

The widow's blind date

Drama. Woman seeks revenge on two old high school classmates who participated in her gang rape when she was 17. 2 acts 2m 1w 1 interior

In Horovitz, I. New England blue: plays of working-class life

Horror plays

y Allman, S. and Pickett, B. Frankenstein unbound
Barker, C. Frankenstein in love
y Booth, R. Where did you spend the night?
Carmichael, F. Frankenstein 1930
Churchill, C. The Skriker
Clapp, T. Dracula
Cross, J. C. Julia of Louvain
Deane, H. Dracula (1924)
Deane, H. and Balderston, J. L. Dracula: the vampire play (1927)
Dietz, S. Dracula
Downing, M. The demon
y Fraser, B. Prom night of the living dead
Moss, R. S. Nightmare : the fright of your life
Nigro, D. The Transylvanian clockworks
Peake, R. B. Presumption
Slout, W. L. The trial of Dr. Jekyll
Wellman, M. Dracula

Horse racing

Aerenson, B. Lighting up the two-year old
Wilson, L. Eukiah

Horses

c Harris, A. Young Black Beauty

Hosanna. Tremblay, M.

Hospitals

Baker, E. A. Face divided
Bumbalo, V. What are Tuesdays like?
Chappell, E. It can damage your health
Hastings, C. The wayward spirit
Hunkins, L. The best of strangers
Kingsley, S. Men in white
Lewis, J. Our boys
Linney, R. Goodbye, Howard
Marshall, G. and Ganz, L. Wrong turn at Lungfish
Mitchell, M. Life support
Mitterer, F. Beyond our understanding
Pintauro, J. Benjamin falling
Pintauro, J. Swans flying
Ricchi, R. A foreboding
Ricchi, R. The promise
Vanderhaeghe, G. Dancock's dance
Vickery, F. A kiss on the bottom
Vickery, F. Roots and wings
See also Psychiatric hospitals

Hostages

Blessing, L. Two rooms
Bynum, R. C. Escapee
Harwood, R. J. J. Farr
McGuinness, F. Someone who'll watch over me

Hot line. May, E.

Hot 'n' throbbing. Vogel, P.

Hotels, taverns, etc.

Anderson, G. Appearances
Arzoomanian, R. The Tack Room
Barteve, R. The orphanage
Berlin, E. The line that's picked up 1000 babes (and how it can work for you!)
Brooks, V. Let's pretend
Cartwright, J. Two
Doyle, R. War
Edwards, G. Old West
Emond, P. Talk about love!
Godber, J. and Thornton, J. Shakers re-stirred
Gurney, A. R. The Wayside Motor Inn
Horovitz, I. The honest-to-god schnozzola
Johnson, T. Insignificance

Hotels, taverns, etc.—*Continued*
LaChiusa, M. J. Eulogy for Mister Hamm
McPherson, C. The weir
Meyer, M. G. Moe's Lucky Seven
Murphy, T. Conversations on a homecoming
O'Neill, E. The iceman cometh
Panych, M. The ends of the earth
Russell, W. Stags and hens
Thomson, K. Barmaids
Vago, S. M. An ordinary woman under stress
Walcott, D. Pantomime

Hotlines (Telephone counseling)
May, E. Hot line

The **hour** of recognition. Schnitzler, A.

The **hour** we knew nothing of each other. Handke, P.

House, Jack
Cherchez la femme. Players Press 1996 20p
Father is concerned with son's "bad habits". 1 act 4m 1 interior

House, Ron, and Shearman, Alan
The scandalous adventures of Sir Toby Trollope. French 1994 112p
Historical farce set in 1784 England. Sentenced to be hanged, tax evader schemes to save his life. 2 acts 7 scenes Variable cast 25 characters settings

House humans. MacIvor, D.

House made of air. Pintauro, J.

House of America. Thomas, E.

The **house** of Bernardo Alba. García Lorca, F.

House of secrets. McKelvey, P.

The **House** of the Seven Gables. Thane, A.

House of wonders. Aspengren, K.

The **house** of yes. MacLeod, W.

The **house** plant. Worboyes, S.

The **houseguests.** Kondoleon, H.

Household moving. See Moving, Household

The **housewarming.** Aldrich, A.

Housman, Alfred Edward, 1859-1936
Stoppard, T. The invention of love

Houston, Velina Hasu
As sometimes in a dead man's face
Set in 1964-1994 Kansas and California. Relationships in multicultural family focus on sister's feelings for adopted brother. 2 acts 6 scenes 1m 3w settings
In Asian American drama; ed. by B. Nelson

Asa ga kimashita (Morning has broken)
First play of trilogy based on author's family. Set in postwar Japan. Family drama about patriarch driven to suicide by loss of land and daughter's involvement with African American soldier. Prologue 8 scenes 5m 5w 1 setting
In The Politics of life: four plays by Asian American women

Kokoro (true heart)
Set in San Diego, California 1985. Marital problems destroy Japanese family. 1m 5w
In But still, like air, I'll rise; ed. by V. H. Houston

The Matsuyama mirror
Drama adapted from ancient Japanese fairy tale. Spirit of dead mother guides girl through troubled times. Music, singing, dancing. Prologue 5 scenes 1 act 1m 8w extra 1 interior
In Short plays for young actors; ed. by C. Slaight and J. Sharrar

Tea
Final play of trilogy based on author's family. Follows Asa ga Kimashita and American dreams. Look at struggles of Japanese war brides in Kansas spans 1945 to 1968. Prelude 4 scenes 1m 4w 1 interior
In Plays for actresses; ed. by E. Lane and N. Shengold
In Unbroken thread; ed. by Roberta Uno

How Anansi helped a fisherman. See Gerke, P. The adventures of Anansi: "How Anansi helped a fisherman"

How else am I supposed to know I'm still alive. Fernandez, E.

How Gertrude stormed the Philosophers' Club. Epstein, M.

How I learned to drive. Vogel, P.

How many to tango? Albert, S. J.

How Santa Claus discovered Christmas. Peterson, M. L.

How the first letter was written. Kipling, R. (dramatization) See Summer, A. The just so letter

How the people got fire. McCullough, L. E.

How the world got wisdom. See Gerke, P. The adventures of Anansi: "How the world got wisdom"

How things happen in three! Cooper, R. M.

How to be an alien. Haylock, D.

How to write a play. Terson, P.

Howard, Ed. See Williams, J. jt. auth.

Howard, John, 1726?-1790
Inchbald, Mrs. Such things are

Howard Crabtree's Whoop-dee-doo! Crabtree, H.

Howe, Tina
Appearances
Slapstick comedy set in women's dressing room of department store. 2w 1 interior
In Plays for actresses; ed. by E. Lane and N. Shengold

Approaching Zanzibar
Adventures of young family driving cross-country to visit aunt dying of cancer in New Mexico. 2 acts 9 scenes 4m 5w 3b 1g 1 setting
In Howe, T. Approaching Zanzibar and other plays

Birth and after birth. French 1997 88p
At birthday party for four year old son, parents try to convince childless friends to have children. 2 acts 3m 2w 1 interior
—Same
In Howe, T. Approaching Zanzibar and other plays
In Women on the verge: 7 avant-garde American plays; ed. by R. C. Lamont

One shoe off. French 1993 90p
Upstate New York farmhouse setting for comedic examination of marital fidelity, careerism and the theater. 2 acts 5 scenes 3m 2w 1 interior
—Same
In Howe, T. Approaching Zanzibar and other plays

Painting Churches
Estranged daughter reassesses relationship with aging parents. 2 acts 5 scenes 1m 2w 1 interior
In Best American plays: 9th series, 1983-1992

Howles, Lynne
The king's highway. Moorley's 1993 30p
Dramatization of John Bunyan's allegorical novel the Pilgrim's progress. Christian and sister Faith journey to Great City. 9 scenes Large mixed cast

Hrosvitha, ca. 935-1002
Linney, R. Three poets: Hrosvitha

Hubert Murray's widow. Harding, M.

Huff, Betty
y Spy for a day
Comedy. Inept secret agents of ICK pitted against those of OUCH in spoof on foreign intrigue. 1 act 7m 5w extras 1 exterior
In The Big book of large-cast plays; ed. by S. E. Kamerman

Huff, Keith
Leon and Joey
Drama with elements of fantasy about twin brothers, one suicidal, the other retarded. 3m 1w 8 scenes 1 setting
In Act One '95

Huggy bear. Mercer, D.

Hughes, Declan
Digging for fire
Black comedy set in Dublin bar about disasterous, booze-soaked college reunion. 4 acts 6 scenes 5m 2w 2 interiors
In Frontline intelligence I; ed. by P. Edwardes
In Hughes, D. Digging for fire & New morning

New morning
Family drama about guilt and redemption. Two sisters seek reconciliation with one another and their past. 3 acts 1m 2w 1 interior
In Hughes, D. Digging for fire & New morning

Hughes, Doug. See Kash, M. jt. auth.

Hughes, Langston
Don't you want to be free?
Folk poems and prose about black history and life in musical comedy form. Music, singing, dancing. Large mixed cast 1 setting
In Black theatre USA [v1]; ed. by J. V. Hatch and T. Shine

The Em-Fuehrer Jones
Short parody of Eugene O'Neill's Emperor Jones. African American boxer embarrasses German dictator. 2m extras 1 exterior
In Lost plays of the Harlem Renaissance; ed. by J. V. Hatch and L. Hamalian

Emperor of Haiti
Historical drama set in 1791. Jean Jacques Dessalines helps overthrow French rule in Haiti. 3 acts 4 scenes Large mixed cast 2 interiors 2 exteriors
In Black drama in America: an anthology; ed. by D. T. Turner

Limitations of life
Parody of film Imitation of life. White maid serves African American family. 1m 2w 1 interior
In Black theatre USA [v2]; ed. by J. V. Hatch and T. Shine

Mulatto
Tragedy about race relations set in Georgia. Problems and attitudes of children of white landowner and African American housekeeper-mistress. 2 acts 3 scenes 10m 2w 1b extras 1 interior
In Black theatre USA [v2]; ed. by J. V. Hatch and T. Shine

Hughes, Langston—*Continued*

Scarlet Sister Barry

Satire about famous white actress who played African American roles in black face. 1w

In Lost plays of the Harlem Renaissance; ed. by J. V. Hatch and L. Hamalian

Simply heavenly

Romantic comedy. Simple loves Joyce, but has several misunderstandings with her until his divorce from his wife finally comes through. Music and singing. 2 acts 18 scenes 11m 7w 5 interiors 1 exterior

In Black comedy: nine plays; ed. by P. F. Jackson and Karimah

Soul gone home

Dead African American youth's spirit accuses prostitute mother of neglect. 3m 1w 1 interior

In Around the world in 21 plays; ed. by L. Swortzell

See also Johnson, J. P. jt. auth.

About

y Satchell, M. Langston Hughes: poet of the people

Hughes, Pam

y Abracadabra, Aladdin! Originally adapted and dramatized from "The Arabian Nights' Entertainment"; book by Tim Kelly; music & lyrics by Pam Hughes. Pioneer Drama Service 1992 39p

Musical dramatization of Aladdin and his wonderful lamp. 10 scenes 7m 13w extras 2 interiors 1 exterior

Hughes, Ted

The wound

Soldiers have supernatural encounter during World War II. 2m 1w extras

In Hughes, T. Difficulties of a bridegroom

Hughes, Veronica

c Strongman meets his match

Based on Japanese folk tale. Women train wrestler for competition in Emperor's tournament. 4 scenes 3m 3w extras 3 exteriors

In Thirty plays from favorite stories; ed. by S. E. Kamerman

Hugo, Victor

Hernani; tr. by Camilla Crosland

Tragedy. Young Spanish woman betrothed to uncle loves nobleman plotting against Charles I of Spain. Verse play. 5 acts 26 scenes 18m 3w extras 3 interiors 2 exteriors

In Hugo, V. Three plays

The king amuses himself (Le roi s'amuse!) tr. by Frederick L. Slous

Tragedy. Innocent daughter of court jester who has encouraged debauchery of Francis I of France is raped by king and killed in trap set by her vengeful father for king. Verse play. 5 acts 23 scenes 17m 4w extras 2 interiors 1 exterior 1 setting

In Hugo, V. Three plays

Ruy Blas; tr. by Camilla Crosland

Tragedy. Innocent servant in love with Spanish queen is used by vengeful noble to trap and punish queen. Verse play. 5 acts 27 scenes 19m 4w extras 4 interiors

In Hugo, V. Three plays

Humai's secret. McCaslin, N.

Human cannon. Bond, E.

Humour helps. Barnes, P.

The **Hunchback** of Notre Dame goes West. Swift, R.

The **hundred** and one Dalmatians. Robbins, G.

Hungary

History—Revolution, 1956

Paice, E. and Woddis, R. World on edge

Hunger. See Fornes, M. I. What of the night?: Hunger

A **hunger** artist. Kafka, F. (dramatization) See Drexler, R. Occupational hazard

The **hungry** earth. Maponya, M.

Hunkins, Lee

The best of strangers

Two women, one white one black exchange confidences while sharing hospital room. 6 scenes 3m 3w 1 interior

In Facing forward; ed. by L. D. Frank

y Freedom is my middle name. Dramatic 1994 52p

Stagecoach Mary takes high school students on a tour of African American history. Singing. 3m 3w 1 setting

Hunt, Mame

Unquestioned integrity: the Hill-Thomas hearings

Docudrama based on Clarence Thomas-Anita Hill Senate hearings. 2m 1w 1 interior

In Voicings: ten plays from the documentary theatre; ed. by A. Favorini

The **hunted.** See O'Neill, E. Mourning becomes Electra: The hunted

Hunter, Maureen

Transit of Venus; a play. Blizzard Pub. 1992 92p

Historical drama set in France 1760-1771 loosely based on life of Guillaume Le Gentil. Astronomer's obsessive attempts to chart the transits of Venus cost him true love. 3 acts 8 scenes 2m 3w 1 interior

Hurlyburly. Rabe, D.

Hurricane roses. Spencer, D.

Hurst, James R. See Hurst, Z. B. jt. auth.

Hurst, Zoe Bell, and Hurst, James R.
y The cowhand's Christmas Carol; or, T'was plum tired of pudding. Pioneer Drama Service 1992 22p

Christmas melodrama. Ranch housekeeper foils villain, helps orphans and finds true love. 2 scenes 3m 3w extras 2 interiors 2 exteriors

Hurston, Zora Neale
The first one

Mythic drama based on biblical story. Noah curses son Ham to be forever black. Music, singing, dancing. 1 act 4m 4w extras 1 exterior

In Black theatre USA [v1]; ed. by J. V. Hatch and T. Shine

Spunk (dramatization) See Wolfe, G. C. Story in Harlem slang

Husband and wife
Albee, E. Edward Albee's Marriage play
Baker, E. A. Face divided
Beaumarchais, P. A. C. de. The marriage of Figaro
Canby, V. After all
Cooke, C. Threat
De Groen, A. The girl who saw everything
Dowling, C. The Marlboro man
Feydeau, G. Going to pot
Feydeau, G. Nothing but the tooth
Fo, D. The open couple
Foote, H. The traveling lady
Garcia Lorca, F. Yerma
Gifford, B. Blackout
Glore, J. The company of heaven
Glover, S. The straw chair
Graham, B. The Champagne Charlie Stakes
Gray, S. Hidden laughter
Gray, S. Man in a side-car
Guare, J. Something I'll tell you Tuesday
Hayes, E. Poison
Hornby, I. One across
Horovitz, I. Acrobats
Ibsen, H. A doll's house
Linney, R. Clair de Lune
Luckham, C. The choice
MacIntyre, T. Sheep's milk on the boil
McGuinness, F. A doll's house
McWeeny, D. and Swan, S. Broken bones
Mitterer, F. Beyond our understanding
Musset, A. de. Caprice
Noonan, J. F. When it comes early
Nunn, J. Punch
O'Neill, E. Warnings
Pinter, H. Ashes to ashes
Pinter, H. Old times
Pirandello, L. The rules of the game
Schisgal, M. The cowboy, the Indian and the fervent feminist
Schwarz-Bart, S. Your handsome captain
Sears, J. Eddie Lee, Eddie Lee
Shaffer, P. The gift of the Gorgon
Smith, W. H. The drunkard
Steinour, M. At Land's End
Stoppard, T. 'M' is for moon among other things
Storey, D. Caring
Storey, D. The restoration of Arnold Middleton
Strindberg, A. The dance of death
Stroppel, F. Domestic violence
Sturner, L. The death of Huey Newton
Thomas, E. East from the Gantry
Treadwell, S. Machinal
Vickery, F. Love forty
Waterhouse, J. and Leach, P. A nest of cuckoos
Weller, M. At home (Split, Part 1)
Welsh, D. Make it happen
Wilhelm, L. Whoppers
Wilson, L. Breakfast at the track
Young, P. Squashed

See also Adultery; Divorce; Family; Marriage

Hush. De Angelis, A.

Hutchins, Pat
The curse of the Egyptian mummy (dramatization) See Conville, D. and Gooderson, D. The curse of the Egyptian mummy

Hutchison, Patrick. See Pruitt, D. jt. auth.

Huth, Angela
The trouble with old lovers. French (London) 1995 61p

Drama about infidelity. Marriage threatened when ex-lovers meet again after more than twenty years. 2 acts 4 scenes 2m 3w 1 interior

Huynh, Quang Nhuong
Dance of the wandering souls

Vietnamese Princess and Chinese prince become involved in their kingdoms' power struggles and wars. 2 acts 13 scenes 10m 1w settings

In But still, like air, I'll rise; ed. by V. H. Houston

Hwang, David Henry
Bondage
A look at race and sexual attraction set in Los Angeles S & M parlor. 1 act 1m 1w 1 interior
In 20/20: twenty one-act plays from twenty years of the Humana Festival
In Asian American drama; ed. by B. Nelson
In The Best American short plays, 1992-1993
In But still, like air, I'll rise; ed. by V. H. Houston
In Hwang, D. H. Trying to find Chinatown and Bondage
The sound of a voice
Stylized tale with folkloric nuances of young samurai's encounter with mysterious woman. 9 scenes 1m 1w 1 setting
In Telling tales: new one-act plays; ed. by E. Lane
Trying to find Chinatown
Lower East Side confrontation between two men explores questions of race, ethnicity and identity. Music. 2m 1 exterior
In Humana Festival '96
In Hwang, D. H. Trying to find Chinatown and Bondage

The **hyacinth** macaw. Wellman, M.

Hyem, Jill
Lorna Doone. French 1997 93p
Dramatization of R. D. Blackmore's historical novel of romance and adventure set in 17th century Exmoor, Devonshire. 2 acts 27 scenes 16m 7w 4g extras 1 setting

Hypochondria
Molière. The hypochondriac
Molière. The imaginary invalid

The **hypochondriac.** Molière

Hypocrisy
Crimp, M. The misanthrope
Ibsen, H. Ghosts
Ibsen, H. Pillars of society
Molière. The misanthrope

Hysteria. Johnson, T.

I

I ain't yo' uncle. Alexander, R.

I am a man. Oyamo

I am a winner. Valle, F.

I am yours. Thompson, J.

I bet your life. Carmichael, F.

I can't remember anything. Miller, A.

I dodici mesi: The twelve months. Gerke, P.

I don't know what I'm doing. Margulies, D.

I had a job I liked. Once. Vanderhaeghe, G.

I hate mothers. Rayfield, J.

I have a dream. Fisher, A.

I love you Anne Murray. See Ledoux, P. and Young, D. Love is strange

I remember you. Boretz, A.

I remember you. Slade, B.

'**I** told you so'. Aynsley, E.

I want my mummy! Reiser, D.

I won't take a bath! Martin, J.

Iago. Jackson, C. B.

Ibsen, Henrik
Brand (adaptation) See Hill, G. Brand
A doll's house; tr. by Kenneth McLeish. Hern Bks. 1994 102p (Drama classics)
Social drama. Woman comes to realization that her married life is a sham and decides to leave family to pursue personal freedom. 3 acts 4m 4w 2b 1g 1 interior
—Same; tr. by William Archer. Players Press 1993 68p
—Same; tr. by Rick Davis and Brian Johnston
In Ibsen, H. Ibsen: four major plays
A doll's house (adaptation) See McGuinness, F. A doll's house
An enemy of the people; tr. by Rick Davis and Brian Johnston
Variant title: A public enemy. Social drama set in 19th century Norway. Idealistic doctor who advocates community water purification is considered hostile to town's financial interests. 5 acts 8m 2w 1b extras 4 interiors
In Ibsen, H. Ibsen: four major plays
An enemy of the people (adaptation) See Nolan, P. T. An enemy of the people
Ghosts; tr. by Rick Davis and Brian Johnston
Tragedy about effects of suppressing disturbing truths. Widow finally faces husband's dissipation and adultery and realizes her son is suffering from hereditary syphilis. 3 acts 3m 2w 1 interior
In Ibsen, H. Ibsen: four major plays
Hedda Gabler; tr. by Rick Davis and Brian Johnston
Tragedy of clever, sophisticated woman bored with dull marriage and social conventions. Her role in lover's death discovered, she shoots herself. 4 acts 3m 4w 1 interior
In Ibsen, H. Ibsen: four major plays

Ibsen, Henrik—*Continued*

The master builder; tr. by Nicholas Rudall
Dee, I. R. 1994 111p (Plays for performance)

Symbolic tragedy. Successful architect believes he attained success unfairly through his strange extrasensory powers and now tries to regain his integrity. 3 acts 4m 3w extras 2 interiors 1 exterior

—Same; tr. by Brian Johnston
In Ibsen, H. Ibsen: four plays

Pillars of society; tr. by Brian Johnston

An exposé of human hypocrisy which attacks the facade of respectability. Leading citizen of small Norwegian town, whose success has been founded on a lie, finally redeems himself. 4 acts 10m 9w extras 1 interior

In Ibsen, H. Ibsen: four plays

Rosmersholm; tr. by Brian Johnston

Tragedy. Strong-minded emancipated woman influences politics of weak-spirited idealistic man. When she confesses her role in his wife's suicide, they commit suicide together. 4 acts 4m 2w 2 interiors

In Ibsen, H. Ibsen: four plays

The wild duck; tr. by Brian Johnston

Symbolic tragedy in which wealthy businessman's son exposes father's corruption to family ruined by his father's past actions. Theme explores confusion between idealism and illusions. 5 acts 12m 3w extras 2 interiors

In Ibsen, H. Ibsen: four plays

The wild duck (adaptation) See Brustein, R. The wild duck

About

Palmer, J. Henrik Ibsen on the necessity of producing Norwegian drama

Parodies, imitations, etc.

Dodson, O. Bayou legend

Icarus. Sanchez, E.

Icarus's mother. Shepard, S.

The **ice**-fishing play. Kling, K.

The **ice** wolf. Kraus, J. H.

The **iceman** cometh. O'Neill, E.

Ichabod. Cole, J. D.

An **ideal** husband. Wilde, O.

Idealism
Brustein, R. The wild duck
Hauptmann, G. Before daybreak
Hill, G. Brand
Ibsen, H. An enemy of the people
Ibsen, H. The wild duck
y Nolan, P. T. An enemy of the people
Reddin, K. The innocents' crusade

Identity (Psychology)
Fo, D. Trumpets and raspberries
Oates, J. C. Ontological proof of my existence
Townsend, S. The great celestial cow

Identity crisis. Burns, K.

The **idiot.** Fishelson, D.

The **idiots** Karamazov. Durang, C.

If angels were mortals ... Petersen, C. A.

If I can't take it with me ... I'm not going to go. Hendrick, B.

If we are women. Glass, J. M.

If you're Glad I'll be Frank. Stoppard, T.

Iizuka, Naomi

Polaroid stories

Adaptation of Ovid's Metamorphoses set in late 1990s. Prologue 1 act 5m 5w 1 setting

In Humana Festival '97

Ikhlasi, Walid

The path; tr. by Olive Kenny, and Thomas G. Ezzy

Semidocumentary drama about hypocrisy and repression in Arab world. 2 acts 14 scenes 2m 1w extras 1 setting

In Modern Arabic drama; ed. by S. K. Jayyusi and R. Allen

Ikke, ikke, nye, nye, nye. Wilson, L.

Iko, Momoko

Gold watch

Set in Pacific Northwest. Tensions within Japanese American family and community preceding World War II internment. 2 acts 5m 2w 1g extras 1 setting

In Unbroken thread; ed. by R. Uno

Ikoli, Tunde

Scrape off the black

Domestic drama about racially mixed family in 1970s London. 2 acts 2m 2w 1 interior

In Black plays: three; ed. by Y. Brewster

Illegal contact. Heiss, R. L.

Illegitimacy
Chinn, J. Home before dark

Illiteracy. See Literacy

Illness
Bamford, S. Scorpio
Maguire, M. The tower
Pintauro, J. Bird of ill omen
Pinter, H. A kind of Alaska
Plowman, G. Philip and Rowena
Potter, D. Joe's ark
Potter, D. Karaoke
Steinour, M. At Land's End
Sutherland, E. Edufa

The **illusion.** Kushner, T.

Ilsa, queen of the Nazi love camp. Brooker, B.

I'm not Rappaport. Gardner, H.

I'm not stupid. Rodriguez, D. E.

The **imaginary** cuckold. Molière

The **imaginary** invalid. Molière

An **imaginary** life. Parnell, P.

An **imaginary** trial of George Washington. Wolman, D.

Imagination
Patrick, R. Love lace

Immortality
Capek, K. The Makropoulos secret
Williams, R. The life of the world to come

Imperceptible mutabilities in the Third Kingdom. Parks, S. L.

Impersonation
Farquhar, G. The beaux' stratagem
Feydeau, G. The dressmaker
Lebow, B. Little Joe Monaghan
Molière. Amphitryon
Molière. The flying doctor
Plautus, T. M. Amphitryon

The **importance** of being Earnest. Harris, A.

The **importance** of being Earnest. Wilde, O.

Imposters and imposture
Pushkin, A. Boris Godunov

In a pig's valise. Overmyer, E.

In an art factory. Frost, R.

In August we play the Pyrenees. Rubio, J. L.

In by the half. Chinn, J.

In celebration. Storey, D.

In Dahomey. Dunbar, P. L. and Shipp, J. A.

In Dahomey. Perry, S.

In fireworks lie secret codes. Guare, J.

In her sight. Mack, C. K.

In mama's house. See Regan, S. Morning star

In my grandmother's purse. Bass, E.

In perpetuity throughout the universe. Overmyer, E.

In plain Arabic. Ramli, L.

In Shakespeare and the Bible. Wilder, T.

In spite of everything! Piscator, E. and Gasbarra, F.

In splendid error. Branch, W.

In the beginning. Ritchie, R.

In the bleak midwinter. Way, C.

In the cemetery. Hardstack, M.

In the company of men. Bond, E.

In the eye of the hurricane. Machado, E.

In the garden of the witch. Williams, B.

In the heart of America. Wallace, N.

In the native state. Stoppard, T.

In the play of summer breezes. Schnitzler, A.

In the ruins. Dear, N.

In the summer house. Bowles, J.

In the wine time. Bullins, E.

"**In** trousers." Finn, W.

In with Alma. Packard, S.

Incas
c Brown, J. The lake at the end of the world

Incest
Baum, T. Cold hands
Berkoff, S. Greek
Dryden, J. Love triumphant
Ford, J. 'Tis pity she's a whore
Hamilton, G. Kissing Marianne
Kane, S. Phaedra's love
MacDonald, B. What we do with it
MacLeod, W. The house of yes
Maguire, M. Phaedra
Olmos, C. Profane games
Pintauro, J. Dirty talk
Sade, Marquis de. Henrietta and St. Clair
Sophocles. Oedipus the King
Taylor, P. Familiar haunts
Thomas, E. House of America
Ward, N. Apart from George
Wilson, L. Home free!

Inchbald, Elizabeth Simpson. See Inchbald, Mrs. 1753-1821

Inchbald, Mrs. 1753-1821
Such things are
Comedy satirizing vulgarity of British in Sumatra. Dramatizes work of philanthropist and prison reformer John Howard. 5 acts 12 scenes epilogue 14m 3w 7 interiors 1 exterior
In The Meridian anthology of Restoration and eighteenth-century plays by women; ed. by K. M. Rogers

The **inchcape** bell. Fitzball, E.

The **incorruptible**. Nowra, L.

The **increased** difficulty of concentration. Havel, V.

Independence. Blessing, L.

India
Dryden, J. Aureng-Zebe
McNally, T. A perfect Ganesh
Tagore, R. The Post Office
y Thane, A. The moonstone

Folklore

See Folklore—India

History—British occupation, 1765-1947

Stoppard, T. In the native state
Stoppard, T. Indian ink

Social life and customs

Mehta, D. Brides are not for burning

Indian ink. Stoppard, T.

The **Indian** princess. Barker, J. N.

The **Indian** wants the Bronx. Horovitz, I.

Indians of North America
Barker, J. N. The Indian princess
Brown, C. Buffalo Hair
Colorado, E. and Colorado, H. 1992: blood speaks
y Dietz, S. The rememberer
Glancy, D. Weebjob
Gomez, T. Inter-tribal
c Hezlep, W. Red Cloud's revenge
y McCaslin, N. The legend of Minna Lamourrie
c McCaslin, N. Mercy in moccasins
c McCaslin, N. A miracle in the Christmas city
c McCullough, L. E. Bird woman of the Shoshones
c McCullough, L. E. Chief Sarah, the Indian Joan of Arc
c McCullough, L. E. Great medicine painter
c McCullough, L. E. The rainbow cradle
c Morris, V. Legend of Pocahontas
Pollock, S. Walsh
Robinson, M. Collateral damage
Shurtz, R. K. Cowboys, Indians and waitresses
Spiderwoman Theater. Sun Moon and Feather

See also Wampanoag Indians

Legends

c Gerke, P. Da-hoos-whee'-whee: The seal-hunting brothers
c Gerke, P. Legend of the seasons
Gerke, P. Star story
c Grauer, R. The boy who tricked the moon
c McCaslin, N. Bluebonnets
c McCaslin, N. Cold face, warm heart
c McCullough, L. E. Gluscabi and his magic game bag
y McCullough, L. E. Greta Nilson's magic mare
c McCullough, L. E. How the people got fire
c McCullough, L. E. Rocky Mountain rendezvous

Wars

See also Red River War, 1874-1875

Canada

Highway, T. Dry Lips oughta move to Kapuskasing
Lill, W. The occupation of Heather Rose
Ryga, G. The ecstasy of Rita Joe
y Sinclair, B. Dreamkeeper
y Suntep Theatre. Wheel of justice
Taylor, D. H. Someday

Indians of South America

Brazil

Hampton, C. Savages

Legends

c McCaslin, N. A gift of music

Indic folklore. See Folklore—Indic

Indonesia
Dryden, J. Amboyna

See also British—Indonesia; Sumatra (Indonesia)

Industrial painters. See Painters, Industrial

The **inexperienced** ghost. Nolan, P. T.

Infancy. Wilder, T.

Infanticide
Graham, S. It's morning
Linney, R. True crimes
Turrini, P. Infanticide

Infants
Durang, C. Baby with the bathwater
Thatcher, K. Emma's child
Wilder, T. Infancy

Infidelities! Van Zandt, B. and Milmore, J.

Informers
Havel, V. Audience

Ingleton, Sue
The passion ... and its deep connection with lemon delicious pudding. Currency Press in association with Playbox Theatre 1995 67p (Current theatre series)
Suburban Australian woman takes voyage of self-discovery through fantastic world of images and events drawn from legends and folktales. 2 acts 63 scenes 2m 5w 1 setting

The **Ingoldsby** legends. Pickering, K.

Ingraffia, Sam
Pasquini the Magnificent
Comedy. Encounter with troubled housewife gives has-been magician new confidence. 2m 1w 1 interior
In Off-Off Broadway Festival plays, 18th ser.

Inherit the wind. Lawrence, J. and Lee, R. E.

Inheritance and succession
Adams, A. A bit of land
Day, D. M. Possession is ...
Dinner, W. Logic upside down
Centlivre, S. A bold stroke for a wife
Farquhar, G. The twin rivals
Granville-Barker, H. The Voysey inheritance
Haywood, D. Twisted tape
Mamet, D. Jolly
Zuberbuehler, A. Fieldstones

Inishmaan (Ireland)
McDonagh, M. The cripple of Inishmaan

The **innkeeper's** daughter. Thompson, L.

Innocence. McGuinness, F.

The **innocents'** crusade. Reddin, K.

Inquest. Freed, D.

Inquisition
Linney, R. Ambrosio
Linney, R. Spain: Torquemada

Insalata mista. Bauer, W.

Insanity
Goethe, J. W. von. Torquato Tasso
Gray, S. The rear column
Hall, W. Jane Eyre
Linney, R. Spain: Anna Rey
Linney, R. Spain: Escobedo de la Aixa
Maturin, C. R. Bertram
Nigro, D. Glamorgan
Nigro, D. Squirrels
Nigro, D. The Transylvanian clockworks
Nigro, D. The weird sisters
O'Neill, E. All God's chillun got wings
Shakespeare, W. and Fletcher, J. Cardenio

Inside. Beim, N.

Inside job. Clemens, B.

Inside out. Russ, A.

The **inside** story. Dawson, J. and Bass, P.

The **inside** story of Dr. Crippen. Dallman, J.

Inside the belly of the beast. Taylor, R.

Insignificance. Johnson, T.

Intellectuals
Campanile, A. The inventor of the horse
Chekhov, A. Uncle Vanya
Chekhov, A. The wood demon
Davies, R. Fortune, my foe
Mitchell, J. August
Nagy, A. The seducer's diary
Osofisan, F. The oriki of a grasshopper
Shawn, W. The designated mourner

Interludes, English
Mankind. A critical edition of the medieval play Mankind
c Swortzell, L. Jack Fuggler

Intermarriage. See Miscegenation

The **internal** teen machine. Francoeur, B.

Internment of Japanese Americans, 1942-1945. See Japanese Americans—Evacuation and relocation, 1942-1945

Interracial marriage
Ikoli, T. Scrape off the black
O'Neill, E. All God's chillun got wings
Roberts, D. Breaking glass
Wilson, L. The gingham dog

Inter-tribal. Gomez, T.

The **interview.** Mamet, D.

The **interview.** Oates, J. C.

Interviewee. Bynum, R. C.

Interviewing
Mamet, D. An interview
Miller, A. The Ryan interview
Oates, J. C. The interview

Into. Carley, D.

Into the woods. Sondheim, S. and Lapine, J.

Inuit
Kraus, J. H. The ice wolf

The **invention** of love. Stoppard, T.

The **inventor** of the horse. Campanile, A.

The **investigation.** Weiss, P.

Investigations. See Courts-martial and courts of inquiry; Trials (Murder)

The **invisible** man. Hill, K.

Involuntary homicide. Abe, K.

Iphigenia (Greek mythology)
Euripides. Iphigenia among the Taurians
Euripides. Iphigenia in Aulis
Goethe, J. W. von. Iphigenia in Tauris

Iphigenia among the Taurians. Euripides

Iphigenia in Aulis. Euripides

Iphigenia in Tauris. Goethe, J. W. von

IRA. See Irish Republican Army

Iraq

History—Zanj Rebellion, 868-883

Al-Madani, 'Izz al-Din. The Zanj Revolution

Ireland, Vicky

c Roald Dahl's The Giraffe and the Pelly and me; a play with music for children; adapted by Vicky Ireland. French (London) 1996 33p

Dramatization of Roald Dahl's fantasy about adventures of boy, giraffe, pelican, and monkey. Music. 2 acts 9 scenes 5m 1w 1b extras 1 setting

Ireland
Barry, S. Boss Grady's boys
Barry, S. The steward of Christendom
Bolger, D. Blinded by the light
Boucicault, D. The Colleen Bawn
Brogan, P. B. Eclipsed
Coghlan, L. Waking
Donnelly, N. A little like paradise
Doyle, R. Brownbread
FitzGibbon, G. The rock station
Friel, B. Wonderful Tennessee
Hendrick, B. If I can't take it with me ... I'm not going to go
Keane, J. B. Moll
Kilroy, T. The seagull
McGuinness, F. The factory girls
Mac Intyre, T. Good evening, Mr Collins
Murphy, T. Bailegangaire
Murphy, T. Conversations on a homecoming
Murphy, T. A thief of a Christmas
O'Casey, S. Cock-a-doodle dandy
O'Donovan, J. Copperfaced Jack
Roche, B. The Cavalcaders
Shaw, B. John Bull's other Island
Synge, J. M. The playboy of the Western World
Synge, J. M. Riders to the sea
Williams, N. A little like paradise
Yeats, W. B. The Countess Cathleen

See also Cork (Ireland); Dublin (Ireland); Inishman (Ireland); Northern Ireland; Sherkin Island (Ireland)

Army

McGuinness, F. Observe the sons of Ulster marching towards the Somme

History—1558-1603

Kilroy, T. The O'Neill

History—1649-1660

Edmundson, H. The clearing

Irene and Lillian forever. Farmer, B.

Irish

Australia

c Davis, J. Moorli and the Leprechauns
Enright, N. Good works

Canada

Reaney, J. The St. Nicholas Hotel, Wm. Donnelly, prop.

England

Donnelly, N. The duty master
Finnegan, S. It's all blarney
Magee, D. Paddywack

United States

Barry, S. White Woman Street
O'Neill, E. A touch of the poet
Phelan, B. Himself

Irish Republican Army
Harding, M. Hubert Murray's widow
Magee, D. Paddywack
Muldoon, P. Six honest serving men
Shields, B. J. Highwire

An **Irish** triangle. Barnes, D.

Iron magnolias. Hillman, B. L.

Iron Tommy. Ryan, J.

Irony. See Satire

Irving, Washington
The legend of Sleepy Hollow (dramatization) See Cole, J. D. Ichabod

Rip Van Winkle—Parodies, imitations, etc.

y Priore, F. V. The return of Rip Van Winkle, Jr.

Is that the bus to Pittsburgh? Toddie, J. L.

Is that you Nancy? Shotlander, S.

Is there a comic in the house? St. John, B.

Is there anybody there? Bisson, P.

Isitt, Debbie
Matilda liar! Warner Chappell Plays 1994 83p
Dark comedy. Compulsive liar living with dysfunctional family experiences sudden change and feels compelled to tell the truth. Prologue 3 acts 2m 3w 1 interior
Nasty neighbours. Warner Chappell Plays 1995 115p
Black comedy set in England. Feud between neighbors escalates in intensity. 2 acts 46 scenes 3m 3w 1 setting
The woman who cooked her husband. Warner Chappell Plays 1993 72p
Black comedy. Woman seeks revenge against philandering husband. Prologue 9 scenes 2m 1w 1 interior

The **Island** of Anyplace. Rocklin, B.

Islands of the Pacific
y Cowell, M. Song for the navigator

Iso tank. Saunders, J.

Isolation. Haynes, H. J.

Israel
Brittney, L. A different way to die
Havis, A. A vow of silence
Tomer, B.-Z. Children of the shadows

It can damage your health. Chappell, E.

It changes every year. Baitz, J. R.

Italian Americans
Chayefsky, P. Marty
Miranda, J. Italian funerals and other festive occasions
Tibbles, G. The turn of the worm

Italian funerals and other festive occasions. Miranda, J.

Italian rum cake. Tasca, J.

Italians
Australia
Pitts, G. Emma

Italy
De Filippo, E. Grand magic
De Filippo, E. The local authority
Fo, D. Trumpets and raspberries
Ford, J. 'Tis pity she's a whore
McCullough, L. E. O thou joyful day
Micone, M. Beyond the ruins
See also Naples (Italy)
Church history—476-1400
Barnes, P. Sunsets and glories
History—15th century
Maeterlinck, M. Monna Vanna
History—16th century
Musset, A. de. Lorenzaccio
Spoor, K. Everything under the sun
History—17th century
Middleton, T. A critical edition of Thomas Middleton's The witch
Middleton, T. The witch
History—20th century
Griffiths, T. Occupations
Politics and government
Fo, D. Can't pay? Won't pay!
Social life and customs—16th century
Machiavelli, N. Clizia
The Revenger's tragedy
Social life and customs—18th century
y Cornthwaite, R. Carlo Goldoni's Villeggiatura
Goldoni, C. Villeggiatura: Adventures in the country
Goldoni, C. Villeggiatura: Back from the country
Goldoni, C. Villeggiatura: Crazy for the country

Ithaka. Benn, G.

It's a bird! It's a plane! It's ... Nerdman?! Sodaro, C.

It's a slippery slope. Gray, S.

It's a wonderful life. Rodgers, J. W.

It's a wonderful life. Sharkey, T. M.

It's all blarney. Finnegan, S.

It's all relative. Labiche, E. and Michel, M.

It's called the Sugar Plum. Horovitz, I.

It's dark up there. See Booth, R. Where did you spend the night?

It's impossible to think of everything. See Musset, A. de. You can't think of everything

It's morning. Graham, S.

It's our town, too. Miller, S.

Ivan IV, the Terrible, Czar of Russia
Barnes, P. Laughter!

Ivanov. Chekhov, A.

Ivanov. Hare, D.

I've got the shakes. Foreman, R.

Ives, David
All in the timing (condensation)
In The Best plays of 1993-1994

Ives, David—*Continued*

Ancient history

Comedy. Unmarried couple decide to stay unmarried. 2 acts 1m 1w 1 setting

In Ives, D. All in the timing: fourteen plays

Degas, c'est moi

Comedy. New York City man decides to be Edgar Degas for a day. 3m 3w 1 setting

In The Best American short plays, 1995-1996

Don Juan in Chicago. Dramatists 1995 116p

Comedy combining Don Juan and Faust legends. Academic must bed different women each day to remain immortal. 3 acts 5m 3w 1 interior

English made simple

Man and woman, attracted to each other, struggle to overcome strictures of banal party talk. 1m 1w 1 interior

In Ives, D. All in the timing: fourteen plays

In Ives, D. The land of Cockaigne and English made simple

Foreplay; or, The art of the fugue

Comedy. Young man and two older manifestations of himself play at miniature golf and seduction. 1 act 3m 3w 1 exterior

In Ives, D. All in the timing: fourteen plays

In Ives, D. Long ago and far away and other short plays

The land of Cockaigne

Dramatic portrayal of American family. Three scenes depict small birthday in Midwestern yard on summer day. 3 scenes 2m 4w 1 exterior

In Ives, D. The land of Cockaigne and English made simple

Long ago and far away

Domestic drama about troubled young Manhattan wife. 2m 2w 1 interior

In Ives, D. All in the timing: fourteen plays

In Ives, D. Long ago and far away and other short plays

Mere mortals

Comedy. Three construction workers on lunch break share amazing confidences. 1 act 3m 1 setting

In Ives, D. All in the timing: fourteen plays

In Ives, D. Long ago and far away and other short plays

The Philadelphia

Comedy. Man in Twilight zone-like state must ask for opposite of what he truly wants. 2m 1w 1 interior

In Ives, D. All in the timing: fourteen plays

In Ives, D. All in the timing: six one-act comedies

Philip Glass buys a loaf of bread

Spoof of a contemporary opera with focus on Philip Glass' work. 1 act 2m 2w 1 interior

In Ives, D. All in the timing: fourteen plays

In Ives, D. All in the timing: six one-act comedies

Seven menus

Comedy about relationships set at restaurant table. Group of friends change, couple by couple and course by course throughout several meals. 1 act 4m 4w 1 interior

In Ives, D. All in the timing: fourteen plays

In Ives, D. Long ago and far away and other short plays

A singular kinda guy

Monologue. Young guy out on Saturday night makes startling revelation. 1m

In Ives, D. All in the timing: fourteen plays

Speed-the-play

Comic condensations of David Mamet's American buffalo, Speed-the-plow, Sexual perversity in Chicago, and Glengarry Glen Ross. 1 act 13m 3w 4 interiors

In Ives, D. All in the timing: fourteen plays

In Ives, D. Long ago and far away and other short plays

Sure thing

Comedy. Young man desperately seeks to impress woman he meets in cafe. 1 act 1m 1w 1 interior

In Ives, D. All in the timing: fourteen plays

In Ives, D. All in the timing: six one-act comedies

In Telling tales: new one-act plays; ed. by E. Lane

The universal language

Comedy. Love blossoms between young woman with stutter and inventor of comic language. 2m 1w 1 interior

In The Best American short plays, 1993-1994

In Ives, D. All in the timing: fourteen plays

In Ives, D. All in the timing: six one-act comedies

Variations on the death of Trotsky

Comedy. Scenes portray Russian revolutionary on day of his assassination. 1 act 2m 1w 1 interior

In Ives, D. All in the timing: fourteen plays

In Ives, D. All in the timing: six one-act comedies

Ives, David—*Continued*
Words, words, words
Comedy. Three monkeys at typewriters try to write Hamlet. 1 act 2m 1w 1 interior
In Ives, D. All in the timing: fourteen plays
In Ives, D. All in the timing: six one-act comedies

J

J. J. Farr. Harwood, R.

J. P. Morgan saves the nation. Larson, J.

Jack and Jill. Martin, J.

Jack and the beanstalk
Parodies, imitations, etc.
c Snipes, L. E. Jack and the wonder beans

Jack and the beanstalk. Mahlmann, L. and Jones, D. C.

Jack and the wonder beans. Snipes, L. E.

Jack Fuggler. Swortzell, L.

Jack the Ripper
Courts, R. Jack's holiday
Dickinson, J. Jack the Ripper, monster of Whitechapel

Jack the Ripper, monster of Whitechapel. Dickinson, J.

Jack the Ripper Murders, London, England, 1888
Dickinson, J. Jack the Ripper, monster of Whitechapel
Pollock, S. Saucy Jack

Jackets. Bond, E.

Jackie. Rasche, D.

Jack's holiday. Courts, R.

Jackson, C. Bernard
Iago
Revisionist look at Shakespeare's Othello in racial terms. 2 acts 15 scenes Variable cast
In The National black drama anthology; ed. by W. King

Jackson, David
c No one will marry a princess with a tree growing out of her head! (A musical fantasy in one act); book & lyrics by Michael Elliot Brill; music and orchestrations by David Jackson. Anchorage Press 1996 59p
Musical fantasy. Princess tries to break evil spell. 3 scenes Variable cast 15 characters 2 interiors

Jackson, Judith Alexa
WOMBmanWARs
Satirical one woman show addresses issues raised by Anita Hill/Clarence Thomas hearings. 1w
In Moon marked and touched by sun; ed. by S. Mahone

Jackson, Keith
c Laffin' school reunion. Pioneer Drama Service 1997 23p
Comedy. Rambunctious class with new teacher. Variable cast 11 characters extras
y Street story. Pioneer Drama Service 1993 18p
Teenager renounces gang life. 8m 8w extras 1 setting
y Three doors to death; or, The choice is yours. Pioneer Drama Service 1995 19p
Audience helps uncover murderer of actor killed during rehearsal of British thriller. 4m 5w 1 interior

Jackson, Marilee
c Unlucky Cinderella
Parody of fairy tale, Cinderella wins prince despite having big feet. 3 scenes 2m 7w 2 interiors
In The Big book of skits; ed. by S. E. Kamerman

Jackson, Marsha A.
Sisters
Drama exploring how two very different African American women confront contemporary social realities. Prologue 2 acts 2w 1 setting
In The National black drama anthology; ed. by W. King

Jackson, Nagle
The quick-change room. Dramatists 1994 64p
Political satire set backstage at Kuzlov Theater, St. Petersburg, Russia, 1991-1992. Rushing to embrace capitalism Chekhov's The three sisters is transformed into American-style musical. 2 acts 27 scenes 5m 5w 1 interior

Jackson, R. Eugene. See Alette, C. The secret garden

Jacob, Eva
c The crowded house
Wise man advises family to bring animals into crowded house. 4 scenes 2m 2w 4b 4g extras 1 interior
In Thirty plays from favorite stories; ed. by S. E. Kamerman

Jacobean drama. See English drama—17th century

Jacob's wake. Cook, M.

Jailbird. Mitterer, F.

Jake's women. Simon, N.

A **Jamaican** airman foresees his death. D'Aguiar, F.

Jamais vu. Campbell, K.

Jamal, Dorothy
The highway. NCEC 1993 30p
Religious play. English townspeople fighting to save old church building face some difficult questions of faith. 4 scenes 8m 4w extras 1 interior

James, Alice, 1848-1892
Sontag, S. Alice in bed

James, Henry, 1843-1916
The turn of the screw (dramatization) See Hatcher, J. The turn of the screw

James, Jesse, 1847-1882
c McCullough, L. E. Jesse James: blood on the saddle

James, JoAnne
c The echo box
Drama about children vacationing in Vancouver Island. Summer marked by reunion, betrayal and reconciliation. Background music. 12 scenes 1b 2g
In James, J. Three quest plays
c Moving day
Best friends separated by one family's move from Calgary to Vancouver. 9 scenes 1b 2g
In James, J. Three quest plays
c Willa and Sam
Best friends reunited after move find time and distance have separated them more profoundly than they thought. 12 scenes 1b 2g
In James, J. Three quest plays

James A. Michener's Sayonara. Fischoff, G.

Janaczewska, Noelle
The history of water/huyền thoại một giòng nu'ó'c. Currency Press 1995 56p
Psychological drama about two women in contemporary Australia. Photographer with English background and Vietnamese translator struggle with duality of their lives and histories. Slide projections. 2w 1 setting

Jane Austen's Northanger Abbey. Francis, M.

Jane Eyre. Hall, W.

Jane Eyre. Vance, C.

Janes, Hugh
Two of a kind. French (London) 1996 58p
Comedy. Rebellious old sailor finds it impossible to adapt to retirement home living. 2 acts 2m 2w 1 setting

Jannuzzi, Luigi
The appointment
Comedy. Man bides time while awaiting his appointment with God. 2m 2w 1 interior
In Off-Off Broadway Festival plays, 20th ser.
With or without you
Romantic comedy. Woman reluctantly meets devoted admirer in restaurant. 1m 1w 1 interior
In Off-Off Broadway Festival plays, 21st ser.

Japan
Abe, K. Involuntary homicide
c Love, D. Kabuki gift
McDonough, J. Butterfly
Oswald, P. Fair ladies at a game of poem cards
Smolensky, S. and Waldrop, J. The Mikado

History—1185-1600

Yoshitsune and the thousand cherry trees

History—17th century

Bond, E. The bundle

History—1945-

Fischoff, G. James A. Michener's Sayonara
Houston, V. H. Asa ga kimashita (Morning has broken)

Japanese

Australia

Broinowski, A. The gap

Canada—Evacuation and relocation, 1942-1945

c Wing, P. A. Naomi's road

Hawaii

Gotanda, P. K. Ballad of Yachiyo

United States

Houston, V. H. Tea
Yamauchi, W. The music lessons

Japanese-Americans
Gotanda, P. K. Day standing on its head
Gotanda, P. K. Fish head soup
Gotanda, P. K. A song for a Nisei fisherman
Gotanda, P. K. The wash
Houston, V. H. Kokoro (true heart)
Iko, M. Gold watch
Nishikawa, L. and Talmadge, V. The gate of heaven
Okita, D. The rainy season
Omata, G. H. S.A.M. I am
Uyehara, D. Hiro
Yamauchi, W. And the soul shall dance

Evacuation and relocation, 1942-1945

Yamauchi, W. 12-1-A

Japanese folklore. See Folklore—Japanese

Jar the floor. West, C. L.

Jarry, Alfred
Ubu cocu
Variant title: Ubu cuckolded; Satirical farce. Ubu commandeers scholar's home and enjoys a reign of absurd terror. Characters can also be enacted by marionettes. Dancing. 5 acts 26 scenes 11m 1w extra 1 interior
In A Dozen French farces; ed. by A. Bermel

Jarvis, Graham. See Dover, M. jt. auth.

Jason (Greek mythology)
Gurney, A. R. The Golden Fleece

Jazz music
Rubess, B. Boom, baby, boom!

Jealousy
Connolly, H. Daddy's gone a-hunting
Robson, J. Mail order bride
Sade, Marquis de. The bedroom
Strindberg, A. The dance of death
Wilder, T. A ringing of doorbells

Jeanne Laisné. Sade, Marquis de

Jefferson, Thomas, 1743-1826
Keithley, G. The best blood of the country
Kingsley, S. The patriots

Jeffrey. Rudnick, P.

Jeffreys, Stephen
A going concern. Hern Bks. 1993 80p
Drama set in 1966 London. Three generations conspire against each other to gain control of ailing family firm. 2 acts 5 scenes 7m 1w 1 interior

The libertine. Hern Bks. 1995 84p
Historical comedy of manners about the Earl of Rochester, confidant of Charles I, and the most notorious rake of his time. Music. Prologue 2 acts 13 scenes 5m 5w extras 1 setting

Jehanne of the witches. Clark, S.

Jelinek, Elfriede
President Evening Breeze
Loosely based on folk play by Johann Nestroy. Political satire on career of Kurt Waldheim. Singing. 3 acts 4m 1w 1 exterior
In New anthology of contemporary Austrian folk plays; ed. by R. H. Lawson

Totenauberg (Death/Valley/Summit)
Drama about politicalization of rhetoric and totalitarianism. Portrays philosopher turned Nazi Martin Heidegger and his student and lover, Hannah Arendt. 1m 1w extras 1 interior
In DramaContemporary: Germany; ed. by C. Weber

Jelly's last jam. Wolfe, G. C.

Jenkin, Len
Careless love. Sun & Moon Press 1993 92p
Existential comedy about search for love and meaning in late 20th century Western society. Music, singing. 4m 4w

c Ramona Quimby. Dramatic 1994 67p
Based on series of novels by Beverly Cleary. Vignettes involving boisterous third grade girl, her family and friends. 30 scenes 4m 6w 1b 3g extras

Jennie's story. Lambert, B.

Jennings, Caleen Sinnette
Sunday dinner. Dramatic 1993 38p
After long period of estrangement three African American sisters, of very different lifestyles, gather for Sunday dinner in their childhood home. 1 act 3w 1 interior

Jenny keeps talking. Greenberg, R.

Jensen, Julie
The total meaning of real life
Girl's journey to commit suicide interrupted by seedy character hawking ten-minute marriages in Las Vegas. 1m 1w 1 interior
In Lucky 13; ed. by R. Shuttleworth

Jensen, Mark
Zombie chick
Teenage girl has ability to raise small animals from the dead. 2w 1 setting
In Lucky 13; ed. by R. Shuttleworth

Jeremy borrows a book. Pflomm, P. N.

Jeremy Whistler, mad scientist. LaBounty, D.

Jerusalem. Gurr, M.

Jery and Betty. Goethe, J. W. von

Jesse James: blood on the saddle. McCullough, L. E.

The **jest.** Netzel, S.

Jest a second! Sherman, J.

Jesus Christ
c Haylock, D. Here is the news: Riot in Nazareth
c Haylock, D. Rejection
c Haylock, D. Whoever
Joseph, C. M. The temptations of Jesus
c McCaslin, N. The Christmas lamb
Wilson, E. A first-born son

Crucifixion

y Aynsley, E. What a weekend!
c Haylock, D. Here is the news: Sad news and amazing news
Mueller, D. A. Eyes upon the cross
Solórzano, C. The crucified
c Stephens, J. The servant king
Warner, F. Moving reflections

Jesus Christ—*Continued*

Nativity

c Anderson, J. The animals' Christmas
Enscoe, L. G. and Enscoe, A. Candles and carols
c Haylock, D. Guardian Angels
c Haylock, D. The nativity scene
c Haylock, D. The shepherd and the psychiatrist
c Haylock, D. The Wallies guide to Christmas
c Haylock, D. A window in the diary
c McCullough, L. E. Bring a torch, Jeannette, Isabella
c McCullough, L. E. Let us go, O shepherds
c McCullough, L. E. We three Kings of Orient are
McDonough, J. Posadas
c Petersen, C. A. If angels were mortal . . .
c Peterson, M. L. How Santa Claus discovered Christmas
c Pound, S. R. The Angels' greatest message
c Thompson, L. The innkeeper's daughter
c Trott, S. Buster come home
Trott, S. Destination Bethlehem
c Trott, S. Did I miss anything important?
c Trott, S. Nocturne
c Trott, S. R.S.V.P.
c Trott, S. Something sacred this way comes
c Trott, S. You don't say!
Vigil, A. Los pastores. The shepherds

Passion

Sahlins, B. The mysteries: The Passion

Resurrection

y Aynsley, E. What a weekend!
c Haylock, D. Here is the news: Sad news and amazing news

Jesus on the oil tank. Sherman, J. M.

The **Jew** of Malta. Marlowe, C.

Jewel. MacLeod, J.

Jewel thieves! Beim, N.

Jewish refugees. See Refugees, Jewish

Jews

Bellon, L. Bonds of affection
Chayefsky, P. Holiday song
Herzberg, J. The wedding party
Mann, E. Annulla
Margulies, D. Lola
Margulies, D. New Year's eve and Kibbutz
Margulies, D. Sight unseen
Margulies, D. What's wrong with this picture?
Schwartz, D. Shenandoah
Sherman, J. The God of Isaac
Tannen, D. An act of devotion
Wasserstein, W. The sisters Rosensweig
See also Antisemitism; Holocaust, Jewish (1933-1945); Holocaust survivors

Australia

Fischer, M. The gay divorcee

Austria

Marans, J. Old wicked songs
Mitterer, F. There's not a finer country

Bronx (New York, N.Y.)

Odets, C. Awake and sing!

Brooklyn (New York, N.Y.)

Braverman, C. The Yiddish Trojan women
Margulies, D. The Loman family picnic
Miller, A. Broken glass
Simon, N. Brighton Beach memoirs
Smith, A. D. Fires in the mirror: Crown Heights, Brooklyn and other identities

Canada

Horovitz, I. Today I am a fountain pen
Ravel, A. Vengeance

Eastern Europe

Ansky, S. The dybbuk
c Ravel, A. Tales from the shtetl: the Sholom Aleichem show

England

Lee, J. A. Coming home
Samuels, D. Kindertransport
Sherman, G. Broken English

Europe, Central

Goldberg, L. Lady of the Castle

France

Grumberg, J.-C. The free zone
Grumberg, J.-C. The workroom
Segal, G. All the tricks but one

Germany

Horovitz, I. Lebensraum
Mead, K. Line of descent
c Watts, I. K. Goodbye Marianne

Hungary

Lerner, M. Kastner

Lithuania

Sobol, J. Adam

Netherlands

y Kops, B. Dreams of Anne Frank

New York (N.Y.)

Baitz, J. R. The substance of fire
Gardner, H. Conversations with my father

Jews—New York (N.Y.)—*Continued*
Klavan, L. Freud's house
Kramer, L. The destiny of me
Pearson, S. Unfinished stories
Regan, S. Morning star
Rice, E. Counsellor-at-law
Richards, G. Dividends
Sherman, J. M. Serendipity and serenity
Tolins, J. The twilight of the Golds

Poland

Barnes, P. The spirit of man: The night of the Sinhat [sic] Torah
Garner, J. The flight into Egypt

Prague (Czech Republic)

Basso, E. The fall of Prague

Queens (New York, N.Y.)

Hardstack, M. In the cemetery

South Africa

Harwood, R. Another time

United States

Behrman, S. N. The cold wind and the warm
Chayefsky, P. The tenth man
Goldstein, J. Martin Night
Greenberg, R. The American plan
Greenspan, D. Dead mother
Hardstack, M. The cure
Hoffman, A. Welcome stranger
Horovitz, I. Unexpected tenderness
Kravitz, A. Just thinking
Lawrence, J. and Lee, R. E. Only in America
Margulies, D. Zimmer
Minjares, J. The king of the kosher grocers
Nishikawa, L. and Talmadge, V. The gate of heaven
Page, E. Aryan birth
Paterson, D. L. Pieces of the sky
Rumble, P. B. Aunt Sophie's latkes
Simon, N. Lost in Yonkers
Uhry, A. Driving Miss Daisy
Uhry, A. The last night of Ballyhoo
Van Zandt, B. and Milmore, J. What the rabbi saw
Zark, J. A body of water: Foreign bodies
Zark, J. A body of water: Shooting souls
Zark, J. A body of water: White days

Ji-da (the bird) Roberts, A. V.

Jiang Qing, 1914-1991
Yamauchi, W. The chairman's wife

Jim Dandy Gilbert, S.

Jingle bells. McCullough, L. E.

Joan of Arc, Saint
Clark, S. Jehanne of the witches

Job hunters. Edward, H. F. V.

The **job** interview. Mauro, R.

Joe Turner's come and gone. Wilson, A.

Joe's ark. Potter, D.

Joe's drum. McGrath, J.

Joey. Margulies, D.

Joey-Boy. Dashow, K.

Johanson, Robert
Charles Dickens' Great expectations. Dramatic 1994 125p

Dramatization of Dickens' classic coming of age tale set in 19th century England. Background music. 2 acts Variable cast 30 characters extras various settings

A tale of two cities. Dramatic 1995 120p

Dramatization of Dickens' romantic tragedy set against the French Revolution. 2 acts 16m 7w 2b 1b extras 1 setting

John, the Baptist
Wilde, O. Salomé

John Henry (Legendary character)
Browne, T. Natural man
Winther, B. John Henry

John Paul II, Pope, 1920-
Fo, D. The Pope and the witch

John and Mary Doe. Durang, C.

John Bull's other Island. Shaw, B.

John the bear. See Vigil, A. Juan Oso. John the bear

Johnny Appleseed. McCaslin, N.

Johnny Appleseed and Willie Crabgrass. McCullough, L. E.

Johnny Pye. Courts, R.

Johnny Pye and the Foolkiller. Benet, S. V. (dramatization) See Courts, R. Johnny Pye

Johnny Tenorio. Morton, C.

Johnson, Catherine
Boys mean business

Portrait of aimless twentysomethings in British seaside town. 3 scenes 3m 2w 1 exterior

In Bush Theatre plays

Johnson, Cindy Lou
The years. Dramatists 1994 74p

Drama about politics of race, gender and sexuality. Interwoven monologues by three generations of Australian aborigine women. 3w 1 setting

Johnson, Eva
What do they call me?
Family prepares for two wedding ceremonies, separated in time by thirteen years. 3 acts 10 scenes 3m 3w
In Australian gay and lesbian plays; ed. by B. Parr

Johnson, Francis Hall
Run little chillun
Drama set in the South depicting religious conflict between two major faiths of early African Americans; the so-called pagan and Baptist. 2 acts 4 scenes 7m 14w 3 interiors 1 exterior
In Lost plays of the Harlem Renaissance; ed. by J. V. Hatch and L. Hamalian

Johnson, Georgia Douglas
A Sunday morning in the South
Racial drama set in 1920s South. Innocent black man lynched for supposedly attacking white woman. 2m 4w 1b extra 1 interior
In Black theatre USA [v1]; ed. by J. V. Hatch and T. Shine

Johnson, James P. and Hughes, Langston
The organizer
Blues opera about attempt to unionize Southern black cotton pickers. Singing. 1 act 5m 2w 1 setting
In Lost plays of the Harlem Renaissance; ed. by J. V. Hatch and L. Hamalian

Johnson, Judith
Somewhere
Drama set 1981 in northwest of England and 1991 in Amsterdam. Explores directionless youth, prostitution, and working-class girl's search for love. 2 parts 6m 4w 2 settings
In Frontline intelligence I; ed. by P. Edwardes

Uganda
Domestic drama set in small English town. Children visit widowed father over Christmas holidays. 2 acts 14 scenes 3m 4w 1 interior
In Frontline intelligence 3; ed. by P. Edwardes

Johnson, Robert, d. 1938
Harris, B. Robert Johnson: trick the Devil

Johnson, Terry
Cries from the mammal house
Following death of patriarchal owner, provincial English zoo is threatened with closure, setting in motion biazarre events forcing characters to explore their social conscience and family guilt. 3 acts 15 scenes 5m 3w 3 interiors
In Johnson, T. Plays: one

Dead funny. Methuen Drama 1994 102p (Methuen modern plays)
Comedy about impotence, sex therapy and English sense of humor. 2 acts 4 scenes 3m 2w 1 interior

Hysteria; or, Fragments of an analysis of an obsessional neurosis. Methuen Drama in association with the Royal Court Theatre 1993 93p (Royal Court writers series)
Comedy set in 1939 London. Sigmund Freud, in state of near hysteria, burns latest publication and is berated by surrealist Salvador Dali. 2 acts 3 scenes 3m 1w 1 interior

Insignificance
Set in 1953 New York City. In luxury hotel bedroom, famous scientist is visited by film star, baseball player and senator, each asking others to make some kind of sacrifice. 2 acts 4m 1w 1 interior
In Johnson, T. Plays: one

Unsuitable for adults
Drama about aggressive feminist comedian and her relationships with fellow performers; a magician, stripper and her philandering boyfriend. 4m 2w 2 acts epilogue 2 interiors
In Johnson, T. Plays: one

Johnston, Christine
c A pig tale. Moorley's 1994 14p
Humorous version of the parable of the prodigal son. Music. 8m extras 1 setting

Joined at the head. Butterfield, C.

A **joke**. Chekhov, A. (dramatization) See Guare, J. The talking dog

The **joke** code. Mamet, D.

Jolly. Mamet, D.

Jonah (Biblical figure)
c Haylock, D. Here is the news: Overseas and underseas news
c Richardson, D. McJonah

Jones, Charles
My Antonia. French 1994 125p
Dramatization of Willa Cather's novel depicting life of Bohemian immigrant girl on Nebraska frontier in 1880s. 2 acts 20 scenes 11m 7w 3b 4g 1 setting
See also Cole, J. D. Ichabod

Jones, Henry Arthur
The middleman
Brilliant potter exploited by profiteering master. 4 acts 12m 6w 3 interiors
In The Lights o' London and other Victorian plays; ed. by M. R. Booth

Jones, Jeffrey M.
Love trouble. Sun & Moon Press 1994 80p (Sun & Moon classics)
Black comedy with stuffed animal protagonist. Fable about parenthood, love and fear of loss. Music, singing. 2m 3w 1 setting

Jones, Leroi. See Baraka, Amiri

Jones, Lisa
Combination skin
Satire on tragic mulatto archetype and assimilationist black artists of the 1980s. Background music. 3m 5w 1 setting
In Contemporary plays by women of color; ed. by K. A. Perkins and R. Uno

Jones, Marie
A night in November. Hern Bks. 1995 48p (New Island/new drama)
Humorous monologue about Protestant tradition in Northern Ireland. Belfast man decides to travel to New York after witnessing sectarian hatred surrounding soccer match. 2 acts 1m

Jones, Martin
Vanishing points. Broadway Play Pub. 1993 86p
Impressionistic murder mystery incorporating psychological spectors, dreams and nightmares. 2 acts 4m 4w 1 setting

Jones, mother, 1830-1930
Gilbert, R. Mother Jones: the most dangerous woman in America
y McCullough, L. E. The most dangerous woman in America

Jones, Rhodessa
Big butt girls, hard-headed women
Series of monologues by women incarcerated in San Francisco City Jail. 4w 1 interior
In Colored contradictions: an anthology of contemporary African-American plays

Jones, Stanleigh H. See Yoshitsune and the thousand cherry trees

Jones, Taffy
c Camping out
Puppet play. Sisters try to scare brothers away from tent. 7 characters
In Jones, T. Old barn puppet plays
c The computer
Puppet play. Farmer neglects chores and family to use new computer. 3 scenes 7 characters
In Jones, T. Old barn puppet plays
c Froggie woggies
Puppet play. Frog encounters trouble when he disregards farmer's advice. 3 scenes 10 characters
In Jones, T. Old barn puppet plays
c Gertie goat
Puppet play. Goat makes amends for chewing farmer's clothing. 2 scenes 3 characters
In Jones, T. Old barn puppet plays
c Gone fishing
Puppet play. Farmer has no luck catching fish. 5 characters
In Jones, T. Old barn puppet plays
c Scarecrows
Puppet play. Friends help scarecrow do his job. 6 characters
In Jones, T. Old barn puppet plays
c Who stole the pie!
Puppet play. Farmer solves mystery of missing blueberry pie. 6 characters
In Jones, T. Old barn puppet plays

Jones, Thomas W.
The wizard of hip
Comedic monologue. African American man expounds on what constitutes "hipness." 2 acts 1m
In Black comedy: nine plays; ed. by P. F. Jackson and Karimah

Joplin, Scott
Overmyer, E. The Heliotrope Bouquet by Scott Joplin & Louis Chauvin

Joselovitz, Ernest, and Bagdasian, Harry Michael
Love by the numbers. French 1995 73p
Romantic comedy. New York City computer honcho falls in love with small town library assistant. 2 acts 6 scenes 5m 4w 1 setting

Joseph, Curt M.
The temptations of Jesus. C.S.S. Pub. Co. 1993 67p
Worship program. Jesus resists temptation in six short dialogues with Satan. 2m

Joseph Dintenfass. Mamet, D.

Joseph in the underground. Basso, E.

Journalists
Bandele, 'B. Marching for Fausa
Blessing, L. Down the road
Elton, B. Silly cow
Gray, O. The torrents
Hare, D. A map of the world
Lucie, D. The shallow end
Nigro, D. Necropolis
Osborne, J. The world of Paul Slickey
Waterhouse, J. The cardboard cavaliers
Williamson, D. Sanctuary

Journey to Gotha. See Musset, A. de. You can't think of everything

Journey to the West. Lee, C. K.

Joyce, Lucia
Hall, F. B. Lucia
Nigro, D. Lucia mad

Joyce, Nora Barnacle, 1884-1951
Nigro, D. Lucia mad

Joyce, William, 1906-1946
Kilroy, T. Double cross

Joyriders. Reid, C.

Juan Oso. John the bear. Vigil, A.

Juarez, Benito
c Vigil, A. La Batalla de Cinco de Mayo. The Battle of Cinco de Mayo

Judah Loew ben Bezalel, ca. 1525-1609
Basso, E. The fall of Prague

Judge and jury. Dunn, M.

Judges
Banville, J. The broken jug
Dunn, M. Judge and jury
Mortimer, J. Edwin
O'Donovan, J. Copperfaced Jack

The **judgment** of Father Martinho. Samtareno, B.

Judith (Biblical figure)
Barker, H. Judith: a parting from the body

Judith: a parting from the body. Barker, H.

Judo
Barnes, P. More than a touch of Zen
Godber, J. Blood, sweat and tears

Judy, George
Antigone. Pioneer Drama Service 1997 64p

Adaptation of Sophocles' drama about battle between public authority and personal conscience that divides city of Thebes. Includes optional prologue. Chorus. 10m 1w 1 setting

The **juiceman** cometh. Spiro, P.

Julia. Rivera, C.

Julia of Louvain. Cross, J. C.

Julie Allardyce. McLean, D.

Julie Johnson. Hammond, W.

Juliet. Linney, R.

July 7, 1994. Margulies, D.

The **jumping** mimuses of Byzantium. Barnes, P.

Jungle rot. Greenland, S.

Junk bonds. Wang, L.

Jupiter (Roman deity)
Dryden, J. Amphitryon
y McCaslin, N. Travelers from Olympus
Molière. Amphitryon
Plautus, T. M. Amphitryon

Jury
Sutton, J. Voir dire

Just a loving touch. Bamford, S.

Just like home. Uys, P.-D.

The **just** so letter. Summer, A.

Just thinking. Kravitz, A.

Justice, Administration of
Aristophanes. Wasps

Justinian, 483?-565, Emperor of the East
Warner, F. Byzantium

Juvenile delinquency
Kingsley, S. Dead end

K

Kaahumanu, Queen, consort of Kamehama I, King of Hawaiian Islands, 1777-1832
Kneubuhl, V. N. The conversion of Ka'ahumanu

Kabuki gift. Love, D.

Kachejian, Greg
y All's well that ends wrong. Bakers Plays 1993 33p

College girls discover relevance of Shakespeare in their lives. 2m 5w 1 interior

Kafka, Franz
A hunger artist (dramatization) See Drexler, R. Occupational hazard

About

Daly, T. Kafka dances

Parodies, imitations, etc.

Clark, S. The trial of Judith K.

Kafka dances. Daly, T.

Kahlo, Frida, 1907-1954
Blecher, H.; Cruz, M. and Rodriguez, R. X. Frida: the story of Frida Kahlo

Kahn, Si. See Gilbert, R. Mother Jones: the most dangerous woman in America

Kai, Nubia
Harvest the frost

African American family reunited following funeral of alcoholic son. 2 acts 3 scenes 5m 3w 1 interior

In The National black drama anthology; ed. by W. King

Kaiser, Georg
From morning to midnight; tr. by J. M. Ritchie

Expressionist tragedy. Provincial German bank clerk embezzles large sum but fails to find happiness in big city. Music. 7 scenes Large mixed cast 5 interiors 2 exteriors

In German expressionist plays; ed. by E. Schurer

Kaiser, Georg—*Continued*

Gas I; tr. by Herman Scheffauer

Sequel to: The coral. Second part of author's expressionistic trilogy dealing with man's problems in industrial society. Background music. 5 acts 15m 4w extras 3 interiors 1 exterior

In German expressionist plays; ed. by E. Schurer

Gas II; tr. by Winifred Katzin

Third part of trilogy. Industrialization brings about collapse of society. 3 acts 16m extras 2 interiors

In German expressionist plays; ed. by E. Schurer

The **Kaisers** of Carnuntum. Harrison, T.

Kalamu ya Salaam

Blk love song #1

Consciousness raising piece about black struggle for racial and cultural identity. 3 scenes 4m 3w extras

In Black theatre USA [v2]; ed. by J. V. Hatch and T. Shine

Kalinoski, Richard

Beast on the moon

Set in 1921-1933 Milwaukee. Armenian photographer and his mail-order bride's lives reverbrate with sorrow of Armenian holocaust. 2 acts 10 scenes 2m 1w 1b 1 interior

In Humana Festival '95

Kander, John

The kiss of the spider woman; book by Terrence McNally; (based on the novel by Manuel Puig); music by John Kander; lyrics by Fred Ebb; directed by Harold Prince. French 1997 85p (French's musical library)

Musical adaptation of Puig's novel about relationship between homosexual and Marxist conspirator incarcerated in brutal Latin American prison. Prologue 2 acts 19 scenes 14m 3w 1 interior

Kiss of the Spider woman (condensation)

In The Best plays of 1992-1993

Kane, Sarah

Blasted

Drama about male carnality and modern warfare. Hotel in civil war ravaged Europe setting for rape, torture and cannibalism. 5 scenes 2m 1w 1 interior

In Frontline intelligence 2; ed. by P. Edwardes

In Kane, S. Blasted & Phaedra's love

Phaedra's love

Drama about incest and unrequited love based on Seneca's classical tragedy. 8 scenes 5m 4w extras 1 setting

In Kane, S. Blasted & Phaedra's love

Kanin, Fay

Goodbye, my fancy

Romantic comedy. Liberal Congresswoman confronts old beau, now an arch-conservative college administrator. 3 acts 4 scenes 8m 11w 1 interior

In Plays by American women, 1930-1960; ed. by J. E. Barlow

Karagiozis baker

Comic Greek folk drama featuring traditional puppet figures. 12m 1 setting

In Myrsiades, Linda S. and Myrsiades, Kostas. Karagiozis. Univ. Press of Ky. 1992

Karaoke. Potter, D.

Karl XII, King of Sweden, 1683-1718. See Charles XII, King of Sweden, 1683-1718

Karna and Kunti. Tagore, R.

Kárpáti, Péter

Everywoman

Comic retelling of medieval Everyman story with female protagonist. 2 acts 8 scenes 6m 5w 1 setting

In Hungarian plays; ed. by L. Upor

Kase-Polisini, Judith

c Southern fried cracker tales. Anchorage Press 1995 42p

Story theater play based on several American folktales. Music, dancing. Variable cast 58 characters

Kash, Marcia, and Hughes, Doug

Who's under where? French 1993 114p

Farce. Chaos reigns when two women rent hotel suite for private showing of their new line of sexy lingerie. 2 acts 5m 2w 1 interior

Kass, Sam Henry

Dice and cards

Back room of social club scene of confrontation between two "wise guys." 2m 1 interior

In Showtime's Act One Festival of one-act plays, 1994

Lusting after Pipino's wife. French 1994 91p

Comedy about war between the sexes. Restaurant owner and best friend bemoan their inability to understand women. 2 acts 32 scenes 2m 2w 1 setting

Kastner, Rudolf. See Kasztner, Reszo, 1906-1957

Kasztener, Reszo, 1906-1957

Lerner, M. Kastner

Katims, Jason

Who made Robert DeNiro king of America?

Unemployed construction worker knocks off successful screenplay while novelist wife struggles with writer's block. 1m 2w 1 interior

In Act One '95

Kaufman, Lynne
Shooting Simone
Drama explores feminist Beauvoir's fifty year relationship with Sartre. Prelude 2 acts 15 scenes 2m 2w 1 setting
In Humana Festival '93

Keane, John B.
Moll. Mercier Press 1991 102p
Comedy about life in Irish county presbytery. 2 acts 6 scenes 5m 2w 1 interior

Kearns, Michael
Myron, a fairy tale in black and white
Drama loosely based on Rostand's Cyrano de Bergerac about African American gay man with AIDS. 20 scenes 3m 1 interior
In Sharing the delirium; ed. by T. Jones

Keating, Barry
y The garbage cantata; book, music & lyrics by Barry Keating; additional material by Jon Lonoff. French 1996 42p
Musical comedy set in garbage dump. Landfill monster runs amok. Variable cast 1 setting

Keatley, Charlotte
My mother said I never should. Methuen Drama in association with the Royal Court Theatre 1995 53p (Royal Court writers series)
Drama about mothers and daughters set in Manchester, Oldham and London England at various times during the 20th century. 3 acts 19 scenes 4w 1 setting

Keaton, Buster, 1895-1966
Higgins, D. Buster Keaton enters into paradise

Keats, Mark
c Peter Salem, Minuteman
Drama about role of Crispus Attucks at Battle of Bunker Hill. 9m 4w 1b 1g extras 1 setting
In The Big book of large-cast plays; ed. by S. E. Kamerman

Keeler, Dawn
Edith Wharton's The house of mirth. French 1995 93p
Adaptation of Edith Wharton's novel about New York society at the beginning of the century. 2 acts 5m 5w 1 extra 1 setting

Keely and Du. Martin, J.

Keene, Daniel
All Souls. Currency Press in association with Playbox Theatre Centre 1995 50p (Current Theatre series)
Drama set in urban landscape on eve of All Souls. Three couples pass under gaze of homeless visionary. 2 acts 15 scenes 2m 3w 1 setting

Keep an eye of Amélie. See Feydeau, G. That's my girl!

The **keepers.** Lebow, B.

Keillor, Garrison
The midlife crisis of Dionysus
Comedy. Greek god of wine confronts middle age. 2m 3w 1 setting
In The Best American short plays, 1993-1994

Keithley, George
The best blood of the country. Mellon Poetry Press 1993 110p
Historical drama about Aaron Burr's confrontations with Jefferson and Hamilton and his participation in conspiracy to conquer territory west of Appalachians. 3 acts 11 scenes 8m 4w extras 3 settings

Kelly, Christopher
Excess baggage. New Playwrights Network 1997 25p
Comedy. Middle-aged couple's life is disrupted due to bureaucratic error. 1 act 2m 3w 1 interior

Kelly, Tim
y Bang! Bang! You're dead; or, What I learned from watching television. Pioneer Drama Service 1993 17p
Parody of television game show in which contestants are tested on their knowledge of handguns. Variable cast 16 characters 1 interior

y Ditch Day. Pioneer Drama Service 1996 52p
Farce. High school students participating in treasure hunt encounter jewel thieves. 2 acts 10 scenes Variable cast 32 characters extras

y Here come the cows; or . . . Never say moo in Mesa. Pioneer Drama Service 1995 39p
Melodrama. Western town threatened by avaricious villain and his scheming partner. 2 acts 3 scenes 5m 7w extras 1 interior

Hide and shriek. Bakers Plays 1994 83p
Farce. City girl hides out in Ozark Mountains hoping to escape fiance's jealous ex-girlfriend. Background music. 2 acts 5 scenes 5m 9w 1 interior

y Hooray for Hollywood. Pioneer Drama Service 1993 53p
Parody. Teenagers seek fame in Hollywood movie industry. Non-musical version of Teens in Tinseltown. 2 acts 7 scenes 12m 16w extras

Renfield of the flies and spiders. Pioneer Drama Service 1993 61p
Parody of Bram Stoker's Dracula. Declared sane, Renfield returns to castle and becomes Dracula's master. 2 acts 6 scenes 7m 16w 1 interior

y That's the spirit! Bakers Plays 1993 86p
Parody. Magician's ghost solves murder mystery. 2 acts 6 scenes 5m 8w 1 interior

Kelly, Tim—*Continued*

c Treachery at Cartilage Creek; or, Our hero has a bone to pick. Pioneer Drama Service 1995 39p

Melodrama set in Old West. Scoundrel schemes to take over town. 2 scenes 4m 6w extras 1 interior

y Trick or treat. Bakers Plays 1995 79p

Halloween comedy. Old house haunted by scarecrow. 2 acts 3 scenes 5m 7w extras 1 interior

y Trouble in Tumbleweed. Pioneer Drama Service 1995 34p

Farce suggested by Nikolai Gogol's The Inspector General. Pinkerton detective arrives in 1880s Arizona Territory to investigate corruption. 2 acts 4 scenes Variable cast 20 characters extras

y Yard sale. Pioneer Drama Service 1995 54p

Comedy. College students organize yard sale to save their boarding house from wrecking ball. 2 acts 3 scenes 10m 18w extras 1 interior

y You can't stamp out love; or, "Oh, my darling, Val Anne Tyne." Pioneer Drama Service 1996 39p

Melodrama. True love triumphs when fraudulent matchmaking scheme is exposed. 2 scenes 4m 8w extras 1 interior

See also Christiansen, A. A monster ate my homework; Christiansen, A. Wash your troubles away; Francoeur, B. Coney Island of Dr. Moreau; Francoeur, B. Gone with the breeze; Francoeur, B. Hee haw hayride; Francoeur, B. The internal teen machine; Francoeur, B. Kilroy was here!; Francoeur, B. A little princess; Francoeur, B. Oz!; Francoeur, B. The secret garden; Francoeur, B. Shakespeare comes to Calamity Creek; Francoeur, B. Snow White and the seven dwarfs; Francoeur, B. Wrangler Ranch; Hughes, P. Abracadabra, Aladdin!; Reiser, D. Alas! Alack! Zorro's back; Reiser, D. Dr. Jekyll ... please don't hyde; Reiser, D. I want my mummy!; Reiser, D. The creepy creeps of Pilgrim Road

Kelly & Donald. Collings, J.

Kelm, Andrew

Black bride

Man deconstructs nursery rhyme. 1m 1 setting

In Solo; ed. by J. Sherman

Kemp, Jenny

The black sequin dress. Currency Press in association with Playbox Theatre 1996 56p (Current theatre series)

Following accident woman lapses into surreal state where money, desire and dreams converge. 2m 4w extras 1 setting

Kemp, Robert

Dalwhinnie. Players Press 1996 28p

Comedy of manners revolving around Edinburgh lawyer, his wife and aristocratic client with marital problems. 1 act 2m 1w 1 interior

A trump for Jericho. Players Press 1996 60p

Comedy set 1843 Edinburgh. Religious dispute between sisters is complicated by arrival of guests. 3 acts 3 scenes 4m 5w 1 interior

Keneally, Thomas

The playmaker (dramatization) See Wertenbaker, T. Our country's good

Kenna, Peter

Mates

Portrait of Australian drag performer. 3m 1w 1 interior

In Australian gay and lesbian plays; ed. by B. Parr

Kennedy, Adam P. and Kennedy, Adrienne

Sleep deprivation chamber. Theatre Communications Group 1996 72p

Autobiographical theater piece about brutal beating of young African American man by police after being charged with minor traffic violation. 3 scenes 3m 1w extras settings

Kennedy, Adrienne

The dramatic circle

Radio play set in 1961 London. While waiting to hear from husband who has disappeared in West Africa, pregnant black American author and sister-in-law do dramatic readings. 3m 2w extras

In Moon marked and touched by sun; ed. by S. Mahone

Funnyhouse of a Negro

Symbolic drama. Black girl with white fixation struggles with guilt and self-hatred. 1 act 6 scenes 2m 6w 1 setting

In Black theatre USA [v2]; ed. by J. V. Hatch and T. Shine

Motherhood 2000

Drama of urban chaos. Mother ponders emotional aftermath of son's senseless beating by policemen nine years earlier. 4m 1w 1 setting

In Plays for the end of the century; ed. by B. Marranca

See also Kennedy, A. P. jt. auth.

Kennedy, Richard

c Hans Christian Andersen's The Snow Queen; a Christmas pageant; adapted by Richard Kennedy; music by Mark Lambert; pictures by Edward S. Gazsi. HarperCollins Pubs. 1996 85p

Christmas pageant based on Hans Christian Andersen's fairy tale. Girl releases boy from spell cast by evil queen. Singing, dancing, music. 2 acts 11 scenes 6m 9w 1b 2g extras

Kennelly, Brendan

Euripides' The Trojan woman. Bloodaxe Bks. 1993 80p

Modern verse version of Euripides' classical Greek tragedy about brutality of war set immediately after fall of Troy. 2m 6w extras 1 setting

Sophocles' Antigone. Bloodaxe Bks. 1996 63p

Adaptation of Sophocle's political tragedy in verse about conflict between need for civil order and demands of ancestral piety. Antigone decides to bury her disgraced brother in opposition to Creon's authority

See also García Lorca, F. Blood wedding

Kenneth. Foxton, D.

The **Kentish** barons. North, F.

Kentucky

Carson, J. A preacher with a horse to ride

y Cole, N. And the tide shall cover the earth

Crutcher, J. and McBride, V. Diggin in: the farm crisis in Kentucky

Schenkkan, R. The courtship of Morning Star

Schenkkan, R. Fire in the hole

Schenkkan, R. God's great supper

Schenkkan, R. The homecoming

Schenkkan, R. Masters of the trade

Schenkkan, R. Tall tales

Schenkkan, R. Ties that bind

Schenkkan, R. The war on poverty

Schenkkan, R. Which side are you on?

The **Kentucky** cycle. See under Schenkkan, Robert

Kenyatta, Kisha

Harriet

One-woman dramatization of life of Harriet Tubman. 1w 1 interior

In Award winning plays v2

Kesselman, Wendy

y Maggie Magalita

Young Hispanic American girl has difficulty communicating with grandmother who speaks only Spanish. Dialogue in Spanish and English 12 scenes 1m 3w extras

In Around the world in 21 plays; ed. by L. Swortzell

The **key.** al-'Ani, Yusuf

Keyboard skills. Bruce, L.

Khan-din, Ayub

East is east. Rev. ed. Hern Bks. 1997 76p

Family drama set in 1970s Salford, England. Five brothers and sister caught between rigid, traditional views of Pakistani father and English mother's laissez-faire approach to life. 2 acts 10 scenes 7m 3w 1 setting

Khmer Rouge

Lipsky, J. The survivor: a Cambodian odyssey

Kidnapping

Beard, J. A. Vladivostok blues

Doyle, R. Brownbread

Fo, D. Abducting Diana

Hornby, I. The price to pay

Martin, J. Keely and Du

Yates, P. Nuances

Kids. Morgan, J.

Kiefer, Nancy

Gwen and Gwen. French 1997 85p

Psychological drama. Disturbed woman's alter ego goads her toward self-destruction. 3 acts 4 scenes 4w 1 interior

Killers. Pernak, A.

Killer's head. Shepard, S.

Killing time. Warner, F.

Killjoy. Mayer, J.

Kilroy, Thomas

Double cross. Gallery Bks. 1994 90p

Drama portraying roles of two Irishmen during WWII. One was Brendan Bracken, aide to Churchill, the other William Joyce, Nazi propagandist "Lord Haw Haw." 2 parts Variable cast 11 characters 2 settings

The O'Neill. Gallery Bks. 1995 74p

Historical drama about life of Irish chieftan and rebel Hugh O'Neill, 2nd Earl of Tyrone. 2 acts 11m 2w extras 1 setting

The seagull. Gallery Bks. 1993 87p

Set in 19th century Ireland. Adaptation of Chekhov's drama about young actresses' tragic love for selfish playwright. 4 acts 6m 4w extras 2 interiors 1 exterior

The secret fall of Constance Wilde. Gallery Bks. 1997 69p

Drama exploring complex relationship between Constance Wilde, her husband Oscar, and his lover, Alfred Douglas. 2 parts 2m 1w extras 1 setting

Talbot's box. Gallery Bks. 1997 63p

Drama set in Dublin exploring life of prayer, fasting and self-mortification lived by saintly former alcoholic Matt Talbot. 2 acts 3m 2w 1 interior

Kilroy was here! Francoeur, B.

Kimchee and chitlins. Wong, E.

A **kind** of Alaska. Pinter, H.

A **kind** of Vesuvius. Plowman, G.

Kindertransport. Samuels, D.

Kindly keep it covered. Freeman, D.

King, Larry L.
The Golden Shadows Old West Museum. Texas Christian Univ. Press 1993 150p (Texas tradition series no20)
Dramatization of short story by Michael Blackman. Bittersweet tale set during 1981 Christmas season about cowboy confined to Texas old age home. Background music. 2 acts 9 scenes 3m 5w 1 interior

King, Martin Luther
c Fisher, A. I have a dream
Stetson, J. The meeting

The **king** amuses himself. Hugo, V.

The **king** and the miller. Holmes, R. V.

The **king** and the queen. Tagore, R.

King Arthur. Dryden, J.

King Arthur. Reakes, P.

King Francis I. Warner, F.

The **king** in the kitchen. Slattery, M. E.

The **king** is the king. Wannus, Sa'dallah

King Kong Palace. Parra, M. A. de la

King Midas and the golden touch. Mahlmann, L. and Jones, D. C.

The **king** of the kosher grocers. Minjares, J.

King-Smith, Dick
The sheep-pig (dramatization) See Wood, D. The sheep-pig

The **king** who hated Christmas. Enscoe, L. G. and Enscoe, A.

Kings and rulers
Gass, K. Claudius
Granville-Barker, H. His majesty
Jarry, A. Ubu cocu
Martin, J. Pomp and circumstance
O'Neill, E. The Emperor Jones
Tagore, R. The cycle of spring
Tagore, R. The king and the queen
Tagore, R. Malini
c Witkiewicz, S. The courageous princess
See also names of Kings and rulers, e.g. George III, King of England

Succession

Ford, J. Perkin Warbeck

The **king's** bean soup. Werner, S.

The **king's** highway. Howles, L.

Kingsley, Sidney
Darkness at noon
Tragic drama about totalitarianism based on Arthur Koestler's novel. Set in Russian prison during Stalinist purges of 1930s. 3 acts 18m 3w extras 17 interiors 1 exterior
In Kingsley, S. Sidney Kingsley: five prizewinning plays
Dead end
Exploration of crime and juvenile delinquency in New York City slums. 3 acts Large mixed cast 1 exterior
In Kingsley, S. Sidney Kingsley: five prizewinning plays
Detective story
Tragic career of policeman to whom duty was an obsession revealed in a typical day at a police station. 3 acts 25m 9w 1 interior
In Kingsley, S. Sidney Kingsley: five prizewinning plays
Men in white
Drama deals with young doctor who must choose between early marriage to wealthy girl or life of service in a hospital. 3 acts 9 scenes 19m 8w 1g extras 8 interiors
In Kingsley, S. Sidney Kingsley: five prizewinning plays
The patriots
Thomas Jefferson, Secretary of State in the chaotic days of the infant Republic, clashes with Alexander Hamilton. Prologue 3 acts 7 scenes 18m 5w extras 6 interiors 1 exterior
In Kingsley, S. Sidney Kingsley: five prizewinning plays

Kipling, Rudyard
How the first letter was written (dramatization) See Summer, A. The just so letter
Mrs. Hauksbee sits out
Volunteer ball in British India setting for intrigue and romance. 5m 4w extras 1 setting
In Kipling, R. Collected stories

Kirby, Margaret
My body. My blood. Currency Press 1996 109p
Drama set in biblical times, late 16th century England and 20th century Australia shortly after ordination of women in Anglican church. Explores role of women in organized religion. 4m 6w extras 1 setting

Kirk, Lynn
y Men and angels
Wealthy young man and cleaning woman discuss price of not pursuing one's dreams. 1m 1w 1 interior
In Eureka! ed. by J. J. Lewis and D. Warren

The **kiss** of the spider woman. Kander, J.

Kiss of the spider woman. Puig, M.

A **kiss** on the bottom. Vickery, F.

Kissing Christine. Shanley, J. P.

Kissing Marianne. Hamilton, G.

Kissinger, Henry, 1923-
Lees, R. Nixon's Nixon

Kitchen, Barry
Halfway up the M3 on the way to Basingstoke. New Playwrights Network 1995 29p

Comedy. English drama group presents original play full of clichéd dialogue. 1 act 5 scenes 3m 5w 1 interior

Kittleson, Ole. See Christiansen, A. A monster ate my homework; Christiansen, A. Wash your troubles away

Kittson, Jean
Escape

Waitress in country roadhouse hungers for new life. 1w 1 interior

In Passion: six new short plays by Australian women; ed. by R. Horin

Klavan, Laurence
Freud's house. Dramatists 1997 20p

Romantic comedy set in Upper West Side synagogue. Man and woman betray each other, ostensibly in name of faith. 1 act 1m 1w 1 setting

—Same
In EST Marathon '95

Klein, Jon
Betty the yeti. Dramatists 1995 69p

Satirical fantasy set in Oregon woods. Environmentalists clash with loggers over future of land. 2 acts 8 scenes 2m 4w 1 exterior

—Same
In Humana Festival '94

Klein, Robin, 1936-
Boss of the pool (dramatization) See Morris, M. Boss of the pool

Kleist, Heinrich von
The broken jug (adaptation) See Banville, J. The broken jug; Morrison, B. The cracked pot

Klíma, Ivan
Games

Responding to murder, partygoers participate in games that strip away conventions of civilized behavior. 2 acts 6m 2w 1 interior

In Czech plays; modern Czech drama; ed. by B. Day

Kling, Kevin
21A

Comedy. One actor portrays driver and passengers on Minneapolis bus. 1m

In 20/20: twenty one-act plays from twenty years of the Humana Festival

The ice-fishing play

Man in middle of frozen lake in Minnesota visited by apparitions from past. 2 acts 6m 1w extras 1 setting

In Humana Festival '93

Klondike fever. McCullough, L. E.

Kluger, Garry Michael
Till death, or whatever, do us part. Players Press 1996 66p

Romantic comedy. Vignettes and anecdotes trace intertwining relationships of two couples over period of years. Background music. 2 acts 2 scenes epilogue 2m 2w 4 interiors

Knee, Allan
The St. Valentine's Day massacre

Ex-lovers rendevous in cafe on St. Valentine's Day. 1m 1w 1 interior

In The Best American short plays, 1995-1996

Kneubuhl, Victoria Nalani
The conversion of Ka'ahumanu

Missionaries come to Hawaiian Islands, convert Queen Kaahumanu. 2 acts 21 scenes 5w 1 setting

In But still, like air, I'll rise; ed. by V. H. Houston

Knights. Aristophanes

Knights and knighthood
Goethe, J. W. von. Goetz von Berlichingen with the iron hand

Knives in hens. Harrower, D.

The **knocky.** Wynne, M.

Knuckle. Hare, D.

Kobler, Flip
Wild dust. French 1994 129p

Comic Western. Mayhem results when society ladies are forced to take refuge in brothel during 1880 dust storm. 2 acts 7 scenes 2m 8w 1 interior

Koch, Kenneth
The banquet

Leading modernist figures attend 1918 banquet in Paris. Singing. 7m 2w extras 1 setting

In Koch, K. The gold standard: a book of plays

The construction of Boston

Experimental verse play collaboration with three modern artists. 5m 1w extras 1 setting

In Koch, K. The gold standard: a book of plays

Koch, Kenneth—*Continued*
The death of Sir Brian Caitskill
Verse play. Father kills daughter's suitor in duel. 4 scenes 6m 1w 1 setting
In Koch, K. The gold standard: a book of plays

Edward and Christine
Experimental play about adventure and passion. 1m 1w
In Koch, K. The gold standard: a book of plays

George Washington crossing the Delaware
Satire on myths surrounding the strategies and heroes of the Revolutionary War. 7 scenes 22m 3w 1b 1 interior 4 exteriors
In Koch, K. The gold standard: a book of plays

The gold standard
Verse play set in Chinese mountain shrine. Two Buddhist monks discuss value of currency. 2m
In Koch, K. The gold standard: a book of plays

A heroine of the Greek resistance
Experimental verse play about the modern age. Variable cast 8 characters
In Koch, K. The gold standard: a book of plays

The Red Robins
Allegorical fantasy in verse adapted from author's novel. Santa Claus and the Easter Bunny battle each other for world supremacy. 3 acts 23 scenes Large mixed cast 3 interiors 15 exteriors
In Koch, K. The gold standard: a book of plays

The strangers from the sea
Experimental verse play based on Swedish legend. 5 scenes Variable cast settings
In Koch, K. The gold standard: a book of plays

Kochanowski, Jan
The dismissal of the Grecian envoys; tr. from the Polish by Charles S. Kochanowski. Players Press 1994 72p
Sixteenth century Polish drama based on Greek myth of Helen and the Trojan War. Prologue epilogue 8m 3w Speaking chorus

Koenig, Laird
The little girl who lives down the lane. Dramatists 1997 71p
Thriller set in 1840 New York farmhouse. Thirteen-year-old British girl hides ghoulish secret. 2 acts 11 scenes 3m 2w

Koestler, Arthur
Darkness at noon (dramatization) See Kingsley, S. Darkness at noon

Kogawa, Joy
Naomi's road (dramatization) See Wing, P. A. Naomi's road

Kokoro (true heart). Houston, V. H.

Kokoschka, Oskar
Murderer of women's hope; tr. by Michael Hamburger
Variant title: Murderer hope of womankind. German expressionist free verse drama set in antiquity about conflict between men and women. Victorious warrior initiates apocalyptic carnage. 1 act 4m 4w 1 exterior
In German expressionist plays; ed. by E. Schurer

Komachi. See Ono, Komachi, 9th century

Kondoleon, Harry
The houseguests. Dramatists 1993 47p
Absurdist comedy about relationship of two couples. 2m 2w 1 setting

Kopit, Arthur
End of the world
First produced 1984 as The assignment. Satire. Playwright commissioned to write play that will save doomed world. Research leads to Pentagon and world of Nukespeak. 3 acts 6m 2w 1b extras 1 setting
In Best American plays: 9th series, 1983-1992

Road to Nirvana
Black comedy. Washed-up Hollywood producers degrade themselves so that rock superstar will allow them to film her autobiography. 2 acts 3m 2w 2 interiors
In A Decade of new comedy: plays from the Humana Festival v1

Kops, Bernard
y Dreams of Anne Frank. French (London) 1993 44p
Drama set in occupied Holland. Jewish girl and family hide from Nazis. Singing. 2 acts 18 scenes 4m 4w 1 setting

Korder, Howard
Fun
Traces two fifteen-year-old boys seeking excitement on Friday night. 10 scenes 6m 1w 1 setting
In 20/20: twenty one-act plays from twenty years of the Humana Festival
In Telling tales: new one-act plays; ed. by E. Lane

The lights. Dramatists 1994 87p
Expressionistic look at problems faced by contemporary American city dwellers. 15 scenes 13m 4w extras 1 setting

Night maneuver. Dramatists 1996 56p
Black comedy. Low-life urban brothers wait to score deal that could change their lives. 3 scenes 2m 1 interior

Korean Americans
Rno, S. Cleveland raining
Wong, E. Kimchee and chitlins

Kornhauser, Barry
This is not a pipe dream. Anchorage Press 1992 46p
Based on early life of Belgian surrealist-painter René Magritte. Background music. 20 scenes 5m 2w 1b

Kottke, Theodore G.
y Deputy Toby
Comedy. Pranks spur sheriff to arrest corrupt mayor. 2 scenes 3m 2w 1 interior
In The Big book of skits; ed. by S. E. Kamerman

Kovacevic, Dusan
The gathering place; tr. by Dennis Barnett. French 1997 109p
Absurdist comedy. Dying professor relays messages from dead to their friends and family members. 2 acts 4 scenes 10m 4w 1 interior

The professional; tr. and adapted by Bob Djurdjevic. French 1996 50p
Political fable set in post-communist Eastern European country. Publisher confronted by member of secret police who surveilled him for previous regime. 3m 1w extras 1 setting

A roaring tragedy; tr. by Vladislava Felbabov. French 1997 74p
Tragic farce about generational conflict and deadly family misunderstandings. 2 acts 6m 3w 1 interior

Kral, Brian
From the life of the bog people
Primitive man exhibited in small Page, Arizona museum. Variable cast 4 characters 1 interior
In Lucky 13; ed. by R. Shuttleworth
y One to grow on. Anchorage Press 1995 51p
Young man recalls birthday he spent with grandfather following parents' divorce. 6 scenes 6m 1w 1b 1 setting

Kramer, Larry
The destiny of me. Hern Bks. 1993 76p
Autobiographical memory play about author/activist/AIDS victim who submits to experimental treatment and recalls growing up Jewish and gay in the 1930s and 1940s. 3 acts 5m 2w
—Same. Plume Bks. 1993 122p
The destiny of me (condensation)
In The Best plays of 1992-1993
The normal heart. Hern Bks. 1993 72p
Dramatizes onset of AIDS epidemic in New York City, the agonizing fight to get political and social recognition of it's problems, and the toll exacted on private lives. 2 acts 16 scenes 13m 1 setting

Kramer, Sherry
David's redhaired death
Fantasy. Love between two women cut short by tragedy. 2 acts 2w 1 interior
In Plays for actresses; ed. by E. Lane and N. Shengold

A permanent signal
Fantasy. Mousy woman visited by sirens. 3w 1 interior
In Facing forward; ed. by L. D. Frank

Kranes, David
Cantrell
Character study of contract killer attempting to live reformed life. 8m 1w 1 setting
In Lucky 13; ed. by R. Shuttleworth

Kraus, Joanna Halpert
y The ice wolf
Fair-haired girl is rejected by Eskimo tribe into which she was born. Prologue 3 acts 7 scenes 5m 2w 2g extras 2 interiors 2 exteriors
In Around the world in 21 plays; ed. by L. Swortzell

Kraus, Joanna Halpert, and Woodward, Greer
Tenure track. Players Press 1992 41p
Behind the scenes look at contemporary university life. 14 scenes 3m 3w

Krausz, Rob. See Bernstein, D. jt. auth.

Kravitz, Alan
Just thinking
Comedy. Jewish boy, not quite bar mitzvahed, fantasizes about his sexual orientation. 2m 1w 1 interior
In Off-Off Broadway Festival plays, 18th ser.

Kringle's window. Medoff, M.

Kroetz, Franz Xaver
Mensch Meier
Laborer inadvertently poisons Alpine lake that consequently causes infant son's illness. 3 acts 20 scenes 1m 1w 1b 1 setting
In Kroetz, F. X. Through the leaves and other plays
The nest
Study of German working-class family shows how society renders its members powerless. 3 acts 27 scenes 2m 2w 1 interior
In Kroetz, F. X. Through the leaves and other plays
Through the leaves
Final version of play published with titles Men's business and A man, a dictionary. Depicts relationship between female butcher and her laborer lover. 11 scenes 1m 1w 1 setting
In Kroetz, F. X. Through the leaves and other plays

Ku Klux Klan
Mann, E. Greensboro

Kudelka, Jan. See Vingoe, M. jt. auth.

Kugler, D. D. See Rose, R. jt. auth.

Kuharski, Janice

c The leopard's noisy drum

Based on African folktale. Clever turtle uses leopard's drum to appease sky god. 3 scenes Unidentified cast 6 characters 1 exterior

In Thirty plays from favorite stories; ed. by S. E. Kamerman

Kuhn, Kevin

Midsummer nights; a rock 'n' roll musical in two acts; music by Kevin Kuhn; book and lyrics by Bryan D. Leys. French 1996 92p (French's musical library)

Musical about 1960s California beach culture follows basic plot of Shakespeare's A midsummer night's dream. Music, singing. Prologue 2 acts 7 scenes 6m 8w 1 setting

Kukla, Don

y Sticks and stones. Bakers Plays 1993 35p

Series of comic skits illustrating dangers of drinking, smoking, and drug use. 2m 1w 1 setting

Kurginian, Sergei

Compensation

Docudrama on Chernobyl disaster. Prologue 17 scenes 2m 5w extra 1 setting

In Voicings: ten plays from the documentary theatre; ed. by A. Favorini

Kurtti, Casey

Catholic school girls

Satirical look at Catholic school life in the 1960s. 2 acts 4w 1 interior

In Plays for actresses; ed. by E. Lane and N. Shengold

Kurtz, Jack

c The ballad of King Windowglass. Bakers Plays 1995 25p

Comedy based on Christmas carol Good King Wencelas. Includes two optional epilogues. Singing. 8m 1w extras

Kurzy of the sea. Barnes, D.

Kushner, Tony

Angels in America: a gay fantasia on national themes. Pt. 1: Millennium approaches. Hern Bks. 1992 90p (Royal National Theatre)

Examines the political, sexual, and religious aspects of contemporary American life set against the AIDS epidemic and the life of Roy Cohn. 32 acts 27 scenes 5m 3w extras 1 setting

—Same. Theatre Communications Group 1993 119p

Angels in America: a gay fantasia on national themes. Pt.2: Perestroika. Hern Bks. 1992 99p (Royal National Theatre)

Drama focusing on affair between AIDS-crossed lovers, marriage between latent homosexual Mormon and his demented wife and last days of Roy Cohn. 5 acts 33 scenes epilogue 6m 2w extras 1 setting

—Same. Theatre Communications Group 1994 158p

Angels in America: millennium approaches (condensation)

In The Best plays of 1992-1993

Angels in America, part II: Perestroika (condensation)

In The Best plays of 1993-1994

A bright room called day. Theatre Communications Group 1994 183p

Political drama set in 1932-1933 Berlin and in 1990 America. Portrays failure of group of intellectuals to prevent Hitler's rise to power. Prologue 2 parts 25 scenes epilogue 5m 6w 1 setting

—Same

In Kushner, T. Plays by Tony Kushner

The illusion. Theatre Communications Group 1994 83p (TCG translations, 6)

Freely adapted from Corneille's The comic illusion. Comedy set in 17th century France about contrite father, who hires magician to conjure up whereabouts of prodigal son. 2 acts 6m 2w 1 setting

—Same

In Kushner, T. Plays by Tony Kushner

Slavs!

Satirical socio-political exploration of life in Soviet Union during Perestroika and after break-up of the Soviet Union set in 1985 Moscow and 1992 Siberia. Prologue 3 acts 8 scenes epilogue 3m 3w 1g 1 setting

In Humana Festival '94

—Same

In Kushner, T. Thinking about the longstanding problems of virtue and happiness

See also Dorfman, A. Widows

Kvetch. Berkoff, S.

Kwahulé, Koffi

That old black magic

Examines racial tensions in American boxing milieu. Music. 12 scenes 11m 2w extras 1 interior

In New French-language plays

Kyd, Thomas

The Spanish tragedy

Elizabethan tragedy of revenge set in 16th century Spain and Portugal. Verse play. 4 acts 29 scenes 15m 3w extras

In Four revenge tragedies; edited by K. E. Maus

Kyle Christopher

The monogamist. Dramatists 1996 70p

Satirical look at legacy of 1960s generation. Fortyish poet, his wife, and their younger lovers explore art, love, and politics in 1991. 2 acts 16 scenes 2m 3w 1 interior

L

L. A. Margulies, D.

L. A. sketches. Mamet, D.

The **La La** Awards. Franco, C. [et al.]

La Roche-Guilhen, Anne de
All-wondrous (Rare-en-tout)
Comedy with ballet and music about charming fop in 17th century London. Prologue 3 acts 2 interludes epilogue Variable cast 1 setting
In The Lunatic lover and other plays; ed. by P. Gethner

Labiche, Eugene
Eating crow; tr. by J. Magruder
Comedy. Penniless dandy with no moral scruples uses flattery and wit to win fortune and hand of girl he loves. 5 acts Large mixed cast 2 exterior 3 interiors
In Three French comedies

Labiche, Eugene, and Delacour, A.
The piggy bank (La cagnotte); tr. by Albert Bermel
Variant title: Pots of money. Farce. Spinster intending secret visit to marriage broker convinces provincial club to spend savings on excursion to Paris. Members are cheated in restaurant, accused of theft and pursued by police. Singing. 5 acts 13m 3w extras 4 interiors 1 exterior
In A Dozen French farces; ed. by A. Bermel

Labiche, Eugène, and Michel, Marc
It's all relative (Les suites d'un premier lit); tr. by Norman R. Shapiro
Farce. Fianceé and father discover prospective bridegroom has middle-aged daughter from previous marriage. 1 act 3m 3w 1 interior
In A Flea in her rear, and other vintage French farces

Labor and laboring classes
Dresser, R. Below the belt

Canada

Fennario, D. Balconville
French, D. Leaving home

Germany

Hauptmann, G. The weavers
Kroetz, F. X. Mensch Meier

Great Britain

c Breeze, N. The Rochdale Pioneers
Chessman, P. et al. Fight for Shelton Bar
Daniels, S. The gut girls
Jones, H. A. The middleman
Storey, D. The contractor

Ireland

McGuinness, F. The factory girls

Scotland

McGrath, J. Blood red roses

United States

Gilbert, R. Mother Jones: the most dangerous woman in America
y McCullough, L. E. The most dangerous woman in America
Wallace, N. Slaughter City

Labor disputes
Toller, E. Masses and man

Labor unions
Carson, J. A preacher with a horse to ride
Johnson, J. P. and Hughes, L. The organizer
Schenkkan, R. Which side are you on?

LaBounty, David
c Jeremy Whistler, mad scientist
Comedy. Boy wreaks havoc with science kit. 1w 1b 1g 1 interior
In The Big book of skits; ed. by S. E. Kamerman

Labour Party (Great Britain)
Hare, D. The absence of war

The **labourers** of Herakles. Harrison, T.

LaChiusa, Michael John
Agnes
Musical. Depressed wheelchair-bound woman persuades stranger to kill her. 1m 2w 1 exterior
In LaChiusa, M. J. Lucky nurse and other short musical plays

Break
Musical about Virgin Mary's visitation with two construction workers. 2m 1w 1 exterior
In LaChiusa, M. J. Lucky nurse and other short musical plays

Eulogy for Mister Hamm
Musical. Residents of flop house band together when they suspect their superintendent may be dead. 2m 2w 1 interior
In LaChiusa, M. J. Lucky nurse and other short musical plays

First Lady suite: Eleanor sleeps here
Musical about Eleanor Roosevelt's relationship with Lorena Hickok and Amelia Earhart. 3w 1 interior
In LaChuisa, M. J. First Lady suite

First Lady suite: Olio
Musical sketch featuring Harry Truman's wife and daughter. 2w
In LaChuisa, M. J. First Lady suite

First Lady suite: Over Texas
Musical set on Air Force One November 22, 1963. White House personal secretary's dream portends tragedy. 1m 4w 1 interior
In LaChuisa, M. J. First Lady suite

LaChiusa, Michael John—*Continued*
First Lady suite: Where's Mamie?
Musical fantasy in which Marian Anderson visits Mamie Eisenhower, alone and unhappy on birthday. 2w
In LaChuisa, M. J. First Lady suite

Hello again; a musical; words and music by Michael John LaChiusa; suggested by the play La ronde by Arthur Schnitzler. Dramatists 1995 78p
Musical. Various characters search for love through the century. 10 scenes 6m 4w settings

Lucky nurse
Musical about troubled life of two nurses, one male one female, lonely woman and guilt-ridden cab driver. 2m 2w 1 setting
In LaChiusa, M. J. Lucky nurse and other short musical plays

Ladies' day. See Aristophanes. Festival time

The **ladies** of the camellias. Garrett-Groag, L.

Ladies' room. See Booth, R. Where did you spend the night?

The **lady** and the commissioner of airports. Rector, M. H.

The **lady** and the mortician. Rector, M. H.

Lady of the camellias. Lang, W.

Lady of the Castle. Goldberg, L.

Lady Strass. Mamet, E.

Lady Windermere's fan. Wilde, O.

The **ladykiller.** Wells, J. S.

L'affaire Tartuffe. Ackerman, M.

Laffin' school. See Castle, G. V. Recess!

Laffin' school reunion. Jackson, K.

Lahr, John
The Manchurian candidate. Dramatists 1993 98p
Based on Richard Condon's novel of political intrigue. 2 acts 9m 5w 31 scenes settings

Laird, Marvin
Ruthless! the musical; book & lyrics by Joel Paley; music by Marvin Laird. French 1995 114p
Musical spoof. Eight-year-old actress will stop at nothing to land coveted role. Music, singing. 2 acts 2 prologues 7 scenes 8w 1 setting

The **lake** at the end of the world. Brown, J.

Lake of illusions. Szyszkowitz, G.

Lake Street extension. Blessing, L.

Lambert, Betty
Jennie's story
Set in rural Canada. Jennie seeks revenge upon priest who impregnated her years ago and then had her sterilized with her mother's approval. 2 acts 8 scenes 2m 2w 2 interiors
In The *CTR* anthology; ed. by A. Filewod

Lambert, Lucien
Sunrise at noon. American version by Norman Stokle. French 1996 102p
American version of French comedy. New York City architect attempts to save his troubled marriage. 2 acts 7 scenes 7m 2w 3 interiors

Lament for Rastafari. White, E.

Lan, David
The ends of the earth. Faber & Faber 1996 80p
Drama set in London and war-torn Balkan country. British geologist, suffering mental breakdown, attempts to save ill daughter. 2 acts 9 scenes 5m 2w 1g 1 setting

Lancashire (England)
Cartwright, J. Road

L'Anconitana: the woman from Ancona. Ruzzante

The **land** of Cockaigne, Ives, D.

The **Land** of Heart's Desire. Yeats, W. B.

The **land** of the astronauts. Foote, H.

Land slides. Leader, J.

The **land,** the animals. Brooker, B.

Landau, Tina
1969; or, Howie takes a trip
In 1969, lonely high school senior takes psychedelic journey towards sexual identity. Music. 5m 2w
In Humana Festival '94

Landlord and tenant
Congdon, C. Boarders
Gray, S. Pig in a poke
Horovitz, I. My old lady
Shepherd, C. Delphiniums
Worboyes, S. The house plant

Landslide for Shakespeare. Dias, E. J.

Lane, Eric
Cater-waiter
Comedy. Two gay waiters at Republican fundraiser in Connecticut. 4 scenes 2m 1 interior
In The Actor's book of gay and lesbian plays; ed. by E. Lane and N. Shengold

Lane, Eric—*Continued*
Dancing on Checkers' grave
Drama set in Long Island pet cemetery. Two teenaged girls—one black, one white—explore their feelings for each other. 2w 1 exterior
In Telling tales: new one-act plays; ed. by E. Lane

Lang, Christine
Amelia and the man. New Playwrights Network 1997 47p
Fate of quarrelling couple's marriage has long range ramifications. 1 act 4m 4w 1 setting

Lang, William
Lady of the camellias. Dramatic 1994 80p
Dramatization of Dumas' romantic tale of beautiful courtesan in love with young aristocrat in 19th century Paris. 2 acts 3m 4w 1 setting

Langley, Rod
The Dunsmuirs: a promise kept. Talonbooks 1992 116p
Second play in author's The Dunsmuirs trilogy. Continues saga about one of Canada's wealthiest, most ruthless and ill-fated families. 2 acts 33 scenes 7m 4w extras

Langston Hughes: poet of the people. Satchell, M.

Language and languages
Ackerman, M. L'affaire Tartuffe
Fornes, M. I. The Danube
Havel, V. The garden party
Havel, V. The memorandum
Horovitz, I. Un drôle de mari français
Stoppard. T. Dogg's Hamlet, Cahoot's Macbeth

A **language** of their own. Yew, C.

Lanquirand, Jacques
Autumn violins (Les violons d'automne); tr. by Albert Bermel
Tragic farce about elderly people caught in love triangle. 3 acts 2m 1w 1 interior
In A Dozen French farces; ed. by A. Bermel

Laodamia, Queen of Epirus. Bernard, C.

Lapin Lapin. Serreau, C.

Lapine, James
Twelve dreams. Rev. ed. Dramatists 1996 63p
Based on actual case study by Carl Jung of ten-year-old girl who predicted her own death through a series of twelve dreams. Music. 2 acts 15 scenes 3m 3w 2g 1 setting
See also Finn, W. jt. auth.; Sondheim, S. jt. auth.

Larbey, Bob
Half an idea. French (London) 1994 38p
Playwrights efforts at serious drama result in antic comedy. 12m 15w 1 setting
A small affair. French (London) 1994 45p
Comedy. Rehearsal for television drama beset with mishaps. 5m 12w 1 interior

Largo desolato. Havel, V.

Larson, Jonathan
J. P. Morgan saves the nation; book and lyrics by Jeffrey M. Jones; music by Jonathan Larson. Sun & Moon Press 1995 106p
Musical about life and times of financier J. P. Morgan. Music, singing, dancing. 4m 1w extras 1 setting
Rent (condensation)
In The Best plays of 1995-1996

Larson, Larry, and Lee, Levi
The salvation of Iggy Scrooge. French 1997 63p
Rock and roll version of Dickens' holiday ghost story. Music, singing. 2 acts Variable cast 25 characters extras
Some things you need to know before the world ends (a final evening with illuminati)
Satirical look at organized religion. Post holocaust sanctuary of church setting for evangelist's final sermon: 'Life is like a basketball game.' 2 acts Variable cast 6 characters 1 interior
In A Decade of new comedy: plays from the Humana Festival v1

Larson, Larry; Lee, Levi, and Wackler, Rebecca
Tent meeting
Satire. Deluded evangelist believes grandson may be the Second Coming. 2 acts 10 scenes 2m 1w 1 setting
In By Southern playwrights; ed. by M. B. Dixon and M. Volansky

Las Vegas (Nev.)
Berlin, E. The Midnight Moonlight Wedding Chapel
Jensen, J. The total meaning of real life

The **last** Apache reunion. Farrell, B.

The **last** bread pudding. Warburton, N.

Last exit before toll. Goldstein, C.

The **last** girl singer. Winer, D. G.

The **last** horizon. McCaslin, N.

The **last** leaf. Henry, O. (dramatization) See Ekstrom, P. An O. Henry Christmas: The last leaf

The **last** Munro. Watson, D.

The **last** night of Ballyhoo. Uhry, A.

Last requests. Shaffer, D.

Last respects. Shaffer, D.

The **last** romantics. Schevill, J.

Last summer in Chulimsk. Vampilov, A.

The **last** ten miles of Avery J. Coping. Delaney, D.

Last things. Barnes, P.

The **last** time I saw Paris. Olfson, L.

The **last** time we saw her. Anderson, J.

The **last** wife. Brittney, L.

The **last** Yankee. Miller, A.

Late bus to Mecca. Cleage, P.

Late frost. McConnell, J.

Late of this address. Hornby, I.

Late Sunday afternoon, early Sunday evening. Toddie, J. L.

The **latent** heterosexual. Chayefsky, P.

Later life. Gurney, A. R.

Latin America
Fornes, M. I. The conduct of life

Latin Americans

North America

Verdecchia, G. Fronteras Americanas (American borders)

Latin drama (Comedy)
Plautus, T. M. Amphitryon
Plautus, T. M. Asses galore
Plautus, T. M. The braggart soldier
Plautus, T. M. The brothers Menaechmus
Plautus, T. M. The captives
Plautus, T. M. The entrepreneur
Plautus, T. M. Epidicus
Plautus, T. M. A funny thing happened on the way to the wedding
Plautus, T. M. The haunted house
Plautus, T. M. The little box
Plautus, T. M. The little Carthaginian
Plautus, T. M. The Persian
Plautus, T. M. The pot of gold
Plautus, T. M. Pseudolus
Plautus, T. M. The rope
Plautus, T. M. The savage slave
Plautus, T. M. Stichus
Plautus, T. M. The thirty-dollar day
Plautus, T. M. Two sisters named Bacchis
Plautus, T. M. The weevil

Latin drama (Tragedy)
Seneca. Thyestes

Latinologues: monologues of the Latin experience. Najera, R.

Latins anonymous. Leschin, L. [et al.]

Latvians

Canada

Rubess, B. Boom, baby, boom!

Laughter! Barnes, P.

Laughter in the shadow of the trees. Prideaux, J.

Laughter on the 23rd floor. Simon, N.

Laughing wild. Durang, C.

Laughton, Verity
The mourning after. Currency Press in association with Playbox Theatre 1996 45p (Current theatre series)

One woman show. Reminiscences of Australian actress and singer. Music, singing. 2 acts 3 scenes 1w 1 setting

Laundromats. See Self-service laundries

Laura Dennis. Foote, H.

Laurents, Arthur
Home of the brave

When several soldiers volunteer for a dangerous mission, Jewish soldier feeling prejudice and guilt develops psychological paralysis. Set in Pacific during World War II. 3 acts 8 scenes 6m 2 interiors 2 exteriors

In Awake and singing: 7 classic plays from the American Jewish repertoire; ed. by E. Schiff

The radical mystique. French 1996 77p

Comedy of manners set in Greenwich Village in late 1960s. Radical-chic fundraiser for Black Panthers. 2 acts 5 scenes 3m 2w 1 interior

Laurier. See Hollingsworth, M. The history of the village of the small huts

Lauro, Shirley
The coal diamond

Female employees of Missouri insurance company conduct lunchtime bridge game. 1 act 4w 1 interior

In Telling tales: new one-act plays; ed. by E. Lane

Lavender years. Beard, P.

Lavrakas, Paul
y Escape from Nemotex. Bakers Plays 1993 32p

Science fiction play about ecological degradation of earth. 9 scenes Variable cast

Lavrakas, Paul—*Continued*

c The princess and the pea. Anchorage Press 1993 35p

Version of classic fairy tale. Princess must pass three tests to prove she is for real. Music. 8 scenes 4m 2w 1 setting

Law, Maggie

Advertising Arnold. New Playwrights Network 1994 16p

Two women respond to newspaper ad from strange, lonely single man. 1 act 1m 2w 1 exterior

Cry wolf. New Playwrights Network 1995 12p

Mystery set in London. Wealthy American businessman caught in web of deceit is accused of rape. 1 act 2m 2w 1 interior

My Johnny. New Playwrights Network 1994 16p

Domineering English woman's ambitions for her son result in his death. 1 act 1m 4w

The **law** of remains. Abdoh, R.

Lawrence, D. H. (David Herbert)

The rocking horse winner (dramatization) See Auden, W. H. and Stern, J. The rocking horse winner

Lawrence, Gertrude, 1898-1952

Morley, S. Noel and Gertie

Lawrence, Jerome, and Lee, Robert E.

Auntie Mame

Comedy based on novel by Patrick Dennis. Young orphan raised by his warmhearted but eccentric aunt. 2 acts 25 scenes Large mixed cast 10 interiors 4 exteriors

In Lawrence, J. and Lee, R. E. Selected plays of Jerome Lawrence and Robert E. Lee

A call on Kuprin

Variant title: Checkmate. Based on novel by Maurice Edelman. American tourist in Russia assigned task of kidnapping old friend. 3 acts 9 scenes 5m 3w extras 4 interiors 4 exteriors

In Lawrence, J. and Lee, R. E. Selected plays of Jerome Lawrence and Robert E. Lee

Diamond orchid

Variant title: Sparks fly upward. Obscure radio actress engineers coup, installs colonel friend as President, becomes First Lady and dominates her Latin-American country. 2 acts 15 scenes 16m 6w extras 11 interiors 1 exterior

In Lawrence, J. and Lee, R. E. Selected plays of Jerome Lawrence and Robert E. Lee

First Monday in October

First woman Supreme Court justice, a conservative clashes with older liberal justice. 2 acts 14m 1w extras 1 setting

In Lawrence, J. and Lee, R. E. Selected plays of Jerome Lawrence and Robert E. Lee

The gang's all here. [Revised version]

Satire on politics. Spineless man is elected to Presidency and takes his corrupt friends with him. 2 acts 5 scenes 15m 4w 4 interiors

In Lawrence, J. and Lee, R. E. Selected plays of Jerome Lawrence and Robert E. Lee

Inherit the wind

Based on Tennessee trial in 1925 when John Thomas Scopes was charged with teaching evolution in the schools. The case hinged on modernist-fundamentalist controversy in Christianity. Includes group singing. 3 acts 5 scenes 23m 7w extras 1 setting

In Lawrence, J. and Lee, R. E. Selected plays of Jerome Lawrence and Robert E. Lee

The night Thoreau spent in jail

Incidents in Thoreau's life at Walden Pond. 2 acts 11m 4w extras 1 setting

In Lawrence, J. and Lee, R. E. Selected plays of Jerome Lawrence and Robert E. Lee

Only in America

Comedy based on book by Harry Golden. Harry's newspaper is so successful he is asked to serve on school board but can't because he was once in prison. 3 acts 18m 6w 1 interior 1 exterior

In Lawrence, J. and Lee, R. E. Selected plays of Jerome Lawrence and Robert E. Lee

Lawrence, Maggie

c 'Twas the night before Columbus Day ... I mean Christmas

Humorous recitation of Moore's classic poem with audience participation. Unidentified cast 9 characters extras

Lawrence, Slingsby. See Lewes, George Henry

Lawyers

Arzoomanian, R. The Tack Room
Elwell, J. S. The act of dating
Frockt, D. L. Hard-boiled
Granville-Barker, H. Farewell to the theatre
Gray, S. Plaintiffs and defendants
Gurney, A. R. Richard Cory
Hare, D. Murmuring judges
Kemp, R. Dalwhinnie
Mamet, D. An interview
McWeeney, D. and Swan, S. Sticks and stones
Rice, E. Counsellor-at-law
Wilder, T. Cement hands
Wilder, T. Queens of France

Lazarus (Biblical figure)

O'Neill, E. Lazarus laughed

Lazarus, John, 1947-
c Night light
Explores strategies brother and sister employ to conquer fear. 2b 1g 1 interior 1 exterior
In Lazarus, J. Not so dumb: four plays for young people

c The Nightingale
Dramatization of Hans Christian Andersen's fairy tale. Beautiful singing nightingale saves emperor from certain death. 2 acts 24 scenes 5m 3w 3 interiors 3 exteriors
In YPThree: three plays from Young People's Theatre

c Not so dumb
Learning disabled students and class "brain" discover they have much in common. 2b 1g 1 interior
In Lazarus, J. Not so dumb: four plays for young people

c Schoolyard games
Portrays power struggles and betrayal among schoolgirls. 3g 1 exterior
In Lazarus, J. Not so dumb: four plays for young people

y Secrets
Teenagers initiated into mysteries of trust, love and sex. 2 acts 2m 2w 2 interiors
In Lazarus, J. Not so dumb: four plays for young people

Lazarus laughed. O'Neill, E.

The **laziest** girl in the world. McCullough, L. E.

The **lazy** ones. McCaslin, N.

Le Prince De Beaumont, Madame. See Francoeur, B. The enchantment of Beauty and the beast.

Le, Quy Duong
Cho doi (Market of lives)
Respected cadre of Vietnamese city forced to face truth about his past during Vietnam War. 5 scenes 7m 4w 1 interior 1 exterior
In Young playwrights; ed. by E. Bray

Leach, Karoline
The mysterious Mr. Love. French (London) 1997 53p
Psychological thriller set in Edwardian England. Fortune hunting confidence man develops genuine feelings for overweight milliner. 2 acts 1m 1w 1 setting

Leach, Patricia. See Waterhouse, J. jt. auth.

Leader, Jessica
y Land slides. Bakers Plays 1993 38p
Teacher helps reclusive girl cut herself free of imaginary friends and join "real" world. 8 scenes 1m 4w 2 interiors

Leading lady. McCaslin, N.

Leaking from every orifice. Dowie, C.

Lear, Edward
Barker, C. Subtle bodies

Learner, Tobsha
The glass mermaid. Currency Press in association with Playbox Theatre 1994 65p (Current theatre series)
Drama set in isolated beach house on Australian coast about grieving and shattered lives left in wake of suicide. 2 acts 17 scenes 2m 3w 1 interior

The gun in history
Three skits about sex and violence. Gun passes through three generations. 3 parts 2m 2w 1 setting
In Passion: six new short plays by Australian women; ed. by R. Horin

Witchplay
Black comedy about suffering, fear and ignorance. Monologue by female Holocaust survivor working as spiritual medium in Australia. 1w 1 setting
In Nimmo, H. and Learner, T. One small step [and] Witchplay

Learning Chinese. See Yew, C. A language of their own

Learning disabilities
c Lazarus, J. Not so dumb

Leaving home. French, D.

Lebanon
Mouawad, W. Wedding day at the Cro-Magnons'

Lebensraum. Horovitz, I.

Lebow, Barbara
The keepers. Dramatists 1995 84p
Drama set in 1850s Maine lighthouse about husband, wife and black woman raised as their daughter. 3 acts 1m 2w 1 interior

Little Joe Monaghan. Dramatists 1995 51p
Drama based on true life adventures of woman cowboy of late 1800s who passed as man for entire adult life. 2 acts 2m 2w 1 interior

Tiny Tim is dead. Dramatists 1993 67p
Christmas with makeshift family of homeless people. 2 acts 3m 2w 1b 1 exterior

Ledoux, Paul, and Smyth, David
Cheatin' hearts. Playwrights Canada 1995 126p
Musical about country music set in Canadian bar. Music, singing. 2 acts 10 scenes 6m 3w 1 interior

Ledoux, Paul, and Young, David
Love is strange
First produced under title: I love you Anne Murray. Romantic obsession and the cult of celebrity are explored in courtroom drama about man on trial for stalking popular singer. Music. 2 acts 6m 1w 1 setting
In The *CTR* anthology; ed. by A. Filewod

Ledwidge, Francis, 1887-1917
MacKenna, J. Faint voices

Lee, Chee Keng
c Journey to the West
Puppet play. Traditional Chinese tale counterpoints contemporary generation gap story. Variable cast 13 characters
In Young playwrights; ed. by E. Bray

Lee, Cherylene
Arthur and Leila
Relationship between Chinese American brother and sister explores conflict between traditional and contemporary American values. 2 acts 9 scenes 1m 1w 3 interiors 1 exterior
In Women playwrights: the best plays of 1993

Lee, Eddie Levi. See Lee, Levi

Lee, Eugene
East Texas hot links. French 1994 85p
Drama set in 1955 about proprietess and habitués of East Texas cafe. 7m 1w 1 interior

Lee, Jeffrey A.
Coming home. New Playwrights Network 1996 60p
Holocaust survivor living in Cornwall reunites with estranged homosexual son dying of AIDS. 5 scenes 3m 2w 1 extra 1 exterior

The execution. New Playwrights Network 1996 20p
Drama set in occupied territory in Europe. Two women and three men, including village priest, face execution as reprisal against train bombing. 1 act 5m 2w 1 setting

Lee, Laurie
Cider with Rosie (dramatization) See Roose-Evans, J. Cider with Rosie

Lee, Leslie
The first breeze of summer
Drama about three generations of African American family in Northeastern city. 2 acts 8m 6w 1 setting
In Classic plays from the Negro Ensemble Company; ed. by P. C. Harrison and G. Edwards

Lee, Levi. See Larson, L. jt. auth.

Lee, Nathaniel
The Princess of Cleves
Restoration comedy in verse satirizing the licentiousness of 17th century Parisian society. Includes songs and dancing with instrumental music. 5 acts 14 scenes 9m 7w extras 3 interiors
In Four Restoration marriage plays; ed. by M. Cordner

Lee, Robert E. See Lawrence, J. jt. auth.

Leech, Michael T.
y The Scarlet Pimpernel
Based on Baroness Orczy novel. English aristocrats rescue French friends. 5 scenes 9m 4w extras 3 interiors 2 exteriors
In The Big book of dramatized classics; ed. by S. E. Kamerman

Lees, Russell
Nixon's Nixon, Dramatists 1996 51p
Political satire. Encounter between Henry Kissinger and Nixon on eve of President's resignation. 2m 1 interior

LeFevre, Adam
Americansaint
Satire. Vatican emisary investigating claims of sainthood arrives in small Vermont town by mistake. 7 scenes Variable cast 4 characters 1 interior 4 exteriors
In Telling tales: new one-act plays; ed. by E. Lane

Waterbabies
Mother investigates YMCA swimming program for her eleven-month-old son. 2w 1 interior
In Humana Festival '97
In Plays for actresses; ed. by E. Lane and N. Shengold

Legacies. See Inheritance and succession

The **legend** of Minna Lamourrie. McCaslin, N.

Legend of Pocahontas. Morris, V.

The **legend** of Sleepy Hollow. Irving, W. (dramatization) See Cole, J. D. Ichabod

The **legend** of the golden coffee bean. Martin, M.

Legend of the lake. Price J. W. and Becker, C.

Legend of the seasons. Gerke, P.

Legends
Barnes, P. The jumping Mimuses of Byzantium
Brenton, H. Faust, parts I & II
Goethe, J. W. von. Faust, part I
Goethe, J. W. von. Faust, part II

England

c Duncombe, P. Robin Hood

Ireland

c McCaslin, N. Maelduin of Arran

Mexico

c Vigil, A. La flor de la Noche Buena. The flower of the Holy Night

Legg, Rodney
Oscar: the Oscar Wilde trials of 1895. Wincanton Press 1993 63p
Dramatization for radio or television of the trials of Oscar Wilde. 21m

Leguizamo, John
Mambo mouth. Bantam Bks. 1993 119p
One man show. Seven satirical portraits of Latino manhood. 1m

Lemon sky. Wilson, L.

Lenin, Vladimir Ilich 1870-1924
Chayefsky, P. The passion of Josef D.

Lennon, Gary
Blackout. French 1997 62p
Alcoholics Anonymous meeting on Christmas Eve. 4m 7w 1 interior

Dates and nuts. French 1997 67p
Romantic comedy. Animal rights activist, dumped by her boyfriend, searches for Mr. Right in dating jungle of New York City. 9 scenes 2m 2w 2 interiors 1 exterior

Lent. Wilcox, M.

Lenten pudding. Pintauro, J.

Leo Baeck. Sylvanus, E.

Leon and Joey. Huff, K.

Leonard, Hugh
Moving. French (London) 1994 82p
Family drama set in small town near Dublin in 1957 and 1987. Household moves reflect family's changing values and relationships. 2 parts 5m 5w 2 interiors

Leonard, Jim
c Crow & Weasel. French 1996 73p
Dramatization of Barry Lopez's coming-of-age tale. Two young animal people travel to Land Where Dreaming Begins. Music. 2 acts Variable cast 1 setting

Leonardo da Vinci, 1452-1519
Barnes, P. Leonardo's Last Supper

Leonardo's Last Supper. Barnes, P.

Leonce and Lena. Büchner, G.

Leonora. Holm, S.

The **leopard's** noisy drum. Kuharski, J.

Lepage, Robert, and Brassard, Marie
Polygraph; translated by Gyllian Raby. Methuen Drama 1997 44p (Methuen modern plays)
Noir thriller set in Quebec city about murder of young woman. Slide projections. 22 scenes 2m 1w 1 setting

—Same
In The *CTR* anthology; ed. by A. Filewod
In Modern Canadian plays v2; ed. by J. Wasserman

The **leprechaum.** Pflomm, P. N.

Lerman, Louis
y The Abolition Flyer
Fictional drama of night John Henry helped out the Underground Railroad. 5m 2w extras
In Plays of black Americans; ed. by S. E. Kamerman

Lerner, Motti
Kastner
Events in life of Hungarian Jewry in 1944 Budapest focuses on Kastner's stand on deportations and later accusation of collaboration with Nazis. Prologue 2 acts 61 scenes epilogue 15m 4w settings
In Israeli Holocaust drama; ed. by M. Taub

Leroux, Gaston
The phantom of the opera (dramatization)
See Hill, K. The phantom of the opera

Parodies, imitations, etc.

y Prior, J. Phantom of the music hall

Lesage, Alain René
Turcaret
Comedy. An infatuated and stingy financier is finally ruined not by the faithless coquette he loved; but his valet, who obtained master's money in order to marry the lady's maid. 5 acts. 8m 5w 1 interior
In Three French comedies

Lesbianism
Anderson, J. The last time we saw her
Campton, D. Permission to cry
Carilli, T. Dolores Street
Carilli, T. Wine country
Chafee, C. Why we have a body
Connolly, H. One careful owner
Dowie, C. Death and dancing
Dowie, C. Drag act
Dowie, C. Leaking from every orifice
Dowie, C. Why is John Lennon wearing a skirt?
Eisenstein, L. At the root
Fischer, M. The gay divorcee
The Five Lesbian Brothers. Brave smiles . . . another lesbian tragedy
Fornes, M. I. Springtime
Fornes, M. I. What of the night?: Springtime
Hammond, W. Julie Johnson
Johnson, E. What do they call me?
Johnson, J. Uganda
Kramer, S. David's redhaired death
Lane, E. Dancing on Checkers' grave
Linney, R. Can can
Lyssa, A. Pinball
Miller, S. It's our town, too
Miller, S. My left breast
Moraga, C. Giving up the ghost
Peters, K. The confirmation
Pintauro, J. Lenten pudding

Lesbianism—*Continued*
Royce, C. Why we have a body
Shotlander, S. Is that you Nancy?
Vogel, P. And baby makes seven
Wiener, S. D. Pavane
Wilson, L. Say De Kooning
See also Homosexuality

Leschin, Luisa, et al.
Latins anonymous
Satirical look at Latinos who reject their cultural heritage. 2 acts 2m 2w 1 setting
In Latins anonymous: two plays

Leslee, Ray
Avenue X; the a cappella musical; books and lyrics by John Jiler; music by Ray Leslee. French 1995 97p
Doo-wop musical set in 1963 Gravesend, Brooklyn. Two singers, one Italian American, one black, try to put together interracial act for talent show. Music, singing. 2 acts 6m 2w 1 setting

The **less** than human club. Mason, T.

Lessing, Gotthold Ehraim
Parodies, imitations, etc.
Barker, H. Minna

Let us go, O shepherds. McCullough, L. E.

Let's be puppets. Pflomm, P. N.

Let's have a hoedown! McCullough, L. E.

Let's pretend. Brooks, V.

Letters
Wong, E. Letters to a student revolutionary

Letters to a student revolutionary. Wong, E.

Letting Lucinda down. Teagarden, J.

Leukemia
Barasch, N. Standing by
Horovitz, I. Strong-man's weak child
McPherson, S. Marvin's room

Leuser, Eleanore
c The big stone
King and his fool devise test to find good leader. 8m 3w 1b 1 exterior
In Thirty plays from favorite stories; ed. by S. E. Kamerman

Levi, Lee. See Larson, L. jt. auth.

Levi, Stephen
y Good morning Miss Vickers. French 1995 134p
Comedy about ghosts and time travel. Five teenagers struggle to break time bubble and escape ghost school. 2 acts 8 scenes Variable cast 10 characters settings
y Merry Christmas Miss Vickers. French 1996 143p
Comedy about ghosts and time travel. Five teens travel back to Christmas 1910. 2 acts 12 scenes Variable cast 12 characters 2 interiors

Levy, Jonathan
Old blues
Singing group, composed of old college chums, reacts to death of one of its members. Singing. 4m 1 interior
In The Best American short plays, 1995-1996

Lewes, George Henry
The game of speculation
Adaptation of Balzac's Mercadet. Comedy about financial manipulation, stock-market gambling and debt. 3 acts 9m 4w 2 interiors
In The Lights o' London and other Victorian plays; ed. by M. R. Booth

Lewis, Ira
Chinese coffee. Dramatists 1995 55p
Drama set in Greenwich Village. Volatile relationship between struggling novelist and photographer best friend comes to a head. 2m 1 interior

Lewis, Jonathan
Our boys. French (London) 1995 71p
Drama set 1984 in English military hospital. Savage war of words among veterans of Northern Ireland troubles and victims of Hyde Park bombing. 2 acts 10 scenes 6m 1 interior

Lewis, Matthew G.
The captive
Monologue by woman imprisoned in asylum following husband's false accusation of madness. 1w 1 interior
In Seven Gothic dramas, 1789-1825
The castle spectre
Gothic ghost story. Heroine liberated from clutches of lustful aristocrat. Music. Prologue 5 acts 12 scenes epilogue 13m 3w 7 interiors 3 exteriors
In Seven Gothic dramas, 1789-1825

Lewis and Clark Expedition, (1804-1806)
c McCullough, L. E. Bird woman of the Shoshones

Lewman, David. See Stites, K. Adventures with young King Arthur

Lewton, Randall
y An alien stole my skateboard. French (London) 1993 66p
Comedy fantasy. English schoolboys combat evil wizard from Tolkein-type planet. 2 acts 18 scenes Variable cast 22 characters settings

Leznoff, Glenda
y The stockbroker and the fairy godmother
Fairy godmother reminds stockbroker of daughter's birthday. 1m 1w 1 interior
In The Big book of skits; ed. by S. E. Kamerman

Libert, Nancy Porta
c The Western Civ rap
History of Western civilization through the Age of Exploration in rap verse. Singing. Variable cast 1 interior
In The Big book of large-cast plays; ed. by S. E. Kamerman

The **libertine.** Jeffreys, S.

Liberty deferred. Silvera, J. D. and Hill, A.

The **librarian.** Prideaux, J.

Librarians
Guare, J. A day for surprises

Libraries
Dean, D. Mama's girl
Hischak, T. Murder on reserve
c Pflomm, P. N. Jeremy borrows a book
c Pflomm, P. N. A visit to the library
Prideaux, J. The librarian

Library lady. Baitz, J. R.

Lichtig, Robin Rice
Queen for a day. Bakers Plays 1994 43p
Twelve-year-old boy copes with alcoholic mother. 2m 1w 1 interior

Licking Hitler. Hare, D.

Liebert, Burt
c A terrible tale of a dreaded dragon. Bakers Plays 1993 35p
Stranger helps save Kingdom and harmless dragon from greedy royal conspirators. Singing, music, audience participation. Variable cast 15 characters extras 2 exteriors

Life after Elvis. Milligan, J.

The **life** and times of Mackenzie King. See Hollingsworth, M. The history of the village of the small huts

The **life** and times of Malcolm X. Davis, T.

Life comes to the old maid. Sawyer, A. V.

Life gap. York, Y.

Life history of the African elephant. Martini, C.

Life in the trees: Chemistry. Butterfield, C.

Life in the trees: No problem. Butterfield, C.

Life in the trees: The last time I saw Timmy Boggs. Butterfield, C.

A **life** in the woods. DeVita, J.

The **life** of stuff. Donald, S.

The **life** of the world to come. Williams, R.

Life science. Panych, M.

Life sentences. Nelson, R.

Life support. Mitchell, M.

A **life** with no joy in it. Mamet, D.

Life without instruction. Clark, S.

Lifelines. Rosenthal, A.

Light of the world. Haylock, D.

A **light** on the landing. Miller, J.

Light on the road to Damascus. Haylock, D.

Light sensitive. Geoghan, J.

Light shadows. Warner, F.

The **lighthouse** keeper's wife. Wilkinson, M. E.

Lighting up the two-year old. Aerenson, B.

Lightning. Pintauro, J.

The **lights.** Korder, H.

The **lights** o' London. Sims, G. R.

Liking, Werewere
The widow Dylemma
Psychological drama. African woman reacts to death of philandering husband. 1w extras
In Plays by women: an international anthology bk2; ed. by N. Shange

Liliuokalani, 1838-1917, Queen of Hawaii
Morris, A. Lili'uokalani

Lill, Wendy
All fall down. Talonbooks 1994 116p
Drama about inquiry into doubtful molestation incident at small town daycare in Nova Scotia. 2 acts 17 scenes 2m 2w extras 2 interiors

The Glace Bay Miners' Museum. Talonbooks 1996 126p
Dramatization of novel by Sheldon Currie. Memory play about ill-fated romance between itinerant musician and Cape Breton coal miner's daughter. 2 acts 14 scenes 3m 2w 1 setting

The occupation of Heather Rose
Monologue. Nurse recounts her harrowing experiences on isolated Canadian Indian reservation. 1w 1 interior
In Modern Canadian plays v2; ed. by J. Wasserman

Lillo, George
The London merchant. Players Press 1996 52p
Variant title: George Barnwell. 18th century English tragedy based on ballad. London merchant's apprentice seduced and ruined by courtesan who leads him to rob employer and murder rich uncle. Prologue 5 acts 13 scenes epilogue 6m 3w extras 5 interiors 3 exteriors

Lily. See Nemeth, S. Sally's shorts: Lily

Lim, Genny

Bitter cane

Drama about gender exploitation and racism focusing on oppression of Chinese laborers on Hawaiian sugarcane plantations. 11 scenes 4m 1w settings

In The Politics of life: four plays by Asian American women; ed. by V. H. Houston

Paper angels

Set in Angel Island Immigrantion Detention Center, San Francisco harbor, 1915. Drama explores problems faced by Chinese immigrants. Prologue 14 scenes 6m 5w 1 setting

In Unbroken thread; ed. by R. Uno

Limbaugh, Rush

Varon, C. Rush Limbaugh in night school

Limitations of life. Hughes, L.

Lin, Maya Ying

Barroga, J. Walls

Lincoln, Abraham, 1809-1865

c DuBois, G. Bind up the nation's wounds

y McCullough, L. E. Abe Lincoln for the defense

y Watson, W. J. Abe Lincoln and the runaways

Lindsay, Norman, 1879-1969

O'Donoghue, J. Abbie and Lou, Norman and Rose

Line. Horovitz, I.

A **line** in the sand. Verdecchia, G. and Youssef, M.

Line of descent. Mead, K.

The **line** that's picked up 1000 babes (and how it can work for you!) Berlin, E.

Linney, Romulus

2. Dramatists 1993 58p

Hitler's second-in-command at the Nuremberg trials. 2 acts 6m 2w extras 1 setting

—Same

In By Southern playwrights; ed. by M. B. Dixon and M. Volansky

In Linney, R. Six plays

Ambrosio. Dramatists 1993 53p

Drama freely adapted from Matthew Gregory Lewis's gothic novel The monk. 16th century monk's sexual crimes set against backdrop of Spanish Inquisition's reign of terror and religious persecution. 19 scenes 5m 2w 1 setting

—Same

In Linney, R. Seventeen short plays

April snow

Bittersweet comedy about aging writer and women who have figured prominently in his life. 1 act 4m 2w 1 interior

In Linney, R. Six plays

Can can

Experimental drama weaves two love stories together, one heterosexual, one lesbian. 1 act 1m 3w 1 setting

In Linney, R. Seventeen short plays

The captivity of Pixie Shedman

Memory play in which young author must exorcise ghosts of his ancestors before embarking on own career. 2 acts 4m 1w 1g 1 interior

In Linney, R. Seventeen short plays

Childe Byron

Dying of cancer and stimulated by drugs, Lord Byron's daughter summons her father to life in attempt to find the truth behind the myth. Background music. Prologue 2 acts 4m 4w 1 setting

In Linney, R. Six plays

A Christmas carol. Dramatists 1996 76p

Dramatization of Dickens' classic holiday ghost story. 2 acts Large mixed cast 1 setting

Clair de Lune

Older, retired couple in Florida reminisce about their hell-raising children. 1m 1w 1 setting

In Linney, R. Seventeen short plays

The death of King Philip

Based on the narrative of Mary Rowlandson, which recalls her capture by the Wampanoag Indians and her fanatical minister husband's vengeance. 1 act 2m 2w 1 setting

In Linney; R. Seventeen short plays

F. M.

Prim creative writing teacher is appalled and then awed by rough, whiskey-drinking author. 1 act 1m 3w

In Linney, R. Six plays

Gold and silver waltz

Autobiographical monologue about author's boyhood and youth. 1m

In Linney, R. Seventeen short plays

Goodbye, Howard

Set in North Carolina hospital, where three rich, aging spinster sisters await news of their brother's death. 1 act 2m 4w 1 interior

In Linney, R. Seventeen short plays

Heathen Valley

Based on author's novel of same title. In 1840s North Carolina, Episcopal bishop attempts to bring religion to isolated Appalachian valley filled with violence, wantonness and poverty. 2 acts 4m 2w 1 setting

In Linney, R. Six plays

El hermano

Cultures clash in San Francisco bar when Hispanic attempts to protect his sisters from advances of two frustrated G.Is. Background music. 1 act 5m 3w 1 interior

In Linney, R. Seventeen short plays

Linney, Romulus—*Continued*

Juliet

Comedic look at mothers and sons. Director and actress debate about how role of Mrs. Alving in Ibsen's Ghosts should be played. 1 act 2m 2w 1 interior

In Linney, R. Seventeen short plays

The love suicide at Schofield Barracks

Revised, one-act version of drama entered in 1968-1972 Play Index. Military inquiry into suicide of American general and wife in Hawaii. 1 act 6m 3w 1 interior

In Linney, R. Seventeen short plays

Mountain memory. Dramatists 1997 53p

Drama about Appalachian life set 1776-1995. 2 acts 5m 3w 1b 1 setting

Paradise

Following mother's death young man visits alcoholic aunt. 1 act 3m 2w 1 interior

In EST marathon, 1994

Sand Mountain

Comprised of: Act one: Sand Mountain matchmaking, about courtship of young woman on Tennessee frontier; Act two: Why the Lord came to Sand Mountain about how divine intervention bestows miracle on impoverished unwed couple. Background music. 2 acts 8m 3w 2b extras 2 interiors

In Linney, R. Seventeen short plays

Shotgun

Lakeside vacation cottage summer 1993 setting for embittered husband's stand on disintegrating marriage. 3m 2w 1 interior

In Humana Festival '94

Songs of love

Comedy. Two nursing home residents decide to marry over objections of their children. 3m 3w 1 interior

In Linney, R. Seventeen short plays

Spain: Anna Rey

Drama set in 1992 about woman psychiatrist researching Spanish treatment of insane in monastery at end of 15th century. 1m 1w extras 1 setting

In Linney, R. Spain

Spain: Escobedo de la Aixa

Set in Spanish monastery in 1480. Abbot converses with madman who thinks he is God. 2m 1 setting

In Linney, R. Spain

Spain: Torquemada

Set in 1490. While questioning couple, Grand Inquisitor unearths past infidelities involving young monk. 4m 1w 1 setting

In Linney, R. Spain

Stars

Present day Manhattan terrace setting for he-she encounter. 1m 1w 1 exterior

In Humana Festival '97

Tennessee

A young couple and their son are visited on their Appalachian mountain farm in North Carolina by an old woman who slips into her youth and acts out her wedding trip to Tennessee and her painful return to the present time and place. 1 act 2m 3w 1b 1 exterior

In Linney, R. Six plays

Three poets: Akhmatova

Set in Moscow, 1953. Anna Akhmatova and other poets interrogated by authorities on political meaning of poem. 1 act 2m 3w 1 interior

In Linney, R. Seventeen short plays

Three poets: Hrosvitha

In 10th century Saxony Mother Superior and censoring monk debate merits of Hrosvitha's verse play Abraham. 2w 3w 1 interior

In Linney, R. Seventeen short plays

Three poets: Komachi

In 9th century Japan Ono No Komachi uses her conflict with prince as material for her poetry. 1m 2w 1 setting

In Linney, R. Seventeen short plays

True crimes. Dramatists 1996 47p

Set in Appalachian Mountains, 1900. Drama revolves around scheming family resorting to murder and infanticide for personal gain. 4m 4w extra 1 setting

Why the Lord come to Sand Mountain

Forms act two of Sand Mountain, entered above

In Linney, R. Seventeen short plays

Yancey

Painfully shy country boy proves he can hold his own against two veteran New York actors. 1 act 2m 1w 1 exterior

In Linney, R. Seventeen short plays

Lion and mouse stories Neuman. C.

Lion in the streets. Thompson, J.

Lions

c Neuman, C. Lion and mouse stories

Lipp, John L.

y Titanic: destination disaster

Drama of 1912 sinking of the steamship. 13m 4w extras 1 setting

In The Big book of large-cast plays; ed. by S. E. Kamerman

Lipsky, Jon

The survivor: A Cambodian odyssey

Dramatization of Haing Ngor's memoir of surviving Khmer Rouge atrocities. 2 acts 3m 3w

In Humana Festival '94

Lisle, Janet Taylor

Afternoon of the elves (dramatization) See York, Y. Afternoon of the elves

Litterbugs. Pflomm, P. N.

The **little** box. Plautus, T. M.

The **little** Carthaginian. Plautus, T. M.

Little drops of rain. Barnes, D.

Little Egypt. Siefert, L.

The **little** fir tree. Woyiwada, A.

The **little** foxes. Hellman, L.

The **little** French lawyer. Fletcher, J. and Massinger, P.

Little gems. See St. John, B. Rubies: Little gems

The **little** ghost. See Plautus, T. M. The haunted house

The **little** girl who lives down the lane. Koenig, L.

Little Joe Monaghan. Lebow, B.

A **little** like drowning. Minghella, A.

A **little** like paradise. Williams, N.

The **little** mermaid. Daugherty, L.

The **little** old sod shanty. McCullough, L. E.

A **little** princess. Francoeur, B.

The **little** red hen. Gerke, P.

Little Red Riding Hood

Parodies, imitations, etc.

Aronson, B. Little Red Riding Hood
c Bisson, P. Little Red Riding Hood
Schenkar, J. M. The universal wolf

Little Red Riding Hood and The three little pigs. Goldberg, M.

Little sister. MacLeod, J.

The **little** squire of Flanders. McCaslin, N.

The **Little** Tommy Parker Celebrated Colored Minstrel show. Brown, C.

Little victories. Prendergast, S.

Little white lies. Booth, J.

Little women. Alcott, L. M. (dramatization) See Morley, O. J. Romance for Jo March

The **little** years. Mighton, J.

The **littlest** ant. Vigil, A.

Live and in color! Vance, D.

Live bed show. Smith, A.

A **live** bird in its jaws. Delisle, J. M.

Live-in witnesses. Bynum, R. C.

Live with it. Moore, E.

Liverpool (England)

Barker, C. Paradise Street
Russell, W. Stags and hens

Lives of the great poisoners. Churchill, C.

Lives of the great waitresses. Shengold, N.

Living creation. Warner, F.

Living curiosities: a story of Anna Swan. Vingoe, M.

Living in this world. See Nemeth, S. Sally's shorts: Living in this world

Livingston, Myrtle Smith

For unborn children

Set in the early 20th century. Black man who was planning to marry white woman bravely faces lynch mob. 1 act 1m 3w extras 1 interior

In Black theatre USA [v1]; ed. by J. V. Hatch and T. Shine

Lloyd, Peter

The scam. Seren 1996 89p

Satirical look at friendship, macho attitudes, class and greed. Two young Welshmen set out to take business world by storm. 7 scenes 4m 1 setting

Lloyd, Richard

c Smut's saga; or, Santa and the Vikings. French (London) 1994 73p

Musical pantomime. Comical adventures of Vikings as they plunder British coastline. Audience participation. 2 acts 10 scenes 13m 4w extras

c Treasure Island, the panto. French (London) 1997 79p

Pantomime based on R. L. Stevenson's adventure classic. Prologue 2 acts 16 scenes Variable cast 19 characters extras

Lloyd Webber, Andrew

Sunset Boulevard; the musical [by] Don Black and Christopher Hampton; music by Andrew Lloyd Webber; based on the screenplay by Billy Wilder, Charles Brackett and D. M. Marshman, Jr. Faber & Faber 1993 103p

Musical adaptation of Wilder's screen classic. Out of work Hollywood screenwriter becomes involved in life of aging silent screen actress. Music, singing. 2 acts 20 scenes 6m 2w 1 setting

Sunset Boulevard (condensation)

In The Best plays of 1994-1995

The **local** authority. De Filippo, E.

Lockie Leonard, human torpedo. Gibbs, P.

The **lodger.** Burke, S.

Lodging houses

Bowles, J. In the summer house
y Kelly, T. Yard sale
McKelvey, P. House of secrets
Pinter, H. Family voices
Shaughnessy, D. The manager
White, P. The ham funeral
Wilson, A. Joe Turner's come and gone

Logic upside down. Dinner, W.

Lola. Margulies, D.

Lola Starr builds her dream home. Gilbert, S.

The **Loman** family picnic. Margulies, D.

London (England)

15th century

Chaurette, N. The queens

17th century

La Roche-Guilhen, A. de. All-wonderous
Middleton, T. A trick to catch the old one
Wallace, N. One flea spare

17th century—Plague

Wallace, N. One flea spare

18th century

Dear, N. The art of success
Godfrey, P. The modern husband
c Webster, P. Dick Turpin
Wertenbaker, T. The grace of Mary Traverse

19th century

Dickinson, J. Jack the Ripper, monster of Whitechapel
Sims, G. R. The lights o' London

20th century

Adamson, S. Clocks and whistles
Berkoff, S. East
Berkoff, S. Greek
Berkoff, S. West
Brenton, H. Berlin Bertie
Butterworth, J. Mojo
Churchill, C. Cloud 9
Churchill, C. The Skriker
Gray, S. The holy terror
Hare, D. Skylight
c Hezlep, W. Tower of London
Johnson, T. Dead funny
Kennedy, A. The dramatic circle
Mead, K. The Anderson
Miller, J. and Miller, S. Consequences
Pinter, H. Victoria Station
Rattigan, T. After the dance
Ravenhill, M. Shopping and fucking
Rensten, M. The skip
Shaw, B. Pygmalion
Stoppard, T. The dissolution of Dominic Boot
Stoppard, T. In the native state
Stoppard, T. Indian ink
Ward, N. The strangeness of others
Wertenbaker, T. Three birds alighting on a field
White, P. The ham funeral

The **London** merchant. Lillo, G.

London suite: Diana and Sidney. Simon, N.

London suite: Going home. Simon, N.

London suite: Settling accounts. Simon, N.

London suite: The man on the floor. Simon, N.

Londonderry (Northern Ireland)
McGuinness, F. Carthaginians

Loneliness
Bamford, S. Who's a pretty boy then?

Lonely hearts. Adams, G.

Lonely planet. Dietz, S.

Lonergan, Kenneth
Betrayed by everyone

West Side Manhattan apartment setting for exchange between two representatives of youth culture. 1 act 1m 1w 1 interior

In Act One '95

The **lonesome** West. McDonagh, M.

Long, John Luther
Madame Butterfly (dramatization) See McDonough, J. Butterfly

Long ago and far away, a winter's tale. Ives, D.

The **long** Christmas dinner. Wilder, T.

Long gone lonesome cowgirls. Dean, P.

Long Island
Pintauro, J. Men's lives

The **long** leather bag. Gerke, P.

Look back in anger. Osborne, J.

Looking for Muruga. Pillay, K.

Loomer, Lisa
c Bocón

Play about opposition to dictatorial power incorporates Latin folkloric characters. Dialogue in English and Spanish. Singing. Prologue 6 scenes Variable cast 25 characters

In ¡Aplauso! Hispanic children's theater; ed. by J. Rosenberg

Loose ends. Vickery, F.

Loose ends. Weller, M.

Loose knit. Rebeck, T.

The **loose** tooth. Pflomm, P. N.

Lopes, Barry Holstun
Crow and Weasel (dramatization) See Leonard, J. Crow & Weasel

López, Eduardo Iván
Spanish eyes
Culture conflict reflected in courtship and marriage of Puerto Rican man and Anglo-American woman. 2 acts 4m 1w extras settings
In Nuestro New York; ed. by J. V. Antush

López, Eva
Marlene
Dramatic fantasy set in East Harlem. Second generation Puerto Rican women reacts to accidental death of girl in barrio. 2w extra 1 exterior
In Nuestro New York; ed. by J. V. Antush

Lord of the flies. Golding, W. (dramatization) See Williams, N. William Golding's Lord of the flies

Lorenzaccio. Musset, A. de

Lorna Doone. Hyem, J.

Los Angeles (Calif.)
Margulies, D. L.A.
Smith, A. D. Twilight: Los Angeles, 1992

Losers. Tricker, C.

Losing father's body. Congdon, C.

Losing it. Davis, R.

The **lost** colony. MacLeod, W.

Lost in a fairy tale. Pflomm, P. N.

Lost in a mall. Martin, J.

Lost in Yonkers. Simon, N.

The **lost** silk hat. Dunsay, E. J. M. D. P.

Lot 13: the bone violin. Wright, D.

Louie. Margulies, D.

Louis, Joe
Schmidt, E. Mr. Rickey calls a meeting

Love, Douglas
c Be kind to your Mother (Earth)
Time-traveling environmentalists attempt to save the Earth. 6 scenes Variable cast 28 characters 1 interior 4 exteriors
In Love, D. Be kind to your Mother (Earth) and Blame it on the wolf
c Blame it on the wolf
Parody. Fairy tale characters testify at trial of wolf charged with eating Red Riding Hood's granny. 9 scenes Variable cast 25 characters 1 setting
In Love, D. Be kind to your Mother (Earth) and Blame it on the wolf
c Holiday in the rain forest
Comedy. Family takes environmentally enlightening vacation to rain forest. 9 scenes Variable cast 16 characters 5 interiors 2 exteriors
In Love, D. Holiday in the rain forest and Kabuki gift
c Kabuki gift
Multicultural comedy in Kabuki style set in ancient Japan. 11 scenes Variable cast 27 characters 6 interiors 2 exteriors
In Love, D. Holiday in the rain forest and Kabuki gift

Love
Adams, G. Lonely hearts
Bamford, S. Just a loving touch
Barasch, N. Standing by
Barnes, D. Water-ice
Barry, P. J. A distance from Calcutta
y Bland, J. The squire's daughter
Boretz, A. I remember you
Butterfield, C. Life in the trees: Chemistry
Chayefsky, P. Middle of the night
Clark, S. Moo
Compton, J. Barefoot
Davies, R. Eros at breakfast
Dietz, S. Trust
Du Maurier, D. September tide
Edmunson, H. Anna Karenina
Fletcher, J. The fair maid of the inn
Fletcher, J. The lover's progress
Gee, S. Never in my lifetime
Gélinas, G. The passion of Narcisse Mondoux
Gill, P. Mean tears
Goethe, J. W. von. Jery and Betty
Gordon, P. Generations apart
Granville-Barker, H. Waste
Guare, J. The talking dog
y Hackett, W. A tale of two cities
Hall, W. Jane Eyre
Hall, W. Mansfield Park
Hampton, C. The philanthropist
Hastings, C. The wayward spirit
Heward, L. Or what's a heaven for?
Horovitz, I. Fighting over Beverley
Jenkin, L. Careless love
Knee, A. The St. Valentine's Day massacre
Kroetz, F. X. Through the leaves
Lang, W. Lady of the camellias
Lill, W. The Glace Bay Miners' Museum
Linney, R. Can can
Linney, R. Songs of love
Lyly, J. Gallathea
Marber, P. After Miss Julie
Marivaux. The triumph of love
McNally, T. Frankie and Johnny in the Clair de Lune
Meyer, M. G. Moe's Lucky Seven
y Morely, O. J. Romance for Jo March
Mueller, L. Violent peace

Love—*Continued*
Musset. A. de. Don't play with love
Nagy, A. The seducer's diary
Nigro, D. Fair Rosamund and her murderer
y Olfson, E. Wuthering Heights
Oswald, P. Fair ladies at a game of poem cards
Paz, O. Rappaccini's daughter
Plowman, G. Beata Beatrix
Plowman, G. Philip and Rowena
Reid, C. Did you hear the one about the Irishman . . . ?
Ricchi, R. The promise
Ritter, E. Automatic pilot
Sade, Marquis de. The haunted tower
Sade, Marquis de. The self-proclaimed philosopher
Sade, Marquis de. The twins
Schnitzler, A. The gallant Cassian
Schwartz, D. Paris and Helen
Shanley, J. P. The red coat
Sierens, A. Drummers
Silver, N. Free will & wanton lust
Smith, A. Live bed show
Sondheim, S. Passion
Storey, R. The saints and apostles
Strauss, B. The tour guide
Szilágyi, A. Unsent letters
Thompson, E. The Valentine Fairy
Upton, J. The shorewatchers' house
Vance, C. Jane Eyre
Wadsworth, S. The triumph of love
Warner, F. A conception of love
Warner, F. Lying figures
Weitz, P. All for one
Weller, M. Loose ends
Wilder, T. Love and how to cure it
y Yates, P. Starlover
See also Comedy—Romantic; Courtship; Marriage

Love, Maternal
Cocteau, J. Les parents terribles

A **love** affair. Mayer, J.

Love affairs. See Adultery; Love

Love allways. Taylor, R. and Bologna, J.

Love and how to cure it. Wilder, T.

Love and shrimp. Markham, S.

Love by the bolt. See Feydeau, G. The dressmaker

Love by the numbers. Joselovitz, E. and Bagdasian, H. M.

Love child. Murray-Smith, J.

The **love** course. See Gurney, A. R. Public affairs: Pt 1 The love course

The **love** for three oranges. Gozzi, C. (adaptation) See Prokofiev, S. The love of three oranges

Love forty. Vickery, F.

Love is strange. Ledoux, P. and Young, D.

Love me slender. Brooks, V.

The **love** of a good man. Barker, H.

The **love** of the nightingale. Wertenbaker, T.

The **love** of three oranges. Prokofiev, S.

The **love** of three oranges. Swortzell, L.

Love off the shelf. Norman, P.

Love poem #98. Taylor, R.

Love seen in laundromat. Benyon, L.

A **love** song for Ulster: The daughter. Morrison, B.

A **love** song for Ulster: The marriage. Morrison, B.

A **love** song for Ulster: The son. Morrison, B.

The **love** suicide at Schofield Barracks. Linney, R.

The **love** talker. Pryor, D.

Love triumphant. Dryden, J.

Love trouble. Jones, J. M.

Love! Valour! Comapssion! McNally, T.

Lovecraft, H. P. (Howard Phillips)
Schevill, J. Lovecraft's follies

Lovecraft's follies. Schevill, J.

The **loved** one. Booth, J.

The **loveliest** afternoon of the year. Guare, J.

Lovepuke. Sarkies, D.

The **lover's** melancholy. Ford, J.

The **lover's** progress. Fletcher, J.

Loves labour wonne. Nigro, D.

Love's light in flight. Moore, C. M.

A **lovesome** thing. McConnell, J.

Lovesong. Fulford, R.

Loving Daniel Boone. Norman, M.

Low level panic. McIntyre, C.

Loyalty
Shepard, S. The mad dog blues

Lucas, Bob. See Finch, C. jt. auth.

Lucas, Craig
Bad dream
Fear of sex and intimacy in age of AIDS. 2m 1 setting
In The Actor's book of gay and lesbian plays; ed. by E. Lane and N. Shengold

Credo
Monologue. Woman, having just broken up with boyfriend, reacts to death of her dog. 1w
In EST Marathon '95
In Plays for actresses; ed. by E. Lane and N. Shengold

The Dying Gaul
First scene of longer play about homosexual writer. 2m 1 extra
In Showtime's Act One Festival of one-act plays, 1994

Missing persons. Dramatists 1996 65p
Revised version of play first produced 1981. Wealthy tenured professor and author spends Thanksgiving attempting to hold together her fractured family. 2 acts 3 scenes 3m 3w 1b 1 interior

Prelude to a kiss
After their honeymoon man discovers his wife's soul has migrated to the body of an old man dying of cancer. 2 acts 2 scenes 8m 4w extras
In The Best of Off-Broadway; ed. by R. Wetzsteon

Throwing your voice
Two New York couples debate morality of owning diamond which may have been mined in South Africa. 2m 2w 1 interior
In Telling tales: new one-act plays; ed. by E. Lane

What I meant was
Set in Columbia, Maryland, 1968. Gay man makes peace with his parents. 2m 2w 1 interior
In Humana Festival '96

Lucia mad. Nigro, D.

Lucie, Doug
Grace. Hern Bks. 1993 74p
Satire set on English country estate about greed and hypocrisy of American evangelists. 8 scenes 4m 4w 1 setting

The shallow end. Methuen Drama in association with the Royal Court Theatre 1997 85p (Royal Court writers series)
Lavish corporate wedding reception setting for black comedy about personal freedom and increasing power of media corporations. 4 acts 16m 3w 3 interiors

Luckham, Claire
The choice. Dramatic 1994 67p
Couple expecting first child learn that baby will have Down syndrome. Slide projections. 2 acts 3m 2w 1 interior

The **lucky** chance. Behn, A.

Lucky nurse. LaChiusa, M. J.

Lucky Peter's journey. Swortzell, L.

Lucky sods. Godber, J.

Ludlow fair. Wilson, L.

Ludwig, Ken
Moon over Buffalo. French 1996 128p
Farce about show business set in 1953. Husband-and-wife acting team in third-rate theatrical company yearn for Hollywood careers. 2 acts 4 scenes 4m 4w 1 setting

Luce, William. See Fischoff, G. James A. Michener's Sayonara

Lucia. Hall, F. B.

Lulu: a monster tragedy. Wedekind, F.

Lumborg, Dennis
One find day. French (London) 1995 48p
One man play. Bureaucratic interference separates British man from wife and family. 2 acts 4 scenes 1m 3 interiors

Lumen. See Warner, F. Maquettes for the requiem: Lumen

Lumumba, Patrice, 1925-1961
Greenland, S. Jungle rot

The **lunatic** lover. Pascal, F.

Lunch. Berkoff, S.

Lunch with Ginger. Norman, M.

Lunden, Jeffrey
Wings (condensation)
In The Best plays of 1992-1993

Lust. The Heather Brothers

Lust. See Fornes, M. I. What of the night?: Lust

Lusting after Pipino's wife. Kass, S. H.

Lying. See Truthfulness and falsehood

Lying figures. Warner, F.

Lyly, John
Campaspe
Comedy set in Athens in 4th century B.C. Alexander falls in love with Theban prisoner but loses her to artist. Prologue 5 acts 19 scenes epilogue 25m 3w extras 1 setting
In Lyly, J. Selected prose and dramatic work

Lyly, John—*Continued*
Gallathea
Elizabethan allegorical pastoral comedy that debates the virtues of love and chastity. Singing. Prologue 5 acts 20 scenes epilogue 12m 9w extras
In Lyly, J. Selected prose and dramatic work

Lynch, May
c Scheherazade
Scheherazade's storytelling so enchants cruel sultan that he spares her life. 3m 7w extras 1 interior
In Thirty plays from favorite stories; ed. by S. E. Kamerman

Lynching
Johnson, G. D. A Sunday morning in the South
Livingston, M. S. For unborn children
Mitchell, J. S. Son-Boy
Seiler, C. Darker brother

Lynette at 3 AM. Anderson, J.

Lynette has beautiful skin. Anderson, J.

Lysander, Per, and Osten, Suzanne
c Medea's children
Experimental play about divorce based on Euripides tragedy. Background music. Prologue 7 scenes 1m 2w 1b 1g 1 extra
In Around the world in 21 plays; ed. by L. Swortzell

Lysistrata. Aristophanes

Lyssa, Alison
Pinball
Comedy relating the myth of Solomon to child custody battle involving a lesbian mother. Prologue 2 acts 11 scenes 2m 4w 4 interiors 1 exterior
In Australian gay and lesbian plays; ed. by B. Parr

Lyssiotis, Tes
Blood moon
Together with A white sports coat and The Forty Lounge Cafe forms loose trilogy about Greek family life in Australia. Four sisters reunited on Greek island to divide possessions of dead mother. 4w 1 setting
In Lyssiotis, T. A white sports coat & other plays

The Forty Lounge Cafe
Drama about cultural differences. Two Greek women, brought to Australia by arranged marriages, adjust to their new milieu. 2 acts 36 scenes 1m 4w extras settings
In Lyssiotis, T. A white sports coat & other plays

A white sports coat
Dramatist struggles to complete commissioned play before birth of her second child. 3m 3w 1 setting
In Lyssiotis, T. A white sports coat & other plays

M

'M' is for moon among other things. Stoppard, T.

The **M** word. Ball, A.

Ma Lien and the magic paintbrush. Gerke, P.

Ma Rainey's black bottom. Wilson, A.

Mac Intyre, Tom
Good evening, Mr Collins
Portrays characters and events surrounding legendary demise of Irish revolutionary Michael Collins. 2 acts 16 scenes 7m 1w 1 setting
In The Dazzling dark: new Irish plays; ed. by F. McGuinness

Sheep's milk on the boil
Postmodern fable set on remote Irish island. Earthy couple observed and interfered with by symbolic characters. Music, singing. 2 acts 16 scenes 3m 2w extras 1 interior
In New plays from the Abbey Theatre, 1993-1995

MacDonald, Ann-Marie
The Arab's mouth. Blizzard Pub. 1996 79p
Gothic drama set 1899 on Scottish Coast. While investigating unexplained happenings at family's ancestral home, scientific-minded woman confronts Freudian analysis, Roman Catholicism, homosexuality, superstition and Egyptian mythology. 2 acts 35 scenes 3m 3w 1 setting

MacDonald, Bruce
What we do with it
Short father-daughter battle for truth regarding memory of incest. 1m 1w 1 interior
In Actors Theatre of Louisville. Ten-minute plays: v3
In Humana Festival '93

MacDonald, Bryden
The weekend healer. Talonbooks 1995 108p
Psychological drama set in Toronto suburb about child sexual abuse. Disappearance of her teenage son forces woman and her estranged mother to share painful memories. 8 scenes 1m 2w 1 setting

Whale riding weather. Talonbooks 1994 127p
Drama set in Toronto explores disintegration of homosexual relationship. 8 scenes 3m 1 interior

Macdonald, Sharman
Borders of paradise
Drama exploring mysteries of young adulthood. Five English boys and two Scottish girls interact on North Devon beach. 2 acts 5m 2w 1 setting
In Macdonald, S. Plays: one

Macdonald, Sharman—*Continued*

When I was a girl, I used to scream and shout. . .

Drama set in Scotland traces lasting effects of repressive mother on daughter and her best friend over span of some thirty years. 2 acts 5 scenes 1m 3w 1 setting

In Macdonald, S. Plays: one

When we were women

Drama set in Scotland during World War II. Village girl, impregnated by serviceman, marries him and discovers he is a bigamist. 2 acts 9 scenes 2m 3w 1 setting

In Macdonald, S. Plays: one

The winter guest

Woman, her widowed daughter and grandson face uncertain future. 2 acts 1m 3w 2b 1 setting

In Macdonald, S. Plays: one

Macedonia

Petsinis, T. The drought

Machado, Eduardo

In the eye of the hurricane

Cuban family suffers when business is confiscated by Fidel Castro's government. 2 acts 4 scenes 7m 4w 1 interior 1 exterior

In A Decade of new comedy: plays from the Humana Festival v1

Machiavelli, Nicolo

Clizia; tr. by Daniel T. Gallagher. Waveland Press 1996 62p

Comedy set in 16th century Italy. Both father and brother fall in love with adopted girl. 5 acts 33 scenes 6m 4w

Machinal. Treadwell. S.

MacIvor, Daniel

2-2-tango

Gay couple explore emotional, physical and spiritual aspects of relationships. Dancing. 3m 1 setting

In Making, out; ed. by R. Wallace

House humans. Coach House Press 1992 93p

In House, a black comedic monologue, anti-hero's resentments and persecution fantasies shape his hallucinatory world. Humans consists of prose stories that may be inserted into monologue. 1m 1 setting

Never swim alone

Drama about men's competitive relationships. 2m 1 w

In MacIvor, D. Never swim alone & This is a play

This is a play

Comic drama about a play about a play. 1m 2w 1 extra

In MacIvor, D. Never swim alone & This is a play

MacIvor, Daniel, and Brooks, Daniel

Here lies Henry. Playwrights Canada 1997 55p

Comedic monologue by gay man. Slide projections. 1m 1 setting

Mack, Carol K.

In her sight

Drama set mainly in 1777 Vienna. Based on case of gifted blind young pianist's treatment by Doctor Franz Anton Mesmer. Music. 23 scenes 5m 2w 1 setting

In Humana Festival '97

The magenta shift

Photographer encounters troubled female token clerk in New York City subway. 2w 1 interior

In The Best American short plays, 1993-1994

MacKenna, John

Faint voices

Ghostly memory play based on life and loves of Irish poet Francis Ledwidge who died in World War I. 1 act 4m 4w 1 setting

In Greatest hits: four Irish one-act plays; ed. by D. Bolger

MacKenzie, William Lyon, 1795-1861

Salutin, R. and Theatre Passe Muraille. 1837: The Farmer's Revolt

The **MacKenzie**-Papineau Rebellion. See Hollingsworth, M. The history of the village of the small huts

MacLaughlin, Wendy

Watermelon boats

Two women who are lifelong friends share their thoughts at three stages of their lives. 2w 1 setting

In 20/20: twenty one-act plays from twenty years of the Humana Festival

MacLeod, Joan

The Hope slide

Natural disaster serves as metaphor for AIDS crisis. Actress travels back in memory to Hope, British Columbia, site of 1965 mountain collapse. 1w

In MacLeod, J. The Hope slide [and] Little sister

Jewel

Woman mourns husband's death. 1w 1 interior

In Solo; ed. by J. Sherman

Little sister

Five teens link self-esteem with personal appearance. 2m 5w 1 setting

In MacLeod, J. The Hope slide [and] Little sister

Toronto, Mississippi

Family life of moderately mentally handicapped 18-year-old Toronto girl. Prologue 2 acts 9 scenes epilogue 2m 2w 1 interior

In Modern Canadian plays v2; ed. by J. Wasserman

MacLeod, Wendy
The house of yes. Dramatists 1996 60p
Black comedy. Incestuous relationship between insane young woman who has modeled herself on Jackie Kennedy and her recently engaged twin brother disrupts Thanksgiving gathering. 11 scenes 2m 3w 2 interiors

The lost colony
Ideals clash when couple vacations with their daughter and her boyfriend. 9 scenes 2m 2w 1 interior
In MacLeod, W. The shallow end and The lost colony

The shallow end
Classmate's death causes teenage girl to examine her friendships and priorities. 8 scenes 4w 1 exterior
In MacLeod, W. The shallow end and The lost colony

MacNeice, Louis
Christopher Columbus
Radio verse play about life of famed explorer. Large mixed cast
In MacNeice, L. Selected plays of Louis MacNeice

The dark tower
Radio play written in response to World War II. Man on parabolic quest is led astray many times but finally confronts absolute evil. Variable cast
In MacNeice, L. Selected plays of Louis MacNeice

He had a date; or, What bearing?
Radio play about World War II sea casualty. As he drowns, voices from Royal Navy man's past sound in his head. Large mixed cast
In MacNeice, L. Selected plays of Louis MacNeice

The mad islands
Radio fantasy about man sailing among strange islands seeking revenge for murder of his father. 14 characters
In MacNeice, L. Selected plays of Louis MacNeice

One for the grave
Symbolic drama based on late medieval morality play Everyman. Satirizes cross commercialism of television. Large mixed cast
In MacNeice, L. Selected plays of Louis MacNeice

Persons from Porlock
Radio play. Artist, exploring cave, confronts death. Various people in his life speak to him as he dies. 7m 3w
In MacNeice, L. Selected plays of Louis MacNeice

Prisoner's progress
Radio parable play about moral, intellectual and spiritual imprisonment. Hero fails in desperate escape attempts from prisoner-of-war camp. 13m 4w extras
In MacNeice, L. Selected plays of Louis MacNeice

They met on Good Friday
Radio play. Depicts conflict between the Viking and native inhabitants of 11th century Ireland. Songs. 12m 5w
In MacNeice, L. Selected plays of Louis MacNeice

Macquarie, Lachlin, 1761-1824
Buzo, A. Macquarie

Mad boy chronicle. O'Brien, M.

The **mad** dog blues. Shepard, S.

Mad forest. Churchill, C.

The **mad** islands. MacNeice, L.

A **mad** world, my masters. Middleton, T.

Madách, Imre
The tragedy of man; tr. by Iain MacLeod. Canongate 1993 189p
Philosophical verse drama about meaning of life. Traces symbolic characters of Eve, Adam, and Lucifer from Biblical times through various historical settings. 15 scenes Large mixed cast 1 setting

Madame Butterfly. Long, J. L. (dramatization) See McDonough, J. Butterfly

Madame collects herself. Barnes, D.

Madame Zena's séance. Hanson, M.E. and Sheldon, D. P.

Madame Zoyka. See Bulgakov, M. Zoyka's apartment

Madam's late mother. See Feydeau, G. My wife's dead mother

Al-Madani, 'Izz al-Din
The Zanj Revolution
Historical drama set in 9th century Southern Iraq. Black "slave" community rebels against racial, social, and economic discrimination. 2 acts 3 scenes 2 interludes 11m 1w 1 setting
In Modern Arabic drama; ed. by S. K. Jayyusi and R. Allen

Madcap Monster Inn. Priore, F. V.

Made for a woman. Ball, A.

Made in Bangkok. Minghella, A.

A **madhouse** in Goa. Sherman, M.

Madison, Dolley, 1768-1849
c McCaslin, N. Daring, darling Dolly

The **madness** of Esme and Shaz. Daniels, S.

The **madness** of George III (condensation). Bennett, A.

The **madness** of Lady Bright. Wilson, L.

The **madness** of misfortune. Sade, Marquis de

The **Madras** House. Granville-Barker, H.

Madrid (Spain)
Valle-Inclan, R. del. Bohemian lights

Maelduin of Arran. McCaslin, N.

Maeterlinck, Maurice
Monna Vanna. Second Renaissance Bks. 1993 102p
Drama about honor and values set in 15th-century Italy. Florentine general who is besieging Pisa promises citizens relief in exchange for night with wife of Pisa's commander. 3 acts 7m 1w extras 3 interiors

Mafia
De Filippo, E. The local authority

Magazine. Saunders, J.

Magee, Daniel
Paddywack. French 1992 115p
Political drama about Irish laborer in London who may be IRA bomber. 2 acts 15 scenes 4m 2w 1 setting

The **magenta** shift. Mack, C. K.

Maggie Magalita. Kesselman, W.

Maggie of the saints. Barnes, D.

Magic
y Bush, M. Aalmauria: Voyage of the dragonfly
y Bush, M. The crystal
c Carlson, N. K. and Chapman, B. The magic pebble
c Golden, G. The magic in me
Havel, V. Temptation
Kushner, T. The illusion
c Mahlmann, L. and Jones, D. C. The table, the donkey and the stick
Martin, S. The zig-zag woman
c Zeder, S. L. Wiley and the Hairy Man

The **magic** in me. Golden, G.

The **magic** pebble. Carlson, N. K. and Chapman, B.

Magicians
c Colón, A. The caravan
Martin, S. Patter for the floating lady
c Surface, M. H. The sorcerer's apprentice

The **magistrate.** Pinero, A. W.

The **magnificent** voyage of Emily Carr. Marchessault, J.

Magnus Fourpenny and the black bear birthday bash. McCulloughs, L. E.

Magritte, René, 1898-1967
Kornhauser, B. This is not a pipe dream

Maguire, Matthew
Phaedra. Sun & Moon Press 1995 77p
Drama set in contemporary United States loosely based on Racine's drama of forbidden love. Upper class family torn apart by violence and erotic desire. 2 acts 3m 3w 1 interior

The tower. Sun & Moon Press 1993 85p
Symbolic drama about modern society's ideals, violence and madness. Woman on operating table dreams, or remembers, that she is secretly rebuilding Tower of Babel. 9 scenes Variable cast 5 characters extras 3 settings

The **Maharajah** is bored. Winther, B.

Mahfuz, 'Isam
The China tree
Symbolic drama. Man found guilty of murder by totalitarian judge. Prologue 12 scenes 4m 1w extras 1 setting
In Modern Arabic drama; ed. by S. K. Jayyusi and R. Allen

Mahlmann, Lewis, and Jones, David Cadwalader
c Aladdin; or, The wonderful lamp
Puppet play based on traditional Arabian nights tale of boy who defeats evil magician. 8 scenes 7 characters
In Mahlmann, L. and Jones, D. C. Plays for young puppeteers

c Ali Baba and the Forty Thieves
Puppet play based on Arabian nights tale. Virtuous Ali Baba battles evil Al Raschid and his forty thieves. 7 scenes 7 characters
In Mahlmann, L. and Jones, D. D. Plays for young puppeteers

c Alice's adventures in Wonderland
Puppet play. Dramatization of several episodes from the fantasy by Lewis Carroll. 8 scenes 16 characters
In Mahlmann, L. and Jones, D. C. Plays for young puppeteers

c Beauty and the Beast
Puppet play based on fairy tale of girl who saves prince from enchantment. 5 scenes 10 characters
In Mahlmann, L. and Jones, D. C. Plays for young puppeteers

c Cinderella
Puppet play based on the traditional fairy tale about mistreated stepdaughter who wins prince. 4 scenes 8 characters
In Mahlmann, L. and Jones, D. C. Plays for young puppeteers

c The Emperor's nightingale
Puppet play dramatization of Hans Christian Andersen's fairy tale about death and beauty. 3 scenes 8 characters
In Mahlmann, L. and Jones, D. C. Plays for young puppeteers

c The Frog Prince
Puppet play. Dramatization of fairy tale by Brothers Grimm about prince who was turned into frog. 3 scenes 6 characters
In Mahlmann, L. and Jones, D. C. Plays for young puppeteers

Mahlmann, Lewis, and Jones, David Cadwalader—*Continued*

c The Gingerbread Boy

Puppet play based on English folk tale. Gingerbread boy runs away from home. 5 scenes 10 characters

In Mahlmann, L. and Jones, D. C. Plays for young puppeteers

c Jack and the beanstalk

Puppet play. Dramatization of story about the boy whose magic beans bring him surprising adventures and wealth. 6 scenes 9 characters

In Mahlmann, L. and Jones, D. C. Plays for young puppeteers

c King Midas and the golden touch

Puppet play version of Greek myth about greed. 3 scenes 7 characters

In Mahlmann, L. and Jones, D. C. Plays for young puppeteers

c The Nutcracker Prince

Puppet play based on the E.T.A. Hoffman fantasy of the enchanted Nutcracker who fights a Mouse King. Music. 4 scenes 10 characters

In Mahlmann, L. and Jones, D. C. Plays for young puppeteers

c Peter Pan

Puppet play adapted from J. M. Barrie's fantasy. 5 scenes 11 characters

In Mahlmann, L. and Jones, D. C. Plays for young puppeteers

c The Pied Piper of Hamelin

Puppet play based on the poem by Robert Browning. When the Mayor refuses to give Pied Piper money agreed on for ridding Hamelin of rats, Pied Piper takes drastic revenge. 3 scenes 9 characters

In Mahlmann, L. and Jones, D. C. Plays for young puppeteers

c Pinocchio

Puppet play based on Collodi's story about mischievous marionette. 8 scenes 13 characters

In Mahlmann, L. and Jones, D. C. Plays for young puppeteers

c Puss-in-Boots

Puppet play based on Perrault's version of classic fairy tale about ingenious cat. 4 scenes 8 characters

In Mahlmann, L. and Jones, D. C. Plays for young puppeteers

c Rapunzel's tower

Puppet play based on traditional fairy tale. Girl with long hair is imprisoned in tower by witch. 6 scenes 8 characters

In Mahlmann, L. and Jones, D. C. Plays for young puppeteers

c The reluctant dragon

Puppet play. Dramatization of Kenneth Grahame's story about a boy who made friends with a dragon and arranged a match for him with St. George. 5 scenes 6 characters

In Mahlmann, L. and Jones, D. C. Plays for young puppeteers

c Rumpelstiltskin

Puppet play based on the Grimms' fairy tale of little man who spins straw into gold. 5 scenes 6 characters

In Mahlmann, L. and Jones, D. C. Plays for young puppeteers

Sleeping Beauty

Puppet play based on classic fairy tale of princess placed under spell by wicked witch. 6 scenes 11 characters

In Mahlmann, L. and Jones, D. C. Plays for young puppeteers

c Snow White and Rose Red

Puppet play based on traditional fairy tale. Sisters help prince turned into bear by wicked dwarf. 3 scenes 8 characters

In Mahlmann, L. and Jones, D. C. Plays for young puppeteers

c Show White and the seven dwarfs

Puppet play based on Grimms' fairy tale about adventures of wicked queen's stepdaughter. 6 scenes 13 characters

In Mahlmann, L. and Jones, D. C. Plays for young puppeteers

c The table, the donkey and the stick

Puppet play based on German folk tale by Grimm Brothers. Magic complicates innkeeper's life. 9 scenes 9 characters

In Mahlmann, L. and Jones, D. C. Plays for young puppeteers

c The tale of Peter Rabbit

Puppet play based on story by Beatrix Potter about rabbit who runs from Mr. McGregor's garden. 5 scenes 10 characters

In Mahlmann, L. and Jones, D. C. Plays for young puppeteers

c Three Billy Goats Gruff

Puppet play based on traditional folk tale. Goats outsmart troll who lives under bridge. 2 scenes 7 characters

In Mahlmann, L. and Jones, D. C. Plays for young puppeteers

c The Wizard of Oz

Puppet play. Dramatization of L. Frank Baum's story about Dorothy who leaves Kansas and meets the Wizard of Oz, the Scarecrow and the Tin Woodsman. 10 scenes 19 characters

In Mahlmann, L. and Jones, D. C. Plays for young puppeteers

Mahon, Derek

Racine's Phaedra. Gallery Bks. 1996 66p

Adaptation of Racine's verse tragedy based on Greek legend. Queen falls in love with stepson. 2 acts 3m 5w 1 setting

The **Mai.** Carr, M.

The **maid** in the mill. Fletcher, J. and Rowley, W.

The **maiden** stone. Munro, R.

Mail order bride. Robson, J.

Majeski, Bill

y A flutter of lace

Comedy skit about role of handkerchiefs in romance stories. Variable cast 10 characters extras

In The Big book of skits; ed. by S. E. Kamerman

Major, Roberta Olsen

c Melodrama at Mayfair Meadows

Melodrama with audience participation. Three maidens tied to railroad tracks by villain. Singing. 2 scenes 4m 4w extras 1 interior 1 exterior

In The Big book of large-cast plays; ed. by S. E. Kamerman

Major Barbara. Shaw, B.

Major Bullshot-Gorgeous. See Plautus, T. M. The braggart soldier

Major Weir. Nigro, D.

Majorca (Spain)

Brooks, V. Let's pretend

Make it happen. Welsh, D.

Make-up. Tasca, J.

Makin' it. Allaway, B.

Making sandwiches. See Pope, R. Sandwiches: Making sandwiches

The **Makropoulos** secret. Capek, K.

Malcolm X, 1925-1965

Davis, T. The life and times of Malcolm X

Riche, R. Malcolm X: message from the grassroots

Stetson, J. The meeting

Malcolm *X:* message from the grassroots. Riche, R.

Malini. Tagore, R.

Malpede, Karen

US

Experimental memory play. Feminist exploration of sexual myth and reality. 11 scenes 1m 1w 1 setting.

In Women on the verge: 7 avant-garde American plays; ed. by R. C. Lamont

Malta

Marlowe, B. The Jew of Malta

Mama drama, by Leslie Ayvazian [et al.]; with original music by The Roches. Revised version. French (London) 1993 96p

A series of pieces about pregnancy, childbirth, and motherhood. 2 acts 5w 1 setting

Mama, I want to sing. Higginsen, V. and Wydro, K.

Mama's girl. Dean, D.

Mambo mouth. Leguizamo, J.

Mamet, David

Almost done

Monologue. Young mother reflects on stories she will pass on to her child. 1w

In Mamet, D. A life with no joy in it, and other plays and pieces

The cryptogram. Dramatists 1995 59p

Dramatic look at unravelling of middle-class family in 1959 through eyes of 10-year-old boy. 3 acts 1m 1w 1b 1 interior

—Same. Vintage Bks. 1995 101p

The cryptogram (condensation)

In The Best plays of 1994-1995

Dodge

Story about origin of man's name changes as it passes to next generation. 2m

In Mamet, D. A life with no joy in it, and other plays and pieces

Edmond

Man abandoning conventional life style, has series of degrading encounters with denizens of New York City underworld. 23 scenes 20m 8w settings

In The Best of Off-Broadway; ed. by R. Wetzsteon

Fish

Two men recall story of fish who traded wishes for immortal soul. 2m

In Mamet, D. A life with no joy in it, and other plays and pieces

Glengarry Glen Ross

Comedy about sharp dealings of small-time, cut-throat real estate salesmen. 2 acts 4 scenes 7m 2 interiors

In Best American plays: 9th series, 1983-1992

Goldberg Street

Radio play about anti-semitism in combat military. 1m 1w

In Fruitful and multiplying; ed. by E. Schiff

An interview

Comedy set in hell. Colloquy between sleazy lawyer and interrogator. 2m 1 setting

In The Best American short plays, 1994-1995

In Death defying acts

The joke code

Two friends have philosophical discussion. Variable cast 2 characters

In Mamet, D. A life with no joy in it, and other plays and pieces

Mamet, David—*Continued*

Jolly

Brother and sister feud over mother's estate. 3 scenes 2m 1w 1 interior

In The Best American short plays, 1992-1993

Joseph Dintenfass

Conversation between older man and young woman. 1m 1w

In Mamet, D. A life with no joy in it, and other plays and pieces

L.A. sketches

Series of five scenes related to entertainment industry. 2m

In Mamet, D. A life with no joy in it, and other plays and pieces

A life with no joy in it

Conversation between ex-lovers. 1m 1w

In Mamet, D. A life with no joy in it, and other plays and pieces

Monologue (February 1990)

Monologue. Self condemnation and perceptions of God. Variable cast 1 character

In Mamet, D. A life with no joy in it, and other plays and pieces

No one will be immune

Man tries to explain why he stopped flight from taking off. 2m

In EST Marathon '95

In Mamet, D. A life with no joy in it, and other plays and pieces

Oleanna. Dramatists 1993 49p

Drama about power, ideology and political correctness. Professor is accused of sexually harassing one of his students. 3 acts 1m 1w 1 interior

—Same. Vintage Bks. 1993 80p

Oleanna (condensation)

In The Best plays of 1992-1993

A perfect mermaid

Fantastic beach encounter. Variable cast 2 characters

In Mamet, D. A life with no joy in it, and other plays and pieces

A scene—Australia

Two women discuss acquaintance who was killed by husband. 2w

In Mamet, D. A life with no joy in it, and other plays and pieces

Sunday afternoon

Conversation between two men interrupted by woman bleeding from kitchen accident. 2m 1w

In Mamet, D. A life with no joy in it, and other plays and pieces

Two enthusiasts

Two friends discuss life, death, God and baseball. Variable cast 2 characters

In Mamet, D. A life with no joy in it, and other plays and pieces

About

Stroppel, F. The Mamet women

Parodies, imitations, etc.

Ives, D. Speed-the-play

The **Mamet** women. Stroppel, F.

Man and superman. Shaw, B.

Man in a side-car. Gray, S.

The **man** of mode. Etherege, G.

Man of the moment. Ayckbourn, A.

The **man** on the floor. See Simon, N. London suite: The man on the floor

The **man**, the rose and silence. Ricchi, R.

The **man** without a country. Hackett, W.

The **manager.** Shaughnessy, D.

The **Manchurian** candidate. Lahr, J.

Mander, Charles

Getting along. French (London) 1994 42p

Comedy. Middle-aged English couple accompanied on annual holiday in south of France by three widowed friends. 3m 2w 1 interior

World première. French (London) 1995 27p

Comedy about tribulations of amateur theatrical group. 3m 4w 1 interior

Manet, Eduardo

Lady Strass

Surreal drama set in Belize. Two thieves break into home of apparently wealthy widow of English businessman. 2m 1w 1 interior

In Playwrights of exile: an international anthology

Manhattan. See New York (N.Y.)—Manhattan

Manhattan love songs—Bronx cheers. Taylor, R. and Bologna, J.

Mankind

A critical edition of the medieval play Mankind. Edwin Mellen Press 1995 152p

15th century English morality play. Allegory dramatizing mercy shown by God to repentant sinners. Verse play in Middle English. 3 scenes Unidentified cast 7 characters

Mann, Emily

Annulla

Original version produced with title: Annulla, Allen: autobiography of a survivor. Television monologues by Holocaust survivor living in London and voice of young American woman. 1w 1 extra

In Fruitful and multiplying; ed. by E. Schiff

In Mann, E. Testimonies: four plays

Mann, Emily—*Continued*
Execution of justice
Docudrama portraying trial of Dan White for murders of San Francisco Mayor George Moscone, and Harvey Milk, city's first openly gay supervisor. Slide projections. 2 acts Large mixed cast 1 setting
In Mann, E. Testimonies: four plays
In Voicings: ten plays from the documentary theatre; ed. by A. Favorini

Greensboro
Docudrama about trial resulting from attack by Ku Klux Klan members and American Nazis on anti-Klan rally in Greensboro, North Carolina, in 1979. 2 acts Variable cast 31 characters 1 setting
In Mann, E. Testimonies: four plays

Having our say. Dramatists 1996 42p
Based on book of reminiscences by Delany sisters portraying 100 years of African-American family life. 2w 1 interior

Still life
Performed in documentary style, depicts the way the Vietnam War has affected a man, his wife, and mistress. Background music. 3 acts 27 scenes 1m 2w 1 interior
In Mann, E. Testimonies: four plays

Manning, Bob
What wasn't said, what didn't happen
Business consultant and seminar leader get involved in personal business. 2m 1w
In Actors Theatre of Louisville. Ten minute plays: v3

Manning, Ned
Close to the bone. Currency Press 1994 63p
Drama about Australian policy of forced adoption. Young woman discovers that she was taken from her aborigine family in the 1960s and raised as white. 2 acts 3m 9w 2g 1 setting

Manns, Darren
y Heart of the land
White men dump rubbish on sacred burial site of Australian aborigines. Background music. 5 scenes 3m 1 exterior
In Young playwrights; ed. by E. Bray

Manny. Margulies, D.

The **man's** shop. Chadwick, C.

Mansfield Park. Hall, W.

Manual of trench warfare. Gorman, C.

Manzi, Warren
Perfect crime. Revised. French 1993 139p
Thriller. Local inspector's obsession with bizarre murder case leads him to suspect husband and wife psychiatrists. 2 acts 7 scenes 4m 1w 1 interior

Mao, Madame. See Jiang Qing, 1914-1991

A **map** of the world. Hare, D.

Maponya, Maishe
The hungry earth
Theatrical piece about aspirations of South African blacks. Singing. Prologue 6 scenes epilogue Variable cast 1 setting
In South African plays; ed. by S. Gray

Mapp, Frances
y The wonderful Wizard of Oz
Based on L. Frank Baum's fantasy about Dorothy and her friends in the Land of Oz. 6 scenes 5m 4w 1g extras 5 interiors
In The Big book of dramatized classics; ed. by S. E. Kamerman

Maquettes for the requiem: Emblems. Warner, F.

Maquettes for the requiem: Lumen. Warner, F.

Maquettes for the requiem: Troat. Warner, F.

Maraini, Dacia
Crime at the tennis club
Dramatization of Alberto Moravia's short story about murder of older woman by four young men. Staged from woman's point of view. 4m 1w 1 interior
In Maraini, D. Only prostitutes marry in May

Dialogue between a prostitute and her client
Psychological drama. Conversation between intellectually perceptive prostitute and man seeking solace in body of woman he doesn't know. 1m 1w 1 interior
In Maraini, D. Only prostitutes marry in May

Dreams of Clytemnestra
Tale of mythic Greek heroine transferred to modern Italy. Passionate woman stands up to male chauvinism. 2 acts 4m 4w extras 1 setting
In Maraini, D. Only prostitutes marry in May

Mary Stuart
Historical drama freely adapted from Schiller's drama. Relationship between Elizabeth I and Mary Queen of Scots. 2 acts 2w 1 setting
In Maraini, D. Only prostitutes marry in May

Marans, Jon
Old wicked songs. Dramatists 1996 71p
Apartment/rehearsal studio in 1986 Vienna, Austria scene of confrontation between elderly music teacher and young neurotic music prodigy from California. Music, singing. 2 acts 8 scenes 2m 1 interior

Old wicked songs (condensation)
In The Best plays of 1996-1997

Marber, Patrick
After Miss Julie. Methuen Drama 1996 47p (Methuen modern plays)
Drama set in English country house 1945. Events of Strindberg's tragic love story transposed to night of Labour Party's landslide victory. 1m 2w 1 interior

Dealer's choice. Methuen Drama 1995 118p (Methuen modern plays)
Weekly poker game setting for exploration of masculine rituals, father-son relationships and nature of obsession. 3 acts 6m 2 interiors

Marc Antony. See Antonius, Marcus

Marcel pursued by the hounds. Tremblay, M.

March of the falsettos. Finn, W. and Lapine, J.

The **march** on Russia. Storey, D.

Marchessault, Jovette
The magnificent voyage of Emily Carr; tr. by Linda Gaboriau. Talonbooks 1992 104p
Impressionistic exploration of life of Canadian artist Emily Carr. 1m 3w 1 interior

Marching for Fausa. Bandele, 'B.

"**Marco** millions." O'Neill, E.

Marco Polo sings a solo. Guare, J.

Marconi, Guglielmo, 1874-1937
c Sussman, D. Mystery of the phantom voice

Mardi Gras. Meilhac, H. and Halévy, L.

Margulies, Donald
Anthony
Monologue. Twelve-year-old boy witnesses woman threatening to jump off apartment building roof. 1b
In Margulies, D. July 7, 1994: short plays and monologues

Death in the family
Uncle phones nephew when distant relative dies. 2m
In Margulies, D. July 7, 1994: short plays and monologues

Father and son
Father and son after mother's death. 2m
In Margulies, D. July 7, 1994: short plays and monologues

First love
Boy and girl in schoolyard. 1b 1g
In Margulies, D. July 7, 1994: short plays and monologues

Found a peanut
Parable. Children (portrayed by adult actors) quarreling over a bag of money found in yard of Brooklyn tenement, glimpse the greed, betrayal and violence of adult life. 1 act 6m 2w 1 exterior
In Margulies, D. Sight unseen and other plays

Homework
Brief sketch about neighborhood youth. 1m 1g
In Margulies, D. July 7, 1994: short plays and monologues

I don't know what I'm doing
Monologue by woman recalling first love. 1w
In Margulies, D. July 7, 1994: short plays and monologues

Joey
Monologue by directionless man in early twenties celebrating his birthday in Chinese restaurant. 1m
In Margulies, D. July 7, 1994: short plays and monologues

July 7, 1994
Examination of female inner-city doctor's life and work. Slide projections. 2m 4w 2 settings
In 20/20: twenty one-act plays from twenty years of the Humana Festival
In Humana Festival '95
In Margulies, D. July 7, 1994: short plays and monologues

L.A.
Los Angeles bar setting for down-on-his-luck movie star's confidences. 1m 1w 1 interior
In Margulies, D. Pitching to the star and other short plays

Lola
Monologue by Polish immigrant woman, survivor of Auschwitz. 1w
In Margulies, D. July 7, 1994: short plays and monologues

The Loman family picnic. Dramatists 1994 63p
Revised version of play first produced 1989. Black comedy about a middle-class Jewish family in 1960s Coney Island preparing for bar mitzvah. Music, singing. 2 acts 9 scenes 2m 2w 1b 1 interior

—Same
In Margulies, D. Sight unseen and other plays

Louie
Monologue by older hearing-impaired man. 1m
In Margulies, D. July 7, 1994: short plays and monologues

Manny
Monologue by 25-year-old petty criminal. 1m
In Margulies, D. July 7, 1994: short plays and monologues

Margulies, Donald—*Continued*

The model apartment

Black comedy about pair of elderly Holocaust survivors, their schizophrenic daughter and her mildly retarded black boyfriend. 16 scenes 2m 2w 1 interior

In Margulies, D. Sight unseen and other plays

New Year's eve and Kibbutz

Two scenes of Jewish life, one set in Flatbush, Queens the other on Israeli Kibbutz in 1972. 2 parts 3m 1w

In Margulies, D. July 7, 1994: short plays and monologues

Pitching to the star

Hollywood writer finds his script and his integrity challenged by television actress. 2m 2w extra 1 interior

In The Best American short plays, 1992-1993

In Margulies, D. Pitching to the star and other short plays

Sight unseen

Successful Jewish American artist visits ex-lover and husband while in London for exhibition. Questions by German reporter force character to deal with issues of artistic integrity, abandoned love, anti-semitism and the legacy of the Holocaust. 2 acts 8 scenes 2m 2w 1 interior

In Fruitful and multiplying; ed. by E. Schiff

In Margulies, D. Sight unseen and other plays

Somnambulist

Brief monologue by woman describing her death. 1w

In Margulies, D. July 7, 1994: short plays and monologues

Space

Man relates story of break-up with girlfriend. 2m 1 interior

In Margulies, D. Pitching to the star and other short plays

What's wrong with this picture?

Comedy. Eccentric Jewish father and son cope with apparent death of wife and mother. 2 acts 3m 3w 1 interior

In Margulies, D. Sight unseen and other plays

Women in motion

Friendship of two women who work and vacation together sours when both show interest in same man. 5 scenes 2w 1 setting

In Margulies, D. Pitching to the star and other short plays

Zimmer

Jewish record store clerk relates tales of growing up in 1960s. Music, singing. 1 act 1m

In Margulies, D. Pitching to the star and other short plays

Los **mariachis** Mexicanos: "The Brementown musicians." Gerke, P.

Mariamme, consort of Herod I, King of Judea, ca 57-ca. 29 B.C.

Cary, E. The tragedy of Miriam, the fair

Marianne. See Musset, A. de. The moods of Marianne

Marionettes: The gallant Cassian. Schnitzler, A.

Marionettes: The great puppet show. Schnitzler, A.

Marionettes: The puppeteer. Schnitzler, A.

Marisol. Rivera, J.

Marius's mule. Sturgess, B.

Marivaux

La dispute; tr. by Timberlake Wertenbaker

Eighteenth century French romantic comedy. As scientific experiment two girls and two boys have been reared in isolation and then released to determine which sex is more egoistic and inconstant. 20 scenes 5m 5w

In Short plays for young actors; ed. by C. Slaight and J. Sharrar

The triumph of love; tr. by James Magruder. Dramatists 1994 57p

Romantic comedy revolving around disguises, mistaken identity and Spartan princess out to woo heir to throne. 3 acts 4m 3w 1 exterior

—Same; tr. by James Magruder

In Three French comedies

The triumph of love (adaptation) See Wadsworth, S. The triumph of love

Markham, Shelly

Love and shrimp; words by Judith Viorst; music by Shelly Markham. French 1993 65p

Musical revue based on Judith Viorst's poetry about middle-aged married women. 2 acts 3w 1 interior

The **Marlboro** man. Dowling, C.

Marlene. López, E.

Marlowe, Christopher

Edward II. Clarendon Press 1994 188p (The Complete works of Christopher Marlowe v3)

Also known as The troublesome reign of and lamentable death of Edward II. Elizabethan historical tragedy in verse. Portrays defeat and murder of homosexual king by powerful barons. 5 acts 24 scenes 27m 2w extras 1 setting

The Jew of Malta. Clarendon Press 1995 127p (The Complete works of Christopher Marlowe v4)

Variant titles: The famous tragedy of the rich Jew of Malta; The rich Jew of Malta. Elizabethan historical tragedy. Once dignified Jewish merchant, unjustly persecuted by hypocritical Christians, degenerates into stock caricature of greedy Jew willing to sacrifice his daughter for gold. Prologue 5 acts 20 scenes 22m 4w extras 1 setting

—Same. Hern Bks. 1994 106p

Marriage
Albee, E. Finding the sun
Armstrong, G. K. Handcuffs
Beard, P. Swingers
Behn, A. Sir Patient Fancy
Beim, N. Dreams
Blessing, L. Two rooms
Booth, J. Friendly affair
Boothe, C. The women
Butterfield, C. Snowing at Delphi
Canetti, V. The Ogre
Chappell, E. Theft
Chayefsky, P. The bachelor party
Connolly, H. One careful owner
Donaghy, T. Northeast local
Durang, C. The marriage of Bette and Boo
Everett, R. Close to the wind
Fannon, C. Green icebergs
Feydeau, G. The dressmaker
Feydeau, G. A flea in her rear
Feydeau, G. That's my girl
Feydeau, G. and Devalliers, M. All my husbands
Firbank, R. The Princess Zoubaroff
Foote, H. The roads to home: The dearest of friends
Foster, N. Wrong for each other
Godber, J. Lucky sods
Godfrey, P. The modern husband
Goldenthal, J. Charley's girl
Goldstein, J. The end
Goluboff, B. My side of the story
Gow, M. Sweet Phoebe
Granville-Barker, H. The Madras House
Gray, S. Dog days
Gray, S. Dutch uncle
Houston, V. H. Kokoro (true heart)
Huth, A. The trouble with old lovers
Lang, C. Amelia and the man
Linney, R. Songs of love
López, E. I. Spanish eyes
MacLeod, W. The lost colony
Mayer, J. A love affair
McDonald, H. Dream of a common language
Miller, A. Broken glass
Morrison, B. A love song for Ulster: The marriage
Oates, J. C. Gulf War
O'Neill, E. Servitude
Osborne, J. Look back in anger
Pearson, C. Divergent lines
Pope, R. Sandwiches: Eating sandwiches
Potter, D. Cream in my coffee
Prideaux, J. Laughter in the shadow of the trees
Rattigan, T. The Browning version
Robinson, R. T. The cover of life
Robson, J. Mail order bride
Rooney, T. Flip
Schnitzler, A. The Bacchanale
Schnitzler, A. The hour of recognition
Schnitzler, A. Marionettes: The puppeteer
Shaw, B. Getting married
Sondheim, S. Company
Southerne, T. The wives' excuse
Stone, T. Whatever you say
Sweet, J. With and without
Taylor, R. Love poem #98
Thompson, E. Zipless
Vickery, F. Spanish lies
The Washtub
Williams, C. Rebecca
Zark, J. A body of water: White days
See also Adultery; Bigamy; Husband and wife; Weddings

The **marriage.** See Morrison, B. A love song for Ulster: The marriage

Marriage brokerage
Labiche, E. and Delacour, A. The piggy bank

The **marriage** of Bette and Boo. Durang, C.

The **marriage** of Figaro. Beaumarchais, P. A. C. de

The **marriage** proposal. See Chekhov, A. The proposal

The **marrying** of Ann-Leete. Granville-Barker, H.

Mars
Greenspan, D. Son of an engineer

Marshall, Garry, and Ganz, Lowell
Wrong turn at Lungfish. French 1994 94p

Tragicomedy. Encounter between dying, blind college professor and street-wise young woman who volunteers to read to him in hospital. 2 acts 5 scenes 2m 2w 1 interior

Marshall, Sheila L.
c The emperor's New Year

Chinese emperor names years after animals who entertain him at celebration of New Year. Unidentified cast 16 characters extras 1 interior

In Thirty plays from favorite stories; ed. by S. E. Kamerman

Martens, Anne Coulter
y The comeback caper

Trial of TV actress accused of theft. 2 scenes 8m 7w extras 2 interiors

In The Big book of large-cast plays; ed. by S. E. Kamerman

Martens, Anne Coulter—*Continued*

c One life to lose

School children learn about life of Nathan Hale. 3m 3w 3b 2g extras

In Great American events on stage; ed. by S. E. Kamerman

Martha and Elvira. Braithwaite, D.

Martin, Jane

The boy who ate the moon

Drama. Adolescent boy visits doctor's office claiming to have eaten the moon. 1m 1w 1 interior

In Martin, J. Collected plays, 1980-1995

Cementville

Comedy. Satiric look at professional wrestling. 2 acts 5m 9w 1 interior

In A Decade of new comedy: plays from the Humana Festival v2

In Martin, J. Collected plays, 1980-1995

Criminal hearts

Comedy set in Chicago. Woman enlists help of female burglar to exact revenge on her pompous, estranged husband. 2 acts 3 scenes 2m 2w extras 1 interior

In Martin, J. Collected plays, 1980-1995

Cul de sac

Drama. Woman exacts grisly revenge on rapist in secluded alleyway. 1w 1 setting

In Martin, J. Collected plays, 1980-1995

Jack and Jill. French 1996 89p

The birth, life, death and rebirth of a relationship is traced in a series of short scenes. 2 acts 1m 1w extras 1 setting

—Same

In Humana Festival '96

Keely and Du. French (London) 1993 77p

Woman, impregnated by rapist is kidnapped by right-to-lifers on her way to abortion clinic. 18 scenes 2m 3w extras 2 interiors

—Same

In Humana Festival '93

In Martin, J. Collected plays, 1980-1995

Middle-aged white guys. French 1995 63p

Comedy set at garbage dump in Midwest. Three brothers toast memory of woman, wife to one and lover to others, who committed suicide. 4m 3w 1 exterior

—Same

In Humana Festival '95

In Martin, J. Collected plays, 1980-1995

Pomp and circumstance

Composer struggles to adapt his identity to become more pleasing to King. 2m 1 interior

In Actors Theatre of Louisville. Ten-minute plays: v3

In Martin, J. Collected plays, 1980-1995

Shasta Rue

Comedic monologue relating how middle-aged black woman and her daughter crash beauty pageant. 1w

In Martin, J. Collected plays, 1980-1995

Summer

Drama. Adolescent girl grows into womanhood while spending summer of 1949 on relatives' Montana ranch. 4m 3w settings

In Martin, J. Collected plays, 1980-1995

Talking with . . .

Series of self-relevatory monologues by obsessive women. 11w

In Martin, J. Collected plays, 1980-1995

Travelin' show

Drama. Small town hasn't been same since traveling show arrived. 1m

In Martin, J. Collected plays, 1980-1995

Vital signs

Over thirty brief monologues form collage of contemporary women. 2 acts 2m 6w

In Martin, J. Collected plays, 1980-1995

Martin, Judith

c Big burger

Family's vacation delayed as they go on wild car chase searching for the Big Burger. Variable cast 6 characters

In Martin, J. Out of the bag

c The big mess

Mother and son confront mess in boy's room. 1w 1b 1 extra

In Martin, J. Out of the bag

c Hands off! don't touch!

Flowers and butterflies scold human for trying to pick or catch them. 1m extras

In Martin, J. Out of the bag

c I won't take a bath!

Boy gives mother hard time about bathing. Singing. Variable cast 5 characters

In Martin, J. Out of the bag

c Lost in a mall

Children separated from parents while shopping. 1m 1w 1b 1g

In Martin, J. Out of the bag

c Sandwich

Two women fight over enormous sandwich. 1m 2w

In Martin, J. Out of the bag

Martin, Lynn
Waltzing De Niro
Young single woman's dream man. Music. 1m 2w
In Showtime's Act One Festival of one-act plays, 1994

Martin, Manuel
c The legend of the golden coffee bean
Mayan girl travels Central America in search of magic coffee bean. Singing, music, dancing, audience participation. 1m 1g 1 setting
In ¡Aplauso! Hispanic children's theater; ed. by J. Rosenberg

Martin, Steve
Patter for the floating lady
Magician's levitation trick allows assistant to attain her freedom from his suffocating love. 1m 2w 1 setting
In Martin, S. Picasso at the Lapin Agile and other plays

Picasso at the Lapin Agile. French 1994 78p
Paris bar in 1904 scene of imaginary meeting between Pablo Picasso and Albert Einstein. 7m 4w 1 interior

—Same
In Martin, S. Picasso at the Lapin Agile and other plays

WASP
Comedy set in idealized 1950s suburbia depicting stereotypical middle-class white Anglo-Saxon protestant family. 5 scenes 3m 3w 4 interiors
In The Best American short plays, 1994-1995
In EST marathon, 1994
In Martin, S. Picasso at the Lapin Agile and other plays

The zig-zag woman
Woman uses magic in desperate search for affection. 3m 1w 1 setting
In Martin, S. Picasso at the Lapine Agile and other plays

Martin Night. Goldstein, J.

Martini, Clem
Life history of the African elephant
Black comedy. Depressed elephant keeper and accident-prone woman discover connection between their tragic pasts. 1 act 5 scenes 2m 1w 1 interior
In Escape acts; ed. by C. Curran

c Swimmers
Young boy and girl cope with family and school life by escaping into shared dream world. 9 scenes 3m 1w 1g
In Playhouse: six fantasy plays for children

Martinique
Césaire, I. Fire's daughters

Martucci, Vinnie. See Blum, G. jt. auth.

Marty. Chayefsky, P.

Marvin's room. McPherson, S.

Marx, Pamela
c The haunting contest
Play in verse for Halloween. Singing. Large mixed cast 1 setting
In Marx, P. Practical plays

c Hearts and tarts
Play in verse featuring nursery rhyme characters. Large mixed cast 1 setting
In Marx, P. Practical plays

c Old Frost's winter adventure
Children celebrate winter holidays including Hanukkah, Chinese New Year, and Christmas around the world. Singing, dancing. Large mixed cast 1 setting
In Marx, P. Practical plays

c The picnic
On picnic, children learn about ecology. Singing. Large mixed cast 1 setting
In Marx, P. Practical plays

c The rainbow people
People of many colors learn the value of cooperation. Large mixed cast 1 setting
In Marx, P. Practical plays

c The troubled Pilgrim
Pilgrims celebrate first Thanksgiving Day. 3 scenes Large mixed cast 2 exteriors
In Marx, P. Practical plays

Mary, Blessed Virgin, Saint
LaChiusa, M. J. Break
Pintauro, J. Fiat
Porter, D. No more Medea

Mary, Queen of Scots, 1542-1587
Maraini, D. Mary Stuart

Mary Maginn. Finnegan, S.

Mary McLeod Bethune, dream maker. Satchell, M.

Mary Stuart. Maraini, D.

Maryland
Race relations
Heelan, K. Distant fires

Masks. Mori, Ō

Mason, Judi Ann
Daughters of the mock
Feminist drama about three generations of African American women from Louisiana. 2 acts 5 scenes 5w 1 setting
In Classic plays from the Negro Ensemble Company; ed. by P. C. Harrison and G. Edwards

Mason, Keith Antar
For black boys who have considered homicide when the streets were too much
Experimental theater piece about street culture of young African American males. 6m 1 exterior
In Colored contradictions: an anthology of contemporary African-American plays

Mason, Paul Nicholas
The discipline committee. Dramatic 1995 72p
Drama set in Ontario residential school for boys. Young female teacher unearths truth behind act of brutality. 2 acts 3m 1w 1 interior

Mason, Timothy
y Ascension day
Teenagers at Bible camp in 1947 Wisconsin feel stifled by small town life. Singing. 26 scenes 4m 5w 1 setting
In New plays from A.C.T.'s young conservatory [v1]

Babylon gardens. Dramatists 1993 76p
Drama set in Greenwich Village. Young bohemian couples strive to adjust to harsh realities of urban life. 2 acts 21 scenes 5m 5w 1 setting

The fiery furnace. Dramatists 1994 71p
Drama set in Wisconsin farm country between 1950 and 1963. Woman and her two grown daughters look for ways to escape their men. 2 acts 4 scenes 2m 3w 1 interior

y The less than human club
Troubled man looks back to 1968, a turbulent year in his life, with hopes of understanding path his life has taken. 20 scenes 4m 4w 1 setting.
In New plays from A.C.T.'s young conservatory v2

Sorry
Romantic comedy. Young man and woman meet when she accidentally shoots him outside her Greenwich Village apartment. 1m 1w 1 interior
In Short plays for young actors; ed. by J. Slaight and J. Sharrar

Massachusetts
History—1775-1865
Warren, M. The Group

Massage. Berkoff, S.

Massage. Wilcox, M.

Masses and man. Toller, E.

Massinger, Philip. See Fletcher, J. The honest man's fortune; Fletcher, J. jt. auth.

Mast, Edward, and Bensinger, Lenore
c Dinosaurus. Anchorage Press 1994 31p
Shadow play. Dinosaurs encounter humans. Music. Variable cast 13 characters extras

Master & Margarita. Van Itallie, J. C.

The **master** builder. Ibsen, H.

Master class. McNally, T.

Mastergate. Gelbart, L.

Masterpiece theatre. Gilbert, S. M. and Gubar, S.

Masters of the trade. Schenkkan, R.

Mastrosimone, William
Extremities
Drama. Violent encounter between rapist and his victim. 2 acts 5 scenes 1m 3w 1 interior
In Mastrosimone, W. William Mastrosimone: collected plays

Nanawatai!
Drama about Soviet invasion of Afghanistan. Speaking chorus. 2 acts 5 scenes 10m 1w 1 setting
In Mastrosimone, W. William Mastrosimone: collected plays

Shivaree
Comedy. Love develops between sheltered hemophiliac youth and itinerant belly dancer. Background music. 2 acts 2m 3w 1 interior
In Mastrosimone, W. William Mastrosimone: collected plays

A stone carver
First produced under title: The understanding. Retired stonemason and son clash when family home is condemned and father refuses to leave. 2m 1w 1 setting
In Mastrosimone, W. William Mastrosimone: collected plays

Sunshine
Stripper flees porn-king spouse and seeks shelter with burned-out paramedic. 3 scenes 2m 1w 2 interiors
In Mastrosimone, W. William Mastrosimone: collected plays

Tamer of horses
Childless couple take on youthful black offender as foster child. 2 acts 8 scenes 2m 1w 1 setting
In Mastrosimone, W. William Mastrosimone: collected plays

The woolgatherer
Dreary Philadelphia apartment setting for encounter between daydreaming, shy salesgirl and hard-working, hard-drinking truck driver. 2 acts 1m 1w 1 interior
In Mastrosimone, W. William Mastrosimone: collected plays

Mataora and Niwareka in the Underworld. Gerke, P.

Match point. Gilroy, F. D.

Maternal love. See Love, Maternal

Mates. Kenna, P.

Mathematics
c Miller, H. L. That figures!
Stoppard, T. Arcadia

Matheus, John Frederick
Black damp
Black and white coal miners of mixed ethnic origins trapped in cave-in. 2 scenes 8m extras 1 setting
In Lost plays of the Harlem Renaissance; ed. by J. V. Hatch and L. Hamalian
'Cruiter
Lured by industrial recruiter, young black man leaves Georgia farm to work in Detroit munitions factory during World War I. 2 scenes 2m 2w 1 interior
In Black theatre USA [v1]; ed. by J. V. Hatch and T. Shine

Matilda liar! Isitt, D.

Matricide
Pedneault, H. Evidence to the contrary

Matsuo, Bashō, 1644-1694
Bond, E. The bundle

The **Matsuyama** mirror. Houston, V. H.

A **matter** of diplomacy. Adam, A.

Matthiessen, Peter
Men's lives (dramatization) See Pintauro, J. Men's lives

Maturin, C. R.
Bertram; or, The castle of St. Aldobrand
Gothic tragedy about evil, madness and murder. Prologue 5 acts 15 scenes epilogue 10m 5w extras 7 interiors 3 exteriors
In Seven Gothic dramas, 1789-1825

Maupassant, Guy de
The necklace (dramatization) See Dias, E. J. The necklace

Mauritius
Johnson, T. Cries from the mammal house

Mauro, Robert
y Formula for romance
Shy young man and woman get conflicting advice about dating. 2m 2w 1 setting
In The Big book of skits; ed. by S. E. Kamerman
y The job interview
Comedy skit about misunderstandings at employment agency. 1m 1w 1 interior
In The Big book of skits; ed. by S. E. Kamerman
c The Mother Goose olympics
Nursery rhyme characters participate in sporting events. 1m 1w extras 1 exterior
In The Big book of large-cast plays; ed. by S. E. Kamerman

The **mauve** tower. Firbank, R.

May, Bob
9th inning wedding. Clark, I. E. 1994 13p
Comedy. Man's teenage daughter and widowed mother both announce engagements. 2 scenes 4m 3w 1 interior

May, Elaine
Hot line
Comedy. Neurotic woman calls suicide crisis hot line. 3m 1w 1 interior
In The Best American short plays, 1994-1995
In Death defying acts

Mayas
c Hezlep, W. Treasure of the Mayans
c Martin, M. The legend of the golden coffee bean

Mayberry, Bob
The catechism of Patty Reed
Focuses on girl who survived ordeal of Donner Party in Sierra Nevada Mountains in 1846-1847. 1m 1w 1g 1 setting
In Lucky 13; ed. by R. Shuttleworth

Mayer, Jerry
Killjoy. French 1994 90p
Romantic comedy thriller. Woman's plans to murder ex-husband go awry. 2 acts 7 scenes 4m 3w 1 interior
A love affair. French 1995 87p
Romantic comedy exploring 38-year marriage. Two pairs of actors play couple at various times from 1953 to 1991. Music. 2m 3w settings

Mayer, Oliver
Blade to the heat. Dramatists 1996 49p
Drama exploring Latino boxing scene of 1959. Fighter's struggle with his sexual identity manifests itself in ring brutality. 7m 1w 1 interior

Mayr, Grace Alicia
c The printer on Queen Street
Drama portraying 17-year-old Ben Franklin's experience as printer. 6m extras 1 interior
In Great American events on stage; ed. by S. E. Kamerman

Mazza, Rita Norton
Parked. French 1994 59p
Dramatic comedy about platonic love between the sexes. Divorced mother of three, freelance artist father, and unfulfilled suburban mom develop relationship as their children play together. 7 scenes 1m 2w extra 1 setting

McBride, Vaughn. See Crutcher, J. jt. auth.

McBurney, Simon, and Wheatley, Mark
The three lives of Lucie Cabrol. Methuen Drama 1995 54p (Methuen modern plays)
Dramatization of John Berger's short story about life, death, and afterlife of French alpine peasant woman. Prologue 2 acts 12 scenes epilogue 5m 2w 1 setting

McCarthy, Cormac

The stonemason. Vintage Bks. 1995 133p (Vintage international)

Drama set in 1970s Louisville, Kentucky about four generations of African American family of stonemasons. 5 acts 35 scenes 6m 5w 1b 1g extras 1 setting

McCaslin, Nellie

c Angel of the battlefield. Players Press 1993 20p

Drama about life of Clara Barton, Civil War nurse and founder of the Red Cross. 3 scenes 3m 6w extras 3 interiors

c The bailiff's wonderful coat. Players Press 1996 24p

Based on Swedish folktale about bailiff's magic coat that adjusts to fit the deserving. 1 act 3 scenes 4m 5w extras 1 interior

c Bluebonnets. Players Press 1993 18p

Based on American Indian legend. Comanche girl sacrifices most prized possession to save her people. 2 scenes 4m 2w 1b 1g extras

c Borrowed trouble. Players Press 1996 14p

Based on folk tale from Denmark about conflict between obstinate husband and wife. 1 act 4m 1w 1 interior

c Brave new banner. Players Press 1993 20p

Betsy Ross sews first American flag. 3m 4w 1 extra 1 interior

c Christmas fiesta. Players Press 1996 18p

Mexican family and their neighbors gather to celebrate Christmas Eve. 3m 1w 2b 1g extras 1 interior

c The Christmas lamb. Players Press 1996 20p

Visit from Christ Child changes life of woodcarver who makes religious icons. 2 scenes 3m 1w 3b 4g 1 extra 1 interior

Clever Marya and the Czar. Players Press 1996 19p

Based on Russian folktale about clever peasant girl who impresses czar with her wisdom. 3 scenes 5m 1w extras 1 interior

c The coins of Lin Foo. Players Press 1996 16p

Based on Chinese folklore. Wise magistrate tricks thief into admitting he stole poor widow's coins. Background music. 3 scenes 1m 1w 2b extras

c Cold face, warm heart. Players Press 1993 19p

Based on Navajo Indian legend. Girl recognizes goodness of brave in spite of his physical ugliness. 3 scenes 7m 6w extras 1 setting

c Daring, darling Dolly. Players Press 1993 20p

Portrays life of Dolley Madison, flamboyant wife of President James Madison. Music. 3 scenes 2m 1w 1b extras 1 interior 2 exteriors

c A gift of music. Players Press 1996 15p

Radio play based on South American Indian legend. Stranger brings music and song to Amazon village. Singing. 3m 1w 1b 1g extras

c Humai's secret. Players Press 1996 19p

Based on Persian legend. Banished son of Shah is returned to throne. 1 act 5m 2w extras

c Johnny Appleseed. Players Press 1996 15p

Based on American legend. Settlers try to persuade aging Johnny Appleseed to settle in their town. 2 scenes 4m 2w 1b 1g 1 extra 1 interior

c The last horizon. Players Press 1993 24p

Drama set shortly after Civil War. Irish immigrant Nellie Cashman makes name for herself as prospector on West Coast and owner of boarding house in Tombstone. 3 scenes 5m 6w extras 2 interiors 1 exterior

c The lazy ones. Players Press 1996 18p

Comedy based on Colombian folk tale. When monkeys take over human work people miss purpose in life. 1 act 3 scenes 4m 3w extras

c Leading lady. Players Press 1993 19p

Drama about life of 19th century actress and dramatist Anna Cora Ogden Mowatt. 2 scenes epilogue 4m 5w extras 1 interior

y The legend of Minna Lamourrie. Players Press 1993 20p

Set in colonial America near Canadian border at time of French and Indian Wars. Legend of white girl who risks her life to keep peace with Indians. 3 scenes 4m 1w 3g extras 2 exteriors

c The little squire of Flanders. Players Press 1996 20p

Betrayed and exiled knight discovers loyal squire is wife in disguise. Singing. 1 act 3 scenes 4m 4w extras 1 interior 1 exterior

c Maelduin of Arran. Players Press 1996 15p

Radio play based on Irish legend. Maelduin encounters natural and supernatural perils in quest for father's killer. 12m 3w

c Mercy in moccasins. Players Press 1993 15p

Dramatizes legend of Pocahontas, Indian maiden, who saves life of English colonist John Smith. 4m 1g extras 1 interior

c A miracle in the Christmas city. Players Press 1993 15p

Adaptation of Moravian Christmas tale set in colonial Pennsylvania. Native American disuaded from attack by holiday spirit. 2m 1w 1b 1g

c Paul Bunyan: lumberjack. Players Press 1996 15p

Based on American folklore. Loggers recount their adventures with legendary lumberjack. 5m extras 1 setting

c Prelude to fame. Players Press 1993 23p

Drama depicting early life of Harriet Beecher Stowe. 3 scenes 5m 3w 3b 3g extras 3 interiors

McCaslin, Nellie—*Continued*

y A straight shooter. Players Press 1993 15p

Fifteen-year-old Annie Oakley wins shooting contest against vaudeville marksman Frank Butler. 5m 2w extras 1 interior

c Three meals a day. Players Press 1996 18p

Comedy based on Dutch folktale. Rascal bargains to work for farmer for three meals a day, all to be eaten at once. 6m 3w extra 1 interior

c Too many cooks. Players Press 1993 20p

Comedic look at rural family life illustrates origin of adage "too many cooks spoil the broth." 2 scenes 2m 3w 3g extras 1 interior

y Travelers from Olympus. Players Press 1996 18p

Adaptation of Greek myth in which an old, impoverished couple generously share their food with hungry travelers who turn out to be Jupiter and Mercury in disguise. 2 scenes 8m 1w 1 interior

c Who laughs last? Players Press 1996 19p

Based on Polish folklore. Retired Jester and wife trick king and queen into providing promised pension. 3 scenes 2m 2w extras 2 interiors

McCauley, Robbie

Sally's rape

Drama about race, privilege and power with audience participation. Two women, one white, one black explore history of rape as tool of oppression. 2w 1 setting

In Black theatre USA [v2]; ed. by J. V. Hatch and T. Shine

In Moon marked and touched by sun; ed. by S. Mahone

McClinton, Marion

Stones and bones

Two African American couples struggle to relate. 2m 2w

In 20/20: twenty one-act plays from twenty years of the Humana Festival

In Actors Theatre of Louisville. Ten-minute plays: v3

In Humana Festival '94

McConnell, Jean

Dancers

Comedy about tea-dancing world of two widows. 2w 1 exterior

In McConnell, J. Deckchairs

Doggies

Comedy about eccentricities of dog owners. 2w 1 exterior

In McConnell, J. Deckchairs

Early blight

Doomed relationship between woman and her elderly mother. 2w 1 exterior

In McConnell, J. Deckchairs

Late frost

Woman finds out best friend had affair with late husband. 2w 1 exterior

In McConnell, J. Deckchairs

A lovesome thing. French (London) 1994 27p

Comedy. Members of English women's club fill in for benefactor's gardener with disastrous results. 8w 1 interior

Shoppers

Comedy. Two well-to-do women shopaholics have surprising secret. 2w 1 exterior

In McConnell, J. Deckchairs

McCullough, L. E.

y Abe Lincoln for the defense

Based on historical 1858 trial. Lincoln defends friend's son against murder charge. 12m 2w 1b extras 1 setting

In McCullough, L. E. Plays of America from American folklore for young actors

y Annie Christmas and the Natchez Trace bandits

Drama based on legendary Mississippi ferry boat navigator and roustabout Annie Christmas. Singing, music. 5m 4w 1b 1g 1 setting

In McCullough, L. E. Plays of America from American folklore for young actors

c Annie Oakley: little sure-shot

Drama based on life and career of sharpshooter in Buffalo Bill's Wild West Show. Singing. 5m 5w 1b 1g extras 1 setting

In McCullough, L. E. Plays of the Wild West v1

c The beggar in the blanket

Based on Vietnamese folktale. Wife uses deception to teach husband true value of friendship and family loyalty. Music. 7m 1w extras 1 setting

In McCullough, L. E. Plays of America from American folklore for children

c Bird woman of the Shoshones

Drama based on life of Sacagawea, Shoshone guide to Lewis and Clark expedition. Singing. 9m 3w extras 1 setting

In McCullough, L. E. Plays of the Wild West v1

c Bring a torch, Jeannette, Isabella

Based on French Christmas carol. Three girls celebrate Nativity on Christmas eve in 1676 Provence. Dancing, singing 2m 3g extras 1 interior

In McCullough, L. E. The plays of the songs of Christmas

McCullough, L. E.—*Continued*

c The buffalo hunters

Old man recalls hunting buffalo in the post Civil War West. Singing, background music. Large mixed cast 1 setting

In McCullough, L. E. Plays of the Wild West v2

c Chief Sarah, the Indian Joan of Arc

Drama based on life of Paiute chief Sarah Winnemucca. Singing. 8m 11w 2g

In McCullough, L. E. Plays of the Wild West v2

c The cobbler's pipe

Christmas drama based on Dutch folklore, set in 1660 New Amsterdam. 4m 2w 1b 1g extras 1 setting

In McCullough, L. E. Plays of America from American folklore for children

c El Corrido de Gregorio Cortez

Based on folk ballad about Mexican American outlaw Gregorio Cortez. Singing. 11m 4w

In McCullough, L. E. Plays of the Wild West v2

c Darling Clementine: a tail of old San Francisco

Historical drama set during California gold rush. Growth of San Francisco from cat's point of view. Singing. Large mixed cast 1 setting

In McCullough, L. E. Plays of the Wild West v1

c Diamonds in the snow

Grandfather recalls 1940s childhood Christmas when he believed in miracles. Singing. 2m 2w 2b 2g 1 interior

In McCullough, L. E. The plays of the songs of Christmas

c Fandango!

Westerners of many cultural backgrounds come together for musical celebration. Singing, music. 9m 5w extras

In McCullough, L. E. Plays of the Wild West v2

y The flames of hell (Les flammes d'enfer)

Drama with roots in Louisiana folklore about Cajun musician tempted by Devil. Singing, music, dancing. 3m extras 1 exterior

In McCullough, L. E. Plays of America from American folklore for young actors

c "Git along, little dogies!"

Cowboys prepare for cattle drive on Old Chisholm Trail. Singing. 8m 2w extras 1 setting

In McCullough, L. E. Plays of the Wild West v1

c The glass mountain

Drama set in 19th century Michigan based on Finnish American folklore. Young man bests brothers to win boss' daughter. Music. 5m 2w extras

In McCullough, L. E. Plays of America from American folklore for children

c The golden spike

First transcontinental railroad is completed in Promontory Point, Utah in 1869. Singing. 16m 2w extras 1 setting

In McCullough, L. E. Plays of the Wild West v1

c Gluscabi and his magic game bag

Based on North American Indian legend. Great Hunter teaches people to respect animals and hunt wisely. Music. 2m 1w 1b extras 1 exterior

In McCullough, L. E. Plays of America from American folklore for children

c Go tell it on the mountain

Stranger resolves Southern family feud during 1898 Christmas holiday. Singing, background music. 7m 5w 1 interior

In McCullough, L. E. The plays of the songs of Christmas

c Good King Wenceslas

Based on traditional Christmas carol. Ruler of Bohemia shows kindness to poor family on St. Stephen's day 931 A.D. Singing. 5m 2w extras 1 setting

In McCullough, L. E. The plays of the songs of Christmas

c Greasepaint and Ginthons: the medicine show comes to town

Patent medicine show comes to Western town in 1880s. Singing. 3m 2w 1b extras

In McCullough, L. E. Plays of the Wild West v2

c Great medicine painter

Drama based on life of George Catlin, painter of American West. Singing. 12m 5w 1 setting

In McCullough, L. E. Plays of the Wild West v1

y Greta Nilson's magic mare (La caballa blanca)

Drama set in 1852 based on Blackfoot tribal legend. Pioneers on Oregon Trail encounter "the Ghost Horse." Music. 8m 3w 1 exterior

In McCullough, L. E. Plays of America from American folklore for young actors

c "Have floss, will travel": the ever-so-true saga of Hiram T. McRoot, frontier dentist

Dentist treats outlaw in Old West. Singing. 6m 1w extras 1 setting

In McCullough, L. E. Plays of the Wild West v2

McCullough, L. E.—*Continued*

c Here we come a-wassailing

Elizabethan English family is entertained by Mummers at Christmas time. Singing. 9m 3w 2b 2g 1 interior

In McCullough, L. E. The plays of the songs of Christmas

c The honest miller

Drama set in 19th century New Mexico incorporating elements from several Mexican-American folktales. 4m 3w extras 1 setting

In McCullough, L. E. Plays of America from American folklore for children

c How the people got fire

Drama based on Maidu tribal legend about origins of fire. Unidentified cast 19 characters extras 1 exterior

In McCullough, L. E. Plays of America from American folklore for children

c Jesse James: blood on the saddle

Drama based on life of Western outlaw. Singing. Large mixed cast 1 setting

In McCullough, L. E. Plays of the Wild West v2

c Jingle bells

James Pierpont of Boston creates his classic holiday song to encourage horse to pull carriage on Christmas day 1857. Singing. 4m 2w 1b 1g extras 1 exterior

In McCullough, L. E. The plays of the songs of Christmas

y Johnny Appleseed and Willie Crabgrass

Based on American folklore. Johnny Appleseed confronts evil cousin who threatens environment. 5m 3w 2g extras 1 setting

In McCullough, L. E. Plays of America from American folklore for young actors

c Klondike fever

Drama in verse based on life of Nellie Cashman, Alaska gold prospector and dogsledder, set 1898. 5m 1w extras 1 setting

In McCullough, L. E. Plays of the Wild West v1

c The laziest girl in the world

Play set in 1890s Boston based on Irish folktale. Fairies help lazy girl find love. Music. 2m 7w extras 1 interior

In McCullough, L. E. Plays of America from American folklore for children

c Let us go, O shepherds

Boy in search of lost lamb leads shepherds to New Mexican desert Nativity on Christmas eve 1701. Singing. 7m 4w 1b 1 exterior

In McCullough, L. E. The plays of the songs of Christmas

c Let's have a hoedown!

Drama showcasing folklore and history found in some 19th century American folk songs. Music, dancing, singing. 4m 1w extras 1 interior

In McCullough, L. E. Plays of America from American folklore for children

c The little old sod shanty

Homesteaders survive hardships in 19th century North Dakota. Singing, dancing. 6m 3w extras 1 setting

In McCullough, L. E. Plays of the Wild West v1

c Magnus Fourpenny and the black bear birthday bash

Based on folklore from Big Thicket region of Texas. Hunter encounters bear's birthday party. Music, singing. 4m 4w extras 1 setting

In McCullough, L. E. Plays of America from American folklore for children

y The most dangerous woman in America

Drama based on life of labor activist Mother Jones. Singing. 10m 2w 1b extras 1 setting

In McCullough, L. E. Plays of America from American folklore for young actors

c The most expensive bonnet in all Indiana

Drama based on folktales set in 1840 Indiana. Captain loses flatboat race because of wife's vanity. Singing. 6m 2w 1b 1g extras 1 setting

In McCullough, L. E. Plays of America from American folklore for children

c Mr. & Mrs. Charlie T. Mule

Dramatization of Appalachian folk tale. Fiddle music breaks spell that turned man and woman into beasts. Music, dancing. 4m 3w 2b 1g extras 1 setting

In McCullough, L. E. Plays of America from American folklore for children

c Ninth Cavalry to the rescue!

General Colin Powell pays tribute to American cavalry soldiers of the Old West. Singing. 8m extras

In McCullough, L. E. Plays of the Wild West v2

c O, Christmas tree

Saint Boniface introduces Christianity to the Teuton people on Christmas eve of 720 A.D. Singing. 5m extras 1 exterior

In McCullough, L. E. The plays of the songs of Christmas

c O thou joyful day

St. Nicholas prevents widower from selling daughters into slavery on Christmas in 320 A.D. Sicily. Singing. 4m 5w 1 interior

In McCullough, L. E. The plays of the songs of Christmas

McCullough, L. E.—*Continued*

c Outlaw gold: the lost treasure of Comanche Creek

Children are intrigued by Western legend of lost treasure. 3m 1b 2g extras 1 setting

In McCullough, L. E. Plays of the Wild West v2

c El paseo del vaquero (The ride of the vaquero)

In 1890 Chicago, cowboy tells children about life of vaqueros, Mexican American cowboys, in 1850 Sante Fe. Singing. 5m 1w 2b 1g 1 setting

In McCullough, L. E. Plays of the Wild West v1

Patches solves a wedding riddle

Based on African American folklore from Georgia Sea Islands. Gullah boy solves riddle and wins hand of governor's daughter. Music. 3m 3w extras 1 setting

In McCullough, L. E. Plays of America from American folklore for children

c Pony Express rider

Present day school children learn about Pony Express of 1860. Singing. 4m 1w 1b 2g extras 1 setting

In McCullough, L. E. Plays of the Wild West v1

c The rainbow cradle

In 1876 Arizona territory, Navajo grandmother relates creation myth. Singing. 4m 4w 1b 1g extras 1 setting

In McCullough, L. E. Plays of the Wild West v1

c Return of the Red Phantom

Play based on American folklore of the sea. Captain and mutineers of 19th century clipper ship return as ghosts. Singing. 5m 2b 1g extras 1 setting

In McCullough, L. E. Plays of America from American folklore for children

c Rocky Mountain rendezvous

Western mountain men, including Jim Beckwourth, tell stories from American Indian folklore. Singing. 9m 3w extras 1 setting

In McCullough, L. E. Plays of the Wild West v2

y The seven Chan brothers of Paiute Pass

Chinese folk tale reset in 1892 American West. Seven identical Chinese brothers struggle against discrimination in mining town. Singing, music. 16m 3w extras 1 setting

In McCullough, L. E. Plays of America from American folklore for young actors

c Shlemazl goes to paradise

Drama based on folklore of Eastern European Jews. Music. 8m 1w extras 1 setting

In McCullough, L. E. Plays of America from American folklore for children

c Silent night

Austrian priest Joseph Mohr creates his classic Christmas carol in 1818 Oberndorf church. Singing. 4m 1w 1b extras

In McCullough, L. E. The plays of the songs of Christmas

y The splendid voyage of Kitty Doyle

Drama based on 1873 maritime incident. Treachery was suspected when The Atlantic sailing from Liverpool to Halifax, foundered upon rocks and lost over 500 passengers. Singing. 6m 4w extras 1 setting

In McCullough, L. E. Plays of America from American folklore for young actors

c Tillie Edelpickel's sack of lies

Drama set in 1776 based on folklore of Pennsylvania Dutch. Clever girl saves brother from British soldiers and aids General Washington. 5m 4w extras 1 setting

In McCullough, L. E. Plays of America from American folklore for children

c Turquoise Tom, the versifying bandit of Old California

Western drama based on life of stagecoach bandit known as Black Bart. Singing. 5m 1w extras 1 setting

In McCullough, L. E. Plays of the Wild West v2

c The twelve days of Christmas

Play in verse based on traditional Christmas carol. Prince gives gifts to princess on Christmas. Singing. 2m 2w extras 1 interior

In McCullough, L. E. The plays of the songs of Christmas

c Vinegar Pete's calico whisker pie

Cowboys suspect cook of baking missing cat in pie. Singing. Variable cast 17 characters

In McCullough, L. E. Plays of the Wild West v2

c We three Kings of Orient are

Based on Christmas carol. Three Kings bring gifts to newborn Jesus. Singing. 8m 2w extras

In McCullough, L. E. The plays of the songs of Christmas

y When people could fly

Drama based on African American folklore. Slaves find strength to endure by harnessing spiritual knowledge within themselves. Singing, music, dancing. 4m 1w extras 1 exterior

In McCullough, L. E. Plays of America from American folklore for young actors

McCullough, L. E.—*Continued*

y "You're live with Bigfoot Wallace!"

Television talk show features legendary American tall tale heroes. 6m 2w extras 1 interior

In McCullough, L. E. Plays of America from American folklore for young actors

c Zebra dun

Based on folk song. Cowboys are surprised by stranger who tames wild horse. Singing. 8m 1 exterior

In McCullough, L. E. Plays of the Wild West v1

McCusker, Paul

Pap's place. Lillenas 1993 59p

Family celebrates last two birthdays of patriarch's life. 2 acts 5m 2w 2 interiors

McDonagh, Martin

The beauty queen of Leenane. Methuen Drama in association with the Royal Court Theatre 1996 60p (Royal Court writers series)

Part of Leenane trilogy. Domestic drama set in Connemara, County Galway. Aging mother's interference in middle-aged daughter's romantic life leads to terrifying act of violence. 9 scenes 2m 2w 1 interior

The cripple of Inishman. Methuen 1997 82p (Methuen modern plays)

First of a projected trilogy to be set on various Aran Islands. Life of crippled adolescent orphan living with aunts on Inishman Island affected by appearance of Hollywood film crew filming 1934 documentary Man of Aran. 2 acts 6 scenes 5m 4w film projection 3 interiors 1 exterior

The lonesome West. Methuen Drama in association with the Royal Court Theatre 1997 69p (Royal Court writers series)

Part of the Leenane trilogy. Domestic drama set in Galway about two brothers living alone following father's death. Young local priest attempts to reconcile brothers before their petty squabbles erupt in violence. 7 scenes 3m 1w 1 interior

A skull in Connemara. Methuen Drama in association with Royal Court Theatre 1997 66p (Royal Court writers series)

Part of the Leenane trilogy. Man hired to disinter bones in Irish village cemetery is rumored to have played role in wife's sudden death seven years earlier. 4 scenes 3m 1w 1 interior

McDonald, Heather

Dream of a common language. French 1993 99p

Set in 1874 Paris. Love story of married couple, both painters. 2 acts 8 scenes 2m 3w 1b 1 exterior

—Same

In Here to stay: five plays from the Women's Project; ed. by J. Miles

Faulkner's bicycle. French 1994 74p

Drama set in Oxford, Mississippi about fear of senility, intellectual isolation and failure. Explores psychological impact of Faulkner's legacy on neighbor and her daughters. 25 scenes 1m 3w 1 setting

McDonough, Jerome

Butterfly. Clark, I. E. 1993 22p

Based on story of Madame Butterfly found in John Luther Long's novella, David Belasco's play, and Puccini's opera. American soldier abandons Japanese sweetheart in World War II Nagasaki. Background music. 3 scenes 6m 4w extras 1 setting

McDonough, Jerome, and Alderete, Betty

c Posadas. Clark, I. E. 1994 26p

Bilingual play in Spanish and English. During Christmas season, Hispanic children re-enact Joseph and Mary's search for shelter. Background music. Variable cast

McDonough, Virginia Miller

y All that glitters . . .

Girl accuses guest of stealing mother's wedding ring. 1m 2w 2g 1 interior

In The Big book of skits; ed. by S. E. Kamerman

McGillivray, David, and Zerlin, Walter

Chase me up Farndale Avenue, s'il vous plaît! French (London) 1994 63p

Comedy. Inept amateur women's drama society stages French farce. Prologues 2 acts 1m 4w 1 interior

The Farndale Avenue Housing Estate Townspeople's Guild Operatic Society's production of The Mikado; music arranged by Sue Van Colle. French (London) 1993 75p

Musical comedy. Inept amateur women's operatic society stages Gilbert and Sullivan's The Mikado. Prologue 2 acts 3m 19w 1 interior

McGovern, Christopher

c The ugly duck; book & lyrics by James Still; music by Christopher McGovern. Anchorage Press 1995 69p

Musical about individuality and perseverance. New York City boy adjusts to life with eccentric aunt in small town Kansas. 12 scenes 1m 1w 3b 1g extras 1 setting

McGrath, John

Blood red roses

Examination of labor-management relations in Scotland during the Thatcher years. 2 acts 22 scenes 3m 3w extras 1 setting

In McGrath, J. Six-pack: plays for Scotland

Border warfare

Historical look at Anglo-Scottish relations from the Dark Ages to the 1990s. Prologue 6 scenes Variable cast 1 setting

In McGrath, J. Six-pack: plays for Scotland

McGrath, John—*Continued*

The Cheviot, the stag and the black, black oil

Political satire presented in form of traditional Highland ceilidh, telling story of capitalistic exploitation of Scottish Highlands. Music, singing. 1 act Variable cast 1 setting

In McGrath, J. Six-pack: plays for Scotland

Joe's drum

Political drama set in 1979 Scotland. Music, singing. 2 acts Variable cast 1 setting

In McGrath, J. Six-pack: plays for Scotland

Out of our heads

Drama about political and social apathy set in 1970s Scotland. Music, singing. 2 acts Variable cast 1 setting

In McGrath, J. Six-pack: plays for Scotland

Random happenings in the Hebrides

Drama about failed politics and compromised hopes set in 1960s Scotland. 2 acts 8 scenes 15m 8w 1 setting

In McGrath, J. Six-pack: plays for Scotland

McGuinness, Frank

Baglady

Monologue by homeless woman haunted by violent past. Singing. 1w

In McGuinness, F. Plays: one

Carthaginians

Drama set in Irish graveyard about Northern Catholic culture. Six people, haunted by memories of Bloody Sunday, await fulfillment of vision. 7 scenes 4m 3w 1 exterior

In McGuinness, F. Plays: one

A doll's house. Faber & Faber 1997 106p

Adaptation of Henrik Ibsen's play in which woman decides to leave family to pursue personal freedom. 3 acts 3m 4w 2b 1 extra 1 interior

The factory girls

Revised version of drama first produced 1982. Five women in Donegal shirt factory decide to confront both management and union in attempt to control their future. 8 scenes 2m 5w 1 setting

In McGuinness, F. Plays: one

Innocence

Drama set in 1606 Rome depicting the artist Caravaggio as agonized, self-destructive, homosexual anarchist. 2 parts 6m 3w 2 interiors

In McGuinness, F. Plays: one

Observe the sons of Ulster marching towards the Somme

Drama about sacrifice made by 36th (Ulster) Division at Battle of the Somme, 1916, and its significance in loyalist Protestant mind. 4 parts 9m 1 exterior 2 interiors

In McGuinness, F. Plays: one

Someone who'll watch over me. French 1994 78p

Comedy-drama. Englishman, Irishman and an American held hostage in Middle East cell help each other face fear, boredom and frustration. Prologue 9 scenes 3m 1 interior

McGullion, Bart

Murdermind. French 1994 111p

Psychological thriller set on Southern estate. Gothic family tale of one hundred fifty years of horror, love, murder and insanity. 2 acts 6 scenes 3m 3w 1 interior

McIntyre, Clare

Low level panic

Three women share their intimate thoughts about pornography, sex and weight problems. 8 scenes 3w extras 1 setting

In McIntyre, C. My heart's a suitcase & Low level panic

My heart's a suitcase

Parable of modern materialism. Two female friends spend weekend in grand, empty seaside flat. 10 scenes 2m 4w 1 interior

In McIntyre, C. My heart's a suitcase & Low level panic

The thickness of skin. Hern Bks. in association with Royal Court Theatre 1996 72p (An Instant Playscript)

Middle-class English family reacts to contemporary social problems. 14 scenes 3m 4w 4 interiors 3 exteriors

McJonah. Richardson, D.

McKee, Julie

The 'far-flung'

Women in provincial New Zealand parish of early 1950s plan pageant to celebrate visit by Queen Elizabeth. 1 act 2 scenes 1m 4w 1 interior

In EST marathon, 1994

McKelvey, Peter

House of secrets. French (London) 1994 74p

Police suspect burglar is lodger from boarding house in rundown London neighborhood. 2 acts 5 scenes 3m 3w 1 interior

McLachlan, Lawrentia, 1866-1953

Whitemore, H. The best of friends

McLaren, Maria

c Seven with one blow. Players Press 1994 24p

Comic retelling of Grimms' fairy tale about tailor's apprentice who gains fame and fortune after killing seven flies with one blow. 3 scenes 7m 3w 2 settings

McLaughlin, Thomas

Greatest hits

Psychological thriller about deadly game of words and deception between two Irish terrorists. 1 act 2m 1 interior

In Greatest hits: four Irish one-act plays; ed. by D. Bolger

McLean, Duncan

Julie Allardyce

Drama set in and around Aberdeen, Scotland. Oil industry provides great wealth but upsets traditional social relationships. Singing. 18 scenes 4m 2w 1 setting

In Made in Scotland; ed. by I. Brown and M. Fisher

McLeod, Kevin R.

Broken hearts

During heart transplant surgery woman communicates with her dead grandmother and heart donor. 3w 1 interior

In Actors Theatre of Louisville. Ten-minute plays: v3

McLure, James

Ghost world. Dramatists 1995 33p

Playwright meets character from one of his abandoned projects on bench in Central Park. 2m 1 exterior

McMahon, James P., and Ryan, Nancy

c Buttonbush. Players Press 1996 31p

Musical comedy. Frogs rescue alligators from captors. 2 acts 3 scenes 1m 2w 3b 4g extras 2 exteriors

McNally, Terrence

And things that go bump in the night

Locked in after dark against nameless enemy, family entices dissenter into home and murders him. 3 acts 4m 2w 1 interior

In McNally, T. Collected plays v2

Andre's mother

Drama set in Central Park about emotional impact of AIDS. Homosexual man encounters his dead lover's mother at memorial service. 1 act 2m 2w 1 exterior

In McNally, T. Andre's mother and other short plays

In Telling tales: new one-act plays; by E. Lane

Bad habits: Dunelawn

Sanatorium uses drugs and gibberish to treat personal neuroses. 1 act 6m 2w 1 setting

In McNally, T. 15 short plays

Bad habits: Ravenswood

Elegant sanatorium tries to cure couples suffering from emotional problems through total permissiveness. 1 act 6m 2w 1 setting

In McNally, T. 15 short plays

Botticelli

Play about the inhumanity of war. 1 act 3m 1 exterior

In McNally, T. 15 short plays

Bringing it all back home

Satire. Societal indifference reflected in family's superficial reaction to son's death in Vietnam. 1 act 3m 3w 1 interior

In McNally, T. 15 short plays

¡Cuba si!

Cuban revolutionary fails in her attempt to start anarchy and revolution in the United States from her Central Park encampment. 1m 5w 1 exterior

In McNally, T. 15 short plays

Dusk

Hunk on beach pursued by two women. 1 act 1m 2w 1 exterior

In By the sea, by the sea, by the beautiful sea

Frankie and Johnny in the Clair de Lune

Romantic comedy. Waitress and short-order cook discover they are in love after what could have been just a one-night stand. Background music. 2 acts 1m 1w extra 1 interior

In Best American plays: 9th series, 1983-1992

Hidden agendas

Satirical look at non-profit arts institutions. Variable cast 13 characters 1 interior

In McNally, T. 15 short plays

In McNally, T. Andre's mother and other short plays

Love! Valour! Compassion! Dramatists 1995 104p

Eight gay men spend three summer holiday weekends at country house in Dutchess County, New York. 3 acts 8m 1 setting

Love! Valour! Compassion! (condensation)

In The Best plays of 1994-1995

Master class. Dramatists 1996 51p

Drama portrays the legendary Maria Callas as she conducts coaching sessions. 2 acts 3m 3w 1 setting

—Same. Plume Bks. 1996 62p

Master class (condensation)

In The Best plays of 1995-1996

Next

Comedy. Reluctant draftee reports for physical to Amazon-like sergeant. 1m 1w 1 interior

In McNally, T. 15 short plays

Noon

Comedy. Practical joker summons group of sex perverts with different hang-ups to an intimate rendezvous. 1 act 3m 2w 1 interior

In McNally, T. 15 short plays

A perfect Ganesh. Dramatists 1994 97p

Comic drama about prejudice, AIDS and suffering. Two middle-aged American women of means travel to India on spiritual journey accompanied by Hindu god Ganesha. 2 acts 10 scenes 2m 2w settings

A perfect Ganesh (condensation)

In The Best plays of 1993-1994

Prelude & Liebestod

Orchestra conductor recalls sexual experiences with man and woman. 3m 2w 1 interior

In McNally, T. 15 short plays

In McNally, T. Andre's mother and other short plays

The Ritz

Comedy set in a men's bathhouse about a fugitive hiding out from a gangster family's vengeance. 2 acts 8m 3w extras 1 interior

In McNally, T. 15 short plays

McNally, Terrence—*Continued*

Street talk

Confrontational monologue about theater in America. 1m 1w

In McNally, T. 15 short plays

In McNally, T. Andre's mother and other short plays

Sweet Eros

Drama. Unsettled young man kidnaps and enslaves unsuspecting girl. 11 scenes 1m 1w 1 interior

In McNally, T. 15 short plays

Where has Tommy Flowers gone?

Tragicomedy. Young anti-hero becomes progressively alienated from life. 2 acts 6m 7w 1 setting

In McNally, T. Collected plays v2

Whiskey

Comedy. Dramatizes interactions of a drunken group of western performers on tour. 1 act 3m 2w extras 1 setting

In McNally, T. 15 short plays

The wibbly, wobbly, wiggly dance that Cleopatterer did

Drama about one-night stand between lonely young man and male hustler. 2m

In McNally, T. 15 short plays

In McNally, T. Andre's mother and other short plays

Witness

A presidential assassination is the focal point of this black comedy depicting violence in America. 3m 1w 1 interior

In McNally, T. 15 short plays

McPherson, Conor

The good thief

Monologue by small-time Irish criminal. 1m

In McPherson, C. This lime tree bower: three plays

Rum and vodka

Monologue. Working class Irish husband loses his job, fights with wife, and spends drunken night with young woman. 1m

In McPherson, C. This lime tree bower: three plays

St Nicholas

Black comedy about obsession, seduction and entrapment. Jaded London theater critic falls for beautiful actress. 2 parts. 1m 1 setting

In McPherson, C. St Nicholas & The weir

This lime tree bower

Hard-boiled suspense yarn. Three men from small Irish seaside town tell overlapping tales of fateful night. 3m 1 setting

In McPherson, C. This lime tree bower: three plays

The weir

Drama set in rural Irish bar. Tables are turned on local men swapping spooky stories in attempt to impress young woman. 4m 1w 1 interior

In McPherson, C. St Nicholas & The weir

McPherson, Scott

Marvin's room. Dramatists 1993 68p

Drama about mental and physical illness. Woman with leukemia selflessly cares for her dysfunctional family. 2 acts 14 scenes 5m 4w 1 setting

McQueen, Noel. See Hark, M. jt. auth.

McWeeny, Drew, and Swan, Scott

Broken bones

Argument between a husband and wife turns violent. 1m 2w 1 interior

In Act One '95

Sticks and stones

Racial prejudices surface when Jewish trial lawyer confronts bigoted policeman client. 2m 1 interior

In Showtime's Act One Festival of one-act plays, 1994

Me and Jezebel. Fuller, E. L.

Me and Mamie O'Rourke. Donoghue, M. A.

Me 'n' Alfred. Beechy High School Drama Club

Mea culpa. Solórzano, C.

Mead, Kathy

After the child. Miller, J. G. 1995 20p

Medium makes contact with spirit of dead child and eases parents' grief. 2m 3w 1 interior

And who will pay the rent? Kenyon-Deane 1995 27p

Scam artists prey on visually impaired old woman living alone in flat. 3 scenes 4w 1 interior

The Anderson. Miller, J. G. 1995 23p

Set in 1940s London. Family gets trapped in blitz. 2m 2w 1 interior

Crying out loud. Kenyon-Deane 1995 22p

Family tries to help woman suffering from agoraphobia. 5w 1 interior

Line of descent. Miller, J. G. 1992 30p

Jewish family fleeing Nazis encounters family escaping from Soviet Union. 1 act 2 scenes 1m 4w 1 interior

The other other woman. Kenyon-Deane 1992 27p

Wife of unfaithful husband joins forces with his ex-mistresses. 2 scenes 6w 1 interior

This common bond. Miller, J. G. 1992 29p

Humorous drama describing convalescence of two attempted suicides. 1 act 2 scenes 1m 1w

Meadows, Karen Jones
Henrietta
Follows relationship between two African American women, one driven by tragedy to assume lunatic pose and the other determined to help her. 2 acts 9 scenes 1m 2w
In The National black drama anthology; ed. by W. King

Mean tears. Gill, P.

Meara, Anne
After-play. Dramatists 1996 58p
Two post-middle-aged couples converse in sleek Manhattan restaurant having just attended latest "must-see" play. 7 scenes 2m 2w 1 interior
After-play (condensation)
In The Best plays of 1994-1995

Meat and two veg. Beard, P.

Medea (Greek mythology)
Churchill, C. Lives of the great poisoners
Durang, C. and Wasserstein, W. Medea
Euripides. Medea
Gurney, A. R. The Golden Fleece
Porter, D. No more Medea

Medea's children. Lysander, P. and Osten, S.

Medical ethics
Kingsley, S. Men in white
Shaw, B. The doctor's dilemma

Medical profession. See Physicians

Medici, Lorenzo de', 1449-1492
Warner, F. Living creation

The **medieval** murders. Chiodo, T.

Medley, Cassandra
Dearborn Heights
Drama about racism and friendship. Two African American women meet for lunch in suburban Detroit diner. 2w 1 interior
In Act One '95
In The Best American short plays, 1995-1996
In EST Marathon '95

Medoff, Mark
y Big Mary
Hanging of circus elephant accused of crime vehicle for examination of racism and bigotry in small Tennessee town in 1916. Music. Large mixed cast 1 setting
In Around the world in 21 plays; ed. by L. Swortzell

The homage that follows. Dramatists 1995 78p
Psychological drama set in Southwest. Events surrounding murder of her substance-abusing TV-star daughter force recently widowed woman to re-examine the past. 2 acts 3m 2w 1 setting

c Kringle's window. Dramatists 1994 64p
Modern Christmas fable about sisters caught in middle of parents' trial separation during holiday season. 2 acts 10 scenes 2m 4w 3b 4g 1 setting

c Stefanie hero. Dramatists 1994 80p
Fantasy adventure. Princess battles evil. 2 acts 15 scenes 8m 8w 1b 1g

Stumps. Dramatists 1995 80p
Violence results when two Vietnam vets set out to make film with porn star and her manipulative "manager." 2 acts 14 scenes 3m 2w 1 setting

Meet my husbands. Carmichael, F.

The **meeting.** Stetson, J.

Meeting ends. Warner, F.

Meetings
Gurney, A. R. The rape of Bunny Stuntz

Megged, Aharon
Hanna Senesh
Drama about Hungarian Jewish underground fighter captured and executed by Nazis during World War II. 2 acts 13m 4w extras 2 interiors
In Israeli Holocaust drama; ed. by M. Taub

Mehta, Dina
Brides are not for burning. Rupa & Co. 1993 94p
Drama about the dowry system still prevalent in contemporary India. 2 acts 8 scenes 8m 3w

Meilhac, Henri, and Halévy, Ludovic
Mardi Gras (La mi-carème); tr. by Norman R. Shapiro
Farce revolving around woman with numerous admirers all converging on Paris hotel for Mardi Gras. 10m 5w 1 setting
In A Flea in her rear, and other vintage French farces

Signor Nicodemo (Tout pour les dames!); tr. by Norman R. Shapiro
Misunderstandings abound when well-meaning, wealthy Italian with poor command of language gets involved in bachelor's financial and emotional problems. 5m 2w 1 interior
In A Flea in her rear, and other vintage French farces

Mein Kampf. Tabori, G.

Meinhof, Ulrike, 1934-1976
Rubess, B. No. here comes Ulrike Meinhof

Melbourne (Australia)
Sewell, S. The garden of granddaughters

Mélesville. See Scribe, E. jt. auth.

Melfi, Mary
Sex therapy. Guernica 1996 118p
Black comedy about group therapist and his patients. 13 scenes 3m 5w 1 interior

Mellor, Kay
A passionate woman. French (London) 1996 56p
Comedy. On morning of son's wedding middle-aged English woman recalls her youth and summons up courage to escape the men who have prevented her from fulfilling her potential. 2 acts 3m 1w 1 setting

Mellow drama. Welsh, D.

Melodrama
Boucicault, D. Octoroon
Carmichael, F. Damsel of the desert
Christiansen, D. M. Who's mining the mercantile?
Fitzball, E. The inchcape bell
y Hurst, Z. B. and Hurst, J. R. The cowhand's Christmas Carol
y Kelly, T. Here come the cows
c Kelly, T. Treachery at Cartilage Creek
y Kelly, T. You can't stamp out love
c Major, R. O. Melodrama at Mayfair Meadows
y Mueller, D. A. Dreadful doings at the cider mill
Sharrocks, M. Sweet Rose of Old Aldgate
Sims, G. R. The lights o' London
Smith, W. H. The drunkard
y St. John, B. Dogsbreath Devereaux, the dastardly doctor
y St. John, B. The fiendish firebug strikes again!
y St. John, B. Heaven help the po'taters!
y St. John, B. Peril on the high seas
c Stanford, J. Snow White—the purdiest gal in the West
y Swift, R. Dirty work on the trail
y Swift, R. The paper bag bandit rides again
y Swift, R. Rascals under the big top

Melodrama at Mayfair Meadows. Major, R. O.

Melville, Herman
Moby Dick (dramatization) See Thane, A. Moby Dick

About

Hall, F. B. Nathaniel in Berkshire

Members of the Road Company Ensemble
Blind desire
Feminist fantasy. Interior world of young Southern woman. Dancing. 2 acts 3w 2m 1 setting
In Alternative roots; ed. by K. deNobriga and V. Anderson

Memoir. Murrell, J.

The **memorandum.** Havel, V.

Memory
Bremner, B. Mrs. Coney
y Harder, E. Rememberin' stuff
Linney, R. Clair de Lune
MacLeod, J. The Hope slide
y Mason, T. The less than human club
Miller, A. I can't remember anything
Murphy, T. Bailegangaire
Murrell, J. Memoir
Nemeth, S. Sally's shorts: Word games
Noonan, J. F. When it comes early
Pintauro, J. Seymour in the very heart of winter
Pinter, H. A kind of Alaska
Sharif, B. My ancestor's house
Wilson, E. C. Cross-dressing in the Depression

Men
Barylli. Buttered bread
Bogosian, E. Drinking in America
Bogosian, E. Men inside
Gurney, A. R. The snow ball
MacIvor, D. Never swim alone
Shanley, J. P. Missing Marisa
Wreggitt, A. and Shaw, R. The wild guys

Men and angels. Kirk, L.

Men in white. Kinglsey, S.

Men inside. Bogosian, E.

Men on the verge of a his-panic breakdown. Reyes, G.

Men without wives. Pintauro, J.

The **Menaechmus** twins. See Plautus, T. M. The brothers Menaechmus

Menander
The double deceiver (adaptation) See Plautus, T. M. Two sisters named Bacchis

Menchú, Rigoberta
Ehn, E. Two altars, ten funerals (all souls)

Menken, Alan
Weird romance: Her pilgrim soul
Musical dramatization of Alan Brennert's short story. Scientist encounters living holograph of woman thought long dead. 1 act 5m 4w 1 setting
In Menken, A. Weird romance
Weird romance: The girl who was plugged in
Musical dramatization of short story by James Tiptree, Jr. Soul of homeless bag lady transplanted into body of gorgeous android. 1 act 4m 3w 1 setting
In Menken, A. Weird romance

Men's lives. Pintauro, J.

Mensch Meier. Kroetz, F. X.

Mental illness
Barnes, P. Nobody here but us chickens
Blessing, L. Independence
Bynum, R. C. Escapee
Collings, J. Kelly & Donald
Cooper, B. Nellie Bly: ten days in a madhouse
Daniels, S. Head-rot holiday
Foote, H. The roads to home: A nightingale
Foote, H. The roads to home: Spring dance
Fraser, B. Wolfboy
Granger, P. Vivien
Greth, R. Halfway
Hall, F. B. Lucia
Hill, G. L. The Black Branch
Kiefer, N. Gwen and Gwen
McNally, T. Bad habits: Dunelawn
McNally, T. Bad habits: Ravenswood
Mead, K. Crying out loud
Munro, R. Fugue
Nigro, D. Lucia mad
Noonan, J. F. Music from down the hill
Pintauro, J. Snow orchid
Poliakoff, S. She's been away
Pollock, S. Getting it straight
Prideaux, J. The librarian
Snodgrass, K. Haiku
Storey, D. The restoration of Arnold Middleton
c York, Y. Afternoon of the elves
See also Depression, Mental; Insanity; Schizophrenia

Mentally handicapped
Barry, P. J. A distance from Calcutta
Harper, T. Requiem for Denys
Huff, K. Leon and Joey
MacLeod, J. Toronto, Mississippi
Morris, M. Boss of the pool
Moxley, G. Danti-Dan
Nave, B. Visiting Oliver
Randall, B. David's mother
Rodriguez, D. E. I'm not stupid
Royce, C. My son Susie
Simon, N. Lost in Yonkers
Stock, J. Star-gazy pie and sauerkraut
Turrini, P. Swine
Wilson, L. Eukiah

Mental hospitals. See Psychiatric hospitals

Mephisto rock. Wells, M.

Mequasset by the sea. Goldenthal, J.

Mercadet. Balzac, H. de

Mercadet. Balzac, H. de. (adaptation) See Lewes, G. H. The game of speculation

Mercati, Cynthia
c Bigger than life! Pioneer Drama Service 1995 26p
Based on American folk tales about Pecos Bill, Sal Fink, Annie Oakley, P. T. Barnum and Sally Cato. Singing, audience participation. 1m 4w 1 exterior
c Cinderella; or, It's okay to be different. Bakers Plays 1994 38p
Children act out alternative versions of Cinderella story. 1b 4g 1 exterior

Mercator. See Plautus, T. M. The entrepreneur

Mercer, David, 1928-1980
An afternoon at the festival
Television play. Scenes of producer's forthcoming film starring his bastard son and third wife interspersed with scenes detailing his private life. 3m 2w 1 extra
In Mercer, D. Plays: two
The Arcata promise
Television play. Destructive relationship of older actor with young inexperienced girl. 2 acts 2m 1w
In Mercer, D. Plays: two
The bankrupt
Television play. Examination of anguished mind of middle aged man, emotionally drained and disoriented. 5m 2w extras
In Mercer, D. Plays: two
The cellar and the almond tree
Television play. Part of Kelvin trilogy. Communist writer in Eastern European country suffers first at hands of Nazis, later at hands of Stalinists. 8m 2w 1b 1g extras
In Mercer, D. Plays: one

Mercer, David, 1928-1980—*Continued*

Duck song

Explores feelings of group of people suddenly stripped of their familiar everyday trappings. 2 acts 3 scenes 5m 2w 1 setting

In Mercer, D. Plays: two

Emma's time

Television play. Part of Kelvin trilogy. Concerns situation of Robert Kelvin's mistress after his death. Flashbacks reveal development of relationship between the young woman and the aging novelist. 7m 5w extras

In Mercer, D. Plays: one

Find me

Television play. Episodes portray life and checkered career of disillusioned, womanizing Polish writer haunted by wartime memories. Focus is on his relationships with English poet, wife of dead comrade encountered during partisan days. 61 scenes 2m 2w extras

In Mercer, D. Plays: two

Flint

Aging English vicar whose agnosticism, political and sexual activities have been subject of continual scandal finds winter of his life transformed by young Irish girl, pregnant and unmarried. 2 acts 10 scenes 9m 3w 2b extras 5 interiors 1 exterior

In Mercer, D. Plays: two

The Governor's lady

Widow of British colonial governor, unable to accept prevailing political and social realities, suffers breakdown. Background music. 8 scenes 4m 2w 1 setting

In Mercer, D. Plays: one

Huggy bear

Satirical television play about reactionary British society. Dysfunctional dentist rejects convention and immerses himself in world of infantile perversion. 3m 5w

In Mercer, D. Plays: two

On the eve of publication

Television play. Part of Kelvin trilogy. Famous aging English Marxist novelist, facing death on eve of publication of latest book, reviews life and relationships with women. 3m 3w extras

In Mercer, D. Plays: one

A suitable case for treatment

Fanciful, nonconformist writer finally decides to make commitment to girlfriend. 5m 4w extras

In Mercer, D. Plays: one

Where the difference begins

Television play. First play of trilogy: The generations. Conflicting political, social and personal values are revealed when college-educated sons of socialist worker visit dying mother. 4m 5w extras

In Mercer, D. Plays: one

The **merchant.** See Plautus, T. M. The entrepreneur

Merchants

c DeFelice, J. The merchants of Dazu

The **merchants** of Dazu. DeFelice, J.

Mercury (Roman deity)

y McCaslin, N. Travelers from Olympus

Mercy in moccasins. McCaslin, N.

Mere mortals. Ives, D.

Merlin (Legendary character)

c Hezlep, W. Merlin's cave

Merlin's cave. Hezlep, W.

Mermaids

Barnes, D. Kurzy of the sea

c Daugherty, L. The little mermaid

Merry Christmas Miss Vickers. Levi, S.

Merry widows. Bisson, P.

Mesmer, Franz Anton, 1734-1815

Mack, C. K. In her sight

Metamorphoses. Siegel, J.

Metamorphosis

Barnes, D. Kurzy of the sea

Metamorphosis. Ovid. (dramatization) See Iizuka, N. Polaroid stories

Mexican Americans

y Alvarez, L. Eddie Mundo Edmundo

Banda, V. H. R. Murder with malice

Colorado, E. and Colorado, H. 1992: blood speaks

Fernandez, E. How else am I supposed to know I'm still alive

c McCullough, L. E. El paseo del vaquero (The ride of the vaquero)

c McCullough, L. E. Let us go, O shepherds

Minjares, J. The king of the kosher grocers

Moraga, C. Giving up the ghost

Moraga, C. Heroes and saints

Morton, C. Johnny Tenorio

Najera, R. A quiet love

Rascon Banda, V. H. Murder with malice

y Soto, G. Novio boy

c Vigil, A. El Dia de los Muertos. The Fiesta of the Day of the Dead

Mexicans

United States

Gaytán, J. G. Fred Menchacha and Filemón

Mexico

y Alvarez, L. Eddie Mundo Edmundo

c Gerke, P. Los mariachis Mexicanos: "The Brementown musicians"

c Hezlep, W. Treasure of the Mayans

c McCaslin, N. Christmas fiesta

Morton, C. The miser of Mexico

Solórzano, C. The crucified

Mexico—*Continued*
History—Conquest, 1519-1540
c Vigil, A. La aparicion de Nuestra Senora de Guadalupe. The miracle of Our Lady of Guadalupe
History—19th century
c Vigil, A. La Batalla de Cinco de Mayo. The Battle of Cinco de Mayo

Meyer, Marlane Gomard
Moe's Lucky Seven
Modern day retelling of story of Adam, Eve, and serpent, set in waterfront bar. Prologue 6 scenes 9m 3w 1 interior
In Women playwrights: the best plays of 1994

Meyer, Michael
The odd women. French (London) 1993 76p
Dramatization of George Gissing's novel set in London and the Lake District in 1888-89. Portrays social conditions of women and beginning of feminist movement. 2 acts 22 scenes 4m 6w 1 setting

Miami (Fla.)
Guare, J. Moon under Miami

Mice
c Neuman, C. A better mousetrap
Neuman, C. Lion and mouse stories

Michaelmas Term. Middleton, T.

Michel, Marc. See Labiche, E. jt. auth.

Michelangelo, Buonarroti, 1475-1564
Spencer, S. Water and wine

Michels, Jeanne, and Murphy, Phyllis
The queen of bingo. Dramatists 1994 59p
Two sisters in their 50s find fun and excitement at church bingo games. 2 acts 1m 2w extras 1 setting

Michener, James
Sayonara (dramatization) See Fischoff, G. James A. Michener's Sayonara

Micone, Marco
Beyond the ruins; tr. from the French by Jill MacDougall. Guernica 1995 78p (Drama series 10)
Drama set in 1972 Montreal and 1987 Italian village. Five members of family reflect cultural and political contradictions inherent in immigration. 19 scenes 3m 2w

Middle age
Barrie, J. M. Rosalind
Goldenthal, J. Mequasset by the sea
Gurney, A. R. Later life
Gurney, A. R. The snow ball
Gurney, A. R. Sylvia
Levy, J. Old blues

Middle-aged white guys. Martin, J.

The **Middle** Ages. Gurney, A. R.

Middle classes
Germany
Sternheim, C. The bloomers
Great Britain
Osborne, J. Look back in anger
Osborne, J. and Creighton, A. Epitaph for George Dillon

Middle distance. Basso, E.

Middle of the night. Chayefsky, P.

The **middleman.** Jones, H. A.

Middleton, Thomas
A critical edition of Thomas Middleton's The witch. Garland 1993 307p (The Renaissance imagination)
17th century tragicomedy about how witchcraft facilitates the revenge of duchess upon her husband, the King of Lombardy. 5 acts 14 scenes 10m 8w extras 1 setting

A mad world, my masters
Jacobean satirical comedy partly in verse about love and intrigue surrounding calculating courtesan. 5 acts 18 scenes 17m 4w extras 1 setting
In Middleton, T. A mad world, my masters and other plays

Michaelmas Term
Jacobean drama about tactics used by city merchants to fleece country squires of their lands. 5 acts 18 scenes 9m 7w 2b extras 1 setting
In Middleton, T. A mad world, my masters and other plays

No wit, no help like a woman's
Jacobean social comedy in which woman disguised as man attempts to aid her brother in wooing wealthy widow. 5 acts 10 scenes 14m 5w 1b 1 interior
In Middleton, T. A mad world, my masters and other plays

A trick to catch the old one
Jacobean comedy of manners. Bankrupt landed gentleman resolves to get estate back from those who fleeced him. 5 acts 17 scenes 16m 5w extras
In Middleton, T. A mad world, my masters and other plays

The witch. Norton 1994 95p (New mermaids)
Note under A critical edition of Thomas Middleton's The witch

Parodies, imitations, etc.
Barker, H. Women beware women
See also The Revenger's tragedy

The **midlife** crisis of Dionysus. Keillor, G.

The **Midnight** Moonlight Wedding Chapel. Berlin, E.

Midsummer nights. Kuhn, K.

Mighton, John

Body and soul. Coach House Press 1994 53p

Surreal comedy-drama about desire, sex, virtual reality, necrophilia, mass media and non-communication. 14 scenes 2m 3w

The little years. Playwrights Canada 1995 69p

Philosophical drama about passage of time and nature of immortality. Dreams and aspirations of three generations of women. 2 acts 9 scenes 1m 4w 1 setting

Migrant labor

Schwarz-Bart, S. Your handsome captain

The **Mikado.** Smolensky, S. and Waldrop, J.

Mikkelsen, Jon

c Resolution revolution. Pioneer Drama Service 1996 28p

Various characters learn how to resolve a conflict. Singing. Variable cast 12 characters

Mikveh

Zark, J. A body of water: White days

Military service, Compulsory

Dunbar-Nelson, A. Mine eyes have seen
McNally, T. Next

Milk, Harvey

Mann, E. Execution of justice
Pruitt, D. and Hutchinson, P. The Harvey Milk show

Milk of paradise. Bingham, S.

The **mill** on the floss. Edmundson, H.

Millan, Jim, and Brooker, Blake

Serpent kills. Playwrights Canada 1994 115p

Drama about Indo-Vietnamese serial killer Charles Sobhraj. 2 acts 77 scenes 3m 2w

Millar, Thomas P.

The Cassandra Complex. Palmer Press 1992 195p

Satirical look at psychoanalytic theory. Prologue 3 acts 5 scenes epilogue 8m 2w 3 settings

Millay, Edna St. Vincent

Aria da capo

Morality play about the futility of war. 1 act 4m 1w 1 interior

In Short plays for young actors; ed. by C. Slaight and J. Sharrar

About

Andrews, B. No wider than the heart

Miller, Arthur

After the fall

Action takes place in memory of protagonist, Quentin. In search for unity of his past experiences he examines relationships with his family and three women he has loved. 2 acts 5m 7w extras 1 setting

In Miller, A. The portable Arthur Miller

The American clock

Series of vignettes depicting America during the Great Depression. Music. 2 acts Large mixed cast 1 setting

In Miller, A. The portable Arthur Miller

Broken glass. Dramatists 1994 88p

Drama set in 1938 Brooklyn deals with Holocaust and anti-semitism in America by focusing on middle-aged Jewish housewife's mysterious paralysis. 2 acts 11 scenes 3m 3w 3 interiors

—Same. Penguin Bks. 1994 161p
—Same
In Miller A. The portable Arthur Miller

The crucible

Witchcraft trials in Salem, Massachusetts in 1692. 4 acts 11m 9w 1g 4 interiors

In Miller, A. The portable Arthur Miller

Death of a salesman

Tragedy. Mediocre salesman, after life of self deception, realizes failure and commits suicide to leave family insurance money. Background music. 2 acts requiem 8m 5w 1 setting

In Miller, A. The portable Arthur Miller

I can't remember anything

New England widow's daily visit to neighbor, her late husband's assistant and best friend reveals the indignities of aging, loss of memory and loneliness. 1 act 1m 1w 1 interior

In Telling tales: new one-act plays; ed. by E. Lane

The last Yankee. Dramatists 1993 39p

Expanded version of the play entered in 1988-1992 Index. State mental hospital setting for encounter between two visiting husbands and their wives. 2 scenes 2m 2w 1 extra 2 interiors

—Same. Penguin Bks. 1994 98p
—Same
In Miller, A. The portable Arthur Miller

The ride down Mount Morgan. Warner Chappell Plays 1995 110p

Tragicomedy set in upstate New York hospital. Bigamous life of wealthy middle-aged Jewish insurance entrepreneur unravels after auto accident. 2 acts 4m 3w 1 interior

Miller, Arthur—*Continued*
The Ryan interview; Or, How it was around here
Woman journalist interviews man on his 100th birthday. 1 act 1m 1w 1 setting
In EST marathon '95

Miller, Brian
Mum's the word. French (London) 1994 46p
Comic murder mystery set in Home Counties. Young wife shoots retired army officer husband with his service revolver. Eccentric relatives arrive. 6 scenes postscript 2m 4w 1 interior

Miller, D. Lee
Origami tears
Widow and ghost of husband. 1m 2w extra 1 interior
In Facing forward; ed by L. D. Frank

Miller, Ev
Morning shows the day. Players Press 1994 59p
Divorced businessman returns to Midwest home town to confront troubled family history. 2 acts 2 scenes 6m 6w 2b 1 extra 1 interior

Up rose a burning man. Players Press 1996 51p
Elderly man's romance with widow withstands children's disapproval. Background music. 2 acts 6m 4w 1 interior

Miller, Helen Louise
c Bandit Ben rides again
Cowboys and Indians cooperate to catch bandit. Singing. 12m 8w
In The Big book of large-cast plays; ed. by S. E. Kamerman

c The Birds' Christmas Carol
Dramatization of episode from Kate Douglas Wiggin's novel. Invalid Carol Bird celebrates Christmas. Chorus. 4 scenes 2m 4w 3b 1g extras 3 interiors
In The Big book of large-cast plays; ed. by S. E. Kamerman

c Name that book!
Characters act out scenes from classic books for TV quiz show. 2m 1w 4b 5g extras 1 interior
In The Big book of large-cast plays; ed. by S. E. Kamerman

c The princess and the pea
Based on Hans Christian Andersen's fairy tale. Ragged girl passes test proving her to be true princess. 2m 7w 1 interior
In Thirty plays from favorite stories; ed. by S. E. Kamerman

c That figures!
Mr. Wizard shows girl importance of mathematics. 2m 2w 1b 3g extra 1 interior
In The Big book of skits; ed. by S. E. Kamerman

Miller, Henry
A winter reunion
Drama set in Harlem church rectory on Christmas Eve. Grandson attempts to reconcile mother and sexton grandfather. 2 scenes 2m 1w 1 interior
In Off-Off Broadway Festival plays, 20th ser.

Miller, Jason
Barrymore's ghost. Dramatists 1997 45p
One-man show about legendary actor John Barrymore. 2 acts 1m 1 setting

Miller, Jim
A light on the landing. New Playwrights Network 1997 27p
Following funeral, family is forced to face unwelcome truths. 1 act 2m 6w 1g 1 interior

Miller, Jim, and Miller, Susan
Consequences. New Playwrights Network 1995 19p
Man meets other troubled souls as he contemplates suicide in London underground station. 6m 4w 1 interior

Miller, Kathryn Schultz
y Red badge of courage. Anchorage Press 1995 33p
Dramatization of Stephen Crane's novel about the Civil War. Singing, music. Variable cast 11 characters 1 setting

Miller, May
Graven images
Based on story in Old Testament Book of Numbers. Young Eliezar, son of Moses and black Ethiopian Zipporah, encounter racial prejudice. 1 act 2m 1w 4b 2g extras 1 setting
In Black theatre USA [v1]; ed. by J. V. Hatch and T. Shine

Miller, Susan
It's our town, too
Loosely based on Thornton Wilder's play Our town. Depicts everyday life of homosexuals and lesbians. 4m 4w 1 extra 1 setting
In The Actor's book of gay and lesbian plays; ed. by E. Lane and N. Shengold
In The Best American short plays, 1992-1993

My left breast
Monologue by gay woman about effects of breast cancer on her emotional well being. 1w
In The Best American short plays, 1993-1994
In Humana Festival '94

Repairs
Thirtysomething married woman, her husband, and her best friend face fear of future. 1m 2w
In Facing forward; ed. by L. D. Frank
See also Miller, J. jt. auth.

Miller, Tim
My queer body
Autobiographical performance piece. Gay man reacts to homophobia and AIDS. 1m
In Sharing the delirium; ed. by T. Jones

Miller, William, 1782-1849
Barnes, P. The end of the world—and after

Milligan, Jason
Clara and the gambler
Comedic send-up of silent screen westerns. 1 act 1m 1w 1 interior
In Milligan, J. Cross country

Class of '77
Home for his high school reunion, Hollywood director of B-grade horror films relives past with old girlfriend. 1 act 1m 1w 1 interior
In Milligan, J. Cross country

Life after Elvis
Comedy. As part of witness protection program Elvis Presley lives with average couple in middle America. 1 act 3m 1w 1 interior
In Milligan, J. Cross country

Money talks
Comedy. Meeting in Manhattan pub turns into blind date from hell. 1 act 2m 1w 1 interior
In Milligan, J. Cross country

The quality of boiled water
Farce. Wall Street hotshot wakes up with strange woman in strange house. 1 act 4m 2w 1 interior
In Milligan, J. Cross country

Road trip
Family drama. Drifter visits brother after long absence. 1 act 2m 1w 1 interior
In Milligan, J. Cross country

Shore leave
Drama set in Tokyo bar. Young sailor harassed by two shipmates after wild night. 1 act 4m 1 interior
In Milligan, J. Cross country

Walking on the moon. French 1997 111p
Satire. Ex-astronaut's celebrity status. 2 acts 21 scenes 7m 3w extras

Milmore, Jane. See Van Zandt, B. jt. auth.

Milner, Arthur
Zero hour
Political drama about American Intervention in Central America. Three American men meet in Costa Rican prison. 7 scenes 3m 1 interior
In The *CTR* anthology; ed. by A. Filewod

Milton, John, 1608-1674
Paradise lost (dramatization) See Dryden, J. The state of innocence and fall of man

Mina tonight! Robertson, H. W.

The **mind** king. Foreman, R.

Mine eyes have seen. Dunbar-Nelson, A.

Mines and mining
Langley, R. The Dunsmuirs: a promise kept
Schenkkan, R. Tall tales

Minghella, Anthony
Cigarettes and chocolate
Radio play about complex love lives of contemporary young people. 3m 5w
In Minghella, A. Plays 2

Days like these
Short monologue by lonely old woman. 1w
In Minghella, A. Plays 2

Hang up
Radio play. Two lovers have meandering telephone conversation. 1m 1w
In Minghella, A. Plays 2

A little like drowning
Drama portraying three generations of Italian Catholic family torn apart by adultery. 2 acts 23 scenes 6m 7w 1 setting
In Minghella, A. Plays 1

Made in Bangkok
Satire. Five Britishers arrive in Bangkok and in time exploit the natives either commercially or physically. 2 acts 17 scenes 5m 1w extras 1 setting
In Minghella, A. Plays 1

Mosaic
Dance text for two women. 2w
In Minghella, A. Plays 2

Two planks and a passion
Set in 14th century York England. Guilds are preparing their mystery plays when they learn that King Richard II will attend the festivities. 2 acts 20 scenes 11m 4w extras 1 setting
In Minghella, A. Plays 1

Whale music
Drama about what happens when university student becomes pregnant and her friends gather round in support. 2 acts 15 scenes 7w extras 1 setting
In Minghella, A. Plays 1

What if it's raining?
Television play about adultery. 5m 4w
In Minghella, A. Plays 2

Minieri, Alan
Your life is a feature film
Comedy. Young man whose entire life has been a film production must struggle to get grip on reality. 3m 2w 1 interior
In Off-Off Broadway Festival plays, 17th ser.

Ministers. See Clergy

Minjares, Joe
The king of the kosher grocers. French 1993 103p
Comedy set in Minneapolis. Old Jewish grocer saves his business with help from black and Mexican American friends. 3 acts 3 scenes 6m 1w 1 interior

Minna. Barker, H.

A **miracle** in the Christmas city. McCaslin, N.

The **miracle** of Our Lady of Guadalupe. See Vigil, A. La aparicion de Nuestra Senora de Guadalupe. The miracle of our Lady of Guadalupe

Miracles
Pope, R. Amazing Grace

Miranda, John
Italian funerals and other festive occasions. French 1996 85p
Comic drama. Faced with impending loss of aged mother, Italian American man, viewing life in operatic terms, explores family history. Prologue 2 acts epilogue 6m 6w interior.

Miranda, Julian E.
c Cornerstone of civil rights
Strike of immigrant workers in colonial Virginia persuaded House of Burgesses to grant vote to non-English colonists. 2 scenes 11m 3w extras 1 interior
In Great American events on stage; ed. by S. E. Kamerman

Mirror mirror on the wall. Booth, J.

The **misanthrope.** Crimp, M.

The **misanthrope.** Molière

Miscegenation
Aldridge, I. The black doctor
Franklin, J. E. Two mens'es daughter
Fugard, A. Statements after an arrest under the immorality act
Hughes, L. Mulatto
Livingston, M. S. For unborn children

The **miser.** Molière.

The **miser.** Molière (adaptation) See Morton, C. The miser of Mexico

The **miser** of Mexico. Morton, C.

Misers
Molière. The miser
Morton, C. The miser of Mexico
Plautus, T. M. The pot of gold

Misha's party. Nelson, R. and Gelman, A.

Misreadings. Beber, N.

Miss Evers' boys. Feldshuh, D.

Miss Honey's young'uns. Franklin, J. E.

Miss Julie. Strindberg, A.

Miss Julie. Strindberg, A. (adaptation) See Marber, P. After Miss Julie

Miss Temptation. Cooperman, D.

The **Miss** Witch contest. Cheatham, V. R.

Missing Marisa. Shanley, J. P.

Missing person. Taylor, P.

Missing persons
Nagy, P. Disappeared

Missing persons. Lucas, C.

Missionaries
Kneubuhl, V. N. The conversion of Ka'ahumanu
Salom, J. Bonfire at dawn

Missouri
Lauro, S. The coal diamond

Mistake. Havel, V.

Mistaken identity
Behn, A. The feigned courtesans
Booth, J. Seeing double
y Cohen, F. Try a little Shakespeare
Feydeau, G. Brothers in crime
Feydeau, G. A flea in her rear
c Hardee, L. The prince and the pauper
Harris, A. The importance of being Earnest
y Harris, A. The prince and the pauper
Marivaux. The triumph of love
Plautus, T. M. Epidicus
Wilde, O. The importance of being Earnest

Mistero buffo comic mysteries. Fo, D.

Misto, John
The shoe-horn sonata. Currency Press 1996 91p
Filming of television documentary reunites two women who in 1945 were freed from Japanese POW camp deep in jungles of Sumatra. 2 acts 14 scenes 2w 2 interiors

Mistress of desire. Vargas Llosa, M.

Mitchell, Joseph S.
Son-Boy
Lynching drama set in Southern States around 1900. African American family faces virulent racism. 3m 2w 1 interior
In Lost plays of the Harlem Renaissance; ed. by J. V. Hatch and L. Hamalian

Mitchell, Julian

August; an adaptation of Chekhov's Uncle Vanya, by Julian Mitchell; from a translation by Tania Alexander. Amber Lane Press 1994 77p

This adaptation of Chekhov's play is set in 1890s North Wales. 4 acts 5m 4w extras 3 interiors 1 exterior

Falling over England. Amber Lane Press 1994 112p

National and personal skeletons unearthed in chronicle of English family from 1945, through the Suez crisis of 1956, to the present. 2 acts 5m 2w 2b 1g 1 setting

Mitchell, Max

Life support

Gay man removes life support from dying lover. 1m 1 interior

In The Best American short plays, 1994-1995

Mitterer, Felix

Abraham

Drama about scourge of AIDS and love between father and son. Prologue 11 scenes 8m 1w extras 4 interiors 2 exteriors

In Mitterer, F. The wild woman and other plays

Beyond our understanding

Husband visits wife in hospital over Christmas holiday. 1 act 4 scenes 1m 1w 1 interior

In Mitterer, F. Siberia and other plays

Children of the Devil

Drama set in 1678 Salzburg. Homeless children become victims of institutional superstition and cruelty. 21 scenes 8m 1w 4b 1g 1 interior

In Mitterer, F. The wild woman and other plays

Dragon thirst; or, The rusty knight; or, Black and white, money and bread, the living and the dead

Allegorical fantasy of good and evil. Prelude 5 scenes 7m 7w extras 2 interiors 3 exteriors

In Mitterer, F. Siberia and other plays

Home

Prodigal son and non-conformist girlfriend, rejected by family, face small town brutality, prejudice and contempt. 5m 3w 1 setting

In Mitterer, F. The wild woman and other plays

Jailbird

Husband visits wife, in prison for attempting to murder him. 1 act 1m 1w 1 interior

In Mitterer, F. Siberia and other plays

No place for idiots

Austrian folk play about greed, power, and inhumanity. Village attempts to forget its past and pursue lucrative future at citizens' expense. 3 acts 6m 3w 1b extras 3 interiors

In Anthology of contemporary Austrian folk plays

One everyman

Modern version of medieval morality play. Wall Street Devil, not content with merely winning, seeks to destroy rivals at all cost. 2 acts Variable cast 1 interior

In Mitterer, F. The wild woman and other plays

Shunted into a siding

Woman visits father-in-law in old people's home. 1 act 1m 1w 1 interior

In Mitterer, F. Siberia and other plays

Siberia

Monologue. Old man struggles for dignity in retirement home. 1m

In Mitterer, F. Siberia and other plays

Stigma

Historical drama about faith and superstition set on European farm in 1830s. 17 scenes 12m 4w extras 1 setting

In Mitterer, F. Siberia and other plays

There's not a finer country

Historical drama set in Austrian village about betrayal of local Jewish citizen to Nazis. 13 scenes 11m 4w extras 1 setting

In Mitterer, F. Siberia and other plays

Wheat on the autobahn

Daughter visits father in psychiatric hospital. 1 act 1m 1w 1 interior

In Mitterer, F. Siberia and other plays

The wild woman

Five woodcutters vie for attentions of mythological wild woman. 18 scenes 5m 1w 1 interior

In Mitterer, F. The wild woman and other plays

Mixed emotions. Baer, R.

Miz Lena's backyard. Villarrubia, J.

Moby Dick. Thane, A.

The **model** apartment. Margulies, D.

The **modern** husband. Godfrey, P.

A **modern** proposal. Tasca, J.

Modernist-fundamentalist controversy

Lawrence, J. and Lee, R. E. Inherit the wind

A **modest** proposal. Tilly

Moe's Lucky Seven. Meyer, M. G.

Mohr, Joseph, 1792-1848
c McCullough, L. E. Silent night

Mojo. Butterworth, J.

The **mojo** and the sayso. Rahman, A.

Molière
Amphitryon; tr. by Richard Wilbur. Dramatists 1995 108p

Adaptation of Plautus' Amphitryon with benefit of alteration made by Jean Rotrou. Jupiter and Mercury disguised as Amphitryon and his slave visit the Roman's home, where Jupiter spends the night with Amphitryon's wife. Comedy ensues when the real pair return. Prologue 3 acts 2m 2w extras 1 exterior

—Same; tr. into English verse and with an afterword by Richard Wilbur. Harcourt Brace & Co. 1995 146p

The flying doctor; tr. by Albert Bermel

Farce. Valet posing as doctor aids lovers and foils father's matchmaking. 1 act 5m 2w 1 setting

In Around the world in 21 plays; ed. by L. Swortzell

The hypochondriac; tr. and introduced by Martin Sorrell. Hern Bks. 1994 102p (Drama classics)

Variant title: The imaginary invalid. Satirical comedy set in 17th century Paris. Hypochondriac wants to marry his daughter to a doctor in order to get free medical care. Music, singing, dancing. Prologues 3 acts 31 scenes interludes 9m 2w 1g 1 interior 2 exteriors

The imaginary cuckold; or, Sganarelle; tr. by Richard Wilbur. Dramatists 1993 38p

Comedy of manners in verse. Misunderstandings and mistaken identity grow more tangled in satire about adultery and young love. 24 scenes 5m 2w extras 1 setting

The imaginary invalid (Le malade imaginaire); tr. by Albert Bermel

Variant title: The hypochondriac, entered above

In A Dozen French farces; ed. by A. Bermel

The misanthrope; tr. by Charles Heron Wall. Players Press 1993 60p

Comedy of manners. Satire on 17th century Parisian society in which hypocrisy plays an important role. 5 acts 29 scenes 8m 3w 1 interior

The misanthrope (adaptation) See Crimp, M. The misanthrope

The miser; tr. by David Chambers. Dramatists 1993 68p

Comedy satirizing miserliness. Set in 17th century Paris. 8m 3w 1 interior

The miser (adaptation) See Morton, C. The miser of Mexico

The school for wives (adaptation) See Nolan, P. T. The school for wives

Tartuffe (adaptation) See Thomas, F. Tartuffe: born again

About

Ackerman, M. L'affaire Tartuffe

Parodies, imitations, etc.

Richardson, A. A fine gentleman

Moll. Keane, J. B.

Moll Flanders. Stiles, G.

Molly. Gray, S.

Molly Pitcher meets the General. Hall, M.

Molly Sweeney. Friel, B.

Mommsen, Theodor, 1817-1903
Müller, H. Mommsen's block

Mommsen's block. Müller, H.

Monaghan, Joe
Lebow, B. Little Joe Monaghan

Monasticism and religious orders
Barnes, P. Noonday demons
Linney, R. Ambrosio

Mondschein, Nikki Leigh
y Hold on!

Telephone conversation. Young woman asks young man for date. 2m 2w 1 setting

In The Big book of skits; ed. by S. E. Kamerman

Money
Granville-Barker, H. The Voysey inheritance
Koch, K. The gold standard
Margulies, D. Found a peanut

Money talks. Milligan, J.

Mongrels. Enright, N.

The **monkey** palace. Bynum, R. C.

Monkeys
Sardou, V. For love or monkey

Monks
Koch, K. The gold standard
See also Monasticism and religious orders

Monologue. Pinter, H.

Monologue (February 1990). Mamet, D.

Monologues
Auden, W. H. The dark valley
Baitz, J. R. Recipe for one
Barnes, P. Confessions of a primary terrestrial mental receiver and communicator: Num III Mark I
Barnes, P. The end of the world—and after

Monologues—*Continued*
Barnes, P. Glory
Barnes, P. The jumping Mimuses of Byzantium
Barnes, P. No end to dreaming
Barnes, P. Revolutionary witness
Barnes, P. Rosa
Barnes, P. The theory and practice of belly-dancing
Barnes, P. Yesterday's news
Bensinger, L. A ghost story
Berkoff, S. Actor
Berkoff, S. Dog
Berkoff, S. Harry's Christmas
Blount, R. Five Ives gets named
Bogosian, E. Drinking in America
Bogosian, E. Fun house
Bogosian, E. Men inside
Bogosian, E. Pounding nails in the floor with my forehead
Bogosian, E. Sex, drugs, rock & roll
Bogosian, E. Voices of America
Callan, L. Homebound
Campbell, K. Pigspurt
Campbell, K. Violin time
Chekhov, A. The dangers of tobacco
Dowie, C. Adult child/dead child
Dowie, C. Drag act
Dowie, C. Leaking from every orifice
Dowie, C. Why is John Lennon wearing a skirt?
Durang, C. Mrs. Sorken
Fyffe, L. The sand
Garnhum, K. Beuys buoys boys
Gaytán, J. G. Fred Menchacha and Filemón
Gilbert, R. Mother Jones: the most dangerous woman in America
Goldenthal, J. Charley's girl
Goldenthal, J. Dance piece
Goldenthal, J. Wife to Tolstoi
Goldstein, C. Last exit before toll
Goldstein, J. Hate
Goldstein, J. Our baby's first seven years
Gray, S. Gray's anatomy
Gray, S. It's a slippery slope
Green, M. Yowl
Harmer, W. What is the matter with Mary Jane?
Hatcher, J. Three viewings
Horovitz, I. Spared
Ives, D. A singular kinda guy
Jones, M. A night in November
Learner, T. Witchplay
Lewis, M. G. The captive
Lill, W. The occupation of Heather Rose
Linney, R. Gold and silver waltz
MacIvor, D. House humans
MacIvor, D. and Brooks, D. Here lies Henry
Mamet, D. Almost done
Mamet, D. Monologue (February 1990)
Margulies, D. Anthony
Margulies, D. I don't know what I'm doing
Margulies, D. Joey
Margulies, D. Lola
Margulies, D. Louie
Margulies, D. Manny
Margulies, D. Somnambulist
Martin, J. Talkin with . . .
McGuinness, F. Baglady
McNally, T. Street talk
McPherson, C. The good thief
McPherson, C. Rum and vodka
McPherson, C. St Nicholas
Miller, S. My left breast
Minghella, A. Days like these
Mitterer, F. Siberia
Müller, H. Mommsen's block
Nelson, R. Flyer
Nemeth, S. Sally's shorts: Black cloud morning New York
Nemeth, S. Sally's shorts: Living in this world
Nemeth, S. Sally's shorts: Pre-nuptial agreement
Nemeth, S. Sally's shorts: Visions of grandeur
Nigro, D. Squirrels
Nigro, D. Within the ghostly mansion's labyrinth
O'Neal, J. and Watkins, N. B. You can't judge a book by looking at the cover: sayings from the life and writings of Junebug Jabbo Jones: v2
Ordway, S. Panicked
Page, E. Aryan birth
y Panych, M. Cost of living
y Panych, M. Life science
Parks, S.-L. Pickling
Pintauro, J. House made of air
Pintauro, J. Parakeet eulogy
Pinter, H. Monologue
Pollock, S. Getting it straight
Ricchi, R. The man, the rose and silence
Royce, C. My son Susie
Schnupp, A. The Harper chronicles
Schwaiger, B. Yes, my führer!
Sheffer, W. Falling man
Shepard, S. Killer's head
Sloate, D. Le radeau de la Comtesse
'Udwan, Mamduh. That's life
y Waddy, L. Shakespeare remembers

Monologues—*Continued*
Wasserstein, W. Workout
Wellman, M. Terminal hip
Wilson, L. Days ahead
Wilson, L. The moonshot tape
Wilson, L. A poster of the cosmos
Wong, E. China doll
Woodward, C. Pretty fire
Woodward, M. B. Day shift
Zell, A. E. Come to leave

Monna Vanna. Maeterlinck, M.

The **monogamist.** Kyle, C.

Monroe, Marilyn, 1926-1962
Cullen, A. Self catering
Mueller, L. American dreamers

Monsieur Beaucaire. Olfson, L.

A **monster** ate my homework. Christiansen, A.

Monsters
Carmichael, F. Frankenstein 1930
y Christiansen, A. A monster ate my homework
y Priore, F. V. Madcap Monster Inn

Montgomery, L. M.
Anne of Green Gables (dramatization) See Sandberg, R. N. Anne of Green Gables; Turner, J. Anne of Green Gables

Montgomery of Alamein, Bernard Law Montgomery, Viscount, 1887-1976
Hagger, N. The warlords

The **month** before the moon. Bassen, L. S.

A **month** in the country. Friel, B.

Montreal (Quebec)
Ackerman, M. L'affaire Tartuffe
Fennario, D. Balconville
Micone, M. Beyond the ruins

The **monument.** Wagner, C.

Moo. Clark, S.

The **moods** of Marianne. Musset, A. de

Moon
Stoppard, T. Another moon called Earth

Moon over Buffalo. Ludwig, K.

Moon over Miami. See Guare, J. Moon under Miami

Moon under Miami. Guare, J.

Moonchildren. Weller, M.

Moonlight. Pinter, H.

The **moonshot** tape. Wilson, L.

The **moonstone.** Thane, A.

Moore, Charles Michael
Love's light in flight

Adulterous affair stirs things up in Michigan town's African American community. 2 acts 17 scenes 5m 4w 1 setting

In The National black drama anthology; ed. by W. King

Moore, Clement Clark, 1779-1863
c Swortzell, L. A visit from St. Nicholas

Moore, Edward
The foundling

18th century English comedy. Rake rescues young woman from rape by "guardian" who bought her as purported foundling from governess. After installing her in father's house under false story, he is tempted to seduce her himself. Singing. Prologue 5 acts 9 scenes epilogue 6m 2w extras

In Moore, E. The foundling and The gamester

The gamester

18th century English tragedy. Downfall of gambler. Singing. Prologue 5 acts 16 scenes epilogue 7m 3w 5 interiors 1 exterior

In Moore, E. The foundling and The gamester

Moore, Elise
Live with it. Blizzard Pub. 1994 75p

Biographical drama about successful London playwright Joe Orton and his jealous lover and murderer Ken Halliwell. 2 acts 14 scenes 2m 1 setting

Moorli and the Leprechaun. Davis, J.

Moose mating. Grae, D.

Moraga, Cherrie
Giving up the ghost

Blank verse play about Chicana lesbian experience. Prologue 12 scenes 3w extras 1 setting

In The Actor's book of gay and lesbian plays; ed. by E. Lane and N. Shengold

Heroes and saints

Mexican American children of small California town die from exposure to pesticides. 2 acts 24 scenes 4m 5w 1g extras 1 setting

In Contemporary plays by women of color; ed. by K. A. Perkins and R. Uno

Moralities, English
Everyman
Mankind. A critical edition of the medieval play Mankind

Moravia, Alberto
Crime at the tennis club (dramatization) See Maraini, D. Crime at the tennis club

More, Sir Thomas, 1478-1535
Barker, H. Brutopia

More than a touch of Zen. Barnes, P.

Moreto, Agustin
Spite for spite; tr. by Dakin Matthews. Smith & Kraus 1995 141p (Great translations for actors)

Romantic verse comedy set in 17th century Spain. Battle of sexes between man who finds himself irresistible and woman who considers herself immovable. 3 acts 5m 4w extras 1 setting

Morgan, J. P., 1867-1943
Larson, J. J. P. Morgan saves the nation

Mori, Ōgai
Masks

Set in 1900s Japan. Play about death and human resolution. Physician discusses illness with patient. 7m 4w extras 1 interior

In Mori, Ō Youth and other stories

Morgan, John
Kids. French (London) 1997 28p

Play about childhood set on playground. Characters, played by adults, reflect on follies of adulthood. 2m 3w 1 exterior

Morley, Olive J.
y Pride and prejudice

Based on Jane Austen's novel set in early 19th century England. Efforts of socially ambitious mother to secure wealthy husbands for her daughters. 3 scenes 3m 8w 2 interiors

In The Big book of dramatized classics; ed. by S. E. Kamerman

y Romance for Jo March

Dramatization of incident from Louisa May Alcott's Little women. Jo March falls in love with German professor. 4 scenes 5m 6w 4g extras 2 interiors 1 exterior

In The Big book of dramatized classics; ed. by S. E. Kamerman

Morley, Sheridan
Noel and Gertie. French (London) 1993 76p

Musical look at private and professional relationship between Gertrude Lawrence and Noel Coward. Music, singing. 2 parts 1m 1w 1 setting

Morning. Horovitz, I.

The **morning** after optimism. Murphy, T.

Morning and evening. Saalbach, A.

Morning coffee. Stroppel, F.

Morning has broken. See Houston, V. H. Asa ga kimashita (Morning has broken)

Morning shows the day. Miller, E.

Morning star. Regan, S.

Morountodun. Osofisan, F.

Morris, Aldyth
Lili'uokalani. Univ. of Hawaii Press 1993 71p

Historical drama about overthrow of Hawaiian Queen Liliuokalani and annexation of the islands by the U.S. 2 acts 2w 1 setting

Morris, Arlene J.
c An American story

Episodes from American history from 1775 to present. Singing. Large mixed cast 1 setting

In The Big book of large-cast plays; ed. by S. E. Kamerman

In Great American events on stage; ed. by S. E. Kamerman

Morris, Mary
Boss of the pool. Currency Press 1993 66p

Dramatization of Robin Klein's novel set in Australia. Adolescent girl embarrassed that her mother works as occupational therapy aid at facility for mentally handicapped. 1m 4w 2 interiors 1 exterior

Two weeks with the Queen. Currency Press 1993 79p

Dramatization of novel by Morris Gleitzman. Tragicomedy about Australian boy who travels to England to speak to Queen about brother's cancer. Background music. 34 scenes Variable cast 27 characters 4 interiors 1 exterior

Morris, Vera
c Thumbelina. Pioneer Drama Service 1997 41p

Based on Hans Christian Andersen's fairy tale about adventures of tiny girl and her animal friends. 2 acts 9 scenes Variable cast 21 characters extras 1 setting

See also Francoeur, B. The enchantment of Beauty and the beast

Morrison, Bill
A love song for Ulster: The daughter

Conclusion of trilogy. Family copes with religious, political and personal issues from 1969-1993. 2 acts 8m 2w 1 interior

In Morrison, B. A love song for Ulster

A love song for Ulster: The marriage

First play in trilogy. Arranged marriage between Protestant and carefree Catholic girl. Music. 2 acts 8m 3w extras 1 interior

In Morrison, B. A love song for Ulster

A love song for Ulster: The son

Second play in trilogy. Family drama covering years 1939-1969. 2 acts 8m 3w 2 interiors

In Morrison, B. A love song for Ulster

Morrison, Blake
The cracked pot. French (London) 1996 63p
Adaptation of Heinrich von Kleist's Der Zerbrochene Krug. Farce about parochial justice set in 1810 Yorkshire village. 2 acts 6 scenes 5m 3w 1 interior

Morrissey, Kim
Dora: a case of hysteria. Hern Bks. 1994 39p
Humorous exploration of Freud's famous case from a feminist perspective. 2 acts 2m 1w 1 interior

Morticians. See Undertakers and undertaking

Mortimer, John
Charles Dickens' A Christmas carol. French (London) 1995 101p
Dramatization of Charles Dickens tale about Scrooge's transformation from skinflint to benefactor. Includes chorus, music and singing. 2 acts 27 scenes Large mixed cast settings

Edwin. French (London) 1984 43p
Comedy. Retired Suffolk judge "tries" neighbor for alleged seduction of his wife. 2 scenes 2m 1w 1 exterior

Mortmain. Parsons, R.

Morton, Carlos
Johnny Tenorio. Players Press 1993 29p
Satire based on Spanish legend of Don Juan, set in modern San Antonio, Texas. Dialogue in Spanish and English. 3m 2w 1 interior

The miser of Mexico. Players Press 1993 47p
Adaptation of The miser by Molière set in 1910 Mexico. 2 acts 7m 4w

Pancho Diablo. Players Press 1993 43p
Satire depicting the Devil as owner of Mexican cantina. Dialogue in Spanish and English. 2 acts Variable cast 18 characters

The savior. Players Press 1993 51p
Drama about martyrdom of Archbishop Oscar Romero, killed in El Salvador for opposing government oppression. 2 acts Variable cast 17 characters extras

Morton, Jelly Roll
Wolfe, G. C. Jelly's last jam

Mosaic. Minghella, A.

Moscow (Russia)
Bulgakov, M. Zoyka's apartment
Findley, T. The stillborn lover
Van Itallie, J.-C. Master & Margarita

Moslems. See Muslims

Mosley, Paul. See Warhurst, M. Peter and the princess

Moss, Roger, S.
Nightmare: the fright of your life. French (London) 1993 66p
Horror tale. Young couple's nightmare begins when they move into converted chapel in English village. 2 acts 6 scenes 2m 2w 1 interior

Mossy Cape. Poole-Carter, R.

The **most** dangerous woman in America. McCullough, L. E.

The **most** expensive bonnet in all Indiana. McCullough, L. E.

The **most** interesting gift of all. Vigil, A.

The **most** massive woman wins. George, M.

The **mother.** Chayefsky, P.

The **mother.** Witkiewicz, S. I.

Mother Courage and her children. Brecht, B.

Mother Goose. Edgar, K.

The **Mother** Goose olympics. Mauro, R.

Mother Hicks. Zeder, S. L.

Mother Jones: the most dangerous women in America. Gilbert, R.

Mother liked it. Hazzard, A.

Mother O. Schevill, J.

The **mother** of us all. Stein, G.

The **mother** tongue. Franks, A.

Motherhood 2000. Kennedy, A.

Mothers
Bill, S. Curtains
Burrill, M. P. They that sit in darkness
Chayefsky, P. The mother
Cocteau, J. Les parents terribles (Indiscretions)
De Filippo, E. Filumena Marturano
Farhoud, A. Game of patience
Groves, W. Good night, sweet mother
Gurney, A. R. Children
Hayes, J. F. Nothing in common
Hendrick, B. If I can't take it with me . . . I'm not going to go
Horovitz, I. Free gift
Mama drama
Mamet, D. Almost done
Serreau, C. Lapin Lapin
Strindberg, A. The pelican

Mothers and daughters
Barnes, D. Maggie of the saints
Barnes, D. She tells her daughter

Mothers and daughters—*Continued*
Bellon, L. Bonds of affection
Blessing, L. Independence
Booth, J. Both worlds
Bowles, J. In the summer house
Cartwright, J. The rise and fall of Little Voice
Césaire, I. Fire's daughters
Chafee, C. Why we have a body
Chinn, J. In by the half
Dean, P. H. The Sty of The Blind Pig
De Angelis, A. Hush
Du Maurier, D. September tide
Franks, A. The mother tongue
García Lorca, F. The house of Bernarda Alba
Gems, P. Deborah's daughter
Glass, J. M. If we are women
Goldenthal, J. Dance piece
Greenberg, R. The American plan
Hare, D. Amy's view
Haywood, D. Twisted tape
Higgins, F. The sweet by 'n' by
Houston, V. H. The Matsuyama mirror
Johnson, E. What do they call me?
Keatley, C. My mother said I never should
Macdonald, S. When I was a girl, I used to scream and shout . . .
Macdonald, S. The winter guest
Martin, J. Shasta Rue
Mason, J. A. Daughters of the mock
Mason, T. The fiery furnace
McConnell, J. Early blight
McConnell, J. Shoppers
McDonagh, M. The beauty queen of Leenane
Medoff, M. The homage that follows
y Morley, O. J. Pride and prejudice
Morris, M. Boss of the pool
y Murray, P. Spitting chips
Murray-Smith, J. Love child
Peters, K. The confirmation
Pintauro, J. Lightning
Reddin, K. Brutality of fact
Reid, C. Tea in a china cup
Royce, C. Why we have a body
Samuels, D. Kindertransport
Simon, N. London suite: Going home
Simon, N. Lost in Yonkers
Snodgrass, K. Haiku
Stone, T. Hello, Ma!
Swedeen, S. The sleep seeker
Taylor, D. H. Someday
Taylor, R. Mudtracks
Thompson, P. Calamity Jane and the fat buffalo moon
Uyehara, D. Hiro
Wilder, T. A ringing of doorbells
Wilson, L. The sand castle
Youngblood, S. Talking bones
Zark, J. A body of water: Foreign bodies

Mothers and sons
Baitz, J. R. It changes every year
Barnes, D. At the roots of the stars
Bozzone, B. Sonny DeRee's life flashes before his eyes
Dove, R. The darker face of the earth
Durang, C. Naomi in the living room
Eisenstein, L. At the root
Foote, H. Talking pictures
Gifford, B. Mrs. Kashfi
Goldstein, J. Our baby's first seven years
Hibbert, G. Tilting ground
Hughes, L. Soul gone home
Kennedy, A. Motherhood 2000
Kennedy, A. P. and Kennedy, A. Sleep deprivation chamber
Law, M. My Johnny
Lichtig, R. R. Queen for a day
Linney, R. Juliet
c Martin, J. The big mess
Mastrosimone, W. Shivaree
Nave, B. Visiting Oliver
Randall, B. David's mother
Ricchi, R. The scandal
Rodriguez, D. E. I'm not stupid
Schevill, J. The last romantics
Schevill, J. Mother O
Sherman, J. M. Women and Wallace
Silverman, J. L. Correct address
Tagore, R. Karna and Kunti
Vickery, F. Loose ends
Ward, N. Trouble sleeping
Watson, A. Final placement
Wilson, L. The sand castles
Witkiewicz, S. I. The mother

Mother's Day
Baitz, J. R. It changes every year

Mothers-in-law
Storey, D. The restoration of Arnold Middleton

Motion picture critics
Gilroy, F. D. Real to reel

Motion picture industry
y Christiansen, A. Teens in Tinseltown
y Francoeur, B. Gone with the breeze
y Kelly, T. Hooray for Hollywood
Shanley, J. P. Four dogs and a bone
Stroppel, F. Package deal

Motion picture producers and directors
Crimp, M. The treatment
Griffin, T. Mrs. Sedgewick's head
Margulies, D. Pitching to the star
Mercer, D. An afternoon at the festival
Milligan, J. Class of '77
Sherman, J. The retreat

Motion pictures
Abdoh, R. The law of remains
Durang, C. A history of the American film
Foote, H. Talking pictures
Gilroy, F. D. Give the bishop my faint regards
Goluboff, B. Big Al
Lloyd Webber, A. Sunset Boulevard
Mercer, D. An afternoon at the festival
Minieri, A. Your life is a feature film
O'Neill, E. The movie man
Osborne, W. and Herrera, A. Smoke & mirrors

The **motor** trade. Foster, N.

Mouawad, Wajdi
Wedding day at the Cro-Magnons'
Eccentric Lebanese family prepares for daughter's wedding while neighborhood is destroyed by bombs. 4 acts 3m 3w 1 interior
In Playwrights of exile: an international anthology

Mound builders
Wilson, L. The mound builders

Mountain language. Pinter, H.

Mountain memory. Linney, R.

Mountain thunder. Pierson, K.

Mountaineering
Booth, J. Both worlds
Watson, D. The last Munro

The **mourning** after. Laughton, V.

Mourning becomes Electra: Homecoming. O'Neill, E.

Mourning becomes Electra: The haunted. O'Neill, E.

Mourning becomes Electra: The hunted. O'Neill, E.

The **movie** man. O'Neill, E.

Moving, Household
Howe, T. Painting Churches
c James, J. Moving day
Leonard, H. Moving

Moving. Leonard, H.

Moving day. James, J.

Moving reflections. Warner, F.

Mowatt, Anna Cora
Fashion; or, Life in New York
Satire on 19th century New York society. Background music. Prologue 5 acts 8 scenes epilogue 8m 5w extras 6 interiors
In Early American drama; ed. by J. H. Richards

Moxley, Gina
Danti-Dan
Drama set summer 1970, ten miles from Cork city. Teenage girl's sexual aggressiveness leads to tragedy for mentally handicapped boy. 2 acts 16 scenes 2m 3w 1 setting
In The Dazzling dark: new Irish plays; ed. by F. McGuinness

Mr. & Mrs. Charlie T. Mule. McCullough, L. E.

Mr A's amazing maze plays. Ayckbourn, A.

Mr. Quigley's revenge. Brett, S.

Mr. Rickey calls a meeting. Schmidt, E.

Mr. Universe. Grimsley, J.

Mrs. Cage. Barr, N.

Mrs. Coney. Bremner, B.

Mrs. Hauksbee sits out. Kipling, R.

Mrs. Kashfi. Gifford, B.

Mrs. Klein (condensation). Wright, N.

Mrs. Sedgewick's head. Griffin, T.

Mrs. Sorken. Durang, C.

Mrs. Warren's profession. Shaw, B.

Mtwa, Percy; Ngema, Mbongeni, and Simon, Barney
Woza Albert!
Political satire about South Africa during apartheid. 26 scenes 2m 1 setting
In Crosswinds; ed. by W. B. Branch

El **muchacho** que mato al gigante. The boy who killed the giant. Vigil, A.

Mudtracks. Taylor, R.

Mueller, Don A.
y Dreadful doings at the cider mill; or, The ballad of sweet Lucy Sweet. Bakers Plays 1993 92p
Melodrama set in 1889 Western town. Woman mayoral candidate helps clean up town. Singing, dancing. 2 acts 10 scenes 6m 5w 1 setting

Mueller, Don A.—*Continued*

Eyes upon the cross. Bakers Plays 1993 86p

Good Friday program. The death of Christ is seen from points of view of various witnesses. Large mixed cast

Mueller, Lavonne

American dreamers

Marilyn Monroe and Carl Sandburg meet in Washington, D.C. hotel. 1m 1w 1 interior

In The Best American short plays, 1995-1996

Jim's Commuter Airlines

Drama about owner of small commuter airline. 1m 1w 1 interior

In Facing forward; ed. by L. D. Frank

Violent peace

Drama depicting tortuous love affair between army brat and her father's aid. 2 acts 1m 1w 1 interior

In Playwriting women; ed. by J. Miles

Mulatto. Hughes, L.

Muldoon, Paul

Six honest serving men. Gallery Press 1995 50p

Verse play set in safe house on Irish border. Six members of IRA cell and widow of chief assess recent developments. 36 scenes 6m 1w 1 interior

Mullane, Michael. See Ross, D. jt. auth.

Müller, Heiner

Mommsen's block

Monologue reflecting on European cultural and political history focusing on German historian Theodor Mommsen. 1m

In DramaContemporary: Germany; ed. by C. Weber

Müller's dancers. Németh, Á.

Mullins, Brighde

Pathological Venus

Set in Nevada eating disorder center. Drama about societal definitions of beauty. 3w 2m 1b 1g extras 1 setting

In Lucky 13; ed. by R. Shuttleworth

Mum's the word. Miller, B.

Munda negra. Greer, B.

Munro, Rona

Fugue

Drama. Dialogue takes place in young secretary's mind as she suffers mental breakdown. Elements of the supernatural are incorporated. 2 acts 4 scenes 4w 1 setting

In Munro, R. Your turn to clean the stair & Fugue

The maiden stone. Hern Bks. 1995 86p

Drama about early 19th century actress and her family in northeast Scotland. 2 acts 18 scenes 3m 4w extras 1 setting

Your turn to clean the stair

Psychological drama about tensions among residents of Edinburgh tenement. 2 acts 2m 3w 1 setting

In Munro, R. Your turn to clean the stair & Fugue

Murder

Abe, K. Involuntary homicide
The Anna Project. This is for you, Anna
Baillie, J. De Monfort
Baker, D. and Cocke, D. Red fox/second hangin'
Baraka, A. Dutchman
Barnes, D. She tells her daughter
Beard, P. Death of a clown
Beard, P. Waiting for Pierrepoint
Blessing, L. Down the road
Blum, G.; Barker, W. and Martucci, V. Clue: the musical
Bond, E. Olly's prison
Booth, J. Mirror mirror on the wall
Booth, J. A question of identity
Brett, S. Murder in play
Büchner, G. Woyzeck
Burns, K. Psycho night at the Paradise Lounge
Burrill, M. P. Aftermath
Chiodo, T. Boardwalk melody hour murders
Chiodo, T. The medieval murders
Chiodo, T. Murder under the big top
Clemens, B. Inside job
Dallman, J. The inside story of Dr. Crippen
De Filippo, E. The local authority
De Geesewell, P. Murder at the asylum
DePietro, P. Death and deceit on the Nile
y DePietro, P. Murder at the prom
Dickins, B. Remember Ronald Ryan
Dickinson, J. Jack the Ripper, monster of Whitechapel
Dover, M. and Jarvis, G. Seconds
Downing, M. The demon
Dubois, R. D. Being at home with Claude
Durbridge, F. Sweet revenge
Enright N. Blackrock
y Enright, N. A property of the clan
Fennario, D. Doctor Thomas Neill Cream: mystery at McGill
Fulford, R. Lovesong
Foote, H. The one-armed man
Fraser, B. The ugly man
Gardiner, D. Weeds in the wheat
Graham, G. The boys
Gray, S. Dutch uncle
Gray, S. Molly

Murder—*Continued*
Gray, S. Stage struck
Harper, T. Rehearsal for murder
Harris, R. C. Abigail
Harrower, D. Knives in hens
Heiss, R. L. Illegal contact
Hischak, T. Murder by the book
Hope, K. Foreign lands
Hornby, I. Murdered, presumed dead
Hornby, I. Wait until the ghost is clear
Hornby, I. Where there's a will . . .
Jones, M. Vanishing points
Klíma, I. Games
Koenig, L. The little girl who lives down the lane
Law, M. Advertising Arnold
Lepage, R. and Brassard, M. Polygraph
Lillo, G. The London merchant
Linney, R. Ambrosio
Mamet, D. A scene—Australia
Maturin, C. R. Bertram
Mayer, J. Killjoy
McGullion, B. Murdermind
McNally, T. And things that go bump in the night
Medoff, M. The homage that follows
Millan, J. and Brooker, B. Serpent kills
Miller, B. Mum's the word
Nagy, P. Butterfly kiss
Nagy, P. Weldon rising
Nelson, T. B. Eye of God
Nigro, D. Ardy Fafirsin
Oates, J. C. Tone clusters
Oliver, D. The case of the dead flamingo dancer
Osborne, W. and Herrera, A. Smoke & mirrors
Parra, M. A. de la. Dostoevski goes to the beach
Pernak, A. Killers
Rascon Banda, V. H. Murder with malice
Reingold, J. Girl gone
Rodriguez, D. E. I'm not stupid
Sands, L. Checkmate
Schenkkan, R. The homecoming
Schnitzler, A. The Green Cockatoo
Sherman, M. Cracks
Sondheim, S. and Furth, G. Getting away with murder
Stoppard, T. The real Inspector Hound
Strindberg, A. Pariah
Strindberg, A. Simoom
Swedeen, S. The sleep seeker
Szyszkowitz, G. Somewhere over the rainbow
y Thane, A. The moonstone
Tissian, G. Night baseball
Triana, J. Night of the assassins
Valle-Inclan, R. de. The head of the Baptist
Vogel, P. Hot 'n' throbbing
Walker, G. F. The art of war
Walker, G. F. Beyond Mozambique
Walker, G. F. Theatre of the film noir
Wallace, N. In the heart of America
Watkins, M. Chicago
Wells, J. S. The ladykiller
Wilde, O. The Duchess of Padua
Williams, C. Rebecca
Wilson, L. Balm in Gilead
Wilson, L. Eukiah
Yew, C. Porcelain
Young, P. Squashed
See also Assassination; Fratricide; Infanticide; Mystery; Trials (Murder)

Murder at Minsing Manor: a nancy boys mystery. Simon, M. and Simon, R.

Murder at the asylum. De Geesewell, P.

Murder at the prom. DePietro, P.

Murder by the book. Hischak, T.

Murder for rent. Robinson, G. and Robinson, C. K.

Murder in play. Brett, S.

Murder in the House of horrors. St. John, B.

A **murder** of crows. Wellman, M.

Murder on reserve. Hischak, T.

Murder on the Orient Express subway. Boiko, C.

Murder under the big top. Chiodo, T.

Murder with malice. Rascon Banda, V. H.

Murdered, presumed dead. Hornby, I.

Murdered to death. Gordon, P.

Murderer hope of womankind. See Kokoschka, O. Murderer the women's hope

Murderer the women's hope. Kokoschka, O.

Murdermind. McGullion, B.

Murmuring judges. Hare, D.

Murmurs. Sickles, S. C.

Murphy, Jimmy
A picture of paradise
Dublin family struggles to avoid homelessness. 2 acts 3m 1w 1 interior 1 exterior
In The Dazzling dark: new Irish plays; ed. by F. McGuinness

Murphy, Phyllis. See Michels, J. jt. auth.

Murphy, Thomas
Bailegangaire
Drama set in 1984 rural Ireland. Allegory about need to exorcise the past to insure future happiness. Woman constantly relives old memory while at same time her granddaughters struggle to come to terms with their limited lives. 2 acts 3w 1 interior
In Murphy, T. Plays: two
Conversations on a homecoming
Comedy set in East Galway pub. Man returns from America for long-awaited reunion with his drinking buddies. 4m 3w 1 interior
In Murphy, T. Plays: two
The Gigli Concert
Irish millionaire undergoing breakdown consults quack calling himself a dynamatologist. 8 scenes 2m 1w 1 interior
In Murphy, T. Plays: three
The morning after optimism
Drama set in dreamlike forest. Fairy tale characters explore relationship between freedom and illusion. 10 scenes 2m 2w 1 exterior
In Murphy, T. Plays: three
The sanctuary lamp
Two unemployed circus performers spend the night in a Catholic church. They discuss their former lives and their feelings about religion. 2 acts 9 scenes 5m 2w 1 interior 1 exterior
In Murphy, T. Plays: three
A thief of a Christmas
Christmas story incorporating elements of Irish folklore. Man challenged to laughing contest. Music. 2 acts 8m 5w extras 1 interior
In Murphy, T. Plays: two

Murphy, Tom. See Murphy, Thomas

Murray, Peta
y Spitting chips. Currency Press 1995 62p
Teenager copes with grief and anger following mother's death. 10 scenes 2m 2w 1 setting

Murray-Smith, Joanna
Flame
Woman encounters dead husband. 1m 1w 1 setting
In Passion: six new short plays by Australian women; ed. by R. Horin
Honour. Currency Press in association with Playbox Theatre 1995 58p (Current Theatre series)
Portrait of a marriage on the rocks. 19 scenes 1m 3w 1 setting
Love child. Currency Press in association with Playbox Theatre 1993 93p (Current theatre series)
Drama explores feelings of young woman seeking natural mother. 2w 1 interior

Murrell, John
Memoir
Sarah Bernhardt's seventy-seventh and last summer. 2 acts 1m 1w 1 exterior
In Heroines; ed. by J. Doolittle

Murrone, Pietrodi. See Celestine V, Pope, Saint, 1215-1296

Museums
Kral, B. From the life of the bog people

Music
Study and teaching
Marans, J. Old wicked songs

Music critics
Harwood, R. Poison pen

Music from down the hill. Noonan, J. F.

Music-halls (Variety-theaters, cabarets, etc.)
Ritter, E. Automatic pilot

The **music** lessons. Yamauchi, W.

Music trade
Guare, J. Muzeeka

The **music** window. Buero-Vallejo, A.

Musical plays. See Musicals

Musical revues, comedies, etc. See Musicals

Musicals
c Adkins, D. Ready steady go
c Alette, C. The secret garden
y Allaway, B. Makin' it
y Allman, S. and Pickett, B. Frankenstein unbound
Arlen, H. Sweet and hot
Bartlett, N. Night after night
Berg, R. AIDS! the musical!
Blum, G.; Barker, W. and Martucci, V. Clue: the musical
Bohmler, C. and Adler, M. Gunmetal blues
c Breeze, N. The Rochdale Pioneers
Bricusse, L. The revenge of Sherlock Holmes
Brooker, B. Ilsa, queen of the Nazi love camp
Burke, J. Swinging on a star
c Carlson, N. K. and Chapman, B. The magic pebble
c Castle, G. V. Recess!
y Cearley, B. Welcome to Nashville
y Christiansen, A. A monster ate my homework
y Christiansen, A. Teens in Tinseltown
y Christiansen, A. Wash your troubles away

Musicals—*Continued*
Clarke, T. The Venetian twins
y Cohen, F. Try a little Shakespeare
c Cole, J. D. Conestoga stories
c Cole, J. D. Ichabod
c Colette, P. and Fritzen, G. Toy camp
c Cooper, R. M. How things happen in three!
Courts, R. Jack's holiday
Courts, R. Johnny Pye
Crabtree, H. Howard Crabtree's Whoop-dee-doo!
Craver, M. and Hardwick, M. Radio gals
c Dawson, J. and Bass, P. The inside story
Dunbar, P. L. and Shipp, J. A. In Dahomey
Durang, C. A history of the American film
Ekstrom, P. An O. Henry Christmas: The gift of the Magi
Ekstrom, P. An O. Henry Christmas: The last leaf
Feuer, J. Eating Raoul
Finch, C. and Lucas, B. Evelyn and the polka king
Finn, W. "In trousers"
Finn, W. and Lapine, J. Falsettoland
Finn, W. and Lapine, J. March of the falsettos
Fischoff, G. James A. Michener's Sayonara
c Flower, M. and Follows, S. Robin's last stand
y Foster, J. Play to win
y Francoeur, B. Coney Island of Dr. Moreau
c Francoeur, B. The enchantment of Beauty and the beast
y Francoeur, B. Gone with the breeze
y Francoeur, B. Hee haw hayride
y Francoeur, B. The internal teen machine
y Francoeur, B. Kilroy was here!
c Francoeur, B. The secret garden
y Francoeur, B. Shakespeare comes to Calamity Creek
c Francoeur, B. Snow White and the seven dwarfs
y Francoeur, B. Wrangler Ranch
Frandsen, E. [et al.] Song of Singapore
y Fraser, B. Prom night of the living dead
Gilbert, S. Capote at Yaddo
c Golden, G. The magic in me
c Hardee, L. The prince and the pauper
c Harder, E. Hey ho, Pinocchio
The Heather Brothers. Lust
Higginsen, V. and Wydro, K. Mama, I want to sing
Hill, K. The phantom of the opera
y Hughes, P. Abracadabra, Aladdin!
Hughes, L. Don't you want to be free?
c Ireland, V. Roald Dahl's The Giraffe and the Pelly and me
c Jackson, D. No one will marry a princess with a tree growing out of her head!
Kander, J. The kiss of the spider woman
y Keating, B. The garbage cantata
Kuhn, K. Midsummer nights
LaChiusa, M. J. Agnes
LaChiusa, M. J. Break
LaChiusa, M. J. Eulogy for Mister Hamm
LaChuisa, M. J. First Lady suite: Eleanor sleeps here
LaChuisa, M. J. First Lady suite: Olio
LaChuisa, M. J. First Lady suite: Over Texas
LaChuisa, M. J. First Lady suite: Where's Mamie?
LaChiusa, M. J. Lucky nurse
Laird, M. Ruthless!
Larson, J. J.P. Morgan saves the nation
Larson, L. and Lee, E. L. The salvation of Iggy Scrooge
Ledoux, P. and Smyth, D. Cheatin' hearts
Leslee, R. Avenue X
Lloyd Webber, A. Sunset Boulevard
Markham, S. Love and shrimp
McGillivray, D. and Zerlin, W. The Farndale Avenue Housing Estate Townspeople's Guild Operatic Society's production of The Mikado
c McGovern, C. The ugly duck
c McMahon, J. P. and Ryan, N. Buttonbush
Menken, A. Weird romance: Her pilgrim soul
Menken, A. Weird romance: The girl who was plugged in
Morley, S. Noel and Gertie
Nassif, R. L. Opal
Newman, M. and Damashek, B. Quilters
Norman, M. The secret garden
Norman, P. Love off the shelf
O'Connor, C. All that he was . . .
Oliver, D. The case of the dead flamingo dancer
Ono, Y. New York rock
Osborne, J. The world of Paul Slickey
Overmyer, E. In a pig's valise
Pattison, J. Dreams from a summer house
Pen, P. Bed and sofa
Perry, S. In Dahomey
c Peterson, L. The wind in the willows
y Polsky, M. E. SATisfaction

Musicals—*Continued*
y Poskitt, K. Henry the Tudor dude
c Poskitt, K. The Rumpelstiltskin racket
y Prior, J. Phantom of the music hall
Pruitt, D. and Hutchison, P. The Harvey Milk show
y Reiser, D. Alas! Alack! Zorro's back
y Reiser, D. The creepy creeps of Pilgrim Road
y Reiser, D. Dr. Jekyll ... please don't hyde
y Reiser, D. I want my mummy!
c Rocklin, B. The Island of Anyplace
y Rowe, D. P. Zombie prom
c Ruch, A. Clarissa's closet
Russ, A. Inside out
Sharkey, T. M. It's a wonderful life
Sherman, A. Hello muddah, hello fadduh!
Silver, J. M. and Boyd, J. A ... my name is still Alice
y Sloyer, G. Ezekiel saw the ... what?
Smolensky, S. and Waldrop, J. The Mikado
Sondheim, S. Company
Sondheim, S. Passion
Sondheim, S. and Lapine, J. Into the woods
Stiles, G. Moll Flanders
c Stites, K. Adventures with young King Arthur
Stoll, D. Teller of tales
Swados, E. Esther
c Swajeski, D. M. The revolution machine
c Valenti, M. Beauty and the beast
Warrender, S. Das barbecü
Wolfe, G. C. Jelly's last jam
c Wood, D. Rupert and the green dragon
c Woyiwada, A. The little fir tree

Musicians
Hare, D. Teeth 'n' smiles
Overmyer, E. The Heliotrope Bouquet by Scott Joplin & Louis Chauvin
Sierens, A. Drummers
West, C. L. Before it hits home
Wolfe, G. C. Jelly's last jam

Muslims
Gallaire, F. You have come back
Sharif, B. My ancestor's house

Musset, Alfred de
Caprice; tr. by Donald Watson
Variant title: A diversion. Domestic comedy set in 1837 France. Count realizes value of faithful wife after experiencing subtle intrigue of another woman. 8 scenes 2m 2w 1 interior
In Musset, A. de. Five plays

Don't play with love (On ne badine pas avec l'amour); tr. by Michael Sadler
Variant titles: Camille and Perdican; No trifling with love. Afraid of love, woman pushes childhood sweetheart into arms of her sister who commits suicide upon learning they still love each other. Speaking chorus. 3 acts 18 scenes 4m 3w extras 4 interior 5 exteriors
In Mussett, A. de. Five plays

Don't trifle with love; tr. by Nagle Jackson
Variant title: Don't play with love, entered above
In Musset, A. de. Fantasio and other plays

Fantasio; tr. by Brian Singleton
Comedy. Impoverished youth becomes king's jester and saves princess from unhappy marriage. Singing. 2 acts 10 scenes 8m 2w extras 4 interiors 4 exteriors
In Musset, A. de. Five plays
—Same; tr. by Richard Howard
In Musset, A. de. Fantasio and other plays

Lorenzaccio; tr. by Donald Watson
Historical drama about assassination of Florentine tyrant Alessandro de Medici by his cousin. 5 acts 39 scenes 30m 4w extras 1 setting
In Musset, A. de. Five plays
—Same; tr. by Paul Schmidt
In Musset, A. de. Fantasio and other plays

The moods of Marianne (Les caprices de Marianne); tr. by Donald Watson
Variant titles: The follies of Marianne; Marianne. Young man dies in vain for love of capricious married woman who falls in love with his best friend. Inspired by Musset's love affair with George Sand. 2 acts 7m 2w extras 1 exterior
In Musset, A. de. Five plays

You can't think of everything; tr. by Michael Feingold
Variant title: It's impossible to think of everything; Journey to Gotha; One can not think of everything. Romantic comedy set in early 19th century France. Absent-minded nobleman courts countess who has same failing. 3m 2w 1 interior
In Musset, A. de. Fantasio and other plays

Muzeeka. Guare, J.

My ancestor's house. Sharif, B.

My Antonia. Jones, C.

My body. My blood. Kirby, M.

My crummy job. Steppling, J.

My head was a sledgehammer. Foreman, R.

My heart's a suitcase. McIntyre, C.

My Johnny. Law, M.

My left breast. Miller, S.

My mother said I never should. Keatley, C.

My mother's eyes. Sebbar, L.

My name, shall I tell you my name? Reid, C.

My night with Reg. Elyot, K.

My old lady. Horovitz, I.

My queer body. Miller, T.

My side of the story. Goluboff, B.

My son Susie. Royce, C.

My thing of love. Gersten, A.

My very own story. Ayckbourn, A.

My wife's dead mother. Feydeau, G.

Myron, a fairy tale in black and white. Kearns, M.

Mysteries and miracle plays
Solórzano, C. The crucified

The **mysteries** and what's so funny? Gordon, D.

The **mysteries:** The Passion. Sahlins, B.

The **mysterious** Mr. Love. Leach, K.

Mystery
Aldrich, A. The housewarming
Bobrick, S. Are you sure?
Bohmler, C. and Adler, M. Gunmetal blues
y Boiko, C. Murder on the Orient Express subway
Booth, J. By whose hand?
Booth, J. Dead on time
Booth, J. Face of evil
Booth, J. Mirror mirror on the wall
Booth, J. Or was he pushed?
Booth, J. A question of identity
Booth, J. Tangled web
Brett, S. Murder in play
Burns, K. Psycho night at the Paradise Lounge
Byerrum, E. A Christmas cactus
Chiodo, T. Boardwalk melody hour murders
Chiodo, T. The medieval murders
Chiodo, T. Murder under the big top
c Conville, D. and Gooderson, D. The curse of the Egyptian mummy
De Geesewell, P. Murder at the asylum
DePietro, P. Death and deceit on the Nile
DePietro, P. The hilarious hillbilly massacre
y DePietro, P. Murder at the prom
Dudley, E. The return of Sherlock Holmes
French, D. Silver dagger
Gardiner, D. Weeds in the wheat
Gordon, P. Murdered to death
Gray, C. The shaken reed
Hare, D. Knuckle
Harper, T. Rehearsal for murder
Harper, T. That's the spirit
Harris, R. C. Abigail
Heiss, R. L. Illegal contact
c Hezlep, W. Treasure of the Mayans
High, B. G. Ambush
Hischak, T. Murder by the book
Hischak, T. Murder on reserve
Hornby, I. Murdered, presumed dead
Hornby, I. The price to pay
Hornby, I. A question of innocence
Hornby, I. Voices
y Jackson, K. Three doors to death
Kelly, T. That's the spirit
Law, M. Cry wolf
Manzi, W. Perfect crime
y Martens, A. C. The comeback caper
Oliver, D. The case of the dead flamingo dancer
Robinson, G. and Robinson, C. K. Murder for rent
Sands, L. Checkmate
Sherman, M. Cracks
St. John, B. 13 past midnight
y St. John, B. Murder in the House of horrors
Stoppard, T. The real Inspector Hound
y Thum, N. B. The Red-headed League
Welsh, D. Make it happen
y Zeder, S. L. The death and life of Sherlock Homes

Mystery of the phantom voice. Sussman, D.

Mystery of the rose bouquet. Puig, M.

The **mystery** school. Selig, P.

Mythology, Classical
Dryden, J. Amphitryon

Mythology, Egyptian
MacDonald, A.-M. The Arab's mouth

Mythology, Greek
Aeschylus. Agamemnon
c Asbrand, K. Pandora's box
c Boiko, C. Persephone
Euripides. Alcestis

Mythology, Greek—*Continued*
Euripides. Bakkhai
Euripides. The children of Heracles
Euripides. The Cyclops
Euripides. Electra
Euripides. Hekabe
Euripides. Hippolytus
Euripides. Iphigenia among the Taurians
Euripides. Iphigenia in Aulis
Euripides. Medea
Euripides. Orestes
Goethe, J. W. von. Iphigenia in Tauris
Goethe, J. W. von. Pandora
Judy, G. Antigone
Kennelly, B. Sophocles' Antigone
Kochanowski, J. The dismissal of the Grecian envoys
c Mahlmann, L. and Jones, D. C. King Midas and the golden touch
y McCaslin, N. Travelers from Olympus
y Nightingale, E. M. Arise, Sparta!
y Olfson, L. The last time I saw Paris
Racine, J. Phaedra
Shaffer, P. The gift of the Gorgon
Sophocles. Antigone
Sophocles. Electra
Sophocles. Oedipus at Colonus
Sophocles. Oedipus the King
Wertenbaker, T. The love of the nightingale
Wilder, T. The drunken sisters

Mythology, Yoruban
Osofisan, F. Esu and the vagabond minstrels

N

Naaman, the Syrian
Aynsley, E. 'I told you so'

Nadine. See Fornes, M. I. What of the night?: Nadine

Nagasaki (Japan)

History—Bombardment, 1945

Tanaka, C. The head of Mary

Nagy, Andras
The seducer's diary
Philosophical tale of seduction and betrayal loosely based on autobiographical writings of Kierkegaard. 2 acts 35 scenes 4m 2w 1 interior
In Hungarian plays; ed. by L. Upor

Nagy, Phyllis
Butterfly kiss. Hern Bks. 1994 49p
Psychological drama set in jail cell explores web of events that led woman to murder. 2 acts 3m 5w 1 interior

Disappeared. French (London) 1995 55p
Twenty-five-year old travel agent disappears after she leaves seedy bar in New York's Hells Kitchen. 2 acts 15 scenes 5m 3w 1 setting
—Same
In Nagy, P. Weldon rising & Disappeared

The scarlet letter. French 1995 88p
Dramatization of Hawthorne's novel about adultery and social ostracism in colonial Massachusetts. 2 acts 4m 3w 1 setting

The Strip. Hern Bks. in association with the Royal Court Theatre 1995 77p
Female impersonator, love-struck repo man and lesbian journalist seek fame in Las Vegas. In England, astrologer, fugitive white supremacists and gay pawnbroker search for justice in Liverpool. 2 acts 5m 5w 1 setting

Trip's cinch
Female academic tries to discover truth behind trial of wealthy young man accused of raping working class woman. 3 scenes 1m 2w
In Humana Festival '94

Weldon rising
Surreal look at homosexuality, poverty, murder and urban life set in Manhattan's meat-packing district. 4m 2w 1 exterior
In Nagy, P. Weldon rising & Disappeared

Najera, Rick
Latinologues: monologues of the Latin experience
Series of nine comic monologues reflecting Hispanic American experience. 9 scenes 6m 3w
In Najera, R. The pain of the macho and other plays

The pain of the macho
Satirical one man show. Linked monologues explore meanings of machismo through diverse characters. Prologue 9 scenes 1m 1 setting
In Najera, R. The pain of the macho and other plays

A quiet love
Autobiographical drama. Cross-generational story of Mexican American family. Prologue 2 scenes 4m 2w 1 setting
In Najera, R. The pain of the macho and other plays

Naked West. Green, M.

The **name** game. Soland, L.

Name that book! Miller, H. L.

Nanawatai! Mastrosimone, W.

Nannies. See Servants

Naomi in the living room. Durang, C.

Naomi's road. Wing, P. A.

Naples (Italy)
De Filippo, E. Filumena Marturano
De Filippo, E. Napoli milionaria
Fletcher, J. and Massinger, P. The double marriage

Napoli milionaria. De Filippo, E.

Narcissism
Marivaux. La dispute

Narcotic addicts
Bullins, E. Goin' a Buffalo
Crowley, M. A breeze from the gulf
Wilson, L. Balm in Gilead

Narcotic habit. See Narcotic addicts

Nasimento, Abdias do
Sortilege II: Zumbi returns
Explores Brazil's black heritage. Variable cast 8 characters extras 1 setting
In Crosswinds; ed. by W. B. Branch

Nashville (Tenn.)
y Cearley, B. Welcome to Nashville

Nassif, Robert Lindsey
Opal; a new musical adventure; based on the childhood diary of Opal Whiteley (aka Françoise D'Orleans) written at age seven, winner of the Richard Rodgers Award. French 1993 118p
Musical based on diary of aristocratic girl who was taken to live in lumber camp after being orphaned in shipwreck off Oregon coast in 1904. Prologue 7 scenes 3m 6w 1g 1 setting

Nasty neighbours. Isitt, D.

Nathaniel in Berkshire. Hall, F. B.

National socialism
Barnes, P. Laughter!
De Boer, L. The Buddha of Ceylon
Garrett-Groag, L. The White Rose
Harwood, R. Taking sides
Mitterer, F. There's not a finer country
Norton-Taylor, R. Nuremberg
Page, E. Aryan birth
Preses, P. and Becher, U. Our Mr. Bockerer
Roth, A. Born guilty
Schwaiger, B. Yes, my führer!
Szyszkowitz, G. Friedmann Puntigam
Unger, H. R. The bell tolls at twelve
y Williams, K. Gran Webster's war

Native son. Wright, R. and Green, P.

Native speech. Overmyer, E.

The **nativity** scene. Haylock, D.

The **natural** daughter. Goethe, J. W. von

Natural man. Browne, T.

The **nature** and purpose of the universe. Durang, C.

Nave, Bill
Visiting Oliver
Woman visits mentally retarded son in institution. 3m 1w 1 interior
In Off-Off Broadway Festival plays, 18th ser.

Navrotsky, Pavel Ivanovich
Fugard, A. A place with the pigs

Nazis. See National socialism

Neary, Jack
c Aladdin and the wonderful lamp. Bakers Plays 1993 47p
Members of royal court act out the Arabian nights tale. 7m 3w extras 1 interior

Nebraska
Cloud, D. O pioneers!

The **necklace.** Dias, E. J.

Necropolis. Nigro, D.

Negative. Oates, J. C.

Negroes. See African Americans; Blacks

Neidermyer, Dan
c The tortoise and the hare race again. Pioneer Drama Service 1996 17p
Environmental message central in retelling of tortoise and hare's race. Unidentified cast 8 characters extras 1 exterior

Neighborliness
Dixon, M. B. and Smith, V. Breaking the chain
Richardson, W. The chip woman's fortune

Neighbors
Beard, P. Meat and two veg
Heggie, I. An experienced woman gives advice
Isitt, D. Nasty neighbours
Yamauchi, W. And the soul shall dance

Neipris, Janet
Brussels sprouts
Ex-lovers meet in academic setting. 1m 1w 1 interior
In Facing forward; ed. by L. D. Frank

Nellie Bly: ten days in a madhouse. Cooper, B.

Nelson, Greg
Castrato. Blizzard Pub. 1993 78p
Psychological drama set in Edmonton about clash of liberal and fundamentalist religious views. Brothers reunited after twelve-year estrangement following sensational suicide of their abusive preacher father. 2 acts 13 scenes 3m 1w

Nelson, Richard
Flyer
First scene from Roots in water. Monologue by Vietnam vet set in 1976. 1m
In Telling tales: new one-act plays; ed. by E. Lane
The General from America. Faber & Faber 1996 92p
Historical drama about Benedict Arnold. 13 scenes 12m 5w extras
Life sentences. Faber & Faber 1993 56p
Story of a couple, a college professor and his girl friend who is twenty years his junior. 2 acts 12 scenes 1m 1w 1 setting
New England. Faber & Faber. 1994 66p
Connecticut farmhouse setting for drama exploring lives of English expatriates reunited for family funeral. 8 scenes 4m 4w 2 interiors
New England (condensation)
In The Best plays of 1995-1996

Nelson, Richard and Gelman, Alexander
Misha's party. Faber & Faber 1993 66p
Comedy set in Moscow 1991. Against backdrop of attempted coup, man attempts to throw himself sixtieth birthday party and grandmother attempts reconciliation with granddaughter. 11 scenes 7m 7w 1 interior

Nelson, Tim Blake
Eye of God. Dramatists 1997 50p
Lonely woman marries disturbed ex-con who ends up killing her. 2 acts 5m 3w 2 interiors

Németh, Ákos
Müller's dancers
Allegory about modern Hungary. Dance troupe falls apart when leader deserts them. Music, dancing. 3m 4w extras 1 setting
In Hungarian plays; ed. by L. Upor

Nemeth, Sally
Sally's shorts: Black cloud morning New York
Monologue. Accidental discovery brightens woman's hellish day. 1w 1 setting
In Nemeth, S. Sally's shorts
Sally's shorts: Lily
During World War I, two sisters banished from small town for being involved with married man. 2w 1 setting
In Nemeth, S. Sally's shorts
Sally's shorts: Living in this world
Monologue. Woman survives in post-apocalyptic city. 1w 1 setting
In Nemeth, S. Sally's shorts
Sally's shorts: Pagan day
Woman's sexual dreams and fantasies. 2w 1 setting
In Nemeth, S. Sally's shorts
Sally's shorts: Pre-nuptial agreement
Monologue. War nurse attends wounded soldier. 1w 1 setting
In Nemeth, S. Sally's shorts
Sally's shorts: The cat act
Dialogue between senile old woman and her caretaker. 2w 1 extra 1 setting
In Nemeth, S. Sally's shorts
Sally's shorts: Visions of grandeur
Monologue. Woman imagines her life as black and white movie. 1w 1 setting
In Nemeth, S. Sally's shorts
Sally's shorts: Word games
While smoking marijuana, two women share memories. 2w 1 setting
In Nemeth, S. Sally's shorts
Water play
Symbolic drama. Two men and woman monitor rising flood waters. Slide projections. 2m 1w 1 setting
In Facing forward; ed. by L. D. Frank

Nephews
Wilson, L. Brontosaurus

Nero, Emperor of Rome, 37-68
Warner, F. Light shadows

Neruda, Pablo
Pintauro, J. House made of air

Nervous breakdown. See Neurasthenia

The **nest.** Kroetz, F. X.

A **nest** of cuckoos. Waterhouse, J. and Leach, P.

A **nest** of dragons. Barnieh, Z.

Nestroy, Johann
As you were; tr. by Geoffrey Skelton. French (London) 1997 22p
Farce. Amorous chaos and duplicity reign in household of wealthy timber merchant and jealous wife. 2m 2w 1 interior

Netherwood. White, P.

Netzel, Sally
c The dark castle. Clark, I. E. 1993 27p
Hero saves princess from evil baron. Audience participation. 2 acts 11 scenes 6m 4w 1 interior 2 exteriors
y The jest. Anchorage Press 1996 32p
Adaptation of subplot of Shakespeare's Twelfth night. Characters trick pompous Malvolio with false love letter. 10 scenes 4m 2w

Neuman, Colleen
c A better mousetrap
Man and woman try to catch mouse. Unidentified cast 3 characters extras
In The Big book of large-cast plays; ed. by S. E. Kamerman
c Lion and mouse stories. Bakers Plays 1993 47p
Three fables featuring animals. Variable cast 42 characters 1 setting

Neurasthenia
Gray, S. The holy terror
Harwood, R. The ordeal of Gilbert Pinfold
Lan, D. The ends of the earth
Murphy, T. The Gigli Concert
Storey, D. Stages
Wilson, L. The madness of Lady Bright

Neutral ground. Stoppard, T.

Never in my lifetime. Gee, S.

Never swim alone. MacIvor, D.

Neville's Island. Firth, T.

New anatomies. Wertenbaker, T.

New England
Linney, R. The death of King Philip
O'Neill, E. Desire under the elms
O'Neill, E. Mourning becomes Electra: Homecoming
O'Neill, E. Mourning becomes Electra: The haunted
O'Neill, E. Mourning becomes Electra: The hunted

New England. Nelson, R.

New-found-land. Stoppard, T.

New France. See Hollingsworth, M. The history of the village of the small huts

New Jersey
Wilder, T. The happy journey to Camden and Trenton

New Mexico
Glancy, D. Weebjob
y Reiser, D. Alas! Alack! Zorro's back

New morning. Hughes, D.

New Orleans (La.)
Calhoun, W. Call it clover
c Church, J. The Pied Piper of New Orleans
Grimsley, J. Mr. Universe

A **new** Punch and Judy. Pflomm, P. N.

The **new** world order. Pinter, H.

New Year
Beard, P. Come the resolution

New Year's eve and Kibbutz. Margulies, D.

New York (N.Y.)
Boothe, C. The women
Chayefsky, P. The mother
Childress, A. Trouble in mind
Courts, R. Jack's holiday
Crimp, M. The treatment
Glowacki, J. Antigone in New York
Hoffman, W. M. As is
Horovitz, I. The Indian wants the Bronx
Ives, D. Degas c'est moi
Kingsley, S. Dead end
Kramer, L. The normal heart
Mamet, D. Edmond
Mowatt, A. C. Fashion
Nagy, P. Weldon rising
O'Neill, E. The iceman cometh
Rebeck, T. Loose knit
Rivera, J. Marisol

Bronx

Brown, M. H. The day the Bronx died
Cruz, M. The have-little
Gilroy, F. D. Any given day
Odets, C. Awake and sing!

Brooklyn

Dizon, L. Till voices wake us
Leslee, R. Avenue X
Margulies, D. Found a peanut
Miller, A. Broken glass.
Pugliese, F. Aven'u boys
Smith, A. D. Fires in the mirror: Crown Heights, Brooklyn and other identities

Greenwich Village

Hansberry, L. The sign in Sidney Brustein's window
Mason, T. Babylon gardens
Mason, T. Sorry
Pintauro, J. Uncle Chick
Witten, M. Washington Square moves

Harlem

Childress, A. Wine in the wilderness
Coleman, R. M. The girl from back home
Edmonds, S. R. Old man Pete
Elder, L. Ceremonies in dark old men
Glover, K. Dancing on moonlight
Hill, A. On Strivers Row
Hughes, L. Simply heavenly
Russell, C. Five on the black hand side
Walker, J. The River Niger
Wolfe, G. C. Story in Harlem slang

Manhattan

Brown, C. The African Company presents Richard III
Chayefsky, P. Middle of the night
Doctorow, E. L. Drinks before dinner
Gardner, H. I'm not Rappaport
Gilroy, F. D. A way with words
Hwang, D. H. Trying to find Chinatown
Ives, D. Long ago and far away, a winter's tale
Johnson, T. Insignificance
Noonan, J. F. The drowning of Manhattan
Oakes, M. and Wells, J. Greenfield blooms

New York (N.Y.)—Manhattan—*Continued*
Paterson, D. L. Dungeons
Pogos, A. Strangers in the night
Rivera, J. Slaughter in the lake
Sánchez, E. Trafficking in broken hearts

Queens

Reilly, C. Astronauts
Richards, G. The root

New York (State)

c Cole, J. D. Ichabod

New York actor. Guare, J.

New York Public Library
Guare, J. A day for surprises

New York rock. Ono, Y.

Newfoundland
Pittman, A. West moon

Newhouse. Rose, R. and Kugler, D. D.

Newman, John Henry
Pickering, K. The parting of friends

Newman, Molly, and Damashek, Barbara
Quilters

Based on The quilters: women and domestic art, by Patricia Cooper and Norma Bradley Allen. Musical depicting frontier life of pioneer woman and her six daughters. Music, singing, dancing. 2 acts 7w extras 1 setting

In Voicings: ten plays from the documentary theatre; ed. by A. Favorini

Newsom, John D.
Dance Saturday night

Drama about racial prejudice set outside community hall in 1890s Prescott, Arizona. 3m 1w 1 setting

In Lucky 13; ed. by R. Shuttleworth

Newspapers
Gray, O. The torrents

Next. McNally, T.

Ngema, Mbongeni. See Mtwa, P. jt. auth.

Nicholas, Saint, Bishop of Myra
McCullough, L. E. O thou joyful day

Nicholas, Denise
Buses

Dream play about civil rights revolving around Mary Ellen Pleasant and Rosa Parks. 2w

In The National black drama anthology; ed. by W. King

Nicholson, John, 1790-1843
Harrison, T. Poetry or bust

Nicol, Ron
c The Snow Queen. French (London) 1997 53p

Based on Hans Christian Andersen's fairy tale. Girl rescues boy from evil enchantress. 2 acts Large mixed cast

Nigeria
Onwueme, O. T. The broken calabash
Onwueme, O. T. Parables for a season
Onwueme, O. T. The reign of Wazobia

Native peoples

See Yorubas

Night after night. Bartlett, N.

Night and her stars (condensation). Greenberg, R.

Night baseball. Tissian, G.

A **night** divided. Pedrero, P.

A **night** in November. Jones, M.

A **night** in the theatre. Casler, L.

Night light. Lazarus, J.

Night maneuver. Korder, H.

Night of the assassins. Triana, J.

The **night** of the missing bridegroom. Wilkinson, L.

The **night** of the Sinhat [sic] Torah. See Barnes, P. The spirit of man: The night of the Sinhat [sic] Torah

Night on Bald Mountain. White, P.

Night seasons. Foote, H.

Night sky. Yankowitz, S.

The **night** Thoreau spent in jail. Lawrence, J. and Lee, R. E.

Night traveler. Salah, 'Abd al-Sabur

Nightclubs. See Music-halls (Variety-theaters, cabarets, etc.)

Nightingale, E. M.
y Arise, Sparta!

Comedy. Dramatization of Greek myth of Helen of Troy. Helen runs away with Paris precipitating war between Sparta and Troy. 3m 1w extras 1 exterior

In The Big book of skits; ed. by S. E. Kamerman

Nightingale, Florence, 1820-1910
y Waddy, L. Florence Nightingale

The **Nightingale.** Lazarus, J.

A **nightingale.** See Foote, H. The roads to home: A nightingale

Nightmare: the fright of your life. Moss, R. S.

Night's candles. Wyld, H.

Nigro, Don
Animia mundi. French 1994 121p

Scenes from life of American poet involved in European intellectual circles of early 20th century. 2 acts 16 scenes 8m 5w 1 setting

Nigro, Don—*Continued*

Ardy Fafirsin. French 1993 110p

Mock-Elizabethan farce based on lurid accounts of sensational murder. Singing. 2 acts 30 scenes 8m 4w 1 setting

Fair Rosamund and her murderer

Romance develops between Henry II's mistress and murderer dispatched to slay her. 1m 1w

In Nigro, D. Glamorgan and other plays

Give us a kiss and show us your knickers

Dark comedy. Young woman entertains roommate's new boyfriend. 1m 2w 1 setting

In Nigro, D. Glamorgan and other plays

Glamorgan

Gothic drama, 18th century woman's heritage of madness and passion through three generations. 2m 3w 1 setting

In Nigro, D. Glamorgan and other plays

Loves labour wonne. French 1995 106p

Comedic drama about literary genius. In drunken reverie Shakespeare muses about his early struggles, rivals, loves, family and characters. 2 acts 14 scenes 9m 5w 1 setting

Lucia mad. French 1993 123p

Drama explores madness of James Joyce's daughter and her doomed love for the young Samuel Beckett. 2 acts 26 scenes 4m 2w

Major Weir

Black comedy. Ghosts of brother and sister executed in Scotland in 1670 for devil worship. 1m 1w interior

In Nigro, D. Glamorgan and other plays

Necropolis

Drama set in eastern European country torn by civil war. Journalist enamored of young female sniper. 1m 1w 1 interior

In Nigro, D. Glamorgan and other plays

Paganini. French 1995 116p

Surreal comedy based on bizarre career of violin virtuoso Nicolo Paganini. 2 acts 20 scenes 7m 5w 1 setting

Squirrels

Demented monologue. Woman gives birth to squirrels. 1w

In Nigro, D. Glamorgan and other plays

The Transylvanian clockworks. French 1996 95p

Gothic horror tale loosely based on B. Stoker's Dracula. Van Helsing travels to London to unravel mystery of Jonathan Harker's dementia. 2 acts 32 scenes 4m 3w 1 setting

The weird sisters

Monologue by woman who believes her unborn twin sister is living inside her skull. 1w

In Nigro, D. Glamorgan and other plays

Within the ghostly mansion's labyrinth

Monologue by lonely old woman who has spent years constructing labyrinthine mansion. 1w

In Nigro, D. Glamorgan and other plays

Nimmo, Heather

One small step

Young married Australian woman explores her relationships and responsibilities as she considers accepting job promotion. 2 acts 1w 1 setting

In Nimmo, H. and Learner, T. One small step [and] Witchplay

Nimmo, Paul

y Will Shakespeare save the King!

Famous speeches and scenes from Shakespeare acted out as part of comic story about bored King and his troupe of players. 1 act Variable cast 1 setting

In Nimmo, P. Will Shakespeare save us! Will Shakespeare save the King!

y Will Shakespeare save us!

Companion piece to title entered above. 1 act Variable cast 1 setting

In Nimmo, P. Will Shakespeare save us! Will Shakespeare save the King!

Nina in the morning. Durang, C.

Nineteen hundred sixty nine. Landau, T.

Ninth Cavalry to the rescue! McCullough, L. E.

Ninth inning wedding. May, B.

The **nip** and the bite. GeBauer, J.

Nishikawa, Lane, and Talmadge, Victor

The gate of heaven

Follows fortunes and friendship of Japanese American soldier and Dachau survivor. 2 acts 14 scenes 2m extras

In Asian American drama; ed. by B. Nelson

Nissen, Kaj

Fair Kirsten; tr. by Julian Garner

Historical monologue by country girl who becomes mistress to King of Denmark. 1w

In New Danish plays; ed. by H. C. Andersen

Nixon, Richard M.

Lees, R. Nixon's Nixon

Nixon's Nixon. Lees, R.

No cycle. Standjofski, H.

No end to dreaming. Barnes, P.

No. here comes Ulrike Meinhof. Rubess, B.

No man's land. Pinter, H.

No means no! Frost R.; Olson, G. and Johnson, L.

No mercy. Congdon, C.

No more Medea. Porter, D.

No one will be immune. Mamet, D.

No one will marry a princess with a tree growing out of her head! Jackson, D.

No place for idiots. Mitterer, F.

No problem. See Butterfield, C. Life in the trees: No problem

No roses around the door. Bamford, S.

No triffling with love. See Musset, A. de. Don't play with love

No wider than the heart. Andrews, B.

No wit, no help like a woman's. Middleton, T.

No worries. Holman, D.

Noah (Biblical figure)
Hurston, Z. N. The first one

Nobody here but us chickens. Barnes, P.

Nocturne. Trott, S.

Noddy. Wood, D.

Noel and Gertie. Morley, S.

Nolan, Paul T.

y An enemy of the people

Adaptation of Henrik Ibsen's play set in 19th century Norway. Doctor who opposes opening of contaminated public baths is ostracized. 2 scenes 8m 2w extras 2 interiors

In The Big book of dramatized classics; ed. by S. E. Kamerman

y The inexperienced ghost

Based on short story by H. G. Wells set 1890 London. Timid ghost haunts matron and niece. 3m 2w 1 interior

In The Big book of dramatized classics; ed. by S. E. Kamerman

y The school for wives

Adaptation of Molière's romantic comedy set in 17th century France. Rich old man intends to marry his young ward despite her love for another. 3 scenes 6m 3w 1 exterior

In The Big book of dramatized classics; ed. by S. E. Kamerman

Noon. McNally, T.

Noonan, John Ford

The drowning of Manhattan

Satire set in future. Congress votes to flood Manhattan. 4m 1w extras 1 interior

In The Best American short plays, 1992-1993

Music from down the hill. French 1995 85p

Two women from dissimilar backgrounds gradually discover their commonality while in upstate New York mental hospital. 2 acts 12 scenes 2w 1 interior

When it comes early

Husband's memories affected by brain surgery. 1m 1w 1 setting

In The Best American short plays, 1995-1996

Noonday demons. Barnes, P.

Norbury, Peter

Valparaiso. New Playwrights Network 1994 20p

Comedy. Man falls in love with seductive mailbox. 2m 1w extras 1 exterior

Norcross, E. Blanche

c Pied Piper's land

Dramatization of Browning's poem about piper who rids town of rats and lures children away when mayor won't pay his fee. 3 scenes 2m 1w 5b 4g extras 3 exteriors

In The Big book of large-cast plays; ed. by S. E. Kamerman

Nordlicht, Lillian

c Cover your eyes and run! Anchorage Press 1995 32p

Young ghost wants to be boy for Halloween. Singing. 2 acts 3 scenes 3m 2w 6b 4g 1 interior

Norm and Ahmed. Buzo, A.

The **normal** heart. Kramer, L.

Norman, Marsha

Loving Daniel Boone

First produced as D. Boone. Cleaning woman in history museum obsessed with Daniel Boone moves back and forth in time from the present to frontier Kentucky of 1778. 2 acts 7m 2w extras 1 setting

In By Southern playwrights; ed. by M. B. Dixon and M. Volansky

Lunch with Ginger

Scene from Trudy Blue, entered below. 1 act 4w 1 interior

In EST marathon, 1994

Norman, Marsha—*Continued*
The secret garden; book and lyrics by Marsha Norman; music by Lucy Simon; based on the novel by Frances Hodgson Burnett. French 1993 136p
Musical set in 1906 India and England. Orphaned girl and invalid cousin are restored to health and happiness as they tend secret garden. Prologue 2 acts 18 scenes 10m 9w 1b 1g extras settings
—Same. Theatre Communications Group 1992 128p
Trudy Blue
Successful female writer embarks on spiritual journey accompanied by main character of her novel, Trudy Blue. Prologue 15 scenes 4m 6w extra 1 setting
In A Decade of new comedy: plays from the Humana Festival v2
In Humana Festival '95

Norman, Philip
Love off the shelf, a musical; book by Roger Hall; lyrics by A. K. Grant; music by Philip Norman. French (London) 1993 78p
Musical parody of romantic novel genre. 2 acts 5 scenes 4m 4w 1 setting

Norman, is that you? Clark, R. and Bobrick, S.

Norsemen. See Northmen

North, Francis
The Kentish barons
Gothic drama with songs. Man must liberate true love from rival castle. 3 acts 10 scenes 6m 4w extras
In Seven Gothic dramas, 1789-1825

North Carolina
Race relations
Mann, E. Greensboro

North Dakota
c McCullough, L. E. The little old sod shanty

North Shore Fish. Horovitz, I.

Northanger Abbey. Austen, J. (dramatization) See Francis, M. Jane Austen's Northanger Abbey

Northeast local. Donaghy, T.

Northern Ireland
Devlin, A. After Easter
Harding, M. Hubert Murray's widow
Jones, M. A night in November
McLaughlin, T. Greatest hits
Reid, C. My name, shall I tell you my name?
See also Belfast (Northern Ireland)

Northmen
c Lloyd, R. Smut's saga
MacNeice, L. They met on Good Friday
O'Brien, M. Mad boy chronicle

Norton-Taylor, Richard
Nuremberg. Hern Bks. 1997 72p
Historical drama using only actual words spoken during 1946 Nuremberg War Crimes Trial. One by one members of Nazi High Command profess their innocence. 16m 1 interior

Norway
Social life and customs—19th century
Hill, G. Brand
Ibsen, H. Pillars of society
Ibsen, H. Rosmersholm

Nose
Abnormalities and deformities
Rostand, E. Cyrano de Bergerac

Not a game for boys. Block, S.

Not as bad as they seem. Barnes, P.

Not so dumb. Lazarus, J.

Nothing but the tooth. Feydeau, G.

Nothing but the truth. Smith, R.

Nothing in common. Hayes, J. F.

Nothing less than a man. Unamuno, M. de. (dramatization) See Dorst, T. Fernando Krapp wrote me this letter: an assaying of the truth

Nottage, Lynn
Poof!
Short sketch of abusive husband obliterated by spontaneous combustion. 2w 1 interior
In Facing forward; ed by L. D. Frank
In Humana Festival '93
In Plays for actresses; ed. by E. Lane and N. Shengold

Nova Scotia
Lill, W. All fall down
Lill, W. The Glace Bay Miners' Museum

Novelists
See also Women authors

Novio boy. Soto, G.

Now you know. Frayn, M.

Nowak, Pawel Marcin
On the island
Young castaway dreams of escape from island while older castaway resigns himself to future of isolation. 3 scenes 2m
In Young playwrights; ed. by E. Bray

Nowra, Louis

Così. Rev. ed. Currency Press 1994 89p

Revised version of play first produced 1992. Drama set in 1971 Melbourne about institutions and ideology. Theatrical director stages Mozart's Così fan tutti in psychiatric hospital. 2 acts 9 scenes 5m 3w 1 interior

Crow. Currency Press in association with The State Theatre Company of South Australia and The Perth Theatre Trust 1994 72p (Current theatre series)

Drama set in 1942 Darwin, Australia. Woman fights government to win back tin mine that is rightfully hers. 2 acts 18 scenes 13m 2w 1 setting

The incorruptible. Currency Press 1995 85p (Current theatre series)

Political drama set in Australia. Having attained high political office, conservative Christian sugar cane farmer is corrupted by power. 2 acts 20 scenes Variable cast 11 characters settings

The temple. Currency Press in association with Playbox Theatre Centre 1993 102p (Current theatre series)

Account of excess and greed of 1980s. Traces career of former slaughterhouse owner who becomes known as takeover king of Australia. 3 acts 19 scenes Variable cast 19 characters

Nuances. Yates, P.

Nuclear warfare

Kopit, A. End of the world

Nukala, Dan

y The write stuff. Bakers Plays 1993 48p

Student faces dreaded spelling test. 6m 7w 1 extra 1 interior

The **numbers** game. Garver, J.

Nunn, Jim

Arrangements. New Playwrights Network 1994 52p

Family secrets revealed at celebration of parents' 50th wedding anniversary. 4 scenes 2m 3w extras 1 interior

c The Pied Piper. New Playwrights Network 1993 21p

Dramatization of poem by Robert Browning about Piper who rids town of rats and lures children away when mayor won't pay his fee. Variable cast 1 setting

Punch. New Playwrights Network 1994 20p

Wife plots to prevent husband from retiring from Punch and Judy puppet show. 1 act 2m 2w 1 interior

Stuck. New Playwrights Network 1994 24p

Comedy. Preparations for surprise church concert for vicar's anniversary go awry. 1 act 4m 6w extras 1 interior

Nunn, Trevor. See Caird, J. jt. auth.

Nuns

Durang, C. Sister Mary Ignatius explains it all for you

Hastings, C. The wayward spirit

Linney, R. Three poets: Hrosvitha

Pope, R. Amazing Grace

Shaffer, D. Sacrilege

Nuremberg. Norton-Taylor, R.

Nuremberg, trial of German war criminals, Nuremberg, Germany, 1945-1946

Linney, R. 2

Norton-Taylor, R. Nuremberg

Nursery rhymes

c Cooper, R. M. How things happen in three!

Kelm, A. Black bride

c Mauro, R. The Mother Goose olympics

c Marx, P. Hearts and tarts

Sampson, L. Old MacDonald's farmyard follies

c Tutt, B. Heart to heart

c Wylie, B. J. The old woman and the pedlar

Nurses and nursing

Blanc, E. S. Wars I have seen

Feldshuh, D. Miss Evers' boys

Hastings, C. The wayward spirit

LaChiusa, M. J. Lucky nurse

Lill, W. The occupation of Heather Rose

Nemeth, S. Sally's shorts: Pre-nuptial agreement

Puig, M. Mystery of the rose bouquet

Ricchi, R. The promise

Steelsmith, M. Wacs in khaki

y Waddy, L. Florence Nightingale

Nursing homes

Adam, A. Between two thieves

See also Old age homes

The **nutcracker** and the Mouse King. Hoffman, E. T. A. (dramatization) See Mahlmann, L. and Jones, D. C. The Nutcracker Prince

The **Nutcracker** Prince. Mahlmann, L. and Jones, D. C.

Nutricia Goodheart's Body Building Construction Company. Simmons, D. W.

Nyswaner, Ron

Reservoir

Religious teenager deals with aftermath of homosexual encounter. 2m 1 exterior

In The Actor's book of gay and lesbian plays; ed. by E. Lane and N. Shengold

O

O, Christmas tree. McCullough, L. E.

O Flatharta, Antoine
Blood guilty
Elderly brothers in remote Irish cottage are terrorized by two young brothers from Dublin. 1 act 4m 1 interior
In EST marathon, 1994
In Greatest hits: four Irish one-act plays; ed. by D. Bolger

An **O.** Henry Christmas: The gift of the Magi. Ekstrom, P.

An **O.** Henry Christmas: The last leaf. Ekstrom, P.

O pioneers! Cloud, D.

O thou joyful day. McCullough, L. E.

Oakes, Michael, and Wells, Jennifer
Greenfield blooms. French 1994 40p
Residents of New York City housing project plant community garden in vacant lot. 3m 4w 1 setting

Oakley, Annie, 1860-1926
y McCaslin, N. A straight shooter
c McCullough, L. E. Annie Oakley: little sure-shot

Oates, Joyce Carol
Black
Surrealistic drama. As career diplomat gives American academic couple tour of top secret bomb shelter their more primitive personalities emerge. 1 act 2m 1w
In Here to stay: five plays from the Women's Project; ed. by J. Miles
In Oates, J. C. The perfectionist and other plays

Gulf War
Underlying tensions revealed when young married couple, recovering from crib death of their baby, entertain husband's business associate and wife. 1 act 6 scenes 2m 2w 1 setting
In Oates, J. C. The perfectionist and other plays

Here she is!
Suburban housewife inexplicably finds herself in beauty contest. 1 act 1m 6w extras
In Oates, J. C. The perfectionist and other plays

Homesick
Explores sexual violence from victim's and rapist's viewpoints. 2 scenes 1m 1w 1 setting
In Oates, J. C. The perfectionist and other plays

The interview
Inept journalist interviews man he believes to be world renowned author. 1 act 2m 1w 1 interior
In The Best American short plays, 1993-1994
In Oates, J. C. The perfectionist and other plays

Negative
Racial stereotypes reversed when young white woman meets her African American college roommate. 1 act 2w 1 interior
In Oates, J. C. The perfectionist and other plays

Ontological proof of my existence
Surrealistic play. Runaway girl, sexually brutalized and incarcerated by 2 men, loses sense of identity and rejects father's rescue attempt. 1 act 3m 1w 1 interior
In Oates, J. C. The perfectionist and other plays

The perfectionist
Comedy of manners set in affluent New Jersey suburb. 2 acts 8 scenes 3m 3w 5 interiors
In Oates, J. C. The perfectionist and other plays

The rehearsal
Insecure actress and HIV-positive gay actor rehearse scene for overbearing director. 1m 1w extra
In Oates, J. C. The perfectionist and other plays

The sacrifice
Woman reacts angrily to break-up of her marriage. 1 act 1m 1w 1 setting
In Oates, J. C. The perfectionist and other plays

Tone clusters
Drama. Middle-aged couple's lives are shattered when son is accused of murder. 9 scenes 1m 1w extra 1 setting
In 20/20: twenty one-act plays from twenty years of the Humana Festival

Obesity
Dierlam, K. Helen Melon at the sideshow

Oblivion: a story of Isabelle Eberhardt. Rubess, B.

O'Brien, John
y Wherefore art thou Juliet? Meriwether 1993 45p
Comedy. High school drama students stage Romeo and Juliet in unconventional manner. 2 acts 9 scenes 7m 9w extras 3 interiors

O'Brien, Judith Tate
Ancestress. Bakers Plays 1994 55p
Reader's theater presentation of biblical story of Abraham. Related in series of poems told from Sarah's point of view. 3m 5w

O'Brien, Michael
Mad boy chronicle. Playwrights Canada 1996 154p
Saga of murder and revenge in 999 A.D. Viking Denmark. Incorporates material from Shakespeare's Hamlet and Saxo's Gesta Danorum. 2 acts 29 scenes 6m 4w extras 1 setting

Observe the sons of Ulster marching towards the Somme. McGuinness, F.

O'Casey, Sean
Cock-a-doodle dandy
Farce. Two young Irish women break away from superstition and bigotry in their village. Irish dialect. Songs with accordion music. 3 scenes 16m 4w 1 exterior
In The Playboy of the Western World and two other Irish plays; ed. by W. A. Armstrong

About

Prince, H. Grandchild of kings

The **occupation** of Heather Rose. Lill, W.

Occupational hazard. Drexler, R.

Occupations. Griffiths, T.

Ocean. See Sea

Ocean dream. Rhodes, N.

Ocean travel
Durang, C. Titanic
Harwood, R. The ordeal of Gilbert Pinfold
y McCullough, L. E. The splendid voyage of Kitty Doyle
y St. John, B. Peril on the high seas

O'Connor, Cindy
All that he was ... ; a new musical; book and lyrics by Larry Johnson; music by Cindy O'Connor. French 1995 86p (French's musical library)
Musical about one man's struggle with AIDS. Deceased serves as host and narrator, invisible to those gathered to pay him final respects. 7m 5w 1 setting

O'Connor, Joseph
Red roses and petrol. Methuen Drama 1995 105p (Methuen modern plays)
Comic drama about Irish family. Children from England and America return to Dublin to be with mother following father's death. 4 acts 3m 3w 1 interior

The **octoroon.** Boucicault, D.

Odd fish. Boyd, P.

Odets, Clifford
Awake and sing!
Life of Jewish family in Depression era Bronx. 3 acts 9 scenes 7m 2w 1 interior
In Awake and singing: 7 classic plays from the American Jewish repertoire; ed. by E. Schiff

The **odd** women. Meyer, M.

O'Donnell, Mark
Strangers on Earth. Dramatists 1993 89p
Dramatization of short story of same title. Five twentysomethings become embroiled in parodies of unrequited love, friendship and ambition. 2 acts 30 scenes 3m 2w 1 setting

O'Donoghue, John
Abbie and Lou, Norman and Rose. Currency Press in association with the Hunter Valley Theatre Company 1993 88p (Current theatre series)
Drama about artistic success and failure set in Australia 1895-1935. Portrays attempts of Louis Stone to establish himself as novelist and his relationship with artist Norman Lindsay and Norman's wife Rose. 2 acts 3m 3w 1 setting

O'Donovan, John
Carlotta
Drama about Bernard Shaw, his wife, sister and Mrs. Patrick Campbell his renowned leading lady. 1m 3w 1 interior
In Donovan, J. Jonathan, Jack, and GBS

Copperfaced Jack
Drama set in 1798 Dublin. Battle of wills between English Lord Justice and convicted Irish revolutionary. 2 acts 3 scenes 13m 5w extras 2 interiors 1 exterior
In Donovan, J. Jonathan, Jack, and GBS

The fiddler and the Dean
Radio play. Imaginary conversations between Jonathan Swift and George Frederick Handel. 2m 1w 1 setting
In Donovan, J. Jonathan, Jack, and GBS

The Shaws of Synge Street
Biographical drama set in 1860's Dublin about youth of Bernard Shaw. 3 acts epilogue 10m 3w extras 2 interiors
In Donovan, J. Jonathan, Jack, and GBS

Odysseus from Vraa. Ornsbo, J.

Oedipus (Greek mythology)
Sophocles. Oedipus at Colonus
Sophocles. Oedipus the King

Oedipus. See Sophocles. Oedipus the King

Oedipus at Colonus. Sophocles

Oedipus Rex. See Sophocles. Oedipus the King

Oedipus the King. Sophocles

Oedipus Tyrants. See Sophocles. Oedipus the King

Off out. Adams, G.

Off the map. Ackerman, J.

The **offering.** Edwards, G.

The **office** party. Godber, J.

Oglesby, Tamsin
Two lips indifferent red
Satirical look at cosmetic surgery and society's images of women. 2 acts 8 scenes 2m 5w settings
In Bush Theatre plays

The **Ogre.** Canetti, V.

Oh, the innocents. Roth, A.

Ohio impromptu. Beckett, S.

OK. Chocrón, I.

O'Kelly, Donald
Asylum! Asylum!
Drama explores plight of Ugandan seeking asylum in Dublin, Ireland. 3 acts 4m 2w 1 interior 1 exterior
In New plays from the Abbey Theatre, 1993-1995

Okita, Dwight,
The rainy season
Gay Japanese American's relationship with his understanding mother and Brazilian lover. Prologue 12 scenes 3m 3w 1 setting
In Asian American drama; ed. by B. Nelson

Old age
Adam, A. Between two thieves
Adam, A. A great occasion
Adamson, S. Grace note
Auden, W. H. The dark valley
Bamford, S. Who's a pretty boy then?
Barnes, P. The jumping Mimuses of Byzantium
Barnes, P. Rosa
Barnes, P. Yesterday's news
Beim, N. Dreams
Bill, S. Curtains
Brand, D. Vine and dandy
Canby, V. After all
Cartwright, J. Bed
Connolly, H. Snakes and ladders
Cook, M. The head, guts and sound bone dance
Delaney, D. The last ten miles of Avery J. Coping
Foote, H. The trip to Bountiful
Gardner, H. I'm not Rappaport
Guare, J. Something I'll tell you Tuesday
Hampton, D. The evergreens
Haywood, D. Twisted tape
Horovitz, I. The 75th
Horovitz, I. My old lady
Horovitz, I. Park your car in Harvard Yard
Howe, T. Painting Churches
Janes, H. Two of a kind
Languirand, J. Autumn violins
Linney, R. Clair de Lune
Linney, R. Goodbye, Howard
McCusker, P. Pap's place
Mead, K. And who will pay the rent?
Mercer, D. Flint
Miller, A. I can't remember anything
Miller, A. The Ryan interview
Miller, E. Up rose a burning man
Minjares, J. The king of the kosher grocers
Mitterer, F. Shunted into a siding
Mitterer, F. Siberia
Nemeth, S. Sally's shorts: The cat act
Ordway, S. Trips
Perry, S. Bookends
Pinter, H. No man's land
Sawyer, A. V. Life comes to the old maid
Shepherd, C. Delphiniums
Simon, M. The old lady's guide to survival
Storey, D. Home
Stubbs, N. The patio window
Tasca, J. Gums
Taylor, A. and Devenish, L. Disturbing the dust
Toddie, J. L. And go to Innisfree
Toddie, J. L. Is that the bus to Pittsburgh?
Toddie, J. L. Late Sunday afternoon, early Sunday evening
Uhry, A. Driving Miss Daisy
Wilcox, M. Lent
Wise, R. Eventide
Ziegler, T. Grace & Glorie

Old age homes
Barry, S. The steward of Christendom
King, L. L. The Golden Shadows Old West Museum
Stoppard, T. A separate peace
White, P. A cheery soul
See also Nursing homes

Old blues. Levy, J.

The **old** boy. Gurney, A. R.

Old Frost's winter adventure. Marx, P.

The **old** lady's guide to survival. Simon, M.

Old MacDonald's farmyard follies. Sampson, L.

Old man Pete. Edmonds, S. R.

Old men. See Old age

Old Mother Hubbard. Reakes, P.

The **Old** One-Two. Gurney, A. R.

The **Old** rust bucket. Furse, J.

Old times. Pinter, H.

Old West. Edwards, G.

Old wicked songs. Marans, J.

The **old** woman and the pedlar. Wylie, B. J.

Old women

See also Old age

The **oldest** profession. Vogel, P.

Oleanna. Mamet, D.

Olfson, Emily

y Wuthering Heights

Based on Emily's Brontë's 18th century novel. 2 scenes 3m 2w 1 interior

In The Big book of dramatized classics; ed. by S. E. Kamerman

Olfson, Lewy

y The admirable Crichton

Adaptation of J. M. Barrie's satire on 19th century class distinction. When a group of aristocrats is shipwrecked on an island the butler takes over. 5m 4w

In The Big book of dramatized classics; ed. by S. E. Kamerman

y Avon calling!

Will Shakespeare in meeting with tough theater impresario Jerry Globe, honors contract by collaborating with would-be playwright Francis Bacon. 4m 1 interior

In The Big book of skits; ed. by S. E. Kamerman

y The last time I saw Paris

When Paris visits Mount Olympus he must decide which of the three goddesses is fairest of the fair. Each of the goddesses tries to bribe the impressionable, bumbling Paris. 1m 3w 1 exterior

In The Big book of skits; ed. by S. E. Kamerman

y Monsieur Beaucaire

First produced as a radio play. Based on novel by Booth Tarkington. Set in 18th century England. French nobleman disguised as barber is scorned by English aristocrats. 4 scenes 6m 4w extras 3 interiors

In The Big book of dramatized classics; ed. by S. E. Kamerman

y The Pickwick papers

Comedy based on incident in Charles Dickens' novel set in 19th century London. Due to misunderstanding, housekeeper sues Pickwick for breach of promise. 4 scenes 11m 2w extras 4 interiors

In The Big book of dramatized classics; ed. by S. E. Kamerman

Oliensis, Adam

Ring of men. Dramatists 1995 28p

Character study set in Central Park. Longtime friendship among three men disrupted by untimely revelation. 2 scenes 3m 1 exterior

Olio. See LaChuisa, M. J. First Lady suite: Olio

Olive and Hilary. Aron, G.

Oliver, Donald

The case of the dead flamingo dancer; book and lyrics by Dan Butler; music by Donald Oliver. French 1997 121p

Musical murder mystery set on East Hampton estate in 1942. Music, singing. 2 acts 4m 4w 1 interior

Olly's prison. Bond, E.

Olmos, Carlos

Propane games

First play in author's Trilogy of games. Absurdist drama about perverted relationship between brother, sister and possibly dead parents. 1m 1w 1 interior

In The Fickle finger of Lady Death and other plays

O'Malley, Mike

Diverting devotion. French 1997 98p

Comedy about old secrets and new loves. Three men approaching thirty gather to attend friend's wedding. 2 acts 9 scenes 3m 4w 2 interiors 1 exterior

Three years from "thirty." French 1996 89p

Comedy drama about group of twenty-seven-year-old friends facing personal and professional decisions. 2 acts 13 scenes 4m 3w 1 setting

Omata, Garrett H.

S.A.M. I am

Romantic comedy explores world of personal ads, interracial dating and dilemmas of single Asian male. 2 acts 13 scenes 4m 3w extras 1 setting

In Asian American drama; ed. by B. Nelson

On a darkling plain. Beim, N.

On Baile's strand. Yeats, W. B.

On hold at 30,000 feet. Burns, K.

On Strivers Row. Hill, A.

On the bum. Bell, N.

On the eve of publication. Mercer, D.

On the fields of France. Cotter, J. S.

On the harmfulness of tobacco. See Chekhov, A. The dangers of tobacco

On the island. Nowak, P. M.

On the ledge. Bleasdale, A.

On the marry-go-round. See Feydeau, G. and Devallieres, M. All my husbands

On the open road. Tesich, S.

On the verge. Overmyer, E.

Once upon a beginning. Perry, E. E.

Once upon a dream. Boiko, C.

Once upon a taxi. Hamlett, C.

One across. Hornby, I.

One-act plays
Adam, A. Between two thieves
Adam, A. Birds of prey
Adam, A. A bit of land
Adam, A. Business meeting
Adam, A. A cameo from Cranford
Adam, A. Castles in the air
Adam, A. Christmas
Adam, A. A great occasion
Adam, A. A matter of diplomacy
Adrian, Y. Flyboy
Alám, S. A. Zookeeper
Albee, E. Finding the sun
y Allard, J. Painted rain
Alvarez, L. Who is chasing whom!
y Avery, A. Stardust melody
Ball, A. Bachelor holiday
Ball, A. The M word
Ball, A. Made for a woman
Ball, A. Power lunch
Ball, A. Your mother's butt
Bamford, S. The answer
Bamford, S. Who's a pretty boy then?
Barnes, D. Three from the earth
Barnes, P. Humour helps
Barnes, P. Last things
Barnes, P. Waiting for a bus
Bartram, F. Tiddley pum
Beard, P. Cliff's edge
Beard, P. Come the resolution
Beard, P. Death of a clown
Beard, P. Lavender years
Beard, P. Swingers
Beard, P. Waiting for Pierrepoint
Beckett, S. Ohio impromptu
Beim, N. The deserter
Beim, N. Inside
Bell, N. Out the window
Berlin, E. The line that's picked up 1000 babes (and how it can work for you!)
Berlin, E. The Midnight Moonlight Wedding Chapel
Bisson, P. Is there anybody there?
Bisson, P. Merry widows
c Bisson, P. Spacenapped
Bisson, P. When the clock strikes
Booth, J. A bit on the other side
Booth, J. Both worlds
Booth, J. By whose hand?
Booth, J. Charley's uncle
Booth, J. Dead on time
Booth, J. Dirty weekend
Booth, J. Echo of applause
Booth, J. Face of evil
Booth, J. 50 . . . and counting
Booth, J. Friendly affair
Booth, J. Little white lies
Booth, J. The loved one
Booth, J. Mirror mirror on the wall
Booth, J. Or was he pushed?
Booth, J. Over his dead body
Booth, J. Season of goodwill
Booth, J. Seeing double
Booth, J. Something on his mind
Booth, J. Your place or mine?
Bower, M. A fitting finish
Bozzone, B. Sonny DeRee's life flashes before his eyes
Bozzone, B. and DiPietro, J. Breast men
Braithwaite, D. Martha and Elvira
Broadhurst, K. The eye of the beholder
Brownell, R. Afterhours
Buchan, A. Conditional surrender
Burrill, M. P. They that sit in darkness
Buzo, A. Norm and Ahmed
Calhoun, W. Affections of an alley cat
Calhoun, W. Call it clover
Caliban, R. Gladiator
Canby, V. After all
Carmichael, F. Damsel of the desert
Carter, J. The twisted mirror
Chekhov, A. The bear
Chekhov, A. The festivities
Chekhov, A. The proposal
Chekhov, A. Swan song
Chekhov, A. The wedding
Chekhov, A. The wedding reception
Childress, A. Wine in the wilderness
Cleveland, R. Tom and Jerry
Coen, D. Tinkle time
Collings, J. Kelly & Donald
Cooke, C. Threat
Corrie, J. Billy Shaw
Corrie, J. A bride for Heatherhill
Coyne, J. S. Did you ever send your wife to Camberwell?
Crawford, D. W. Borrowed plumage
Cruz, M. Telling tales
Curran, C. Senetta Boynton visits the Orient
Davies, R. Eros at breakfast
Dean, D. Mama's girl
Dinner, W. Logic upside down
Dowling, C. The Marlboro man
Dunbar, D. A song for Robbie
Dunbar-Nelson, A. Mine eyes have seen
Dunsany, E. J. M. D. P. The glittering gate
Dunsany, E. J. M. D. P. The lost silk hat
Durang, C. The actor's nightmare

One-act plays—*Continued*
Durang, C. Death comes to us all, Mary Agnes
Durang, C. 'dentity crisis
Durang, C. The nature and purpose of the universe
Durang, C. Sister Mary Ignatius explains it all for you
Edward, H. F. V. Job hunters
Eisenstein, L. At the root
c Evans, L. Gran
Farmer, B. Irene and Lillian forever
Feydeau, G. Brothers in crime
Feydeau, G. Nothing but the tooth
Firbank, R. A disciple from the country
c Fisher, A. I have a dream
Fo, D. One was nude and one wore tails
Fo, D. The virtuous burglar
Foote, H. The roads to home: A nightingale
Foote, H. The roads to home: The dearest of friends
Foote, H. The roads to home: Spring dance
Fornes, M. I. Springtime
Freeman, D. Creeps
Friedman, R. All for art
Fuentes, C. Orchids in the moonlight
Fugard, A. Statements after an arrest under the immorality act
y Fuson, D. Clippings
Fyffe, L. The sand
Gaines-Shelton, R. A. The church fight
Gambaro, G. Bad blood
Goethe, J. W. von. Brother and sister
Goldstein, J. Our baby's first seven years
Goluboff, B. The other five percent
Granger, P. Vivien
Granville-Barker, H. Farewell to the theatre
Granville-Barker, H. Rococo
Granville-Barker, H. Vote by ballot
Greenberg, R. The author's voice
Gregor, H. Freedom! Freedom!
Gurney, A. R. The comeback
Gurney, A. R. The David show
Gurney, A. R. The Golden Fleece
Gurney, A. R. The Old One-Two
Gurney, A. R. The problem
Gurney, A. R. Public affairs: Pt 1 The love course
Gurney, A. R. Public affairs: Pt 2 The opening meeting
Gurney, A. R. The rape of Bunny Stuntz
Guyer, M. The American century
Hall, F. B. Nathaniel in Berkshire
Hallman, B. The women of Theta Kappa
Hampton, C. Treats
Hardstack, M. The cure
Hardstack, M. In the cemetery
Hare, D. The bay at Nice
Haubold, C. The big black Box
Havel, V. Protest
y Haynes, H. J. Isolation
Haywood, D. Twisted tape
High, B. G. Ambush
Hill, G. L. The Black Branch
Hogg, F. A. Afternoon at Tavern MacTavish
Hornby, I. One across
Hornby, I. Situation vacant
House, J. Cherchez la femme
Houston, V. H. The Matsuyama mirror
Huff, K. Leon and Joey
Hurston, Z. N. The first one
Hwang, D. H. Bondage
Hwang, D. H. The sound of a voice
Ives, D. Foreplay
Ives, D. Mere mortals
Ives, D. The Philadelphia
Ives, D. Philip Glass buys a loaf of bread
Ives, D. Seven menus
Ives, D. Sure thing
Ives, D. The universal language
Ives, D. Variations on the death of Trotsky
Ives, D. Words, words, words
y Jackson, K. Street story
Jennings, C. S. Sunday dinner
Johnson, J. P. and Hughes, L. The organizer
Kalamu ya Salaam. Blk love song #1
Katims, J. Who made Robert DeNiro king of America?
Kelly, C. Excess baggage
y Kelly, T. Bang! Bang! You're dead
Kemp, R. Dalwhinnie
Kennedy, A. Funnyhouse of a Negro
Kitchen, B. Halfway up the M3 on the way to Basingstoke
Klavan, L. Freud's house
Korder, H. Fun
Lane, E. Dancing on Checker's grave
Lang, C. Amelia and the man
Lauro, S. The coal diamond
Law, M. Advertising Arnold
Law, M. Cry wolf
Law, M. My Johnny
Lee, J. A. The execution
LeFevre, A. Americansaint
Lim, G. Paper angels
Linney, R. April snow
Linney, R. Can can
Linney, R. F.M.
Linney, R. El hermano
Linney, R. Juliet

One-act plays—*Continued*
Linney, R. The love suicide at Schofield Barracks
Linney, R. Paradise
Linney, R. Songs of love
Linney, R. Tennessee
Linney, R. Three poets: Akhmatova
Linney, R. Yancey
Livingston, M. S. For unborn children
Lonergan, K. Betrayed by everyone
Lucas, C. Throwing your voice
MacKenna, J. Faint voices
Margulies, D. July 7, 1994
Margulies, D. Zimmer
Marivaux. La dispute
Martin, L. Waltzing De Niro
c Martin, M. The legend of the golden coffee bean
Martini, C. Life history of the African elephant
Matheus, J. F. 'Cruiter
c McCaslin, N. The bailiff's wonderful coat
c McCaslin, N. Borrowed trouble
c McCaslin, N. Brave new banner
c McCaslin, N. The Christmas lamb
c McCaslin, N. Daring, darling Dolly
c McCaslin, N. A gift of music
c McCaslin, N. Humai's secret
c McCaslin, N. The lazy ones
c McCaslin, N. Leading lady
y McCaslin, N. The legend of Minna Lamourrie
c McCaslin, N. The little squire of Flanders
c McCaslin, N. Paul Bunyan: lumberjack
y McCaslin, N. A straight shooter
c McCaslin, N. Too many cooks
McClinton, M. Stones and bones
McGrath, J. The Cheviot, the stag and the black, black oil
McKee, J. The 'far-flung'
McLaughlin, T. Greatest hits
McNally, T. Bad habits: Dunelawn
McNally, T. Bad habits: Ravenswood
McNally, T. Bringing it all back home
McNally, T. Noon
McNally, T. Whiskey
McWeeny, D. and Swan, S. Broken bones
McWeeny, D. and Swan, S. Sticks and stones
Mead, K. Line of descent
Mead, K. This common bond
Menken, A. Weird romance: Her pilgrim soul
Menken, A. Weird romance: The girl who was plugged in
Millay, E. St. V. Aria da capo
Miller, A. I can't remember anything
Miller, A. The Ryan interview
Miller, J. A light on the landing
Miller, J. and Miller, S. Consequences
Miller, M. Graven images
Milligan, J. Clara and the gambler
Milligan, J. Class of '77
Milligan, J. Life after Elvis
Milligan, J. Money talks
Milligan, J. The quality of boiled water
Milligan, J. Road trip
Milligan, J. Shore leave
Mitterer, F. Beyond our understanding
Mitterer, F. Jailbird
Mitterer, F. Shunted into a siding
Mitterer, F. Wheat on the autobahn
Molière. The flying doctor
Nave, B. Visiting Oliver
y Nimmo, P. Will Shakespeare save the King!
y Nimmo, P. Will Shakespeare save us!
Norman, M. Lunch with Ginger
Norman, M. Trudy Blue
c Nunn, J. The Pied Piper
Nunn, J. Punch
Nunn, J. Stuck
Oakes, M. and Wells, J. Greenfield blooms
Oates, J. C. Gulf War
Oates, J. C. Here she is!
Oates, J. C. The interview
Oates, J. C. Negative
Oates, J. C. Ontological proof of my existence
Oates, J. C. The rehearsal
Oates, J. C. The sacrifice
O Flatharta, A. Blood guilty
O'Neill, E. Abortion
O'Neill, E. Fog
O'Neill, E. The movie man
O'Neill, E. Recklessness
O'Neill, E. The sniper
O'Neill, E. Thirst
O'Neill, E. Warnings
O'Neill, E. The web
O'Neill, E. A wife for a life
Osofisan, F. The oriki of a grasshopper
Owen, K. Black, green, white and gold
Parks, S. L. Devotees in the garden of love
Paz, O. Rappaccini's daughter
Pearson, C. Divergent lines
Pearson, C. Scruples, agents, and Wilfred
Pierson, K. Mountain thunder
Pinter, H. Mountain language
y Polsky, M. E. Act of Will
y Polsky, M. E. SATisfaction
Pope, R. Sandwiches: Eating sandwiches

One-act plays—*Continued*
Pope, R. Sandwiches: Making sandwiches
Quayle, T. Bein Lochaber
Rattigan, T. The Browning version
Rattigan, T. Harlequinade
Ravel, A. Vengeance
Real, C. Why the Beach Boys are like opera
Rector, M. H. The lady and the commissioner of airports
Rector, M. H. The lady and the mortician
Reddin, K. Throwing smoke
Reddin, K. You belong to me
Ricchi, R. The appointment
Ricchi, R. A foreboding
Ricchi, R. The man, the rose and silence
Ricchi, R. The promise
Ricchi, R. The scandal
Richardson, A. A fine gentleman
Richardson, W. The chip woman's fortune
y Rideout, G. Texas boy
Rivera, J. Slaughter in the lake
Rodriguez, D. E. I'm not stupid
Roland, B. Feet of clay
Rowan, A. A. A stitch in time
Rumble, P. B. Aunt Sophie's latkes
Ruzzante. The veteran
Ruzzante. Weasel
Sade, Marquis de. The bedroom
Sade, Marquis de. The haunted tower
Sade, Marquis de. The self-proclaimed philosopher
Sadler, C. and Pemberton, S. Christmas balls
Schisgal, M. The artist and the model
Schisgal, M. The artist and the model/2
Schisgal, M. The cowboy, the Indian and the fervent feminist
Schisgal, M. Extensions
Schisgal, M. Sexaholics
Schnitzler, A. The Bacchanale
Schnitzler, A. The big scene
Schnitzler, A. The Green Cockatoo
Schnitzler, A. The hour of recognition
Schnitzler, A. Paracelsus
Schnitzler, A. Marionettes: The puppeteer
c Schurman-O'Connor, K. At the bus stop
c Schurman-O'Connor, K. Billy's problem
c Schurman-O'Connor, K. Ghoul Scout camp
c Schurman-O'Connor, K. Grandma Rusnak
Schurman-O'Connor, K. The Wizard of Zoz
Schwartz, S. Vito on the beach
Scotland, J. Day of wrath
Scotland, J. A surgeon for Lucinda
Sears, J. Eddie Lee, Eddie Lee
Sessions, G. The return of spring
Shaffer, D. Last respects
Shanley, J. P. Kissing Christine
Shanley, J. P. Missing Marisa
Shanley, J. P. The red coat
Shanley, J. P. The wild goose
Sharrocks, M. Sweet Rose of Old Aldgate
Shaughnessy, D. The manager
Sheeler, W. Vortex
Shepherd. C. Delphiniums
Sherman, J. M. Women and Wallace
Shine, T. Contribution
Simon, N. London suite: Diana and Sidney
Simon, N. London suite: Going home
Simon, N. London suite: Settling accounts
Simon, N. London suite: The man on the floor
y Slaight, B. High tide
y Slaight, B. The open road
y Slaight, B. Sightings and High tide
Snodgrass, K. Haiku
Solórzano, C. Crossroads
Solórzano, C. The crucified
Spiro, P. The juiceman cometh
St. John, B. Rubies: Heirlooms
St. John, B. Rubies: Little gems
Stoppard, T. New-found-land
Stoppard, T. Dirty linen
Strindberg, A. Miss Julie
Strindberg, A. Pariah
Strindberg, A. Simoom
Strugess, B. Marius's mule
c Summer, A. The just so letter
y Swift, R. The paper bag bandit rides again
Szyszkowitz, G. Commander Carrigan
Taylor, P. Familiar haunts
Taylor, P. Missing person
Taylor, P. A redheaded man
Taylor, R. Inside the belly of the beast
Teagarden, J. Birds
Teagarden, J. Letting Lucinda down
Terson, P. How to write a play
Thompson, G. M. A time to go home
Toddie, J. L. And go to Innisfree
Toddie, J. L. Is that the bus to Pittsburgh?
Toddie, J. L. Late Sunday afternoon, early Sunday evening
Toomer, J. Balo
Tremblay, M. Marcel pursued by the hounds

One-act plays—*Continued*
Trenholme, H. Fell blow
Vogel, P. How I learned to drive
Walker, D. The affairs of Dilys Willis
Walker, D. A quiet night in
Walker, D. Triangle
Walker, S. Come on up
Warner, F. Maquettes for the requiem: Emblems
Warner, F. Maquettes for the requiem: Lumen
Warner, F. Maquettes for the requiem: Troat
Waterhouse, J. The cardboard cavaliers
Waterhouse, J. and Leach, P. Frank's feathered friend
Waterhouse, J. and Leach, P. A nest of cuckoos
Watson, A. Final placement
Weller, M. Abroad (Split, Part 2)
Weller, M. At home (Split, Part 1)
Weller, M. Loose ends
Wells, M. Mephisto rock
Welsh, D. Make it happen
y Welsh, D. Mellow drama
Whyte, P. Tuesday, eight-fifteen
Wilde, O. Salomé
Wilder, T. Childhood
Wilder, T. The drunken sisters
Wilder, T. Infancy
Wilder, T. The long Christmas dinner
Wilder, T. Love and how to cure it
Wilder, T. Pullman car Hiawatha
Wilder, T. Queens of France
Wilkinson, M. E. The lighthouse keeper's wife
Williams, G. Rain
Williams, S.-A. Home
Willmott, K. and Averill, R. T-Money & Wolf
Wilson, L. This is the rill speaking
Windwick, N. D. A father's daughter
Wise, R. Eventide
Wise, R. Sound choice
Wise, R. When one door closes
c Witkiewicz, S. I. Cockroaches
Wood, P. Faint sound of a bell
Yates, P. Nuances
y Yates, P. Starlover
Young, P. Squashed
Zoshchenko, M. Crime and punishment
Zuberbuehler, A. Fieldstones

The **one**-armed man. Foote, H.

One can not think of everything. See Musset, A. de. You can't think of everything

One careful owner. Connolly, H.

One child at a time. Pickering, K.

One everyman. Mitterer, F.

One fine day. Lumborg, D.

One flea spare. Wallace, N.

One for the grave. MacNeice, L.

One for the road. Pinter, H.

One hundred women. Halvorson, K.

One life to lose. Martens, A. C.

One minute play. Durang, C.

One monkey don't stop no show. Evans, D.

One-900-desperate. Durang, C.

One question. Stone, T.

One shoe off. Howe, T.

One-sided triangle. Smith, S.

One small step. Nimmo, H.

One to grow on. Kral, B.

One under. Horovitz, I.

One was nude and one wore tails. Fo, D.

O'Neal, John, and Watkins, Nayo Barbara

You can't judge a book by looking at the cover: sayings from the life and writings of Junebug Jabbo Jones: v2

Monologue about migration of African Americans from deep South to industrial North. Prologue 2 acts epilogue 1m

In Alternate roots; ed. by K. deNobriga and V. Anderson

O'Neill, Eugene

Abortion

Tragedy. College athlete commits suicide when girl he betrayed dies as result of abortion. 1 act 4m 3w extras 1 interior

In O'Neill, E. Ten "lost" plays

All God's chillun got wings

Tragedy. Study of racial hatred focusing on white woman who marries black lawyer and goes mad. 2 acts 7 scenes 3m 4w extras 1 interior 2 exteriors

In O'Neill, E. The hairy ape and All God's chillun got wings
In O'Neill, E. Nine plays

"Anna Christie"

Drama about ex-prostitute's relationships with her Swedish father and Irish sailor lover. 4 acts 11m 2w 3 interiors

In O'Neill, E. The Emperor Jones; "Anna Christie"; The hairy ape

Desire under the elms

Tragedy of farm life set in 19th century New England centers on son's passion for tyrannical father's third wife. 3 parts 12 scenes 8m 3w extras 1 setting

In O'Neill, E. Nine plays

O'Neill, Eugene—*Continued*

The Emperor Jones

Tragedy. Black tyrant, in West Indies, overthrown by natives. 8 scenes 4m 1w extras 1 interior 5 exteriors

In O'Neill, E. The Emperor Jones; "Anna Christie"; The hairy ape
In O'Neill, E. Nine plays

Fog

Tragedy. Adrift in lifeboat, poet and businessman argue about life. Rescuers claim dead child's cries guided them in fog. 1 act 3m 1w extras 1 exterior

In O'Neill, E. Ten "lost" plays

The great God Brown

Symbolic drama about conflict between artistic and materialistic ambitions of an architect. Prologue 4 acts 11 scenes epilogue 9m 5w extras 5 interiors 1 exterior

In O'Neill, E. Nine plays

The hairy ape

Symbolic tragedy about man's search for identity. Expressionistic play about stoker on transatlantic liner. 8 scenes 6m 2w extras 4 interiors 2 exteriors

In O'Neill, E. The Emperor Jones; "Anna Christie"; The hairy ape
In O'Neill, E. The hairy ape & All God's chillun got wings
In O'Neill, E. Nine plays

The iceman cometh. Hern Bks. 1993 142p (Royal National Theatre)

Thoughts and actions of a group of derelicts, habitues of a cheap New York saloon. 4 acts 16m 3w 1 interior

Lazarus laughed

Pageantlike drama focusing on the risen Lazarus who is deified throughout Roman Empire. When executed by burning, Lazarus' laughter rises above flames in reaffirmation of life. Speaking chorus. 4 acts 8 scenes Large mixed case settings

In O'Neill, E. Nine plays

"Marco millions"

Satire on materialism and religion centering on figure of Marco Polo. Prologue 3 acts 11 scenes epilogue Large mixed cast settings

In O'Neill, E. Nine plays

Mourning becomes Electra: Homecoming

Beginning of author's trilogy based on Aeschylus' Oresteia. Incest and adultery plague pre-Civil War New England family. 4 acts 7m 2w 1 setting

In O'Neill, E. Nine plays
In O'Neill, E. Three plays

Mourning becomes Electra: The haunted

Concluding play in author's trilogy about guilt-ridden New England family focuses on incestuous relationship between brother and sister. 4 acts 5 scenes 7m 2w 1 setting

In O'Neill, E. Nine plays
In O'Neill, E. Three plays

Mourning becomes Electra: The hunted

Second play in trilogy about tragic history of New England family beset by murder and suicide. 5 acts 7m 5w 1 setting

In O'Neill, E. Nine plays
In O'Neill, E. Three plays

The movie man

Comedy set in Mexico. In return for material support motion picture company can photograph rebel army in action. 1 act 5m 1w 1 interior

In O'Neill, E. Ten "lost" plays

Recklessness

Tragedy. Vengeful husband sends chauffeur, wife's lover, to death in defective automobile. 1 act 2m 3w extras 1 interior

In O'Neill, E. Ten "lost" plays

Servitude

Self-sacrificing wife mistakenly thinks egocentric husband loves a troubled woman who is influenced by his plays. 3 acts 4m 2w 1b 1g 1 interior

In O'Neill, E. Ten "lost" plays

The sniper

Tragedy set in Belgium. Portrayal of wartime destruction, panic, and death. 1 act 8m 1 interior

In O'Neill, E. Ten "lost" plays

Strange interlude

Psychological drama. Woman whose lover is dead finds fulfillment with three different men. 9 acts 5m 3w 4 interiors 2 exteriors

In O'Neill, E. Nine plays
In O'Neill, E. Three plays

Thirst

Tragedy. Adrift on life raft, dancer, gentleman, and mulatto sailor die after much suffering. 1 act 2m 1w 1 exterior

In O'Neill, E. Ten "lost" plays

A touch of the poet. Hern Bks. 1993 99p (Royal National Theatre)

Truculent, hard drinking, pretentious Irish immigrant in Massachusetts stands in way of daughter's marriage to an American. Irish dialect. 4 acts 7m 3w 1 interior

Warnings

Tragedy. Urged by wife and terrified of dire poverty, deaf wireless operator stays on job with dire consequences. 1 act 2 scenes 5m 2w 3g 1 interior 1 exterior

In O'Neill, E. Ten "lost" plays

The web

Tragedy. Tubercular prostitute is unjustly jailed for murdering escaped convict who protected her from pimp. 1 act 5m 1w 1 interior

In O'Neill, E. Ten "lost" plays

A wife for a life

Tragedy set in Arizona desert. Young gold miner falls in love with wife of man who becomes his friend. 1 act 3m 1 exterior

In O'Neill, E. Ten "lost" plays

Parodies, imitations, etc.

Hughes, L. The Em-Fuehrer Jones

The **O'Neill.** Kilroy, T.

Only a game. Younghusband, C.

Only in America. Lawrence, J. and Lee, R. E.

The **only** true history of Lizzie Finn. Barry, S.

Ono, Komachi, 9th century
Linney, R. Three poets: Komachi

Ono, Yoko
New York rock; written and composed by Yoko Ono. French 1994 62p
Allegorical rock musical traces legacy of random violence through one generation of New York family. 2 acts 31 scenes 8m 2w

Ontario
Horovitz, I. Today, I am a fountain pen
Robinson, M. Colonial tongues

Ontological proof of my existence. Oates, J. C.

Onwueme, Osonye Tess
The broken calabash
Drama set in Nigerian village. Love triumphs over discrimination and women question subjugation to outmoded traditions. Dancing. Prologue 7 scenes epilogue 7m 4w extras 1 setting
In Onwueme, O. T. Three plays
Parables for a season
Explores role of women in traditional African society. Speaking chorus, music. Prologue 5 scenes 6m 8w 1 setting
In Onwueme, O. T. Three plays
The reign of Wazobia
Nigerian woman's reign as regent threatens traditional village power structure. Music, singing. dancing. Prologue 6 scenes 5m 7w extras 1 setting
In Onwueme, O. T. Three plays
Tell it to women. Wayne State Univ. Press 1997 211p (African American life series)
Epic drama critiques western feminist movement from rural African perspective. 4m 8m 1g 1 setting

Opal. Nassif, R. L.

The **open** boat. Clapp, T.

The **open** couple. Fo, D.

The **open** road. Slaight, B.

The **opening** meeting. See Gurney, A. R. Public affairs: Pt 2 The opening meeting

Opera
Hill, K. The phantom of the opera
Ives, D. Philip Glass buys a loaf of bread
Nowra, L. Così

Opera singers. See Singers

Operation Desert Storm, 1991. See Persian Gulf War, 1991

Operation sidewinder. Shepard, S.

Oppenheimer, J. Robert, 1904-1967
Congdon, C. No mercy

Or was he pushed? Booth, J.

Or what's a heaven for? Heward, L.

Orchids in the moonlight. Fuentes, C.

Orczy, Emmuska, Baroness, 1865-1947
The Scarlet Pimpernel (dramatization) See Leech, M. T. The Scarlet Pimpernel

Ordeal at Valley Forge. Van Horn, B.

The **ordeal** of Gilbert Pinfold. Harwood, R.

An **ordinary** day. Fo, D.

An **ordinary** woman under stress. Vago, S. M.

Ordway, Sally
Panicked
Monologue by troubled woman. 1w
In Facing forward; ed. by L. D. Frank
Trips
Two seventy-year-old women bide their time in retirement apartment complex. 2w 1 setting
In Facing forward; ed. by. L. D. Frank

O'Reilly, James
Work
Profiles three people at various levels of employment. 1m 1 setting
In Solo; ed. by J. Sherman

Orestes (Greek mythology)
Euripides. Electra
Euripides. Iphigenia among the Taurians
Euripides. Orestes
Goethe, J. W. von. Iphigenia in Tauris
Sophocles. Electra

The **organizer.** Johnson, J. P. and Hughes, L.

Origami tears. Miller, D. L.

The **original** Last Wish Baby. Seebring, W.

The **oriki** of a grasshopper. Osofisan, F.

Orloff, Rich
The whole shebang
Satire. Graduate student defends universe he created. Variable cast 6 characters 1 interior
In The Best American short plays, 1994-1995

Ornsbo, Jess

Odysseus from Vraa

Comedy based on The Odyssey. Contemporary Odysseus returns to wife who runs boarding house full of parasitic lodgers, and petty criminal son fathered by someone else. 2 acts 16 scenes 11m 4w 1 setting

In New Danish plays; ed. by H. C. Andersen

The **orphan.** Rabe, D.

The **orphan** muses. Bouchard. M. M.

The **orphanage.** Barteve, R.

Orphans

McDonaugh, M. The cripple of Inishmaan

c Sandberg, R. N. Anne of Green Gables

y Turner, J. Anne of Green Gables

Orr, Mary

The wisdom of Eve. Revised. Dramatists 1994 99p

Adapted from story of same title, later the basis for film: All about Eve. Unscrupulous ingenue's rise to stardom. 2 acts 5m 5w 1 setting

Orton, Joe

Moore, E. Live with it

Osborne, John

Déjàvu

Social drama. Jimmy Porter, protagonist of Look back in anger, in bitter middle age denounces contemporary liberalism. 2 acts 4 scenes 3m 2w 1 interior

In Osborne, J. Plays: one

Look back in anger

Angry young man from working class rails against complacency of post-war English society. Tormented upper-class wife leaves him, but they are reconciled after she loses child. Music. 3 acts 5 scenes 3m 2w 1 interior

In Osborne, J. Plays: one

The world of Paul Slickey

Musical satire about gossip columnist. Music, singing, dancing. 2 acts 11 scenes Large mixed cast 2 interiors

In Osborne, J. Plays: one

Osborne, John and Creighton, Anthony

Epitaph for George Dillon

Drama set in 1950s England. Despairing author/actor makes changes in play to insure financial success. By settling in middle-class suburbia, he writes his own epitaph. 3 acts 4 scenes 5m 4w 1 interior

In Osborne, J. Plays: one

Osborne, Will, and Herrera, Anthony

Smoke & mirrors. French 1993 113p

Comic murder mystery. Power-hungry producer-director lures screenwriter into scheme to get rid of film star. 2 acts 3 scenes 4m 1w 1 interior

Oscar: The Oscar Wilde trials of 1895. Legg, R.

Osment, Philip

The dearly beloved. French (London) 1993 93p

First play in author's trilogy about life in Devon, England. Successful television producer's return to rural home town creates domestic turmoil. 4 acts 4m 5w 1 interior 3 exteriors

—Same

In Osment, P. Plays: 1

Flesh and blood. Methuen Drama in association with Method & Madness 1996 110p (Methuen fast track playscript)

Completes author's Devon plays trilogy. Jealousies and resentments fester among two brothers and sister on remote farm. Thirty years later unexpected visitor brings feud to climax. 2 parts 15 scenes 2m 2w 1 setting

—Same

In Osment, P. Plays: 1

What I did in the holidays. French (London) 1995 105p

Second of author's Devon plays. Tragi-comedy set summer of 1963 on dilapidated farm. Eleven-year-old boy copes with puberty and family tensions. 6 scenes 4m 3w 1b 1 setting

—Same

In Osment, P. Plays: 1

Osofisan, Femi

Birthdays are not for dying

Tragedy strikes as young African man attempts to assume leadership of late father's business. 6m 2w 1 interior

In Osofisan, F. The oriki of a grasshopper and other plays

Esu and the vagabond minstrels

Theater piece about divinity who, in Yoruba world concept, mediates between gods and humans. Music. 4 parts Variable cast 1 setting

In Osofisan, F. The oriki of a grasshopper and other plays

Morountodun

Celebratory theater piece based on Yoruba oral legend of Moremi. 16 scenes Variable cast 1 setting

In Osofisan, F. The oriki of a grasshopper and other plays

The oriki of a grasshopper

Practical dilemmas confront radical intellectual in Third World country. 1 act 2m 1w 1 interior

In Osofisan, F. The oriki of a grasshopper and other plays

Osten, Suzanne. See Lysander, P. jt. auth.

Osterman, Georg

Brother truckers. French 1993 122p

Melodramatic parody of 1940s film noir set in contemporary New York City about man trying to become successful in garbage business. 2 acts 13 scenes 5m 4w extras 1 setting

Oswald, Debra
Gary's house. Currency Press in association with Playbox Theatre 1996 83p (Current theatre series)
Family struggles to rise above status of born losers in remote Australian bush block. 2 acts 27 scenes 3m 2w 1 setting

Oswald, Peter
Fair ladies at a game of poem cards. Methuen Drama 1996 90p
Verse drama based on 18th century puppet play by Chikamatsu Monzaemon. Two pairs of lovers threatened with death by jealous lord. 11 scenes 7m 4w 1b extras 1 setting

The **other** five percent. Goluboff, B.

The **other** other woman. Mead, K.

Other people. Saunders, G.

Other people's money: the ultimate seduction. Sterner, J.

Otherwise engaged. Gray, S.

Otway, Thomas
The soldiers' fortune
Restoration comedy about adultery and political revenge focusing on discontented wife and her elderly husband. Prologue 5 acts 12 scenes epilogue 7m 3w 1b extras 5 interiors 2 exteriors
In Four Restoration marriage plays; ed. by M. Cordner

Our baby's first seven years. Goldstein, J.

Our boys. Lewis, J.

Our country's good. Wertenbaker, T.

Our day out. Russell, W.

Our lan'. Ward, T.

Our Mr. Bockerer. Presses, P. and Becher, U.

Our song. Waterhouse, K.

Out of our heads. McGrath, J.

Out the window. Bell, N.

Outlaw gold: the lost treasure of Commanche Creek. McCullough, L. E.

Outlaws
c McCullough, L. E. El Corrido de Gregorio Cortez
c McCullough, L. E. Jesse James: blood on the saddle
c McCullough, L. E. Turquoise Tom, the versifying bandit of Old California
Shepard, S. The unseen hand

Outlaws. Wasserman, E. H.

Outrageous. Tasca, J.

Over his dead body. Booth, J.

Over Texas. See LaChuisa, M. J. First Lady suite: Over Texas

Over the checkerboard. Carmichael, F.

Over the hill. Slabolepszy, P.

Overland Journeys to the Pacific
See also Donner Party

Overmyer, Eric
Don Quixote de La Jolla. Broadway Play Pub. 1993 74p
Travesty of Cervantes' classic. Music. 2m 2w 1b 1 setting

Dark rapture
Play revolves around morally corrupt characters scheming to get their hands on parcel of cash. 2 acts 16 scenes 6m 3w settings
In Overmyer, E. Eric Overmyer: collected plays

The Heliotrope Bouquet by Scott Joplin & Louis Chauvin. Broadway Play Pub. 1993 68p
Ragtime great Scott Joplin haunted by his past. Music. 6m 5w 2 parts
—Same
In Overmyer, E. Eric Overmyer: collected plays

In a pig's valise
Musical send-up of Raymond Chandler school of hard-boiled detective fiction. Music, singing, dancing. 2 acts 7m 3w 1 setting
In Overmyer, E. Eric Overmyer: collected plays

In perpetuity throughout the universe
Dark comedy looks at paranoid reality created by group of ghost writers. 37 scenes 3m 3w 1 setting
In Overmyer, E. Eric Overmyer: collected plays

Native speech
Set in the future. Disc jockey provides view of degenerate civilization. 2 acts 8m 3w extras 1 interior
In Overmyer, E. Eric Overmyer: collected plays

On the verge; or, The geography of yearning
Three intrepid Victorian lady explorers become disoriented as the surrounding rainforest reveals artifacts from the future. 2 acts 22 scenes 1m 3w 1 setting
In Overmyer, E. Eric Overmyer: collected plays

Overseas and underseas news. See Haylock, D. Here is the news: Overseas and underseas news

Overtime. Connolly, H.

Overtime. Gurney, A. R.

Ovid
Metamorphosis (dramatization) See Iizuka, N. Polaroid stories

Owen, Ken
Black, green, white and gold. New Playwrights Network 1996 23p
Native houseboy causes problems for British soldier stationed in West Africa during WW II. 1 act 5m 1 interior

The **owl** killer. Dean, P. H.

Oxford University. See University of Oxford

Oyamo
I am a man. Applause 1995 94p
Drama set in 1968 Memphis about strike by African-American sanitation workers just prior to assassination of Martin Luther King, Jr. 2 acts 14m 2w extras 1 setting

Oz! Francoeur, B.

P

Pacific Union. Buzo, A.

Pacino, Al
Goluboff, B. Big Al

Package deal. Stroppel, F.

Packard, Steven
In with Alma
Drama set in small Midwestern town. Sterile husband tries to keep wife's pregnancy secret. 4m 1w 1 exterior
In Off-Off Broadway Festival plays, 21st ser.

Paddywack. Magee, D.

Pagan day. See Nemeth, S. Sally's shorts: Pagan day

Paganini, Nicolo, 1782-1840
Nigro, D. Paganini

Page, Elizabeth
Aryan birth
Monologue. American Jewish man has affair with daughter of Nazi. 1m 1 setting
In The Best American short plays, 1992-1993

Pageants
DuBois, W. E. B. Star of Ethiopia
c Kennedy, R. Hans Christian Andersen's The snow queen
Mueller, D. A. Eyes upon the cross
United States Food Administration. Why we are at war

Paice, Eric, and Woddis, Roger
World on edge
Living newspaper account of Suez Crisis and 1956 Hungarian Revolution. 2 acts Variable cast
In Voicings: ten plays from the documentary theatre; ed. by A. Favorini

The **pain** of the macho. Najera, R.

Painted rain. Allard, J.

Painters
Broadhurst, K. The eye of the beholder
Childress, A. Wine in the wilderness
Howe, T. Painting Churches
McDonald, H. Dream of a common language
See also Artists and names of painters, e.g. Kahlo, Frida

Painters, Industrial
Stoppard, T. Albert's bridge

Painting Churches. Howe, T.

Paintings
Hare, D. The bay at Nice
Shamas, L. Portrait of a nude

Pakistanis
Sharif, B. My ancestor's house

England

Khan-Din, A. East is east

Pale horse. Penhall, J.

Pales Matos, Luis
La elegia del Saltimbanqui (dramatization) See Colón, A. The caravan

Palestinian Arabs
Balalin Company of Jerusalem. Darkness
Havis, A. A vow of silence
Verdecchia, G. and Youssef, M. A line in the sand

Palmer, Greg
c The falcon. Anchorage Press 1993 44p
Dramatization of Russian folk tale Fenist, the bright falcon. Fantastic adventures of young farm girl. Singing. 3m 3w 1 setting

Palmer, John
Henrik Ibsen on the necessity of producing Norwegian drama
In dramatic lecture Henrik Ibsen argues that theatrical canon is proof of nationhood. 2m 1w 1 setting
In The *CTR* anthology; ed. by A. Filewod

Pam-Grant, Susan
Curl up and dye
Black comedy set in South African beauty salon. Five mixed race women find strictures of aparthied more powerful than their common interests. 2 acts 5w 1 interior
In South Africa plays; ed. by S. Gray

Pancho Diablo. Morton, C.

Pandora. Goethe, J. W. von

Pandora's box. Asbrand, K.

Pangaean dreams a shamanic journey. Rosenthal, R.

Panic in the palace. Swintz, M.

Panicked. Ordway, S.

Pantaloon. Barrie, J. M.

Pantomime. Walcott, D.

Pantomimes
c Bisson, P. Simple Simon
c Duncombe, P. Robin Hood
c Green, M. Spring the king
c Lloyd, R. Treasure Island, the panto
Schnitzler, A. The transformation of Pierrot
Schnitzler, A. The veil of Pierrette
c Staite, J. Cinderella - the sequel
Staite, J. Goldilocks and the three Martians
c Webster, P. Babes in the wood
c Webster, P. Dick Turpin

Pantomimes with music
c Bisson, P. Little Red Riding Hood
c Brown, A. Sleeping Beauty
c Cregan, D. Aladdin
c Dolmen, C. and Dolmen, J. The three little pigs
c Edgar, K. Aladdin
c Edgar, K. Mother Goose
c Lloyd, R. Smut's saga
c Reakes, P. Dick Turpin
c Reakes, P. King Arthur
c Reakes, P. Old Mother Hubbard
c Robbins, N. Snow White
c Wakefield, C. The sleeping beauty
c Warhurst, M. Peter and the princess

Panych, Morris
y 2B WUT UR
Comic drama about adolescence set in teenage boy's imagination. 3m 3w 1 setting
In Panych, M. Other schools of thought

y Cost of living
Monologue by adolescent male about awkwardness and absurdities of teenage life. 1m
In Panych, M. Other schools of thought

The ends of the earth. Talonbooks 1993 140p
Black comedy about paranoia and fear set in seedy hotel run by deaf man and murderous blind woman. 2 acts 3m 2w 1 setting

y Life science
Monologue by high school girl reacting to death of homeless man. Slide projections. 1w
In Panych, M. Other schools of thought

Vigil. Talonbooks 1996 77p
Black comedy. Shallow, self-centered man finds himself in life and death situation. 2 acts 37 scenes 1m 1w

Paper angels. Lim, G.

The **paper** bag bandit rides again. Swift, R.

The **paper** rose. Valle-Inclán, R. del

Papineau Rebellion. See Canada—History—Rebellion, 1837-1838

Pap's place. McCusker, P.

Parables
Abe, K. The green stockings
Baitz, J. R. Coq au vin
Bond, E. The bundle
Cook, M. The head, guts and sound bone dance
MacNeice, L. The dark tower
MacNeice, L. Prisoner's progress
Margulies, D. Found a peanut
Richardson, D. Party night (the great feast)
Storey, D. The contractor
Walker, G. F. Rumours of our death
See also individual parables, e.g. Prodigal son (Parable)

Parables for a season. Onwueme, O. T.

Paracelsus. Schnitzler, A.

Paradise. Linney, R.

Paradise Drive. Way, C.

Paradise follies. Taylor, R. and Bologna, J.

Paradise lost (dramatization) See Dryden, J. The state of innocence and fall of man

Paradise Street. Barker, C.

Parakeet eulogy. Pintauro, J.

Paranoia
Panych, M. The ends of the earth

Parapsychology
Glore, J. The company of heaven

Parent and child
Adrian, Y. Flyboy
Allen, R. J. What to name your baby
y Aston, M. Fossils!
Brooks, V. Penny Blue
Churchill, C. Blue heart: Heart's desire
Crawford, D. W. Borrowed plumage
Crawford, J. L. Facelifting at St. Viators
Crowley, M. A breeze from the gulf
Durang, C. Baby with the bathwater
Everett, R. Present from the past
Foote, H. The young man from Atlanta
c Griffiths, D. That's the way to do it
Guyer, M. The American century
Howe, T. Birth and after birth
Howe, T. Painting Churches
Houston, V. H. As sometimes in a dead man's face
Hughes, L. Mulatto
Labiche, E. and Michel, M. It's all relative
Lucas, C. What I meant was
MacDonald, B. The weekend healer
MacLeod, W. The lost colony
Mazza, R. N. Parked
Miller, H. A winter reunion
Olmos, C. Profane games
Osofisan, F. Birthdays are not for dying
Plautus, T. M. The captives
Poliakoff, S. Playing with trains
Quayle, T. Bein Lochaber
Ross, A. Feet
Royce, C. My son Susie
Sawyer, A. V. Life comes to the old maid
Sherman, G. Broken English
y Sod, T. and Grant, S. Three wishes
Spencer, D. Hurricane roses
Taylor, P. Missing person
Terry, M. Fireworks
Tibbetts, M. Bottles with baskets on
Vickery, F. Roots and wings
Weller, M. Spoils of war
Wilder, T. Childhood
Wilder, T. Infancy
Wright, D. Lot 13: the bone violin
Wright, D. Watbanaland
See also Conflict of generations; Family; Fathers and daughters; Fathers and sons; Mothers and daughters; Mothers and sons

Parentcraft. Smith, S.

Les **parents** terribles (Indiscretions). Cocteau, J.

Pariah. Strindberg, A.

Paris (France)
19th century
Ayckbourn, A. Wolf at the door
Foxton, D. Caught on the hop
Labiche, E. and Delacour, A. The piggy bank
McDonald, H. Dream of a common language
Séjour, V. The brown overcoat
20th century
Kaufman, L. Shooting Simone
Martin, S. Picasso at the Lapin Agile
Sebbar, L. My mother's eyes
Walker, G. F. Theatre of the film noir
20th century—Riot, 1968
Griffiths, T. The party

Paris and Helen. Schwartz, D.

The **park.** Ursell, G.

Park your car in Harvard Yard. Horovitz, I.

Parked. Mazza, R. N.

Parker, Neil. See Ross, D. jt. auth.

Parker, Ron
y Under the influence. Clark, I. E. 1993 42p
Family members and friends of alcoholics and drug abusers relate their experiences. Variable cast 15 characters 1 setting

Parks, Rosa, 1913-
Nicholas, D. Buses

Parks, Suzan-Lori
The America play. Dramatists 1995 48p
Experimental theater piece on black identity, theater, and American history. 2 acts 8 scenes 3m 3w 1 setting
—Same
In Parks, S.-L. The America play and other works

Betting on the Dust Commander
Experimental play about language and marriage. Slide projections. 1m 1w 1 setting
In Parks, S.-L. The America play and other works

The death of the last black man in the whole entire world
Experimental drama depicting life and times of composite African-American couple. Variable cast
In Moon marked and touched by sun; ed. by S. Mahone
In Parks, S.-L. The America play and other works
In Women on the verge: 7 avant-garde American plays; ed. by R. C. Lamont

Parks, Suzan-Lori—*Continued*
Devotees in the garden of love
Satiric look at courtship, love and marriage. 3w 1 exterior
In 20/20: twenty one-act plays from twenty years of the Humana Festival
In Parks, S.-L. The America play and other works
Imperceptible mutabilities in the Third Kingdom. Sun & Moon Press 1995 68p
Surreal experimental work addresses issues of black history and identity. 4 parts 2m 3w
—Same
In The Best of Off-Broadway; ed. by R. Wetzsteon
In Colored contradictions: an anthology of contemporary African-American plays
In Parks, S.-L. The American play and other works
Pickling
Monologue. Experimental memory play. 1w
In Parks, S.-L. The America play and other works
Venus. Theater Communications Group 1997 165p
Historical drama about racial and sexual exploitation focusing on the Venus Hottentot, an African woman exhibited as freak in 19th century Europe because of her enormous buttocks. Music, singing. 31 scenes 2m 2w extras 1 setting

Parks
y Ursell, G. The park

Parnell, Peter
Flaubert's latest. Dramatists 1993 89p
Flaubert returns to life to visit blocked writer struggling to complete unfinished Flaubert novel. 2 acts 6 scenes 5m 3w 1 exterior
An imaginary life. Dramatists 1995 83p
Fantasy and reality collide when divorced middle-aged playwright, faced with his own mortality, searches for fictional solutions to his problems. 2 acts 6m 1w 1 setting

Parodies
y Boiko, C. Belinda and the Beast
y Boiko, C. Murder on the Orient Express subway
y Christiansen, A. Teens in Tinseltown
Gilbert, S. Lola Starr builds her dream home
Hughes, L. Limitations of life
y Kelly, T. Bang! Bang! You're dead
y Kelly, T. Hooray for Hollywood
y Kelly, T. That's the spirit!
c Love, D. Blame it on the wolf
McGillivray, D. and Zerlin, W. Chase me up Farndale Avenue, s'il vous plaît!
Osterman, G. Brother truckers
y Priore, F. V. Madcap Monster Inn
c Reakes, P. King Arthur
Simon, M. and Simon, R. Murder at Minsing Manor: a nancy boys mystery
y Sodaro, C. It's a bird! It's a plane! It's . . . Nerdman?!
Steelsmith, M. Wacs in khaki
Stroppel, F. The Mamet women
y Swift, R. Attack of the giant grasshoppers

Parra, Marco Antonio de la
Dostoevski goes to the beach
Private investigator descendant of Russian writer living in Chile accuses transnational magnate of murder. 2 acts 30 scenes 8m 4w 1 setting
In Parra, M. A. de la. The theatre of Marco Antonio de la Parra
Every young woman's desire (El deseo de toda ciudadana)
Intruder's physical and psychological subjugation of woman mirrors authoritarian regime's coersive methods. 7 scenes 3m 2w extras 1 setting
In Parra, M. A. de la. The theatre of Marco Antonio de la Parra
King Kong Palace; or, Tarzan's exile
Drama about betrayal featuring characters from popular culture. 4 acts 18 scenes 4m 4w 1 setting
In Parra, M. A. de la. The theatre of Marco Antonio de la Parra
The raw, the cooked, and the rotten (Lo crudo, lo cocido, lo podrido)
Political drama about Chile during Pinochet regime. 4m 1w 1 interior
In Parra, M. A. de la. The theatre of Marco Antonio de la Parra
Secret obscenities (La secreta obscenidad de cada dia)
Political drama about indecency, corruption and torture. Two exhibitionists perform act of terrorism. 2m 1 setting
In Parra, M. A. de la. The theater of Marco Antonio de la Parra

Parris-Bailey, Linda
Dark cowgirls and prairie queens
Performance piece about role of African American women on Western frontier. Singing. 2 acts 5w 1 setting
In Alternate roots; ed. by K. deNobriga and V. Anderson

Parsley, Roger
Brideshead revisited. French (London) 1994 87p
Dramatization of Waugh's satirical novel about young man's emotional involvement with eccentric aristocratic Roman Catholic family. 2 acts 31 scenes 5m 3w extras 1 setting

Parsons, Nicholas
Dead heart. Currency Press in association with Black Swan and Belvoir St. Theatre by arrangement with the National Institute of Dramatic Art and the Festival of Perth 1994 98p (Current theatre series)
Drama set in small aborigine community explores complex issues facing both black and white Australians in 1990s. 2 acts 10m 2w extras 1 setting

Parsons, Richard
Dead end
Seemingly law-abiding woman visited by government inspector. 1m 1w extra 1 interior
In Parsons, R. Rialto; Mortmain; Dead end

Mortmain
Widow on mission to locate all names in husband's diary. 1m 1w 1 interior
In Parsons, R. Rialto; Mortmain; Dead end

Rialto
Elderly widow cleverly manipulates smarmy confidence man to suit her purposes. 1m 1w 1 exterior
In Parsons, R. Rialto; Mortmain; Dead end

Parties
See also Balls (Parties); Entertaining

The **parting** of friends. Pickering, K.

The **party.** Griffiths, T.

Party night (the great feast). Richardson, D.

Party time. Pinter, H.

Pascal, Françoise
The lunatic lover (L'amoureux extravagant)
Farce set in 17th century Lyons about two pairs of lovers, their wily servants and lunatic poet. 4m 3w 1 exterior
In The Lunatic lover and other plays; ed. by P. Gethner

El **paseo** del vaquero (The ride of the vaquero). McCullough, L. E.

Pasquini the Magnificent. Ingraffia, S.

Passion. Sondheim, S.

The **passion** ... and its deep connection with lemon delicious pudding. Ingleton, S.

Passion and sin. Alianak, H.

Passion killers. Godber, J.

The **passion** of Josef D. Chayefsky, P.

The **passion** of Narcisse Mondoux. Gélinas, G.

A **passion** play. Barnes, D.

Passion plays. See Mysteries and miracle plays

A **passionate** woman. Mellor, K.

Passione d'amore. Scola, E. (adaptation) See Sondheim, S. Passion

Pastoral drama
Lyly, J. Gallathea

Patches solves a wedding riddle. McCullough, L. E.

Paternity
Mortimer, J. Edwin

Paterson, David L.
Dungeons. French 1995 85p
Comedy drama. Corporate-climbing yuppie and two homeless people wait to be rescued after steam pipe explosion in midtown Manhattan. 2m 1w 1 interior

Finger painting in a Murphy bed. French 1995 75p
Romantic comedy set in Queens, New York. Needy young man plots to destroy sister's budding romance out of fear of losing her. 4 scenes 2m 1w 1 interior

Pieces of the sky. French 1996 89p
Drama set in Nebraska diner during World War II. Friendship develops between middle-aged mother of soldier fighting in Europe and town's Jewish mailman. 2 acts 5 scenes 4m 1w 1 interior

The **path.** Ikhlasi, Walid

Pathological Venus. Mullins, B.

Patient A. Blessing, L.

The **patio** window. Stubbs, N.

Patricide
Schenkkan, R. The homecoming

Patrick, Robert
Love lace
Using their imagination, man and woman journey to historical and mythical locations in effort to enrich their relationship. 1m 1w
In Short plays for young actors; ed. by C. Slaight and J. Sharrar

Patriotism
c Hackett, W. The man without a country

The **patriots.** Kingsley, S.

Patter for the floating lady. Martin, S.

Pattison, John

Dreams from a summer house; a musical play; book and lyrics by Alan Ayckbourn; music by John Pattison. French (London) 1997 87p

Romantic musical fantasy. Characters from Beauty and the Beast create havoc with lives of contemporary English family. Music, singing. 2 acts 5m 3w 1 exterior

Paul, Jeremy

The secret of Sherlock Holmes. Players Press 1996 59p

Mystery based on characters created by Conan Doyle. Focuses on friendship that develops between Holmes and Watson. 2 acts 2m 1 interior

Paul Bunyan: lumberjack. McCaslin, N.

Paul Robeson. Dean, P. H.

Paull, Sylvia Lee

The Rainclouds study the Ten Commandments. Clark, I. E. 1993 29p

Worship program. Father explains the Ten Commandments to his children. 10 scenes 2m 1w 1b 1g 1 setting

Pavane. Wiener, S. D.

Pawley, Thomas

The tumult and the shouting

Drama set in Virginia. African American college professor forced into retirement. Music. 3 acts 11 scenes 10m 4w extras 1 setting

In Black theatre USA [v2]; ed. by J. V. Hatch and T. Shine

Paz, Octavio

Rappaccini's daughter

Poetic drama about love, death and loss of innocence based on Nathaniel Hawthorne's short story. Prologue 9 scenes epilogue 3m 3w 1 setting

In Latin American plays; ed. by S. Doggart

Peace

Aristophanes. Acharnians
Aristophanes. Lysistrata
Aristophanes. Peace

Peace in our time. Cadman, L.

Peaches. Grosso, N.

Peake, R. B.

Presumption; or, The fate of Frankenstein

Dramatization of Shelley's horror classic. 3 acts 11 scenes 10m 4w extras 5 interiors 6 exteriors

In Seven Gothic dramas, 1789-1825

A **pearl** of great price. Adam, A.

Pearson, Chris

Divergent lines. New Playwrights Network 1996 16p

Wife's new career in advertising puts strain on marriage. 1 act 1m 1w 1 interior

Scruples, agents and Wilfred. New Playwrights Network 1997 27p

Real estate employees anxious over impending layoff. 1 act 3m 1w 1 interior

Pearson, Sybille

Unfinished stories. Dramatists 1993 72p

Family drama set in New York about Jewish doctor who fled Germany in 1930s, his son, grandson and ex-daughter-in-law. 5 scenes 3m 1w 1 setting

—Same

In Women playwrights: the best plays of 1992

Watching the dog

Comedy set in veterinarian's office waiting room in New York City. 2m 4w extra 1 interior

In Facing forward; ed. by L. D. Frank

Peasantry

France

McBurney, S. and Wheatley, M. The three lives of Lucie Cabrol

Ireland

Synge, J. M. The playboy of the Western World

Pecong. Carter, S.

Pedneault, Hélène

Evidence to the contrary; tr. by Linda Gaboriau. NuAge 1993 62p (Performance series)

Psychological drama. Policeman interrogates woman accused of killing her mother. Videotape. 3 parts 3w 1m 1 setting

Pedophilia

Crowley, M. For reasons that remain unclear

Vogel, P. How I learned to drive

Pedrero, Paloma

The color of August

Successful woman artist confronts woman with whom she shares painful past. 2w 1 interior

In Pedrero, P. Parting gestures

A night divided

Actress seduces Bible salesman. 1m 1w 1 extra 1 exterior

In Pedrero, P. Parting gestures

The voucher

Divorcing couple fight over custody of dog. 1m 1w 1 interior

In Pedrero, P. Parting gestures

The **pelican.** Strindberg, A.

Pelonero, Edna

Family names

Farce. Receptionist encounters husband's mistress. 2w 1 interior

In Off-Off Broadway Festival plays, 19th ser.

Peloponnesian War, 431-404 B.C. See Greece—History—Peloponnesian War, 431-404 B.C.

Pemberton, Sue. See Sadler, C. jt. auth.

Pen, Polly

Bed and sofa; a silent movie opera; music by Polly Pen; libretto by Laurence Klaven; based on the film by Abram Room. Dramatists 1997 52p

Chamber opera farce set in 1920s Moscow based on Russian silent film. Wife falls in love with husband's friend who is sharing their one-room apartment. Music, singing. 2m 1w 1 interior

Pendleton, Austin

Booth. French 1944 108p

First produced with title: Booth is back. Traces the turbulent relationship between Junius Brutus Booth and his son Edwin as they travel across America in 1850s. 3 acts 9 scenes 5m 3w 1 setting

Uncle Bob. Dramatists 1995 58p

Drama set in Greenwich Village. Reclusive man with AIDs visited by nephew determined to care for him. 2m 1 interior

Penhall, Joe

Pale horse. Methuen Drama in association with the Royal Court Theatre 1995 72p (Royal Court writers series)

Urban drama about identity and mortality. Widower plunges himself into London underworld and is implicated in horrific crime. 2 acts 20 scenes 3m 2w extras 1 setting

—Same

In Penhall, J. Some voices & Pale horse

Some voices

Tragedy set in West London. Young schizophrenic desperately tries to reassimilate after stay in mental hospital. 2 acts 18 scenes 4m 1w 1 setting

In Frontline intelligence 3; ed. by P. Edwardes

In Penhall, J. Some voices & Pale horse

Pennies from heaven. Potter, D.

Penny, Rob

Good black don't crack

Family drama set in Pittsburgh during 1972 Christmas holiday. Single African American mother of three teenagers makes commitment to younger lover. 2 acts 16 scenes 3m 5w 3 interiors

In The National black drama anthology; ed. by W. King

Penny Blue. Brooks, V.

Pennsylvania Dutch

c McCaslin, N. A miracle in the Christmas city

Pentecost. Edgar, D.

People annihilation. Schwab, W.

Perfect crime. Manzi, W.

A **perfect** Ganesh. McNally, T.

A **perfect** match. Charles, R.

A **perfect** mermaid. Mamet, D.

Perfect pie. Thompson, J.

The **perfectionist.** Oates, J. C.

Performers. See Entertainers

Pericles, 499-429 B.C.

Warner, F. Healing nature

Peril on the high seas. St. John, B.

Perkin Warbeck. Ford, J.

A **permanent** signal. Kramer, S.

Permission to cry. Campton, D.

Pernak, Adam

Killers. French (London) 1993 71p

Drama about after-effects of murder. Man imprisoned for crime passionnel while his fighter pilot brother is lauded as patriotic hero. Prologue 2 acts 10 scenes 6m 4w 1 setting

Peron, Eva, 1919-1952

Lawrence, J. and Lee, R. E. Diamond orchid

Perrault, Charles

Cinderella (dramatization) See D'Arcy, A. Cinderella

Puss in boots (dramatization) See Bush, M. Puss in boots; Elfenbein, J. A. Puss-in-boots; Foxton, D. The real story of Puss in boots; Gerke, P. Chat botté: Puss-in-boots; Mahlmann, L. and Jones, D. C. Puss-in-boots

Perry, E. Eugene

y Once upon a beginning. Bakers Plays 1994 32p

Comedy based on Biblical stories of Adam and Eve, Noah, and Samson and Delilah. 4m 3w

Perry, Scott

Bookends. French (London) 1997 34p

Two men on park bench discuss indignities of aging. 2m 1 exterior

Perry, Shauneille

In Dahomey

Version of musical farce first produced 1902 with book by Jesse Shipp. Fraudulent scheme by black syndicate to sell land in Dahomey as haven for dissatisfied American blacks. 2 acts 4 scenes 7m 4w 1 setting

In The National black drama anthology; ed. by W. King

Persa. See Plautus, T. M. The Persian

Persephone. Boiko, C.

The **Persian.** Plautus, T. M.

Persian Gulf War, 1991
Verdecchia, G. and Youssef, M. A line in the sand

The **Persians.** Auletta, R.

The **personal** peace. See Aristophanes. Acharnians

Personality, Disorders of
Hare, D. Plenty

Persons from Porlock. MacNeice, L.

Peschina, Helmut
Straight as a corkscrew (Ich doch nicht)
Married man considers sex with male acquaintance. 2m 1 setting
In Seven contemporary Austrian plays; ed. by R. H. Lawson

Peter and the princess. Warhurst, M.

Peter Pan. Caird, J. and Nunn, T.

Peter Pan. Mahlmann, L. and Jones, D. C.

Peter Panto. Webster, P.

Peter Rabbit and me. Harris, A.

Peter Salem, Minuteman. Keats, M.

Peters, Kier
The confirmation. Sun & Moon Press 1993 63p (American theater in literature)
Arrival of woman's lesbian lover sets in motion series of ridiculous encounters which lead mother and sisters to reveal true feelings for one another. 4 acts 5w 1 setting

Petersen, Candyce A.
c If angels were mortal . . . Pioneer Drama Service 1996 24p
Complications arise in heaven as angels await the birth of Christ. Background music. 3 scenes Variable cast 8 characters extras 2 interiors

Peterson, Liz
c The wind in the willows; dramatized by Liz Peterson from Kenneth Grahame's classic children's book; music: Liz Peterson; lyrics: Liz Peterson and Kenneth Grahame; musical consultant: George Banhalmi. Anchorage Press 1993 50p
Musical dramatization of Grahame's classic animal tale. 12 scenes Variable cast 14 characters 1 setting

Peterson, Louis
Take a giant step
Middle-class black teenager confronts racial prejudice in 1950s New England. 2 acts 6 scenes 9m 7w 7 interiors
In Black drama in America: an anthology; ed. by D. T. Turner
In Black theatre USA [v2]; ed. by J. V. Hatch and T. Shine

Peterson, Martin L.
c How Santa Claus discovered Christmas
Worship program. Santa Claus discovers religious significance of Christmas. Singing. 8 scenes 3m 2w 2b 1g extras 1 setting
In Christmas plays for young audiences

Peterson, Mary Nygaard
c The soup stone
Based on folktale. Hungry traveler convinces hosts that he can make soup from a stone. 2 scenes 2m 3w 2b 1g extras 1 interior 1 exterior
In Thirty plays from favorite stories; ed. by S. E. Kamerman

Petroleum industry
McLean, D. Julie Allardyce

Petsinis, Tom
The drought. Currency Press in association with La Mama Theatre 1994 55p (Current theatre series)
Drama about tensions surrounding migration and return. Macedonian-born Australian, having failed to find his fortune, returns to drought-stricken village of his birth. 3 acts 15 scenes 4m 4w

Pflomm, Phyllis Noe
c Autumn leaves
Puppet play about autumn. 5 characters
In Pflomm, P. N. Puppet plays plus
c The busy Santa
Puppet play. Snowman helps Santa solve problem. 5 characters
In Pflomm, P. N. Puppet plays plus
c Clever pets
Puppet play about child's attempts to train parrot and dog. 3 characters
In Pflomm, P. N. Puppet plays plus
c Couch potatoes
Puppet play about watching too much television. 3 characters
In Pflomm, P. N. Puppet plays plus
c Fishing
Puppet play. Boy and girl go fishing. 4 characters
In Pflomm, P. N. Puppet plays plus
c Five little snowmen
Puppet play about winter. 6 characters
In Pflomm, P. N. Puppet plays plus
c Gracie's garden
Puppet play. Father and daughter plant magic garden. 2 characters
In Pflomm, P. N. Puppet plays plus
c Halloween ghosts
Puppet play. Children go trick-or-treating on Halloween. 4 characters
In Pflomm, P. N. Puppet plays plus

Pflomm, Phyllis Noe—*Continued*

c Jeremy borrows a book

Puppet play. Boy learns how to care for library books. 6 characters

In Pflomm, P. N. Puppet plays plus

c The leprechaun

Puppet play based on Irish folklore. Leprechauns encounter Paddy's pig. 5 characters

In Pflomm, P. N. Puppet plays plus

c Let's be puppets

Puppet play with audience participation. Puppet characters demonstrate hand puppet manipulation. Alternate endings for preschool to kindergarten and elementary grades. 2 acts 2 characters

In Pflomm, P. N. Puppet plays plus

c Litterbugs

Puppet play. Flyswatter teaches children not to litter. 3 characters

In Pflomm, P. N. Puppet plays plus

c The loose tooth

Puppet play. Boy loses baby tooth and gets money from tooth fairy. 3 characters

In Pflomm, P. N. Puppet plays plus

c Lost in a fairy tale

Puppet play. Goldilocks asks other fairy tale characters for help in finding her way home. 9 characters

In Pflomm, P. N. Puppet plays plus

c A new Punch and Judy

Nonviolent version of traditional puppet play. Punch tricks and bothers adversaries with feather duster. 9 characters

In Pflomm, P. N. Puppet plays plus

c The picnic

Puppet play. Woodland animals eat girl's picnic lunch but boy offers to share his. 6 characters

In Pflomm, P. N. Puppet plays plus

c Ryan's hat

Puppet play. Boy finds missing hat. 4 characters

In Pflomm, P. N. Puppet plays plus

c Silvie the substitute reindeer

Puppet play. Female reindeer substitutes for sick Prancer. 4 characters

In Pflomm, P. N. Puppet plays plus

c The talent show

Puppet play about talent show contestants. 8 characters

In Pflomm, P. N. Puppet plays plus

c The Thanksgiving bear

Puppet play. Bear is disappointed when friends say they can't come to his Thanksgiving dinner. 5 characters

In Pflomm, P. N. Puppet plays plus

c The Valentine bouquet

Puppet play about girl's generosity on Valentine's Day. 5 characters

In Pflomm, P. N. Puppet plays plus

c Vegetables

Puppet play in verse. Doctor hypnotizes boy to persuade him to eat vegetables. 3 characters

In Pflomm, P. N. Puppet plays plus

c A visit to the library

Puppet play. Boy and girl learn about public library. 4 characters

In Pflomm, P. N. Puppet plays plus

c Witches and ghosts

Puppet play. On Halloween witch and ghost compete to be scariest. 2 characters

In Pflomm, P. N. Puppet plays plus

Phaedra (Greek mythology)
Racine, J. Phædra

Phaedra. Maguire, M.

Phaedra, Racine, J. (adaptation) See Mahon, D. Racine's Phaedra

Phaedra. Seneca. (adaptation) See Kane, S. Phaedra's love

Phaedra's love. Kane, S.

Phantom of the music hall. Prior, J.

The **phantom** of the opera. Hill, K.

Phelan, Brian
Himself. Warner Chappell Plays 1994 105p

Drama. On lecture tour of United States Irish actor becomes involved with mysterious Christian movement. 2 acts 10 scenes 5m 2w

Philadelphia (Pa.)
Bullins, E. In the wine time

The **Philadelphia.** Ives, D.

The **philanthropist.** Hampton, C.

Philemon
Emporus (adaptation) See Plautus, T. M. The entrepreneur

Philip, Sachem of the Wampanoags, d. 1679
Linney, R. The death of King Philip

Philip and Rowena. Plowman, G.

Philip Glass buys a loaf of bread. Ives, D.

Philomela (Greek mythology)
Wertenbaker, R. The love of the nightingale

Philosophers
Havel, V. Largo desolato

Philosophy
Barker, H. All he fears
Epstein, M. How Gertrude stormed the Philosophers' Club
Madách, I. The tragedy of man

Philosophy—*Continued*
O'Neill, E. Servitude
Stoppard, T. Arcadia

Phobias
See also Agoraphobia

Phonetics
Shaw, B. Pygmalion

Photographers
Kalinoski, R. Beast on the moon
Lewis, I. Chinese coffee
Shengold, N. Finger food

Phrynichus, 5th cent. B.C. See Harrison, T. The labourers of Herakles

Phyllis and Xenobia. Durang, C.

Physical. Thomas, B.

Physically handicapped
y Allard, J. Painted rain
Barnes, P. More than a touch of Zen
Bell, N. Out the window
Calhoun, W. Call it clover
Corthron, K. Come down burning
Hastings, C. The wayward spirit
LaChiusa, M. J. Agnes
McDonagh, M. The cripple of Inishmaan
Sanchez, E. Icarus
Thatcher, K. Emma's child
Williams, G. Rain
Zauner, F. Ch. A handful of earth
See also Blind; Cerebral palsy; Deaf

Physicians
Aldridge, I. The black doctor
Baitz, J. R. The end of the day
Benn, G. Ithaka
Bennett, A. Habeas corpus
Blanc, E. S. Wars I have seen
Brown, W. W. The escape
Fennario, D. Doctor Thomas Neill Cream: mystery at McGill
Ibsen, H. An enemy of the people
Kingsley, S. Men in white
Mori, Ō. Masks
y Nolan, P. T. An enemy of the people
Pollock, D. Doc
Schnitzler, A. Paracelsus
Shaw, G. B. The doctor's dilemma
y St. John, B. Dogsbreath Devereaux, the dastardly doctor
See also Women physicians

Pianists
Harwood, R. Another time
Roth, A. Oh, the innocents

Picasso, Pablo
Martin, S. Picasso at the Lapin Agile

Picasso at the Lapin Agile. Martin, S.

Pickering, Kenneth
The Ingoldsby legends; or, Mirth and marbels. Miller, J. G. 1994 48p

Based on legends by English clergyman Richard Barham who wrote under pseudonym Thomas Ingoldsby. Devil tries to misuse Barham's macabre stories to capture his soul. 2 acts Variable cast

One child at a time; music by Philip Bass. Miller, J. G. 1994 45p

Depicts plight of children in developing world. Music. 19 scenes Variable cast

The parting of friends. Miller, J. G. 1994 63p

Drama based on life of Cardinal John Henry Newman, leader of the Oxford Movement who converted to Catholicism in 1845. Background music. 3 acts Variable cast 26 characters

See also Dawson, J. and Bass, P. The inside story

Pickett, Bob. See Allman, S. jt. auth.

Pickett, James Carroll
Queen of Angels

Experimental black comedy about gay identity and AIDS. Music, singing. Prologue 2 acts 35 scenes 8m extras 1 setting

In Sharing the delirium; ed. by T. Jones

Pickling. Parks, S.-L.

The **Pickwick** papers. Olfson, L.

The **picnic**. Marx, P.

The **picnic**. Pflomm, P. N.

Picnic time. Cooper, J. B.

A **picture** of paradise. Murphy, J.

Pieces of the sky. Paterson, D. L.

The **Pied** Piper. Nunn, J.

Pied Piper of Hamelin
c Mahlmann, L. and Jones, D. C. The Pied Piper of Hamelin
c Norcross, E. B. Pied Piper's land
c Nunn, J. The Pied Piper

The **Pied** Piper of New Orleans. Church, J.

Pied Piper's land. Norcross, E. B.

Pierson, Kenn
Mountain thunder. Univ. of South Dakota Press 1993 63p (The Wayne S. Knutson Dakota playwriting project v4)

One man show based on writings of South Dakota cowboy poet Badger Clark. 1m 1 setting

Pig in a poke. Gray, S.

A **pig** tale. Johnston, C.

The **piggy** bank. Labiche, E. and Delacour, A.

Pigs

c Wood, D. Babe, the sheep-pig

Pig's ear. Cullen, A.

Pigspurt. Campbell, K.

Pikser, Jeremy

Revolution in Cleveland (dramatization) See Griffiths, T. Real dreams

Pilgrims (New Plymouth Colony)

c Marx, P. The troubled Pilgrim

The **Pilgrim's** progress. Bunyan, J. (dramatization) See Howles, L. The king's highway

A **pillar** of the church. Richardson, W.

Pillars of society. Ibsen, H.

Pillay, Kriben

Looking for Muruga. Asoka Theatre Publs. 1995 57p (Playscript no.4)

Cross-cultural drama set in post-aparthied Africa about topics ranging from Marxism and mythology to love and magic. 2 acts 3m 1 setting

Pimps

Wilson, L. Balm in Gilead

Pinball. Lyssa, A.

The **pinballs.** Harris, A.

Pinero, Arthur Wing

The magistrate

Farce. Concealment of woman's real age causes her embarrassment in second marriage. 3 acts 4 scenes 12m 4w 3 interiors

In Pinero, A. W. Trelawny of the 'Wells' and other plays

The schoolmistress

Farcical view of Victorian social structure set in London seminary for young ladies. Action revolves around secret marriage and principal's theatrical ambitions. 3 acts 9m 7w 3 interiors

In Pinero, A. W. Trelawny of the 'Wells' and other plays

The second Mrs. Tanqueray

Woman with a past marries above her station, is rejected by society and by stepdaughter and driven to suicide. 4 acts 7m 4w 2 interiors

In Pinero, A. W. Trelawny of the 'Wells' and other plays

Trelawny of the 'Wells'

Comedy about the beginning of realism in the English theater focusing on the career and marital problems of young actress. 4 acts 10m 8w extras 3 interiors

In Pinero, A. W. Trelawny of the 'Wells' and other plays

Pinnock, Winsome

Talking in tongues

Drama set in London and in Jamaica about social and sexual miscegenation. Prologue 2 acts 12 scenes 4m 8w 1 interior 1 exterior

In Black plays: three; ed. by Y. Brewster

Pinocchio. Mahlmann, L. and Jones, D. C.

Pinocchio. Roca, M.

Pinocchio commedia. Simons, J.

Pintauro, Joe

Benjamin falling

From hospital bed man envisions own death. 1m 1 interior

In Pintauro, J. Metropolitan operas

Bird of ill omen

Drama. Terminally ill deaf man visits prostitute in Manhattan whorehouse. 1m 1w extra 1 interior

In Pintauro, J. Metropolitan operas

Birds in church

Drama. Two Catholic priests attempting to catch birds flying about their church discuss questions of theology. 2m 1 interior

In Pintauro, J. Metropolitan operas

Bus stop diner

Comedy. Playwright persuaded to help fix appallingly bad play by opening night. 3m 1 interior

In Pintauro, J. Metropolitan operas

Butterball

Absurdist commentary on American life in the late 20th century. Background music. 2m 3w 1 interior

In Pintauro, J. Metropolitan operas

Charlie's farewell

Brief sketch about death. 2m 1 setting

In Pintauro, J. Metropolitan operas

Dawn

Tensions arise when man, accompanied by sister and wife gather at beach to scatter mother's ashes. 1 act 1m 2w 1 exterior

In By the sea, by the sea, by the beautiful sea

Dirty talk

Drama. Young man has sex change and returns to hometown and seduces his/her father. Music, dancing. 2m 1w 1 interior

In Pintauro, J. Metropolitan operas

Easter night

Drama. Easter dinner strained by recent loss of loved one. Background music. 2m 2w 1 interior

In Pintauro, J. Metropolitan operas

Fiat

Drama about nature of reality. Customer claiming to be the Virgin Mary visits hairdresser. Background music, singing. 1m 1w 1 interior

In Pintauro, J. Metropolitan operas

Pintauro, Joe—*Continued*

Frozen dog

Drama. Roman Catholic priest discovers another priest is gay and in love with him. 2m 1 interior

In Pintauro, J. Metropolitan operas

Fur hat

Drama. Divorced couple, unexpectedly reunited, insult and berate each other with truths neither can deny. 1m 1w 1 interior

In Pintauro, J. Metropolitan operas

His dish

Drama about sibling rivalry. Middle-aged man rejects his brother's new wife out of jealousy. 2m 1w 1 interior

In Pintauro, J. Metropolitan operas

House made of air

Pablo Neruda's wife tells of poet's last days. 1w 1 setting

In Pintauro, J. Metropolitan operas

Lenten pudding

Drama. Old lesbian aunt abandoned by family. 2w 1 exterior

In Pintauro, J. Metropolitan operas

Lightning

Experimental piece. Abandoned wife is left to run farm and raise daughter on her own. 2w 1 exterior

In Pintauro, J. Metropolitan operas

Men without wives

Drama. Father and son, both widowers, commiserate with each other. 2m 1 interior

In Pintauro, J. Metropolitan operas

Men's lives. Dramatists 1994 61p

Drama based on Peter Mathiessen's book. Explores fate of fishing family on East End of Long Island. 7m 1w 1 setting

Parakeet eulogy

Priest reflects on death. 1m 1 setting

In Pintauro, J. Metropolitan operas

Reindeer soup. Dramatists 1996 47p

Hallucinatory portrait of dysfunctional family. 4m 2w 2g 1 setting

—Same

In New plays from A.C.T.'S young conservatory [v1]

Rex

Black comedy. Woman serves pheasant she ran over for dinner. Background music. 1m 1w 1 interior

In Pintauro, J. Metropolitan operas

Rosen's son

Drama. Elderly Jewish man comes to terms with his dead son's homosexual lover. 3m 1 interior

In The Actor's book of gay and lesbian plays; ed. by E. Lane and N. Shengold

In Pintauro, J. Metropolitan operas

Rules of love

Drama. Priest attempts to reconcile his sexual feelings with rules of his vocation. 1m 1w 1 interior

In Pintauro, J. Metropolitan operas

Seymour in the very heart of winter

Drama. On Christmas Eve, depressed middle-aged woman shares memories with young lover. 2m 1w 1 interior

In Pintauro, J. Metropolitan operas

Snow orchid. Dramatists 1997 66p

Domestic drama. After spending time in rehab following suicide attempt, manic-depressive man clashes with agoraphobic wife and homosexual son. 2 acts 7 scenes 4m 1w 1 interior

Soft dude

Drama. Sexually dysfunctional adults, victims of childhood abuse, cannot overcome fear of intimacy. 1m 1w 1 interior

In Pintauro, J. Metropolitan operas

Swans flying

Impressionistic theater piece. Hospital patient hears sound of swans flying. Background music. 1m 2w 1 interior

In Pintauro, J. Metropolitan operas

Ten-dollar drinks

Variant title: Five-dollar drinks. Drama. Two rival actresses meet for drinks. 2w 1 interior

In Pintauro, J. Metropolitan operas

Two eclairs

Woman learns younger sister is having affair with husband. Background music. 1m 1w extra 1 interior

In Pintauro, J. Metropolitan operas

Uncle Chick

Drama set in Greenwich Village. Young homosexual attempts to seduce his uncle. 2m 1 interior

In Pintauro, J. Metropolitan operas

Watchman of the night

Drama examines emotional similarities between hetero- and homosexual relationships. Offstage voices. 2m extras 1 interior

In Pintauro, J. Metropolitan operas

Pintauro, Joseph. See Pintauro, Joe

Pinter, Harold

Ashes to ashes. Grove Press 1997 85p

Drama about personal and political violence. Husband relentlessly questions wife about her abusive ex-lover. 1m 1w 1 setting

Betrayal

Adulterous love affair between woman and husband's best friend shown in stages, from 1977 back to 1968 inception. 9 scenes 3m 1w 7 interiors

In Pinter, H. Plays: four

Family voices

Radio play. Unrelated voices of mother, father and son reflect complexity of familial relationships. 2m 1w 1 setting

In Pinter, H. Plays: four

A kind of Alaska

Woman awakes after twenty nine years in coma induced by sleeping sickness. 1m 2w 1 interior

In Pinter, H. Plays: four

Pinter, Harold—*Continued*
Monologue
Monologue in which old man shares his memories with empty chair. 1m
In Pinter, H. Plays: four
Moonlight. Dramatists 1996 37p
Dysfunctional family contends with dying husband and father. 4m 3w 1 setting
—Same. Faber & Faber 1993 80p
Mountain language
Drama. Four brief scenes illustrate inherent brutality of state-enforced oppression. 4 scenes 6m 2w
In Pinter, H. Plays: four
In Telling tales: new one-act plays; ed. by E. Lane
The new world order
Political sketch about superpower viciousness and hypocrisy. 3m
In Pinter, H. Party time and The new world order
In Pinter, H. Plays: four
No man's land
Tragicomedy involving two elderly men trapped in no man's land between their present reality (where they are in effect captives of two younger servants) and their faultily remembered past. 2 acts 4m 1 interior
In Pinter, H. Plays: four
Old times
Behind the conversation of reminiscing married couple and visiting female friend they have not seen for twenty years lurk suggestions of frightening past. Singing. 2 acts 1m 2w 2 interiors
In Pinter, H. Plays: four
One for the road
Study of political terror set in unnamed totalitarian state. Interrogator torments tortured prisoner and his imprisoned wife and son. 2m 1w 1b 1 interior
In Pinter, H. Plays: four
Party time
Television play. Stylish bourgeoisie attend elegant cocktail party while sinister military presence shields them from poverty and dissent. 5m 4w extras
In Pinter, H. Party time and The new world order
Precisely
Satirical sketch. Two men discuss accuracy of generally accepted number of victims ascribed to historical event. 2m
In Pinter, H. Plays: four
Victoria Station
Humorous exchange between lost taxi driver and dispatcher. 2m 1 setting
In Pinter, H. Plays: four

Pirandello, Luigi
The rules of the game; in a new version by David Hare. Absolute Classics 1993 64p
Husband, wife and her lover caught in triangle of desire, jealousy and revenge. 3 acts 9m 2w extras 3 interiors

Pirates
c Caird, J. and Nunn, T. Peter Pan
c Staite, J. Cinderella - the sequel
y York, M. A. Treasure Island

Piscator, Erwin, and Gasbarra, Felix
In spite of everything!
Historical review of Berlin workers' revolutionary politics from 1914 to 1919. Contains film clips. 24 scenes Large mixed cast
In Voicings: ten plays from the documentary theatre; ed. by A. Favorini

Pitbull. See Berkoff, S. Dog

Pitcher, Molly, 1754-1832
c Hall, M. Molly Pitcher meets the General

The **pitchfork** Disney. Ridley, P.

Pitching to the star. Margulies, D.

Pittman, Al
West moon. Breakwater 1995 63p
Drama set in mid-1960s Newfoundland. Dead explore social, political, moral, and theological issues facing Canadians in isolated coastal community. 2 parts 6m 4w extra 1 setting

Pitts, Graham
Emma. Currency Press in association with Playbox Theatre 1996 52p (Current theatre series)
Dramatic adaptation of Emma; a translated life by Michael Bosworth and Emma Ciccotosto who migrated to Australia from Italy in 1939. Music, singing. 2 acts 1m 3w extras 1 setting

Pix, Mary
The Spanish wives
Romantic comedy mocking importance of virginity and male fears of cuckoldry. Prologue 3 acts 15 scenes epilogue 7m 4w 5 interiors
In The Meridian anthology of Restoration and eighteenth-century plays by women; ed. by K. M. Rogers

Pizza: a love story. Bernstein, J.

A **place** where love is. Wiener, S. D.

A **place** with the pigs. Fugard, A.

Plague

London, 1665

See London (England)—17th century—Plague

Plagues
Barnes, P. Red noses

The **plain** dealer. Wycherley, W.

Plaintiffs and defendants. Gray, S.

Plantation life
Aiken, G. L. Uncle Tom's cabin
Dove, R. The darker face of the earth

Plastic surgery. See Surgery, Plastic

Plautus, Titus Maccius
Amphitryon; tr. by Constance Carrier
Latin comedy based on Greek mythology. Theban general cuckolded by Jupiter
In Plautus, T. M. Plautus: the comedies v1

Asses galore (Asinaria); tr. by Fred Chappell
Variant title: The comedy of asses. Based on play by Demophilus about father-son rivalry for affection of beautiful courtesan
In Plautus, T. M. Plautus: the comedies v3

The braggart soldier (Miles gloriosus); tr. by Erich Segal
Variant titles: The braggart warrior; The Swaggering soldier; Major Bullshot-Gorgeous. Farcical verse play about vain and lecherous Roman soldier
In Plautus, T. M. Four comedies
In Plautus, T. M. Plautus: the comedies v1

The braggart warrior; tr. by Robert Wind
In Plautus, T. M. Three comedies

The brothers Menaechmus (Menaechmi); tr. by Erich Segal
Farcical Latin drama about complications arising from man's search for long lost identical twin brother
In Plautus, T. M. Four comedies

—Same; tr. by Palmer Bovie
In Plautus, T. M. Plautus: the comedies v4

The captives (Captivi); tr. by Richard Moore
Variant title: The prisoners. Latin comedy. To secure exchange for son captured in war Hegio buys two enemy captives, one of whom turns out to be another son stolen years ago
In Plautus, T. M. Plautus: the comedies v1

Casina: tr. by Robert Wind
Variant title: A funny thing happened on the way to the wedding, entered below
In Plautus, T. M. Three comedies

The entrepreneur (Mercator); tr. by George Garrett
Variant title: The merchant. Comedy based on Philemon's Emporus. Father buys courtesan not knowing she is his son's mistress
In Plautus, T. M. Plautus: the comedies v2

Epidicus; tr. by Constance Carrier
Latin comedy of intrigue revolving around scheming slaves, mistaken identity and father's reunion with long-lost illegitimate daughter
In Plautus, T. M. Plautus: the comedies v3

A funny thing happened on the way to the wedding (Casina); tr. by Richard Beacham
Latin comedy. Old gentleman tries to marry off beautiful slave girl to his servant in order to get her for himself, while his son attempts similar scheme
In Plautus, T. M. Plautus: the comedies v1

The haunted house (Mostellaria); tr. by Erich Segal
Comedy. Adventure of a cunning, mercenary slave attempting to conceal profligacy of master's son. Verse play
In Plautus, T. M. Four comedies

—Same; tr. by Palmer Bovie
In Plautus, T. M. Plautus: the comedies v3

The little box (Cistellaria); tr. by R. H. W. Dillard
Variant title: The casket. Fragments of Plautus' comedy as augmented by the translator
In Plautus, T. M. Plautus: the comedies v4

The little Carthaginian (Poenulus); tr. by Janet Burroway
Latin comedy in verse. Young man rescues lovely girl from loathsome pimp who is about to sell her into prostitution
In Plautus, T. M. Plautus: the comedies v3

The Persian (Persa); tr. by Palmer Bovie
Variant title: The girl form Persia. Latin comedy about Athenian slave's love for courtesan
In Plautus, T. M. Plautus: the comedies v4

The pot of gold (Aulularia); tr. by Erich Segal
Latin comedy about a miser, his seduced daughter and miser's effort to protect his gold
In Plautus, T. M. Four comedies

—Same; tr. by Palmer Bovie
In Plautus, T. M. Plautus: the comedies v2

Pseudolus; tr. by Richard Beacham
Latin comedy in verse. Cunning slave helps his master's son get the girl he wants
In Plautus, T. M. Plautus: the comedies v4

Plautus, Titus Maccius—*Continued*
The rope (Rudens); tr. by Constance Carrier
Latin comedy in verse about a girl stolen from her father and adventures that befall them both before they are reunited
In Plautus, T. M. Plautus: the comedies v2
—Same; tr. by Robert Wind
In Plautus, T. M. Three comedies
The savage slave (Truculentus); tr. by James Tatum
Comedy. Three men vie for attentions of scheming courtesan
In Plautus, T. M. Plautus: the comedies v2
Stichus; tr. by Carol Poster
Latin comedy about two sisters who marry rich brothers
In Plautus, T. M. Plautus: the comedies v4
The thirty-dollar day (Trinummus); tr. by Daniel Mark Epstein
Variant title: A three-dollar day. Latin comedy. Son who squandered father's property tries to restore family's honor when sister needs dowry
In Plautus, T. M. Plautus: the comedies v3
Two sisters named Bacchis (Bacchides); tr. by James Tatum
Variant title: The two Bacchides. Comedy set in Athens adapted from Menander's The double deceiver. Two young men slavishly devoted to two courtesans who will do anything for money
In Plautus, T. M. Plautus: the comedies v2
The weevil (Curculio); tr. by Henry Taylor
Latin comedy about a parasite who uses stolen ring to rescue girl his master loves from pimp who is about to sell her
In Plautus, T. M. Plautus: the comedies v1

Play for germs. Horovitz, I.

The **play** of Daniel. Auden, W. H.

Play to win. Foster, J.

Play within a play
Bennett, A. Forty years on
Brett, S. Murder in play
Brewer, E. and Toksvig, S. The pocket dream
y Christiansen, A. A monster ate my homework
Davis, R. The (revised) travelling Cinderella show
c Davis, R. The travelling Jekyll & Hyde show
Dietz, S. Private eyes
Gerstenberg, A. The pot boiler
Harper, T. Rehearsal for murder
Hayman, R. Playing the wife
y Jackson, K. Three doors to death
Kitchen, B. Halfway up the M3 on the way to Basingstoke
Kushner, T. The illusion
Linney, R. Tennessee
MacIvor, D. This is a play
McGillivray, D. and Zerlin, W. Chase me up Farndale Avenue, s'il vous plaît!
McGillivray, D. and Zerlin, W. The Farndale Avenue Housing Estate Townspeople's Guild Operatic Society's Production of The Mikado
c Mercati, C. Cinderella
Minghella, A. Two planks and a passion
c Neary, J. Aladdin and the wonderful lamp
y Nimmo, P. Will Shakespeare save the King!
y Nimmo, P. Will Shakespeare save us!
y O'Brien, J. Wherefore art thou Juliet?
Parnell, P. An imaginary life
Pinero, A. W. Trelawny of the 'Wells'
y Polsky, M. E. Act of will
y Prior, J. Phantom of the music hall
Rattigan, T. Harlequinade
y Rayfield, J. I hate mothers
Rubens, B. Hijack
Sadler, C. and Pemberton, S. Christmas balls
Schnitzler, A. The Green Cockatoo
c Simons, J. Pinocchio commedia
Smith, M. L. An evening of culture: Faith County II, the saga continues
Solórzano, C. And death brought forth the light
Stoppard, T. The real Inspector Hound
y Swift, R. The Hunchback of Notre Dame goes West
Tagore, R. The cycle of spring
y Welsh, D. Mellow drama
Wertenbaker, T. Our country's good
Witkiewicz, S. I. The mother

The **playboy** of the Western World. Synge, J. M.

Playhouse creatures. De Angelis, A.

Playing bare. Champagne, D.

Playing the wife. Hayman, R.

Playing with trains. Poliakoff, S.

Playland. Fugard, A.

The **playmaker.** Keneally, T. (dramatization) See Wertenbaker, T. Our country's good

Plays in verse
Addison, J. Cato
Aeschylus. Agamemnon
Aeschylus. Seven against Thebes
Anderson, M. Richard and Anne
Aristophanes. Acharnians
Aristophanes. Birds
Aristophanes. The clouds
Aristophanes. Festival time
Aristophanes. Frogs
Aristophanes. Knights
Aristophanes. Lysistrata
Aristophanes. Peace
Aristophanes. Wasps
Auletta, R. The Persians
Bau, T. Cold hands
c Bennett, R. Rumpelstiltskin
c Bennett, R. The shoemaker and the elves
Berkoff, S. Sink the Belgrano!
Bird, R. M. The gladiator
Cary, E. The tragedy of Mariam, the fair
Chapman, G. The revenge of Bussy d'Ambois
Dove, R. The darker face of the earth
Dryden, J. All for love
Dryden, J. Aureng-Zebe
Dryden, J. Cleomenes the Spartan heroe
Dryden, J. King Arthur
Dryden, J. Love triumphant
Dryden, J. The state of innocence and fall of man
Dunlap, W. Andre
Euripides. Alcestis
Euripides. Bakkhai
Euripides. The children of Heracles
Euripides. The Cyclops
Euripides. Electra
Euripides. Hekabe
Euripides. Hippolytus
Euripides. Iphigenia among the Taurians
Euripides. Iphigenia in Aulis
Euripides. Medea
Euripides. Orestes
Euripides. Suppliant women
Everyman
c Fisher, A. Harriet Tubman—the second Moses
Fletcher, J. and Massinger, P. The elder brother
Fletcher, J. and Massinger, P. The little French lawyer
Fletcher, J. and Massinger, P. The prophetess
Fletcher, J. and Rowley, W. The maid in the mill
Ford, J. The broken heart
Ford, J. The lover's melancholy
Ford, J. Perkin Warbeck
Ford, J. 'Tis pity she's a whore
García Lorca, F. Yerma
Goethe, J. W. von. Faust, part I
Goethe, J. W. von. Faust, part II
Goethe, J. W. von. Iphigenia in Tauris
Goethe, J. W. von. The natural daughter
Goethe, J. W. von. Pandora
Goethe, J. W. von. Torquato Tasso
Hagger, N. The warlords
Harrison, T. The Kaisers of Carnuntum
Harrison, T. The labourers of Herakles
Harrison, T. Poetry or bust
Hill, G. Brand
Hughes, L. Don't you want to be free?
Hugo, V. Hernani
Hugo, V. The king amuses himself
Hugo, V. Ruy Blas
Judy, G. Antigone
Kennelly, B. Euripides' The Trojan woman
Kennelly, B. Sophocles' Antigone
Koch, K. The construction of Boston
Koch, K. The death of Sir Brian Caitskill
Koch, K. The gold standard
Koch, K. A heroine of the Greek resistance
Koch, K. The Red Robins
Koch, K. The strangers from the sea
Kochanowski, J. The dismissal of the Grecian envoys
Kokoschka, O. Murderer the women's hope
Kushner, T. The illusion
Kyd, T. The Spanish tragedy
Lee, N. The Princess of Cleves
c Librert, N. P. The Western Civ rap
MacNeice, L. Christopher Columbus
Madách, I. The tragedy of man
Mahon, D. Racine's Phaedra
Mankind. A critical edition of the medieval play Mankind
Marlowe, C. Edward II
Marlowe, C. The Jew of Malta
c Marx, P. The haunting contest
c Marx, P. Hearts and tarts
c McCullough, L. E. Klondike fever
McCullough, L. E. The twelve days of Christmas
c McCullough, L. E. Vinegar Pete's calico whisker pie
Middleton, T. A mad world, my masters
Middleton, T. Michaelmas Term
Middleton, T. No wit, no help like a woman's
Middleton, T. A trick to catch the old one

Plays in verse—*Continued*
Molière. The imaginary cuckold
Moreto, A. Spite for spite
Muldoon, P. Six honest serving men
O'Brien, J. T. Ancestress
c Pflomm, P. N. Vegetables
Plautus, T. M. The braggart soldier
Plautus, T. M. The haunted house
Plautus, T. M. The little Carthaginian
Plautus, T. M. Pseudolus
Plautus, T. M. The rope
Pushkin, A. Boris Godunov
Racine, J. Phædra
The Revenger's tragedy
Sade, Marquis de. The bedroom
Sade, Marquis de. Jeanne Laisné
Sade, Marquis de. The shyster
Sade, Marquis de. The twins
Sahlins, B. The mysteries: The Passion
Salah, 'Abd al-Sabur. Night traveler
Schnitzler, A. Paracelsus
Schwartz, D. Choosing company
Schwartz, D. Dr. Bergen's belief
Schwartz, D. Paris and Helen
Schwartz, D. Shenandoah
Schwartz, D. Venus in the back room
Seneca. Thyestes
Shakespeare, W. and Fletcher, J. Cardenio
Sophocles. Antigone
Sophocles. Electra
Sophocles. Oedipus at Colonus
Sophocles. Oedipus the King
Spoor, K. Everything under the sun
c Thompson, L. The innkeeper's daughter
Tourneur, C. The atheist's tragedy
Warner, F. Byzantium
Warner, F. Healing nature
Warner, F. King Francis I
Warren, M. The Group
Wilde, O. A Florentine tragedy
Wilde, O. La sainte courtisane
y Wood, B . The green snake and the beautiful lily
Yeats, W. B. The Countess Cathleen
Yeats, W. B. The Land of Heart's Desire
Yeats, W. B. On Baile's strand

Playwrights. See Dramatists

Pleasant, Mary Ellen
Nicholas, D. Buses

The **pleasure** man. West, M.

Plenty. Hare, D.

Plowman, Gillian
Beata Beatrix. French (London) 1995 22p
Troubled man and woman meet in art gallery. 3m 4w 1 interior

Close to Croydon. French (London) 1996 21p
Man and woman develop relationship while trapped in train wreck. 2m 2w 1 interior

A kind of Vesuvius. French (London) 1994 32p
Three men cope with effects of unemployment on themselves and their families. 3m 1 interior

Philip and Rowena. French (London) 1996 28p
Drama set in hospice. Terminally ill man and woman discover friendship, romance, and consolation with each other. 3m 4w 1 interior

Umjana Land. French (London) 1995 31p
Aspiring suburban romance writer's wife, lover and sister find common bond. 3m 4w 1 interior

Pocahontas
Barker, J. N. The Indian princess
c McCaslin, N. Mercy in moccasins
c Morris, V. Legend of Pocahontas

The **pocket** dream. Brewer, E. and Toksvig, S.

The **poet** and the women. See Aristophanes. Festival time

Poetry or bust. Harrison, T.

Poets
Adamson, S. Clocks and whistles
Friedman, R. All for art
Kyle, C. The monogamist
Nigro, D. Anima mundi
O'Neill, E. Fog
Valle-Inclan, R. del. Bohemian lights
See also Women poets; also names of poets, e.g. Cyrano de Bergerac, Savanien; Housman, Alfred Edward

Pogos, Abe
Strangers in the night. Currency Press in association with Playbox Theatre 1996 53p (Current theatre series)
Drama follows young writer's descent into hell as he researches New York City's red light district. 2 acts 11 scenes 4m 2w 5 interiors 2 exteriors

Pohl, Klaus
The beautiful stranger
Political drama set in reunited Germany. Depicts hostility and violence directed against foreigners. 5 acts 17 scenes 7m 2w 1 setting
In DramaContemporary: Germany; ed. by C. Weber

Poison. Hayes, E.

Poison pen. Harwood, R.

Poker
Gaminara, W. According to Hoyle
Marber, P. Dealer's choice

Poland

Politics and government

Stoppard, T. Squaring the circle

Polaroid stories. Iizuka, N.

Poles

Great Britain

Mercer, D. Find me

United States

Glowacki, J. Home section
See also Polish Americans

Poliakoff, Stephen
Blinded by the sun
Drama revolving around scientific fraud in English university. 2 acts 11 scenes 4m 4w 1 setting
In Poliakoff, S. Blinded by the sun & Sweet panic

Breaking the silence
Drama based upon experience of Poliakoff family during cataclysmic upheavals of Russian Revolution. 2 acts 6 scenes 5m 2w 1 interior
In Poliakoff, S. Plays: two

Playing with trains
Drama set in England. Entrepreneur endangers his relationship with son and daughter when he embarks on self-aggrandizing campaign against British inertia. 2 acts 15 scenes 6m 2w
In Poliakoff, S. Plays: two

She's been away
Television play. With closure of home for mentally ill, woman returns to her family after forty year absence. 19m 11w
In Poliakoff, S. Plays: two

Sweet panic
Child psychologist stalked by patient's mother. 2 acts 8 scenes 3m 3w 1 setting
In Poliakoff, S. Blinded by the sun & Sweet panic

Police
Pedneault, H. Evidence to the contrary

Australia

Shearer, J. The family

Canada

Vanderhaeghe, G. I had a job I liked. Once.

Chicago (Ill.)

Smith, C. Freefall

Dallas (Tex.)

Rascon Banda, V. H. Murder with malice

England

Yates, P. Nuances

Ireland

Barry, S. The steward of Christendom
Stembridge, G. The gay detective

New York (N.Y.)

Guare, J. Cop-out
Shields, B. J. Highwire

Paris

Courteline, G. The police chief's an easygoing guy

United States

Tissian, G. Night baseball
See also Detectives

The **police** chief's an easygoing guy. Courteline, G.

Polish Americans
Margulies, D. Lola

Polish drama

16th century

Kochanowski, J. The dismissal of the Grecian envoys

Political conventions
Vidal, C. The best man

Political prisoners
Pinter, H. One for the road
See also Hostages

Politicians. See Politics, Practical

Politics
Barker, H. The power of the dog
Bond, E. Jackets
Gems, P. Deborah's daughter
Granville-Barker, H. His majesty
Pinter, H. Party time
Rayson, H. Competitive tenderness

Politics, Practical
Bennett, A. Getting on
Graham, B. Belmont Avenue Social Club
Gurney, A. R. The old boy
Gurney, A. R. Public affairs: Pt2 The opening meeting
Hansberry, L. The sign in Sidney Brustein's window
Tasca, J. Make-up
Vidal, C. The best man

Pollock, Sharon
Doc
Grown woman returns home to confront memories of anguished childhood as daughter of alcoholic mother and workaholic doctor/father. Singing. 2 acts 2m 3w 1 setting
In Modern Canadian plays v2; ed. by J. Wasserman

Pollock, Sharon—*Continued*
Getting it straight
Monologue. Thoughts of woman suffering from mental illness. 1w 1 setting
In Heroines; ed. by J. Doolittle

c Prairie dragons
Drama incorporating elements of Chinese folklore. Two young women face prejudice and adversity on the Canadian prairie. Variable cast 7 characters 1 exterior
In Playhouse: six fantasy plays for children

Saucy Jack. Blizzard Pub. 1994 60p
Drama implicating Prince Albert Victor and his tutor in the Jack the Ripper murders. 2 acts 3m 1w 1 interior

Walsh
Historical drama depicting Sitting Bull's exile in Canada after the massacre at Little Big Horn. Background music. Prologue 2 acts 11m 1w 1 setting
In Modern Canadian plays v1; ed. by J. Wasserman

Polo, Marco 1254-1323?
O'Neill, E. "Marco millions"

Polsky, Milton E.
y Act of will. Players Press 1996 18p
Comedy. Shakespeare's ghost helps English teacher adapt Macbeth for school pageant. 4m 6w extras 1 setting

y SATisfaction. Players Press 1996 30p
Musical introduction to Scholastic Aptitude Tests. Prologue 1 act 1m 1w

Polygraph. Lepage, R. and Brassard, M.

Pomo Afro Homos
Dark fruit
Performance piece about African American gay men. Variable cast settings
In Staging gay lives; ed. by J. M. Clum

Pomp and circumstance. Martin, J.

Pony Express rider. McCullough, L. E.

Poof! Nottage, L.

Poole-Carter, Rosemary
y Mossy Cape. Clark I.E. 1994 27p
Dramatic blending of King Lear legend and the Cinderella story set in the American South. Spurned daughter acquires cape with magic powers. Music. 2 acts 8 scenes 4m 6w extras 1 interior 2 exteriors

The **poor** beggar and the fairy godmother. Allais, A.

Poor Super Man. Fraser, B.

Pope, Rena
Amazing Grace. New Playwrights Network 1993 16p
When woman accidentally moves church statue while dusting, nuns believe it was a miracle. Background music. 5w 1 interior

Sandwiches: Eating sandwiches
Homemakers' ironic conversation in dying man's hospital room. 1 act 7w 1 extra 1 interior
In Pope, R. Sandwiches

Sandwiches: Making sandwiches
Friction arises between bride's mother and new mother-in-law in aftermath of wedding. 1 act 6w 1 interior
In Pope, R. Sandwiches

The **Pope** and the witch. De la Tour, A.

The **Pope** and the witch. Fo, D.

Pope Joan. Rubess, B.

Porcelain. Yew, C.

Pornography
Mastrosimone, W. Sunshine
Pogos, A. Strangers in the night
Vogel, P . Hot 'n' throbbing
Wellman, M. 7 blowjobs

Porter, Deborah
Flowers
Canadian female quintuplets strive to find singular identities after childhood of celebrity. 2 parts 5w 1 setting
In Porter, D. Flowers & No more Medea

No more Medea
Comedy. Virgin Mary and Medea view modernity. 2w extras 1 setting
In Porter, D. Flowers & No more Medea

Portia Coughlan. Carr, M.

Portrait of a nude. Shamas, L.

The **portrait** the wind the chair. York, Y.

Portugal
Santareno, B. The judgment of Father Martinho

Posadas. McDonough, J. and Alderete, B.

Poskitt, Kjartan
y Henry the Tudor dude. French (London) 1995 77p
Musical comedy based on life of King Henry VIII. 2 acts 15 scenes Large mixed cast

c The Rumpelstiltskin racket; a musical play. French (London) 1996 85p
Musical parody of Grimms' fairy tale about dwarf who helps girl spin straw into gold. 2 acts 19 scenes Variable cast 11 characters extras

Pospisil, Craig
Somewhere in between. Dramatists 1996 62p
Episodic comedy about man's attempts to overcome his feelings of isolation. 10 scenes 3m 3w 1 setting

Possession is . . . Day, D. M.

The **possibilities.** Barker, H.

Possible maps. Riche, E.

The **Post** Office. Tagore, R.

Postal service
c McCullough, L. E. Pony Express rider

A **poster** of the cosmos. Wilson, L.

The **pot** boiler. Gerstenberg, A.

The **pot** of gold. Plautus, T. M.

Pots of money. See Labiche, E. and Delacour, A. The piggy bank

Potter, Beatrix
The tale of Peter Rabbit (dramatization) See Harris, A. Peter Rabbit and me; Mahlmann, L. and Jones, D. C. The tale of Peter Rabbit

About

c Robinette, J. The adventures of Peter Rabbit and his friends

Potter, Dennis
Blue remembered hills
Television play. Adult actors portray seven English children left disastrously to their own devices. 5m 2w
In Potter, D. Blue remembered hills and other plays

Cold Lazarus
Television satire set 400 years in future. Author's cryogenically preserved head and chemically induced memories exploited for commercial purposes. Large mixed cast
In Potter, D. Karaoke and Cold Lazarus

Cream in my coffee
Television play about loving wife and her cranky, genuinely unlovable husband. 8m 6w
In Potter, D. Blue remembered hills and other plays

Joe's ark
Television play. Ill woman attempts to face death head on while those around her evade or ignore the subject. 8m 3w
In Potter, D. Blue remembered hills and other plays

Karaoke
Television play. Fact and fiction collide when terminally ill screenwriter, unhappy with director of his latest project, starts drinking heavily. Large mixed cast
In Potter, D. Karaoke and Cold Lazarus

Pennies from heaven. Faber & Faber 1996 247p
Six part television drama set in 1930s England. Amorous and geographical adventures of sheet music salesman. Large mixed cast

Pound, Ezra, 1885-1972
Hall, F. B. Ezra's Noh for Willie

Pound, Sandra R.
c The Angels' greatest message
Angels prepare to announce birth of Christ. 3 scenes Variable cast 12 characters extras
In Christmas plays for young audiences

Pounding nails in the floor with my forehead. Bogosian, E.

Poverty
Barnes, D. The death of life
Burrill, M. P. They that sit in darkness
Corthron, K. Come down burning
Cruz, M. The have-little
Farmer, B. Irene and Lillian forever
Fornes, M. I. What of the night?: Hunger
Franklin, J. E. Christchild
Gill, P. Cardiff East
Hauptmann, G. The weavers
y Kirk, L. Men and angels
c Kurtz, J. The ballad of King Windowglass
LaChiusa, M. J. Eulogy for Mister Hamm
Murphy, J. A picture of paradise
Pickering, K. One child at a time
y Pintauro, J. Reindeer soup
Richardson, W. The chip woman's fortune
Sade, Marquis de. The madness of misfortune
Shaw, B. Major Barbara
Spiderwoman Theater. Sun Moon and Feather
Ward, N. The strangeness of others
York, Y. Life gap

Powell, Colin L.
c McCullough, L. E. Ninth Cavalry to the rescue!

Power (Social sciences)
Barker, H. The Europeans: struggles to love
Fornes, M. I. The conduct of life
Gregor, H. Freedom! Freedom!
Mamet, D. Oleanna
Parra, M. A. de la. Every young woman's desire
Pinter, H. One for the road

The **power** and the glory. Wilhelm, L.

Power failure. Gelbart, L.

Power lunch. Ball, A.

The **power** of the dog. Barker, H.

Practical politics. See Politics, Practical

Prague (Czech Republic)
Basso, E. The fall of Prague
Havel, V. Protest

Prairie dragons. Pollock, S.

Prayer meeting. Caldwell, B.

Prayers of Sherkin. Barry, S.

A **preacher** with a horse to ride. Carson, J.

Precisely. Pinter, H.

Pregnancy
Allen, R. J. What to name your baby
Brogan, P. B. Eclipsed
Butterfield, C. Snowing at Delphi
y Deverell, R. Switching places
Fernandez, E. How else am I supposed to know I'm still alive
Lyssiotis, T. A white sports coat
Mama drama
Minghella, A. Whale music
Packard, S. In with Alma
Rivera, J. The winged man
y Sod, T. and Grant, S. Three wishes
Tolan, K. Approximating mother
Vogel, P. And baby makes seven
y Walker, G. F. Tough!
Zark, J. A body of water: Shooting souls

Prejudices and antipathies
Bell, H. Fortune
Buzo, A. Norm and Ahmed
y Coo, C. Removing the glove
c Davis, J. Moorli and the Leprechauns
Laurents, A. Home of the brave
c Marx, P. The rainbow people
McWeeny, D. and Swan, S. Sticks and stones
y Medoff, M. Big Mary
Newsom, J. D. Dance Saturday night
Pohl, K. The beautiful stranger
Uhry, A. The last night of Ballyhoo
Wellman, M. Sincerity forever
c Wing, P. A. Naomi's road
Wong, E. Kimchee and chitlins
See also Antisemitism; Race discrimination

Prelude & Liebestod. McNally, T.

Prelude to a kiss. Lucas, C.

Prelude to fame. McCaslin, N.

Prendergast, Shaun
c Little victories. French (London) 1994 40p

Right-of-passage drama with elements of the fantastic. Widowed mother's new boyfriend gives boy popular computer game about death. 2 acts 2m 2w extras 1 setting

Pre-nuptial agreement. See Nemeth, S. Sally's shorts: Pre-nuptial agreement

The **present.** Ward, N.

Present from the past. Everett, R.

Preses, Peter, and Becher, Ulrich
Our Mr. Bockerer

Folk play. Austrian butcher resists cooperating with Nazis during World War II. 3 acts 13 scenes 13m 7w extras 4 interiors 4 exteriors

In Anthology of contemporary Austrian folk plays

President Evening Breeze. Jelinek, E.

Presley, Elvis, 1935-1977
Milligan, J. Life after Elvis

Presumption. Peake, R. B.

Pretenders. See Imposters and imposture

Pretty fire. Woodard, C.

Price, Jody Wyatt
c Dora and the Pheelguds from the future. Pioneer Service 1996 15p

Girl travels through time, learns respect for others. Variable cast 7 characters

c Rocket recycle. Pioneer Drama Service 1996 15p

Two educational plays about reusing, reducing and recycling. Grades k-3 version has 1m 1w; grades 4-6 version has 3 scenes 2m 3w

Price, Jody Wyatt, and Becker, Christopher
c Legend of the lake. Pioneer Drama Service 1996 14p

Two educational plays about water conservation. Grades k-3 version has 3 characters; grades 4-6 version has 6 characters

The **price** to pay. Hornby, I.

Prichard, Rebecca
Essex girls

Portrays five upperschool girls in Essex, England. 2 acts 5w extra 2 interiors

In Coming on strong: new writing from the Royal Court Theatre

Pricone, Steven
c A tree grows in Hollywood

Trees honored with academy awards. Large mixed cast 1 setting

In The Big book of skits; ed. by S. E. Kamerman

Pride and prejudice. Morley, O. J.

Prideaux, James
Abraham Lincoln dies at Versailles

Prideaux, James—*Continued*

Drama set 1889 in gardens of Versailles. 16-year-old grandson of late president meets woman who attended Gettysburg address. 1m 2w 1 exterior

In Prideaux, J. Laughter in the shadow of the trees and other plays

Elephants

Drama set in Rome, 108 A.D. Young man reacts to brutality witnessed in coliseum. 2m 1 exterior

In Prideaux, J. Laughter in the shadow of the trees and other plays

Laughter in the shadow of the trees

Distinguished critic, slipping into state of dementia, cared for by supportive wife. 1m 2w 1 setting

In Prideaux, J. Laughter in the shadow of the trees and other plays

The librarian

Drama set in mental institution. Librarian driven to act of violence when her beloved library was closed. 1m 2w 1 interior

In Prideaux, J. Laughter in the shadow of the trees and other plays

Requiem for us

Middle-aged couple await end of time. 1m 1w

In Prideaux, J. Laughter in the shadow of the trees and other plays

Priests

Barnes, P. Red noses
Bumbalo, V. Show
Doyle, R . Brownbread
Hill, G. Brand
McDonagh, M. The lonesome West
Pintauro, J. Birds in church
Pintauro, J. Frozen dog
Pintauro, J. Parakeet eulogy
Pintauro, J. Rules of love
Solórzano, C. Mea culpa
Turrini, P. Death and the Devil

The **primary** English class. Horovitz, I.

Prince, Harold

Grandchild of kings. French 1993 125p

Dramatization of autobiographical writings of Irish dramatist Sean O'Casey. 2 acts 6m 2w 1 setting

The **prince** and the pauper. Hardee, L.

The **prince** and the pauper. Harris, A.

Prince Edward Island

c Sandberg, R. N. Anne of Green Gables
y Turner, J. Anne of Green Gables

Princes

c Mahlmann, L. and Jones, D. C. The Frog Prince

The **princess** and the pea. Lavrakas, P.

The **princess** and the pea. Miller, H. L.

The **Princess** of Cleves. Lee, N.

The **Princess** Zoubaroff. Firbank, R.

Princesses

c Lavrakas, P. The princess and the pea
c Medoff, M. Stefanie hero

The **printer** on Queen Street. Mayr, G. A.

Printer's measure. Chayefsky, P.

Printing

Chayefsky, P. Printer's measure

Prior, Frank V.

y Madcap Monster Inn

Parody of horror stories. Hotel visited by werewolves, Dracula, and other monsters. 3m 1w 1b extras

In The Big book of skits; ed. by S. E. Kamerman

y The return of Rip Van Winkle, Jr.

Parody of Washington Irving's Rip Van Winkle. Rip's son awakes in the 20th century to find he owes back taxes. 2 scenes 5m 1w 1 interior

In The Big book of skits; ed. by S. E. Kamerman

c Spooks on strike!

Dissatisfied ghosts strike on Halloween. 3 scenes 6m 2w 1 interior

In The Big book of skits; ed. by S. E. Kamerman

Prior, Judith

y Phantom of the music hall. Players Press 1996 47p

Musical parody of Gaston Leroux's Phantom of the Opera. 3 acts 5m 6w extras 1 interior

Prisoner. Bell, J. A.

The **prisoner** of Zenda. Francis, M.

Prisoners

Caliban, R. Gladiator
Corthron, K. Cage rhythm
Griffiths, T. Who shall be happy . . . ?
Havel, V. Mistake
Herbert, J. Fortune and men's eyes
Jones, R. Big butt girls, hard-headed women
Kander, J. The kiss of the spider woman
Milner, A. Zero hour
Misto, J. The shoe-horn sonata
Plautus, T. M. The captives
Puig, M. Kiss of the spider woman
Robinson, M. Collateral damage

Prisoners—*Continued*
Wertenbaker, T. Our country's good
Willmott, K. and Averill, R. T-Money & Wolf
Yeaton, D. Helen at risk
See also Hostages; Political prisoners

The **prisoners.** See Plautus, T. M. The captives

Prisoner's progress. MacNeice, L.

The **Prisoner's** Song. Foote, H.

Prisons
Inchbald, Mrs. Such things are
Mitterer, F. Jailbird
Yeaton, D. Helen at risk

Private eyes. Dietz, S.

A **private** moment. Gregg, S.

Private view. See Havel, V. Unveiling

The **problem.** Gurney, A. R.

A **procession** of shades. Schnitzler, A.

Procne (Greek mythology)
Wertenbaker, T. The love of the nightingale

Prodigal son (Parable)
c Johnston, C. A pig tale

Profane games. Olmos, C.

The **professional.** Kovacevic, D.

Professional foul. Stoppard, T.

Professor Bernhardi. Schnitzler, A.

Professor Taranne. Adamov, A.

Professors. See College teachers; Teachers

Prokofiev, Sergei
The love of three oranges (L'amour de trois oranges); tr. by Albert Bermel
Libretto from Carlo Gozzi's scenario L'amore delle tre melarance. Fairy tale about melancholy prince, magic, oranges and redemption of princess. 4 acts 5 scenes Large mixed cast
In A Dozen French farces; ed. by A. Bermel

Prom night of the living dead. Fraser, B.

Prometheus (Greek mythology)
Goethe, J. W. von. Prometheus

Promiscuity
Plautus, T. M. The savage slave

The **promise.** Ricchi, R.

A **promise** kept. See Langley, R. The Dunsmuirs: a promise kept

Propaganda
Kilroy, T. Double cross
British
Hare, D. Licking Hitler

Properly processed. Brittney, L.

A **property** of the clan. Enright, N.

The **prophetess.** Fletcher, J. and Massinger, P.

The **prophet's** cloak. Cross, J.

The **proposal.** Chekhov, A.

Proserpina (Roman deity)
Goethe, J. W. von. Proserpina

Prostitutes
Ayckbourn, A. Communicating doors
Barnes, D. A passion play
Barnes, P. Yesterday's news
Bullins, E. Goin' a Buffalo
De Filippo, E. Filumena Marturano
Dubois, R. D. Being at home with Claude
Gifford, B. Tricks
Horovitz, I. The honest-to-god schnozzola
Hughes, L. Soul gone home
Kobler, F. Wild dust
Maraini, D. Dialogue between a prostitute and her client
Pintauro, J. Bird of ill omen
Shuttleworth, R. This is dead level
Taylor, R. Love poem #98
Vogel, P. The oldest profession
West, M. Sex
Wilcox, M. Rents
Wilson, L. Thymus vulgaris
Yates, P. Nuances
See also Courtesans; Prostitution

Prostitution
Adams, G. Off out
Berkoff, S. Massage
Bulgakov, M. Zoyka's apartment
Heise, K. and Heise, D. Clarence Darrow in hell
Johnson, J. Somewhere
O'Neill, E. "Anna Christie"
O'Neill, E. The web
Plautus, T. M. The little Carthaginian
Shaw, B. Mrs. Warren's profession
Wedekind, F. Lulu: a monster tragedy
Wilder, T. In Shakespeare and the Bible
Wilson, L. Balm in Gilead

Protest. Havel, V.

Pruitt, Dan, and Hutchison, Patrick
The Harvey Milk show
Musical revue based on life of San Francisco gay activist Harvey Milk. Prologue 2 acts epilogue 7m 3w
In Staging gay lives; ed. by J. M. Clum

Pryor, Deborah
The love talker
Drama incorporating legend, folklore, myth and the supernatural focusing on two sisters in rural Virginia. 1m 3w 1 setting
In 20/20: twenty one-act plays from twenty years of the Humana Festival

Pseudolus. Plautus, T. M.

Psychiatric hospitals
Clark, S. Saint Frances of Hollywood
De Geesewell, P. Murder at the asylum
Foote, H. The roads to home: Spring dance
McNally, T. Bad habits: Dunelawn
McNally, T. Bad habits: Ravenswood
Miller, A. The last Yankee
Mitterer, F. Wheat on the autobahn
Nowra, L. Così
Storey, D. Home

Psychiatrists
Ball, A. Your mother's butt
Brittney, L. A different way to die
Champagne, S. Away from me
Gray, S. Stage struck
Lapine, J. Twelve dreams
Manzi, W. Perfect crime
Rodriguez, D. E. I'm not stupid
Wilson, L. Say De Kooning

Psycho night at the Paradise Lounge. Burns, K.

Psychoanalysis
Durang, C. 'dentity crisis
Millar, T. P. The Cassandra Complex

Psychologists
Melfi, M. Sex therapy
Poliakoff, S. Sweet panic

Psychology
Gurney, A. R. The problem

Psychotherapy
Durang, C. Beyond therapy

Pterodactyls. Silver, N.

Public affairs: Pt2 The opening meeting. Gurney, A. R.

Public baths

Norway

Ibsen, H. An enemy of the people
y Nolan, P. T. An enemy of the people

A **public** enemy. See Ibsen, H. An enemy of the people

Publishers and publishing
Baitz, J. R. The substance of fire
Gray, S. The holy terror
Kovacevic, D. The professional
Rubens, B. Hijack

Puccini, Giacomo
Madame Butterfly (adaptation) See Mcdonough, J. Butterfly

Puerto Ricans
Rivera, C. Julia

New York (N.Y.)

Alám, S. A. Zookeeper
Cruz, M. The have-little
Gonzalez, R. The boiler room
López, E. Marlene
Rodriguez, Y. Rising sun, falling star
Tirado, C. Some people have all the luck
Valle, F. I am a winner

United States

López, E. I. Spanish eyes

Puerto Rico
Suarez, R. R. The betrothal

Pugliese, Frank
Aven'u boys. Broadway Play Pub. 1994 89p
Drama about racial and sexual violence among Italian American urban poor in Brooklyn's Bensonhurst. Prologue 2 acts 20 scenes epilogue 3m 3w 1 setting

The talk
Four brothers talk following mother's funeral. 4m 1 setting
In Act One '95

Puig, Manuel
Kiss of the spider woman; tr. by Allan Baker
Set in Buenos Aires jail. Attempts by secretly pardoned homosexual offender to extract information from Marxist revolutionary cellmate dissolve when false friendship becomes real. 2 acts 9 scenes 2m 1 interior
In Puig, M. Kiss of the spider woman and two other plays

Kiss of the spider woman (adaptation) See Kander, J. The kiss of the spider woman

Mystery of the rose bouquet; tr. by Allan Baker
Psychological drama set in exclusive clinic. Depressed elderly autocratic woman patient forges bond with middle-aged nurse. 2 acts 2w 1 interior
In Puig, M. The kiss of the spider woman and two other plays

Puig, Manuel—*Continued*
Under a mantle of stars; tr. by Ronald Christ
From voyeuristic, oedipal sex to domestic farce this drama pits psychology of nostalgia against personal politics. 2 acts 2m 3w 1 setting
In Puig, M. Kiss of the spider woman and two other plays

Pullman car Hiawatha. Wilder, T.

Pullman cars. See Railroads—Sleeping cars

Punch. Nunn, J.

Punch and Judy; illustrated by Cruikshank; edited [by] William-Alan Landes. Players Press 1995 39p
Traditional puppet play. Punch confronts adversaries with his hitting stick. 3 acts 4 scenes 13 characters extras

Punch and Judy. Svanoe, B.

Punch and Judy, A new. See Pflomm, P. N. A new Punch and Judy

Punch and Judy: their tragical comedy, their comical tragedy. Swortzell, L.

The **puppeteer.** See Schnitzler, A. Marionettes: The puppeteer

The **puppets.** Solórzano, C.

Puppets and puppet-plays
Barker, H. All he fears
c Jones, T. Camping out
c Jones, T. The computer
c Jones, T. Froggie woggies
c Jones, T. Gertie goat
c Jones, T. Gone fishing
c Jones, T. Scarecrows
c Jones, T. Who stole the pie!
Karagiozis baker
c Lee, C. K. Journey to the West
c Mahlmann, L. and Jones, D. C. Aladdin
c Mahlmann, L. and Jones, D. C. Ali Baba and the Forty Thieves
c Mahlmann, L. and Jones, D. C. Beauty and the Beast
c Mahlmann, L. and Jones, D. C. Cinderella
c Mahlmann, L. and Jones, D. C. The Emperor's nightingale
c Mahlmann, L. and Jones, D. C. The Frog Prince
c Mahlmann, L. and Jones, D. C. The Gingerbread Boy
c Mahlmann, L. and Jones, D. C. Jack and the beanstalk
c Mahlmann, L. and Jones, D. C. King Midas and the golden touch
c Mahlmann, L. and Jones, D. C. The Nutcracker Prince
c Mahlmann, L. and Jones, D. C. Peter Pan
c Mahlmann, L. and Jones, D. C. The Pied Piper of Hamelin
c Mahlmann, L. and Jones, D. C. Pinocchio
c Mahlmann, L. and Jones, D. C. Puss-in-Boots
c Mahlmann, L. and Jones, D. C. Rapunzel's tower
c Mahlmann, L. and Jones, D. C. The reluctant dragon
c Mahlmann, L. and Jones, D. C. Rumpelstiltskin
Mahlmann, L. and Jones, D. C. Sleeping Beauty
c Mahlmann, L. and Jones, D. C. Snow White and Rose Red
c Mahlmann, L. and Jones, D. C. Snow White and the seven dwarfs
c Mahlmann, L. and Jones, D. C. The table, the donkey and the stick
c Mahlmann, L. and Jones, D. C. The tale of Peter Rabbit
c Mahlmann, L. and Jones, D. C. Three Billy Goats Gruff
c Mahlmann, L. and Jones, D. C. The Wizard of Oz
Nunn, J. Punch
c Pflomm, P. N. Autumn leaves
c Pflomm, P. N. The busy Santa
c Pflomm, P. N. Clever pets
c Pflomm, P. N. Couch potatoes
c Pflomm, P. N. Fishing
c Pflomm, P. N. Five little snowmen
c Pflomm, P. N. Gracie's garden
c Pflomm, P. N. Halloween ghosts
c Pflomm, P. N. Jeremy borrows a book
c Pflomm, P. N. The leprechaun
c Pflomm, P. N. Let's be puppets
c Pflomm, P. N. Litterbugs
c Pflomm, P. N. The loose tooth
c Pflomm, P. N. Lost in a fairy tale
c Pflomm, P. N. A new Punch and Judy
c Pflomm, P. N. Ryan's hat
c Pflomm, P. N. Silvie the substitute reindeer
c Pflomm, P. N. The talent show
c Pflomm, P. N. The Thanksgiving bear
c Pflomm, P. N. The Valentine bouquet
c Pflomm, P. N. Vegetables
c Pflomm, P. N. A visit to the library
c Pflomm, P. N. Witches and ghosts
Punch and Judy
Schnitzler, A. Marionettes: The great puppet show

Puppets and puppet-plays—*Continued*
Solórzano, C. The puppets
c Swortzel, L. Punch and Judy: their tragical comedy, their comical tragedy
Yoshitsune and the thousand cherry trees

Purim
Swados, E. Esther

Puritans
Nagy, P. The scarlet letter
y Thane, A. The House of the Seven Gables

The **purple** flower. Bonner, M. O.

Pushkin, Alexander
Boris Godunov

Historical tragedy in blank verse, set in Russia from 1598-1605. Boris Godunov, suspected of having caused murder of rightful heir to throne, becomes Czar, only to be deposed later by imposter. 23 scenes 27m 5w extras

In An Anthology of Russian literature; ed. by N. Rzhevsky

The captain's daughter (dramatization) See Bland, J. The squire's daughter

Puss in boots. Perrault, C. (dramatization) See Bush, M. Puss in boots; Elfenbein, J. A. Puss-in-boots; Foxton, D. The real story of Puss in boots; Gerke, P. Chat botté: Puss-in-boots; Mahlmann, L. and Jones, D. C. Puss-in-boots

Puss in boots. Bush, M.

Puss-in-boots. Elfenbein, J. A.

Puss-in-Boots. Mahlmann, L. and Jones, D. C.

Pygmalion. Shaw, B.

Pyle, Mary Thurman
c Clever Peter

Young man uses magic bottle to win princess. 4 scenes 7m 4w 2b 2g 1 interior 1 exterior

In Thirty plays from favorite stories; ed. by S. E. Kamerman

Q

The **quality** of boiled water. Milligan, J.

A **quarrel** of sparrows. Duff, J.

Quayle, Tom
Bein Lochaber. New Playwrights Network 1995 21p

Scottish sheep farmer reconciles with embittered daughter and son. 1 act 2m 1w 1 interior

Quartermaine's terms. Gray, S.

The **Queen** and I. Townsend, S.

Queen for a day. Lichtig, R. R.

Queen of Angels. Pickett, J. C.

The **queen** of bingo. Michels, J. and Murphy, P.

Queens
Bernard, C. Laodamia, Queen of Epirus
See also names of queens, e.g., Elizabeth I, Queen of England

Queens
New York (N.Y.)
See New York (N.Y.)—Queens

The **queens.** Chaurette, N.

The **Queen's** garden. Aoki, B. W.

Queens of France. Wilder, T.

A **question** of identity. Booth, J.

A **question** of innocence. Hornby, I.

The **quick**-change room. Jackson, N.

A **quiet** love. Najera, R.

A **quiet** night in. Walker, D.

Quills. Wright, D.

Quilters. Newman, M. and Damashek, B.

Quiltmakers
Newman, M. and Damashek, B. Quilters

Quinn, Laura
Well done poets

Two drunken female college students and waiter discuss women poets. 1m 2w 1 interior

In Facing forward; ed. by L. D. Frank

Quinton, Everett
William Shakespeare's A midsummer night's dream. French 1995 99p

Adaptation of Shakespeare's comedy incorporating sexual cross-casting and visual gags. 5 acts 10 scenes 10m 5w 1 setting

Quiz shows
y Dias, E. J. Landslide for Shakespeare
Feffer, S. The wizards of quiz
c Miller, H. L. Name that book!

R

R.A.W. ('cause I'm a woman). Son, D.

R.S.V.P. Trott, S.

Rabbits
c Mahlmann, L. and Jones, D. C. The tale of Peter Rabbit

Rabe, David

The basic training of Pavlo Hummel

Life and death of an American soldier with United States Army in Vietnam. 2 acts 15m 4w extras 1 setting

In Rabe, D. The Vietnam plays v1

Hurlyburly

Dramatic comedy chronicles post-Vietnam War American lives among jaded jet set in Los Angeles. 3 acts 6 scenes 4m 3w 1 setting

In Best American plays: 9th series, 1983-1992

The orphan

Symbolic drama using Oresteia as framework. Links violence of Manson family members with American presence in Vietnam. 2 acts 7m 9w 1 setting

In Rabe, D. The Vietnam plays v2

Sticks and bones

Anti-war play attacking American society. Blind Vietnam War veteran is driven to suicide by insensitive, hypocritical family. 2 acts 5m 2w 1 interior

In Rabe, D. The Vietnam plays v1

Streamers

American soldiers about to be sent to Vietnam get involved in dispute over homosexuality in which one of them is killed. 2 acts 3 scenes 10m extra 1 interior

In Rabe, D. The Vietnam plays v2

Those the river keeps. French 1994 131p

Drama featuring supporting character from the author's play Hurlyburly. Former mob hitman desperately struggles to escape his past. 2 acts 5 scenes 2m 2w 1 setting

Race discrimination

Miller, M. Graven images

Parks, S. L. Venus

Smith, A. D. Aye aye I'm integrated

Race relations

Owen, K. Black, green, white and gold

See also African Americans; and Race relations under names of places, e.g. South Carolina—Race relations; Southern States—Race relations

Rachel. Grimké, A. W.

Racine, Jean

Phædra; tr. by Robert Bruce Boswell. Players Press 1993 56p

Tragedy in verse. French neo-classic version of the Greek legend about queen who falls in love with stepson. 5 acts 30 scenes 3m 5w extras

Phaedra (adaptation) See Mahon, D. Racine's Phaedra

Racine's Phaedra. Mahon, D.

Le **radeau** de la Comtesse. Sloate, D.

The **radiator.** See Schevill, J. Shadows of memory: The radiator

The **radical** mystique. Laurents, A.

Radio

Bogosian, E. Talk radio

Schooleman, S. and Sewell, C. The stars within

Radio announcing. See Disc jockeys

Radio broadcasting

Craver, M. and Hardwick, M. Radio gals

Radio gals. Craver, M. and Hardwick, M.

Radio operators

O'Neill, E. Warnings

Radio plays

Auden, W. H. The dark valley

Auden, W. H. and Stern, J. The rocking horse winner

Barnes, P. Acting exercise

Barnes, P. Confessions of a primary terrestrial mental receiver and communicator: Num III Mark I

Barnes, P. The end of the world—and after

Barnes, P. Glory

Barnes, P. The jumping Mimuses of Byzantium

Barnes, P. No end to dreaming

Barnes, P. Rosa

Barnes, P. The theory and practice of belly-dancing

Barnes, P. Yesterday's news

Bolt, C. Compañeras

Cooper, B. Nellie Bly: ten days in a madhouse

Dear, N. In the ruins

Finnegan, S. Wild grass

Graham, S. Track thirteen

Gray, S. The holy terror

Griffiths, L. The Duchess: pieces of Wallis Simpson

Hughes, T. The wound

Kennedy, A. The dramatic circle

Legg, R. Oscar: the Oscar Wilde trials of 1895

MacNeice, L. Christopher Columbus

MacNeice, L. The dark tower

MacNeice, L. He had a date

MacNeice, L. The mad islands

MacNeice, L. Persons from Porlock

MacNeice, L. Prisoner's progress

MacNeice, L. They met on Good Friday

c McCaslin, N. A gift of music

c McCaslin, N. Maelduin of Arran

Mamet, D. Goldberg Street

Minghella, A. Cigarettes and chocolate

Minghella, A. Hang up

Nissen, K. Fair Kirsten

O'Donovan, J. The fiddler and the Dean

Radio plays—*Continued*
Pinter, H. Family voices
Reid, C. My name, shall I tell you my name?
Rubess, B. No. here comes Ulrike Meinhof
Rubess, B. Oblivion: a story of Isabelle Eberhardt
Stoppard, T. Albert's bridge
Stoppard, T. Artist descending a staircase
Stoppard, T. The dissolution of Dominic Boot
Stoppard, T. The dog it was that died
Stoppard, T. If you're Glad I'll be Frank
Stoppard, T. In the native state
Stoppard, T. 'M' is for moon among other things
Stoppard, T. Where are they now?
Sylvanus, E. Leo Baeck
Thompson, P. Calamity Jane and the fat buffalo moon
Vingoe, M. Living curiosities: a story of Anna Swan
Ward, N. Trouble sleeping

Rael, Elsa. See Valenti, M. Beauty and the beast

Rahman, Aishah
The mojo and the sayso
African American family drama portraying effects of police brutality upon victim's survivors. 2 acts 3 scenes 3m 1w 1 interior
In Black theatre USA [v2]; ed. by J. V. Hatch and T. Shine
In Moon marked and touched by sun; ed. by S. Mahone

Railroads
c McCullough, L. E. The golden spike
Accidents
Plowman, G. Close to Croydon
Sleeping cars
Wilder, T. Pullman car Hiawatha
Stations
Solórzano, C. Crossroads
Graham, S. Track thirteen
Travel
Salah, 'Abd al-Sabur. Night traveler

Rain. Williams, G.

The **rainbow** cradle. McCullough, L. E.

The **rainbow** people. Marx, P.

The **Rainclouds** study the Ten Commandments. Paul, S. L.

Rainey, Ma 1886-1939
Wilson, A. Ma Rainey's black bottom

The **rainy** season. Okita, D.

Rais, Gilles de, 1404-1440
Clark, S. Jehanne of the witches

Raised in captivity. Silver, N.

A **raisin** in the sun. Hansberry, L.

Rame, Ranca. See Fo, D. The open couple; Fo, D. An ordinary day

Ramlī, Līnīn
In plain Arabic; tr. by Esmat Allouba. American Univ. in Cairo Press 1994 102p (Modern Arabic writing)
Satirical drama about lack of Arab unity. Palestinian student in London disappears and his colleagues representing fourteen Arab states fail to agree on course of action. Prologue 2 acts 14 scenes epilogue Large mixed cast 1 setting

Ramly, Lenin. See Ramī, Līnīn

Ramona Quimby. Jenkin, L.

Ramsey, Erik
Acetylene
Death of rigidly righteous husband threatens sanity of poorly educated woman. 2m 1w 1 setting
In Award winning plays v2

Randall, Bob
David's mother. French 1993 112p
Comic drama about divorced New Yorker and her autistic son. 2 acts 10 scenes 3m 5w 1 interior

Random happenings in the Hebrides. McGrath, J.

Randy's house. Clum, J. M.

Rankers
Barnes, P. The spirit of man: From sleep and shadow

Ranson, Rebecca
Blood on blood
Woman has long-standing affair with husband's brother. 2m 1w 1 setting
In Alternate roots; ed. by K. deNobriga and V. Anderson

Rape
y Bush, M. The emerald circle
Carlos, L. White chocolate for my father
Clark, S. Life without instruction
Crawford, D. W. Borrowed plumage
Enright, N. Blackrock
y Frost, R.; Olson, G. and Johnson, L. No means no!
Graham, G. The boys
Horovitz, I. The widow's blind date
Law, M. Cry wolf
Linney, R. Ambrosio
Martin, J. Cul de sac
Martin, J. Keely and Du

Rape—*Continued*
Mastrosimone, W. Extremities
McCauley, R. Sally's rape
McNally, T. Sweet Eros
Nagy, P. Trip's cinch
Oates, J. C. Homesick
Rubess, B. and Cooper, B. Thin ice
Teagarden, J. Birds

The **rape** of Bunny Stuntz. Gurney, A. R.

Rappaccini's daughter. Paz, O.

Rapunzel. Bush, M.

Rapunzel. Thane, A.

Rapunzel's tower. Mahlmann, L. and Jones, D. C.

Rascals under the big top. Swift, R.

Rasche, David
Jackie
New York actor meets LA agent. 1m 1w 1 interior
In Showtime's Act One Festival of one-act plays, 1994

Rascon Banda, Victor Hugo
Murder with malice
Docudrama depicting circumstances surrounding death of Chicano boy at hands of Dallas, Texas police. 26 scenes 8m 2w 1 setting
In The Fickle finger of Lady Death and other plays

Rats
c Ellison, L. Utter garbage
Horovitz, I. Rats

Rattigan, Terence
After the dance. Hern Bks. 1995 85p
Drama set in Mayfair about moral vacuity of British intelligensia on brink of World War II. High-living hard-drinking writer simultaneously involved with suicidal wife and earnest young woman. 3 acts 4 scenes 8m 5w extras 1 interior

The Browning version
Unpopular classics master at English public school unable to connect with students or his adulterous wife. 1 act 5m 2w 1 interior
In Rattigan, T. The Browning version and Harlequinade

French without tears. Hern Bks. 1995 80p
Comedy set on Riviera in 1930s. Young British diplomats attempt to learn French amid many romantic distractions. 3 acts 5 scenes 7m 3w 1 interior

Harlequinade
Farce about British theatrical company. Egos clash during production of Romeo and Juliet. 1 act 10m 5w 1 interior
In Rattigan, T. The Browning version and Harlequinade

The Winslow boy. Hern Bks. 1994 96p
Drama based on real-life court case of young British naval cadet unjustly accused of theft. 3 acts 7m 4w 1 interior

Ravel, Aviva
c Tales from the shtetl: the Sholom Aleichem show. Pioneer Drama Service 1994 50p
Dramatization of seven short stories by Sholem Aleichem about poor Jewish community in Eastern Europe. Music, singing. Prologue 7 scenes epilogue Variable cast 35 characters 1 setting

Vengeance
Holocaust survivor, posing as nurse to old woman, seeks to avenge parents' betrayal. Background music. 2w 1 interior
In Escape acts; ed. by C. Curran

Ravenhill, Mark
Shopping and fucking. Methuen Drama in association with the Royal Court Theatre and Out of Joint 1997 89p (Royal Court writers series)
Satiric look at commodity culture in which money rules. Five young Londoners engulfed by drugs, sex and lack of values. 14 scenes 3m 2w 1 setting

The **raw,** the cooked, and the rotten. Parra, M. A. de la

Rayfield, James
y I hate mothers. Bakers Plays 1993 22p
Actress in high school play complains about being typecast as mother. 1m 2w 1 interior

Rayment, Mark. See Du Maurier, D. September tide

Rayson, Hannie
Competitive tenderness. Currency Press in association with Playbox Theatre 1996 130p (Current theatre series)
Farce about government reform set in Australian city. Satirical look at bureaucracy, corruption and romance. 2 acts 59 scenes 4m 4w extras

Falling from grace. Currency Press in association with Playbox Theatre 1994 69p (Current theatre series)
Unexpected events severely test friendship among forty-year-old women, juggling careers, children and lovers. 2 acts 31 scenes 2m 6w

Ready steady go. Adkins, D.

Reakes, Paul
c Dick Turpin. French (London) 1995 100p
Pantomime with music. Legendary highwayman's adventures in 18th century England. 2 acts 14 scenes 9m 3w extras 1 setting

c King Arthur. French (London) 1997 89p
Musical pantomime which parodies King Arthur legend. Prologue 2 acts 12 scenes 5m 5w extras 2 interiors 4 exteriors

Reakes, Paul—*Continued*
c Old Mother Hubbard. French (London) 1993 88p
Musical pantomime. Old Mother Hubbard and her children are magically transported to the Old West. 2 acts 12 scenes Large mixed cast 1 interior 3 exteriors

Real, Carole
Why the Beach Boys are like opera
Romantic yearnings and relationships of thirtysomething group. 8 scenes 4m 3w
In Act One '95

Real dreams. Griffiths, T.

Real estate business
Mamet, D. Glengarry Glen Ross
Pearson, C. Scruples, agents and Wilfred
Wise, R. Some do, some don't

The **real** Inspector Hound. Stoppard, T.

The **real** story of Puss in boots. Foxton, D.

Real to reel. Gilroy, F. D.

Reality
Durang, C. The actor's nightmare

Reaney, James
The St. Nicholas Hotel, Wm. Donnelly, prop.
Part II of trilogy: The Donnellys. A stage coach feud sparks off a chain of violence that results in the murder of Michael Donnelly. Singing, chorus. 3 acts Large mixed cast 1 interior 1 setting
In Modern Canadian plays v1; ed. by J. Wasserman

The **rear** column. Gray, S.

Rebecca. Williams, C.

Rebeck, Theresa
The family of Mann. French 1995 118p
Satirical look at television sitcom executives. 2 acts 28 scenes 4m 3w 1 interior
—Same
In Women playwrights: the best plays of 1994
Loose knit. French (London) 1994 111p
Set in present-day New York City. Five women in their 30s gather to knit while their lives unravel. 2 acts 9 scenes 2m 5w 1 setting
Spike heels
Romantic comedy of manners set in Boston explores contemporary relations between the sexes. 2 acts 2 scenes 2m 2w 2 interiors
In Women playwrights: the best plays of 1992
Sunday on the rocks. French 1996 112p
Comedy. Female housemates drink, joke, and argue about difficulties of making moral decisions in complex world. 2 acts 5 scenes 4w 1 exterior

Recess! Castle, G. V.

Recipe for one. Baitz, J. R.

Recklessness. O'Neill, E.

Recluses
Anderson, E. That all of us should be fed
Frost, R. A way out
Shawn, W. Aunt Dan and Lemon
Wilson, L. The rimers of Eldritch
See also Hermits

The **recollections** of a furtive nudist. Campbell, K.

Recording instruments. See Tape recorders

The **recruiting** officer. Farquhar, G.

Rector, Margaret Hayden
The lady and the commissioner of airports. Players Press 1993 12p
Comedy. Attractive elderly widow clashes with Los Angeles airport administrator. 1 act 1m 1w
The lady and the mortician. Players Press 1993 11p
Romantic comedy. While planning her own funeral, aging widow develops friendship with funeral director. 1 act 1m 1w 1 interior

Red badge of courage. Miller, K. S.

Red Cloud, 1822-1909
c Hezlep, W. Red Cloud's revenge

Red Cloud's revenge. Hezlep, W.

The **red** coat. Shanley, J. P.

Red Cross. Shepard, S.

Red fox/second hangin'. Baker, D. and Cocke, D.

The **Red**-headed League. Thum, N. B.

Red noses. Barnes, P.

Red River War, 1874-1875
Brown, C. Buffalo Hair

The **Red** Robins. Koch, K.

Red roses and petrol. O'Connor, J.

Reddin, Keith
Black snow. Dramatists 1993 65p
Dramatization of Mikhail Bulgakov's unfinished satiric novel. Misadventures of playwright confronting artistic hypocrisy, government oppression, and labyrinthine theater bureaucracy. 2 acts 37 scenes 11m 4w extras 1 setting
Brutality of fact. Dramatists 1995 64p
Black comedy about relationships between mothers and daughters in terminally dysfunctional family. 2 acts 15 scenes 2m 5w 1g 1 setting

Reddin, Keith—*Continued*

The innocents' crusade. Dramatists 1993 62p

Elements of absurdism and naturalism in play about youth who starts crusade to promote idealism and total honesty. 2 acts 18 scenes Variable cast 15 characters 4 interiors 5 exteriors

Throwing smoke

Comedy. Minor league baseball players desert during game, leaving too few players to finish and a dejected coach. 1 act 7m 1 setting

In Telling tales: new one-act plays; ed. by E. Lane

You belong to me

Wife and husband and two friends have murder on the mind. 2m 2w 1 setting

In Act One '95

Redevelopment. Havel, V.

A **redheaded** man. Taylor, P.

Redmond, Sandra. See Adkins, D. Ready steady go

Redwood curtain. Wilson, L.

Reform, Social. See Social problems

Refugees

Glowacki, J. Antigone in New York

Mead, K. Line of descent

Refugees, Haitian

Sunde, K. Haiti (a dream)

Refugees, Jewish

Samuels, D. Kindertransport

Refuse and refuse disposal

c Pflomm, P. N. Litterbugs

Regan, Sylvia

Morning star

Also produced under titles: The golden door and In mama's house. Follows fortunes of Jewish emigrant family in New York City 1910-1931. Music. 3 acts 6 scenes 8m 5w 1 setting

In Awake and singing: 7 classic plays from the American Jewish repertoire; ed. by E. Schiff

The **rehearsal.** Oates, J. C.

Rehearsal for murder. Harper, T.

Reid, Christina

The belle of the Belfast city

Drama. Bawdy matriarch presides over reunion of three generations of her Belfast family. Singing. 2 acts 8 scenes 6m 5w 3 interiors

In Reid, C. Plays: 1

Clowns

Sequel to Joyriders set on eve of IRA ceasefire. Belfast youth confront the past and prepare for uncertain future. Music, singing. 2 acts 3 scenes 3m 4w 1 setting

In Reid, C. Plays: 1

Did you hear the one about the Irishman . . . ?

Drama. Conflict among three Belfast families related by marriage but divided by religion, has tragic results for young lovers. Variable cast 11 characters 1 setting

In Reid, C. Plays: 1

Joyriders

Drama set in Belfast. Though bound by pessimism, younger generation, having grown up without hope adjust with grace and good humor to their lot. Music. 2 acts 8 scenes 2m 3w 4 interiors

In Reid, C. Plays: 1

My name, shall I tell you my name?

Radio play set simultaneously in Derry old people's home and London's Holloway prison. Explores intransigent nature of Protestant patriotism in Northern Ireland. 1m 1w extra

In Reid, C. Plays: 1

Tea in a china cup

Domestic chronicle of humor, prejudice, affection and courage woven around Belfast Protestant family between 1939 and 1972. 2 acts 7m 8w 1 setting

In Reid, C. Plays: 1

The **reign** of Wazobia. Onwueme, O. T.

Reilly, Claudia

Astronauts

Comedy about love and ambition in life of parochial school music teacher and his neighbors in Forest Hills, Queens. 2 acts 5 scenes 2m 3w 1 setting

In A Decade of new comedy: plays from the Humana Festival v1

The **reincarnation** of Jaimie Brown. Alvarez, L.

Reindeer soup. Pintauro, J.

Reingold, Jacquelyn

Dear Kenneth Blake

Young Cambodian American woman seeks out homeless man she sees on television. 1m 1w 1 setting

In The Best American short plays, 1994-1995

In EST marathon, 1994

Girl gone. Dramatists 1995 78p

Dancer in New York City topless bar becomes obsessed with finding friend's murderer. 3m 5w 1 setting

—Same

In Women playwrights: the best plays of 1994

Reiser, Dave

y Alas! Alack! Zorro's back! Book by Tim Kelly; music & lyrics by David Reiser. Pioneer Drama Service 1995 40p

Musical comedy set in Old New Mexico. Man impersonating his hero Zorro, saves town from dastardly villain. 2 scenes 5m 6w extras 2 interiors

Reiser, Dave—*Continued*

y The creepy creeps of Pilgrim Road; book by Tim Kelly; music and lyrics by Dave Reiser. Pioneer Drama Service 1993 67p

Musical farce. Macabre family enters All-American Street contest. 2 acts 6 scenes 10m 15w extras 1 interior

y Dr. Jekyll ... please don't hyde! Book by Tim Kelly; music & lyrics by David Reiser. Pioneer Drama Service 1995 29p

Musical parody of Robert Louis Stevenson's story about doctor with dual personality. 5m 8w extras 1 setting

y I want my mummy! by Tim Kelly; music & lyrics by David Reiser. Pioneer Drama Service 1995 27p

Musical comedy. Monsters conceive plan to avoid eviction from castle. 5m 7w 1 interior

Reiss, Jay

Awkward silence

Comedic account of blind date. 2m 1w 1 interior

In Off-Off Broadway Festival plays, 19th ser.

Rejection. Haylock, D.

Religion

Barnes, D. Maggie of the saints
Burris, A. M. You mus' be bo'n ag'in
Duff, J. A quarrel of sparrows
Durang, C. The Book of Leviticus Show
Durang, C. The nature and purpose of the universe
Gregor, H. The Spanish cape
Hill, G. Brand
Jamal, D. The highway
Johnson, F. H. Run little chillun
Kemp, R. A trump for Jericho
Larson, L. and Lee, L. Some things you need to know before the world ends (a final evening with the illuminati)
Linney, R. Heathen Valley
Lucie, D. Grace
Nelson, G. Castrato
Nyswaner, R. Reservoir
Phelan, B. Himself
Ramsey, E. Acetylene
Richardson, W. A pillar of the church
Schnitzler, A. Professor Bernhardi
Sherman, J. M. Jesus on the oil tank
Tagore, R. Malini
Tasca, J. Deus-X
Williams, G. Rain

Religious belief. See Faith

Relocation of Japanese Americans, 1942-1945. See Japanese Americans—Evacuation and relocation, 1942-1945

The **reluctant** dragon. Mahlmann, L. and Jones, D. C.

The **reluctant** dragon. Surface, M. H.

Remarriage

Gurney, A. R. Children

Remember Ronald Ryan. Dickins, B.

The **rememberer.** Dietz, S.

Rememberin' stuff. Harder, E.

Remembering Aunt Jemima: a menstrual show. Clarke, B. and Dickerson, G.

Removing the glove. Coo, C.

Renfield of the flies and spiders. Kelly, T.

Rensten, Mary

The skip. French (London) 1995 17p

Comedy. Homeless women and antique dealers fight over Victorian chamber pot. 5w 1 exterior

Village day. New Playwrights Network 1995 75p

Choice of guest celebrity for church festival causes conflict in English village. 3 acts 7 scenes 5m 9w extras 1 interior

Rent (condensation). Larson, J.

Rents. Wilcox, M.

Repairs. Miller, S.

Reporters and reporting

Walker, G. F. The art of war

Requiem for Denys. Harper, T.

Requiem for us. Prideaux, J.

Reservoir. Nyswaner, R.

Resistance to government. See Government, Resistance to

Resolution revolution. Mikkelsen, J.

Restaurants, lunchrooms, etc.

Guard, J. New York actor
Holsclaw, D. The baddest of boys
Lee, E. East Texas hot links
Medley, C. Dearborn Heights
Ribman, R. The cannibal masque
Rooney, T. Flaming idiots
Wilson, A. Two trains running

The **restoration** of Arnold Middleton. Storey, D.

The **retreat.** Sherman, J.

The **return** of Rip Van Winkle, Jr. Priore, F. V.

The **return** of Sherlock Holmes. Dudley, E.

The **return** of spring. Sessions, G.

Return of the Red Phantom. McCullough, L. E.

Reunions
Bassen, L. S. The month before the moon
Farrell, B. The last Apache reunion
Horovitz, I. The 75th
Horovitz, I. Hopscotch
Milligan, J. Class of '77
Stoppard, T. Where are they now?
Visdei, A. Class photo
See also Family reunions

Revenge
The Anna Project. This is for you, Anna
Ayckbourn, A. The revengers' comedies
Brett, S. Mr. Quigley's revenge
Carter, S. Pecong
Chapman, G. The revenge of Bussy d'Ambois
Durbridge, F. Sweet revenge
Euripides. Medea
Fletcher, J. The sea voyage
Ford, J. The broken heart
Gray, S. Stage struck
Harris, R. Dead guilty
Horovitz, I. The widow's blind date
Hugo, V. The king amuses himself
Isitt, D. The woman who cooked her husband
Kyd, T. The Spanish tragedy
MacNeice, L. The mad islands
Martin, J. Cul de sac
Mastrosimone, W. Extremities
Middleton, T. A critical edition of Thomas Middleton's The witch
Middleton, T. The witch
O'Brien, M. Mad boy chronicle
Ravel, A. Vengeance
The Revenger's tragedy
Schenkkan, R. Final passages
Seneca. Thyestes
Shepard, S. Simpatico
Stoppard, T. Teeth
Strindberg, A. Simoom
Thain, P. Black widow
Tissian, G. Night baseball
Walker, G. F. Zastrozzi: the master of discipline
West, M. The pleasure man
See also Vendetta

The **revenge** of Bussy d'Ambois. Chapman, G.

The **revenge** of Sherlock Holmes. Bricusse, L.

The **revengers'** comedies. Ayckbourn, A.

The **Revenger's** tragedy
Jacobean tragedy in verse set in 16th century Italy. Revenge taken by young man upon degenerate duke who poisoned his mistress.. 5 acts 20 scenes 11m 3w extras 1 setting
In Four revenge tragedies; edited by K. E. Maus

Revolution in Cleveland. Pikser, J. (dramatization) See Griffiths, T. Real dreams

The **revolution** machine. Swajeski, D. M.

The **(revised)** travelling Cinderella show. Davis, R.

Revolutionaries. See Revolutionists

Revolutionary witness. Barnes, P.

Revolutionists
Gregor, H. Freedom! Freedom!
Griffiths, T. Occupations
Griffiths, T. Real dreams
McNally, T. ¡Cuba si!
O'Donovan, J. Copperfaced Jack

Rex. Pintauro, J.

Reyes, Guillermo
Chilean holiday
Set in working class district of Santiago, Chile 1975. Second anniversary of Pinochet's coup exposes family's irreconcilable political differences. Prologue 2 acts 3 scenes 3m 3w 1 extra 1 setting
In Humana Festival '96

Men on the verge of a his-panic breakdown
Monologues by gallery of gay Hispanic men. 1m
In Staging gay lives; ed. by J. M. Clum

Reynolds, Jean
Dance with me
Comedy about adultery and love triangles. 1m 2w 2 interiors
In Women playwrights: the best plays of 1995

Rhodes, Nancy
Ocean dream
Girl has fantastic encounter on beach. 2g 1 setting
In Facing forward; ed. by L. D. Frank

Rialto. Parsons, R.

Ribman, Ronald
Buck
Idealism of cable television employees is slowly destroyed by demands of commercialism. Background music. 2 acts 5 scenes 13m 3w extras 3 interiors
In Ribman, R. The rug merchants of chaos, and other plays

Ribman, Ronald—*Continued*

The cannibal masque

Black comedy. Restaurant scene in 1923 Bavaria. Music. 3m 1w 1 interior

In The Best American short plays, 1994-1995

The rug merchants of chaos

Comedy about frenzied quest for riches set on ship off coast of South Africa. Two couples willing to risk everything for another shot at success. 2 acts 4 scenes 3m 2w 1 interior 1 exterior

In Ribman, R. The rug merchants of chaos, and other plays

Sweet table at the Richelieu

Satiric look at self obsessed patrons of metaphorical luxury spa. 3 scenes 7m 7w 2 interiors 1 exterior

In Ribman, R. The rug merchants of chaos, and other plays

Ricchi, Renzo

The appointment

Father's attempts to reveal to middle-aged son that he has only short time to live. 1 act 2m 1 setting

In Ricchi, R. Five one-act plays

A foreboding

While visiting granddaughter in hospital man relates painful tale of lost love. 1 act 1m 1w 1 interior

In Ricchi, R. Five one-act plays

The man, the rose and silence

Monologue. Man speculates on silence, poetry and beauty. 1 act 1m

In Ricchi, R. Five one-act plays

The promise

Elderly male hospital patient discusses death and love with vibrant young nurse. 1 act 2m 1w 1 interior

In Ricchi, R. Five one-act plays

The scandal

Psychological drama. Mother left alone following deaths of two sons and husband's grief-induced madness. 1 act 8 scenes 4m 2w extras 1 setting

In Ricchi, R. Five one-act plays

Rice, Elmer

Counsellor-at-law

Prominent New York Jewish lawyer faces professional crisis as marriage unravels. 3 acts 9 scenes 19m 9w 2 interiors

In Awake and singing: 7 classic plays from the American Jewish repertoire; ed. by E. Schiff

Rich and famous. Guare, J.

The **rich** Jew of Malta. See Marlowe, C. The Jew of Malta

Richard II, King of England, 1367-1400

Minghella, A. Two planks and a passion

Richard III, King of England, 1452-1485

Anderson, M. Richard and Anne

Richard and Anne. Anderson, M.

Richard Cory. Gurney, A. R.

Richards, Gary

Dividends. French 1995 64p

Comedy drama. Explores generation gap between struggling Jewish artist and his ailing grandfather. 2 acts 2m 1w 1 setting

The root. French 1993 95p

Drama set in Queens, New York. Man wants out of arrangement with shady acquaintances that turned his auto body business into chop shop for stolen cars. 2 acts 5 scenes 4m 1 interior

Richardson, Alan

A fine gentleman. Players Press 1996 30p

Comedy in Scottish dialect inspired by Molière's Le sicilien. Set 1763, lovers scheme to elope despite uncle's opposition. 1 act 3m 3w 1 extra 1 interior

Richardson, Dave

c McJonah. Moorley's 1994 11p

Humorous retelling of biblical story. McJonah is called as missionary to Edinburgh. Singing. 2m 1w extras

Party night (the great feast). Moorley's 1994 11p

Religious play based on Biblical parable. When rich decline invitation to opening of new Caribbean hotel, poor and sick take their places. Background music. 4m 2w extras

Richardson, Willis

The chip woman's fortune

Folk-drama. Poor black mother and son give savings to unemployed friends to avoid repossession of friends' Victrola. Background music. 1 act 2m 3w extras 1 interior

In Black drama in America: an anthology; ed. by D. T. Turner

The deacon's awakening

Women in African American deacon's family want right to vote. 2m 3w 1 interior

In Black theatre USA [v1]; ed. by J. V. Hatch and T. Shine

A pillar of the church

African American father in fundamentalist Christian family refuses to allow daughter to finish high school. 1m 4w 1 interior

In Lost plays of the Harlem Renaissance; ed. by J. V. Hatch and L. Hamalian

Riche, Edward

Possible maps

Man imagines life of deceased cartographer father. Slide projections. 1m 1 setting

In Solo; ed. by J. Sherman

Riche, Robert

Malcolm X: message from the grassroots. French 1994 135p

Drama based on life of black militant leader. 2 acts 17 scenes 12m 4w 1b extras settings

Rickey, Branch, 1881-1965
Schmidt, E. Mr. Rickey calls a meeting

Ridd, Karen
Bolt, C. Compañeras

The **ride** down Mount Morgan. Miller, A.

Rideout, George
y Texas boy
Drama about adolescence set in 1964 Ontario. Canadian girl and teenager from Texas share confidences. 1m 1w 1 exterior
In Escape acts; ed. by C. Curran

Riders to the sea. Synge, J. M.

Ridley, Philip
The fastest clock in the universe. Methuen Drama 1992 83p (Methuen new theatrescript)
Vain, manipulative homosexual's attempted seduction of young man erupts in violence when unexpected visitor arrives. 2 acts 3m 2w 1 interior
—Same
In Ridley, P. Plays: 1

Ghost from a perfect place. Methuen Drama 1994 77p (Methuen modern plays)
Black comedy set in London's East End. Gangleader from 1960s returns after absence of twenty five years and confronts present day gang more vicious than anything in his past. 2 acts 2m 3w 1 interior
—Same
In Ridley, P. Plays: 1

The pitchfork Disney
Black comedy. Twenty-eight-year old twin brother and sister suffer from, and revel in grotesque dreams and fantasies. 3m 1w 1 interior
In Ridley, P. Plays: 1

Riff raff. Fishburne, L.

Rimbaud, Arthur, 1854-1891
Hampton, C. Total eclipse

The **rimers** of Eldritch. Wilson, L.

Ring of men. Oliensis, A.

A **ringing** of doorbells. Wilder, T.

Rintoul, Harry
Brave hearts
Homosexual rancher with AIDS is comforted by alcoholic former lover. Background music. 2m 1 exterior
In Making, out; ed. by R. Wallace

Riot in Nazareth. See Haylock, D. Here is the news: Riot in Nazareth

Ripe conditions. Allen, C.

The **rise** and fall of Little Voice. Cartwright, J.

Rising sun, falling star. Rodriguez, Y.

Ritchie, Anna Cora Ogden Mowatt, 1819-1870
c McCaslin, N. Leading lady

Ritchie, Rebecca
In the beginning
Satire. Documentary filmmaker interviews Eve and previously unknown "first woman." 3w
In Facing forward; ed. by L. D. Frank

Rites and ceremonies
Teagarden, J. Birds

Ritter, Erika
Automatic pilot
Comedienne in Toronto night club breaks off love affair with decent man because she can only do her act when she feels unhappy. 2 acts 13 scenes 3m 1w 1 setting
In Modern Canadian plays v1; ed. by J. Wasserman

Ritual suicide. See Suicide

The **Ritz.** McNally, T.

The **rivals.** Sheridan, R. B.

The **River** Niger. Walker, J.

Rivera, Carmen
Julia
Puerto Rican woman's odyssey from illiteracy to talented amateur poet. 14 scenes 2w 1b extras settings
In Nuestro New York; ed. by J. V. Antush

Rivera, José
Cloud tectonics
Man picks up pregnant hitchhiker on stormy night in Los Angeles after which time stops and supernatural forces take over. 2m 1w 1 interior
In Humana Festival '95
In Rivera, J. Marisol and other plays

Each day dies with sleep
Elements of surrealism, expressionism and magic-realism combine in drama about triangle of father, daughter, and son-in-law. 2 acts 24 scenes 2m 1w 1 setting
In Rivera, J. Marisol and other plays

Marisol. Dramatists 1994 60p
Drama set in New York City. Young Catholic Latina woman saved by angel as she is about to be attacked by mugger. 2 acts 10 scenes 1m 4w extras 1 setting
—Same
In Nuestro New York; ed. by J. V. Antush
In Rivera, J. Marisol and other plays

Slaughter in the lake
Drama set in Central Park about strained friendship between two middle-aged editors. 2m 1 exterior
In Telling tales: new one-act plays; ed. by E. Lane

Rivera, José—*Continued*
Tape
Character forced to listen to tape recording of his/her lies. Unidentified cast 2 characters 1 interior
In Actors Theatre of Louisville. Ten-minute plays v3
In Humana Festival '93
The winged man
Magic realism incorporated in a tale of teenage pregnancy set in suburbia. 7 scenes 1m 3w 1 setting
In Plays for actresses; ed. by E. Lane and N. Shengold

The **rivers** under the earth. Wilder, T.

Rno, Sung
Cleveland raining
Questions of identity and artistic ability motifs in play about Korean American brother and sister. Prologue in 2 scenes 2 acts 18 scenes epilogue 2m 2w 1 setting
In But still, like air, I'll rise; ed. by V. H. Houston

Road. Cartwright, J.

The **road** to Nineveh. Wilhelm, L.

Road to Nirvana. Kopit, A.

Road trip. Milligan, J.

The **roads** to home: A nightingale. Foote, H.

The **roads** to home: Spring dance. Foote, H.

The **roads** to home: The dearest of friends. Foote, H.

Roald Dahl's The Giraffe and the Pelly and me. Ireland, V.

A **roaring** tragedy. Kovacevic, D.

Robbins, Glyn
c The hundred and one Dalmatians. French (London) 1997 62p
Dramatization of novel by Dodie Smith. Dogs foil plot of evil woman and rescue kidnapped puppies. Prologue 2 acts 11 scenes Unidentified cast 26 characters extras 5 interiors 3 exteriors

Robbins, Norman
c Snow White. French (London) 1996 63p
Pantomime based on Grimms' fairy tale about jealous queen's stepdaughter. This version includes a ghost, fairy, and court jester. Singing, dancing. Prologue 2 acts 12 scenes 10m 4w extras 1 setting

Robert I, King of Scotland, 1274-1329
Silver, R. S. The hert o Scotland

Robert Johnson: trick the Devil. Harris, B.

Roberts, Amy Vanessa
c Ji-da (the bird)
Magic bird teaches Australian aborigine children to protect their spirits. Background music. Prelude 3 acts 9 scenes finale 4m 5w 1b 1g extras 1 exterior
In Young playwrights; ed. by E. Bray

Robertson, H. W.
Mina tonight! French 1996 99p
Satire about outrageous South Carolina cable access talk show. 2 acts 3 scenes 5m 4w 1 interior

Roberts, Dmae
Breaking glass
Cultural and generational problems in family with strong-willed, controlling Chinese mother, American born Amerasian children and caucasian father. 2m 3w
In But still, like air, I'll rise; ed. by V. H. Houston

Robeson, Paul, 1898-1976
Dean, P. H. Paul Robeson
Schmidt, E. Mr. Rickey calls a meeting

Robin Hood (Legendary character)
c Duncombe, P. Robin Hood
c Flower, M. and Follows, S. Robin's last stand
c Webster, P. Babes in the wood

Robinette, Joseph
c The adventures of Peter Rabbit and his friends. Dramatic 1994 71p
Dramatizations of five Beatrix Potter tales are interwoven with scenes from life of their creator. 2 acts Variable cast 43 characters extras 1 interior 1 exterior

Robin's last stand. Flower, M. and Follows, S.

Robinson, Bill, 1878-1949
Schmidt, E. Mr. Rickey calls a meeting

Robinson, Charles Knox. See Robinson, G. jt. auth.

Robinson, Giovanna, and Robinson, Charles Knox
Murder for rent. French 1994 124p
Comic murder mystery. United Nations interpreter finds that apartment of her dreams comes at deadly cost. 2 acts 5 scenes 4m 4w 1 interior

Robinson, Jackie, 1919-1972
y Foster, J. Play to win
Schmidt, E. Mr. Rickey calls a meeting

Robinson, Mansel
Collateral damage. Blizzard Pub. 1994 57p
Drama about culture clash and oppression. Canadian husband and wife, imprisoned for unknown crime, joined in cell by bilingual North American Indian woman. 1m 2w 1g 1 interior
Colonial tongues. Playwrights Canada 1995 95p
Drama set in small northern Ontario town in 1967 and 1995. Family confronts social and economic changes. 2 acts 3m 2w 1 setting

Robinson, R. T.
The cover of life. French 1996 96p
Comic drama set in 1943 rural Louisiana. Three young brides struggle to achieve sense of self-worth. 2 acts 20 scenes 1m 6w settings

Robson, James
Beulah. French (London) 1995 59p
Family drama set in old folks' estate in North Yorkshire town. Family secrets surface as father nears death. 2 acts 7 scenes 4m 6w 1 interior

Falling short. French (London) 1996 63p
Romantic comedy. Philandering London fiction editor bets he can tell absolute truth for an entire day. 2 acts 6 scenes 7m 4w extras 1 interior

Mail order bride. French (London) 1996 71p
Drama set on Yorkshire farm. Jealous sister attempts to sabotage marriage between brother and Filipino woman he met through video dating service. 2 acts 10 scenes 2m 3w 1 interior

Roca, Maristella
c Pinocchio
Dramatization of Carlo Collodi's story of the marionette who becomes a real boy. 2 acts 44 scenes Variable cast 41 characters 1 setting
In YPThree: plays from Young People's Theatre

The **Rochdale** Pioneers. Breeze, N.

Roche, Billy
The Cavalcaders. Hern Bks. 1994 67p
Small Irish town setting for memory play about shoemaker who sings with barbershop quartet. 2 acts 4m 2w 1 interior

Rochelle, R.
y Alice in Wonderland
Dramatization of Lewis Carroll's fantasy. Background music. 7m 2w 1g extra
In The Big book of dramatized classics; ed. by S. E. Kamerman

Rochester, John Wilmot, 2nd Earl of
Jeffreys, S. The libertine

The **rock** garden. Shepard, S.

Rock music
y Bush, M. Rockway Cafe
Butterworth, J. Mojo
Dietz, S. Trust
Wells, M. Mephisto rock
y Yates, P. Starlover

The **rock** station. FitzGibbon, G.

Rocket recycle. Price, J. W.

The **rocking** horse winner. Auden, W. H. and Stern, J.

Rocklin, Barry
c The Island of Anyplace, by Charles Marz; music by Barry Rocklin. French 1996 38p
Musical fantasy about nature of theatrical experience. Music, singing. 4m 3w 1 setting

Rockway Cafe. Bush, M.

Rocky Mountain rendezvous. McCullough, L. E.

Rococo. Granville-Barker, H.

Rodgers, James, W.
It's a wonderful life. Dramatic 1994 69p
Adaptation of classic holiday tale of small town idealist and his guardian angel. 2 acts 12m 10w 2b 2g 1 setting

Rodriguez, David E.
I'm not stupid
Woman murders mentally handicapped son and blames son's psychiatrist. 3 scenes 2m 1w 2 interiors
In Telling tales: new one-act plays; ed. by E. Lane

Rodriguez, Robert X. See Blecher, H. jt. auth.

Rodriguez, Yolanda
Rising sun, falling star
Drama set on New York City's Lower East Side. Deleterious effect of drugs on Puerto Rican family. 2 acts 5 scenes 7m 2w 1 interior
In Nuestro New York; ed. by J. V. Antush

Rodriguez Solis, Eduardo
The fickle finger of Lady Death
Satirical drama set in and around Mexico City. Lady Death witnesses contemporary society's deadly sins: gluttony, lust, jealousy, drunkenness, nosiness, obsessive weight loss and addiction to television. 5m 3w 1 setting
In The Fickle finger of Lady Death and other plays

Rokuro. Anderson, P.

Roland, Betty
Feet of clay
Social comedy about male possessiveness. Australian sculptor struggles to control his sexual fantasies. 1 act 2m 2w 1 interior
In Playing the past: three plays by Australian women; ed. by K. Kilner and S. Tweg

The **role** of Della. Wooten, J. J.

Rollo, Duke of Normandy. Fletcher, J. and Massinger, P.

Romance for Jo March. Morley, O. J.

Romania
Churchill, C. Mad forest

Romanov, House of
Barker, H. Hated nightfall

Rome
Plautus, T. M. The braggart soldier
History—Civil War, 49-48 B.C.
Addison, J. Cato
History—Servile Wars, 135-71 B.C.
Bird, R. M. The gladiator
History—Empire, 30 B.C.-284 A.D.
Barbier, M.-A. Arria and Paetus
O'Neill, E. Lazarus laughed
Prideaux, J. Elephants
Warner, F. Light shadows
Warner, F. Moving reflections
Warner, F. Virgil and Caesar
History—Empire, 284-476
Fletcher, J. and Massinger, P. The prophetess

Rome. Barker, H.

Romero, Oscar A., 1917-1980
Morton, C. The savior

La **ronde.** Schnitzler, A. (adaptation) See LaChiusa, M. Hello again

Roommates
Saunders, G. Other people

Rooney, Tom
Flaming idiots. French 1993 100p
Farce. Chaos reigns when two postal clerks open restaurant. 2 acts 5 scenes 6m 2w 1 interior
Flip. French 1993 84p
Anniversary party setting for portrayal of hypocrisy among present day middle-class American professionals. 4m 4w interior

Roose-Evans, James
Cider with Rosie. French (London) 1994 59p
Dramatization of Laurie Lee's autobiography. Depicts poet's childhood in Cotswold village. 2 acts 5m 4w 1 setting

Roosevelt, Eleanor
LaChuisa, J. M. First Lady suite: Eleanor sleeps here

The **root.** Richards, G.

Rooted. Buzo, A.

Roots and wings. Vickery, F.

The **rope.** Plautus, T. M.

Rosa. Barnes, P.

Rosalind. Barrie, J. M.

Rose, Arthur. See Terry, J. E. H. jt. auth.

Rose, Richard, and Kugler, D. D.
Newhouse
Drama about political and social effects of sexually transmitted plague on Canadian society. Freely adapted from works by Tirso de Melina, Sophocles, Molière, Seneca and Diderot. 2 acts 35 scenes Variable cast 20 characters extras 1 setting
In The *CTR* anthology; ed. by A. Filewod

Rosei, Peter
Blameless
Depicts how media popularizes and trivializes current social problems. 4 acts 3m 3w extras
In New anthology of contemporary Austrian folk plays; ed. by R. H. Lawson

Rosemary with Ginger. Baker, E. A.

Rosenberg, Ethel
Freed, D. Inquest

Rosenberg, Joe
c El gato sin amigos—The cat who had no friends
Based on story by Teresita Gomez Valleyjo. Cat gains friends by learning not to be lazy. Dialogue in English and Spanish. Music, dancing, masks, audience participation. Unidentified cast 5 characters extras 1 setting
In ¡Aplauso! Hispanic children's theater; ed. by J. Rosenberg

Rosenberg, Julius
Freed, D. Inquest

Rosen's son. Pintauro, J.

Rosenthal, Amy
Lifelines. French (London) 1997 17p
Wrong number initiates long distance telephone relationship between man and woman plagued by love troubles. 3 scenes 1m 1w 1 setting

Rosenthal, Rachel
Pangaean dreams a shamanic journey
Experimental eco-feminist performance piece. Video projections. 1w 1 setting
In Plays for the end of the century; ed. by B. Marranca

Rosmersholm. Ibsen, H.

Ross, Aden
Feet
Poverty-stricken couple with infant wander backroads of Utah. 1m 1w 1 exterior
In Lucky 13; ed. by R. Shuttleworth

Ross, Betsy
c McCaslin, N. Brave new banner

Ross, Jennifer
Anne Marie's bedroom
Ruminations of heavily tattooed woman. 1w 1 interior
In Solo; ed. by J. Sherman

Rostand, Edmond
Cyrano de Bergerac; tr. by John Murrell. Blizzard Pub. 1995 157p
French poet of the 17th century handicapped by long nose strives to secure the happiness of the woman he loves. 5 acts Large mixed cast 2 interiors 3 exteriors
—Same; tr. by Charles Marowitz. Smith & Kraus 1995 195p (Great translations for actors series)

Roth, Ari
Born guilty. French 1994 109p
Based on Peter Sichrovsky's compilation of interviews with children of Nazi and SS officials. Journalist's obsessive quest to uncover who killed his grandmother. Prologue 21 scenes Variable cast 4m 3w 1 setting
Oh, the innocents. French 1996 100p
Comedy. Young piano teacher becomes involved with student's mother, an aspiring jazz singer. 2 parts 15 scenes 4m 1w 1g

Rough justice. Frisby, T.

Round the world with class six. Warburton, N.

The **rover.** Behn, A.

Rowan, Alex A.
A stitch in time. Players Press 1996 19p
Comedy in Scottish dialect. Wife, mother-in-law, and daughter refuse to shorten man's trousers but have second thoughts. 1m 3w 1 interior

Rowe, Dana P.
y Zombie prom; a musical; music by Dana P. Rowe; book and lyrics by John Dempsey; based on a story by John Dempsey & Hugh Murphy. French 1996 115p
Girl meets zombie in musical set in 1950s at Enrico Fermi High. 2 acts 8 scenes 5m 5w extras settings

Rowland, Elsi
c A baker's dozen
Based on English folk tale. In 16th century village baker is put on trial for cheating customers. 14m 5w extras 1 interior
In Thirty plays from favorite stories; ed. by S. E. Kamerman

Rowley, William. See Fletcher, J. jt. auth.

The **Roy** Murphy show. Buzo, A.

A **royal** affair. Santeiro, L.

Royal Air Force. See Great Britain—Royal Air Force

Royce, Cheryl
My son Susie
Monologue by man raised by severely retarded parents. 1m extras
In Women playwrights: the best plays of 1993

Rubens, Bernice
Hijack. French 1993 86p
Cautionary comedy. Aspiring novelist kidnaps publisher and reads aloud his novel that reflects duplicity of publisher's life. 2 acts 6 scenes 2m 2w 1 interior

Rubess, Banuta
Boom, baby, boom!
Latvian woman discovers bohemian life in 1959 Toronto jazz club. Music. 37 scenes 3m 3w extras 1 setting
In The *CTR* anthology; ed. by A. Filewod
No. here comes Ulrike Meinhof
Radio play based on life of German revolutionary Ulrike Meinhof. Background music. 22 scenes 11m 6w
In Adventures for (big) girls; ed. by A. Jansen
Oblivion: a story of Isabelle Eberhardt
Radio play based on life of Isabelle Eberhardt, 19th century Swiss-born writer who, disguised as a man, wandered North African desert. Background music. 15 scenes 13m 4w 1b 1g
In Adventures for (big) girls; ed. by A. Jansen
Pope Joan
Historical comedy based on legend of female pope. 2 acts 12 scenes 3m 3w 1 setting
In New Canadian drama

Rubess, Banuta, and Cooper, Beverley
Thin ice
Four teenagers struggle with values, myths and stereotypes that encourage sexual coercion. 19 scenes 2m 2w
In Wanna play?

Rubies: Heirlooms. St. John, B.

Rubies: Little gems. St. John, B.

Rubio, José López
In August we play the Pyrenees (Celos del aire); tr. by Marion Peter Holt. Estreno 1992 66p (Estreno collection of contemporary Spanish plays 2)
Bourgeois comedy about hypocrisy and infidelity. Play-within-a-play staged to reconcile young couple summering in elderly couple's mountain home. 3 acts 4m 3w 1 interior

Ruch, Alan
c Clarissa's closet, by Monica Long Ross; music and lyrics by Alan Ruch. Anchorage Press 1996 46p
Musical. Imaginary characters emerge from girl's messy closet. 1m 2w 1b 1g extras 1 interior

Rudens. See Plautus, T. M. The rope

Rudnick, Paul
Jeffrey. Dramatists 1995 77p
Comedy about gay New York actor so afraid of AIDS he decides to give up sex. 2 acts 7m 1w 1 setting
—Same. Plume Bks. 1994 89p

Rudnick, Paul—*Continued*
Jeffrey (condensation)
In The Best plays of 1992-1993

The **rug** merchants of chaos. Ribman, R.

Rugby football
Godber, J. Up 'n' under II
Slabolepszy, P. Over the hill

Rules of love. Pintauro, J.

The **rules** of the game. Pirandello, L.

The **ruling** class. Barnes, P.

Rum and vodka. McPherson, C.

Rumble, P. Barry
Aunt Sophie's latkes. Players Press 1995 12p

Comedy. Aunt confuses ingredients for potato pancakes for Hanukkah dinner. 1 act 2w 1 interior

Rummage sales
Townsend, S. Bazaar & rummage

Rumours. Simon, N.

Rumours of our death. Walker, G. F.

Rumpelstiltskin. Bennett, R.

Rumpelstiltskin. Mahlmann, L. and Jones, D. C.

The **Rumpelstiltskin** racket. Poskitt, K.

Run little chillun. Johnson, F. H.

Runaways (Children)
Oates, J. C. Ontological proof of my existence

Runaways (Youth)
y Blacker, T. Homebird
Foxton, D. Kenneth
Hodgson, S. Tunnel vision
Sánchez, E. Trafficking in broken hearts

Running
Horovitz, I. The great Labor Day classic

Rupert and the green dragon. Wood, D.

Rupert Street Lonely Hearts Club. Harvey, J.

Rush Limbaugh in night school. Varon, C.

Russ, Adryan
Inside out; book by Doug Haverty; music by Adryan Russ; lyrics by Adryan Russ & Doug Haverty. French 1996 82p

Musical. Women in therapy group reveal their fears and insecurities. Music, singing. 2 acts 6w 1 setting

Russell, Bill
Elegies for angels, punks and raging queens; music by Janet Hood. French 1996 101p

Celebration of lives of AIDS victims told in free verse monologues with blues, jazz and rock score. Music. Large mixed cast 1 setting

Russell, Charlie
Five on the black hand side

Portrays the joys and sorrows of a Harlem family—the father a barber, mother a rebelling housewife, daughter about to wed, son a militant. 3 acts 6 scenes 12m 7w 1 setting

In Black comedy: nine plays; ed. by P. F. Jackson and Karimah
In Black drama in America: an anthology; ed. by D. T. Turner

Russell, Willy
Breezeblock Park

Comedy of manners about suffocating effect of possessions and possessiveness on working-class Liverpudlian family. 2 acts 5m 4w 2 interiors

In Russell, W. Plays: 1

Educating Rita

Comedy set in present-day England. Disillusioned English professor and student examine their feelings about education, life and each other. 2 acts 15 scenes 1m 1w 1 interior

In Russell, W. Plays: 1

y Our day out

Comedy following adventures of class of fourteen-year-olds on school trip in Wales. Music, singing. 2 acts Variable cast 29 characters 1 setting

In Russell, W. Plays: 1

Stags and hens

Comedy set in the bathrooms of tacky Liverpool club, where bride-to-be begins to question her plans, to the horror of her friends. 2 acts 7m 5w 1 interior

In Russell, W. Plays: 1

Russia
Edmundson, H. Anna Karenina
Fishelson, D. The brothers Karamazov
Fishelson, D. The idiot
Reddin, K. Black snow
Zoshchenko, M. Crime and punishment

History—16th century

Barnes, P. Laughter!

History—1533-1605

Pushkin, A. Boris Godunov

History—Nicholas I, 1825-1855

Edmundson, H. War and peace

History—Revolution, 1917-1921

Barker, H. Hated nightfall
Chayefsky, P. The passion of Josef D.
Poliakoff, S. Breaking the silence

Russia—*Continued*

Politics and government

Kushner, T. Slavs!
Lawrence, J. and Lee, R. E. A call on Kuprin
Linney, R. Three poets: Akhmatova
Nelson, R. and Gelman, A. Misha's party
Sewell, S. Traitors
Wilde, O. Vera

Social conditions

Brustein, R. The cherry orchard
Chekhov, A. The cherry orchard
Chekhov, A. Three sisters
Vampilov, A. Duck-hunting
Vampilov, A. Last summer in Chulimsk

Social life and customs

y Bland, J. The squire's daughter
Chekhov, A. The bear
Chekhov, A. Ivanov
Chekhov, A. The seagull
Chekhov, A. Uncle Vanya
Chekhov, A. The wedding
Chekhov, A. The wedding reception
Chekhov, A. The wood demon
Friel, B. A month in the country
Gorky, M. The summer people
Hare, D. Ivanov

Ruthless! Laird, M.

Ruy Blas. Hugo, V.

Ruzzante, 1502?-1542

L'Anconitana: the woman from Ancona [by] Ruzante (Angelo Beolco); tr. by Nancy Dersofi. Univ. of Calif. Press 1994 173p

Comedy about love, deception and social class set in 16th century Padua. 2 prologues 5 acts 19 scenes 5m 5w 1 setting

The veteran (Parlamento de Ruzante)

Tragicomedy set in 1520s Venice. Paduan peasant, returning from wars, attempts to convince wife to return to him. 1 act 2m 1w 1 exterior

In Ruzzante. The veteran and Weasel

Weasel (Bilora)

Tragicomedy set in 1520s Venice. Paduan peasant murders wealthy usurper of wife's affections. 1 act 4m 1w 1 exterior

In Ruzzante. The veteran and Weasel

Ryan, James

Iron Tommy

Men attend workshop. 6m 1w

In Showtime's Act One Festival of one-act plays, 1994

Ryan, Nancy. See McMahon, J. P. jt. auth.

Ryan, Ronald, 1925-1967

Dickins, B. Remember Ronald Ryan

The **Ryan** interview. Miller, A.

Ryan's hat. Pflomm, P. N.

Ryga, George

The ecstasy of Rita Joe

Drama. Young Canadian Indian woman is rejected by white society for her refusal to accept degraded social status. Singing. 2 acts 13m 4w extras 1 setting

In Modern Canadian plays v1; ed. by J. Wasserman

S

S.A.M. I am. Omata, G. H.

Saalbach, Astrid

Morning and evening; tr. by Malene S. Madsen

Drama about fragmented nature of contemporary society. Characters' ill-defined personalities make communication impossible. 2 acts 6 scenes 3m 4w 1g 1 setting

In New Danish plays; ed. by H. C. Andersen

Saba, James

c A tree with arms. Anchorage Press 1997 77p

Play set in suburban backyard about rivalry between two builders of tree houses. 2 acts 10 scenes 6b 5g 1 exterior

Sacagawea b. 1786

c McCullough, L. E. Bird woman of the Shoshones

Sachar, Louis

c There's a boy in the girl's bathroom

Based on Louis Sachar's novel. Troubled boy learns to believe in himself with help of school counselor. Puppets. 2 acts 21 scenes Variable cast 14 characters 1 setting

In Seattle Children's Theatre: six plays for young audiences; ed. by M. Smith

Sachon, Susan

c Beauty and the beast. New Playwrights Network 1996 46p

Based on fairy tale by the Brothers Grimm. A woman's love breaks spell which turned prince into beast. Background music, dancing. 2 acts 10 scenes 5m 5w extras 1 interior 3 exteriors

Sackville-West, V. (Victoria), 1892-1962

Atkins, E. Vita & Virginia

The **sacrifice.** Oates, J. C.

Sacrifice. Tagore, R.

Sacrilege. Shaffer, D.

Sacrilege. Valle-Inclán, R. del

Sad news and amazing news. See Haylock, D. Here is the news: Sad news and amazing news

Sade, Marquis de

The bedroom; or, Certified folly

Free verse comedy about unfaithful wife set in 18th century Paris. 1 act 2m 2w 1 interior

In Sade, Marquis de. The plays of the Marquis de Sade v1

Count Oxtiern; or, The dangers of debauchery

Prose drama. Swedish nobleman, an inveterate rake, seduces and abducts Colonel's daughter and has her beloved imprisoned on false charges. 3 acts 7m 2w 1 interior

In Sade, Marquis de. The plays of the Marquis de Sade v1

The haunted tower

Opéra-comique. Young infantry officer banishes rival to haunted tower and weds baron's daughter. Singing. 1 act 3m 2w extras 1 interior

In Sade, Marquis de. The plays of the Marquis de Sade v1

Henrietta and St. Clair; or, The power of blood

Gothic melodrama set in 18th century France about incestuous relationship between brother and sister ignorant of their parentage. 5 acts 24 scenes 5m 5w 2 interiors 1 exterior

In Sade, Marquis de. The plays of the Marquis de Sade v2

Jeanne Laisné; or, The siege of Beauvais

Verse tragedy about heroine of 1472 siege of Beauvais, France. 5 acts 16m 2w extras 1 exterior

In Sade, Marquis de. The plays of the Marquis de Sade v2

The madness of misfortune

Variant title: The virtuous criminal. Prose drama. Impoverished French aristocrat living in London commits crime to provide for beloved wife and son. 3 acts 19 scenes 3m 2w extras 2 interiors 1 exterior

In Sade, Marquis de. The plays of the Marquis de Sade v1

The self-proclaimed philosopher

Comedy about pretense, graft and manipulation employed in games of love. 1 act 3m 2w extras 1 interior

In Sade, Marquis de. The plays of the Marquis de Sade v2

The shyster; or, The magistrate of long ago

Verse comedy set in 1774 Paris. Instead of regulating public morality magistrate becomes instrumental in its corruption. 5 acts 25 scenes 10m 1w extras 3 interiors

In Sade, Marquis de. The plays of the Marquis de Sade v1

Truth and treason

Melodrama about incarceration, greed, lust, and deception set in 18th century France. 3 acts 14 scenes 4m 3w extras 1 interior

In Sade, Marquis de. The plays of the Marquis de Sade v2

The twins; or, Difficult choices

Verse comedy set in 18th century France. Lady's maid runs interference between her twin mistresses and their suitors. 2 acts 21 scenes 3m 5w 1 interior

In Sade, Marquis de. The plays of the Marquis de Sade v2

About

Wright, D. Quills

Sadism

Walker, G. F. Beyond Mozambique

Sadler, Coleen, and Pemberton, Sue

Christmas balls. New Playwrights Network 1996 26p

Farce. Substitute stage crew makes shambles of serious Christmas play. 1 act 4m 2w 1 interior

Sahlins, Bernard

The mysteries: The Passion. Dee, I. R. 1993 55p (Plays for performance)

Modern English adaptation of medieval mystery plays depicting passion of Christ. Large mixed cast 1 setting

Saigon: year of the cat. Hare, D.

Sailors. See Seamen

Saint Frances of Hollywood. Clark, S.

Saint Petersburg (Russia)

Hare, D. The bay at Nice

La **sainte** courtisane. Wilde, O.

The **saints** and apostles. Storey, R.

Salaam, Kalamu ya. See Kalamu ya Salaam

Salah, 'Abd al-Sabur

Night traveler; tr. by Mohammed Inani and Anselm Hollo

Absurdist verse play set on train about individual faced with tyrannical authority. 2m extras 1 setting

In Modern Arabic drama; ed. by S. K. Jayyusi and R. Allen

Salem's daughter. Sodaro, C.

Sales personnel and selling

Chadwick, C. The man's shop

Hollinger, M. Two-part invention

Mamet, D. Glengarry Glen Ross

Miller, A. Death of a salesman

Potter, D. Pennies from heaven

Wise, R. When one door closes

Salesmen. See Sales personnel and selling

Salim, 'Ali

The comedy of Oedipus: you're the one who killed the beast

Political satire set in ancient Greece loosely based on Oedipus myth. Symbolic look at Nasser's rule in Egypt. 3 acts 11 scenes 6m 1w extras 1 setting

In Modern Arabic drama; ed. by S. K. Jayyusi and R. Allen

Sally's rape. McCauley, R.

Sally's shorts: Black cloud morning New York. Nemeth, S.

Sally's shorts: Lily. Nemeth, S.

Sally's shorts: Living in this world. Nemeth, S.

Sally's shorts: Pagan day. Nemeth, S.

Sally's shorts: Pre-nuptial agreement. Nemeth, S.

Sally's shorts: The cat act. Nemeth, S.

Sally's shorts: Visions of grandeur. Nemeth, S.

Sally's shorts: Word games. Nemeth, S.

Salomé. Wilde, O.

Salten, Felix

Bambi (dramatization) See DeVita, J. A life in the woods

Salvation Army

Shaw, B. Major Barbara

The **salvation** of Iggy Scrooge. Larson, L. and Lee, E. L.

Salutin, Rick, and Theatre Passe Muraille

1837: The Farmers' Revolt

Historical drama focusing on the role of William Lyon MacKenzie in the Canadian Rebellion of 1837. Background music. 2 acts 23 scenes Large mixed cast 1 setting

In Modern Canadian plays v1; ed. by J. Wasserman

Same time, another year. Slade, B.

Salom, Jaime

Bonfire at dawn; tr. by Phyllis Zatlin. Estreno 1992 66p (Estreno contemporary Spanish plays 1)

Historical tableau based on the life and passion of Fray Bartolomé de las Casas who sailed with Colombus and participated in Spain's colonization of New World. 4 acts 11m 4w 1 setting

Sampson, Lu

c Old McDonald's farmyard follies

Nursery rhyme characters on Old MacDonald's farm. Singing. 1m 3w 1b extras 1 exterior

In The Big book of skits; ed. by S. E. Kamerman

Samuels, Diane

Kindertransport. Hern Bks. 1995 88p

Moving back and forth in time, drama depicts traumatic after effects of Holocaust on Jewish girl evacuated from Hitler's Germany to London prior to start of war. 2 acts 4 scenes 1m 5w 1 interior

Samuel's major problem. Foreman, R.

Samurai

Hwang, D. H. The sound of a voice

San Francisco (Calif.)

c McCullough, L. E. Darling Clementine: a tail of old San Francisco

Sánchez, Edwin

Icarus

Beauty, ugliness, reality, dreams, and symbolism motifs in drama about group of dysfunctional individuals seeking redemption. 3m 2w 1 exterior

In Humana Festival '97

Trafficking in broken hearts

Portrays Times Square hustlers and runaways. 3m extras 1 setting

In The Actor's book of gay and lesbian plays; ed. by E. Lane and N. Shengold

Sancta Susanna. Stramm, A.

Sanctuary. Williamson, D.

The **sanctuary** lamp. Murphy, T.

The **sand.** Fyffe, L.

The **sand** castle. Wilson, L.

Sand Mountain. Linney, R.

The **sandalwood** box. Wellman, M.

Sandberg, R. N.

c Anne of Green Gables. Anchorage Press 1995 78p

Dramatization of L. M. Montgomery's novel about adventures of orphan girl adopted by elderly brother and sister on Prince Edward Island farm. 2 acts 21 scenes 2m 3w 1b 2g 2 interiors 6 exteriors

—Same

In Seattle Children's Theatre: six plays for young audiences; ed. by M. Smith

Sandburg, Carl, 1878-1967

Mueller, L. American dreamers

Sandock, Frank

y Campaign fever

Politics of popularity in high school election. 3 scenes 5m 5w extras 1 interior

In The Big book of large-cast plays; ed. by S. E. Kamerman

Sands, Leslie
Checkmate. French 1993 102p
Murder mystery. British television star suspected of foul play in wife's death. 2 acts 4 scenes 3m 2w extras 1 interior

Sandwich. Martin, J.

Sandwiches: Eating sandwiches. Pope, R.

Sandwiches: Making sandwiches. Pope, R.

Santa Claus
c Chatfield, R. The great Santa kidnap
c Peterson, M. L. How Santa Claus discovered Christmas
c Pflomm, P. N. The busy Santa
c Pflomm, P. N. Silvie the substitute reindeer

Santareno, Bernardo
The judgment of Father Martinho; tr. and introduced by Celso Lemos de Oliveira. Gávea-Brown 1994 134p
Portuguese village priest stands up to hierarchy of Catholic Church in behalf of his parishioners. 2 acts 11m 5w extras 1 setting

Santeiro, Luis
A royal affair. Dramatists 1995 65p
Illegal immigrant's experiences with royalty, romance and fantasy convince her to return to family in Honduras. 2 acts 32 scenes Variable cast 7 characters

Santiago, Héctor
c The day they stole all the colors; tr. by J. Rosenberg
Punch and Judy style adventure spoof about intergalactic pirates. Singing, music, puppets. Prologue 8 scenes Variable cast 16 characters extras 1 setting
In ¡Aplauso! Hispanic children's theater; ed. by J. Rosenberg

Sanyasi. Tagore, R.

Sarah (Biblical figure)
O'Brien, J. T. Ancestress

Sarajevo (Bosnia and Herzegovina)
Stefanovski, G. Sarajevo: tales from a city

Sarajevo: tales from a city. Stefanovski, G.

Sardou, Victorien
For love or monkey (L'ecureuil); tr. by Norman R. Shapiro
Farce set in 19th century Paris. Escaped monkey helps two young people find love. 3m 1w 1g 1 interior
In A flea in her rear, and other vintage French farces

Sarkies, Duncan
y Lovepuke
Comedy exploring relationship concerns of contemporary young adults. Background music. 4m 4w
In Young playwrights; ed. by E. Bray

Sartin, Laddy
Catfish moon. Dramatists 1997 70p
Three middle-aged men attempt to recapture friendship and settle disputes on overnight fishing trip. 2 acts 4 scenes 3m 1w 1 exterior

Sartre, Jean Paul, 1905-1980
Kaufman, L. Shooting Simone

Satan and Simon Desoto. Sod, T.

Satchell, Mary
y Daniel Hale Williams, pioneer surgeon
Drama based on life of well-known 19th century black surgeon. 4 scenes 5m 4w 3 interiors
In Plays of black Americans; ed. by S. E. Kamerman
y Langston Hughes: poet of the people
Depicts life of influential African American poet. 4 scenes 6m 5w 1b extras 3 interiors 1 exterior
In The Big book of large-cast plays; ed. by S. E. Kamerman
In Plays of black Americans; ed. by S. E. Kamerman
y Mary McLeod Bethune, dream maker
Deals with beginnings of Bethune's dream to create college for blacks. 3 scenes epilogue 4m 6w extras 3 interiors
In Plays of black Americans; ed. by S. E. Kamerman
y The secret gifts
High school students meet heroes from African American history while preparing for Black History Week. 6m 6w 1 interior
In The Big book of large-cast plays; ed. by S. E. Kamerman

Satire
Abe, K. The ghost is here
Aristophanes. Acharnians
Aristophanes. The clouds
Aristophanes. Frogs
Aristophanes. Knights
Aristophanes. Peace
Aristophanes. Wasps
Ayckbourn, A. Man of the moment
Baitz, J. R. The end of the day
Ball, A. The M word
Ball, A. Made for a woman
Ball, A. Power lunch
Ball, A. Your mother's butt
Barnes, P. The bewitched
Barnes, P. Clap hands here comes Charlie
Barnes, P. Laughter!
Barnes, P. Leonardo's Last Supper
Barnes, P. Noonday demons
Barnes, P. The ruling class
Bays, C. L. Five visits from Mr. Whitcomb

Satire—*Continued*
Beard, J. A. Vladivostok blues
Bennett, A. Forty years on
Berkoff, S. Decadence
Berkoff, S. Sink the Belgrano!
Bjorneboe, J. The bird lovers
Bleadsdale, A. On the ledge
Blount, R. That dog isn't fifteen
Bogosian, E. Fun house
Bogosian, E. Pounding nails in the floor with my forehead
Bond, E. In the company of men
Breslin, J. Contract with Jackie
Brittney, L. Properly processed
Brooker, B. Ilsa, queen of the Nazi love camp
Brooker, B. Tears of a dinosaur
Brown, B. All things considered
Bulgakov, M. Zoyka's apartment
Burney, F. The Witlings
Burris, A. M. You mus' be bo'n ag'in
Buzo, A. The Roy Murphy show
Caldwell, B. Prayer meeting
Campanile, A. The big bun
Campanile, A. The inventor of the horse
Campanile, A. War
Champagne, D. Playing bare
Chayefsky, P. The latent heterosexual
Chekhov, A. The dangers of tobacco
Chekhov, A. Ivanov
Chekhov, A. The wedding reception
Coen, A. Tinkle time
Congdon, C. Tales of the lost Formicans
y Coo, C. Removing the glove
y Cornthwaite, R. Carlo Goldoni's Villeggiatura
Crimp, M. The misanthrope
Crimp, M. The treatment
Davies, R. Fortune, my foe
Dear, N. The art of success
De la Tour, A. The Pope and the witch
y Deverell, R. Switching places
Dietz, S. Halcyon days
Durang, C. Beyond therapy
Durang, C. The Book of Leviticus Show
Durang, C. 'dentity crisis
Durang, C. John and Mary Doe
Durang, C. Laughing wild
Durang, C. The marriage of Bette and Boo
Durang, C. The nature and purpose of the universe
Durang, C. 1-900-desperate
Durang, C. Sister Mary Ignatius explains it all for you
Durang, C. The Vietnamization of New Jersey
Elton, B. Gasping
Elton, B. Silly cow
Essmann, J. Artificial reality
Feydeau, G. My wife's dead mother
Finley, K. The theory of total blame
Fo, D. Abducting Diana
Fo, D. Accidental death of an anarchist
Fo, D. Trumpets and raspberries
y Fontaine, R. Graduation address
Francis, M. Jane Austen's Northanger Abbey
Franco, C. et al. The LA LA Awards
Gaines-Shelton, R. A. The church fight
Gay, J. Beggar's opera
Gelbart, L. Mastergate
Gelbart, L. Power failure
Gilbert, S. M. and Gubar, S. Masterpiece theatre
Gill, P. Mean tears
Godber, J. Bouncers: 1990's REMIX
Goldoni, C. Villeggiatura: Adventures in the country
Goldoni, C. Villeggiatura: Back from the country
Goldoni, C. Villeggiatura: Crazy for the country
Gray, S. Gray's anatomy
Gray, S. Hidden laughter
Gray, S. The holy terror
Griffiths, T. Real dreams
Guare, J. Cop-out
Guare, J. Moon under Miami
Guare, J. Muzeeka
Guare, J. Rich and famous
Gurney, A. R. The dining room
Gurney, A. R. The Old One-Two
Gurney, A. R. Scenes from American life
Hare, D. Ivanov
Harris, A. The importance of being Earnest
Hauptmann, G. The beaver coat
Havel, V. The garden party
Havel, V. The increased difficulty of concentration
Havel, V. The memorandum
Havel, V. Unveiling
Hill, A. On Strivers Row
Horovitz, I. Morning
Hughes, L. Scarlet Sister Barry
Jackson, J. A. WOMBmanWARs
Jackson, N. The quick-change room
Jarry, A. Ubu cocu
Jelinek, E. President Evening Breeze
Jones, L. Combination skin
Klein, J. Betty the yeti
Koch, K. George Washington crossing the Delaware

Satire—*Continued*
Kopit, A. End of the world
Kushner, T. Slavs!
Kyle, C. The monogamist
Larson, L. and Lee, L. Some things you need to know before the world ends (a final evening with the illuminati)
Larson, L.: Lee, L. and Wackler, R. Tent meeting
Lawrence, J. and Lee, R. E. The gang's all here
Lee, N. The Princess of Cleves
Lees, R. Nixon's Nixon
Leguizamo, J. Mambo mouth
Leschin, L. et al. Latins Anonymous
Lloyd, P. The scam
Lucie, D. Grace
Lumborg, D. One fine day
MacNeice, L. One for the grave
Martin, J. Cementville
McGrath, J. The Cheviot, the stag and the black, black oil
McNally, T. Bad habits: Dunelawn
McNally, T. Bad habits: Ravenswood
McNally, T. Bringing it all back home
McNally, T. Hidden agendas
Mercer, D. Huggy bear
Middleton, T. A critical edition of Thomas Middleton's The witch
Middleton, T. The witch
Molière. The hypochondriac
Molière. The imaginary cuckold
Molière. The imaginary invalid
Molière. The misanthrope
Molière. The miser
Morrissey, K. Dora: a case of hysteria
Morton, C. Johnny Tenorio
Morton, C. The miser of Mexico
Morton, C. Pancho Diablo
Mowatt, A. C. Fashion
Mtwa, P.; Ngema, M. and Simon, B. Woza Albert!
Najera, R. The pain of the macho
Noonan, J. F. The drowning of Manhattan
Oglesby, T. Two lips indifferent red
y Olfson, L. The admirable Crichton
O'Neill, E. "Marco millions"
Orloff, R. The whole shebang
Parsley, R. Brideshead revisited
Pintauro, J. Butterball
Potter, D. Cold Lazarus
Ramlī, L. In plain Arabic
Rayson, H. Competitive tenderness
Rebeck, T. The family of Mann
Reddin, K. Black snow
Ritchie, R. In the beginning
Robertson, H. W. Mina tonight!
Rodriguez Solis, E. The fickle finger of Lady Death
Salim, 'Ali. The comedy of Oedipus: you're the one who killed the beast
Schnitzler, A. Professor Bernhardi
Schuyler, G. S. The yellow peril
Seebring, W. The original Last Wish Baby
Shadwell, T. The virtuoso
Shanley, J. P. Four dogs and a bone
Shaw, B. Arms and the man
Shaw, B. The doctor's dilemma
Shaw, B. Getting married
Shaw, B. John Bull's other Island
Shaw, B. Major Barbara
Shaw, B. Mrs. Warren's profession
Shepard, S. The mad dog blues
Shepard, S. Operation sidewinder
Sheridan, R. B. The rivals
Sheridan, R. B. The school for scandal
Sherman, M. A madhouse in Goa
Sherman, M. Cracks
Siegel, J. Metamorphoses
Slabolepszy, P. Over the hill
Smolensky, S. and Waldrop, J. The Mikado
Spiro, P. The juiceman cometh
Sterner, J. Other people's money: the ultimate seduction
Stoppard, T. After Magritte
Stoppard, T. Albert's bridge
Stoppard, T. Artist descending a staircase
Stoppard, T. The dog it was that died
Stoppard, T. If you're Glad I'll be Frank
Stoppard, T. A separate peace
Stoppard, T. Where are they now?
y Suntep Theatre. Wheel of justice
Tasca, J. Make-up
Tasca, J. A modern proposal
Thomas, F. Tartuffe: born again
Townsend, S. The Queen and I
Tuttle, J. The hammerstone
Tyler, R. The contrast
Unger, H. R. The bell tolls at twelve
Vance, D. Live and in color!
Van Itallie, J.-C. Master & Margarita
Varon, C. Rush Limbaugh in night school
Vidal, C. The best man
Wannus, Sa'dallah. The king is the king
Ward, D. T. Day of absence
Warren, M. The Group
Wasserstein, W. Workout
Watkins, M. Chicago
Wellman, M. 7 blowjobs

Satire—*Continued*
Wellman, M. Sincerity forever
Wellman, M. Whirligig
Wertenbaker, T. Three birds alighting on a field
Wilde, O. The importance of being Earnest
Wilkinson, L. The night of the missing bridegroom
Williams, R. The life of the world to come
Williamson, D. Dead white males
Wilson, L. Victory on Mrs. Dandywine's island
Wolfe, G. C. The colored museum
Wreggitt, A. and Shaw, R. The wild guys
See also Comedy; Farces

SATisfaction. Polsky, M. E.

Satyric drama, Greek. See Greek drama (Satyr play)

Saucy Jack. Pollock, S.

Saunders, Geoff
Other people. French (London) 1994 22p
Drama depicting chaotic half hour in lives of four argumentative roommates. 2m 2w 1 interior

Saunders, Jennifer
Birthday
Television play. Episode from popular BBC satirical series. 4m 4w
In Saunders, J. Absolutely fabulous

Fashion
Television play. Episode from popular BBC satirical series. 1m 5w
In Saunders, J. Absolutely fabulous

France
Television play. Episode from popular BBC satirical series. 1m 6w
In Saunders, J. Absolutely fabulous

Iso tank
Television play. Episode from popular BBC satirical series. 5m 9w
In Saunders, J. Absolutely fabulous

Magazine
Television play. Episode from popular BBC satirical series. 1m 9w
In Saunders, J. Absolutely fabulous

The **sausage** eaters. Starosta, S.

The **savage** slave. Plautus, T. M.

Savages. Hampton, C.

The **savior.** Morton, C.

Savonarola, Girolamo, 1452-1498
Warner, F. Living creation

Sawyer, Anne V.
Snow stars
Homeless old couple spend snowy night together. 1m 1w 1 exterior
In Off-Off Broadway Festival plays, 20th ser.

Saxony

History—To 1423

Linney, R. Three poets: Hrosvitha

Say De Kooning. Wilson, L.

Saying yes. Gambaro, G.

Sayonara. Michener, J. (dramatization) See Fischoff, G. James A. Michener's Sayonara

The **scam.** Lloyd, P.

The **scandal.** Ricchi, R.

The **scandalous** adventures of Sir Toby Trollope. House, R. and Shearman, A.

Scanlan, Michael
c Give and take. Bakers Plays 1993 57p
Play about generosity and greed based on folklore from around the world. Music. 2 acts Variable cast 38 characters extras

Scanlon, Patricia
What is this everything?
Dream play in surrealist setting. Child/woman and philosopher poet communicate their existential crises. Background music. 8 scenes 2m 1w 1 setting
In Woman playwrights: the best plays of 1992

Scarecrows. Jones, T.

The **scarlet** letter. Nagy, P.

The **Scarlet** Pimpernel. Leech, M. T.

Scarlet Sister Barry. Hughes, L.

A **scene** — Australia. Mamet, D.

Scenes from American life. Gurney, A. R.

Schaaf, Albert K.
y Hassle in the castle
Parody of Sleeping Beauty. Maid tries to stop prince from kissing sleeping princess. 3m 2w extras 1 interior
In The Big book of skits; ed. by S. E. Kamerman

y Your money cheerfully refunded
Customer returns defective toy robot to department store. Unidentified cast 2 characters 1 interior
In The Big book of skits; ed. by S. E. Kamerman

Schario, Christopher
c A Christmas carol. Dramatists 1996 44p
Dramatization of Dickens' classic Christmas story. 5m 2w 1 setting

Schave, Ellsworth

A Texas romance. French 1996 72p

Comedy set in small Texas town in 1928. Romance reenters life of widow of philandering husband. 2 acts 4 scenes 1m 2w 1 exterior

Scheffer, Will

Falling man

Monologue by gay ballroom dancer plummeting to his death. 1m extra 1 setting

In The Actor's book of gay and lesbian plays; ed. by E. Lane and N. Shengold

In EST marathon, 1994

Scheherazade. Lynch, M.

Schenkar, Joan M.

The universal wolf

Experimental play. Feminist version of Little Red Riding Hood. Slide projections. 1m 2w extra 1 setting

In Women on the verge: 7 avant-garde American plays; ed. R. C. Lamont

Schenkkan, Robert

The courtship of Morning Star

Second play in cycle is set in 1776 Southeastern Kentucky. Rowen, kidnaps Cherokee girl whose tribe was ravaged by smallpox. 1 act 6 scenes 1m 1w 1 extra

In Schenkkan, R. The Kentucky cycle, Pt 1, #2

Final passages. Dramatists 1993 71p

Ghost story set in 1878 off coast of Nova Scotia about love, betrayal, madness, and revenge. Mystery surrounds fate of crew of apparently abandoned ship. 2 acts 26 scenes 7m 1w extras 1 setting

Fire in the hole

Seventh play in cycle is set in 1920. Rowen family members face dangers of coal mining and unfair labor practices. 1 act 12 scenes 9m 4w 1b extras 1 setting

In Schenkkan, R. The Kentucky cycle, Pt 2, #2

God's great supper

Fifth play in cycle is set in 1861. Rowen family now poor sharecroppers avenge themselves on members of family that acquired their land. 1 act Large mixed cast 1 setting

In Schenkkan, R. The Kentucky cycle, Pt 1, #5

The homecoming

Third play in cycle is set in 1792. Rowen brings home black slave woman and is killed by. son. Neighbor is also murdered for his land. 1 act 2 scenes 3m 3w 2 exteriors

In Schenkkan, R. The Kentucky cycle, Pt 1, #3

The Kentucky cycle (condensation)

In The Best plays of 1993-1994

Masters of the trade

First play in cycle following fortunes of Kentucky family. Set in 1775 Eastern Kentucky. Rowen, an Irish indentured servant swindles and murders in effort to survive hostile environment. 1 act 5m extras 1 exterior

In Schenkkan, R. The Kentucky cycle, Pt 1 #1

Tall tales

Sixth play in cycle is set in 1890, this episode involves mineral rights to Rowen land and dire consequences for beautiful valley. Prologue 1 act 3 scenes epilogue 3m 3w 1 setting

In The Best American short plays, 1993-1994

In Schenkkan, R. The Kentucky cycle, Pt 2, #1

Ties that bind

Fourth play in cycle is set in 1819. This episode centers on Patrick Rowen's efforts to retain his land rights. 1 act 7m 2w 1 extra

In Schenkkan, R. The Kentucky cycle, Pt 1, #4

The war on poverty

Final play in cycle is set in 1975 on original Rowen homestead. Ghosts of Rowens' past rise and family curse is laid to rest. 1 act 5m 1 exterior

In Schenkkan, R. The Kentucky cycle, Pt 2, #4

Which side are you on?

Eighth play in cycle is set in Howsen County 1954. Joshua Rowen, powerful union leader cuts deal that compromises mine safety. 1 act 7 scenes Large mixed cast

In Schenkkan, R. The Kentucky cycle, Pt 2, #3

Schevill, James

The last romantics

Autobiographical drama about last vestiges of 19th-century romanticism within group of 1950s intellectuals. Conservative Episcopalian woman's second marriage to noted plant pathologist. 2 acts 29 scenes 3m 2w extra 1 setting

In Schevill, J. 5 plays 5

Lovecraft's follies

Experimental drama about relationship between science and art in rapidly changing world. Prologue 2 acts 6 scenes Large mixed cast 1 setting

In Schevill, J. 5 plays 5

Mother O; or, The last American mother

Experimental drama incorporating music of Cole Porter and dances of Martha Graham. Mother copes with linguistic obsessions of schizophrenic son. Prologue 2 acts 25 scenes 3m 1w 1 setting

In Schevill, J. 5 plays 5

Shadows of memory: Ape-God; or, Who killed Dian Fossey?

Dramatic look at life and death of primatologist Dian Fossey. 10 scenes 1m 2w extras 1 setting

In Scheville, J. 5 plays 5

Schevill, James—*Continued*
Shadows of memory: The radiator
Drama about novelist, poet and playwright Djuna Barnes. 11 scenes 1m 2w 1 setting
In Schevill, J. 5 plays 5

The ushers; or, Lies, accusations, curses, exorcisms
Experimental drama about aimless drift of contemporary American society. Variable cast 1 setting
In Schevill, J. 5 plays 5

Schiller, Friedrich, 1759-1805
Mary Stuart (adaptation) See Maraini, D. Mary Stuart

Schisgal, Murray
The artist and the model
Aging artist sketching young female nude model reflects on life. 1m 1w 1 interior
In The Best American short plays, 1994-1995
In Schisgal, M. Sexaholics and other plays

The artist and the model/2
Woman artist reflects on choices she has made while making nude sketch of best friend's son. 1m 1w 1 interior
In Schisgal, M. Sexaholics and other plays

The cowboy, the Indian and the fervent feminist
Unemployed executive seeks refuge in fantasy life in Old West. 2m 1w 1 interior
In The Best American short plays, 1992-1993
In Schisgal, M. Sexaholics and other plays

Extensions
Husband and wife vaudeville team in desparate straits. 1m 1w
In EST marathon, 1994
In Schisgal, M. Sexaholics and other plays

Sexaholics
Couples' sex lives before and after advent of AIDS. 2 scenes 1m 1w 1 interior
In Schisgal, M. Sexaholics and other plays

Schizophrenia
Margulies, D. The model apartment
Penhall, J. Some voices
Schevill, J. Mother O

Schmidt, Ed.
Mr. Rickey calls a meeting. French 1994 93p
Drama about race relations in 1947 America. Joe Louis, Paul Robeson, "Bojangles" Robinson, Jackie Robinson and Dodgers owner Branch Rickey meet to discuss integrating baseball. 6m 1 interior

Schmidt, W. F.
The Explorators Club. Bakers Plays 1994 70p
Comedy. Complications ensue when club refuses to admit woman. 2 acts 6m 2w 1 interior

Schnitzler, Arthur
The Bacchanale; tr. by G. J. Weinberger
Drama set in Salzburg train station. Author's misuse of language causes strain in his marriage. 2m 1w extras 1 interior
In Schnitzler, A. Professor Bernhardi and other plays

The big scene; tr. by G. J. Weinberger
Recently reconciled actor and wife argue about past infidelities. 1 act 3m 2w extras 1 interior
In Schnitzler, A. Professor Bernhardi and other plays

Fink and Fliederbusch; tr. by G. J. Weinberger
Comedy about questionable ethics of rival journalists. 3 acts 14m 1w extras 2 interiors 1 exterior
In Schnitzler, A. Professor Bernhardi and other plays

The Green cockatoo; tr. by G. J. Weinberger
Tragic play-within-a-play set in France on eve of Revolution. Jealousy motivates murder in seedy tavern. 1 act 17m 5w extras
In Schnitzler, A. Paracelsus and other one-act plays

The hour of recognition; tr. by G. J. Weinberger
After years of pretense, Viennese physician and his wife acknowledge emptiness of their marriage. 1 act 3m 2w 1 interior
In Schnitzler, A. Professor Bernhardi and other plays

In the play of summer breezes; tr. by G. J. Weinberger
Various members of famous sculptor's entourage express feelings of jealousy, loneliness, fear of aging and worldly resignation. 3 acts 6m 5w 1 exterior
In Schnitzler, A. The final plays

Marionettes: The gallant Cassian; tr. by G. J. Weinberger
Unfaithful suitor destroyed by his own arrogance. Brave cousin saves jilted woman. 1 act 3m 1w 1 interior
In Schnitzler, A. Paracelsus and other one-act plays

Marionettes: The great puppet show; tr. by G. J. Weinberger
Puppet play set in Viennese amusement park about reality and illusion. 1 act 12m 5w extras 1 exterior
In Schnitzler, A. Paracelsus and other one-act plays

Schnitzler, Arthur—*Continued*
Marionettes: The puppeteer; tr. by G. J. Weinberger
Husband and wife visited by old friend whose practical joke led to their marriage. 1 act 2m 1w 1b extra 1 interior
In Schnitzler, A. Paracelsus and other one-act plays
Paracelsus; tr. by G. J. Weinberger
Verse play set in 16th century Basel about reality, medicine and hypnotism. 1 act 11 scenes 4m 2w 1 interior
In Schnitzler, A. Paracelsus and other one-act plays
A procession of shades; tr. by J. G. Weinberger
Drama about writer's ethics and the institutionalized double standard of behavior for men and women. 9 scenes Large mixed cast setting
In Schnitzler, A. The final plays
Professor Bernhardi; tr. by G. J. Weinberger
Satirical drama about anti-semitism and rift between science and religion. Prominent Jewish physician in Vienna becomes center of controversy when he refuses to permit Catholic priest to visit dying girl. 5 acts 19m 1w extras 5 interiors
In Schnitzler, A. Professor Bernhardi and other plays
La ronde (adaptation) See LaChiusa, M. Hello again
The transformation of Pierrot; tr. by G. J. Weinberger
Pantomime with traditional commedia dell'arte figures about love, betrayal and revenge. Prelude 6 scenes 8m 2w extras 1 setting
In Schnitzler, A. Paracelsus and other one-act plays
The veil of Peirrette; tr. by G. J. Weinberger
Pantomime set in early 19th century Vienna. Play-within-a-play about love, dreams, and reality. 3 scenes 6m 3w extras 1 setting
In Schnitzler, A. Paracelsus and other one-act plays
The word; tr. by G. J. Weinberger
Tragicomedy on irresponsible use of language. 5 acts 15m 6w 5 interiors
In Schnitzler, A. The final plays

Schnupp, Al
The Harper chronicles
Series of interrelated monologues about residents of small Virginia town. Variable cast 33 characters

The **school** for scandal. Sheridan, R. B.

The **school** for wives. Nolan, P. T.

Schooleman, Susan, and Sewell, Christopher
The stars within. French 1994 89p
Comedy. Overweight radio talk show astrologer and Lutheran minister attracted to each other during on-the-air debate. 2 acts 8 scenes 2m 2w extras 3 interiors

The **schoolmistress.** Pinero, A. W.

Schools
c Bentley-Fisher, T. Friends
c Castle, G. V. Recess!
y Dietz, S. The rememberer
c Jackson, K. Laffin' school reunion
c Lazarus, J. Not so dumb
y Leader, J. Land slides
y Nukala, D. The write stuff
c Sachar, L. There's a boy in the girls' bathroom
y Smith, R. Nothing but the truth

Australia
Enright, N. St. James Infirmary
c Holman, D. No worries

Canada
Mason, P. N. The discipline committee

England
Bennett, A. Forty years on
Chinn, J. After September
Chinn, J. Albert make us laugh
Gray, S. Quartermaine's terms
Rattigan, T. The Browning version
Rattigan, T. The Winslow boy
Stoppard, T. Where are they now?
c Warburton, N. Round the world with class six
Williams, N. Class enemy

Germany
y Williams, K. Gran Webster's war

South Africa
Baitz, J. R. The film society

Schoolyard games. Lazarus, J.

Schreiber, William
Burgoo! French 1994 45p
One man show about Senator Alben Barkley of Kentucky who served as Truman's Vice President. 1m 1 setting

Schurman-O'Connor, Kathleen
c At the bus stop
Children come to defense of lonely boy when older schoolmates bully him. 3 scenes 3w 5b 3g 1 exterior
In Schurman-O'Connor, K. One-act plays for children
c Billy's problem
Boy tries to tell family he has accidentally broken window, but no one will listen to him. 4m 2w 2b 2g 1 setting
In Schurman-O'Connor, K. One-act plays for children
c Ghoul Scout camp
Girls tell ghost stories around campfire. 2w 9g 1 exterior
In Schurman-O'Connor, K. One-act plays for children

Schurman-O'Connor, Kathleen—*Continued*

c The Grandma Rusnak

Grandmother babysits ten grandchildren. 2w 3b 7g 1 setting

In Schurman-O'Connor, K. One-act plays for children

c The Wizard of Zoz

Fantasy. Princesses are saved from witches' clutches by Wizard and long-lost brother. 2 scenes 3m 7w 2 interiors

In Schurman-O'Connor, K. One-act plays for children

Schuyler, George S.

The yellow peril

Satire about race. Bedroom farce about light skinned Afro-American con artist/madam. 6m 3w 1 interior

In Lost plays of the Harlem Renaissance; ed. by J. V. Hatch and L. Hamalian

Schwab, Erner

People annihilation; or, My liver is senseless (Volksvernichtung oder meine Leber ist Sinnlos)

Experimental drama about language and family. 2m 5w 3 interiors

In Seven contemporary Austrian plays; ed. by R. H. Lawson

Schwaiger, Brigitte

Yes, my Führer! (Führer, Befiehl!)

Monologue by pro-Nazi Austrian woman. 1w

In Seven contemporary Austrian plays; ed. by R. H. Lawson

Schwartz, Delmore

Choosing company

Verse play about New York abortion scandal incorporating themes of alienation, personal dissociation and materialism in American society. 4m 1w 1 setting

In Schwartz, D. Shenandoah and other verse plays

Dr. Bergen's belief

Drama with passages in blank verse. Physician searching for motivation behind daughter's suicide reexamines his faith. 3m 2w extras 1 setting

In Schwartz, D. Shenandoah and other verse plays

Paris and Helen

Verse play. Variation on famous love triangle of Paris, Helen and Menelaus in the Iliad. 3m 4w 1 setting

In Schwartz, D. Shenandoah and other verse plays

Shenandoah

Verse play about naming of Jewish male child. 9m 8w 1b 1 setting

In Schwartz, D. Shenandoah and other verse plays

Venus in the back room

Existential verse play. Having made Faustian pact with homosexual, man gambles for his freedom. 4m 1w extras 1 setting

In Schwartz, D. Shenandoah and other verse plays

Schwartz, Samuel

Vito on the beach

Homosexual boxer and portrait artist reveal they are HIV positive. 2m 1 exterior

In Telling tales: new one-act plays; ed. by E. Lane

Schwarz-Bart, Simone

Your handsome captain

Drama about emotional toll of economic exile. Haitian migrant worker in Guadeloupe listens to cassette his wife has sent him. Music, singing, dancing. 1 act 4 scenes 1m extra 1 interior

In Plays by women: an international anthology bk3; ed. by N. Shange

Science fiction

Anderson, P. Rokuro

y Ayckbourn, A. Callisto 5

c Bisson, P. Spacenapped

y Boiko, C. Escape to the blue planet

Congdon, C. Tales of the lost Formicans

Gross, T. D. Them ... within us

Guyer, M. The American century

Hill, K. The invisible man

y Lavrakas, P. Escape from Nemotex

Menken, A. Weird romance: Her pilgrim soul

Menken, A. Weird romance: The girl who was plugged in

c Price, J. W. Dora and the Pheelguds from the future

y Ullom, S. Geeks do come from outer space

Wellman, M. Whirligig

Scientists

Angwin, F. Beryllium

Field, B. Boundary Waters

Havel, V. Temptation

Lawrence, J. and Lee, R. E. A call on Kuprin

Poliakoff, S. Blinded by the sun

Shadwell, T. The virtuoso

Scola, Ettore, b. 1931

Passione d'amore (adaptation) See Sondheim, S. Passion

Scorpio. Bamford S.

Scotland, James

Day of wrath. Players Press 1996 24p

Fifteenth century Scottish pilgrims suddenly discover that the Judgement Day is at hand. Background music, dancing. 1 act 1 scene 1 setting 5m 3w 1 extra

Scotland, James—*Continued*
A surgeon for Lucinda. Players Press 1996 28p
Comedy in Scottish dialect set 1760 Glasgow. Daughter of tobacco lord schemes to marry tax agent, her father's mortal enemy. 1 act 6m 3w 1 interior

Scotland
Corrie, J. A bride for Heatherhill
Donald, S. The life of stuff
y Gollobin, L. B. Selkie
Kemp, R. A trump for Jericho
MacDonald, A.-M. The Arab's mouth
Macdonald, S. When I was a girl, I used to scream and shout...
Macdonald, S. When we were women
McGrath, J. Blood red roses
McGrath, J. Border warfare
McGrath, J. Joe's drum
McGrath, J. Out of our heads
McGrath, J. Random happenings in the Hebrides
McLean, D. Julie Allardyce
Munro, R. The maiden stone
Quayle, T. Bein Lochaber
Silver, R. S. The hert o Scotland
Sloate, D. Countess in Thistleland
See also Edinburgh (Scotland)

Economic conditions

McGrath, J. The Cheviot, the stag and the black, black oil

History—18th century

Glover, S. The straw chair

Scotland Road. Hatcher, J.

Scots

Canada

Langley, R. The Dunsmuirs: a promise kept

Scott, Robert Falcon, 1868-1912
Vingoe, M. and Kudelka, J. Hooligans

Scrape off the black. Ikoli, T.

Scribe, Eugène
A glass of water; tr. by Robert Cornthwaite. Smith & Kraus 1995 89p (Great translations for actors series)
Historical drama set in 18th century England. Romantic intrigue in court of Queen Anne. 3 acts 5 scenes 4m 3w extras 3 interiors

Scribe, Eugène, and Mélesville
The castrata (Le soprano); tr. by Norman R. Shapiro
Farce set in 18th century Rome. Penniless young soprano posing as castrata, gains access to Cardinal's palace. 1 act 4m 2w extras 1 interior
In A Flea in her rear, and other vintage French farces

Scribe's paradox. Feingold, M.

Scruples, agents and Wilfred. Pearson, C.

Sculptors
Roland, B. Feet of clay
Schnitzler, A. In the play of summer breezes

Sea
O'Neill, E. "Anna Christie"
Synge, J. M. Riders to the sea

Sea of Cortez. Steppling, J.

The **sea** voyage. Fletcher, J. and Massinger, P.

Seagirl. Elitzig, F.

The **seagull.** Chekhov, A.

The **seagull.** Kilroy, T.

The **seal**-hunting brothers. See Gerke, P. Da-hoos-whee'-whee: The seal-hunting brothers

Seals (Animals)
Cowan, C. A woman from the sea

Seamen
Clapp, T. The open boat
Cook, M. Jacob's wake
Furse, J. The old rust bucket
c McCullough, L. E. Return of the Red Phantom
O'Neill, E. "Anna Christie"
y Thane, A. Moby Dick
y York, M. A. Treasure Island

Sears, Joe
Eddie Lee, Eddie Lee. French 1993 36p
Comedy about rocky marriage of rodeo-riding drunk. 1m 2w interior
See also Williams, J. jt. auth.

The **season** at Sarsaparilla. White, P.

Season of goodwill. Booth, J.

Sebbar, Leïla
My mother's eyes
Teenaged girl of Algerian descent arrested and held in Paris metro station. 4m 2w 1 interior
In Playwrights of exile: an international anthology

The **second** maiden's tragedy. See Shakespeare, W. and Fletcher, J. Cardenio

Seconds. Dover, M. and Jarvis, G.

The **secret** diary of Adrian Mole aged 13¾. Townsend, S.

The **secret** fall of Constance Wilde. Kilroy, T.

The **secret** garden. Alette, C.

The **secret** garden. Francoeur, B.

The **secret** garden. Norman, M.

The **secret** gifts. Satchell, M.

The **secret** life. Granville-Barker, H.

Secret obscenities. Parra, M. A. de la

The **secret** of Sherlock Holmes. Paul, J.

The **secret** rapture. Hare, D.

Secrets. Lazarus, J.

The **seducer's** diary. Nagy, A.

Seduction
Lillo, G. The London merchant
Pedrero, P. A night divided
Pintauro, J. Uncle Chick
Wilson, L. Ikke, ikke, nye, nye, nye

Seebring, William
The original Last Wish Baby
Satirical look at contemporary society. Baby born without heart. Variable cast
In The Best American short plays, 1995-1996

Seeing double. Booth, J.

Segal, Gilles
All the tricks but one. French 1993 80p
Comic drama about life and death set in 1944 Vichy, France. Jewish vaudeville comic develops fondness for grandson of theater director. 2 acts 10 scenes 6m 2w 1b extras 1 exterior

Seidel, Georg
Carmen Kittel
Tragic plight of young working-class woman in socialist East Germany of the 1980s. 2 acts 16 scenes 5m 6w extras
In Drama Contemporary: Germany; ed. by C. Weber

Seiler, Conrad
Darker brother
Anti-lynching drama set in South. Prison scenes blend with those of comic fantasy as falsely accused African American man faces lynch mob. 10 scenes 19m 6w extras 1 setting
In Lost plays of the Harlem Renaissance; ed. by J. V. Hatch and L. Hamalian

Séjour, Victor
The brown overcoat
Parisian coquette discards suitor, a baron, when her interest in him becomes as faded as his overcoat. 9 scenes 1m 2w 1 interior
In Black theatre USA [v1]; ed. by J. V. Hatch and T. Shine

The **self**-begotten. Wellman, M.

Self catering. Cullen, A.

The **self**-proclaimed philosopher. Sade, Marquis de

Self-service laundries
Benyon, L. Love seen in laundromat

Selig, Paul
The mystery school
Three monologues by women on religion, alcoholism and mental illness. 3w
In The Best American short plays, 1995-1996

Selkie. Gollobin, L. B.

Seminars
Anderson, J. Tough choices for the new century: a seminar for responsible living

Seneca
Phaedra (adaptation) See Kane, S. Phaedra's love
Thyestes; tr. and introduced by Caryl Churchill. Hern Bks. 1995 42p
Classical Latin play in verse about tragedy of the House of Argas. Atreus, avenging himself for hurts inflicted by his brother, Thyestes, slays his nephews and serves them for dinner to their unsuspecting father. Speaking chorus

Senesh, Hannah, 1921-1944
Megged, A. Hanna Senesh

Senetta Boynton visits the Orient. Curran, C.

A **separate** peace. Stoppard, T.

Separation (Law)
Gotanda, P. K. The wash
Weller, M. Abroad (Split, Part 2)

September revisited. Coles, E.

September tide. Du Maurier, D.

Seremba, George
Come good rain. Blizzard Pub. 1993 57p
Autobiographical drama set in Uganda during murderous regimes of Idi Amin and Milton Obote. Account of author's politicalization, abduction and torture. 2 acts Large mixed cast

Serendipity and serenity. Sherman, J. M.

Sergent, Shirley
Father's prize Poland china. French 1996 89p
Farce. Gigolo disrupts lives of women in farm family. 2 acts 4 scenes 3w extras 1 setting

Serpas, Stephen
Waning crescent moon. Bakers Plays 1993 35p
Drama about the coming of age of two teenage boys set in the contemporary Midwest. 2m 1w 1 setting

Serpent kills. Millan, J. and Brooker, B.

Serreau, Coline
Lapin Lapin
Comedy. Woman succeeds in keeping dysfunctional family from total collapse. 2 acts 10 scenes 5m 5w extras 1 interior
In Plays by women: an international anthology bk 3; ed. by N. Shange

The **servant** king. Stephens, J.

Servants
Beaumarchais, P. A. C. de. The marriage of Figaro
Coles, E. September revisited
Feydeau, G. Nothing but the tooth
Hugo, V. Ruy Blas
LeSage, A. R. Turcaret
y Olfson, L. The admirable Crichton
Pinter, H. No man's land
Plautus, T. M. Pseudolus
Tilly. A modest proposal

Service stations
Ackermann, J. Stanton's Garage

Servitude. O'Neill, E.

Sessions, Graham
The return of spring. New Playwrights Network 1996 30p

Rebellious young woman returns to family after disappointing love affair. 1 act 2m 3w 1 setting

Settling accounts. See Simon, N. London suite: Settling accounts

Seven against Thebes. Aeschylus

The **seven** ages of Dan. Avery, C.

Seven blowjobs. Wellman, M.

The **seven** Chan brothers of Paiute Pass. McCullough, L. E.

Seven guitars. Wilson, A.

Seven menus. Ives, D.

The **seven** streams of the River Ota. Bernier, E.

Seven with one blow. McLaren, M.

The **seventy** fifth. Horovitz, I.

Sewell, Anna
Black Beauty (dramatization) See Harris, A. Young Black Beauty

Sewell, George
Speak of the devil. Players Press 1994 55p

Comedy. Single woman upsets landlord and neighbors by taking zany characters into her home. 2 acts 6 scenes 4m 2w 1 interior

Sewell, Stephen
The garden of granddaughters. Currency Press in association with Playbox Theatre 1993 78p (Current theatre series)

Domestic comedy set in Melbourne about world renowned conductor, his daughters and granddaughters. 2 acts 25 scenes 2m 5w 2g 1 setting

Traitors. Currency Press 1995 103p

Drama set in 1927 Leningrad and Moscow about personal and political paranoia resulting from rise of totalitarianism. Prologue 3 acts epilogue 3m 3w 1 setting

Sex
Alianak, H. Passion and sin
Barker, H. Judith: a parting from the body
Berkoff, S. Massage
Congdon, C. Casanova
Delisle, J. M. A live bird in its jaws
y Deverell, R. Switching places
Dryden, J. Love triumphant
Ensler, E. Floating Rhoda and the glue man
Fornes, M. I. Enter the night
Fraser, B. The ugly man
Granville-Barker, H. The Madras House
Griffiths, L. A game of inches
Hwang, D. H. Bondage
Johnson, T. Dead funny
Learner, T. The gun in history
Linney, R. Paradise
Malpede, K. US
Mamet, D. Edmond
McIntyre, C. Low level panic
McNally, T. Noon
McNally, T. Prelude & Liebestod
Mighton, J. Body and soul
Moxley, G. Danti-Dan
Nemeth, S. Sally's shorts: Pagan day
Pintauro, J. Soft dude
Ravenhill, M. Shopping and fucking
Rebeck, T. Spike heels
Rubess, B. and Cooper, B. Thin ice
Schisgal, M. Sexaholics
Silverstein, S. Dreamers
y Sod, T. and Grant, S. Three wishes
Valle-Inclán, R. del. Blood pact
Valle-Inclán, R. del. The head of the Baptist
Vargas Llosa, C. Orchids in the moonlight
Ward, N. The present
Ward, N. The strangeness of others
Wedekind, F. Lulu: a monster tragedy
Wedekind, F. Spring awakening
West, M. The pleasure man
West, M. Sex
Wilcox, M. Massage
Youngblood, S. There are many houses in my tribe

Sex. West, M.

Sex change. See Transsexuality

Sex crimes
Oates, J. C. Ontological proof of my existence

Sex, drugs, rock & roll. Bogosian, E.

Sex role
c Artist, V. A. The clever Maakafi

Sex role—*Continued*
Berc, S. A girl's guide to the Divine Comedy: a trilogy
Churchill, C. Cloud 9
Lebow, B. Little Joe Monaghan
c Pollock, S. Prairie dragons

Sex therapy. Melfi, M.

Sexaholics. Schisgal, M.

Sextet (yes). Wilson, L.

Sexual abuse
Baum, T. Cold hands
Blessing, L. Lake Street extension
Daniel, S. Beside herself

Sexual harassment
Mamet, D. Oleanna
Sherman, J. M. Sophistry

Sexually transmitted diseases
Horovitz, I. Play for germs
Rose, R. and Kugler, D. D. Newhouse

Seymour in the very heart of winter. Pintauro, J.

Shadow pantomimes and plays
c Mast, E. and Bensinger, L. Dinosaurus

Shadows. Sharpe, T.

Shadows of memory: Ape-God. Schevill, J.

Shadows of memory: The radiator. Schevill, J.

Shadwell, Thomas
The virtuoso
Seventeenth century satire of the scientists of the day and particularly the newly founded Royal Society of London. Prologue 5 acts 19 scenes epilogue 9m 7w extras 4 interiors 3 exteriors
In The Sensational Restoration; ed. by H. J. Jensen

Shaffer, Diane
Last requests
Woman with terminal cancer arranges meeting with recently estranged lifelong love. 1 act 4m 3w 1 interior
In Shaffer, D. Solace at twilight
Last respects
Man dying of cancer flees hospital to smoke one last cigarette in park where he has been groundskeeper. 1 act 14 scenes 5m 4w 1 setting
In Shaffer, D. Solace at twilight
Sacrilege. French 1996 100p
Outspoken Roman Catholic nun challenges Vatican to open priesthood to women. 2 acts 13 scenes 6m 3w settings
—Same
In Women playwrights: the best plays of 1995

Shaffer, Peter
The gift of the Gorgon. Viking 1993 93p
Drama incorporating mythological elements set 1975 to 1993 on Greek island of Thera. Dialectic between playwright obsessed with murder and revenge and his wife who champions fairness and mercy. 3 acts 4 scenes 7m 10w extras

Shahjahan, Emperor of India, ca. 1592-1666
Dryden, J. Aureng-Zebe

The **shaken** reed. Gray, C.

Shakers re-stirred. Godber, J. and Thornton, J.

Shakespeare, William
Antony and Cleopatra (adaptation) See Dryden, J. All for love

About

y Atkins, G. William of Stratford
Beim, N. Shakespeare revisited
y Kachejian, G. All's well that ends wrong
Nigro, D. Loves labour wonne
y Polsky, M. E. Act of will
y Waddy, L. Shakespeare remembers
Williamson, D. Dead white males

Parodies, imitations, etc.

Annie G. Something rotten in Denmark
y Avery, C. The seven ages of Dan
Blessing, L. Fortinbras
Brewer, E. and Toksvig, S. The pocket dream
Chaurette, N. The queens
y Cohen, F. Try a little Shakespeare
y Francoeur, B. Shakespeare comes to Calamity Creek
Gass, K. Claudius
Gurney, A. R. Overtime
Jackson, C. B. Iago
Kuhn, K. Midsummer nights
y Netzel, S. The jest
y Nimmo, P. Will Shakespeare save the King!
y Nimmo, P. Will Shakespeare save us!
y O'Brien, J. Wherefore are thou Juliet?
y Olfson, L. Avon calling!
Quinton, E. William Shakespeare's A midsummer night's dream
Smith, M. L. An evening of culture: Faith County II, the saga continues
Stoppard, T. Dogg's Hamlet, Cahoot's Macbeth
Vogel, P. Desdemona
Warburton, N. The Droitwich discovery
Whelan, P. Shakespeare country

Shakespeare, William, and Fletcher, John 1579-1625

Cardenio; or, The second maiden's tragedy; [edited by] Charles Hamilton. Glenbridge Pub. 1994 275p

Authorship disputed; has also been attributed to Chapman, Massinger, Tourneur and most frequently Thomas Middleton. Jacobean tragedy in verse. Psychotic King in love with corpse of beautiful woman. 5 acts 12 scenes 8m 3w settings

Shakespeare comes to Calamity Creek. Francoeur, B.

Shakespeare country. Whelan, P.

Shakespeare remembers. Waddy, L.

Shakespeare revisited. Beim, N.

Shakin' the mess outta misery. Youngblood, S.

The **shallow** end. Lucie, D.

The **shallow** end. MacLeod, W.

Shamas, Laura

Portrait of a nude. Dramatic 1995 74p

Drama traces history of socio-political response to Goya's masterpiece "Naked Maya" from its creation in 1798 Spain to contemporary America. 2 acts 4 scenes Variable cast 20 characters 1 setting

Shank, Adele Edling

67201

Post office employees carry on adulterous affair. 1w 1w 1 interior

In Facing forward; ed. by L. D. Frank

Dry smoke

Woman testifies about suspicious fire. Tape recording. 1w extra 1 interior

In Facing forward; ed. by L. D. Frank

Shanley, John Patrick

Four dogs and a bone

Satirical comedy about people in motion picture industry. 2 acts 4 scenes 2m 2w 1 setting

In Shanley, J. P. Four dogs and a bone and The wild goose

Kissing Christine

Romantic comedy. Woman recovering from horrific accident and man in troubled marriage meet for unusual first date. 1 act 1m 1w 1 interior

In Humana Festival '96

In Shanley, J. P. Missing/Kissing

Missing Marisa

Comedy. Two men discuss woman who loved and abandoned them both. 1 act 2m 1 interior

In Humana Festival '96

In Shanley, J. P. Missing/Kissing

The red coat

Teenage boy lays in wait outside party to tell girl he loves her. 1m 1w 1 exterior

In Telling tales: new one-act plays; ed. by E. Lane

The wild goose

Absurdist comedy about relations between woman and two men. 2m 1w

In Shanley, J. P. Four dogs and a bone and The wild goose

The **shaper.** Steppling, J.

Sharif, Bina

My ancestor's house

Pakistani woman returns to family home during mother's mortal illness. Background music. 2 acts 4 scenes epilogue 3m 5w extras

In Contemporary plays by women of color; ed. by K. A. Perkins and R. Uno

Sharkey, Thomas M.

It's a wonderful life; a new musical based on the Frank Capra film; and the original story by Philip Van Doren Stern; book, music and lyrics by Thomas M. Sharkey; original piano arrangements by Jack Sharkey; orchestration & vocal arrangements by David J. Blackburn. French 1993 100p

Musical based on film about whimsical angel saving despairing do-gooder. 2 acts 9m 4w settings

Sharpe, Ted

Shadows. New Playwrights Network 1994 12p

Comedy. As couple tries to sell house they are visited by ghost of previous owner. 3m 2w 1 interior

The **sharpshooters.** Bynum, R. C.

Sharrocks, Monica

Calling in. New Playwrights Network 1997 60p

Comedy set in British town awaiting Queen's visit. Woman delays leaving husband to plan daughter's wedding. 3m 5w 1 interior

Sweet Rose of Old Aldgate. New Playwrights Network 1997 36p

Melodrama. Parents sell secretly betrothed maiden to villainous thief. 1 act 10 scenes 6m 7w 1 setting

Shasta Rue. Martin, J.

Shaughnessy, Darrin

The manager. French 1994 70p

Comedy. College student fends off advances of lusty female manager of his boarding house. 1 act 2m 2w 1 interior

Shaw, Bernard

Arms and the man

Satirical comedy. Episode during 19th century Serbo-Bulgarian War involving conflict between romantic and realistic views of war and heroism. 3 acts 5m 3w 2 interiors 1 exterior

In Shaw, B. Arms and the man and John Bull's other island

Shaw, Bernard—*Continued*

Caesar and Cleopatra

Historical comedy. Aging Caesar teaches young Cleopatra to be queen while battling opponents in Egypt during Roman Civil War. Prologue 5 acts 8 scenes 11m 4w extras 3 interiors 6 exteriors

In Shaw, B. George Bernard Shaw: selected plays

The doctor's dilemma. Players Press 1996 75p

Satire on medical profession. Doctor faces conflict between medical ethics and his love for wife of tubercular artist. 5 acts 11m 4w 3 interiors 1 exterior

Getting married. Players Press 1995 79p

Social comedy. Young couple's impending wedding provokes discussion of inadequacies of marriage as an institution, satirizing particular attitudes. 7m 5w extras 1 interior

Heartbreak House

Old sea captain takes a dim view of early 20th century English society. Music. 3 acts 6m 4w 1 setting

In Shaw, B. George Bernard Shaw: selected plays

John Bull's other island

Satirical comedy about Anglo-Irish relations. Ambitious Englishman decides to run for Parliament in Ireland. 4 acts 6 scenes 10m 2w 2 interiors 3 exteriors

In Shaw, G. Arms and the man and John Bull's other island

Major Barbara

Philosophical comedy. Idealistic daughter of munitions manufacturer joins Salvation Army, but father's realistic arguments create ironic reversal in her views of capitalism and poverty. 3 acts 10m 5w 1 interior 2 exteriors

In Shaw, B. George Bernard Shaw: selected plays

Man and superman

Philosophical romantic comedy. Modernized version of the Don Juan legend portraying man as quarry, woman as hunter. Incidental music. 4 acts 6 scenes 11m 5w extras 1 interior 3 exteriors

In Shaw, B. George Bernard Shaw: selected plays

Mrs. Warren's profession

Satirical comedy exposing hypocritical British society which condemns women it drives into prostitution. Well-raised daughter learns mother heads brothel syndicate. 4 acts 4m 2w 2 interiors 2 exteriors

In Shaw, B. George Bernard Shaw: selected plays

Pygmalion

Comedy of manners set in London and based on Pygmalion legend. A British professor of phonetics transforms a slatternly Covent Garden flower girl into the semblance of a duchess. 5 acts 4m 6w extras 4 interiors 2 exteriors

In Great Irish plays

In Shaw, B. George Bernard Shaw: selected plays

An unsocial socialist (dramatization) See Hatcher, J. Smash

About

O'Donovan, J. Carlotta

O'Donovan, J. The Shaws of Synge Street

Whitemore, H. The best of friends

Shaw, George Bernard. See Shaw, Bernard

Shaw, Rebecca. See Wreggitt, A. jt. auth.

Shawn, Wallace

Aunt Dan and Lemon

Banality of society's evil portrayed through relationship between two women, one a young recluse obsessed with Nazi atrocities and the other an eccentric, opinionated professor. Variable cast 12 characters 1 interior

In The Best of Off-Broadway; ed. by R. Wetzsteon

The designated mourner. Noonday Press 1997 103p

Drama about self, art and political oppression. Three interwoven monologues by renowned intellectual, his daughter, and her husband, a former English-literature student. 2 parts 2m 1w 1 setting

The **Shaws** of Synge Street. O'Donovan, J.

She dupes to conquer. Courteline, G.

She needs me. Stone, T.

She stoops to conquer. Goldsmith, O.

She tells her daughter. Barnes, D.

Shearer, Jill

The family. Currency Press 1995 79p

Drama set in Brisbane, Australia. Policewoman, newly appointed to Internal Investigations, uncovers long-buried case implicating her police officer father as accessory to corruption. 2 acts 3m 4w 1 setting

Shearman, Alan. See House, R. jt. auth.

Sheeler, Wade

Vortex. French 1997 38p

Drama set atop Cathedral Rock in Sedona, Arizona. Man on run from vengeful criminals encounters apparent new-age visionary. 1 act 2m 1 exterior

The **sheep**-pig. King-Smith, D. (dramatization) See Wood, D. Babe, the sheep-pig

Sheep's milk on the boil. MacIntyre, T.

Shelley, Mary Wollstonecraft

Frankenstein (dramatization) See Carmichael, F. Frankenstein 1930; Peake, R. B. Presumption

Shenandoah. Schwartz, D.

Shengold, Nina

Finger food

Comedy. Encounter between food photographer and hand model. 1m 1w 1 interior

In Telling tales: new one-act plays; ed. by E. Lane

Lives of the great waitresses

Comedy. Four actresses working as waitresses. 4w 1 interior

In Plays for actresses; ed. by E. Lane and N. Shengold

Shepard, Sam

4-H Club

Three psychologically crippled roommates react to contemporary society. 1 scene 3m 1 interior

In Shepard, S. The unseen hand and other plays

Back bog beast bait

Unsavory characters turn into animals that reflect their basic instincts. 3 scenes 3m 3w extra 1 interior

In Shepard, S. The unseen hand and other plays

Buried child. Rev. ed. Dramatists 1997 75p

Visit from grandson no one remembers and accidental unearthing of dark secret might help farm family purge itself of guilt. 3 acts 5m 2w 1 interior

Chicago

Symbolic play about loss and identity. 4m 3w 1 interior

In Shepard, S. The unseen hand and other plays

Cowboys #2

Two aimless cowboys, at the end of their resources, make feeble attempts at communicating with each other. 2m 1 setting

In Shepard, S. The unseen hand and other plays

Forensic and the navigators

Experimental theater drama about the paranoia of our times. Two revolutionaries attempt to liberate inmates of a concentration camp. 4m 1w 1 setting

In Shepard, S. The unseen hand and other plays

Fourteen hundred thousand

Black comedy about books and reading. 3m 2w 1 interior

In Shepard, S. The unseen hand and other plays

The holy ghostly

Confrontation between spiritually dead but mechanically alive father who unsuccessfully resists ghost of death and disaffected son who fears the same fate. Singing. 1 scene 3m 1w extra 1 exterior

In Shepard, S. The unseen hand and other plays

Icarus's mother

Symbolic drama about fear in the nuclear age. 3m 1w 1 exterior

In Shepard, S. The unseen hand and other plays

Killer's head

Monologue by prisoner awaiting execution. 1m

In Shepard, S. The unseen hand and other plays

The mad dog blues

Satirical farce about the misadventures encountered by a group of fickle friends while hunting for a hidden treasure. Music, singing, dancing. Prologue 2 acts 6m 3w extra

In Shepard, S. The unseen hand and other plays

Operation sidewinder

Satiric comedy. Political allegory on the dehumanizing effects of American technology. Air Force computer in form of huge snake escapes into American forest. Music and singing interludes by rock group. 2 acts 12 scenes 18m 3w extras

In Shepard, S. The unseen hand and other plays

Red Cross

Surreal look at physical ailments. 1m 2w 1 interior

In Shepard, S. The unseen hand and other plays

The rock garden

A woman reminisces about her husband, a man talks of making a rock garden, and a teenage boy describes his sexual encounters. The final scene was performed as part of Oh! Calcutta! 3 scenes 2m 1w extra 1 interior

In Shepard, S. The unseen hand and other plays

Simpatico. Dramatists 1995 99p

Revenge tragicomedy in film noir style. 3 acts 7 scenes 3m 3w 1 interior

States of shock

Allegorical drama set during future war. Friction between Colonel and disabled veteran reflects failed relationships between fathers and sons. 3m 2w 1 interior

In Shepard, S. States of shock; Far north; Silent tongues

The unseen hand

Set in surrealistic wasteland of the nightmare future. Three former 19th century desperadoes are summoned by single oppressed thought-controlled individual to help fight dehumanized system. 5m 1 setting

In Shepard, S. The unseen hand and other plays

Parodies, imitations, etc.

Durang, C. A stye of the eye

Shepherd, Catherine

Delphiniums

Drama set in Australian rooming house. Pensioner's desire for secure future frustrated by her vindictive landlady. 1 act 1m 4w 1 interior

In Playing the past: three plays by Australian women; ed. by K. Kilner and S. Tweg

The **shepherd** and the psychiatrist. Haylock, D.

Shepherd on the rocks. White, P.

Shepherds

c Haylock, D. The shepherd and the psychiatrist

c McCullough, L. E. Let us go, O shepherds

The **shepherds.** See Vigil, A. Los pastores. The shepherds

Sheridan, Richard Brinsley

The rivals. Hern Bks. 1994 98p (Drama classics)

Romantic comedy of manners set in 18th century England. Army captain woos young woman whose fortune will be forfeited if she marries without the consent of her aunt. Prologue 5 acts 14 scenes epilogue 8m 4w 1b extras 1 setting

The school for scandal. Players Press 1995 84p

Comedy of manners set in 18th century London. True love triumphs over malicious gossip. Singing. Prologue 5 acts 14 scenes epilogue 11m 4w extras 6 interiors

—Same

In Great Irish plays

Sherkin Island (Ireland)

Barry, S. Prayers of Sherkin

Sherlock's veiled secret. Brown, K. C.

Sherman, Allan. See Bernstein, D. and Krausz, R. Hello muddah, hello fadduh!

Sherman, Geraldine

Broken English. French 1996 93p

Black comedy set in post-war London. Jewish refugee couple brings teenage daughter home from orphanage where she has been raised as British school girl. 2 acts 4 scenes 1m 3w 1 setting

Sherman, James

The God of Isaac. French 1995 76p

Comedy about search for spiritual identity set in Chicago and Skokie, Illinois. Young Jewish man reacts to threatened neo-Nazi demonstration. 2 acts 3m 3w 1 setting

Jest a second! Dramatists 1996 75p

Comedy set in Chicago. Divorced man announces he is gay at mother's birthday celebration. 2 acts 3 scenes 4m 2w 1 interior

Sherman, Jason

The retreat. Playwrights Canada 1996 113p

Comedy set 1993 in Toronto and at artist's retreat in Canadian Rockies. Film producer drawn to young Jewish woman's screenplay about false Messiah. 2 acts 18 scenes 3m 1w 2 interiors

Three in the back, two in the head. Playwrights Canada 1995 78p

Drama set in the Pentagon about ultimate cost of state and personal secrets. 14 scenes 4m 1w 1 exterior

Sherman, Jonathan Marc

Jesus on the oil tank

Small rural community thrown into turmoil when image of Christ appears on side of soybean oil tank. 18 scenes 12m 1w 1 setting

In Sherman, J. M. Three short plays

Serendipity and serenity

Comic coming-of-age tale of Manhattan Jewish boy. 13 scenes 4m 4w 1 setting

In Sherman, J. M. Three short plays

Sons and fathers

Absurdist look at how disturbed young man copes with mother's death. 8 scenes 3m 2w 1 setting

In Sherman, J. M. Three short plays

Sophistry. Dramatists 1995 57p

Drama set on New England college campus. Tenured male professor accused of sexual harrassment by male student. 2 acts 18 scenes 5m 3w settings

Women and Wallace

Black comedy. Mother's suicide sends son into period of mental and emotional confusion. Prologue 20 scenes epilogue 1m 8w 1 setting

In Telling tales: new one-act plays; ed. by E. Lane

Wonderful time. Dramatists 1997 49p

Cynical film student convinces free spirited American studies major to accompany him to friend's wedding. 20 scenes 3m 2w settings

Sherman, Martin

Cracks. French (London) 1993 45p

Trendy California party setting for murder mystery with elements of satire. 2 acts 5 scenes 5m 4w 1 interior

A madhouse in Goa

Satirical drama in two parts set on Greek islands. Acts are entitled: A table for a king and Keeps rainin' all the time. Examines personal, sexual, social and political deceptions. 2 parts 7m 3w 2 exteriors

In Staging gay lives; ed. by J. M. Clum

Some sunny day. Amber Lane Press 1996 93p

Drama set in 1942 Cairo about lust and international intrigue. Cultures clash as British nationals pursue love in society awash in secrecy. 2 acts 3m 3w 1 interior

Sherwood. Bynum, R. C.

She's been away. Poliakoff, S.

Shields, Brian James

Highwire

Corrupt New York City cop leans on Irish bartender to recruit for IRA. 2m 1w 1 interior

In Off-Off Broadway Festival plays, 19th ser.

Shields, Carol

Thirteen hands. Blizzard Pub. 1993 61p

Four women combat feelings of loneliness, fear, and isolation by meeting weekly at bridge club. Intimacy they

Shields, Carol—*Continued*
form is passed on to next generation. 2 acts 4w 1 interior

Shields, Carol, and Shields, Catherine
Fashion, power, guilt and the charity of families. Blizzard Pub. 1995 64p
Government bureaucrats attempt to legislate end to loneliness by creating ideal suburban family unit. Music. 2 acts 11 scenes 3m 2w 1 setting

Shields, Catherine. See Shields, Carol, jt. auth.

Shin, Rob
The art of waiting
Theater piece on theme of racism. Large mixed cast
In Asian American drama; ed. by B. Nelson

Shine, Ted
Contribution
Black grandmother, unable to join demonstrations, reveals to grandson her own method of aiding struggle for civil rights. 1m 2w 1 interior
In Black comedy: nine plays; ed. by P. F. Jackson and Karimah
In Black theatre USA [v2]; ed. by J. V. Hatch and T. Shine

Shining souls. Hannan, C.

The **ship.** Césaire, M.

Shipmasters
O'Neill, E. "Anna Christie"

Ships
Schenkkan, R. Final passages

Shipwrecks
Clapp, T. The open boat
Nowak, P. M. On the island
O'Neill, E. Warnings

Shivaree. Mastrosimone, W.

Shlemazl goes to paradise. McCullough, L. E.

The **shoe.** Solórzano, C.

The **shoe**-horn sonata. Misto, J.

The **shoemaker** and the elves. Bennett, R.

Shoemakers
c Bennett, R. The shoemaker and the elves

The **shoemakers.** Witkiewicz, S. I.

Sholem Aleichem. See Ravel, A. Tales from the shtetl: the Sholom Aleichem show

Shoo fly pudding. Hoppenstedt, E. M.

Shooting gallery. Horovitz, I.

Shooting rats. Turrini, P.

Shooting Simone. Kaufman, L.

Shooting souls. See Zark, J. A body of water: Shooting souls

Shoppers. McConnell, J.

Shopping and fucking. Ravenhill, M.

Shopping bag ladies. See Homeless

Shore leave. Milligan, J.

Shores, Del
Daughters of the Lone Star State. French 1993 107p
Comedy set in Texas. Women's service organization prepares for Christmas holiday. Singing. 2 acts 11w 1 interior

The **shorewatchers'** house. Upton, J.

Shotgun. Linney, R.

Shotlander, Sandra
Is that you Nancy?
Satirical look at lesbian lives featuring portrayal of Gertrude Stein. 11w 1 setting
In Australian gay and lesbian plays; ed. by B. Parr

Show. Bumbalo, V.

Showdown at the 3-R Ranch. Gallanar, I.

Shunted into a siding. Mitterer, F.

Shurtz, Raymond King
c Amy's attic. Anchorage Press 1997 56p
Girl discovers magic trunk in grandmother's attic. Variable cast 1 setting

Cowboys, Indians and waitresses
Comic-drama about nature of war. Vietnam vet challenges Navajo Indian to drunken slug-fest. 2m 1w extra 1 interior
In Off-Off Broadway Festival plays, 17th ser.

Shuttleworth, Red
This is dead level
Drama set in Nevada hotel room. Discussion between man and prostitute interrupted by arrival of hooker's husband. 2m 2w 1 interior
In Lucky 13; ed. by R. Shuttleworth

The **shyster.** Sade, Marquis de

Siamese twins
Gregg, S. A private moment

Siberia. Mitterer, F.

Sichrovsky, Peter
Born guilty (dramatization) See Roth, A. Born guilty

Sickles, Scott C.
Murmurs
Coming-of-age drama. Two teenage boys find comfort in each other. 2m 1 interior
In Off-Off Broadway Festival plays, 21st ser.

Siefert, Lynn
Little Egypt. Dramtists 1995 63p
Romantic comedy. Amorous entanglements of mother and two grown daughters in small town Illinois. 2 acts 29 scenes 3m 3w 1 setting

The **siege** of Vienna. Turrini, P.

Siegel, June
Metamorphoses
Satire. Three women relate tales of fantastic male transformations. 3w 1 setting
In Facing forward; ed. by L. D. Frank

Siempre en mi corazón. Colón, O. A.

Sierens, Arne
Drummers
Son's music teacher forces impoverished woman to recall great love of her youth. 1m 1w 1 interior
In Dutch and Flemish plays; ed. by D. Couling

Sight unseen. Margulies, D.

Sightings. Slaight, B.

The **sign** in Sidney Brustein's window. Hansberry, L.

Signal driver. White, P.

Signor Nicodemo. Meilhac, H. and Halévy, L.

Silent night. McCullough, L. E.

Silly cow. Elton, B.

The **silly** villagers. See Gerke, P. Ne hölmöläiset: The silly villagers

Silver, Joan Micklin, and Boyd, Julianne
A ... my name is still Alice; a musical review; conceived by Joan Micklin Silver and Juilianne Boyd. French 1993 91p (French's musical library)
Sequel to A ... my name is Alice. Feminist revue exploring women in 1990s. 2 acts 5w

Silver, Nicky
Fat men in skirts. Dramatists 1994 84p
Black comedy about incest, cannibalism, adultery, matricide, insanity and transvestism. 3 acts Variable cast 6 characters 2 interiors 1 exterior
—Same
In Silver, N. Etiquette and vitriol
Fit to be tied. Dramatists 1997 71p
Farcical comedy revolving around relationship of troubled wealthy homosexual, his mother and beautiful youth working as angel at Radio City music show. 2 acts 6 scenes 3m 1w 1 interior
The food chain. Dramatists 1996 67p
Black comedy set in New York City about love, sex, loneliness and importance of being thin. 3 scenes 3m 2w 2 interiors
—Same
In Silver, N. Etiquette and vitriol
Free will & wanton lust
Explores contemporary relationships in contrasting styles of Noel Coward and Bertolt Brecht. 2 acts 2m 3w 2 interiors
In Silver, N. Etiquette and vitriol
Pterodactyls. Dramatists 1994 81p
Black comedy about family afflicted with AIDS, alcoholism, and emotional coldness. 2 acts 3 scenes 3m 2w 1 interior
—Same
In Silver, N. Etiquette and vitriol
Raised in captivity. Dramatists 1995 89p
Black comedy about guilt, redemption and self-punishment. Twin brother and sister reunited following mother's funeral. 2 acts 10 scenes 3m 2w 4 interiors 1 exterior
—Same. Theatre Communications Group 1995 114p

Silver, Robert S.
The hert o Scotland. [amended and expanded ed] Scottish Cultural Press 1995 73p
Historical drama about Robert the Bruce's role in medieval Scotland's struggle for independence from England. 3 acts 15 scenes 25m 5w 1 setting

Silver dagger. French, D.

Silver face. Valle-Inclan, R. del

Silvera, John D. and Hill, Abram
Liberty deferred
Living newspaper history of African American experience from advent of slavery to 1930s. Large mixed cast
In Black theatre USA [v1]; ed. by J. V. Hatch and T. Shine

Silverman, Judd Lear
Correct address
Drama. Having been barred from funeral by deceased's mother, gay man converses with ghost of lover who died of AIDS. 2m 1 interior
In Off-Off Broadway Festival plays, 17th ser.

Silverstein, Shel
Dreamers
Two men discuss their erotic dreams. 2m 1 interior
In The Best American short plays, 1992-1993

Silvie the substitute reindeer. Pflomm, P. N.

Simmons, David W.
c Be smart! Don't start! Pioneer Drama Service 1996 13p
Two versions of same play, one for children in grades k-3, the other 4-6. Physician provides girl with information that helps her resist peer pressure to use drugs. 2m 1b 1g 1 interior

Simmons, David W.—*Continued*

c Nutricia Goodheart's Body Building Construction Company. Pioneer Drama Service 1996 18p

Construction foreman learns how to build a strong healthy body. Variable cast 7 characters

Simon, Barney. See Mtwa, P. jt. auth.

Simon, Lucy. See Norman, M. The secret garden

Simon, Mayo

The old lady's guide to survival. Dramatic 1994 66p

Two women from very different backgrounds cope with problems associated with aging. 2 acts 10 scenes 2w

Walking to Waldheim. Dramatic 1995 47p

Bittersweet comedy about six mourners on way to funeral. 3m 3w 1 setting

Simon, Michael, and Simon, Richard

Murder at Minsing Manor: a nancy boys mystery. French 1996 107p

Sexual mis-identities featured in campy take-off on stereotypes of juvenile detective fiction. 2 acts 3 scenes 8m 2w 1 setting

Simon, Neil

Brighton Beach memoirs

First play in author's semi-autobiographical trilogy about growing up in Depression era Brooklyn. 2 acts 3m 4w 1 setting

In Best American plays: 9th series, 1983-1992

Jake's women. French 1993 112p

Successful writer works through midlife crisis in series of conversations, real and imagined, with women in his life. 2 acts 2 scenes 1m 7w 1 interior

—Same. Random House 1994 131p

Laughter on the 23rd floor. French 1995 103p

Set in office on 23rd floor of 57th Street New York City building in 1953. Comedy about team of writers working on TV comedy show. 2 acts 3 scenes 7m 2w 1 interior

—Same. Random House 1995 114p

Laughter on the 23rd floor (condensation)

In The Best plays of 1993-1994

London suite: Diana and Sidney

Comedy. Meeting him for first time since divorce actress comes to realization that she still loves her bisexual ex-husband. 1m 2w 1 interior

In Simon, N. London suite

London suite: Going home

Comedy. Vacationing American daughter encourages widowed mother to spend last evening in London with wealthy, unmarried Scotsman. 2w 1 interior

In Simon, N. London suite

London suite: Settling accounts

Comedy. Inebriated Welsh writer holds long-time business manager at gun-point when he catches him absconding to Buenos Aires with his money. 2m 1 interior

In Simon, N. London suite

London suite: The man on the floor

Comedy. American couple search for lost Wimbledon tickets while hotel tries to move them from suite to accommodate movie star Kevin Costner. 3m 2w 1 interior

In Simon, N. London suite

Lost in Yonkers. French 1992 110p

Domestic tragicomedy set in 1942. Portrait of dysfunctional Jewish family centered around icy matriarch and her mildly retarded daughter. 2 acts 8 scenes 4m 3w 1 interior

Rumours. [Revised acting edition] French (London) 1997 75p

Farce about wedding anniversary party for deputy mayor of New York that goes awry because of series of domestic crises. 2 acts 5m 5w 1 interior

Simon, Richard. See Simon, M. jt. auth.

Simon, Shirley

c The tiger and the Brahman

Based on folktale from India. Jackal outwits tiger who wants to eat Brahman. Unidentified cast 5 characters 1 exterior

In Thirty plays from favorite stories; ed. by S. E. Kamerman

Simons, Johnny

c Pinocchio commedia. Clark, I. E. 1993 30p

Harlequinade version of Collodi's story of the marionette who wished to be human. 2 acts 6m 2w 1 setting

Simonson, Eric

Bang the drum slowly. Dramatists 1995 77p

Dramatization of Mark Harris' novel set in 1956 about New York Mammoths baseball club. Team responds to Afro-American catcher slowly dying of Hodgkin's disease. 2 acts 15m 2w 1 interior

Simoom. Strindberg, A.

Simpatico, David

Wish fulfillment

Tragicomedy. Various scenarios in which son discloses his homosexuality to father. 2m

In Showtime's Act One Festival of one-act plays, 1994

Simpatico. Shephard, S.

Simple Simon. Bisson, P.

Simply disconnected. Gray, S.

Simply heavenly. Hughes, L.

Simpson, Ed

The comet of St. Loomis. French 1995 110p

Comedy. Lonely motel owner in small town Pennsylvania visited by old high school classmate. 2 acts 4m 2w 1 exterior

Sims, George Robert
The lights o' London
Victorian melodrama contrasting country innocence and city experience. Disowned son and lass he loves undergo trying times in London. 5 acts 11 scenes 18m 8w settings
In The Lights o' London and other Victorian plays; ed. by M. R. Booth

Sin
Solórzano, C. The Angel's forty winks

Sinai Campaign, 1956
Paice, E. and Woddis, R. World on edge

Sincerity forever. Wellman, M.

Sinclair, Bruce
y Dreamkeeper
Series of dream sequences regarding past and future of Canadian Indians. Singing, dancing. 5 scenes 1m 1w 1 setting
In Eureka! ed. by J. J. Lewis and D. Warren

Sing this. Dashow, K.

Singapore
Frandsen, E. et al. Song of Singapore

Singers
Ayckbourn, A. A chorus of disapproval
Chinn, J. Something to remember you by
Dean, P. H. The Sty of The Blind Pig
Higginsen, V. and Wydro, K. Mama, I want to sing
Ledoux, P. and Young, D. Love is strange
Levy, J. Old blues
McNally, T. Master class
Roche, B. The Cavalcaders
Roth, A. Oh, the innocents
Scribe, E. and Mélesville. The castrata
Whelan, P. Shakespeare country
Winer, D. G. The last girl singer
y Yates, P. Starlover

Singing
Wilson, A. Seven guitars

Single and proud. Stroppel, F.

Single men
Law, M. Advertising Arnold
Stroppel, F. Single and proud

Single women
Adam, A. A cameo from Cranford
Adam, A. Castles in the air
Booth, J. Over his dead body
Carter, J. The twisted mirror
y Charles, R. A perfect match
Dean, P. H. The Sty of The Blind Pig
García Lorca, F. The house of Bernarda Alba
Martin, L. Waltzing De Niro
Real, C. Why the Beach Boys are like opera
Rebeck, T. Loose knit
Sewell, G. Speak of the devil
Stroppel, F. Single and proud
Wilson, L. Victory on Mrs. Dandywine's island

A **singular** kinda guy. Ives, D.

Sink the Belgrano! Berkoff, S.

Sins of the father. Smith, L.

Sir Patient Fancy. Behn, A.

Sirens (Mythology)
Kramer, S. Permanent signal

Sister Mary Ignatius explains it all for you. Durang, C.

Sisters
Ackermann, J. The batting cage
Aron, G. Olive and Hilary
Baker, E. A. Rosemary with Ginger
Barnes, D. The dove
Booth, J. Little white lies
Brandl, D. Vine and dandy
Brenton, H. Berlin Bertie
Butterfield, C. Life in the trees: The last time I saw Timmy Boggs
Butterfield, C. Where the truth lies
Chekhov, A. Three sisters
Day, D. M. Possession is . . .
De Angelis, A. Hush
Durang, C. Phyllis and Xenobia
Gallagher, M. Bedtime
Greenberg, R. Jenny keeps talking
Harding, N. This year, next year
Hare, D. The secret rapture
Hughes, D. The morning
Jennings, C. S. Sunday dinner
Kemp, R. A trump for Jericho
Linney, R. Goodbye, Howard
Lyssiotis, T. Blood moon
Mann, E. Having our say
c Medoff, M. Kringle's window
Michels, J. and Murphy, P. The queen of bingo
Nemeth, S. Sally's shorts: Lily
Peters, K. The confirmation
Pintauro, J. Two eclairs
Plautus, T. M. Stichus
Plautus, T. M. Two sisters named Bacchis
Porter, D. Flowers
Pryor, D. The love talker

Sisters—*Continued*
Royce, C. Why we have a body
St. John, B. Rubies: Heirlooms
St. John, B. Rubies: Little gems
Thompson, J. I am yours
Tibbles G. The turn of the worm
Visdei, A. Always together
Wasserstein, W. The sisters Rosensweig
Wiener, S. D. A place where love is
c York, Y. The portrait the wind the chair

Sisters. Jackson, M. A.

The **sisters** Rosensweig. Wasserstein, W.

Sitting Bull, Dakota Chief, 1831-1890
Pollock, S. Walsh

Situation vacant. Hornby, I.

Six Canterbury tales. Thomas, E. and Redmond, B.

Six honest serving men. Muldoon, P.

Skin. Biswas, N.

The **skip.** Rensten, M.

The **Skriker.** Churchill, C.

A **skull** in Connemara. McDonagh, M.

Skylight. Hare, D.

Slabolepszy, Paul
Over the hill
Satire about white middle-class racial attitudes focusing on South African rugby team. 1 act 2m 1w 1 interior
In South Africa plays; ed. by S. Gray

Slade, Bernard
I remember you. French 1994 106p
Romantic comedy. Cocktail lounge performer discovers his current love interest is daughter of woman he had passionate affair with twenty-five years ago. Music, singing. 2 acts 6 scenes 2m 2w 2 interiors

Same time, another year. French 1996 112p
Sequel to: Same time, next year. Romantic comedy. Extra marital affair conducted one weekend a year in Northern California seaside cottage from 1976-1993. 2 acts 6 scenes 1m 1w 1 interior

You say tomatoes. French 1994 118p
Comedy about differences in manners, morals and attitudes between Great Britain and the U.S. Relationship develops between brash New York woman film producer and reclusive British mystery writer. 2 acts 6 scenes 2m 2w 2 interiors

Slag. Hare, D.

Slaight, Brad
y Class action. Bakers Plays 1995 61p
Series of scenes from lives of high school students. 25 scenes 3m 4w

—Same
In New plays from A.C.T.'S young conservatory v2

y High tide
Chance meeting with two girls on California beach helps two young surfers deal with friend's death. 1 act 3m 2w 1 exterior
In New plays from A.C.T.'S young conservatory [v1]
In Slaight, B. Sightings and High tide

y The open road
Teenage boy, inspired by passions of Walt Whitman's poetry, decides to impersonate him. 2m 1w 1 interior
In Short plays for young actors; ed. by C. Slaight and J. Sharrar

y Sightings
Teenage girl, dating self-important stud, hides her true feelings for eccentric friend. 1 act 2m 1w extras 1 exterior
In New plays from A.C.T.'S young conservatory [v1]
In Slaight, B. Sightings and High tide

Slam dunk. Hibberd, J.

Slander. See Gossip

Slattery, Margaret E.
c The king in the kitchen
Peasant wins princess by guessing what the king has cooked. 4m 4w 1 interior
In Thirty plays from favorite stories; ed. by S. E. Kamerman

Slaughter City. Wallace, N.

Slaughter in the lake. Rivera, J.

Slave ship. Baraka, A.

Slave-trade
Baraka, A. Slave ship

Slavery
Bird, R. M. The gladiator
Hughes. L. Emperor of Haiti
Plautus, T. M. A funny thing happened on the way to the wedding

United States

Aiken, G. L. Uncle Tom's cabin
Alexander, R. I ain't yo' uncle
y Asher, S. F. A woman called Truth
Boucicault, D. Octoroon
Branch, W. In splendid error
Brown, W. W. The escape
c Davis, O. Escape to freedom
Dove, R. The darker face of the earth
c Fisher, A. Harriet Tubman—the second Moses

Slavery—United States—*Continued*
Graham, S. It's morning
Hall, F. B. Dance of the Eland
y Lerman, L. The Abolition Flyer
y McCullough, L. E. When people could fly
c Sodaro, C. Freedom train
y Watson, W. J. Abe Lincoln and the runaways

Slaves. See Slavery

Slavs! Kushner, T.

Sled. Thompson, J.

Sleep deprivation chamber. Kennedy, A. P. and Kennedy, A.

The **sleep** seeker. Swedeen, S.

Sleeping arrangements. Booth, J.

Sleeping Beauty. Brown, A.

Sleeping beauty. Edgar, K.

Sleeping Beauty. Mahlmann, L. and Jones, D. C.

The **sleeping** beauty. Wakefield, C.

Sleeping-cars. See Railroads—Sleeping cars

Sleeping dog. Gray, S.

Sloate, Daniel
Countess de Kitchen
Experimental playlet. Woman washes dishes. 1m 1w 1 interior
In Sloate, D. The Countess cycle
Countess in Courtland
Surreal courtroom scene. 2m 1w extras 1 interior
In Sloate, D. The Countess cycle
Countess in Thistleland
Fantasy about sex roles set on Scottish moor. 3m 1w extras 1 setting
In Sloate, D. The Countess cycle
Le radeau de la Comtesse
Monologue by woman reveals artifice behind theatrical experience. 1m 1w 1 setting
In Sloate, D. The Countess cycle
Suddenly, a foot
Surreal playlet. Man asks Countess for advice about daughter's unusual problem. 1m 2w 1 interior
In Sloate, D. The Countess cycle

Slout, William L.
The trial of Dr. Jekyll. Borgo Press 1993 75p
Dramatization of R. L. Stevenson's The strange case of Dr. Jekyll and Mr. Hyde. In attempt to determine extent of his guilt Jekyll fantasizes himself on trial. 2 acts 8m 2w 1 interior

Sloyer, Gary
y Ezekiel saw the . . . what? Book and lyrics by Kirk R. Brown; music by Gary Sloyer. Pioneer Drama Service 1993 27p
Contemporary musical about Biblical prophet Ezekiel. 1m 1w extras 1 setting

Slums
Bullins, E. In the wine time

A **small** affair. Larbey, B.

A **small** family business. Ayckbourn, A.

Small town life. See Country life

Smash. Hatcher, J.

The **smelly** feet. Vigil, A.

Smith, Anna Deavere
Aye aye aye I'm integrated
Look at absurdist aspects of racial discrimination in America. 1w
In Here to stay: five plays from the Women's Project; ed. by J. Miles
Fires in the mirror: Crown Heights, Brooklyn and other identities. Dramatists 1997 141p
Theater piece about racial tension following 1991 death of black child and Hasidic scholar in Crown Heights, Brooklyn. 1w 1 setting
Twilight: Los Angeles, 1992. Anchor Bks. 1994 265p
One woman performance dealing with riots in South-Central Los Angeles following the Rodney King trial. 1w
Twilight: Los Angeles, 1992 (condensation)
In The Best plays of 1993-1994

Smith, Arthur
Live bed show. Warner Chappel Plays 1995 63p
Comic exploration of modern relationships. 1m 1w 1 setting

Smith, Barbara L.
Butterscotch. French 1997 88p
Comic drama set in small town Pennsylvania. Vintage car serves as common bond between restaurant critic and his future father-in-law. 2 acts 9 scenes 3m 2w 1 setting

Smith, Beatrice S.
c Adams for the defense
John Adams agrees to defend British soldier who participated in Boston Massacre. 3m 2w 1 interior
In Great American events on stage; ed. by S. E. Kamerman

Smith, Cedric. See Winter, J. jt. auth.

Smith, Charles
Freefall. French 1994 96p
Drama set in 1991 Chicago about two African American brothers, one a career criminal the other a cop. 2 acts 10 scenes 3m 1w

Smith, Dodie
The hundred and one Dalmatians (dramatization) See Robbins, G. The hundred and one Dalmatians

Smith, Joanna Murray. See Murray-Smith, Joanna

Smith, John, 1580-1631
c McCaslin, N. Mercy in moccasins
c Morris, V. Legend of Pocahontas

Smith, Leo
Sins of the father. French (London) 1992 24p
Married man manipulated into leaving his wife by amoral mistress. 7 scenes 1m 2w 1 setting

Smith, Mark Landon
An evening of culture: Faith County II, the saga continues. Bakers Plays 1994 62p
Comedy. Small Southern town stages production of Shakespeare's Romeo and Juliet. 2 acts 3 scenes 3m 5w 1 interior

Smith, Ronn
y Nothing but the truth. Avon Flare 1997 154p
Dramatization of Avi's documentary novel. Ninth-grader's suspension for humming "The star-spangled banner" during homeroom becomes national news story. Prologue. 2 acts 18 scenes Variable cast 38 characters 1 setting

Smith, Stephen
One-sided triangle. French (London) 1994 27p
Drama. British youth becomes involved in Thai heroin trade. 2m 1w 1 exterior

Parentcraft. French (London) 1996 28p
Comedy. Four expectant mothers and one father await midwife who will give them their first "parentcraft" class. 1m 4w 1 interior

Smith, Val
The gamblers. French 1993 89p
Suspense drama about marriage, money and power set aboard riverboat in antebellum South. Unhappy wife schemes to cheat wealthy husband of his fortune. 2 acts 23 scenes 5m 1w 1 setting

See also Dixon, M. B. jt. auth.

Smith, William Henry
The drunkard; or, The fallen saved
Downward path of young husband and father and his bitter struggle against demon rum. 4 acts 18 scenes 13m 5w 1g extras 6 interiors 6 exteriors
In Early American drama; ed. by J. H. Richards

Smoke & mirrors. Osborne, W. and Herrera, A.

Smoking
y Kukla, D. Sticks and stones

Smolensky, Sheila, and Waldrop, Jerry
The Mikado. Pioneer Drama Service 1994 39p
Adaption of Gilbert and Sullivan's satiric operetta set in ancient Japan. 2 acts 3 scenes 7m 6w extras 1 exterior

Smut's saga. Lloyd, R.

Smyth, David. See Ledoux, P. jt. auth.

The **snake.** See Gerke, P. La culebra: "The snake"

Snakes and ladders. Connolly, H.

Snelgrove, Michael
Bums on seats. French (London) 1997 66p
Satirical look at production of new play by provincial English theatre. 2 acts 6m 6w 1 interior

The **sniper.** O'Neill, E.

Snipes, Larry E.
c Jack and the wonder beans. Anchorage Press 1996 43p
Appalachian version of the traditional tale Jack and the beanstalk. Singing, music, audience participation. Variable cast 8 characters 1 setting

Snodgrass, Katherine
Haiku
Mother facing blindness concerned about welfare of disturbed, poetically gifted daughter. 3w 1 setting
In Telling tales: new one-act plays; ed. by E. Lane

The **snow** ball. Gurney, A. R.

Snow orchid. Pintauro, J.

The **Snow** Queen. Andersen, H. C. (dramatization) See Kennedy, R. Hans Christian Andersen's The Snow Queen; Nicol, R. The Snow Queen

Snow stars. Sawyer, A. V.

Snow White. Robbins, N.

Snow White and Rose Red. Mahlmann, L. and Jones, D. C.

Snow White and the seven dwarfs. Grimm, J. and Grimm, W. (dramatization) See Francoeur, B. Snow White and the seven dwarfs; Mahlmann, L. and Jones, D. C. Snow White and the seven dwarfs; Robbins, N. Snow White

Snow White—the purdiest gal in the West. Stanford, J.

The **Snow** Witch. Dixon, D.

Snowing at Delphi. Butterfield, C.

The **snows** of Kilimanjaro. Harnetiaux, B.

So tell me about this guy. Whiskeyman, D.

Sobhraj, Charles, 1944-
Millan, J. and Brooker, B. Serpent kills

Sobol, Joshua
Adam
Part of author's Vilna triology. Holocaust drama focuses on critical moment in life of Vilna ghetto. Prologue 18 scenes 8m 4w 1 setting
In Israeli Holocaust drama; ed. by R. Jenkins

Soccer
Jones, M. A night in November

Social classes
Flanagan, H. and Clifford, M. E. Can you hear their voices?
Toller, E. Masses and man
Wesley, R. The talented tenth

Social conflict
Barker, H. The love of a good man

Social distinction. See Class distinction

Social problems
Bennett, A. Enjoy
Doctorow, E. L. Drinks before dinner
Shaw, B. Major Barbara

Social reform. See Social problems

Social workers
Barnes, P. Rosa

Socialism
c Breeze, N. The Rochdale Pioneers
Finnegan, S. Comrade Brennan
Griffiths, T. The party
Hatcher, J. Smash

Socrates
Aristophanes. The clouds
Emery, S. W. Apology
Emery, S. W. Crito
Emery, S. W. Euthyphro

Sod, Ted
Satan and Simon Desoto
Dark comedy set in Seattle. HIV positive gay man sells soul to Devil. 2 acts 4m 1w settings
In Sharing the delirium; ed. by T. Jones

Sod, Ted, and Grant, Suzanne
y Three wishes. Meriwether 1993 36p
Musical fable. Pregnant teenager is granted three wishes by fairy godsister. 12 scenes Variable cast 13 characters

Sodaro, Craig
y Blind date
Teenage sisters foil spy at aunt's apartment. 2 scenes 2m 4w 1 interior
In The Big book of skits; ed. by S. E. Kamerman

c Freedom train
Family helps slaves escape to freedom on Underground Railroad. 4m 4w 1b 1g 1 interior
In Great American events on stage; ed. by S. E. Kamerman
In Plays of black Americans; ed. by S. E. Kamerman

y It's a bird! It's a plane! It's . . . Nerdman?! Pioneer Drama Service 1993 42p
Parody of Superman. Superhero combats crime wave. 2 acts 6 scenes 12m 10w 1 interior

y Salem's daughter. Pioneer Drama Service 1997 47p
Victim of Salem witch trials returns to haunt present day high school girls. 2 acts 6 scenes 7w extras 2 interiors 1 exterior

Soft dude. Pintauro, J.

Soland, Lisa
The name game. French 1995 105p
Comedy set in L.A. Kidnapped woman, her abductor and her policeman boyfriend form romantic triangle. 2 acts 9 scenes 2m 1w 1 interior

Soldiers

American

Bell, J. A. Prisoner
Bynum, R. C. The sharpshooters
Cotter, J. S. On the fields of France
Fischoff, G. James A. Michener's Sayonara
Fuller, C. A soldier's play
Laurents, A. Home of the brave
Linney, R. El hermano
Nemeth, S. Sally's shorts: Pre-nuptial agreement
Rabe, D. The basic training of Pavlo Hummel
Rabe, D. Streamers
Steelsmith, M. Wacs in khaki
Szyszkowitz, G. Commander Carrigan
Wallace, N. In the heart of America

Australian

Gorman, C. Manual of trench warfare

British

Armstrong, I. Fallen heroes
y Bond, E. Tuesday
Gee, S. Never in my lifetime
Lewis, J. Our boys
Macdonald, S. When we were women
Owen, K. Black, green, white and gold

Canadian

Vanderhaeghe, G. Dancock's dance
Verdecchia, G. and Youssef, M. A line in the sand

Soldiers—*Continued*

German

Büchner, G. Woyzeck

Irish

Dowling, C. The Marlboro man

Roman

Plautus, T. M. The braggart soldier

Russian

Edmundson, H. War and peace

South African

Akerman, A. Somewhere on the border

The **soldiers'** fortune. Otway, T.

A **soldier's** play. Fuller, C.

Solidarity (Trade union)
Stoppard, T. Squaring the circle

Solis, Eduardo Rodriguez. See Rodriguez Solis, Eduardo

Solomon, King of Israel
Lyssa, A. Pinball

Solórzano, Carlos

And death brought forth the light

Play-within-a-play exploration of political corruption in Spanish-American country. 5m 1w extras 1 interior

In Solórzano, C. Crossroads and other plays

The Angel's forty winks

Woman struggles with guardian angel who forces her to admit to and expiate her sins. 1m 1w 1 interior

In Solórzano, C. Crossroads and other plays

Crossroads

Symbolic play about man who fails to recognize the woman he has long been waiting for. 1 act 2m 1w 1 exterior

In Solórzano, C. Crossroads and other plays

The crucified

Variant title: The crucifixion. Drunken Mexican villagers identify with roles in Good Friday passion play and carry out real crucifixion. 1 act 3 scenes 8m 4w 1 interior

In Solórzano, C. Crossroads and other plays

The hands of God

Spanish American woman, at instigation of Devil, steals from church after she and husband are defrauded of their land. 3 acts 5m 3w 2b 1g 1 exterior

In Solórzano, C. Crossroads and other plays

Mea culpa

Drama about Catholic concepts of guilt and responsibility. Elderly bishop hears man's confession. 2m extras 1 interior

In Solórzano, C. Crossroads and other plays

The puppets

Symbolic puppet play based on traditional Mexican Holy Saturday custom. 8 characters 1 setting

In Solórzano, C. Crossroads and other plays

The shoe

Adolescent boy struggles to realize his independence. 1m extra 1 setting

In Solórzano, C. Crossroads and other plays

Some assembly required. Strickland, E.

Some do, some don't. Wise, R.

Some people have all the luck. Tirado, C.

Some sunny day. Sherman, M.

Some things you need to know before the world ends (a final evening with the illuminati). Larson, L. and Lee, L.

Some voices. Penhall, J.

Someday. Taylor, D. H.

Someone from Assisi. Wilder, T.

Someone who'll watch over me. McGuinness, F.

Something cloudy, something clear. Williams, T.

Something I'll tell you Tuesday. Guare, J.

Something on his mind. Booth, J.

Something rotten in Denmark. Annie G.

Something sacred this way comes. Trott, S.

Something to remember you by. Chinn, J.

Somewhere. Johnson, J.

Somewhere in between. Pospisil, C.

Somewhere on the border. Akerman, A.

Somewhere over the rainbow. Szyszkowitz, G.

Somme, 1st Battle of the, 1916
McGuinness, F. Observe the sons of Ulster marching towards the Somme

Somnambulist. Margulies, D.

Son, Diana

R.A.W. ('cause I'm a woman)

Experimental theater piece in which Asian American women react to sexual stereotypes. Background music, slides. 4w

In Contemporary plays by women of color; ed. by K. A. Perkins and R. Uno

The **son.** Hasenclever, W.

The **son**. See Morrison, B. A love song for Ulster: The son

Son-Boy. Mitchell, J. S.

Son of an engineer. Greenspan, D.

Sondheim, Stephen

Company; a musical comedy; music and lyrics by Stephen Sondheim; book by George Furth. Theatre Communications Group 1996 118p

Musical comedy on the shortcomings and realities of marriage as shown in the lives of five couples and their mutual friend, a bachelor whom they try to persuade to enter into matrimony. 2 acts 11 scenes 6m 8w extras settings

Passion; a musical; music and lyrics by Stephen Sondheim; book and direction by James Lapine. Theatre Communications Group 1994 131p

Musical based on Ettore Scola's film Passione d'amore and Iqinioi Uqo Tarchetti's novel Fosca. Dark tale set in 19th century Italy about woman's obsessive love for unavailable man. 16 scenes 10m 4w 1 setting

Passion (condensation)

In The Best plays of 1993-1994

Sondheim, Stephen, and Furth, George

Getting away with murder. Theatre Communications Group 1997 123p

Comedy thriller about Pulitzer prize-winning psychiatrist-author who brings together in group therapy seven individuals each personifying a capital sin. Alternate ending appended. 2 acts 8m 3w extras 1 interior

Sondheim, Stephen, and Lapine, James

Into the woods

Cinderella, Little Red Riding Hood, Jack and the Beanstalk, and other famous fairy tales interwoven with story of baker and his wife whose longing for a child is thwarted by a witch. 2 acts 8 scenes 8m 13w 1b 1g settings

In Best American plays: 9th series, 1983-1992

A **song** for a Nisei fisherman. Gotanda, P. K.

A **song** for Robbie. Dunbar, D.

Song for the navigator. Cowell, M.

The **song** of Jacob Zulu. Yourgrau, T.

Song of Singapore. Frandsen, E. et al.

Song of the oak—El canto del roble. Conboy, R.

Songs of love. Linney, R.

Sons and fathers. Sherman, J. M.

Sonny DeRee's life flashes before his eyes. Bozzone, B.

Sontag, Susan

Alice in bed. Farrar Straus Giroux 1993 117p

Dramatic fantasy based on life of Alice James, brilliant but troubled sister of Henry and William. 8 scenes 4m 6w 1 setting

Sophistry. Sherman, J. M.

Sophists (Greek philosophy)

Aristophanes. The clouds

Sophocles

Antigone. Players Press 1995 38p

Greek tragedy in verse. Disaster follows refusal of Creon, King of Thebes to permit burial of his enemy Antigone's brother. Speaking chorus

Antigone; tr. by David Grene

In Sophocles. The Theban plays

Antigone (adaptation) See Judy, G. Antigone; Kennelly, B. Sophocles' Antigone

Electra; tr. by E. A. Heary. Players Press 1995 40p

Greek classical tragedy in verse. Based on the legend telling how Orestes and Electra, children of Agamemnon, avenged their father's murder

—Same; tr. by Nicholas Rudall. Dee, I. R. 1993 70p (Plays for performance)

Oedipus at Colonus; tr. by David Grene

Greek classical tragedy in verse. Conclusion to Oedipus saga. Oedipus, pursued by Creon, miraculously passes from this world to become guardian spirit of Athens

In Sophocles. The Theban plays

Oedipus the King; tr. by David Grene

Variant titles: Oedipus; Oedipus Rex; Oedipus Tyranos. Greek classical tragedy in verse. Oedipus, King of Thebes, is powerless to escape curse of earlier crime. Speaking chorus

In Sophocles. The Theban plays

Sophocles' Antigone. Kennelly, B.

The **Sorcerer's** apprentice. Surface, M. H.

Sorensen, Kathy

y An endangered species: waking up. French 1994 55p

Drama. Group of high school students discover they are spreading HIV virus through heterosexual sex. 3m 4w 1 setting

Sorry. Mason, T.

Sortilege II: Zumbi returns. Nascimento, A. do

Soto, Gary

y Novio boy. Harcourt Brace & Co. 1997 78p

Play about misery and joy of young love in Mexican American community. 7 scenes 4m 4w extras 1 setting

Soul
See also Transmigration

Soul gone home. Hughes, L.

Sound choice. Wise, R.

The **sound** of a voice. Hwang, D. H.

The **soup** stone. Peterson, M. N.

The **South.** See Southern States

South Africa
Baitz, J. R. The film society
Fugard, A. Valley song
Harwood, R. Another time
Maponya, M. The hungry earth
Pillay, K. Looking for Muruga
See also Cape Town (South Africa)

Race relations

Baitz, J. R. A fair country
Fugard, A. Playland
Fugard, A. Statements after an arrest under the immorality act
Harwood, R. Tramway Road
Ntwa, P.; Ngema, M. and Simon, B. Woza Albert!
Pam-Grant, S. Curl up and dye
Slabolepszy, P. Over the hill
Yourgrau, T. The song of Jacob Zulu

South Africans

England

Uys, P.-D. Just like home

South Carolina

Race relations

Burrill, M. P. Aftermath

Southern fried cracker tales. Kase-Polisini, J.

Southern States
Bynum, R. C. Sherwood
Dewberry, E. Flesh and blood
Hellman, L. The little foxes
McCullough, L. E. Go tell it on the mountain
Smith, M. L. An evening of culture: Faith County II, the saga continues
Ward, D. T. Day of absence
Williams, S.-A. Home

Race relations

Brown, W. W. The escape
Fuller, C. A soldier's play
Hughes, L. Mulatto
Johnson, G. D. A Sunday morning in the South
Mitchell, J. S. Son-Boy
Uhry, A. Driving Miss Daisy

Southerne, Thomas
The wives' excuse; or, Cuckolds make themselves

Restoration comedy about dissolution of hollow marriage. Prologue 5 acts 13 scenes epilogue 8m 5w extras settings

In Four Restoration marriage plays; ed. by M. Cordner

Soyinka, Wole
Death and the King's Horseman

Tragedy based on events of 1946 in Oyo, Nigeria. English Colonial officer intervenes to prevent ritual suicide of Yoruba chief. Choral speaking. 5 acts 9m 3w extras 1 setting

In Crosswinds; ed. by W. B. Branch

Space. Margulies, D.

Spacenapped. Bisson, P.

Spain
Dryden, J. Love triumphant
Valle-Inclan, R. del. Divine words

History—9th century

Linney, R. Three poets: Komachi

History—House of Austria, 1516-1700

Barnes, P. The bewitched
Fletcher, J. and Rowley, W. The maid in the mill
Hugo, V. Hernani

History—Civil War, 1936-1939

Blanc, E. S. Wars I have seen
Bond, E. Human cannon

Social life and customs

Beaumarchais, P.-A. C. de. The barber of Seville
Fletcher, J. and Massinger, P. The Spanish curate
García Lorca, F. The house of Bernarda Alba

Spain: Anna Rey. Linney, R.

Spain: Escobedo de la Aixa. Linney, R.

Spain: Torquemada. Linney, R.

The **Spanish** cape. Gregor, H.

The **Spanish** curate. Fletcher, J. and Massinger, P.

Spanish eyes. López, E. I.

Spanish lies. Vickery, F.

The **Spanish** tragedy. Kyd, T.

The **Spanish** wives. Pix, M.

Spared. Horovitz, I.

Sparks fly upward. See Lawrence, J. and Lee, R. E. Diamond orchid

Spastics. See Cerebral palsy

Speak of the devil. Sewell, G.

Speech

See also Phonetics

Speeches, addresses, etc.

y Fontaine, R. Graduation address

Speed-the-play. Ives, D.

The **spelling** bee. Vassallo, P.

The **spelling** of Coynes. Tasca, J.

Spence, Eulalie

Undertow

Set in early 20th century Harlem. Black couple's unhappy marriage further disrupted when husband's former mistress appears. 2m 3w 1 interior

In Black theatre USA [v1]; ed. by J. V. Hatch and T. Shine

Spencer, David

Hurricane roses

Television screens, soliloquy, inner monologues and hallucinations incorporated into drama about young British man battling cynically corrupt society. 2m 2w 1 setting

In Frontline intelligence 2; ed. by P. Edwardes

Spencer, Stanley, 1891-1959

Gems, P. Stanley

Spencer, Stuart

Blue stars

Limousine driver offers lonely housewife free trip. 2m 1w 1 interior

In The Best American short plays, 1993-1994

Water and wine

Deals with the identification of the Laocoon by Michelangelo Buonarroti and Giuliano Da Sangallo. 4m 1 interior

In Act One '95

In EST Marathon '95

Spiders

c Turner, J. The white spider's gift

Spiderwoman Theater

Sun Moon and Feather

Drama based on autobiographical stories of poor American Indian women. Background music. 3w 1 setting

In Contemporary plays by women of color; ed. by K. A. Perkins and R. Uno

Spies

Dunlap, W. André

Freed, D. Inquest

y Huff, B. Spy for a day

y Sodaro, C. Blind date

Stoppard, T. The dog it was that died

Stoppard, T. Hapgood

Stoppard, T. Neutral ground

Spike heels. Rebeck, T.

Spinsters. See Single women

The **spirit** of man: A hand witch of the second stage. Barnes, P.

The **spirit** of man: From sleep and shadow. Barnes, P.

The **spirit** of man: The night of the Sinhat [sic] Torah. Barnes, P.

Spirits

Chayefsky, P. The tenth man

Spiritualism

c Hanson, M. E. and Sheldon, D. P. Madame Zena's séance

Mead, K. After the child

Spiro, Peter

The juiceman cometh

Satire on health-consciousness set in juice bar. 3m 1w 1 interior

In Act One '95

Spite for spite. Moreto, A.

Spitting chips. Murray, P.

The **splendid** voyage of Kitty Doyle. McCullough, L. E.

Spoiled. Gray, S.

Spoils of war. Weller, M.

Spooks on strike! Priore, F. V.

Spoor, Keith

Everything under the sun. New Playwrights Network 1995 60p

Verse play with music. Galileo promotes theory that Earth orbits sun despite opposition from Catholic Church and the Inquisition. 2 acts 7 scenes epilogue 9m 2w

Sports

See also Television broadcasting of sports

Spreading the news. Gregory, L.

Spring awakening. Wedekind, F.

Spring dance. See Foote, H. The roads to home: Spring dance

Spring the king. Green, M.

Springtime. Fornes, M. I.

Spunk. Hurston, Z. N. (dramatization) See Wolfe, G. C. Story in Harlem slang

Spy for a day. Huff, B.

Squaring the circle. Stoppard, T.

Squashed. Young, P.

The **squire's** daughter. Bland, J.

Squirrels. Nigro, D.

Sroka, Jerry, and Fleming, John
Dying for laughs. French 1996 101p
Comedy. Television writing team gets more than bargained for when they become involved with dipsomaniac comedienne. 2 acts 4 scenes 5m 2w 1 interior

St. Germain, Mark
Camping with Henry & Tom. French 1995 83p
Henry Ford and Thomas Edison invite President Harding on camping trip in July 1921. 2 acts 4m 1 exterior

Camping with Henry & Tom (condensation)
In The Best plays of 1994-1995
See also Courts, R. Jack's holiday

St. James Infirmary. Enright, N.

St. John, Billy
13 past midnight. Bakers Plays 1994 87p
Comedy. Cast of TV soap opera gathers for murder mystery game party. 2 acts 5 scenes 7m 9w 1 interior

y Dogsbreath Devereaux, the dastardly doctor; or, Nurses! Foiled again! Pioneer Drama Service 1993 49p
Melodrama. Greedy, scheming doctor sets sights on rich widow. Variable cast 16 characters 1 interior

y The fiendish firebug strikes again! or, There'll be a hot time in the old town tonight. Pioneer Drama Service 1993 39p
Melodrama set 1915. Firefighter hero foils villainous factory owner. 7m 6w extras 1 setting

y Heaven help the po'taters! or, I'd-a-hoe the potatoes but they just won't grow. Pioneer Drama Service 1994 42p
Melodrama set in 1898 Idaho. Villainous lawyer withholds water rights from potato farmers during drought. 8 scenes 8m 8w 1b 4g extras

y Here comes the judge! Pioneer Drama Service 1993 56p
Comedy. Hostage situation takes place in courtroom presided over by zany judge. 2 acts 10m 12w extras 1 interior

Is there a comic in the house? French 1995 103p
Comedy set in boarding house for stand-up comics. 2 acts 6m 7w extras 1 interior

y Murder in the House of horrors. Pioneer Drama Service 1995 53p
Ancient Egyptian ruins setting for comic murder mystery revolving around stolen jewels. Audience participation. 2 acts 8m 7w extras 1 interior

y Peril on the high seas; or, "Let's get together and do launch." Pioneer Drama Service 1996 60p
Melodrama set in 1920s. Villains plot to kidnap heiress on ocean voyage. Background music, offstage voices. 2 acts 10 scenes 5m 9w extras 1 setting

Rubies: Heirlooms
Drama set in Birmingham, Alabama, spring of 1990. Twin sisters and their cousins attend high school reunion. 1 act 2m 4w 1 interior
In St. John, B. Rubies

Rubies: Little gems
Set in 1960 Birmingham, Alabama. Follows high school days of twin sisters and their cousins. 1 act 2m 4w 1 interior
In St. John, B. Rubies

St Nicholas. McPherson, C.

The **St.** Nicholas Hotel, Wm. Donnelly, prop. Reaney, J.

St. Petersburg (Russia)
See Saint Petersburg (Russia)

The **St.** Valentine's Day massacre. Knee, A.

Stage directions. Horovitz, I.

Stage struck. Gray, S.

Stages. Storey, D.

Stags and hens. Russell, W.

Staite, Jackie
c Cinderella - the sequel; or, "How I ran away to join a pirate ship and found true happiness." New Playwrights Network 1997 51p
Comedy pantomime. Cinderella decides Prince is boring and runs away to band of pirates. Prologue 2 acts 4 scenes Large mixed cast 2 exteriors

Goldilocks and the three Martians. New Playwrights Network 1996 62p
Pantomime. Goldilocks visits Mrs. Mars. Music, singing, 2 acts 6 scenes large mixed cast 1 interior 4 exteriors

Stalin, Joseph, 1879-1953
Chayefsky, P. The passion of Josef D.

The **stand**-in. Curran, K.

Standard of the breed. Steppling, J.

Standards & practices. Baitz, J. R.

Standing by. Barasch, N.

Standjofski, Harry
Anton
Dramatic comedy about wealth focusing on bourgeois family in 1989 Montreal. 15 scenes 2m 3w extras 1 setting
In Standjofski, H. Urban myths: Anton & No cycle

Standjofski, Harry—*Continued*
No cycle
Cycle of five stories on religious themes based on traditional Noh Theatre of Japan. Slide projections. Music, singing. 2m 3w 1 setting
In Standjofski, H. Urban myths: Anton & No cycle

Stanford, Janet
c Snow White—the purdiest gal in the West; a melodramatic comedy; music by Carol Gulley. French (London) 1997 39p
Melodramatic retelling of fairy tale set in Old West. Singing. 2 acts Variable cast 12 characters 1 setting

Stanley, Sir Henry Morton, 1841-1904
Gray, S. The rear column

Stanley. Gems, P.

The **Stanley** Parkers. Aron, G.

Stanton's Garage. Ackermann, J.

Star-gazy pie and sauerkraut. Stock, J.

Stardust melody. Avery, A.

Starhemberg, Heinrich von. See Gregor, Henry

Starlover. Yates, P.

Starosta, Stephen
The sausage eaters
Black comedy about family life. 2m 3w 1 interior
In The Best American short plays, 1992-1993

Star of Ethiopia. DuBois, W. E. B.

Star story. Gerke, P.

Stars. Linney, R.

The **stars** within. Schooleman, S. and Sewell, C.

The **state** of innocence and fall of man. Dryden, J.

Statements after an arrest under the immorality act. Fugard, A.

States of shock. Shepard, S.

Steele, Richard
The conscious lovers. Players Press 1996 62p
Romantic comedy about young man who does not wish to marry the woman his father has chosen for him. Songs. Prologue 5 acts 11 scenes epilogue 8m 5w 5 interiors 2 exteriors

Steelsmith, Mary
Wacs in khaki. Players Press 1996 18p
Experiences of three American army nurses. 3w

Stefanie hero. Medoff, M.

Stefanovski, Goran
Sarajevo: tales from a city
Impressionistic scenes of war-torn city. 41 scenes 6m 3w 1 setting
In Balkan blues: writing out of Yugoslavia; ed. by J. Labon

Stein, Gertrude
The mother of us all
Experimental theater piece about Susan B. Anthony. Singing. Prologue 2 acts 11 scenes Large mixed cast 1 setting
In Plays by American women, 1930-1960; ed. by J. E. Barlow

Three sisters who are not sisters
Experimental theater piece about murder. 3 acts 5 scenes 2m 3w 1 interior
In Around the world in 21 plays; ed. by L. Swortzell

About

Shotlander, S. Is that you Nancy?

Steinour, Marcus
At Land's End
Dying woman wants assurances that husband will remarry. 1m 1w 1 interior
In Off-Off Broadway Festival plays, 21st ser.

Stella. Goethe, J. W. von

Stembridge, Gerard
The gay detective. New Island Bks./Hern Bks. 1996 80p
Film noir-like exploration of loyalty, betrayal and sexual desire focusing on homosexual Dublin police sergeant. 2 acts 6m 1w 1 setting

Stempel, Herbert
Feffer, S. The wizards of quiz

The **Stendhal** syndrome. Strijards, F.

Stenning, Stephen. See Fo, D. Abducting Diana

Stephen & Mr. Wilde. Bartley, J.

Stephens, John
c The servant king. Moorley's 1993 27p
Religious drama about crucifixion of Christ. Singing. 6 scenes Large mixed cast

Stepping off a cloud. Cocek, C.

Steppling, John
My crummy job
Three losers in dead-end jobs. 2m 1w 1 setting
In Steppling, J. Sea of Cortez and other plays

Sea of Cortez
Drama about illness, family, pornography and lack of communication in contemporary society. 2 acts 7m 1w 1 setting
In Steppling, J. Sea of Cortez and other plays

Steppling, John—*Continued*
The shaper
Drama about failed dreams set in rundown California surfboard shop. 2 acts 14 scenes 3m 3w 1 setting
In Steppling, J. Sea of Cortez and other plays

Standard of the breed
Escaping failed relationship, young L.A. woman visits dog breeder's desert home outside Las Vegas. 2 acts 3m 2w 1 setting
In Steppling, J. Sea of Cortez and other plays

Stern, Philip Van Doren
It's a wonderful life (dramatization) See Rodgers, J. W. It's a wonderful life; Sharkey, T. M. It's a wonderful life

Sterne, Lawrence
The life and opinions of Tristram Shandy (dramatization) See Buchan, A. Conditional surrender

Sterner, Jerry
Other people's money: the ultimate seduction
Satire on capitalist mentality. Corporate raider attempts to take over moribund mom-and-pop company. 2 acts 4m 2w 2 interiors
In Best American plays: 9th series, 1983-1992

Sternheim, Carl
The bloomers
Variant title: The underpants. First play in author's trilogy about the Maske family. Comedy set in Germany. Middle class woman loses underpants, to the horror of her family. 4 acts 3m 2w 1 interior
In German expressionist plays; ed. by E. Schurer

Stetson, Jeff
The meeting
Meeting between Malcolm X and Martin Luther King, Jr. 1 act 3m 1 interior
In The National black drama anthology; ed. by W. King

Stevenson, Robert Louis
The strange case of Dr. Jekyll and Mr. Hyde (dramatization) See Slout, W. L. The trial of Dr. Jekyll

About

Stoll, D. Teller of tales

Parodies, imitations, etc.

Davis, R. The travelling Jekyll & Hyde show
c Lloyd, R. Treasure Island, the panto
y Reiser, D. Dr. Jekyll ... please don't hyde

The **steward** of Christendom. Barry, S.

Stichus. Plautus, T. M.

Stickland, Eugene
Some assembly required. Coteau Bks. 1995 71p
Black comedy. Christmas Eve with dysfunctional Canadian family. 2 acts 22 scenes 3m 2w 3 interiors

Stickney, Phyllis Yvonne
Big Momma 'n 'em
One actress portrays five different African American women. 1w
In Black comedy: nine plays; ed. by P. F. Jackson Karimah

Sticks and bones. Rabe, D.

Sticks and stones. Kukla, D.

Sticks and stones. McWeeney, D. and Swan, S.

Stigma. Mitterer, F.

Stiles, George
Moll Flanders; a musical; book by Claire Luckham; lyrics by Paul Leigh; music by George Stiles; based on the novel by Daniel Defoe. French (London) 1994 73p
Musical dramatization of Defoe's picaresque novel. Adventures of lusty and strong-willed woman in 17th century England. Music, singing. 2 acts 31 scenes 5m 4w extras 1 setting

Still, James
Jack and the wonder beans (dramatization) See Snipes, L. E. Jack and the wonder beans
See also McGovern, C. The ugly duck

Still life. Mann, E.

The **stillborn** lover. Findley, T.

A **stitch** in time. Rowan, A. A.

Stites, Kevin
c Adventures with young King Arthur; a musical for young audiences; book and lyrics by David Lewman; music by Kevin Stites. Dramatic 1995 54p
Musical. Merlin magically transports brother and sister back in time to teach young Arthur a lesson. 8 scenes 7m 2w 3 interiors 1 exterior

Stock, James
Blue night in the heart of the West
Innocent Scottish traveller falls into clutches of fiendish Iowa farm family. 2 acts 12 scenes 2m 2w extras 1 interior
In Stock, J. Star-gazy pie

Stock, James—*Continued*

Star-gazy pie and sauerkraut

Drama about eugenics ranging from 19th century Cornwall asylum and Nazi Germany to contemporary Cornish fishing village and California. Bankrupt fisherman with mentally handicapped son meets Germanic woman with similarly afflicted granddaughter. 2 acts 14 scenes 4m 4w extras 1 setting

In Stock, J. Star-gazy pie

Stock exchange

Wang, L. Junk bonds

The **stockbroker** and the fairy godmother. Leznoff, G.

Stoker, Bram

Dracula (dramatization) See Clapp, T. Dracula; Deane, H. Dracula (1924); Deane, H. and Balderston, J. L. Dracula: the vampire play (1927); Dietz, S. Dracula; Wellman, M. Dracula

Parodies, imitations, etc.

Bisson, P. When the clock strikes
Kelly, T. Renfield of the flies and spiders
Nigro, D. The Transylvanian clockworks
Wellman, M. Dracula

Stokle, Norman. See Lambert, L. Sunrise at noon

Stoll, David

Teller of tales; a musical adventure from the life of Robert Louis Stevenson; book and lyrics by Neil Wilkie; music by David Stoll. French 1996 199p (French's musical library)

Musical based on life of 19th century Scottish novelist, poet, and essayist. 2 acts 26 scenes 12m 7w 1g extras settings

Stone, Louis, 1871-1935

O'Donoghue, J. Abbie and Lou, Norman and Rose

Stone, Trude

Hello, Ma!

Telephone conversations between widow and her adult daughter. 2w 1 setting

In Stone, T. Hello, Ma! and other plays

One question

Comedy. Widow asks widower to marry her. 1m 1w 1 interior

In Stone, T. Hello, Ma! and other plays

She needs me

Comedy. Widow tries to convince neighbor to join her in Florida. 2w 1 interior

In Stone, T. Hello, Ma! and other plays

Whatever you say

Comedy. After fifty years of marriage woman wants divorce because of broken promise. 1m 1w 1 interior

In Stone, T. Hello, Ma! and other plays

A **stone** carver. Mastrosimone, W.

Stone soup. Thain, P.

The **stonemason.** McCarthy, C.

Stones and bones. McClinton, M.

The **stonewater** rapture. Wright, D.

Stoop. Wilson, L.

Stoppard, Tom

After Magritte

Satire. Three witnesses provide absurd explanation of mundane event. 3m 2w

In Stoppard, T. Plays: one
In Stoppard, T. The real Inspector Hound and other entertainments

Albert's bridge

Radio satire. Young philosophy graduate becomes obsessed with job as solitary bridge painter. Efficiency expert's attempt to compensate for flaw in painting schedule brings disaster. 10m 2w

In Stoppard, T. Plays: two

Another moon called Earth

Television play linking moral absolutes, meaning of history, marital problems and moon-landings. 3m 1w extras

In Stoppard, T. The television plays, 1965-1984

Arcadia. Faber & Faber 1993 97p

Dramatic comedy set in English country house concurrently in present day and 1809. Landscape gardening, poetry, chaos theory, sex, and the end of the world are among topics discussed in exploration of clash between classical order and romantic ardor. 2 acts 7 scenes 8m 3w 1 setting

—Same. French 1993 106p

Arcadia (condensation)

In The Best plays of 1994-1995

Artist descending a staircase

Radio satire. Ambiguous tape recording leads two old artists to mutual accusation of murdering third friend. Flashbacks reveal friends' modern art theories and love triangle involving blind girl. 6m 1w

In Stoppard, T. Plays: two

Dirty linen

Comedy lampooning House of Commons' investigations into sexual indiscretions of a number of members. 1 act 6m 2w 1 interior

In Stoppard, T. Plays: one
In Stoppard, T. The real Inspector Hound and other entertainments

The dissolution of Dominic Boot

Radio drama about desperation. Man runs up escalating taxi-fare and dashes about London in search of funds. 6m 4w

In Stoppard, T. Plays: two

Stoppard, Tom—*Continued*

The dog it was that died

Absurdist radio play about divided loyalties. Both English and Russians manipulate bewildered agent. 9m 3w

In Stoppard, T. Plays: two

Dogg's Hamlet, Cahoot's Macbeth

Two plays, both experimental adaptations of Shakespeare and dependent upon each other in performance, are linked together by sections exploring possibilities of language. 2 parts Large mixed cast 1 setting

In Stoppard, T. Plays: one

In Stoppard, T. The real Inspector Hound and other entertainments

Hapgood. Broadway ed. Faber & Faber 1997 77p

Woman who runs British counter-espionage agency searches for source of information leak. 2 acts 12 scenes 8m 1w 5 interiors 2 exteriors

Hapgood (condensation)

In The Best plays of 1994-1995

If you're Glad I'll be Frank

Radio satire. Man tries to rescue long-lost wife from efficiency-mad phone company where she is voice of time service. Interior monologues express her thoughts on time and personal entrapment. 7m 5w

In Stoppard, T. Plays: two

In the native state

Radio play set in colonial India and London explores cultural and political legacies India and England have given each other from 1930 to the present. 9m 4w extras

In Stoppard, T. Plays: two

Indian ink. Faber & Faber 1995 83p

Drama based on author's radio play In the native state about cultural and political legacies of colonialism. Follows lives of British poet, Indian artist and their descendents from 1930s India to 1980s London. 2 acts 11m 4w extras 2 interiors

—Same. French (London) 1995 82p

The invention of love. Faber & Faber 1997 106p

Scenes from life of homosexual poet and classical scholar A. E. Housman. 2 acts 19m 1w extras 1 setting

'M' is for moon among other things

Radio play about barren, middle-aged marriage. 1m 1w

In Stoppard, T. Plays: two

Neutral ground

Television play loosely based on Sophocles' Philoctetes. East-West intelligence organizations do battle. 6m 1w 1b extras

In Stoppard, T. The television plays, 1965-1984

New-found-land

Two Home Office officials consider case of American seeking British citizenship. 1 act 2m 1 interior

In Stoppard, T. Plays: one

In Stoppard, T. The real Inspector Hound and other entertainments

Professional foul

Television comedy. English philosophy professor in Prague for a convention encounters government repression: his former student is imprisoned for political dissent. 17m 1w 1b extras

In Stoppard, T. The television plays, 1965-1984

The real Inspector Hound

Farce. Two drama critics become involved on stage in a murder mystery play. 5m 3w 1 interior

In Stoppard, T. Plays: one

In Stoppard, T. The real Inspector Hound and other entertainments

A separate peace

Television play. Man seeking secure, restful, anonymous existence in nursing home is driven out by staff which cannot accept presence of admittedly healthy person. 19 scenes 2m 4w 2 interiors

In Stoppard, T. The television plays, 1965-1984

Squaring the circle

Television drama depicting the rise and fall of the Solidarity Movement in Poland. 11m extras

In Stoppard, T. The television plays, 1965-1984

Teeth

Television play. Cuckolded dentist extracts revenge on wife's lover. 2m 3w

In Stoppard, T. The television plays, 1965-1984

Where are they now?

Radio satire intercutting dinner at British school with reunion 24 years later. One "old boy" expresses memories of cruelty and unhappiness as exaggeratedly one-sided as others' happy nostalgia. 13m

In Stoppard, T. Plays: two

Storey, David, 1933-

Caring

Drama about conflict between life and art. Entertainers view their marriage as series of negotiations. 1m 1w 1 setting

In Storey, D. Plays: one

The contractor

Parable set in England about capitalism, social change and artistic creation. Workers painstakingly erect wedding tent. 3 acts 9m 3w 1 exterior

In Storey, D. Plays: two

Home

Mental home scene of conversation between two male and two female inmates. 2 acts 3 scenes 3m 2w 1 setting

In Storey, D. Plays: one

In celebration

Three educated sons of coal miner return to provincial Yorkshire home to celebrate parents' 40th anniversary. 2 acts 4 scenes 5m 2w 1 interior

In Storey, D. Plays: one

The march on Russia

Family tensions surface when three adult children

Storey, David, 1933—*Continued*
arrive to help parents celebrate their 60th anniversary. 2 acts 4 scenes 3m 3w 1 interior
In Storey, D. Plays: two

The restoration of Arnold Middleton
Provincial school master on verge of breakdown, is torn between dependence on wife and attraction to mother-in-law. 3 acts 6 scenes 2m 4w 1 interior
In Story, D. Plays: two

Stages
Following mental breakdown, working-class artist is visited by family, friends and memories of the past. 1m 4w 1 interior
In Storey, D. Plays: one

Storey, Raymond
The saints and apostles. Playwrights Canada 1993 91p
Contemporary love story set in Canada. Modern relationships and fear of intimacy in age of HIV infection. 2 acts 3m 2w 1 setting

The **storm.** See Fletcher, J. and Massinger, P. The sea voyage

Story in Harlem slang. Wolfe, G. C.

Storytelling
c Ayckbourn, A. My very own story
c Ayckbourn, A. This is where we came in
Baker, D. and Cocke, D. Red fox/second hangin'
c Lynch, M. Scheherazade
Mamet, D. Dodge
c Schurman-O'Connor, K. Ghoul Scout camp

Stowe, Harriet Beecher
Uncle Tom's cabin (dramatization) See Aiken, G. Uncle Tom's cabin
About
Alexander, R. I ain't yo' uncle
c McCaslin, N. Prelude to fame

Straight as a corkscrew. Peschina, H.

A **straight** shooter. McCaslin, N.

Stramm, August
Sancta Susanna
Expressionist drama dealing with erotic mysticism. Variable cast
In German expressionist plays; ed. by E. Schurer

Strand, Richard
The death of Zukasky
Farce. When sales associates find supervisor dead they scheme for his job. 7 scenes 4m 1w 1 interior
In A Decade of new comedy: plays from the Humana Festival v2

The **strange** case of Dr. Jekyll and Mr. Hyde. Stevenson, R. L. (dramatization) See Slout, W. L. The trial of Dr. Jekyll

The **strange** illness. Crump, R.

Strange interlude. O'Neill, E.

The **strangeness** of others. Ward, N.

Strangers don't drink coffee. Diyab, Mahmud

The **strangers** from the sea. Koch, K.

Strangers in the night. Pogos, A.

Strangers on Earth. O'Donnell, M.

Straparola, Giovani Francesco. See Francoeur, B. The enchantment of Beauty and the beast

Strauss, Botho
The tour guide
Symbolic drama. Middle-aged German teacher on sabbatical in Greece, has doomed affair with mysterious young tour guide. 2 acts 23 scenes 3m 3w
In DramaContemporary: Germany; ed. by C. Weber

The **straw** chair. Glover, S.

Streamers. Rabe, D.

Streep, Meryl
Cullen, A. Self catering

Street singers. See Singers

Street story. Jackson, K.

Street talk. McNally, T.

Strelich, Thomas
Dog logic. French 1993 86p
Black comedy set in California desert. Eccentric owner of run-down pet cemetery fights developers who want to turn property into shopping mall. 2 acts 8 scenes 2m 2w 1 exterior

Strijards, Frans
The Stendhal syndrome
Widow hosts funeral party for wealthy financier who has killed himself. 2 acts 6m 6w 1 interior
In Dutch and Flemish plays; ed. by D. Couling

Strikes and lockouts
Griffiths, T. Occupations
c Miranda, J. E. Cornerstone of civil rights
Oyamo. I am a man

Strindberg, August
Carl XII; tr. by Joe Martin
Expressionist drama about Sweden's doomed militarist King Karl XII. 5 acts Large mixed cast settings
In Strindberg, A. Strindberg—other sides

Strindberg, August—*Continued*
The dance of death; tr. by Joe Martin
Comprises first of a two-part drama. Frustrated army captain, stationed on isolated Swedish island, and his once promising ex-actress wife, approach silver wedding anniversary with mutual hatred. New officer's arrival precipitates ironic reconciliation. 4 acts 2m 1w extras 1 setting
In Strindberg, A. Strindberg—other sides
The ghost sonata; tr. by Joe Martin
Fantasy in symbolic form about the hidden guilt and failure of lives that lack the grace of God or man. 3 scenes 8m 7w extras 2 interiors 1 exterior
In Strindberg, A. Strindberg—other sides
Lucky Peter's journey (adaptation) See Swortzell, L. Lucky Peter's journey
Miss Julie; tr. by Truda Stockenström. Dee, I. R. 1996 62p
Tragedy. Social problems of class distinction in 19th century Sweden exemplified in the relations between wealthy young woman and her manservant. Singing and dancing chorus. 1 act 1m 2w extras 1 interior
Miss Julie (adaptation) See Marber, P. After Miss Julie
Pariah; tr. by Joe Martin
Drama of intellectual one-upmanship between murderer and blackmailer. 1 act 2m 1 interior
In Strindberg, A. Strindberg—other sides
The pelican; tr. by Joe Martin
Tragedy. Cruel mother, who mistreats son and daughter, and loves daughter's husband is forced into suicide when son sets house ablaze. The brother and sister also perish in the conflagration, but die experiencing their first happiness. 3 scenes 2m 3w 1 setting
In Strindberg, A. Strindberg—other sides
Simoom; tr. by Joe Martin
Set in Algeria ca. 1890. Arab girl destroys French soldier to avenge lover's death. 1 act 2m 1w 1 interior
In Strindberg, A. Strindberg—other sides
The stronger; tr. by Joe Martin
Social comedy. Wife versus "the other woman." 3w 1 interior
In Strindberg, A. Strindberg—other sides

About

Hayman, R. Playing the wife

The **Strip**. Nagy, P.

Strong-man's weak child. Horovitz, I.

The **stronger**. Strindberg, A.

Strongman meets his match. Hughes, V.

Stroppel, Frederick
Domestic violence
Comedy. Perfect wife drives husband away. 1m 1w 1 interior
In Stroppel, F. Single and proud & other plays
Fortune's fools. French 1995 107p
Comedic look at contemporary love and marriage. About-to-be wed couple watches as relationship develops between two members of wedding party. 2 acts 2m 2w 1 setting
A good man. French 1994 108p
Black comedy about funeral director's disastrous day. 2 acts 4 scenes 5m 4w 1 interior
The Mamet women
Comic power scene between two women written à la David Mamet. 2w 1 interior
In Stroppel, F. Single and proud & other plays
Morning coffee
Drama. Unmarried couple separates after five year relationship. 1m 1w 1 interior
In Stroppel, F. Single and proud & other plays
Package deal
Comedy. Battle of wits between film actress and conniving agent. 2w 1 interior
In Stroppel, F. Single and proud & other plays
Single and proud
Comedy. Young man, woman and 60-year-old grandmother attend singles seminar. 1m 3w 1 interior
In Stroppel, F. Single and proud & other plays

Stubbs, Norman
The patio window. French 1994 17p
Retired teacher returns to beloved home and garden after six month stay in nursing home. 2m 2w 1 interior

Stuck. Nunn, J.

Students
y Barrie, S. Carrying the calf
y Dias, E. J. Landslide for Shakespeare
Fuerstenberg, A. Blind dates
Landau, T. 1969
y Polsky, M. E. SATisfaction
y Sorensen, K. An endangered species: waking up
See also College students

Stumps. Medoff, M.

Sturges, Bob
Marius's mule. New Playwrights Network 1996 27p
Comedy. Foibles and infidelities of two Oxford dons. 3m 2w 1 interior

Sturner, Lynda
The death of Huey Newton
Husband and wife recall 1960s student activism. 1m 1w 1 interior
In Facing forward; ed. by L. D. Frank

The **Sty** of The Blind Pig. Dean, P. H.

A **stye** of the eye. Durang, C.

Styx and Bones. Dickinson, S.

Suarez, Roberto Rodriguez
The betrothal (El-Casorio)
Drama about arranged marriage in rural Puerto Rican fishing village. 3 acts 3m 7w extras
In Nuestro New York; ed. by J. V. Antush

Substance abuse
y Kukla, D. Sticks and stones

The **substance** of fire. Baitz, J. R.

Subtle bodies. Barker, C.

Surburban life
Gurney, A. R. The rape of Bunny Stuntz
White, P. The season at Sarsaparilla

SubUrbia. Bogosian, E.

Subways
Baraka, A. Dutchman

Such great hope. Aba, N.

Such things are. Inchbald, Mrs.

Such things only happen in books. Wilder, T.

Suddenly, a foot. Sloate, D.

Suicide
Barnes, D. The death of life
Barnes, D. Humour helps
Beard, P. Cliff's edge
Behrman, S. N. The cold wind and the warm
Boucicault, D. Octoroon
Brown, B. All things considered
Cocteau, J. Les parents terribles (Indiscretions)
Connolly, H. Overtime
Foote, H. The young man from Atlanta
Gilroy, F. D. Match point
Granville-Barker, H. Waste
Gray, S. Man in a side-car
Groves, W. Good night, sweet mother
Gurney, A. R. Richard Cory
Horovitz, I. One under
Ibsen, H. Rosmersholm
Learner, T. The glass mermaid
Linney, R. The love suicide at Schofield Barracks
Mead, K. This common bond
Miller, A. Death of a salesman
Miller, J. A light on the landing
Nelson, G. Castrato
Pintauro, J. Fiat
Sherman, J. M. Women and Wallace
y Slaight, B. High tide
Soyinka, W. Death and the King's Horseman
Strijards, F. The Stendhal syndrome
Strindberg, A. The pelican
Ward, N. Apart from George
Way, C. Paradise Drive
Weller, M. Fishing
Wiechmann, B. Feeding the moonfish
Wilde, O. The Duchess of Padua

A **suitable** case for treatment. Mercer, D.

Sullivan, Sir Arthur, 1842-1900
The Mikado (adaptation) See Smolensky, S. and Waldrop, J. The Mikado

Sumatra (Indonesia)
Inchbald, Mrs. Such things are

Summer, Andrea
c The just so letter. New Playwrights Network 1996 18p
Set in Neolithic times. Comedy based on Rudyard Kipling's How the first letter was written from his Just so stories. 7m 7w extras 1 setting

Summer. Martin, J.

Summer folk. See Gorky, M. The summer people

Summer homes
Gurney, A. R. What I did last summer

The **summer** people. Gorky, M.

Sun Moon and Feather. Spiderwoman Theater

Sunday afternoon. Mamet, D.

Sunday dinner. Jennings, C. S.

A **Sunday** morning in the South. Johnson, G. D.

Sunday on the rocks. Rebeck, T.

Sunde, Karen
Haiti (a dream)
Haitian husband and wife in overcrowded sailboat journeying toward Florida. 2 scenes 2m 2w 1 setting
In Facing forward; ed. by L. D. Frank

Sunken treasure. See Buried treasure

Sunrise at noon. Lambert, L.

Sunset Boulevard. Lloyd Webber, A.

Sunsets and glories. Barnes, P.

Sunshine. Mastrosimone, W.

Suntep Theatre
y Wheel of justice
Satire in form of television game show. Christopher Columbus tried by Canadian Indians for discovering North America. Variable cast 12 characters 1 setting
In Eureka! ed by J. J. Lewis and D. Warren

Super Dooper Man. Hatton, T. J.

Supernatural
Bennett, T. Dark rituals
Gifford, B. Mrs. Kashfi
Hughes, T. The wound
McPherson, C. The weir

Superstition
MacDonald, A.-M. The Arab's mouth
Mitterer, F. Stigma
O'Casey, S. Cock-a-doodle dandy
Sutherland, E. Edufa
See also Exorcism

Supple, Tim
c Grimm tales. Faber & Faber 1996 128p
Dramatization of eight fairy tales from The Brothers Grimm as adapted by Carol Ann Duffy. Music. 4m 3w

Suppliant women. Euripides

Supreme Court. See United States—Supreme Court

Al Surayyiʿ, ʿAbd al-ʿAziz
The bird has flown; tr. by Salwa Jabsheh and Thomas G. Ezzy
Drama about differences between European and traditional Arabic culture. Son of Arab father and Anglo-Indian mother travels from England to meet Kuwaiti family. 3 acts 6 scenes 7m 4w 1 interior 1 exterior
In Modern Arabic drama; ed. by S. K. Jayyusi and R. Allen

Sure thing. Ives, D.

Surface, Mary Hall
c The reluctant dragon. Anchorage Press 1997 66p
Based on story by Kenneth Grahame. Boy helps peace-loving dragon avoid battle with St. George. Singing. 10 scenes 5m 2w 1b 2 exteriors
c The sorcerer's apprentice. Anchorage Press 1994 45p
Sorcerer and apprentice must learn to use their magical powers wisely. 4 scenes Unidentified cast 6 characters 1 interior

A **surgeon** for Lucinda. Scotland, J.

Surgery, Plastic
Oglesby, T. Two lips indifferent red

Surrealism
Bamford, S. The answer
Bynum, R. C. Live-in witnesses
Bynum, R. C. The monkey palace
Chinn, J. Something to remember you by
Dallman, J. The inside story of Dr. Crippen
Gonzalez, R. The boiler room
Green, M. Dreams of a drunken Quaker
Harding, M. Hubert Murray's widow
Kemp, J. The black sequin dress
Languirand, J. Autumn violins
Oates, J. C. Ontological proof of my existence
Parks, S. L. Imperceptible mutabilities in the Third Kingdom
Scanlon, P. What is this everything?
Shepard, S. Red Cross
Sloate, P. Countess in Courtland
Sloate, D. Suddenly, a foot
Walker, G. F. Theatre of the film noir
Warner, F. Lying figures
See also Experimental theater

Surrounded by water. Garnhum, K.

Survival (after airplane accidents, shipwrecks, etc.)
Firth, T. Neville's Island
Fletcher, J. The sea voyage
y Olfson, L. The admirable Crichton
O'Neill, E. Fog
O'Neill, E. Thirst

The **survivor:** a Cambodian odyssey. Lipsky, J.

Sussman, David
c Mystery of the phantom voice. Pioneer Drama Service 1996 29p
Children learn how sound travels by meeting Alexander Graham Bell and Guglielmo Marconi. Singing. 5m 3w 1 setting

Sutherland, Efua
Edufa
Tragedy. Man's attempt to help beloved ailing wife stirs up conflict between superstitious tribal beliefs and modern medicine. Singing speaking chorus. Prologue 3 acts 9 scenes 4m 3w extras 1 interior
In Crosswinds; ed. by W. B. Branch

Sutton, Joe
Voir dire. Dramatists 1996 80p
Racial issues engulf New York jury as it deliberates case of prominent black man accused of buying crack. Prologue 7 scenes epilogue 1m 5w extras 1 interior

Suzie Goo: private secretary. Gilbert, S.

Svanoe, Bill
Punch and Judy. Dramatists 1996 60p
Comedy about friendship that develops between recently divorced socialite and unsuccessful woman author she employs to help her write novel. 2 acts 6 scenes 3w 1 interior

Swados, Elizabeth
Esther
Musical retelling the Purim story of how Esther saved the Jews from the evil Haman. 2 acts 3m 3w extras 1 setting
In Fruitful and multiplying; ed. by E. Schiff

The **swaggering** soldier. See Plautus, T. M. The braggart soldier

Swajeski, Donna Marie
c The revolution machine. Players Press 1996 20p
Musical profile of John Dickinson, who refused to sign Declaration of Independence, but helped write U.S. Constitution. 3m 3w

Swan, Anna, 1846-1888
Vingoe, M. Living curiosities: a story of Anna Swan

Swan, Scott. See McWeeny, D. jt. auth.

The **swan.** Egloff, E.

Swan song. Chekhov, A.

Swans flying. Pintauro, J.

Swartz, L. Don
y Halloween dreams. Bakers Plays 1993 92p
Fear of serial killer puts damper on farm family's Halloween festivities. 2 acts 4 scenes 9m 6w 1 interior

y Halloween screams. French 1995 114p
Comic thriller. Theater group transforms community center's basement into Halloween spook house. 2 acts 5 scenes 2m 1w 1g extras 1 interior

Swedeen, Staci
The sleep seeker
Mother's death and unbearable guilt lead to woman's breakdown. 1m 5w 1 setting
In Facing forward; ed. by L. D. Frank

Sweden
Social life and customs
Strindberg, A. Miss Julie

Sweet, Jeffrey
American enterprise (condensation)
In The Best plays of 1993-1994

The value of names
Drama set in present about lingering effect of Hollywood blacklist on two performers; one testified against the other before House Committee on Un-American Activities. 2m 1w 1 exterior
In 20/20: twenty one-act plays from twenty years of the Humana Festival
In Fruitful and multiplying; ed. by E. Schiff

With and without. Dramatists 1997 68p
Husband and wife's intervention in friends marriage reveals fault lines in their own. 4 scenes 2m 2w 1 setting

Sweet and hot. Arlen, H.

The **sweet** by 'n' by. Higgins, F.

Sweet Eros. McNally, T.

Sweet panic. Poliakoff, S.

Sweet Phoebe. Gow, M.

Sweet revenge. Durbridge, F.

Sweet Rose of Old Aldgate. Sharrocks, M.

Sweet table at the Richelieu. Ribman, R.

Swift, Jonathan, 1667-1745
O'Donovan, J. The fiddler and the Dean
Parodies, imitations, etc.
Wilder, T. Youth

Swift, Robert
y Attack of the giant grasshoppers; or, "Leaf me alone." Pioneer Drama Service 1993 27p
Parody of horror movies. High school is invaded by giant grasshoppers. 2 scenes 8m 13w extras 1 interior

y Dirty work on the trail; or, Go slow with the Pony Express. Pioneer Drama Service 1993 41p
Melodrama. Cowboy hero foils villain's plan to defraud Pony Express. 2 scenes 4m 8w extras 1 setting

y The Hunchback of Notre Dame goes West; or "Oh, bury me not in old Paree." Pioneer Drama Service 1993 25p
Comedy. High School production of Hunchback of Notre Dame becomes intertwined with Western spoof. 2 scenes 7m 14w extras

y The paper bag bandit rides again; or, ... Behind the cheap mask. Pioneer Drama Service 1994 27p
Melodrama. Sheriff impersonates bandit. 3 scenes 7m 13w extras 1 setting

y Rascals under the big top; or, The ring's around Miss Rosie. Pioneer Drama Service 1995 25p
Melodrama set in Wild West. Roustabout saves circus from unscrupulous ringmaster. Background music. 7m 15w extras

Swimmers. Martini, C.

Swimming
c Martini, C. Swimmers

Swindlers and swindling
Middleton, T. Michaelmas Term
Wilder, T. Queens of France

Swine. Turrini, P.

Swingers. Beard, P.

Swinging on a star. Burke, J.

Swintz, Martha
c Panic in the palace
Confusion reigns at princess' first birthday celebration. 7m 5w extras 1 interior
In Thirty plays from favorite stories; ed. by S. E. Kamerman

Switching places. Deverell, R.

Swoop. Wellman, M.

Swortzell, Lowell
c Jack Fuggler
Adaptation of anonymous 16th century English interlude about abuse of power. Hapless servant manipulated by trickster. 3m 2w 1 exterior
In Around the world in 21 plays; ed. by L. Swortzell

c The love of three oranges
Adaptation of 1761 scenario of fairy tale play by Carlo Gozzi. Prince overcomes witch's spell. 2 acts 6 scenes 6m 5w extras
In Around the world in 21 plays; ed. by L. Swortzell

y Lucky Peter's journey
Freely adapted from Strindberg's allegory. Innocent young man on quest of self-discovery. 7 scenes 17m 4w extras 4 interiors 3 exteriors
In Around the world in 21 plays; ed. by L. Swortzell

c Punch and Judy: their tragical comedy, their comical tragedy
Adaptation of traditional puppet play. Punch battles the Devil and is reunited with Judy. 12 characters
In Around the world in 21 plays; ed. by L. Swortzell

c A visit from St. Nicholas; or, The night before Christmas
Story of the creation of Clement Moore's 1822 Christmas classic. 2m 4w 1 interior
In Around the world in 21 plays; ed. by L. Swortzell

Sydney (Australia)
Christian, B. Blue murder
White, P. Big toys
White, P. A cheery soul
White, P. The season at Sarsaparilla

Sylvanus, Erwin
Leo Baeck. Lang, P. 1996 151p (Literature and the sciences of man v10)
Radio play about faith and endurance of Rabbi Baeck while prisoner in Theresienstadt. 9m extras

Sylvia. Gurney, A. R.

Sylvia's wedding. Chinn, J.

Symbolism
Barnes, D. Five thousand miles
Barnes, D. Three from the earth
Bernier, E. The seven streams of the River Ota
Bond, E. Coffee
Bonner, M. O. The purple flower
Brustein, R. The wild duck
Césaire, I. The ship
Chekhov, A. The seagull
Diyab, Mahmud. Strangers don't drink coffee
Farag, A. 'Ali Janah al-Tabrizi and his servant Quffa
Foote, A. The land of the astronauts
Foote, A. The one-armed man
Friel, B. Wonderful Tennessee
Gala, A. The Bells of Orleans
Guare, J. Marco Polo sings a solo
Haubold, C. The big black Box
Havel, V. Temptation
Hill, G. Brand
Ibsen, H. The master builder
Ibsen, H. The wild duck
Kennedy, A. Funnyhouse of a Negro
Mac Intyre, T. Sheep's milk on the boil
MacLeod, J. The Hope slide
MacNeice, L. One for the grave
Madách, I. The tragedy of man
Maguire, M. The tower
Mahfuz, 'Isam. The China tree
Mercer, D. Duck song
Nelson, T. B. Eye of God
Nemeth, S. Water play
O'Neill, E. The great God Brown
Rabe, D. The orphan
Sanchez, E. Icarus
Shepard, S. Chicago
Shepard, S. Icarus's mother
Solórzano, C. Crossroads
Strauss, B. The tour guide
Strindberg, A. The pelican
Toller, E . Masses and man
Turrini, P. Death and the Devil
Yeats, W. B. The Countess Cathleen
See also Expressionism

Synagogues
Chayefsky, P. The tenth man

Synge, John Millington
The playboy of the Western World. Players Press 1966 68p
Folk comedy about Irish peasant life. Young braggart who thinks he killed his father is made much of in remote village to which he flees, but is ultimately deflated. Singing. 3 acts 7m 5w extras 1 interior

—Same
In Great Irish plays
In The Playboy of the Western World and two other Irish plays; ed. by W. A. Armstrong

Synge, John Millington—*Continued*
Riders to the sea
Tragedy about relentless malignity of the sea toward Irish fisherfolk. 1m 3w extras 1 interior
In Great Irish plays

Syphilis
Ibsen, H. Ghosts

Szilágyi, Andor
Unsent letters
Surreal love story. Two people meet, fall in love, then part. 2 acts 9 scenes 1m 1w 1 setting
In Hungarian plays; ed. by L. Upor

Szumigalski, Anne
Z: a meditation on opprression, desire and freedom. Coteau Bks. 1995 68p
Theatrical piece about Holocaust set in concentration camp during World War II and in memorial garden in 1960s. Incorporates poetry, music and dance. Prologue 2 acts 2m 3w extras 1 setting

Szyszkowitz, Gerald
Commander Carrigan
Drama set 1961 in Saigon airport terminal about growing American involvement in Vietnam. 1 act 8 scenes 4m 1 interior
In Szyszkowitz, G. Five plays

Comrade Briggemann
Drama set in Halle, East Germany. Portrays lives of group of intellectuals shortly after construction of Berlin Wall and then thirty years later, following collapse of communism. 2 acts 13 scenes 3m 1w 1 interior
In Szyszkowitz, G. Five plays

Friedemann Puntigam; or, The delicate art of losing one's memory
Austrian folk play. Woman comes to terms with Austria's World War II legacy. 7 acts 32 scenes 14m 2w extras
In Anthology of contemporary Austrian folk plays

Grillparzer; or, The three sisters
Tragicomedy set in Vienna 1826 to 1830. Three sisters secretly hope to wed famous Austrian writer. 5 acts 20 scenes 2m 3w 2 interiors
In Szyszkowitz, G. Five plays

Lake of illusions
Five Austrian women struggle to shape successful careers. 5 acts 28 scenes 5w 1 interior 2 exteriors
In Szyszkowitz, G. Five plays

Somewhere over the rainbow
Drama set in Central Europe. Waitress embarks on life of sex, lies and murder. 7 acts 9m 7w 1 setting
In Szyszkowitz, G. Five plays

T

T-Money & Wolf. Willmott, K. and Averill, R.

Table for one? Haywood, C.

The **table,** the donkey and the stick. Mahlmann, L. and Jones, D. C.

Tabori, George
Mein Kampf
Allusions, Biblical legends, Talmudic arguments, folklore and elements of silent movie farce combine in drama about Hitler's early years in Vienna as struggling artist. 5 acts 4m 2w extras 1 interior
In DramaContemporary: Germany; ed. by C. Weber

The **Tack** Room. Arzoomanian, R.

Tagore, Rabindranath
Chitra
Lyrical drama based on story from the Mahabharata about physical and spiritual beauty in relationship between man and woman. 3m 1w extras
In Tagore, R. The collected poems and plays

The cycle of spring
King, beset by problems, looks to traditional drama for inspiration. Singing. Prelude 4 acts Large mixed cast 1 setting
In Tagore, R. The collected poems and plays

Karna and Kunti
Symbolist drama based on episode from Sanskrit epic Mahabharata about chance encounter between mother and son. 1m 1w 1 setting
In Tagore, R. The collected poems and plays

The king and the queen
King faces rebellion and queen's displeasure. 2 acts 9m 3w 1 setting
In Tagore, R. The collected poems and plays

Malini
Religious differences divide kingdom. 2 acts 2m 3w 2 exteriors
In Tagore, R. The collected poems and plays

The Post Office; tr. by Krishna Dutta and Andrew Robinson. St. Martin's Press 1996 52p
Young boy in India, confined to his bedroom with an incurable disease, dreams of worldly adventures. 2 acts 8m 1b 1g extras 1 interior
—Same
In Tagore, R. The collected poems and plays

Sacrifice
Drama depicting sacrifice as ritual propitiation and death as triumphal new beginning. 4m 1w 1g extras 1 interior
In Tagore, R. The collected poems and plays

Tagore, Rabindranath—*Continued*
Sanyasi; or, The ascetic
Hindu ascetic observes villagers mundane concerns. Variable cast 1 setting
In Tagore, R. The collected poems and plays

Taikeff, Stanley
Dolorosa Sanchez
Drama student's performance inadvertently dramatizes Aristotlean principles for professor. 1m 1w 1 interior
In Off-Off Broadway Festival plays, 21st ser.

Tailoring
Grumberg, J.-C. The workroom

Take a giant step. Peterson, L.

Takeda, Izumo. See Yoshitsune and the thousand cherry trees

Taking liberties. Carley, D.

Taking sides. Harwood, R.

Talbot, Matthew, 1865-1952
Kilroy, T. Talbot's box

Talbot's box. Kilroy, T.

The **tale** of Peter Rabbit. Mahlmann, L. and Jones, D. C.

The **tale** of Peter Rabbit. See Harris, A. Peter Rabbit and me

A **tale** of two cities. Francis, M.

A **tale** of two cities. Hackett, W.

A **tale** of two cities. Johanson, R.

A **tale** of two cities. Ross, D.; Parker, N. and Mullane, M.

A **tale** told. See Wilson, L. Talley & Son

The **talent** show. Pflomm, P. N.

The **talented** tenth. Wesley, R.

Tales from the shtetl: the Sholom Aleichem show. Ravel, A.

Tales of King Arthur. Chambers, J.

Tales of the lost Formicans. Congdon, C.

The **talk.** Pugliese, F.

Talk about love! Emond, P.

Talk radio. Bogosian, E.

Talk-story. Barroga, J.

Talking bones. Youngblood, S.

The **talking** dog. Guare, J.

Talking in tongues. Pinnock, W.

Talking pictures. Foote, H.

Talking with ... Martin, J.

Tall Betsy and the crackerbarrel tales. Wheeler, J. and Hartsfield, M. G.

Tall tales. Schenkkan, R.

Talley & Son. Wilson, L.

Tamer of horses. Mastrosimone, W.

Tangled garden. Crawford, D. W.

Tangled web. Booth, J.

Tannen, Deborah
An act of devotion
Elderly Jewish man and daughter visit Warsaw and explore family history. 1m 1w 1 interior
In The Best American short plays, 1993-1994

Tape. Rivera, J.

Tape recorders
Rivera, J. Tape

Tarchetti, Iginio Ugo
Fosca (dramatization) See Sondheim, S. Passion

Tarkington, Booth
Monsieur Beaucaire (dramatization) See Olfson, L. Monsieur Beaucaire

Tartuffe: born again. Thomas, F.

Tasca, Jules
Deus-X
Black comedy. Scientist discovers gland in brain that determines whether or not one is religious. 4m 2w 1 interior
In Tasca, J. Outrageous! and other comedies

Extraction
Black comedy. Dentists react violently when vaccine is discovered to eliminate tooth decay. 3m 1w extra 1 interior
In Tasca, J. Outrageous! and other comedies

Gums
Comedy about senior citizens' football league. 2m 1 setting
In Tasca, J. Outrageous! and other comedies

Italian rum cake
Comedy. Wives of two rival mob bosses enter baking contest causing trouble for local politician serving as judge. 7m 3w
In Tasca, J. Outrageous! and other comedies

Tasca, Jules—*Continued*
Make-up
Satire. Candidate for senator made-over by two slick political advisors. 2m 1w 1 interior
In Tasca, J. Outrageous! and other comedies

A modern proposal
Satire set in year 2075. Because of over-population hungry people are eating priests and missionaries. 1m 1 interior
In Tasca, J. Outrageous! and other comedies

Outrageous
Arson results when black family moves into white suburban Boston neighborhood. 7m 1w 1 setting
In Tasca, J. Outrageous! and other comedies

The spelling of Coynes
Comedy. Hoping to inherit her money, housepainter schemes to marry 80-year-old woman. 1m 2w 1 interior
In The Best American short plays, 1994-1995

Tassi, Agostino, ca. 1580-1644
Clark, S. Life without instruction

Tasso, Torquato, 1544-1595
Goethe, J. W. von. Torquato Tasso

Tattooing
Ross, J. Anne Marie's bedroom

Tax evasion
Chayefsky, P. The latent heterosexual

Taxicabs
Pinter, H. Victoria Station
Stoppard, T. The dissolution of Dominic Boot

Taylor, Ariette, and Devenish, Luke
Disturbing the dust. Currency Press in association with Playbox Theatre Centre 1994 51p
Memory play. Elderly English ballerina looks back on life of acclaim. 3m 5w 1 setting

Taylor, Drew Hayden
Someday. Fifth House 1993 81p
Drama set in Ojibwa community in central Ontario. Mother and daughter, separated by children's aid workers 35 years ago, reunited at Christmastime. 2 acts 1m 3w 1 interior 1 exterior

Taylor, Peter
Familiar haunts
Brother and sister visited by ghost of dead father. 1 act 2m 1w 1 interior
In Taylor, P. The oracle at Stoneleigh Court

Missing person
Mother and father visited by ghost of son killed in action. 1 act 2m 1w 1 interior
In Taylor, P. The oracle at Stoneleigh Court

A redheaded man
Daughter's ghost facilitates reconciliation between old man and illegitimate grandson. 1 act 3m 1w 1 interior
In Taylor, P. The oracle at Stoneleigh Court

Taylor, Regina
Between the lines
Set from late 1970s to present, scenes follow lives of two college friends. 46 scenes 3m 5w extras settings
In Humana Festival '95

Inside the belly of the beast
Exploration of contemporary African American life. Prologue 1 act 14 scenes 3m 5w 1 setting
In Taylor, R. The ties that bind

Love poem #98
Film noir-type scene about married man's obsession with prostitute. Variable cast 3 characters 1 setting
In Actors Theatre of Louisville. Two-minute plays: v3

Mudtracks
Three generations of African American women victimized by men. 1 act 16 scenes 4m 3w 1 setting
In EST marathon, 1994

Watermelon rinds
Originally produced as part of double bill titled Various small fires. Absurdist comedy about African American family politics. 6 scenes 3m 5w 1 interior
In The Best American short plays, 1992-1993
In A Decade of new comedy: plays from the Humana Festival v2
In Humana Festival '93
In Taylor, R. The ties that bind

Taylor, Renée, and Bologna, Joseph
Acts of love and other comedies
Six comic vignettes about contemporary romance. 5m 4w extras
In Taylor, R. and Bologna, J. Love allways

Barry, Betty and Bill
Comedy. Estranged husband interrupts wife's date. 2m 1w 1 interior
In The Best American short plays, 1993-1994

Comedies in apple blossom time
Presented on television under title: Three for two. Three short romantic comedies. 4m 3w extras
In Taylor, R. and Bologna, J. Love allways

Taylor, Renée, and Bologna, Joseph— *Continued*
Love allways
Five comic vignettes about middle-aged lovers. 6m 5w
In Taylor, R. and Bologna, J. Love allways
Manhattan love songs—Bronx cheers
Comedy exploring four relationships in contemporary New York. 6m 4w
In Taylor, R. and Bologna, J. Love allways
Paradise follies
Five brief romantic comedies set in island vacation spots. 9m 6w extras
In Taylor, R. and Bologna, J. Love allways

Tea. Houston, V. H.

Tea in a china cup. Reid, C.

Teachers
Adamov, A. Professor Taranne
Beber, N. Misreadings
Bennett, A. Forty years on
Chinn, J. After September
c Cole, J. D. Ichabod
Donnelly, N. The duty master
Gray, S. Quartermaine's terms
Gray, S. Spoiled
Hampton, C. The philanthropist
Hare, D. Slag
Harvey, J. Babies
Horovitz, I. Park your car in Harvard Yard
Linney, R. F.M.
Rattigan, T. The Browning version
Reilly, C. Astronauts
Shaw, B. Pygmalion
Storey, D. The restoration of Arnold Middleton
Townsend, S. Groping for words
Trenholme, H. Fell blow
Wilde, P. What's wrong with angry?
See also College teachers

Teagarden, Jay
Birds. New Playwrights Network 1995 29p
In parallel stories set in present and in 19th century Cornwall. Shamanistic rituals help victims of sexual abuse. 1 act 8 sections Variable cast 9 characters
Letting Lucinda down. New Playwrights Network 1995 31p
Comedy. Upwardly mobile professional couple discover strange girl in their house. 1 act 2m 2w 1 interior

Tears of a dinosaur. Brooker, B.

The **tears** of my sister. Foote, H.

Technology and civilization
Kaiser, G. Gas I
Kaiser, G. Gas II
Shepard, S. Operation sidewinder
Witkiewicz, S. I. They

Teenagers. See Youth

Teens in Tinseltown. Christiansen, A.

Teeth. Stoppard, T.

Teeth 'n' smiles. Hare, D.

Telephone
Durang, C. 1-900-desperate
Rosenthal, A. Lifelines
Stone, T. Hello, Ma!
Stoppard, T. If you're Glad I'll be Frank

Telephone counseling. See Hotlines (Telephone counseling)

Televangelists
Thomas, F. Tartuffe: born again

Television
Brittney, L. Have a nice day
Rebeck, T. The family of Mann
Ribman, R. Buck
Sroka, J. and Fleming, J. Dying for laughs
Williams, N. Harry and me

Television broadcasting of sports
Buzo, A. The Roy Murphy show

Television plays
Barnes, P. Bye bye Columbus
Barnes, P. More than a touch of Zen
Barnes, P. Nobody here but us chickens
Barnes, P. Not as bad as they seem
Barnes, P. Revolutionary witness
Barnes, P. The spirit of man: A hand witch of the second stage
Barnes, P. The spirit of man: From sleep and shadow
Barnes, P. The spirit of man: The night of the Sinhat [sic] Torah
Berkoff, S. Dahling you were marvellous
Bond, E. Olly's prison
y Bond, E. Tuesday
Chayefsky, P. The bachelor party
Chayefsky, P. The big deal
Chayefsky, P. Holiday song
Chayefsky, P. Marty
Chayefsky, P. The mother
Chayefsky, P. Printer's measure
y Foote, H. The dancers
Foote, H. The tears of my sister
Foote, H. Tomorrow
Foote, H. The trip to Bountiful [television play]

Television plays—*Continued*
Gifford, B. Blackout
Gifford, B. Mrs. Kashfi
Gifford, B. Tricks
Gray, S. The caramel crisis
Gray, S. Man in a side-car
Gray, S. Pig in a poke
Gray, S. Plaintiffs and defendants
Gray, S. Sleeping dog
Gray, S. Spoiled
Gray, S. Two Sundays
Griffiths, T. Hope in the year two
Hare, D. Licking Hitler
Hare, D. Saigon: year of the cat
Harwood, R. The guests
Havel, V. Audience
Havel, V. Unveiling
Legg, R. Oscar: the Oscar Wilde trials of 1895
Margulies, D. Pitching to the star
Mercer, D. An afternoon at the festival
Mercer, D. The bankrupt
Mercer, D. The cellar and the almond tree
Mercer, D. Emma's time
Mercer, D. Find me
Mercer, D. Huggy bear
Mercer, D. On the eve of publication
Mercer, D. A suitable case for treatment
Mercer, D. Where the difference begins
Minghella, A. What if it's raining?
Pinter, H. Monologue
Pinter, H. Party time
Poliakoff, S. She's been away
Potter, D. Blue remembered hills
Potter, D. Cold Lararus
Potter, D. Cream in my coffee
Potter, D. Joe's ark
Potter, D. Karaoke
Potter, D. Pennies from heaven
Saunders, J. Birthday
Saunders, J. Fashion
Saunders, J. France
Saunders, J. Iso tank
Saunders, J. Magazine
Stoppard, T. Another moon called Earth
Stoppard, T. Neutral ground
Stoppard, T. Professional foul
Stoppard, T. A separate peace
Stoppard, T. Squaring the circle
Stoppard, T. Teeth

Television programs
Bartram, F. Tiddley pum
y Bush, M. Rockway Cafe
Durang, C. The Book of Leviticus Show
y Kelly, T. Bang! Bang! You're dead
Larbey, B. A small affair
y McCullough, L. E. "You're live with Bigfoot Wallace"
Robertson, H. W. Mina tonight!
Rosei, P. Blameless
St. John, B. 13 past midnight

Tell it to women. Onwueme, O. T.

Teller of tales. Stoll, D.

Telling tales. Cruz, M.

Temperance
Smith, W. H. The drunkard

The **temple.** Nowra, L.

Temptation. Havel, V.

The **temptations** of Jesus. Joseph, C. M.

Ten dilemmas. Barker, H.

Ten-dollar drinks. Pintauro, J.

Ten lost years. Winter, J. and Smith, C.

Tenants. See Landlord and tenant

Tennessee
Linney, R. Sand Mountain
y Medoff, M. Big Mary

Tennessee. Linney, R.

Tent meeting. Larson, L.; Lee, L. and Wackler, R.

The **tenth** man. Chayefsky, P.

Tenure. Wine, B.

Tenure track. Kraus, J. H. and Woodward, G.

Terminal Cafe. Tuttle, J.

Terminal hip. Wellman, M.

Terminal terror. Burns, K.

A **terrible** tale of a dreaded dragon. Liebert, B.

Terrorism
Blessing, L. Two rooms
Fo, D. Trumpets and raspberries
McLaughlin, T. Greatest hits
Parra, M. A. de la. Secret obscenities
Yourgrau, T. The song of Jacob Zulu

Terry, J. E. Harold, and Rose, Arthur
The return of Sherlock Holmes (adaptation) See Dudley, E. The return of Sherlock Holmes

Terry, Megan
Breakfast serial
Exploration of gender roles. Violent youth preys on young boys. 1m 3w 1 exterior
In Facing forward; ed. by L. D. Frank

Terry, Megan—*Continued*
Fireworks
Children learn of parents' impending divorce during Independence Day Celebration. 1m 1b 1g
In 20/20: twenty one-act plays from twenty years of the Humana Festival

Terson, Peter
y How to write a play
Comedy about playwriting. 1 act 2m extras
In Around the world in 21 plays; ed. by L. Swortzell

Teschke, Holger
The appeasement
Termination of employment interview. Variable cast 2 characters 1 interior
In Actors Theatre of Louisville. Ten-minute plays: v3

Tesh, Jane
c Breakfast at the Bookworm Cafe
Bookworms use books to foil evil termites. 8m 3w extras 1 interior
In The Big book of large-cast plays; ed. by S. E. Kamerman

Tesich, Steve
Arts & leisure. French 1997 66p
Dark comedy. Self absorbed drama critic confronted by alienated women in his life. Prologue 6 scenes 1m 4w

On the open road. French 1993 73p
Black comedy about future of mankind. Adventures of two men fleeing civil war. 2 acts 11 scenes 4m 1b 1g 1 setting

Tesori, Jeanine
Violet (condensation)
In The Best plays of 1996-1997

Tess of the d'Urbervilles. Fry, M.

Texas
Callan, L. Homebound
Crawford, D. W. Tangled garden
Foote, H. The chase
Foote, H. Dividing the estate
Foote, H. The habitation of dragons
Foote, H. The land of the astronauts
Foote, H. Laura Dennis
Foote, H. Night seasons
Foote, H. The one-armed man
Foote, H. The Prisoner's Song
Foote, H. The roads to home: A nightingale
Foote, H. The roads to home: Spring dance
Foote, H. The roads to home: The dearest of friends
Foote, H. Talking pictures
Foote, H. The tears of my sister
Foote, H. The traveling lady
Foote, H. The trip to Bountiful
Foote, H. The widow Claire
Foote, H. The young man from Atlanta
King, L. L. The Golden Shadows Old West Museum
Lee, E. East Texas hot links
Shores, D. Daughters of the Lone Star State
Williams, J.; Sears, J. and Howard, E. A Tuna Christmas

Texas boy. Rideout, G.

A **Texas** romance. Schave, E.

Textile weavers. See Weavers

Thailand
Smith, S. One-sided triangle

Thain, Paul
Black widow. French (London) 1996 83p
Drama set in 1909 England. Lord's daughter sets out to exact terrible revenge on father's killers. 2 acts 4m 6w

c Stone soup. French (London) 1993 41p
Allegory of modern society based on ancient folk tale. Woman feeds needy villagers with magical soup. 7m 8w 2b 2g 1 exterior

Thane, Adele
y The House of the Seven Gables
Dramatization of Nathaniel Hawthorne's novel set in Salem Village, Massachusetts. Puritan family suffers for mistakes of ancestors. 5 scenes 9m 5w extras 2 interiors 2 exteriors
In The Big book of dramatized classics; ed. by S. E. Kamerman

y Moby Dick
Based on Herman Melville's novel of 19th century sea captain obsessed with white whale. 2 scenes 9m 1b extras 1 setting
In The Big book of dramatized classics; ed. by S. E. Kamerman

y The moonstone
Based on mystery by Wilkie Collins set in 1799 India and England about theft of diamond. 5 scenes 9m 5w 2b extras 4 interiors 1 exterior
In The Big book of dramatized classics; ed. by S. E. Kamerman

c Rapunzel
Based on fairy tale by Brothers Grimm. With prince's help, Rapunzel is freed from tower where she had been imprisoned by witch. 3 scenes 2m 3w 1b 4g 1 interior 1 exterior
In Thirty plays from favorite stories; ed. by S. E. Kamerman

Thanks. Dashow, K.

The **Thanksgiving** bear. Pflomm, P. N.

Thanksgiving Day
c Marx, P. The troubled Pilgrim
c Pflomm, P. N. The Thanksgiving bear

That all of us should be fed. Anderson, E.

That dog isn't fifteen. Blount, R.

That figures! Miller, H. L.

That old black magic. Kwahulé, K.

Thatcher, Kristine
Emma's child. Dramatists 1997 79p
Couple in their 40s arrange to adopt teenager's baby but when child is born with severe hydrocephalus all their lives change. 3 acts 12 scenes 3m 8w 1 setting
—Same
In Women playwrights: the best plays of 1995

Thatcher's children. Griffiths, T.

That's life. 'Udwan, Mamduh

That's my girl. Feydeau, G.

That's the spirit. Harper, T.

That's the spirit! Kelly, T.

That's the way to do it. Griffiths, D.

Theater
Albee, E. Edward Albee's fragments
Barker, H. Uncle Vanya
Bell, N. On the bum
Berkoff, S. Dahling you were marvellous
Brown, C. The African Company presents Richard III
Casler, L. A night in the theatre
Champagne, D. Playing bare
y Cheatham, V. R. Broadway hit
Childress, A. Trouble in mind
Crane, R. Under the stars
Dashow, K. Sing this
Dashow, K. Top of 16
Durang, C. Mrs. Sorken
Feingold, M. Scribe's paradox
Jackson, N. The quick-change room
Linney, R. Juliet
Ludwig, K. Moon over Buffalo
Mander, C. World première
c McCaslin, N. Leading lady
McNally, T. Street talk
McPherson, C. St Nicholas
Meara, A. After-play
Orr, M. The wisdom of Eve
Palmer, J. Henrik Ibsen on the necessity of producing Norwegian drama
Pintauro, J. Bus stop diner
Prince, H. Grandchild of kings
Reddin, K. Black snow
Snelgrove, M. Bums on seats
Warburton, N. Distracted globe
Warburton, N. The last bread pudding
Wellman, M. The bad infinity
Wellman, M. Crowbar
y Wells, J. S. Competition piece
West, M. The pleasure man
Wilder, T. Love and how to cure it

England

Annie G. Something rotten in Denmark
De Angelis, A. Playhouse creatures
Harwood, R. The dresser
Pinero, A. W. Trelawny of the 'Wells'

Theater critics
Tesich, S. Arts & leisure

Theatre of the film noir. Walker, G. F.

Theatre Passe Muraille. See Salutin, R. jt. auth.

Theft
Beim, N. Jewel thieves!
Solórzano, C. The hands of God
Tremblay, M. Les belles soeurs

Theft. Chappel, E.

Them . . . within us. Gross, T. D.

The **theory** and practice of belly-dancing. Barnes, P.

The **theory** of total blame. Finley, K.

There are many houses in my tribe. Youngblood, S.

There's a boy in the girls' bathroom. Sachar, L.

There's not a finer country. Mitterer, F.

Theseus (Greek mythology)
Euripides. Hippolytus

Thesmophoriazusai. See Aristophanes. Festival time

They. Witkiewicz, S. I.

They met on Good Friday. MacNeice, L.

They that sit in darkness. Burrill, M. P.

The **thickness** of skin. McIntyre, C.

A **thief** of a Christmas. Murphy, T.

Thieves
Barnes, D. A passion play
Chappell, E. Theft
Dunsany, L. The glittering gate
Gay, J. Beggar's opera
Hauptmann, G. The beaver coat
Manet, E. Lady Strass
Middleton, T. A mad world, my masters
c Witkiewicz, S. I. The courageous princess

Thin ice. Rubess, B. and Cooper, B.

The **third** death. Gregor, H.

Thirteen bells of Boglewood. Bush, M.

Thirteen hands. Shields, C.

Thirteen past midnight. St. John, B.

Thirst. O'Neill, E.

The **thirty**-dollar day. Plautus, T. M.

Thirty Years War, 1618-1648
Brecht, B. Mother Courage and her children

This common bond. Mead, K.

This is a play. MacIvor, D.

This is dead level. Shuttleworth, R.

This is for you, Anna. The Anna Project

This is not a pipe dream. Kornhauser, B.

This is the rill speaking. Wilson, L.

This is where we came in. Ayckbourn, A.

This lime tree bower. McPherson, C.

This year, next year. Harding, N.

Thomas, Buddy
Physical. French 1994 85p
Comedy set in New England college town. Man's carefully planned evening of romance ruined by unexpected visitor. 2 acts 2m 2w 1 interior

Thomas, Clarence
Hunt, M. Unquestioned integrity: the Hill-Thomas hearings

Thomas, Colin
y Flesh and blood
Drama exploring relationship between troubled high-school student and his older gay brother who has AIDS. 18 scenes 3m 1w 1 setting
In Making, out; ed. by R. Wallace

Thomas, Eberle, and Redmond, Barbara
y Six Canterbury tales. Anchorage Press 1993 70p
Dramatization of six tales from Chaucer's Canterbury tales, about fourteenth century pilgrims travelling from London to Canterbury. 13 scenes 4m 2w 1 setting

Thomas, Edward
East from the Gantry
Paranoid, gun-wielding husband cross-examines wife about her drunkenness and alleged infidelities. 2m 1w 1 interior
In Frontline intelligence I; ed. by P. Edwardes
In Thomas, E. Three plays

Flowers of the dead red sea
Two men in Welsh slaughterhouse locked in conflict of assertion and denial while world crumbles around them. 2m 1 interior
In Thomas, E. Three plays

House of America
Drama about dysfunctional Welsh family. Fantasy life inspired by Kerouac's On the road leads to incest and murder. 3 acts 3m 2w 1 setting
In Thomas, E. Three plays

Thomas, Freyda
Tartuffe: born again; translated and adapted by Freyda Thomas. French 1997 130p
Adaptation of Molière's play. Set in TV studio in present day Baton Rouge, Louisiana with Tartuffe as scheming, deposed televangelist. 2 acts 6m 5w 1 interior

Thomas, Thom
Without apologies. French 1995 94p
Comedy set in 1933 London. Follows fortunes of family featured in Oscar Wilde's The importance of being Earnest. 2 acts 4 scenes 3m 3w 1 interior

Thompson, Ernest
The Valentine Fairy
First title in author's Valentines for two trilogy. Fairy comes to single woman's aid. 1m 1w 1 interior
In The Best American short plays, 1992-1993

Zipless
Second part of Valentines for two trilogy. Satirical exploration of contemporary marriage. 1m 1w 1 setting
In The Best American short plays, 1993-1994

Thompson, G. M.
A time to go home. Dramatic 1995 41p
Drama about death and dying. Four teenagers killed by drunk driver find themselves in sanctuary of church where they discuss their feelings. 1 act 13m 13w 1 interior

Thompson, Judith
I am yours
Drama. Two sisters struggle to find love while battling their own psychological torments. 2 acts 36 scenes 3m 3w 1 setting
In Modern Canadian plays v2; ed. by J. Wasserman

Lion in the streets. Coach House Press 1992 62p
Psychological drama featuring ghost of murdered young girl. Women cope with cancer, poverty, childcare and weight problems. 2 acts 2m 4w 1 setting

Perfect pie
Small town woman sends tape to deceased childhood friend. 1w 1 interior
In Solo; ed. by J. Sherman

Sled. Playwrights Canada 1997 130p
Drama about violence and national identity set in Toronto and Canadian North. Singing. 3 acts 47 scenes 4m 3w 1 setting

Thompson, Laura

c The innkeeper's daughter. Moorley's 1994 11p

Religious drama in verse. Birth of Christ as viewed by daughter of innkeeper. 8m 2w 1 setting

Thompson, Peggy

Calamity Jane and the fat buffalo moon

Radio play based on life of Calamity Jane, her relationships with Wild Bill Hickok, and with the daughter she gave up for adoption. 25 scenes 6m 5w

In Adventures for (big) girls; ed. by A. Jansen

Thomson, Katherine

Barmaids. Currency Press in association with Belvoir Street Theatre 1992 58p (Current theatre series)

Drama set in Australian saloon about two barmaids with refined sense of service and loyalty. Prologue 2 acts 12 scenes 2w 1 interior

Thoreau, Henry David, 1817-1862

Lawrence, J. and Lee, R. E. The night Thoreau spent in jail

Thornton, Jane. See Godber, J. jt. auth.

Those the river keeps. Rabe, D.

Threat. Cooke, C.

Three Billy Goats Gruff. Mahlmann, L. and Jones, D. C.

Three birds alighting on a field. Wertenbaker, T.

A **three**-dollar day. See Plautus, T. M. The thirty-dollar day

Three doors to death. Jackson, K.

Three for two. See Taylor, R. and Bologna, J. Comedies in apple blossom time

Three from the earth. Barnes, D.

The **three** golden hairs of Grandfather Know All. See Gerke, P. Tri zlate vlasy Deda Vseveda: "The three golden hairs of Grandfather Know All"

Three hotels. Baitz, J. R.

Three in the back, two in the head. Sherman, J.

Three Little Pigs

Parodies, imitations, etc.

c Cheatham, V. R. The Three Little Pigs and friends

The **three** little pigs. Dolmen, C. and Dolmen, J.

The **Three** Little Pigs and friends. Cheatham, V. R.

The **three** lives of Lucie Cabrol. McBurney, S. and Wheatley, M.

Three meals a day. McCaslin, N.

The **three** musketeers. Hall, W.

Three out. Bartel, R.

The **three** pieces of good advice. Vigil, A.

Three poets: Akhmatova. Linney, R.

Three poets: Hrosvitha. Linney, R.

Three poets: Komachi. Linney, R.

Three sisters. Chekhov, A.

Three sisters who are not sisters. Stein, G.

Three tall women. Albee, E.

Three viewings. Hatcher, J.

Three wishes. Sod, T. and Grant, S.

Three years from "thirty." O'Malley, M.

Throckmorton, Susan L.

c The forest bride

Farmer's son wins princess and breaks spell that turned her into mouse. 5 scenes 5m 1w extras 1 exterior

In Thirty plays from favorite stories; ed. by S. E. Kamerman

Through the leaves. Kroetz, F. X.

Throwing smoke. Reddin, K.

Throwing your voice. Lucas, C.

Thum, Nancy B.

y The Red-headed League

Mystery based on Arthur Conan Doyle's short story featuring Sherlock Holmes. 3 scenes 7m 1 interior 2 exteriors

In The Big book of dramatized classics; ed. by S. E. Kamerman

Thumbelina. Morris, V.

Thyestes (Greek mythology)

Seneca. Thyestes

Thymus vulgaris. Wilson, L.

Tibbetts, Mike

Bottles with baskets on. French (London) 1996 30p

On eve of her wedding, English woman discovers long-buried secret about her parents' marriage. 2m 2w 1 interior

Tibbles, George

The turn of the worm. French 1997 80p

Comedy. Lessons learned by all when two street kids move in with feuding elderly Italian American sisters. 2 acts 4 scenes 2m 3w 1 interior

Tiddley pum. Bartram, F.

Ties that bind. Schenkkan, R.

The **tiger** and the Brahman. Simon, S.

Till death, or whatever, do us part. Kluger, G. M.

Till voices wake us. Dizon, L.

Tillie Edelpickel's sack of lies. McCullough, L. E.

Tilly

A modest proposal; tr. by Richard Miller. UBU Repertory Theater Publs. 1994 65p

Racial confrontation results when bigoted, provincial French couple is visited by adult daughter and her African manservant. 3 scenes 2m 3w 1 interior

Tilting ground. Hibbert, G.

Time

y Bernardi, P. and Havens, D. Twice upon a time

Stoppard, T. If you're Glad I'll be Frank

Time of my life. Ayckbourn, A.

Time out. Dashow, K.

Time quest. Ford, K.

A **time** to go home. Thompson, G. M.

Time travel

Ayckbourn, A. Communicating doors

Barker, C. Paradise Street

y Levi, S. Good morning Miss Vickers

y Levi, S. Merry Christmas Miss Vickers

Tim'll fix it. Hornby, I.

The **tinder** box. Whelan, P.

Tinkle time. Coen, D.

Tinniswood, Peter

The village fête. French (London) 1995 86p

Domestic drama set in London and rural village. Handyman helps family of misfits come to terms with themselves. 2 acts 4m 4w 1 interior 1 exterior

Tiny Tim is dead. Lebow, B.

Tiptree, James

The girl who was plugged in (dramatization) See Menken, A. Weird romance: The girl who was plugged in

Tirado, Cándido

Some people have all the luck

Psychological portrait of young Puerto Rican man in Bronx, New York. Incorporates fantastic elements. 2 acts 2m 3w 1 setting

In Nuestro New York; ed. by J. V. Antush

'Tis pity she's a whore. Ford, J.

Tissian, Gabriel

Night baseball

Drama about race relations and violence set in working-class Philadelphia neighborhood. Police avenge murder of young man by brutalizing blacks. 6m 1 interior

In The Best American short plays, 1992-1993

Titanic (Steamship)

Durang, C. Titanic

Hatcher, J. Scotland Road

y Lipp, J. L. Titanic: destination disaster

Titanic (condensation). Yeston, M.

Titanic: destination disaster. Lipp, J. L.

To the dogs. Barnes, D.

Tobago

Walcott, D. Pantomime

Tobin, Scott

y Cotton girls. Bakers Plays 1993 28p

Drama set at 1959 county fair. Three teenage girls exchange confidences on graduation night. 3w 1 setting

Tod, the boy Tod. Wilks, T.

Today, I am a fountain pen. Horovitz, I.

Toddie, Jean Lenox

And go to Innisfree. French 1995 30p

Older woman facing important decision receives advice from the child she was and the middle-aged matron she became. 1 act 3w 1 exterior

Is that the bus to Pittsburgh?

Comic drama set in Pittsburgh community garden. Old woman, middle aged-man and young woman share their hopes and dreams. 1m 2w 1 exterior

In Toddie, J. L. Late Sunday afternoon, early Sunday evening and Is that the bus to Pittsburgh?

Late Sunday afternoon, early Sunday evening

Seventy-year-old woman, bored with her sedate life, tells granddaughter of travel plans. 2w 1 interior

In Toddie, J. L. Late Sunday afternoon, early Sunday evening and Is that the bus to Pittsburgh?

Tolan, Kathleen

Approximating mother

Comedy. Two pregnant women friends from New York City and pregnant Midwestern teenager discuss pros and cons of parenting, motherhood and adoption. 12 scenes 2m 5w 1 setting

In Playwriting women; ed. by J. Miles

Tolins, Jonathan

The twilight of the Golds. French 1994 105p

New York Jewish family deals with homosexuality. Woman debates aborting fetus she knows will be gay. 2 acts 6 scenes 3m 2w 1 setting

Toller, Ernst
Masses and man
Symbolic drama. Woman reacts to social upheaval caused by anti-war strike. Variable cast 1 setting
In German expressionist plays; ed. by E. Schurer

Tolstoy, Leo
Anna Karenina (dramatization) See Edmundson, H. Anna Karenina
War and peace (dramatization) See Edmundson, H. War and peace

Tom and Jerry. Cleveland, R.

Tom Sawyer, whitewasher. Hackett, W.

Tomer, Ben-Zion
Children of the shadows
Set in 1955 Israel. Psychological problems of two Holocaust survivors. 2 acts 11 scenes 7m 2w extras settings
In Israeli Holocaust drama; ed. by M. Taub

Tomorrow. Foote, H.

Tomorrow! Havel, V.

Tone clusters. Oates, J. C.

Tony n' Tina's wedding, by Artificial Intelligence; conceived by Nancy Cassaro; created by Thomas Michael Allen [et al.] French 1994 147p
Comedy. Audience members are invited guests at wedding and reception. 15m 11w 2 interiors

Too many cooks. McCaslin, N.

Toomer, Jean
Balo
Vignette about a religious black farming family in Georgia in 1924. Music, singing. 1 act 7m 2w extras
In Black theatre USA [v1]; ed. by J. V. Hatch and T. Shine

Tooth and consequences. See Feydeau, G. Nothing but the tooth

Top of 16. Dashow, K.

Topol, Josef
Cat on the rails
Drama set in railway station on outskirts of Prague. Two lovers wait for train that never comes. 3m 1w 1b setting
In Czech plays; modern Czech drama; ed. by B. Day

Torgov, Morley
A good place to come from (dramatization) See Horovitz, I. Today, I am a fountain pen

Toronto (Ont.)
Bartley, J. Stephen & Mr. Wilde
Rubess, B. Boom, baby, boom!

Toronto, Mississippi. MacLeod, J.

Torquato Tasso. Goethe, J. W. von

Torquemada, Tomas de, 1420-1498
Linney, R. Spain: Torquemada

The **torrents.** Gray, O.

The **tortoise** and the hare race again. Neidermyer, D.

Torture
Mitterer, F. Children of the Devil

Total eclipse. Hampton, C.

The **total** meaning of real life. Jensen, J.

Totalitarianism
Dorfman, A. Widows
Fo, D. Accidental death of an anarchist
Gambaro, G. Bad blood
Gregor, H. The third death
Havel, V. The garden party
Havel, V. Largo desolato
Havel, V. Redevelopment
Havel, V. Temptation
Jelinek, E. Totenauberg (Death/Valley/Summit)
Kovacevic, D. The professional
Mahfuz, 'Isam. The China tree
Pinter, H. Mountain language
Pinter, H. One for the road
Seremba, G. Come good rain
Sewell, S. Traitors
Stoppard, T. Professional foul

Totenauberg (Death/Valley/Summit). Jelinek, E.

Touch. Demchuk, D.

A **touch** of the poet. O'Neill, E.

Tough! Walker, G. F.

Tough choices for the new century: a seminar for responsible living. Anderson, J.

The **tour** guide. Strauss, B.

Tourist trade
Hogg, F. A. Afternoon at Tavern MacTavish

Tourneur, Cyril
The atheist's tragedy; or, The honest man's revenge
Jacobean verse tragedy. Atheist devises complicated scheme to steal brother's fortune. Music. 5 acts 21 scenes 9m 4w 9 interiors 4 exteriors
In Four revenge tragedies; ed. by K. E. Maus
See also The Revenger's tragedy

The **tower.** Maguire, M.

Tower of London. Hezlep, W.

The **towne** without a tale. Enscoe, L. G. and Enscoe, A.

Townsend, Sue

Bazaar & rummage

Comedy about neurotic do-gooder, trainee social worker and three agoraphobics who venture out of their homes to rummage sale. 2 acts 6w 1 interior

In Townsend, S. Plays: 1

The great celestial cow

Indian woman who joins husband in England loses her sense of identity when faced with local prejudices. 2 acts 26 scenes 2m 6w extras settings

In Townsend, S. Plays: 1

Groping for words

Teacher of adult literacy class in England convinces school caretaker to learn to read. 2 acts 17 scenes 2m 2w 2 interiors

In Townsend, S. Plays: 1

The Queen and I. French (London) 1994 83p

Satirical look at failings of British welfare state and the pretensions of the royal family. 2 acts 19 scenes 4m 5w extras 1 setting

The Queen and I: the play with songs. Methuen Drama in association with the Royal Court Theatre 1994 117p (Royal Court writers series)

Version of the title entered above with the addition of several songs

The secret diary of Adrian Mole aged 13¾

Play based on the author's novel of the same title about trials and tribulations of adolescent boy. Music, singing. 2 acts Variable cast 18 characters 1 setting

In Townsend, S. Plays: 1

Womberang

Comedy. Free spirit brings joy and anarchy to grim waiting-room of gynecology clinic. 1 act 2m 8w 1 interior

In Townsend, S. Plays: 1

Toy camp. Collette, P. and Fritzen, G.

Toys

c Collete, P. and Fritzen, G. Toy camp

Track thirteen. Graham, S.

Trading-stamps

Tremblay, M. Les belles soeurs

Traffic accidents

Horovitz, I. It's called the Sugar Plum

Trafficking in broken hearts. Sánchez, E.

Tragedy

Addison, J. Cato
Aldridge, I. The black doctor
Ansky, S. The dybbuk
Barbier, M.-A. Arria and Paetus
Barker, H. Minna
Barker, H. Ten dilemmas
Bernard, C. Laodamia, Queen of Epirus
Bird, R. M. The gladiator
Bond, E. Coffee
Brecht, B. Mother Courage and her children
Brenton, H. Faust, parts I & II
Brustein, R. The wild duck
Büchner, G. Danton's death
Büchner, G. Woyzeck
Chapman, G. The revenge of Bussy d'Ambois
Chekhov, A. Ivanov
Chekhov, A. The seagull
Crowley, M. A breeze from the gulf
Dryden, J. All for love
Dryden, J. Aureng-Zebe
Dryden, J. Cleomenes the Spartan heroe
Dunlap, W. André
Elder, L. Ceremonies in dark old men
Fletcher, J. and Massinger, P. Rollo, Duke of Normandy
Foote, H. The chase
Foote, H. Tomorrow
Ford, J. The broken heart
Ford, J. The lover's melancholy
Ford, J. Perkin Warbeck
Ford, J. 'Tis pity she's a whore
Freed, D. Inquest
French, D. Leaving home
Fry, M. Tess of the d'Urbervilles
García Lorca, F. Blood wedding
García Lorca, F. The house of Bernarda Alba
García Lorca, F. Yerma
Goethe, J. W. von. Clavigo
Goethe, J. W. von. Egmont
Goethe, J. W. von. Faust, part I
Goethe, J. W. von. The natural daughter
Goethe, J. W. von. Stella
Goethe, J. W. von. Torquato Tasso
Graham, S. It's morning
Granville-Barker, H. Waste
Hare, D. Ivanov
Hare, D. Plenty
Hauptmann, G. The weavers
Hughes, L. Mulatto
Hugo, V. Hernani
Hugo, V. The king amuses himself
Hugo, V. Ruy Blas
Ibsen, H. Ghosts
Ibsen, H. Hedda Gabler
Ibsen, H. The master builder
Ibsen, H. Rosmersholm
Ibsen, H. The wild duck
Kaiser, G. From morning to midnight
Kennelly, B. Sophocles' Antigone
Kilroy, T. The seagull

Tragedy—*Continued*
Kingsley, S. Darkness at noon
Kokoschka, O. Murderer the women's hope
Kyd, T. The Spanish tragedy
Lee, N. The Princess of Cleves
Lillo, G. The London merchant
Mahon, D. Racine's Phaedra
Marlowe, C. Edward II
Marlowe, C. The Jew of Malta
McDonough, J. Butterfly
Mead, K. The Anderson
Miller, A. Death of a salesman
Moore, E. The gamester
O'Neill, E. Abortion
O'Neill, E. All God's chillun got wings
O'Neill, E. Desire under the elms
O'Neill, E. The Emperor Jones
O'Neill, E. The hairy ape
O'Neill, E. Mourning becomes Electra: Homecoming
O'Neill, E. Mourning becomes Electra: The haunted
O'Neill, E. Mourning becomes Electra: The hunted
O'Neill, E. Recklessness
O'Neill, E. Thirst
O'Neill, E. Warnings
O'Neill, E. The web
O'Neill, E. A wife for a life
Osofisan, F. Birthdays are not for dying
Rabe, D. The orphan
Racine, J. Phædra
The Revenger's tragedy
Shakespeare, W. and Fletcher, J. Cardenio
Strindberg, A. The dance of death
Strindberg, A. Miss Julie
Strindberg, A. The pelican
Sutherland, E. Edufa
Synge, J. M. Riders to the sea
Tourneur, C. The atheist's tragedy
Treadwell, S. Machinal
Walker, J. The River Niger
Wedekind, F. Lulu: a monster tragedy
Wedekind, F. Spring awakening
White, P. Night on Bald Mountain
Wilde, O. The Duchess of Padua
Wilde, O. A Florentine tragedy
Wilde, O. Salomé
Wilde, O. Vera
Wilson, L. The rimers of Eldritch
See also Greek Drama (Tragedy); Latin drama (Tragedy); Tragicomedy

The **tragedy** of man. Madách, I.

The **tragedy** of Mariam, the fair. Cary, E.

Tragicomedy
Ayckbourn, A. Wildest dreams
Bennett, R. Funerals and circuses
Buzo, A. Rooted
Cartwright, J. Road
Chekhov, A. The wood demon
Desjardins, M.-C. The favorite minister
Fletcher, J. The fair maid of the inn
Fletcher, J. The honest man's fortune
Ford, J. The lover's melancholy
Horovitz, I. It's called the Sugar Plum
Horovitz, I. Park your car in Harvard Yard
Horovitz, I. Shooting gallery
Kovacevic, D. A roaring tragedy
McNally, T. Where has Tommy Flowers gone?
Middleton, T. A critical edition of Thomas Middleton's The witch
Middleton, T. The witch
Morris, M. Two weeks with the Queen
Pinter, H. No man's land
Plautus, T. M. Amphitryon
Ruzzante. The veteran
Ruzzante. Weasel
Schnitzler, A. The word
Shepard, S. Simpatico
Simon, N. Lost in Yonkers
Szyszkowitz, G. Grillparzer
Valle-Inclan, R. del. Bohemian lights
Valle-Inclan, R. del. Divine words
Valle-Inclan, R. del. Silver face
Zuberbuehler, A. Fieldstones

Traitors. Sewell, S.

Tramway Road. Harwood, R.

The **transformation** of Pierrot. Schnitzler, A.

Transit of Venus. Hunter, M.

Transmigration
Lucas, C. Prelude to a kiss

Transsexuality
Pintauro, J. Dirty talk

Transvestism
Tremblay, M. Hosanna

The **Transylvanian** clockworks. Nigro, D.

Travelers
Curran, C. Senetta Boynton visits the Orient
Howe, T. Approaching Zanzibar

Travelers from Olympus. McCaslin, N.

Travelin' show. Martin, J.

The **traveling** lady. Foote, H.

The **travelling** Jekyll & Hyde show. Davis, R.

Travelling north. Williamson, D.

Treachery at Cartilage Creek. Kelly, T.

Treadwell, Sophie
Machinal. Royal National Theatre/Hern Bks. 1993 83p
Expressionist drama about woman who murders her husband to escape loveless marriage. 9 scenes 21m 7w 2 setting

Treasure Island. York, M. A.

Treasure Island, the panto. Lloyd, R.

Treasure of the Mayans. Hezlep, W.

Treasure trove. See Buried treasure

The **treatment.** Crimp, M.

Treats. Hampton, C.

The **tree.** Garro, E.

A **tree** grows in Hollywood. Pricone, S.

A **tree** with arms. Saba, J.

Trees
c Conboy, R. Song of the oak—El canto del roble
c Pricone, S. A tree grows in Hollywood

Trelawny of the 'Wells.' Pinero, A. W.

Tremblay, Michel
Les belles soeurs
French Canadian woman in poor neighborhood wins one million trading-stamps and invites female relatives, friends and neighbors to pasting-in party. 2 acts 15w 1 interior
In Modern Canadian plays v1; ed. by J. Wasserman

La Duchesse de Langeais
Monologue by drunken old 'queen' who after forty years of male prostitution, has been rejected and abandoned. 2 acts 1w
In Solo; ed. by J. Sherman

Hosanna
Homosexual transvestite, humiliated by practical joke, assesses his life and relationship with lover. 2 acts 2m 1 interior
In Heroines; ed. by J. Doolittle

Marcel pursued by the hounds; tr. by John Van Burek and Bill Glassco. Talonbooks 1996 80p
Teenage boy turns to sister for protection after witnessing brutal crime. 1 act 1m 5w 1 setting

Trenholme, Hilary
Fell blow. New Playwrights Network 1995 17p
Pushed to breaking point by difficult pupils in inner city English school, teacher arranges hiking trip with colleagues. 1 act 3m 3w 1 exterior

Tri zlate vlasy Deda Vseveda: "The three golden hairs of Grandfather Know All." Gerke, P.

The **trial** of Dr. Jekyll. Slout, W. L.

The **trial** of Judith K. Clark, S.

Trials
Alexander, R. I ain't yo' uncle
Anderson, G. Appearances
Banville, J. The broken jug
Bjorneboe, J. The bird lovers
Freed, D. Inquest
Frisby, T. Rough justice
Gilbert, S. Drag queens on trial
Heise, K. and Heise, D. Clarence Darrow in hell
Lawrence, J. and Lee, R. E. Inherit the wind
Ledoux, P. and Young, D. Love is strange
Legg, R. Oscar: the Oscar Wilde trials of 1895
Mann, E. Greensboro
y Martens, A. C. The comeback caper
Miller, A. The crucible
Mitterer, F. Children of the Devil
Morrison, B. The cracked pot
Nagy, P. Trip's cinch
Rattigan, T. The Winslow boy
Ryga, G. The ecstasy of Rita Joe
Slout, W. L. The trial of Dr. Jekyll
y Suntep Theatre. Wheel of justice
c Wolman, D. An imaginary trial of George Washington

Trials (Genocide)
See also War crime trials

Trials (Murder)
Fuller, C. A soldier's play
Mann, E. Execution of justice
y McCullough, L. E. Abe Lincoln for the defense
Treadwell, S. Machinal

Trials (War crimes). See War crime trials

Triana, José
Night of the assassins
Three siblings plot murder of their parents. 2 acts 1m 2w 1 interior
In Latin American plays; ed. by S. Doggart

Triangle. Walker, D.

Trick or treat. Kelly, T.

A **trick** to catch the old one. Middleton, T.

Tricker, Carole
Losers. New Playwrights Network 1995 64p
Comedy. Chaos results when members attempt to save job of weight-loss club leader. 2 acts 3 scenes 2m 8w 1 interior

Tricks. Gifford, B.

Trinummus. See Plautus, T. M. The thirty-dollar day

The **trip** to Bountiful. Foote, H.

Trips. Ordway, S.

Trip's cinch. Nagy, P.

Tristam Shandy. See Buchan, A. Conditional surrender

The **triumph** of love. Marivaux

The **triumph** of love. Wadsworth, S.

Troat. See Warner, F. Maquettes for the requiem: Troat

Trojan War
Euripides. Iphigenia in Aulis
Kennelly, B. Euripides' The Trojan woman
Kochanowski, J. The dismissal of the Grecian envoys

Trophies. Wooten, J. J.

The **Tropical** Breeze Hotel. Conde, M.

Trotsky, Leon
Ives, D. Variations on the death of Trotsky

Trott, Steve
c Buster come back
Worship program. Runaway dogs debate pros and cons of freedom while children contemplate significance of Christ's nativity. Singing, music. Large mixed cast
In Trott, S. Destination Bethlehem: seven Christmas plays for young people

c Destination Bethlehem
Worship program. Children learn about four journeys made on occasion of first Christmas. Singing. Large mixed cast
In Trott, S. Destination Bethlehem: seven Christmas plays for young people

c Did I miss anything important?
Worship program. Various Biblical characters fail to recognize God's deliverance. Singing. Large mixed cast
In Trott, S. Destination Bethlehem: seven Christmas plays for young people

c Nocturne
Worship program. Stargazers learn meaning of Christ's birth. Singing. Large mixed cast
In Trott, S. Destination Bethlehem: seven Christmas plays for young people

c R.S.V.P.
Worship program. Grandmother's Christmas cards come to life and form nativity scene. Singing. 1m 1w extras
In Trott, S. Destination Bethlehem: seven Christmas plays for young people

c Something sacred this way comes
Worship program. Girl asks many questions as she awaits birth of Messiah. Singing. 2m 1w 1b extras
In Trott, S. Destination Bethlehem: seven Christmas plays for young people

c You don't say!
Worship program. Series of mime skits about word of God. Singing, mime. Variable cast
In Trott, S. Destination Bethlehem: seven Christmas plays for young people

Trouble in mind. Childress, A.

Trouble in Tumbleweed. Kelly, T.

Trouble sleeping. Ward, N.

The **trouble** with old lovers. Huth, A.

The **troubled** Pilgrim. Marx, P.

The **troublesome** reign of and lamentable death of Edward II. See Marlowe, C. Edward II

Truculentus. See Plautus, T. M. The savage slave

Trudy Blue. Norman, M.

True crimes. Linney, R.

Truman, Bess Wallace, 1885-1982
LaChuisa, M. J. First Lady suite: Olio

Truman, Margaret, 1924-
LaChuisa, M. J. First Lady suite: Olio

A **trump** for Jericho. Kemp, R.

Trumpets and raspberries. Fo, D.

Trust. Dietz, S.

Truth, Sojourner, d. 1883
y Asher, S. F. A woman called Truth

Truth and treason. Sade, Marquis de

Truthfulness and falsehood
Booth, J. Little white lies
y Hannay, R. Windows
Hare, D. Licking Hitler
See also Honesty

Try a little Shakespeare. Cohen, F.

Trying to find Chinatown. Hwang, D. H.

Tuberculosis
Mori, Ō Masks

Tubman, Harriet, 1815-1913
c Fisher, A. Harriet Tubman—the second Moses
Kenyatta, K. Harriet

Tuesday. Bond, E.

Tuesday, eight-fifteen. Whyte, P.

Tumbling after. See Martin, J. Jack and Jill

The **tumult** and the shouting. Pawley, T.

A **Tuna** Christmas. Williams, J.; Sears, J. and Howard, E.

Tunnel vision. Hodgson, S.

Turcaret. LeSage, A. R.

Turgenev, Ivan
A month in the country (adaptation) See Friel, B. A month in the country

The **turn** of the screw. Hatcher, J.

The **turn** of the worm. Tibbles, G.

Turner, Jamie
y Anne of Green Gables
Based on L. M. Montgomery's novel about orphan girl adopted by elderly brother and sister on Prince Edward Island. 5 scenes 3m 5w 1g 1 interior
In The Big book of dramatized classics; ed. by S. E. Kamerman
c The white spider's gift
Dramatization of South American folktale. Spider helps youth win chieftain's daughter in marriage. 3 scenes 6m 7w extras 1 setting
In Thirty plays from favorite stories; ed. by S. E. Kamerman

Turquoise Tom, the versifying bandit of Old California. McCullough, L. E.

Turrini, Peter
Alpine glow; tr. by Richard Dixon. Ariadne Press 1994 69p (Studies in Austrian literature, culture, and thought. Translation series)
Symbolic drama about guilt and redemption. Encounter between blind ex-Nazi and has-been actress posing as prostitute. 13 scenes 3m 1w extras 1 setting
—Same
In Seven contemporary Austrian plays; ed. by R. H. Lawson
Death and the Devil
Symbolic drama. Disillusioned priest sets out on journey to discover sin. 11 scenes 12m 3w extras
In Turrini, P. Shooting rats, other plays and poems
Infanticide
Unfortunate, alienated young woman murders her infant child. 3m 1w 1 setting
In Turrini, P. Shooting rats, other plays and poems
Shooting rats
Couple alienated from consumer society. 1m 1w 1 setting
In Turrini, P. Shooting rats, other plays and poems
The siege of Vienna
Drama about contemporary Austrian society. 2 acts 7m 3w extras 1 setting
In Turrini, P. Shooting rats, other plays and poems
Swine
Austrian folk play. Farmer's mentally handicapped son treated as swine by townspeople. 3m 2w 1b
In Anthology of contemporary Austrian folk plays

Tutors and tutoring
Barker, H. Hated nightfall

Tutt, Barbara
c Heart to heart
Knave of Hearts returns tarts to Queen of Hearts on Valentine's Day. 1m 2w extras 1 setting
In The Big book of skits; ed. by S. E. Kamerman

Tuttle, Jon
The hammerstone. Dramatists 1995 82p
Satiric look at mid-life crises of two professors at small Southwestern college. Prologue 2 acts 8 scenes 3m 3w 1 setting
Terminal Cafe. Dramatists 1996 84p
Drama about greed and corruption set in small New Mexico town, 1941 to 1945. Mine safety compromised to produce more coal for Los Alamos. Prologue 2 acts 4 scenes epilogue 6m 3w 1 setting

Twain, Mark
The adventures of Tom Sawyer (dramatization) See Hackett, W. Tom Sawyer, whitewasher
The prince and the pauper (dramatization) See Hardee, L. The prince and the pauper; Harris, A. The prince and the pauper

'Twas the night before Columbus Day . . . I mean Christmas. Lawrence, M.

Twelve-1-A. Yamauchi, W.

The **twelve** days of Christmas. McCullough, L. E.

Twelve dreams. Lapine, J.

The **twelve** months. See Gerke, P. I dodici mesi: The twelve months

Twenty one A. Kling, K.

Twice upon a time. Bernardi, P. and Havens, D.

Twilight: Los Angeles, 1992. Smith, A. D.

The **twilight** of the Golds. Tolins, J.

The **twin** Menaechmi. See Plautus, T. M. The brothers Menaechmus

The **twin** rivals. Farquhar, G.

Twins
Booth, J. A question of identity
Booth, J. Seeing double
Carr, M. Portia Coughlan
Césaire, I. Fire's daughters
Clarke, T. The Venetian twins
y Cohen, F. Try a little Shakespeare
Huff, K. Leon and Joey
MacLeod, W. The house of yes
Plautus, T. M. The brothers Menaechmus
Ridley, P. The pitchfork Disney
Sade, Marquis de. The twins
St. John, B. Rubies: Heirlooms

The **twisted** mirror. Carter, J.

Twisted tape. Haywood, D.

Two. Cartwright, J.

Two. Linney, R.

Two-2-tango. See MacIvor, D. 2-2-tango

Two altars, ten funerals (all souls). Ehn, E.

Two-b wut ur. Panych, M.

The **two** Bacchides. See Plautus, T. M. Two sisters named Bacchis

Two eclairs. Pintauro, J.

Two enthusiasts. Mamet, D.

Two ladies take tea. Barnes, D.

Two lips indifferent red. Oglesby, T.

Two mens'es daughter. Franklin, J. E.

Two of a kind. Janes, H.

Two-part invention. Hollinger, M.

Two planks and a passion. Minghella, A.

Two rooms. Blessing, L.

Two sisters named Bacchis. Plautus, T. M.

Two Sundays. Gray, S.

Two trains running. Wilson, A.

Two weeks with the Queen. Morris, M.

Tyler, Royall
The contrast

Post Revolutionary War satire set in New York dealing with the superiority of the social ideals of the new American nation over those of the most brilliant European societies. Singing. Prologue 5 acts 10 scenes 5m 4w extras 3 interiors 1 exterior

In Early American drama; ed. by J. H. Richards

Tyndale, William, d. 1536
Anderson, J.-S. Tyndale's dream

Tyndale's dream. Anderson, J.-S.

Tyron, Hugh O'Neill, 2nd Earl of
Kilroy, T. The O'Neill

U

Ubu cocu. Jarry, A.

Ubu cuckolded. See Jarry, A. Ubu cocu

'Udwan, Mamduh
That's life

Monologue. Dictatorial attitude of Syrian husband and father representative of authoritarianism in other aspects of Arab life. 1m 1 interior

In Modern Arabic drama; ed. by S. K. Jayyusi and R. Allen

Uganda
Seremba, G. Come good rain

Uganda. Johnson, J.

Ugandans

Ireland

O'Kelly, D. Asylum! Asylum!

The **ugly** duck. McGovern, C.

The **ugly** man. Fraser, B.

Uhry, Alfred
Driving Miss Daisy

Set in Atlanta, Georgia from 1948 to 1973. Explores relationship between crotchety elderly Jewish widow and her black chauffeur. 2m 1w 1 setting

In Best American plays: 9th series, 1983-1992

The last night of Ballyhoo. Theater Communications Group 1997 99p

Comedy drama about interethnic prejudice set in 1939 Atlanta. Family prepares for German-Jewish community's top social event. 2 acts 13 scenes 3m 4w 2 interiors

The last night of Ballyhoo (condensation)
In The Best plays of 1996-1997

Ulfeldt, Leonora Christina, 1621-1698
Holm, S. Leonora

Ullom, Shirley
y Geeks do come from outer space. Meriwether 1993 20p
Comedy. Aliens observe behavior of high school students. 4 scenes 10m 9w 1 interior 1 exterior

Ulster (Northern Ireland and Ireland)
McGuinness, F. Observe the sons of Ulster marching towards the Somme
Morrison, B. A love song for Ulster: The daughter
Morrison, B. A love song for Ulster: The marriage
Morrison, B. A love song for Ulster: The son

The **ultimate** bliss. Chocrón, I.

Umjana Land. Plowman, G.

Unamuno, Miguel de
Nothing less than a man (dramatization) See Dorst, T. Fernando Krapp wrote me this letter: an assaying of the truth

Uncle Bob. Pendleton, A.

Uncle Chick. Pintauro, J.

Uncle Tom's cabin. Aiken, G. L.

Uncle Vanya. Barker, H.

Uncle Vanya. Chekhov, A.

Uncle Vanya. Chekhov, A. (adaptation) See Mitchell, J. August

Uncles
Margulies, D. Death in the family
Pendleton, A. Uncle Bob
Vogel, P. How I learned to drive

Under a mantle of stars. Puig, M.

Under the influence. Parker, R.

Under the stars. Crane, R.

Underground railroad
Aiken, G. L. Uncle Tom's cabin
Braithwaite, D. Martha and Elvira
c Sodaro, C. Freedom train

The **underpants.** See Sternheim, C. The bloomers

Undertakers and undertaking
Barnes, P. Leonardo's Last Supper
Dickinson, S. Styx and Bones
Rector, M. H. The lady and the mortician
Warner, F. Lying figures

Undertow. Spence, E.

Underwear, perfume and crash helmet. Gurr, M.

Unemployed
Foote, H. The Prisoner's Song
Kroetz, F. X. Mensch Meier
Plowman, G. A kind of Vesuvius
Teschke, H. The appeasement

Unexpected tenderness. Horovitz, I.

Unfinished stories. Pearson, S.

Unger, Heinz R.
The bell tolls at twelve
Satirical Austrian folk play. Inhabitants of Styrian village refuse to cooperate with Nazi occupiers. 4 acts 10m 3w extras 1 exterior
In New anthology of contemporary Austrian folk plays; ed. by R. H. Lawson

United Nations
Buzo, A. Pacific union

United States
Air Force
Glore, J. The company of heaven
Shepard, S. Operation sidewinder

Army

McNally, T. Next

Army—Military life

Fuller, C. A soldier's play
Rabe, D. Streamers

Army—Officers

y Hackett, W. The man without a country
Linney, R. The love suicide at Schofield Barracks

Central Intelligence Agency

Greenland, S. Jungle rot
Sherman, J. Three in the back, two in the head

Constitution

c Brown, C. J. The Constitution is born

Federal Bureau of Investigation

Guare, J. Moon under Miami

History

c Blum, R. California wax museum
c Morris, A. J. An American story

History—Colonial period

Barker, J. N. The Indian princess
Miller, A. The crucible
c Miranda, J. E. Cornerstone of civil rights
c Smith, B. S. Adams for the defense

History—French and Indian War, 1755-1763

y McCaslin, N. The legend of Minna Lamourrie

History—Revolution

c Boiko, C. Yankees vs. Redcoats
Dunlap, W. André
c Hall, M. Molly Pitcher meets the General

United States—History—Revolution—*Continued*
c Keats, M. Peter Salem, Minuteman
Koch, K. George Washington crossing the Delaware
c McCaslin, N. Brave new banner
Nelson, R. The General from America
c Swajeski, D. M. The revolution machine
c Van Horn, B. Ordeal at Valley Forge

History—1783-1865

Kingsley, S. The patriots

History—1801-1809

Keithley, G. The best blood of the country

History—War with Mexico, 1845-1848

Lawrence, J. and Lee, R. E. The night Thoreau spent in jail

History—Civil War

Bynum, R. C. The sharpshooters
c DuBois, G. Bind up the nation's wounds
Graham, S. It's morning
y Miller, K. S. Red badge of courage
Schenkkan, R. God's great supper
c Wartski, M. C. The birthday guests

History—1865-1898

Glover, K. Coming of the Hurricane

History—1901-1953

Miller, A. The American clock

Navy

Milligan, J. Shore leave

Race relations

Baraka, A. Dutchman
Barry, L. The good times are killing me
Brown, M. H. The day the Bronx died
Childress, A. Trouble in mind
Childress, A. Wine in the wilderness
Feldshuh, D. Miss Evers' boys
Franklin, J. E. Miss Honey's young'uns
Grimké, A. W. Rachel
Harrison, P. C. The great MacDaddy
Hughes, L. Limitations of life
Hughes, L. Scarlet Sister Barry
Jones, L. Combination skin
Kennedy, A. P. and Kennedy, A. Sleep deprivation chamber
Kwahulé, K. That old black magic
Leslee, R. Avenue X
Mann, E. Having our say
McCauley, R. Sally's rape
Medley, C. Dearborn Heights
Oates, J. C. Negative
Rahman, A. The mojo and the sayso
Schmidt, E. Mr. Rickey calls a meeting
Seiler, C. Darker brother
Shin, R. The art of waiting
Smith, A. D. Aye aye aye I'm integrated
Smith, A. D. Fires in the mirror: Crown Heights, Brooklyn and other identities
Smith, A. D. Twilight: Los Angeles, 1992
Son, D. R.A.W. ('cause I'm a woman)
Sutton, J. Voir dire
Tasca, J. Outrageous
Tissian, G. Night baseball
Wong, E. Kimchee and chitlins
Wright, R. and Green, P. Native son

Social life and customs—19th century

c McCullough, L. E. Go tell it on the mountain

Social life and customs—20th century

Chayefsky, P. The mother
Gurney, A. R. The dining room
Gurney, A. R. Scenes from American life
Pintauro, J. Butterball

Supreme Court

Lawrence, J. and Lee, R. E. First Monday in October

United States Food Administration
Why we are at war

Patriotic pageant urging African Americans to support nation's entry into World War I. Music. Variable cast

In Black theatre USA [v1]; ed. by J. V. Hatch and T. Shine

The **universal** language. Ives, D.

The **universal** wolf. Schenkar, J. M.

University of Oxford
Warner, F. A conception of love

Unlucky Cinderella. Jackson, M.

Unmarried couples
Anderson, J. Lynette at 3 AM
Bailey, M. Going all the way
Ives, D. Ancient history
Linney, R. Sand Mountain
Nelson, R. Life sentences
Stroppel, F. Morning coffee

Unquestioned integrity: the Hill-Thomas hearings. Hunt, M.

The **unseen** hand. Shepard, S.

Unsent letters. Szilágyi, A.

An **unsocial** socialist. Shaw, B. (dramatization) See Hatcher, J. Smash

Unsuitable for adults. Johnson, T.

Unveiling. Havel, V.

Up and running! Benfield, D.

Up 'n' under II. Godber, J.

Up rose a burning man. Miller, E.

Upton, Judy

Ashes and sand

Drama about violent girl gang in English seaside resort. 3 acts 6 scenes 3m 4w 1 setting

In Frontline intelligence 3; ed. by P. Edwardes

Bruises

Domestic drama set in British coastal town. Father passes on inheritance of drunken cruelty to his son. 3 acts 5 scenes 2m 3w 1 setting

In Upton, J. Bruises & The shorewatchers' house

The shorewatchers' house

Drama set in English coastal village awaiting construction of nuclear plant. Three entangled lovers struggle to escape their obsessive fears. 2 acts 5 scenes 2m 2w 1 interior

In Upton, J. Bruises & The shorewatchers' house

Ursell, Geoffrey

y The park

Apartment dweller resists eviction and leads movement to preserve local park. 2 scenes Variable cast 11 characters extras 1 interior 1 exterior

In Eureka! ed. by J. J. Lewis and D. Warren

Us. Malpede, K.

The **ushers.** Schevill, J.

Utopias

Aristophanes. Birds

Utter garbage. Ellison, L.

Uyehara, Denise

Hiro

Spirit of dead daughter visits Japanese American family. 2 acts 11 scenes 1m 3w extra 1 setting

In Asian American drama; ed. by B. Nelson

Uys, Pieter-Dirk

Just like home

Meditation on exile focusing on South Africans living in 1980s London. 2 acts 3m 1w 1 interior

In South African plays; ed. by S. Gray

V

Vacations

Ackermann, J. The batting cage

Vago, Sandra Marie

Connie & Sabrina in waiting. French 1994 85p

Following death of her friend woman looks back on their years together. 2 acts Variable cast 14 characters 1 setting

An ordinary woman under stress. French 1996 81p

Comedy. Wealthy woman leaves husband of thirty years and checks into hotel scheduled to be razed. 2 acts 3m 3w extras 1 interior

Valenti, Michael

c Beauty and the beast; a musical for children; music by Michael Valenti; lyrics by Elsa Rael; book by Peter del Valle & John Ahearn. French 1994 53p

Musical dramatization of classic fairy tale about prince released from spell through love of beautiful maiden. 2 acts 9 scenes 4m 3w 2 interiors 4 exteriors

The **Valentine** bouquet. Pflomm, P. N.

The **Valentine** fairy. Thompson, E.

Valentine's Day

c Marx, P. Hearts and tarts

c Pflomm, P. N. The Valentine bouquet

c Tutt, B. Heart to heart

Valle, Fred

I am a winner

Farce set in New York City. Puerto Rican man wins lottery. 2 acts 3 scenes 5m 1w 1 interior

In Nuestro New York; ed. by J. V. Antush

Valle-Inclán, Ramón del

Blood pact

Virgin, forced into unwanted sexual union by greedy mother, fights to save her virtue for ideal love. 3m 2w 1 interior

In Valle-Inclán, R. del. Savage acts

Bohemian lights

Episodic tragicomedy about corruptive nature of urban life. Poor blind poet sets out with opportunistic friend to try his luck in streets of Madrid. 15 scenes Large mixed cast 1 setting

In Valle-Inclán, R. del. Three plays

Divine words

Tragicomedy. Theater of the absurd. The decadence of modern day civilization with all its cruelty, brutality and horrors, set against idyllic Galician countryside. 3 acts 20 scenes Large mixed cast 1 interior 8 exteriors 3 settings

In Valle-Inclán, R. del. Three plays

The head of the Baptist

Seductive woman convinces thief to murder outlaw. 2m 1w extras 1 setting

In Valle-Inclán, R. del. Savage acts

The paper rose

Greedy man who abused dying wife perishes in moment of necrophiliac abandon. 5m 5w extras

In Valle-Inclán, R. del. Savage acts

Sacrilege

Aged criminal sentenced to death by fellow cutthroats. 7m 1 setting

In Valle-Inclán, R. del. Savage acts

Valle-Inclán, Ramón del—*Continued*
Silver face
First play in The Savage plays trilogy. Hallucinatory vision of family representing way of life that conflicts violently with late 19th and early 20th century. 3 acts 17 scenes Large mixed cast 1 interior 2 exteriors
In Valle-Inclán, R. del. Three plays

Vallejo, Teresita Gomez
El gato sin amigos (dramatization) See Rosenberg, J. El gato sin amigos—The cat who had no friends

Valley song. Fugard, A.

Valparaiso. Norbury, P.

The **value** of names. Sweet, J.

Vampilov, Aleksandr
Duck-hunting
Variant title: Duck shooting. Suicidal thoughts affecting Soviet engineer bored with job and unhappy with marriage gone stale dispelled by vodka and urge to hunt. 3 acts 6m 4w 1 setting
In Vampilov, A. Duck-hunting [and] Last summer in Chulimsk

Last summer in Chulimsk
Drama set in Siberia during communist rule. Explores issues of history, conscience, rape and native peoples. 2 acts 4 scenes 6m 3w 1 setting
In Vampilov, A. Duck-hunting [and] Last summer in Chulimsk

Vampires
Clapp, T. Dracula
Deane, H. Dracula (1924)
Deane, H. and Balderston, J. L. Dracula: the vampire play (1927)
Dietz, S. Dracula
Wellman, M. Dracula
Wellman, M. Dracula [another play]
Wellman, M. Swoop

Van Doren, Charles Lincoln, 1926-
Feffer, S. The wizards of quiz

Van Itallie, Jean-Claude
Master & Margarita; or, The Devil comes to Moscow. Dramatists 1995 69p
Dramatization of Bulgakov's novel set in Stalin's Moscow. 2 acts 22 scenes Large mixed cast settings

Van Zandt, Billy, and Milmore, Jane
Infidelities! French 1993 84p
Revised version of play entered in Play Index 1988-1992. Romantic comedy. Playwright and aspiring soap opera actress cope with their bi-coastal romance. 2 acts 5m 4w 1 setting

What the rabbi saw. French 1996 89p
Slapstick farce about infidelity set in posh New York City hotel minutes before scheduled wedding. 2 acts 7m 4w 1 interior

Vance, Charles
Jane Eyre. French (London) 1996 71p
Dramatization of Charlotte Brontë's classic love story set in 1840s Yorkshire. 2 acts 9 scenes 4m 7w 1 interior

Vance, Danitra
Live and in color!
Satiric one woman show about African American women. 2 parts epilogue 1w 1 setting
In Moon marked and touched by sun; ed. by S. Mahone

Vancouver (B.C.)
c James, J. The echo box

Vanderhaeghe, Guy
Dancock's dance. Blizzard Pub. 1996 71p
Shell shocked and confined to Saskatchewan insane asylum, WWI veteran cannot escape his conscience which takes shape as ghostly apparition of dead soldier. 2 acts 21 scenes 5m 1w 1 interior

I had a job I liked. Once. Fifth House 1992 89p
Drama about justice set in Saskatchewan police station. Interrogation of young man accused of crime involving wealthy teenage girl. 2 acts 3 scenes 4m 1w 1 interior

Vanishing points. Jones, M.

Vanuatu
Campbell, K. Jamais vu

Vargas Llosa, Mario
Mistress of desires
Drama set in Peruvian bar. Fantasy and reality intermingle in play about love, desire, taboo, greed, and role of women in male-dominated society. 2 acts 15 scenes 4m 2w 1 setting
In Latin American plays; ed. by S. Doggart

Variations on the death of Trotsky. Ives, D.

Varon, Charlie
Rush Limbaugh in night school. Dramatists 1997 49p
One man show framed as public television documentary. Satirical look at conservative politics. 2 acts 1m 1 setting

Vasilisa Prekrasnaia: "Vasilisa the beautiful." Gerke, P.

Vasilisa the beautiful. See Gerke, P. Vasilisa Prekrasnaia: "Vasilisa the beautiful"

Vassallo, Philip
The spelling bee
Comedy. Encounter between two young men, one black and one white, each victimized by same crime. 2m 1 setting
In Off-Off Broadway Festival plays, 19th ser.

Vegetables. Pflomm, P. N.

The **veil** of Pierrette. Schnitzler, A.

Vendetta
McNally, T. The Ritz
Reaney, J. The St. Nicholas Hotel, Wm. Donnelly, prop.
See also Revenge

The **Venetian** twins. Clarke, T.

Vengeance. Ravel, A.

Venice (Italy)
Goldoni, C. The coffee shop

Venus. Parks, S. L.

Venus in the back room. Schwartz, D.

Vera. Wilde, O.

Verdecchia, Guillermo
Fronteras Americanas (American borders). Coach House Press 1993 79p

One-man theater piece about Latin experience in North America. 2 acts 1m

Verdecchia, Guillermo, and Youssef, Marcus
A line in the sand. Talonbooks 1997 127p

Drama about psychological and cultural roots of war. Canadian soldier and teenage Palestinian black-marketeer meet in Qatari desert during Operation Desert Storm. Includes alternate version of act 2. 3 acts 10 scenes 3m 1 exterior

Verlaine, Paul, 1844-1896
Hampton, C. Total eclipse

The **veteran.** Ruzzante

Veterans
Hall, P. D-Day
Shepard, S. States of shock

Veterans (Vietnamese conflict, 1961-1975)
Barroga, J. Walls
Cadman, L. Peace in our time
Durang, C. The Vietnamization of New Jersey
Mann, E. Still life
Medoff, M. Stumps
Rabe, D. Sticks and bones
Shurtz, R. K. Cowboys, Indians and waitresses
Wilson, L. Redwood curtain

Veterans (World War, 1914-1918)
Vanderhaeghe, G. Dancock's dance

Via Reggio revisited. Hall, F. B.

Vickery, Frank
Biting the bullet. French (London) 1997 92p

Comedy set in Wales. Abandoned wife refuses to let husband return when he has second thoughts. 2 acts 10 scenes 2m 3w 1 interior

Erogenous zones. French (London) 1994 84p

Depicts triangle of overlapping relationships. Homosexual is in love with flatmate who is having affair with woman married to philandering husband. 2 acts 3 scenes 3m 2w 1 setting

Green favours. French (London) 1994 19p

Romantic comedy. Man and woman in gardening club, both married, find themselves attracted to each other. 1m 1w 1 interior

A kiss on the bottom. French (London) 1995 59p

Prequel to Loose-ends. Bittersweet comedy about three women being treated for cancer in East Glamorgan, Wales hospital. 2 acts 5 scenes 5w extras 1 interior

Loose ends. French (London) 1995 72p

Comedy. Sequel to A kiss on the bottom. Overly protective mother meddles in son's and daughter's love life. 2 acts 2m 3w 1 interior

Love forty. French (London) 1997 70p

On their 40th anniversary unhappily married couple agree to persevere. 2 acts 2m 2w 1 interior

Roots and wings. French (London) 1997 74p

Comedy. Couple learns son is gay while visiting him in hospital after car crash. 2 acts 3 scenes 3m 3w 1 setting

Spanish lies. French (London) 1993 83p

Comedy. Husband and wife hope to reinvigorate flagging marriage with anniversary trip to their honeymoon hotel in Majorca. 2 acts 5 scenes 3m 4w 1 setting

Victoria Station. Pinter, H.

Victory on Mrs. Dandywine's island. Wilson, L.

Vidal, Gore
The best man. Rev. ed. Dramatists 1996 81p

Political satire. Two candidates, one honorable and one ruthless, struggle for their party's presidential nomination. 3 acts 7 scenes 12m 5w extras 2 interiors

Vienna (Austria)
Barker, H. The Europeans: struggles to love
Marans, J. Old wicked songs
Szyszkowitz, G. Grillparzer
Tambori, G. Mein Kampf

Vietnam
Huynh, Quang Nhuong. Dance of the wondering souls
y Le, Q. D. Cho doi (Market of lives)

Vietnam Veterans Memorial (Washington, D.C.)
Barroga, J. Walls
Cadman, L. Peace in our time

Vietnamese

Australia

Janaczewska, N. The history of water/huyền thoại một giòng nu'ó'c

Vietnamese Conflict, 1961-1975
Hare, D. Saigon: year of the cat
y Le, Q. D. Cho doi (Market of lives)
Mann, E. Still life
Rabe, D. The basic training of Pavlo Hummel
Rabe, D. The orphan
Rabe, D. Streamers
Szyszkowitz, G. Commander Carrigan

Prisoners and prisons

Bell, J. A. Prisoner

Protest movements

Enright, N. St. James Infirmary

The **Vietnamization** of New Jersey. Durang, C.

The **view** from here. Dulaney, M.

Vigil, Angel

c La aparicion de Nuestra Senora de Guadalupe. The miracle of Our Lady of Guadalupe

Portrays origins of Hispanic Feast Day of Our Lady of Guadalupe which begins Christmas season. 6 scenes 3m 2w 1 interior 1 exterior

In Vigil, A. ¡Teatro! Hispanic plays for young people

c La Batalla de Cinco de Mayo. The Battle of Cinco de Mayo

Historical drama in which Mexican government headed by President Benito Juarez defeats French in 1862. 7 scenes 18m 1 setting

In Vigil, A. ¡Teatro! Hispanic plays for young people

c Blanca flor. White flower

Based on Hispanic folklore. Young lovers reunited through magic and transformation. 10 scenes 4m 2w extras 1 setting

In Vigil, A. ¡Teatro! Hispanic plays for young people

c El Dia de los Muertos. The Fiesta of the Day of the Dead

Mexican American family celebrates The Day of the Dead. 4 scenes 2m 2w 1b 1g 1 setting

In Vigil, A. ¡Teatro! Hispanic plays for young people

c La estrella de oro. The gold star

Based on Hispanic folklore. Mistreated young girl befriended by magical guardian. 10 scenes 2m 5w extras 1 setting

In Vigil, A. ¡Teatro! Hispanic plays for young people

c La flor de la Noche Buena. The flower of the Holy Night

Mexican miracle legend of how poinsettia got its red leaves. 5 scenes 1w 2m 1b 2g extra 1 setting

In Vigil, A. ¡Teatro! Hispanic plays for young people

c The foolish Coyote

Based on Hispanic fable. Owl outwits foolish coyote. 4 scenes Unidentified cast 9 characters 1 setting

In Vigil, A. ¡Teatro! Hispanic plays for young people

c Juan Oso. John the bear

Drama based on Hispanic folklore. Adventures of youth with strength of bear. Singing. 5 scenes 5m 5w extras 1 setting

In Vigil, A. ¡Teatro! Hispanic plays for young people

c The littlest ant

Based on Hispanic fable. Cumulative tale about lazy ant. 3 scenes Unidentified cast 15 characters 1 setting

In Vigil, A. ¡Teatro! Hispanic plays for young people

c The most interesting gift of all

Based on Hispanic folklore. Three brothers compete for woman's hand in marriage. 9 scenes 5m 3w 1 setting

In Vigil, A. ¡Teatro! Hispanic plays for young people

c El muchacho que mato al gigante. The boy who killed the giant

Based on Hispanic folklore. Boy rescues princess from giant with help from the animal kingdom. 8 scenes Unidentified cast 15 characters extras 1 setting

In Vigil, A. ¡Teatro! Hispanic plays for young people

c Los pastores. The shepherds

Nativity play based on traditional Hispanic folklore. 4 scenes 10m 2w 1 setting

In Vigil, A. ¡Teatro! Hispanic plays for young people

c The smelly feet

Based on Hispanic fable. Feuding lion and bear outwitted by fox. 3 scenes Unidentified cast 9 characters 1 setting

In Vigil, A. ¡Teatro! Hispanic plays for young people

c The three pieces of good advice

Drama based on folktale from the Hispanic Southwest about the gaining of wisdom through experience. 7 scenes 8m 3w extra 2 settings

In Vigil, A. ¡Teatro! Hispanic plays for young people

Vigil. Panych, M.

Vikings. See Northmen

Village day. Rensten, M.

The **village** fête. Tinniswood, P.

Villarrubia, Jan
Miz Lena's backyard. Dramatic 1994 54p
Drama about death and loss set in 1989 New Orleans. Widow creates fantasy world to escape facing personal problems. 8 scenes 3m 1w 1 exterior

Villeggiatura: Adventures in the country. Goldoni, C.

Villeggiatura: Back from the country. Goldoni, C.

Villeggiatura: Crazy for the country. Goldoni, C.

Villon, François, b. 1431
Fischerova, D. Dog and wolf

Vine and dandy. Brandl, D.

Vinegar Pete's calico whisker pie. McCullough, L. E.

Vingoe, Mary
Living curiosities: a story of Anna Swan
Radio play based on life of Anna Swan, who was displayed in P.T. Barnum's circus. Background music. 16 scenes 9m 8w
In Adventures for (big) girls; ed. by A. Jansen

Vingoe, Mary, and Kudelka, Jan
Hooligans
Drama based on diaries and writings of dancer Isadora Duncan, poet Sergei Esenin, explorer Robert Falcon Smith, historian Kathleen Bruce, and scenic designer Edward Gordon Craig. 3m 2w
In New Canadian drama 6

Violence
Aba, N. Such great hope
Alianak, H. Passion and sin
Ball, A. Made for a woman
Barker, H. Minna
y Barrie, S. Carrying the calf
Barteve, R. The orphanage
y Bond, E. Tuesday
Burke, S. The lodger
Carson, J. A preacher with a horse to ride
Dryden, J. Amboyna
Farhoud, A. Game of patience
y Foon, D. War
Fraser, B. Wolfboy
y Gallagher, M. Windshook
Glover, K. Dancing on moonlight
y Haynes, H. J. Isolation
Hibberd, J. Slam dunk
Horovitz, I. The Indian wants the Bronx
Horovitz, I. The widow's blind date
Isitt, D. Nasty neighbours
Kennedy, A. Motherhood 2000
Learner, T. The gun in history
Mack, C. K. The magenta shift
Maguire, M. Phaedra
Mann, E. Still life
Margulies, D. Manny
Mason, P. N. The discipline committee
Mastrosimone, W. Extremities
McGuinness, F. Carthaginians
McNally, T. Witness
Medoff, M. Stumps
Mouawad, W. Wedding day at the Cro-Magnons'
Oates, J. C. Homesick
O Flatharta, A. Blood guilty
Oliensis, A. Ring of men
Ono, Y. New York rock
Pinter, H. Ashes to ashes
Prideaux, J. Elephants
Pugliese, F. Aven'u boys
Reid, C. Did you hear the one about the Irishman . . . ?
Ridley, P. The fastest clock in the universe
Ridley, P. Ghost from a perfect place
Taylor, R. Mudtracks
Terry, M. Breakfast serial
Thompson, J. Sled
Upton, J. Ashes and sand
Valle-Inclan, R. del. Silver face
Wellman, M. Harm's way
White, P. Netherwood
Williams, N. William Golding's Lord of the flies

Violent peace. Mueller, L.

Violet (condensation). Tesori, J.

Violin time. Campbell, K.

Violinists
Wright, D. Lot 13: the bone violin
See also Paganini, Nicolo

Viorst, Judith. See Markham, S. Love and shrimp

Virgil
Warner, F. Virgil and Caesar

Virgil and Caesar. Warner, F.

Virginia
c Miranda, J. E. Cornerstone of civil rights
History
Barker, J. N. The Indian princess

Virtual reality
Mighton, J. Body and soul

The **virtuoso.** Shadwell, T.

The **virtuous** burglar. Fo, D.

The **virtuous** criminal. See Sade, Marquis de. The madness of misfortune

Visdei, Anca

Always together

Two sisters, a playwright and an actress, separated by Iron Curtain. 2w 1 setting

In Plays by women: an international anthology bk3; ed. by N. Shange

Class photo

Woman, after self imposed exile of twenty years in Paris, revisits native Bucharest and organizes high school reunion. 7 scenes 6m 4w settings

In Playwrights of exile: an international anthology

Visions of grandeur. See Nemeth, S. Sally's shorts: Visions of grandeur

A **visit** from St. Nicholas. Swortzell, L.

A **visit** to the library. Pflomm, P. N.

Visiting Oliver. Nave, B.

Visually handicapped

Mead, K. And who will pay the rent?

Vita & Virginia. Atkins, E.

Vital signs. Martin, J.

Vito on the beach. Schwartz, S.

Vivien. Granger, P.

Vladivostok blues. Beard, J. A.

Vogel, Paula

And baby makes seven

Timid gay man shares apartment with two lesbians, one of whom is expecting his child. 2 Prologues 2 acts 14 scenes epilogue 1m 2w 1 interior

In Vogel, P. The Baltimore waltz and other plays

The Baltimore waltz

Dramatic comedy set in Baltimore, Maryland hospital. Imaginary trip to Europe shared by sister and brother vehicle for comments on attitudes toward AIDS. 30 scenes 2m 1w 1 setting

In The Actor's book of gay and lesbian plays; ed. by E. Lane and N. Shengold

In Vogel, P. The Baltimore waltz and other plays

In Women playwrights: the best plays of 1992

Desdemona. Dramatists 1994 51p

Revisionist version of Shakespeare's Othello with feminist undertones. Desdemona portrayed as free-thinking strumpet. Prologue 30 scenes 3w 1 interior

—Same

In Plays for actresses; ed. by E. Lane and N. Shengold

In Vogel, P. The Baltimore waltz and other plays

Hot 'n' throbbing

Drama about domestic violence. Feminist who writes erotica to support herself and her teenage children is murdered by husband after obtaining restraining order against him. 3m 3w 1 setting

In Vogel, P. The Baltimore waltz and other plays

In Women playwrights: the best plays of 1994

How I learned to drive. Dramatists 1997 60p

Middle-aged man's obsession with wife's teenaged niece. 1 act 1m 1w extras

How I learned to drive (condensation)

In The Best plays of 1996-1997

The oldest profession

Social drama about feminization of poverty set in 1980 New York. Four prostitutes in their 70's and their madam discuss their fees, clients and cost of living. 5w 1 setting

In Vogel, P. The Baltimore waltz and other plays

Vogelstein, Cherie

Date with a stranger

Manhattan diner setting for exploration of contemporary relationships. 2m 1w 1 interior

In The Best American short plays, 1993-1994

Voices. Hornby, I.

Voices of America. Bogosian, E.

Voir dire. Sutton, J.

Vonnegut, Kurt

Miss Temptation (dramatization) See Cooperman, D. Miss Temptation

Vortex. Sheeler, W.

Vote by ballot. Granville-Barker, H.

The **voucher.** Pedrero, P.

A **vow** of silence. Havis, A.

Voyage of the dragonfly. See Bush, M. Aalmauria: Voyage of the dragonfly

Voyage to the sonorous land. Handke, P.

Voyages and travels

Césaire, I. The ship

The **Voysey** inheritance. Granville-Barker, H.

Vreeland, Diana

Hampton, M. and Wilson, M. L. Full gallop

The **vultures.** See Ayckbourn, A. Wolf at the door

W

Wackler, Rebecca. See Larson, L. jt. auth.

Wacs in khaki. Steelsmith, M.

Waddy, Lawrence

y Florence Nightingale. Players Press 1996 27p

Pioneering nurse Florence Nightingale recounts her career in series of monologues and flashbacks. 2 acts 2 scenes 3m 2w 1 interior

y Shakespeare remembers. Players Press 1994 40p

Monologue. William Shakespeare looks back upon his life and work. 2 acts 1m 1 interior

Wadsworth, Stephen

The triumph of love. French 1993 102p

Adaptation of Marivaux's light comedy set in ancient Greece. Princess, disguised as man, infiltrates philosopher's retreat. 3 acts 35 scenes 5m 4w extra 1 exterior

Wagner, Colleen

The monument. Playwrights Can. Press 1996 88p

Philosophical play about ambiguities of morality and justice. Young soldier convicted of war crimes "rescued" by woman from enemy side. 8 scenes 1m 1w 1 setting

Wagner, Richard, 1813-1883

Parodies, imitations, etc.

Warrender, S. Das barbecü

Wait until the ghost is clear. Hornby, I.

Waiters

Lane, E. Cater-waiter

Waiting for a bus. Barnes, P.

Waiting for Pierrepoint. Beard, P.

Waitresses

Godber, J. and Thornton, J. Shakers restirred

Kittson, J. Escape

Shengold, N. Lives of the great waitresses

Woodward, M. B. Day shift

A **wake** for Donald. Hood, E.

Wakefield, Colin. See Edgar, K. Aladdin; Edgar, K. Mother Goose; Edgar, K. The sleeping beauty

Waking. Coghlan, L.

Walcott, Derek

Dream on Monkey Mountain

Nightmare vision of West Indian charcoal-burner. Includes music, dancing, and male chorus. Prologue 2 parts 6 scenes epilogue 7m 1w extras 1 interior 4 exteriors

In Classic plays from the Negro Ensemble Company; ed. by P. C. Harrison and G. Edwards

Pantomime

In Tobago, British actor-hotel owner and "servant" plan show for hotel guests. Ensuing conflicts reflect problems of postcolonial life. Singing, dancing. 2 acts 2m 1 exterior

In Crosswinds; ed. by W. B. Branch

Waldrop, Jerry. See Smolensky, S. jt. auth.

Wales

Mitchell, J. August

Way, C. In the bleak midwinter

See also Cardiff (Wales)

Walk about the villages. Handke, P.

Walker, David

The affairs of Dilys Willis. New Playwrights Network 1997 19p

Housewife obsessed with cleaning confronts vacuum cleaner salesman. 3m 2w 1 interior

A quiet night in. New Playwrights Network 1997 16p

Couple's evening is interrupted by armed animal rights advocates. 1 act 2m 2w 1 interior

Triangle. New Playwrights Network 1997 20p

Divorced man's romantic weekend plans disrupted by appearance of long-absent teenaged daughter. 1 act 1m 2w 1 interior

Walker, George F.

The art of war

Concluding play in author's Power play trilogy. Reporter meets arch-enemy face to face representing battle between art and artlessness. Prologue 4m 2w 8 scenes 1 exterior

In Walker, G. F. Shared anxiety

Better living

Prequel to Criminals in love, entered below. Thought dead, man returns home forcing his wife and daughters to allow him to resume authority. 2 acts 3m 4w

In Walker, G. F. Shared anxiety

Beyond Mozambique

On porch of decaying colonial house in Mozambique, six characters, including ex-Nazi doctor and junkie priest, act out real and imagined roles as chaos of surrounding jungle gradually engulfs them. 6 scenes 4m 2w 1 exterior

In Walker, G. F. Shared anxiety

Criminals in love

Two innocent teenagers in urban wasteland find themselves transformed into armed terrorists. 1 act 9 scenes 3m 3w settings

In Walker, G. F. Shared anxiety

Escape from happiness. Coach House Press 1992 126p

Absurdist comedy about eccentric urban blue-collar family entangled with drug dealing, pornography and police corruption. 6 scenes 5m 5w 1 interior

—Same

In Walker, G. F. Shared anxiety

Rumours of our death

Black comedy about colonialism. 25 scenes 5m 3w 1 setting

In The *CTR* anthology; ed. by A. Filewod

Walker, George F.—*Continued*
Theatre of the film noir
Surreal comedy about morality and guilt set in 1944 Paris. Suspects in murder of Resistance fighter include Communists looking for martyr, young man's psychopathic homosexual lover, and his collaborationist sister. 12 scenes 4m 1w 1 setting
In Walker, G. F. Shared anxiety

y Tough!
Young, single pregnant woman and her girlfriend confront father of child. 1m 2w 1 exterior
In Walker, G. F. Shared anxiety

Zastrozzi: the master of discipline
Exploration of good and evil in turn-of-the-century Italy as amoral, sadistic criminal seeks revenge upon feeble-minded impressionist painter. Prologue 10 scenes 4m 2w 1 setting
In Modern Canadian plays v2; ed. by J. Wasserman
In Walker, G. F. Shared anxiety

Walker, Joseph
The River Niger
Domestic drama set in Harlem. Tensions develop when idealistic son returns from military service to face his militant neighborhood friends. Background bass music. 3 acts 8m 3w extras 1 interior
In Classic plays from the Negro Ensemble Company; ed. by P. C. Harrison and G. Edwards

Walker, Robert. See Fo, D. Can't pay? Won't pay!

Walker, Sylvia
Come on up. New Playwrights Network 1997 36p
Comedy. Women in heaven await the arrival of their husbands. Background music. 1 act 3 scenes 1m 3w 1 interior

Walking on the moon. Milligan, J.

Walking to Waldheim. Simon, M.

Wallace, Naomi
In the heart of America
Critique of American racism, militarism, and homophobia. Sister seeks truth about murder of her gay soldier brother. 11 scenes 3m 2w settings
In Staging gay lives; ed. by J. M. Clum

One flea spare
Set in plague-infested 1665 London. Wealthy elderly couple quarantined with 12-year-old girl and young sailor. 2 acts 21 scenes 3m 1w 1g 1 setting
In Bush Theatre plays
In Humana Festival '96

Slaughter City. Faber & Faber 1996 91p
Drama about workers in American textile factory. Prelude 2 acts 28 scenes 5m 3w 1 setting

The **Wallies** guide to Christmas. Haylock, D.

Walls. Barroga, J.

Walsh. Pollock, S.

Waltzing De Niro. Martin, L.

Wampanoag Indians
Linney, R. The death of King Philip

Wanda's visit. Durang, C.

Wandering. Wilson, L.

Wang, Lucy
Junk bonds
Look at world of wheeling and dealing bond traders. 2 acts 12 scenes 4m 1w extras 1 setting
In But still, like air, I'll rise; ed. by V. H. Houston

Waning crescent moon. Serpas, S.

Wannus, Sa'dallah
The king is the king
Satirical look at political power and social differences. Arab merchant tricked into believing he is king. Puppets prologue 4 interludes 5 scenes 10m 3w extras 1 setting
In Modern Arabic drama; ed. by S. K. Jayyusi and R. Allen

Wanted: one fair damsel. Dunham, S.

War
Akerman, A. Somewhere on the border
Barker, H. The love of a good man
Brecht, B. Mother Courage and her children
Campanile, A. War
Edgar, D. Pentecost
Kane, S. Blasted
Lee, J. A. The execution
MacNeice, L. The dark tower
MacNeice, L. Prisoner's progress
McNally, T. Botticelli
Millay, E. St. V. Aria da capo
Nigro, D. Necropolis
O'Neill, E. The sniper
Shepard, S. States of shock
Stefanovski, G. Sarajevo
Tesich, S. On the open road
Warner, F. Killing time
See also names of specific wars, e.g. Trojan War; Vietnamese Conflict, 1961-1975; World War, 1939-1945

War. Campanile, A.

War. Doyle, R.

War. Foon, D.

War and peace. Edmundson, H.

War crime trials
Weiss, P. The investigation

War criminals
Harwood, R. The handyman
Linney, R. 2
Wagner, C. The monument
Willmott, K. and Averill, R. T-Money & Wolf

The **war** on poverty. Schenkkan, R.

Warbeck, Perkin, 1474-1499
Ford, J. Perkin Warbeck

Warburton, N. J.
Distracted globe. French (London) 1994 37p
Comedy. After show party for cast and crew of amateur production of Hamlet. 2m 4w 1 interior

Warburton, Nick
The Droitwich discovery. French (London) 1996 31p
Comedy. Ghost of Shakespeare's brother accuses the bard of literary thievery. 3m 3w 1 interior

The last bread pudding. French (London) 1997 25p
Comedy about nature of theatrical experience. Amateur group meets to discuss new play. 2m 4w extra 1 interior

c Round the world with class six. French (London) 1995 20p
British school children reenact Sir Francis Drake's 1577 sea voyage. Variable cast 7 characters 1 interior

Ward, Douglas Turner
Day of absence
Satirical comedy. Havoc reigns for day in Southern town when all blacks mysteriously disappear. 10 scenes 16m 6w extras 1 setting
In Black comedy: nine plays; ed. by P. F. Jackson and Karimah
In Black theatre USA [v2]; ed. by J. V. Hatch and T. Shine

Ward, Nick
Apart from George
Domestic drama set in East Anglia. Unemployed man, having incestuous relationship with daughter, commits suicide. 3 acts 28 scenes 3m 2w settings
In Ward, N. Plays: one

The present
Variant title: Danny Rule. Black comedy. Australian youth fascinated with and threatened by adult sexuality. Music. 2 acts 11 scenes 2m 2w settings
In Ward, N. Plays: one

The strangeness of others
Adultery, blackmail, family betrayals, homelessness, petty criminality and political hypocrisy in contemporary London. 5 acts 62 scenes 11m 8w settings
In Ward, N. Plays: one

Trouble sleeping
Radio play set in East Anglia. Life of middle-aged man living with mother forever altered when aunt visits with strange young woman. 2 acts 19 scenes 1m 3w
In Ward, N. Plays: one

Ward, Theodore
Big white fog
Seeking solutions to racial and economic problems before and during the Depression, members of black family in Harlem turn to Garveyism, capitalism and socialism/communism. 3 acts 8 scenes 10m 6w extras 1 interior
In Black theatre USA [v1]; ed. by J. V. Hatch and T. Shine

Our lan'
Historical drama. Group of freed slaves struggle to build new life on island off Georgia coast. 2 acts 10 scenes Large mixed cast 1 interior 1 exterior
In Black drama in America: an anthology; ed. by D. T. Turner

Warhol, Andy, 1928?-1987
Abdoh, R. The law of remains

Warhurst, Melvyn
c Peter and the princess. New Playwrights Network 1994 52p
Pantomime with music and audience participation. Commoner wooing princess is prince in disguise. Singing. 2 acts 16 scenes 6m 4w extras 4 interiors 5 exteriors

The **warlords.** Hagger, N.

Warner, Francis
Byzantium
Verse play about rule of Roman Emperor Justinian. 2 acts 30 scenes epilogue 13m 3w extras 1 setting
In Warner, F. Agora v1

A conception of love
University of Oxford setting for 20th century love story with mythological overtones. 2 acts 24 scenes epilogue 5m 3w 1 setting
In Warner, F. Agora v2

Healing nature: the Athens of Pericles
Verse drama. Portrayal of Athens during Pericles' time provides historical account of his experiment with democracy. Prologue 4 acts 23 scenes epilogue 17m 4w extras 2 settings
In Warner, F. Agora v1

Killing time
Second play in Requiem trilogy. Experimental play about war using human brain as setting. 2 acts 19 scenes 3m 2w 1 setting
In Warner, F. Agora v2

King Francis I. Smythe/Dufour Eds. 1995 105p (Oxford theater texts 12)
First installment in author's Europa tetralogy. Historical verse play. Portrayal of François I as King, warrior, husband, lover, religious bigot and patron of the arts. 2 acts 2 prologues 30 scenes epilogue 12m 7w extras 1 setting

Warner, Francis—*Continued*
Light shadows
Concluding play in Roman trilogy portrays life in Nero's court of mid-sixties A.D. 13 scenes 9m 2w 1 setting
In Warner, F. Agora v1

Living creation
Drama set in Renaissance Florence portraying civic and religious conflicts of the Medicis and Savonarola and the artistic career of Botticelli. Prologues 2 acts 35 scenes epilogue 11m 9w extras 1 setting
In Warner, F. Agora v1

Lying figures
First play in Requiem trilogy. Surrealistic comedy about love, life and death in the 20th century. 4 acts 3m 3w 1 interior 1 exterior
In Warner, F. Agora v2

Maquettes for the requiem: Emblems
Experimental play. Non-sequitur conversational attempts at communication between actor and actress. 1 act 1m 1w 1 setting
In Warner, F. Agora v2

Maquettes for the requiem: Lumen
Theater of the absurd play about marriage. 1 act 1m 2w 1 setting
In Warner, F. Agora v2

Maquettes for the requiem: Troat
Experimental play about how different generations view sex and gender issues. 1 act 2m 1w 1b 1 setting
In Warner, F. Agora v2

Meeting ends
Concluding play of Requiem trilogy. Experimental theater. Puns, poetry and sex are ingredients of these formally patterned scenes, which contrast the grotesque with the lyrical, and the symbolic with the banal. Prologue 2 acts 18 scenes epilogue 2m 3w 1 setting
In Warner, F. Agora v2

Moving reflections
Second play in Roman trilogy explores state's relations with Christianity. Depicts Empire's role in crucifixion of Christ. 3 prologues 2 acts 24 scenes 7m 4w 3 settings
In Warner, F. Agora v1

Virgil and Caesar. Smythe/Dufour Eds. 1993 95p (Oxford theatre texts)
First play in author's Roman trilogy. Historical play set in Rome and Brundisium 29 B.C.-19 B.C., about tensions between pragmatism of politics and idealistic vision of the poet. 2 acts 44 scenes epilogue 13m 3w 2 settings

—Same
In Warner, F. Agora v1

Warnings. O'Neill, E.

Warren, Dianne
Club Chernobyl. Coteau Bks. 1994 70p (Florence James series 6)
Theater of absurd comedy set in nightclub on night that the world might end. Music. 2 acts 3m 3w 1 interior

Warren, Mercy
The Group
Satire dealing with English king's abrogation of Massachusetts charter and his appointment of a Tory upper house. Verse play. Prologue 2 acts 2 scenes 15m 2 interiors
In The Meridian anthology of Restoration and eighteenth-century plays by women; ed. by K. M. Rogers

Warrender, Scott
Das barbecü; book and lyrics by Jim Luigs; music by Scott Warrender. French 1995 116p
Retelling of Wagner's "Ring" cycle as country western musical spoof. 2 acts 19 scenes 5m settings

Wars I have seen. Blanc, E. S.

Warsaw (Poland)
Tannen, D. An act of devotion

Wartski, Maureen Crane
c The birthday guests
Union and confederate soldiers seeking shelter in Kentucky home find they have much in common. 3 scenes 3m 3w 1 interior
In Great American events on stage; ed. by S. E. Kamerman

The **wash.** Gotanda, P. K.

Wash your troubles away. Christiansen, A.

Washington, George, 1732-1799
c Hall, M. Molly Pitcher meets the General
Koch, K. George Washington crossing the Delaware
c Wolman, D. An imaginary trial of George Washington

Washington Square moves. Witten, M.

The **Washtub** (Le curvier); tr. by Albert Bermel
Medieval French farce. Shrew releases husband from contracted chores when she nearly drowns in washtub and saving her is not in contract. 1m 2w 1 exterior
In A Dozen French farces; ed. by A. Bermel

Wasp. Martin, S.

Wasps. Aristophanes

Wasserman, E. G.
Outlaws
Outlaw-cowboy shoot-out. Variable cast 5 characters 1 setting
In Actors Theatre of Louisville. Ten-minute plays: v3

Wasserstein, Wendy
The sisters Rosensweig. Dramatists 1997 84p
Comedy. Three middle-aged, Brooklyn-born Jewish sisters gather in London to celebrate eldest's birthday. 2 acts 7 scenes 4m 4w 1 interior
—Same. French (London) 1996 60p
—Same. Harcourt Brace & Co. 1993 109p
The sisters Rosensweig (condensation)
In The Best plays of 1992-1993
Workout
Satiric monologue by overachieving, have-it-all woman of the 90s. 1w
In Facing forward; ed. by L. D. Frank
In Plays for actresses; ed. by E. Lane and N. Shengold
See also Durang, C. jt. auth.

Waste. Granville-Barker, H.

Watbanaland. Wright, D.

Watching the dog. Pearson, S.

Watchman of the night. Pintauro, J.

Water
Pollution
Ibsen, H. An enemy of the people
Kroetz, F. X. The nest
y Nolan, P. T. An enemy of the people

Water and wine. Spencer, S.

Water-ice. Barnes, D.

Water play. Nemeth, S.

Waterbabies. LeFevre, A.

Waterhouse, John
The cardboard cavaliers. New Playwrights Network 1996 23p
Farce. Homeless family interviewed by TV journalist. 1 act 2m 2w extras
There's an angel in my closet (dramatization) See Waterhouse, J. and Leach, P. Frank's feathered friend

Waterhouse, John, and Leach, Patricia
Frank's feathered friend. New Playwrights Network 1996 19p
Farce based on John Waterhouse's story There's an angel in my closet. Incompetant angel substitutes for Angel of Death. Background music. 3m 1w 1 interior
A nest of cuckoos. New Playwrights Network 1995 28p
Based on short story by John Waterhouse. Domestic peace between husband and wife shattered by bizarre behavior of lodgers. 1 act 3m 1w 1 extra

Waterhouse, Keith
Our song. French (London) 1993 68p
Dramatization of author's novel about middle-aged married executive's tempestuous love affair with woman half his age. Prologue 2 acts 24 scenes epilogue 4m 3w 1 setting

Watermelon boats. MacLaughlin, W.

Watermelon rinds. Taylor, R.

Watkins, Maurine
Chicago. Southern Ill. Univ. Press 1997 xxxii, 158p
Satirical comedy about imprisoned murderesses awaiting trial in 1920s Chicago. Prologue 3 acts 5 scenes 7m 8w extras 3 interiors

Watson, Ara
Final placement
Mother, guilty of child abuse, attempts to regain custody of son who has been put up for adoption by courts. 1 act 2w 1 interior
In Telling tales: new one-act plays; ed. by E. Lane

Watson, Dave
The last Munro. French (London) 1997 18p
Young climbing couple faces future with renewed hope after encounter with widower atop Scottish mountain. 2m 1w 1 exterior

Watson, Wenta Jean
y Abe Lincoln and the runaways
Variant title: Abe and the runaways. Young Abe Lincoln helps two runaway slaves. Background music. 7m 4w 1 setting 1 exterior
In Plays of black Americans; ed. by S. E. Kamerman

Watts, Irene Kirstein
Goodbye Marianne. Anchorage Press 1997 36p
Drama set in 1938 Berlin. Young Jewish girl is sent by parents to Canada to escape Nazi terror. 8 scenes Variable cast 7 characters 1 setting

Waugh, Evelyn
Brideshead revisited (dramatization) See Parsley, R. Brideshead revisited
The ordeal of Gilbert Pinfold (dramatization) See Harwood, R. The ordeal of Gilbert Pinfold

Way, Charles
Dead man's hat
Exploration of myths of American west. Stranger arrives at remote Wyoming homestead and helps mother and daughter save their ranch. Music, singing. 2 acts 3m 2w extras 1 setting
In Way, C. Three plays
In the bleak midwinter
Contemporary version of medieval mystery play set in Wales. 2 acts 14 scenes 2m 2w 1 setting
In Way, C. Three plays

Way, Charles—*Continued*

Paradise Drive

Domestic drama following British family through 1980s. Upwardly mobile daughter marries for money and artist son commits suicide. 4 acts 6 scenes 2m 2w 1 interior

In Way, C. Three plays

A **way** out. Frost, R.

A **way** with words. Gilroy, F. D.

The **Wayside** Motor Inn. Gurney, A. R.

The **wayward** spirit. Hastings, C.

We three Kings of Orient are. McCullough, L. E.

We won't pay! We won't pay! See Fo, D. Can't pay? Won't pay!

Wealth

Brustein, R. The wild duck

Godber, J. Lucky sods

Ibsen, H. The wild duck

y Kirk, L. Men and angels

Ribman, R. The rug merchants of chaos

Standjofski, H. Anton

Weasel. Ruzzante

Weavers

Hauptmann, G. The weavers

The **web.** O'Neill, E.

Webster, John, 1580?-1625? See Fletcher, J. The fair maid of the inn

Webster, Peter

c Babes in the wood

Pantomime. Robin Hood and Maid Marion rescue King's children from kidnappers. Singing. 2 acts 7 scenes 6m 6w extras 2 interiors 2 exteriors

In Webster, P. Dick Turpin and Babes in the wood

c Dick Turpin

Pantomime. Escapades of adventurer and suspected thief in 18th century London. Singing. 2 acts 9 scenes 7m 4w extras 5 interiors 2 exteriors

In Webster, P. Dick Turpin and Babes in the wood

c Peter Panto. Warner Chappel Plays 1996 74p

Based on J. M. Barrie's dramatic fantasy Peter Pan. Adventures of children who run away to Never Land to escape growing up. Singing. 2 acts 12 scenes 3m 2w 3b 1g extras 2 interiors 3 exteriors

The **wedding.** Chekhov, A.

Wedding day at the Cro-Magnons.' Mouawad, W.

The **wedding** party. Herzberg, J.

The **wedding** reception. Chekhov, A.

Weddings

Ball, A. Five women wearing the same dress

Barker, C. Subtle bodies

Berlin, E. The Midnight Moonlight Wedding Chapel

Blackwood, G. L. Futures

Bonal, D. A country wedding

Chekhov, A. The wedding

Chekhov, A. The wedding reception

Chinn, J. Sylvia's wedding

García Lorca, F. Blood wedding

Herzberg, J. The wedding party

Jensen, J. The total meaning of real life

Johnson, C. L. The years

Lucie, D. The shallow end

Mouawad, W. Wedding day at the Cro-Magnons'

Pope, R. Sandwiches: Making sandwiches

Sharrocks, M. Calling in

Storey, D. The contractor

Stroppel, F. Fortune's fool

Tony n' Tina's wedding

Van Zandt, B. and Milmore, J. What the rabbi saw

Wedekind, Frank

The first Lulu; tr. by Eric Bentley. Applause 1994 207p

Another-version of Lulu: a monster tragedy

Lulu: a monster tragedy; tr. by Edward Bond and Elizabeth Bond-Pablé

Translation of Wedekind's original which was later reworked as Earth spirit and Pandora's box. Set in 1890s Berlin, Paris and London. Life of Lulu, amoral woman of sexually voracious appetite. 5 acts 14m 3w settings

In Wedekind, F. Plays: one

Spring awakening: a children's tragedy; tr. by Edward Bond and Elisabeth Bond-Pablé

Variant title: Spring's awakening. Tragedy results as three adolescents seek to balance their natural sexual desires with the dictates of repressive and hypocritical society. 3 acts 19 scenes Large mixed cast 7 interiors 6 exteriors

In Wedekind, F. Plays: one

Weebjob. Glancy, D.

Weeds in the wheat. Gardiner, D.

The **weekend** healer. MacDonald, B.

The **weevil.** Plautus, T. M.

Weight lifting

Horovitz, I. Strong-man's weak child

The **weir.** McPherson, C.

Weird romance: Her pilgrim soul. Menken, A.

Weird romance: The girl who was plugged in. Menken, A.

The **weird** sisters. Nigro, D.

Weiss, Matthew

Hesh. Dramatists 1995 80p

Violent family saga set in Bronx and Westchester County, New York, 1974-1991. Son makes effort to reconcile with estranged father. 2 acts 11 scenes 3m 2w 1 setting

Weiss, Peter

The investigation

Condensation of court record of trial of eighteen Germans accused of crimes at Auschwitz. 28m 2w 1 interior

In Voicings: ten plays from the documentary theatre; ed. by A. Favorini

Weitz, Paul

All for one. French 1995 101p

Comic drama set in Los Angeles. Weekend reunion of three childhood friends sabotaged by ambition and unrequited love. 2 acts 3m 2w 1 interior

Welcome stranger. Hoffman, A.

Welcome to Four Way: the town that time forgot. Brown, K. R.

Welcome to Nashville. Cearley, B.

Weldon rising. Nagy, P.

Well done poets. Quinn, L.

Weller, Michael

Abroad (Split, Part 2)

Originally produced as a one act play under title: Split. The dissolution of Carol and Paul's marriage forces their friends to reassess modern relationships. 7 scenes 4m 3w 3 interiors 1 exterior

In Weller, M. Five plays

At home (Split, Part 1)

To their friends, Carol and Paul are the perfect couple, although at home their marriage is disintegrating. 1 act 1m 1w 1 interior

In Weller, M. Five plays

c Dogbrain; a play for children. Dramatists 1997 45p

Naughty six-year-old boy conjures Dogbrain, reflection of his meaner self. Audience participation version included in inserts. Variable cast 9 characters 1 setting

Fishing

Two young married couples and friend suffer shattered dreams and must face unattractive truths about themselves when business venture collapses. 2 acts 4 scenes 5m 2w 1 interior 2 exteriors

In Weller, M. Five plays

Loose ends

Drama. Couple, the product of 1960s counter culture, find their relationship deteriorating against the conflicting social pressures of 1970s. 1 act 8 scenes 7m 4w 4 interiors 4 exteriors

In Weller, M. Five plays

Moonchildren

Originally produced under title: Cancer. Comedy explores aimless lives of senior year college students in communal co-ed apartment. 2 acts 7 scenes 12m 3w 1 interior

In Weller, M. Five plays

Spoils of war

Drama chronicles desperate attempts of sixteen-year-old boy to reconcile his divorced parents. 2 acts 3m 3w settings

In Best American plays: 9th series, 1983-1992

Wellman, Mac

7 blowjobs

Satirical look at U.S. senator's anti-pornography campaign. 2 acts 3 scenes 2m 2w extras 1 interior

In Wellman, M. The bad infinity: eight plays

The bad infinity

Explores shopworn conventions of modern society focusing on geopolitics, fashion, professional sports, crime, international banking, art, economics and the theater. 12 scenes 7m 2w extras 4 interiors 1 exterior

In Wellman, M. The bad infinity: eight plays

Cellophane

Experimental theater piece about language. Variable cast

In Plays for the end of the century; ed. by B. Marranca

Cleveland

Drama about adolescent girl's dreams. Music. 7 scenes 5m 7w 1 setting

In Short plays for young actors; ed. by C. Slaight and J. Sharrar

Crowbar

Broadway's Victory Theater setting for piece about urban decay and fate of contemporary theater. 6m 4w extras 1 interior

In Wellman, M. The bad infinity: eight plays

Dracula

Version of Bram Stoker's erotic vampire tale. 6m 4w extras 1 setting

In Wellman, M. The bad infinity: eight plays

Dracula [another play]

Drama set in 1899 Transylvania. Stoker's classic vampire story serves as catalyst for exploration of Victorian sexuality. 2 acts 6m 3w extras 2 settings

In Wellman, M. The land beyond the forest: Dracula and Swoop

Wellman, Mac—*Continued*

Harm's way

Dramatic meditation on American culture of violence. Gunfighter hero revealed to be nothing more than glorified psychopath and serial killer. 11 scenes 11m 2w extras 1 setting

In Wellman, M. The bad infinity: eight plays

The hyacinth macaw

Woman's marginal existence in sinister backwater town disrupted by stranger with apocalyptic message. 2 acts 6 scenes 3m 2w 1 setting

In Wellman, M. Two plays

A murder of crows

Drama about language and contemporary life. Young woman escapes humiliating life through meteorological prophecy. 9 scenes 3m 3w extras 1 setting

In Wellman, M. Two plays

The sandalwood box

Experimental drama. Troubled woman reacts to human cruelty. 2w extras

In The Best American short plays, 1995-1996

The self-begotten

Portrayal of corrupt senator. 2m 1w 1 setting

In Wellman, M. The bad infinity: eight plays

Sincerity forever

Satiric play about fears, prejudices, anger and sexual impulses of small town American youth. 8 scenes 5m 3w extras 1 setting

In Grove new American theater: ed. by M. Feingold

Swoop

Three vampires featured in Dracula transplanted from Victorian era to present day New York metropolitan area. 1m 3w 1 setting

In Wellman, M. The land beyond the forest: Dracula and Swoop

Terminal hip

Monologue decrying effects of advertising, television, and politics on American culture. 1m

In Wellman, M. The bad infinity: eight plays

Whirligig

Satirical look at society. Girl confronts space aliens in bus station. 2 acts 2m 4w 2 interiors

In Wellman, M. The bad infinity: eight plays

Wells, H. G.

The inexperienced ghost (dramatization) See Nolan, P. T. The inexperienced ghost

The invisible man (dramatization) See Hill, K. The invisible man

Parodies, imitations, etc.

y Francoeur, B. Coney Island of Dr. Moreau

Wells, Jennifer. See Michael, J. jt. auth.

Wells, John S.

y Competition piece. French 1993 43p

Comedy. High school drama students engage in one-act play competition. 6m 13w

The ladykiller. French 1997 38p

Comedy. Man turns into serial killer when wife switches to vegetarian diet. 1m 1w 1 interior

Wells, Mike

Mephisto rock. New Playwrights Network 1994 28p

Members of fading rock band offered come-back by mysterious manager. 1 act 5m 1 interior

Welsh, David

Make it happen. New Playwrights Network 1996 26p

Thriller set in 1980s. Unemployed yuppie and wife scheme to profit from his faked death. 1 act 4 scenes 4m 2w 1 interior

y Mellow drama. New Playwrights Network 1995 20p

Farce. Disastrous errors occur in staging of a melodrama. Music. Variable cast 10 characters 1 setting

Wenceslaus

c McCullough, L. E. Good King Wenceslas

Werner, Sally

c The king's bean soup

Beggar finds missing ingredient for King's soup. Variable cast 12 characters 1 interior

In Thirty plays from favorite stories; ed. by S. E. Kamerman

Wertenbaker, Timberlake

The break of day. Faber & Faber 1995 97p

Three women and their partners face the coming century with feelings of unease and dissatisfaction. 2 acts 12m 7w extras 1 setting

The grace of Mary Traverse

Picaresque drama. Misadventures of young woman seeking emancipation in 18th century London. 4 acts 19 scenes 5m 3w extras 1 setting

In Wertenbaker, T. Plays: one

The love of the nightingale

Drama based on Greek myth of Procne and Philomela depicting victimization of women. Chorus. 21 scenes Large mixed cast

In Wertenbaker, T. Plays: one

New anatomies

European woman alienated from society flees to Algerian desert. Singing. 2 acts 12 scenes 5w settings

In Wertenbaker, T. Plays: one

Wertenbaker, Timberlake—*Continued*
Our country's good
Drama based on Thomas Keneally's novel The playmaker, about civilizing influence of theater. Convicts in 18th century Australia enact Farquhar's The recruiting officer under guidance of their jailers. 2 acts 22 scenes Variable cast 22 characters 1 setting
In Wertenbaker, T. Plays: one

Three birds alighting on a field. Dramatic 1993 85p
Satire on English art establishment of late 1980s. 2 acts 21 scenes 12m 12w 1 setting
—Same
In Wertenbaker, T. Plays: one
See also Marivaux. La dispute

Wesley, Richard
The talented tenth
Explores world of college-educated, upwardly mobile, African American corporate types. 22 scenes 4m 3w extra settings
In Crosswinds; ed. by W. B. Branch

West, Cheryl L.
Before it hits home. Dramatists 1993 72p
Drama about bisexual Afro-American jazz musician who has contracted AIDS virus. Prologue 2 acts 4m 5w 1b 1 setting
—Same
In Colored contradictions: an anthology of contemporary African-American plays

Jar the floor
Drama depicting conflict among four generations of African American women. 2 acts 4 scenes 5w 1 interior
In Women playwrights: the best plays of 1992

West, Mae, 1892-1980
The drag
Comedy about homosexual society in 1920s New York City. 3 acts 4 scenes 11m 5w 1b extras 2 interiors
In West, M. Three plays by Mae West

The pleasure man
Comic drama about lust and theatrical life. Rakish actor castrated by avenging brother of one of his sexual victims. 3 acts 5 scenes Large mixed cast 3 interiors
In West, M. Three plays by Mae West

Sex
Comic drama about prostitution and sexual relations set in Montreal, Trinidad and Connecticut. 3 acts 6 scenes 12m 6w extras 3 interiors
In West, M. Three plays by Mae West

West (U.S.)
y Boiko, C. Belinda and the Beast
y Francoeur, B. Shakespeare comes to Calamity Creek
y Francoeur, B. Wrangler Ranch
c Gallanar, I. Showdown at the 3-R Ranch
Green, M. Naked West
c Kelly, T. Treachery at Cartilage Creek
y Kelly, T. Trouble in Tumbleweed
Kobler, F. Wild dust
c McCaslin, N. The last horizon
c McCullough, L. E. Annie Oakley: little sure-shot
c McCullough, L. E. The buffalo hunters
c McCullough, L. E. Chief Sarah, the Indian Joan of Arc
c McCullough, L. E. El Corrido de Gregorio Cortez
c McCullough, L. E. Darling Clementine: a tail of old San Francisco
c McCullough, L. E. Fandango!
c McCullough, L. E. "Git along, little dogies!"
c McCullough, L. E. The golden spike
c McCullough, L. E. Greasepaint and Ginthons: the medicine show comes to town
c McCullough, L. E. Great medicine painter
c McCullough, L. E. "Have floss, will travel": the ever-so-true saga of Hiram T. McRoot, frontier dentist
c McCullough, L. E. Jesse James: blood on the saddle
c McCullough, L. E. Ninth Cavalry to the rescue!
c McCullough, L. E. Outlaw gold: the lost treasure of Commanche Creek
c McCullough, L. E. El paseo del vaquero (The ride of the vaquero)
c McCullough, L. E. Pony Express rider
c McCullough, L. E. The rainbow cradle
c McCullough, L. E. Rocky Mountain rendezvous
y McCullough, L. E. The seven Chan brothers of Paiute Pass
c McCullough, L. E. Turquoise Tom, the versifying bandit of Old California
c McCullough, L. E. Vinegar Pete's calico whisker pie
c McCullough, L. E. Zebra dun
c Miller, H. L. Bandit Ben rides again
Milligan, J. Clara and the gambler
c Reakes, P. Old Mother Hubbard
c Stanford, J. Snow White—the purdiest gal in the West
y Swift, R. Rascals under the big top

West. Berkoff, S.

West Africa
Bandele, 'B. Marching for Fausa

West Indians

England

White, E. Lament for Rastafari

United States

White, E. Lament for Rastafari

West Indies
O'Neill, E. The Emperor Jones
Walcott, D. Dream on Monkey Mountain

West moon. Pittman, A.

Westerhout, Gart
c The Zeem dream

Children dream of being saved from Horrible Hogglewart on Planet Zeem. Singing. 5 scenes 2b 2g extras 1 interior 1 exterior

In The Big book of large-cast plays; ed. by S. E. Kamerman

The **Western** Civ rap. Libert, N. P.

Whale music. Minghella, A.

Whale riding weather. MacDonald, B.

Whaling
y Thane, A. Moby Dick

Wharton, Edith
The house of mirth (dramatization) See Keeler, D. Edith Wharton's The house of mirth

What a weekend! Aynsley, E.

What are Tuesdays like? Bumbalo, V.

What do they call me? Johnson, E.

What I did in the holidays. Osment, P.

What I did last summer. Gurney, A. R.

What I meant was. Lucas, C.

What if it's raining? Minghella, A.

What is the matter with Mary Jane? Harmer, W.

What is this everything? Scanlon, P.

What of the night?: Hunger. Fornes, M. I.

What of the night?: Lust. Fornes, M. I.

What of the night?: Nadine. Fornes, M. I.

What of the night?: Springtime. Fornes, M. I.

What she found there. Glore, J.

What the rabbi saw. Van Zandt, B. and Milmore, J.

What to name your baby. Allen, R. J.

What wasn't said, what didn't happen. Manning, B.

What we do with it. MacDonald, B.

Whatever you say. Stone, T.

What's wrong with angry? Wilde, P.

What's wrong with this picture? Margulies, D.

Wheat on the autobahn. Mitterer, F.

Wheatley, Mark. See McBurney, S. jt. auth.

Wheatley, Phillis, 1753-1784
Hall, F. B. Dance of the eland

Wheel of justice. Suntep Theatre

Wheeler, Jacque, and Hartsfield, Mariella Glenn
c Tall Betsy and the crackerbarrel tales. Players Press 1993 29p

Drama based on Mariella Glenn Hartsfield's Tall Betsy and Dunce Baby: South Georgia folktales. Friendly ghost enjoys telling and listening to traditional tales with local townsfolk. Music, singing. 5m 6w

Whelan, Peter
Divine right. Warner Chappell Plays 1996 120p

Drama set in 2000 examining debate on future of British monarchy. 2 acts 22 scenes 18m 11w 1 setting

The herbal bed. Warner Chappell Plays 1996 123p

Drama based on actual events in 1613 Stratford-on-Avon. Shakespeare's eldest daughter, a physician's wife, is publicly accused of having sexual liaison with married neighbor. 2 acts 5 scenes 5m 3w 1 interior 1 exterior

Shakespeare country. Warner Chappell Plays 1993 89p

Modern day updating of A midsummer night's dream. American country singer arrives in Stratford-on-Avon seeking to authenticate claim that he is descendant of Shakespeare. Music, singing. 2 acts 4 scenes 8m 3w 1 setting

c The tinder box. French (London) 1995 64p

Dramatization of Hans Christian Anderson's story. Soldier loses fortune but with help of magical tinder box marries King's daughter and finds peace and happiness. Singing, music. 2 acts 22 scenes 4m 6w extras

When I was a girl, I used to scream and shout . . . Macdonald, S.

When it comes early. Noonan, J. F.

When one door closes. Wise, R.

When people could fly. McCullough, L. E.

When the clock strikes. Bisson, P.

When we were women. Macdonald, S.

Where are they now? Stoppard, T.

Where did you spend the night? Booth, R.

Where has Tommy Flowers gone? McNally, T.

Where the difference begins. Mercer, D.

Where the truth lies. Butterfield, C.

Where there's a will... Hornby, I.

Wherefore art thou Juliet? O'Brien, J.

Where's Mamie? See LaChuisa, M. J. First Lady suite: Where's Mamie?

Which side are you on? Schenkkan, R.

Whirligig. Wellman, K.

Whiskey. McNally, T.

Whiskeyman, Dolores

So tell me about this guy

Two women exchange confidences. 2w 1 interior

In Actors Theatre of Louisville. Ten-minute plays: v3

White, Daniel James

Mann, E. Execution of justice

White, Edgar

Lament for Rastafari

Deals with journey, both spiritual and physical, of West Indian family from Commonwealth to England and finally America. Background music. 3 acts 36 scenes 8m 7w 1 setting

In Crosswinds; ed. by W. B. Branch

White, Patrick

Big toys

Drama set in 1979 Sydney about social and political corruption. Draws on melodrama, caricature, parody and music to express its themes. 3 acts 2m 1w 1 setting

In White, P. Collected plays v2

A cheery soul

Comedy set in old ladies home in Sydney. Residents' antics involve clergyman. Chorus. 3 acts 8 scenes 7m 19w 2b 3g settings

In White, P. Collected plays v1

The ham funeral

Set in a drab London lodginghouse of late 1910s. Death of landlord provides widow with opportunity for a lovely funeral. 2 acts 10 scenes 6m 4w 1 setting

In White, P. Collected plays v1

Netherwood

Parable of good and evil set in 1970s Australia. City couple confronted with violence when they move to country to care for group of misfits. 6m 6w 1 setting

In White, P. Collected plays v2

Night on Bald Mountain. Currency Press in association with State Theatre Co. of South Australia 1996 98p (Current theatre series)

Tragedy set in New South Wales. Curious lives of solitary female goatkeeper, disaffected professor, his alcoholic wife and nurse. 3 acts 3 scenes 5m 4w 1 interior 2 exteriors

—Same

In White, P. Collected plays v1

The season at Sarsaparilla

Explores domestic life of three families in Sydney suburb. 2 acts 7m 5w 2g 1 setting

In White, P. Collected plays v1

Shepherd on the rocks

Drama set in Australia about contemporary social and religious values. Disgraced cleric-turned-vaudevillean examines modern mores. Music. 14 scenes Variable cast 21 characters 1 setting

In White, P. Collected plays v2

Signal driver

Two supernatural beings take an allegorical look at the romantic aspirations and material disappointments suffered by suburban Australians. 3 acts 2m 2w 1 setting

In White, P. Collected plays v2

White chocolate for my father. Carlos, L.

White days. See Zark, J. A body of water: White days

White flower. See Vigil, A. Blanca flor. White flower

The **White** Rose. Garrett-Groag, L.

The **white** spider's gift. Turner, J.

A **white** sports coat. Lyssiotis, T.

White Woman Street. Barry, S.

Whitechapel murders, 1888. See Jack the Ripper Murders, London, England, 1888

Whiteley, Opal Stanley

Nassif, R. L. Opal

Whitemore, Hugh

The best of friends. French 1993 66p

Friendship spanning years 1924 through 1962. Adapted from the letters and writings of Dame Laurentia McLachlan, Sir Sydney Cockerell and George Bernard Shaw. 2 acts 2m 1w 2 interiors

Whitman, Walt, 1819-1892

y Slaight, B. The open road

Who is chasing whom! Alvarez, L.

Who killed Richard Cory. See Gurney, A. R. Richard Cory

Who laughs last? McCaslin, N.

Who made Robert DeNiro king of America? Katims, J.

Who shall be happy . . . ? Griffiths, T.

Who stole the pie! Jones, T.

Whoever. Haylock, D.

The **whole** shebang. Cook, P.

The **whole** shebang. Orloff, R.

Whoppers. Wilhelm, L.

Who's a pretty boy then? Bamford, S.

Who's mining the mercantile? Christiansen, D. M.

Who's under where? Kash, M. and Hughes, D.

Why Anansi lives in ceilings. See Gerke, P. The adventures of Anansi: "Why Anansi lives in ceilings"

Why is John Lennon wearing a skirt? Dowie, C.

Why the Beach Boys are like opera. Real, C.

Why the Lord come to Sand Mountain. Linney, R.

Why we are at war. United States Food Administration

Why we have a body. Chafee, C.

Why we have a body. Royce, C.

Whyte, Paterson
Tuesday, eight-fifteen. Players Press 1996 22p
Comedy in Scottish dialect. Women's theatrical group copes with real-life drama. 7w 1 interior

The **wibbly,** wobbly, wiggly dance that Cleopatterer did. McNally, T.

The **widow** Claire. Foote, H.

The **widow** Dylemma. Liking, W.

Widowers
Chayefsky, P. Middle of the night
Pintauro, J. Men without wives
Watson, D. The last Munro

Widows
Adam, A. Christmas
Bisson, P. Merry widows
Du Maurier, D. September tide
Foote, H. The trip to Bountiful
Foote, H. The widow Claire
Hibbert, G. Tilting ground
Hood, E. A wake for Donald
Liking, W. The widow Dylemma
Manet, E. Lady Strass
McConnell, J. Dancers
Mercer, D. The Governor's lady
Miller, D. L. Origami tears
Murray-Smith, J. Flame
Parsons, R. Mortmain
Parson, R. Rialto
Rector, M. H. The lady and the commissioner of airports
Rector, M. H. The lady and the mortician
Schave, E. A Texas romance
Stone, T. She needs me
Uhry, A. Driving Miss Daisy
Villarrubia, J. Miz Lena's backyard
Wilcox, M. Accounts
Woodward, M. B. Day shift

Widows. Dorfman, A.

The **widow's** blind date. Horovitz, I.

Wiechmann, Barbara
Feeding the moonfish
Young man, haunted by father's suicide, finds comfort with teenager whose mother killed father in self-defense. 1m 1w extras 1 exterior
In Telling tales: new one-act plays; ed. by E. Lane

Wiener, Sally Dixon
Pavane
Child forever alters lives of two gay couples. 2m 2w 1 setting
In Off-Off Broadway Festival plays, 20th ser.

A place where love is
Woman returns to rural home of older sister and dying father. 1m 2w 1 interior
In Facing forward; ed. by L. D. Frank

Wife abuse
Crimp, M. The treatment
McWeeny, D. and Swan, S. Broken bones
Vogel, P. Hot 'n' throbbing

A **wife** for a life. O'Neill, E.

Wife to Tolstoi. Goldenthal, J.

Wiggins, Kate Douglas
The Birds' Christmas Carol (dramatization) See Miller, H. L. The Birds' Christmas Carol

Wilcox, Michael
Accounts
Widow with two sons, one homosexual, struggles to survive on Scottish farm. 2 parts 4m 1w
In Wilcox, M. Plays: 1

Lent
Drama about adolescence and old age set at British boys school during Easter holiday 1956. 2 parts 3m 2w 1 setting
In Wilcox, M. Plays: 1

Wilcox, Michael—*Continued*
Massage
Drama set in 1986 West London about exploitative sex and pedophilia. 2 acts 2m 1w 1 interior
In Wilcox, M. Plays: 1
Rents
Set in Edinburgh. Comic portrayal of youthful homosexuals trying to survive by prostitution and odd jobs. 2 acts 5m various settings
In Wilcox, M. Plays: 1

The **wild** duck. Brustein, R.

The **wild** duck. Ibsen, H.

Wild dust. Kobler, F.

The **wild** goose. Shanley, J. P.

Wild grass. Finnegan, S.

The **wild** guys. Wreggitt, A. and Shaw, R.

Wilde, Constance, 1858-1898
Kilroy, T. The secret fall of Constance Wilde

Wilde, Oscar
The Duchess of Padua
Murder and suicide in 16th century Italy. Tragedy results when Duchess allows lover to be convicted of crime she committed. 5 acts 10m 2w extras 4 interiors 1 setting
In Wilde, O. The complete Oscar Wilde
A Florentine tragedy
Fragment of unfinished play. Love, intrigue, and violent death in medieval Florence. 2m 1w 1 interior
In Wilde, O. The complete Oscar Wilde
An ideal husband
Social comedy. 19th century British government official's marriage and career are threatened by woman eager to regain social position. 4 acts 9m 6w 3 interiors
In Wilde, O. The complete Oscar Wilde
In Wilde, O. Lady Windermere's fan; Salome; A woman of no importance; An ideal husband; The importance of being Earnest
The importance of being Earnest
Drawing room comedy exposing quirks and foibles of Victorian society with plot revolving around amorous pursuits of two young men who face social obstacles when they woo young ladies of quality. 3 acts 6m 4w 2 interiors
In Wilde, O. The complete Oscar Wilde
In Wilde, O. Lady Windermere's fan; Salome; A woman of no importance; An ideal husband; The importance of being Earnest
The importance of being Earnest (adaptation) See Harris, A. The importance of being Earnest
Lady Windermere's fan. Players Press 1994 56p
Comedy of manners about 19th century English society. Woman with a past returns, saving daughter from ruin. 4 acts 7m 9w 3 interiors
—Same
In Wilde, O. The complete Oscar Wilde
In Wilde, O. Lady Windermere's fan; Salome; A woman of no importance; An ideal husband; The importance of being Earnest
La sainte courtisane; or, The woman covered with jewels
Courtesan from Alexandria becomes a Christian convert when she visits a godly hermit. 3m 1w 1 exterior
In Wilde, O. The complete Oscar Wilde
Salome
Tragedy. Salome dances for Herod Antipas and as her reward claims head of John the Baptist. 1 act 11m 2w extras 1 exterior
In Wilde, O. The complete Oscar Wilde
In Wilde, O. Lady Windermere's fan; Salome; A woman of no importance; An ideal husband; The importance of being Earnest
Vera; or, The Nihilists
Tragedy. In 19th century Russia, Vera, a Nihilist, seeking revenge for her brother's imprisonment, plots to kill the Czar. Prologue 4 acts 14m 1w extras 4 interiors
In Wilde, O. The complete Oscar Wilde
A woman of no importance
Social comedy. Young Englishman's courtship of rich American orphan is complicated by the reappearance of his father after a twenty-five year absence. 4 acts 8m 7w 3 interiors 1 exterior
In Wilde, O. The complete Oscar Wilde
In Wilde, O. Lady Windermere's fan; Salome; A woman of no importance; An ideal husband; The importance of being Earnest

About

Bartley, J. Stephen & Mr. Wilde
Kilroy, T. The secret fall of Constance Wilde
Legg, R. Oscar: the Oscar Wilde trials of 1895

Parodies, imitations, etc.

Thomas, T. Without apologies

Wilde, Patrick

What's wrong with angry?

Student and teacher at British Catholic high school face pressures from homophobic society. 2 acts 27 scenes 8m 4w settings

In Staging gay lives; ed. by J. M. Clum

Wilder, Thornton

Bernice

Second play in the Seven deadly sins cycle. Ex-con, abandoned by family, turns to African American maid for advice. 3m 1w 1 interior

In Wilder, T. The collected short plays of Thornton Wilder v1

Cement hands

Concluding play of the Seven deadly sins cycle. Young woman discovers wealthy fiancé's miserly ways. 3m 1w 1 interior

In Wilder, T. The collected short plays of Thornton Wilder v1

Childhood

Children's view of adult world expressed through make believe. 1 act 1m 1w 1b 2g 1 exterior

In Wilder, T. The collected short plays of Thornton Wilder v1

The drunken sisters

First play in the Seven deadly sins cycle. Satyr play. Apollo, god of the sun tricks the three sisters of fate into releasing death-hold on King Admetus. 1 act 1m 3w

In Wilder, T. The collected short plays of Thornton Wilder v1

The happy journey to Camden and Trenton

Variant titles: Happy journey; The happy journey to Trenton and Camden. Farce about family automobile trip between Newark and Camden, New Jersey in the 1930's. 1 act 3m 3w

In Short plays for young actors; ed. by C. Slaight and J. Sharrar

In Wilder, T. The collected short plays of Thornton Wilder v1

In Shakespeare and the Bible

Fifth play in the Seven deadly sins cycle. Former madam entertains estranged niece and lawyer fiancé. 1m 3w 1 interior

In Wilder, T. The collected short plays of Thornton Wilder v1

Infancy

Two women pushing baby-buggies in park demonstrate complete lack of understanding of nature and needs of infants. 1 act 3m 2w 1 exterior

In Wilder, T. The collected short plays of Thornton Wilder v1

The long Christmas dinner

Fantasy. Ninety years of family life recalled during Christmas dinner. 1 act 4m 5w extra 1 interior

In Wilder, T. The collected short plays of Thornton Wilder v1

Love and how to cure it

Lovesick youth dissuaded from using gun on stage of London theater. 1 act 2m 2w 1 interior

In Wilder, T. The collected short plays of Thornton Wilder v1

Pullman car Hiawatha

Fantasy. Actions and thoughts of passengers travelling in Pullman car. 1 act 7m 5w extras 1 interior

In Wilder, T. The collected short plays of Thornton Wilder v1

Queens of France

Satire. Lawyer swindles women in 1869 New Orleans. 1 act 1m 3w extras 1 interior

In Wilder, T. The collected short plays of Thornton Wilder v1

A ringing of doorbells

Fourth play in the Seven deadly sins cycle. Elderly widow compelled to assist mother-daughter con artists despite their attempt to trick her. 4w 1 interior

In Wilder, T. The collected short plays of Thornton Wilder v1

The rivers under the earth

Family drama about relationship between father and daughter. 2m 2w 1 exterior

In Wilder, T. The collected short plays of Thornton Wilder v1

Someone from Assisi

Sixth play in the Seven deadly sins cycle. Visiting priest encounters old flame on visit to convent. 1m 2w 1g 1 interior

In Wilder, T. The collected short plays of Thornton Wilder v1

Such things only happen in books

Comedy. Author living in New Hampshire village fails to recognize wealth of fictional material all around him. 3m 1w 1 interior

In Wilder, T. The collected short plays of Thornton Wilder v1

The wreck on the Five-twenty-five

Third play in the Seven deadly sins cycle. Stroke of good fortune causes suburban accountant to reexamine his life. 2m 2w 1 interior

In The Best American short plays, 1994-1995

In EST Marathon '95

In Wilder, T. The collected short plays of Thornton Wilder v1

Youth

Forty-six-year old Lemuel Gulliver washes ashore on island inhabited by the young. 3m 2w extras 1 exterior

In Wilder, T. The collected short plays of Thornton Wilder v1

Parodies, imitations, etc.

Miller, S. It's our town, too

Wildest dreams. Ayckbourn, A.

Wiley and the Hairy Man. Zeder, S. L.

Wilhelm, Le
Cherry blend with vanilla
Comedy. Confession from husband's ghost helps widow get over prolonged bereavement. 1m 2w 1 exterior
In Off-Off Broadway Festival plays, 19th ser.
Life comes to the old maid
Comedy. Reclusive old woman visited by young girl with startling memories. 2w 1 interior
In Off-Off Broadway Festival plays, 20th ser.
The power and the glory
Originally produced as Windows of the world. Drama set in elevator. One woman helps another deal with her insecurities. 2w
In Off-Off Broadway Festival plays, 18th ser.
The road to Nineveh
Lonely man and woman meet in snowbound Tennessee restaurant on Christmas Eve. 2m 1w 1 interior
In Off-Off Broadway Festival plays, 17th ser.
Whoppers
Comedy. Husband and wife engaged in ridiculous argument while fishing. 1m 1w 1 setting
In Off-Off Broadway Festival plays, 21st ser.

Wilkinson, Linden
The night of the missing bridegroom
Satire. Woman loses husband on wedding night. 3m 1w 1 setting
In Passion: six new short plays by Australian women; ed. by R. Horin

Wilkinson, Mary E.
The lighthouse keeper's wife
Symbolic drama about lonely, repressive life of wife of lighthouse keeper on island off coast of Northern Australia. 1 act 1m 1w 1 exterior
In Playing the past: three plays by Australian women; ed. by K. Kilner and S. Tweg

Wilks, Talvin
Tod, the boy Tod
Drama about assimilated young African American man suffering from cultural schizophrenia. Prologue 2 acts 15 scenes 6m 1w 1 interior
In Colored contradictions: an anthology of contemporary African-American plays; ed. by H. J. Elam, Jr. and R. Alexander
In The National black drama anthology; ed. by W. King

Will Shakespeare save the King! Nimmo, P.

Will Shakespeare save us! Nimmo, P.

Willa and Sam. James, J.

William Golding's Lord of the flies. Williams, N.

William of Stratford. Atkins, G.

William Shakespeare's A midsummer night's dream. Quinton, E.

Williams, Alan
The cockroach trilogy
Man recalls counterculture of 1960s. 1m 1 interior
In Solo; ed. by J. Sherman

Williams, Bryan
y In the garden of the witch. Bakers Plays 1993 63p
Friendship with unconventional woman neighbor benefits troubled suburban teenagers. Singing. 7 scenes 2m 2w 1g 1 exterior

Williams, Clifford
Rebecca. French (London) 1994 67p
Adaptation of Daphne du Maurier's stage version of her novel. Psychological melodrama set in Cornwall. Second wife slowly uncovers husband's tragic and unhappy past. 2 acts 6 scenes 8m 3w extras 1 interior

Williams, Daniel Hale, 1856-1931
y Satchell, M. Daniel Hale Williams, pioneer surgeon

Williams, Garry
A death in Bethany
Husband tries to achieve reconciliation with wife he deserted. 2m 1w 1 interior
In Showtime's Act One Festival of one-act plays, 1994
Rain
Psychological drama set on farm during drought. Farmer, wheelchair-bound since accident, rails against God. 1 act 2m 3w 1 setting
In EST marathon '95

Williams, Jaston; Sears, Joe, and Howard, Ed
A Tuna Christmas. French 1995 105p
Holiday sequel to authors' Greater Tuna. Satirical look at residents of third-smallest hamlet in Texas. May be played with from two to twenty actors. 2 acts 7 scenes Variable cast 1 setting
A Tuna Christmas (condensation)
In The Best plays of 1994-1995

Williams, Keith
y Gran Webster's war. Miller, J. G. 1995 82p
Dramatic portrayal of school life in Nazi Germany. Music. Prologue 5 acts 21 scenes Large mixed cast settings

Williams, Niall

A little like paradise

Comedy about regeneration of small western Irish town. 2 acts 4m 3w 2 settings

In New plays from the Abbey Theatre, 1993-1995

Williams, Nigel

Class enemy. Faber & Faber 1995 82p

Drama set in South London school. Class of anarchic teenage boys. 2 acts 7m 1 interior

Harry and me. Faber & Faber 1995 90p

Comedy. Producer and researcher desperately try to save failing television chat show. 2 acts 2m 1w 1 interior

William Golding's Lord of the flies. Faber & Faber 1996 130p

Dramatization of Golding's allegory about group of boys stranded on island who revert to savagery and ritual murder. 3 acts 2m 11b 1 setting

Williams, Rod

The life of the world to come

Satirical look at American lust for eternal life and enormous profits. 2 acts 7m 1w 1 interior

In Frontline intelligence 2; ed. by P. Edwardes

Williams, Samm-Art

Home

Young African American man leaves South Carolina farm to build new life in north, but eventually returns home. Singing. 1 act 1m 2w 1 setting

In Classic plays from the Negro Ensemble Company; ed. by P. C. Harrison and G. Edwards

Williams, Tennessee

Something cloudy, something clear. Dramatists 1995 63p

Autobiographical play set in 1940 Provincetown, Cape Cod. Homosexual playwright on verge of success meets his first great love. 2 parts 3 scenes 5m 3w 1 interior

—Same. New Directions 1995 85p

Parodies, imitations, etc.

Durang, C. Desire, desire, desire

Durang, C. For whom the Southern belle tolls

Williamson, David, 1942-

The club

Turning point in history of professional football club. 2 acts 6m

In Williamson, D. Collected plays v2

Dead white males. Currency Press 1995 99p

Academic satire aimed at political correctness, poststructuralism, radical feminism and multiculturalism. Australian coed and trendy critic cope with Shakespeare's legacy. 2 acts 5m 6w 1 setting

The department

Drama exploring antics at departmental staff meeting of technical college in Victoria, Australia, 1967. 2pts 8m 2w 1 setting

In Williamson, D. Collected plays v2

A handful of friends [Revised version]

Drama explores artistic and professional integrity. Australian academic and wife newly returned from United States discover filmmaker friend has based his new film on their lives. 2 acts 8 scenes 2m 3w 1 setting

In Williamson, D. Collected plays v2

Sanctuary. Currency Press in association with Playbox Theatre Centre 1994 48p

Drama set in Queensland, Australia. Retired internationally renowned investigative journalist beset by intrepid young biographer. Slide projections. 2 acts 2m 1 setting

Travelling north

Drama set in New South Wales. Aging radical couple faces mortality. 2 acts 33 scenes 4m 4w settings

In Williamson, D. Collected plays v2

Willie & Esther. Bronson, J. G.

Willmott, Kevin, and Averill, Ric

T-Money & Wolf. Dramatic 1994 54p

Nazi war criminal and young gang member incarcerated in Newark, New Jersey jail. 1 act 19 scenes Variable cast 22 characters 1 setting

Wilson, August

Joe Turner's come and gone

Drama set in 1911 Pittsburgh boardinghouse. Southern blacks attempt to adjust to their new environment. 2 acts 10 scenes 6m 5w 1 setting

In Best American plays: 9th series, 1983-1992

In Crosswinds; ed. by W. B. Branch

Ma Rainey's black bottom

Recording session by black blues great Ma Rainey for white-owned studio, setting for exploration of racial relations and conflicts. 2 acts 8m 2w 1 interior

In Black drama in America: an anthology; ed. by D. T. Turner

Seven guitars. Dutton 1996 107p

Drama set in black neighborhood of Pittsburgh, 1948. Chronicle of final days in life of blues singer. 2 acts 14 scenes 4m 3w 1 exterior

—Same. French 1996 121p

Seven guitars (condensation)

In The Best plays of 1995-1996

Two trains running. Plume 1992 110p

Drama set in 1969 Pittsburgh restaurant, part of cycle about black experience in America. 2 acts 8 scenes 6m 1w 1 interior

Wilson, Edward

A first-born son. New Playwrights Network 1995 56p

Life of Christ related in style of medieval mystery play. Singing. Prelude 3 acts 10 scenes Variable cast

Wilson, Erin Cressida

Cross-dressing in the Depression

Man looks back on his 1930s Depression boyhood. 1m 1w 1b 1 setting

In Women playwrights: the best plays of 1993

Wilson, Lanford

Abstinence

Comedic look at Manhattan's "smart set." Chaos reigns at charity party for Liars Anonymous. 2m 3w 1 interior

In Wilson, L. Lanford Wilson: 21 short plays

Balm in Gilead

In underground world of sex and sordidness narcotics pusher defaults and is killed. Includes singing and song with score. 2 acts 16m 8w extras 1 setting

In Wilson, L. Collected plays, 1965-1970

A betrothal

Comedy. Two frustrated flower breeders plan to crossbreed their two would-be champions into an unbeatable strain. 1m 1w 1 interior

In Wilson, A. Lanford Wilson: 21 short plays

Breakfast at the track

Early morning conversation between husband and wife. 1m 1w 1 interior

In Wilson, L. Lanford Wilson: 21 short plays

Brontosaurus

Middle-aged antiques dealer confronted by callowness of youth in person of her college student nephew. 1m 2w 1 setting

In Wilson, L. Lanford Wilson: 21 short plays

Burn this

Romantic comedy. Dancer falls in love with married brother of recently deceased dancing partner. 2 acts 3m 1w 1 interior

In Best American plays: 9th series, 1983-1992

Day

Local gardener on beach during lunch hour encounters yuppie sexpot. 1 act 1m 2w 1 exterior

In By the sea, by the sea, by the beautiful sea

Days ahead

Monologue. Man reflects on passage of time and lost love. 1m 1 interior

In Wilson, L. Four short plays

In Wilson, L. Lanford Wilson: 21 short plays

Eukiah

Mentally handicapped teenager is murdered after overhearing criminal plan to steal race horses. 2m 1 interior

In 20/20: twenty one-act plays from twenty years of the Humana Festival

In Wilson, L. Lanford Wilson: 21 short plays

The family continues

Experimental piece about theatrical characterization. 2m 2w 1 setting

In Wilson, L. Lanford Wilson: 21 short plays

The gingham dog

Breakup of a marriage between a white Southern liberal and black girl from Harlem. 2 acts 2m 2w 1 interior

In Wilson, L. Collected plays, 1965-1970

The Great Nebula in Orion

Conversation between two women reveals emptiness of their lives. 2w 1 interior

In Wilson, L. Lanford Wilson: 21 short plays

Home free!

Incestuous brother and sister inhabit fantasy world. 1m 1w 1 interior

In Wilson, L. Lanford Wilson: 21 short plays

Ikke, ikke, nye, nye, nye

Comedic look at telephone seduction. 1m 1w 1 interior

In Wilson, L. Lanford Wilson: 21 short plays

Lemon sky

Seventeen-year-old boy's unsuccessful attempt to establish a meaningful relationship with preoccupied father. 3 acts 2m 3w 2b 1 setting

In Wilson, L. Collected plays, 1965-1970

Ludlow fair

Comedy. Hysterical young woman tells roommate about relationship with larcenous boyfriend. 2w 1 interior

In Wilson, L. Lanford Wilson: 21 short plays

The madness of Lady Bright

Set in New York City. Mental breakdown of lonely homosexual. Background music. 2m 1w 1 interior

In Wilson, L. Four short plays

In Wilson, L. Lanford Wilson: 21 short plays

The moonshot tape

Monologue. In interview with unseen high school journalist, author tells of her revenge upon stepfather who sexually abused her. 1w 1 interior

In Wilson, L. Lanford Wilson: 21 short plays

Wilson, Lanford—*Continued*

The mound builders. Dramatists 1996 78p

Two archeologists, their families and assistants dig in Southern Illinois for cultural history of Indian mound builders. Interplay of characters and contrast of Indian versus present culture is accentuated. 2 acts 2 scenes 3m 3w 1g 1 setting

A poster of the cosmos

Drama. Homosexual suspected of killing AIDS afflicted lover makes taped statement in police station. 1m 1 interior

In Wilson, L. Lanford Wilson: 21 short plays

Redwood curtain. Dramatists 1995 54p

Successful 17-year-old concert pianist, daughter of GI and Vietnamese woman, searches for biological father among Vietnam veterans living in northern California redwood forest. 3 scenes 1m 2w 1 setting

The rimers of Eldritch

Tragedy set in American Middle West. Prying small town recluse killed by woman when he interferes in attack on crippled girl. 2 acts 2 scenes 7m 11w 1 setting

In Wilson, L. Collected plays, 1965-1970

The sand castle; or, There is a tavern in the town

Set in beach house on California coast. Widow summers with her college-aged children and friends. 3m 3w 1b 1 setting

In Wilson, L. Collected plays, 1965–1970

Say De Kooning

Hamptons summer house scene of interaction between artist and two female lovers. 1m 2w 1 interior

In Wilson, L. Four short plays

In Wilson, L. Lanford Wilson: 21 short plays

Sextet (yes)

Exploration of intertwined relationships among six characters. 3m 3w

In Wilson, L. Lanford Wilson: 21 short plays

Stoop

Three aging women on stoop of city brownstone converse in aftermath of catastrophic event. 3w 1 exterior

In Wilson, L. Lanford Wilson: 21 short plays

Talley & Son. Dramatists 1995 81p

Earlier version produced under title: A tale told. Third play in Talley family cycle. Business decisions pit Eldon Talley against both his father and his older son. 2 acts 6m 6w 1 interior

This is the rill speaking

Play for voices. Evocation of life in small Ozark community. 3m 3w 1 exterior

In Wilson, L. Four short plays

In Wilson, L. Lanford Wilson: 21 short plays

Thymus vulgaris

Reunion between hard-living, long-suffering mother and her one-time prostitute daughter portrays life and dreams of two perennial losers. 1m 2w 1 interior

In Wilson, L. Lanford Wilson: 21 short plays

Wandering

Young man faces pressures to conform. 2m 1w

In Wilson, L. Lanford Wilson: 21 short plays

See also Chekhov, A. Three sisters

Wilson, Mary Louise. See Hampton, M. jt. auth.

The **wind** in the willows. Peterson, L.

The **wind** pearl. See Gerke, P. Feng zhenzhu: The wind pearl

A **window** in the diary. Haylock, D.

Window of opportunity. Augustine, J.

Windows. Hannay, R.

Windows of the world. See Wilhelm, L. The power and the glory

Windshook. Gallagher, M.

Windsor, Wallis Warfield, 1896-1986

Griffiths, L. The Duchess: pieces of Wallis Simpson

Windwick, Norman D.

A father's daughter. New Playwrights Network 1994 12p

Drama set in 19th century Orkney Islands. Young woman, facing social and economic pressures, finds strength in father's legacy. 1 act 4m 2w 1 interior

Wine, Bill

Tenure. Players Press 1993 62p

Comedic look at contemporary college faculty relationships. Two candidates for tenure are also personally involved. 2 acts 10m 5w 1 setting

Wine country. Carilli, T.

Wine in the wilderness. Childress, A.

Winer, Deborah Grace

The last girl singer. French 1997 81p

Reclusive film siren, currently a cabaret singer in Spain, manipulated by ex-husband and wealthy socialite neighbor. Singing. 18 scenes 1m 2w 1 setting

Wing, Paula Adele
c Naomi's road
Based on Joy Kogawa's novel. Child questions injustice of Canada's internment of Japanese Canadians in World War II. Singing. 2 acts Variable cast 16 characters 1 setting
In YPThree: three plays from Young People's Theatre

The **winged** man. Rivera, J.

Wings (condensation). Lunden, J.

The **Winslow** boy. Rattigan, T.

Winter, Jack, and Smith, Cedric
Ten lost years
Drama about effects of the Great Depression on Canadians. Singing. 34 scenes 6m 4w 1 setting
In The *CTR* anthology; ed. by A. Filewod

The **winter** guest. Macdonald, S.

A **winter** reunion. Miller, H.

Winther, Barbara
c The dreadful dragon of Utrecht
Chimney sweep saves Dutch city from dragon. 2 scenes Variable cast 8 characters extras 1 exterior
In Thirty plays from favorite stories; ed. by S. E. Kamerman

y John Henry
Adaptation of ballad about black folk hero. 3 scenes 7m 3w extras 1 interior
In Plays of black Americans; ed. by S. E. Kamerman

c The Maharajah is bored
Based on a Hindu folktale which dramatizes conflict between poor and rich in India as they try to please the Maharajah. Background music. 4m 2w extras 1 exterior
In Thirty plays from favorite stories; ed. by S. E. Kamerman

Winton, Tim
Lockie Leonard, human torpedo (dramatization) See Gibbs, P. Lockie Leonard, human torpedo

Wireless operators. See Radio—Operators

The **wisdom** of Eve. Orr, M.

Wise, Rob
Eventide
Comedy about four residents of old age home. 1 act 4w
In Wise, R. A bit of three-by-one

Some do, some don't. New Playwrights Network 1994 44p
Comedy. Old woman outwits unscrupulous real estate agent. 2 acts 14 scenes 4m 6w 3 interiors

Sound choice
Committee selects play for drama festival. 1 act 2m 3w 1 interior
In Wise, R. A bit of three-by-one

When one door closes
Comedy about garage sale. 1 act 4m 3w 1 exterior
In Wise, R. A bit of three-by-one

Wise child. Gray, S.

The **wise** men had it easy. Enscoe, L. G. and Enscoe, A.

Wiseman, Adele
Crackpot (dramatization) See Wyatt, R. Crackpot

Wish fulfillment. Simpatico, D.

Wishbones. Coxon, L.

Wit and humor
See also Satire

The **witch.** Middleton, T.

Witchcraft
Barnes, P. The spirit of man: A hand witch of the second stage
Bush, M. Hansel and Gretel, little brother and sister
c Bush, M. Rapunzel
Middleton, T. A critical edition of Thomas Middleton's The witch
Middleton, T. The witch
Miller, A. The crucible
c Thane, A. Rapunzel
c Wood, D. The witches
c Zeder, S. L. Mother Hicks

The **witches.** Wood, D.

Witches and ghosts. Pflomm, P. N.

Witchplay. Learner, T.

With and without. Sweet, J.

With or without you. Jannuzzi, L.

Within the ghostly mansion's labyrinth. Nigro, D.

Without apologies. Thomas, T.

Witkiewicz, Stanislaw Ignacy
c Cockroaches
Comedy. Town threatened by cockroaches. 1 act 4 scenes 4m extras
In Around the world in 21 plays; ed. by L. Swortzell

c Comedies of family life
Four short comedies about family life. 3 acts 5 scenes Variable cast 1 setting
In Around the world in 21 plays; ed. by L. Swortzell

Witkiewicz, Stanislaw Ignacy—*Continued*
c The courageous princess
King's daughter kills to save father from executioner. 4 acts 15 scenes 6m 2w extras 1 setting
In Around the world in 21 plays; ed. by L. Swortzell
The mother
Theater of the absurd play within a play both parodies and extends theatrical naturalism of Ibsen and Strindberg. Portrays unstable relationship between bourgeois mother and son. 2 acts epilogue 7m 6w extras 2 interiors
In Witkiewicz, S. I. The mother & other unsavory plays
The shoemakers
Philosophical tirades, invented obscenities, and ironic parodies in an orgy of lust, madness and cruelty portray end of Western civilization. 3 acts 9m 1w extras 1 interior
In Witkiewicz, S. I. The mother & other unsavory plays
They
Deals in bizarrely farcical terms with crushing of the individual and of art by mechanized totalitarian society. 2½ acts 10m 6w extras 1 interior
In Witkiewicz, S. I. The mother & other unsavory plays

The **Witlings.** Burney, F.

Witness. McNally, T.

Witten, Matthew
Washington Square moves. Dramatists 1995 75p
Urban misfits who congregate in Greenwich Village's Washington Square Park set world's record for most consecutive hours playing chess. 2 acts 6 scenes 5m 2w 1 setting

The **wives'** excuse. Southerne, T.

The **wizard** of hip. Jones, T. W.

The **Wizard** of Oz. Baum, L. F. (dramatization) See Francoeur, B. Oz!; Mahlmann, L. and Jones, D. C. The Wizard of Oz; Mapp, F. The wonderful Wizard of Oz

The **Wizard** of Zoz. Schurman-O'Connor, K.

The **wizards** of quiz. Feffer, S.

Woddis, Roger. See Paice, E. jt. auth.

Wolf at the door. Ayckbourn, A.

Wolfboy. Fraser, B.

Wolfe, George C.
The colored museum
Series of satirical sketches comment on contemporary blacks. Singing. 2m 3w extra 1 setting
In Black comedy: nine plays; ed. by P. F. Jackson and Karimah
In Black theatre USA [v2]; ed. by J. V. Hatch and T. Shine
Jelly's last jam; book and direction by George C. Wolfe; lyrics by Susan Birkenhead; music by Jelly Roll Morton; additional music & adaptation by Luther Henderson; introduction by John Lahr. Theatre Communications Group 1993 99p
Musical about life of black musician Jelly Roll Morton. Prologue 2 acts 12 scenes Large mixed cast settings
Story in Harlem slang
Dramatization of episode in Zora Neale Hurston's story Spunk, about life in Harlem. 1m 1w extras 1 setting
In Telling tales: new one-act plays; ed. by E. Lane

Wolman, Diana
c An imaginary trial of George Washington
Imaginary trial of George Washington by the Crown. Historical figures are witnesses. 15m 3w extras 1 interior
In Great American events on stage; ed. by S. E. Kamerman

A **woman** called Truth. Asher, S. F.

The **woman** from Ancona. See Ruzzante. L'Anconitana: the women from Ancona

A **woman** from the sea. Cowan, C.

A **woman** of no importance. Wilde, O.

Woman stand-up. Durang, C.

The **woman** who cooked her husband. Isitt, D.

A **woman's** comedy. Herst, B.

Womberang. Townsend, S.

WOMBmanWARs. Jackson, J. A.

Women
Acworth, E. Composing Venus
Albee, E. Three tall women
Augustine, J. Window of opportunity
Barbier, M.-A. Arria and Paetus
y Barrie, S. Carrying the calf
Barry, S. The only true history of Lizzie Finn
Barylli, G. Honeymoon
Bond, E. Human cannon
Braverman, C. The Yiddish Trojan women
Brittney, L. Failed investments
Brooks, V. Love me slender
Butterfield, C. Where the truth lies
Carlos, L. White chocolate for my father
Carr, M. The Mai
Clarke, B. and Dickerson, G. Re/membering Aunt Jemima: a menstrual show
Colorado, E. and Colorado, H. 1992: blood speaks
Corthron, K. Cage rhythm

Women—*Continued*
Daniels, S. Beside herself
Daniels, S. The madness of Esme and Shaz
Dunn, M. Five tellers dancing in the rain
Durang, C. Nina in the morning
Elisha, R. Choice
Epstein, M. How Gertrude stormed the Philosophers' Club
Farhoud, A. Game of patience
Finnegan, S. Mary Maginn
c Foote, H. The roads to home: A nightingale
Garro, E. The tree
Glass, J. M. If we are women
Graffigny, F. D. D. de. Cenia
Hallman, B. The women of Theta Kappa
Heggie, I. An experienced woman gives advice
Horovitz, I. North Shore Fish
Jones, R. Big butt girls, hard-headed women
Kirby, M. My body. My blood
Lambert, B. Jennie's story
Lewis, M. G. The captive
López, E. Marlene
Macdonald, S. When I was a girl, I used to scream and shout...
Mama drama
Markham, S. Love and shrimp
Martin, J. Cul de sac
Martin, J. Summer
Martin, J. Talkin with...
Martin, J. Vital signs
McCauley, R. Sally's rape
McDonald, H. Faulkner's bicycle
McGuinness, F. The factory girls
McIntyre, C. Low level panic
McKee, J. The 'far-flung'
Misto, J. The shoe-horn sonata
Murphy, T. Bailegangaire
Murray-Smith, J. Honour
Nagy, P. Butterfly kiss
Pam-Grant, S. Curl up and dye
Pinnock, W. Talking in tongues
Poliakoff, S. She's been away
Rebeck, T. Sunday on the rocks
Russ, A. Inside out
Shields, C. Thirteen hands
Siegel, J. Metamorphoses
Silver, J. M. and Boyd, J. A ... my name is still Alice
Simon, M. The old lady's guide to survival
Son, D. R.A.W. ('cause I'm a woman)
Steelsmith, M. Wacs in khaki
Stickney, P. Y. Big Momma 'n 'em
Strindberg, A. The stronger
Svanoe, B. Punch and Judy
Szyszkowitz, G. Lake of illusions
Tremblay, M. Les belles soeurs
Vago, S. M. Connie & Sabrina in waiting
Walker, G. F. Better living
Wasserstein, W. Workout
Wertenbaker, T. The break of day
Wertenbaker, T. The love of the nightingale
West, C. L. Jar the floor
Wilhelm, L. The power and the glory
Wilson, L. The Great Nebula in Orion
Wyatt, R. Crackpot
See also Single women; Widows

Psychology

Barnes, D. The dove
Barr, N. Mrs. Cage
Brittney, L. A different way to die
Broinowski, A. The gap
Carr, M. Portia Coughlan
Christian, B. Blue murder
Cocek, C. Stepping off a cloud
Colón, O. A. Siempre en mi corazón
Conde, M. The Tropical Breeze Hotel
Daniels, S. Head-rot holiday
Devlin, A. After Easter
Dulaney, M. The view from here
Durang, C. Woman stand-up
Friel, B. Molly Sweeney
Gillis, C. Caveman rainbow
Greth, R. Halfway
Griffiths, L. A game of inches
Guare, J. The talking dog
Hammond, W. Julie Johnson
Harrison, J. Holidays
Hatcher, J. Scotland Road
Hatcher, J. The turn of the screw
Hope, K. Foreign lands
Ingleton, S. The passion ... and its deep connection with lemon delicious pudding
Kemp, J. The black sequin dress
Kiefer, N. Gwen and Gwen
Kramer, S. David's redhaired death
Kramer, S. Permanent signal
Liking, W. The widow Dylemma
Lucas, C. Credo
Lucas, C. Missing persons
MacLeod, J. Jewel
Members of the road company ensemble. Blind desire
Mighton, J. The little years
Murray-Smith, J. Love child
Oates, J. C. Here she is!
Oates, J. C. The sacrifice
Oglesby, T. Two lips indifferent red
O'Neill, E. Strange interlude
Ordway, S. Panicked

Women— Psychology —*Continued*
Pedneault, H. Evidence to the contrary
Pintauro, J. Seymour in the very heart of winter
Porter, D. Flowers
Ramsey, E. Acetylene
Ross, J. Anne Marie's bedroom
Selig, P. The mystery school
Spencer, S. Blue stars
Swedeen, S. The sleep seeker
Thatcher, K. Emma's child
Thompson, J. I am yours
Thompson, J. Lion in the streets
Thompson, J. Perfect pie
Toddie, J. L. And go to Innisfree
Treadwell, S. Machinal
Turrini, P. Infanticide
Vickery, F. Biting the bullet
Wilkinson, M. E. The lighthouse keeper's wife
York, Y. Life gap
Zark, J. A body of water: Shooting souls

Relation to other women

Adam, A. Business meeting
Bassen, L. S. The month before the moon
Boothe, C. The women
Braithwaite, D. Martha and Elvira
Butterfield, C. Joined at the head
Butterfield, C. Life in the trees: No problem
Cinoman, S. Fitting rooms
Cleage, P. Late bus to Mecca
Coles, E. September revisited
Coxon, L. Wishbones
Dean, P. Long gone lonesome cowgirls
Donoghue, M. A. Me and Mamie O'Rourke
Farmer, B. Irene and Lillian forever
Fernandez, E. How else am I supposed to know I'm still alive
Goldenthal, J. Mequasset by the sea
Halvorson, K. One hundred women
Hunkins, L. The best of strangers
Jackson, M. A. Sisters
Janaczewska, N. The history of water/huyền thoại một giòng nu'ó'c
MacLaughlin, W. Watermelon boats
Margulies, D. Women in motion
Martin, J. Criminal hearts
McIntyre, C. My heart's a suitcase
Mead, K. The other other woman
Meadows, K. J. Henrietta
Miller, S. Repairs
Minghella, A. Whale music
Noonan, J. F. Music from down the hill
Pedrero, P. The color of August
Pintauro, J. Ten-dollar drinks
Pope, R. Sandwiches: Eating sandwiches
Pope, R. Sandwiches: Making sandwiches
Rayson, H. Falling from grace
Rebeck, T. Loose knit
Shawn, W. Aunt Dan and Lemon
Tolan, K. Approximating mother
Townsend, S. Womberang
Tremblay, M. Les belles soeurs
Vickery, F. A kiss on the bottom
Whyte, P. Tuesday, eight-fifteen
Ziegler, T. Grace & Glorie

Social conditions

Brogan, P. B. Eclipsed
Chinn, J. Home before dark
Chislett, A. Yankee notions
Cleage, P. Flyin' west
Corthron, K. Come down burning
Daniels, S. The gut girls
Edmundson, H. The mill on the floss
Fo, D. The open couple
Fo, D. An ordinary day
Fornes, M. I. What of the night?: Nadine
Francis, M. Jane Austen's Northanger Abbey
Fry, M. Tess of the d'Urbervilles
Gallaire, F. You have come back
Glover, S. Bondagers
Gotanda, P. K. Ballad of Yachiyo
Ibsen, H. A doll's house
Ibsen, H. Hedda Gabler
Ibsen, H. Rosmersholm
Johnson, T. Unsuitable for adults
Lyssiotis, T. The Forty Lounge Cafe
Maraini, D. Dreams of Clytemnestra
McGuinness, F. A doll's house
Mehta, D. Brides are not for burning
Mellor, K. A passionate woman
Meyer, M. The odd women
Nimmo, H. One small step
Onwueme, O. T. The broken calabash
Onwueme, O. T. Parables for a season
Onwueme, O. T. The reign of Wazobia
Onwueme, O. T. Tell it to women
Overmyer, E. On the verge
Parks, S. L. Venus
Pinero, A. W. The second Mrs. Tanqueray
Robinson, R. T. The cover of life
Seidel, G. Carmen Kittel
Shaw, B. Mrs. Warren's profession
Strindberg, A. Miss Julie
Townsend, S. The great celestial cow
'Udwan, Mamduh. That's life
Vargas Llosa, C. Orchids in the moonlight

Women—Social Conditions—*Continued*
Wallace, N. One flea spare
Wertenbaker, T. The grace of Mary Traverse
Wong, E. Letters to a student revolutionary

Suffrage

Richardson, W. The deacon's awakening

The **women.** Boothe, C.

Women and Wallace. Sherman, J. M.

Women artists
Boretz, A. I remember you
Garner, J. The flight into Egypt
Pedrero, P. The color of August

Women at the Thesmophoria. See Aristophanes. Festival time

Women authors
Bensinger, L. A ghost story
Butterfield, C. Joined at the head
Curran, C. Senetta Boynton visits the Orient
Gray, S. Man in a side-car
Kennedy, A. The dramatic circle
Norman, M. Trudy Blue
Sherman, J. The retreat
Wilson, L. The moonshot tape

Women beware women. Barker, H.

Women in a playground. Durang, C.

Women in motion. Margulies, D.

Women in politics
Kanin, F. Goodbye, my fancy

Women judges
Lawrence, J. and Lee, R. E. First Monday in October

The **women** of Theta Kappa. Hallman, B.

Women photographers
Janaczewska, N. The history of water/huyền thoại một giòng nu'ó'c

Women physicians
Margulies, D. July 7, 1994

Women poets
Linney, R. Three poets: Akhmatova
Linney, R. Three poets: Hrosvitha
Linney, R. Three poets: Komachi
Rivera, C. Julia
See also names of women poets, e.g. Millay, Edna St. Vincent

Women's Liberation Movement
See also Feminism

Wonderful Tennessee. Friel, B.

Wonderful time. Sherman, J. M.

The **wonderful** Wizard of Oz. Mapp, F.

Wong, Anna May, 1907-1961
Wong, E. China doll

Wong, Elizabeth
China doll

Monologue by Chinese American actress Anna May Wong. 1w 1 interior

In Contemporary plays by women of color; ed. by K. A. Perkins and R. Uno

Kimchee and chitlins

Play explores conflicts between African Americans and Korean Americans in New York City. 2 acts Variable cast 1 setting

In But still, like air, I'll rise; ed. by V. H. Houston

Letters to a student revolutionary

Chinese woman and Chinese American woman chafe against societies that confine them. 1 act epilogue 3m 3w 1 setting

In Unbroken thread; ed. by Roberta Uno

In Women on the verge: 7 avant-garde American plays; ed. by R. C. Lamont

Wood, Benedict
y Goethe's fairy tale The green snake and the beautiful lily. Temple Lodge 1993 43p

Verse play dramatization of Goethe's fairy tale about how the rational and sensuous sides of human nature may fall into harmony. Snake sacrifices himself for well-being of community. 2 Prologues 2 acts 11 scenes 8m 5w extras

Wood, David
c Babe, the sheep-pig. French (London) 1997 51p

Dramatization of Dick King-Smith's The sheep-pig. Pig on English farm becomes famous. 2 acts Variable cast 2 settings

c Noddy. French (London) 1995 67p

Fantasy based on Enid Blyton's novels about adventures of wooden boy. Music, puppets, audience participation. 2 acts 12 scenes Variable cast 18 characters extras

c Rupert and the green dragon; a musical play; book, music and lyrics by David Wood. French (London) 1997 68p

Musical based on Rupert stories and characters by Mary Tourtel and Alfred Bestall. Magic adventures of bear and his animal friends. Puppets. 2 acts 13 scenes 1 setting Unidentified cast 15 characters extras

Wood, David—*Continued*
c The witches. French (London) 1993 57p
Based on Roald Dahl's novel. Boy and grandmother foil witches' plot to turn children into mice. Puppets. 2 acts 13 scenes Variable cast 22 characters extras 9 interiors 2 exteriors

Wood, Patricia
Faint sound of a bell. Players Press 1996 31p
Comedy. Scottish author's home is haunted by three ghosts. 1 act 4 scenes 2m 6w 1 interior

The **wood** demon. Chekhov, A.

Woodard, Charlayne
Pretty fire. Plume Bks. 1995 53p
Autobiographical one woman show about African American life. 1w 1 setting

Woodward, Greer. See Kraus, J. H. jt. auth.

Woodward, Meredith Bain
Day shift
Monologue by widowed waitress in small British Columbia town. 1w 1 interior
In Escape acts; ed. by C. Curran

Woolf, Virginia, 1882-1941
Atkins, E. Vita & Virginia

The **woolgatherer.** Mastrosimone, W.

The Wooster Group
Frank Dell's The temptation of St. Antony
Experimental theater piece about magic and spiritualism drawing inspiration from Flaubert, Lenny Bruce, Lafcadio Hearn, Ingmar Bergman and others. 5m 4w
In Plays for the end of the century; ed. by B. Marranca

Wooten, John J.
The role of Della
Comedy. Actresses at audition. 3w 1 interior
In Plays for actresses; ed. by E. Lane and N. Shengold

Trophies. Dramatists 1994 77p
Family tragedy. Young actor clashes with estranged father following accident that left younger brother mildly brain damaged. 2 acts 5 scenes 3m 2w 1 interior

Worboyes, Sally
The house plant. French (London) 1995 27p
Black comedy. Domestic war between young couple and their wily elderly tenant. 1m 2w extras 1 setting

The **word.** Schnitzler, A.

Word games. See Nemeth, S. Sally's shorts: Word games

Words, words, words. Ives, D.

Work. O'Reilly, J.

Workout. Wasserstein, W.

The **workroom.** Grumberg, J.-C.

The **world** of Paul Slickey. Osborne, J.

World on edge. Paice, E. and Woddis, R.

World première. Mander, C.

World War, 1914-1918
McGuinness, F. Observe the sons of Ulster marching towards the Somme
United States Food Administration. Why we are at war

Aerial operations

Gray, J. Billy Bishop goes to war

Armistice

Guare, J. Home fires

France

Harwood, R. After the lions

United States

Nemeth, S. Sally's shorts: Lily

World War, 1939-1945
Blanc, E. S. Wars I have seen
Hagger, N. The warlords
Hare, D. Plenty
Hughes, T. The wound
Kilroy, T. Double cross

Atrocities

Weiss, P. The investigation

Africa

Owen, K. Black, green, white and gold

Austria

Preses, P. and Becher, U. Our Mr. Bockerer
Szyszkowitz, G. Friedmann Puntigam

Canada

Horovitz, I. Today, I am a fountain pen

Egypt

Sherman, M. Some sunny day

Evacuation of civilians

See also Japanese Americans—Evacuation and relocation, 1942-1945

France

Beim, N. The deserter
Grumberg, J.-C. The free zone
Grumberg, J.-C. The workroom
Segal, G. All the tricks but one

Germany

Mead, K. Line of descent

Great Britain

Harding, N. This year, next year
Hare, D. Licking Hitler
Mead, K. The Anderson

Japan

McDonough, J. Butterfly

World War, 1939-1945—*Continued*
Pacific Ocean
Laurents, A. Home of the brave
Prisoners and prisons
Megged, A. Hanna Senesh
Scotland
Macdonald, S. When we were women
Sumatra (Indonesia)
Misto, J. The shoe-horn sonata
United States
y Francoeur, B. Kilroy was here!
Gurney, A. R. What I did last summer
c Hark, M. and McQueen, N. Civilians stay put
Paterson, D. L. Pieces of the sky
Tuttle, J. Terminal Cafe

World War II. See Hollingsworth, M. The history of the village of the small huts

Worship programs
Enscoe, L. G. and Enscoe, A. Call for the lights and sing!
Enscoe, L. G. and Enscoe, A. Candles and carols
Enscoe, L. G. and Enscoe, A. The great Gemdale Christmas tree ornament factory
Enscoe, L. G. and Enscoe, A. The king who hated Christmas
Ensoce, L. G. and Enscoe, A. The towne without a tale
Enscoe, L. G. and Enscoe, A. The wise men had it easy
c Haylock, D. Christian olympics
c Haylock, D. Don't care, won't care, couldn't care less
c Haylock, D. The flaming fiery furnace
c Haylock, D. Follow the leader
c Haylock, D. Guardian angels
c Haylock, D. Here is the news: Good news and bad news
c Haylock, D. Here is the news: Overseas and underseas news
c Haylock, D. Here is the news: Riot in Nazareth
c Haylock, D. Here is the news: Sad news and amazing news
c Haylock, D. How to be an alien
c Haylock, D. Light of the world
c Haylock, D. Light on the road to Damascus
c Haylock, D. The nativity scene
c Haylock, D. Rejection
c Haylock, D. The shepherd and the psychiatrist
c Haylock, D. The Wallies guide to Christmas
c Haylock, D. Whoever
c Haylock, D. A window in the diary
Joseph, C. M. The temptations of Jesus
Paul, S. L. The Rainclouds study the Ten Commandments
Peterson, M. L. How Santa Claus discovered Christmas
c Trott, S. Buster come home
c Trott, S. Destination Bethlehem
c Trott, S. Did I miss anything important?
c Trott, S. Nocturne
c Trott, S. R.S.V.P.
c Trott, S. Something sacred this way comes
c Trott, S. You don't say!

Woudstra, Karst
Burying the dog
Black comedy about stressful relationship between two brothers and their partners. 2m 1w 1 interior
In Dutch and Flemish plays; ed. by D. Couling

The **wound.** Hughes, T.

Wounds to the face. Barker, H.

Woyiwada, Allison
c The little fir tree; a musical for primary children; based on the story by Hans Christian Andersen; script, music, and lyrics by Allison Woyiwada. Players Press 1994 14p
Lonely fir is ecstatic when chosen for Christmas tree. 2 scenes Unidentified cast 17 characters extras 1 interior 1 exterior

Woyzeck. Büchner, G.

Woza Albert! Mtwa, P.; Ngema, M. and Simon, B.

Wrangler Ranch. Francoeur, B.

The **wreck** on the Five-twenty-five. Wilder, T.

Wreggitt, Andrew, and Shaw, Rebecca
The wild guys. Blizzard Pub. 1994 63p
Satirical look at four men on "wildman" weekend in remote forest setting. Singing. 2 acts 12 scenes 4m 1 setting

Wrestling
c Hughes, V. Strongman meets his match
Martin, J. Cementville

Wright, Doug
Lot 13: the bone violin
Fantastic tale of violin prodigy. 3m 2w 1 setting
In The Best American short plays, 1994-1995

Wright, Doug—*Continued*

Quills. Dramatists 1994 82p

Black humor and grotesque exaggeration used to depict Marquis de Sade's final years in Charenton Asylum. 2 acts 25 scenes 4m 2w 3 interiors

The stonewater rapture

Teenagers struggle with conflict between religious faith and peer pressure from hostile classmates. 2 scenes 1m 1w 1 setting

In Short plays for young actors; ed. by C. Slaight and J. Sharrar

Watbanaland. Dramatists 1995 69p

Drama about spiritual, physical and sexual hunger. Nursery school teacher desperate to have child pressures bond trader husband, unaware that he has fathered brain-damaged child with secretary. 2 acts 25 scenes 3m 3w 1 setting

Wright, Nicholas

Mrs. Klein (condensation)

In The Best plays of 1995-1996

Wright, Richard, and Green, Paul

Native son

Dramatization of Richard Wright's novel set in 1930s Chicago slum. Black youth commits murder, is defended by communist lawyer, and condemned to death. 10 scenes 13m 6w extras 9 interiors 1 exterior

In Black theatre USA [v2]; ed. by J. V. Hatch and T. Shine

The **write** stuff. Nukala, D.

Writers. See Authors

Writing

c Summer, A. The just so letter

Wrong for each other. Foster, N.

Wrong turn at Lungfish. Marshall, G. and Ganz, L.

Wuthering Heights. Olfson, L.

Wyatt, Rachel

Crackpot. Playwrights Canada 1995 145p

Dramatization of Adele Wiseman's novel about life of strong-willed Canadian woman from 1912 to 1942. Prologue 2 acts 46 scenes 8m 5w 1 setting

Wycherley, William

The country wife (adaptation) See The Heather Brothers. Lust

The plain dealer

Restoration comedy of manners. Plain-speaking sea captain finds that he has been cheated of his love and money and sets out to avenge himself. Prologue 5 acts 8 scenes epilogue 18m 15w extras

In The Sensational Restoration; ed. by H. J. Jensen

Wydro, Ken. See Higginsen, V. jt. auth.

Wyld, Hazel

Night's candles. French (London) 1994 21p

Drama set in "hereafter." Divorced elderly actors recall happy times before their careers drew them apart. 3m 2w 1 exterior

Wylie, Betty Jane

c The old woman and the pedlar

Based on nursery rhyme about old woman's search for identity. Variable cast 7 characters

In Playhouse: six fantasy plays for children

Wynne, Michael

The knocky

Domestic drama set on housing estate in 1994 Birkenhead, England. 2 acts 4 scenes 7m 4w 3b 1 setting

In Coming on strong: new writing from the Royal Court Theatre

X

Xerxes I, King of Persia, 519-465 or 4 B.C.

Auletta, R. The Persians

Y

Yamauchi, Wakako

12-1-A

Japanese American family sent to incarceration camp during World War II. 2 acts 7 scenes 6m 6w 1 setting

In The Politics of life: four plays by Asian American women

And the soul shall dance

Dramatization of author's short story about two Japanese families on neighboring farms. 2 acts 9 scenes 2m 3w 1g

In Yamauchi, W. Songs my mother taught me

The chairman's wife

Events in life of Mao Tse-tung's widow. 2 acts 6m 3w 1 setting

In The Politics of life: four plays by Asian American women

The music lessons

Dramatization of author's short story entitled In heaven and earth. Japanese farm family in 1935 Imperial Valley, California. 2 acts 10 scenes 4m 4w 1 setting

In Unbroken thread; ed. by Robert Uno

In Yamauchi, W. Songs my mother taught me

Yancey. Linney, R.

Yankee dawg you die. Gotanda, P. K.

Yankee notions. Chislett, A.

Yankees vs. Redcoats. Boiko, C.

Yankowitz, Susan
Night sky
Metaphorical drama about language, thinking, and the universe. Woman astronomer suffers from aphasia after an automobile accident. 9 scenes 3m 3w 1 setting
In Playwriting women; ed. by J. Miles

Yard sale. Kelly, T.

Yates, Peter
Nuances. New Playwrights Network 1996 32p
Policeman's son is implicated in abduction of young prostitute. 1 act 10 scenes 2m 4w 1 setting
y Starlover. New Playwrights Network 1996 34p
Female rock singer's dreams of stardom and love come into conflict with reality. Singing. 5m 4w 1 interior

The **years.** Johnson, C. L.

Yeaton, Dana
Helen at risk
Short scene set in prison. Mask-making class turns deadly. 2m 1w 1 interior
In Actors Theatre of Louisville. Ten-minute plays: v3
In Humana Festival '95

Yeats, William Butler
The Countess Cathleen
Verse play. Earlier version of author's symbolic Irish drama Cathleen-ni Houlihan, about old woman's role in the Irish Rebellion of 1798. Singing. 5 scenes 5m 3w extras 2 interiors 1 exterior
In The Playboy of the Western World and two other Irish plays; ed. by W. A. Armstrong
The Land of Heart's Desire
Verse play based on Irish folklore. 3m 2w 1g 1 interior
In Great Irish plays
On Baile's strand
Verse play based on Irish legend. Blind man relates tragic tale of Cuchulain. Singing. 1 act 5m 1w 1 interior
In Great Irish plays

The **yellow** peril. Schuyler, G. S.

Yep, Laurence
c Dragonwings. Dramatists 1993 51p
Drama based on the author's novel of same title set in early 20th century San Francisco. Chinese boy helps father realize his dream of building flying machine. 9 scenes 4m 1w extra 1 setting
—Same
In Around the world in 21 plays; ed. by L. Swortzell

Yerma. García Lorca, F.

Yes, my Führer! Schwaiger, B.

Yesterday's news. Barnes, P.

Yeston, Maury
Titanic (condensation)
In The Best plays of 1996-1997

Yew, Chay
A language of their own
Originally two separate pieces entitled Learning Chinese and Broken English. Series of monologues and dialogues explore homosexual relationship. 2m
In But still, like air, I'll rise; ed. by V. H. Houston
In Yew, C. Porcelain and A language of their own
Porcelain
Exploration of crime of passion. Nineteen-year-old Asian homosexual confesses to shooting lover in London public lavatory. 29 scenes 1m extras 1 setting
In Staging gay lives; ed. by J. M. Clum
In Yew, C. Porcelain and A language of their own

Yiddish drama
Ansky, S. The dybbuk

The **Yiddish** Trojan women. Braverman, C.

York, Marjorie Ann
y Treasure Island
Dramatization of Robert Louis Stevenson's novel. 8m extras
In The Big book of dramatized classics; ed. by S. E. Kamerman

York, Y.
c Afternoon of the elves
Based on novel by Janet Taylor Lisle. Girl shares elf fantasy with troubled friend secretly caring for mentally ill mother. 2 acts 16 scenes 1m 2w 4g 1 interior 2 exteriors
In Around the world in 21 plays; edited by L. Swortzell
In Seattle Children's Theatre: six plays for young audiences; ed. by M. Smith
Life gap
Wealthy woman attempts to help fatherless tenement family. 21 scenes 1m 3w 1b 1 setting
In Facing forward; ed. by L. D. Frank
c The portrait the wind the chair
Drama about latchkey children. Two sisters create kingdom of imagination to help them cope with their fears. 2 acts 1m 1w 1g 1 interior
In Seattle Children's Theatre: six plays for young audiences; ed. by M. Smith

York (England)
Minghella, A. Two planks and a passion

Yoruban mythology. See Mythology, Yoruban

Yorubas
Soyinka, W. Death and the King's Horseman

Yoshitsune and the thousand cherry trees; tr. by Stanleigh H. Jones, Jr. Columbia Univ. Press 1993 286p (Translations from the Asian classics)
Puppet play set in 12th century Japan written by 18th century playwriting team of Takeda Izumo, Miyoshi Shōraku, and Namiki Senryū. Adventures of fugitive on run from henchmen dispatched by jealous brother. Prologue 5 acts 15 scenes Large mixed cast

You belong to me. Reddin, K.

You can swim in the Danube—but the water is too cold. See Fornes, M. I. The Danube

You can't judge a book by looking at the cover: sayings from the life and writings of Junebug Jabbo Jones: v2. O'Neal, J. and Watkins, N. B.

You can't stamp out love. Kelly, T.

You can't think of everything. Musset, A. de.

You don't say! Trott, S.

You have come back. Gallaire, F.

You mus' be bo'n ag'in. Burris, A. M.

You say tomatoes. Slade, B.

You should be so lucky. Busch, C.

Young, David
Glenn. Coach House Press 1992 126p
Dramatic exploration of music, ideas and life of iconoclastic pianist Glenn Gould. Music. 2 acts 4m 1 setting
See also Ledoux, P. jt. auth.

Young, Peter
Squashed. New Playwrights Network 1996 20p
Man's plan to murder nagging wife goes awry. 1 act 1m 1w

Young Black Beauty. Harris, A.

The **young** man from Atlanta. Foote, H.

Youngblood, Shay
Shakin' the mess outta misery. Dramatic 1994 45p
Young black girl's coming of age in 1960s South. 2 acts 10 scenes 8w 1 setting
—Same
In Colored contradictions: an anthology of contemporary African-American plays; ed. by H. J. Elam, Jr. and R. Alexander

Talking bones. Dramatic 1994 50p
Three generations of African American women turn to ancestral voices for guidance. 7 scenes 3w 2m 1 interior

There are many houses in my tribe
Exploration of African American sexuality and community. Variable cast 2 characters
In The Actor's book of gay and lesbian plays; ed. by E. Lane and N. Shengold

Younghusband, Carol
c Only a game. French (London) 1996 38p
Boy's visit to magical land teaches him that cheating is wrong. Variable cast 16 characters extras

Your handsome captain. Schwarz-Bart, S.

Your life is a feature film. Minieri, A.

Your money cheerfully refunded. Schaaf, A. K.

Your mother's butt. Ball, A.

Your obituary is a dance. Cummings, B.

Your place or mine? Booth, J.

Your turn to clean the stair. Munro, R.

"You're live with Bigfoot Wallace." McCullough, L. E.

Yourgrau, Tug
The song of Jacob Zulu. Arcade Pub. 1993 106p
Political drama incorporating folk play elements. Young black South African driven by apartheid's brutality to commit terrorist act. Singing, dancing. 2 acts 20 scenes 15m 1w 1 setting

Youssef, Marcus. See Verdecchia, G. jt. auth.

Youth
Bent, S. Bad company
Berkoff, S. West
Bogosian, E. SubUrbia
Coyle, K. Corner boys
y Foon, D. War
y Foote, H. The dancers
y Fraser, B. Prom night of the living dead
y Fuerstenberg, A. Blind dates
Godber, J. Bouncers: 1990's REMIX
Grosso, N. Peaches
Hibberd, J. Slam dunk
Johnson, C. Boys mean business
Linney, R. Gold and silver waltz
Lonergan, K. Betrayed by everyone
Macdonald, S. Borders of paradise
Margulies, D. Homework
McNally, T. Where has Tommy Flowers gone?
y Nukala, D. The write stuff

Youth—*Continued*
Osborne, J. Look back in anger
Prichard, R. Essex girls
Reid, C. Clowns
Reid, C. Joyriders
Rivera, J. The winged man
Rubess, B. and Cooper, B. Thin ice
y Sarkies, D. Lovepuke
Serpas, S. Waning crescent moon
y Walker, G. F. Tough!
Wellman, M. Cleveland
Wellman, M. Sincerity forever
Wilson, L. The sand castles
Wright, D. The stonewater rapture
Wynne, M. The knocky

Youth. Wilder, T.

Yowl. Green, M.

Z

Z: a meditation on oppression, desire and freedom. Szumigalski, A.

Zaire. See Congo (Democratic Republic)

The **Zanj** Revolution. Al-Madani, 'Izz al-Din

Zara Spook and other lures. Ackermann, J.

Zark, Jenna
A body of water: Foreign bodies
Young woman joins Jewish burial society and comes to terms with mother's death. 3 scenes 4w 1 interior
In Zark, J. A body of water

A body of water: Shooting souls
Woman preparing for Rosh Hashanah along with her religious community finds herself unhappily pregnant for sixth time. 2m 4w 1 interior
In Zark, J. A body of water

A body of water: White days
Young Jewish wife hopes to strengthen marriage by participating in ancient bathing ritual. Prologue 3 scenes 2m 3w 3 interiors
In Zark, J. A body of water

Zastrozzi: the master of discipline. Walker, G. F.

Zauner, Friedrich Ch.
A handful of earth
Austrian folk drama set at turn-of-the century. Wife of crippled farmer achieves financial goals but destroys family in the process. 5 scenes 3m 3w extras 1 interior
In In New anthology of contemporary Austrian folk plays; ed. by R. H. Lawson

Zebra dun. McCullough, L. E.

Zeder, Suzan L.
y The death and life of Sherlock Holmes. Anchorage Press 1994 80p
Drama based on several Holmes/Watson mysteries and Doyle's own life. 2 acts 12 scenes Variable cast 12 characters 3 interiors 2 exteriors

c Mother Hicks
Drama about witchcraft set in 1935 Illinois. Homeless girl befriends unusual woman and deaf man. Background music. 2 acts 6m 4w 1b 1 setting
In Seattle Children's Theatre: six plays for young audiences; ed. by M. Smith

c Wiley and the Hairy Man. Collins Educ. 1994 90p
Based on Southern folktale. With courage and resourcefulness boy outsmarts sinister Hairy Man. 1 act 2m 1w extra 1 setting

—Same
In Around the world in 21 plays; ed. by L. Swortzell

The **Zeem** dream. Westerhout, G.

Zell, Allison Eve
Come to leave
Monologue. Woman explores meaning of death. 1w
In Women playwrights: the best plays of 1994

Zenobia, Queen of Palmyra
Dear, N. Zenobia

Zerlin, Walter. See McGillivray, D. jt. auth.

Zero hour. Milner, A.

Ziegler, Tom
Grace & Glorie. French 1997 88p
Comedy. Transplanted New York do-gooder helps 90-year-old woman live out her final hours in Blue Ridge Mountain cabin. 2 acts 5 scenes 2w 1 interior

The **zig**-zag woman. Martin, S.

Zimmer. Margulies, D.

Zindel, Paul
y Every seventeen minutes the crowd goes crazy!
Sardonic comedy about modern family abandoned by their parents. Music. 7m 6w 1b 1 interior
In New plays from A.C.T.'s young conservatory

Zipless. Thompson, E.

Zombie chick. Jensen, M.

Zombie prom. Rowe, D. P.

Zookeeper. Alám, J. S.

Zoos

c Dawson, J. and Bass, P. The inside story
Johnson, T. Cries from the mammal house

Zoshchenko, Mikhail

Crime and punishment

Comedy about director of Soviet cooperative enterprise engaged in petty larceny. 1 act 7m 1w 1 interior

In An Anthology of Russian literature; ed. by N. Rzhevsky

Zoyka's apartment. Bulgakov, M.

Zuberbuehler, Alan

Fieldstones. Players Press 1996 28p

Tragicomedy about two brothers and an inheritance. 1 act 2m 1 interior

Part II

Cast Analysis

This section is designed to locate plays by type and number of players or readers. It is divided into these six sections: (1) all male cast (2) all female cast (3) mixed cast (4) puppet plays (5) unidentified cast (6) variable cast. Unidentified cast is used for non-human characters. Variable cast is used when roles can be acted by either male or female characters, or when an actor can take several parts, so that the exact number of the cast is not easily ascertainable.

Under each type of cast the arrangement is by total number of characters in ascending order. A mixed cast of over thirty-six characters is designated as large. "Extras" indicates that the play requires extra players for non-speaking parts or chorus.

Under Mixed Cast the arrangement is first by the total of characters in the cast, then by type of character from small to large number in this order: men, women, boys, girls, extras. For example, a four-character play for a cast of one man and three women (1m 3w), would precede one for two men and two women (2m 2w); then would follow two men and two boys (2m 2b), two boys and two girls (2b 2g), and three men and one woman (3m 1w).

The symbol *c* denotes a play intended for children through grade six. A *y* indicates material for grades seven through twelve approximately.

MIXED CAST

8 characters (4m 4w)

Wasserstein, W. The sisters Rosensweig

In the sample entry above, Wendy Wasserstein's play *The sisters Rosensweig* has a mixed cast of eight characters, four men and four women. Consult the author entry in Part I for information about the source of the play.

MALE CAST

1 character (1m)

Baitz, J. R. Broadway
Baitz, J. R. Standards & practices
Barnes, P. Confessions of a primary terrestrial mental receiver and communicator: Num III Mark I
Barnes, P. The end of the world—and after
Barnes, P. Glory
Barnes, P. The jumping Mimuses of Byzantium
Barnes, P. No end to dreaming
Berkoff, S. Actor
Berkoff, S. Dog
Berkoff, S. Harry's Christmas
Blount, R. Five Ives get named
Bogosian, E. Fun house
Bogosian, E. Men inside
Bogosian, E. Pounding nails in the floor with my forehead
Bogosian, E. Sex, drugs, rock & roll
Bogosian, E. Voices of America
Brooker, B. Changing bodies
Campbell, K. Jamais vu
Campbell, K. Pigspurt
Campbell, K. The recollections of a furtive nudist
Campbell, K. Violin time
Chekov, A. The dangers of tobacco
Essmann, J. Artificial reality
Fulford, R. Lovesong
Garnhum, K. Beuys buoys boys
Garnhum, K. Surrounded by water
c Gaytán, J. G. Fred Menchacha and Filemón

MALE CAST—*Continued*
Goldstein, J. Hate
Gray, S. Gray's anatomy
Gray, S. It's a slippery slope
Green, M. Yowl
Horovitz, I. Spared
Ives, D. A singular kinda guy
Jones, M. A night in November
Jones, T. W. The wizard of hip
Kelm, A. Black bride
Kling, K. 21A
Leguizamo, J. Mambo mouth
Linney, R. Gold and silver waltz
Lumborg, D. One fine day
MacIvor, D. House humans
MacIvor, D. and Brooks, D. Here lies Henry
Margulies, D. Joey
Margulies, D. Louie
Margulies, D. Manny
Margulies, D. Zimmer
Martin, J. Travelin' show
McPherson, C. The good thief
McPherson, C. Rum and vodka
McPherson, C. St Nicholas
Miller, J. Barrymore's ghost
Miller, T. My queer body
Mitchell, M. Life support
Mitterer, F. Siberia
Müller, H. Mommsen's block
Najera, R. The pain of the macho
Nelson, R. Flyer
Page, E. Aryan birth
y Panych, M. Cost of living
Pierson, K. Mountain thunder
Pintauro, J. Benjamin falling
Pintauro, J. Parakeet eulogy
Pinter, H. Monologue
O'Neal, J. and Watkins, N. B. You can't judge a book by looking at the cover: sayings from the life and writings of Junebug Jabbo Jones: v2
O'Reilly, J. Work
Reyes, G. Men on the verge of a his-panic breakdown
Ricchi, R. The man, the rose and silence
Riche, E. Possible maps
Schreiber, W. Burgoo!
Shepard, S. Killer's head
Tasca, J. A modern proposal
'Udwan, Mamduh. That's life
Varon, C. Rush Limbaugh in night school
Verdecchia, G. Fronteras Americanas (American borders)
y Waddy, L. Shakespeare remembers
Wellman, M. Terminal hip
Williams, A. The cockroach trilogy
Wilson, L. Days ahead
Wilson, L. A poster of the cosmos

1 character (1b)

Margulies, D. Anthony

1 character and extras (1m extras)

Bogosian, E. Drinking in America
Campanile, A. War
Diyab, Mahmud. Strangers don't drink coffee
Haubold, C. The big black Box
Royce, C. My son Susie
Schwarz-Bart, S. Your handsome captain
Sheffer, W. Falling man
Solórzano, C. The shoe
Yew, C. Porcelain

2 characters (1m 1b)

Dear, N. In the ruins

2 characters (2m)

Alám, J. S. Zookeeper
Aron, G. The Stanley Parkers
Bamford, S. The answer
Barnes, P. Acting exercise
Barnes, P. Nobody here but us chickens
Beard, P. Death of a clown
Beckett, S. Ohio impromptu
Beim, N. Shakespeare revisited
Boakye, P. Boy with beer
Bumbalo, V. Show
Buzo, A. Norm and Ahmed
Cadman, L. Peace in our time
Caldwell, B. Prayer meeting
Chekhov, A. Swan song
Collings, J. Kelly & Donald
Cotter, J. S. On the fields of France
Dashow, K. Sing this
Dean, P. H. Paul Robeson
Demchuk, D. Touch
Dietz, S. Lonely planet
DiPietro, J. Executive dance
Donaghy, T. The dadshuttle
Duberstein, H. The cord and the track
Dunsany, L. The glittering gate
Ellison, K. The Harry and Sam dialogues
FitzGibbon, G. The rock station
Gambaro, G. Saying yes
Goluboff, B. Big Al
Goluboff, B. My side of the story
Gotanda, P. K. Yankee dawg you die
Gray, J. Billy Bishop goes to war
Green, M. Dreams of a drunken Quaker
Griffiths, T. Who shall be happy . . . ?
Hamilton, G. Kissing Marianne
Havel, V. Audience
Havel, V. Protest

MALE CAST—*Continued*

Hollinger, M. Two-part invention
Horovitz, I. The former one-on-one basketball champion
Horovitz, I. Play for germs
Hwang, D. H. Trying to find Chinatown
Joseph, C. M. The temptations of Jesus
Kass, S. H. Dice and cards
Koch, K. The gold standard
Korder, H. Night maneuver
Lane, E. Cater-waiter
Lees, R. Nixon's Nixon
Lewis, I. Chinese coffee
Linney, R. Spain: Escobedo de la Aixa
Lucas, C. Bad dream
Mamet, D. Dodge
Mamet, D. Fish
Mamet, D. An interview
Mamet, D. L.A. sketches
Mamet, D. No one will be immune
Marans, J. Old wicked songs
Margulies, D. Death in the family
Margulies, D. Father and son
Margulies, D. Space
Martin, J. Pomp and circumstance
McLaughlin, T. Greatest hits
McLure, J. Ghost world
McNally, T. The wibbly, wobbly, wiggly dance that Cleopatterer did
McWeeney, D. and Swan, S. Sticks and stones
Miller, A. The last Yankee
Moore, E. Live with it
Mtwa, P.; Ngema, M. and Simon, B. Woza Albert!
Nowak, P. M. On the island
Nyswaner, R. Reservoir
Parra, M. A. de la. Secret obscenities
Paul, J. The secret of Sherlock Holmes
Pendleton, A. Uncle Bob
Perry, S. Bookends
Peschina, H. Straight as a corkscrew
Pintauro, J. Birds in church
Pintauro, J. Charlie's farewell
Pintauro, J. Frozen dog
Pintauro, J. Men without wives
Pintauro, J. Uncle Chick
Pinter, H. Precisely
Pinter, H. Victoria Station
Prideaux, J. Elephants
Puig, M. Kiss of the spider woman
Ricchi, R. The appointment
Rintoul, H. Brave hearts
Rivera, J. Slaughter in the lake
Schwartz, S. Vito on the beach
Shanley, J. P. Missing Marisa
Sheeler, W. Vortex
Shepard, S. Cowboys #2
Sickles, S. C. Murmurs
Silverman, J. L. Correct address
Silverstein, S. Dreamers
Simon, N. London suite: Settling accounts
Simpatico, D. Wish fulfillment
Stoppard, T. New-found-land
Strindberg, A. Pariah
Tasca, J. Gums
Thomas, E. Flowers of the dead red sea
Tremblay, M. Hosanna
Vassallo, P. The spelling bee
Walcott, D. Pantomime
Williamson, D. Sanctuary
Wilson, L. Eukiah
Yew, C. A language of their own
Zuberbuehler, A. Fieldstones

2 characters and extras (2m extras)

Barnes, P. Noonday demons
Emery, S. W. Crito
Emery, S. W. Euthyphro
Frost, R. A way out
Fugard, A. Playland
Hughes, L. The Em-Fuehrer Jones
Lucas, C. The Dying Gaul
Nishikawa, L. and Talmadge, V. The gate of heaven
Pintauro, J. Watchman of the night
Salah,'Abd al-Sabur. Night traveler
Solórzano, C. Mea culpa
y Terson, P. How to write a play

3 characters (3m)

Arzoomanian, R. The Tack Room
Baitz, J. R. Coq au vin
Baker, D. and Cocke, D. Red fox/second hangin'
Ball, A. Bachelor holiday
Barnes, P. More than a touch of Zen
Barnes, P. The spirit of man: The night of the Sinhat [sic] Torah
Barylli, G. Buttered bread
Beim, N. The deserter
Blessing, L. Lake Street extension
Block, S. Not a game for boys
Bozzone, B. and DiPietro, J. Breast men
Broadhurst, K. The eye of the beholder
Bynum, R. C. The sharpshooters
Caliban, R. Gladiator
Cleveland, R. Tom and Jerry
Crowley, M. For reasons that remain unclear
Dashow, K. He ain't heavy
Dashow, K. Time out
Dresser, R. Below the belt

MALE CAST—*Continued*

Fishburne, L. Riff raff
Foote, H. The one-armed man
Foster, A. Chemical reactions
Gilbert, S. Drag queens in outer space
Glowacki, J. Home section
Hardstack, M. In the cemetery
Hibberd, J. Slam dunk
Horovitz, I. The Indian wants the Bronx
Ives, D. Mere mortals
Kearns, M. Myron, a fairy tale in black and white
MacDonald, B. Whale riding weather
MacIvor, D. 2-2-tango
y Manns, D. Heart of the land
McGuinness, F. Someone who'll watch over me
McNally, T. Botticelli
McPherson, C. This lime tree bower
Milner, A. Zero hour
Oliensis, A. Ring of men
O'Neill, E. A wife for a life
Pillay, K. Looking for Muruga
Pintauro, J. Bus stop diner
Pintauro, J. Rosen's son
Pinter, H. The new world order
Plowman, G. A kind of Vesuvius
Shepard, S. 4-H Club
Stetson, J. The meeting
Verdecchia, G. and Youssef, M. A line in the sand

3 characters and extras (3m extras)

Anderson, P. Rokuro
Farag, A. 'Ali Janah al-Tabrizi and his servant Quffa
y McCullough, L. E. The flames of hell
Sánchez, E. Trafficking in broken hearts

4 characters (4m)

Aerenson, B. Lighting up the two-year old
Dubois, R. D. Being at home with Claude
Firth, T. Neville's Island
y Foon, D. War
Gilbert, S. Drag queens on trial
Godber, J. Bouncers: 1990's REMIX
Green, M. Naked West
House, J. Cherchez la femme
Levy, J. Old blues
Lloyd, P. The scam
Milligan, J. Shore leave
O Flatharta, A. Blood guilty
y Olfson, L. Avon calling!
Pinter, H. No man's land
Pugliese, F. The talk
Richards, G. The root
Spencer, S. Water and wine
St. Germain, M. Camping with Henry & Tom
Szyszkowitz, G. Commander Carrigan
c Witkiewicz, S. Cockroaches
Wreggitt, A. and Shaw, R. The wild guys
Yew, C. A language of their own
Young, D. Glenn

4 characters and extras (4m extras)

Benn, G. Ithaka
Cullen, M. The cut

5 characters (5m)

Dunsany, E. J. M. D. P. The lost silk hat
Gaminara, W. According to Hoyle
Gorman, C. Manual of trench warfare
Graham, B. Belmont Avenue Social Club
Harrison, T. The labourers of Herakles
Havel, V. Mistake
Herbert, J. Fortune and men's eyes
Owen, K. Black, green, white and gold
Schenkkan, R. The war on poverty
Shepard, S. The unseen hand
Warrender, S. Das barbecü
Wells, M. Mephisto rock
Wilcox, M. Rents

5 characters and extras (5m extras)

Clapp, T. The open boat
c McCaslin, N. Paul Bunyan: lumberjack
c McCullough, L. E. O, Christmas tree
Schenkkan, R. Masters of the trade

6 characters (6m)

Barry, S. White Woman Street
Bond, E. In the company of men
Butterworth, J. Mojo
Coen, D. Tinkle time
Elyot, K. My night with Reg
Gray, S. The rear column
Harwood, R. J. J. Farr
Heelan, K. Distant fires
Laurents, A. Home of the brave
Lewis, J. Our boys
Marber, P. Dealer's choice
Mason, K. A. For black boys who have considered homicide when the streets were too much
Schmidt, E. Mr. Rickey calls a meeting
Tissian, G. Night baseball
Williamson, D. The club

6 characters and extras (6m extras)

c Mayr, G. A. The printer on Queen Street

7 characters (7m)

Akerman, A. Somewhere on the border
Brown, C. The Little Tommy Parker Celebrated Colored Minstrel Show

MALE CAST—*Continued*

Mamet, D. Glengarry Glen Ross
Reddin, K. Throwing smoke
y Thum, N. B. The Red-headed League
Valle-Inclán, R. del. Sacrilege
Williams, N. Class enemy

7 characters and extras (7m extras)

Bond, E. Coffee

8 characters (8m)

Brown, C. Buffalo Hair
y McCullough, L. E. Zebra dun
McNally, T. Love! Valour! Compassion!
O'Neill, E. The sniper

8 characters and extras (8m extras)

Johnston, C. A pig tale
Matheus, J. F. Black damp
c McCullough, L. E. Ninth Cavalry to the rescue!
Pickett, J. C. Queen of Angels
y York, M. A. Treasure Island

9 characters (9m)

Crabtree, H. Howard Crabtree's Whoop-dee-doo!
Crowley, M. The boys in the band
McGuinness, F. Observe the sons of Ulster marching towards the Somme

9 characters and extras (9m extras)

Emery, S. W. Apology
Sylvanus, E. Leo Baeck

10 characters and extra (10m extra)

Rabe, D. Streamers

11 characters (11m)

Griffiths, T. Comedians

11 characters and extras (7m 4w extras)

Chislett, A. Yankee notions

11 characters and extras (11m extras)

Stoppard, T. Squaring the circle

12 characters (12m)

Fuller, C. A soldier's play
Karagiozis baker

13 characters (2m 11b)

Williams, N. William Golding's Lord of the flies

13 characters (13m)

Stoppard, T. Where are they now?

13 characters and extras (13m extras)

c Brown, C. J. The Constitution is born

14 characters and extras (14m extras)

y Hackett, W. The man without a country

15 characters (15m)

Warren, M. The Group

16 characters (16m)

Norton-Taylor, R. Nuremberg

16 characters and extras (16m extras)

Kaiser, G. Gas II

17 characters (17m)

c Boiko, C. Yankees vs. Redcoats

18 characters (18m)

c Vigil, A. La Batalla de Cinco de Mayo. The Battle of Cinco de Mayo

21 characters (21m)

Legg, R. Oscar: the Oscar Wilde trials of 1895

FEMALE CAST

1 character (1w)

Auden, W. H. The dark valley
Barnes, P. Rosa
Barnes, P. The theory and practice of belly-dancing
Barnes, P. Yesterday's news
Bensinger, L. A ghost story
Callan, L. Homebound
Cleage, P. Chain
Cocek, C. Stepping off a cloud
Dowie, C. Adult child/dead child
Dowie, C. Drag act
Dowie, C. Leaking from every orifice
Dowie, C. Why is John Lennon wearing a skirt?
Durang, C. Mrs. Sorken
Durang, C. Woman stand-up
Eisenstein, L. At the root
Fyffee, L. The sand
Gilbert, R. Mother Jones: the most dangerous woman in America
Gillis, C. Caveman rainbow
Goldenthal, J. Charley's girl
Goldenthal, J. Dance piece
Goldenthal, J. Wife to Tolstoi
Goldstein, C. Last exit before toll
Goldstein, J. Our baby's first seven years
Greenberg, R. Jenny keeps talking
Griffiths, L. A game of inches
Harmer, W. What is the matter with Mary Jane?
Harwood, R. The guests
Hughes, L. Scarlet Sister Barry
Jackson, J. A. WOMBmanWARs
Kenyatta, K. Harriet
Kittson, J. Escape
Laughton, V. The mourning after
Learner, T. Witchplay
Lewis, M. G. The captive

FEMALE CAST—*Continued*

Lill, W. The occupation of Heather Rose
Lucas, C. Credo
MacLeod, J. The Hope slide
MacLeod, J. Jewel

1 character (1w)

Mamet, D. Almost done
Margulies, D. I don't know what I'm doing
Margulies, D. Lola
Margulies, D. Somnambulist
Martin, J. Cul de sac
Martin, J. Shasta Rue
McGuinness, F. Baglady
Miller, S. My left breast
Minghella, A. Days like these
Nemeth, S. Sally's shorts: Black cloud morning New York
Nemeth, S. Sally's shorts: Living in this world
Nemeth, S. Sally's shorts: Pre-nuptial agreement
Nemeth, S. Sally's shorts: Visions of grandeur
Nigro, D. Squirrels
Nigro, D. The weird sisters
Nigro, D. Within the ghostly mansion's labyrinth
Nimmo, H. One small step
Nissen, K. Fair Kirsten
Ordway, S. Panicked
y Panych, M. Life science
Parks, S.-L. Pickling
Pintauro, J. House made of air
Pollock, S. Getting it straight
Rosenthal, R. Pangaean dreams a shamanic journey
Ross, J. Anne Marie's bedroom
Schwaiger, B. Yes, my Führer!
Smith, A. D. Aye aye aye I'm integrated
Smith, A. D. Fires in the mirror: Crown Heights, Brooklyn and other identities
Smith, A. D. Twilight: Los Angeles, 1992
Stickney, P. Y. Big Momma 'n 'Em
Thompson, J. Perfect pie
Tremblay, M. La Duchesse de Langeais
Vance, D. Live and in color!
Wasserstein, W. Workout
Wilson, L. The moonshot tape
Wong, E. China doll
Woodard, C. Pretty fire
Woodward, M. B. Day shift
Zell, A. E. Come to leave

1 character and extras (1w extras)

Dierlam, K. Helen Melon at the sideshow
Fischer, M. The gay divorcee
Goethe, J. W. von. Proserpina
Greth, R. Curtain call
Hampton, M. and Wilson, M. L. Full gallop
Liking, W. The widow Dylemma
Mann, E. Annulla
Shank, A. E. Dry smoke

2 characters (2w)

Anderson, E. That all of us should be fed
Atkins, E. Vita & Virginia
Augustine, J. Window of opportunity
Baker, E. A. Rosemary with Ginger
Barnes, P. Humour helps
Barnes, D. An Irish triangle
Barnes, D. Little drops of rain
Barnes, D. She tells her daughter
Barnes, D. Two ladies take tea
Beber, N. Food
Beber, N. Misreadings
Braithwaite, D. Martha and Elvira
Broinowski, A. The gap
Carter, J. The twisted mirror
Cleage, P. Late bus to Mecca
Dean, P. Long gone lonesome cowgirls
Dewberry, E. Head on
Durang, C. Phyllis and Xenobia
Durang, C. Women in a playground
Farmer, B. Irene and Lillian forever
Franklin, J. E. Two mens'es daughter
Fuller, E. L. Me and Jezebel
Garro, E. The tree
Greth, R. Halfway
Hayes, J. F. Nothing in common
Horovitz, I. Free gift
Howe, T. Appearances
Jackson, M. A. Sisters
Janaczewska, N. The history of water
Jensen, M. Zombie chick
Kramer, S. David's redhaired death
LaChuisa, M. J. First Lady suite: Olio
LaChuisa, M. J. First Lady suite: Where's Mamie?
Lane, E. Dancing on Checkers' grave
LeFevre, A. Waterbabies
Mack, C. K. The magenta shift
MacLaughlin, W. Watermelon boats
Mamet, D. A scene - Australia
Mann, E. Having our say
Maraini, D. Mary Stuart
Margulies, D. Women in motion
McCauley, R. Sally's rape
McConnell, J. Dancers
McConnell, J. Doggies
McConnell, J. Early blight
McConnell, J. Late frost

FEMALE CAST—*Continued*

McConnell, J. Shoppers
Medley, C. Dearborn Heights
Minghella, A. Mosaic
Misto, J. The shoe-horn sonata
Morris, A. Lili'uokalani
Murray-Smith, J. Love child
Nemeth, S. Sally's shorts: Lily
Nemeth, S. Sally's shorts: Pagan day
Nemeth, S. Sally's shorts: Word games
Nicholas, D. Buses
Noonan, J. F. Music from down the hill
Nottage, L. Poof!
Oates, J. C. Negative
Ordway, S. Trips
Pedrero, P. The color of August
Pelonero, E. Family names
Pintauro, J. Lenten pudding
Pintauro, J. Lightning
Pintauro, J. Ten-dollar drinks
Puig, M. Mystery of the rose bouquet
Ravel, A. Vengeance
Rumble, P. B. Aunt Sophie's latkes
Sawyer, A. V. Life comes to the old maid
Simon, N. London suite: Going home
Simon, M. The old lady's guide to survival
Stone, T. Hello, Ma!
Stone, T. She needs me
Stroppel, F. The Mamet women
Stroppel, F. Package deal
Thomson, K. Barmaids
Toddie, J. L. Late Sunday afternoon, early Sunday evening
Visdei, A. Always together
Watson, A. Final placement
Whiskeyman, D. So tell me about this guy
Wilhelm, L. The power and the glory
Wilson, L. The Great Nebula in Orion
Wilson, L. Ludlow fair
Ziegler, T. Grace & Glorie

2 characters (2g)

Gallagher, M. Bedtime
Rhodes, N. Ocean dream

2 characters and extras (2w extras)

Fernandez, E. How else am I supposed to know I'm still alive
Hall, F. B. The book of herself
López, E. Marlene
Nemeth, S. Sally's shorts: The cat act
Porter, D. No more Medea
Wellman, M. The sandalwood box

3 characters (2w lg)

Blount, R. That dog isn't fifteen

3 characters (3w)

Barnes, D. At the roots of the stars
Barnes, D. The dove
Barylli, G. Honeymoon
Farhoud, A. Game of patience
Hare, D. Slag
High, B. G. Ambush
Jennings, C. S. Sunday dinner
Johnson, E. What do they call me?
Kramer, S. Permanent signal
LaChuisa, M. J. First Lady suite: Eleanor sleeps here
Markham, S. Love and shrimp
McLeod, K. R. Broken hearts
Murphy, T. Bailegangaire
Parks, S. L. Devotees in the garden of love
Ritchie, R. In the beginning
Selig, P. The mystery school
Siegel, J. Metamorphoses
Snodgrass, K. Haiku
Spiderwoman Theater. Sun Moon and Feather
Steelsmith, M. Wacs in khaki
Strindberg, A. The stronger
Svanoe, B. Punch and Judy
y Tobin, S. Cotton girls
Toddie, J. L. And go to Innisfree
Vogel, P. Desdemona
Wilson, L. Stoop
Wooten, J. J. The role of Della

3 characters and extras (3w extras)

McIntyre, C. Low level panic
Moraga, C. Giving up the ghost
Sergent, S. Father's prize Poland China

4 characters (4w)

The Anna Project. This is for you, Anna
y Barrie, S. Carrying the calf
Blessing, L. Independence
Carilli, T. Dolores Street
Chafee, C. Why we have a body
y Curran, K. T. The First Time Club
Colorado, E. and Colorado, H. 1992: blood speaks
George, M. The most massive woman wins
Glass, J. M. If we are women
Godbar, J. and Thornton, J. Shakers restirred
Hope, K. Foreign lands
Jones, R. Big butt girls, hard-headed women
Keatley, C. My mother said I never should
Kiefer, N. Gwen and Gwen
Kurtti, C. Catholic school girls

FEMALE CAST—*Continued*

Lauro, S. The coal diamond
Lyssiotis, T. Blood moon
MacLeod, W. The shallow end
Mead, K. And who will pay the rent?
Munro, R. Fugue
Norman, M. Lunch with Ginger
Rebeck, T. Sunday on the rocks
Royce, C. Why we have a body
Shengold, N. Lives of the great waitresses
Shields, C. Thirteen hands
Son, D. R.A.W. ('cause I'm a woman)
Wilder, T. A ringing of doorbells
Wise, R. Eventide
Zark, J. A body of water: Foreign bodies

4 characters and extras (4w extras)

Césaire, I. Fire's daughters
Coles, E. September revisited

5 characters (5w)

Adam, A. Birds of prey
Booth, J. Friendly affair
Booth, J. Or was he pushed?
Bower, M. A fitting finish
Carilli, T. Wine country
Clarke, B. and Dickerson, G. Re/membering Aunt Jemima: a menstrual show
De Angelis, A. Playhouse creatures
Dunn, M. Five tellers dancing in the rain
The Five Lesbian Brothers. Brave smiles ... another lesbian tragedy
Kneubuhl, V. N. The conversion of Ka'ahumanu
Mama drama
Mason, J. A. Daughters of the mock
Mead, K. Crying out loud
Pam-Grant, S. Curl up and dye
Parris-Bailey, L. Dark cowgirls and prairie queens
Peters, K. The confirmation
Pope, R. Amazing Grace
Porter, D. Flowers
Rensten, M. The skip
Silver, J. M. and Boyd, J. A ... my name is still Alice
Szyszkowitz, G. Lake of illusions
Vogel, P. The oldest profession
Wertenbaker, T. New anatomies
West, C. L. Jar the floor

5 characters and extras (5w extras)

Booth, J. By whose hand?
Goldenthal, J. Mequasset by the sea
Prichard, R. Essex girls
Vickery, F. A kiss on the bottom

6 characters (6w)

Adam, A. Business meeting
Adam, A. A cameo from Cranford
Adam, A. A great occasion
Chaurette, N. The queens
Cinoman, S. Fitting rooms
Cunningham, L. Beautiful bodies
Day, D. M. Possession is ...
Mead, K. The other other woman
Pope, R. Sandwiches: Making sandwiches
Russ, A. Inside out
Townsend, S. Bazaar & rummage

6 characters and extras (6w extras)

Glover, S. Bondagers

7 characters (7w)

Brooks, V. Love me slender
Carlos, L. White chocolate for my father
y Hamlett, C. Hairum-scarum
Hillman, B. L. Iron magnolias
Whyte, P. Tuesday, eight-fifteen

7 characters and extras (7w extras)

Adam, A. Between two thieves
Minghella, A. Whale music
Newman, M. and Damashek, B. Quilters
Pope, S. Sandwiches: Eating sandwiches
y Sodaro, C. Salem's daughter

8 characters (8w)

Adam, A. Castles in the air
Adam, A. Christmas
Brogan, P. B. Eclipsed
Daniels, S. The madness of Esme and Shaz
Hallman, B. The women of Theta Kappa
Laird, M. Ruthless!
McConnell, J. A lovesome thing
Youngblood, S. Shakin' the mess outta misery

8 characters and extras (8w extras)

Corthron, K. Cage rhythm

11 characters (2w 9g)

c Shurman-O'Connor, K. Ghoul Scout camp

11 characters (11w)

Martin, J. Talkin with ...
Shores, D. Daughters of the Lone Star State
Shotlander, S. Is that you Nancy?

15 characters (15w)

Tremblay, M. Les belles soeurs

Large cast

Booth, C. The women

MIXED CAST

2 characters (1m 1w)

Albee, E. Edward Albee's Marriage play
Albert, S. J. How many to tango?
Anderson, J. The last time we saw her
Anderson, J. Tough choices for the new century: a seminar for responsible living
Angwin, F. Beryllium
Baitz, J. R. Three hotels
Ball, A. The M word
Ball, A. Made for a woman
Ball, A. Your mother's butt
Barasch, N. Standing by
Barnes, D. Five thousand miles
Barnes, D. To the dogs
Barnes, P. Last things
Barr, N. Mrs. Cage
Bell, N. Out the window
Benyon, L. Love seen in laundromat
Berkoff, S. Decadence
Berkoff, S. Lunch
Breslin, J. Contract with Jackie
Bronson, J. G. Willie & Esther
y Bruce, M. Car crazy
Bynum, R. C. Live-in witnesses
Cahill, S. Ballycastle
Calhoun, W. Affections of an alley cat
Campton, D. The evergreens
Canby, V. After all
Cardinal, V. J. The Colorado catechism
Cartwright, J. Two
Conde, M. The Tropical Breeze Hotel
Cummings, B. Your obituary is a dance
Durang, C. DMV tyrant
Durang, C. Funeral parlor
Durang, C. Laughing wild
Durang, C. One minute play
Ekstrom, P. An O. Henry Christmas: The gift of the Magi
Fo, D. The open couple
Foster, N. Wrong for each other
Frost, R. In an art factory
Fugard, A. A place with the pigs
Fugard, A. Valley song
Gans, S. and Charney, J. A Chekhov concert
Gélinas, G. The passion of Narcisse Mondoux
Gilroy, F. D. Real to reel
Glore, J. What she found there
Godber, J. April in Paris
Gow, M. Sweet Phoebe
Graybill, C. Go look
Guare, J. Cop-out
Guare, J. A day for surprises
Gurney, A. R. The Golden Fleece
Gurney, A. R. The problem
Hatcher, J. The turn of the screw
Hayes, E. Poison
c Haylock, D. A window in the diary
Horovitz, I. The 75th
Horovitz, I. Acrobats
Horovitz, I. Hopscotch
Horovitz, I. It's called the Sugar Plum
Hwang, D. H. Bondage
Hwang, D. H. The sound of a voice
Ives, D. Ancient history
Ives, D. English made simple
Ives, D. Sure thing
Jannuzzi, L. With or without you
Jensen, J. The total meaning of real life
y Kirk, L. Men and angels
Klavan, L. Freud's house
Knee, A. The St. Valentine's Day massacre
Koch, K. Edward and Christine
Kroetz, F. X. Through the leaves
Leach, K. The mysterious Mr. Love
Lee, C. Arthur and Leila
y Leznoff, G. The stockbroker and the fairy godmother
Linney, R. Clair de Lune
Linney, R. Stars
Lonergan, K. Betrayed by everyone
MacDonald, B. What we do with it
Malpede, K. US
Mamet, D. Goldberg Street
Mamet, D. Joseph Dintenfass
Mamet, D. A life with no joy in it
Mamet, D. Oleanna
Maraini, D. Dialogue between a prostitute and her client
Margulies, D. L.A.
Martin, J. The boy who ate the moon
Mason, T. Sorry
Mastrosimone, W. The woolgatherer
y Mauro, R. The job interview
McNally, T. Next
McNally, T. Street talk
McNally, T. Sweet Eros
Mead, K. This common bond
Miller, A. I can't remember anything
Miller, A. The Ryan interview
Milligan, J. Clara and the gambler
Milligan, J. Class of '77
Minghella, A. Hang up
Mitterer, F. Beyond our understanding
Mitterer, F. Jailbird
Mitterer, F. Shunted into a siding
Mitterer, F. Wheat on the autobahn
Morley, S. Noel and Gertie
Mueller, L. American dreamers
Mueller, L. Jim's commuter airlines
Mueller, L. Violent peace

MIXED CAST—*Continued*
Murray-Smith, J. Flame
Murrell, J. Memoir
Neipris, J. Brussels sprouts
Nelson, R. Life sentences
Nigro, D. Fair Rosamund and her murderer
Nigro, D. Major Weir
Nigro, D. Necropolis
Noonan, J. F. When it comes early
Oates, J. C. Homesick
Oates, J. C. The sacrifice
Olmos, C. Profane games
Panych, M. Vigil
Parks, S.-L. Betting on the Dust Commander
Parsons, R. Mortmain
Parsons, R. Rialto
Patrick, R. Love lace
Pearson, C. Divergent lines
Pedrero, P. The voucher
Pintauro, J. Fiat
Pintauro, J. Fur hat
Pintauro, J. Rix
Pintauro, J. Rules of love
Pintauro, J. Soft dude
Pinter, H. Ashes to ashes
y Polsky, M. E. SATisfaction
c Price, J. W. Rocket recycle (k-3)
Prideaux, J. Requiem for us
Rasche, D. Jackie
Rector, M. H. The lady and the commissioner of airports
Rector, M. H. The lady and the mortician
Reingold, J. Dear Kenneth Blake
Ricchi, R. A foreboding
y Rideout, G. Texas boy
Rosenthal, A. Lifelines
Ross, A. Feet
Russell, W. Educating Rita
Sawyer, A. V. Snow stars
Schisgal, M. The artist and the model
Schisgal, M. The artist and the model/2
Schisgal, M. Extensions
Schisgal, M. Sexaholics
Shank, A. E. 67201
Shanley, J. P. Kissing Christine
Shanley, J. P. The red coat
Shengold, N. Finger food
Sierens, A. Drummers
Sinclair, B. Dreamkeeper
Slade, B. Same time, another year
Sloate, D. Countess de Kitchen
Sloate, D. Le radeau de la Comtesse
Smith, A. Live bed show
Solórzano, C. The Angel's forty winks
Steinour, M. At Land's End
Stone, T. One question
Stone, T. Whatever you say
Stoppard, T. `M' is for moon among other things
Storey, D. Caring
Stroppel, F. Domestic violence
Stroppel, F. Morning coffee
Sturner, L. The death of Huey Newton
Szilágyi, A. Unsent letters
Tagore, R. Karna and Kunti
Taikeff, S. Dolorosa Sanchez
Tannen, D. An act of devotion
Thompson, E. The Valentine Fairy
Thompson, E. Zipless
Turrini, P. Shooting rats
Vickery, F. Green favours
Wagner, C. The monument
Weller, M. At home (Split, Part 1)
Wells, J. S. The ladykiller
Wilhelm, L. Whoppers
Wilkinson, M. E. The lighthouse keeper's wife
Wilson, L. A betrothal
Wilson, L. Breakfast at the track
Wilson, L. Home free!
Wilson, L. Ikke, ikke, nye, nye, nye
Wright, D. The stonewater rapture
Young, P. Squashed

2 characters (1m 1g)

Margulies, D. Homework
c Martin, M. The legend of the golden coffee bean

2 characters (1b 1g)

Margulies, D. First love

2 characters and extras (1m 1w extras)

Angwin, F. Beryllium
Bell, N. Drive
Dowling, C. The Marlboro man
y Garver, J. The numbers game
Granville-Barker, H. Farewell to the theatre
Hamlett, C. Once upon a taxi
Horovitz, I. Park your car in Harvard Yard
Hurston, N. Z. Story in Harlem slang
Jelinek, E. Totenauberg (Death/Valley/Summit)
Linney, R. Spain: Anna Rey
Martin, J. Jack and Jill
c Mauro, R. A. The Mother Goose olympics
McNally, T. Frankie and Johnny in the Clair de Lune
Oates, J. C. The rehearsal
Oates, J. C. Tone clusters

MIXED CAST—*Continued*
Parsons, R. Dead end
Pedrero, . A night divided
Pintauro, J. Bird of ill omen
Pintauro, J. Two eclairs
Reid, C. My name, shall I tell you my name?
Schenkkan, R. The courtship of Morning Star
y Sloyer, G. Ezekial saw the ... what?
c Trott, S. R.S.V.P.
Vogel, P. How I learned to drive
Wiechmann, B. Feeding the moonfish
Wolfe, G. C. Story in Harlem slang

2 characters and extras (1w 1b extras)

c Martin, J. The big mess

3 characters (1m 1w 1b)

y Allard, J. Painted rain
Allen, R. J. What to name your baby
Kroetz, F. X. The nest
Mamet, D. The cryptogram
Wilson, E. C. Cross-dressing in the Depression

3 characters (1m 1w 1g)

Mayberry, B. The catechism of Patty Reed
c York, Y. The portrait the wind the chair

3 characters (1m 1b 1g)

Terry, M. Fireworks

3 characters (1w 1b 1g)

c LaBounty, D. Jeremy Whistler, mad scientist

3 characters (1m 2w)

y Avery, A. Stardust melody
Baker, E. A. Face divided
Barker, H. Judith: a parting from the body
Barnes, D. Water-ice
Barrie, J. M. Rosalind
Beard, P. Lavender years
Booth, J. Both worlds
Booth, J. The loved one
Booth, J. Mirror mirror on the wall
Butterfield, C. Life in the trees: No problem
y Charles, R. A perfect match
Cowan, C. A woman from the sea
Curran, C. Senetta Boynton visits the Orient
Dean, P. H. The owl killer
Dixon, M. B. and Smith, V. Breaking the chain
Durang, C. Canker sores and other distractions
Durang, C. Naomi in the living room
Fornes, M. I. Springtime
Fornes, M. I. What of the night?: Springtime
Gilroy, F. D. Match point
Gregory, L. Spreading the news
Groves, W. Good night, sweet mother
Halvorson, K. One hundred women
Hatcher, J. Three viewings
c Haylock, D. The shepherd and the psychiatrist
Hornby, I. One across
Horovitz, I. My old lady
Howe, T. Painting Churches
Hughes, D. The morning
Hughes, L. Limitations of life
Katims, J. Who made Robert DeNiro king of America?
LaChiusa, M. J. Agnes
Law, M. Advertising Arnold
Linney, R. Three poets: Komachi
MacDonald, B. The weekend healer
Mann, E. Still life
Marber, P. After Miss Julie
c Martin, J. Sandwich
Martin, L. Waltzing De Niro
Martin, S. Patter for the floating lady
McNally, T. Dusk
McWeeny, D. and Swan, S. Broken bones
Meadows, K. J. Henrietta
Miller, S. Repairs
Nagy, P. Trip's cinch
Nigro, D. Give us a kiss and show us your knickers
Pintauro, J. Dawn
Pintauro, J. Swans flying
Pinter, H. A kind of Alaska
Pinter, H. Old times
Prideaux, J. Abraham Lincoln dies at Versailles
Prideaux, J. Laughter in the shadow of the trees
Prideaux, J. The librarian
Quinn, L. Well done poets
y Rayfield, J. I hate mothers
Reynolds, J. Dance with me
Schave, E. A Texas romance
Schevill, J. Shadows of memory: The radiator
Sears, J. Eddie Lee, Eddie Lee
Séjour, V. The brown overcoat
Shepard, S. Red Cross
Simon, N. London suite: Diana and Sidney
Sloate, D. Suddenly, a foot
Smith, L. Sins of the father
Tasca, J. The spelling of Coynes

MIXED CAST—*Continued*
Toddie, J. L. Is that the bus to Pittsburgh?
Triana, J. Night of the assassins
Vogel, P. And baby makes seven
Walker, D. Triangle
y Walker, G. F. Tough!
Warner, F. Maquettes for the requiem: Emblems
The Washtub
Wiener, S. D. A place where love is
Wilhelm, L. Cherry blend with vanilla
Williams, S.-A. Home
Wilson, L. Brontosaurus
Wilson, L. Day
Wilson, L. Redwood curtain
Wilson, L. Say De Kooning
Wilson, L. Thymus vulgaris
Winer, D. G. The last girl singer

3 characters (1b 2g)

c James, J. The echo box
c James, J. Moving day
c James, J. Willa and Sam

3 characters (2m 1w)

Allais, T. The poor beggar and the fairy godmother
Allen, C. Ripe conditions
Anderson, J. Lynette at 3 AM
Anderson, J. Lynette has beautiful skin
Barnes, D. The death of life
Barnes, P. Not as bad as they seem
Barnes, P. The spirit of man: From sleep and shadow
Barnes, P. Waiting for a bus
Beard, P. Cliff's edge
Beard, P. Meat and two veg
Berkoff, S. Massage
Blessing, L. Down the road
Blessing, L. Patient A
Bozzone, B. Sonny DeRee's life flashes before his eyes
Brooker, B. Ilsa, queen of the Nazi love camp
Brooker, B. The land, the animals
Brooker, B. Tears of a dinosaur
y Bruce, M. Caveman blues
Butterfield, C. Life in the trees: Chemistry
Calhoun, W. Call it clover
Chekhov, A. The bear
Chekhov, A. The proposal
Chocrón, I. OK
Chocrón, I. The ultimate bliss
Clemens, B. Inside job
Coleman, R. M. The girl from back home
Connor, T. A couple with a cat
Crowley, M. A breeze from the gulf
Dean, P. H. Dink's blues
Delisle, J. M. A live bird in its jaws
Egloff, E. The swan
Elwell, J. S. The art of dating
Emond, P. Talk about love!
Fols, C. Buck Simple
Foreman, R. The mind king
Foreman, R. Samuel's major problem
Fornes, M. I. Enter the night
Friedman, R. All for art
Friel, B. Molly Sweeney
Frockt, D. L. Hard-boiled
Fugard, A. Statements after an arrest under the immorality act
Geoghan, J. Light sensitive
Gifford, B. Blackout
Gilroy, F. D. Fore!
Gilroy, F. D. Give the bishop my faint regards
Gilroy, F. D. A way with words
Goluboff, B. The other five percent
Granger, P. Vivien
Gray, S. Wise child
Greenberg, R. The author's voice
Griffiths, T. Hope in the year two
Gurney, A. R. The Old One-Two
Gurney, A. R. Public affairs: Pt2 The opening meeting
Guyer, M. The American century
Hampton, C. Treats
Harding, A. Blood and honour
Hare, D. Skylight
Harrison, J. Holidays
Harrower, D. Knives in hens
Havel, V. Unveiling
Hibbert, G. Tilting ground
Hood, E. A wake for Donald
Horovitz, I. Lebensraum
Horovitz, I. Shooting gallery
Horovitz, I. Un drôle de mari français
Horovitz, I. The widow's blind date
Hunt, M. Unquestioned integrity: the Hill-Thomas hearings
Ingraffia, S. Pasquini the Magnificent
Isitt, D. The woman who cooked her husband
Ives, D. The Philadelphia
Ives, D. The universal language
Ives, D. Variations on the death of Trotsky
Ives, D. Words, words, words
Kane, S. Blasted
Kemp, R. Dalwhinnie
Kravitz, A. Just thinking
y Kukla, D. Sticks and stones
LaChiusa, M. J. Break

MIXED CAST—*Continued*

Languirand, J. Autumn violins
Larson, L.; Lee, L. and Wackler, R. Tent meeting
Lepage, R. and Brassard, M. Polygraph
Lichtig, R. R. Queen for a day
Linney, R. Yancey
MacIvor, D. Never swim alone
Mamet, D. Jolly
Mamet, D. Sunday afternoon
Manet, E. Lady Strass
Manning, B. What wasn't said what didn't happen
Martini, C. Life history of the African elephant
Mastrosimone, W. A stone carver
Mastrosimone, W. Sunshine
Mastrosimone, W. Tamer of horses
Mercer, D. The Arcata promise
Miller, H. A winter reunion
Milligan, J. Money talks
Milligan, J. Road trip
Morrissey, K. Dora: a case of hysteria
Mortimer, J. Edwin
Nemeth, S. Water play
Oates, J. C. Black
Oates, J. C. The interview
O'Donovan, J. The fiddler and the Dean
O'Neill, E. Thirst
Osofisan, F. The oriki of a grasshopper
Palmer, J. Henrik Ibsen on the necessity of producing Norwegian drama
Paterson, D. L. Dungeons
Paterson, D. L. Finger painting in a Murphy bed
Pen, P. Bed and sofa
Pintauro, J. Dirty talk
Pintauro, J. His dish
Pintauro, J. Seymour in the very heart of winter
Pinter, H. Family voices
Quayle, T. Bein Lochaber
Ramsey, E. Acetylene
Ranson, R. Blood on blood
Reiss, J. Awkward silence
Ricchi, R. The promise
Richards, G. Dividends
Rivera, J. Cloud tectonics
Rivera, J. Each day dies with sleep
y Rodriguez, D. E. I'm not stupid
Ruzzante. The veteran
Scanlon, P. What is this everything?
Schisgal, M. The cowboy, the Indian and the fervent feminist
Serpas, S. Waning crescent moon
Shanley, J. P. The wild goose
Shawn, W. The designated mourner
Shields, B. J. Highwire
Slabolepszy, P. Over the hill
Slaight, B. The open road
Smith, S. One-sided triangle
Soland, L. The name game
Solórzano, C. Crossroads
Spencer, S. Blue stars
Steppling, J. My crummy job
Strindberg, A. Simoom
Sweet, J. The value of names
Tasca, J. Make-up
Taylor, P. Familiar haunts
Taylor, P. Missing person
Taylor, R. and Bologna, J. Barry, Betty and Bill
Thomas, E. East from the Gantry
Uhry, A. Driving Miss Daisy
Vogel, P. The Baltimore waltz
Vogelstein, C. Date with a stranger
Watson, D. The last Munro
Wellman, M. The self-begotten
White, P. Big toys
Whitemore, H. The best of friends
Wilcox, M. Massage
Wilde, O. A Florentine tragedy
Wilhelm, L. The road to Nineveh
Williams, G. A death in Bethany
Williams, N. Harry and me
Wilson, L. Days ahead
Wilson, L. The madness of Lady Bright
Woudstra, K. Burying the dog
Yeaton, D. Helen at risk
c Zeder, S. Wiley and the Hairy Man

3 characters (2m 1g)

Bynum, R. C. The monkey palace

3 characters (2b 1g)

c Lazarus, J. Night light
c Lazarus, J. Not so dumb

3 characters and extras (1m 2w extras)

Butterfield, C. Joined at the head
Finch, C. and Lucas, B. Evelyn and the polka king
Fuentes, C. Orchids in the moonlight
Hall, F. B. Via Reggio revisited
MacIvor, D. This is a play
Mazza, R. N. Parked
Michels, J. and Murphy, P. The queen of bingo
Miller, D. L. Origami tears
Schenkar, J. M. The universal wolf
Schevill, J. Shadows of memory: Ape-God
Strindberg, A. Miss Julie
c Tutt, B. Heart to heart
Worboyes, S. The house plant

MIXED CAST—*Continued*

3 characters and extras (2m 1w extras)

al-'Ani, Yusuf. The key
c Bennett, R. The shoemaker and the elves
Bohmler, C. and Adler, M. Gunmetal blues
Fo, D. An ordinary day
Foreman, R. My head was a sledgehammer
Hughes, T. The wound
Iklasi, Walid. The path
Kilroy, T. The secret fall of Constance Wilde
Norbury, P. Valparaiso
c Richardson, D. McJonah
Schnitzler, A. The Bacchanale
Shepard, S. The unseen hand
Shurtz, R. K. Cowboys, Indians and waitresses
y Slaight, B. Sightings and high tide
Sloate, D. Countess in Courtland
Strindberg, A. The dance of death
Valle-Inclán, R. del. The head of the Baptist
Zeder, S. Wiley and the Hairy Man

3 characters and extras (2w 1b extras)

Rivera, C. Julia

4 characters (1m 1w 1b 1g)

c Martin, J. Lost in a mall

4 characters (1m 2w 1g)

Robinson, M. Collateral damage
Wilder, T. Someone from Assisi

4 characters (1m 3w)

Ackermann, J. The batting cage
Albee, E. Three tall women
Aldrich, A. The housewarming
Barnes, D. Madame collects herself
Bisson, P. Merry widows
Biswas, N. Skin
Bouchard, M. M. The orphan muses
Compton, J. Barefoot
Cruz, M. The have-little
Davis, R. The (revised) Travelling Cinderella show
c Davis, R. The travelling Jekyll & Hyde show
Dewberry, E. Flesh and blood
Dulaney, M. The view from here
Finn, W. "In trousers"
Foote, H. The roads to home: A nightingale
Foreman, R. I've got the shakes
Glover, S. The straw chair
Hatcher, J. Scotland Road
Haywood, D. Twisted tape
Houston, V. H. As sometimes in a dead man's face
Linney, R. Can can
Linney, R. F.M.
Macdonald, S. When I was a girl, I used to scream and shout . . .
Mastrosimone, W. Extremities
McDonald, H. Faulkner's bicycle
Murray-Smith, J. Honour
O'Donovan, J. Carlotta
y Olfson, L. The last time I saw Paris
Overmyer, E. On the verge
Pryor, D. The love talker
Rivera, J. The winged man
Rowan, A. A. A stitch in time
Sherman, G. Broken English
Stroppel, F. Single and proud
Taylor, D. H. Someday
Terry, M. Breakfast serial
Turrini, P. Infanticide
Walker, S. Come on up
Ward, N. Trouble sleeping
Wellman, M. Swoop
Wilder, T. The drunken sisters
Wilder, T. In Shakespeare and the Bible

4 characters (2m 1w 1b)

Crawford, J. L. Facelifting at St. Viators
Kalinoski, R. Beast of the moon
Pinter, H. One for the road
Warner, F. Maquettes for the requiem: Troat

4 characters (2m 1b 1g)

c Simmons, D. W. Be smart! Don't start!

4 characters (2m 2w)

Adams, G. Lonely hearts
Adams, G. Off out
Allen, R. J. Blue cities
Baitz, J. R. It changes every year
Baker, E. A. A dead man's apartment
Ball, A. Power lunch
Barry, P. J. And Fat Freddy's blues
Beard, P. Swingers
Beard, P. Waiting for Pierrepoint
Beim, N. Dreams
Beim, N. Jewel thieves!
Bellon, L. Bonds of affection
Berkoff, S. Greek
Blessing, L. Two rooms
Boretz, A. I remember you
Brittney, L. A different way to die
Butterfield, C. Life in the trees: The last time I saw Timmy Boggs
Bynum, R. C. Escapee
Carley, D. Into
Carmichael, F. Coming apart

MIXED CAST—*Continued*
Cooke, C. Threat
Corrie, J. A bride for Heatherhill
y Deverell, R. Switching places
Donaghy, T. Northeast local
Donoghue, M. A. Me and Mamie O'Rourke
Durang, C. For whom the Southern belle tolls
Edwards, G. The offering
Ekstrom, P. An O. Henry Christmas: The last leaf
Feydeau, G. My wife's dead mother
Foote, H. The Prisoner's Song
Foote, H. The roads to home: The dearest of friends
Foster, N. The motor trade
Friedman, S. Freedom days
Gersten, A. My thing of love
Godber, J. Lucky sods
Goldberg, L. Lady of the Castle
c Goldberg, M. Little Red Riding Hood and The three little pigs
Gonzalez, R. The boiler room
Gray, S. Dog days
Greenspan, D. Son of an engineer
Gregg, S. A private moment
Gross, T. D. Them ... within us
Gurney, A. R. The cocktail hour
Gurney, A. R. The fourth wall
Gurney, A. R. Later life
Gurney, A. R. The Middle Ages
Gurney, A. R. Public affairs: Pt 1 The love course
Gurney, A. R. Sylvia
Hare, D. The bay at Nice
Hayman, R. Playing the wife
Haywood, C. Table for one?
Horovitz, I. Fighting over Beverley
Ikoli, T. Scrape off the black
Ives, D. Long ago and far away, a winter's tale
Ives, D. Philip Glass buys a loaf of bread
Janes, H. Two of a kind
Jannuzzi, L. The appointment
Kass, S. H. Lusting after Pipino's wife
Kaufman, L. Shooting Simone
Kluger, G. M. Till death, or whatever, do us part
Kondoleon, H. The houseguests
Kroetz, F. X. Mensch Meier
LaChiusa, M. J. Eulogy for Mister Hamm
LaChiusa, M. J. Lucky nurse
Lambert, B. Jennie's story
Law, M. Cry wolf
y Lazarus, J. Secrets
Learner, T. The gun in history
Lebow, B. Little Joe Monaghan
Lennon, G. Dates and nuts
Leschin, L. [et al.] Latins anonymous
Linney, R. The death of King Philip
Lucas, C. Throwing your voice
Lucas, C. What I meant was
MacLeod, J. Toronto, Mississippi
MacLeod, W. The lost colony
Margulies, D. The model apartment
Margulies, D. Sight unseen
Marshall, G. and Ganz, L. Wrong turn at Lungfish
Matheus, J. F. 'Cruiter
y Mauro, R. Formula for romance
McClinton, M. Stones and bones
McDonagh, M. The beauty queen of Leenane
McNally, T. Andre's mother
McNally, T. A perfect Ganesh
Mead, K. The Anderson
Meara, A. After-play
y Mondschein, N. L. Hold on!
Moss, R. S. Nightmare: the fright of your life
Murphy, T. The morning after optimism
y Murray, P. Spitting chips
Musset, A. de. Caprice
Nestroy, J. As you were
Nunn, J. Punch
Oates, J. C. Gulf War
Osment, P. Flesh and blood
Pintauro, J. Easter night
Plowman, G. Close to Croydon
Rabe, D. Those the river keeps
Rebeck, T. Spike heels
Reddin, K. You belong to me
Rno, S. Cleveland raining
Roland, B. Feet of clay
Rubens, B. Hijack
Rubess, B. and Cooper, B. Thin ice
Sade, marquis de. The bedroom
Shanley, J. P. Four dogs and a bone
Shaughnessy, D. The manager
Shuttleworth, R. This is dead level
Slade, B. I remember you
Slade, B. You say tomatoes
Spencer, D. Hurricane roses
Strelich, T. Dog logic
Stroppel, F. Fortune's fool
Stubbs, N. The patio window
Sunde, K. Haiti (a dream)
Sweet, J. With and without
Teagarden, J. Letting Lucinda down
Thomas, B. Physical
Tibbetts, M. Bottles with baskets on
Townsend, S. Groping for words

MIXED CAST—*Continued*
Upton, J. The shorewatchers' house
Vickery, F. Love forty
Walker, D. A quiet night in
Ward, N. The present
Way, C. In the bleak midwinter
Way, C. Paradise Drive
White, P. Signal driver
Wiener, S. D. Pavane
Wilder, T. Love and how to cure it
Wilder, T. The rivers under the earth
Wilder, T. The wreck on the Five-twenty-five
Wilson, L. The family continues
Wilson, L. The gingham dog

4 characters (3m 1g)

Horovitz, I. Strong-man's weak child

4 characters (3m 1w)

Baer, R. Mixed emotions
Barnes, D. Three from the earth
Barnes, P. Leonardo's Last Supper
Barnes, P. Revolutionary witness
Barnes, P. The spirit of man: A hand witch of the second stage
Barrie, J. M. Pantaloon
Beim, N. On a darkling plain
Brittney, L. Properly processed
Bynum, R. C. Interviewee
c Carlisle, B. The Crane wife
Coghlan, L. Waking
c Colón, A. The caravan
Connolly, H. One careful owner
Donaghy, T. Down the shore
Durang, C. The Hardy Boys and the mystery of where babies come from
Epstein, M. How Gertrude stormed the Philosophers' Club
Foote, H. The roads to home: Spring dance
Fornes, M. I. The Danube
Foster, N. The affections of May
c Gallanar, I. Showdown at the 3-R Ranch
Gilbert, S. Capote at Yaddo
Glowacki, J. Antigone in New York
Goethe, J. W. von. Brother and sister
Gray, S. Stage struck
Hall, P. D-Day
Harwood, R. Tramway Road
Horovitz, I. One under
Huff, K. Leon and Joey
Hughes, L. Soul gone home
Johnson, T. Hysteria
Kenna, P. Mates
Marchessault, J. The magnificent voyage of Emily Carr
Margulies, D. New Year's eve and Kibbutz
Martin, S. The zig-zag woman
Mason, P. N. The discipline committee
May, E. Hot line
McDonagh, M. The lonesome West
McDonagh, M. A skull in Connemara
McNally, T. Witness
Mellor, K. A passionate woman
Milligan, J. Life after Elvis
Murphy, J. A picture of paradise
Nave, B. Visiting Oliver
Nelson, G. Castrato
Newsom, J. D. Dance Saturday night
Oates, J. C. Ontological proof of my existence
Pearson, C. Scruples, agents and Wilfred
Pearson, S. Unfinished stories
Pedneault, H. Evidence to the contrary
Pinter, H. Betrayal
Pollock, S. Saucy Jack
Rahman, A. The mojo and the sayso
Ribman, R. The cannibal masque
Ridley, P. The pitchfork Disney
Ritter, E. Automatic pilot
Sartin, L. Catfish moon
Schevill, J. Mother O
Schnitzler, A. Marionettes: The gallant Cassian
Shepard, S. Icarus's mother
Sherman, J. The retreat
Silver, N. Fit to be tied
Smith, C. Freefall
Spiro, P. The juiceman cometh
Szyszkowitz, G. Comrade Briggemann
Taylor, P. A redheaded man
Thomas, C. Flesh and blood
Uys, P.-D. Just like home
Villarrubia, J. Miz Lena's backyard
Waterhouse, J. and Leach, P. Frank's feathered friend
Wilde, O. La sainte courtisane
Wilder, T. Bernice
Wilder, T. Cement hands
Wilder, T. Such things only happen in books
Wilkinson, L. The night of the missing bridegroom
Wilson, L. Burn this

4 characters (2w 2b)

Barnes, D. Maggie of the saints

4 characters (3w 1m)

Aron, G. Olive and Hilary

4 characters and extras (1m 1w 2b extras)

c McCaslin, N. The coins of Lin Foo

MIXED CAST—*Continued*

4 characters and extras (1m 3w extras)

Gala, A. The Bells of Orleans
Harris, R. Dead guilty
y Kesselman, W. Maggie Magalita
Livingston, M. S. For unborn children
Pitts, G. Emma
Synge, J. M. Riders to the sea
Uyehara, D. Hiro
Wilder, T. Queens of France

4 characters and extras (2m 1w 1b extras)

c McCaslin, N. Daring, darling Dolly
c McCullough, L. E. Gluscabi and his magic game bag
Schnitzler, A. Marionettes: The puppeteer
c Trott, S. Something sacred this way comes

4 characters and extras (2m 1w extras)

y Swartz, L. D. Halloween screams

4 characters and extras (2m 2w extras)

y Bartel, R. 3 out
Burns, K. On hold at 30,000 feet
Casler, L. A. A night in the theatre
Chekhov, A. The anniversary
Chekhov, A. The festivities
Connolly, H. Daddy's gone a-hunting
Dean, P. H. The Sty of The Blind Pig
Dover, M. and Jarvis, G. Seconds
Durang, C. Business lunch at the Russian Tea Room
Durang, C. Wanda's visit
Finnegan, S. Wild grass
Firbank, R. The mauve tower
Franco, C. [et al.] The LA LA Awards
Grae, D. Moose mating
Guare, J. Muzeeka
Lill, W. All fall down
Margulies, D. Pitching to the star
Martin, J. Criminal hearts
c McCaslin, N. Who laughs last?
c McCullough, L. E. The twelve days of Christmas
Mercer, D. Find me
Miller, A. The last Yankee
Molière. Amphitryon
Parks, S. L. Venus
c Prendergast, S. Little victories
Schooleman, S. and Sewell, C. The stars within
Stock, J. Blue night in the heart of the West
Waterhouse, J. The cardboard cavaliers
Wellman, M. 7 blowjobs

4 characters and extras (3m 1w extras)

Baraka, A. Dutchman
Bynum, R. C. Sherwood
Goethe, J. W. von. Jery and Betty
Gotanda, P. K. Fish head soup
c Hamlett, C. Face value
c Hatton, T. J. Super Dooper Man
Kennedy, A. P. and Kennedy, A. Sleep deprivation chamber
Kovacevic, D. The professional
y Nightingale, E. M. Arise, Sparta!
O'Neill, E. Fog
Sloate, D. Countess in Thistleland
Stoppard, T. Another moon called Earth
Tagore, R. Chitra
Tasca, J. Extraction
Turrini, P. Alpine glow
Waterhouse, J. and Leach, P. A nest of cuckoos

4 characters and extras (2b 2g extras)

c Westerhout, G. The Zeem dreamz

5 characters (1m 1w 1b 2g)

Wilder, T. Childhood

5 characters (1m 2w 2g)

y McDonough, V. M. All that glitters . . .

5 characters (1m 3w 1b)

York, Y. Life gap

5 characters (1m 3w 1g)

Hammond, W. Julie Johnson

5 characters (1m 4w)

Bisson, P. When the clock strikes
Braverman, C. The Yiddish Trojan women
Brittney, L. Failed investments
Chinn, J. In by the half
Ehn, E. Two altars, ten funerals (all souls)
Houston, V. H. Tea
LaChuisa, M. J. First Lady suite: Over Texas
Law, M. My Johnny
y Leader, J. Land slides
McGillivray, D. and Zerlin, W. Chase me up Farndale Avenue, s'il vous plaît!
McKee, J. The 'far-flung'
Mead, K. Line of descent
c Mercati, C. Bigger than life!
Mighton, J. The little years
Morris, M. Boss of the pool
Richardson, W. A pillar of the church
Shepherd, C. Delphiniums
Smith, S. Parentcraft
Storey, D. Stages
Tesich, S. Arts & leisure

MIXED CAST—*Continued*

5 characters (1w 2b 2g)

c Bentley-Fisher, T. Friends

5 characters (1b 4g)

c Mercati, C. Cinderella

5 characters (2m 1w 1b 1g)

c Bush, M. Ghost of the river house
c McCaslin, N. A miracle in the Christmas city
Paul, S. L. The Rainclouds study the Ten Commandments

5 characters (2m 2w 1b)

Margulies, D. The Loman family picnic
Overmyer, E. Don Quixote de La Jolla

5 characters (2m 2w 1g)

y Williams, B. In the garden of the witch

5 characters (2m 3w)

Adam, A. A matter of diplomacy
Adam, A. A pearl of great price
Allen, W. Central Park West
Aronson, B. Little Red Riding Hood
Bamford, S. Who's a pretty boy then?
Barnes, D. Kurzy of the sea
Barry, P. J. A distance from Calcutta
Bennett, T. Dark rituals
Booth, J. Seeing double
Brenton, H. Berlin Bertie
Brittney, L. The last wife
Brochu, J. Fat chance
Bruce, L. Keyboard skills
y Bush, M. Rockway Cafe
Carmichael, F. Damsel of the desert
Chinn, J. Something to remember you by
Cocteau, J. Les parents terribles (Indiscretions)
Coxon, L. Wishbones
Coyne, J. S. Did you ever send your wife to Camberwell?
Cullen, A. Self catering
Daly, T. Kafka dances
Dashow, K. Top of 16
Durang, C. The actor's nightmare
Durang, C. Baby with the bathwater
Durang, C. 'dentity crisis
Eichelberger, E. Dasvedanya Mama
Elisha, R. Choice
Foreman, R. Eddie goes to Poetry City (Part one: Seattle version)
Fornes, M. I. The conduct of life
Foxton, D. Caught on the hop
Fraser, B. Poor Super Man
Godber, J. Blood, sweat and tears
Gregor, H. Freedom! Freedom!
Guare, J. Something I'll tell you Tuesday
Gurney, A. R. Children
Hall, F. B. Dance of the Eland
c Haylock, D. The nativity scene
Hazzard, A. Mother liked it
Hodgson, S. Tunnel vision
Hornby, I. Late of this address
Horovitz, I. Faith
Hunter, M. Transit of Venus
Huth, A. The trouble with old lovers
Isitt, D. Matilda liar!
Jones, J. M. Love trouble
Keillor, G. The midlife crisis of Dionysus
Kelly, C. Excess baggage
Kyle, C. The monogamist
Learner, T. The glass mermaid
Linney, R. Three poets: Akhmatova
Linney, R. Three poets: Hrosvitha
Macdonald, S. When we were women
MacLeod, W. The house of yes
Mason, T. The fiery furnace
Mastrosimone, W. Shivaree
Mayer, J. A love affair
Mead, K. After the child
Mighton, J. Body and soul
Morgan, J. Kids
Moxley, G. Danti-Dan
Munro, R. Your turn to clean the stair
Nigro, D. Glamorgan
Parks, S. L. Imperceptible mutabilities in the Third Kingdom
Pintauro, J. Butterball
Pollock, D. Doc
c Price, J. W. Rocket recycle
Puig, M. Under a mantle of stars
Reid, C. Joyriders
Reilly, C. Astronauts
Richardson, W. The deacon's awakening
Ridley, P. Ghost from a perfect place
Roberts, D. Breaking glass
Robson, J. Mail order bride
Sessions, G. The return of spring
Silver, N. Free will & wanton lust
Spence, E. Undertow
Standjofski, H. No cycle
Starosta, S. The sausage eaters
Stein, G. Three sisters who are not sisters
Stoppard, T. Teeth
Strindberg, A. The pelican
Szyszkowitz, G. Grillparzer
Tagore, R. Malini
Tibbles, G. The turn of the worm
Tilly. A modest proposal
Tirado, C. Some people have all the luck
Upton, J. Bruises
Vickery, F. Biting the bullet

MIXED CAST—*Continued*

Vickery, F. Loose ends
Warner, F. Meeting ends
Williams, G. Rain
Williamson, D. A handful of friends
Wilson, J. Abstinence
Wilson, L. Victory on Mrs. Dandywine's island
Wise, R. Sound choice
Zark, J. A body of water: White days

5 characters (3m 1w 1b)

Finn, W. March of the falsettos
Topol, J. Cat on the rails

5 characters (3m 1w 1g)

c Martini, C. Swimmers
Sardou, V. For love or monkey
Wallace, N. One flea spare

5 characters (3m 2w)

Adamson, S. Clocks and whistles
Armstrong, G. K. Handcuffs
Bailey, M. Going all the way
Baitz, J. R. The substance of fire
Beard, P. Come the resolution
Berkoff, S. East
Berkoff, S. Kvetch
Bernstein, J. Pizza: a love story
Booth, J. Echo of applause
Burns, K. Terminal terror
y Bush, M. The emerald circle
Buzo, A. Rooted
Carley, D. Taking liberties
Champagne, D. Playing bare
Chappell, E. Theft
Childress, A. Wine in the wilderness
Clark, R. and Bobrick, S. Norman, is that you?
Connolly, H. Overtime
Danowski, C. Family values
Dietz, S. Private eyes
Dresser, R. Gun-shy
Durang, C. John and Mary Doe
Durang, C. Nine in the morning
Elton, B. Silly cow
Everett, R. Present from the past
Fannon, C. Green icebergs
Farrell, B. Forty-four, Sycamore
Feingold, M. Scribe's paradox
Fo, D. Can't pay? Won't pay!
y Fontaine, R. Graduation address
Foreman, R. Eddie goes to Poetry City (Part two: New York version)
Fornes, M. I. What of the night?: Hunger
Gill, P. Mean tears
Goethe, J. W. von. Torquato Tasso
Goldstein, J. Martin Night
Gow, M. Furious
Graham, B. The Champagne Charlie Stakes
Gray, S. Spoiled
Greenberg, R. The American plan
Guare, J. In fireworks lie secret codes
Harvey, J. Beautiful thing
Harvey, J. Rupert Street Lonely Hearts Club
Holsclaw, D. The baddest of boys
Horovitz, I. Morning
Howe, T. Birth and after birth
Howe, T. One shoe off
Ibsen, H. Ghosts
Johnson, C. Boys mean business
Johnson, T. Dead funny
Kilroy, T. Talbot's box
Koenig, L. The little girl who lives down the lane
Kopit, A. Road to Nirvana
y Kottke, T. G. Deputy Toby
Laurents, A. The radical mystique
Lill, W. The Glace Bay Miners' Museum
Linney, R. Paradise
Linney, R. Shotgun
Luckham, C. The choice
Mander, C. Getting along
McNally, T. Noon
McNally, T. Prelude & Liebestod
Medoff, M. The homage that follows
Medoff, M. Stumps
Members of the Road Company Ensemble. Blind desire
Micone, M. Beyond the ruins
Millan, J. and Brooker, B. Serpent kills
Minieri, A. Your life is a feature film
Mitchell, J. S. Son-Boy
Morton, C. Johnny Tenorio
Musset, A. de. You can't think of everything
y Nolan, P. T. The inexperienced ghost
O'Donnell, M. Strangers on Earth
y Olfson, E. Wuthering Heights
Osborne, J. Déjàvu
Osborne, J. Look back in anger
Oswald, D. Gary's house
Panych, M. The ends of the Earth
Ravenhill, M. Shopping and fucking
Ribman, R. The rug merchants of chaos
Ridley, P. The fastest clock in the universe
Robinson, M. Colonial tongues
Sanchez, E. Icarus
Schnitzler, A. The hour of recognition
Sharpe, T. Shadows
Shepard, S. Fourteen hundred thousand

MIXED CAST—*Continued*
Shepard, S. States of shock
Sherman, A. Hello muddah, hello fadduh!
Sherman, J. M. Sons and fathers
Sherman, J. M. Wonderful time
Shields, Carol, and Shields, Catherine. Fashion, power, guilt and the charity of families
Silver, N. The food chain
Silver, N. Pterodactyls
Silver, N. Raised in captivity
Simon, N. London suite: The man on the floor
y Slaight, B. High tide
c Smith, B. S. Adams for the defense
Smith, B. L. Butterscotch
Steppling, J. Standard of the breed
Sternheim, C. The bloomers
Stickland, E. Some assembly required
Stoppard, T. After Magritte
Storey, D. Home
Storey, R. The saints and apostles
Sturgess, B. Marius's mule
c Swortzell, L. Jack Fuggler
Thomas, E. House of America
Tolins, J. The twilight of the Golds
Valle-Inclán, R. del. Blood pact
Vickery, F. Erogenous zones
c Vigil, A. La aparicion de Nuestra Senora de Guadalupe. The miracle of Our Lady of Guadalupe
Vingoe, M. and Kudelka, J. Hooligans
y Waddy, L. Florence Nightingale
Walker, D. The affairs of Dilys Willis
Wallace, N. In the heart of America
Ward, N. Apart from George
Warner, F. Killing time
Weiss, M. Hesh
Weitz, P. All for one
Wellman, M. The hyacinth macaw
Wilcox, M. Lent
Wilder, T. Infancy
Wooten, J. J. Trophies
Wright, D. Lot 13: the bone violin
Wyld, H. Night's candles
Youngblood, S. Talking bones

5 characters (3w 1b 1g)

Corthron, K. Come down burning

5 characters (4m 1w)

Barnes, D. The beauty
Bays, C. L. Five visits from Mr. Whitcomb
Chadwick, C. The man's shop
Corbitt, W. Crying holy
Davies, R. Eros at breakfast
Edwards, G. Old West
y Foster, J. Play to win
c Gallanar, I. Showdown at the 3-R Ranch
Goethe, J. W. von. Iphigenia in Tauris
Hardstack, M. The cure
Harris, B. Robert Johnson: trick the Devil
Harrison, T. The Kaisers of Carnuntum
Horovitz, I. Line
Jelinek, E. President Evening Breeze
Johnson, T. Insignificance
Kennedy, A. Motherhood 2000
Lim, G. Bitter cane
Linney, R. Spain: Torquemada
Manzi, W. Perfect crime
Maraini, D. Crime at the tennis club
c McCaslin, N. Borrowed trouble

5 characters (4m 1g)

Hampton, C. Alice's adventures under ground
McPherson, C. The weir
Millay, E. St. V. Aria da capo
Osborne, W. and Herrera, A. Smoke & mirrors
Packard, S. In with Alma
Parra, M. A. de la. The raw, the cooked, and the rotten
Paterson, D. L. Pieces of the sky
Penhall, J. Some voices

5 characters (4m 1w)

Pintauro, J. Snow orchid
Ruzzante. Weasel
Schwartz, D. Choosing company
Shepard, S. Forensic and the navigators
Sherman, J. Three in the back, two in the head
Sod, T. Satan and Simon Desoto
Strand, R. The death of Zukasky
Vanderhaeghe, G. I had a job I liked. Once.
Walker, G. F. Theatre of the film noir
Wilcox, M. Accounts

5 characters and extras (1m 2w 1b lg extras)

Hall, F. B. Emily's play
c Lysander, P. and Osten, S. Medea's children
c Ruch, A. Clarissa's closet

5 characters and extra (1m 3w 1b extra)

Durang, C. 1-900-desperate
c Sampson, L. Old MacDonald's farmyard follies

5 characters and extras (1m 4w extras)

c D'Arcy, A. Cinderella
Lyssiotis, T. The Forty Lounge Cafe
Rivera, J. Marisol

MIXED CAST—*Continued*

5 characters and extras (2m 1w 1b 1g extras)

c Hezlep, W. Merlin's cave
c Vigil, A. La fior de la Noche Buena. The flower of the Holy Night

5 characters and extras (2m 2w 1b extras)

y Harris, A. The pinballs

5 characters and extras (2m 2w 1g extras)

Ayckbourn, A. Henceforward . . .

5 characters and extras (2m 3w extras)

y Bond, E. At the inland sea
Brittney, L. Have a nice day
Crane, R. Under the stars
Hall, F. B. Lucia
Higginsen, V. and Wydro, K. Mama, I want to sing
Martin, J. Keely and Du
Nunn, J. Arrangements
O'Neill, E. Recklessness
Richardson, W. The chip woman's fortune
Standjofski, H. Anton
Szumigalski, A. Z: a meditation on oppression, desire and freedom
Wolfe, G. C. The colored museum

5 characters and extras (2m 3g extras)

c McCullough, L. E. Bring a torch, Jeannette, Isabella

5 characters and extras (3m 1w 1b extras)

y Priore, F. V. Madcap Monster Inn

5 characters and extras (3m 2w extras)

Dean, D. Mama's girl
c Elfenbein, J. A. Puss-in-boots
Gray, S. Molly
Greer, B. Munda negra
Guare, J. Home fires
Hall, F. B. Nathaniel in Berkshire
Harwood, R. Another time
Kennedy, A. The dramatic circle
Lee, J. A. Coming home
MacIntyre, T. Sheep's milk on the boil
McNally, T. Whiskey
Mercer, D. An afternoon at the festival
Parra, M. A. de la. Every young woman's desire
Penhall, J. Pale horse
Sade, Marquis de. The haunted tower
Sade, Marquis de. The madness of misfortune
Sade, Marquis de. The self-proclaimed philosopher
Sands, L. Checkmate
y Schaaf, A. K. Hassle in the castle
Schevill, J. The last romantics
Schnitzler, A. The big scene
Schwartz, D. Dr. Bergen's belief
Way, C. Dead man's hat
Wilder, T. Youth

5 characters and extras (4m 1g extras)

c McCaslin, N. Mercy in moccasins

5 characters and extras (4m 1w extras)

Berkoff, S. Sink the Belgrano!
Feydeau, G. "Hey, cut out the parading around stark naked!"
Gilbert, S. Lola Starr builds her dream home
Gilbert, S. Suzie Goo: private secretary
Larson, J. J.P. Morgan saves the nation
López, E. I. Spanish eyes
Mahfuz, 'Isam. The China tree
c McCullough, L. E. Let's have a hoedown!
y McCullough, L. E. When people could fly
Noonan, J. F. The drowning of Manhattan
O'Neill, E. The Emperor Jones
Schwartz, D. Venus in the back room
Shepard, S. The holy ghostly
Wang, L. Junk bonds
c Yep, L. Dragonwings

6 characters (1m 1w 2b 2g)

c Hezlep, W. Red Cloud's revenge
c Hezlep, W. Tower of London

6 characters (1m 3w 1b 1g)

Bush, M. Hansel and Gretel, little brother and sister

6 characters (1m 3w 2b)

Macdonald, S. The winter guest

6 characters (1m 5w)

Ball, A. Five women wearing the same dress
Day, J. Come back for light refreshments after the service
Harding, N. This year, next year
Houston, V. H. Kokoro (true heart)
McNally, T. ¡Cuba si!
Samuels, D. Kindertransport
Saunders, J. Fashion
Swedeen, S. The sleep seeker
Tremblay, M. Marcel pursued by the hounds

6 characters (2m 1w 2b 1g)

c Hezlep, W. Treasure of the Mayans

6 characters (2m 2w 1b 1g)

c Vigil, A. El Dia de los Muertos. The Fiesta of the Day of the Dead

MIXED CAST—*Continued*

6 characters (2m 3w 1b)

Durang, C. Sister Mary Ignatius explains it all for you
Linney, R. Tennessee
McDonald, H. Dream of a common language

6 characters (2m 3w 1g)

Barteve, R. The orphanage
Yamauchi, W. And the soul shall dance

6 characters (2m 4w)

Ackermann, J. Zara Spook and other lures
Christian, B. Blue murder
Cleage, P. Flyin' west
Corrie, J. Billy Shaw
De Groen, A. The girl who saw everything
Dietz, S. Trust
Dunbar, D. A song for Robbie
Foote, H. The tears of my sister
Gee, S. Never in my lifetime
Godfrey, P. A bucket of eels
Gurney, A. R. What I did last summer
Hare, D. The secret rapture
Hornby, I. Dream, lover!
Ives, D. The land of Cockaigne
Klein, J. Betty the yeti
Linney, R. Goodbye, Howard
Lyssa, A. Pinball
Margulies, D. July 7, 1994
McIntyre, C. My heart's a suitcase
Miller, B. Mum's the word
y Sodaro, C. Blind date
St. John, B. Rubies: Heirlooms
St. John, B. Rubies: Little gems
Stoppard, T. A separate peace
Storey, D. The restoration of Arnold Middleton
c Swortzell, L. A visit from St. Nicholas
Thompson, J. Lion in the streets
Warburton, N. J. Distracted globe
Wellman, M. Whirligig
Yates, P. Nuances
Zark, J. A body of water: Shooting souls

6 characters (3m 1w 1b 1g)

Barker, H. The possibilities

6 characters (3m 1w 2b)

c Weller, M. Dogbrain

6 characters (3m 2w 1b)

Adrian, Y. Flyboy
Césaire, I. The ship
GeBauer, J. The nip and the bite
Lebow, B. Tiny Tim is dead
Turrini, P. Swine

6 characters (3m 2w 1g)

Ackermann, J. Off the map
Fornes, M. I. What of the night?: Nadine
Yeats, W. B. The Land of Heart's Desire

6 characters (3m 3w)

Adamson, S. Grace note
Alianak, H. Passion and sin
Arlen, H. Sweet and hot
Armstrong, I. Fallen heroes
y Asher, S. F. A woman called Truth
Ayckbourn, A. Communicating doors
Bamford, S. Just a loving touch
Bamford, S. Scorpio
Bartram, F. Tiddley pum
Benfield, D. Anyone for breakfast?
Benfield, D. A fly in the ointment
Benfield, D. Up and running!
Berlin, E. The line that's picked up 1000 babes (and how it can work for you)
Berlin, E. The Midnight Moonlight Wedding Chapel
y Bland, J. The squire's daughter
Bobrick, S. Are you sure?
Booth, J. Charley's uncle
Booth, J. Dead on time
Booth, J. Face of evil
Booth, J. Little white lies
Booth, J. A question of identity
Booth, J. Something on his mind
Booth, J. Tangled web
Booth, J. Your place or mine?
Brooks, V. Let's pretend
Brooks, V. Penny Blue
Buchan, A. Conditional surrender
Buero-Vallejo, A. The music window
Burns, K. Identity crisis
Burrill, M. F. Aftermath
Busch, C. You should be so lucky
Butterfield, C. Snowing at Delphi
Cartwright, J. The rise and fall of Little Voice
Chiodo, T. The medieval murders
c Clapp, P. The girl whose fortune sought her
c Cooper, R. M. How things happen in three!
Coyle, K. Corner boys
Crawford, D. W. Borrowed plumage
De Angelis, A. Hush
De Boer, L. The Buddha of Ceylon
Dias, E. J. The necklace
Downing, M. The demon
DuMaurier, D. September tide
Enright, N. Good works
Everett, R. Close to the wind
Fraser, B. Wolfboy

MIXED CAST—*Continued*
French, D. Silver dagger
Friel, B. Wonderful Tennessee
Godfrey, P. The modern husband
Granville-Barker, H. Rococo
Granville-Barker, H. Vote by ballot
Grosso, N. Peaches
Gurney, A. R. A Cheever evening
Gurney, A. R. The dining room
Gurney, A. R. The old boy
Gurr, M. Jerusalem
Gurr, M. Underwear, perfume and crash helmet
y Hannay, R. Windows
Hare, D. Amy's view
Hill, G. L. The Black Branch
Hornby, I. Wait until the ghost is clear
Horovitz, I. The great Labor Day classic
Hunkins, L. The best of strangers
y Hunkins, L. Freedom is my middle name
Isitt, D. Nasty neighbours
Ives, D. Degas, c'est moi
Ives, D. Foreplay
Johnson, C. L. The years
Kraus, J. H. and Woodward, G. Tenure track
Labiche, E. and Michel, M. It's all relative
Linney, R. Songs of love
Lipsky, J. The survivor: A Cambodian odyssey
Lyssiotis, T. A white sports coat
MacDonald, A.-M. The Arab's mouth
Maquire, M. Phaedra
Margulies, D. What's wrong with this picture?
Martin, S. WASP
McGullion, B. Murdermind
McKelvey, P. House of secrets
McNally, T. Bringing it all back home
McNally, T. Master class
Miller, A. Broken glass
Mouawad, W. Wedding day at the Cro-Magnons'
Oates, J. C. The perfectionist
O'Connor, J. Red roses and petrol
O'Donoghue, J. Abbie and Lou, Norman and Rose
Okita, D. The rainy season
Overmyer, E. In perpetuity throughout the universe
c Palmer, G. The falcon
c Panych, M. 2B WUT UR
Parks, S.-L. The America play
Paz, O. Rappaccini's daughter
Poliakoff, S. Sweet panic
Pospisil, C. Somewhere in between
Pugliese, F. Aven'u boys
Rubess, B. Pope Joan
Schenkkan, R. The homecoming
Schenkkan, R. Tall tales
Sewell, S. Traitors
Shepard, S. Simpatico
Sherman, J. The God of Isaac
Sherman, M. Some sunny day
Siefert, L. Little Egypt
Simon, M. Walking to Waldheim
Steppling, J. The shaper
Storey, D. The march on Russia
Strauss, B. The tour guide
c Swajeski, D. M. The revolution machine
Thomas, T. Without apologies
Thompson, J. I am yours
Trenholme, H. Fell blow
Tuttle, J. The hammerstone
Vickery, F. Roots and wings
Vogel, P. Hot 'n' throbbing
Walker, G. F. Criminals in love
Warburton, N. The Droitwich discovery
Warner, F. Lying figures
Warren, D. Club Chernobyl
c Wartski, M. C. The birthday guests
Weller, M. Spoils of war
Wilder, T. The happy journey to Camden and Trenton
Wilson, L. Sextet (yes)
Wilson, L. This is the rill speaking
Wong, E. Letters to a student revolutionary
Wright, D. Watbanaland
Yankowitz, S. Night sky

6 characters (4w 1w 1g)

Linney, R. The captivity of Pixie Shedman
Roth, A. Oh, the innocents

6 characters (4m 1b 1g)

Tesich, S. On the open road

6 characters (4m 2w)

Adam, A. A bit of land
Annie, G. Something rotten in Denmark
Baitz, J. R. The end of the day
Baitz, J. R. The film society
Barroga, J. Talk-story
Barry, P. J. Down by the ocean
Bartley, J. Stephen & Mr. Wilde
Basso, E. Middle distance
Berkoff, S. Brighton beach scumbags
Berry, W. The cool of the day
Boyd, P. Odd fish
Burke, S. The lodger
Byerrum, E. A Christmas cactus
Champagne, S. Away from me

MIXED CAST—*Continued*
Chappel, E. Haunted
Duff, J. A quarrel of sparrows
Durang, C. Beyond therapy
Durang, C. Titanic
Field, B. Boundary Waters
Finley, K. The theory of total blame
Fo, D. Elizabeth: almost by chance a woman
Gambaro, G. Bad blood (La malasangre)
Gray, S. Dutch uncle
Greenspan, D. Dead mother
Gurney, A. R. The comeback
Harwood, R. Taking sides
c Haylock, D. Here is the news: Overseas and underseas news
Heggie, I. An experienced woman gives advice
Herst, B. A woman's comedy
Ibsen, H. Rosmersholm
Johnson, T. Unsuitable for adults
Linney, R. April snow
Linney, R. Heathen Valley
Magee, D. Paddywack
McLean, D. Julie Allardyce
McNally, T. And things that go bump in the night
Mercer, D. The Governor's lady
Milligan, J. The quality of boiled water
Nagy, A. The seducer's diary
Nagy, P. Weldon rising
Najera, R. A quiet love
y Netzel, S. The jest
Nigro, D. Lucia mad
O'Kelly, D. Asylum! Asylum!
Pogos, A. Strangers in the night
Roche, B. The Cavalcaders
Sadler, C. and Pemberton, S. Christmas balls
Schnitzler, A. Paracelsus
Sebbar, L. My mother's eyes
Sewell, G. Speak of the devil
Shaw, B. Mrs. Warren's profession
Sherman, J. Jest a second!
Simpson, E. The comet of St. Loomis
Sterner, J. Other people's money: the ultimate seduction
Tasca, J. Deus-X
y Thomas, E. and Redmond, B. Six Canterbury tales
Vargas Llosa, C. Orchids in the moonlight
Walker, G. F. The art of war
Walker, G. F. Beyond Mozambique
Walker, G. F. Zastrozzi: the master of discipline
Welsh, D. Make it happen
Windwick, N. D. A father's daughter
Wright, D. Quills

6 characters (5m 1w)

Auletta, R. The Persians
Berkoff, S. Acapulco
Bumbalo, V. What are Tuesdays like?
Chappell, E. It can damage your health
Firth, T. The end of the food chain
Fo, D. Accidental death of an anarchist
Goldstein, J. The end
Gray, S. The common pursuit
Dorst, T. Fernando Krapp wrote me this letter: an assaying of the truth
Gurney, A. R. The David show
Mitterer, F. The wild woman
O'Neill, E. The movie man
O'Neill, E. The web
y Priore, F. V. The return of Rip Van Winkle, Jr.
Smith, V. The gamblers
Valle, F. I am a winner
Vanderhaeghe, G. Dancock's dance
Yeats, W. B. On Baile's strand
Yep, L. Dragonwings

6 characters and extras (1m 1w 3b 1g extras)

c McGovern, C. The ugly duck

6 characters and extras (1m 5w extras)

Sutton, J. Voir dire

6 characters and extras (2m 4w extras)

Dixon, D. The Snow Witch
Kemp, J. The black sequin dress
Pearson, S. Watching the dog
Warburton, N. The last bread pudding

6 characters and extras (3m 1w 1b 1g extras)

c McCaslin, N. A gift of music

6 characters and extras (3m 2w 1b extras)

c McCullough, L. E. Greasepaint and Ginthons: the medicine show comes to town

6 characters and extras (3m 3w extras)

Abe, K. The green stockings
y Coo, C. Removing the glove
Dallman, J. The inside story of Dr. Crippen
Elton, B. Gasping
Enright, N. Mongrels
Finnegan, S. Mary Maginn
Gomez, T. Inter-tribal
Holm, S. Leonora
c Holman, D. No worries
c Hughes, V. Strongman meets his match
y Hurst, Z. B. and Hurst, J. R. The cowhand's Christmas Carol

MIXED CAST—*Continued*

c McCullough, L. E. Patches solves a wedding riddle
McGrath, J. Blood red roses
Mercer, D. On the eve of publication
Reyes, G. Chilean holiday
Richardson, A. A fine gentleman
Rosei, P. Blameless
Rubess, B. Boom, baby, boom!
Shepard, S. Back bog beast bait
Swados, E. Esther
Vago, S. M. An ordinary woman under stress
Zauner, F. Ch. A handful of earth

6 characters and extras (3m 1b 2g extras)

c McCullough, L. E. Outlaw gold: the lost treasure of Commanche Creek

6 characters and extras (4m 1w 1b extras)

c McCullough, L. E. Silent night

6 characters and extras (4m 1w 1g extras)

Tagore, R. Sacrifice

6 characters and extras (4m 2w extras)

Aynsley, E. 'I told you so'
Bell, H. Fortune
y Boiko, C. Murder on the Orient Express subway
Brewer, E. and Toksvig, S. The pocket dream
Crump, R. The strange illness
Finnegan, S. Comrade Brennan
Glancy, D. Weebjob
Gray, S. Man in a side-car
Hall, F. B. Ezra's Noh for Willie
Hogg, F. A. Afternoon at Tavern MacTavish
c Lavrakas, P. The Princess and the pea
Ricchi, R. The scandal
Richardson, D. Party night (the great feast)
Scribe, E. and Mélesville. The castrata
Tambori, G. Mein Kampf
c Vigil, A. Blanca flor. White flower
c Winther, B. The Maharajah is bored

6 characters and extras (5m 1w extras)

Bamford, S. No roses around the door
c Bennett, R. Rumpelstiltskin
Koch, K. The construction of Boston
McCaslin, N. Clever Marya and the Czar
c McCullough, L. E. Klondike fever
c McCullough, L. E. Turquoise Tom, the versifying bandit of Old California
Minghella, A. Made in Bangkok
Solórzano, C. And death brought forth the light

c Throckmorton, S. L. The forest bride
c Grauer, R. The boy who tricked the moon

7 characters (1m 2w 4g)

c York, Y. Afternoon of the elves

7 characters (1m 6w)

Robinson, R. T. The cover of life
Saunders, J. France

7 characters (1w 6b)

y Hackett, W. Tom Sawyer, whitewasher

7 characters (2m 1w 1b 3g)

Beim, N. Inside

7 characters (2m 3w 1b 1g)

Franklin, J. E. Christchild

7 characters (2m 3w 2b)

Wilson, L. Lemon sky

7 characters (2m 4w 1g)

y Cole, N. And the tide shall cover the earth

7 characters (2m 5w)

Bolger, D. April Bright
Booth, J. 50 . . . and counting
Butterfield, C. Where the truth lies
DePietro, P. The hilarious hillbilly massacre
Firbank, R. A disciple from the country
Ingleton, S. The passion . . . and its deep connection with lemon delicious pudding
y Kachejian, G. All's well that ends wrong
Keene, D. All Souls
MacLeod, J. Little sister
McGuinness, F. The factory girls
Oglesby, T. Two lips indifferent red
Schwab, W. People annihilation
Tolan, K. Approximating mother

7 characters (3m 3w 1b)

y Alvarez, L. Eddie Mundo Edmundo
Bremner, B. Mrs. Coney
Feydeau, G. Going to pot
Glore, J. The company of heaven
Lucas, C. Missing persons
Wilson, L. The sand castle
Kushner, T. Slavs!
Wilson, L. The mound builders

7 characters (3m 4w)

Baum, T. Cold hands
Blackwood, G. L. Futures
Bonal, D. Beware the heart
Booth, J. Dirty weekend
Booth, J. Over his dead body

MIXED CAST—*Continued*
Brown, K. C. Sherlock's veiled secret
Brownell, R. Afterhours
Burke, J. Swinging on a star
Chen, K. Eating chicken feet
Chinn, J. Sylvia's wedding
Chiodo, T. Murder under the big top
Clark, S. The trial of Judith K.
Craver, M. and Hardwick, M. Radio gals
Dinner, W. Logic upside down
c DuBois, G. Bind up the nation's wounds
Durang, C. A stye of the eye
Durang, C. and Wasserstein, W. Medea
Edmundson, H. The mill on the floss
Ensler, E. Floating Rhoda and the glue man
Franks, A. The mother tongue
y Gollobin, L. B. Selkie
Gotanda, P. K. Ballad of Yachiyo
Graham, G. The boys
Harper, T. Christmas isn't for families
Higgins, F. The sweet by 'n' by
Hornby, I. Murdered, presumed dead
Hornby, I. The price to pay
Hornby, I. Tim'll fix it!
Ibsen, H. Hedda Gabler
Johnson, J. Uganda
Lang, W. Lady of the camellias
Mander, C. World première
McIntyre, C. The thickness of skin
Oakes, M. and Wells, J. Greenfield blooms
O'Malley, M. Diverting devotion
Plowman, G. Beata Beatrix
Plowman, G. Philip and Rowena
Plowman, G. Umjana Land
Reid, C. Clowns
Schwartz, D. Paris and Helen
Shearer, J. The family
Simon, N. Brighton Beach memoirs
y Slaight, B. Class action
y Sorensen, K. An endangered species: waking up
Uhry, A. The last night of Ballyhoo
Upton, J. Ashes and sand
Vickery, F. Spanish lies
Walker, G. F. Better living

7 characters (4m 3w)

Ayckbourn, A. Time of my life
Beard, J. A. Vladivostok blues
Bennett, A. Getting on
Booth, J. Sleeping arrangements
Brown, B. All things considered
y Bush, M. The crystal
y Bush, M. 13 bells of Boglewood
Congdon, C. Tales of the lost Formicans
Crawford, D. W. Tangled garden
Dickinson, S. Styx and Bones
Feydeau, G. Brothers in crime
Findley, T. The stillborn lover
Finn, W. and Lapine, J. Falsettoland
Fo, D. The virtuous burglar
Fraser, B. The ugly man
Freeman, D. Kindly keep it covered
French, D. Leaving home
Furse, J. The old rust bucket
y Gallagher, M. Windshook
Gardiner, D. Weeds in the wheat
Gardner, H. I'm not Rappaport
Garner, J. The flight into Egypt
Gelbart, L. Power failure
Gerstenberg, A. The pot boiler
Glover, K. Dancing on moonlight
Godber, J. The office party
Godber, J. Passion killers
Graffigny, F. D. D. de. Cenia
Gray, S. Butley
Greig, D. The architect
Grimsley, J. Mr. Universe
Hampton, C. The philanthropist
Harwood, R. After the lions
c Haylock, D. Here is the news: Riot in Nazareth
c Haylock, D. Here is the news: Sad news and amazing news
Horovitz, I. Unexpected tenderness
Ibsen, H. The master builder
Marivaux. The triumph of love
Martin, J. Middle-aged white guys
Martin, J. Summer
May, B. 9th inning wedding
Mayer, J. Killjoy
McGuinness, F. Carthaginians
Menken, A. Weird romance: The girl who was plugged in
Miller, A. The ride down Mount Morgan
Murphy, T. Conversations on a homecoming
Nagy, P. The scarlet letter
Nigro, D. The Transylvanian clockworks
O'Malley, M. Three years from "thirty"
Pascal, F. The lunatic lover
y Perry, E. E. Once upon a beginning
Pinter, H. Moonlight
Rabe, D. Hurlyburly
Real, C. Why the Beach Boys are like opera
Rebeck, T. The family of Mann
c Rocklin, B. The Island of Anyplace
Rubio, J. L. In August we play the Pyrenees
Shaffer, D. Last requests
Shepard, S. Chicago
Simon, N. Lost in Yonkers

MIXED CAST—*Continued*

c Supple, T. Grimm tales
Taylor, R. Mudtracks
Thompson, J. Sled
c Valenti, M. Beauty and the beast
Waterhouse, K. Our song
Williams, N. A little like paradise
Wilson, A. Seven guitars
Wise, R. When one door closes

7 characters (5m 2w)

Barnes, D. A passion play
Brown, C. The African Company presents Richard III
Chocrón, I. Clipper
Cook, M. Jacob's wake
y Cowell, M. Song for the navigator
Davis, O. Escape to freedom
Elder, L. Ceremonies in dark old men
Fo, D. Abducting Diana
Fo, D. One was nude and one wore tails
Gifford, B. Tricks
Gray, S. Otherwise engaged
Gray, S. Quartermaine's terms
Gray, S. Simply disconnected
Gray, S. Sleeping dog
Harvey, J. Boom bang-a-bang
c Haylock, D. Here is the news: Good news and bad news
Horovitz, I. The honest-to-god Schnozzola
Horovitz, I. Unexpected tenderness
Hughes, D. Digging for fire
Johnson, J. P. and Hughes, L. The organizer
Kash, M. and Hughes, D. Who's under where?
Keane, J. B. Moll
Kramer, L. The destiny of me
Landau, T. 1969
Lee, J. A. The execution
Linney R. Ambrosio
Macdonald, S. Borders of paradise
Mack, C. K. In her sight
McBurney, S. and Wheatley, M. The three lives of Lucie Cabrol
McCusker, P. Pap's place
Meilhac, H. and Halévy, L. Signor Nicodemo
Mercer, D. Duck song
Molière. The flying doctor
Murphy, T. The sanctuary lamp
Phelan, B. Himself
Poliakoff, S. Breaking the silence
Potter, D. Blue remembered hills
Rabe, D. Sticks and bones
Rattigan, T. The Browning version
c Schario, C. A Christmas carol
Shepard, S. Buried child
Sroka, J. and Fleming, J. Dying for laughs
Storey, D. In celebration
Weller, M. Fishing
Witten, M. Washington Square moves
Feffer, S. The wizards of quiz
Feldshuh, D. Miss Evers' boys
Gilbert, S. Jim Dandy

7 characters (6m 1w)

Koch, K. The death of Sir Brian Caitskill
Korder, H. Fun
Ledoux, P. and Young, D. Love is strange
Minjares, J. The king of the kosher grocers
Muldoon, P. Six honest serving men
Parnell, P. An imaginary life
Ryan, J. Iron Tommy
Stembridge, G. The gay detective
Stoppard, T. Artist descending a staircase
Wilks, T. Tod, the boy Tod
Wilson, A. Two trains running

7 characters and extras (1m 3w 2b 1g extras)

Burrill, M. They that sit in darkness

7 characters and extras (1m 6w extras)

Oates, J. C. Here she is!

7 characters and extras (2m 2w 1b 2g extras)

Barker, H. Hated nightfall

7 characters and extras ((2m 3w 1b 1g extras)

Grimké, A. W. Rachel

7 characters and extras (2m 4w 1b extras)

Johnson, G. D. A Sunday morning in the South

7 characters and extras (2m 5w extras)

y DePietro, P. Murder at the prom
Kurginian, S. Compensation
c Vigil, A. La estrella de oro. The gold star

7 characters and extras (3m 1w 2b 1g extras)

c McCaslin, N. Christmas fiesta

7 characters and extras (3m 2w 1b 1g extras)

c Boiko, C. A dog's best friend
Mullins, B. Pathological Venus

7 characters and extras (3m 3w 1b extras)

Gifford, B. Mrs. Kashfi

7 characters and extras (3m 4w extras)

Andrews, B. No wider than the heart
Booth, J. Season of goodwill
Churchill, C. Blue heart: Heart's desire
Fry, M. Tess of the d'Urbervilles
Griffiths, T. Thatcher's children

MIXED CAST—*Continued*

Hendrick, B. If I can't take it with me . . . I'm not going to go
c McCaslin, N. Brave new banner
Munro, R. The maiden stone
Németh, Á. Müller's dancers
O'Neill, E. All God's chillun got wings

7 characters and extras (4m 3w extras)

c Artist, V. A. The clever judge
c Artist, V. A. The clever Maakafi
Barker, H. The Europeans: struggles to love
De Pietro, P. Death and deceit on the Nile
Dizon, L. Till voices wake us
Edmonds, S. R. Old man Pete
Gems, P. Deborah's daughter
Horovitz, I. The primary English class
Ibsen, H. The master builder
Kalamu ya Salaam. Blk love song #1
c McCaslin, N. The lazy ones
c McCullough, L. E. The honest miller
Musset, A. de. Don't play with love
Omata, G. H. S.A.M. I am
O'Neill, E. Abortion
Sade, Marquis de. Truth and treason
Scribe, E. A glass of water
Sutherland, E. Edufa
Taylor, R. and Bologna, J. Comedies in apple blossom time
Wesley, R. The talented tenth

7 characters and extras (5m 1w 1b extras)

c Ireland, V. Roald Dahl's The Giraffe and the Pelly and me

7 characters and extras (5m 1w 1g extras)

c Ayckbourn, A. Mr A's amazing maze plays

7 characters and extras (5m 2w extras)

Barker, H. Minna
Bennett, A. Forty years on
Congdon, C. Dog opera
D'Aguiar, F. A Jamaican airman foresees his death
Dietz, S. Dracula
Goethe, J. W. von. Prometheus
Hare, D. Knuckle
y Lerman, L. The Abolition Flyer
c McCaslin, N. Humai's secret
y McCaslin, N. A straight shooter
c McCullough, L. E. The glass mountain
c McCullough, L. E. Good King Wenceslas
Mercer, D. The bankrupt
Molière. The imaginary cuckold

7 characters and extras (6m 1w extras)

Bartlett, N. Night after night
Courteline, G. The police chief's an easygoing guy
Kling, K. The ice-fishing play
c McCullough, L.E. "Have floss, will travel": the ever-so-true saga of Hiram T. McRoot, frontier dentist
Salim, 'Ali. The comedy of Oedipus: you're the one who killed the beast

8 characters (1m 7 w)

Bank, D. Halfway home
Carr, M. The Mai
Simon, N. Jake's women

8 characters (2m 2w 2b 2g)

c McCullough, L. E. Diamonds in the snow

8 characters (2m 3w 1b 2g)

c Sandberg, R. N. Anne of Green Gables

8 characters (2m 5w 1g)

Reddin, K. Brutality of fact

8 characters (2m 6w)

Bassen, L. S. The month before the moon
Churchill, C. Blue heart: Blue kettle
Daniels, S. The gut girls
Harris, R. C. Abigail
Kennedy, A. Funnyhouse of a Negro
Martin, J. Vital signs
Rayson, H. Falling from grace
Wood, P. Faint sound of a bell

8 characters (3m 3w 2g)

Lapine, J. Twelve dreams

8 characters (3m 4w 1g)

Saalbach, A. Morning and evening

8 characters (3m 5w)

Bill, S. Curtains
Booth, J. A bit on the other side
Brett, S. Murder in play
Carmichael, F. Don't mention my name
Clark, S. Moo
Colón, O. A. Siempre en mi corazón
Durang, C. Desire, desire, desire
Evans, D. One monkey don't stop no show
Gotanda, P. K. The wash
Gray, C. The shaken reed
Jones, L. Combination skin
King, L. L. The Golden Shadows Old West Museum
Kitchen, B. Halfway up the M3 on the way to Basingstoke
Mahon, D. Racine's Phaedra
Melfi, M. Sex therapy
Mercer, D. Huggy bear

MIXED CAST—*Continued*

Minghella, A. Cigarettes and chocolate
Nagy, P. Butterfly kiss
O'Brien, J. T. Ancestress
Penny, R. Good black don't crack
Randall, B. David's mother
Reingold, J. Girl gone
Sade, Marquis de. The twins
Sharrocks, M. Calling in
Smith, M. L. An evening of culture: Faith County II, the saga continues
Taylor, A. and Devenish, L. Disturbing the dust
Taylor, R. Inside the belly of the beast
Taylor, R. Watermelon rinds

8 characters (4m 2w 1b 1g)

O'Neill, E. Servitude

8 characters (4m 3w 1b)

Horovitz, I. Today I am a fountain pen
Osment, P. What I did in the holidays

8 characters (4m 4w)

Ackermann, J. Stanton's Garage
Albee, E. Edward Albee's fragments
Albee, E. Finding the sun
Ayckbourn, A. Family circles
Barry, S. Boss Grady's boys
Bernard, C. Laodamia, Queen of Epirus
c Boswell, L. Beauty and the beast
Carmichael, F. I bet your life
Carmichael, F. Over the checkerboard
Cartwright, J. Bed
y Cearley, B. Welcome to Nashville
c Church, J. The Pied Piper of New Orleans
Clark, S. Jehanne of the witches
y Cook, P. The whole shebang
Dunbar-Nelson, A. Mine eyes have seen
c Dunham, S. Wanted: one fair damsel
Fennario, D. Balconville
Frayn, M. Now you know
Gray, S. Close of play
c Griffiths, D. Flavio's disgrace
Gurney, A. R. Scenes from American life
Harper, T. Rehearsal for murder
Harper, T. Requiem for Denys
Harwood, R. A family
Havel, V. The increased difficulty of concentration
Heiss, R. L. Illegal contact
Hornby, I. Where there's a will ...
Ives, D. Seven menus
Jenkin, L. Careless love
Jones, M. Vanishing points
Kokoschka, O. Murderer the women's hope
y Kops, B. Dreams of Anne Frank
Lang, C. Amelia and the man
Linney, R. Childe Byron
Lucie, D. Grace
Ludwig, K. Moon over Buffalo
MacKenna, J. Faint voices
y Mason, T. The less than human club
Nelson, R. New England
Norman, P. Love off the shelf
Oliver, D. The case of the dead flamingo dancer
Parra, M. A. de la. King Kong Palace
Petsinis, T. The drought
Poliakoff, S. Blinded by the sun
Robinson, G. and Robinson, C. K. Murder for rent
Rooney, T. Flip
y Sarkies, D. Lovepuke
Saunders, J. Birthday
Sherman, J. M. Serendipity and serenity
c Slattery, M. E. The king in the kitchen
Tinniswood, P. The village fête
Wasserstein, W. The sisters Rosensweig
Williamson, D. Travellng north
Yamauchi, W. The music lessons

8 characters (5m 2w 1b)

Kornhauser, B. This is not a pipe dream
Surface, M. H. The reluctant dragon

8 characters (5m 2w 1g)

Lan, D. The ends of the earth

8 characters (5m 3w)

Alvarez, L. The reincarnation of Jaimie Brown
Ayckbourn, A. Wildest dreams
Barry, S. The only true history of Lizzie Finn
Bisson, P. Is there anybody there?
Blum, G.; Barker, W. and Martucci, V. Clue: the musical
y Cheatham, V. R. Broadway hit
Cooper, J. B. Picnic time
Coyne, J. Exploding love
Crews, H. Blood issue
Donald, S. The life of stuff
Edmundson, H. The clearing
Frisby, T. Rough justice
Gray, S. Hidden laughter
Guare, J. New York actor
Harding, M. Hubert Murray's widow
Harwood, R. The handyman
Havel, V. Largo desolato
Havel, V. Temptation
y Haynes, H. J. Isolation
Ives, D. Don Juan in Chicago
Johnson, T. Cries from the mammal house

MIXED CAST—*Continued*
Kai, N. Harvest the frost
c Lazarus, J. The Nightingale
Linney, R. El hermano
Mitterer, F. Home
Morrison, B. The cracked pot
Nagy, P. Disappeared
Nelson, T. B. Eye of God
Nowra, L. Cosi
O'Neill, E. Strange interlude
Parnell, P. Flaubert's latest
Pattison, J. Dreams from a summer house
Pendleton, A. Booth
Rodriguez Solis, E. The fickle finger of Lady Death
Shaw, G. B. Arms and the man
Sherman, J. M. Sophistry
Stoppard, T. The real Inspector Hound
c Sussman, D. Mystery of the phantom voice
c Vigil, A. The most interesting gift of all
Walker, G. F. Rumours of our death
Wallace, N. Slaughter City
Warner, F. A conception of love
Whelan, P. The herbal bed
Williams, T. Something cloudy, something clear

8 characters (6m 2w)

Baitz, J. R. A fair country
Bent, S. Bad company
Cooney, R. Funny money
Deane, H. and Balderston, J. L. Dracula: the vampire play (1927)
Durang, C. The Vietnamization of New Jersey
Farrell, B. The last Apache reunion
Goethe, J. W. von. Clavigo
Greig, D. Europe
Griffiths, T. Occupations
Guare, J. Marco Polo sings a solo
Handke, P. Voyage to the sonorous land
Harwood, R. Poison pen
Klíma, I. Games
Kushner, T. The illusion
Leslee, R. Avenue X
Lloyd Webber, A. Sunset Boulevard
Margulies, D. Found a peanut
McNally, T. Bad habits: Dunelawn
McNally, T. Bad habits: Ravenswood
O'Neill, E. The hairy ape
Osofisan, F. Birthdays are not for dying
Pinter, H. Mountain language
Poliakoff, S. Playing with trains
Prince, H. Grandchild of kings
c Priore, F. V. Spooks on strike!
Rooney, T. Flaming idiots
Schmidt, W. F. The Explorators Club
c Simons, J. Pinocchio commedia
Stoppard, T. Dirty linen

8 characters (7m 1w)

Buzo, A. The Roy Murphy show
Garrett-Groag, L. The white rose
Glover, K. Coming of the Hurricane
c Hall, M. Molly Pitcher meets the General
c Holmes, R. V. The king and the miller
Jeffreys, S. A going concern
Lee, E. East Texas hot links
Mac Intyre, T. Good evening, Mr Collins
Mayer, O. Blade to the heat
Pintauro, J. Men's lives
Rudnick, P. Jeffrey
Steppling, J. Sea of Cortez
Tasca, J. Outrageous
Walcott, D. Dream on Monkey Mountain
Williams, R. The life of the world to come
Zoshchenko, M. Crime and punishment

8 characters and extra (2m 2w 1b 3g extra)

c Miller, H. L. That figures!

8 characters and extras (2m 3w 1b 2g extras)

c Sandberg, R. N. Anne of Green Gables

8 characters and extras (2m 3w 2b 1g extras)

c Peterson, M. N. The soup stone

8 characters and extras (2m 3w 3g extras)

c McCaslin, N. Too many cooks

8 characters and extras (2m 6w extras)

Kennelly, B. Euripides' The Trojan woman
Townsend, S. The great celestial cow

8 characters and extras (3m 2w 2b 1g extras)

Peterson, M. L. How Santa Claus discovered Christmas

8 characters and extra (3m 5w extra)

Aspengren, K. House of wonders
Bass, G. H. Black masque: the passion of darkie's bones
Carter, S. Pecong
c Edgar, K. Mother Goose
Goethe, J. W. von. Stella
Racine, J. Phaedra
Sharif, B. My ancestor's house
Taylor, R. Between the lines

8 characters and extras (4m 1w 1b 2g extras)

c McCullough, L. E. Pony Express rider

8 characters and extras (4m 1w 3g extras)

y McCaslin, N. The legend of Minna Lamourrie

MIXED CAST—*Continued*

c McCaslin, N. Bluebonnetsc McCaslin, N. Johnny Appleseed
c McCullough, L. E. The cobbler's pipe
c McCullough, L. E. Jingle bells

8 characters and extras (4m 4w extras)

Berc, S. A girls' guide to the Divine Comedy: a trilogy
Clark, S. Saint Frances of Hollywood
y Dias, E. J. Landslide for Shakespeare
Edmundson, H. Anna Karenina
c Francoeur, B. OZ!
Hurston, Z. N. The first one
Linney, R. True crimes
c Major, R. O. Melodrama at Mayfair Meadows
Maraini, D. Dreams of Clytemnestra
c McCaslin, N. The little squire of Flanders
c McCullough, L. E. Magnus Fourpenny and the black bear birthday bash
Miller, S. It's our town, too.
Rayson, H. Competitive tenderness
y Soto, G. Novio boy
Stock, J. Star-gazy pie and sauerkraut

8 characters and extras (5m 2w 1g extras)

Iko, M. Gold watch

8 characters and extras (5m 2b 1g extras)

c McCullough, L. E. Return of the Red Phantom

8 characters and extras (5m 3w extras)

Crimp, M. The misanthrope
Crimp, M. The treatment
Dietz, S . Halcyon days
Kushner, T. Angels in America: Pt.1: Millennium approaches
Lawrence, J. and Lee, R. E. A call on Kuprin
Parsley, R. Brideshead revisited
Scotland, J. Day of wrath
Wellman, M. Sincerity forever
Wertenbaker, T. The grace of Mary Traverse
Yeats, W. B. The Countess Cathleen

8 characters and extras (6m 1w 1b extras)

y Kral, B. One to grow on
Stoppard, T. Neutral ground

8 characters and extras (6m 2w extras)

Capek, K. The Makropoulos secret
Kushner, T. Angels in America: Pt.2: Perestroika
Linney, R. 2
y McCullough, L. E. "You're live with Bigfoot Wallace"
Moore, E. The foundling
O'Neill, E. The hairy ape
c Witkiewicz, S. The courageous princess

8 characters and extras (7m 1w extras)

Frost, R. The guardeen
Maeterlinck, M. Monna Vanna
c McCullough, L. E. The beggar in the blanket
Schenkkan, R. Final passages

9 characters (1m 8w)

Sherman, J. M. Women and Wallace

9 characters (2m 5w 2g)

Sewell, S. The garden of granddaughters

9 characters (2m 6w 1g)

Miller, J. A light on the landing

9 characters (2m 7w)

Horovitz, I. North Shore Fish
Jackson, M. Unlucky Cinderella
c Miller, H. L. The princess and the pea

9 characters (3m 5w 1g)

y Turner, J. Anne of Green Gables

9 characters (3m 6w)

Congdon, C. Boarders

9 characters (4m 3w 1b 1g)

c Davis, J. Moorli and the Leprechaun

9 characters (4m 5w)

Butterfield, C. Joined at the head
Carmichael, F. Meet my husbands
Chindo, T. Boardwalk melody hour murders
Daniels, S. Beside herself
c DeVita, J. A life in the woods
Faulkner, A. For England and King George
Gregor, H. The Spanish cape
Hornby, I. The cat's away
Hornby, I. Hello.... Is there any body there?
y Jackson, K. Three doors to death
Kemp, R. A trump for Jericho
y Mason, T. Ascension day
McCullough, L. E. O thou joyful day
Osment, P. The dearly beloved
Wertenbaker, T. Three birds alighting on a field

9 characters (5m 1w 2b 1g)

c McCullough, L. E. El Paseo del Vaquero (the ride of the vaquero)

9 characters (5m 1w 3b)

Cook, M. The head, guts and sound bone dance

MIXED CAST—*Continued*

9 characters (5m 3w 1b)

Congdon, C. No mercy
Linney, R. Mountain memory

9 characters (5m 4w)

Barker, H. Uncle Vanya
Barry, S. The steward of Christendom
Bogosian, E. SubUrbia
Chekhov, A. Uncle Vanya
Connolly, H. Snakes and ladders
Delaney, D. The last ten miles of Avery J. Coping
Dunn, M. Judge and jury
Feydeau, G. Nothing but the tooth
Foote, H. The young man from Atlanta
Golden, E. Great expectations
Gotanda, P. K. Day standing on its head
Gray, S. The caramel crisis
c Griffiths, D. That's the way to do it
Harris, A. The importance of being Earnest
Joselovitz, E. and Bagdasian, H. M. Love by the numbers
McDonagh, M. The cripple of Inishmaan
McPherson, S. Marvin's room
Menken, A. Weird romance: Her pilgrim soul
Minghella, A. What if it's raining?
Moore, C. M. Love's light in flight
y Olfson, L. The admirable Crichton
Osborne, J. and Creighton, A. Epitaph for George Dillon
Robertson, H. W. Mina tonight!
Roose-Evans, J. Cider with Rosie
Russell, W. Breezeblock Park
y Satchell, M. Daniel Hale Williams, pioneer surgeon
Shaffer, D. Last respects
Sherman, M. Cracks
Stroppel, F. A good man
Van Zandt, B. and Milmore, J. Infidelities
White, P. Night on Bald Mountain
The Wooster Group. Frank Dell's The temptation of St. Antony
y Yates, P. Starlover

9 characters (6m 3w)

Childress, A. Trouble in mind
Cooperman, D. Miss Temptation
Desjardins, M.-C. The favorite minister
Gilroy, F. D. Any given day
Gurney, A. R. Overtime
Hansberry, L. The sign in Sidney Brustein's window
Harrison, T. Poetry or bust
Havel, V. The garden party
Kovacevic, D. A roaring tragedy
Ledoux, P. and Smyth, D. Cheatin' hearts
Linney, R. The love suicide at Schofield Barracks
McGuinness, F. Innocence
Najera, R. Latinologues: monologues of the Latin experience
y Nolan, P. T. The school for wives
Overmyer, E. Dark rapture
Schuyler, G. S. The yellow peril
Scotland, J. A surgeon for Lucinda
Shaffer, D. Sacrilege
Stefanovski, G. Sarajevo: tales from a city
Tuttle, J. Terminal Cafe
Vampilov, A. Last summer in Chulimsk
Yamauchi, W. The chairman's wife

9 characters (7m 2w)

Balalin Company of Jerusalem. Darkness
Berkoff, S. West
Godber, J. Up 'n' under II
Hare, D. Fanshen
Highway, T. Dry Lips oughta move to Kapuskasing
Lambert, L. Sunrise at noon
Odets, C. Awake and sing!
O'Neill, E. Mourning becomes Electra: Homecoming
O'Neill, E. Mourning becomes Electra: The haunted
Pohl, K. The beautiful stranger
Rodriguez, Y. Rising sun, falling star
Sade, Marquis de. Count Oxtiern
Simon, N. Laughter on the 23rd floor
c Stites, K. Adventures with young King Arthur

9 characters (8m 1w)

Bleadsdale, A. On the ledge
Campanile, A. The big bun
Clum, J. M. Randy's house
Kranes, D. Cantrell
y McCaslin, N. Travelers from Olympus
Stoppard, T. Hapgood

9 characters and extras (1m 8w extras)

Houston, V. H. The Matsuyama mirror

9 characters and extras (2m 1w 4b 2g extras)

Miller, M. Graven images

9 characters and extras (2m 7w extras)

c McCullough, L. E. The laziest girl in the world

9 characters and extras (3m 2w 3b 1g extras)

c Webster, P. Peter Panto

MIXED CAST—*Continued*

9 characters and extras (3m 3w 2b 1g extras)

c Alette, C. The secret garden

9 characters and extras (3m 4w 2b extras)

McGuinness, F. A doll's house

9 characters and extras (3m 6w extras)

Hornby, I. Voices
c McCaslin, N. Angel of the battlefield

9 characters and extras (4m 1w 2b 2g extras)

c Carlson, N. K. and Chapman, B. The magic pebble

9 characters and extras (4m 5w extras)

c Asbrand, K. Pandora's box
c McCaslin, N. The bailiff's wonderful coat
c McCaslin, N. Leading lady
Mercer, D. Where the difference begins
Townsend, S. The Queen and I
Wilder, T. The long Christmas dinner

9 characters and extras (5m 2w 2g extras)

Kraus, J. H. The ice wolf

9 characters and extras (5m 3w 1b extras)

Hansberry, L. A raisin in the sun

9 characters and extras (5m 4w extras)

y Frost, R; Olson, G. and Johnson, L. No means no!
Kane, S. Phaedra's love
Kipling, R. Mrs. Hauksbee sits out
c McCullough, L. E. Tillie Edelpickel's sack of lies
Mercer, D. A suitable case for treatment
Mitchell, J. August
Moreto, A. Spite for spite
Osterman, G. Brother truckers
Pinter, H. Party time
Stiles, G. Moll Flanders
Taylor, R. and Bologna, J. Acts of love and other comedies
Tyler, R. The contrast
Wadsworth, S. The triumph of love

9 characters and extras (6m 2w 1b extras)

Kopit, A. End of the world
Segal, G. All the tricks but one

9 characters and extras (6m 3w extras)

Foote, H. The trip to Bountiful
c Hark, M. and McQueen, N. Civilians stay put
Heise, K. and Heise, D. Clarence Darrow in hell
Lillo, G. The London merchant
c McCaslin, N. Three meals a day
c McCullough, L. E. The little old sod shanty
Schnitzler, A. The veil of Pierrette
Shepard, S. The mad dog blues
Wellman, M. Dracula

9 characters and extras (7m 2w extras)

Abe, K. The ghost is here
Bogosian, E. Talk radio
Gray, S. Two Sundays
Hare, D. Licking Hitler
Koch, K. The banquet
Musset, A. de. The moods of Marianne
Norman, M. Loving Daniel Boone
Schenkkan, R. Ties that bind
Tomer, B.-Z. Children of the shadows
Toomer, J. Balo
Wellman, M. The bad infinity

9 characters and extras (8m 1w extras)

Beaumarchais, P.-A. C. de. The barber of Seville
Courteline, G. Boubouroche
c Kurtz, J. The ballad of King Windowglass
c McCullough, L. E. Shlemazl goes to paradise
Mitterer, F. Abraham

10 characters (1m 9w)

Saunders, J. Magazine

10 characters (2m 3w 1b 4g)

c Thane, A. Rapunzel

10 characters (2m 4w 3b 1g)

c Miller, H. L. The Birds' Christmas Carol

10 characters (2m 8w)

Chayefsky, P. The mother
Kobler, F. Wild dust
Townsend, S. Womberang
Tricker, C. Losers

10 characters (3m 6w 1g)

Nassif, R. L. Opal

10 characters (3m 7w)

Bingham, S. Milk of paradise
y Foote, H. The dancers
Shurman-O'Connor, K. The Wizard of Zoz

10 characters (4m 2w 2b 2g)

c Shurman-O'Connor, K. Billy's problem

10 characters (4m 4w 1b 1g)

c Sodaro, C. Freedom train

10 characters (4m 5w 1b)

West, C. L. Before it hits home

10 characters (4m 5w 1g)

Foote, H. The traveling lady

10 characters (4m 6w)

Feydeau, G. The dressmaker

MIXED CAST—*Continued*
Feydeau, G. A fitting confusion
Franklin, J. E. Miss Honey's young'uns
Gaines-Shelton, R. A. The church fight
Hornby, I. A question of innocence
Kirby, M. My body. my blood
Meyer, M. The odd women
Robson, J. Beulah
Sontag, S. Alice in bed
Thain, P. Black widow
Wise, R. Some do, some don't

10 characters (5m 2w 2b 1g)

Mitchell, J. Falling over England

10 characters (5m 2w 3g)

O'Neill, E. Warnings

10 characters (5m 4w 1g)

Ayckbourn, A. Man of the moment

10 characters (5m 5w)

Bernier, E. The seven streams of the River Ota
c Cheatham, V. R. The Miss Witch contest
Cullen, A. Pig's ear
Doust, P. Cold Comfort Farm
Durang, C. The marriage of Bette and Boo
Gordon, P. Murdered to death
Harnetiaux, B. The snows of Kilimanjaro
Hatcher, J. Smash
Hischak, T. Murder on reserve
Houston, V. H. Asa ga kimashits (Morning has broken)
Jackson, N. The quick-change room
Jeffreys, S. The libertine
Leonard, H. Moving
Marivaux. La dispute
Mason, T. Babylon gardens
Nagy, P. The Strip
Orr, M. The wisdom of Eve
Ruzzante. L'Anconitana: the woman from Ancona
Sade, Marquis de. Henrietta and St. Clair
Simon, N. Rumours
Walker, G. F. Escape from happiness

10 characters (6m 3w 1b)

Handke, P. Walk about the villages

10 characters (6m 4w)

c Ayckbourn, A. This is where we came in
Barker, H. Ego in Arcadia
Cooney, M. Cash on delivery!
Dear, N. The art of success
Durbridge, F. Sweet revenge
Gass, K. Claudius
Griffiths, L. The Duchess: pieces of Wallis Simpson
Gurney, A. R. The Wayside Motor Inn
Hannan, C. Shining souls
Harper, T. That's the spirit
Hellman, L. The little foxes
Johnson, J. Somewhere
LaChiusa, M. J. Hello again
Machiavelli, N. Clizia
Miller, E. Up rose a burning man
Miller, J. and Miller, S. Consequences
c Netzel, S. The dark castle
Pernak, A. Killers
Shaw, B. Heartbreak House
Stoppard, T. The dissolution of Dominic Boot
Taylor, R. and Bologna, J. Manhattan love songs—Bronx cheers
Vampilov, A. Duck-hunting
Visdei, A. Class photo
White, P. The ham funeral
Wilde, O. The importance of being Earnest
Winter, J. and Smith, C. Ten lost years

10 characters (7m 2w 1b)

y Bond, E. Tuesday

10 characters (7m 3w)

Bolt, C. Compañeras
Courts, R. Johnny Pye
Curran, K. The stand-in
Dashow, K. Thanks
Davies, R. Fortune, my foe
Dudley, E. The return of Sherlock Holmes
Durang, C. Diversions
Foote, H. The trip to Bountiful [television play]
Garrett-Groag, L. The ladies of the camellias
y Hark, M. and McQueen, N. George Washington Carver
Khan-Din, A. East is east
MacNeice, L. Persons from Porlock
c McLaren, M. Seven with one blow
Moore, E. The gamester
O'Neill, E. A touch of the poet
Overmyer, E. In a pig's valise
Pruitt, D. and Hutchison, P. The Harvey Milk show
Rattigan, T. French without tears
Sherman, M. A madhouse in Goa
Tasca, J. Italian rum cake

10 characters (8m 2w)

Addison, J. Cato
Banda, V. H. R. Murder with malice

MIXED CAST—*Continued*
Foote, H. The widow Claire
Frandsen, E. [et al.] Song of Singapore
Griffin, T. Mrs. Sedgewick's head
Hasenclever, W. The son
Millar, T. P. The Cassandra Complex
Morrison, B. A love song for Ulster: The daughter
Ono, Y. New York rock
Rascon Banda, V. H. Murder with malice
Simon, M. and Simon, R. Murder at Minsing Manor: a nancy boys mystery
Slout, W. L. The trial of Dr. Jekyll
c Thompson, L. The innkeeper's daughter
Williamson, D. The department
Wilson, A. Ma Rainey's black bottom

10 characters (9m 1w)

Bauer, W. Insalta mista
Freeman, D. Creeps

10 characters and extras (1m 2w 3b 4g extras)

c McMahon, J. P. and Ryan, N. Buttonbush

10 characters and extras (2m 4w 2b 2g extras)

c Hamlett, C. Boarder skirmish

10 characters and extras (3m 7w extras)

Burnham, Y. Everywoman: a modern morality play
García Lorca, F. Blood wedding
c Lynch, M. Scheherazade
Suarez, R. R. The betrothal

10 characters and extras (4m 3w 2b 1g extras)

c McCullough, L. E. Mr. and Mrs. Charlie T. Mule

10 characters and extras (4m 4w 1b 1g extras)

c McCullough, L. E. The rainbow cradle

10 characters and extras (4m 5w 1b extras)

c Bisson, P. Simple Simon

10 characters and extras (4m 5w 1g extras)

Moraga, C. Heroes and saints

10 characters and extras (4m 6w extras)

c Edgar, K. The sleeping beauty
c Kelly, T. Treachery at Cartilage Creek
Norman, M. Trudy Blue
Nunn, J. Stuck
y Polsky, M. E. Act of will
y Poole-Carter, R. Mossy Cape
y Satchell, M. Mary McLeod Bethune, dream maker
Shaw, B. Pygmalion
c Whelan, P. The tinder box

10 characters and extras (5m 3w 2g extras)

y McCullough, L. E. Johnny Appleseed and Willie Crabgrass

10 characters and extras (5m 4w 1g extras)

y Mapp, F. The wonderful Wizard of Oz

10 characters and extras (5m 5w extras)

Gurney, A. R. The snow ball
Keeler, D. Edith Wharton's The house of mirth
c Reakes, P. King Arthur
y Rowe, D. P. Zombie prom
c Sachon, S. Beauty and the beast
y Sandock, F. Campaign fever
Serreau, C. Lapin Lapin
Valle-Inclán, R. del. The paper rose
c Vigil, A. Juan Oso. John the bear

10 characters and extras (6m 2w 1b 1g extras)

McCullough, L. E. The most expensive bonnet in all Indiana

10 characters and extras (6m 3w 1b extras)

Mitterer, F. No place for idiots

10 characters and extras (6m 4w extras)

Baillie, J. De Monfort
Barker, H. Ten dilemmas
Edgar, K. Aladdin
Fennario, D. Doctor Thomas Neill Cream: mystery at McGill
Goldsmith, O. She stoops to conquer
c Green, M. Spring the king
Hare, D. A map of the world
Kilroy, T. The seagull
y McCullough, L. E. The splendid voyage of Kitty Doyle
McDonough, J. Butterfly
North, F. The Kentish barons
O'Brien, M. Mad boy chronicle
y Olfson, L. Monsieur Beaucaire
Pittman, A. West moon
c Warhurst, M. Peter and the princess
Wellman, M. Crowbar
Wellman, M. Dracula

10 characters and extras (7m 2w 1g extras)

y Rochelle, R. Alice in Wonderland

10 characters and extras (7m 3w extras)

Baraka, A. Slave ship
Brustein, R. The wild duck
Chekhov, A. The wedding
Chekhov, A. The wedding reception
Clarke, T. The Venetian twins
Dryden, J. King Arthur
Fitzball, E. The inchcape bell
Fo, D. The Pope and the witch
Milligan, J. Walking on the moon
c Neary, J. Aladdin and the wonderful lamp
Turrini, P. The siege of Vienna

MIXED CAST—*Continued*
y Winther, B. John Henry

10 characters and extras (8m 1b 1g extras)

Tagore, R. The Post Office

10 characters and extras (8m 2w extras)

Barker, C. Frankenstein in love
Cross, J. The prophet's cloak
c McCullough, L. E. "Git along, little dogies!"
c McCullough, L. E. We three Kings of Orient are
Musset, A. de. Fantasio
y Nolan, P. T. An enemy of the people
Schnitzler, A. The transformation of Pierrot

10 characters and extras (9m 1w extras)

Hampton, C. Savages
Witkiewicz, S. I. The shoemakers

10 characters and extras (9m 1b extras)

y Thane, A. Moby Dick

11 characters (1m 10w)

Chinn, J. After September

11 characters (2m 2w 3b 4g)

c Medoff, M. H. Kringle's window

11 characters (2m 9w)

Hischak, T. Murder by the book

11 characters (3m 8w)

y Morley, O. J. Pride and prejudice
Thatcher, K. Emma's child

11 characters (3w 5b 3g)

c Shurman-O'Connor, K. At the bus stop

11 characters (4m 4w 2b 1g)

Ibsen, H. A doll's house

11 characters (4m 5w 1b 1g)

Doctorow, E. L. Drinks before dinner

11 characters (4m 6w 1b)

Fornes, M. I. What of the night?: Lust

11 characters (4m 7w)

Acworth, E. Composing Venus
Lennon, G. Blackout
Vance, C. Jane Eyre

11 characters (5m 4w 1b 1g)

y McCullough, L. E. Annie Christmas and the Natchez Trace bandits

11 characters (5m 6w)

Gems, P. Stanley
Kushner, T. A bright room called day
c Wheeler, J. and Hartsfield, M. G. Tall Betsy and the crackerbarrel tales
Williamson, D. Dead white males

11 characters (6m 4w 1b)

c Zeder, S. L. Mother Hicks

11 characters (6m 5w)

Banville, J. The broken jug
Bennett, A. Habeas corpus
Brandl, D. Vine and dandy
Carr, M. Portia Coughlan
Foote, H. Talking pictures
Kárpáti, P. Everywoman
Lim, G. Paper angels
y Mueller, D. A. Dreadful doings at the cider mill
Overmyer, E. The Heliotrope Bouquet by Scott Joplin & Louis Chauvin
Reid, C. The belle of the Belfast city
Schnitzler, A. In the play of summer breezes
Taylor, R. and Bologna, J. Love allways
Thomas, F. Tartuffe: born again
Thompson, P. Calamity Jane and the fat buffalo moon
Wilson, A. Joe Turner's come and gone

11 characters (6b 5g)

c Saba, J. A tree with arms

11 characters (7m 4w)

Deane, H. Dracula (1924)
y Gibbs, P. Lockie Leonard, human torpedo
y Le, Q. D. Cho doi (Market of lives)
Machado, E. In the eye of the hurricane
Martin, S. Picasso at the Lapin Agile
Morton, C. The miser of Mexico
Perry, S. In Dahomey
Pinero, A. W. The second Mrs. Tanqueray
Pix, M. The Spanish wives
Rattigan, T. The Winslow boy
Al-Surayyi', 'Abd al-'Aziz. The bird has flown
Van Zandt, B. and Milmore, J. What the rabbi saw
Warner, F. Moving reflections
y Watson, W. J. Abe Lincoln and the runaways
Weller, M. Loose ends

11 characters (8m 3w)

Clark, S. Life without instruction
Finnegan, S. It's all blarney
Foote, H. The chase
Goethe, J. W. von. The natural daughter
Goldoni, C. Villeggiatura: Crazy for the country
Gray, S. The holy terror
Greenland, S. Jungle rot
Harwood, R. The dresser

MIXED CAST—*Continued*

Kochanowski, J. The dismissal of the Grecian envoys
y McCullough, L. E. Greta Nilson's magic mare
Mehta, D. Brides are not for burning
Molière. The misanthrope
Molière. The miser
Morrison, B. A love song for Ulster: The son
Potter, D. Joe's ark
Shakespeare, W. and Fletcher, J. Cardeno
Stoppard, T. Arcadia
Whelan, P. Shakespeare country

11 characters (9m 2w)

Chayefsky, P. The big deal
Spoor, K. Everything under the sun
Warner, F. Light shadows

11 characters (10m 1w)

Havis, A. A vow of silence
Huynh, Quang Nhuong. Dance of the wandering souls
Judy, G. Antigone
Mastrosimone, W. Nanawatai!

11 characters and extras (3m 1w 3b 4g extras)

c McCaslin, N. The Christmas lamb

11 characters and extras (3m 3w 3b 2g extras)

c Martens, A. C. One life to lose

11 characters and extras (4m 5w 1b 1g extras)

c Roberts, A. V. Ji-da (the bird)

11 characters and extras (5m 3w 2b 1g extras)

Solórzano, C. The hands of God

11 characters and extras (5m 6w extras)

c McCaslin, N. The last horizon
y Prior, J. Phantom of the music hall
y Reiser, D. Alas! Alack! Zorro's back
Seidel, G. Carmen Kittel

11 characters and extras (6m 5w extras)

Enright, N. Blackrock
y Frankel, R. The Decade Club
y Hoppenstedt, E. M. Shoo fly pudding
c Swortzell, L. The love of three oranges

11 characters and extras (7m 3w 1b extras)

Feydeau, G. and Devalliers, M. All my husbands
Otway, T. The soldiers' fortune

11 characters and extras (7m 3w 1g extras)

y Atkins, G. William of Stratford
c Brown, J. The lake at the end of the world

11 characters and extras (7m 4w extras)

Chayefsky, P. Holiday song
c Cole, J. D. Ichabod
Gotanda, P. K. A song for a Nisei fisherman
Guare, J. Moon under Miami
Langley, R. The Dunsmuirs: a promise kept
Onwueme, O. T. The broken calabash
Robson, J. Falling short
c Webster, P. Dick Turpin

11 characters and extras (8m 2w 1b extras)

Ibsen, H. An enemy of the people

11 characters and extras (8m 3w extras)

Ackerman, M. L'affaire Tartuffe
Centlivre, S. A bold stroke for a wife
Chayefsky, P. The latent heterosexual
Gray, S. Plaintiffs and defendants
McNally, T. The Ritz
Morrison, B. A love song for Ulster: The marriage
O'Neill, E. Desire under the elms
Overmyer, E. Native speech
Sondheim, S. and Furth, G. Getting away with murder
c Tesh, J. Breakfast at the Bookworm Cafe
c Vigil, A. The three pieces of good advice
Walker, J. The River Niger
Williams, C. Rebecca

11 characters and extras (9m 2w extras)

Dunlap, W. André
c Fisher, A. I have a dream
Pirandello, L. The rules of the game

11 characters and extras (10m 1w extras)

Sade, Marquis de. The shyster

12 characters (2w 3b 7g)

c Shurman-O'Connor, K. Grandma Rusnak

12 characters (3m 9w)

Chayefsky, P. Middle of the night

12 characters (4m 8w)

Pinnock, W. Talking in tongues

12 characters (5m 7w)

c Daugherty, L. The little mermaid
y Reiser, D. I want my mummy!
Wellman, M. Cleveland

12 characters (6m 6w)

c Adkins, D. Ready steady go
Churchill, C. Cloud 9
Devlin, A. After Easter
Dickinson, J. Jack the Ripper, monster of Whitechapel

MIXED CAST—*Continued*
Durang, C. Death comes to us all, Mary Agnes
Flanagan, N. Burning time
Grumberg, J.-C. The workroom
Hastings, C. The wayward spirit
Heward, L. Or what's a heaven for?
Miranda, J. Italian funerals and other festive occasions
y Satchell, M. The secret gifts
Snelgrove, M. Bums on seats
Strijards, F. The Stendhal syndrome
White, P. Netherwood
Wilson, L. Talley & Son
Yamauchi, W. 12-1-A

12 characters (7m 4w 1b)

Grumberg, J.-C. The free zone

12 characters (7m 4w 1b)

c McCullough, L. E. Let us go, O shepherds

12 characters (7m 5w)

Barry, S. Prayers of Sherkin
Bennett, R. Funerals and circuses
Chayefsky, P. The bachelor party
Dryden, J. Love triumphant
Friel, B. A month in the country
Granville-Barker, H. The secret life
c McCullough, L. E. Go tell it on the mountain
Nigro, D. Paganini
O'Connor, C. All that he was . . .
O'Neill, E. Mourning becomes Electra: The hunted
Russell, W. Stags and hens
Stoppard, T. If you're Glad I'll be Frank

12 characters (8m 3w 1b)

c Leuser, E. The big stone

12 characters (8m 4w)

Barker, H. Women beware women
Behrman, S. N. The cold wind and the warm
Dryden, J. Amphitryon
Nigro, D. Ardy Fafirsin
Parra, M. A. de la. Dostoevski goes to the beach
Sobol, J. Adam
Solórzano, C. The crucified
Wilde, P. What's wrong with angry?

12 characters (9m 2w 1g)

Molière. The hypochondriac
Molière. The imaginary invalid

12 characters (9m 3w)

Griffiths, T. Real dreams
Meyer, M. G. Moe's Lucky Seven
Stoppard, T. The dog it was that died
Storey, D. The contractor
Tagore, R. The king and the queen

12 characters (10m 2w)

Basso, E. Joseph in the underground
Branch, W. In splendid error
Hare, D. Teeth 'n' smiles
Shaw, G. B. John Bull's other Island
Stoppard, T. Albert's bridge
c Vigil, A. Los pastores. The shepherds

12 characters (11m 1w)

Brown, M. H. The day the Bronx died
Al-Madani, 'Izz al-Din. The Zanj Revolution
Pollock, S. Walsh

12 characters and extras (2m 1w 4b 5g extras)

c Miller, H. L. Name that book!

12 characters and extras (2m 1w 5b 4g extras)

c Norcross, E. B. Pied Piper's land

12 characters and extras (2m 2w 4b 4g extras)

c Jacob, E. The crowded house

12 characters and extras (4m 8w extras)

y Christiansen, A. Wash your troubles away
y Kelly, T. You can't stamp out love
y Swift, R. Dirty work on the trail

12 characters and extras (5m 5w 1b 1g extras)

c McCullough, L. E. Annie Oakley: little sure-shot

12 characters and extras (5m 7w extras)

y Kelly, T. Here come the cows
y Kelly, T. Trick or treat
Miller, A. After the fall
Onwueme, O. T. The reign of Wazobia

12 characters and extras (6m 4w 2g extras)

Dryden, J. All for love

12 characters and extras (6m 5w 1b extras)

y Satchell, M. Langston Hughes: poet of the people

12 characters and extras (6m 6w extras)

Burris, A. M. You mus' be bo'n ag'in
Gilbert, M. Environment
c Webster, P. Babes in the wood

12 characters and extras (7m 4w 1b extras)

Oswald, P. Fair ladies at a game of poem cards

12 characters and extras (7m 5w extras)

Guare, J. Four baboons adoring the sun
The Heather Brothers. Lust
y Huff, B. Spy for a day
Mercer, D. Emma's time

MIXED CAST—*Continued*

Shaw, G. B. Getting married
c Swintz, M. Panic in the palace
Synge, J. M. The playboy of the Western World
Wilder, T. Pullman car Hiawatha

12 characters and extras (8m 2w 1b 1g extras)

Mercer, D. The cellar and the almond tree

12 characters and extras (8m 4w extras)

Dryden, J. King Arthur
Farquhar, G. The constant couple
Fletcher, J. and Massinger, P. The little French lawyer
Fletcher, J. and Massinger, P. The prophetess
Jamal, D. The highway
Keithley, G. The best blood of the country
Lucas, C. Prelude to a kiss

12 characters and extras (9m 3w extras)

Büchner, G. Leonce and Lena
Bullins, E. Goin' a Buffalo
Dryden, J. Amboyna
c Duncombe, P. Robin Hood
Fletcher, J. The honest man's fortune
Havel, V. The memorandum
c McCullough, L. E. Bird woman of the Shoshones
c McCullough, L. E. Rocky mountain rendezvous
c Reakes, P. Dick Turpin
Soyinka, W. Death and the King's Horseman

12 characters and extras (10m 2w extras)

Campanile, A. The inventor of the horse
Doyle, R. Brownbread
Gelbart, L. Mastergate
Parsons, N. Dead heart
Wilde, O. The Duchess of Padua

12 characters and extras (11m 1w extras)

Hare, D. Saigon: year of the cat
Jarry, A. Ubu cocu

13 characters (4m 5w 3b 1g)

Howe, T. Approaching Zanzibar

13 characters (4m 8w 1g)

Onwueme, O. T. Tell it to women

13 characters (4m 9w)

Cooper, B. Nellie Bly: ten days in a madhouse
Foote, H. Dividing the estate

13 characters (5m 8w)

Foote, H. Laura Dennis
y Kelly, T. That's the spirit!

13 characters (6m 7w)

Burney, F. The Witlings
Congdon, C. Losing father's body
McNally, T. Where has Tommy Flowers gone?
Minghella, A. A little like drowning
Sharrocks, M. Sweet Rose of Old Aldgate
c Van Horn, B. Ordeal at Valley Forge

13 characters (7m 6w)

Ayckbourn, A. A chorus of disapproval
Ayckbourn, A. A small family business
Brown, K. R. Welcome to Four Way: the town that time forgot
Chekhov, A. The seagull
Foote, H. Night seasons

13 characters (8m 4w 1b)

Hauptmann, G. The beaver coat

13 characters (8m 5w)

De Filippo, E. Filumena Marturano
LeSage, A. R. Turcaret
Miller, A. Death of a salesman
Nigro, D. Anima mundi
Regan, S. Morning star
Steele, R. The conscious lovers
Wyatt, R. Crackpot

13 characters (9m 2w 2b)

Gardner, H. Conversations with my father

13 characters (9m 4w)

Chekhov, A. The wood demon
Havel, V. Redevelopment
y Leech, M. T. The Scarlett Pimpernel
Lewes, G. H. The game of speculation
Sharkey, T. M. It's a wonderful life
Tourneur, C. The atheist's tragedy

13 characters (10m 3w)

Bennett, A. Enjoy
Büchner, G. Woyzeck
Hare, D. The absence of war

13 characters (11m 2w)

Barker, H. The love of a good man
Bolger, D. Blinded by the light
Francis, M. The prisoner of Zenda
Gray, O. The torrents
O'Neill, E. "Anna Christie"

13 characters (12m 1w)

Chayefsky, P. The tenth man
y Eleder, M. V. The Count of Monte Cristo
Sherman, J. M. Jesus on the oil tank

MIXED CAST—*Continued*

13 characters and extras (5m 8w extras)

y Reiser, D. Dr. Jekyll ... please don't hyde

13 characters and extras (6m 5w 1b 1g extras)

McCarthy, C. The stonemason

13 characters and extras (6m 7w extras)

Donnelly, N. The duty master
Donnelly, N. A little like paradise
Harvey, J. Babies
y Nukala, D. The write stuff
St. John, B. Is there a comic in the house?
c Turner, J. The white spider's gift

13 characters and extras (7m 5w 1g extras)

c Bisson, P. Little Red Riding Hood

13 characters and extras (7m 6w extras)

Aldridge, I. The black doctor
c Cregan, D. Aladdin
Durang, C. The idiots Karamazov
c McCaslin, N. Cold face, warm heart
Smolensky, S. and Waldrop, J. The Mikado
y St. John, B. The fiendish firebug strikes again!
Witkiewicz, S. I. The mother

13 characters and extras (8m 3w 2b extras)

Linney, R. Sand Mountain

13 characters and extras (8m 4w 1b extras)

Sheridan, R. B. The rivals

13 characters and extras (8m 5w extras)

Bandele, 'B. Marching for Fausa
Behn, A. The feigned courtesans
Brustein, R. The cherry orchard
Fischerova, D. Dog and wolf
c Flower, M. and Follows, S. Robin's last stand
Godfrey, P. The blue ball
Mowatt, A. C. Fashion
Murphy, T. A thief of a Christmas
Rattigan, T. After the dance
Southerne, T. The wives' excuse
y Wood, B. The green snake and the beautiful lily

13 characters and extras (9m 4w extras)

Balzac, H. de. Mercadet
Barroga, J. Walls
Stoppard, T. In the native state
Farquhar, G. The twin rivals

13 characters and extras (10m 2w 1b extras)

Hughes, L. Mulatto
y McCullough, L. E. The most dangerous woman in America

13 characters and extras (10m 3w extras)

Bjorneboe, J. The bird lovers
Bond, E. Olly's prison
Fletcher, J. The sea voyage
Fletcher, J. and Massinger, P. The elder brother
Goldoni, C. The coffee shop
O'Donovan, J. The Shaws of Synge Street
Unger, H. R. The bell tolls at twelve
Wannus, Sa'dallah. The king is the king

13 characters and extras (11m 2w extras)

Barnes, P. Heaven's blessings
Fletcher, J. and Massinger, P. The double marriage
Kilroy, T. The O'Neill
Kwahulé, K. That old black magic
y Olfson, L. The Pickwick papers
Wellman, M. Harm's way
Wilde, O. Salomé

14 characters (3m 9w 2g)

Manning, N. Close to the bone

14 characters (5m 9w)

Kelly, T. Hide and shriek
Martin, J. Cementville
Saunders, J. Iso tank

14 characters (6m 6w 1b 1g)

c Hanson, M. E. and Sheldon, D. P. Madame Zena's séance

14 characters (6m 8w)

Chayefsky, P. Marty
Gordon, D. The mysteries and what's so funny?
Graham, S. It's morning
Kuhn, K. Midsummer nights
Onwueme, O. T. Parables for a season

14 characters (7m 4w 3b)

Wynne, M. The knocky

14 characters (7m 5w 2g)

White, P. The season at Sarsaparilla

14 characters (7m 6w 1b)

y Zindel, P. Every seventeen minutes the crowd goes crazy!

14 characters (7m 7w)

Abdoh, R. The law of remains
Bullins, E. In the wine time
De Geesewell, P. Murder at the asylum
Nelson, R. and Gelman, A. Misha's party
Ribman, R. Sweet table at the Richelieu

14 characters (8m 1w 4b 1g)

Mitterer, F. Children of the Devil

MIXED CAST—*Continued*

14 characters (8m 6w)

Herzberg, J. The wedding party
Lee, L. The first breeze of summer
Potter, D. Cream in my coffee

14 characters (9m 5w)

Chekhov, A. Three sisters
Crutcher, J. and McBride, V. Diggin in: the farm crisis in Kentucky
c Francoeur, B. Snow White and the seven dwarfs
Hare, D. Plenty
Lahr, J. The Manchurian candidate
Nigro, D. Loves labour wonne

14 characters (10m 4w)

Adamov, A. Professor Taranne
Barker, C. Paradise Street
Dryden, J. Aureng-Zebe
Kovacevic, D. The gathering place
Sondheim, S. Passion

14 characters (13m 1w)

Kramer, L. The normal heart

14 characters and extras (4m 6w 1b 3g extras)

c Jenkin, L. Ramona Quimby

14 characters and extras (5m 3w 3b 3g extras)

c McCaslin, N. Prelude to fame

14 characters and extras (5m 5w 2b 2g extras)

Christiansen, D. M. Who's mining the mercantile?

14 characters and extras (5m 9w extras)

Baldwin, J. The amen corner
Rensten, M. Village day
y St. John, B. Peril on the high seas

14 characters and extras (6m 6w 2b extras)

Miller, E. Morning shows the day

14 characters and extras (6m 8w extras)

y Booth, R. Where did you spend the night?
c Golden, G. The magic in me
Sondheim, S. Company

14 characters and extras (7m 5w 2b extras)

Cary, E. The tragedy of Mariam, the fair

14 characters and extras (7m 7w extras)

Mitterer, F. Dragon thirst
c Summer, A. The just so letter

14 characters and extras (8m 6w extras)

Blanc, E. S. Wars I have seen
Cartwright, J. Road

14 characters and extras (9m 3w 2b extras)

Mercer, D. Flint

14 characters and extras (9m 4w 1b extras)

Schenkkan, R. Fire in the hole

14 characters and extras (9m 5w extras)

Chayefsky, P. Printer's measure
Chekhov, A. The cherry orchard
c McCullough, L. E. Fandango!
O'Neill, E. The great God Brown
y Thane, A. The House of the Seven Gables

14 characters and extras (10m 4w extras)

c Chambers, J. Tales of King Arthur
Farquhar, G. The recruiting officer
Hoffman, W. M. As is
Pawley, T. The tumult and the shouting
Peake, R. B. Presumption
Robbins, N. Snow White

14 characters and extras (11m 3w extras)

y Allman, S. and Pickett, B. Frankenstein unbound
c Miranda, J. E. Cornerstone of civil rights
The Revenger's tragedy

14 characters and extras (12m 2w extras)

Bird, R. M. The gladiator

14 characters and extras (13m 1w extras)

Edward, H. F. V. Job hunters

15 characters (3m 2w 6b 4g)

c Nordlicht, L. Cover your eyes and run!

15 characters (6m 7w 1b 1g)

Firbank, R. The Princess Zoubaroff

15 characters (7m 4w 2b 2g)

c Pyle, M. T. Clever Peter

15 characters (7m 8w)

Reid, C. Tea in a china cup

15 characters (8m 7w)

y Blacker, T. Homebird
White, E. Lament for Rastafari
Wilde, O. A woman of no importance

15 characters (9m 6w)

y Davis, R. Losing it
Durang, C. A history of the American film
Edmundson, H. War and peace
Fishelson, D. The idiot
Goldoni, C. Villeggiatura: Adventures in the country
y Swartz, L. D. Halloween dreams
Wilde, O. An ideal husband

15 characters (10m 5w)

Griffiths, T. The party

MIXED CAST—*Continued*
Meilhac, H. and Halevy, L. Mardi Gras
Quinton, E. William Shakespeare's A midsummer night's dream
Rattigan, T. Harlequinade
Shaw, B. Major Barbara
Wine, B. Tenure

15 characters (11m 4w)

Blessing, L. Fortinbras
Hoffman, A. Welcome stranger
c McCullough, L. E. El Corrido de Gregorio Cortez
Ornsbo, J. Odysseus from Vraa
Salom, J. Bonfire at dawn
Shaw, G. B. The doctor's dilemma

15 characters (12m 3w)

c McCaslin, N. Maelduin of Arran
Weller, M. Moonchildren

15 characters (13m 2w)

Nowra, L. Crow

15 characters and extras (5m 3w 7b extras)

Euripides. Suppliant women

15 characters and extras (5m 6w 4g extras)

y Morley, O. J. Romance for Jo March

15 characters and extras (5m 10w extras)

Bowles, J. In the summer house

15 characters and extras (7m 8w extras)

Watkins, M. Chicago

15 characters and extras (8m 7w extras)

y Martens, A. C. The comeback caper
y St. John, B. Murder in the House of horrors
Strindberg, A. The ghost sonata

15 characters and extras (9m 4w 1b 1g extras)

c Keats, M. Peter Salem, Minuteman

15 characters and extras (9m 6w extras)

Boucicault, D. The Colleen Bawn
Taylor, R. and Bologna, J. Paradise follies

15 characters and extras (10m 5w extras)

Feydeau, G. A flea in her rear
Fletcher, J. The fair maid of the inn
Hampton, C. Total eclipse
Maturin, C. R. Bertram

15 characters and extras (11m 4w extras)

Drexler, R. Occupational hazard
Ford, J. 'Tis pity she's a whore
Lawrence, J. and Lee, R. E. The night Thoreau spent in jail
Minghella, A. Two planks and a passion
Mitterer, F. There's not a finer country
Reddin, K. Black snow
Shaw, B. Caesar and Cleopatra
Sheridan, R. B. The school for scandal
Stoppard, T. Indian ink

15 characters and extras (12m 2w 1b extras)

y McCullough, L. E. Abe Lincoln for the defense

15 characters and extras (12m 3w extras)

Ibsen, H. The wild duck

15 characters and extras (13m 2w extras)

Turrini, P. Death and the Devil

15 characters and extras (14m 1w extras)

Bell, J. A. Prisoner
Lawrence, J. and Lee, R. E. First Monday in October
Schnitzler, A. Fink and Fliederbusch
Wilde, O. Vera

16 characters (6m 7w 3g)

Bates, H. E. The darling buds of May

16 characters (6m 10w)

Hill, A. On Strivers Row

16 characters (7m 9w)

Churchill, C. The Skriker
Rabe, D. The orphan
St. John, B. 13 past midnight
Wilde, O. Lady Windermere's fan

16 characters (9m 3w 2b 2g)

c McCullough, L. E. Here we come a-wassailing

16 characters (9m 7w)

Burns, K. Psycho night at the Paradise Lounge
Peterson, L. Take a giant step
Pinero, A. W. The schoolmistress
Szyszkowitz, G. Somewhere over the rainbow

16 characters (10m 5w 1g)

Beaumarchais, P. A. C. de. The marriage of Figaro

16 characters (10m 6w)

y Avery, C. The seven ages of Dan
Carmichael, F. Frankenstein 1930
Doyle, R. War
Goldoni, C. Villeggiatura: Back from the country
Granville-Barker, H. Waste
Gregor, H. The third death

16 characters (11m 5w)

Foote, H. The habitation of dragons

16 characters (12m 4w)

De la Tour, A. The Pope and the witch
Fishelson, D. The brothers Karamazov

MIXED CAST—*Continued*
Pinero, A. W. The magistrate

16 characters (13m 3w)

Ives, D. Speed-the-play
Lewis, M. G. The castle spectre
Warner, F. Virgil and Caesar

16 characters (14m 2w)

Buzo, A. Macquarie
Fo, D. Trumpets and raspberries

16 characters (15m 1w)

Yourgrau, T. The song of Jacob Zulu

16 characters and extras (6m 10w extras)

c Francoeur, B. The enchantment of Beauty and the beast

16 characters and extras (7m 9w extras)

y O'Brien, J. Wherefore art thou Juliet?

16 characters and extras (8m 8w extras)

Francis, M. Jane Austen's Northanger Abbey
Gill, P. Cardiff East
y Jackson, K. Street story

16 characters and extras (9m 5w 2b extras)

y Thane, A. The moonstone

16 characters and extras (9m 7w extras)

Hall, W. Mansfield Park
Lee, N. The Princess of Cleves
Shadwell, T. The virtuoso

16 characters and extras (10m 6w extras)

c Hardee, L. The prince and the pauper
Ward, T. Big white fog
Witkiewicz, S. I. They

16 characters and extras (11m 5w extras)

Barker, H. Brutopia
Santareno, B. The judgment of Father Martinho
Shaw, B. Man and superman

16 characters and extras (12m 2w 1b 1g extras)

c Bisson, P. Spacenapped

16 characters and extras (12m 4w extras)

Ford, J. The lover's melancholy
y Hackett, W. A tale of two cities
Mitterer, F. Stigma

16 characters and extras (13m 3w extras)

Barnes, P. Bye bye Columbus
Fletcher, J. The lover's progress
Labiche, E. and Delacour, A. The piggy bank
Ribman, R. Buck
Warner, F. Byzantium

16 characters and extras (14m 2w extras)

Barnes, P. Laughter!

Oyamo. I am a man
Szyszkowitz, G. Friedman Puntigam

17 characters (5m 12w)

Larbey, B. A small affair

17 characters (7m 7w 2b 1g)

y Dietz, S. The rememberer

17 characters (9m 7w 1b)

Granville-Barker, H. The Voysey inheritance

17 characters (9m 8w)

Vingoe, M. Living curiosities: a story of Anna Swan

17 characters (11m 6w)

Beckett, S. Eleuthéria
Rubess, B. No. here comes Ulrike Meinhof

17 characters (12m 5w)

Harwood, R. The ordeal of Gilbert Pinfold
MacNeice, L. They met on Good Friday
c McCullough, L. E. Great medicine painter

17 characters (14m 3w)

Inchbald, Mrs. Such things are
Kander, J. The kiss of the spider woman
Wedekind, F. Lulu: a monster tragedy

17 characters (15m 2w)

Simonson, E. Bang the drum slowly

17 characters and extras (7m 10w extras)

Shaffer, P. The gift of the Gorgon

17 characters and extras (8m 9w extras)

Etherege, G. The man of mode

17 characters and extras (9m 5w 3b extras)

Bricusse, L. The revenge of Sherlock Holmes

17 characters and extras (10m 7w extras)

Dove, R. The darker face of the earth. Completely rev. 2nd ed.

17 characters and extras (11m 5w 1b extras)

West, M. The drag

17 characters and extras (11m 6w extras)

c Boiko, C. Once upon a dream
Clapp, T. Dracula
Farquhar, G. The beaux' stratagem

17 characters and extras (12m 4w 1b extras)

Riche, R. Malcolm X: message from the grassroots

17 characters and extras (12m 5w extras)

Barker, J. N. The Indian princess

MIXED CAST—*Continued*

Nelson, R. The General from America
Schnitzler, A. Marionettes: The great puppet show
Vidal, C. The best man

17 characters and extras (13m 4w extras)

Fletcher, J. and Massinger, P. The Spanish curate
Hall, W. The three musketeers
Hare, D. Ivanov
Hill, K. The invisible man
Korder, H. The lights
y Lipp, J. L. Titanic: destination disaster
c Lloyd, R. Smut's saga
MacNeice, L. Prisoner's progress
Megged, A. Hanna Senesh
Ryga, G. The ecstasy of Rita Joe

17 characters and extras (15m 2w extras)

Chayefsky, P. The passion of Josef D.

18 characters (7m 11w)

Wilson, L. The rimers of Eldritch

18 characters (8m 8w 1b 1g)

c Medoff, M. Stefanie hero

18 characters (9m 8w 1b)

Schwartz, D. Shenandoah

18 characters (10m 8w)

Feydeau, G. An absolute turkey

18 characters (11m 7w)

Hughes, L. Simply heavenly

18 characters (12m 6w)

Ayckbourn, A. Wolf at the door
y Cornthwaite, R. Carlo Goldoni's Villeggiatura
Jones, H. A. The middleman

18 characters (14m 4w)

Anderson, G. Appearances

18 characters and extras (5m 11w 1b 1g extras)

c Francoeur, B. The secret garden

18 characters and extras (6m 9w 1b 2g extras)

c Kennedy, R. Hans Christian Andersen's The snow queen

18 characters and extras (8m 10w extras)

Chekhov, A. Ivanov

18 characters and extras (9m 7w 2b extras)

Middleton, T. Michaelmas Term

18 characters and extras (9m 8w 1b extras)

Foote, H. The land of the astronauts

18 characters and extras (10m 8w extras)

c Ayckbourn, A. My very own story
Barker, C. Subtle bodies
Middleton, T. A critical edition of Thomas Middleton's The witch
Middleton, T. The witch
Pinero, A. W. Trelawny of the 'Wells'
Tanaka, C. The head of Mary

18 characters and extras (11m 7w extras)

Behn, A. The rover

18 characters and extras (12m 6w extras)

Bond, E. Jackets
West, M. Sex

18 characters and extras (13m 5w extras)

O'Donovan, J. Copperfaced Jack

18 characters and extras (15m 3w extras)

y Aynsley, E. What a weekend!
Foote, H. Tomorrow
Goethe, J. W. von. Egmont
Kyd, T. The Spanish tragedy
c Wolman, D. An imaginary trial of George Washington

18 characters and extras (16m 2w extras)

c McCullough, L. E. The golden spike
Sade, Marquis de. Jeanne Laisné

19 characters (6m 13w)

y Wells, J. S. Competition piece

19 characters (7m 8w 2b 2g)

c Thain, P. Stone soup

19 characters (8m 11w)

Kanin, F. Goodbye, my fancy

19 characters (10m 9w)

Hauptmann, G. Before daybreak
y Ullom, S. Geeks do come from outer space

19 characters (11m 8w)

Cloud, D. O pioneers!
Ward, N. The strangeness of others

19 characters (12m 7w)

Russell, C. L. Five on the black hand side

19 characters (13m 4w 1b 1g)

Rubess, B. Oblivion: a story of Isabelle Eberhardt

19 characters (15m 4w)

Freed, D. Inquest
Granville-Barker, H. His majesty
Lawrence, J. and Lee, R. E. The gang's all here
Lerner, M. Kastner

19 characters (16m 3w)

Lucie, D. The shallow end
O'Neill, E. The iceman cometh

MIXED CAST—*Continued*

19 characters and extras (5m 6w 2b 6g extras)

c Morris, V. Legend of Pocahontas

19 characters and extras (10m 9w extras)

Ibsen, H. Pillars of society

19 characters and extras (12m 7w extras)

Behn, A. The lucky chance
Warner, F. King Francis I
Wertenbaker, T. The break of day

19 characters and extras (13m 5w 1g extras)

Smith, W. H. The drunkard

19 characters and extras (13m 6w extras)

Ford, J. The broken heart
Francis, M. A tale of two cities
Wright, R. and Green, P. Native son

19 characters and extras (14m 5w extras)

Berkoff, S. Dahling you were marvellous
c Rowland, E. A baker's dozen

19 characters and extras (15m 4w extras)

Dunbar, P. L. and Shipp, J. A. In Dahomey
Fletcher, J. and Rowley, W. The maid in the mill
Kaiser, G. Gas I
Rabe, D. The basic training of Pavlo Hummel

19 characters and extras (16m 3w extras)

y McCullough, L. E. The seven Chan brothers of Paiute Pass

19 characters and extras (17m 1w 1b extras)

Stoppard, T. Professional foul

20 characters (12m 8w)

c Miller H. L. Bandit Ben rides again

20 characters (14m 5w 1b)

Middleton, T. No wit, no help like a woman's

20 characters (14m 6w)

Boucicault, D. Octoroon
De Filippo, E. The local authority
Granville-Barker, H. The marrying of Ann-Leete

20 characters (16m 4w)

O'Casey, S. Cock-a-doodle dandy

20 characters and extras (7m 13w extras)

y Hughes, P. Abracadabra, Aladdin!
y Swift, R. The paper bag bandit rides again

20 characters and extras (8m 12w extras)

García Lorca, F. The house of Bernarda Alba

20 characters and extras (11m 9w extras)

Carson, J. A preacher with a horse to ride
De Filippo, E. Grand magic

20 characters and extras (12m 7w 1g extras)

Stoll, D. Teller of tales

20 characters and extras (13m 7w extras)

Preses, P. and Becher, U. Our Mr. Bockerer

20 characters and extras (15m 5w extras)

Barker, H. The power of the dog

20 characters and extras (19m 1w extras)

Schnitzler, A. Professor Bernhardi
Stoppard, T. The invention of love

21 characters (7m 14w)

Johnson, F. H. Run little chillun

21 characters (8m 11w 2g)

c McCullough, L. E. Chief Sarah, the Indian Joan of Arc

21 characters (10m 11w)

y Beechy High School Drama Club. Me 'n' Alfred

21 characters (11m 9w 1g)

Miller, A. The crucible

21 characters (15m 6w)

Schnitzler, A. The word

21 characters and extras (7m 14w extras)

y Swift, R. The Hunchback of Notre Dame goes West

21 characters and extras (8m 8w 1b 4g extras)

y St. John, B. Heaven help the po'taters!

21 characters and extras (8m 13w extras)

y Swift, R. Attack of the giant grasshopper

21 characters and extras (10m 9w 1b 1g extras)

Norman, M. The secret garden

21 characters and extras (10m 11w extras)

Canetti, V. The Ogre

21 characters and extras (12m 9w extras)

Dove, R. The darker face of the earth
Lyly, J. Gallathea

21 characters and extras (15m 6w extras)

y Boiko, C. Belinda and the Beast
Cowley, H. P. The belle's stratagem

21 characters and extras (16m 5w extras)

Middleton, T. A trick to catch the old one

MIXED CAST—*Continued*

21 characters and extras (17m 4w extras)

Graham, S. Track thirteen
Hugo, V. The king amuses himself (Le roi s'amuse!)
Middleton, T. A mad world, my masters
y Swortzell, L. Lucky Peter's journey
Warner, F. Healing nature

21 characters and extras (18m 3w extras)

Hugo, V. Hernani
Kingsley, S. Darkness at noon
Shepard, S. Operation sidewinder

22 characters (3m 19w)

McGillivray, D. and Zerlin, W. The Farndale Avenue Housing Estate Townswomen's Guild Operatic Society's production of The Mikado

22 characters (8m 14w)

Barry, L. The good times are killing me

22 characters (12m 10w)

y Sodaro, C. It's a bird! It's a plane! It's . . . Nerdman?!

22 characters (17m 5w)

Barnes, P. The ruling class

22 characters and extras (7m 15w extras)

y Swift, R. Rascals under the big top

22 characters and extras (8m 14w extras)

Dorfman, A. Widows

22 characters and extras (10m 12w extras)

y St. John, B. Here comes the judge!

22 characters and extras (12m 10w extras)

Edgar, D. Pentecost

22 characters and extras (16m 6w extras)

Lawrence, J. and Lee, R. E. Diamond orchid
Ward, D. T. Day of absence

22 characters and extras (17m 5w extras)

Schnitzler, A. The Green Cockatoo

23 characters (8m 13w 1b 1g)

Sondheim, S. and Lapine, J. Into the woods

23 characters (12m 11w)

Ayckbourn, A. The revengers' comedies
Bulgakov, M. Zoyka's apartment

23 characters (15m 8w)

McGrath, J. Random happenings in the Hebrides

23 characters (18m 5w)

Hill, G. Brand

23 characters and extras (7m 16w extras)

Kelly, T. Renfield of the flies and spiders

23 characters and extras (18m 5w extras)

Kingsley, S. The patriots

23 characters and extras (19m 3w 1b extras)

Goethe, J. W. von. Goetz von Berlichingen with the iron hand

23 characters and extras (19m 4w extras)

Hugo, V. Ruy Blas

24 characters (6m 17w 1b)

García Lorca, F. Yerma

24 characters (12m 12w)

Wertenbaker, T. Three birds alighting on a field

24 characters (14m 10w)

Alexander, R. I ain't yo' uncle

24 characters (18m 6w)

Lawrence, J. and Lee, R. E. Only in America

24 characters (19m 5w)

Barnes, P. Sunsets and glories

24 characters and extras (15m 9w extras)

Behn, A. Sir Patient Fancy

24 characters and extras (16m 8w extras)

Wilson, L. Balm in Gilead

24 characters and extras (18m 6w extras)

Horovitz, I. Henry Lumper

24 characters and extras (20m 4w extras)

Chapman, G. The revenge of Bussy d'Ambois

24 characters and extras (21m 3w extras)

Fletcher, J. and Massinger, P. Rollo, Duke of Normandy

24 characters and extras (22m 2w extras)

Dear, N. Zenobia

25 characters (8m 17w)

Granville-Barker, H. The Madras House

25 characters (11m 7w 3b 4g)

Jones, C. My Antonia

25 characters and extras (9m 16w extras)

y Christiansen, A. Teens in Tinseltown

25 characters and extras (10m 15w extras)

y Reiser, D. The creepy creeps of Pilgrim Road

25 characters and extras (19m 6w extras)

Seiler, C. Darker brother

26 characters (12m 10w 2b 2g)

Rodgers, J. W. It's a wonderful life

26 characters (13m 13w)

Thompson, G. M. A time to go home

MIXED CAST—*Continued*

26 characters (15m 11w)

Tony n' Tina's wedding

26 characters (18m 8w)

Sims, G. R. The lights o' London

26 characters (22m 3w 1b)

Koch, K. George Washington crossing the Delaware

26 characters and extras (14m 12w extras)

Gay, J. Beggar's opera

26 characters and extras (16m 7w 2b 1g extras)

Johanson, R. A tale of two cities

26 characters and extras (16m 9w 1g extras)

Feydeau, G. That's my girl

26 characters and extras (22m 4w extras)

Marlowe, C. The Jew of Malta

27 characters (12m 15w)

Larbey, B. Half an idea

27 characters (23m 4w)

Bond, E. The bundle

27 characters and extras (9m 18w extras)

y Francoeur, B. Wrangler Ranch

27 characters and extras (16m 7w 4g extras)

Hyem, J. Lorna Doone

27 characters and extras (24m 3w extras)

Ford, J. Perkin Warbeck

28 characters (19m 9w)

Rice, E. Counsellor-at-law

28 characters (20m 7w 1b)

Aiken, G. L. Uncle Tom's cabin

28 characters (20m 8w)

Mamet, D. Edmond

28 characters (21m 7w)

Treadwell, S. Machinal

28 characters and extras (10m 18w extras)

y Kelly, T. Yard sale

28 characters and extras (12m 16w extras)

y Kelly, T. Hooray for Hollywood

28 characters and extras (19m 8w 1g extras)

Kingsley, S. Men in white

28 characters and extras (23m 5w extras)

Ansky, S. The dybbuk

28 characters and extras (25m 3w extras)

Lyly, J. Campaspe

29 characters (18m 11w)

Whelan, P. Divine right

29 characters and extras (14m 15w extras)

Chinn, J. Home before dark

29 characters and extras (17m 12w extras)

Flanagan, H. and Clifford, M. E. Can you hear their voices?

29 characters and extras (27m 2w extras)

Marlowe, C. Edward II

30 characters (19m 11w)

Poliakoff, S. She's been away

30 characters (25m 5w)

Silver, R. S. The hert o Scotland

30 characters (28m 2w)

Weiss, P. The investigation

30 characters and extras (11m 19w extras)

y Francoeur, B. Kilroy was here!

30 characters and extras (23m 7w extras)

Lawrence, J. and Lee, R. E. Inherit the wind

30 characters and extras (26m 4w extras)

Browne, T. Natural man

31 characters (7m 19w 2b 3g)

White, P. A cheery soul

32 characters and extras (27m 5w extras)

Pushkin, A. Boris Godunov

33 characters and extras (18m 15w extras)

Wycherley, W. The plain dealer

34 characters (25m 9w)

Kingsley, S. Detective story

34 characters and extras (14m 20w extras)

Brett, S. Mr. Quigley's revenge

34 characters and extras (30m 4w extras)

Musset, A. de. Lorenzaccio

Large cast

y Allaway, B. Makin' it
Anderson, M. Richard and Anne
Barker, C. Colossus
Barker, C. Crazyface
Barker, C. The history of the Devil
Barker, H. Rome
Barnes, P. The bewitched
Barnes, P. Clap hands here comes Charlie
Barnes, P. Red noses
Basso, E. The fall of Prague
Behn, A. The emperor of the moon
Blecher, H.; Cruz, M. and Rodriquez, R. X. Frida: the story of Frida Kahlo
c Blum, R. California wax museum
Bonal, D. A country wedding
Bond, E. Human cannon

MIXED CAST—*Continued*
Brecht, B. Mother Courage and her children
c Breeze, N. The Rochdale Pioneers
Brenton, H. Faust, parts I & II
c Brown, A. Sleeping Beauty
Brown, W. W. The escape
Büchner, G. Danton's death
c Caird, J. and Nunn, T. Peter Pan
Chayefsky, P. Gideon
y Christiansen, A. A monster ate my homework
Churchill, C. Mad forest
Congdon, C. Casanova
Davis, T. The life and times of Malcolm X
Dickins, B. Remember Ronald Ryan
Dodson, O. Bayou legend
Doust, P. Amphibious spangulatos
DuBois, W. E. B. Star of Ethiopia
Fischoff, G. James A. Michener's Sayonara
y Francoeur, B. Coney Island of Dr. Moreau
Francoeur, B. Gone with the breeze
y Francoeur, B. Hee haw hayride
y Fraser, B. Prom night of the living dead
Gilbert, S. M. and Gubar, S. Masterpiece theatre
Goethe, J. W. von. Faust, part I
Goethe, J. W. von. Faust, part II
Goethe, J. W. von. Pandora
Gorky, M. The summer people
Hagger, N. The warlords
Hall, W. Jane Eyre
Handke, P. The hour we knew nothing of each other
Hare, D. Murmuring judges
Hauptmann, G. The weavers
Haylock, D. The flaming fiery furnace
c Haylock, D. Light on the road to Damascus
c Haylock, D. Whoever
Hill, K. The phantom of the opera
Hollingsworth, M. The history of the village of the small huts
Howles, L. The king's highway
Hughes, L. Don't you want to be free?
Hughes, L. Emperor of Haiti
Kaiser, G. From morning to midnight
Kingsley, S. Dead end
Koch, K. The Red Robins
Labiche, E. M. Eating crow
Lawrence, J. and Lee, R. E. Auntie Mame
Linney, R. A Christmas carol
MacNeice, L. Christopher Columbus
MacNeice, L. He had a date
MacNeice, L. One for the grave
Madách, I. The tragedy of man
Mann, E. Execution of justice
c Marx, P. The haunting contest
c Marx, P. Hearts and tarts
c Marx, P. Old Frost's winter adventure
c Marx, P. The picnic
c Marx, P. The rainbow people
c Marx, P. The troubled Pilgrim
c McCullough, L. E. The buffalo hunters
c McCullough, L. E. Darling Clementine: a tail of old San Francisco
c McCullough, L. E. Jesse James: blood on the saddle
y Medoff, M. Big Mary
Miller, A. The American clock
c Morris, A. J. An American story
Mortimer, J. Charles Dickens' A Christmas carol
Mueller, D. A. Eyes upon the cross
c Nicol, R. The Snow Queen
O'Neill, E. Lazarus laughed
O'Neill, E. "Marco millions"
Osborne, J. The world of Paul Slickey
Piscator, E. and Gasbarra, F. In spite of everything!
y Poskitt, K. Henry the Tudor dude
Potter, D. Cold Lazarus
Potter, D. Karaoke
Potter, D. Pennies from heaven
c Pricone, S. A tree grows in Hollywood
Prokofiev, S. The love of three oranges
Ramlī, L. In plain Arabic
c Reakes, P. Old Mother Hubbard
Reaney, J. The St. Nicholas Hotel, Wm. Donnelly, prop.
Rostand, E. Cyrano de Bergerac
Russell, B. Elegies for angels, punks and raging queens
Sahlins, B. The mysteries: The Passion
Salutin, R. and Theatre Passe Muraille. 1837: The Farmers' Revolt
Schenkkan, R. God's great supper
Schenkkan, R. Which side are you on?
Schevill, J. Lovecraft's follies
Schnitzler, A. A procession of shades
Seremba, G. Come good rain
Shin, R. The art of waiting
Silvera, J. D. and Hill, A. Liberty deferred
c Staite, J. Cinderella - the sequel
Staite, J. Goldilocks and the three Martians
Stein, G. The mother of us all

MIXED CAST—*Continued*

c Stephens, J. The servant king
Stoppard, T. Dogg's Hamlet, Cahoot's Macbeth
Strindberg, A. Carl XII
Tagore, R. The cycle of spring
c Trott, S. Buster come home
Trott, S. Destination Bethlehem
c Trott, S. Did I miss anything important?
c Trott, S. Nocturne
Valle-Inclan, R. del. Bohemian lights
Valle-Inclan, R. del. Divine words
Valle-Inclan, R. del. Silver face
Van Itallie, J.-C. Master & Margarita
Ward, T. Our lan'
Wedekind, F. Spring awakening
Wertenbaker, T. The love of the nightingale
West, M. The pleasure man
y Williams, K. Gran Webster's war
Wolfe, G. C. Jelly's last jam
Yoshitsune and the thousand cherry trees

PUPPETS

2 characters

c Pflomm, P. N. Gracie's garden
c Pflomm, P. N. Let's be puppets
c Pflomm. P. N. Witches and ghosts

3 characters

c Bass, E. In my grandmother's purse
c Jones, T. Gertie goat
c Pflomm, P. N. Clever pets
c Pflomm, P. N. Couch potatoes
c Pflomm, P. N. Litterbugs
c Pflomm, P. N. The loose tooth
c Pflomm, P. N. Vegetables

4 characters

c Pflomm, P. N. Fishing
c Pflomm, P. N. Halloween ghosts
c Pflomm, P. N. Ryan's hat
c Pflomm, P. N. Silvie the substitute reindeer
c Pflomm, P. N. A visit to the library

5 characters

c Jones, T. Gone fishing
c Pflomm, P. N. Autumn leaves
c Pflomm, P. N. The busy Santa
c Pflomm, P. N. The leprechaun
c Pflomm, P. N. The Thanksgiving bear
c Pflomm, P. N. The Valentine bouquet

6 characters

c Jones, T. Scarecrows
c Jones, T. Who stole the pie!
c Mahlmann, L. and Jones, D. C. The Frog Prince
c Mahlmann, L. and Jones, D. C. The reluctant dragon
c Mahlmann, L. and Jones, D. C. Rumpelstiltskin
c Pflomm, P. N. Five little snowmen
c Pflomm, P. N. The picnic

7 characters

c Jones, T. Camping out
c Jones, T. The computer
c Mahlmann, L. and Jones, D. C. Ali Baba and the Forty Thieves
c Mahlmann, L. and Jones, D. C. Aladdin
c Mahlmann, L. and Jones, D. C. King Midas and the golden touch
c Mahlmann, L. and Jones, D. C. Three Billy Goats Gruff

8 characters

c Mahlmann, L. and Jones, D. C. Cinderella
c Mahlmann, L. and Jones, D. C. The Emperor's nightingale
c Mahlmann, L. and Jones, D. C. Puss-in-Boots
c Mahlmann, L. and Jones, D. C. Rapunzel's tower
c Mahlmann, L. and Jones, D. C. Snow White and Rose Red
c Pflomm, P. N. The talent show
Solórzano, C. The puppets

9 characters

c Mahlmann, L. and Jones, D. C. Jack and the beanstalk
c Mahlmann, L. and Jones, D. C. The Pied Piper of Hamelin
c Mahlmann, L. and Jones, D. C. The table, the donkey and the stick
c Pflomm, P. N. Lost in a fairy tale
c Pflomm, P. N. A new Punch and Judy

10 characters

c Jones, T. Froggie woggies
c Mahlmann, L. and Jones, D. C. Beauty and the Beast
c Mahlmann, L. and Jones, D. C. The Gingerbread Boy
c Mahlmann, L. and Jones, D. C. The Nutcracker Prince
c Mahlmann, L. and Jones, D. C. The tale of Peter Rabbit

10 characters and extras

y Harris, A. The prince and the pauper

PUPPETS—*Continued*

11 characters

c Mahlmann, L. and Jones, D. C. Peter Pan
Mahlmann, L. and Jones, D. C. Sleeping Beauty

12 characters

c Swortzell, L. Punch and Judy: their tragical comedy, their comical tragedy

13 characters

c Mahlmann, L. and Jones, D. C. Pinocchio
c Mahlmann, L. and Jones, D. C. Snow White and the seven dwarfs

16 characters

c Mahlmann, L. and Jones, D. C. Alice's adventures in Wonderland

17 characters

Barker, H. All he fears

19 characters

c Mahlmann, L. and Jones, D. C. The Wizard of Oz

UNIDENTIFIED CAST

2 characters

Alvarez, L. Who is chasing whom!
Rivera, J. Tape
y Schaaf, A. K. Your money cheerfully refunded

3 characters

c Gerke, P. The adventures of Anansi: "Why Anansi lives in ceilings"
Horovitz, I. Rats

3 characters and extras

c Neuman, C. A better mousetrap

4 characters

c Conboy, R. Song of the oak—El canto del roble

4 characters and extras

y Ayckbourn, A. Callisto 5

5 characters

c Simon, S. The tiger and the Brahman

5 characters and extras

c Rosenberg, J. El gato sin amigos—The cat who had no friends

6 characters

c Kuharski, J. The leopard's noisy drum
c Surface, M. H. The sorcerer's apprentice

7 characters

Mankind. A critical edition of the medieval play Mankind

7 characters and extras

c Ellison, L. Utter garbage

8 characters and extras

c Neidermyer, D. The tortoise and the hare race again

9 characters

c Cheatham, V. R. The Three Little Pigs and friends
c Vigil, A. The foolish coyote
c Vigil, A. The smelly feet

9 characters and extras

c Lawrence, M. 'Twas the night before Columbus day . . . I mean Christmas

12 characters

c Dolmen, C. and Dolmen, J. The three little pigs

12 characters and extras

c Chatfield, R. The great Santa kidnap

13 characters

Punch and Judy

13 characters and extras

c Collette, P. and Fritzen, G. Toy camp

14 characters

MacNeice, L. The mad islands

15 characters

y Bernardi, P. and Havens, D. Twice upon a time
c Vigil, A. The littlest ant

15 characters and extras

c Vigil, A. El muchacho que mato al gigante. The boy who killed the giant
c Wood, D. Rupert and the green dragon

16 characters and extras

Marshall, S. L. The emperor's New Year

17 characters and extras

c Woyiwada, A. The little fir tree

19 characters and extras

c McCullough, L. E. How the people got fire

26 characters and extras

c Robbins, G. The hundred and one Dalmatians

VARIABLE CAST

Aoki, B. W. The Queen's garden
Arent, A. Ethiopia

VARIABLE CAST—*Continued*

Auden, W. H. and Stern, J. The rocking horse winner
Berg, R. AIDS! the musical!
Bonner, M. O. The purple flower
Chessman, P. [et al.] Fight for Shelton bar
Churchill, C. Lives of the great poisoners
y Cohen, F. Try a little Shakespeare
Cross, J. C. Julia of Louvain
Cruz, M. Telling tales
Dryden, J. The state of innocence and fall of man
Enscoe, L. G. and Enscoe, A. Call for the lights and sing!
Enscoe, L. G. and Enscoe, A. Candles and carols
Enscoe, L. G. and Enscoe, A. The great Gemdale Christmas tree ornament factory
Enscoe, L. G. and Enscoe, A. The king who hated Christmas
Enscoe, L. G. and Enscoe, A. The towne without a tale
Enscoe, L. G. and Enscoe, A. The wise men had it easy
c Fisher, A. Harriet Tubman—the second Moses
Fo, D. Mistero buffo comic mysteries
Ford, K. Time quest
Freeman, B.; Branner, D. and Gupton, E. Fierce love
y Fuerstenberg, A. Blind dates
c Gerke, P. The adventures of Anansi: "How Anansi helped a fisherman"
c Gerke, P. Chat botté: Puss-in-boots
c Gerke, P. La culebra: "The snake"
c Gerke, P. Da-hoos-whee'-whee: The seal-hunting brothers
c Gerke, P. Drakesbill
Gerke, P. East of the sun and west of the moon
c Gerke, P. Feng zhen-zhu: The wind pearl
c Gerke, P. The firebird, the horse of power, and Czarevna Vasilisa
c Gerke, P. The great bear
c Gerke, P. I dodici mesi: The twelve months
c Gerke, P. Legend of the seasons
c Gerke, P. The little red hen
c Gerke, P. The long leather bag
c Gerke, P. Ma Lien and the magic paintbrush
c Gerke, P. Los mariachis Mexicanos: "The Brementown musicians"
Gerke, P. Mataora and Niwareka in the Underworld
c Gerke, P. Star story
c Gerke, P. Tri zlate vlasy Deda Vseveda: "The three golden hairs of Grandfather Know All"
c Gerke, P. Vasilisa Prekrasnaia: "Vasilisa the beautiful"
Guare, J. Rich and famous
Gurney, A. R. Richard Cory
y Harder, E. Rememberin' stuff
c Haylock, D. Follow the leader
c Haylock, D. Light of the world
c Haylock, D. Rejection
Higgins, D. Buster Keaton enters into paradise
Jackson, C. B. Iago
y Keating, B. The garbage cantata
Koch, K. The strangers from the sea
La Roche-Guilhen, A. de. All-wondrous
y Lavrakas, P. Escape from Nemotex
c Leonard, J. Crow & Weasel
c Libert, N. P. The Western Civ rap
MacNeice, L. The dark tower
Maponya, M. The hungry earth
c McDonough, J. and Alderete, B. Posadas
McGrath, J. Border warfare
McGrath, J. The Cheviot, the stag and the black, black oil
McGrath, J. Joe's drum
McGrath, J. Out of our heads
Mitterer, F. One everyman
y Nimmo, P. Will Shakespeare save the King!
y Nimmo, P. Will Shakespeare save us!
c Nunn, J. The Pied Piper
Osofisan, F. Esu and the vagabond minstrels
Osofisan, F. Morountodun
Paice, E. and Woddis, R. World on edge
Parks, S.-L. The death of the last black man in the whole entire world
Pickering, K. One child at a time
Pomo Afro Homos. Dark fruit
Prior, J. Girls night out
Schevill, J. The ushers
Seebring, W. The original Last Wish Baby
c Shurtz, R. K. Amy's attic
Stramm, A. Sancta Susanna
Tagore, R. Sanyasi
Toller, E. Masses and man
c Trott, S. You don't say!
United States Food Administration. Why we are at war
Wellman, M. Cellophane
Williams, J.; Sears, J. and Howard, E. A Tuna Christmas
Wilson, E. A first-born son

VARIABLE CAST—*Continued*

c Witkiewicz, S. Comedies of family life
Wong, E. Kimchee and chitlins
c Wood, D. Babe, the sheep-pig

1 character

Mamet, D. Monologue (February 1990)

2 characters

Mamet, D. A perfect mermaid
Mamet, D. Two enthusiasts
Teschke, H. The appeasement
Youngblood, S. There are many houses in my tribe

3 characters

c Haylock, D. Guardian Angels
c Price, J. W. and Becker, C. Legend of the lake
Taylor, R. Love poem #98

4 characters

Dashow, K. Joey-Boy
Kral, B. From the life of the bog people
LeFevre, A. Americansaint

5 characters

Campton, D. Permission to cry
c Martin, J. I won't take a bath!
Wasserman, E. H. Outlaws

5 characters and extras

Maguire, M. The tower

6 characters

c Haylock, D. How to be an alien
c Haylock, D. The Wallies guide to Christmas
Larson, L. and Lee, L. Some things you need to know before the world ends (a final evening with the illuminati)
c Martin, J. Big burger
Orloff, R. The whole shebang
c Price, J. W. and Becker, C. Legend of the lake
Silver, N. Fat men in skirts

7 characters

y Bush, M. Aalmauria: Voyage of the dragonfly
c Bush, M. Rapunzel
Durang, C. The Book of Leviticus Show
Hornby, I. Situation vacant
c Pollock, S. Prairie dragons
c Price, J. W. Dora and the Pheelguds from the future
Roth, A. Born guilty
Santeiro, L. A royal affair
c Simmons, D. W. Nutricia Goodheart's Body Building Construction Company
c Warburton, N. Round the world with class six
c Watts, I. K. Goodbye Marianne
Wylie, B. J. The old woman and the pedlar

7 characters and extras

y Horitz, T. Good King Wenceslas and the Chancellor of Bohemia

8 characters

y Enright, N. A property of the clan
Gordon, P. Generations apart
c Haylock, D. Christian olympics
Koch, K. K. A heroine of the Greek resistance
c Snipes, L. E. Jack and the wonder beans

8 characters and extras

Nascimento, A. do. Sortilege II: Zumbi returns
c Petersen, C. A. If angels were mortal . . .
c Winther, B. The dreadful dragon of Utrecht

9 characters

Daniels, S. Head-rot holiday
Teagarden, J. Birds
Weller, M. Dogbrain

9 characters and extras

y Fuson, D. Clippings

10 characters

Abe, K. Involuntary homicide
y Aston, M. Fossils!
c Barnieh, Z. A nest of dragons
c DeFelice, J. The merchants of Dazu
c Foxton, D. The real story of Puss in boots
c Haylock, D. Don't care, won't care, couldn't care less
y Levi, S. Good morning Miss Vickers
y Welsh, D. Mellow drama

10 characters and extras

y Majeski, B. A flutter of lace

11 characters

y Boiko, C. Escape to the blue planet
Durang, C. The nature and purpose of the universe
Kilroy, T. Double cross
y Miller, K. S. Red badge of courage
Nowra, L. The incorruptible
Reid, C. Did you hear the one about the Irishman . . . ?

11 characters and extras

c Boiko, C. Persephone
c Jackson, K. Laffin' school reunion
c Poskitt, K. The Rumpelstiltskin racket
y Ursell, G. The park

12 characters

c Bush, M. Puss in boots

VARIABLE CAST—*Continued*

y Levi, S. Merry Christmas Miss Vickers
c Mikkelsen, J. Resolution revolution
Shawn, W. Aunt Dan and Lemon
c Stanford, J. Snow White—the purdiest gal in the West
y Suntep Theatre. Wheel of justice
c Werner, S. The king's bean soup
y Zeder, S. L. The death and life of Sherlock Holmes

12 characters and extras

c Castle, G. V. Recess!
c Harris, A. Young Black Beauty
c Pound, S. R. The Angels' greatest message

13 characters

Aba, N. Such great hope
c Lee, C. K. Journey to the West
McNally, T. Hidden agendas
y Sod, T. and Grant, S. Three wishes

13 characters and extras

c Anderson, J. The animals' Christmas
c Mast, E. and Bensinger, L. Dinosaurus

14 characters

Elitzig, F. Seagirl
c Sachar, L. There's a boy in the girls' bathroom
c Peterson, L. The wind in the willows
Vago, S. M. Connie & Sabrina in waiting

15 characters

Chinn, J. Albert make us laugh
c Jackson, D. No one will marry a princess with a tree growing out of her head!
y Parker, R. Under the influence
Reddin, K. The innocents' crusade

15 characters and extras

c Harder, E. Hey ho, Pinocchio
c Liebert, B. A terrible tale of a dreaded dragon

16 characters

Gallaire, F. You have come back
c Harris, A. Peter Rabbit and me
y Kelly, T. Bang! Bang! You're dead
c Love, D. Holiday in the rain forest
y St. John, B. Dogsbreath Devereaux, the dastardly doctor
c Wing, P. A. Naomi's road

16 characters and extras

Feuer, J. Eating Raoul
c Santiago, H. The day they stole all the colors
c Younghusband, C. Only a game

17 characters

c Bush, M. The boy who left home to find out about the shivers
c McCullough, L. E. Vinegar Pete's calico whisker pie
Morton, C. The savior

17 characters and extras

Havel, V. Tomorrow!

18 characters

Morton, C. Pancho Diablo
Townsend, S. The secret diary of Adrian Mole aged $13\frac{3}{4}$

18 characters and extras

c Wood, D. Noddy

19 characters

Nowra, L. The temple

19 characters and extras

c Lloyd, R. Treasure Island, the panto

20 characters

Anderson, J.-S. Tyndale's dream
c Conville, D. and Gooderson, D. The curse of the Egyptian mummy
c Evans, L. Gran
Shamas, L. Portrait of a nude

20 characters and extras

y Kelly, T. Trouble in Tumbleweed
Rose, R. and Kugler, D. D. Newhouse

21 characters

White, P. Shepherd on the rocks

21 characters and extras

c Morris, V. Thumbelina

22 characters

y Lewton, R. An alien stole my skateboard
Wertenbaker, T. Our country's good
Willmott, K. and Averill, R. T-Money & Wolf

22 characters and extras

c Wood, D. The witches

23 characters

Foxton, D. Kenneth
y Francoeur, B. The internal teen machine

24 characters and extras

y Clark, R. J. Fighting for myself

25 characters

House, R. and Shearman, A. The scandalous adventures of Sir Toby Trollope
c Loomer, L. Bocón
c Love, D. Blame it on the wolf

25 characters and extras

Buzo, A. Pacific Union

VARIABLE CAST—*Continued*

Larson, L. and Lee, E. L. The salvation of Iggy Scrooge

26 characters

Pickering, K. The parting of friends

26 characters and extras

c Dawson, J. and Bass, P. The inside story

27 characters

Courts, R. Jack's holiday
c Love, D. Kabuki gift
Morris, M. Two weeks with the Queen

28 characters

c Love, D. Be kind to your Mother (Earth)

29 characters

y Russell, W. Our day out

30 characters

Barker, H. Wounds to the face

30 characters and extras

y Francoeur, B. Shakespeare comes to Calamity Creek
Johanson, R. Charles Dickens' great expectations

31 characters

Mann, E. Greensboro

32 characters and extras

y Kelly, T. Ditch Day

33 characters

Schnupp, A. The Harper chronicles

35 characters

Bell, N. On the bum
c Ravel, A. Tales from the shtetl: the Sholom Aleichem show

38 characters

y Smith, R. Nothing but the truth

38 characters and extras

c Scanlan, M. Give and take

41 characters

c Roca, M. Pinocchio

42 characters

c Cole, J. D. Conestoga stories
c Neuman, C. Lion and mouse stories

43 characters and extras

c Robinette, J. The adventures of Peter Rabbit and his friends

58 characters

c Kase-Polisini, J. Southern fried cracker tales

Part III

List of Collections Indexed

This is an author-title list of play collections, plays issued or bound together, and composite works containing plays. Separately published plays are described in Part I.

3 plays. Crowley, M.

4 new plays. Foote, H.

4 short plays. Wilson, L.

5 plays 5. Schevill, J.

6 award winning plays. Beim, N.

15 short plays. McNally, T.

20/20: twenty one-act plays from twenty years of the Humana Festival; edited by Michele Volansky and Michael Bigelow Dixon; foreword by Jon Jory. Smith & Kraus 1995 374p (Contemporary playwrights series)
ISBN 1-880399-98-9 LC 95-45877

27 short plays. Durang, C.

A

Abe, Kōbō
Three plays; translated and with an introduction by Donald Keene. Columbia Univ. Press 1993 233p
ISBN 0-231-08280-0 LC 93-36358

Absolutely fabulous. Saunders, J.

Act One '95; the complete plays; edited by Marisa Smith; foreword by Risa Bramon Garcia and Jerry Levine. Smith & Kraus 1996 278p (Contemporary playwrights series)
ISBN 1-880339-97-0

Volume for 1994 entered under Showtime's Act One Festival of one-act plays, 1994

The **Actor's** book of gay and lesbian plays; edited by Eric Lane and Nina Shengold. Penguin Bks. 1995 544p
ISBN 0-14-024552-9 LC 95-339

Actors Theatre of Louisville
20/20: twenty one-act plays from twenty years of the Humana Festival. See 20/20: twenty one-act plays from twenty years of the Humana Festival
By Southern playwrights. See By Southern playwrights
A Decade of new comedy. See A Decade of new comedy
Humana Festival . . . See Humana Festival . . .
Ten-minute plays: v3; from Actors Theatre of Louisville; edited by Michael Bigelow Dixon and Michele Volansky with a foreword by Jon Jory. French 1995 259p
ISBN 0-573-62602-2 LC 95-223620
Earlier volumes entered in previous volumes of Play Index

Adventures for (big) girls; seven radio plays; edited by Ann Jansen. Blizzard Pub. 1993 xx, 172p
ISBN 0-921368-32-1 LC 94-125822

Agora. Warner, F.

Alcestis and other plays. Euripides

Alexander, Robert
(ed.) Colored contradictions: an anthology of contemporary African-American plays. See Colored contradictions: an anthology of contemporary African-American plays

All in one universe. Anderson, P.

All in the timing: fourteen plays. Ives, D.

All in the timing: six one-act comedies. Ives, D.

Allen, Richard James
What to name your baby. Paper Bark Press in association with Tasdance 1995 40p
ISBN 0-646-23747-0
Contents: What to name your baby; Blue cities

Allen, Roger
(ed.) Modern Arabic drama. See Modern Arabic drama

Alternate roots; plays from the Southern theater; edited by Kathie DeNobriga and Valetta Anderson. Heinemann 1994 340p
ISBN 0-435-08632-4

The **America** play and other works. Parks, S.-L.

Andersen, Hans Christian, 1951-
(ed.) New Danish plays. See New Danish plays

Anderson, Poul
All in one universe. TOR Bks. 1996 304p
ISBN 0-312-85873-6 LC 95-39773
"A Tom Doherty Associates book"
Analyzed for play only

Anderson, Valetta
(ed.) Alternate roots. See Alternate roots

Andre's mother and other short plays. McNally, T.

Ansky, S.
The dybbuk and other writings; edited and with an introduction by David G. Roskies; translations by Golda Werman. Schocken Bks. 1996 c1992 220p (Library of Yiddish classics)
ISBN 0-8052-1070-9 LC 91-52619
Analyzed for play only

Anthology of contemporary Austrian folk plays by Veza Canetti [et al.]; translated and with an afterword by Richard Dixon. Ariadne Press 1993 397p (Studies in Austrian literature, culture, and thought. Translation series)
ISBN 0-929497-67-8 LC 93-18742

An **Anthology** of Russian literature; from earliest writings to modern fiction; introduction to a culture; edited by Nicholas Rzhevsky. Sharpe, M. E. 1996 587p
ISBN 1-56324-421-7 LC 95-42684

Antush, John V.
(ed.) Nuestro New York. See Nuestro New York

¡Aplauso! Hispanic children's theater; edited by Joe Rosenberg. Piñata Bks. 1995 274p
ISBN 1-55885-136-4 LC 94-36005
Partially analyzed

Approaching Zanzibar and other plays. Howe, T.

April Bright & Blinded by the light. Bolger, D.

Aristophanes
Plays; introduced by Michael Walton; translated and introduced by Kenneth McLeish. Methuen 1993 2v (Methuen world classics)
ISBN v1 0-413-66900-9; v2 0-413-66910-6
Contents: Plays: one: Acharnians; Knights; Peace; Lysistrata
Plays: two: Wasps; Clouds; Birds; Festival time (Thesmophoriazousai); Frogs

Arms and the man and John Bull's other island. Shaw, B.

Armstrong, W. A.
(ed.) The Playboy of the Western World and two other Irish plays. See The Playboy of the Western World and two other Irish plays

Around the world in 21 plays; theatre for young audiences; edited by Lowell Swortzell. Applause 1996 690p
ISBN 1-55783-263-3 LC 96-30499

The **art** of success & In the ruins. Dear, N.

Asian American drama: 9 plays from the multiethnic landscape; edited by Brian Nelson. Applause 1997 421p
ISBN 1-55783-314-1 LC 97-27054

At the roots of the stars: the short plays. Barnes, D.

Auden, W. H.
Libretti, and other dramatic writings by W. H. Auden, 1939-1973; edited by Edward Mendelson. Princeton Univ. Press. 1993 xxxvi, 755p (Complete works of W. H. Auden)
ISBN 0-691-03301-3 LC 92-18681
At head of title: W. H. Auden and Chester Kallman
Partially analyzed

Australian gay and lesbian plays; edited by Bruce Parr. Currency Press 1996 384p
ISBN 0-86819-455-7

Awake and singing: 7 classical plays from the American Jewish repertoire; edited and with an introduction by Ellen Schiff. Mentor 1995 636p
ISBN 0-451-62869-1 LC 94-77538

Award winning plays v2. Acetylene, by Erik Ramsey [and] Harriet, by Kisha Kenyatta. French 1995 50p
ISBN 0-573-62600-6
"Co-winners, American College Theatre Festival Short Play Award program"

Ayckbourn, Alan
Plays: one; introduced by the author. Faber & Faber 1995 562p (Contemporary classics)
ISBN 0-571-17680-1
Contents: A chorus of disapproval; A small family business; Henceforward ... ; Man of the moment

B

Babes and brides. Berlin, E.

The **bad** infinity. Wellman, M.

Baitz, Jon Robin
The substance of fire and other plays. Theatre Communications Group 1993 172p
ISBN 1-55936-052-6 LC 92-16985
Three hotels: plays and monologues. Theatre Communications Group 1994 85p
ISBN 1-55936-085-2 LC 93-51492

Baker, Edward Allan
A dead man's apartment; Rosemary with Ginger; Face divided; three plays. Dramatists 1996 83p
ISBN 0-8222-1513-6

The **bald** trilogy. Campbell K.

Balderston, John L. See Deane, H., jt. auth.

Balkan blues: writing out of Yugoslavia; edited by Joanna Labon. Northwestern Univ. Press 1995 268p
ISBN 0-8010-1325-2
Analyzed for play only

Ball, Alan
Five one-act plays. Dramatists 1994 110p
LC 94-163126
Contents: Made for a woman; Bachelor holidays; Power lunch; The M word; Your mother's butt

The **Baltimore** waltz and other plays. Vogel, P.

Barker, Clive
Forms of heaven; three plays. HarperPrism 1996 378p
ISBN 0-06-105270-1 LC 96-31921
Incarnations; three plays. HarperPrism 1995 366p
ISBN 0-06-105244-2 LC 96-37118

Barker, Harley Granville-. See Granville-Barker, Harley

Barker, Howard
Collected plays v2-3. Calder, J./Riverrun Press 1993-1996 2v
ISBN v2 0-7145-4182-6; v3 0-7145-4279-2 LC 88-36769
Contents: v2 The love of a good man; The possibilities; Brutopia; Rome; Uncle Vanya; Ten dilemmas
v3 The power of the dog; The Europeans; Women beware women; Minna; Judith; Ego in Arcadia

Barker, Howard—*Continued*

Hated nightfall [and] Wounds to the face. Calder, J./Riverrun Press 1994 80p (Playscript 120)

ISBN-0-7145-4270-0 LC 93-42638

Barlow, Judith E.

(ed.) Plays by American women, 1930-1960. See Plays by American women, 1930-1960

Barnes, Djuna

At the roots of the stars: the short plays; edited and with an introduction by Douglas Messerli. Sun & Moon Press 1995 190p (Sun & Moon classics 53)

ISBN 1-55713-160-0 LC 95-36297

Barnes, Peter

Corpsing; four one-act plays. French (London) 1996 58p

ISBN 0-573-100006-3

Contents: Humour helps; Waiting for a bus; Acting exercise; Last things

Plays. Methuen 1996 3v (Methuen world dramatists)

ISBN v1 0-413-62180-4; v2 0-413-68030-4; v3 0-413-69980-3

Plays: one first published 1989

Contents Plays: one: The ruling class; Leonardo's Last Supper; Noonday demons; The bewitched; Laughter!; Barnes' people: eight monologues

Plays: two: Red noses; The spirit of man; Nobody here but us chickens; Sunsets and glories; Bye bye Columbus

Plays: three: Clap hands here comes Charlie; Heaven's blessings; Revolutionary witness

Barry, Sebastian

The only true history of Lizzie Finn; The steward of Christendom; White Woman Street; three plays. Methuen 1995 181p (Methuen modern plays)

ISBN 0-413-69890-4

Plays: 1; introduced by Fintan O'Toole with a preface by the author. Methuen 1997 301p (Methuen contemporary dramatists)

ISBN 0-413-71120-X

Contents: Boss Grady's boys; Prayers of Sherkin; White Woman Street; The only true history of Lizzie Finn; The steward of Christendom

Basso, Eric

The Golem triptych; a dramatic trilogy by Eric Basso; with incidental music composed & arranged by the author. Asylum Arts 1994 372p

ISBN 1-878580-15-9 LC 93-70300

Be kind to your Mother (Earth) and Blame it on the wolf. Love, D.

Beaumont, Francis, and Fletcher, John, 1579-1625

The dramatic works in the Beaumont and Fletcher canon. General editor: Fredson Bowers. Cambridge Univ. Press 1994-1996 2v

ISBN v9 0-521-36188-5; v10 0-521-36189-3 LC 66-74421

Earlier volumes entered in previous volumes of Play Index

Contents: v9: The sea voyage; The double marriage; The prophetess; The little French lawyer; The elder brother; The maid in the mill

v10: The honest man's fortune; Rollo, Duke of Normandy; The Spanish curate; The lover's progress; The fair maid of the inn

Behn, Aphra

The rover; The feigned courtesans; The lucky chance; The emperor of the moon; edited with an introduction by Jane Spencer. Oxford 1995 400p (World's classics)

ISBN 0-19-282248-9 LC 95-5205

Beim, Norman

Six award winning plays. Newconcept Press 1995 251p

ISBN 0-931231-06-X LC 94-40724

Contents: On a darkling plain; Shakespeare revisited; Dreams; Inside; Jewel thieves!; The deserter

Bennett, Alan

Plays: one; introduced by the author. Faber & Faber 1996 333p (Contemporary classics)

ISBN 0-571-17745-X

Contents: Forty years on; Getting on; Habeas corpus; Enjoy

Berkoff, Steven

The collected plays v1-2. Faber & Faber 1994 2v

ISBN v1 0-571-16903-1; v2 0-571-17102-8

Contents: v1 East; West; Greek; Sink the Belgrano!; Massage; Lunch

v2 Decadence; Kvetch; Acapulco; Harry's Christmas; Brighton beach scumbags; Dahling you were marvellous; Dog; Actor

Berlin, Eric

Babes and brides: two one-act plays. French 1993 121p

ISBN 0-573-62103-9

Best American plays: 9th series, 1983-1992; edited by Clive Barnes; introduction by Clive Barnes; biographical introductions by Lori Weinless. Crown 1993 526p

ISBN 0-517-57452-7 LC 57-12830

Earlier volumes in this series entered in previous volumes of Play Index

Contents: Brighton Beach memoirs, by N. Simon; Painting Churches, by T. Howe; Glengarry Glen Ross, by D. Mamet; End of the world, by A. Kopit; Hurlyburly, by D. Rabe; As is, by W. M. Hoffman; I'm not Rappaport, by H. Gardner; The widow Claire, by H. Foote; Burn this, by L. Wilson; Into the woods, by S. Sondheim and J. Lapine; Frankie and Johnny in the Clair de Lune, by T. McNally; Joe Turner's come and gone, by A. Wilson; The cocktail hour, by A. R. Gurney; Spoils of war, by M. Weller; Other people's money: the ultimate seduction, by J. Sterner; Driving Miss Daisy, by A. Uhry

The **Best** American short plays, 1992/1993-1995/1996; edited by Howard Stein and Glenn Young. Applause 1993-1997 4v

ISBN 0067-6284

Earlier volumes entered in previous volumes of Play Index

Contents: 1992-1993: Little Red Riding Hood, by B. Aronson; The Tack Room, by R. Arzoomanian; Show, by V. Bumbalo; A couple with a cat, by T. Connor; Bondage, by D. H. Hwang; Jolly, by D. Mamet; Pitching to the star, by D. Margulies; It's our town, too, by S. Miller; The drowning of Manhattan, by J. F. Noonan; Aryan birth, by E. Page; The cowboy, the Indian and the fervent feminist, by M. Schisgal; Dreamers, by S. Silverstein; The sausage eaters, by S. Starosta; Watermelon rinds, by R. Taylor; The Valentine Fairy, by E. Thompson; Night baseball, by G. Tissian

1993-1994: Window of opportunity, by J. Augustine; Barry, Betty, and Bill, by R. Taylor and J. Bologna; Come down burning, by K. Corthron; For whom the southern belle tolls, by C. Durang; The universal language, by D. Ives; The midlife crisis of Dionysus, by G. Keillor; The magenta shift, by C. K. Mack; My left breast, by S. Miller; The interview, by J. C. Oates; Tall tales from the Kentucky cycle, by R. Schenkkan; Blue stars, by S. Spencer; An act of devotion, by D. Tannen; Zipless, by E. Thompson; Date with a stranger, by C. Vogelstein

1994-1995: A stye of the eye, by C. Durang; Buck simple, by C. Fols; Two mens'es daughter, by J. E. Franklin; An interview, by D. Mamet; WASP, by S. Martin; Hot line, by E. May; Life support, by M. Mitchell; The whole shebang, by R. Orloff; Dear

The **Best** American short plays, 1992/1993-1995/1996—*Continued*

Kenneth Blake, by J. Reingold; The cannibal masque, by R. Ribman; The artist and the model, by M. Schisgal; The spelling of Coynes, by J. Tasca; The wreck on the five-twenty-five, by T. Wilder; Lot: 13 the bone violin, by D. Wright

1995-1996: Fitting rooms, by S. Cinoman; Scribe's paradox, by M. Feingold; Home section, by J. Glowacki; Degas c'est moi, by D. Ives; The St. Valentine's Day massacre, by A. Knee; Old blues, by J. Levy; Dearborn Heights, by C. Medley; American dreamers, by L. Mueller; When it comes early, by J. F. Noonan; The original Last Wish Baby, by W. Seebring; The mystery school, by P. Selig; The sandalwood box, by M. Wellman

The **Best** of Off-Broadway, eight contemporary Obie-winning plays; edited and with an introduction by Ross Wetzsteon. Mentor 1994 441p

ISBN 0-451-62865-9 LC 93-79101

The **Best** plays of 1992-1993/1996-1997; edited by Otis L. Guernsey, Jr. and Jeffrey Sweet; illustrated with photographs and with drawings by Hirschfeld. Limelight Eds. 1993-1997 5v illus

"The Otis Guernsey Burns Mantle Theater yearbook"

Earlier volume entered in previous volumes of Play Index. Analyzed for condensed versions of plays only

Contents: 1992-1993: The destiny of me, by L. Kramer; The sisters Rosensweig, by W. Wasserstein; Oleana, by D. Mamet; Joined at the head, by C. Butterfield; Jeffrey, by P. Rudnick; Wings, by J. Lunden; Kiss of the spider woman, by J. Kander; Angels in America: Millenium approaches, by T. Kushner; Later life, by A. R. Gurney

1993-1994: A perfect Ganesh, by T. McNally; The madness of George III, by A. Bennett; The Kentucky cycle, by R. Schenkkan; Laughter on the 23rd floor, by N. Simon; Angels in America: part II: Perestroika, by T. Kushner; All in the timing, by D. Ives; Three tall women, by E. Albee; Twilight: Los Angeles, 1992, by A. D. Smith; Passion, by S. Sondheim; SubUrbia, by E. Bogosian; American enterprise, by J. Sweet

1994-1995; Love! Valour! Compassion! by T. McNally; Sunset Boulevard, by A. L. Webber; Hapgood, by T. Stoppard; ATuna Christmas, by J. Williams; J. Sears, and E. Howards; The young man from Atlanta, by H. Foote; Camping with Henry & Tom, by M. St. Germain; After-play, by A. Meara; Arcadia, by T. Stoppard; The cryptogram, by D. Mamet; Night and her stars, by R. Greenberg

1995-1996: Mrs. Klein, by N. Wright; Master class, by T. McNally; New England, by R. Nelson; Valley song, by A. Fugard; Molly Sweeney, by B. Friel; Rent, by J. Larson; A fair country, by J. R. Baitz; Seven guitars, by A. Wilson; The skriker, by C. Churchill; Curtains, by S. Bill

1996-1997: Old wicked songs, by J. Marans; Skylight, by D. Hare; The last night of Ballyhoo, by A. Uhry; Violet, by J. Tesori; Titanic, by M. Yeston; How I learned to drive, by P. Vogel

Big Al and My side of the story. Goluboff, B.

The **Big** book of dramatized classics; 25 adaptations of favorite novels, stories, and plays for stage and round-the-table reading; edited by Sylvia E. Kamerman. Plays, Inc. 1993 388p

ISBN 0-8238-0299-X LC 93-3387

The **Big** book of large-cast plays; 27 one-act plays for young actors; edited by Sylvia E. Kamerman. Plays, Inc. 1994 351p

ISBN 0-8238-0302-3 LC 94-32725

The **Big** book of skits; 36 short plays for young actors; edited by Sylvia E. Kamerman. Plays, Inc. 1996 263p

ISBN 0-8238-0304-X LC 95-48020

Big-time women from way back when. Playwrights Canada 1993 236p

ISBN 0-88754-493-2

A **bit** of three-by-one. Wise, R.

Black comedy: nine plays; a critical anthology; with interviews and essays edited by Pamela Faith Jackson and Karimah. Applause 1997 499p

ISBN 1-55783-278-1 LC 97-9500

Black drama in America: an anthology; edited and with an introduction by Darwin T. Turner. 2nd ed. Howard Univ. Press 1994 xxxvi, 736p

ISBN 0-88258-062-0 LC 92-42322

Black plays: three; selected and introduced by Yvonne Brewster. Methuen 1995 280p (Methuen new theatrescripts)

ISBN 0-413-69130-6

Contents: Boy with beer, by P. Boakye; Munda negra, by B. Greer; Scrape off the black, by T. Ikoli; Talking in tongues, by W. Pinnock; A Jamaican airman foresees his death, by F. D'Aguiar

Black theatre USA [v1-2]; plays by African Americans; edited by James V. Hatch and Ted Shine. Rev. and expanded ed. Free Press 1996 2v

ISBN v1 0-684-082306-3; v2 0-684-82307-1 LC 95-40329

Partially analyzed

Contents: [v1] The early period, 1847-1938; [v2] The recent period, 1935-today

Blanc, Esther Silverstein

Wars I have seen; the play, in three acts with selected short stories. Volcano Press 1996 126p

ISBN 0-912078-80-4 LC 93-060727

Analyzed for play only

Blasted & Phaedra's love. Kane, S.

Blessing, Lee

Patient A and other plays; five plays. Heinemann 1995 255p

ISBN 0-435-08662-6 LC 95-2412

Contents: Two rooms; Down the road; Fortinbras; Lake Street extension; Patient A

Blinded by the sun & Sweet panic. Poliakoff, S.

Blood wedding and Yerma. Garcia Lorca, F.

Blue heart. Churchill, C.

Blue remembered hills and other plays. Potter, D.

A **body** of water. Zark, J.

Bogosian, Eric

The essential Bogosian: Talk radio, Drinking in America, Funhouse, & Men inside. Theatre Communications Group 1994 228p

ISBN 1-55936-082-8 LC 93-51493

Bolger, Dermot

April Bright & Blinded by the light; two plays. New Island Bks./Hern Bks. 1997 205p

ISBN 1-874597-59-6

(ed.) Greatest hits: four Irish one-act plays. See Greatest hits: four Irish one-act plays

Bologna, Joseph See Taylor, R. jt. auth.

Bond, Edward
Plays: 5. Methuen Drama 1995 428p (Methuen contemporary dramatists)
ISBN 0-413-70390-8
Contents: Human cannon; The bundle; Jackets; In the company of men

Bondagers & The straw chair. Glover, S.

A **book** of travelling shows. Davis, R.

Branch, William B.
(ed.) Crosswinds. See Crosswinds

Bray, Errol
(ed.) Young playwrights. See Young playwrights

Brewster, Yvonne
(ed.) Black plays: three. See Black plays: three

Brooker, Blake
Ilsa, queen of the Nazi love camp and other plays; edited by Joyce Doolittle. RDC Press 1993 179p
ISBN 0-88995-105-5 LC 93-17565

Brown, Ian
(ed.) Made in Scotland. See Made in Scotland

Brownbread and War. Doyle, R.

The **Browning** version and Harlequinade. Rattigan, T.

Bruises & The shorewatchers' house. Upton, J.

Büchner, Georg
Complete plays, Lenz and other writings; translated with an introduction and notes by John Reddick. Penguin Bks. 1993 306p
ISBN 0-14-044586-2
Analyzed for plays only

A **bucket** of eels & The modern husband. Godfrey, P.

Burns, Kitty
If God wanted us to fly he would have given us wings! French 1996 91p
ISBN 0-573-66030-1

Bush, Max
Plays for young audiences; featuring The emerald circle and other plays; edited by Roger Ellis. Meriwether 1995 383p
ISBN 1-56608-011-8 LC 95-2382

Bush Theatre plays; preface by Terry Johnson; introduced by Dominic Dromgoole. Faber & Faber 1996 345p
ISBN 0-571-17813-8
Contents: Keyboard skills, by L. Bruce; Boys mean business, by C. Johnson; Two lips indifferent red, by T. Oglesby; One flea spare, by N. Wallace

But still, like air, I'll rise; new Asian American plays; edited by Velina Hasu Houston; foreword by Roberta Uno. Temple Univ. Press 1997 520p (Asian American history and culture)
ISBN 1-56639-537-2 LC 96-48729

Butterfield, Catherine
Life in the trees. French 1995 94p
ISBN 0-573-69527-X

Buzo, Alex
Norm & Ahmed and other plays. Currency Press 1993 140p
ISBN 0-86819-007-1

By Southern playwrights; plays from Actors Theatre of Louisville; Michael Bigelow Dixon and Michele Volansky, editors; foreword by Jon Jory. Univ. Press of Ky. 1996 240p
ISBN 0-8131-1967-1 LC 95-42493

By the sea, by the sea, by the beautiful sea, by Joe Pintauro, Lanford Wilson and Terrence McNally. Dramatists 1996 70p
ISBN 0-8222-1507-1 LC 162424

Bynum, R. Cary
Six short plays. St. Johann Press 1993 177p
ISBN 1-878282-12-3 LC 93-29396

C

Campanile, Achille
The inventor of the horse and two other short plays; translated and with an introduction by Francesco Loriggio. Guernica 1995 117p (Drama series 7)
ISBN 0-920717-07-7 LC 94-75323

Campbell, Ken
The bald trilogy; with drawings by Eve Stewart. Methuen 1995 298p
ISBN 0-413-69080-6
Contents: The recollections of a furtive nudist; Pigspurt; Jamais vu

Canetti, Veza
Anthology of contemporary Austrian folk plays. See Anthology of contemporary Austrian folk plays

Carilli, Theresa
Women as lovers (two plays). Guernica 1996 269p (Drama series 11)
ISBN 1-55071-007-9 LC 93-81345

Carley, Dave
Taking liberties & Into. Playwrights Canada 1993 95p
ISBN 0-88754-512-2

Carlo Goldoni's Villeggiatura trilogy. Goldoni, C.

Carter Harrison, Paul. See Harrison, Paul Carter

Cartwright, Jim
Plays: 1. Methuen 1996 269p (Methuen contemporary dramatists)
ISBN 0-413-70230-8
Contents: Road; Bed; Two; The rise and fall of Little Voice
Two & Bed. Methuen 1994 81p (Methuen modern plays)
ISBN 0-413-68330-3

Chayefsky, Paddy
The stage plays. Applause 1994 438p (Collected works of Paddy Chayefsky)
ISBN 1-55783-192-0 LC 94-23040
The television plays. Applause 1994 277p (Collected works of Paddy Chayefsky)
ISBN 1-55783-191-2 LC 94-185485

Chekhov, Anton
Chekhov: four plays; translated by Carol Rocamora. Smith & Kraus 1996 239p (Great translations series)
ISBN 1-57525-065-9 LC 96-36228
Chekhov: the major plays; English versions by Jean-Claude van Itallie. Applause 1995 204p
ISBN 1-55783-162-9 LC 94-27070
Chekhov's major plays. Univ. Press of America 1996 328p
ISBN 0-7618-0564-8 LC 96-43305
The plays of Anton Chekhov; a new translation by Paul Schmidt. HarperCollins Pubs. 1997 387p
ISBN 0-06-018705-0 LC 96-42456
Uncle Vanya and other plays; translated by Betsy Hulick. Bantam Bks. 1994 408p (A Bantam classic)
ISBN 0-553-21427-6

Chekhov: four plays. Chekhov, A.

Chekhov: the major plays. Chekhov, A.

Chekhov's major plays. Chekhov, A.

Chocrón, Isaac
Three plays by Isaac Chocrón; translation and critical study by Barbara Younoszai and Rossi Irausquin-Johnson; with a foreword by Isaac Chocrón. Lang, P. 1995 234p (Taft Memorial Fund and University of Cincinnati studies in Latin American, Chicano, and U.S. Latin theater v4)
ISBN 0-8204-2320-3 LC 94-17357

Christmas plays for young audiences. Clark I. E. 1994 52p ('Stage magic' play)
ISBN 0-88680-391-8

Churchill, Caryl
Blue heart. Hern Bks. 1997 69p
ISBN 1-85459-327-7

Classic plays from the Negro Ensemble Company; Paul Carter Harrison & Gus Edwards, editors. Univ. of Pittsburgh Press 1995 594p
ISBN 0-8229-3882-0 LC 95-3825

Clum, John M.
(ed.) Staging gay lives. See Staging gay lives

Collected plays. White, P.

The **collected** plays v1-2. Berkoff, S.

Collected plays v2. Foote, H.

Collected plays v2. McNally, T.

Collected plays v2. Williamson, D.

Collected plays v2, 1974-1983. Gurney, A. R.

Collected plays v2-3. Barker, H.

Collected plays, 1965-1970. Wilson, L.

Collected plays, 1980-1995. Martin, J.

The **collected** plays of Ronald Harwood. Harwood, R.

The **collected** poems and plays. Tagore, R.

Collected poems, prose, & plays. Frost, R.

The **collected** short plays of Thornton Wilder v1. Wilder, T.

Collected stories. Kipling, R.

Colored contradictions: an anthology of contemporary African-American plays; edited by Harry J. Elam, Jr. and Robert Alexander. Plume Bks. 1996 643p

ISBN 0-452-27497-4 LC 96-15948

Coming on strong: new writing from the Royal Court Theatre; preface by Stephen Daldry; introduction by Dominic Tickell. Faber & Faber 1995 280p

ISBN 0-571-17678-X

Contents: Peaches, by N. Grosso; The knocky, by M. Wynne; Essex girls, by R. Prichard; Corner boys, by K. Coyle

Complete full-length plays, 1975-1995. Durang C.

The **complete** Oscar Wilde. Wilde, O.

Complete plays. Firbank, R.

Complete plays, Lenz and other writings. Büchner, G.

Congdon, Constance

Tales of the lost Formicans and other plays. Theatre Communications Group 1994 297p

ISBN 1-55936-083-6 LC 93-51495

Contemporary plays by women of color; an anthology; edited by Kathy A. Perkins and Roberta Uno. Routledge 1996 322p

ISBN 0-415-11377-8 LC 95-07465

Corpsing. Barnes, P.

The **Countess** cycle. Sloate, D.

Cox, Jeffrey N.

(ed.) Seven Gothic dramas, 1789-1825. See Seven Gothic dramas, 1789–1825

Cross country. Milligan, J.

Crossroads and other plays. Solórzano, C.

Crosswinds: an anthology of black dramatists in the diaspora; edited and with an introduction by William B. Branch. Indiana Univ. Press 1993 416p (Blacks in the diaspora)

ISBN 0-253-31260-4 LC 92-26648

Crowley, Mart

3 plays. Alyson Publs. 1996 350p

ISBN 1-55583-357-8 LC 96-13206

Contents: The boys in the band; A breeze from the gulf; For reasons that remain unclear

The ***CTR*** anthology; fifteen plays from Canadian Theatre Review; edited by Alan Filewod. Univ. of Toronto Press 1993 xx, 683p

ISBN 0-8020-6812-X

Curran, Colleen

(ed.) Escape acts. See Escape acts

Cyclops; Alcestis; Medea. Euripides

Czech plays; modern Czech drama; selected and introduced by Barbara Day. Hern Bks. 1994 224p (International collection)
ISBN 1-85459-074-X LC 94-127607

D

The **dadshuttle** and Down the shore. Donaghy, T.

Daniels, Sarah
Plays: two; introduced by the author. Methuen 1994 338p (Methuen world classics)
ISBN 0-413-69040-7 LC 95-199175
Contents: The gut girls; Beside herself; Head-rot holiday; The madness of Esme and Shaz

Dashow, Ken
Da-show must go on; (six plays about love, death, and bad acting). Dramatists 1996 144p
ISBN 0-8222-1535-7

Da-show must go on. Dashow, K.

Davies, Robertson
Fortune, my foe & Eros at breakfast; two plays. Simon & Pierre 1993 126p
ISBN 0-88924-241-0

Davis, Russell
A book of travelling shows; two short plays for a general audience. Bakers Plays 1995 81p
LC 96-137225

The **Dazzling** dark: new Irish plays; selected and introduced by Frank McGuinness. Faber & Faber 1996 311p
ISBN 0-571-17770-0
Contents: Danti-Dan, by G. Moxley; A picture of paradise, by J. Murphy; Good evening, Mr Collins, by T. Mac Intyre; Portia Coughlan, by M. Carr

A **dead** man's apartment; Rosemary with Ginger; Face divided. Baker, E. A.

Dean, Philip Hayes
Moloch blues. Dramatists 1996 68p
ISBN 0-8222-1514-4
Contents: The owl killer; Dink's blues

Deane, Hamilton, and Balderston, John L.
Dracula; the ultimate, illustrated edition of the world-famous vampire play; edited and annotated by David J. Skal. St. Martins Press 1993 151p
ISBN 0-312-09278-4 LC 92-44421
Contents: Dracula (1924) by H. Deane; Dracula: the vampire play (1927) by H. Deane and J. L. Balderston

Dear, Nick
The art of success & In the ruins. Rev. ed. Methuen 1994 99p (Methuen modern plays)
ISBN 0-413-68230-7

Death defying acts; 3 one-act comedies. French 1996 125p
ISBN 0-573-69539-3

Contents: An interview, by D. Mamet; Hotline, by E. May; Central Park West, by W. Allen

A **Decade** of new comedy; plays from the Humana Festival v1-2; edited by Michael Bigelow Dixon and Michele Volansky; foreword by Jon Jory; introduction by Wendy Wasserstein. Heinemann 1996 2v
ISBN v1 0-435-07013-4; v2 0-435-07017-7

Deckchairs. McConnell, J.

De Filippo, Eduardo
Four plays; The local authority, Grand magic, Filumena Marturano, translated by Carlo Ardito; Napoli milionaria, adapted by Peter Tinniswood; with an introduction by Carlo Ardito. Methuen 1992 362p (Methuen world dramatists)
ISBN 0-413-66620-4

The **definitive** Simon Gray I-IV. Gray, S.

DeNobriga, Kathie
(ed.) Alternate roots. See Alternate roots

Destination Bethlehem: seven Christmas plays for young people. Trott, S.

Dick Turpin and Babes in the wood. Webster, P.

Difficulties of a bridegroom. Hughes, T.

Digging for fire & New morning. Hughes, D.

Dixon, Michael Bigelow
(ed.) Actors Theatre of Louisville. Ten-minute plays: v3
(ed.) By Southern playwrights. See By Southern playwrights
(ed.) A Decade of new comedy. See A Decade of new comedy
(ed.) Humana Festival '96. See Humana Festival '96
(ed.) Humana Festival '97. See Humana Festival '97

Doggart, Sebastian
(ed.) Latin American plays. See Latin American plays

Donaghy, Tom
The dadshuttle and Down the shore. Dramatists 1995 71p
ISBN 0-8222-1432-6 LC 95-176257

Doolittle, Joyce
(ed.) Heroines. See Heroines
(ed.) Playhouse: six fantasy plays for children. See Playhouse: six fantasy plays for children

Dowie, Claire
Why is John Lennon wearing a skirt and other stand-up theatre plays. Methuen 1996 156p (Methuen modern plays)
ISBN 0-413-71090-4

Doyle, Roddy
Brownbread and War. Penguin Bks. 1994 215p
ISBN 0-14-023115-3
Also available from Minerva

A **Dozen** French farces; medieval to modern; edited and translated by Albert Bermel. Limelight Eds. 1997 405p
ISBN 0-87910-092-3 LC 97-3325

Dracula. Deane, H. and Balderston, J. L.

Dramacontemporary: Germany; plays by Brotho Strauss [et al.]; edited by Carl Weber. Johns Hopkins Univ. Press 1996 276p (PAJ books)
ISBN 0-8018-5279-X LC 95-41870

The **dramatic** works in the Beaumont and Fletcher canon. Beaumont, F. and Fletcher, J.

Dreams of a drunken Quaker; Naked West & Yowl. Green, M.

Dryden, John
The works of John Dryden v12, 16; plays. Univ. of Calif. Press 1994-1996 2v
ISBN v12 0-520-08247-8; v16 0-520-08766-6 LC 55-7149
Earlier volumes entered in previous volumes of Play Index
Contents: v12: Amboyna; The state of innocence; Aureng-Zebe
v16: King Arthur: Cleomenes; Love triumphant

Duck-hunting [and] Last summer in Chulimsk. Vampilov, A.

Durang, Christopher
27 short plays. Smith & Kraus 1995 419p (Contemporary playwrights series)
ISBN 1-880399-89-X LC 95-39321
Complete full-length plays, 1975-1995. Smith & Kraus 1996 425p (Contemporary playwrights series)
ISBN 1-57525-017-9 LC 96-51133
Durang/Durang. Dramatists 1996 139p
ISBN 0-8222-1460-1
Sister Mary Ignatius explains it all for you and The actor's nightmare; two plays by Christopher Durang. Dramatists 1995 71p
ISBN 0-8222-1035-5 LC 96-208095

Dutch and Flemish plays; selected by Della Couling. Hern Bks. in association with Theater Instituut Nederland 1997 295p (International collection)
ISBN 1-85459-289-0
Contents: The Buddha of Ceylon, by L. De Boer; The wedding party, by J. Herzberg; Drummers, by A. Sierens; Burying the dog, by K. Woudstra; The Stendhal syndrome, by F. Struards

The **dybbuk** and other writings. Ansky, S.

E

Early American drama; edited and with an introduction and notes by Jeffrey H. Richards. Penguin Bks. 1997 512p
ISBN 0-14-043588-5 LC 96-49410

Early verse drama and prose plays. Goethe, J. W. von

Edwardes, Pamela
(ed.) Frontline intelligence 1-3. See Frontline intelligence 1-3

Edwards, Gus
(ed.) Classic plays from the Negro Ensemble Company. See Classic plays from the Negro Ensemble Company

Ekstrom, Peter
An O. Henry Christmas; a Christmas musical adaptation, music & lyrics by Peter Ekstrom. French 1955 69p (French's musical library)
ISBN 0-573-69572-5 LC 96-130941
Consists of two one-act musicals

Elam, Harry J.
(ed.) Colored contradictions: an anthology of contemporary African-American plays. See Colored contradictions: an anthology of contemporary African-American plays

Emery, S. W.
Plato's Euthyphro, Apology, and Crito; arranged for dramatic presentation from the Jowett translation with choruses. Univ. Press of America 1996 79p
ISBN 0-7618-0170-7 LC 95-44385

The **Emperor** Jones; "Anna Christie"; The hairy ape. O'Neill, E.

Engelman, Liz
(ed.) Humana Festival '96. See Humana Festival '96
(ed.) Humana Festival '97. See Humana Festival '97

Enscoe, L. G. and Enscoe, Annie
Joy to the world! a variety collection of six Christmas programs for the church family. Meriwether 1994 238p
ISBN 1-56608-005-3 LC 94-23107

Eric Overmyer: collected plays. Overmyer, E.

Escape acts; seven Canadian one-acts; edited by Colleen Curran. NuAge Eds. 1992 191p (Performance series)
ISBN 0-921833-21-0

The **essential** Bogosian. Bogosian, E.

EST marathon, 1994; one-act plays; edited by Marisa Smith. Smith & Kraus 1995 224p (Contemporary playwrights series)
ISBN 1-880399-83-0 LC 95-2287

EST marathon '95; the complete one-act-plays; edited by Marisa Smith; introduction by Curt Dempster. Smith & Kraus 1995 213p (Contemporary playwrights series)
ISBN 1-880399-85-7 LC 95-3921

Etiquette and vitriol: The food chain and other plays. Silver, N.

Eureka! seven one-act plays for secondary schools; selected by Jacquie Johnston Lewis and Dianne Warren. Coteau Bks. 1994 174p
ISBN 1-55050-059-7

Euripides
Alcestis and other plays; translated by John Davie; introduction and notes by Richard Rutherford. Penguin Bks. 1996 193p
ISBN 0-14-044643-5

Cyclops; Alcestis; Medea; edited and translated by David Kovacs. Harvard Univ. Press 1994 427p (Loeb classical library)
ISBN 0-674-99560-0 LC 93-821

Europe & The architect. Greig, D.

Ezra's Noh for Willie and other plays. Hall, F. B.

F

Facing forward; edited and with an introduction by Leah D. Frank. Broadway Play Pub. 1995 502p
ISBN 0-88145-112-6

Falsettos. Finn, W.

Fantasio and other plays. Musset, A. de

Farquhar, George
The recruiting officer and other plays. Oxford 1995 399p (World's classics)
ISBN 0-19-282249-7 LC 95-2971
Contents: The constant couple; The twin rivals; The recruiting officer; The beaux' stratagem

Farrell, Bernard
Forty-four, Sycamore & The last Apache reunion. Mercier Press 1995 166p
ISBN 1-85635-124-6 LC 96-100482

Faust I & II. Goethe, J. W. von

Favorini, Attilio
(ed.) Voicings: ten plays from the documentary theatre. See Voicings: ten plays from the documentary theatre

Feingold, Michael
(ed.) Grove new American theater. See Grove new American theater

Feydeau, Georges
Five by Feydeau; translated by J. Paul Marcoux. Lang, P. 1994 283p (Studies in French theatre v2)
ISBN 0-8204-2390-4 LC 93-34669

The **Fickle** finger of Lady Death and other plays; translated by Carlos Morton. Lang P. 1996 133p (Taft Memorial Fund and University of Cincinnati studies in Latin American, Chicano, and U.S. Latino theatre v5)
ISBN 0-8204-2525-7 LC 94-37489

Fifteen short plays. McNally, T.

Filewod, Alan
(ed.) The *CTR* anthology. See The *CTR* anthology

The **final** plays. Schnitzler, A.

Finn, William
Falsettos; "Falsettos" "March of the falsettos" and "Falsettoland" by William Finn and James Lapine and "In trousers" by William Finn; with an afterword by Frank Rich. Plume Bks. 1993 246p
ISBN 0-452-27072-3 LC 92-45375

Finnegan, Seamus
It's all blarney: four plays. Harwood Acad. Pubs. 1995 145p (Contemporary theatre studies v8)
ISBN 3-7186-5555-1
Contents: Wild grass; Mary Maginn; It's all blarney; Comrade Brennan

Firbank, Ronald
Complete plays; edited with an introduction by Steven Moore. Dalkey Archive Press 1994 130p
ISBN 1-56478-047-3 LC 93-36133

First Lady suite. LaChuisa, M. J.

Fish head soup and other plays. Gotanda, P. K.

Fisher, Mark
(ed.) Made in Scotland. See Made in Scotland

Five by Feydeau. Feydeau, G.

Five one-act plays. Ball, A.

Five one-act plays. Ricchi, R.

Five plays. Musset, A. de

Five plays. Szyszkowitz, G.

Five plays. Weller, M.

Five plays 5. Schevill, J.

Flavio's disgrace [and other plays]. Griffiths, D.

A **Flea** in her rear; or, Ants in her pants and other vintage French farces! English versions by Norman R. Shapiro. Applause 1994 479p (Tour de farce v4)
ISBN 1-55783-165-3 LC 94-3164

Fletcher, John, 1579-1625. See Beaumont, F. jt. auth.

Flowers & No more Medea. Porter, D.

Fo, Dario
Plays; with an introduction by series editor Stuart Hood. Methuen 1992-1997 2v (Methuen world dramatists)
ISBN v1 0-413-15420-3; v2 0-413-68020-7

Contents: Plays: one: Mistero buffo comic mysteries; Accidental death of an anarchist; Trumpets and raspberries; The virtuous burglar; One was nude and one wore tails

Plays: two: Can't pay? Won't pay!; Elizabeth: almost by chance a woman; The open couple; An ordinary day

Foote, Horton
4 new plays. Smith & Kraus 1993 22p (Contemporary playwrights series)
ISBN 0-880399-41-5 LC 93-33306

Collected plays v2. Smith & Kraus 1996 216p (Contemporary playwrights series)
ISBN 1-57525-019-5 LC 93-33306

Horton Foote's three trips to Bountiful; edited by Barbara Moore and David G. Yellin. Southern Methodist Univ. Press 1993 259p
ISBN 0-87074-326-0 LC 91-52779

Includes teleplay, stageplay and screenplay

The tears of my sister; The Prisoner's Song; The one-armed man and The land of the astronauts. Dramatists 1993 103p

Ford, John
'Tis pity she's a whore and other plays; edited by Marion Lomax. Oxford 1995 378p (World's classics)
ISBN 0-19-282253-5 LC 94-47318

Contents: The lover's melancholy; The broken heart; 'Tis pity she's a whore; Perkin Warbeck

Foreman, Richard
My head was a sledgehammer; six plays. Overlook Press 1995 322p
ISBN 0-87951-9 LC 94-37369

Forms of heaven. Barker, C.

Fortune, my foe & Eros at breakfast. Davies, R.

Forty-four, Sycamore & The last Apache reunion. Farrell, B.

Foster, Norm
The motor trade & The affections of May. Playwrights Canada 1993 215p
ISBN 0-88754-491-6

The **foundling** and The Gamester. Moore, E.

Four baboons adoring the sun and other plays. Guare, J.

Four comedies. Plautus, T. M.

Four dogs and a bone and The wild goose. Shanley, J. P.

Four new plays. Foote, H.

Four plays. De Filippo, E.

Four plays. Goldstein, J.

Four Restoration marriage plays; edited by Michael Cordner with Ronald Clayton. Oxford 1995 1x, 439p (World's classics)
ISBN 0-19-812163-6 LC 95-221028

Contents: The soldier's fortune, by T. Otway; The Princess of Cleves, by N. Lee; Amphitryon; or, The two Sosias, by J. Dryden; The wives' excuse; or, Cuckolds make themselves, by T. Southerne

Four revenge tragedies; edited with an introduction by Katharine Eisaman Maus. Oxford 1995 426p (World's classics)
ISBN 0-19-282633-6 LC 94-8005

Contents: The Spanish tragedy, by T. Kyd; The revenger's tragedy; The revenge of Bussy d'Ambois, by G. Chapman; The athiest's tragedy, by C. Tournier

Four short plays. Wilson, L.

Frank, Leah D.
(ed.) Facing forward. See Facing forward

Fraser, Brad
The wolf plays. NeWest Press 1993 252p (Prairie plays series 12)
ISBN 0-920897-49-5

Contents: Wolfboy; Prom night of the living dead

The **free** zone and The workroom. Grumberg, J.-C.

Frontline intelligence I-3; new plays for the nineties; edited and introduced by Pamela Edwardes. Methuen 1993-1995 3v (Methuen theatrescripts)
ISBN v1 0-413-67680-3; v2 0-413-69880-8; v3 0-413-69430-5

Contents: v1 Hush, by A. De Angelis; Digging for fire, by D. Hughes; Somewhere, by J. Johnson; East from the Gantry, by E. Thomas

v2; Blasted, by S. Kane; Foreign lands, by K. Hope; Hurricane roses, by D. Spencer; The life of the world to come, by R. Williams

v3; Europe, by D. Greig; Uganda, by J. Johnson; Some voices, by J. Penhall; Ashes and sand, by J. Upton

Frost, Robert
Collected poems, prose, & plays. Lib. of America 1995 1036p
ISBN 1-883011-06-X LC 94-43693
Analyzed for plays only

Fruitful and multiplying; 9 contemporary plays from the American Jewish repertoire edited and with an introduction by Ellen Schiff. Mentor 1996 522p
ISBN 0-451-62870-5

Fugard, Athol
Playland and A place with the pigs; two plays. Theatre Communications Group 1993 100p
ISBN 1-55936-070-4 LC 93-11834

G

Garcia Lorca, Federico
Blood wedding and Yerma; translations by Langston Hughes and W. S. Merwin; introduction by Melia Bensussen. Theatre Communications Group 1994 135p (TCG translations)
ISBN 1-55936-080-1 LC-93-51498
Three plays; Blood wedding, Yerma, The house of Bernarda Alba; the new authorized English translations by Michael Dewell and Carmen Zapata; introduction by Christopher Maurer. Farrar, Straus & Giroux 1993 303p
ISBN 0-374-52332-0 LC 91-44230

Gelbart, Larry
Mastergate and Power failure; 2 political satires for the stage. Applause 1994 199p
ISBN 1-55783-177-7 LC 94-1204

George Bernard Shaw: selected plays. Shaw, B.

Gerke, Pamela
Multicultural plays for children. Smith & Kraus 1996 2v (Young actors series)
ISBN v1 1-57525-005-5; v2 1-57525-006-3 LC 96-164
Contents: v1 Grades k-3; v2 Grades 4-6

German expressionist plays; edited by Ernst Schurer. Continuum 1997 322p (German library v66)
ISBN 0-8264-0911-2 LC 96-37251

Gethner, Perry
(ed.) The Lunatic lover and other plays. See The Lunatic lover and other plays

Gifford, Barry
Hotel room trilogy. Univ. Press of Miss. 1995 76p
ISBN 0-87805-776-5 LC 94-23776
Contents: Tricks; Blackout; Mrs. Kashfi

Gilbert, Ronnie
Ronnie Gilbert on Mother Jones; face to face with the most dangerous woman in America. Conari Press 1993 123p
ISBN 0-943233-48-8 LC 93-17099

Gilbert, Sky
Painted, tainted, sainted; four plays. Playwrights Canada 1996 275p
ISBN 0-88754-550-5 LC 97-122470
Contents: Drag queens on trial; Drag queens in outer space; Suzie Goo: Private secretary; Jim Dandy

Gilroy, Frank D.
A way with words: five one act plays. French (London) 1993 135p
ISBN 0-573-69396-X

Glamorgan and other plays. Nigro, D.

Glover, Sue
Bondagers & The straw chair. Methuen 1997 150p (Methuen modern plays)
ISBN 0-413-71210-9

Godber, John
Lucky sods & Passion killers. Methuen 1995 215p (Methuen modern plays)
ISBN 0-413-70170-0

Godfrey, Paul
A bucket of eels & The modern husband; introduced by the author. Methuen 1995 143p (Methuen modern plays)
ISBN 0-413-68830-5

Goethe, Johann Wolfgang von
Early verse drama and prose plays; edited by Cyrus Hamlin and Frank Ryder; translated by Robert M. Browning [et al.] Princeton Univ. Press. 1995 298p (Goethe's collected works v7)
ISBN 0-691-04342-6 LC 94-23913
Faust I & II; edited and translated by Stuart Atkins. Princeton Univ. Press 1994 329p (Goethe's collected works v2)
ISBN 0-691-03656-X LC 94-27617
Plays; edited by Frank G. Ryder. Continuum 1993 xxviii, 241p (German library v20)
ISBN 0-8264-0716-1 LC 92-25103
Contents: Egmont; Iphigenia in Tauris; Torquato Tasso
Verse plays and epic; edited by Cyrus Hamlin and Frank Ryder; translated by Michael Hamburger, Hunter Hannum, and David Luke. Princeton Univ. Press 1995 318p (Goethe's collected works v8)
ISBN 0-691-04343-4 LC 94-40896

The **gold** standard: a book of plays. Koch, K.

Goldenthal, Jolene
Mequasset by the sea and other plays. Andrew Mountain Press 1996 64p
ISBN 0-916897-24-9 LC 96-41538

Goldoni, Carlo
Carlo Goldoni's Villeggiatura trilogy; translated by Robert Cornthwaite. Smith & Kraus 1994 202p (Great translations for actors series)
ISBN 1-880399-69-5

Goldstein, Joshua
Four plays; with a foreword by Howard Stein; illustrations by Neil Welliver and Marilene Phipps. Solomon Press 1993 213p
ISBN 0-934623-50-3 LC 93-35987

The **Golem** triptych. Basso, E.

Goluboff, Bryan
Big Al and My side of the story. Dramatists 1993 45p

Goodman, Robyn
(ed.) Women playwrights: the best plays of 1992. See Women playwrights: the best plays of 1992

Gotanda, Philip Kan
Fish head soup and other plays; introduction by Michael Omi. Univ. of Wash. Press 1995 258p
ISBN 0-295-97417-6 LC 95-18878

Granville-Barker, Harley
Plays; with an introduction by Margery Morgan. Methuen 1993-1994 2v (Methuen world classics)
ISBN v1 0-413-67530-0; v2 0-413-67980-2

Contents: Plays: one: The Voysey inheritance (1934 revision); Waste (1926 revision); The secret life; Rococo; Vote by ballot

Plays: two: The marrying of Ann Leete; The Madras House (1825 revision); His Majesty; Farewell to the theatre

Gray, Simon
The definitive Simon Gray I-IV. Faber & Faber 1992-1993 4v
ISBN v1 0-571-16223-1; v2 0-571-16240-1; v3 0-571-16453-6; v4 0-571-16659-8

Gray, Stephen
(ed.) South African plays. See South African plays

Great American events on stage; 15 plays to celebrate America's past; edited by Sylvia E. Kamerman. Plays, Inc. 1996 231p
ISBN 0-8238-0305-8 LC 96-32197

Great Irish plays. Gramercy Bks. 1995 712p
ISBN 0-517-12429-7 LC 95-19796

Contents: The beaux' stratagem, by G. Farquhar; She stoops to conquer, by O. Goldsmith; The school for scandal, by R. B. Sheridan; The Colleen Bawn, by D. Boucicault; The importance of being Earnest, by O. Wilde; Pygmalion, by G. B. Shaw; Spreading the news, by Lady Gregory; The rising of the moon, by Lady Gregory; The land of heart's desire, by W. B. Yeats; On Baile's strand, by W. B. Yeats; Riders to the sea, by J. M. Synge; The playboy of the Western World, by J. M. Synge

Greatest hits: four Irish one-act plays; edited by Dermot Bolger. New Island Bks./Hern Bks. 1997 120p
ISBN 1-874597-61-8

Contents: Blood guilty, by A. Ó Flatharta; The Marlboro man, by C. Dowling; Greatest hits, by T. McLaughlin; Faint voices, by J. MacKenna

Green, Michael
Dreams of a drunken Quaker; Naked West & Yowl; two plays & a rant. AB Collector Pub. 1992 89p
ISBN 1-895466-02-4

Gregor, Henry
Prince & plays by Henry Gregor (Prince Starhemberg); translated by Harvey I. Dunkle. Ariadne Press 1996 366p (Studies in Austrian literature, culture, and thought. Translation series)
ISBN 0-929497-82-1 LC 95-4996

Analyzed for plays only

Greig, David
Europe & The architect. Methuen 1996 195p (Methuen modern plays)
ISBN 0-413-70880-2

Griffiths, David
c Flavio's disgrace [and other plays]; a masked commedia. Collins Educ. 1993 90p (Upstagers)
ISBN 0-00-330305-5

Griffiths, Trevor
Hope in the year two and Thatcher's children. Faber & Faber 1994 114p
ISBN 0-571-17308-X

Plays: one; introduced by the author. Faber & Faber 1996 344p (Contemporary classics)
ISBN 0-571-17742-5

Grove new American theater; edited and with an introduction by Michael Feingold. Grove Press 1993 386p
ISBN 0-8021-3278-2 LC 91-38276

Grumberg, Jean-Claude
The free zone and The workroom; translated from the French by Catherine Temerson; preface by Michael R. Marrus. Ubu Repertory Theater Publs. 1993 246p
ISBN 0-913745-40-5 LC 93-060152

Guare, John
Four baboons adoring the sun and other plays. Vintage Bks. 1993 188p
ISBN 0-679-74510-6 LC 92-50637

The war against the kitchen sink. Smith & Kraus 1996 192p (Collected works v1)
ISBN 1-57525-031-4 LC 96-22835

Gurney, A. R.
Collected plays v2, 1974-1983. Smith & Kraus 1997 342p (Collected works v2)
ISBN 1-57525-027-6
"Contemporary playwrights series"

Later life and two other plays: The snow ball and The old boy. Plume Bks. 1994 288p
ISBN 0-452-27251-3 LC 93-48843

Nine early plays, 1961-1973. Smith & Kraus 1995 252p (Collected works v1)
ISBN 1-880399-88-1 LC 95-19638
"Contemporary playwrights series"

H

The **hairy** ape & All God's chillun got wings. O'Neill, E.

Hall, Francis Ben
Ezra's Noh for Willie and other plays. Mountain Press 1996 180p
ISBN 0-9625313-6-7 LC 96-094377

Hamalian, Leo
(ed.) Lost plays of the Harlem Renaissance, 1920-1940. See Lost plays of the Harlem Renaissance, 1920-1940

Hampton, Christopher
Plays: one; introduced by the author. Faber & Faber 1997 338p (Contemporary classics)
ISBN 0-571-17834-0

Handke, Peter
Voyage to the sonorous land; or, The art of asking and The hour we knew nothing of each other; translated by Gitta Honegger. Yale Univ. Press 1996 110p
ISBN 0-300-06274-5

Hansberry, Lorraine
A raisin in the sun and The sign in Sidney Brustein's window; Robert Nemiroff, editor; with a new foreword by Jewell Handy Gresham Nemiroff, a note by Robert Nemiroff, and critical essays by Amiri Baraka and Frank Rich. Vintage Bks. 1995 340p
ISBN 0-679-75531-4 LC 95-8917

Hardstack, Michael
The last laugh; two one-act plays. French 1993 86p
ISBN 0-573-69397-8 LC 93-221198

Hare, David
Plays; introduced by the author. Faber & Faber 1996-1997 2v (Contemporary classics)
ISBN v1 0-571-17741-7; v2 0-571-17835-9

Contents: Plays: one: Slag; Teeth 'n' smiles; Knuckle; Licking Hitler; Plenty

Plays: two: Fanshen; A map of the world; Saigon; The bay at Nice; The secret rapture

Harrison, Paul Carter
(ed.) Classic plays from the Negro Ensemble Company. See Classic plays from the Negro Ensemble Company

Harrison, Tony
Plays: three; introduced by Michael Kustow. Faber & Faber 1996 152p (Contemporary classics)
ISBN 0-571-17966-5

Contents: Poetry or bust; The Kaisers of Carnuntum; The labourers of Herakles

Harvey, Jonathan
Rupert Street Lonely Hearts Club & Boom bang-a-bang. Methuen Drama 1995 200p (Methuen modern plays)
ISBN 0-413-70450-5

Harwood, Ronald
The collected plays of Ronald Harwood. Faber & Faber 1993 278p
ISBN 0-571-17001-3

Plays: two. Faber & Faber 1995 336p
ISBN 0-571-17401-9

Contents: Taking sides; Poison pen; Tramway Road; The ordeal of Gilbert Pinfold; After the lions; The guests

Hatch, James V.
(ed.) Black theatre USA. See Black theatre USA
(ed.) Lost plays of the Harlem Renaissance, 1920-1940. See Lost plays of the Harlem Renaissance, 1920-1940

Hated nightfall [and] Wounds to the face. Barker, H.

Hauptmann, Gerhart
Plays; edited by Reinhold Grimm and Caroline Molina y Vedia. Continuum 1994 227p (German library v57)
ISBN 0-8264-0762-9 LC 93-30334

Havel, Václav
Selected plays, 1963-83/1984-87. Faber & Faber 1992-1994 2v
ISBN v1 0-571-16059-X; v2 0-571-17211-3 LC 95-143753

Haylock, Derek
Plays on the word; Christian drama for churches, schools and youth groups. National Soc./Church House Pub. 1993 144p
ISBN 0-7151-4824-9

Hello, Ma! and other plays. Stone, T.

Here to stay: five plays from the Women's Project; edited by Julia Miles. Applause 1997 276p
ISBN 1-557813-315-X LC 97-28470

Heroines; three plays [by] John Murrell, Sharon Pollock [and] Michel Tremblay; edited by Joyce Doolittle. RDC Press 1993 191p
ISBN 0-88995-081-4

Holiday in the rain forest and Kabuki gift. Love, D.

Hope in the year two and Thatcher's children. Griffiths, T.

The **Hope** slide [and] Little sister. MacLeod, J.

Horin, Ros
(ed.) Passion: six new short plays by Australian women. See Passion: six new short plays by Australian women

Horovitz, Israel
New England blue: plays of working-class life. Smith & Kraus 1995 370p (Collected works v2)
ISBN 1-880399-86-5 LC 93-46378
"Contemporary playwrights series"
The primary English class and six new plays. Smith & Kraus 1997 328p (Collected works v3)
ISBN 0-57525-118-3 LC 93-46378
"Contemporary playwrights series"
Sixteen short plays. Smith & Kraus 1993 414p (Collected works v1)
ISBN 1-880399-51-2 LC 93-46378
"Contemporary playwrights series"

Horton Foote's three trips to Bountiful. Foote, H.

Hotel room trilogy. Gifford, B.

Houston, Velina Hasu
(ed.) But still, like air, I'll rise. See But still, like air, I'll rise

Howe, Tina
Approaching Zanzibar and other plays. Theatre Communications Group 1995 211p
ISBN 1-55936-104-2 LC 94-44575

Hughes, Declan
Digging for fire & New morning; introduced by the author. Methuen 1994 116p (Methuen modern plays)
ISBN 0-413-68250-1

Hughes, Ted

Difficulties of a bridegroom. Picador USA 1995 159p

ISBN 0-312-14587-X

Analyzed for play only

Hugo, Victor

Three plays; translated by C. Crosland and F. L. Slous. Fertig 1995 338p

ISBN 0-86527-418-5 LC 93-11420

Contents: Hernani; The king amuses himself; Ruy Blas

Humana Festival

20/20: twenty one-act plays from twenty years of the Humana Festival. See 20/20: twenty one-act plays from twenty years of the Humana Festival

A Decade of new comedy. See A Decade of new comedy

Humana Festival '93: the complete plays; edited by Marisa Smith. Smith & Kraus 1993 247p (Plays for actors)

ISBN 1-880399-37-7

Humana Festival '94: the complete plays; edited by Marisa Smith. Smith & Kraus 1994 367p (Contemporary playwrights series)

ISBN 1-880399-56-3 LC 94-19395

Humana Festival '95: the complete plays; edited by Marisa Smith. Smith & Kraus 1995 370p (Contemporary playwrights series)

ISBN 1-880399-92-X LC 95-37497

Humana Festival '96: the complete plays; edited by Michael Bigelow Dixon and Liz Engelman. Smith & Kraus 1996 356p (Contemporary playwrights series)

ISBN 1-57525-033-0

Humana Festival '97: the complete plays; edited by Michael Bigelow Dixon and Liz Engelman. Smith & Kraus 1997 356p (Contemporary playwrights series)

ISBN 1-57525-114-0

Hungarian plays; new drama from Hungary: selected and introduced by László Upor. Hern Bks. 1996 242p (International collection)

ISBN 1-85459-144-0

Contents: The seducer's diary, by A. Nagy; Unsent letters, by A. Szilágyi; Müller's dancers, by A. Németh; Everywoman, by P. Kárpáti

Hwang, David Henry

Trying to find Chinatown and Bondage. Dramatists 1996 47p

ISBN 0-8222-1552-7

I

Ibsen, Henrik

Ibsen: four major plays; translated by Rick Davis and Brian Johnston. Smith & Kraus 1995 286p (Great translations for actors)

ISBN 0-880399-67-9 LC 95-13632

Ibsen: four plays; translated by Brian Johnston. Smith & Kraus 1996 295p (Great translations series)

ISBN 0-57525-064-0 LC 96-36230

Ibsen: four major plays. Ibsen, H.

Ibsen: four plays. Ibsen, H.

If God wanted us to fly he would have given us wings! Burns, K.

Ilsa, queen of the Nazi love camp and other plays. Brooker, B.

Incarnations. Barker, C.

The **inventor** of the horse and two other short plays. Campanile, A.

Israeli Holocaust drama; edited and with an introduction by Michael Taub. Syracuse Univ. Press 1995 332p
ISBN 0-8156-2673-8 LC 95-10506

It's all blarney: four plays. Finnegan, S.

Ives, David

All in the timing: fourteen plays. Vintage Bks. 1995 313p
ISBN 0-679-75928-X LC 94-27357

All in the timing: six one-act comedies. Dramatists 1994 98p
ISBN 0-8222-1396-6

The land of Cockaigne and English made simple. Dramatists 1995 67p
ISBN 0-8222-1470-9

Long ago and far away and other short plays. Dramatists 1994 103p
ISBN 0-8222-1397-4

J

Jackson, Pamela Faith

(ed.) Black comedy: nine plays. See Black comedy: nine plays

James, Joanne

Three quest plays. Red Deer College Press in association with Players Press 1996 128p
ISBN 0-88734-682-0 LC 96-26703

Jansen, Ann

(ed.) Adventures for (big) girls. See Adventures for (big) girls

Jayyusi, Salma Khadra

(ed.) Modern Arabic drama. See Modern Arabic drama

Jensen, H. James

(ed.) The Sensational Restoration. See The Sensational Restoration

Johnson, Terry

Plays: one; with an introduction by Rob Ritchie. Methuen 1993 209p (Methuen world classics)
ISBN 0-413-68200-5

Contents: Insignificance; Unsuitable for adults; Cries from the mammal house

Jonathan, Jack, and GBS. O'Donovan, J.

Jones, Taffy

Old barn puppet plays; seven plans for 10-minute puppetry experiences for children 5-8. McFarland & Co. 1997 154p
ISBN 0-7864-0327-6 LC 97-11198

Jones, Therese
(ed.) Sharing the delirium. See Sharing the delirium

Joy to the world! Enscoe, L. G. and Enscoe, A.

July 7, 1994: short plays and monologues. Margulies, D.

K

Kamerman, Sylvia E.
(ed.) The Big book of dramatized classics. See The Big book of dramatized classics
(ed.) The Big book of large-cast plays. See The Big book of large-cast plays
(ed.) The Big book of skits. See The Big book of skits
(ed.) Great American events on stage. See Great American events on stage
(ed.) Plays of black Americans. See Plays of black Americans

Kane, Sarah
Blasted & Phaedra's love. Methuen 1996 97p (Methuen modern plays)
ISBN 0-413-70940-X

Karaoke and Cold Lazarus. Potter, D.

Karimah
(ed.) Black comedy: nine plays. See Black comedy: nine plays

The **Kentucky** cycle. Schenkkan, R.

Kilner, Kerry
(ed.) Playing the past: three plays by Australian women. See Playing the past: three plays by Australian women

King, Woodie
(ed.) The National black drama anthology. See The National black drama anthology

Kingsley, Sidney
Sidney Kingsley: five prizewinning plays; with introductions by Sidney Kingsley; edited by Nena Couch. Ohio State Univ. Press 1995 407p (Theatre studies)
ISBN 0-8142-0665-4 LC 95-10843

Kipling, Rudyard
Collected stories; selected and introduced by Robert Gottlieb. Knopf 1994 911p (Everyman's library)
ISBN 0-679-43592-1 LC 94-5854
Analyzed for play only

Kiss of the spider woman and two other plays. Puig, M.

Koch, Kenneth
The gold standard: a book of plays. Knopf 1996 263p
ISBN 0-670-45082-3 LC 96-26169

Kroetz, Franz Xaver
Through the leaves and other plays; translated by Roger Downey. Theatre Communications Group 1992 162p (TSG translations)
ISBN 1-55936-044-5 LC 92-3954

Kushner, Tony
Plays by Tony Kushner. Broadway Play Pub. 1994 159p
ISBN 0-88145-102-9
Thinking about the longstanding problems of virtue and happiness; essays, a play, two poems and a prayer. Theatre Communications Group 1995 224p
ISBN 1-44536-100-X LC 95-4988
Analyzed for play only
Also available from Hern Bks.

L

Labon, Joanna
(ed.) Balkan blues: writing out of Yugoslavia. See Balkan blues: writing out of Yugoslavia

LaChuisa, Michael John
First Lady suite; a musical. Dramatists 1995 81p
ISBN 0-8222-1408-3
Contents: Over Texas; Where's Mamie?; Olio; Eleanor sleeps here
Lucky nurse and other short musical plays; words and music by Michael John LaChiusa. Dramatists 1993 various paging

Lamont, Rosette C.
New French-language plays. See New French-language plays
(ed.) Women on the verge: 7 avant-garde American plays. See Women on the verge: 7 avant-garde American plays

The **land** beyond the forest: Dracula and Swoop. Wellman, M.

The **land** of Cockaigne and English made simple. Ives, D.

Landes, William-Landes
(ed.) Punch and Judy. See Punch and Judy

Lane, Eric
(ed.) The Actor's book of gay and lesbian plays. See The Actor's book of gay and lesbian plays
(ed.) Plays for actresses. See Plays for actresses
(ed.) Telling tales: new one-act plays. See Telling tales: new one-act plays

The **last** laugh. Hardstack, M.

Late Sunday afternoon, early Sunday evening and Is that the bus to Pittsburgh? Toddie, J. L.

Later life and two other plays: The snow ball and The old boy. Gurney, A. R.

Latin American plays; new drama from Argentina, Cuba, Mexico, and Peru; selected, translated and introduced by Sebastian Doggart. Hern Bks. in association with Visiting Arts 1996 230p (International collection)
ISBN 1-85459-249-1
Contents: Rappaccini's daughter, by O. Paz; Night of the assassins, by J. Triana; Saying yes, by G. Gambaro; Orchids in the moonlight, by C. Fuentes; Mistress of desires, by M. Vargas Llosa

Latins anonymous: two plays. Arte Publico Press 1996 103p
ISBN 1-55885-172-0 LC 96-26649

Laughter in the shadow of the trees and other plays. Prideaux, J.

Lawrence, Jerome, and Lee, Robert E.
Selected plays of Jerome Lawrence and Robert E. Lee; edited by Alan Woods; foreword by Norman Cousins. Ohio State Univ. Press 1994 579p
ISBN 0-8142-0646-8 LC 94-15894

Lawson, Richard H.
(ed.) Seven contemporary Austrian plays. See Seven contemporary Austrian plays

Lazarus, John, 1947-
Not so dumb; four plays for young people. Coach House Press 1993 204p
ISBN 0-88910-453-0

Lee, Robert, E. See Lawrence, J. jt. auth.

Lewis, Jacquie Johnston
(ed.) Eureka! See Eureka!

Libretti, and other dramatic writings by W. H. Auden, 1939-1973. Auden, W. H.

Life in the trees. Butterfield, C.

A **life** with no joy in it and other plays and pieces. Mamet, D.

The **Lights** o' London and other Victorian plays; edited by Michael R. Booth. Oxford 1995 xxxiii, 251p (World classics)
ISBN 0-19-282736-7 LC 96-107131

Contents: The inchcape bell; or, The dumb sailor boy, by E. Fitzball; Did you ever send your wife to Camberwell? by J. S. Coyne; The game of speculation, by G. H. Lewes; The lights o' London, by G. R. Sims; The middleman, by H. A. Jones

Linney, Romulus
Seventeen short plays. Smith & Kraus 1992 276p (Plays for actors)
ISBN 1-880399-21-0 LC 92-27781

Six plays. Theatre Communications Group 1993 318p
ISBN 1-59936-054-2; 1-59936-053-4 LC 92-15893

Spain. Dramatists 1994 54p
ISBN 0-8222-1376-1 LC 94-162661

London suite. Simon, N.

Long ago and far away and other short plays. Ives, D.

Lost plays of the Harlem Renaissance, 1920-1940; edited by James V. Hatch and Leo Hamalian. Wayne State Univ. Press 1996 467p (African-American life series)
ISBN 0-8143-2580-7 LC 96-29052

Love, Douglas
Be kind to your Mother (Earth) and Blame it on the wolf; two original plays. HarperFestival 1993 71p
ISBN 0-06-021106-7 LC 92-4624

Holiday in the rain forest and Kabuki gift. HarperCollins Pubs. 1994 83p
ISBN 0-06-024276-0 LC 93-41615

Love allways. Taylor, R. and Bologna, J.

A **love** song for Ulster. Morrison, B.

Lucky 13; short plays about Arizona, Nevada, and Utah; edited by Red Shuttleworth. Univ. of Nev. Press 1995 186p (Western literature series)
ISBN 0-87417-263-2 LC 94-48932

Lucky nurse and other short musical plays. LaChiusa, M. J.

Lucky sods & Passion killers. Godber, J.

The **Lunatic** lover and other plays by French women of the 17th and 18th centuries; edited by Perry Gethner. Heinemann (Portsmouth) 1994 344p
ISBN 0-435-08637-5 LC 93-47317

Lyly, John
Selected prose and dramatic work; edited and introduced by Leah Scragg. Fyfield Bks. 1997 189p
ISBN 1-85754-309-2
Analyzed for plays only

Lyssiotis, Tes
A white sports coat & other plays; edited by Carolyn Pickett. Currency Press 1996 160p
ISBN 0-86819-456-5

M

MacDonald, Sharman
Plays: one; introduced by the author. Faber & Faber 1995 353p (Contemporary classics)
ISBN 0-571-17621-6
Contents: When I was a girl, I used to scream and shout... ; When we were women; The winter guest; Borders of paradise

MacIvor, Daniel
Never swim alone & This is a play; 2 plays. Playwrights Canada 1993 101p
ISBN 0-88754-524-6

MacLeod, Joan
The Hope slide [and] Little sister. Coach House Press 1994 117p
ISBN 0-88910-463-8

MacLeod, Wendy
The shallow end and The lost colony. Dramatists 1993 55p

MacNeice, Louis
Selected plays of Louis MacNeice; edited by Alan Heuser and Peter McDonald. Clarendon Press 1993 413p
ISBN 0-19-811245-9 LC 93-19748

A **mad** world, my masters and other plays. Middleton, T.

Made in Scotland; an anthology of new Scottish plays; selected and introduced by Ian Brown and Mark Fisher. Methuen 1995 238p (Methuen new theatrescripts)
ISBN 0-413-69180-2
Contents: The cut, by M. Cullen; The life of stuff, by S. Donald; Bondagers, by S. Glover; Julie Allardyce, by D. McLean

Mahlmann, Lewis, and Jones, David Cadwalader
Plays for young puppeteers; 25 puppet plays for easy performance. Plays, Inc. 1993 328p
ISBN 0-8238-0298-1 LC 92-38529

Mahone, Sydne
(ed.) Moon marked and touched by sun. See Moon marked and touched by sun

Making, out; plays by gay men; edited by Robert Wallace. Coach House Press 1992 349p
ISBN 0-88910-434-4

Mamet, David
A life with no joy in it and other plays and pieces. Dramatists 1994 132p
ISBN 0-8222-1321-4 LC 95-118215

Mann, Emily
Testimonies: four plays. Theatre Communications Group 1997 330p
ISBN 1-55936-117-4 LC 96-7092

Maraini, Dacia
Only prostitutes marry in May (four plays); edited and with an introduction by Rhoda Helfman Kaufman. Guernica 1994 378p (Drama series 9)
ISBN 0-920717-81-0 LC 93-77802

Margulies, Donald
July 7, 1994: short plays and monologues. Dramatists 1997 109p
ISBN 0-8222-1568-3

Pitching to the star and other short plays. Dramatists 1993 95p
LC 93-227047

Sight unseen and other plays. Theatre Communications Group 1995 347p
ISBN 1-55936-103-4 LC 95-45984

Marisol and other plays. Rivera, J.

Marranca, Bonnie
(ed.) Plays for the end of the century. See Plays for the end of the century

Martin, Jane
Collected plays, 1980-1995. Smith & Kraus 1995 346p (Collected works v 1)
ISBN 1-57525-022-5 LC 95-30492
"Contemporary playwrights series"

Martin, Judith
Out of the bag; the Paper Bag Players book of plays; illustrated by Seymour Chwast. Hyperion Bks. for Children 1997 48p
ISBN 0-7868-1061-0 LC 94-46006

Martin, Steve
Picasso at the Lapin Agile and other plays. Grove Press 1996 150p
ISBN 0-8021-1595-0 LC 96-13222
Contents: Picasso at the Lapin Agile; The zig-zag woman; Patter for the floating lady; WASP

Marx, Pamela
Practical plays; illustrated by Cyd Moore. GoodYearBooks 1993 129p
ISBN 0-673-36049-0

Mastergate and Power failure. Gelbart, L.

Mastrosimone, William
William Mastrosimone: collected plays. Smith & Kraus 1993 346p (Plays for actors)
ISBN 1-880399-32-6 LC 93-40471
"Contemporary playwrights series"

Maus, Katharine Eisaman
(ed.) Four revenge tragedies. See Four revenge tragedies

McConnell, Jean
Deckchairs. French (London) 1995 55p
ISBN 0-573-10003-9

McCullough, L. E.
Plays of America from American folklore for children. Smith & Kraus 1996 161p (Young actors series)
ISBN 1-57525-040-3 LC 96-1702
Plays of America from American folklore for young actors. Smith & Kraus 1996 164p (Young actors series)
ISBN 1-57525-040-3 LC 96-6172
The plays of the songs of Christmas. Smith & Kraus 1996 131p (Young actors series)
ISBN 1-57525-062-4 LC 96-22834
Plays of the Wild West. Smith & Kraus 1997 2v (Young actors series)
ISBN v1 1-57525-104-3; v2 1-57525-105-1 LC 97-14729
Contents: v1 Grades k-3; v2 Grades 4-6

McGrath, John
Six-pack: plays for Scotland. Polygon 1996 460p
ISBN 0-7486-6201-4 LC 96-161397

McGuinness, Frank
(ed.) The Dazzling dark: new Irish plays. See The Dazzling dark: new Irish plays
Plays: one; introduced by the author. Faber & Faber 1996 399p (Contemporary classics)
ISBN 0-571-17740-9
Contents: The factory girls; Observe the sons of Ulster marching towards the Somme; Innocence; Carthaginians; Baglady

McIntyre, Clare
My heart's a suitcase & Low level panic. Hern Bks. 1994 120p
ISBN 1-85459-246-7

McNally, Terrence
15 short plays. Smith & Kraus 1994 373p (Contemporary playwrights series)
ISBN 1-880399-34-2 LC 94-10070
Andre's mother and other short plays. Dramatists 1995 52p
ISBN 0-8222-1419-9
Collected plays v2. Smith & Kraus 1996 165p (Contemporary playwrights series)
ISBN 1-57525-093-4 LC 94-10070

McPherson, Conor

St Nicholas & The weir; two plays. New Island Bks./Hern Bks. in association with the Bush Theatre 1997 97p

ISBN 1-85459-347-1

This lime tree bower: three plays. New Island Bks./Hern Bks. in association with the Bush Theatre 1996 124p

ISBN 1-85459-299-8

Contents: Rum and vodka; The good thief; This lime tree bower

Menken, Alan

Weird romance; two one-act musicals of speculative fiction. Music by Alan Menken; lyrics by David Spencer. "The girl who was plugged in" book by Alan Brennert and David Spencer, based on the story by James Tiptree, Jr. "Her pilgrim soul" book by Alan Brennert, based on his original story. French 1993 124p

ISBN 0-573-68136-8

Mequasset by the sea and other plays. Goldenthal, J.

Mercer, David, 1928-1980

Plays; with an introduction by Stuart Laing. Methuen 1990-1994 2v (Methuen world classics)

ISBN v1 0-413-63450-7; v2 0-413-65200-9

Contents: Plays: one: Where the difference begins; A suitable case for treatment; The Governor's lady; On the eve of publication; The cellar and the almond tree; Emma's time; After Haggerty

Plays: two: Flint; The bankrupt; An afternoon at the festival; Duck song; The Arcata promise; Find me; Huggy bear

The **Meridian** anthology of Restoration and eighteenth-century plays by women; Katharine M. Rogers, editor. Meridian 1994 560p

ISBN 0-452-01110-8 LC 93-39368

Metropolitan operas. Pintauro, J.

Middleton, Thomas

A mad world, my masters and other plays; edited and with an introduction by Michael Taylor. Oxford 1995 xxvi, 389p (World's classics)

ISBN 0-19-282255-1 LC 95-4309

Contents: A mad world, my masters; Michaelmas Term; A trick to catch the old one; No wit, no help like a woman's

Miles, Julia

(ed.) Here to stay. See Here to stay

(ed.) Playwriting women. See Playwriting women

Miller, Arthur

The portable Arthur Miller; original introduction by Harold Clurman; revised edition edited, with an introduction by Christopher Bigsby. Penguin Bks. 1995 575p (Viking portable library)

ISBN 0-14-024709-2 LC 95-9485

Milligan, Jason

Cross country; seven more one-act plays. French 1993 170p

ISBN 0-573-69426-5 LC 94-136827

Minghella, Anthony
Plays. Methuen 1992-1997 2v (Methuen contemporary dramatists)
ISBN v1 0-413-66580-1; v2 413-71520-5
Contents: Plays: 1 Made in Bangkok; Whale music; A little like drowning; Two planks and a passion
Plays: 2 Cigarettes and chocolate; Hang up; What if it's raining?; Truly, madly, deeply [screenplay]; Mosaic; Days like these

Missing/Kissing. Shanley, J. P.

Mitterer, Felix
Siberia and other plays. Ariadne Press 1994 374p (Studies in Austrian literature culture, and thought. Translation series)
ISBN 0-929497-68-6 LC 93-34857
The wild woman and other plays; translated by Todd C. Hanlin and Heidi Hutchinson; afterword by Todd C. Hanlin. Ariadne Press 1995 439p (Studies in Austrian literature, culture, and thought. Translation series)
ISBN 1-57241-002-7 LC 94-43185

Modern Arabic drama; an anthology; edited by Salma Khadra Jayyusi and Roger Allen. Introduction by M. M. Badawi. Indiana Univ. Press 1995 416p (Indiana series in Arab and Islamic studies)
ISBN 0-253-32897-7 LC 94-49178

Modern Canadian plays v1-2; edited by Jerry Wasserman. 3rd ed. Talonbooks 1993-1994 2v
ISBN v1 0-88922-239-4; v2 0-88922-340-8

Moloch blues. Dean, P. H.

Moon marked and touched by sun; plays by African-American women; edited by Sydne Mahone. Theatre Communications Group 1994 406p
ISBN 1-55936-065-8 LC 91-11831
Partially analyzed

Moore, Edward
The foundling; a comedy, and The gamester; a tragedy; edited with an introduction and notes by Anthony Amberg. Univ. of Del. Press 1995 446p
ISBN 0-87413-530-3 LC 94-41277

Mori, Ōgai
Youth and other stories; edited by J. Thomas Rimer. Univ. of Hawaii Press 1994 526p (SHAPS library of translations)
ISBN 0-8248-1600-5 LC 93-38737
Analyzed for play only

Morrison, Bill
A love song for Ulster; a trilogy. Hern Bks. 1994 176p
ISBN 1-85459-260-2

Morton, Carlos
(ed.) The Fickle finger of Lady Death and other plays. See The Fickle finger of Lady Death and other plays

The **mother** & other unsavory plays. Witkiewicz, S. I.

The **motor** trade & The affections of May. Foster, N.

Much, Rita
(ed.) New Canadian drama 6. See New Canadian drama 6

Multicultural plays for children. Gerke, P.

Munro, Rona
Your turn to clean the stair & Fugue. Hern Bks. 1995 121p
ISBN 1-85459-248-3

Murphy Thomas
Plays; with an introduction by Fintan O'Toole. Methuen 1993-1994 2v (Methuen world classics)
ISBN v2 0-413-67560-2; v3 0-413-68350-8 LC 93-222005
Contents: Plays: two: Conversations on a homecoming; Bailegangaire; A thief of a Christmas
Plays: three: The morning after optimism; The sanctuary lamp; The Gigli concert

Murphy, Tom. See Murphy, Thomas

Musset, Alfred de
Fantasio and other plays; translated by Michael Feingold [et al.] introduction by Amlin Gray. Theatre Communications Group 1993 xxiii, 272p (TCG translations)
ISBN 1-55936-066-6 LC 92-44012
Five plays; edited and introduced by Claude Schumacher. Methuen 1995 318p (Methuen world classics)
ISBN 0-413-69240-X
Contents: The moods of Marianne; Fantasio; Lorenzaccio; Don't play with love; Caprice

My head was a sledgehammer. Foreman, R.

My heart's a suitcase & Low level panic. McIntyre, C.

N

Nagy, Phyllis
Weldon rising & Disappeared. Methuen 1996 116p (Methuen modern plays)
ISBN 0-413-70150-6

Najera, Rick
The pain of the macho and other plays. Arte Publico Press 1997 151p
ISBN 1-55885-190-9 LC 96-39820

The **National** black anthology; eleven plays from America's leading African-American theaters; edited by Woodie King, Jr. Applause 1995 515p
ISBN 1-55783-219-6 LC 95-34945

Nemeth, Sally
Sally's shorts; an evening of short plays. Dramatists 1995 59p
ISBN 0-8222-1454-7

Never swim alone & This is a play. MacIvor, D.

New anthology of contemporary Austrian folk plays; edited by Richard H. Lawson. Ariadne Press 1996 354p (Studies in Austrian literature, culture, and thought. Translation series)
ISBN 1-57241-020-5 LC 95-53209

New Canadian drama 6; Rita Much, editor. Borealis Press 1993 166p

ISBN 0-88887-093-0

Earlier volumes entered in previous volumes of Play Index

Contents: Hooligans, by M. Vingoe; Pope Joan, by B. Rubess

New Danish plays; selected and with an introduction by Hans Christian Andersen. Norvik Press 1996 262p

ISBN 1-870041-32-1

New England blue: plays of working-class life. Horovitz, I.

New French-language plays; Martinique, Quebec, Ivory Coast, Belgium. Preface by Rosette C. Lamont. UBU Repertory Theater Publs. 1993 346p

ISBN 0-913745-41-3 LC 93-60694

New plays from A.C.T.'s young conservatory [v1]-2; edited by Craig Slaight. Smith & Kraus 1993-1996 2v (Young actors series)

ISBN v1 1-880399-25-3; v2 1-880399-73-3

Contents: v1 Ascension day, by T. Mason; Windshook, by M. Gallagher; Reindeer soup, by J. Pintauro; Sightings, by B. Slaight; High tide, by B. Slaight

v2 Eddie Mundo Edmundo, by L. Alvarez; Class action, by B. Slaight; The less than human club, by T. Mason; Every seventeen minutes the crowd goes crazy!, by P. Zindel

New plays from the Abbey Theatre, 1993-1995 [by] Michael Harding [et al.]; edited and with an introduction by Christopher FitzSimon and Sanford Sternlicht. Syracuse Univ. Press 1996 315p (Irish studies)

ISBN 0-8156-2699-1 LC 95-53289

Nigro, Don

Glamorgan and other plays. French 1996 163p

ISBN 0-573-69591-1 LC 96-164064

Nimmo, Heather, and Learner, Tobsha

One small step [and] Witchplay. Currency Press 1995 92p

ISBN 0-86819-418-2

Nimmo, Paul

Will Shakespeare save us! Will Shakespeare save the King! two one act-plays. Players Press 1996 55p

ISBN 0-88734-658-8 LC 96-28290

Nine early plays, 1961-1973. Gurney, A. R.

Nine plays. O'Neill, E.

Norm & Ahmed and other plays. Buzo, A.

Not so dumb. Lazarus, J.

Nuestro New York; an anthology of Puerto Rican plays; edited and with an introduction by John V. Antush. Mentor 1994 566p

ISBN 0-451-62868-3

O

An **O.** Henry Christmas. Ekstrom, P.

Oates, Joyce Carol

The perfectionist and other plays. Ecco Press 1995 246p

ISBN 0-88001-400-8 LC 94-17484

O'Donovan, John
Jonathan, Jack, and GBS; four plays about Irish history and literature; edited by Robert Hogan; with a reminiscence by James Plunkett. Univ. of Del. Press 1993 225p
ISBN 0-87413-452-8 LC 91-51141

Off-Off Broadway Festival plays, 17th ser.: The road to Nineveh, by Le Wilhelm; Correct address, by Judd Lear Silverman; Cowboys, Indians, & waitresses, by Raymond King Shurtz; Homebound, by Lyndall Callan; Your life is a feature film, by Alan Minieri. French 1993 160p
ISBN 0-573-69393-5

Off-Off Broadway Festival plays, 18th ser.: Last exit before toll, by Carrie Goldstein; Peace in our time, by Larry Cadman; Something rotten in Denmark, by Annie G.: How many to tango? by Sandra J. Albert; Visiting Oliver, by Bill Nave; The power and the glory, by Le Wilhelm; Just thinking, by Alan H. Kravitz; Pasguini the Magnificent, by Sam Ingraffia. French 1994 187p
ISBN 0-573-69437-0

Off-Off Broadway Festival plays, 19th ser.: Family names, by Edna Pelonero; Cherry blend with vanilla, by Le Wilhelm; Awkward silence, by Jay Reiss; Nothing in common, by Jennifer Fell Hayes; The spelling bee, by Philip Vassallo; Highwire, by Brian Shields; Pizza: a love story, by Julianne Bernstein. French 1995 143p
ISBN 0-573-69501-6

Off-Off Broadway Festival plays, 20th ser.: Pavane, by Sally Dixon Wiener; The art of dating, by Jeffrey Scott Elwell; Snow stars, by Anne V. Sawyer; Life comes to the old maid, by Le Wilhelm; The appointment, by Luigi Jannuzzi; A winter reunion, by Henry Miller. French 1996 165p
ISBN 0-573-60248-4

Off-Off Broadway Festival plays, 21st ser.; Whoppers, by Le Wilhelm; Dolorosa Sanchez, by Stanley Taikeff; At land's end, by Marcus L. Steinour; In with Alma, by Steven Packard; With or without you, by Luigi Jannuzzi; Murmurs, by Scott C. Sickles; Ballycastle, by Sylvia Cahill. French 1997 137p
ISBN 0-573-60250-6

Old barn puppet plays. Jones, T.

One-act plays for children. Schurman-O'Connor, K.

One small step [and] Witchplay. Nimmo, H. and Learner, T.

O'Neill, Eugene
The Emperor Jones; "Anna Christie"; The hairy ape. Vintage Bks. 1995 198p (Vintage international)
ISBN 0-679-76395-3

The hairy ape & All God's chillun got wings; introduction by Christine Dymkowski. Hern Bks. 1993 85p
ISBN 1-85459-151-7

Nine plays; selected by the author. Modern Lib. 1993 829p
ISBN 0-679-60045-0 LC 92-27149

Ten "lost" plays. Dover Publs. 1995 303p
ISBN 0-486-28367-4 LC 94-37321

O'Neill, Eugene—*Continued*
Three plays. Vintage Bks. 1995 424p (Vintage international)
ISBN 0-679-76396-1
Contents: Desire under the elms; Strange interlude; Mourning becomes Electra

Only prostitutes marry in May. Maraini, D.

The **only** true history of Lizzie Finn; The steward of Christendom; White Woman Street. Barry, S.

Onwueme, Osonye Tess
Three plays. Wayne State Univ. Press 1993 173p (African-American life series)
ISBN 0-8143-2444-4 LC 92-47582
Contents: The broken calabash; Parables for a season; The reign of Wazobia

The **oracle** at Stoneleigh Court. Taylor, P.

The **oriki** of a grasshopper and other plays. Osofisan, F.

Osborne, John
Plays: one; introduced by the author. Faber & Faber 1996 375p (Contemporary classics)
ISBN 0-571-17766-2
Contents: Look back in anger; Epitaph for George Dillon; The world of Paul Slickey; Déjavu

Osment, Philip
Plays: 1; introduced by the author; with a preface of Mike Alfreds. Methuen 1997 342p (Methuen contemporary dramatists)
ISBN 0-413-71070-X

Osofisan, Femi
The oriki of a grasshopper and other plays; with an introduction by Abiola Irele. Howard Univ. Press 1995 195p
ISBN 0-88258-181-3 LC 95-6636

Other schools of thought. Panych, M.

Out of the bag. Martin, J.

Outrageous! and other comedies. Tasca, J.

Overmyer, Eric
Eric Overmyer: collected plays. Smith & Kraus 1993 317p (Plays for actors)
ISBN 1-880399-33-4 LC 93-15915

P

The **pain** of the macho and other plays. Najera, R.

Painted, tainted, sainted. Gilbert, S.

Panych, Morris
Other schools of thought. Talonbooks 1994 125p
ISBN 0-88922-346-7

Paracelsus and other one-act plays. Schnitzler, A.

Parks, Suzan-Lori
The America play and other works. Theatre Communications Group 1994 199p
ISBN 1-55936-091-7 LC 94-26687

Parr, Bruce
(ed.) Australian gay and lesbian plays. See Australian gay and lesbian plays

Parra, Marco Antonio de la
The theatre of Marco Antonio de la Parra; translations and commentary; translated and edited by Charles Philip Thomas. Lang, P. 1995 363p (Taft Memorial Fund and University of Cincinnati studies in Latin American, Chicago, and U.S. Latino theatre v2)
ISBN 0-8204-2141-3 LC 93-8865

Parsons, Richard
Rialto; Mortmain; Dead end; three plays. French (London) 1993 48p
ISBN 0-573-10001-2 LC 94-204564

Parting gestures. Pedrero, P.

Party time and the new world orderr Pinter, H.

Passion: six new short plays by Australian women; edited by Ros Horin. Currency Press in association with Griffin Theatre 1994 130p (Current theatre series)
ISBN 0-86819-423-9

Patient A and other plays. Blessing, L.

Pedrero, Paloma
Parting gestures; three plays; translated by Phyllis Zatlin. Estreno 1994 63p (Estreno contemporary Spanish plays 6)
ISBN 0-9631212-5-1

Penhall, Joe
Some voices & Pale horse. Methuen 1996 163p (Methuen modern plays)
ISBN 0-413-70440-8

The **perfectionist** and other plays. Oates, J. C.

Pflomm, Phyllis Noe
Puppet plays plus; hand puppet plays for two puppeteers. Scarecrow Press 1994 244p
ISBN 0-8108-2738-7 LC 94-4875
Partially analyzed

Picasso at the Lapin Agile and other plays. Martin, S.

Pinero, Arthur Wing
Trelawny of the 'Wells' and other plays; edited with an introduction by J. S. Bratton. Oxford 1995 326p (World's classics)
ISBN 0-19-282568-2 LC 94-12320
Contents: The magistrate; The schoolmistress; The second Mrs. Tanqueray; Trelawny of the 'Wells'

Pintauro, Joseph
Metropolitan operas; 27 short plays. Dramatists 1997 227p
ISBN 0-8222-1508-X LC 97-162422

Pinter, Harold
Party time and The new world order; two plays. Grove Press 1993 60p
ISBN 0-8021-3352-5 LC 93-28859

Plays: four. New and rev. ed. Faber & Faber 1993 423p
ISBN 0-571-17303-9
Contents: Old times; No man's land; Betrayal; Monologue; Family voices; A kind of Alaska; Victoria Station; Precisely; One for the road; Mountain language; The new world order

Pitching to the star and other short plays. Margulies, D.

Plato's Euthyphro, Apology, and Crito. Emery, S. W.

Plautus, Titus Maccius

Four comedies; translated, with an introduction and notes, by Erich Segal. Oxford 1996 242p (World's classics)

ISBN 0-19-283108-9 LC 96-44849

Contents: The braggard soldier; The brothers Menaechmus; The haunted house; The pot of gold

Plautus: the comedies; edited by David R. Slavitt and Palmer Bovie. John Hopkins Univ. Press 1995 4v (Complete Roman drama in translations)

ISBN v1 0-8018-5070-3; v2 0-8018-5056-8; v3 0-8018-5067-3; v4 0-8018-5072-X LC 94-45317

Three comedies; translated by Robert Wind. Univ. Press of America 1995 222p

ISBN 0-8191-9815-3 LC 94-41092

Plautus: the comedies. Plautus, T. M.

The **Playboy** of the Western World and two other Irish plays; introduced by W. A. Armstrong. Penguin 1997 224p

ISBN 0-14-018878-9

Contents: The Countess Cathleen, by W. B. Yeats; The playboy of the Western World, by J. M. Synge; Cock-a-doodle dandy, by S. O'Casey

Playhouse: six fantasy plays for children; edited by Joyce Doolittle. RDC Press 1989 202p (Northern lights books for children)

ISBN 0-88995-028-8

Playing the past: three plays by Australian women; edited by Kerry Kilner & Sue Tweg; introduced by Kerry Kilner. Currency Press in association with the National Centre for Australian Studies and the Australian Drama Project 1995 54p (Current theatre series; Australian drama project series no.1)

ISBN 0-86819-449-2

Playland and A place with the pigs. Fugard, A.

Plays. Aristophanes

Plays. Barnes, P.

Plays. Fo, D.

Plays. Goethe, J. W. von

Plays. Hauptmann, G.

Plays. Mercer, D.

Plays. Minghella, A.

Plays. Murphy, T.

Plays. Storey, D.

Plays: 1. Barry, S.

Plays: 1. Cartwright, J.

Plays: 1. Osment, P.

Plays: 1. Reid, C.

Plays: 1. Ridley, P.

Plays: 1. Russell, W.

Plays: 1. Townsend, S.

Plays: 1. Wilcox, M.

Plays: 5. Bond, E.

Plays by American women, 1930-1960; edited and with an introduction by Judith E. Barlow. Applause 1994 542p
ISBN 1-55783-164-5 LC 94-7760

Plays by Tony Kushner. Kushner, T.

Plays by women: an international anthology bk2-3; preface by Ntozake Shange. Ubu Repertory Theater Publs. 1994-1996 2v
ISBN 0-913745-42-1 LC 89-142722
Earlier volume entered in previous volume of Play Index

Plays for actresses; edited by Eric Lane and Nina Shengold. Vintage Bks. 1997 626p
ISBN 0-679-77281-2 LC 96-53573

Plays for the end of the century; edited, with an introduction, by Bonnie Marranca. Johns Hopkins Univ. Press 1996 380p (PAJ books)
ISBN 0-8018-5107-6 LC 96-21936

Plays for young audiences. Bush, M.

Plays for young puppeteers. Mahlmann, L. and Jones, D. C.

Plays: four. Pinter, H.

Plays of America from American folklore for children. McCullough, L. E.

Plays of America from American folklore for young actors. McCullough, L. E.

The **plays** of Anton Chekhov. Chekhov, A.

Plays of black Americans; the black experience in America, dramatized for young people; edited by Sylvia E. Kamerman. New expanded ed. Plays, Inc. 1994 154p
ISBN 0-8238-0301-5 LC 94-9314

The **plays** of the Marquis de Sade. Sade, Marquis de

The **plays** of the songs of Christmas. McCullough, L. E.

Plays of the Wild West. McCullough, L. E.

Plays on the word. Haylock, D.

Plays: one. Ayckbourn, A.

Plays: one. Bennett, A.

Plays: one. Granville-Barker, H.

Plays: one. Griffiths, T.

Plays: one. Hampton, C.

Plays: one. Hare, D.

Plays: one. Johnson, T.

Plays: one. Macdonald, S.

Plays: one. McGuinness, R.

Plays: one. Osborne, J.

Plays: one. Stoppard, T.

Plays: one. Ward, N.

Plays: one. Wedekind, F.

Plays: one. Wertenbaker, T.

Plays: three. Harrison, T.

Plays: two. Daniels, S.

Plays: two. Harwood, R.

Plays: two. Poliakoff, S.

Playwrights of exile: an international anthology. Ubu Repertory Theater Publs. 1997 442p
ISBN 0-913745-48-0 LC 94-012045

Playwriting women; 7 plays from the Women's Project; edited and with an introduction by Julia Miles. Heinemann 1992 325p
ISBN 0-435-08617-0 LC 92-24090

Poliakoff, Stephen
Blinded by the sun & Sweet panic. Methuen 1996 239p (Methuen modern plays)
ISBN 0-413-70700-8

Plays: two; introduced by the author. Methuen 1994 408p (Methuen world classics)
ISBN 0-413-68660-4

Contents: Breaking the silence; Playing with trains; She's been away; Century [screenplay]

The **Politics** of life: four plays by Asian American women; edited and with an introduction and commentaries by Velina Hasu Houston. Temple Univ. Press 1993 274p (Asian American history and culture)
ISBN 1-56639-000-1 LC 92-13090

Pope, Rena
Sandwiches; two one-act plays. New Playwrights Network 1994 24p
ISBN 0-86319-33-7

Porcelain and A language of their own. Yew, C.

The **portable** Arthur Miller. Miller, A.

Porter, Deborah
Flowers & No more Medea. Playwrights Canada 1994 119p
ISBN 0-88754-526-2 LC 94-230022

Potter, Dennis
Blue remembered hills and other plays. Faber & Faber 1996 189p
ISBN 0-571-17906-1

Karaoke and Cold Lazarus; with an introduction by the author. Faber & Faber 1996 392p
ISBN 0-571-17478-7

Practical plays. Marx, P.

Prideaux, James
Laughter in the shadow of the trees and other plays. Dramatists 1996 81p
ISBN 0-8222-1512-8

The **primary** English class and six new plays. Horovitz, I.

Prince & plays. Gregor, H.

Professor Bernhardi and other plays. Schnitzler, A.

Puig, Manuel
Kiss of the spider woman and two other plays. Norton 1994 192p
ISBN 0-393-31148-1 LC 94-6549

Puppet plays plus. Pflomm, P. N.

Purkiss, Diane
(ed.) Renaissance women. See Renaissance women

R

Rabe, David
The Vietnam plays. Grove Press 1993 2v
ISBN v1 0-8021-3313-4; v2 0-8021-3345-2 LC 92-37145
Contents: v1 The basic training of Pavlo Hummel; Sticks and bones
v2: Streamers; The orphan

A **raisin** in the sun and The sign in Sidney Brustein's window. Hansberry, L.

Rattigan, Terence
The Browning version and Harlequinade; introduced by Dan Rebellato. Hern Bks. 1994 95p
ISBN 1-85459-202-5

The **real** Inspector Hound and other entertainments. Stoppard, T.

The **recruiting** officer and other plays. Farquhar, G.

Reid, Christina
Plays: 1; with an introduction by Maria M. Delgado. Methuen 1997 343p (Methuen contemporary dramatists)
ISBN 0-413-71220-6
Contents: Tea in a china cup; Did you hear the one about the Irishman ...?; Joyriders; The belle of the Belfast city; My name, shall I tell you my name?; Clowns

Renaissance women; the plays of Elizabeth Cary; the poems of Aemilia Lanyer; edited with introduction and notes by Diane Purkiss. Pickering & Chatto 1994 lviii, 338p (Pickering women's classics)
ISBN 1-85196-029-5 LC 94-36863
Analyzed for play only

Rialto; Mortmain; Dead end. Parsons, R.

Ribman, Ronald
The rug merchants of chaos and other plays. Theatre Communications Group 1992 177p
ISBN 1-55936-050-X LC 92-2568

Ricchi, Renzo
Five one-act plays; introduced and translated by Renzo D'Agnillo, UCD Dept. of Italian 1996 111p
ISBN 1-898473-51-X

Richards, Jeffrey H.
(ed.) Early American drama. See Early American drama

Ridley, Philip
Plays: 1; with an introduction by the author. Methuen 1997 243p (Methuen contemporary dramatists)
ISBN 0-413-71100-5
Contents: The Pitchfork Disney; The fastest clock in the universe; Ghost from a perfect place

Rivera, José
Marisol and other plays. Theatre Communications Group 1997 184p
ISBN 1-55936-136-0 LC 97-5736

Rogers, Katharine M.
(ed.) The Meridian anthology of Restoration and eighteenth-century plays by women. See The Meridian anthology of Restoration and eighteenth-century plays by women

Ronnie Gilbert on Mother Jones. Gilbert, R.

Rosenberg, Joe
(ed.)¡Aplauso! Hispanic children's theater See ¡Aplauso! Hispanic children's theater

The **Rover:** The feigned courtesan; The lucky chance; The emperor of the moon. Behn, A.

Rubies. St. John, B.

The **rug** merchants of chaos and other plays. Ribman, R.

Rupert Street Lonely Hearts Club & Boom bang-bang. Harvey, J.

Russell, Willly
Plays: 1; with an introduction by the author. Methuen 1996 359p (Methuen contemporary dramatists)
ISBN 0-413-70220-0
Contents: Breezeblock Park; Our day out; Stags and hens; Educating Rita

Ruzzanate, 1502?-1542
The veteran (Parlamento de Ruzante) and Weasel (Bilora); two one-act Renaissance plays [by] Angelo Beolco (Ruzante); translated, with an introduction, notes and bibliography by Ronnie Ferguson. Lang, P. 1995 140p (Studies in Italian culture. Literature in history v17)
ISBN 0-8204-2700-4 LC 94-41317

Rzhevsky, Nicholas
(ed.) An Anthology of Russian literature. See An Anthology of Russian literature

S

Sade, Marquis de
The plays of the Marquis de Sade; translated and edited by John Franceschina and Ben Ohmart. Hollowbrook Pub. 1993 2v
ISBN v1 0-89341-708-4; v2 0-89341-710-6 LC 92-17131

Sally's shorts. Nemeth, S.

Sandwiches. Pope, R.

Saunders, Jennifer
Absolutely fabulous. Pocket Bks. 1993 165p
ISBN 0-671-52714-2

Savage acts. Valle-Inclán, R. del

Schenandoah and other verse plays. Schwartz, D.

Schenkkan, Robert
The Kentucky cycle. Dramatists 1994 264p
ISBN 0-8222-1309-5
Also available from Plume Bks.

Schevill, James
5 plays 5. Swallow Press/Ohio Univ. Press 1993 367p
ISBN 0-8040-0967-8 LC 92-39580

Schiff, Ellen
(ed.) Awake and singing: 7 classic plays from the American Jewish repertoire. See Awake and singing: 7 classic plays from the American Jewish repertoire
(ed.) Fruitful and multiplying. See Fruitful and multiplying

Schisgal, Murray
Sexaholics and other plays. Dramatists 1995 109p
ISBN 0-8222-1438-5 LC 95-176196

Schnitzler, Arthur
The final plays; translated and with an afterword by G. J. Weinberger. Ariadne Press 1996 289p (Studies in Austrian literature, culture, and thought. Translation series)
ISBN 1-57241-029-9 LC 96-1918
Paracelsus and other one-act plays; translated by G. J. Weinberger; afterword by Herbert Lederer. Ariadne Press 1994 220p (Studies in Austrian literature, culture, and thought. Translation series)
ISBN 0-929497-96-1 LC 94-21539
Professor Bernhardi and other plays; translated by G. J. Weinberger; afterword by Jeffrey B. Berlin. Ariadne Press 1993 379p (Studies in Austrian literature, culture, and thought. Translation series)
ISBN 0-929497-70-8 LC 93-7274

Schurer, Ernst
(ed.) German expressionist plays. See German expressionist plays

Schurman-O'Connor, Kathleen
One-act plays for children. Clark, I. E. 1993 52p
ISBN 0-88680-384-5
Contents: Billy's problem; Ghoul Scout camp; At the bus stop; Grandma Rusnak; The Wizard of Zoz

Schwartz, Delmore
Shenandoah and other verse plays; edited and with an introduction by Robert Phillips. BOA Eds. 1992 165p
ISBN 0-918526-91-4 LC 91-73276

Sea of Cortez and other plays. Steppling, J.

Seattle Children's Theatre: six plays for young audiences; Marisa Smith, editor. Smith & Kraus 1997 308p (Young actors series)
ISBN 1-57525-008-X LC 96-18740

Selected plays, 1963-83/1984-87. Havel, V.

Selected plays of Jerome Lawrence and Robert E. Lee. Lawrence, J. and Lee, R. E.

Selected prose and dramatic work. Lyly, J.

The **Sensational** Restoration; edited with notes and commentary by H. James Jensen. Indiana Univ. Press 1996 450p (Indiana masterpiece editions)
ISBN 0-253-33049-1 LC 96-1727

Seven contemporary Austrian plays; edited by Richard H. Lawson. Ariadne Press 1995 283p (Studies in Austrian literature, culture, and thought. Translation series)
ISBN 1-57241-071-5 LC 95-14086

Seven Gothic dramas, 1789-1825; edited with an introduction by Jeffrey N. Cox. Ohio Univ. Press 1992 425p
ISBN 0-8214-1015-6 LC 91-31262

Seventeen short plays. Linney, R.

Sexaholics and other plays. Schisgal, M.

Shaffer, Diane

Solace at twilight; two one-act plays. French 1997 120p
ISBN 0-573-62638-3

The **shallow** end and The lost colony. MacLeod, W.

Shange, Ntozake

(ed.) Plays by women: an international anthology bk 2-3. See Plays by women: an international anthology bk2-3

Shanley, John Patrick

Four dogs and a bone and The wild goose. Dramatists 1995 75p
ISBN 0-8222-1400-8 LC 95-166409

Missing/Kissing. Dramatists 1997 60p
ISBN 0-8222-1590-X

Shared anxiety. Walker, G. F.

Sharing the delirium; second generation AIDS plays and performances; selected and introduced by Therese Jones. Heinemann 1994 342p
ISBN 0-435-08633-2 LC 93-44972

Contents: The baddest of boys, by D. Holsclaw; Myron, a fairy tale in black and white, by M. Kearns; Queen of angels, by J. C. Pickett; Satan and Simon DeSoto, by T. Sod; AIDS! the musical! by R. Berg; What are Tuesdays like?, by V. Bumbalo; My queer body, by T. Miller

Sharrar, Jack

(ed.) Short plays for young actors. See Short plays for young actors

Shaw, Bernard

Arms and the man and John Bull's other island; with an introduction by Stanley and Rodelle Weintraub. Bantam Bks. 1993 258p
ISBN 0-553-21421-7

Shaw, Bernard—*Continued*
George Bernard Shaw: selected plays. Gramercy Bks. 1996 690p (Great Irish plays)
ISBN 0-517-12428-9
Contents: Mrs. Warren's profession; Caesar and Cleopatra; Man and superman; Major Barbara; Pygmalion; Heartbreak House

Shengold, Nina
(ed.) The Actor's book of gay and lesbian plays. See The Actor's book of gay and lesbian plays
(ed.) Plays for actresses. See Plays for actresses

Shepard, Sam
States of shock; Far north; Silent tongue. Vintage Bks. 1993 202p
Analyzed for play only; Far north and Silent tongue are screenplays

The unseen hand and other plays. Vintage Bks. 1996 383p
ISBN 0-679-76789-4 LC 95-47723

Sherman, Jonathan Marc
Three short plays. Dramatists 1995 105p
ISBN 0-8222-1372-9 LC 95-192123
Contents: Serendipity and serenity; Sons and fathers; Jesus on the oil tank

Shine, Ted
(ed.) Black theatre USA. See Black theatre USA

Short plays for young actors; Craig Slaight and Jack Sharrar, editors. Smith & Kraus 1995 xx, 267p (Young actors series)
ISBN 1-880399-74-1 LC 95-26295

Shooting rats, other plays and poems. Turrini, P.

Showtime's Act One Festival of one-act plays, 1994; edited by Marisa Smith. Smith & Kraus 1995 253p (Contemporary playwrights series)
ISBN 1-880399-96-2 LC 95-22540

Shuttleworth, Red
(ed.) Lucky 13. See Lucky 13

Siberia and other plays. Mitterer, F.

Sidney Kingsley: five prizewinning plays. Kingsley, S.

Sight unseen and other plays. Margulies, D.

Sightings and High tide. Slaight, B.

Silver, Nicky
Etiquette and vitriol: The food chain and other plays. Theatre Communications Group 1996 300p
ISBN 1-55936-123-9 LC 96-35078

Simon, Neil
London suite; a comedy. French 1996 104p
ISBN 0-573-69509-1

Single and proud & other plays. Stroppel, F.

Sister Mary Ignatius explains it all for you and The actor's nightmare. Durang, C.

Six award winning plays. Beim, N.

Six-pack: plays for Scotland. McGrath, J.

Six plays. Linney, R.

Six short plays. Bynum, R. C.

Sixteen short plays. Horovitz, I.

Slaight, Brad
Sightings and High tide; two one act plays. Bakers Plays 1993 64p

Slaight, Craig
(ed.) New plays from A.C.T.'s young conservatory. See New plays from A.C.T.'s young conservatory
(ed.) Short plays for young actors. See Short plays for young actors

Sloate, Daniel
The Countess cycle; (five plays). Guernica 1995 182p (Drama series 6)
ISBN 0-920717-78-0 LC 96-120851

Smith, Marisa
(ed.) Act One '95. See Act One '95
(ed.) EST marathon 1994. See EST marathon 1994
(ed.) EST marathon '95. See EST marathon '95
(ed.) Humana Festival . . . See Humana Festival . . .
(ed.) Showtime's Act One Festival of one-act plays, 1994. See Showtime's Act One Festival of one-act plays, 1994
(ed.) Women playwrights: the best plays of . . . See Women playwrights: the best plays of . . .

Solace at twilight. Schaffer, D.

Solo; edited by Jason Sherman. Coach House Press 1993 303p
ISBN 0-88910-449-2

Solórzano, Carlos
Crossroads and other plays; translated and edited by Francesca Colecchia. Fairleigh Dickinson Univ. Press 1993 148p
ISBN 0-8386-3485-0 LC 91-58941

Some voices & Pale horse. Penhall, J.

Songs my mother taught me. Yamauchi, W.

Sophocles
The Theban plays; translated by David Grene; with an introduction by Charles Segal and notes by James Hogan. Knopf 1994 221p (Everyman's library)
ISBN 0-679-43132-2 LC 94-5984
Contents: Oedipus the King; Oedipus at Colonus; Antigone

South African plays; edited with an introduction by Stephen Gray. Hern Bks. 1993 241p
ISBN 1-85459-148-7
Contents: Somewhere on the border, by A. Akerman; The hungry earth, by M. Maponya; Curl up and dye, by S. Pam-Grant; Over the hill, by P. Slabolepszy; Just like home, by P.-D. Uys

Spain. Linney, R.

St. John, Billy
Rubies. Bakers Plays 1993 71p

St Nicholas & The weir. McPherson, C.

The **stage** plays. Chayefsky, P.

Staging gay lives; an anthology of contemporary gay theater; edited by John M. Clum; foreword by Tony Kushner. Westview Press 1996 471p
ISBN 0-8133-2504-8 LC 95-23652

Standjofski, Harry
Urban myths: Anton & No cycle. NuAge Eds. 1992 111p (Performance series)
ISBN 0-921833-15-6

Star-gazy pie. Stock, J.

Starhemberg, Heinrich von. See Gregor, Henry

States of shock; Far north; Silent tongue. Shepard, S.

Stein, Howard
(ed.) The Best American short plays, 1992/1993-1995/1996. See The Best American short plays, 1992/1993-1995/1996

Steppling, John
Sea of Cortez and other plays; with an appreciation by Martin Epstein. Sun & Moon Press 1996 182p (Sun & Moon classics)
ISBN 1-55713-237-2 LC 96-31616

Stock, James
Star-gazy pie; two plays. Hern Bks. 1995 160p
ISBN 1-85459-293-9 LC 96-161398
Contents: Blue night in the heart of the West; Star-gazy pie and sauerkraut

Stone, Trude
Hello, Ma! and other plays. French 1996 91p
ISBN 0-573-69524-5

Stoppard, Tom
Plays; introduced by the author. Faber & Faber 1996 2v (Contemporary classics)
ISBN v1 0-571-17765-4; v2 0-571-17977-0
Contents: Plays: one: The real Inspector Hound; After Magritte; Dirty linen; New-found-land; Dogg's Hamlet, Caboot's Macbeth

Plays: two: The dissolution of Dominic Boot; 'M' is for moon among other things; If you're Glad I'll be Frank; Albert's bridge; Where are they now?; Artist decending a staircase; The dog it was that died; In the native state

The real Inspector Hound and other entertainments. Faber & Faber 1993 211p
ISBN 0-571-16571-0

The television plays, 1965-1984. Faber & Faber 1993 264p
ISBN 0-571-16568-0; 0-571-16570-2

Storey, David, 1933-
Plays; with an introduction by the author. Methuen 1992-1994 2v (Methuen world classics)
ISBN v1 0-413-67350-2; v2 0-413-68610-8
Contents: Plays: one: The contractor; Home; Stages; Caring

Plays: two: The restoration of Arnold Middleton; In celebration; The march on Russia

Strindberg, August
Strindberg—other sides; seven plays; translated and introduced by Joe Martin; with a foreword by Björn Meidal. Lang, P. 1997 382p
ISBN 0-8204-3691-7 LC 96-54508

Strindberg—other sides. Strindberg, A.

Stroppel, Frederick
Single and proud & other plays. French 1993 112p
ISBN 0-573-69411-7

The **substance** of fire and other plays. Baitz, J. R.

Swortzell, Lowell
(ed.) Theatre for young audiences: around the world in 21 plays. See Theatre for young audiences: around the world in 21 plays

Szyszkowitz, Gerald
Five plays; translated by Todd C. Hanlin, Heidi L. Hutchinson, Joseph G. McVeigh; preface by Peter Turrini; afterword by Joseph G. McVeigh. Ariadne Press 1993 344p (Studies in Austrian literature, culture, and thought. Translation series)
ISBN 0-929497-69-4 LC 93-18743

T

Tagore, Rabindranath
The collected poems and plays. Collier Bks. 1993 466p
ISBN 0-02-082455-6 LC 92-33702

Taking liberties & Into. Carley D.

Tales of the lost Formicans and other plays. Congdon, C.

Tasca, Jules
Outrageous! and other comedies. French 1997 92p
ISBN 0-573-62631-6

Taub, Michael
(ed.) Israeli Holocaust drama. See Israeli Holocaust drama

Taylor, Peter
The oracle at Stoneleigh Court; stories. Knopf 1993 323p
ISBN 0-679-41990-X LC 92-54283
Analyzed for plays only

Taylor, Regina
The ties that bind; a pair of one-act plays. Dramatic 1995 70p
ISBN 0-87129-519-9 LC 96-106918
Contents: Watermelon rinds; Inside the belly of the beast

Taylor, Renée, and Bologna, Joseph
Love allways. French 1933 230p
ISBN 0-573-69398-6 LC 94-136672

The **tears** of my sister; The Prisoner's Song; The one-armed man and The land of the astronauts. Foote, H.

¡Teatro! Hispanic plays for young people. Vigil, A.

The **television** plays. Chayefsky, P.

The **television** plays. Stoppard, T.

Telling tales: new one-act plays; edited by Eric Lane. Penguin Bks. 1993 417p
ISBN 0-14-048237-7 LC 92-23876

Ten "lost" plays. O'Neill, E.

Ten-minute plays: v3. Actors Theatre of Louisville

Testimonies: four plays. Mann, E.

The **theatre** of Marco Antonio de la Parra. Parra, M. A. de la

The **Theban** plays. Sophocles

Thirty plays from favorite stories; royalty-free dramatizations of myths, folktales, and legends from around the world; edited by Sylvia E. Kamerman. Plays, Inc. 1997 291p
ISBN 0-8238-03-6-6 LC 97-1039

This lime tree bower: three plays McPherson, C.

Thomas, Edward, 1961-
Three plays; edited by Brian Mitchell. Seren Bks. [distributed by Dufour Eds.] 1994 216p (Seren drama)
ISBN 1-85411-113-2 LC 95-219904

Three French comedies; translated and with an introduction by James Magruder. Yale Univ. Press 1996 180p
ISBN 0-300-06276-1 LC 95-40001
Contents: Turcaret, by LeSage; The triumph of love, by Marivaux; Eating crow, by Labiche

Three hotels; plays and monologues. Baitz, J. R.

Three plays. Abe, K.

Three plays. Crowley, M.

Three plays. Hugo, V.

Three plays. O'Neill, E.

Three plays. Onwueme, O. T.

Three plays. Thomas, E.

Three plays. Valle-Inclan, R. del

Three plays. Way, C.

Three plays: Blood wedding, Yerma, The house of Bernarda Alba. Garcia Lorca, F.

Three plays by Isaac Chocrón. Chocrón, I.

Three plays by Mae West. West, M.

Three quest plays. James, J.

Three short plays. Sherman, J. M.

Through the leaves and other plays. Kroetz, F. X.

The **ties** that bind. Taylor, R.

'Tis pity she's a whore and other plays. Ford, J.

Toddie, Jean Lenox
Late Sunday afternoon, early Sunday evening and Is that the bus to Pittsburgh? two one-act plays. French 1994 62p
ISBN 0-573-62265-5

Townsend, Sue
Plays: 1. Methuen 1996 321p (Methuen contemporary dramatists)
ISBN 0-413-70250-2
Contents: Womberang; Bazaar & rummage; Groping for words; The great celestial cow; The secret diary of Adrian Mole aged 13¾

Trott, Steve
Destination Bethlehem: seven Christmas plays for young people. Baker Bks. 1993 64p
ISBN 0-8010-8906-9 LC 93-19352

Trying to find Chinatown and Bondage. Hwang, D. H.

Turrini, Peter
Shooting rats, other plays and poems; translated and with an afterword by Richard Dixon. Ariadne Press 1996 211p (Studies in Austrian literature, culture, and thought. Translation series)
ISBN 0-929497-98-8 LC 95-50543
Analyzed for plays only

Tweg, Sue
(ed.) Playing the past: three plays by Australian women. See Playing the past: three plays by Australian women

Twenty seven short plays. Durang, C.

Twenty/twenty: twenty one-act plays from twenty years of the Humana Festival. See 20/20: twenty one-act plays from twenty years of the Humana Festival

Two & Bed. Cartwright, J.

Two plays. Wellman, M.

U

Unbroken thread; an anthology of plays by Asian American women; edited by Roberta Uno. Univ. of Mass. Press 1993 328p
ISBN 0-87023-855-8 LC 93-21858

Uncle Vanya and other plays. Chekhov, A.

Uno, Roberta
(ed.) Unbroken thread. See Unbroken thread

The **unseen** hand and other plays. Shepard, S.

Upton, Judy
Bruises & The shorewatchers' house. Methuen 1996 114p (Methuen modern plays)
ISBN 0-413-70430-0

Urban myths. Standjofski, H.

V

Valle-Inclán, Ramón del
Savage acts; four plays; translated by Robert Lima. Estreno 1993 65p (Estreno collection of contemporary Spanish plays 3)
ISBN 0-9631212-2-7 LC 92-75690

Three plays; translated and introduced by Maria M. Delgado. Methuen 1993 273p (Methuen world classics)
ISBN 0-413-67090-2
Cover title: Plays: one
Contents: Divine words; Bohemian lights; Silver face

Vampilov, Alexsandr
Duck-hunting [and] Last summer in Chulimsk; two plays; translated by Patrick Miles. Bramcote Press 1994 158p
ISBN 0-9517853-3-8

Verse plays and epic. Goethe, J. W. von

The **Veteran** (Parlamento de Ruzante) and Weasel (Bilora). Ruzzante

The **Vietnam** plays. Rabe, D.

Vigil, Angel
¡Teatro! Hispanic plays for young people. Teacher Ideas Press 1996 169p
ISBN 1-56308-371-X LC 96-15593

Villeggiatura trilogy, Carlo Goldoni's. Goldoni, C.

Vogel, Paula
The Baltimore waltz and other plays. Theatre Communications Group 1996 296p
ISBN 1-55936-109-3 LC 95-45986

Voicings: ten plays from the documentary theatre; edited and with an introduction by Attilio Favorini. Ecco Press 1995 376p
ISBN 0-88001-397-4 LC 94-44190

Volansky, Michele
(ed.) Actors Theatre of Louisville. Ten-minute plays: v3
(ed.) By Southern playwrights. See By Southern playwrights
(ed.) A Decade of new comedy. See A Decade of new comedy

Voyage to the sonorous land. Handke, P.

W

Walker, George F.
Shared anxiety; selected plays. Coach House Press 1994 503p
ISBN 0-88910-472-7

Wanna play? 3 plays for high school. Playwrights Canada 1994 215p
ISBN 0-88754-495-9

Contents: Carrying the calf, by S. Barrie; Blind dates, by A. Fuerstenberg; Thin ice, by B. Rubess and B. Cooper

The **war** against the kitchen sink. Guare, J.

Ward, Nick
Plays: one; introduced by the author. Faber & Faber 1995 311p (Faber contemporary classics)
ISBN 0-571-17681-X LC 96-145139

Contents: The present; Apart from George; The strangeness of others; Trouble sleeping

Warner, Francis
Agora; an epic. Smythe 1994 2v
ISBN 0-86140-374-6 (set)

Warren, Dianne
(ed.) Eureka! See Eureka!

Wars I have seen. Blanc, E. S.

Wasserman, Jerry
(ed.) Modern Canadian plays. See Modern Canadian plays

Way, Charles
Three plays; edited by Brian Mitchell. Seren Bks. [distributed by Dufour Eds.] 1994 208p (Seren drama)
ISBN 1-85411-114-0 LC 96-121385
Contents: Dead man's hat; Paradise Drive; In the bleak midwinter

A **way** with words. Gilroy, F. D.

Weber, Carl
(ed.) DramaContemporary: Germany. See DramaContemporary: Germany

Webster, Peter
Dick Turpin and Babes in the wood; two pantomimes. Warner Chappell Plays 1996 99p
ISBN 0-85676-226-1

Wedekind, Frank
Plays: one; translated and introduced by Edward Bond and Elsabeth Bond-Pablé. Methuen 1993 212p (Methuen world classics)
ISBN 0-413-67540-8
Contents: Spring awakening: a children's tragedy; Lulu: a monster tragedy

Weird romance. Menken, A.

Weldon rising & Disappeared. Nagy, P.

Weller, Michael
Five plays. Theatre Communications Group 1997 244p
ISBN 1-55936-143-3

Wellman, Mac
The bad infinity; eight plays. Johns Hopkins Univ. Press 1994 277p (PAJ bks)
ISBN 1-55713-197-X

The land beyond the forest: Dracula and Swoop. Sun & Moon Press 1995 99p (American theater in literature)
ISBN 1-55713-228-3 LC 95-25658

Two plays; A murder of crows and The hyacinth macaw. Sun & Moon Press 1994 167p (American theater in literature)
ISBN 0-8018-4687-0 LC 93-1911

Wertenbaker, Timberlake
Plays: one; introduced by the author. Faber & Faber 1996 445p
ISBN 0-571-17743-3

West, Mae, 1892-1980
Three plays by Mae West; edited by Lillian Schlissel. Routledge 1997 246p
ISBN 0-415-90932-5 LC 97-24425
Contents: Sex; The drag; The pleasure man

Wetzsteon, Ross
(ed.) The Best of Off-Broadway. See The Best of Off-Broadway

What to name your baby. Allen, R. J.

White, Patrick
Collected plays. Currency Press 1985-1994 2v (Australian dramatists series)
ISBN v1 0-86819-124-8; v2 0-86819-305-4

A **white** sports coat & other plays. Lyssiotis, T.

Why is John Lennon wearing a skirt and other stand-up theatre plays. Dowie, C.

Wilcox, Michael
Plays: 1; with an introduction by the author. Methuen 1997 265p (Methuen contemporary dramatists)
ISBN 0-413-71110-2
Contents: Rents; Accounts; Lent; Massage

The **wild** woman and other plays. Mitterer, F.

Wilde, Oscar
The complete Oscar Wilde. Crescent Bks. 1995 861p
ISBN 0-517-12073-9
Analyzed for plays only
Lady Windermere's fan; Salome; A woman of no importance; An ideal husband; The importance of being Earnest; edited with an introduction by Peter Raby. Oxford 1995 368p (World's classics)
ISBN 0-19-282246-2

Wilder, Thornton
The collected short plays of Thornton Wilder v1; edited by Donald Gallup and A. Tappan Wilder; with additional material by F. J. O'Neil. Theatre Communications Group 1997 323p
ISBN 1-55936-138-7 LC 97-7734

Will Shakespeare save us! Will Shakespeare save the King! Nimmo, P.

William Mastrosimone: collected plays. Mastrosimone, W.

Williamson, David, 1942-
Collected plays v2. Currency Press 1993 249p (Australian dramatists series)
ISBN 0-86819-287-2

Wilson, Lanford
Collected plays, 1965-1970. Smith & Kraus 1996 274p (Contemporary playwrights series)
ISBN 1-57525-026-8 LC 96-1909
Four short plays. Dramatists 1994 92p
Contents: Days ahead; The madness of Lady Bright; This is the rill speaking; Say De Kooning
Lanford Wilson: 21 short plays. Smith & Kraus 1993 268p (Contemporary playwrights series)
ISBN 0-880399-31-8

Wise, Rob
A bit of three-by-one; three one-act plays. New Playwrights Network 1995 48p
ISBN 0-86319-355-2
Contents: Eventide; When one door closes; Sound choice

Witkiewicz, Stanisław Ignacy
The mother & other unsavory plays; including The shoemakers and They; edited and translated by Daniel Gerould and C. S. Durer; foreword by Jan Kott. Applause 1993 246p
ISBN 1-55783-139-4 LC 93-7013

The **wolf** plays. Fraser, B.

Women as lovers. Carilli, T.

Women on the verge: 7 avant-garde American plays; edited and with an introduction by Rosette C. Lamont. Applause 1993 366p
ISBN 1-55783-148-3 LC 93-11557

Women playwrights: the best plays of 1992; edited by Robyn Goodman and Marisa Smith. Smith & Kraus 1992 242p
ISBN 1-880399-22-9

Women playwrights: the best plays of 1993; edited by Marisa Smith. Smith & Kraus 1994 222p (Contemporary playwrights series)
ISBN 1-880399-45-8 LC 94-10071

Women playwrights: the best plays of 1994; edited by Marisa Smith. Smith & Kraus 1995 354p (Contemporary playwrights series)
ISBN 1-880399-84-9

Women playwrights: the best plays of 1995; introduction by Ellen Burstyn; edited by Marisa Smith. Smith & Kraus 1996 278p (Contemporary playwrights series)
ISBN 1-57525-035-7 LC 94-10071

Women's Project
Here to stay. See Here to stay

The **works** of John Dryden. Dryden, J.

Y

Yamauchi, Wakako
Songs my mother taught me; stories, plays, and memoir; edited and with an introduction by Garrett Hongo; afterword by Valerie Miner. Feminist Press 1994 257p
ISBN 1-55861-086-3 LC 93-45383
Analyzed for plays only

Yew, Chay
Porcelain and A language of their own; two plays. Grove Press 1997 230p
ISBN 0-8021-3500-5 LC 96-47068

Young, Glenn
(ed.) The Best American short plays, 1992/1993-1995/1996. See The Best American short plays, 1992/1993-1995/1996

Young playwrights; eleven new plays; edited by Errol Bray. Currency Press 1994 242p
ISBN 0-86819-415-8

Your turn to clean the stair & Fugue. Munro, R.

Youth and other stories. Mori, Ō.

YPThree: three plays from Young People's Theatre. Playwrights Canada 1994 300p
ISBN 0-88754-475-4

Z

Zark, Jenna
A body of water. Dramatists 1994 110p
ISBN 0-8222-1390-7 LC 95-154578

Part IV

Directory of Publishers and Distributors

AB collector pub. AB collector publishing, 5835 Grant St., Halifax, Nova Scotia, Can. B3H 1C9

Absolute Classics. See Absolute Press

Absolute Press. Absolute Press, Scarborough House, 29 James St. W., Bath BA1 2BT, Eng.

Amber Lane Press. Amber Lane Press, Cheorl House, Church St., Charlbury, Oxford OX7 3PR, Eng.

American Univ. in Cairo Press. American University in Cairo Press, 113 Sharia Kasr el Ainy, Cairo

Anchor Bks. (NY) Anchor Books, 1540 Broadway, New York, N.Y. 10036-4094

Anchorage Press. Anchorage Press, Inc., P.O. Box 8067, New Orleans, La. 70182

Andrew Mountain Press. Andrew Mountain Press, P.O. Box 340353, Hartford, Conn. 06134

Applause. Applause Theatre Book Publishers, 211 W. 71st St., New York, N.Y. 10023

Arcade Pub. Arcade Publishing, 141 5th Ave., New York, N.Y. 10010

Ariadne Press. Ariadne Press, 270 Goins Ct., Riverside, Calif. 92507

Arte Publico Press. Arte Publico Press, University of Houston, 4800 Calhoun, Houston, Tex. 77204-2090

Asoka Theatre Publs. Asoka Theatre Publishers, University of Durban-Westvill, Dept. of Drama, Private Bag X54001, Durban 4000, S. Africa

Asylum Arts Pub. Asylum Arts Publishing, 5847 Sawmill Rd., Paradise, Calif. 95969-5333

Avon Bks. Avon Books, 1350 Ave. of the Americas, 2nd Floor, New York, N.Y. 10019

Avon Flare. See Avon Bks.

Baker Bk. House. Baker Book House, 6030 E. Fulton Rd., Ada, Mich. 49301

Baker Bks. See Baker Bk. House

Bakers Plays. Baker's Plays, 100 Chauncy St., Boston, Mass. 02111

Bantam Bks. Bantam Books, 1540 Broadway, New York, N.Y. 10036

Blizzard Pub. Blizzard Publishing, 73 Furby St., Winnipeg, Man., Can. R3C 2A2

Bloodaxe Bks. Bloodaxe Books, Ltd., P.O. Box 1SN, Newcastle upon Tyne NE99 1SN, Eng.

BOA Eds. BOA Editions, Ltd., 260 East Ave., Rochester, N.Y. 14604

Bolchazy-Carducci Pub. Bolchazy-Carducci Publishers, 1000 Brown St., Unit 101, Wauconda, Ill. 60084

Borealis Press. Borealis/Tecumseh Presses Ltd., 9 Ashburn Dr., Ottawa, Ont., Can. K2E 6N4

Borgo Press. The Borgo Press, P.O. Box 2845, San Bernardino, Calif. 92406-2845

Bramcote Press. Bramcote Press, 27 Seven Oaks Crescent, Bramcote Hills, Nottingham NG9 3FW, Eng.

Breakwater. Breakwater Books Ltd., 100 Water St., P.O. Box 2188, St. John's, Nfld., Can. A1C 6E6

Broadway Play Pub. Broadway Play Publishing Inc., 56 E. 81st St., New York, N.Y. 10028-0202

Calder Publs. Calder Publications Ltd., 126 Cornwall Road, London SE1 8TQ, Eng.

Cambridge Univ. Press. Cambridge University Press, Edinburgh Bldg., Shaftesbury Rd., Cambridge CB2 2RU, Eng.
US address: 40 W. 20th St., New York, N.Y. 10011-4211

Canongate Bks. Canongate Books Ltd., 14 High St., Edinburgh EH1 1TE, Scotland

Canongate Press. See Canongate Bks.

Chicago Hist. Bookworks. Chicago Historical Bookworks, 831 Main St., Evanston, Ill. 60202

Clarendon Press. See Oxford Univ. Press

Clark, I. E. I. E. Clark, Inc., P.O. Box 246, Schulenberg, Tex. 78956-0246

Coach House Bks. Coach House Books, 401 Huron St., Toronto, Ont., Can. M5S 2G5

Coach House Press. See Coach House Bks.
Collier Bks. Collier Books, 1230 Ave. of the Americas, New York, N.Y. 10020
Collins Educ. Collins Educational, 77–85 Fulham Palace Rd., Hammersmith, London W6 8JB, Eng.
Columbia Univ. Press. Columbia University Press, 562 W. 113th St., New York, N.Y. 10025
Continuum. The Continuum Publishing Group, 370 Lexington Ave., Suite 1700, New York, N.Y. 10017
Co-operative Union. Co-operative Union Ltd., Holyoake House, Hanover St., Manchester M60 OAS, Eng.
C.S.S. Pub. Co. C.S.S. Publishing Company, Inc., 517 S. Main St., P.O. Box 4503, Lima, Ohio 45804-4503
Coteau Bks. See Thunder Creek Pub. Co-op.
Crescent Bks. See Random House Value Pub.
Crown. Crown Publishing Group, 201 E. 50th St., New York, N.Y. 10022
Currency Press. The Currency Press Pty., Ltd., 330 Oxford St., P.O. Box 452, Paddington, N.S.W. 2021, Aust.

Dalkey Archive Press. The Dalkey Archive Press, Illinois State University, Campus Box 4241, Normal, Ill. 61790-4241
Dee, I. R. Ivan R. Dee, Inc. 1332 N. Halsted St., Chicago, Ill. 60622-2632
Dramatic. Dramatic Publishing Company, 311 Washington St., Woodstock, Ill. 60098
Dramatists. Dramatists Play Service, Inc., 440 Park Ave. S., New York, N.Y. 10016
Dover Publs. Dover Publications Inc., 31 E. 2nd St. Mineola, N.Y. 11501
Dufour Eds. Dufour Editions, P.O. Box 7, Chester Springs, Pa. 19425-0007
Dutton. Dutton, 375 Hudson St., New York, N.Y. 10014-3657

Ecco Press. Ecco Press, 100 W. Broad St., Hopewell, N.J. 08525
Edwin Mellen Press. The Edwin Mellen Press, P.O. Box 450, Lewiston, N.Y. 14092-0450
Element. Element Books, Ltd., The Old School House, The Courtyard, Bell St., Shaftesbury, Dorset SP7 8BP, Eng.
US address: P.O. Box 830, Rockport, Mass. 01966
Estreno. Estreno, 350 N. Burrowes Bldg., University Park, Pa. 16802
Excalibur Press of London. Excalibur Press of London, 4–6 Effie Rd., London SW6 1TD, Eng.

Faber & Faber. Faber & Faber, Ltd., 3 Queen Sq., London WC1N 3AU, Eng.
US address: 53 Shore Rd., Winchester, Mass. 01890-2821
Fairleigh Dickinson Univ. Press. Fairleigh Dickinson University Press, 440 Forsgate Dr., Cranbury, N.J. 08512
Farrar Straus Giroux. Farrar, Straus & Giroux, 19 Union Sq. W., New York, N.Y. 10003
Feminist Press. The Feminist Press at the City Univ. of N.Y., City College, Wingate Bldg. Convent Ave. at 138th St., New York, N.Y. 10031
Fertig. Howard Fertig, Inc., Publisher, 80 E. 11th St., New York, N.Y. 10003
Fifth House. Fifth House, 6125-11th St. S. E., No. 9, Calgary , Alta., Can. T2H 2L6
Foxrock. Foxrock, Inc., 61 4th Ave., 3rd Floor, New York, N.Y. 10003
Free Press. Free Press, 1230 Ave. of the Americas, New York, N.Y. 10020
French. Samuel French, Inc., 45 W. 25th St., New York, N.Y. 10036
French (London). Samuel French, Ltd., 52 Fitzroy St., London W1P 6JR, Eng.
Fyfield Bks. Fyfield Books, Conavon Ct., 12–16 Blackfriars St., Manchester M3 5BQ, Eng.

Gallery Bks. Gallery Books, The Gallery Press, Loughcrew, Oldcastle, County Meath, Ireland
Garland. Garland Publishing, Inc., 717 5th Ave., Suite 2500, New York, N.Y. 10022
Gávea-Brown. Gávea-Brown Publications, Dept. of Portuguese and Brazilian Studies, Brown University, Providence, Rhode Island 02912
Glenbridge Pub. Glenbridge Publishing, Ltd., 6010 W. Jewell Ave., Lakewood, Colo. 80232-7106
GoodYearBooks. GoodYearBooks, 1900 E. Lake Ave., Glenview, Ill. 60025
Gramercy Bks. See Random House Value Pub.
Grove/Atlantic. Grove/Atlantic, 841 Broadway, New York, N.Y. 10003-4793
Grove Press. See Grove/Atlantic
Guernica. Guernica Editions, Inc., P.O. Box 117, Station P, Toronto, Ont. Can. M5S 2S6
US address: 1814 San Pablo, Berkeley, Calif. 94702

Harcourt Brace & Co. Harcourt Brace & Company, 525 B St., Suite 1900, San Diego, Calif. 92101

HarperCollins Pubs. HarperCollins Publishers, 10 E. 53rd St., New York, N.Y. 10022-5299

HarperFestival. See HarperCollins Pubs.

HarperPrism. See HarperCollins Pubs.

Harvard Univ. Press. Harvard University Press, 79 Garden St., Cambridge, Mass. 02138

Heinemann. Heinemann, 361 Hanover St., Portsmouth, N.H. 03801

Hern Bks. Nick Hern Books, 14 Larden Rd., London W3 7ST, Eng.

Heuer. Heuer Publishing Company, 210 Dows Bldg., Cedar Rapids, Iowa 52406

Howard Univ Press. Howard University Press, 1240 Randolph St. N. E., Washington, D.C. 20017

Hyperion Bks. Hyperion, 114 5th Ave., New York, N.Y. 10011

Indiana Univ. Press. Indiana University Press, 601 N. Morton St., Bloomington, Ind. 47404-3797

International Pocket Lib. International Pocket Library, 17 Station St., P.O. Box 843, Brookline Village, Mass. 02147

Johns Hopkins Univ. Press. The Johns Hopkins University Press, 2715 N. Charles St., Baltimore, Md. 21218-4319

Kenyon-Deane. Kenyon-Deane, Ltd., 10 Station Rd., Industrial Estate, Colwall, Malvern, Worcestershire WR12 6RN, Eng.

Knopf. Alfred A. Knopf Inc., 201 E. 50th St., New York, N.Y. 10022

Lang, P. Verlag Peter Lang AG, Jupiterstr. 15, CH-3015 Bern, Switzerland
US address: 275 7th Ave., 28th Floor, New York, N.Y. 10001-6708

Left Hand Bks. Left Hand Books, Station Hill Rd., Barrytown, N.Y. 12507

Lib. of America. The Library of America, 14 E. 60th St., New York, N.Y. 10022

Lillenas. Lillenas Publishing Company, P.O. Box 419527, Kansas City, Mo. 64141

Limelight Eds. Limelight Editions, 118 E. 30th St., New York, N.Y. 10016

McFarland & Co. McFarland & Co., Inc., Publishers, P.O. Box 611, Jefferson, N.C. 28640-0611

Mellen Poetry Press. See Edwin Mellen Press

Mentor. Mentor, 375 Hudson St., New York, N.Y. 10014-3657

Mercier Press. Mercier Press, Ltd., P.O. Box 5, 5 French Church St., Cork, Ireland

Meridian Bks. (NY) Meridian Books, 375 Hudson St., New York, N.Y. 10014-3657

Meridian Theatre Co. Meridian Theatre Company, 11–12 Marlboro St., Cork, Ireland
US distributor: Dufour Eds.

Meriwether. Meriwether Publishing, Ltd., 885 Elkton Dr., Colorado Springs, Colo. 80907

Methuen. Methuen & Company, Ltd., Michelin House, 81 Fulham Road, London SW3 6RB, Eng.
US distributor: Heinemann

Methuen Drama. See Methuen

Miller, J. G. J. Garnet Miller Ltd., 10 Station Rd., Industrial Estate, Colwall, Malvern, Worcestershire WR13 6RN, Eng.

Minerva. Minerva, 20 Vauxhall Bridge Rd., London SW1V 2SA, Eng.

Modern Lib. The Modern Library, 201 E. 50th St., 22nd Floor, New York, N.Y. 10022

Moorley's. Moorley's Bible & Bookshop, 23 Park Rd., Ilkeston, Derbyshire DE7 5DA, Eng.

Mountain Press. Mountain Press Publishing Company, 1301 S. 3rd W., Missoula, Mont. 59801

National Christian Educ. Council. National Christian Education Council, 1020 Bristol Road, Selly Oak, Birmingham B29 6LB, Eng.

National Society/Church House Publishing, Church House, Great Smith St., London SW1P 3NZ, Eng.

NCEC. See National Christian Educ. Council

New Directions. New Directions Publishing Corporation, 80 8th Ave., New York, N.Y. 10011

New Island Bks./Hern Bks. See Hern Bks.

New Playwrights Network. New Playwrights' Network, 4 Brocklehurst Manor, 25 Brocklehurst Ave., Macclesfield, Cheshire SK10 2RX, Eng.

Newconcept Press. Newconcept Press, Inc., P.O. Box 124, Emerson, N.J. 07630

NeWest Press. NeWest Press, 201, 8540-109th St., Edmonton, Alta., Can. T6G 1E6

Noonday Press. Noonday Press, 19 Union Sq. W., New York, N.Y. 10003

Northwestern Univ. Press. Northwestern University Press, 625 Colfax St., Evanston, Ill. 60208-4210

Norton. W. W. Norton & Co. Inc., 500 5th Ave., New York, N.Y. 10010
Norvik Press. Norvik Press, University of East Anglia/EUR, Norwich NR4 7TJ, Eng. Eds.
US distributor: Dufour
NuAge Eds. NuAge Editions, Concordia Univ., English Dept., 1435 Drummond St., Montreal, Que., Can. H3G 1W4

Oberon Bks. Oberon Books, 521 Caledonian Rd., London N7 9RH, Eng.
Ohio State Univ. Press. Ohio State University Press, 1070 Carmack Rd., 180 Pressey Hall, Columbus, Ohio 43210-1002
Ohio Univ. Press. Ohio University Press, Scott Quadrangle, Athens, Ohio 45701
Overlook Press. The Overlook Press, 386 W. Broadway, 4th Floor, New York, N.Y. 10012
Oxford Univ. Press. Oxford University Press, Great Clarendon St., Oxford OX2 6DP, Eng.
US address: 198 Madison Ave., New York, N.Y. 10016

Palmer Press. Palmer Press, 659 Clyde Avenue, No. 23, West Vancouver, B.C., Can. V7T 1C8
Pantheon Bks. Pantheon Books, Inc., 201 E. 50th St., New York, N.Y. 10022
Paper Bark Press. Paper Bark Press, P.O. Box 59, Brooklyn, N.S.W. 2083, Aust.
Penguin. Penguin Putnam, 375 Hudson St., New York, N.Y. 10014
Picador. Picador, Pan Bks. Ltd., 25 Eccleston Pl., London SW1W 9NF, Eng.
US address: 175 5th Ave., New York, N.Y. 10010
Pickering & Chatto. Pickering & Chatto Publishers, Ltd., 21 Bloomsbury Way, London WC1A 2TH, Eng.
Piñata Bks. See Arte Publico Press
Pioneer Drama Service. Pioneer Drama Service, Inc., P.O. Box 4267, Englewood, Colo. 80155-4267
Players Press. Players Press, Inc., P.O. Box 1132, Studio City, Calif. 91614-0132
Plays, Inc. Plays, Inc., 120 Boylston St., Boston, Mass. 02116
Playwrights. Playwrights Publishing Company, 70 Nottingham Rd., Burton Joyce, Nottingham NG14 5AL, Eng.
Playwrights Canada. Playwrights Canada Press, 54 Wolseley St., 2nd Floor, Toronto, Ont., Can. M5T 1A5
Plume Bks. Plume Books, 375 Hudson St., New York, N.Y. 10014
Pocket Bks. Pocket Books, Simon & Schuster Bldg., 1230 Ave. of the Americas, New York, N.Y. 10020
Polygon. Polygon, 22 George Sq., Edinburgh EH8 9LF, Scotland
Princeton Univ. Press. Princeton University Press, 41 William St., Princeton, N.J. 08540

Random House. Random House, Inc., 201 E. 50th St., New York, N.Y. 10022
Random House Value Pub. Random House Value Publishing, Inc., 40 Engelhard Ave., Avenel, N.J. 07001
Red Deer College Press. Red Deer College Press, 56 Avenue & 32nd St., Red Deer, Alta., Can. T4N 5H5
RDC Press. See Red Deer College Press
Riverrun Press. Riverrun Press, 1170 Broadway, Room 807, New York, N.Y. 10001
Routledge. Routledge, 11 New Fetter Lane, London EC4P 4EE, Eng.
US address: 29 W. 35th St., New York, N.Y. 10001-2299
Royal National Theatre. See Hern Bks.
Rupa & Co. Rupa & Co., 15 Bankim Chatterjee St., P.O. Box 12333, Calcutta 700073, India
Rutgers Univ. Press. Rutgers University Press, Bldg. 4161, Livingston Campus, New Brunswick, N.J. 08903-5062

Salmon Pub. Salmon Publishing Ltd., Knocksedan House, 123 Baldoyle Industrial Estate, Baldoyle, Dublin 13, Ireland
US distributor: Dufour Eds.
Scarecrow Press. Scarecrow Press Inc., 4720 Boston Way, Lanham, Md. 20706
Schocken Bks. Schocken Books, 201 E. 50th St., New York, N.Y. 10022
Scottish Cultural Press. Scottish Cultural Press, Unit 14, Leith Walk Business Centre, 130 Leith Walk, Edinburgh EH6 5DT, Eng.
Second Renaissance Bks. Second Renaissance Books, 110 Copperwood Way, Oceanside, Calif. 92054
Seren Bks. Seren Books, 2 Wyndham St., 1st Floor, Bridgend, Mid Glamorgan CF31 1EF, Wales
Simon & Pierre. Simon & Pierre Publishing Company Ltd., 8 Market St., Suite 200, Toronto, Ont., Can., M5E 1M6
Sister Vision. Sister Vision, Black Women

and Women of Colour Press, P.O. Box 217, Station 'E', Toronto, Ont., Can. M6H 4E2
Smith & Kraus. Smith & Kraus, Inc., 1 Main St., Lyme, N.H. 03768
Smythe. Colin Smythe, Ltd., P.O. Box 6, Gerrards Cross, Buckinghamshire SL9 8XA, Eng.
Solomon Press. Solomon Press, 98–12 86th Ave., Suite 2, Rego Park, N.Y. 11374
Southern Ill. Univ. Press. Southern Illinois University Press, P.O. Box 3697, Carbondale, Ill. 62902-3697
Southern Methodist Univ. Press. Southern Methodist University Press, P.O. Box 415, Dallas, Tex. 75275
St. Johann Press. St. Johann Press, 315 Schraalenburgh Rd., Haworth, N.J. 07641
St. Martin's Press. St. Martin's Press, Inc., 175 5th Ave., New York, N.Y. 10010
Story Line Press. Story Line Press, Three Oaks Farm, Brownsville, Or. 97327-9718
Sun & Moon Press. Sun & Moon Press, 6026 Wilshire Blvd., Los Angeles, Calif. 90036
Swallow Press. See Ohio Univ. Press
Syracuse Univ. Press. Syracuse University Press, 1600 Jamesville Ave., Syracuse, N.Y. 13244-5160

Talonbooks. Talonbooks, #104-3100 Production Way, Burnaby, B.C., Can. V5A 4R4
Teacher Ideas Press. Teacher Ideas Press, P.O. Box 6633, Englewood, Colo. 80155-6633
Temple Lodge. Temple Lodge Publishing, 51 Queen Caroline St., Hammersmith, London W6 9QL, Eng.
Temple Univ. Press. Temple University Press, 1601 N. Broad St., Univ. Services Bldg., Room 306, Philadelphia, Pa. 19122
Texas Christian Univ. Press. Texas Christian University Press, P.O. Box 298300, Fort Worth, Tex. 76129
Theatre Communications Group. Theatre Communications Group, Inc., 355 Lexington Ave., New York, N.Y. 10017
Thunder Creek Pub. Co-op. Thunder Creek Publishing Co-op, 401–2206 Dewdney Ave., Regina, Sask., Can. S4R 1H3
TOR Bks. TOR Books, 175 5th Ave., New York, N.Y. 10010

Ubu Repertory Theater Publs. Ubu Repertory Theater Publications, 15 W. 28th St., New York, N.Y. 10001
UCD Dept. of Italian. Department of Italian, University College, Dublin 4, Ireland
Univ. of Calif. Press. University of California Press, 2120 Berkeley Way, Berkeley, Calif. 94720
Univ. of Del. Press. University of Delaware Press, 440 Forsgate Dr., Cranbury, N.J. 08512
Univ. of Hawaii Press. University of Hawaii Press, 2840 Kolowalu St., Honolulu, Hawaii 96822
Univ. of Mass. Press. University of Massachusetts Press, Box 429, Amherst, Mass. 01004-0429
Univ. of Nev. Press. University of Nevada Press, Mail Stop 166, Reno, Nev. 89557-0076
Univ. of South Dakota Press. University of South Dakota Press, 414 E. Clark St., Vermillion, South Dakota 57069-2390
Univ. of Washington Press. University of Washington Press, P.O. Box 50096, Seattle, Wash. 98145-5096
Univ. Press of America. University Press of America, Inc., 4720 Boston Way, Lanham, Md. 20706
Univ. Press of Ky. University Press of Kentucky, 663 S. Limestone St., Lexington, Ky. 40508-4008
Univ. Press of Miss. University Press of Mississippi, 3825 Ridgewood Rd., Jackson, Miss. 39211-6492

Viking. See Penguin
Vintage Bks. Vintage Books, 201 E. 50th St., New York, N.Y. 10022
Volcano Press. Volcano Press, Inc., P.O. Box 270, Volcano, Calif. 95689-0270

Warner Bks. Warner Books, Time & Life Bldg., 1271 Ave. of the Americas, New York, N.Y. 10020
Warner Chappell Plays. Warner Chappell Plays, 129 Park St., London W1Y 3FA, Eng.
Waveland Press. Waveland Press Inc., P.O. Box 400, Prospect Heights, Ill. 60070
Wayne State Univ. Press. Wayne State University Press, Leonard N. Simons Bldg., 4809 Woodward Ave., Detroit, Mich. 48201-1309
Westview Press. Westview Press Inc., 5500 Central Ave., Boulder, Colo. 80301-2877
Wincanton Press. Wincanton Press, National School, North St., Wincanton, Somerset BA9 9AT, Eng.

Yale Univ. Press. Yale University Press, 302 Temple St., New Haven, Conn. 06520